1995

THAILAND & BURMA HANDBOOK

THIRD EDITION

Editors *Joshua Eliot, Jane Bickersteth,*
Jonathan Miller and Georgina Matthews
Cartographer *Sebastian Ballard*

In the time of King Ramkhamhaeng, this land of
Sukhothai is thriving. In the water there is fish, in the
fields there is rice...so the people of Sukhothai praise him.
Inscription no.1, 1292 AD.

TRADE & TRAVEL *Handbooks*

Trade & Travel Publications Ltd
6 Riverside Court, Lower Bristol Road, Bath BA2 3DZ, England
Telephone 01225 469141 Fax 01225 469461

©Trade & Travel Publications Ltd., September 1994

ISBN 0 900751 55 X   ISSN 1352-786X

CIP DATA: A catalogue record for this book is available from the British Library

In North America, published by

PASSPORT BOOKS
a division of *NTC Publishing Group*

4255 West Touhy Avenue
Lincolnwood (Chicago), Illinois 60646-1975, USA

ISBN   0-8442-8981-7

Library of Congress Catalog Card Number 94-66054

Passport Books and colophon are registered trademarks of NTC Publishing Group

WARNING: While every endeavour is made to ensure that the facts printed in this book are correct at the time of going to press, travellers are cautioned to obtain authoritative advice from consulates, airlines, etc, concerning current travel and visa requirements and conditions before embarking. The publishers cannot accept legal responsibility for errors, however caused, that are printed in this book.

Cover illustration by Suzanne Evans
Printed and bound in Great Britain by Clays Ltd., Bungay, Suffolk

CONTENTS

TRADE & TRAVEL
HANDBOOKS

"A travel guide business that looks set to sweep the world."
The Independent

"The **India Handbook** (formerly the South Asian Handbook) has reminded me of how much I do not know about the sub-continent!"
Mark Tully, BBC India correspondent

"More info - less blah."
Readers's letter, Germany

"By far the best, most comprehensive guides: in a class of their own. Unreservedly recommended - a Handbook will pay for itself many times over."
Journey Latin America

"On Bible thin paper with distinctive covers. The miraculous result is that they are, at the same time, sturdy, exhaustive and light-weight."
Fort Lauderdale Sun Sentinel

"Mines of information and free of pretentiousness: make other guidebooks read like Butlins brochures."
Bookshop review

"Accurate and reliable down to the minutest detail. Amazingly so."
Reader's letter, Canada

"By far the most informative guide to Burma published in recent years. Miraculously, the information appears to be up-to-date, rare for books in this genre."
Far Eastern Economic Review

PREFACE

The former *Thailand, Indochina and Burma Handbook* has been split into two this year. This volume covers Thailand and Burma (Myanmar), while a second deals with the three countries of Indochina – Vietnam, Laos and Cambodia.

The editors have travelled to both Burma and Thailand during 1994 to research the new *Thailand and Burma Handbook*. Burma has been thoroughly revised and the section on Northeast Thailand, the great 'undiscovered' region of the Thai Kingdom, has also been substantially expanded and revised.

In the case of Burma, the most significant change for travellers has been the decision by the authorities to allow visitors to re-new visas and extend their stay from 2 to 4 weeks. There is also the likelihood that 4 week visas to Burma will be granted soon. The decision to open the country to more tourists for longer seems to be driven, primarily, by the pressing need to generate foreign exchange. The regime still views tourists as potentially corrosive and destabilising. On this theme, all three volumes dealing with Southeast Asia have a new section examining the effects of tourism on peoples and cultures (see page 54). In the case of Thailand, 1994 saw the opening of the first bridge spanning the lower reaches of the Mekong River in April, linking the town of Nong Khai (in Northeast Thailand) with Vientiane in Laos. In time, this should considerably boost tourism links between the two countries. Although still in its nascent

stages, there is the intention to develop a tourism nexus that combines Thailand, Laos, Vietnam and China, opening-up a whole range of overland routes that have been closed to foreigners since before World War II.

At a political level, 1993 and 1994 have been relatively quiet years for Thailand and Burma (although not necessarily for the inhabitants of those countries). The gradual undermining of the fragile Chuan coalition government in Thailand raises the prospect of an early election. In the case of Burma, although at an international level it may still be viewed as almost a 'terrorist' state, there has been a slow re-incorporation of the country back into the mainstream of regional (ASEAN) politics. Like the alignment of the members of ASEAN with the reviled Khmers Rouges, this is driven by the realities of politics and business in the region, not by humanitarian concerns. The opposition politician Aung San Suu Kyi remains under house arrest.

We are grateful to all those people who have taken the time and trouble to send us letters, and they are acknowledged at the end of each *Information for Visitors* section. However, we would particularly like to thank Zoe and Ian Creasey-Osmond for their work and support in Thailand, Boris Santosi for information on Vietnam, Sally Burbage for her helpful notes from Thailand, and Violaine Brisou for her work in Burma.

The Editors
Durham

TRADE & TRAVEL
Handbooks
1995

Award-winning guidebooks for all independently minded travellers. This annually updated series of impeccable accuracy and authority now covers over 120 countries, dependencies and dominions from Latin America and the Caribbean across the globe to Africa, India and Southeast Asia.

Practical, pocket sized and excellent value - **Handbooks** take you further.

South American Handbook

Mexico & Central American Handbook

Caribbean Islands Handbook

India Handbook (formerly South Asian Handbook)

Thailand & Burma Handbook

Vietnam, Laos & Cambodia Handbook

Indonesia, Malaysia & Singapore Handbook

North African Handbook
includes Andalucía (Moorish southern Spain)

East African Handbook
includes Zanzibar, Madagascar and the Seychelles

Write for our latest catalogue
Trade & Travel, 6 Riverside Court, Lower Bristol Road, Bath BA2 3DZ, England.
Tel 01225 469141   Fax 01225 469461

"More information - less blah!"

THE EDITORS

Joshua Eliot

Joshua has had a long-standing interest in Asia. He was born in Calcutta, grew up in Hong Kong, has a PhD in Thai agricultural geography from the University of London, and lectures on Southeast Asia. He is the author of a book on the geography of the region and has written well over 30 papers and articles on Southeast Asia. He has lived and conducted research in Thailand, Sumatra and Laos and has travelled extensively in the region over a period of more than 10 years. He speaks Thai, and some Lao and Indonesian.

Jane Bickersteth

Jane is an artist by training and has travelled widely in the region, particularly in Thailand and Indonesia, over a period of over ten years. She spent a year in the region with her young son researching the first edition of this guide and has held exhibitions of work inspired by her travels in Southeast Asia.

Georgina Matthews

Georgina is a professional guidebook editor. She has published books for Nicholson and Dorling Kindersley and has a particular interest in Burma, Laos and Cambodia. She has travelled to the region regularly and spent a year in the field researching the first edition of this guide.

Jonathan Miller

Jonathan is a journalist with the BBC World Service and based in Phnom Penh. Formerly he worked in London. He was raised in Malaysia and Singapore and before joining the BBC was a foreign correspondent in the region contributing pieces for such newspapers and magazines as *The Economist*, the *Asian Wall Street Journal*, *South*, and the *Daily Telegraph*. He speaks Malay, knows Malaysia and Singapore intimately, and returns regularly to the region on assignment.

MAP SYMBOLS

International Border		State Capital	□
State / Province Border		Other town	o
Main Road (National Highway)	**Rt 15**	Bus Station	B
Other Road		Hospital	H
Jeepable Road, Track, Trek, Path, Ferry		Key Number	27
Railway & Station		Airport	
Contours (approx)		Bridge	
River	*Mekong River*	Mountain	
Fortified wall		Waterfall	
Built up area		National Park, Wildlife Park, Bird Sanctuary	♦
Lake, Reservoir		Archaeological Site	▲
Sand Bank, Beach		Church / Cathedral	
National Park, Garden, Stadium		Hindu Temple	
		Mosque	
		Pagoda	
		Stupa	

T V I

INTRODUCTION AND HINTS

CONTENTS

General note The advice given below represents a regional summary of more detailed information provided in the *Information for visitors* sections of each country entry.

Before you go

Documents

● **Passports**

Passports should be valid for at least 6 months from the day of entry. Visitors intending to stay for an extended period or those visiting a number of countries should ensure their passports are valid for even longer than this. Also ensure there is sufficient space for entry and exit stamps. Details of visa formalities are given in the relevant *Information for visitors* sections. Passports should be carefully looked after. Those on a low budget, should keep their passport and other valuables in a money-belt, hidden beneath clothing. In hotels, keep valuables in a safe deposit box. In case of theft, keep a photocopy of your passport and other important documents in a separate place.

● **Visas for Burma**

Bangkok is the easiest city to obtain visas for Burma, as well as the countries of Indochina (Vietnam, Laos and Cambodia). Note that obtaining a visa can take considerable time.

● **ISIC**

Anyone in full-time education is entitled to an International Student Identity Card (ISIC). These are issued by student travel offices and travel agencies across the world and offer special rates on all forms of transport and other concessions and services. The ISIC head office is: ISIC Association, Box 9048, 1000 Copenhagen, Denmark, T (45) 33 93 93 03.

When to go

● **Best time to visit**

The Thai authorities have recently announced that they no longer have an 'off-season' for tourism. This attempt to even-out arrivals has not, however, changed the pattern of the seasons. In general, the dry season in both Thailand and Burma extends from Nov to Mar, and the wet season from May/Jun to Oct (see rainfall chart, page 31). Nearer the equator – in South Thailand – this division is far less distinct. However, it is possible to travel throughout the year in most areas, and the low season for visitors has the advantage of discounted hotel rates.

● **Climate**

See page 30.

Health

See page 19.

Money

● **Travellers' cheques**

If travelling to Burma, travellers' cheques denominated in US$ are most useful. In Thailand, travellers' cheques denominated in most major currencies can be easily changed. Because transaction charges are often calculated per travellers' cheque, it is best to take mostly high value cheques (e.g. US$100). A small amount of cash (in US$) can also be useful in an emergency. Keep it separate from your travellers' cheques.

What to take

Travellers usually tend to take too much. Almost everything is available in towns and cities in Thailand – and often at a lower price than in the West. But in Burma the reverse is true: many goods are hard, if not impossible, to find and relatively expensive to buy. See the relevant section in the *Information for visitors* section for more details on what to take to Burma.

Suitcases are not appropriate if you are intending to travel overland by bus. A backpack, or even better a travelpack (where the straps can be zipped out of sight), is recommended. Travelpacks have the advantage of being hybrid backpacks-suitcases; they can be carried on the back for easy porterage, but they can also be taken into hotels without the owner being labelled a 'hippy'. Note however, that for serious hikers, a backpack with an internal frame is still by far the better option for longer treks.

In terms of clothing, dress in Southeast Asia is relatively casual – even at formal functions. Suits are not necessary except in a very few of the most expensive restaurants. There is a tendency, rather than to take inappropriate articles of clothing, to take too many of the same article. Laundry services are cheap, and the turnaround rapid.

● **Checklist:**
Bumbag
Earplugs
Insect repellent and/or mosquito net, electric mosquito mats, coils
International driving licence
Photocopies of essential documents
Short wave radio
Spare passport photographs
Sun protection cream
Sunglasses
Swiss Army knife
Torch
Umbrella
Wipes (*Damp Ones*, *Baby Wipes* or equivalent)
Zip-lock bags

Those intending to stay in budget accommodation might also include:
Cotton sheet sleeping bag
Money belt
Padlock (for hotel room and pack)
Student card
Towel
Toilet paper

● **Health kit**
Antiacid tablets
Anti-diarrhoea tablets
Anti-malaria tablets
Anti-infective ointment
Condoms
Contraceptives
Dusting powder for feet
First aid kit and disposable needles
Flea powder
Sachets of rehydration salts
Tampons
Travel sickness pills
Water sterilising tablets

EXCHANGE RATES (AUGUST 1994)

	US$	£	DM
Burma (kyat)	5.88	9.03	3.70
Thailand (baht)	25.03	38.46	15.75

NB: the Kyat (Burma) exchange rate is the official rate. The black market rate is more than ten times higher.

Getting there

Air

It is possible to fly direct to several Southeast Asian destinations from Europe and Australasia, the west coast of North America, as well as from the Gulf and South Asia, Japan and Hong Kong. The major destination is Bangkok. Many airlines offer non-stop flights from European cities. The scheduled flying time from London to Bangkok is 12 hrs on direct flights, but may be up to 20 hrs on flights with more than one stop. Many of the world's top airlines fly the Southeast Asian routes and standards are therefore high. Onward reservations should be reconfirmed at every stage. Within Southeast Asia there is a wide range of flight connections on internal airlines.

Non-stop flights to Bangkok are readily available from Europe, Australasia, South Asia (Delhi, Karachi, Colombo, Dhaka and Kathmandu) and from Dubai. From North America's west coast there are flights direct from Los Angeles and Vancouver. From Japan, Hong Kong and the Philippines there are frequent flights.

Stop-overs and round the world tickets It is possible to arrange several stop-overs in Southeast Asia on round the world (RTW) and other longer distance tickets. RTW tickets allow you to fly in to Bangkok and out from another international airport such as Singapore or Kuala Lumpur. Different travel agents organise different deals. *Trailfinders* of London, one of the world's biggest agencies, has a range of discounted deals. Contact at 194 Kensington High St, London W8 7RG, T (071) 938-3366

● **Regional travel**

Tickets can be purchased locally, and paid for in local currency, but this is not a particularly cheap option.

Bangkok has become the principal air travel hub for Burma (Myanmar). There are direct flights from Bangkok to Rangoon. There are numerous flights between Singapore and Bangkok, and these 2 cities are also well-connected with Kuala Lumpur. Travel links out of Burma are limited.

● **Discounts**

It is possible to obtain significant discounts, especially outside European holiday times, most notably in London, even on non-stop flights. Shop around and book early. It is also possible to get discounts from Australasia, South Asia and Japan. Mid-July to mid-August is the peak season and most expensive although all airlines have different seasonal rates.

● **Airline security**

International airlines vary in their arrangements and requirements for security, in particular, the carrying of equipment like radios, tape-recorders and laptop computers. It is advisable to ring the airline in advance to confirm their current regulations. **Note that internal airlines often have different rules from the international carriers.**

In this Handbook, further details on air links to and from each country, arrival and departure regulations, airport taxes, customs regulations and security arrangements for air travel are outlined in the relevant *Information for visitors* sections.

Sea

Few people arrive in mainland Southeast Asia by sea. There are no regular passenger ships to Thailand or Burma. Ships do dock in Singapore and there are regular ferries linking Thailand and Malaysia. For those interested in booking a passage on a cargo ship travelling to the region, contact the *Strand Cruise and Travel Centre*, Charing Cross Shopping Concourse, The Strand, London WC2N 4HZ, T (071) 836-6363, F (071) 497-0078.

Overland

There are road links between Thailand and Laos via the border crossing at Nong

Khai (Northeastern Thailand) to Vientiane. In April 1994 the first bridge over the lower reaches of the Mekong River opened here (see page 343). Overland links between Thailand and Cambodia are not yet open. The border between Burma and Thailand at Mae Sai has recently been opened. The most commonly used border is that between Thailand and Malaysia. Regular buses and trains ply this route. See the relevant *Information for visitors* sections for further details.

When you arrive

Appearance

Southeast Asians admire neatness and cleanliness. They find it difficult to understand how some Westerners – by definition wealthy – can dress so poorly and untidily. By dressing well, you will be accorded more respect and face fewer day-to-day difficulties. Women, particularly, should also dress modestly. Short skirts and bare shoulders are regarded as unacceptable except in beach resorts and one or 2, more cosmopolitan, cities. Both men and women should be particularly sure to dress appropriately if visiting a religious site – a Buddhist temple or mosque for example.

Confidence tricksters

The most common 'threat' to tourists is from confidence tricksters: people selling fake gems and antiques, informal currency exchange services offering surprisingly good rates, and card sharps. Confidence tricksters are, by definition, extremely convincing and persuasive. Time is cheap in Southeast Asia, and people are willing to invest long hours lulling tourists into a false sense of security. Be suspicious of any offer that seems too good to be true. That is probably what it is.

Courtesy

As a general rule, Southeast Asians admire a calm and considered approach to all aspects of life. Open anger or shows of temper should be avoided. Causing another person to 'lose face' is not recommended, and status – particularly in terms of age – should be accorded due respect.

Drugs

Drugs (narcotics) are available in Southeast Asia, particularly in Thailand. However, penalties are harsh. In Thailand there are scores of former tourists overstaying their visas in prisons across the country. Do not agree to take anything out of Thailand without knowing exactly what it is.

Personal safety

So far as visitors are concerned, violence against the person is rare in Southeast Asia. If attacked, do not try to resist – firearms are widespread.

Theft is far more common than violence. Thieves favour public transport; confidence tricksters frequent popular tourist destinations. Personal valuables – money, travellers' cheques, passports, jewellery – should be kept safe. Do not leave valuables in hotel rooms; place them in a safe deposit box if possible, or keep them with you. A money-belt, concealed beneath clothing, is the safest way to carry valuables. Generally, the cheaper the mode or class of transport or hotel, the more likely thieves will be at work. Drugging of tourists on buses and trains by offering doped food does occur, particularly in Thailand. Simple common sense is the best defence.

Police

Report any incident that involves you or your possessions. Tourist Police operate in Thailand and are particularly geared to the problems of tourists. In Burma there are no such dedicated tourist police. Nonetheless, report any incident. In general, police will act promptly and properly. Local people throughout the region are proud of their country's reputation and are often all too willing to help a foreigner in trouble.

Prisoners Abroad

Prisoners Abroad, a UK charity, was formed to help people who fall foul of the law in foreign countries, where sentencing can be much harsher than at home. If you or a friend do get into trouble, you can contact Prisoners Abroad at 72-82 Rosebury Ave, London EC1R 4RR, T 071 833 3467, F 071 833 3467 (F +4471 833 3467 if outside the UK).

Sensitive areas

In Thailand, visitors should be careful when visiting border areas in the North and West, and on the frontier with Cambodia. In Burma, travel is carefully controlled. The government there is fighting a number of low-intensity wars against ethnic minorities.

Tipping

Tipping is not customary in Southeast Asia except in more expensive hotels and restaurants. It is also common for a 10% service charge and government tax (usually of 10%-11%) to be added on to bills in more expensive hotels and restaurants.

Women travelling alone

Women travelling alone face greater difficulties than men or couples. The general advice given above should be observed even more carefully. Young Southeast Asian women rarely travel without a partner, so it is regarded as strange for Western women to do so. Western women are often believed to be of easy virtue – a view perpetuated by Hollywood and in local films, for example. To minimise the pestering that will occur, dress modestly – particularly in the Muslim areas of S

MAPS OF MAINLAND SOUTHEAST ASIA

A decent map is an indispensable aid to travelling. Although maps are usually available locally, it is sometimes useful to buy a map prior to departure to plan routes and itineraries. Below is a select list of maps. Scale is provided in brackets.

Regional maps: Bartholomew Southeast Asia (1:5,800,000); Nelles Southeast Asia (1:4,000,000); Hildebrand Thailand, Burma, Malaysia and Singapore (1:2,800,000).

Country maps: Bartholomew Thailand (1:1,500,000); Bartholomew Vietnam, Laos and Cambodia (1:2,000,000); Nelles Burma (1:1,500,000); Nelles Thailand (1:1,500,000); Nelles Vietnam, Laos and Cambodia (1:1,500,000).

City maps: Nelles Bangkok.

Other maps: Tactical Pilotage Charts (TPC, US Airforce) (1:500,000); Operational Navigational Charts (ONC, US Airforce) (1:500,000). Both of these are particularly good at showing relief features (useful for planning treks); less good on roads, towns and facilities.

Locally available maps: maps are widely available in Thailand and many are given out free, although the quality of information is sometimes poor. Town maps are available in Burma, although their accuracy is sometimes dubious and they can be out-of-date.

Map shops: in London, the best selection is available from Stanfords, 12-14 Long Acre WC2E 9LP, T (071) 836-1321; also recommended is McCarta, 15 Highbury Place, London N15 1QP, T (071) 354-1616.

Thailand. Comments, sometimes derogatory, will be made however carefully you dress and act; simply ignore them. Toiletries such as tampons are widely available in main towns and cities in Thailand, but not in Burma.

Where to stay

Accommodation

The main towns and tourist destinations in Thailand offer a wide range of accommodation. Some of the finest hotels in the world are to be found in the Kingdom and are moderately priced by Western standards. Mid-range and budget accommodation are also generally of a relatively good standard. However, outside the main towns and tourist areas, accommodation can be surprisingly limited – restricted to one or 2 'Chinese' hotels with neither budget places for backpackers, nor more expensive establishments. Paradoxically therefore, it can become more expensive the further one ventures off the tourist 'trail'.

In Burma, accommodation is far more limited. First class hotels are only

---

TRAVELLING WITH CHILDREN & BABIES IN SOUTHEAST ASIA

Many people are daunted by the prospect of taking a child to Southeast Asia. Naturally, it is not something which is taken on lightly; travelling is slower and more expensive and there are additional health risks for the child or baby. But it can be a most rewarding experience, and with sufficient care and planning, it can also be safe. Children are excellent passports into a local culture. You will also receive the best service, and help from officials and members of the public when in difficulty.

Children in Southeast Asia are given 24-hour attention by parents, grandparents and siblings. They are rarely left to cry and are carried for most of the first 8 months of their lives – crawling is considered animal-like. A non-Asian child is still something of a novelty and parents may find their child frequently taken off their hands, even mobbed in more remote areas (particularly in Thailand). This can be a great relief (at mealtimes, for instance) or most alarming. Some children love the attention, others react against it; it is best simply to gauge your own child's reactions.

Accommodation At the hottest time of year, air-conditioning may be essential for a baby or young child's comfort. This rules out many of the cheaper hotels, but a/c accommodation is available in all but the most out-of-the-way spots. When the child is bathing, be aware that the water could carry parasites, so avoid letting him or her drink it.

Transport Public transport may be a problem; trains are fine but long bus journeys are restrictive and uncomfortable. Hiring a car is undoubtedly the most convenient way to see a country with a small child. Back-seatbelts are rarely fitted but it is possible to buy child-seats in capital cities.

Food & drink The advice given in the health section on food and drink (see page 24) should be applied even more stringently where young children are concerned. Be aware that expensive hotels may have squalid cooking conditions; the cheapest street stall is often more hygienic. Where possible, try to watch food being prepared. Stir-fried vegetables and rice or noodles are the best bet; meat and fish may be pre-cooked and then left out before being re-heated. Fruit can be bought cheaply right across Southeast Asia: papaya, banana and avocado are all excellent sources of nutrition, and can be self-peeled ensuring cleanliness. Powdered milk is also available throughout the region, although most brands have added sugar. But if taking a baby, breast-feeding is strongly recommended. Powdered food can be bought in most towns – the quality may not be the same as equivalent foods bought in the West, but it is perfectly adequate for short periods. Bottled water and fizzy drinks are also sold widely. If your child is at the 'grab everything and put it in mouth' stage, a damp cloth and some *dettol* (or equivalent) are useful. Frequent wiping of hands and tabletops can help to minimize the chance of infection.

Sunburn NEVER allow your child to be exposed to the harsh tropical sun without protection. A child can burn in a matter of minutes. Loose cotton-clothing, with long sleeves and legs and a sun-hat are best. High-factor sun-protection cream is essential.

Disposable nappies These can be bought in Thailand, but are often expensive. If you are staying any length of time in one place, it may be worth taking Terry's (cloth) nappies. All you need is a bucket and some double-strength nappy cleanse (simply soak and rinse). Cotton nappies dry quickly in the heat and are generally more comfortable for the baby or child. They also reduce rubbish – many countries are not geared to the disposal of nappies. Of course, the best way for a child to be is nappy-free – like the local children.

Baby products Many Western baby products are now available in Southeast Asia: shampoo, talcum powder, soap and lotion. Baby wipes can be difficult to find.

Emergencies Babies and small children deteriorate very rapidly when ill. A travel insurance policy which has an air ambulance provision is strongly recommended. When planning a route, try to stay within 24 hours' travel of a hospital with good care and facilities. Many expatriats fly to Singapore for medical care, which has the best doctors and facilities in the region.

Check-list:
Baby wipes
Calpol
Dettol (or other disinfectant)
First aid kit
Flannel
Immersion element for boiling water
Kalvol and/or *Snuffle Babe* or equivalent for colds
Milupa for under-one-year-olds
Mug/bottle/bowl/spoons
Nappy cleanse, double-strength
ORS (Oral Rehydration Salts) such as *Dioralyte*, widely available in Thailand, and the most effective way to alleviate diarrhoea (it is not a cure)
Portable baby chair, to hook onto tables; this is not essential but can be very useful
Sarong or backpack for carrying child (and/or light weight collapsible buggy)
Sterilising tablets (and an old baby-wipes container for sterilising bottles, teats, utensils)
Sudocrem, or equivalent, for nappy rash and other skin complaints
Sunblock, factor 15 or higher
Sunhat
Terry's (cloth) nappies, liners, pins and plastic pants
Thermometer
Zip-lock bags for carrying snacks, powdered food, wet flannel.

Suggested reading: Pentes, Tina and Truelove, Adrienne (1984) *Travelling with children to Indonesia and South-East Asia*, Hale & Iremonger: Sydney. Wheeler, Maureen *Travel with children*, Lonely Planet: Hawthorne, Australia.

to be found in Rangoon, the capital. Service, facilities and value for money are generally poor in comparison to Thailand. Budget accommodation likewise is limited. Some cheaper hotels may refuse to offer foreigners a room.

The price categories of accommodation (in US$) used in this book are listed in the local currency in the relevant *Information for visitors* sections, together with a brief summary of the facilities to be expected.

Camping

Camping is becoming increasingly popular in Thailand. Most national parks offer camping facilities, although these are often rudimentary compared with the West. Outside national parks however, there are very few dedicated camping grounds. Southeast Asians find it strange that anyone should want to camp out when it is possible to stay in a hotel. In Burma there are no camping grounds.

Food and drink

Food

Food in Thailand is generally good, and excellent value for money. Although care regarding what you eat and where you eat it is obviously recommended, levels of hygiene are reasonable. The incidence of tourists suffering from serious stomach upsets is far less than, say, in South Asia. All towns have local restaurants and stalls serving cheap, tasty and nourishing dishes. Most towns will also have their requisite Chinese restaurant, so it is usually possible to order food that is not spicy-hot. Details on local cuisines are contained in each *Information for visitors* section.

In tourist areas and more expensive hotels in Thailand, Western food is also widely available. This ranges from fast food outlets like McDonalds, Pizza Hut and Kentucky Fried Chicken, to top class French and Italian restaurants. In areas popular with backpackers, so-called travellers' food is also available: dishes such as chocolate fudge cake, pancakes, fruit shakes (or 'smoothies') and garlic toast.

As with accommodation, the situation in Burma is rather different. In Rangoon and a handful of other towns, the choice is reasonable. Generally, local dishes are excellent, but Western food is often poor. Ingredients – particularly meat – are sometimes of poor quality. Outside the main towns, restaurants can be few and far between, and the food inferior. Western food is not widely available.

Across the region, fruit can be a lifesaver. It is varied, cheap, exotic, safe to eat (if peeled oneself) and delicious. A list of the more exotic Southeast Asian fruits is given in the box on page 17. More details on food and restaurants in each country are contained in the relevant *Information for visitors* sections.

Drink

Alcoholic drinks and soft drinks such as Coca-cola and 7-Up are available in Thailand, and just Coca-cola in Burma, where it has recently become available. Locally brewed beers (light lagers) are comparatively expensive. Tea and coffee are available in all countries of mainland Southeast Asia.

Water

Bottled water is easily obtainable in Thailand and Burma. It is not advisable to drink water straight from the tap.

Getting around

Air

Domestic airlines link major towns and cities. In Thailand, services are efficient and safe, although considerably more expensive than the overland alternatives. In Burma, the domestic airline's

DISTINCTIVE FRUITS OF SOUTHEAST ASIA

Custard apple (or sugar apple) Scaly green skin, squeeze the skin to open the fruit and scoop out the flesh with a spoon. Season: Jun-Sept.

Durian (*Durio zibethinus*) A large prickly fruit, with yellow flesh, about the size of a football. Infamous for its pungent smell. While it is today regarded by many visitors as simply revolting, early Europeans (16th-18th centuries) raved about it, possibly because it was similar in taste to Western delicacies of the period. Borri (1744) thought that "God himself, who had produc'd that fruit". But by 1880 Burbridge was writing: "Its odour - one scarcely feels justified in using the word 'perfume' - is so potent, so vague, but withal so insinuating, that it can scarcely be tolerated inside the house". Banned from public transport in Singapore and hotel rooms throughout the region, and beloved by most Southeast Asians (where prize specimens can cost a week's salary), it has an alluring taste if the odour can be overcome. Some maintain it is an addiction. Durian-flavoured chewing gum, ice cream and jams are all available. Season: May-Aug.

Jackfruit Similar in appearance to durian but not so spiky. Yellow flesh, tasting slightly like custard. Season: Jan-Jun.

Mango (*Mangifera indica*) A rainforest fruit which is now cultivated. Widely available in the West; in Southeast Asia there are hundreds of different varieties with subtle variations in flavour. Delicious eaten with sticky rice and a sweet sauce (in Thailand). The best mangoes in the region are considered to be those from South Thailand. Season: Mar-Jun.

Mangosteen (*Garcinia mangostana*) An aubergine-coloured hard shell covers this small fruit which is about the size of a tennis ball. Cut or squeeze the purple shell to reach its sweet white flesh which is prized by many visitors above all others. In 1898, an American resident of Java wrote, erotically and in obvious ecstasy: "The five white segments separate easily, and they melt on the tongue with a touch of tart and a touch of sweet; one moment a memory of the juiciest, most fragrant apple, at another a remembrance of the smoothest cream ice, the most exquisite and delicately flavoured fruit-acid known - all of the delights of nature's laboratory condensed in that ball of *neige parfumée*". Southeast Asians believe it should be eaten as a chaser to durian. Season: Apr-Sept.

Papaya (*Carica papaya*) A New World Fruit that was not introduced into Southeast Asia until the 16th century. Large, round or oval in shape, yellow or green-skinned, with bright orange flesh and a mass of round, black seeds in the middle. The flesh, in texture and taste, is somewhere between a mango and a melon. Some maintain that it tastes 'soapy'. Season: Year round.

Pomelo A large round fruit the size of anything from an ostrich egg to a football, with thick, green skin, thick pith, and flesh not unlike that of the grapefruit, but less acidic. Season: Aug-Nov.

Rambutan (*Nephelium lappaceum*) The bright red and hairy rambutan - *rambut* is the Malay word for 'hair' - with its slightly rubbery but sweet flesh is a close relative of the lychee of southern China and tastes similar. The Thai word for rambutan is *ngoh*, which is the nickname given by Thais to the fuzzy-haired Negrito aboriginals in the southern jungles. Season: May-Sept.

Salak (*Salacca edulis*) A small pear-shaped fruit about the size of a large plum with a rough, brown, scaly skin (somewhat like a miniature pangolin) and yellow-white, crisp flesh. It is related to the sago and rattan trees.

Tamarind (*Tamarindus indicus*) Brown seedpods with dry brittle skins and a brown tart-sweet fruit which grow on a tree introduced into Southeast Asia from India. The name is Arabic for 'Indian date'. The flesh has a high tartaric acid content and is used to flavour curries, jams, jellies and chutneys as well as for cleaning brass and copper. Elephants have a predilection for tamarind balls. Season: Dec-Feb.

safety record is poor and international standards are not met.

Train

Both Thailand and Burma have passenger railways. Travelling third class is often the cheapest way to get from A to B, while first class (a/c) is more comfortable (and safer) than travelling by bus (although usually slower). **NB**: security can be a problem on long-distance train journeys.

Road

Road is the main mode of transport in the region. **Buses** link nearly all towns, however small. In Thailand roads are good, and air-conditioned 'VIP' buses are available on the more popular routes. These are considerably cheaper than travelling by air. Non a/c buses and other vicarious forms of transport are cheaper still, but usually slower and more uncomfortable. In Burma tourists are constrained and/or discouraged from using buses, although limited use is possible (see relevant *Information for visitors* sections). **NB**: Security can be a problem on long-distance bus journeys.

Car hire

Cars for self-drive hire are available in Thailand, where motorists drive on the left. But road 'courtesy' is not a feature of the country, and larger vehicles expect smaller ones to give way, even where the latter may have right of way. More common than self-drive, is for visitors to hire a car and driver. This is possible in Burma and Thailand.

Hitchhiking and cycling

This is not common in Southeast Asia. However there are increasing numbers of visitors who tour Thailand by **bicycle**.

It is strongly recommended that cyclists arrange their route on minor roads; drivers use the hard shoulder.

Boat

Boats are not a mode of transport frequently used by visitors – although rivers are important arteries of communication. Ferries link islands such as the Thai island of Koh Samui with the mainland and there is also some river transport – for example on rivers in North Thailand and in Burma.

Communications

Language

English is widely spoken in tourist areas. Off the tourist track, it is useful to be able to speak a few words of the local language, although in Thailand there will nearly always be someone who will help translate. English is spoken in Burma by many of the older generation, but few of the young.

Short wave radio guide

British Broadcasting Corporation (BBC, London) *Southeast Asian service* 3915, 6195, 9570, 9740, 11750, 11955, 15360; *Singapore service* 88.9MHz; *East Asian service* 5995, 6195, 7180, 9740, 11715, 11750, 11945, 11955, 15140, 15280, 15360, 17830, 21715.

Voice of America (VoA, Washington) *Southeast Asian service* 1143, 1575, 7120, 9760, 9770, 15185, 15425; *Indonesian service* 6110, 11760, 15425.

Radio Beijing *Southeast Asian service (English)* 11600, 11660.

Radio Japan (Tokyo) *Southeast Asian service (English)* 11815, 17810, 21610.

HEALTH INFORMATION

CONTENTS

The following information has been compiled by Dr David Snashall, Senior Lecturer in Occupational Health, United Medical Schools of Guy's and St Thomas' Hospitals and Chief Medical Adviser, Foreign and Commonwealth Office, London.

The traveller to Southeast Asia is inevitably exposed to health risks not encountered in North America, Western Europe or Australasia. These countries have tropical climates; nevertheless the acquisition of true tropical disease by the visitor is probably conditioned as much by the rural nature and standard of hygiene of the countries concerned than by the climate. There is an obvious difference in health risks between the business traveller who tends to stay in international class hotels in large cities and the backpacker trekking through rural areas. There are no hard and fast rules to follow; you will often have to make your own judgements on the healthiness or otherwise of your surroundings.

The quality of medical care is highly variable. Away from the main cities it can be very poor indeed. In Thailand, medical care is adequate for most ailments and there are good hospitals in Bangkok; for more serious complaints visitors are advised to go to Singapore or elsewhere outside the region. In Burma doctors may speak English, but the likelihood of finding this and a good standard of care diminishes very rapidly as you move away from the big cities. In these countries – and especially in rural areas – there are systems and traditions of medicine wholly different from the Western model and you may be confronted with less orthodox forms of treatment such as herbal medicine and acupuncture. At least you can be sure that local practitioners have a lot of experience with the particular diseases of their region. If you are in a city it may be worthwhile calling on your embassy to provide a list of recommended doctors.

If you are a long way away from medical help, a certain amount of self administered medication may be necessary and you will find many of the drugs available have familiar names. However, always check the date stamping (sell-by date) and buy from reputable pharmacists because the shelf life of some items, especially vaccines and antibiotics, is markedly reduced in hot conditions. Unfortunately, many locally produced drugs are not subjected to quality control procedures and so can be unreliable. There have, in addition, been cases of substitution of inert materials for active drugs. With the following precautions and advice you should keep as healthy as usual. Make local enquiries about health risks if you are apprehensive and take the general advice of European or North American families who have lived or are living in the area.

Before you go

Take out medical insurance. You should also have a dental check-up, obtain a spare glasses prescription and, if you suffer from a long-standing condition, such as diabetes, high blood pressure, heart/lung disease or a nervous disorder, arrange for a check-up with your doctor who can at the same time provide you with a letter explaining details of your medical disorder. Check the current practice for malaria prophylaxis (prevention) for the countries you intend to visit.

Inoculations

Smallpox vaccination is no longer required. Neither is cholera vaccination, despite the fact that the disease occurs – but not at present in epidemic form – in these countries. Yellow fever vaccination is not required either, although you may be asked for a certificate if you have been in a country affected by yellow fever immediately before travelling to Southeast Asia. The following vaccinations are recommended:

Typhoid (monovalent): one dose followed by a booster one month later. Immunity from this course lasts 2-3 years. An oral preparation is also available.

Poliomyelitis: this is a live vaccine generally given orally but a full course consists of 3 doses with a booster in tropical regions every 3-5 years.

Tetanus: one dose should be given, with a booster at 6 weeks and another at 6 months. Ten yearly boosters thereafter are recommended.

Meningitis and Japanese B encephalitis (JVE): there is an extremely small risk of these rather serious diseases; both are seasonal and vary according to region. Meningitis can occur in epidemic form; JVE is a viral disease transmitted from pigs to man by mosquitos. For details of the vaccinations, consult a travel clinic. Children should, in addition to the above, be properly protected against diphtheria, whooping cough, mumps and measles. Teenage girls, if they have not had the disease, should be given a rubella (German measles) vaccination. Consult your doctor for advice on BCG inoculation against tuberculosis: the disease is still common in the region.

Infectious hepatitis (jaundice)

This is common throughout Southeast Asia. It seems to be frequently caught by travellers. The main symptoms are stomach pains, lack of appetite, nausea, lassitude and yellowness of the eyes and skin. Medically speaking there are 2 types: the less serious but more common is *hepatitis A* for which the best protection is careful preparation of food, the avoidance of contaminated drinking water and scrupulous attention to toilet hygiene. Human normal immunoglobulin (gammaglobulin) confers considerable protection against the disease and is particularly useful in epidemics. It should be obtained from a reputable source and is certainly recommended for travellers who intend to travel and live rough. The injection should be given as close as possible to your departure and as the dose depends on the likely time you are to spend in potentially infected areas, the manufacturers' instructions should be followed. A vaccination against hepatitis A has recently become generally available and seems to be safe and effective. Three shots are given over 6 months and confer excellent protection against the disease for up to 10 years. Eventually this vaccine is likely to supersede the use of gammaglobulin.

The other, more serious, version is *hepatitis B* which is acquired as a sexually transmitted disease, from a blood transfusion or an injection with an unclean needle, or possibly by insect bites. The symptoms are the same as hepatitis A but the incubation period is much longer.

You may have had jaundice before or you may have had hepatitis of either type before without becoming jaundiced, in which case it is possible that you could be immune to either hepatitis A or B (or C or a number of other letters). This immunity can be tested for before you travel. If you are not immune to hepatitis B already, a vaccine is available (3 shots over 6 months) and if you are not immune to hepatitis A already, then you should consider having gammaglobulin or a vaccination.

AIDS

This is increasingly prevalent in Southeast Asia. Thus, it is not wholly confined to the well known high risk sections of the population i.e. homosexual men, intravenous drug abusers, prostitutes and the children of infected mothers. Heterosexual transmission is probably now the dominant mode of infection and so the main risk to travellers is from casual sex. The same precautions should be taken as when encountering any sexually transmitted disease. In some Southeast Asian countries, Thailand is an example, almost the entire population of female prostitutes is HIV positive and in other parts intravenous drug abuse is common. The AIDS virus (HIV) can be passed via unsterile needles which have been previously used to inject an HIV positive patient, but the risk of this is very small indeed. It would, however, be sensible to check that needles have been properly sterilized or disposable needles used. The chance of picking up hepatitis B in this way is much more of a danger. Be wary of carrying disposable needles. Customs officials may find them suspicious. The risk of receiving a blood transfusion with blood infected with the HIV virus is greater than from dirty needles because of the amount of fluid exchanged. Supplies of blood for transfusion are supposed to be screened for HIV in all reputable hospitals so the risk should be small. Catching the virus which causes AIDS does not necessarily produce an illness in itself; the only way to be sure if you feel you have been put at risk is to have a blood test for HIV antibodies on your return to a place where there are reliable laboratory facilities. However, the test does not become positive for many weeks.

Common problems

Heat and cold

Full acclimatization to tropical temperatures takes about 2 weeks and during this period it is normal to feel relatively apathetic, especially if the humidity is high. Drink plenty of water (up to 15 litres a day are required when working physically hard in the tropics). Use salt on your food and avoid extreme exertion. Tepid showers are more cooling than hot or cold ones. Large hats do not cool you down but do prevent sunburn. Remember that, especially in highland areas, there can be a large and sudden drop in temperature between sun and shade and between night and day so dress accordingly. Loose-fitting cotton clothes are best for hot weather. Warm jackets and woollens are often necessary after dark at high altitude.

Intestinal upsets

Practically nobody escapes tummy upsets, so be prepared for them. Most of the time intestinal upsets are due to the insanitary preparation of food. Do not eat uncooked fish, vegetables or meat (especially pork), fruit without the skin (always peel fruit yourself), or food that is exposed to flies (particularly salads). Tap water may be unsafe, especially in the monsoon seasons and the same goes for stream water or well water. Filtered or bottled water is usually available and safe but you cannot rely on it. If your hotel has a **central** hot water supply, this is safe to drink after cooling. Ice should be made from boiled water but rarely is, so stand your glass on the ice cubes instead of putting them in the drink. Dirty water should first be strained through a filter bag (available from camping shops) and then boiled or treated. Bringing the water to a rolling boil at sea level is sufficient. In the highlands, you have to boil the water a bit longer to ensure that all the microbes are killed. Various sterilizing methods can be used and there are proprietary preparations containing chlorine or iodine compounds. Pasteurised or heat-treated milk is now fairly widely available as is ice cream and yoghurt produced by the same methods. Unpasteurised milk products, including cheese, are sources of tuberculosis, brucellosis, listeria and food poisoning germs. You can render fresh milk safe by heating it to 62°C for 30 mins followed by rapid cooling or by boiling. Matured or processed cheeses are safer than fresh varieties.

Fish and shellfish are popular foods in mainland Southeast Asia but can be the source of health problems. Shellfish which are eaten raw will transmit food poisoning or hepatitis if they have been living in contaminated water. Certain fish accumulate toxins in their bodies at certain times of the year, which give rise to illness when they are eaten. The phenomenon known as 'red tide' can also affect fish and shellfish which eat large quantities of tiny sea creatures and thereby become poisonous. The only way to guard against this is to keep as well informed as possible about fish and shellfish quality in the area you are visiting. Most countries impose a ban on fishing in periods when red tide is prevalent, although this is often flouted.

Diarrhoea is usually the result of food poisoning, but can occasionally result from contaminated water. There are various causes – viruses, bacteria, protozoa (like amoeba), salmonella and cholera organisms. It may take one of several forms coming on suddenly or rather slowly. It may be accompanied by vomiting or severe abdominal pain, and the passage of blood or mucus (when it is called dysentery).

All kinds of diarrhoea, whether or not accompanied by vomiting, respond favourably to the replacement of water and salts taken as frequent small sips of some kind of rehydration solution. There are proprietary preparations consisting of sachets of oral rehydration electrolyte powder which are dissolved in water, or make up your own by adding half a teaspoonful of salt (3.5 grams) and

4 tablespoons of sugar (40 grams) to a litre of boiled water. If it is possible to time the onset of diarrhoea to the minute, then it is probably viral or bacterial and/or the onset of dysentery. The treatment in addition to rehydration is Ciprofloxacin (500 mgs every 12 hours). The drug is now widely available as are various similar ones.

If the diarrhoea has come on slowly or intermittently, then it is more likely to be protozoal, i.e. caused by amoeba or giardia, and antibiotics will have no effect. These cases are best treated by a doctor as should any diarrhoea continuing for more than 3 days. If there are severe stomach cramps, the following drugs may help: Loperamide (*Imodium, Arret*) and Diphenoxylate with Atropine (*Lomotil*). The drug usually used for giardia or amoeba is Metronidazole (*Flagyl*).

The lynchpins of treatment for diarrhoea are rest, fluid and salt replacement, antibiotics such as Ciprofloxacin for the bacterial types, and special diagnostic tests and medical treatment for amoeba and giardia infections. Salmonella infections and cholera can be devastating diseases and it would be wise to get to a hospital as soon as possible if these were suspected. Fasting, peculiar diets and the consumption of large quantities of yoghurt have not been found useful in calming travellers' diarrhoea or in rehabilitating inflamed bowels. Oral rehydration has, especially in children, been a lifesaving technique and as there is some evidence that alcohol and milk might prolong diarrhoea they should probably be avoided during, and immediately after, an attack. There are ways of preventing travellers' diarrhoea for short periods of time when visiting these countries by taking antibiotics but these are ineffective against viruses and, to some extent, against protozoa. This technique should not be used other than in exceptional circumstances. Some preventatives such as Enterovioform can have serious side effects if taken for long periods.

Insects

These can be a great nuisance. Some, of course, are carriers of serious diseases such as malaria, dengue fever or filariasis and various worm infections. The best way of keeping mosquitos away at night is to sleep off the ground with a mosquito net and to burn mosquito coils containing Pyrethrum. Aerosol sprays or a 'flit gun' may be effective as are insecticidal tablets which are heated on a mat which is plugged into the wall socket (if taking your own, check the voltage of the area you are visiting so that you can take an appliance that will work; similarly, check that your electrical adaptor is suitable for the repellent plug; note that they are widely available in the region).

You can, in addition, use personal insect repellent of which the best contain a high concentration of diethyltoluamide (DET). Liquid is best for arms and face (take care around eyes and make sure you do not dissolve the plastic of your spectacles). Aerosol spray on clothes and ankles deter mites and ticks. Liquid DET suspended in water can be used to impregnate cotton clothes and mosquito nets. The latter are now available in wide mesh form which are lighter to carry and less claustrophobic to sleep under.

If you are bitten, itching may be relieved by cool baths and anti-histamine tablets (take care with alcohol or when driving), corticosteroid creams (great care – never use if any hint of septic poisoning) or by judicious scratching. Calamine lotion and cream have limited effectiveness and anti-histamine creams have a tendency to cause skin allergies and are therefore not generally recommended. Bites which become infected (a common problem in the tropics) should be treated with a local antiseptic or antibiotic cream such as Cetrimide, as

should infected scratches. Skin infestations with body lice, crabs and scabies are unfortunately easy to pick up. Use gamma benzene hexachloride for lice and benzyl benzoate for scabies. Crotamiton cream alleviates itching and also kills a number of skin parasites. Malathion lotion is good for lice but avoid the highly toxic full strength Malathion which is used as an agricultural insecticide.

Malaria

Malaria is prevalent in Southeast Asia and remains a serious disease. You are advised to protect yourself against mosquito bites as above and to take prophylactic (preventative) drugs. Start taking the tablets a few days before exposure and continue to take them 6 weeks after leaving the malarial zone. Remember to give the drugs to babies and children, pregnant women also.

The subject of malaria prevention is becoming more complex as the malaria parasite becomes immune to some of the older drugs. Nowhere is this more apparent than in Southeast Asia – especially parts of Laos and Cambodia and contiguous areas of Thailand. In particular, there has been an increase in the proportion of cases of falciparum malaria which are resistant to the normally used drugs. It would not be an exaggeration to say that we are near to the situation where some cases of malaria will be untreatable with presently available drugs.

Some of the prophylactic drugs can cause side effects, especially if taken for long periods of time, so before you travel you must check with a reputable agency the likelihood and type of malaria in the countries which you intend to visit. Take their advice on prophylaxis but be prepared to receive conflicting advice. Because of the rapidly changing situation in the Southeast Asian region, the names and dosage of the drugs have not been included here. But Chloroquine

CHILDREN AND BABIES

Younger travellers seem to be more prone to illness abroad, but that should not put you off taking them. More preparation is necessary than for an adult and perhaps a little more care should be taken when travelling to remote areas where health services are primitive. This is because children can become more rapidly ill than adults (they often recover more quickly however). For more practical advice on travelling with children and babies see page 14.

Diarrhoea and vomiting are the most common problems so take the usual precautions, but more intensively. Make sure all basic childhood **vaccinations** are up to date as well as the more exotic ones. Children should be properly protected against diphtheria, whooping cough, mumps and measles. If they have not had the disease, teenage girls should be given rubella (german measles) vaccination. Consult your doctor for advice on BCG inoculation against tuberculosis: the disease is still common in the region. Protection against mosquitos and drug prophylaxis against malaria is essential. Many children take to "foreign" food quite happily. Milk in Southeast Asia may be unavailable outside big cities. Powdered milk may be the answer; breast feeding for babies even better.

Upper respiratory infections such as colds, catarrh and middle ear infections are common – antibiotics could be carried against the possibility. **Outer ear infections** after swimming are also common – antibiotic ear drops will help.

The treatment of **diarrhoea** is the same as for adults except that it should start earlier and be continued with more persistence. Children get dehydrated very quickly in the tropics and can become drowsy and uncooperative unless cajoled to drink water or juice plus salts. Oral rehydration has been a lifesaving technique in children.

Protect children against the sun with a hat and high factor tanning lotion. Severe sunburn at this age may well lead to serious skin cancer in the future.

and Proguanil may still be recommended for the countries where malaria is still fully sensitive; while Doxycycline, Mefloquine and Quinghaosu are presently being used in resistant areas. Quinine, Halofamtrine and tetracycline drugs remain the mainstays of treatment.

It is still possible to catch malaria even when taking prophylactic drugs, although this is unlikely. If you do develop symptoms (high fever, shivering, severe headache, and sometimes diarrhoea) seek medical advice immediately. The risk of the disease is obviously greater the further you move from the cities into rural areas, with primitive facilities and standing water.

Sunburn & heat stroke

The burning power of the tropical sun is phenomenal, especially in highland areas. Always wear a wide-brimmed hat, and use some form of sun cream or lotion on untanned skin. Normal temperate zone suntan lotions (protection factors up to 7) are not much good. You need to use the types designed specifically for the tropics or for mountaineers or skiers, with a protection factor between 7 and 15 or higher. Glare from the sun can cause conjunctivitis so wear sunglasses, particularly on beaches.

There are several varieties of heat stroke. The most common cause is severe dehydration. Avoid this by drinking lots of non-alcoholic fluid, and adding salt to your food.

Snake and other bites & stings

If you are unlucky enough to be bitten by a venomous snake, spider, scorpion, centipede or sea creature, try (within limits) to catch or kill the animal for identification. Reactions to be expected are shock, swelling, pain and bruising around the bite, soreness of the regional lymph glands, nausea, vomiting and fever. If in addition any of the following symptoms should follow closely, get the victim to a doctor without delay: numbness, tingling of the face, muscular spasms, convulsions, shortness of breath or haemorrhage. Commercial snakebite or scorpion-sting kits may be available but these are only useful against the specific type of snake or scorpion for which they are designed. The serum has to be given intravenously so is not much good unless you have had some practice in making injections into veins. If the bite is on a limb, immobilize it and apply a tight bandage between the bite and the body, releasing it for 90 seconds every 15 minutes. Reassurance of the victim is very important because death from snake bite is very rare. Do not slash the bite area and try to suck out the poison because this sort of heroism does more harm than good. Hospitals usually hold stocks of snake-bite serum. The best precaution is not walk in long grass with bare feet, sandals, or in shorts.

When swimming in an area where there are poisonous fish such as stone or scorpion fish (also called by a variety of local names) or sea urchins on rocky coasts, tread carefully or wear plimsolls/trainers. The sting of such fish is intensely painful. This can be relieved by immersing the injured part of the body in water as hot as you can bear for as long as it remains painful. This is not always very practical and you must take care not to scald yourself, but it does work. Avoid spiders and scorpions by keeping your bed away from the wall, look under lavatory seats and inside your shoes in the morning. In the rare event of being bitten, consult a doctor.

Other afflictions

Remember that **rabies** is endemic in many Southeast Asian countries. If bitten by a domestic animal, try to have it captured for observation and see a doctor at once. Treatment with human diploid vaccine is now extremely effective and worth seeking out if the likelihood of having contracted rabies is high. A course of anti-rabies vaccine before leaving home might be a good idea.

Dengue fever is present in most of the countries of Southeast Asia. It is a viral disease transmitted by mosquito and causes severe headaches and body pains. Complicated types of dengue known as haemorrhagic fevers occur throughout Asia but usually in persons who have caught the disease a second time. Thus, although it is a very serious type it is rarely caught by visitors. There is no treatment, you must just avoid mosquito bites.

Intestinal worms are common and the more serious ones, such as hook worm can be contracted by walking barefoot on infested earth or beaches.

Influenza and **respiratory diseases** are common, perhaps made worse by polluted cities and rapid temperature and climatic changes – accentuated by air-conditioning.

Prickly heat is a very common itchy rash, best avoided by frequent washing and by wearing loose clothing and is helped by the use of talcum powder, allowing the skin to dry thoroughly after washing.

Athlete's foot and other **fungal infections** are best treated by sunshine and a proprietary preparation such as Tolnaftate.

Hangovers can be bad in the tropics as alcohol accentuates dehydration. The best way to avoid them is by drinking several litres of water if you have been drinking.

When you return home

On returning home, remember to take anti-malarial tablets for 6 weeks. If you have had attacks of diarrhoea, it is worth having a stool specimen tested in case you have picked up amoebic dysentery. If you have been living rough, a blood test may also be worthwhile to detect worms and other parasites.

Basic supplies

See page 10.

Further health information

Information regarding country-by-country malaria risk can be obtained from the World Health Organization (WHO) or in Britain from the Ross Institute, London School of Hygiene and Tropical Medicine, Keppel Street, London WCIE 7HT which also publishes a highly recommended book: *The preser-vation of personal health in warm climates.* The Centres for Disease Control (CDC) in Atlanta, Georgia, USA will provide equivalent information. The organization MASTA (Medical Advisory Service for Travellers Abroad) also based at the London School of Hygiene and Tropical Medicine (T 071 631-4408) will provide up-to-date country-by-country information on health risks. Further information on medical problems overseas can be obtained from the new edition of *Travellers health, how to stay healthy abroad,* edited by Richard Dawood (Oxford University Press, 1992). This revised and updated edition is highly recommended, especially to the intrepid traveller. A more general publication, with hints on health and much more besides, is John Hatt's recommended new edition of *The tropical traveller* (Penguin, 1993).

SOUTHEAST ASIAN REALM

CONTENTS

MAINLAND & ISLAND SOUTHEAST ASIA

A name to conjure with

Since the end of the Second World War, the term 'Southeast Asia' has come to be widely used to describe that portion of the world that lies between India, China and Australasia. Early Chinese and Japanese traders and mariners referred to the area as *Nanyang* or *Nangyo* (both meaning the 'Southern Seas'), while Indian texts talked of a *Suvarnabhumi* ('Land of Gold') or *Suvarnadvipa* ('Island of Gold'), and Persian and Arab accounts of *Zir-e Bad* (the lands 'Below the Wind(s)'). However all the terms employed are loose and indistinct. In the first 2 cases, the terms merely describe Southeast Asia with respect to its geographical position vis à vis China and Japan. *Suvarnabhumi* and *Suvarnadvipa* – the El Dorados of the East – meanwhile probably only related to the Malay Peninsula, Sumatra, and possibly Java and parts of Burma. *Zir-e Bad* just made reference to the lands sailors arrived at by sailing E on the monsoon winds.

During the colonial period, Southeast Asia graduated to the status of a region – albeit still loose and ill-defined – virtually by default. To the Western colonial powers, it was that area which lay between the 2 cultural superpowers of China and India. The terms used to describe it indicate that it was viewed very much as a residual region: Further India, Chin-India, Little China, Indochina, the Indian Archipelago, the Far Eastern Tropics, and the Tropical Far East. In this way, Southeast Asia became defined either as an appendage of India, or as a tropical extension of China and Japan. The terms also indicate the extent to which the region has been overshadowed by its more illustrious neighbours, India and China.

The first use in English of the term 'Southeast Asia' may have been when the Reverend Howard Malcolm, an American from Boston, published a book with the title *Travels in South-Eastern Asia* in 1839. He describes the area covered by his book as including 'all the region between China and the Bay of Bengal, southward of the Thibet Mountains'. Although Malcolm, as well as a handful of anthropologists and other scholars, began to write about 'Southeast Asia' towards the middle of the 19th century, the colonial period prevented the further evolution of a Southeast Asian 'identity'. As Portugal, Britain, France, Holland and Spain (and later the United States) divided the region between themselves, leaving only Thailand with its independence, so the countries of the region became orientated toward one or other of the colonial powers. Economically, politically and to an extent, culturally, the countries' concerns and interests were focused outwards, beyond the region, postponing, for nearly a century, the development of a Southeast Asian regional identity.

It was not until the 1940s that the term Southeast Asia began to be more widely used again in English. In response to the Japanese invasion of Southeast Asia, wartime British and

American leaders Churchill and Roosevelt created the South-East Asia Command (SEAC) in 1943, placing it under the leadership of Lord Louis Mountbatten. The creation of SEAC brought the term Southeast Asia into widespread and general usage. This was greatly accentuated by the onset of the Second Indochinese War in Vietnam in 1965, and growing US involvement in that war. The media coverage of the 'War in Southeast Asia', and particularly television coverage, brought the region to the attention of the public across the globe.

LAND AND LIFE

A region that has lost its heart to the sea

It is not so much the land, but the sea, which dominates Southeast Asia. At the heart of the region are the shallow waters of the South China Sea. During the last Ice Age, 15,000 years ago (when sea levels were considerably lower than they are today), much of this would have been exposed, linking the islands of Sumatra, Java and Borneo, and forming a Southeast Asian continent. In a quite literal sense therefore, Southeast Asia lost its heart to the sea. But the drowning of the once sprawling land mass has had one important side-effect: it has made the region uniquely accessible by sea. The region has a longer coastline than any other area of comparable size. It is no accident therefore that Southeast Asia's early history is one based upon maritime empires and trade.

The geological evolution of Southeast Asia

Originally, the world consisted of just 2 supercontinents: Gondwanaland to the S, and Laurasia to the N. Through a process of 'continental drift' whereby the earth's continental plates slide over and under each other, sections of Gondwanaland and Laurasia have broken away and ploughed

across the oceans to take up their present positions. In the case of Southeast Asia this 'rifting' has been particularly complex. Over a period of 350 million years, successive fragments of Gondwanaland have detached themselves and drifted northwards eventually to collide with the other supercontinent, Laurasia. This process explains the peculiar spider-like shape of the Indonesian island of Sulawesi which consists of 2 halves that did not collide until the Miocene (15 million years ago).

Each fragment of Southeast Asia became a 'Noah's Ark' of plants and animals isolated from outside disturbance. The effect of this isolation can be seen reflected in the remarkable change in the fauna of the region from the Indo-Malayan zoological realm in the N, to the Austro-Malayan in the S. The point

HEAT AND LUST: COLONIAL IMPRESSIONS

Many colonial visitors were tempted to see a link between the hot climate and the Southeast Asian character. In 1811, John Joseph Stockdale, a British publisher, ascribed what he saw as the "wantonness" of Javanese women to the warm temperatures. The British administrator William Marsden wrote in the same year that the Sumatran tradition of polygamy was based on the "influence of a warm atmosphere upon the passions of men" and the "cravings of other disordered appetites". Nor were the judgemental links between climate and activity restricted purely to people: Robert Mac Micking a British traveller who visited the Philippines in the mid 19th century wrote that because of the heat the Filipino dog did not have the same "strength or swiftness, nor is he of equal courage, sincerity and gentleness of character" to those faithful hounds back home.

of change from one to the other is known as Wallace's Line. This runs approximately N to S between the Indonesian islands of Bali and Lombok and then through the Makassar Strait, and is named after one of Victorian England's greatest naturalists, Alfred Russel Wallace. It was Wallace, working in the former Dutch East Indies, who encouraged Charles Darwin to publish his seminal *Origin of species by means of natural selection*. For, independently of Darwin, Wallace too arrived at a theory of natural selection and coincidentally sent the pa-

per outlining his ideas to Darwin in England. Darwin was appalled that his work might be eclipsed, but nevertheless acted entirely properly. Papers by both men were presented to a meeting of the Linnean Society in London in 1858, where they provoked surprisingly little reaction. One year later, in 1859, The *Origin of species* was published.

Despite Southeast Asia's complex geological origins, it is clearly demarcated from the regions that surround it. To the N are the highlands of Burma, Thailand, Laos and Vietnam which form

FIELDS IN THE FOREST – SHIFTING CULTIVATION

Shifting cultivation, also known as slash-and-burn agriculture or swiddening, as well as by a variety of local terms, is one of the characteristic farming systems of Southeast Asia. It is a low-intensity form of agriculture, in which land is cleared from the forest through burning, cultivated for a few years, and then left to regenerate over 10-30 years. It takes many forms, but an important distinction can be made between shifting field systems where fields are rotated but the settlement remains permanently sited, and migratory systems where the shifting cultivators shift both field (swidden) and settlement. The land is usually only rudimentarily cleared, tree stumps being left in the ground, and seeds sown in holes made by punching the soil with a dibble stick.

For many years, shifting cultivators were regarded as 'primitives' who follow an essentially primitive form of agriculture and their methods were contrasted unfavourably with 'advanced' settled rice farmers. There are still many government officials in Southeast Asia who continue to adhere to this mistaken belief, arguing that shifting cultivators are the principal cause of forest loss and soil erosion. They are, therefore, painted as the villains in the region's environmental crisis, neatly sidestepping the considerably more detrimental impact that commercial logging has had on Southeast Asia's forest resources.

Shifting cultivators have an intimate knowledge of the land, plants and animals on which they depend. One study of a Dayak tribe, the Kantu' of Kalimantan (Borneo), discovered that households were cultivating an average of 17 rice varieties and 21 other food crops each year in a highly complex system. Even more remarkably, Harold Conklin's classic 1957 study of the Hanunóo of the Philippines – a study which is a benchmark for such work even today – found that they identified 40 types and subtypes of rocks and minerals when classifying different soils. The shifting agricultural systems are usually also highly productive in labour terms, allowing far more leisure time than farmers using permanent field systems.

But shifting cultivation contains the seeds of its own extinction. Extensive, and geared to low population densities and abundant land, it is coming under pressure in a region where land is becoming an increasingly scarce resource, where patterns of life are dictated by an urban-based elite, and where populations are pressing on the means of subsistence.

a natural barrier with China and India. Running from western Burma southwards through Sumatra and Java and finally northwards to Sulawesi and the Philippines, the region is bounded by a series of deep-sea trenches. These mark the point at which the earth's plates plunge one beneath the other and are zones of intense volcanic activity. Indonesia alone has about 300 volcanoes, of which 200 have been active in historical times, and 127 are active today. The volcanic activity of the area was most dramatically displayed when Krakatau (Krakatoa), located in the Sunda Straits between Java and Sumatra, erupted in 1883. Today, Anak Krakatoa (Child of Krakatoa) and the other remaining islands, are a reserve where scientists have been able to record the recolonization by plants and animals of an island that had effectively died.

Climate

At sea level, **temperatures** are fairly uniform, both across the region and through the year. With the exception of the NE corner of Vietnam, annual average sea-level temperatures are close to 26°C. Travelling N and S from the equator, seasonal variations do become more pronounced. Therefore, while Singapore, virtually on the equator, has a monthly average temperature which varies by a mere 1.5°C, Sittwe (Akyab) in Burma which is 2,600 km to the N – has a monthly average which ranges across 7°C. The sea can also have a significant moderating effect. For example, Mandalay, on the same latitude as Sittwe but over 400 km inland, has a monthly average which spans 10°C. But these figures are monthly averages: before the onset of the SW monsoon in Apr or May, temperatures during the day in the Dry Zone of Burma and in Northeastern Thailand can reach a debilitating 40°C or more. At times like this nothing moves; even the farmers remain in the shade.

Altitude has the greatest effect on temperature, and in the highlands of the region it can become distinctly cool. It is not surprising that the colonial powers built hill retreats in these areas: in the Cameron Highlands and at Fraser's Hill on the Malay Peninsula, at Brastagi in Sumatra (Indonesia), at Mymyo in Burma, and Dalat in southern Vietnam. In the Cameron Highlands, with its rose gardens, afternoon teas and half-timbered houses and log fires, it is easy to believe you are in rural England.

Patterns of **rainfall** in the region are more complex. They vary considerably both across the region and through the year, and seasonality – both for the farmer and the visitor – is linked to rainfall, not to temperature. The pattern of rainfall is intimately related to the monsoons, a term which is taken from the Arabic word *mawsim*, meaning 'season'.

Much of island Southeast Asia experiences what is termed an 'equatorial monsoon' climate. Annual rainfall usually exceeds 2,000 mm and can be as high as 5,000 mm. Close to the equator rainfall *tends* to be distributed evenly through the year, and there is no marked dry season. However, travelling N and S from the equator, the dry season becomes more pronounced, and rainfall concentrated in one or 2 seasonal peaks. This pattern of rainfall is determined by 2 monsoons: the NE and the SW monsoons. The NE monsoon, prevails from Nov/Dec to Feb/Mar and forms the wet season. While the SW monsoon, extends from Jun to Aug/Sept and brings dry conditions to the area.

In mainland Southeast Asia, rainfall tends to be less than in the archipelago (less than 1500 mm), and more seasonally concentrated with the dry season in many places extending over 5 or 6 months. In comparison with island Southeast Asia, the seasons on the mainland are generally reversed. The NE monsoon from Nov to Mar brings cool, dry air to Thailand, Burma and much of Indochina. During this period rainfall may be very low indeed. Just before the SW monsoon arrives in Jun, the heating of the land can lead to torrential thunderstorms – referred to in Burma and Thailand as 'mango rains'. The SW monsoon corresponds with the period of heaviest rainfall, and over much of the mainland 80%-97% of the year's rain falls between the months of May and Oct.

It should be emphasized that local wind systems and the shadowing effects of mountains often distort this generalized pattern of rainfall. Nonetheless, like the English, Southeast Asians talk endlessly

about the weather. The seasons – and this means rain – determine the very pattern of life in the region. Rice cultivation, and its associated festivals, is dependent in most areas on the arrival of the rains, and religious ceremonies are timed to coincide with the seasons. Kampoon Boontawee in his novel *Luuk Isan* (Child of the Northeast) about village life in the Northeastern region of Thailand writes: "When Koon and Jundi and their fathers arrived at the *phuyaiban*'s [headman's] house, the men were talking about what they always talked about – the lack of rain and the lack of food in the village".

SOUTHEAST ASIA: MONTHLY RAINFALL AND TEMPERATURE

		Jan	Feb	Mar	Apr	May	Jun	Jul	Aug	Sep	Oct	Nov	Dec
Singapore	°C	25.5	26	26.5	27	27	27	27	27	26.5	26.5	26	26
1°N, 104°E, 10m	mm	216	155	165	175	183	170	172	216	180	208	254	264
Cameron Hgh	°C	18.5	18.5	19.5	19.5	19.5	19	19	19	19	18.5	18.5	18
5°N, 101°E, 4500m	mm	152	132	162	312	267	127	122	198	213	328	307	246
Sittwe	°C	21	22.5	26	28.5	29	28	27	27	27.5	27.5	25.5	22
20°N, 93°E, 20m	mm	3	5	13	50	348	1255	1364	1080	625	294	127	15
Rangoon	°C	25	26	29	30.5	29	27	26.5	26.5	27	27.5	26.5	25
17°N, 93°E, 18m	mm	5	5	7	35	307	467	546	500	381	178	71	7
Saigon	°C	26	27	29	29.5	29	28	27	28	27	27	26.5	26
11°N, 107°E, SL	mm	17	2	15	48	221	333	307	282	343	272	114	63
Kupang	°C	25.5	26	26.5	26.5	26.5	25	24.5	25.5	26	26.5	26	26.5
10°S, 124°E, 48m	mm	572	361	107	41	2	43	2	2	2	180	104	266
Hanoi	°C	16.5	16.5	19.5	22.5	26.5	28.5	28.5	28.5	27	25.5	21.5	19
21°N, 106°E, SL	mm	30	40	46	71	193	244	289	317	305	111	61	30
Lashio	°C	15.5	17	21.5	24	25	25	24.5	24.5	24.5	22.5	19	16
23°N, 98°E, 2802m	mm	8	8	15	56	175	249	305	323	198	144	68	22
Luang Prab'ng	°C	20.5	22.5	25.5	28	29	28.5	28	28	28	26	23	21
20°N, 102°E, 942m	mm	15	17	30	109	162	155	231	300	165	78	30	13

☐ denotes hot season   ■ denotes wet season

Temperatures are in degrees Celsius, rainfall in mm. Note that the 'rainy' and 'hot' seasons are relative to the prevailing climate in each area. Near the equator the distinction between 'wet' and 'dry' seasons is less pronounced.

The Southeast Asian landscape

On the mainland, mountains, valleys and rivers run N-S. The great rivers of the region are found here: the Irrawaddy, Sittang, Salween, Chao Phraya, Mekong and the Red rivers. It is along these river valleys that people have settled in the greatest numbers, exploiting the rich alluvial soils and the abundance of water by cultivating wet rice. Except for narrow bands of lowland – for example, along the Vietnamese coast – much of the remainder of the mainland is mountainous. Here, tribal peoples such as the Hmong of N Thailand and Laos, and the Karen of Burma support themselves through shifting cultivation. One of the challenges facing the region is how to protect these people and their way of life – and the forests themselves – when population pressure is growing and commercialization spreading.

In island Southeast Asia there are few favourable areas for human settlement. Much of the lowland in places such as eastern Sumatra and southern Borneo is swamp, and rivers are short, offering only limited scope for rice cultivation. The highland areas are cloaked in forest, and their traditional inhabitants such as the Dayaks of the island of Borneo and the tribes of Irian Jaya practise shifting cultivation like their brothers on the mainland. But, the islands are not entirely devoid of areas with significant agricultural potential. The fertile volcanic soils of central Java for example have supported a large population for hundreds of years. Today Java's population is nearly 110 million, and agricultural population densities in some areas exceed 2,000 people/sq km. Taking advantage of the abundance of rain and the rich soils, farmers grow up to 3 crops of rice each year.

Tropical forests

Across Southeast Asia from N Burma through the arc of the Indonesian islands eastwards to Irian Jaya, tropical rainforest – of which there are 13 different types – predominates. Southeast Asia supports the largest area of tropical rainforest in the world outside Latin America. The core areas, located on the islands of Borneo and New Guinea and in Peninsular Malaysia, are possibly the most diverse of all the world's terrestrial ecosystems. In a single hectare of Malayan rainforest there may be as many as 176 species of tree with a diameter of 10 cm or more, and island Southeast Asia as a whole contains 25,000 species of flowering plant – 10% of the world's flora. It is because of this bewildering diversity that environmentalists claim the forest resource must be preserved. And not just because mankind has a moral duty, but also because the forests are an invaluable genetic and pharmaceutical warehouse. Currently over 10% of all prescription drugs are derived from tropical forest products, and the great majority of species have yet to be named and recorded, let alone chemically investigated.

Water for life: wet rice cultivation

Rice probably spread into Southeast Asia from a core area which spanned the highlands from Assam (India) to N Vietnam. Some of the earliest evidence of agriculture in the world has been uncovered in and around the village of Ban Chiang in Northeastern Thailand, and also from Bac-son in N Vietnam. However archaeologists are far from agreed about the dating and significance of the evidence. Some believe that rice may have been cultivated as early as 7,000 BC; others say it dates back no further than 3,000-2,000 BC.

By the time the first Europeans arrived in the 15th century the crop was well-established as the staple for the region. Only on the dry islands of Timor and N Maluku (in Indonesia) did the environment preclude its cultivation.

Today other staples such as taro (a root crop) and sago (produced from the sago palm) are frowned upon, being widely regarded as 'poor man's food'. The im-

portance of rice can be seen reflected in the degree to which culture and crop have become intermeshed, and in the mythology and ceremony associated

THE CYCLE OF WET RICE CULTIVATION

There are an estimated 120,000 rice varieties. Rice seed – either selected from the previous harvest or, more commonly, purchased from a dealer or agricultural extension office – is soaked overnight before being sown into a carefully prepared nursery bed. Today farmers are likely to plant one of the Modern Varieties or MVs bred for their high yields.

The nursery bed into which the seeds are broadcast (scattered) is often a farmer's best land, with the most stable water supply. After a month the seedlings are up-rooted and taken out to the paddy fields. These will also have been ploughed, puddled and harrowed, turning the heavy clay soil into a saturated slime. Traditionally buffalo and cattle would have performed the task; today rotavators, and even tractors are becoming more common. The seedlings are transplanted into the mud in clumps. Before transplanting the tops of the seedlings are twisted off (this helps to increase yield) and then they are pushed in to the soil in neat rows. The work is back-breaking and it is not unusual to find labourers – both men and women – receiving a premium – either a bonus on top of the usual daily wage or a free meal at midday, to which marijuana is sometimes added to ease the pain.

After transplanting, it is essential that the water supply is carefully controlled. The key to high yields is a constant flow of water, regulated to take account of the growth of the rice plant. In 'rain-fed' systems where the farmer relies on rainfall to water the crop, he has to hope that it will be neither too much nor too little. Elaborate ceremonies are performed to appease the rice goddess and to ensure bountiful rainfall.

In areas where rice is grown in irrigated conditions, farmers need not concern themselves with the day-to-day pattern of rainfall, and in such areas 2 or even 3 crops can be grown each year. But such systems need to be carefully managed, and it is usual for one man to be in charge of irrigation. In Bali he is known as the *klian subak*, in North Thailand as the *hua naa muang fai*. He decides when water should be released, organizes labour to repair dykes and dams and to clear channels, and decides which fields should receive the water first.

Traditionally, while waiting for the rice to mature, a farmer would do little except weed the crop from time to time. He and his family might move out of the village and live in a field hut to keep a close eye on the maturing rice. Today, farmers also apply chemical fertilisers and pesticides to protect the crop and ensure maximum yield. After 90-130 days, the crop should be ready for harvesting.

Harvesting also demands intensive labour. Traditionally, farmers in a village would secure their harvesters through systems of reciprocal labour exchange; now it is more likely for a harvester to be paid in cash. After harvesting, the rice is threshed, sometimes out in the field, and then brought back to the village to be stored in a rice barn or sold. It is only at the end of the harvest, with the rice safely stored in the barn, that the festivals begin. As Thai farmers say, having rice in the barn is like having money in the bank.

THE UNIVERSAL STIMULANT – THE BETEL NUT

Throughout the countryside in Southeast Asia, and in more remote towns, it is common to meet men and women whose teeth are stained black, and gums red, by continuous chewing of the 'betel nut'. This, though, is a misnomer. The betel 'nut' is not chewed at all: the 3 crucial ingredients that make up a betel 'wad' are the nut of the areca palm (*Areca catechu*), the leaf or catkin of the betel vine (*Piper betle*), and lime. When these 3 ingredients are combined with saliva they act as a mild stimulant. Other ingredients (people have their own recipes) are tobacco, gambier, various spices and the gum of *Acacia catechu*. The habit, though also common in South Asia and parts of China, seems to have evolved in Southeast Asia and it is mentioned in the very earliest chronicles. The lacquer betel boxes of Burma and Thailand, and the brass and silver ones of Indonesia, illustrate the importance of chewing betel in social intercourse. Galvao in his journal of 1544 noted: "They use it so continuously that they never take it from their mouths; therefore these people can be said to go around always ruminating". Among Westernized Southeast Asians the habit is frowned upon: the disfigurement and ageing that it causes, and the stained walls and floors that result from the constant spitting, are regarded as distasteful products of an earlier age. But beyond the elite it is still widely practised.

with its cultivation. The American anthropologist DeYoung, who worked in a village in Central Thailand in the late 1950s, writes that the farmer:

> "...reverences the crop he grows as a sentient being; he marks its stages of growth by ceremonies; and he propitiates the spirit of the soil in which it grows and the good or evil spirits that may help or harm it. He considers rice to possess a life spirit (*kwan*) and to grow much as a human being grows; when it bears grain, it has become 'pregnant' like a mother, and the rice is the seed or child of the Rice Goddess".

Wet rice, more than any other staple crop, is dependent on an ample and constant supply of water. The links between rice and water, wealth and poverty, and abundance and famine are clear. Throughout the region, there are numerous rituals and songs which honour the 'gift of water' and dwell upon the vagaries of the monsoon. Water-throwing festivals, designed to induce abundant rainfall, are widespread, and if they do not have the desired effect villagers will often resort to magic. The struggle to ensure a constant supply of water can also be seen reflected in the sophisticated irrigation systems of Northern Thailand, Bali and Java. Less obvious, but no less ingenious and complex, farmers without the benefits of irrigation have also developed sophisticated cultivation strategies designed to maintain production through flood and drought.

People and land

An Indian king is reported to have said to a man boasting about the extent of the lands ruled by the King of Siam: "It is true, I admit, that they are greater in extent than mine, but then the King of Golconda is a king of men, while your king is only king of forests and mosquitoes". Southeast Asia has always been relatively land-rich when compared with India and China. In 1600 the population of the region was probably about 20 million, and even by 1800 this had only increased to 30 million. Except for a few areas such as the island of Java and the Red River Delta of Vietnam, the region was sparsely populated. Forests and wildlife abounded, and the inhabitants at times had great trouble maintaining their small areas of 'civilized space'. Even today local words for 'forest' also often imply 'wild' and 'uncivilized'.

The wealth of forest resources has meant that most buildings – even those of the richest nobles and merchants – have always been constructed of wood, bamboo and other forest products. The only exception to this rule was in the construction of religious edifices. In these, stone and brick were used, no doubt signifying the permanence of faith, and the impermanence of men. Today the building skills of the early civilizations of Southeast Asia can be seen reflected in the temples of Prambanan and Borobudur (Java), Angkor (Cambodia), Champa (Vietnam), Sukhothai and Ayutthaya (Thailand), and Pagan (Burma). In most cases the temples stand stark and isolated, which accentuates their visual impact. However, when they were built they would have been surrounded by wooden houses, shops and the bustle and infrastructure of an ancient ceremonial city. These have now rotted away in the region's humid climate.

The abundance of land in Southeast Asia during historical times meant that people were very highly valued. A king's wealth was not measured in terms of the size of his kingdom, but the number of people that came under his control. Land was not 'owned' in the usual sense; ownership was transitory and related to utilization. When a farmer stopped cultivating a piece of land it would revert to the ownership of the sultan or king, but ultimately to God. The value of people becomes clear in the art of warfare in the region. In general, the objective was not to gain land, but to capture prisoners who could then be carried off to become slaves on the victorious king's land. This principle held true for the great kingdoms of Burma, Siam and Cambodia and the remotest tribes of

Borneo. At times entire villages would be transported into captivity. Battles rarely led to many casualties. There was much noise, but little action, and the French envoy Simon de la Loubère in his 17th century account of Siam wrote: "Kill not is the order, which the King of Siam gives his troops, when he sends them into the field".

PRE-COLONIAL HISTORY

Prehistory

Histories are never simple, cut and dried affairs, and Southeast Asia's prehistory must rank among the most confused. Not only is the evidence available to archaeologists fragmentary and highly dispersed (partly because the humid conditions promote rapid decay), but it has also been subject to multiple interpretations. At the core of the debate, is the question as to whether Southeast Asia was a cultural 'receptacle' or a 'hearth' of civilization in itself. In other words, have people, technologies and cultures diffused into the region from the outside, or has Southeast Asia evolved a 'personality' independent of such influences? Ultimately the answer must be one of degree, not of kind.

Racial groups and migrations

The bulk of Southeast Asia's population are Southern Mongoloid. However there are small numbers of Negritos and Melanesians still living in the region; the Semang and Sakais of Malaysia, for example. However, these true indigenous inhabitants of Southeast Asia have been overwhelmed and marginalized by more recent arrivals. First, from about 5000 BC, there began a gradual southerly migration of Southern Mongoloids from southern China and eastern Tibet. This did not occur in a great wave, as at one time postulated, but as a slow process of displacement and replacement.

Later, during the early centuries of the Christian era, the political consolidation of the Chinese empire displaced increasing numbers of Deutero-Malays, as well as Tais, Khmers, Mons, Burmans, Viets and the various hill tribes of the mainland. These groups, the ancestors of the present populations of Thailand, Burma, Indochina, Malaysia and Indonesia, used the great river valleys of the region – the Mekong, Irrawaddy, Salween and Chao Phraya – as their routes S.

Southeast Asia has therefore represented a fragmented land bridge between Asia and Australasia into and through which successive racial groups have filtered. The original inhabitants of the region have all but disappeared.

Most have been absorbed into the racial fabric of more recent arrivals; many others have been displaced into the highlands or out of the region altogether. The Melanesians for example now inhabit islands in the Pacific including New Guinea, while remnant Proto-Malays include the forest-dwelling Dayaks of Borneo and the Bataks of Sumatra.

Not only did these more recent migrants physically displace the earlier inhabitants, they also displaced them culturally. They brought with them knowledge of metallurgy, rice cultivation, the domestication of livestock, and new religious beliefs. But these cultural elements were not incorporated wholesale and unchanged. The nature of the

---

In Siddhartha's Footsteps: A Short History Of Buddhism

Buddhism was founded by Siddhartha Gautama, a prince of the Sakya tribe of Nepal, who probably lived between 563 and 483 BC. He achieved enlightenment and the word *buddha* means 'fully enlightened one', or 'one who has woken up'. Siddhartha Gautama is known by a number of titles. In the W, he is usually referred to as *The Buddha*, i.e. the historic Buddha (but not just Buddha); more common in Southeast Asia is the title *Sakyamuni*, or Sage of the Sakyas (referring to his tribal origins).

Over the centuries, the life of the Buddha has become part legend, and the Jataka tales which recount his various lives are colourful and convoluted. But, central to any Buddhist's belief is that he was born under a *sal* tree (*Shorea robusta*), that he achieved enlightenment under a bodhi tree (*Ficus religiosa*) in the Bodh Gaya Gardens, that he preached the First Sermon at Sarnath, and that he died at Kusinagara (all in India or Nepal).

The Buddda was born at Lumbini (in present-day Nepal), as Queen Maya was on her way to her parents' home. She had had a very auspicious dream before the child's birth of being impregnated by an elephant, whereupon a sage prophesied that Siddhartha would become either a great king or a great spiritual leader. His father, being keen that the first option of the prophesy be fulfilled, brought him up in all the princely skills (at which Siddhartha excelled) and ensured that he only saw beautiful things, not the harsher elements of life.

Despite his father's efforts Siddhartha saw 4 things while travelling between palaces – a helpless old man, a very sick man, a corpse being carried by lamenting relatives, and an ascetic, calm and serene as he begged for food. These episodes made an enormous impact on the young prince, and he renounced his princely origins and left home to study under a series of spiritual teachers. He finally discovered the path to enlightenment at the Bodh Gaya Gardens in India. He then proclaimed his thoughts to a small group of disciples at Sarnath, near Benares, and continued to preach and attract followers until he died at the age of 81 at Kusinagara.

Southeast Asian environment, the abundance of land and food, and the passage of time, have all served to allow the development of a distinctly Southeast Asian cultural heritage.

The historic period: water for communication

Southeast Asia's fragmented geography has made the region remarkably accessible. Winds tend to be moderate and the abundance of wood close to the shoreline has enabled ship-building to flourish. This has had 2 effects: on the one hand, it has meant that Southeast Asia has felt the effects of successive seaborne invasions, and on the other that different parts of the region have been in surprisingly close contact with one another. This is reflected in commonalities of language, particularly in the archipelago, and in the universality of cultural traits such as the chewing of betel nut. During the historic period there have been 5 major infusions of culture and technology into Southeast Asia – all of which have left their imprint on the region: Indianization, Chinese influences, Buddhism, Islam and Westernization.

1. The Indianization of Southeast Asia
From the beginning of the 1st century AD, the allure of gold and spices brought Indian traders to the region. Although they were not on a proselytizing mission – they came to make money

---

In the First Sermon at the deer park in Sarnath, the Buddha preached the Four Truths, which are still considered the root of Buddhist belief and practical experience. These are the 'Noble Truth' that suffering exists, the 'Noble Truth' that there is a cause of suffering, the 'Noble Truth' that suffering can be ended, and the 'Noble Truth' that to end suffering it is necessary to follow the 'Noble Eightfold Path' – namely, right speech, livelihood, action, effort, mindfulness, concentration, opinion and intention.

Soon after the Buddha began preaching, a monastic order – the *Sangha* – was established. As the monkhood evolved in India, it also began to fragment as different sects developed different interpretations of the life of the Buddha. An important change was the belief that the Buddha was transcendent: he had never been born, nor had he died; he had always existed and his life on earth had been mere illusion. The emergence of these new concepts helped to turn what up until then was an ethical code of conduct, into a religion. It eventually led to the appearance of a new Buddhist movement, Mahayana Buddhism which split from the more traditional Theravada 'sect'.

Despite the division of Buddhism into 2 sects, the central tenets of the religion are common to both. Specifically, the principles pertaining to the Four Noble Truths, the Noble Eightfold Path, the Dependent Origination, the Law of Karma and nirvana. In addition, the principles of non-violence and tolerance are also embraced by both sects. In essence, the differences between the 2 are of emphasis and interpretation. Theravada Buddhism is strictly based on the original Pali Canon, while the Mahayana tradition stems from later Sanskrit texts. Mahayana Buddhism also allows a broader and more varied interpretation of the doctrine. Other important differences are that while the Thervada tradition is more 'intellectual' and self-obsessed, with an emphasis upon the attaining of wisdom and insight for oneself, Mahayana Buddhism stresses devotion and compassion towards others.

THE PRACTICE OF ISLAM: LIVING BY THE PROPHET

Islam is an Arabic word meaning 'submission to God'. As Muslims often point out, it is not just a religion but a total way of life. The main Islamic scripture is the Koran or Quran, the name being taken from the Arabic *al-qur'an* or 'the recitation'. The Koran is divided into 114 *sura*, or 'units'. Most scholars are agreed that the Koran was partially written by the Prophet Mohammad. In addition to the Koran there are the hadiths, from the Arabic word *hadith* meaning 'story', which tell of the Prophet's life and works. These represent the second most important body of scriptures.

The practice of Islam is based upon 5 central tenets, known as the Pillars of Islam: Shahada (profession of faith), Salat (worship), Zakat (charity), *saum* (fasting) and Haj (pilgrimage). The mosque is the centre of religious activity. The 2 most important mosque officials are the *imam* – or leader – and the *khatib* or preacher – who delivers the Friday sermon.

The **Shahada** is the confession, and lies at the core of any Muslim's faith. It involves reciting, sincerely, 2 statements: 'There is no god, but God', and 'Mohammad is the Messenger [Prophet] of God'. A Muslim will do this at every **Salat**. This is the daily prayer ritual which is performed 5 times a day, at sunrise, midday, mid-afternoon, sunset and at night. There is also the important Friday noon worship. The Salat is performed by a Muslim bowing and then prostrating himself in the direction of Mecca (in Indonesian *kiblat*, in Arabic *qibla*). In hotel rooms throughout Indonesia, Malaysia and Brunei, there is nearly always a little arrow, painted on the ceiling – or sometimes inside a wardrobe – indicating the direction of Mecca and labelled kiblat. The faithful are called to worship by a mosque official. Beforehand, a worshipper must wash to ensure ritual purity. The Friday midday service is performed in the mosque and includes a sermon given by the *khatib*.

A third essential element of Islam is **Zakat** – charity or alms-giving. A Muslim

– this resulted in the introduction of Hindu-Buddhist culture and the so-called 'Indianization' of Southeast Asia. 'Indianization' was the result not of the immigration of large number of Indians; rather the gradual infusion of an Indian cultural tradition introduced by small numbers of traders and priest-scholars. Given the nature of the contact, it is not surprising that the Indian influence was geographically uneven. Northern Vietnam – then under Chinese suzerainty – was never affected. Elsewhere however, kings quickly adopted and adapted elements of the Indian cultural tradition. For example, the cult of the *deva raja* – or 'god king'- in which the ruler claimed to be a reincarnation of Siva or Vishnu (or to be a Bodhisattva – a future Bud-

dha) was used to legitimate kingship. Pagan (Burma) and Angkor (Cambodia), 2 of the greatest archaeological sites in the world, bear testament to the power and influence of these 'Indianized' empires.

2. Chinese influences

At the same time as this 'Indianization' was underway, Imperial China was also beginning to intensify its links with the region. This was prompted in the 5th century AD by the Jin Dynasty's loss of access to the central Asian caravan routes which brought luxury goods from the West. In response, maritime trading routes through the Southeast Asian archipelago were developed by the Chinese. Tribute-bearing missions from the states of Southeast Asia to the Chinese

is supposed to give up his 'surplus' (according to the Koran); through time this took on the form of a tax levied according to the wealth of the family. In Indonesia there is no official Zakat as there is in Saudi Arabia, but good Muslims are expected to contribute a tithe to the Muslim community. In Bahasa Indonesia, *zakat* is translated as 'obligatory alms'.

The fourth pillar of Islam is **saum** or fasting. The daytime month-long fast of Ramadan is a time of contemplation, worship and piety – the Islamic equivalent of lent. Muslims are expected to read one-thirtieth of the Koran each night. Muslims who are ill or on a journey have dispensation from fasting, but otherwise they are only permitted to eat during the night until "so much of the dawn appears that a white thread can be distinguished from a black one".

The **Haj** or Pilgrimmage to the holy city of Mecca in Saudi Arabia is required of all Muslims once in their lifetime if they can afford to make the journey and are physically able to. It is restricted to a certain time of the year, beginning on the 8th day of the Muslim month of Dhu-I-Hijja. Men who have been on the Haj are given the title *Haji*, and women *hajjah*.

The Koran also advises on a number of other practices and customs, in particular the prohibitions on usury, the eating of pork, the taking of alcohol, and gambling. In Indonesia, these are not strictly interpreted. Islamic banking laws have not been introduced, drinking is fairly widespread – although not in all areas – and the national lottery might be interpreted as a form of gambling. There is quite a powerful Islamic revival in Malaysia – as well as in Brunei and Indonesia – which is attempting to change what is perceived as the rather lax approach to Islamic prohibitions. For example, there is an effort to have the national lottery abolished.

The use of the veil in its most extreme form is not common in Indonesia but is becoming *de rigeur* in Brunei and in areas of Malaysia. The Koran says nothing about the need for women to veil, although it does stress the necessity of women dressing modestly.

court became more common and the settlement of Chinese in the region increased as the area grew in commercial importance. In turn, the cultural impact of China also became more pronounced. Chinese medical theory, technology, cloth, games, music, and calligraphy were all assimilated to a greater or lesser degree. The Chinese diplomat Chou Ta-kuan who visited the city of Angkor in 1296 notes in his journal the large number of his countrymen who had arrived in the city and were gradually being absorbed into the social fabric of the kingdom:

"The Chinese who follow the sea as a profession take advantage of their being in this country to dispense with wearing clothes. Rice is easy to obtain, women are easy to find, the houses are easy to run, personal property is easy to come by, commerce is easy to engage in. Thus there are constantly those who direct themselves towards this country".

3. Buddhism

By the early part of the second millennium the elitist cult of the god-king had become corrupt and degenerate, and was in decline on the mainland. At the same time a third infusion of culture was underway. During the early part of the 12th century, Burmese Buddhist monks travelled to Ceylon and came in contact with Theravada Buddhism (the 'Way of the Elders'). They returned to Burma with news of this populist faith and aggressively spread the word. Unlike the deva raja cult it was an inclusive, rather than an exclusive religion, and it found a willing and receptive audience among the common people. By the 15th century Theravada Buddhism was the dominant religion across much of the mainland – in Burma, Thailand, Laos, and Cambodia.

Buddhism shares the belief, in common with Hinduism, in rebirth. A person goes through countless lives and the experience of one life is conditioned by the acts in a previous one. This is the Law of Karma (act or deed, from Pali *kamma*), the law of cause and effect. But, it is not, as commonly thought in the West, equivalent to fate.

For most people, nirvana is a distant goal, and they merely aim to accumulate merit by living good lives and performing good deeds such as giving alms to monks. In this way the layman embarks on the Path to Heaven. It is also co.. ion for a layman to become ordained, at some point in his life (usually as a young man), for a 3 month period during the Buddhist Rains Retreat.

Monks should endeavour to lead stringently ascetic lives. They must refrain from murder, theft, sexual intercourse, untruths, eating after noon, alcohol, entertainment, ornament, comfortable beds and wealth. They are allowed to own only a begging bowl, 3 pieces of clothing, a razor, needle, belt and water filter. They can only eat food that they have received through begging. Anyone who is male, over 20, and not a criminal can become a monk.

Theravada Buddhism (Hinayana)

The 'Way of the Elders', is believed to be closest to Buddhist as it originally developed in India. It is often referred to by the term 'Hinayana' (Lesser Vehicle), a disparaging name foisted onto Theravadans by Mahayanists. This form of Buddhism is the dominant contemporary religion in the mainland Southeast Asian countries of Thailand, Cambodia, Laos and Burma.

In Theravadan Buddhism, the his-

toric Buddha, Sakyamuni, is revered above all else and most images of the Buddha are of Sakyamuni. Importantly, and unlike Mahayana Buddhism, the Buddha image is only meant to serve as a meditation aid. In theory, it does not embody supernatural powers, and it is not supposed to be worshipped. But, the popular need for objects of veneration has meant that most images *are* worshipped. Pilgrims bring flowers and incense, and prostrate themselves in front of the image. This is a Mahayanist influence which has been embraced by Theravadans.

Mahayana Buddhism

In the 1st century AD a new movement evolved in South India. Initially the differences between this and the 'original' Theravada tradition were not great. But in time the 2 diverged, with the 'new' tradition gaining converts at the expense of its rival. Eventually, a new term was coined – Mahayana Buddhism or the Greater Vehicle. Although the schism is usually presented as a revolutionary development, a gradual evolution is more accurate. The most important difference between Mahayana and Theravada Buddhism is that the principal aim of Mahayana Buddhism should not be to attain enlightenment only for oneself, but to reach Bodhisattvahood (someone who embodies the essence of enlightenment) and then to remain on earth to assist others in their quest for nirvana.

Mahayana Buddhism was a response to a popular appeal for a more approachable and accessible religion – in India, at the time, the Hindu gods Siva and Vishnu were attracting substantial numbers of followers and Buddhism had to respond in some way. Monks were no longer required to retire from everyday life in their ultimately selfish quest for nirvana; they were to lead active lives in the community. And, no longer was there just one distant historic Buddha to look up to; there was a pantheon of Buddhas and Bodhisattvas, all objects of veneration, worship and prayer. Now, Buddhas and Bodhisattvas such as the Buddhas Amitabha, Vajrapani, Vairocana and Avalokitsvara (all various reincarnations of the Buddha) could actively intervene in the world for the betterment of mankind. Within Mahayana Buddhism there was a vast growth in doctrine (contained in the *sutras*) which accompanied this dramatic growth in the numbers of Buddhas and Bodhisattvas.

Mahayana Buddhism became the dominant form of Buddhism practiced in Northern Asia (China and Japan), and also in ancient Cambodia and Indonesia. Today, in Southeast Asia, it is most widely practiced in Vietnam where it has, in most instances, fused with the Chinese 'religions', Taoism and Confucianism.

4. Islam

In island Southeast Asia, a similar displacement of an elitist Hindu-Buddhist religion by a popular religion was underway. In this case however it was Arab and Indian traders who introduced Islam to the area, and this religion has always had strong links with coastal locations and maritime trading routes. Like Theravada Buddhism on the mainland, Islam spread rapidly and by the time the Spanish had begun to colonize the Philippines during the mid- to late-16th century it had diffused northwards as far as the Philippine island of Mindanao.

5. Western cultural influences

The fifth cultural infusion, and one that continues, was that associated with the colonization of Southeast Asia by Portugal, Spain, Holland, Great Britain, France and the United States. Their activities also created the conditions that would promote the immigration of large numbers of Chinese (and to a lesser extent Indians) from the end of the 19th century and into the 20th. In the 1890s for example, up to 150,000 Chinese were arriving annually in Singapore alone. Today the Chinese in Peninsular Malaysia make up a third of the total population. Much of Southeast Asia has been so integrated into the world economy that it comes as a genuine surprise to many first-time visitors. Words like Coca-Cola, Pepsi, Marlboro and Levi's all enter a Southeast Asian's vocabulary at an early age. Many Thais believe that 'supermarket' is a word of Thai origin; while everywhere advertisements entice Southeast Asians to buy Western consumer goods. Even in isolated Indochina and Burma, Western products are highly prized and a mark of success: Johnny Walker Red Label whisky and 555 cigarettes in Burma, jeans in Vietnam, cassette recorders and Western music in Cambodia.

Local genius

Because of these successive cultural infusions over the past 2,000 years, there has been a tendency to emphasize the degree to which the inhabitants of Southeast Asia have been moulded by external cultural influences. They have; but foreign cultural elements have also been adapted and tailored to meet the needs and preferences of the people. Islam in Central Java, for example, includes many elements of Buddhism, Hinduism and Sufi mysticism – religious precursors to Islam on the island. The same is true of Theravada Buddhism in Thailand, which incorporates a large number of essentially animist and Brahmanical elements. The important role of women in Southeast Asian society for example, reflects a tradition which has survived the diffusion of different religions – where women are accorded lesser roles – into the region. Historically at least, this was most clearly reflected in the role of women in sexual relations (see box).

PENIS BALLS AND SEXUAL ROLES IN HISTORICAL SOUTHEAST ASIA

One notable feature of Southeast Asian society is the relative autonomy of women. This is most clearly illustrated in sexual relations. As the historian Anthony Reid writes in his book *Southeast Asia in the age of commerce 1450-1680*: "Southeast Asian literature of the period leaves us in little doubt that women took a very active part in courtship and lovemaking, and demanded as much as they gave by way of sexual and emotional gratification". He then goes on to describe the various ways – often involving painful surgery – that men would try to satisfy their partners. Metal pins, for example, were inserted into the penis, and wheels, studs and spurs attached as accessories to increase the female's pleasure. Alternatively, metal balls or bells, sometimes made of gold or ivory, would be inserted beneath the skin of the penis. Numerous early European visitors expressed their astonishment at the practice. Tome Pires, the 16th century Portuguese apothecary observed that Pegu lords in Burma "wear as many as 9 gold ones [penis bells], with beautiful treble, contralto and tenor tones, the size of the Alvares plums in our country; and those who are too poor...have them in lead...Malay women rejoice greatly when the Pegu men come to their country... [because of] their sweet harmony". Whereas in Africa, genital surgery was, and is, often intended to suppress pleasure for women or increase it for men, in Southeast Asia the reverse was the case. The surgery described above was also widely practiced – in Burma, Siam, Makassar, among the Torajans of Sulawesi, and Java.

The major empires

Southeast Asia has witnessed the development of dozens of states since the turn of the Christian era. In several cases their power and artistic accomplishments can still be seen reflected in the magnificence of the buildings that have survived. There can be few regions in the world offering the visitor such varied and glorious reminders of past civilizations. The Victorian naturalist Joseph Jukes on seeing the Hindu temples at Malang in East Java, and in a characteristically long Victorian sentence, records:

"The imagination became busy in restoring their fallen glories, in picturing large cities, adorned with temples and palaces, seated on the plain, and in recalling the departed power, wealth and state of the native kingdom that once flourished in a land so noble, so beautiful, and so well-adapted for its growth and security" (1847).

A broad – although rather simplistic – distinction can be drawn between those Southeast Asian empires which drew their power and their wealth from maritime trade, and those which were founded on agricultural production.

Maritime empires

Southeast Asia straddles the trade route between East and West. From the early years of the Christian era through to the colonial period, a succession of indigenous empires exploited these trade links with Europe, the Middle East, China and Japan, deriving wealth, power and prestige from their ability to control maritime trade. Foremost among them were Funan (Cambodia, 1st-6th century), and Srivijaya (Sumatra, 7th-13th century).

With its capital near Palembang in SE Sumatra, Srivijaya was in a strategic location to control trade through the 2 most important straits in Southeast Asia: the Strait of Melaka between the Malay peninsula and Sumatra, and the Sunda Strait between Sumatra and Java. Palembang offered seafarers an excellent harbour and repair facilities. The kings also used their wealth to build an impressive fleet with which they suppressed piracy in the Strait of Melaka. Srivijaya's empire expanded so fast that by the 9th century it included much of Sumatra, western Java, the Malay peninsula and the eastern portion of Borneo. In total, Srivijaya was the dominant power in the area for 350 years, from 670 AD to 1025.

Trade not only brought wealth to these maritime states. It also resulted in a fusion of Indian and Southeast Asian cultural traditions, a fact reflected in the legend of Funan's origins. Local legend records that a great Indian Brahmin with the name Kaundinya, acting on the instructions of a dream, sailed to the coast of Vietnam carrying with him a bow and arrow. On arriving, he shot the arrow and where it landed, he established the future capital of Funan. Following this act, Kaundinya married the princess Soma, daughter of the local King of the Nagas. The legend symbolizes the union between Indian and local cultural traditions – the *naga* representing indigenous fertility rites and customs, and the arrow, the potency of Hinduism.

Land-based empires

In addition to Funan and Srivijaya, Southeast Asia also witnessed the development of empires whose wealth was based upon the exploitation of the land, and in particular the cultivation of wet rice. Angkor (Cambodia, 9th-15th century), and the Sailendra dynasty (Java, mid 8th-10th century) are both examples of such empires.

Angkor's power was derived from a coincidence of environmental wealth, human genius, and religious belief. The location of Angkor, close to the Tonle Sap or Great Lake meant that it had access to sufficient water to grow a surplus of rice large enough to support an extensive court, army and religious hierarchy. At the same time, it is also usually claimed that the kings of Angkor built an irrigation network of immense complexity – able to irrigate over 5 million hectares of land, and producing 3 to 4 crops of rice each year. This is now subject to dispute, with scholars arguing that the tanks at Angkor were not for agricultural, but for urban use. The third element contributing to Angkor's success was the legitimacy provided to its kings by the deva raja cult. As long as the king was accepted as divine, as a *chakravartin* or ruler of the universe, by all his subjects and the vassal states and princes under his control, then the empire would remain stable. This was the case from the 9th to the 15th centuries: for over 600 years Angkor lay at the centre of the grandest empire in Southeast Asia. King Jayavarman VII (1181-1219) for example built the famous Bayon, as well as around 200 hospitals and rest houses, and 20,000 shrines. There were an estimated 300,000 priests and monks. It is said that Ta Phrom – just one of the temples in the complex at Angkor – required 79,365 people from 3,140 villages to build it. In 1864 the French explorer Henri Mouhot declared Angkor to be "grander than anything of Greece or Rome".

Like the rulers of Angkor, the kings of the Sailendra dynasty in island Southeast Asia, derived their wealth and power from agriculture. Exploiting the year-long rains, warmth, and fertile volcanic soil of Java, a substantial surplus of rice was produced. This fed a large court and a series of impressive monuments were built. The Sailendras were patrons of Buddhism, and they attracted Buddhist scholars from all over Asia to their court. It also seems that the kings were linked through marriage with the rulers of Srivijaya.

Of all the monuments of the Sailendra period none is more imposing than Borobudur built between 778 AD and 824 – to many the single greatest temple in all of Southeast Asia. This colossal monument, located on the Kedu Plain, represented the cosmological and spiritual centre of Sailendra power. Along its terraces, in row upon row of superbly executed reliefs (some 2,000 of them), the Sailendra world order is depicted: the 9 previous lives of the Gautama Buddha, princes and carpenters, dancers and fishermen. Borobudur was a religious justification for Sailendra rule, and at the same time gave the kings religious authority over Srivijaya. Johann Scheltema, a German traveller, on seeing Java's monuments wrote at the beginning of this century that they were: "...eloquent evidence of that innate consciousness which moves men to propitiate the principle of life by sacrifice in temples as gloriously divine as mortal hand can raise".

COLONIAL HISTORY

Early European contact: the allure of spices (16-18th century)

During the course of the 15th century, the 2 great European maritime powers of the time, Spain and Portugal, were exploring sea routes to the E. Two forces were driving this search: the desire for profits, and the drive to envangelize. At the time, even the wealthy in Europe had to exist on pickled and salted fish and meat during the winter months (fodder crops for winter feed were not grown until the 18th century). Spices to flavour what would otherwise be a very monotonous diet were greatly sought after and commanded a high price. This was not just a passing European fad. An Indian Hindu wrote that: "When the palate revolts against the insipidness of rice boiled with no other ingredients, we dream of fat, salt and spices".

Of the spices, cloves and nutmeg originated from just one location, the Moluccas (Maluku) – the Spice Islands of eastern Indonesia. Perhaps because of their value, spices and their places of origin were accorded mythical status in

Europe. The 14th century French friar Catalani Jordanus claimed for example that the clove flowers of Java produced an odour so strong it killed "every man who cometh among them, unless he shut his mouth and nostrils".

It was in order to break the monopoly on the spice trade held by Venetian and Muslim Arab traders that the Portuguese began to extend their possessions eastwards. This finally culminated in the capture of the port of Melaka by the Portuguese seafarer Alfonso de Albuquerque in Jun 1511. The additional desire to spread the Word of God is clear in the speech that Albuquerque made before the battle with the Muslim sultan of Melaka, when he exorted his men, stressing:

"...the great service which we shall perform to our Lord in casting the Moors out of this country and of quenching the fire of the sect of Mohammet so that it may never burst out again hereafter".

From their base in Melaka, the Portuguese established trading relations with the Moluccas, and built a series of forts across the region: at Bantam (Banten), Flores, Ternate, Tidore, Timor and Ambon (Amboyna).

As the Portuguese were sailing E to Southeast Asia, the Spanish, from their possessions in South America, were sailing W. It was in order to prevent clashes between the 2 powers that a Papal Bull of 1493 divided the world along a line just W of the Azores: everywhere to the W of this line was left for the Spanish, and everything to the E of it for the Portuguese. Unfortunately, the Pope remained convinced that the earth was flat and never envisaged the 2 powers meeting in Southeast Asia. This occurred when Ferdinand Magellan arrived in the Philippines in 1521 having crossed the Pacific – in a remarkable feat of seamanship. After a short period of conflict, the 2 protagonists settled their differences, the Portuguese leaving the Philippines to the Spanish, and the Spanish agreeing not to interfere in the Moluccas.

By the late 16th century, Portuguese influence in Southeast Asia was waning. Their empire was over-extended, and the claim that Portuguese seafarers were helping to introduce Christianity to the infidels of the region sat uneasily next to the barbaric methods they employed. Francis Xavier, the canonized Catholic missionary, is said to have been so appalled by the debauchery and vice of Melaka that when he left he shook the sand from his shoes, vowing never to return to the cursed city again. The Portuguese were supplanted by the Dutch in the region who, by 1616, had established 15 trading posts and gained control of the spice trade.

But despite these advances, in many respects the European presence was peripheral. The motivation was to secure spices and to make money, not to extend territorially. The stupendous lost city of Angkor in Cambodia for example, was not extensively reported upon until the French naturalist Henri Mouhot published the diary of his 1861 visit 3 years later.

Intensification of the European presence (19th-20th century)

At the beginning of the 19th century, a number of developments markedly increased European interest in the colonization of Southeast Asia. Most important, was the region's new-found economic potential. Europe's industrial revolution led to increased demand for industrial raw materials, while at the same time companies were looking for markets for their manufactured goods. Southeast Asia was in a position to provide the first of these at the beginning, and as the region's development proceeded, the second too. Allied to these developments, there were also a number of technological advances which considerably shortened the journey to Southeast Asia. The opening of the Suez canal in 1869 precluded the dangerous trip around Cape of Good Hope, while the development of the steamship slashed days off the journey. The active spread of Christianity was once again firmly on the agenda, and European governments found it hard not to interfere when zealous missionaries and their converts were persecuted by local leaders. This was especially true in Vietnam where missionaries had been periodically persecuted from the early 17th century. This reached its height during the reigns of the Vietnamese emperors Minh Mang (1820-41), Thieu Tri (1841-47) and Tu Duc (1847-83). Minh Mang, for example, issued a decree in 1833 ordering churches to be destroyed and made profession of the Catholic faith a capital offence. French ecclesiastical magazines contained vivid accounts of the torture and murder of French missionaries, and the clamour raised by the French public ultimately led to the invasion and colonization of Vietnam by France.

The effect of these developments was that over a relatively short space of time – about 45 years, between 1825 and 1870 – all of Southeast Asia with the exception of Siam (the old name for Thailand) fell under European control. More detailed discussion about the final subjugation of the region is contained in the introductory sections dealing with the individual countries. In essence however, there were 2 sets of rivalries: between the French and the British on the mainland, and between the Dutch and the British in the archipelago. The local empires had neither the economic power, military might nor, in many cases, the political skills to withstand the Europeans.

The impact of the colonial period in Southeast Asia

The impact of the colonial period extended far beyond mere political domination. Southeast Asia was irreparably affected economically, socially, culturally, even physically. More to the point, these effects are still visible today in the region's economic and social fabric.

The principal effect of the colonial period was to alter the economic basis of life in Southeast Asia. In brief, a process of commercialization was set in train. Huge areas of land were cleared in the river deltas of the region and planted to rice. Along the Irrawaddy in Burma for example, the area under rice cultivation increased from 400,000 hectares in 1855, to 4 million hectares by 1930. This process was pioneered by large numbers of individual peasants responding to the new economic opportunities provided by the presence of the colonial powers. This was even the case in independent Thailand, where the king could do little to constrain the economic influence of the West.

Even more dramatically, Western-financed estates growing plantation crops such as rubber and coffee were widely established. In Malaysia, the area planted to rubber – a crop which was only introduced to the region in the late 19th century – increased from a paltry 137 hectares in 1897, to 1.4 million hectares by 1939. These estates used immigrant labour, imported machinery, they were managed by Europeans, financed by foreign capital, and exported all their production. They formed 'enclaves', completely separate from the local, traditional, economy.

Nor did the economic effects of the colonial period merely affect agriculture. The Western powers also needed minerals and timber to fuel their industrial revolutions. Most spectacularly, tin-mining expanded. The introduction of the steam chain-bucket dredge, steam pumps, and new drilling methods revolutionized the tin industry. By the later 1930s, Indonesia, Thailand and Malaya were supplying 60% of the world's tin.

Not surprisingly, this process of commercialization deeply affected the inhabitants of the region. Farmers were inexorably drawn into the cash economy. Seeds and fertilizers were purchased in increasing quantities, money was borrowed, labour hired, land rented and surplus production sold. The process of commercialization not only undermined the traditional self-sufficiency of the Southeast Asian village, it also affected the social fabric of the village. People became dependent on economic developments in the international economy. This was thrown into stark perspective during the Great Depression of the early 1930s when the price of rubber halved, and then halved again, between 1929 and 1932. Rice farmers had their land repossessed as money lenders foreclosed on their loans. Riots broke out across the region as dispossessed peasants demonstrated their anger and frustration.

The exploitation of Southeast Asia's natural resources entailed the improvement of communications and transport infrastructure. As a result, a network of roads and railways were built. However these did not serve all areas equally. Mainly they linked areas of export commodity production with the outside world. In the same way, although the colonial presence led to a dramatic growth in the number and size of urban settlements, these occupied different locations and had different *raisons d'être* from their indigenous precursors. The great port cities of Singapore, Georgetown (Penang), Batavia (Jakarta), Rangoon, Saigon, even Bangkok developed in order to funnel export commodities out of the region, and manufactured imports in. Likewise, many inland towns owed their existence to the export commodities that were produced in the surrounding areas such as Taiping and Sungei Ujong (now Seremban), both Malayan towns that grew on the back of the tin trade.

Another feature of modern Southeast Asia, which has its roots in the colonial period, is their multi-racial make-up. These groups, although they lived (and continued to live) in close proximity to one another, rarely mixed. The most striking example of a plural society is Malaysia where 32% of the population of Peninsular Malaysia are Chinese, 8% Indian, and nearly 60% Malay. The explanation for this heterogeneous population lies in the demand for labour during the colonial period. For the colonial authorities found it extremely hard to recruit sufficient local labour to work on the plantations, in the tin mines, and in the other export industries. The logical solution was to import labour from abroad. From the end of the 19th century, hundreds of thousands of Chinese and Indians arrived in Malaya. It was usually these immigrants' intention to return to their mother countries, but many stayed on – sometimes because they were too poor to leave, sometimes because they wished to keep an eye on the wealth that they had accumulated. The immigration of 'indentured' labourers was greatest in British Malaya: between 1909 and 1940 some 16 million Indians and Chinese arrived in Malaya. Today Malaysia's total population is only 18 million.

The Second World War and the Japanese interregnum

Prior to the outbreak of the Second World War, the strains of commercialization, domination by foreign powers, and the often heavy-handed and insensitive behaviour of colonial officials had engendered only a limited reaction from the local populations. Nationalist movements lacked focus, and charismatic leaders were needed to add coherence and direction to nascent independence movements. Rather ironically, this was provided by a Western-educated Southeast Asian elite. Men such as Sukarno of Indonesia and Ho Chi Minh of Vietnam, travelled abroad for their further education, were introduced to notions of self-government and nationhood, and read works by Marx, Lenin, Locke and Rousseau. But even with the establishment of a handful of nationalist parties prior to the outbreak of the Second World War, they were regarded as only a minor irritation by the colonial powers. Few would have dreamt that within so short a space of time – less than a decade in most cases – the countries of Southeast Asia would have achieved independence.

The war changed the nature of the relationship between the colonial powers and the people that they ruled. In the space of less than 6 months, virtually the entire region was over-run by Japanese forces. In Dec 1941, the Japanese landed in Northern Malaya, having already taken control of French Indochina; on 11th Jan, Kuala Lumpur fell; on 15th Feb, Singapore capitulated; on 7th Mar, Rangoon was abandoned; and on 8th Mar, the Dutch surrendered in Indonesia. This was the darkest period of the entire war for the Allies. However, not only did the Japanese demonstrate the military fallibility of the colonial powers in a style that could not have been more compelling; they were also Asian. The war made independence inevitable – and sooner rather than later. The colonial powers were drained and exhausted; they had lost much of their credibility; and they returned to find that the fragmented nationalist parties of the pre-war years had grown in size, influence and authority. Burma was granted independence in 1948, Indonesia in 1949, Cambodia in 1953, North Vietnam and Laos in 1954, South Vietnam in 1955, Malaya in 1957, and Singapore in 1963. Brunei only attained full independence in 1984.

MODERN SOUTHEAST ASIA

From the end of the Vietnam War until, roughly, 1992, the Southeast Asian region was effectively divided into 2 groups of countries. On the one hand there were the market economies of the Association of Southeast Asian Nations (ASEAN). These include Thailand, Malaysia, Indonesia, Singapore and Brunei, as well as the Philippines. And on the other there were the Communist/socialist countries of Indochina – Vietnam, Laos and Cambodia – and Burma. These 2 sets of countries embraced contrasting economic and political ideologies. The countries of ASEAN followed – simplistically-speaking – the Western, capitalist, consumer-orientated path to economic success, although they have tended to look to Japan, rather than to Europe or America, as their role model. At the same time they have tended to side with the West politically. In contrast, the countries of Indochina and Burma embraced a socialist or Communist vision of reconstruction and development. They supported the former Soviet Union or China in the East-West conflict, except Burma which followed a policy of nonalignment and self-sufficiency.

This neat division of Southeast Asia into two blocs, always somewhat dubious, has gradually broken down since the late 1980s, so that today it is increasingly hard to sustain in any meaningful sense. Vietnam and Laos may remain explicitly 'Communist', but beneath the vacant terminology the differences are narrowing month-by-month. Politically too, the countries of ASEAN and Indochina have undergone a significant process of rapprochement. Whereas a mere five years ago, the Vietnamese were lobbing shells onto Thai territory to attack Khmers Rouges forces barracked there, the countries now exchange business delegations and senior ministers. And whereas the Lao and Thai armies fought a vicious little war in 1987-88 over some disputed territory near Ban Rom Khlao in the north of Thailand, 1994 saw the opening of the first bridge over the upper reaches of the Mekong River by the King of Thailand and the President of Laos (see page 343). In short, for the first time in recent history, there is the possibility that the Southeast Asian region might be a 'united' area of 400 million people. Former Thai prime minister Chatichai Choonhaven referred to this massive potential market as *Suwannaphume* or a 'Golden Land'. In so doing he was harking back to an earlier era when the great trading ports of the Malay Archipelago – places like Meleka (Malacca) and Aceh – were critical conduits in the fabulously wealthy trade in spices from the Moluccas, silks from China, camphor and ivory from the forests of Southeast Asia, and gold, silver and gemstones from Burma and the Spanish Main.

Southeast Asia in the world economy

In a special report in 1993, *The Economist* predicted that "It is now liklier than not that the most momentous public event in the lifetime of anybody reading this survey will turn out to have been the modernisation of Asia". A rate of economic growth unprecedented in human history is transforming not just Asia, but the balance of global economic power, and by extension political and military power. The countries of Southeast Asia are a central component in this global transformation. Those that comprise the Association of Southeast Asian Nations are among the fastest-growing economies in the world. Since 1965 they have achieved average annual rates of growth of over 6%, and they are seen by many analysts to represent a second tier of 'dragons' or 'tigers': countries which are basing their success on aggressive, export-orientated industrial growth in the way Japan, South Korea, Taiwan and Hong Kong did before them. Although the countries of Indochina – Vietnam, Laos and Cambodia – are currently among some of the poorest in the world, they too, and particularly

Vietnam, are perceived to be on the brink of a potential economic 'miracle'. From the Italian roof-top restaurants of Singapore, the clubs of Bangkok or the manicured golf greens of Malaysia, it is hard to believe that a mere 30 years ago these countries had incomes which put them on a par with India and the countries of Africa. Now, in terms of purchasing power parity (i.e. what average incomes are worth in real terms), they eclipse – or seem about to eclipse – such developed countries as Spain and Ireland. The economic success of Asia has altered the way people perceive the countries concerned and the process of development. What, for example, does the 'Third World' mean if some of the countries that comprise this Third World have higher standards of living than countries in the First World? In short, the ideology of Third Worldism, at least over large areas of Asia, is dead. Nor are the countries and their leaders willing to follow meekly the lead of the West. Individuals like Prime Minister Mahathir Mohamad of Malaysia confront assumptions about their and their countries' place in the world almost monthly, attacking the West for its cultural imperialism, latent superiority, and remnant colonial assumptions. With the Malaysian economy, and others in the region, growing so rapidly, Mahathir finds he is in a strong position to lecture to the West. China's rejection of U.S. President Bill Clinton's attempts to link the renewal of Most Favoured Nation trading status (MFN) with human rights is the most obvious example of the waning power of the West to dictate terms, and the growing confidence of Asia. In May 1994, Clinton accomplished the biggest 'U' turn of his presidency, and de-linked MFN and human rights. It is hard to believe that any Chinese leader would have 'lost face' so completely.

Asian drama

This optimism among the countries of Asia is remarkable when set against the landscape of the 1960s. In 1965 the Swedish economist and Nobel Prize winner Gunnar Myrdal wrote a massive, 2,200 page, two-volume study of Asia entitled *Asian drama*. It is a down-beat and depressing study, which predicted famine and revolution rather than growth and prosperity. Although it is now too easy to reject this seminal work as excessively pessimistic, at the time the volumes seemed prescient to most people, and were lauded as such. In Southeast Asia, the Vietnam War was escalating, Thailand was facing its own growing insurgency problem, Indonesia had experienced revolution and a bloodbath, Burma's formerly vibrant economy was in disarray, populations were growing out of control, and most people were mired in poverty.

The first country in Southeast Asia to break this mould was **Singapore** (along with the other newly industrialising economies of East Asia, Taiwan, South Korea and Hong Kong). When the island-state achieved self government in 1959, it was in a woeful condition with high unemployment, a decaying urban core, political unrest and no manufacturing base to speak of. Today Singapore is one of the wealthiest countries in the world. Average per capita incomes exceed US$12,000 and far-sighted planning has given the city a futuristic feel.

Thailand, Indonesia and Malaysia have had to support sizeable poor rural populations and have enjoyed rather less stratospheric rates of economic growth. Nonetheless, they have still progressed at a speed which would be the envy of many Latin American and African countries. The proportion of the population living in absolute poverty has decreased from 60% to 15% between 1970 and 1990 in Indonesia, and from 26% to 16% over the same period in the

THE ASIAN WAY

The flogging of the American 18-year old Michael Fay in Singapore has led to a great deal of debate about the 'Asian Way'. The low crime levels in Singapore are unfavourably contrasted with the war zones that constitute the centres of some U.S. cities, and it has been asked whether the West in general has allowed the rights of individuals to undermine those of wider society to such an extent that the protection of the majority has been ignored. In short, an abstract principle has got in the way of common sense. The support that the Singapore government received from ordinary Americans for the thrashing of an Amercan boy guilty, some would say, of no more than high jinks, illustrates the frustration that many Westerners feel with the high crime rates in their own countries.

The inability to stop, let along reverse, the seeming inexorable rise in crime in the West is contrasted with the apparent peaceful situation in Asia. Have Asians got it right? Is the West, as former Prime Minister of Singapore Lee Kuan Yew appears to believe, decadent and rotten to its very core? It is on this basis that Asian values are promoted and a great deal of collective navel gazing has ensued.

Asian values – often thought to be Confucianist – are seen to embody such things as respect for elders and the law, hardwork, and recognition that the needs of society may transcend those of the individual. These values are reflected, so the argument goes, in rapid economic growth, low crime rates, stability and rising prosperity. Unfortunately, or perhaps fortunately, this view of Asia, and of the Asian success story, is hugely simplistic.

First, Asia is so diverse that to talk about a single set of Asian values is nonsense. When Asian politicians try, they descend into pronouncements of such crassness as to be almost embarrassing. Second, Asia is not crimeless. Singapore has a low crime rate (Asian commentator Ian Buruma defines the city state as a "huge tropical boarding school", easy to police by the 'nanny' state there), but the

case of Thailand. These four countries of Southeast Asia – Singapore, Malaysia, Thailand and Indonesia – were among the world's 13 most successful developing countries in the years 1965-1990 (four of the others were also Asian, namely Taiwan, Hong Kong, South Korea and China). The rates of growth achieved led to an 8-fold increase in real GDP, a doubling of output every 8 years.

The countries of **Indochina and Burma** may be part of the same region as those of ASEAN, but until the late 1980s they belonged to a different world. They pursued a path to development which aped the experience of the other command economies, and like the others largely failed in the attempt. In the space of 15 years, Vietnam declined from being the greatest military power in the region, to become an economic disaster. The countries of Indochina and Burma are now having to contend with an entirely new global landscape. They have responded to economic stagnation and the general failure of their socialist programmes of development by introducing increasingly reformist economic policies. In Laos, the government talks of *chin thanakan mai* or 'new thinking', while in Vietnam there is *doi moi* or 'renovation' – both Southeast Asian equivalents to the former Soviet Union's *perestroika*. This new outlook embraces the market, foreign investment, incentives and private ownership. Even Burma, still a maverick state, has had to turn to outside investment and expertise to revitalize its moribund economy. But it would be wrong to see Vietnam, Laos,

murder rate in Thailand is, in fact, higher than in the U.S. While at the same time countries like China, Hong Kong and Japan face organised crime syndicates that are far more influential than any which operate in Europe, and corruption is endemic in some countries. Ian Buruma argues that in some of Asia's authoritarian states murder, theft, torture and larceny are institutionalised: rather than individuals doing these things to other individuals, the state does it to those members of its population who try and buck the trend. Events in Burma in 1988 (and since – in 1994 the US government was moving towards imposing economic sanctions on Burma, viewing it effectively as a gangster regime), and in Indonesia and Thailand in 1991 go to show, in Buruma's view, that "crime" has become a "state enterprise". Although this does not mean that the Asian experience should be rejected out of hand as fraudulent, all is not roses in the Asian garden and many Americans would find it suffocating to live in Singapore, for example, where the press is lack-lustre and one-dimensional in the extreme and chewing gum is outlawed for its supposed anti-social tendencies. As Buruma writes, "the firm smack of discipline always sounds sweeter when it lands on someone else's bum."

Despite the claims that Asia is different, some Asian politicians are actively trying to prevent Westernization occurring. At the end of May 1994, the Singapore parliament debated the Maintenance of Parents Bill which would allow parents to sue their children if they did not support them financially in retirement. As the *Straits Times* put it in an editorial supporting the Bill, there is a danger that the younger generation "will grow up self-absorbed, middle-class and very likely, Westernized in reflex. In that milieu, financial support for parents as a time-honoured tradition would whither". There are many other signs that Asia is not impervious to the social trends evident in the West: divorce, crime, drug addiction and so on are all on the rise, just as incomes, level of education and life expectancy are too.

Cambodia and Burma as just a short step behind the countries of ASEAN. As *The Economist* put it in 1993:

"The reality that can be seen, touched, heard and on occasion sniffed is that the average Vietnamese, Lao, Cambodian or Burmese is dirt-poor. Bangkok's street vendors peddle fake designer watches to foreign tourists; Hanoi's mend odd bits of ancient machinery for other townsfolk, or give them shaves and haircuts in front of cracked pieces of mirror."

The city and countryside

Development in the West has been evolutionary rather than revolutionary. In Southeast Asia the reverse has been the case. Progress has been bewilderingly fast and has resulted in the uneven distribution of wealth. The contrast between city and countryside provides

tangible evidence of this. For the visitor, the capital cities of the region can be thoroughly exhausting, with hot and humid climates, noise and bustle, and often appalling traffic conditions. Away from the cities in the countryside, landscape and life tend to be much more in keeping with the popular view of Southeast Asia – rice, buffaloes, tropical forests, traditional festivals and ceremonies. Superficially, rural life seems to reflect traditional patterns and processes. But, in the same way that the modern cities embody many traditional elements, so the traditional countryside is rapidly modernizing. Beneath the surface, the technology of agriculture and the aspirations and outlook of farmers have changed dramatically. Improving communications in the form of better

THE ASIAN MIRACLE: WHY IT HAPPENED – THE STORY ACCORDING TO THE WORLD BANK

In 1993, the World Bank published a study which tried to make sense of the Asian economic success story, with the title *The East Asian miracle: economic growth and public policy*. The unprecedented rate of economic growth in Asia, including in a number of Southeast Asian countries, demanded an explanation so that other, less fortunate regions of the world might also embark on this road to fortune. Of course, not everyone is so sanguine about Asia's success, past or future. These critics point to, for example, human rights violations, poor working conditions, widening rural-urban disparities, environmental degradation on a monumental scale, the exploitation of child labour, and corrupt and corrosive government.

Although the World Bank study begins by pointing out that there is no 'recipe' for success, it does highlight a number of critical elements which countries and governments need, in their view, to get right. As the World Bank puts it, the so-called High Performing Asian Economies or HPAEs (including Singapore, Malaysia, Thailand and Indonesia) "achieved high growth by getting the basics right". Not all the below can be applied to all the countries in question all of the time; nonetheless, they represent a check list of 'right' policies and government.

● *The principle of shared growth*: although the countries of Asia are not, in most cases, democracies, their governments have tried to ensure that the fruits of development have been relatively widely shared. This is particularly true in the case of the 'dragons' (including Singapore) where rapid growth has been achieved with relative equity. This has helped to establish the legitimacy of their governments and usually won the support of the populations at large – despite the fact that those governments may still be authoritarian in complexion.

● *Investment in physical capital*: the countries of Asia have, in general, been saving and investing a greater proportion of their total wealth than countries in any other region of the world. This includes both private and public investment, but is most

roads and transport, and radio and television, have meant that farmers are aware of developments in the wider world. Today they wish to provide for their families the benefits of modern health care and education, and this has necessitated that they embrace the cash economy.

But, the process of development has not always been devoid of tensions and frictions. In the forested areas of Southeast Asia, tribal groups such as the Hmong of Thailand and the upriver Dayak tribes of Sarawak have suffered both economically and culturally as a dominant, Western-style consumer culture has impinged on their lives. Some groups have tried to fight the process of commercialization, often in league with

foreign environmentalist groups. A large segment of the population has also become economically marginalized – despite the rapid economic growth. In the cities, there are millions of slum dwellers and squatters, living without clean water, medical care and education and subsisting in the informal sector. In rural areas, farmers have been pushed off their land as population has begun to press upon the land resource, and as the commercialization of producton has led to the accumulation of land in the hands of a small number of wealthy landowners. The resulting army of landless peasants have been forced to work for wages of perhaps a dollar a day on other people's fields.

dramatic in terms of private investment (the World Bank, as one might expect, views private investment as more efficient and effective in promoting growth).

● *Investment in human capital*: although the proportion of spending allotted to education is not very much higher in Asia than elsewhere in the developing world, this money has been primarily allocated to primary and secondary schooling, not to higher education. Among developing countries, the families of most of those entering higher education can pay for it anyway, and need little government support; the best way to improve general levels of education is by targetting primary and secondary schooling. Asian governments have also tended to educate girls nearly as well as boys.

● *Allowing the market to determine prices*: as one might expect from the World Bank, the report also highlights the importance of allowing the market to determine the price of labour, capital and goods. The Bank skipped around the tendency for Asian governments to intervene in economic decision-making (with the exception of Hong Kong) by arguing that this was judicious intervention which reinforced, rather than tried to buck, the market.

● *That vital intagible*: Lee Kuan Yew, former prime minister of Singapore, visited Vietnam – one of the poorest countries in the world with a per capita income of US220 – and pronounced that the country's prospects were bright because it had that 'vital intangible'. Economists talk rather less poetically in terms of Total Factor Productivity (TFP). In effect, this is what cannot be explained in a country's growth by looking at such variables as investment in physical and human capital. The former Soviet Union, on paper, should have grown as fast as Singapore and South Korea. As is now abundantly clear, it did not. The problem is identifying this ghostly missing catalyst.

● *Creating a business-friendly environment*: the countries have usually welcomed foreign investment and have sought to create the conditions in which foreign companies can thrive. They have also created a cadre of efficient technocrats to manage the economy.

The politics of economic success

Politically, the market economies of AS-EAN have also moved gradually – but often haltingly – towards more representative government. Thailand now has a democratically elected prime minister and government, and President Suharto of Indonesia seems to accept that greater pluralism in the political system is inevitable. But for groups like the New York-based *Human Rights Watch Asia* (formerly, *Asia Watch*) there is much to decry in terms of human rights violations and freedom of expression. They point, for example, to Singapore's heavy-handed government and attempts at social engineering, to Indonesia's 'genocide' in East Timor and control over political opposition, and to Malaysia's treatment of its tribal peoples. The countries of Indochina (but not Burma, which is widely viewed as a gangster state), have not received the same human rights attention as those of ASEAN, perhaps due to a legacy of guilt over the war in Indochina. Pushing such guilt aside, it is clear that although market-orientated economic reform or *perestroika* may have been embraced with alacrity, there has been litte concomitant *glasnost* in the political system. With the exception of Cambodia, the ruling parties have retained a tight hold on the reins of power. They appear unwilling to allow greater plurality of political expression, and outspoken critics are quickly silenced. Whether these countries will be able to maintain the delicate balancing act of allowing greater economic freedom while denying their people any significant political freedom is a moot point.

This last sentence highlights a major difference in opinion between the West and Asia. There seem to be two key issues here, which are almost irreconcileable. First, many Asians, and particularly its political leaders, maintain that Western human rights pressure groups are trying to impose Western cultural values on Asia. They argue that these values are inappropriate in the Asian cultural context, and that this is just another form of imperialism (see box, page 50). The sanctity of the individual, so important in the West, is replaced in Asia by the group (or wider society). The second bone of contention concerns whether democracy really is the answer. It has been argued that the West's problem is that democracy stifles government by giving multitudes of special interest groups too much say. The result is that government cannot govern, and that good government is replaced by the government of appeasement. Lee Kuan Yew, former prime minister of Singapore and a key spokesman for the Asian realm was quoted at the end of 1993 as saying: "Americans believe that out of contention, out of the clash of different ideas and ideals, you get good government. That view is not shared in Asia."

TOURISM: COUNTING THE COSTS

"Tourism is like fire. It can either cook your food or burn your house down". This sums up the ambivalent attitude that many people have regarding the effects of tourism. It is the largest foreign exchange earner in countries like Thailand, and the world's largest single industry; yet many people in receiving countries would rather tourists go home.

Tourism is seen to be the cause of polluted beaches, rising prices, loose morals, consumerism, and much else besides.

The word 'tourist' is derived from 'travail', meaning work or torment. Travail, in turn, has its roots in the Latin word *tripalium*, which was a three-pronged instrument of torture. For many people struggling through the back of beyond in countries like Vietnam or Indonesia this etymology should strike a chord. And yet, as *The Economist* pointed out in a survey of the industry in 1991:

> "The curse of the tourist industry is that it peddles dreams: dreams of holidays where the sun always shines, the children are always occupied, and where every evening ends in the best sex you have ever had. For most of its modern life, this has been matched by a concomitant dreaminess on the part of its customers. When asked, most tourists tell whopping lies about what they want on holiday..." (Economist, 1991).

Most international tourists come from a handful of wealthy countries. Half from just five countries (the USA, Germany, the UK, Japan and France) and 80% from 20 countries. This is why many see tourism as the new 'imperialism', imposing alien cultures and ideals on sensitive and unmodernised peoples. The problem, however, is that discussions of the effects of tourism tend to degenerate into simplifications. Different destinations will be affected in different ways; these effects are likely to vary over time; and different groups living in a particular destination will feel the effects of tourism in different ways and to varying degrees. At no time or place can tourism (or any other influence) be categorised as uniformly 'good' or 'bad'. Tourism can take an Australian backpacker on US$5 a day to villages in the Northern hills of Thailand, an American tourist to luxury hotels in the city state of Singapore where a room can cost over US$200 a night, and a Malaysian Muslim to the southern Thai cities of Hat Yai and Songkhla on a long weekend.

Searching for culture

Southeast Asia is one of the richest cultural areas in the world, and many tourists are attracted to the region because of its exotic peoples: the hill 'tribes' of Northern Thailand, the Hindu Balinese, and the Dayaks of Borneo, for example. When cultural erosion is identified, the tendency is to blame this on tourists and tourism. Turner and Ash have written that tourists are the "suntanned destroyers of culture", while Bugnicourt argues that tourism:

> "...encourages the imitation of foreigners and the downgrading of local inhabitants in relation to foreign tourists; it incites the pillage of art work and other historical artefacts; it leads to the degeneration of classical and popular dancing, the profanation and vulgarization of places of worship, and the perversion of religious ceremonies; it creates a sense of inferiority and a cultural demoralization which 'fans the flames of anti-development' through the acquisition of undesirable cultural traits" (1977).

The problem with views like this is that they assume that change is bad, and that indigenous cultures are unchanging. It makes local peoples victims of change, rather than masters of their own destinies. It also assumes that tourism is an external influence, when in fact it quickly becomes part of the local landscape. Cultural change is inevitable and on-going, and 'new' and 'traditional' are only judgements, not absolutes. Thus new cultural forms can quickly become key markers of tradition. Tourists searching for an 'authentic' experience are assuming that tradition is tangible, easily identifiable and unchanging. It is none of these.

Thai hill people wearing American baseball caps are assumed to have succumbed to Western culture. But such changes really say next to nothing about an individual's strength of identity. There are also problems with identifying cultural erosion, let alone linking it

specifically with tourism, rather than with the wider processes of 'modernisation'. This is exemplified in the case of Bali where tourism is paraded by some as the saviour of Balinese culture, and by others as its destroyer. Michel Picard in his paper "'Cultural tourism' in Bali" (1992) writes:

> "No sooner had culture become the emblematic image of Bali [in the 1920s] than foreign visitors and residents started fearing for its oncoming disappearance. ...the mere evocation of Bali suggested the imminent and dramatic fall from the 'Garden of Eden': sooner of later, the 'Last Paradise' was doomed to become a 'Paradise Lost'" (Picard,1992:77).

Yet the authorities on Bali are clearly at a loss as to how to balance their conflicting views:

> "...the view of tourism held by the Balinese authorities is blatantly ambivalent, the driving force of a modernisation process which they welcome as ardently as they fear. Tourism in their eyes appears at once the most promising source of economic development and as the most subversive agent for the spread of foreign cultural influences in Bali" (Picard,1992:85).

Tourist art: fine art, degraded art

Tourist art, both material (for instance, sculpture) and non-material (like dances) is another issue where views sharply diverge. The mass of inferior 'airport' art on sale to tourists demonstrates, to some, the corrosive effects of tourism. It leads craftsmen and women to mass-produce second rate pieces for a market that appreciates neither their cultural or symbolic worth, nor their aesthetic value. Yet tourism can also give value to craft industries that would otherwise be undermined by cheap industrial goods. The geographer Michael Parnwell has argued that in the poor Northeast of Thailand, the craft tradition should be allied with tourism to create vibrant rural industries. The

TOURISM DEVELOPMENT GUIDELINES

● Tourism should capitalise on local features (cultural and natural) so as to promote the use of local resources.

● Attention should be given to the type of tourist attracted. A mix of mass and individual will lead to greater local participation and better balance.

● Tourist development should be integrated with other sectors. Coordination between agencies is crucial.

● Facilities created should be made available to locals, at subsidised rates if necessary.

● Resources such as beaches and parks must remain in the public domain.

● Different tourists and tourist markets should be exploited so as to minimize seasonal variations in arrivals and employment.

● A tourist threshold should be identified and adhered to.

● Environmental impact assessments and other surveys must be carried out.

● Provision of services to tourists must be allied with improvements in facilities for locals.

● Development should be focused in areas where land use conflicts will be kept to a minimum.

● Supplies, where possible, should be sourced locally.

● Assistance and support should be given to small-scale, local entrepreneurs.

corrosive effects of tourism on arts and crafts also assumes that artists and craftsmen are unable to distinguish between fine pieces and pot-boilers. Many produce inferior pieces for the tourist market while continuing to produce for local demand, the former effectively subsidising the latter.

Some researchers have also shown how there is a tendency for culture to be 'invented' for tourists, and for this to then become part of 'tradition'. Michel Picard has shown in the case of Bali how dances developed for tourists are now paraded as paragons of national cultural heritage. The same is true of art, where the anthropologist Lewis Hill of the Centre for South-East Asian Studies at the University of Hull has demonstrated how objects made for the tourist market in one period are later enthusiastically embraced by the host community.

Environment and tourism

The environmental deterioration that is linked to tourism is due to a destination area exceeding its 'carrying capacity' as a result of overcrowding. But carrying capacity, though an attractive concept, is notoriously difficult to pin down in any exact manner. A second dilemma facing those trying to encourage greater environmental consciousness is the co-called 'tragedy of the commons', better described in terms of Chinese restaurants. When a group of people go to a Chinese restaurant with the intention of sharing the bill, each customer will tend to order a more expensive dish than he or she would normally do - on the logic that everyone will be doing the same, and the bill will be split. In tourism terms, it means that hotel owners will always built those few more bungalows or that extra wing, to maximise their profits, reassured in the knowledge that the environmental costs will be shared among all hotel owners. So, despite most operators appreciating that over-development may 'kill the goose that lays the golden eggs', they do so anyway. Pattaya, the beach resort on Thailand's eastern seaboard, is a classic example. By the late 1980s, the sea off the resort's beaches was too polluted to safely swim. In short, tourism contains the seeds of its own destruction.

But many developing countries have few other development opportunities. Those in Southeast Asia are blessed with beautiful landscapes and exotic cultures, and tourism is a cheap development option. Other possibilities cost more to develop and take longer to take-off. It is also true that 'development', however it is achieved, has cultural and environmental implications. For many,

A Tourism Checklist

Costs	Benefits
vulnerable to external developments - e.g. oil price rises, 1991 Gulf War	diversifies an economy and is usually immune to protectionism
	requires few technical and human resources and is a 'cheap' development option
	requires little infrastructure
erodes culture by debasing it; strong cultures overwhelm sensitive ones (often tribal)	gives value to cultures and helps in their preservation
leads to moral pollution with rising crime and prostitution	changing social norms are not due solely, or even mostly, to tourism
often concentrated in culturally and environmentally sensitive areas, so effects are accentuated	helps to develop marginal areas that would otherwise 'miss out' on development
lack of planning and management causes environmental problems	poor planning and management is not peculiar to tourism and can be rectified
foreigners tend to dominate; costs of involvement are high so local people fail to become involved and benefit	costs of involvement can be very low; tourism is not so scale-dependent as other industries
tourism increases local inequalities	
jobs are usually seasonal and low-skilled	
economic leakages mean revenue generated tends to accrue to foreign multi-nationals	leakage is less that with many other industries; local involvement generally greater and value added is significant
tourism is not sustainable; tourism ultimately destroys tourism because it destroys those attributes that attracted tourists in the first place	tourism is not monolithic; destination areas evolve and do not have to suffer decay

tourism is the least environmentally corrosive of the various options open to poor countries struggling to achieve rapid economic growth.

Suggested reading and tourism pressure groups

In the UK, **Tourism Concern** aims to "promote greater understanding of the impacts of tourism on host communities and environments", "to raise awareness of the forms of tourism that respect the rights and interests of [local] people", and to "work for change in current tourism practice". Annual membership is £15.00 which includes subscription to their magazine *In Focus*. Tourism Concern, Froebel College, Roehampton Lane, London SW15 5PU, T (081) 878-9053.

The most up-to-date book examining tourism in Southeast Asia is: Hitchcock, Mike *et al.* (edits.) (1993) *Tourism in South-East Asia*, Routledge: London.

SOUTHEAST ASIA: SUGGESTED READING AND LISTENING

Magazines

Asiaweek (weekly). A light weight *Far Eastern Economic Review*; rather like a regional *Time* magazine in style.

The Far Eastern Economic Review (weekly). Authoritative Hong Kong-based regional magazine; their correspondents based in each country provide knowledgeable, in-depth analysis particularly on economics and politics, sometimes in rather a turgid style (although a change of editor has meant some lightening in style).

Books

Buruma, Ian (1989) *God's dust*, Jonathan Cape: London. Enjoyable journey through Burma, Thailand, Malaysia and Singapore along with the Philippines, Taiwan, South Korea and Japan; journalist Buruma questions how far culture in this region has survived the intrusion of the West.

Cambridge History of Southeast Asia (1992). Two volume edited study, long and expensive with contributions from most of the leading historians of the region. A thematic and regional approach is taken, not a country one, although the history is fairly conventional. Published by Cambridge University Press: Cambridge.

Caufield, C. (1985) *In the rainforest*, Heinemann: London. This readable and well-researched analysis of rainforest ecology and the pressures on tropical forests is part-based in the region.

Clad, James (1989) *Behind the myth: business, money and power in Southeast Asia*, Unwin Hyman: London. Clad, formerly a journalist with the *Far Eastern Economic Review*, distilled his experiences in this book; as it turned out, rather disappointingly – it is a hotchpotch of journalistic snippets.

Conrad, Joseph (1900) *Lord Jim*, Penguin: London. The tale of Jim, who abandons his ship and seeks refuge from his guilt in Malaya, earning the sobriquet Lord.

Conrad, Joseph (1915) *Victory: an island tale*, Penguin: London. Arguably Conrad's finest novel, based in the Malay Archipelago.

Conrad, Joseph (1920) *The rescue*, Penguin: London. Set in the Malay Archipelago in the 1860s; the hero, Captain Lingard, is forced to choose between his Southeast Asian friend and his countrymen.

Dumarçay, Jacques (1991) *The palaces of South-East Asia: architecture and customs*, OUP: Singapore. A broad summary of palace art and architecture in both mainland and island Southeast Asia.

Fenton, James (1988) *All the wrong places: adrift in the politics of Asia*, Penguin: London. British journalist James Fenton skilfully and entertainingly recounts his experiences in Vietnam, Cambodia, the Philippines and Korea.

Fraser-Lu, Sylvia (1988) *Handwoven textiles of South-East Asia*, OUP: Singapore. Well-illustrated, large-format book with informative text.

Higham, Charles (1989) *The archaeology of mainland Southeast Asia from 10,000 BC to the fall of Angkor*, Cambridge University Press: Cambridge. Best summary of changing views of the archaeology of the mainland.

Keyes, Charles F. (1977) *The golden peninsula: culture and adaptation in mainland Southeast Asia*, Macmillan: New York. Academic, yet readable summary of the threads of continuity and change in Southeast Asia's culture.

King, Ben F. and Dickinson, E.C. (1975) *A field guide to the birds of South-East Asia*, Collins: London. Best regional guide to the birds of the region.

Osborne, Milton (1979) *Southeast Asia: an introductory history*, Allen & Unwin: Sydney. Good introductory history, clearly written, published in a portable paperback edition.

Rawson, Philip (1967) *The art of Southeast Asia*, Thames & Hudson: London. Portable general art history of Cambodia, Vietnam, Thailand, Laos, Burma, Java and Bali; by necessity, rather superficial.

Reid, Anthony (1988) *Southeast Asia in the age of commerce 1450-1680: the lands below the winds*, Yale University Press: New Haven. Perhaps the best history of everyday life in Southeast Asia, looking at such themes as physical well-being, material culture and social organization.

Reid, Anthony (1993) *Southeast Asia in the age of commerce 1450-1680: expansion and crisis*, Yale University Press: New Haven. Volume 2 in this excellent history of the region.

Rigg, Jonathan (1991) *Southeast Asia: a region in transition*, Unwin Hyman: London. A thematic geography of the ASEAN region, providing an insight into some of the major issues affecting the region today.

SarDesai, D.R. (1989) *Southeast Asia: past and present*, Macmillan: London. Skilful but at times frustratingly thin history of the region from the 1st century to the withdrawal of US forces from Vietnam.

Savage, Victor R. (1984) *Western impressions of nature and landscape in Southeast Asia*, Singapore University Press: Singapore. Based on a geography PhD thesis, the book is a mine of quotations and observations from Western travellers.

Steinberg, D.J. *et al.* (1987) *In search of Southeast Asia: a modern history*, University of Hawaii Press: Honolulu. The best standard history of the region; it skilfully examines and assesses general processes of change and their impacts from the arrival of the Europeans in the region.

Wallace, Alfred Russel (1869) *The Malay Archipelago: the land of the orang-utan and the bird of paradise; a narrative of travel with studies of man and nature*, Macmillan: London. A classic of natural history writing, recounting Wallace's 8 years in the archipelago and now reprinted.

Young, Gavin (1991) *In search of Conrad*, Hutchinson: London. This well-known travel writer retraces the steps of Conrad; part travel-book, part fantasy, it is worth reading but not up to the standard of his other books.

Radio

The BBC World Service's *Dateline East Asia* provides probably the best news and views on Asia. Also with a strong Asia focus are the broadcasts of the ABC (Australian Broadcasting Corporation).

THAILAND

CONTENTS

INTRODUCTION

In May 1992, the sight of Thai King Bhumibol scolding the Supreme Commander of the Armed Forces General Suchinda following the massacre of pro-democracy demonstrators on the streets of Bangkok, as if he were a wayward child, was a stark reminder that Thailand – literally, the 'Land of the Free' – was not just another Asian economic success story. Despite the rapid growth, frenetic stock exchange, high-rise towers and sophisticated restaurants and clubs of Bangkok, Thailand is a country with a rich seam of tradition which can make even the commonplace, unusual. Politicians consult the spirits for advice, new banks only open after elaborate Brahmanic rites, rituals are performed to summon rain and the King is revered above all else. It is the enticing mix of beaches, hilltribes, Buddhist monasteries, ruined cities and tropical forests which draws 5 million visitors a year to Thailand.

The kingdom is an up-and-coming regional economic powerhouse: in the six years to 1994, Thailand's economy grew by almost 10% each year. Some developed countries are no longer providing aid, claiming that Thailand has outgrown such support. Inevitably, the rapid pace of change has brought with it social, economic and environmental conflicts. Bangkok is overstretched, its transport system on the verge of collapse, while deforestation is such that the government felt impelled to impose a nationwide logging ban at the beginning of 1989. In the poor Northeast, incomes have stagnated, causing social tensions to become more acute, and in the Central Plains, land is now so scarce that landless farmers are being forced to migrate to the squatter communities of the capital in search of work.

Tourism has brought its own problems – 80% of freshwater wells in the Phi Phi National Park are contaminated because of the sheer numbers using the island's limited services. Some educated Thais also blame tourists for the explosion of the sex industry, and the proliferation of AIDS (see page 101). But despite such tensions, politicians, workers and academics alike are generally optimistic about Thailand's future, believing that most hurdles are surmountable – with hard work and a touch of good fortune. This optimism about the future is all the more remarkable given that in the 1970s, when the Communist Party of Thailand was at its most powerful and Vietnam, Laos and Cambodia had all 'fallen' to Communist governments, Thailand was widely touted as the next 'domino' to fall. Unfortunately, this confidence in the future suffered a rude blow in May 1992 when demonstrations in the capital were

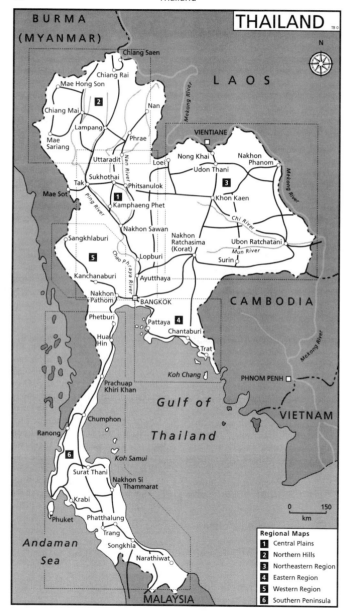

FROM *BAAN* TO *CHANGWAT*: THAILAND'S ADMINISTRATIVE DIVISIONS

Below the region there are a series of further administrative subdivisions. First, the *changwat* or province, of which there are 75, each with a governor at its head. Below the province is the *amphoe* or district, numbering 722 in all, each headed by a *nai amphoe* or district officer. Then comes the *tambon*, a 'commune' of villages, of which there are 7,109, each with a *kamnan* in charge. And finally, the lowest level of administration is the *mubaan*, the village, of which there are 64,450 each headed by a democratically elected *phuuyaibaan* or village head.

---

brutally suppressed by the army. Only the King's intervention prevented further bloodshed, forcing Prime Minister Suchinda Kraprayoon to step down and flee the country (see page 112). With elections held in September 1992, it might appear that Thailand is once again on a democratic path – but many are worried that the army remains a potent force, ready to intervene should events (as the army sees them) warrant.

Environment

The regions of Thailand

Thailand covers an area of 0.5 million square kilometres (about the size of France) and has a population of 58 million (1993) growing at 1.5% each year. It shares its borders with Burma (Myanmar), Laos, Cambodia and Malaysia. Administratively, the country is divided into five main regions: the North, Northeast, Central Plains, South and the Bangkok Metropolitan Region. Two smaller, additional regions are also sometimes identified: the East and West. Each of these seven regions has its own distinctive geographical character.

The **Central region** is Thailand's 'rice bowl', encompassing the wide and fertile Central Plains: this is the economic and cultural heartland of the Thai nation. The construction of dams, and the spread of irrigation in the region has enabled Thailand to become, and remain, the world's largest rice exporter. Yet most farms remain small, family

owned affairs. Towards the southern extremity of the Central Plains lies the **Bangkok Metropolitan Region**. With an official population of nearly 6 million (unofficially somewhere between 7 and 10 million), and supporting both the greatest density of businesses and the key institutions of government, this metropolis is the country's economic and political hub.

The **North** is Thailand's largest region, and includes the Kingdom's second city of Chiang Mai. It is a mountainous region with narrow river valleys, and supports most of the minority hilltribes. The area was not incorporated fully into the Thai state until the 19th century. Doi Pha Hom Pok, the country's highest peak at 2300 m, is located in Chiang Mai Province.

The **Northeast** or '**Isan**' is the second largest, and poorest, region of Thailand. It is also known as the Khorat Plateau and is harsh environmentally. The people of the Northeast speak a dialect of Thai – *Lao* – and they are culturally distinct in terms of food, dress and ritual. Most are rice farmers living in over 25,000 villages.

Just S of the Northeast, sandwiched between the sea and the Damrek range of hills, is the **Eastern region**. This has become an overspill area for Bangkok, with businesses moving to take advantage of cheaper land and less congested infrastructure. The Eastern region also contains the renowned seaside resort of Pattaya.

To the W of the Central Plains and Bangkok is the **Western region**. Until recently this was a relatively undeveloped, mountainous and largely forested area. But over the past 10-20 years, pioneer agriculturalists and logging companies have moved into the West, clearing large tracts of forest, and planting the land with cash crops such as sugar-cane and cassava. Despite these developments, the beautiful mountains which rise up towards the border with Burma still remain relatively unspoilt. Towns here have a 'frontier' atmosphere.

Thailand's seventh region is the **South**, which stretches 1,150 km S to the border with Malaysia. The far South has more in common with island Southeast Asia than mainland Southeast Asia; the climate is tropical, many of the inhabitants are Malay, Islam is widely practiced, and rubber is the dominant crop. Most visitors travel to the South to visit the beach resorts of Koh Samui, Phuket, Koh Phi Phi, Hua Hin and Koh Phangan.

Climate

Thailand lies within the humid tropics and remains hot throughout the year. Mean temperatures vary between 24°C in the far N to 29°C in the Central region, while rainfall ranges from 1,200 mm in parts of the Northeast to over 4,000 mm in some parts of the South (e.g. Ranong) and East (e.g. Khlong Yai, Chantaburi). Far more important than mean figures are seasonal fluctuations in rainfall and, to a lesser extent, temperature. With the exception of the southern isthmus, which receives rainfall throughout the year, Thailand has a dry season which stretches from Nov to Apr corresponding with the period of the NE monsoon, and a wet season from May to Oct, corresponding with the SW monsoon.

The distinction between the dry and the rainy seasons is most pronounced in the Northeast where as much as 98% of

rain falls between Apr and Oct. The dry season can be divided into two, cool and hot. During the cool season in the North, from Dec to Feb, it can become distinctly chilly, with temperatures falling to as low as 7°C at night. The hot season runs between Mar and Jun and temperatures may exceed 40°C before the cooling rains arrive towards the end of the period. But for much of the time and in most places, it is hot whatever the month. The French diplomat La Loubère, who visited Thailand in the 17th century, was convinced that the hot climate 'effiminated the courage' and noticed that the mere sight of a sword would put 100 Thais to flight. (For best time to visit see page 490.)

Generalized seasons

Hot Season Mar to May, dry with temperatures 27°C-35°C, but can be in the 40s for extended periods.

Wet or rainy season Jun to Oct, wet with lower temperatures (due to the cooling effect of the rain and increased cloud cover) 24°C-32°C, but higher humidity.

Cool season Nov to Feb, when conditions are at their most pleasant, with little rain and temperatures ranging from 18°C-32°C.

Seasons in the South Similar weather to that of the Malay peninsula with hot, humid and sunny weather most of the year. Chance of rain at any time, although more likely during the period of the two monsoons, May-Oct (particularly on W side of the peninsula) and Nov-Apr (particularly on E coast).

NB: For monthly rainfall and temperature charts for Bangkok and Chiang Mai see pages 125 and 229 respectively.

Thailand's water crisis

In 1994 Thailand experienced its worst water crisis for many years. The rains in 1993 were fitful and by the beginning of the following year, the country's dams were at only a third of their normal level. Two of the largest storage dams are the

Town and Province	Region	Height above sea	Annual Temp °C			Av Rainfall mm	% rain falling May-Oct
			Max	Min	Av		
Bangkok	C	3m	39.9	9.9	28.1	1418	86%
Lopburi	C	14m	41.8	8.4	28.1	1239	87%
Chiang Mai	N	314m	41.5	6.0	25.8	1268	89%
Mae Hong Son	N	417m	42.0	6.0	26.2	1256	92%
Korat	NE	189m	43.4	4.9	27.1	1197	82%
Udon Thani	NE	181m	43.9	2.5	26.8	1367	88%
Kanchanaburi	W	29m	43.5	5.5	27.8	984	81%
Chantaburi	E	5m	40.8	8.9	27.2	3164	89%
Sattahip	E	56m	40.5	12.3	29.0	1366	65%
Nakhon Si Thammarat	S	7m	37.7	17.1	27.4	2491	39%
Narathiwat	S	4m	36.4	17.1	27.0	2644	41%

TEMPERATURE AND RAINFALL: SELECTED TOWNS

Sirikit and the Bhumibol (named after the Queen and King of Thailand respectively, see page 218), which by March 1994 were at their lowest levels ever. Officials at the Royal Irrigation Department estimate that 7 billion m³ are needed to see the farmers of the Central Plains through the dry season; at the time the dams contained only 1.2 billion m³ between them. The water shortage may so reduce the flow of the Chao Praya River that salt water could intrude upstream and destroy many of the productive market gardens and orchards that line its course.

The crisis has lead to a debate over why Thailand, a country which most people would imagine is blessed with water, should suddenly finds itself faced with the prospect of rationing. As with many environmental discussions in the country, there has been a tendency to look for scapegoats and short-term solutions to a complex and deep-seated problem. Of the varying explanations, the most commonly stated are:

A drier climate brought on by excessive deforestation. Although rainfall was down on the average in 1993, there is no evidence (yet) that Thailand is experiencing a fundamental change in its climate.

Deforestation means less water reaches the dams. This is also unlikely, although deforestation does have an effect in another way. Forests act as sponges, absorbing water during storm periods and making it available for agriculture. The clearing of forests is likely to have caused farmers to use more irrigation water, thereby exerting additional demands on the water supply network.

Dry season cropping is spreading, requiring more water. This is the most convincing of the longer-term explanations. Many more farmers are cultivating rice and other crops during the dry season. These need irrigation water, placing additional demands on the irrigation system.

Farmers are wasteful of water. Although it is difficult to 'blame' farmers, usually the poorest segment of Thailand's population, there is evidence that the water provided to them is used inefficiently. Farmers' irrigation water is heavily subsidised, and so there is a reduced incentive to cultivate crops which are less demanding than wet rice, or to grow wet rice using water more efficiently.

Urban consumers and industry are using more water. This is not a major reason for the crisis. 90% of water is used by farmers; only 4% by domestic users and 6% by industry. Rationing urban consumers is unlikely to have much of an effect on the crisis.

Water supply is poorly managed. Most of Thailand's large dams are designed to be multi-purpose projects. Specifically, they are meant to provide hydro-power and water for irrigation. But they come under the control of the Electricity Generating Authority of Thailand (EGAT) who tend to release water to meet the power needs of industry and urban consumers. This means a great deal of water is 'wasted' during the wet season when it is not needed for agriculture, lowering water levels in the dams and raising the chances of shortages later on.

Identifying a range of explanations of the problem is one thing; but highlighting and then implementing solutions is quite another. The range of solutions mentioned include:

Build more dams. This is unlikely on two counts. First, the environmental movement in Thailand is such that a major dam building programme is highly unlikely. Second, most of the most obvious locations for the construction of large dams have already been exploited. The remainder are either too heavily settled or too valuable environmentally (see page 387).

Price water for agriculture more realistically. This would provide an incentive to farmers to use water more efficiently. But farmers are an influential lobby and have grown use to free water. The battle to implement such a solution would not be easy, especially as Prime Minister Chuan has set 'rural development' as one of the key stones of his administration's aims.

Encourage farmers to grow dryland crops.

This is already occurring. A careful system of subsidies would cause farmers to stop growing rice and planting maize, soybean and other crops in its place.

Ration domestic users and industry. This became the immediate solution. But it will not solve the underlying problem and is mainly intended as a political salve.

Flora and fauna

Flora

Thailand's dominant natural vegetation is **tropical forest**. In the S, parts of the W, and in pockets such as Chanthaburi province in the E, this means 'jungle' or tropical rain forest. Tigers, elephants, banteng (wild ox), sambar (deer) and tapirs still roam the lowland forests, although not in great numbers. Thailand's forests have been depleted to a greater extent than in any other country in Southeast Asia (with the exception of Singapore). In 1938, 70% of Thailand's land area was forested; by 1961 this had been reduced to just over one half. Today, undisturbed forest accounts for only a little more than 15% of the land area. The Royal Forestry Department still insists on a figure of over 20% and puts the area of National Reserve Forest at 40% – despite the fact that over large areas not a single tree remains standing. The causes of this spectacular, and depressing, destruction of Thailand's forests are numerous: simple population growth (in 1911, the Kingdom had a population of just 8 million, today it is nearly 60 million), commercial logging, commercialization and the spread of cash cropping, and dam construction. Cronyism and corruption which is part and parcel of logging across the region, has also marred the management of Thailand's forests. In late 1988 such was the public outcry after floods in the south killed 300 people – and whose severity was linked in the public imagination to deforestation – that a nation-

THAILAND'S ORCHIDS: A BLOOMING BUSINESS

Thailand's forests, wetlands and grasslands support over 1,000 varieties of orchid (there are between 17,000 and 30,000 species worldwide, and another 30,000 registered hybrids) and the country has become Southeast Asia's largest exporter of the blooms. In 1991, flower exports – mostly orchids – earned US$80 million. The industry began in the 1950s, but only really expanded in the mid-1980s as orchid farms were established around Bangkok. Of the various genuses, the most popular is *Dendrobium* which is particularly suited to Thailand's seasonal climate and has the added attraction of blooming throughout the year.

In 1987, official exports of orchid flowers totalled less than US$15 million; in 1991 the figure was more than double this (the true figure is thought to be at least twice as high again). Over half of these exports go to Japan – where customers have a particular predilection for pink and purple blooms – 20%-25% to Europe, and 15%-20% to the US. A problem that has prevented an even more dramatic increase in exports is a lack of air-freight space. But even with such healthy growth, there are fears that a change of fashion in Japan might undermine the market. The price of the popular pink *Sonia dendrobium* has already declined from ฿5-6 to ฿2-3 per bloom.

wide logging ban was introduced in Jan 1989. Few doubt though that deforestation continues.

The tropical rain forests of Thailand, although not comparable with those of Malaysia and Indonesia, have a high diversity of species, exceeding 100/ha in some areas. In total, it is estimated that Thailand supports 20,000-25,000 species of plant.

In the North and the Northeast the vegetation is adapted to a climate with a dry season which may stretch over 6 months. For this reason, the forests are less species-rich than the forests of the South. In many cases they are also highly degraded due to encroachment by loggers and farmers. Other sub-types of tropical forest in Thailand include *semi-evergreen forest* (in the Peninsula and north, along the border with Burma), *dry evergreen forest* (in the wetter parts of the Northeast and the North), *mixed deciduous* and *dry dipterocarp savanna forest* (mostly in the Northeast and parts of the northern Central Plains).

Fauna

Thailand's fauna is even more threatened than its forests. Of the kingdom's 282 species of mammal, 40 are endangered. For its birds, the picture is equally gloomy: 190 endangered species out of 928. And for the country's reptiles and amphibians, there are 37 endangered species out of 405. A century ago, wild elephants and tigers roamed the Bang Kapi area east of Bangkok—now it is over-run with shopping malls. It was only in 1960 that a law was enacted protecting wild animals.

Thailand supports a rich and varied fauna, partly because it lies on the boundary between several zoogeographic regions: the Indochinese, Indian and Sundaic (Malesia). It also lies on a crossroads between N and S, acting as a waystation for animals dispersing N from the Sundaic islands, and S from the Asian mainland. The problem in trying to maintain the country's biodiversity (both flora and fauna) is that most of its national parks and wildlife sanctuaries are thought to be too small to be sustainable. A single male tiger, for example, needs about 50 sq km of forest to survive; some of Thailand's parks are less than 100 sq km in area.

THE SIAMESE CAT

The Siamese cat was originally found only in Siam. Although the charcoal grey breed – in Thai called the *si sawat* – is best known, there are also three other types of Siamese cat: the cream-coloured seal point, the blue point, and the Burmese. Unlike other cats, the Siamese cat is said to like water and be an excellent swimmer. The kink in the tail that used also to be characteristic of the Siamese cat is rare today and is regarded in Thailand as a mark of good luck. It is said that the Siamese cat comes from the town of Korat in the Northeast.

Mammals

During the 1980s some of Thailand's endangered species of mammal disappeared entirely. The Javan and Sumatran rhinoceros, the kouprey (*Bos sauveli*, the largest cattle in the world), wild water buffalo and the Eld's deer (*Cervus eldi*) are probably all extinct in Thailand, or on the verge of extinction. The world's last Schomburgk's deer (*Cervus schomburgki*) was kept as a pet in the grounds of a Buddhist monastery in Samut Sakhon province before being clubbed to death by a drunk in 1938. The reasons for this pattern of extermination are not difficult to fathom: destruction of habitat and over-hunting (see below). Thailand does have national legislation protecting rare species from hunting, capturing and trade, but too often the legislation is ignored and even officials have actively flouted the law, sometimes hunting in national parks. Of Thailand's 282 species of mammal, 40 are listed in the International Union for the Conservation of Nature and Natural Resources (IUCN) Red List of Endangered Species. These include the pileated gibbon (*Hylobates pileatus*), the clouded leopard (*Neofelis nebulosa*), the Malayan tapir (*Tapirus indicus*) and the tiger (*Panthera tigris*). Indeed, almost all Thailand's large mammals are in danger of extinction in the country.

Birds

Birdlife in Thailand is also under severe pressure. Birds' habitats are being destroyed, pollution is increasing, and hunting is barely controlled. Even in Thailand's national parks, a lack of resources and widespread corruption, mean that bird populations are under threat.

Thirty years ago about half of the country was forested, of which 80% has now disappeared. Birds are also hunted by farmers for food and virtually any size and shape of bird is considered fair game. The rarer and more colourful species are hunted by collectors for the bird trade – for which Thailand is a centre. It is not unusual to walk in the countryside and neither see nor hear a bird of any type. Three of Thailand's birds are listed by the IUCN as threatened with extinction: the giant ibis (*Pseudibis gigantea*), Chinese egret (*Egretta eulophotes*), and the white-winged wood duck (*Cairina scutulata*); many others have had their populations decimated.

In total, Thailand has 928 species of bird – more than double the number found in Europe – which account for a tenth of the world's species. This richness of birdlife is due to the varied nature of Thailand's habitats and the country's position at the junction of 3 zoological realms. The country is also an important wintering area for migrant birds from the northern latitudes.

Reptiles

Thailand supports an impressive and varied population of snakes. In total there are 298 reptile and 107 amphibian species, of which 37 are regarded as endangered. The closest most people come to a snake (at least knowingly) is at Bangkok's Red Cross Snake Farm or at the snake farm near the floating market in Thonburi. If bitten see page 25.

The large **non-venomous** pythons are active around dusk and kill their prey by constriction. The reticulated python (*Python reticulatus*) can grow to a length of 15 m and although non-venomous their bites are powerful. Stories about reticulated pythons swallowing people are difficult to substantiate. One report in a Calcutta newspaper in 1927 stated that a Burmese salesman, Maung Chit Chine, had been swallowed while on a hunting trip; his partners found his hat and the snake, asleep, nearby. They killed the python and cut it open to reveal Maung's body inside. Other smaller pythons include the blood python (*Python curtus*) and rock python (*Python molurus bivittatus*).

Some of the most beautiful non-venomous snakes in Thailand are the racers (genus Elaphe and Gonyosoma). They live in a variety of habitats, and because they are diurnal are often seen. The visually striking, gold-coloured copperhead racer (*Elephe radiata*) can grow to a length of 2 m and lives in open grasslands; the bright green, red-tailed racer (*Gonyosoma oxycephalum*) lives in trees. It can also grow to 2m and is easily identified by its brown tail. Other snakes found in Thailand include the rat snakes (genus Zaocys and Ptyas), the beautiful whip-like bronzebacks (genus Dendrelaphis), and the keelbacks (sub-family Natricinae).

But it is the dread – often misplaced – of the **venomous species** which make them the most fascinating of snakes. There are two types: the front-fanged (more venomous) and back-fanged (mildly venomous) snakes. The latter include whip snakes (genus Ahaetulla and Dryophiops), water snakes (subfamily Homalopsinae), and cat snakes (genus Boiga). The former include cobras, the best known of which is the king cobra (*Ophiophagus hannah*), common Chinese cobra (*Naja naja atra*) and the monocled cobra (*Naja naja kaouthia*). The king cobra is said to be the longest venomous snake in the world; it has been known to reach lengths of up to 6 m. It is also among the most dangerous due to its aggressive nature. One specimen shot in the mountains of Nakhon Si Thammarat in 1924 measured 5.6 m. Their venom is a very powerful neurotoxin, and victims can be dead within half an hour. It has even been claimed that elephants have died after being bitten, the snake puncturing the soft skin at the tip of the trunk. King cobras are found throughout the country, in most habitats. It should be emphasized that despite their aggressiveness, few people die from cobra bites in Thailand.

The venom of **sea snakes** (family Hydrophiidae) is even more powerful than that of cobras, and the common sea snake's (*Enhydrina schistosa*) is said to be the most toxic of any snake. Fortunately, sea snakes are not particularly aggressive, and it is rare for swimmers to be bitten. 22 species have been found in the waters of Southeast Asia, and all bar one (*Laticauda colubrina*, which lays its eggs in rock crevices) produce their young live. They grow to a length of 2 m and feed on fish.

Snakes of the viper family (*Viperidae*) grow to a length of 1 m, and the kraits (genus Bungarus) to 2 m. Vipers are easily identifiable by their arrow-shaped heads. The vipers' long fangs, their position at the front of the mouth, and their aggressiveness, makes them more dangerous than other more poisonous species. The Malayan pit viper (*Agkistrodon rhodostoma*) and Pope's pit viper (*Trimeresurus popeiorum*) are both highly irritable. Kraits, though possessing a toxic venom which has been known to kill, are of sleepy temperament and rarely attack unless provoked. The banded krait (*Bungarus fasciatus*), with its black and yellow striped body, is very distinctive.

Insects

Insects are not usually at the top of a visitor's agenda to Thailand. But, as with the kingdom's birds and flora, the country also has a particularly rich insect population due to its position at a crossroads between different, and varied, zoogeographic zones. There are over 1,400 species of butterfly and moth (*Lepidoptera*), including one of the world's largest moths, the giant atlas (*Attacus atlas*) which has a wing span of up to 28 cm. Beetles are even more numerous, although how numerous is not known: one single sq km of the Thung Yai-Huai Kha Khaeng area was found to support 10,000 species alone.

Marine life

Thailand's coastline abuts onto both the Indian Ocean (Andaman Sea) and the South China Sea (Gulf of Thailand) and therefore has marine flora and fauna characteristic of both regions. In the Gulf, 850 species of open-water fish have been identified including tuna, of which Thailand is the world's largest exporter. In the Andaman Sea, game fish such as blue and black marlin, barracuda, sailfish and various sharks are all present.

Among sea mammals, Thailand's shores provide nesting sites for four species of sea turtle: the huge leatherback, green, Ridley's and the hawksbill turtle. The latter is now very rare, while a fifth species, the loggerhead turtle, has disappeared from Thailand's shores and waters. Other marine mammals include 30 species of sea snake, the saltwater crocodile (which may now be extinct), three species of dolphin, and the dugong or sea cow.

Coral reefs probably contain a richer profusion of life than any other ecosystem – even exceeding the tropical rainforest in terms of species diversity. Those in Thailand's Andaman Sea are among the finest in the region – and maritime parks like the Surin and Similan islands have been gazetted to help protect these delicate habitats. Although the country's reefs remain under-researched, 210 species of hard coral and 108 coral reef fish have so far been identified in the Andaman Sea. Literally tens of thousands of other marine organisms including soft corals, crustacea, echinoderms and worms, would have to be added to this list to build up a true picture of the ecosystem's diversity.

Recommended reading

Boonsong Lekagul and J.A. McNeely (1988) *Mammals of Thailand*, Association for the Conservation of Wildlife. For keen ornithologists Boonsong Lekagul and Edward Cronin's (1974) *Bird guide of Thailand*, Association for the Conservation of Wildlife: Bangkok; a newer publication is Boonsong Lekagul and Philip Round's (1991) *The birds of Thailand*, Sahakarn Bhaet: Bangkok. Boonsong Lekagul et

---

THE FOREST IN THE MARKET

A walk around almost any up-country market will reveal not just an abundance of familiar fruits, vegetables, fish, meats and consumer goods, but also a range of 'forest products'. Grubs, beetles, frogs, roots, and turtles are sold—usually for the pot. Among the various insects the most common is the large *maeng da*, a beetle which may be 5 cm long. *Maeng da* are caught at night: nets are strung up and powerful lights used to attract the insects. But because of extensive deforestation *maeng da* have become a luxury item; a single beetle costs ฿6 or more. They are deep fried and usually served with chilli. The name *maeng da* is also the Thai term for pimp, and for the prehistoric horseshoe crab. In all three cases the reason is the same: the male of the species latches on to the female and allows her to carry and support him.

al's (1977) *Fieldguide to the butterflies of Thailand*, Association for the Conservation of Wildlife: Bangkok. Available from most large bookshops in Bangkok.

National parks

In 1961 Khao Yai became Thailand's first national park although King Ramkhamhaeng of Sukhothai created a royal reserve in the 13th century, and the grounds of Buddhist wats have always provided havens for wildlife. Today, 63 parks cover over 25,000 sq km spread throughout the kingdom, encompassing all the principal ecological zones. Including Thailand's 32 wildlife sanctuaries (which cover another 22,000 sq km), and 48 non-hunting areas, over 11% of Thailand's land area is protected in some way. Though impressive on paper, this does not mean that there are nearly 50,000 square kilometres of protected forest, grassland, swamp and sea. Settled and shifting agriculturalists live in many parks, illegal logging is widespread (though better controlled today than in the 1980s), and poaching continues to be a problem. Poor pay, lack of manpower and corruption, all contribute to the difficulties of maintaining the integrity of these 'protected' areas. Park rangers for example are provided with no uniform or equipment and are paid only ฿70/day – hardly conditions or a salary on which to build commitment or motivation. Even so, 40 park wardens have been murdered doing their job.

There seems to have been an increase of late in public awareness towards wildlife and the environment. Certainly, there have been some notable successes: the logging ban of 1990, the shelving of the plan to build the Nam Choan dam in the contiguous Huai Kha Khaeng and Tha Thungna National Parks (see page 387), and a far wider environmental awareness amongst the Thai population. But the battle is far from won. Loggers, poachers, and tree plantation companies wield enormous financial and political power. In 1990, such was the exasperation of Sueb Makasathien, the highly regarded director of the incomparable Huai Kha Khaeng Wildlife Sanctuary, that he committed suicide. It is generally agreed that Sueb killed himself because he was unable to prevent corrupt officials, loggers and poachers from degrading his park – 2,400 sq km of the finest forest in all Southeast Asia (Sueb was hoping to get the sanctuary accepted as a World Heritage area by UNESCO). Tourism has also left its mark on the parks. Khao Yai is now so popular as a weekend trip from Bangkok that its capacity has been exceeded, while coastal and island marine parks suffer from refuse littered beaches and campsites.

In 1993 the Tourist Authority of Thailand (TAT) suggested that they take over control of some of Thailand's national parks from the National Parks Division of the Royal Forestry Department. Environmentalists, perhaps unsurprisingly, were outraged. Having promoted, in their eyes, the ruination of some of the Kingdom's finest coastal areas, here was the TAT intending to do the same to a few areas of wilderness left. To be fair, the TAT also have a case: many of the parks are woefully poorly protected, and the money from tourism, could held fund a better parks service. Koh Samet and Koh Phi Phi, both national parks, are – illegally – covered with bungalow developments. Khao Yai, Thailand's first park, has hotels and golf courses within its area. The Thaplan national park in the NE is extensively logged by army-backed interests. The attractions for the TAT are clear. Thailand is widely – and in some senses unfairly – perceived as 'over-touristed'. The parks are new, unspoilt (to a degree) and can be used to cash in on the eco-tourism, environmentalism and general greenery that pervades the tourism industry. Although the opponents to the TAT's intentions have so far won the argument, the debate is probably a sterile one. The

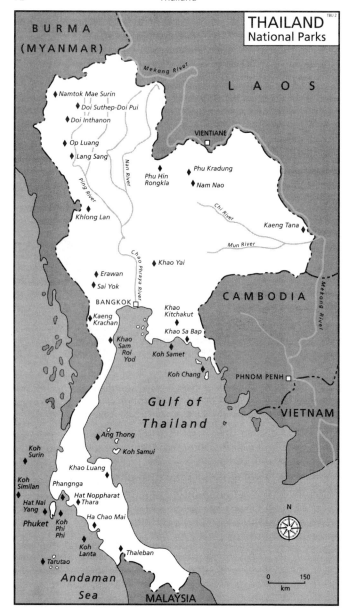

THAILAND
National Parks
TBU 2

BURMA
(MYANMAR)

LAOS

Mekong River

♦ *Namtok Mae Surin*
♦ *Doi Suthep-Doi Pui*
♦ *Doi Inthanon*
♦ *Op Luang*
♦ *Lang Sang*

VIENTIANE □

Nan River
Ping River

♦ *Phu Kradung*
♦ *Phu Hin Rongkla*
♦ *Nam Nao*

Chi River
♦ *Kaeng Tana*

♦ *Khlong Lan*

Mun River

♦ *Khao Yai*

♦ *Erawan*
♦ *Sai Yok*

Chao Phraya River

CAMBODIA

BANGKOK □

♦ *Kaeng Krachan*

♦ *Khao Kitchakut*

♦ *Khao Sam Roi Yod*

♦ *Khao Sa Bap*

♦ *Koh Samet*

♦ *Koh Chang*

Mekong River

PHNOM PENH □

Gulf of Thailand

VIETNAM

Koh Surin
♦

♦ *Ang Thong*
♥ *Koh Samui*

Koh Similan
♦

♦ *Khao Luang*

♦ *Phangnga*
♦ *Hat Noppharat Thara*

Hat Nai Yang
♦

♦ *Ha Chao Mai*

Phuket
♦ *Koh Phi Phi*

♦ *Koh Lanta*

♦ *Thaleban*

Tarutao

N

Andaman Sea

0   150
km

MALAYSIA

national parks, as they stand, are being ruined by poor management; the question is whether the TAT might provide better management.

National park facilities

Most national parks have a park office with wardens (often not English-speaking), bungalows and dormitories for hire, camping grounds, and trails (not always well-marked). Bungalows in the more popular parks – Khao Yai, Phu Kradung, Doi Inthanon, Nam Nao, Doi Suthep and Erawan – are often booked-up, so advance booking is recommended. For reservations contact: Reservation Office, National Parks Division, Royal Forest Department, Phanhonyothin Rd, Bangkhen, Bangkok B 5794842/ 5790529; or telephone park offices given in the relevant sections.

Recommended reading

Gray, D., Pipprell, C. and Graham, M. (1991) *National parks of Thailand*, Industrial Finance Corporation of Thailand: Bangkok.

History

Prehistory

Research since the end of World War II has shown Thailand to be a 'hearth' – or core area – in Southeast Asian prehistory. Discoveries at archaeological sites such as Ban Chiang in the Northeast (see page 334), Non Nok Tha in the North, and Ban Kao in the West have revealed evidence of early agriculture (possibly, 7000 BC) – particularly rice cultivation – pottery (3500 BC) and metallurgy (2500 BC). Although heated argument over the significance and the dating of the finds continues, there is no doubt that important technologies were being developed and disseminated from an early date. These finds have altered the view of this part of the world from being a 'receptacle' for outside influences to being an area of innovation in its own right.

Today, the population of Thailand is made up of Tai-speaking peoples. For long, it has been thought that the Tai migrated from southern China about 2,000 years ago, filtering down the valleys and along the river courses that cut N-S down the country. These migrants settled in the valleys of N Thailand, on the Khorat Plateau, and in parts of the lower Chao Phraya basin. Even at this early date there was a clear division between hill and lowland people. The lowland Tai mastered the art of wet rice cultivation (see page 32), supporting large populations and enabling powerful states and impressive civilizations to evolve. In the highlands, people worked with the forest, living in small itinerant groups, eking out a living through shifting cultivation (see page 29) or hunting and gathering. In exchange for metal implements, salt and pottery, the hill peoples would trade natural forest products: honey, resins such as lac, wild animal skins, ivory and herbs. Even today, lowland 'civilized' Thais view the forest (*pa*) as a wild place (*thuan*), inhabited by spirits and hill peoples. This is reflected in the words used to denote 'civilized' lowland Thais – *Khon Muang*, People of the Town – and 'barbaric' upland people – *Khon Pa*, People of the Forest.

Mon, Srivijayan and Khmer influences

Dvaravati

Before the Tais emerged as the dominant force in the 13th century, Thailand was dominated by Mon and Khmer peoples. The Mon kingdom of Dvaravati was centred close to Bangkok, with cities at modern day Uthong and Nakhon Pathom. Dvaravati relics have also been found in the N and NE, along what are presumed to have been the trade routes between Burma E to Cambodia, N to Chiang Mai and NE to the Khorat Plateau and Laos. Dvaravati lasted from the 6th to the 11th century. Only the tiny

Mon kingdom of Haripunjaya, with its capital at Lamphun in the N, managed to survive annexation by the powerful Khmer empire and remained independent until the 13th century. The state of Dvaravati was an artistic and political outlier of the Mon empire of Burma. Unfortunately, virtually nothing of the architecture of the Dvaravati period remains. Buildings were constructed of laterite blocks, faced with stucco (a mixture of sand and lime) and, apparently, bound together with vegetable glue. In Thailand, only the stupa of Wat Kukut outside Lamphun gives an indication of Dvaravati architecture (it was last rebuilt in 1218, see page 228). Dvaravati sculpture is much better

THAI KINGS

Period	King	Dates
Khmer (Lopburi)	Suryavarman II	1113-1150
	Jayavarman VII	1181-1219
	Indravarman II	1220-1243
Chiang Mai (selected)	Mengrai	?-1317
	Tiloka	1442-1488
Sukhothai (selected)	Intradit	1238-1270?
	Ramkhamhaeng	1275-1317
	Lo Thai	?1327-?1346
	Li Thai	1347-1368
Ayutthaya (selected)	Ramathibodi I (aka King Uthong)	1350-1369
	Boromraja I	1370-1388
	Boromraja II	1424-1448
	Boromtrailokant	1448-1488
	Naresuan	1590-1605
	Prasat Thong	1630-1656
	Narai	1656-1688
	Boromkot	1733-1758
	Suriyamarin	1758-1767
Thonburi	General Taksin	1767-1782
Bangkok	Ramatobodi (Rama I)	1782-1809
	Phra Phutthaloetla (Rama II)	1809-1824
	Phra Nangklao (Rama III)	1824-1851
	Mongkut (Rama IV)	1851-1868
	Chulalongkorn (Rama V)	1868-1910
	Vajiravudh (Rama VI)	1910-1925
	Prajadhipok (Rama VII)	1925-1935
	Ananda Mahidol (Rama VIII)	1935-1945
	Bhumibol (Rama IX)	1945-present

represented and the National Gallery in Bangkok has some fine examples. The sculptors of the period drew their inspiration from India's late-Gupta cave temples, rendering human form almost supernaturally.

Srivijaya

The powerful Srivijayan empire, whose capital was at Palembang in Sumatra, extended its control over S Thailand from the 7th to the 13th century. Inscriptions and sculptures dating from the Srivijayan period have been found near the modern Thai towns of Chaiya and Sating Phra in Surat Thani and Songkhla provinces. They reveal an eclectic mixture of Indian, Javanese, Mon and Khmer artistic influences, and incorporate both Hindu and Mahayana Buddhist iconography. Probably the best examples of what little remains of Srivijayan architecture in Thailand are Phra Boromthat and a sanctuary at Wat Kaeo, both in Chaiya (see page 443).

The Khmers

Of all the external empires to impinge on Thailand before the rise of the Tai, the most influential was the Khmer. Thailand lay on the fringes of the Angkorian Kingdom, but nonetheless many Thai towns are Khmer in origin: That Phanom, Sakhon Nakhon, and Phimai in the NE; Lopburi, Suphanburi and Ratburi in the lower central plain; and Phitsanulok, Sawankhalok and Sukhothai in the upper central plain.

The period of Khmer inspiration is referred to as 'Lopburi', after the Central Thai town of the same name which was a Khmer stronghold. The peak of the Khmer period in Thailand lasted from the 11th to the 13th century, corresponding with the flowering of the Angkorian period in Cambodia. However, antiquities have been found that date back as far as the 7th and 8th century AD. The most impressive architectural remains are to be found in the Northeastern region: Phimai, not far from Nakhon Ratchasima (Korat) (see page 303), and Muang Tham (page 300) and Phanom Rung (page 299), both S of Buriram. As Cambodia's treasures are still relatively expensive and hard to get to, these 'temple cities' are a substitute, giving some idea of the economic power and artistic brilliance of the Khmer period.

The Tais

The Tai did not begin to exert their dominance over modern Thailand until the 12th to 13th centuries. By then they had taken control of Lamphun in the north, founded Chiang Mai, established the Sukhothai Kingdom in the Yom River valley, and gained control of the southern peninsula. From the 13th century onwards, the history of Thailand becomes a history of the Tai people.

An important unit of organization among the Tai was the *muang*. Today, muang is usually translated as 'town'. But it means much more than this, and to an extent defies translation. The muang was a unit of control, and denoted those people who came under the sway of a *chao* or lord. In a region where people were scarce but land was abundant, the key to power was to control manpower, and thereby to turn forest into riceland. At the beginning of the 13th century, some Tai lords began to extend their control over neighbouring muang, forging kingdoms of considerable power. In this way, the Tai began to make a history of their own, rather than merely to be a part of history.

Chiang Mai or Lanna Thai

In Northern Thailand, various Tai chiefs began to expand at the expense of the Mons. The most powerful of these men was **King Mengrai**, born in October 1239 at Chiang Saen. It is said that Mengrai, concerned that the constant warring and squabbling between the lords of the North was harming the population, took it upon himself to unite the region under one king – himself. En-

THAI, SIAMESE OR TAI?

Is a Thai, a Tai? And is this the same as a Siamese? Sometimes. Thai here is used to mean a national of Thailand. Prior to World War II, Thailand was known as Siam, a name by which Europeans had referred to the kingdom from the 16th century. However, in 1939 Prime Minister Phibun Songkhram decided a change was in order, largely because he wished to disassociate his country from the past, but also because of his xenophobia towards the Chinese community. The name he chose is a more direct translation of the Thai term *prathet Thai* (literally 'country of Thailand') and firmly established Thailand as the country of the Tais (see below). Nonetheless, because the change is associated with the right-wing Phibun government, some academics still refuse to use the new name and talk, rather pointlessly, of Siam. Tai here is used to refer to the Tai-speaking peoples who are found not just in Thailand but also in Burma, Laos and Southern China. Some Thais are not Tai (for example the Malay-speaking Thais of the South), while many Tais are not Thais. As David Wyatt writes in his *Thailand: a short history*:

"The modern Thai may or may not be descended by blood from the late-arriving Tai. He or she may instead be the descendant of still earlier Mon or Khmer inhabitants of the region, or of much later Chinese or Indian immigrants. Only over many centuries has a 'Thai' culture, a civilization and identity, emerged as the product of interaction between Tai and indigenous and immigrant cultures."

tranced by the legendary wealth of Haripunjaya, Mengrai spent almost a decade hatching a plot to capture this powerful prize. He sent one of his scribes – Ai Fa – to ingratiate himself with the King of Haripunjaya, and having done this encouraged the scribe to sow seeds of discontent. By 1280, the king of Haripunjaya was alienated from his court and people and in 1281, Mengrai attacked with a huge army and took the city without trouble. Mengrai then set about uniting his expansive, new kingdom. This was helped to a significant degree by the propagation of Ceylonese Theravada Buddhism, which transcended tribal affiliations and helped to create a new identity of Northern Thai. The Lanna (literally, 'Million Rice-fields') Thai Kingdom created by Mengrai was to remain the dominant power in the North until the mid 16th century.

In 1296, Mengrai built a new capital which he named Chiang Mai, or 'New Town' (see page 229). The art of this era is called Chiang Saen and dates from the 11th century. It is still in evidence throughout the N – in Chiang Saen, Chiang Mai, Lamphun and Lampang – and shows strong stylistic links with Indian schools of art (see page 89).

Sukhothai

South of Chiang Mai, at the point where the rivers of the N spill out onto the wide and fertile Central Plains, a second Thai kingdom was evolving during the 13th century: the Sukhothai Kingdom. Its most famous king was **Ramkhamhaeng (1275-1317)** or 'Rama the Brave' who gained his name, so it is said, after defeating an enemy general in elephant combat at the age of 19. When Ramkhamhaeng ascended to the throne in 1275, Sukhothai was a relatively small kingdom occupying part of the upper Central Plain. When he died in 1317, extensive swathes of land came under the King of Sukhothai's control, and only King Mengrai of Lanna and King Ngam Muang of Phayao could be regarded as his equals. But King Ramkhamhaeng is remembered as much for his artistic achievements as for his raw power. Under Khmer tutelage, he devised the Thai writing system and also made a number of administrative reforms. The inscription No. 1 from his reign is regarded as the first work of Thai literature, and contains the famous lines:

'In the time of King Ramkhamhaeng, this land of Sukhothai is thriving. In the water there is fish, in the fields there is rice. The lord of the realm does not levy toll on his subjects for travelling the roads; they lead their cattle to trade or ride their horses to sell; whoever wants to trade in elephants does so; whoever wants to trade in horses, does so; whoever wants to trade in silver and gold, does so. When any commoner or man of rank dies, his estate – his elephants, wives, children, granaries, rice, retainers and groves of areca and betel – is left in its entirety to his son. ... When [the King] sees someone's rice he does not covet it, when he sees someone's wealth he does not get angry... He has hung a bell in the opening of the gate over there: if any commoner in the land has a grievance which sickens his belly and gripes his heart, and which he wants to make known to his ruler and lord, it is easy; he goes and strikes the bell which the King has hung there; King Ramkhamhaeng, the ruler of the kingdom, hears the call; he goes and questions the man, examines the case, and decides it justly for him. So the people of this *muang* [city/state] of Sukhothai praise him'.

Although the kingdom of Sukhothai owed a significant cultural and artistic debt to the Khmers, by the 13th century the Tais of Sukhothai were beginning to explore and develop their own interpretations of politics, art and life. The kingdom promoted Theravada Buddhism, sponsoring missionary monks to spread the word. For many Thais today, the Sukhothai period – which lasted a mere 200 years – represents the apogée, the finest flowering of Thai brilliance. A visit to the ruins of Sukhothai or its sister city of Si Satchanalai reinforces this (see pages 203-214).

Ayutthaya

In the middle of the 14th century, Sukhothai's influence began to be challenged by another Thai kingdom, Ayutthaya. Located over 300 km S, on the Chao Phraya River, Ayutthaya was the successor to the Mon kingdom of Lavo (Lopburi). It seems that from the 11th century, Tais began to settle in the area and were peacefully incorporated into the Mon state where they gradually gained greater influence. Finally, in 1350, a Tai lord took control of the area, and founded a new capital at Ayutthaya. This kingdom would subsequently be known as Siam. From 1350, Ayutthaya began to extend its power S as far as Nakhon Si Thammarat, and E to Cambodia, raiding Angkor in the late 14th century and taking the city in 1432. The palace was looted and the Khmers abandoned their capital, fleeing eastwards towards present-day Phnom Penh. Although Sukhothai and Ayutthaya initially vied with one another for supremacy, Ayutthaya proved the more powerful. In 1438, King Boromraja II placed his seven year old son, Ramesuan (later to become King Boromtrailokant) on the throne, signalling the end of Sukhothai as an independent power.

During the Ayutthayan period, the basis of Thai common law was introduced by King Ramathibodi (1350-1369), who drew upon the Indian Code of Manu, while the powerful King Boromtrailokant (1448-1488) centralized the administration of his huge kingdom and introduced various other civil, economic and military reforms. Perhaps the most important was the *sakdi naa* system in which an individual's social position was related to the size of his landholdings. The heir apparent controlled 16,000 ha, the highest official, 1,600 ha, the lowest commoner, 4 ha. A code of conduct for royalty was also introduced, with punishments again linked to position: princes of high rank who had violated the law were to be bound by gold fetters, those of lower rank by silver. The execution of a member of the royal family was, it has been said, carried out by encasing them in a sack and either beating them to death with scented sandalwood clubs or having them trampled by white elephants. Even kicking a palace door would, in theory, lead to the amputation of the offending foot.

By King Boromtrailokant's reign, Ayutthaya had extended its control over 500,000 sq km, and the capital had a population of 150,000. Although the art of Ayutthaya is not as 'pure' as that of Sukhothai, the city impressed 16th and 17th century European visitors. The German surgeon Christopher Fryke remarked that "there is not a finer City in all India". Perhaps it was the tiger and elephant fights which excited the Europeans so much. The elephants (regarded as noble and representing the state) were expected to win by tossing the tiger (regarded as wild and representing disorder) repeatedly into the air. The fact that the tigers were often tied to a stake or attacked by several elephants at once must have widened the odds against them (in Vietnam it was reported that tigers sometimes had their claws removed and jaws sewn together). Despite the undoubted might of Ayutthaya and the absolute power that lay within each monarch's grasp, kings were not, in the main, able to name their successors. Blood was not an effective guarantee to kingship and a strong competitor could easily usurp a rival even though he might – on paper – have a better claim to the throne. As a result, the history of Ayutthaya is peppered with court intrigues, bloody succession struggles, and rival claims.

From the 16th through to the 18th centuries, the fortunes of the Ayutthayan Kingdom were bound up with those of Burma. Over a 220-year period, the Burmese invaded on no less than 6 occasions. The first time was in 1548 when the Burmese king of Pegu, Tabengshweti encircled the capital. King Mahachakrapat only survived the ensu-

ing battle when one of his wives drove her elephant in front of an approaching warrior. Elephants figured heavily in war and diplomacy during the Ayutthayan period: Tabengshweti justified his invasion by pointing out that he had no white elephants, the holiest of beasts (the Buddha's last reincarnation before his enlightenment was as a white elephant). The Ayutthayan king meanwhile had a whole stable of them, and was not willing to part with even one. Although this attack failed, in 1569, King Bayinnaung mounted another invasion and plundered the city, making Ayutthaya a vassal state. When the Burmese withdrew to Pegu, they left a ravaged countryside, devoid of people, and large areas of riceland returned to scrub and forest. But, a mere 15 years later, Prince Naresuan re-established Thai sovereignty and began to lay the foundations for a new golden age in which Ayutthaya would be more powerful and prosperous than ever before (see page 200).

The 17th century saw a period of intense commercial contact with the Dutch, English and French. In 1608, Ayutthaya sent a diplomatic mission to the Netherlands and in 1664 a trading treaty was concluded with the Dutch. Even as early as the 17th century, Thailand had a flourishing prostitution industry. In the 1680s an official was given a monopoly of prostitution in the capital; he used 600 women to generate considerable state revenues. The kings of Ayutthaya also made considerable use of foreigners as advisers and ministers at the court. The most influential such family was founded by two Persian brothers who arrived at the beginning of the 17th century. However, the best known was the Greek adventurer Constantine Phaulcon, who began his life in the East as a mere cabin boy with the East India Company and rose to become one of King Narai's (1656-1688) closest advisers and one of the kingdom's most influential officials before being executed in 1688 (see page 194). He was implicated in a plot with the French against King Narai and his execution heralded 100 years of relative isolation as the Thais became wary of, and avoided close relations with, the West.

The height of Ayutthaya's power and glory is often associated with the reign of King Boromkot (literally, 'the King in the urn [awaiting cremation]', as he was the last sovereign to be honoured in this way). Boromkot ruled from 1733 to 1758 and he fulfilled many of the imagined pre-requisites of a great king: he promoted Buddhism and ruled effectively over a vast swathe of territory. But, in retrospect, signs of imperial senility were beginning to materialize even as Ayutthaya's glory was approaching its zenith. In particular, King Boromkot's sons began to exert their ambitions. Prince Senaphithak, the eldest, went so far as to have some of the king's officials flogged; in retaliation, one of the aggrieved officials revealed that the prince had been having an affair with one of Boromkot's 3 queens. He admitted to the liaison and was flogged to death along with his lover.

The feud with Burma was renewed in 1760 when the Burmese King Alaungpaya invaded Thailand. His attack was repulsed after one of the seige guns exploded, seriously injuring the Burmese king. He died soon afterwards during the arduous march back to Pegu. Three years later, his successor, King Hsinbyushin raised a vast army and took Chiang Mai, Lamphun and Luang Prabang (Laos). By 1765, the Burmese were ready to mount a second assault on Ayutthaya. Armies approached from the north and west and at the beginning of 1766 met up outside the city, from where they laid seige to the capital. King Suriyamarin offered to surrender, but King Hsinbyushin would hear nothing of it. The city fell after a year, in 1767. David Wyatt writes:

"The Burmese wrought awful desolation. They raped, pillaged and plundered and led tens of thousands of captives away to Burma. They put the torch to everything flammable and even hacked at images of the Buddha for the gold with which they were coated. King Suriyamarin is said to have fled the city in a small boat and starved to death ten days later."

The city was too damaged to be renovated for a second time, and the focus of the Thai state moved southwards once again – to Thonburi, and from there to Bangkok.

Bangkok and the Rattanakosin period

After the sacking of Ayutthaya, **General Taksin** moved the capital 74 km S to Thonburi, opposite Bangkok. Taksin's original name was Sin. Proving himself an adept administrator, he was appointed Lord of Tak (a city in the upper Central Plain), or Phraya Tak. Hence his name Tak-sin. From Thonburi, Taksin successfully fought successive Burmese invasions, until the stress caused his mental health to deteriorate to the extent that he was forced to abdicate in 1782. A European visitor wrote in a letter that "He [Taksin] passed all his time in prayer, fasting, and meditation, in order by these means to be able to fly through the air". He became madder by the month and on April 6th 1782, a group of rebels marched on Thonburi, captured the king and asked one of Taksin's generals, Chao Phya Chakri, to assume the throne. The day that Chao Phya Chakri became King Ramatobodi, April 6th, remains a public holiday in Thailand – Chakri Day – and marks the beginning of the current Chakri Dynasty. Worried about the continuing Burmese threat, Rama I (as Chao Phya Chakri is known) moved his capital to the opposite, and safer, bank of the Chao Phraya River, where he began the process of consolidating his kingdom. By the end of the century, the Burmese threat had dissipated, and the Siamese were once again in a position to lead the Tai world.

During Rama II's reign (1809-1824), a new threat emerged to replace the Burmese: that of the Europeans. In 1821, the English East India Company sent John Crawfurd as an envoy to Siam to open up trading relations. Although the king and his court remained unreservedly opposed to unfettered trade, Crawfurd's visit served to impress upon those more prescient Siamese where the challenges of the 19th century would lie.

Rama II's death and succession illustrates the dangers inherent in having a claim to the throne of Siam, even in the 19th century. The court chronicles record that in 1824 Prince Mongkut was ordained as a monk because the death of a royal white elephant indicated it was an 'ill-omened time'. Historians believe that Rama II, realizing his death was imminent, wished to protect the young prince by bundling him off to a monastery, where the robes of a monk might protect him from court intrigues.

Rama III's reign (1824-1851) saw an invasion by an army led by the Lao King Anou. In 1827, Anou took Nakhon Ratchasima on the edge of the Central Plain and was within striking distance of Bangkok before being defeated. After their victory, the Siamese marched on Vientiane, plundering the city and subjugating the surrounding countryside. In 1829, King Anou himself was captured and transported to Bangkok, where he was displayed to the public. Anou died shortly after this humiliation – it is assumed, of shame. There were also ructions at the court in Bangkok: in 1848 Prince Rakrannaret was found guilty of bribery, corruption, homosexuality and treason, and Rama III had him beaten to death with sandalwood clubs, in time honoured Thai fashion.

The 19th century was a dangerous time for Siam. Southeast Asia was being methodically divided between Britain, France and Holland as they scrambled for colonial territories. The same fate may have befallen Siam, had it not been blessed with two brilliant kings: King Mongkut (Rama IV 1851-1868) and King Chulalongkorn (Rama V 1868-1910).

Mongkut was a brilliant scholar. He learnt English and Latin and when he sat his oral Pali examination performed brilliantly. Indeed, his 27 years in a monastery allowed him to study the religious texts to such depth that he concluded that all Siamese ordinations were invalid. He established a new sect based upon the stricter Mon teachings, an order which became known as the *Thammayutika* or 'Ordering Adhering to the Dharma'. To distinguish themselves from those 'fallen' monks who made up most of the Sangha, they wore their robes with both shoulders covered. Mongkut derisively called the main Thai order – the *Mahanikai* – the 'Order of Long-standing Habit'.

But Mongkut was not an otherwordly monk with scholarly inclinations. He was a rational, pragmatic man who well appreciated the economic and military might of the Europeans. He recognized that if his kingdom was to survive he would have to accept and acquiesce to the colonial powers, rather than try to resist them. He did not accede to the throne until he was 47, and it is said that during his monastic studies he realized that if China, the Middle Kingdom, had to bow to Western pressure, then he would have to do the same.

He set about modernizing his country along with the support of other modern-thinking princes. He established a modern ship-building industry, trained his troops in European methods and studied Western medicine. Most importantly, in 1855 he signed the Bowring Treaty with Britain, giving British merchants access to the Siamese market and setting in train a process of agricultural commercialization and the clearing of the vast Central Plains for rice cultivation. As Wyatt writes: "At the stroke of a pen, old Siam faced the thrust of a surging economic and political power with which they were unprepared to contend or compete". Mongkut's meeting with Bowring illustrates the lengths to which he went to meet the West on its own terms: he received the British envoy and offered him port and cigars from his own hand, an unheard of action in Thai circles.

Unfortunately, in the West, Mongkut is not known for the skilful diplomacy which kept at bay expansionist nations considerably more powerful than his own, but for his characterization in the film *The King and I* (in which he is played by Yul Brynner). Poorly adapted from Anna Leonowens's own distorted accounts of her period as governess in the Siamese court, both the book and the film offend the Thai people. According to contemporary accounts, Mrs Leonowens was a bad tempered lady obviously given to flights of fantasy. She never became a trusted confidant of King Mongkut who scarcely needed her limited skills and there is certainly no evidence to indicate that he was attracted to her sexually. It appears that she was plain in appearance.

King Mongkut died on 1st October 1863 and was succeeded by his 15 year old son **Chulalongkorn**. However, for the next decade a regent controlled affairs of state and it was not until 1873, when Chulalongkorn was crowned for a second time, that he could begin to mould the country according to his own vision. The young king quickly showed himself to be a reformer like his father – for in essence Mongkut had only just begun the process of modernization. Chulalongkorn set about updating the monarchy by establishing ministries and ending the practise of prostration. He also accelerated the process of economic development by constructing roads, railways, schools and hospitals. The opium trade was regulated, court procedures streamlined and slavery finally completely abolished in 1905. Although a number of princes were sent

abroad to study – Prince Rajebuidirekrit went to Oxford – Chulalongkorn had to also rely on foreign advisors to help him undertake these reforms. In total he employed 549 foreigners – the largest number being British, but also Dutch, Germans, French and Belgians. Chulalongkorn even held fancy dress parties at New Year and visited Europe twice. These visits included trips to the poor East End of London and showed Chulalongkorn that for all the power of Britain and France, they were still unable to raise the living standards of a large part of the population much above subsistence levels.

These reforms were not introduced without difficulty. The *Hua Boran* – or 'The Ancients' – as the King derogatorily called them, strongly resisted the changes and in late December 1874 Prince Wichaichan attempted to take the royal palace and usurp the king. The plot was thwarted at the last possible moment, but it impressed upon Chulalongkorn that reform could only come slowly. Realizing he had run ahead of many of his subjects in his zeal for change, he reversed some of his earlier reforms, and toned-down others. Nevertheless, Siam remained on the path to modernization – albeit progressing at a rather slower pace. As during Mongkut's reign, Chulalongkorn also managed to keep the colonial powers at bay. Although the king himself played a large part in placating the Europeans by skilful diplomacy and by presenting an image of urbane sophistication, he was helped in this respect by a brilliant minister of foreign affairs: Prince Devawongse (1858-1923) who controlled Siam's foreign relations for 38 years.

The fundamental weakness of the Siamese state in the face of the European powers was illustrated in the dispute with France over Laos. Despite attempts by Prince Devawongse to manufacture a compromise, the French forced Siam to cede Laos to France in

1893 and to pay compensation – even though they had little claim to the territory. As Mao could have it, power grows out of the barrel of a gun, and Chulalongkorn could not compete with France in military might. It is said that after this humiliation, the king retired from public life, broken in spirit and health. In 1909, the British chipped away at more of Siam's territory, gaining rights of suzerainty over the Malay states of Kelantan, Terengganu, Kedah and Perlis. In total, Siam relinquished nearly 500,000 sq km of territory to maintain the integrity of the core of the nation. King Chulalongkorn died on 24th October 1910, sending the whole nation into deep and genuine mourning.

The 20th Century The kings that were to follow Mongkut and Chulalongkorn could not have been expected to have had such illustrious, brilliant reigns. Absolute kingship was becoming increasingly incompatible with the demands of the modern world, and the kings of Thailand were resisting the inevitable. Rama VI, **King Vajiravudh** (1910-1925), was educated at Oxford and Sandhurst Military Academy and seemed well prepared for kingship. However he squandered much of the wealth built up by Chulalongkorn and ruled in a rather heavy-handed, uncoordinated style. He did try to inculcate a sense of 'nation' with his slogan 'nation, religion, king', but seemed more interested in Western theatre and literature than in guiding Siam through a difficult period in its history. He died at the age of only 44, leaving an empty treasury.

Like his older brother, **King Prajadhipok** (Rama VII 1925-1935), was educated in Europe: at Eton, the Woolwich Military Academy and at the Ecole Superieure de Guerre in France. But he never expected to become king and was thrust onto the throne at a time of great strain. Certainly, he was more careful with the resources that his treasury had to offer, but could do little to prevent the

country being seriously affected by the Great Depression of the 1930s. The price of rice, the country's principal export, declined by two-thirds and over the same two-year period (1930-32) land values in Bangkok fell by 80%. The economy was in crisis and the government appeared to have no idea how to cope. In February 1932, King Prajadhipok told a group of military officers:

"The financial war is a very hard one indeed. Even experts contradict one another until they become hoarse. Each offers a different suggestion. I myself know nothing at all about finances, and all I can do is listen to the opinions of others and choose the best. I have never experienced such a hardship; therefore if I have made a mistake I really deserve to be excused by the officials and people of Siam."

The people, both the peasantry and the middle class, were dissatisfied by the course of events and with their declining economic position. But neither group was sufficiently united to mount a threat to the King and his government. Nevertheless, Prajadhipok was worried: there was a prophesy linked to Rama I's younger sister Princess Narinthewi which predicted that the Chakri dynasty would survive for 150 years, and end on 6th April 1932.

The Revolution of 1932

The date itself passed without incident, but just 12 weeks later on 24th June a clique of soldiers and civilians staged a **coup d'état** while the king was holidaying at the seaside resort of Hua Hin. This episode is often called the Revolution of 1932, but it was not in any sense a revolution involving a large rump of the people. It was orchestrated by a small élite, essentially for the elite. The king accepted the terms offered to him, writing:

"I have received the letter in which you invite me to return to Bangkok as a constitutional monarch. For the sake of peace; and in order to save useless bloodshed; to avoid confusion and loss to the country;

and, more, because I have already considered making this change myself, I am willing to co-operate in the establishment of a constitution under which I am willing to serve."

However, King Prajadhipok had great difficulty adapting to his lesser role, and falling out with the military, he abdicated in favour of his young nephew, Prince Ananda Mahidol in 1935. The Prince at the time was only 10 years old, and at school in Switzerland, so the newly created National Assembly appointed 2 princes to act as regents. From this point until after World War II the monarchy was only partially operative. Ananda was out of the country for most of the time, and the civilian government took centre stage. Ananda was not to physically reoccupy the throne until December 1945 and just 6 months later he was found dead in bed, a bullet through his head. The circumstances behind his death have never been satisfactorily explained and it remains a subject on which Thais are not openly permitted to speculate. Books investigating the death are still banned in Thailand.

While the monarchy receded from view, the civilian government was going through the intrigues and power struggles which were to become such a feature of the future politics of the country. The 2 key men at this time were the army officer Phibun Songkhram, and the left-wing idealist lawyer Pridi Panomyong. Between them they managed to dominate Thai politics until 1957.

When **Prime Minister Pridi Panomyong** tried to introduce a socialist economic programme in 1933, pushing for the state control of the means of production, he was forced into exile in Europe. This is often seen as the beginning of the tradition of authoritarian, right-wing rule in Thailand, although to be fair Pridi's vision of economic and political reform was poorly thought through and rather romantic. Nonetheless, with Pridi in Paris – at least for a

while – it gave the more conservative elements in the government the chance to promulgate an anti-communist law, and thereby to usher in a period of ultra-nationalism. Anti-Chinese propaganda became more shrill, with some government positions being reserved for ethnic Tais. In 1938 the populist writer Luang Wichit compared the Chinese in Siam with the Jews in Germany, and thought that Hitler's policies might be worth considering for his own country.

This shift in policy can be linked to the influence of one man: **Luang Phibun Songkhram**. Born of humble parents in 1897, he worked his way up through the army ranks and then into politics. He became Prime Minister in 1938 and his enduring influence makes him the most significant figure in 20th century Thai politics. Under his direction, Siam became more militaristic, xenophobic, as well as 'religiously' nationalistic, avidly pursuing the reconversion of Siamese Christians back to Buddhism. As if to underline these developments, in 1939, Siam adopted a new name: Thailand. Phibun justified this change on the grounds that it would indicate that the country was controlled by Thais and not by the Chinese or any other group.

World War II and post-War Thailand

During World War II, Phibun Songkhram sided with the Japanese who he felt sure would win. He saw the war as an opportunity to take back some of the territories lost to the West. In 1940, Thai forces invaded Laos and Western Cambodia. A year later, the Japanese used the kingdom as a launching pad for their assaults on the British in Malaya and Burma. Thailand had little choice but to declare war on the Allies and to agree a military alliance with Japan in Dec 1941. As allies of the Japanese, Phibun's ambassadors were instructed to declare war on Britain and the United States. However, the ambassador in Washington, Seni Pramoj refused to deliver the declaration (he considered it illegal) and Thailand never formally declared war on the US. In Thailand itself, Pridi who had returned as regent to the young monarch King Ananda, helped to organize the Thai resistance – the Free Thai Movement. They received help from the US. Office of Strategic Services (OSS) and the British Force 136, and also from many Thais. As the tide of the war turned in favour of the allies, so Prime Minister Phibun was forced to resign. He spent a short time in gaol in Japan, but was allowed to return to Thailand in 1947.

After the war, Seni Pramoj, Thailand's ambassador in the US, became Prime Minister. He was soon followed by Pridi Panomyong as Prime Minister, who had gathered a good deal of support due to the role he played during the conflict. However, in 1946 King Ananda was mysteriously found shot dead in his royal apartments and Pridi was implicated in a plot. He was forced to resign, so enabling Phibun to become Prime Minister once again – a post he kept until 1957. Phibun's fervent anti-Communism quickly gained support in the US, who contributed generous amounts of aid as the country became a front-line state in the battle against the 'red tide' which seemed to be engulfing Asia. Phibun's closest brush with death occurred in June 1951. He was leading a ceremony on board a dredge, the *Manhattan*, when he was taken prisoner and transferred to the Thai navy flagship the *Sri Ayutthaya*. The airforce and army stayed loyal to Phibun, and planes bombed the ship. As it sank, the Prime Minister was able to swim to safety. The attempted coup resulted in 1,200 dead – mostly civilians. For the navy, it has meant that ever since it has been treated as the junior member of the armed forces, receiving far less resources than the army and airforce.

Prime Minister Phibun Songkhram was deposed following a coup d'état in 1957, and was replaced by **General Sarit Thanarat**. General Sarit established the National Economic Development Board (now the National Economic and Social Development Board) and introduced Thailand's first 5 year national development plan in 1961. He was a tough, uncompromising leader and following his death in 1965 was replaced by another General – Thanom Kitticachorn. With the war in Indochina escalating, Thanom allowed US planes to be based in Thailand from where they went on bombing missions over the Lao panhandle and Vietnam. In 1969 a general election was held, which Thanom won, but as the political situation in Thailand deteriorated, so Prime Minister Thanom declared martial law. After bloody student riots around Bangkok's Thammasat University campus in 1973, during which the army and right-wing 'scouts' killed several hundred students, Thanom was forced to resign and left the country. During the demonstrations, Thanom lost the support of the army: the Commander-in-Chief, General Krit Sivara, was unwilling to send his troops out to quell the disturbances while Thanom, apparently, was quite willing to kill thousands if necessary.

Following the riots, Thailand entered a period of turbulent democratic politics until 1976, when the army felt impelled to step in once again. The **Communist Party of Thailand (CPT)** was gaining increasing support and Thailand seemed, to many, to be going the same way as the countries of Indochina. Other Thais wryly commented that neighbouring countries need not worry because the Vietnamese army would never make it through Bangkok's already appalling traffic. In 1976 Tanin Kraivixien was installed as Prime Minister. The next year he was succeeded by Kriangsak Chomanan.

By the late 1970s the ranks of the CPT

had swelled to about 14,000 armed guerillas. However, with the ascendancy of Prem Tinsulanond to the premiership in 1980 and a rapidly changing global political environment, the CPT fragmented and quickly lost support. Its leaders were divided between support for China and the Cambodian Khmers Rouges on the one hand, and the Soviet Union and Vietnam on the other. When the government announced an amnesty in 1980, many of the students who had fled into the forests and hills following the riots of 1973, returned to mainstream politics, exhausted and disenchanted with revolutionary life. In true Thai style, they were forgiven and reintegrated into society.

Prem Tinsulanond presided over the most stable period in Thai politics since the end of World War II. He finally resigned in 1988, and by then Thailand – or so most people thought – was already beginning to outgrow the habit of military intervention in civilian politics. Chatichai Choonhaven replaced Prem after general elections in 1988, by which time the country was felt to be more stable and economically prosperous than at any time in recent memory. During his reign, the present King Bhumibol has played a crucial role in maintaining social stability while the political system has been in turmoil. He is highly revered by his subjects, and has power – which he is careful not to over-exercise – far beyond that which his constitutional position allows (see box).

The widely held belief that the Thai political system had come of age proved ill-founded. In February 1991, with Prime Minister Chatichai daring to challenge the armed forces in various ways, General Suchinda Kraprayoon led a coup d'état which toppled the civilian government. Thailand has now had 17 coups or attempted coups since 1945, and over the 60 years since the original coup of 1932, army strongmen have been in power for no less than 49 years.

Art and architecture

The various periods of Thai art and architecture were characterised by their own distinctive styles as shown in the table below. For illustration, see Buddha heads page 97 and Buddha images page 95.

One of the problems with reconstructing the artistic heritage of any Southeast Asian civilization is that most buildings were built of wood. Wood was abundant, but it also rotted quickly in the warm and humid climate. Although there can be no doubt that fine buildings made of wood were constructed by the various kingdoms of Thailand, much of the art that remains, and on which our appreciation is built, is made of stone, brick or bronze.

Dvaravati style (c. 6th-11th centuries)

The Dvaravati kingdom is rather an enigma to art historians. Theravada Buddhist objects have been unearthed in various parts of the Central Plains which date from the 6th century onwards, among them coins with the inscription 'the merit of the king of Dvaravati'. The capital of this kingdom was probably Nakhon Pathom and it is thought that the inhabitants were Mon in origin, and also spoke Mon. The kingdom covered much of Lower Burma and Central Thailand and may have been influential from as early as the 3rd century to as late as the 13th.

Dvaravati Buddha images show stylistic similarities with Indian Gupta and post-Gupta images (4th-8th centuries), and with pre-Pala (also Indian) images (8th-11th centuries). Most are carved in stone, with only small images cast in bronze. Standing images tend to be presented in the attitude of vitarkamudra (see page 94), and later carvings show more strongly indigenous facial features: a flatter face, prominent eyes, thick nose and lips. Fragments of red paint have been discovered on some images, leading art historians to believe that the carvings would originally have been painted.

Also characteristic of Dvaravati art are terracotta sculptures – some intricately carved (such as those found at Nakhon Pathom and exhibited in the museum there) – carved bas-reliefs and stone Wheels of Law. As well as Nakhon Pathom, Dvaravati art has also been discovered at Uthong in Suphanburi province, and Muang Fa Daed in Kalasin (Northeastern region). But perhaps the finest and most complete remnants of the Dvaravati tradition are found in the Northern town of Lamphun, formerly Haripunjaya (see below).

Haripunjaya style (7th-13th centuries)

It seems that during the 7th century the Dvaravati-influenced inhabitants of Lopburi (Lavo) migrated N to found a new city: Haripunjaya, now called Lamphun (see page 227). Although the art of this Mon outlier was influenced by the Indian Pala tradition, as well as by Khmer styles, it maintained its independence long after the rest of the Dvaravati kingdom had been subsumed by the stronger Tai kingdoms. Indeed, it was not until the late 13th century that Haripunjaya was conquered by the Tais, and as a result is probably the oldest preserved city in Thailand.

PERIODS IN THAI ART AND HISTORY

Period	Date	Location	Peoples/Influence
Pre-Tai States			
Dvaravati	C6th-11th	Central: Uthong, Nakhon Pathom	Mon
Haripunjaya	C7th-13th	North: Lamphun	Mon
Srivijaya	C8th-13th	South: Chaiya, Sating Phra	Srivijaya
Khmer/Lopburi (Lavo)	C7th-14th	Northeast: Phimai, Phanom Rung; Central: Lopburi; also East	Mon/Khmer
Tai States			
Chiang Saen	C11th-18th	North: Lampang, Lamphun	Tai
Chiang Mai		Chiang Mai	Chiang Saen
Sukhothai	C13th-15th	North-Central: Sukhothai, Si Satchanalai	Tai
Ayutthaya	1350-1767	Central: Ayutthaya	Tai
Thonburi	1767-1782	Central: Thonburi	Tai
Bangkok	1782-	Central: Bangkok	Tai

Srivijaya (8th-13th centuries)

The Srivijayan empire was a powerful maritime empire which extended from Java northwards into Thailand, and had its capital at Palembang in Sumatra. Like Dvaravati art, Srivijayan art was also heavily influenced by Indian traditions, in particular Gupta, post-Gupta and Pala-Sena. It seems likely that this part of Thailand was on the trade route between India and China and as a result local artists were well aware of Indian styles. A problem with characterizing the art of this period – which spanned 5 centuries – is that it is very varied.

Srivijaya was a Mahayana Buddhist empire, and numerous Avalokitesvara Bodhisattvas have been found, in both stone and bronze, at Chaiya (see page 443). Some of these are wonderfully carved, and particularly notable is the supremely modelled bronze Avalokitesvara (8th century, 63 cm high) unearthed at Chaiya and now housed in the National Museum in Bangkok. In fact, so much Srivijayan art has been discovered around this town that some experts went so far as to argue that Chaiya, and not Palembang, was the capital of Srivijaya. Unfortunately however, there are few architectural remnants from the period. Two exceptions are Wat Phra Boromthat and Wat Kaeo, both at Chaiya (see page 443).

Khmer or Lopburi style (7th-14th centuries)

Khmer art has been found in the Eastern, Central and Northeastern regions of the country, and is closely linked to the art and architecture of Cambodia. It is usually referred to as Lopburi style because the town of Lopburi in the Central Plains is assumed to have been a centre of the Khmer empire in Thailand (see page 192). The art is Mahayana Buddhist in inspiration and stylistic changes mirror those in Cambodia. In Thailand, the period of Khmer artistic influence begins with the reign of Suryavarman I (1002-1050) and includes Muang Tham, Prasat Phranomwan and the beginnings of Phanom Rung; Phimai, the most visited of the Khmer Shrines was built during the reign of the

TBU 65
VLC 136

KHMER - style PRANG

LATERITE

Many of the Khmer monuments that lie scattered across the S provinces of the Northeast are made of laterite. This red, porous and pock-marked stone is actually an iron-bearing soil. The easily quarried soil was cut into large blocks and left to harden upon exposure to the air.

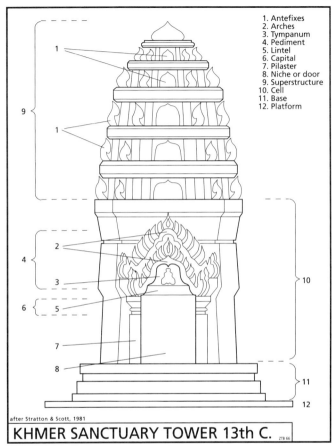

1. Antefixes
2. Arches
3. Tympanum
4. Pediment
5. Lintel
6. Capital
7. Pilaster
8. Niche or door
9. Superstructure
10. Cell
11. Base
12. Platform

after Stratton & Scott, 1981

KHMER SANCTUARY TOWER 13th C. ZTB 66

great King Jayavarman VII (1181-1217).

Lopburi Buddhas are authoritative, with flat, square faces, eyebrows that form almost a straight line, and a protuberance on the crown of the head signifying enlightenment. They are the first Buddhas to be portrayed in regal attire, as the Khmers believed that the king, as a *deva raja* (god king) was, himself divine. They were carved in stone or cast in bronze. Sadly, many of the finer Khmer pieces have been smuggled abroad. Khmer temples in Thailand abound and some are

among the most magnificent in Southeast Asia. The biggest are those of the Northeastern region, including Phimai, Muang Tham and Phanom Rung, although Khmer architecture is also to be found as far afield as Lopburi and at Muang Kao outside Kanchanaburi.

Chiang Saen or Chiang Mai style (c.11th-18th centuries)

This period marks the beginning of Tai art. Earlier works were derivative, being essentially the art of empires and

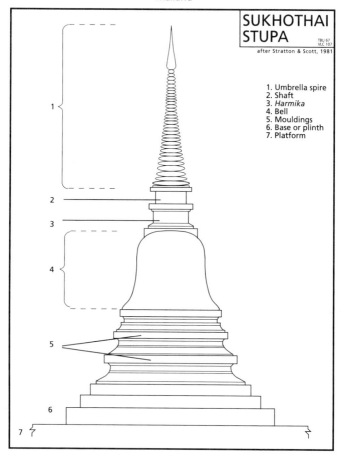

SUKHOTHAI
STUPA
TBU 67
VLC 107
after Stratton & Scott, 1981

1. Umbrella spire
2. Shaft
3. *Harmika*
4. Bell
5. Mouldings
6. Base or plinth
7. Platform

kingdoms whose centres of power lay beyond the country – Cambodia, Sumatra and Burma.

There are generally thought to be 2 styles within this Northern tradition: the Chiang Saen and Chiang Mai (or Later Chiang Saen) schools. The Chiang Saen style, in which the Buddha is portrayed with a round face, arched eyebrows and prominent chin, is stylistically linked to the Pala art of India. Nevertheless, local artists incor-

porated their own vision and produced unique and beautiful images. The earliest date from around the 11th century, and their classification refers to the ancient town of Chiang Saen where many of the finest pieces have been found. The second style is known as Later Chiang Saen or, less confusingly, Chiang Mai. The influence of Sukhothai can be seen in the works from this period: oval face, more slender body, and with the robe over the left shoulder. Images date from the middle of the 14th century.

Buddha images from both of the Northern periods were carved in stone or semi-precious stone, and cast in bronze. The most famous Buddha of all, the Emerald Buddha housed in Wat Phra Kaeo, Bangkok, may have been carved in Northern Thailand during the Late Chiang Saen/Chiang Mai period, although this is not known for certain.

Architecturally, the Northern school began to make a pronounced contribution from the time of the founding of the city of Chiang Mai in 1296. Perhaps the finest example from this period – indeed some people regard them as the finest buildings in all Thailand – is the incomparable Wat Lampang Luang, outside the town of Lampang in the North (see page 224).

Sukhothai style (late 13th-early 15th centuries)

The Sukhothai Buddha is one of the first representations of the Ceylonese Buddha in Siam, the prototypes being from Anuradhapura, Sri Lanka (Ceylon). The Buddha is usually represented in the round, either seated cross-legged in the attitude of subduing Mara; or the languid, one-foot forward standing position, with one hand raised, in the attitude of giving protection as the enlightened one descends from the Tavatimsa Heaven. Most were cast in bronze, as Thailand is noticeably lacking in good stone. Some art historians have also argued that Sukhothai artists disliked the violence of chiselling stone, maintaining that as peaceful Thais and good Buddhists they would have preferred the art of modelling bronze. This is fanciful in the extreme.

For the seated Buddha, the surfaces are smooth and curved, with an oval head and elongated features, small hair curls, arched eyebrows, and a hooked nose. His smile conveys inner content-

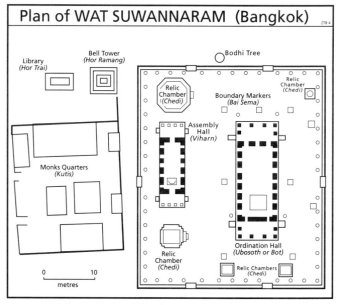

Plan of WAT SUWANNARAM (Bangkok)   ZTB 4

Library
(Hor Trai)

Bell Tower
(Hor Ramang)

Bodhi Tree

Relic Chamber
(Chedi)

Relic Chamber
(Chedi)

Boundary Markers
(Bai Sema)

Assembly Hall
(Viharn)

Monks Quarters
(Kutis)

Ordination Hall
(Ubosoth or Bot)

Relic Chamber
(Chedi)

Relic Chambers
(Chedi)

0   10

metres

ment. The head is topped by a tall flame-like motif or *ketumula*. The shoulders are broad and the waist is narrow. The length of cloth hanging over the left shoulder drops quite a long way down to the navel and terminates in a notched design.

The graceful walking Buddha – perhaps the greatest single artistic innovation of the Sukhothai period – features rather strange projecting heels (which follows the ancient writings describing

the Buddha's physical appearance). Toes are all the same length and the soles of his feet are flat. The figure is almost androgenous in appearance – this was Buddha depicted having achieved enlightenment, which meant that sexual characteristics no longer existed. The finest examples were produced in the decades immediately prior to Ayutthaya conquering the city in 1438. Steve van Beek and Luca Tettoni write in *The arts of Thailand*:

THE THAI WAT

There is no English equivalent of the Thai word *wat*. It is usually translated as either monastery or temple, although neither is correct. It is easiest to get around this problem by calling them wats. They were, and remain to some extent, the focus of the village or town; they serve as places of worship, education, meeting and healing. Without a wat, a village cannot be viewed as a 'complete' community. The wat is a relatively new innovation. Originally, there were no wats, as monks were wandering ascetics. It seems that although the word 'wat' was in use in the 14th century, these were probably just shrines, and were not monasteries. By the late 18th century, the wat had certainly metamorphosed into a monastery, so sometime in the intervening four centuries, shrine and monastery had united into a whole.

● Royal wats, or *wat luang* – of which there are only 186 in the country – can usually be identified by the use of the prefixes *Rat, Raja* or *Racha* in their names. This indicates royal patronage. Wats that contain important relics also have the prefix *Maha* or *Great* – e.g. in Wat Mahathat. Community wats make up the rest and number about 30,000. Although wats vary a great deal in size and complexity, there is a traditional layout to which most conform.

● Wats are usually separated from the secular world by **two walls**. Between these outer and inner walls are found the **monks quarters** or dormitories (*kutis*), perhaps a **bell tower** (*hor rakang*) that is used to toll the hours and to warn of danger and, in larger complexes, schools and other administrative buildings. Traditionally the *kutis* were placed on the S side of the wat. It was believed that if the monks slept directly in front of the principal Buddha image they would die young; if they slept to the left they would become ill; and if they slept behind it there would be discord in the community of monks. This section of the compound is known as the *sanghavasa* or *sanghawat* (i.e. for the Sangha, the monkhood).

● The inner wall, which in bigger wats often takes the form of a **gallery** or cloister (*phra rabieng*) lined with Buddha images, represents the division between the worldly and the holy, the sacred and the profane. It is used as a quiet place for meditation. This part of the wat compound is known as the *buddhavasa* or *phutthawat* (i.e. for the Buddha). Within the inner courtyard, the holiest building is the **ordination hall** or *bot/ubosoth*, reserved for monks only. This is built on consecrated ground, and has a ring of 8 stone tablets or boundary markers (*bai* *sema*), sometimes contained in mini-pavilions, arranged around it at the cardinal and subcardinal points and shaped like stylized leaves of the bodhi tree, often carved with representations of Vishnu, Siva, Brahma or Indra, or of nagas. Buried in the ground beneath the bai sema are *luuk nimit* – stone spheres – and sometimes gold and jewellery. The bai sema mark the limit of earthly power – within the stones, not even a king can issue orders. The ordination hall is characteristically a large, rectangular building with high walls and multiple sloping roofs covered in glazed clay tiles (or wood tiles, in the North). At each end of the roof are *chofaa*, literally 'bunches of sky', which represent garuda grasping two nagas in its talons. Inside, often through elaborately carved and inlaid doors, is a Buddha image. There may also be numerous subsidiary images. The inside walls of the bot may be decorated with murals depicting the Jataka tales or scenes from Buddhist and Hindu cosmology. Like the Buddha, these murals are meant to serve as meditation aids. It is customary for pilgrims to remove their shoes on entering any Buddhist building (or private house for that matter) although in state ceremonies, officials in uniform are not required to do so.

● The other main building within the inner courtyard is the **assembly hall** or **viharn**, but not all wats have one, and some may have more than one. Architecturally this is often indistinguishable from the bot. It contains the wat's principal Buddha images. The main difference between the bot and viharn is that the latter does not stand on consecrated ground, and can be identified by the absence of any bai sema – stone tablets – set around it. The viharn is for more general use than the bot and unlike the bot is rarely locked. Both bot and viharn are supposed to face water, because the Buddha himself was facing a river when he achieved enlightenment under the bodhi tree. If there is no natural body of water, the monks may dig a pond. In the late Ayutthayan period, the curved lines of the bot and viharn were designed to symbolize a boat.

Also found in the inner courtyard may be a number of other structures. Among the more common are *chedis*, bell-shaped **relic chambers** with tapering spires. In larger wats these can be built on a massive scale (such as the one at Nakhon Pathom, see page 379), and contain holy relics of the Buddha himself. More often, chedis are smaller affairs containing the ashes of royalty, monks or pious lay people. A rarer Khmer architectural feature sometimes found in Thai wats is the *prang*, also a relic chamber (see page 88). The best known of these angular corn-cob-shaped towers is the one at Wat Arun in Bangkok (see page 148).

● Another rarer feature is the **library** or scripture repository (*hor trai*), usually a small, tall-sided building where the Buddhist scriptures can be stored safely, high off the ground. *Salas* are open-sided **rest pavilions** which can be found anywhere in the wat compound; the *sala kan parian* or **study hall** is the largest and most impressive of these and is almost like a bot or viharn without walls. Here the monks say their prayers at noon.

● It seems that wats are often short-lived. Even great wats, if they lose their patronage, are deserted by their monks and fall into ruin. Unlike Christian churches, they depend on constant support from the laity; the wat owns no land or wealth, and must depend on gifts of food to feed the monks and money to repair and expand the fabric of its buildings.

MUDRAS AND THE BUDDHA IMAGE

An artist producing an image of the Buddha does not try to create an original piece of art; he is trying to be faithful to a tradition which can be traced back over centuries. It is important to appreciate that the Buddha image is not merely a work of art but an object of, and for worship. Sanskrit poetry even sets down the characteristics of the Buddha – albeit in rather unlikely terms: legs like a deer, arms like an elephant's trunk, a chin like a mango stone and hair like the stings of scorpions. The Pali texts of Theravada Buddhism add the 108 auspicious signs, long toes and fingers of equal length, body like a banyan tree and eyelashes like a cow's. The Buddha can be represented either sitting, lying (indicating *paranirvana*), or standing, and (in Thailand) occasionally walking. He is often represented standing on an open lotus flower: the Buddha was born into an impure world, and likewise the lotus germinates in mud but rises above the filth to flower. Each image will be represented in a particular *mudra* or 'attitude', of which there are 40. The most common are:

Abhayamudra – dispelling fear or giving protection; right hand (sometimes both hands) raised, palm outwards, usually with the Buddha in a standing position.

Varamudra – giving blessing or charity; the right hand pointing downwards, the palm facing outwards, with the Buddha either seated or standing.

Vitarkamudra – preaching mudra; the ends of the thumb and index finger of the right hand touch to form a circle, symbolizing the Wheel of Law. The Buddha can either be seated or standing.

Dharmacakramudra – 'spinning the Wheel of Law'; a preaching mudra symbolizing the teaching of the first sermon. The hands are held in front of the chest, thumbs and index fingers of both joined, one facing inwards and one outwards.

Bhumisparcamudra – 'calling the earth goddess to witness' or 'touching the earth'; the right hand rests on the right knee with the tips of the fingers 'touching ground', thus calling the earth goddess Dharani/Thoranee to witness his enlightenment and victory over Mara, the king of demons. The Buddha is always seated.

Dhyanamudra – meditation; both hands resting open, palms upwards, in the lap, right over left.

Other points of note:
Vajrasana – yogic posture of meditation; cross-legged, both soles of the feet visible.

Virasana – yogic posture of meditation; cross-legged, but with the right leg on top of the left, covering the left foot (also known as *paryankasana*).

Buddha under Naga – a common image in Khmer art; the Buddha is shown seated in an attitude of meditation with a cobra rearing up over his head. This refers to an episode in the Buddha's life when he was meditating; a rain storm broke and Nagaraja, the king of the nagas (snakes), curled up under the Buddha (7 coils) and then used his 7-headed hood to protect the Holy One from the falling rain.

Buddha calling for rain – a common image in Laos; the Buddha is depicted standing, both arms held stiffly at the side of the body, fingers pointing downwards.

Bhumisparcamudra – calling the earth goddess to witness. Sukhothai period, 13th-14th century.

Dhyanamudra – meditation. Sukhothai period, 13th-14th century.

Abhayamudra – dispelling fear or giving protection. Lopburi Buddha, Khmer style 12th century.

Vitarkamudra – preaching, "spinning the Wheel of Law". Dvaravati Buddha, 7th-8th century, seated in the "European" manner.

Abhayamudra – dispelling fear or giving protection; subduing Mara position. Lopburi Buddha, Khmer style 13th century.

ZTB 201

"Sukhothai sculpture suggests a figure in the process of dematerializing, half way between solid and vapour. He doesn't walk so much as float. He doesn't sit, he levitates, and belies his masculine nature which should be hard and inflexible. Even his diaphanous robes ... portray a Buddha which has already shed the trappings of this world."

The initial influence upon Sukhothai art was the Khmer style of architecture, in, for example, the distinctive 'prang' shape (see illustration, page 88). Subsequent stupas can be classified into 3 styles: first, the Ceylonese bell-shaped style (see illustration, page 90), with a square base surrounded by caryatids, above which is another base with niches containing Buddha images (Wat Chang Lom, Si Satchanalai, is a good example). Second, the lotus bud chedi, examples of which can be found at Wat Mahathat, Wat Trapang Ngoen and Wat Chedi Jet Thaew (Si Satchanalai). Other examples in N Thailand can be found at Kamphaeng Phet, Tak, Phitsanulok and Chiang Mai. Third, the stupa style believed to be derived from the Srivijayan stupa, which consists of a square base, above which is a square main body, superimposed with pedestals, containing niches within which are standing Buddha images. Above the main body are bell-shaped *andas* of reducing size. Examples of this style can be found on the corner stupas at Wat Mahathat and some subsiduary stupas at Wat Chedi Jet Thaew (Si Satchanalai). Mention should be made of the mondop, built in place of the stupa on a square plan and always containing a large Buddha image. A good example is Wat Sri Chum (Sukhothai). It is said that the stupa 'evolved' as the Buddha lay dying. One of the disciples, Ananda, asked how they might remember the Enlightened One after his death, to which the Buddha replied it was the doctrine, not himself, that should be remembered. As this reply was clearly unsatisfactory to his distraught followers, the Buddha added that after cremation a relic of his body might be placed within a mound of earth – which, over time, became the stupa.

Ayutthayan style (mid 14th-mid 18th centuries)

Both the art and architecture of this period can be split into 4 sub-periods spanning the years from 1350 to 1767 when Ayutthaya was sacked by the Burmese.

As far as Ayutthayan Buddha images are concerned, for much of the time the artists of the city drew upon the works of other kingdoms for inspiration. To begin with, Uthong Buddhas were popular (themselves drawing upon Khmer prototypes). Then, from the mid-15th century, Sukhothai styles became highly influential – although the images produced looked rather lifeless and are hardly comparable with the originals. In the mid-16th century, when Cambodia came under Thai control, Ayutthayan artists looked to, and imitated, Khmer sculpture (identifiable by the double lips and indistinct moustache). Finally, in the Late Ayutthayan period, a home-grown but rather fussy style arose, with the Buddha often portrayed crowned.

The first of the 4 sub-periods of Ayutthayan architecture commenced in 1350 and may have been influenced by the prang of Wat Phra Sri Ratana Mahathat in Lopburi, though prangs at Ayutthaya are slightly taller. The second period (1488-1629) is dominated by the round Ceylonese-style stupa, the major example of this being Wat Phra Sri Samphet. During the third period (the first half of the 17th century), the King sent architects to Cambodia to study the architectural characteristics of the Khmer monuments. As a result, the prang became fashionable again – Wat Watthanaram and Wat Chumphon (Bang Pa-In) were built at this time. The final period was from 1732 until the sacking

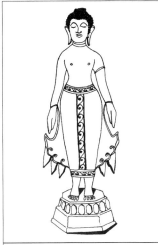

The Buddha 'Calling for Rain'

of Ayutthaya by the Burmese in 1767. The many-rabbeted chedis were popular during this period, although less new building was constructed as King Boromkot was more interested in restoring existing buildings. Most of the viharns and ubosoths have long since perished. What remains dates mainly from the Late Ayutthayan period.

Bangkok style (late 18-20th centuries)

The Bangkok or Rattanakosin period dates from the founding of the Chakri dynasty in 1782. But, initially at least, the need for Buddha images was met not by making new ones, but by recovering old ones. King Rama I ordered that images be collected from around his devastated kingdom and be brought to Bangkok – 1,200 in all – and they were then distributed to the various wats (see,

FACES OF THE BUDDHA: 7TH TO 15TH CENTURY

Sukhothai School, 14th century.

Uthong School, late 14th and early 15th century.

Dvaravati School, 7th to 8th century.

Lopburi School, 13th century.

Haripunjaya School, 13th century.

Punishments in the eight Buddhist hells, commonly found on murals behind the principal Buddha image in the bot.

Adapted from Hallet, Holt (1980) *A thousand miles on an elephant in the Shan States*,
William Blackwood: Edinburgh.

for example the fine array at Wat Pho, page 133).

It is generally accepted that the Buddhas produced during the Bangkok era are, on the whole, inferior and rather lifeless in appearance. Initially they followed the Uthong and Ayutthayan traditions. King Mongkut (1851-1868) did 'commission' a new style: these Buddhas are more lively in style, with carefully carved robes. But Mongkut's new-style Buddha did not catch on, and more often than not old images were merely copied.

Architecturally, there is a similar following of previous styles rather than any new and significant developments. During the first 3 reigns (1782-1851), the prang (e.g. Wat Rakhang, see page 150 and Wat Arun, page 148) and redented chedi (e.g. Wat Pho, see page 133) were popular, as were Ayutthayan-style viharns and ubosoths. Also, during the third reign, the influence of Chinese art becomes quite pronounced. Other oddities include the early 20th century Wat Nivet Thamaprawat at Bang Pa-in which is Gothic in inspiration (see page 190), and Wat Benchamabophit in Bangkok which is a fusion of eastern and western styles (see page 152). In general, Rattanakosin wat buildings are airier and less ornate than those of Ayutthaya.

Thai murals

Like sculptural art in Thailand, paintings – usually murals – were devotional works. They were meant to serve as meditation aids and therefore tended to follow established 'scripts' that any pilgrim could 'read' with ease: the *Ramakien*, the *jataka* tales and the *Traiphum* (*Three Worlds*). Most such murals are found, appropriately, on the interior walls of bots and viharns. Unfortunately, there are no murals to compete in antiquity with carvings in stone, although they were certainly produced during the Sukhothai period and probably much earlier. The use of paint on dry walls (frescoes are painted onto wet plaster and survive much better) made the works susceptible to damp and heat. None has survived that pre-dates the Ayutthaya period and only a handful are more than 150 years old.

The sequence of the murals tend to follow a particular pattern: beneath the windows on the long walls, are episodes from the Buddha's life; behind the principal Buddha image, the Three Worlds – heaven, earth and hell (see illustration); and on the end wall facing the Buddha the contest with Mara. But, in amongst these established themes, the artist was free to incorporate scenes from everyday life, animals, plants and local tales and myths. These are often the most entertaining sections. All were portrayed without perspective using simple lines and blocks of uniform colour, with no use of shadow and shading.

Culture and life

People

Women in Thai society

Although the logic of Buddhism relegates women to a subordinate position, women in Thailand have considerable influence. In the rural North and Northeast, land is usually inherited by the female members of a household, and husbands reside with their wives. It is common to find the wife controlling the finances in a family, determining where and how much fertilizer to buy, and even giving her husband an 'allowance'. This has been noted for centuries: in 1433 the Chinese Muslim traveller Ma Huan recorded: "It is their [Siamese] custom that all affairs are managed by their wives...all trading transactions great and small". Although in public the role of the man is accentuated, in private, equality of the sexes or the reverse is more usually the case. In the fields, ploughing is usually done by men, but other tasks are equally shared – and often women do more than their fair share.

This contrast between the overt position of women in Thai society, and their underlying role is a recurring theme. At one level, it appears that the cause of women's liberation has not proceeded very far: minor wives (*mia noi*) are still common, and while a man can divorce his wife on grounds of adultery, a woman cannot divorce her husband. Prostitution is illegal – but only the prostitute, not her client, is interpreted as breaking the law. Yet, female traders and businesswomen are well represented – indeed there are thought to be more female than male traders. Their influential role in private enterprise is partly because they are still largely excluded from high office in the public sector and as a result, ambitious women are forced to enter the private sector.

The relative strength of the woman's role even extends to sexual relations. Ma Huan's 15th century account of Siam, noted how men would have penis balls inserted under their foreskin to increase their partner's pleasure: "If it is the king...or a great chief or a wealthy man, they use gold to make hollow beads, inside which a grain of sand is placed...They make a tinkling sound, and this is regarded as beautiful" (see page 42).

It is quite common in Thailand for young children to be given to another family member to be raised. This usually occurs because the parents feel that they are unable to raise the child properly due to economic difficulties, and he or she would have a better life opportunity in another household. But this is not to say that family ties are weak and even non-familiar ties are expressed in family terms: a patron is a *phor liang*

19th century mural of a Thai woman wearing a *pha sin*; note the stylized 'axe' cushion in the background.

('nurturing father'), his clients are *luuk nong* ('younger siblings').

The oldest industry: prostitution in Thailand

Embarrassingly for many Thais, their country is often synonymous in foreigner's minds with prostitution and sex tourism, and now with AIDS (see box). That prostitution is big business cannot be denied: various estimates put the numbers of women employed in the industry at between 200,000 and 2 million. This means that somewhere between 2% and 20% of the female population aged between 15 and 34 are employed in some 60,000 brothels. Despite the ubiquitousness of the prostitute in Thai life, the government and the public took offence when Longman's published a *Dictionary of English language and culture* in 1993 with an entry for Bangkok that read: "it is famous for its temples and other beautiful buildings, and is also often mentioned as a place where there are lots of prostitutes". Longman's have agreed to edit the entry in their next edition. Although the growth of prostitution is usually associated with the arrival of large numbers of GIs on 'Rest & Recreation' during the Vietnam War, and after that with the growth of sex tourism, it is an ancient industry. In the 1680s for example, an official was granted a licence to run the prostitution monopoly in Ayutthaya, using 600 women who had been captured and enslaved.

Prostitution has been illegal since 1960 – although only the pimp and the prostitute are liable for prosecution. The act makes it a crime to 'promiscuously [render] sexual services for renumeration', and police have interpreted this as applying only to the provider of such services, not the recipient. Nonetheless, the scale of prostitution indicates that the police turn a blind eye to the industry – and at the same time no doubt gain financial reward. There is a

THE MODERN SCOURGE: AIDS

Thailand has a massive, and growing AIDS crisis on its hands: it is now official. The first person to be tested HIV positive in Thailand was in 1984; now there are 400,000-600,000 infected, and the World Health Organization believes 8-9 million people are at risk. Initially the Thai government played down the problem, fearing that it would harm the tourist industry, the country's largest foreign exchange earner. After all, they reasoned, 70% of visitors are male (1992 was designated Ladies Visit Thailand Year); could this be only by chance? But it is now accepted that the problem is of crisis proportions, and Thailand's anti-AIDS programme is the largest and most innovative of its kind in Southeast Asia. The programme is headed by the charismatic Mechai Viravaidhya who was the former head of Thailand's family planning programme: condoms in Thailand are even known as 'mechais'. Experts claim Mechai's success so far in raising AIDS consciousness in Thailand is unparalleled in the developing world.

The problem does not lie with the tourist industry, but with the culture of prostitution in Thailand. It is a way of life, and there are thought to be anywhere between 200,000 and 2 million prostitutes. Although data is sketchy, 14% of prostitutes are thought to be infected, and safe sex – until recently – was rarely practiced except in brothels geared to tourists. The National AIDS committee launched a '100% condom campaign' in April 1991 to rectify the situation – threatening to shut down brothels that do not comply. It seems that, at last, prostitutes and their customers are responding to these threats and encouragements. What is most extraordinary is the geographical dispersal of the disease. A staggering 15% of army conscripts from the North – mostly country people – tested HIV positive recently. This reflects the prevalence of prostitution, and the mobility of Thais. Now that girls from neighbouring countries – Burma, Laos, Cambodia and southern China – are being attracted or forced into the industry, the disease is being spread across international borders.

brothel or 'tea house' in every town, no matter how small. Farmers are trucked in from the countryside, and every male 'fresher' (first year university undergraduate) is taken to a brothel by the older students as part of their initiation into university life. One survey recorded that 95% of all men over 21 had slept with a prostitute; another put the figure at 75%. Girls in these 'tea houses' are paid ฿30-50 (US$1.25-US$2) per customer, and Pamela DaGrossa writes: "The women I interviewed told me that prostitutes in these brothels [for Thais] are not required to participate in the actual sex act in any way except for lying on their backs. The men expect and receive no more. It is even rumoured that some more experienced prostitutes

read newspapers while they 'work'".

In the North and the Northeast, families 'sell' their daughters for between ฿10,000 and ฿30,000. But for families mired in poverty, and for daughters who are expected to help their parents, this is not seen as reprehensible. One father in Phayao Province in the North explained: "I didn't sell my daughter...she saw me suffer, she saw the family suffer, and she wanted to help". Some people maintain that the subordinate role of women in Buddhism, means that there is less stigma attached to becoming a prostitute. In some villages, having a daughter who has 'gone south' as it is euphemistically termed, is viewed as a good thing. The benefits are clear. As Sanitsuda Ekachai writes: "Riam has given her father more than a house, a television set, a refrigerator and a stereo. She has made him someone in the village. He was once a landless peasant, one of those who sat in the back row at village meetings. Now he sits at the front..."

With incomes in Thailand rising, the flesh trade has looked to neighbouring countries for girls. It is estimated that there are 20,000 Burmese women in Thai brothels, with 10,000 new recruits joining their ranks each year. Asia Watch believes there is "clear evidence of direct official involvement in every stage of the trafficking process". There are also women working in the trade from Yunnan (South China), Laos and Cambodia.

A disturbing development is the apparent spread of child prostitution and the attraction of paedophiles to Thailand where under-age girls and boys are more available than in Western countries. There has been a spate of 'outings' of foreign paedophiles who have found their names splashed across the national and international media. Over the last few years there has been an increase in cooperation between the Thai police force and overseas forces, especially in Europe. Under Thai law, sex with a girl under 15 is illegal. The police estimated in 1990 that there were 100,000 under-age prostitutes in the Kingdom; but Sanphasit Koompraphant, the director of the Centre for the Protection of Children's Rights, puts the figure at 800,000. This latter figure seems to be grossly inflated, and designed more to impress on people the seriousness of the issue than to be based on any accurate survey. It would mean that nearly one in five girls aged 7-15 are engaged in prostitution, or one in ten boys and girls. The difficulty of effectively dealing with the problem is that the police are, in some cases, in league with those who traffic in under-age prostitutes. Their small salaries also makes them easy targets for corruption, and they are paid to overlook

brothels where child sex occurs. A second difficulty concerns where the problem lies. Much of the media attention has been on foreign (ie *farang*) paedophiles. But the police are the first to admit that, in terms of numbers, Thai men and their activities are more of a problem.

Minorities in Thailand: the Chinese, Thai Malays and Lao

The Chinese Anything between 9% and 15% of the population of Thailand is thought to be Sino-Thai (depending on how 'Chinese' is defined). Hundreds of thousands emigrated from China during the 19th and early 20th centuries, escaping the poverty and lack of opportunity in their homeland. In Thailand they found a society and a religion which was inclusive rather than exclusive. Forced to learn Thai to communicate with the ruling classes (rather than English, French or Dutch as in neighbouring colonial countries) they were relatively quickly and easily assimilated into Thai society. They took Thai names, married Thai women, converted to Buddhism – although they were not required to renounce ancestor worship – and learnt Thai: in short, they became Thai. As elsewhere in the region, these Chinese immigrants proved to be remarkably adept at moneymaking and today control a disproportionate slice of businesses. At times, the Chinese have felt the hot breath of Tai nationalism; in 1914 King Rama VI wrote an essay under the *nom de plume* Atsawaphaahu entitled *The Jews of the East* blaming many of his country's problems on the Chinese. Even today, it is common for government documents to maintain that the plight of the farmer is due to the unscrupulous practices of Chinese traders and moneylenders.

Although the Chinese have been well assimilated into the fabric of the nation, Bangkok still supports a large Chinatown. Here, the Chinese language can be heard spoken, shop signs are in Chinese, and

Chinese cultural and religious traits are clearly in evidence (see page 145).

Thai Malays Of the various minority ethnic and religious groups in Thailand, the Thai Malays and Thai Muslims have often felt most alienated from the Thai nation. Not only do many in the southern 4 provinces of the country speak Malay rather than Thai, but the majority are also Muslim rather than Buddhist. The fact that the government has sometimes been rather heavy-handed in its approach to their welfare and citizenship gave great impetus to the growth of the Communist Party of Thailand (CPT) in the S during the 1960s and 1970s. Relations are far better today, but it is still true that few have been recruited into the civil service or army, and schools in the S still give lessons in Thai and present an essentially 'Tai' view of the country. The Islamic revival in Southeast Asia has brought the issue of Muslim disaffection in the South to the fore once again. The King has done more than most to incorporate the Thai Malays into the fabric of the nation by presenting awards for Koranic study and by regularly visiting the region and staying in his newly-built palace at Narathiwat.

The Lao The largest, and least visible, 'minority' group in Thailand are the Lao of the Northeastern region who constitute nearly a third of the total population. The region and its people are also referred to as 'Isan' (meaning northeastern) and they are often regarded by Central Thais as being the equivalent of 'country bumpkins'. Their linguistic and cultural distinctiveness, and the patronizing attitude of the central authorities, led considerable numbers of the population of the Northeast, as in the South, to support the CPT during the 1960s and 1970s. The murder, by the police, of prominent Northeastern politicians during this period also did little to help integrate Northeasterners into the fabric of Thailand. Although the situation has since stabilized, and separatist sentiments are much reduced, the Northeast is still the poorest and least developed part of the country, with the highest incidence of poverty, malnutrition and child mortality. As a result, the government invests considerable resources in trying to develop the area, the most significant recent effort being *Isan Khiaw* – or the Green Northeast – programme, which is attempting to reforest the plateau.

Hilltribes Thailand's assorted hilltribes, concentrated in the north and west, number over half a million people. For more background information, see page 275.

Religion

The Thai census records that 94% of the population is Buddhist. In Thailand's case, this means Theravada Buddhism, also known as Hinayana Buddhism. Of the other 6% of the population, 3.9% are Muslims (living predominantly in the south of the country), 1.7% Confucianists (mostly Chinese Thais living in Bangkok), and 0.6% Christians (mostly hilltribe people living in the North). Though the king is designated the protector of all religions, the constitution stipulates that he must be a Buddhist.

Theravada Buddhism was introduced into Southeast Asia in the 13th century, when monks trained in Ceylon (Sri Lanka) returned actively to spread the word. As a universal and a popular religion it quickly gained converts and spread rapidly amongst the Tai. Theravada Buddhism, from the Pali word *thera* ('elders'), means the 'way of the elders' and is distinct from the dominant Buddhism practiced in India, Mahayana Buddhism or the 'Greater Vehicle'. The sacred language of Theravada Buddhism is Pali rather than Sanskrit, Bodhisattvas (future Buddhas) are not given much attention, and emphasis is placed upon a precise and 'fundamental' interpretation of the Buddha's teachings, as they were

THE ORIGINAL SIAMESE TWINS

Twin brothers, In and Junn, were born in a village 100 km SW of Bangkok in 1811. They were no ordinary twins however: linked together at the chest, they travelled the world as a two-man, one-body, freak show. In and Junn were the original Siamese twins. They performed for Czar Alexander of Russia, Queen Victoria and other notables, demonstrating gymnastic feats.

They married Latin American twins and managed, despite the obvious difficulties, to father 21 children. Displaying themselves to high society in Europe and America (they became U.S. citizens), the twins became wealthy men owning land in Thailand and houses around the world. But, although physically tied to one another, they drifted apart. By all accounts, In was introverted and calm; Junn short-tempered and volatile. Junn also became a heavy drinker. As they grew older, life together became almost intolerable and they fought, even threatening to kill one another. Much of their lives was spent trying to find a surgeon who might be able to separate them. In 1873 In caught pneumonia and died; Junn died a matter of hours afterwards.

Junn and In's life is recounted in Irving and Amy Wallace's *The two*.

originally recorded. For a general account of Buddhism see page 36.

Buddhism, as it is practiced in Thailand, is not the 'other-worldly' religion of Western conception. Ultimate salvation – enlightenment, or *nirvana* – is a distant goal for most people. Thai Buddhists pursue the **Law of Karma**, the reduction of suffering. Meritorious acts are undertaken and demeritorious ones avoided so that life, and more particularly future life, might be improved. Outside many wats it is common to see caged birds or turtles being sold: these are purchased and set free, and in this way the liberator gains merit. 'Karma' is often thought of in the West as 'fate'. It is not. It is true that previous karma determines a person's position in society, but there is still room for individual action – and a person is ultimately responsible for that action. It is the law of cause and effect.

It is important to draw a distinction between 'academic' Buddhism, as it tends to be understood in the West, and 'popular' Buddhism, as it is practiced in Thailand. In Thailand, Buddhism is a 'syncretic' religion: it incorporates elements of Brahmanism, animism and ancestor worship. Amulets are worn to protect against harm and are often sold in temple compounds (see page 142). Brahmanistic 'spirit' houses can be found outside most buildings. In the countryside, farmers have what they consider to be a healthy regard for the spirits (*phi*) and demons that inhabit the rivers, trees and forests. Astrologers are widely consulted by urban and rural dwellers alike. It is these aspects of Thai Buddhism which help to provide worldly assurance, and they are perceived to be complementary, not in contradiction, with Buddhist teachings. But Thai Buddhism is not homogeneous. There are deep scriptural and practical divisions between 'progressive' monks and the *sangha* (the monkhood) hierarchy, for example.

Every village in Thailand will contain a 'temple', 'monastery' or *wat* (the word does not translate accurately) of which there are nearly 30,000 supporting a population of almost 340,000 monks and novices. Large wats may have up to 600 monks and novices, but most in the countryside will have less than 10, many only 1 or 2. The wat represents the mental heart of each community, and most young men at some point in their lives will become ordained as monks, usually during the Buddhist Rains Retreat, which stretches from Jul to Oct. Previously this period represented the only opportunity for a young man to gain an education and to learn how to read. The surprisingly high literacy rate in Thailand before universal education was introduced (although some would maintain that this was hardly *functional* literacy) is explained by the presence of temple education.

Today, **ordination into the monkhood** is seen as an opportunity to study the Buddhist scriptures, to prepare for a responsible moral life, to become 'ripe'. Farmers sometimes still say that just as a girl who cannot weave is 'raw' (*dip*) and not yet 'ripe' (*suk*) for marriage, so the same is true of a man who has not entered the monkhood. An equally important reason for a man to become ordained is so that he can accumulate merit for his family, particularly for his mother, who as a woman cannot become ordained. The government still allows civil servants to take leave, on full pay, to enter the monkhood for 3 months. Women gain merit by making offerings of food each morning to the monks and by performing other meritorious deeds. They can also become nuns. In 1399, the Queen of Sukhothai prayed that through such actions she might be fortunate enough to be 'reborn as a male'. Lectures on Buddhism and meditation classes are held at the World Fellowship of Buddhists in Bangkok (see page 171).

The intrusion of modern life and mores into the *wat* has created considerable tensions for the *sangha* in Thailand, reflected in a growing number of scandals including a monk who was caught having sex with a corpse. At the beginning of 1994 one respected monk, with a large and influential following, Phra Yantra Amaro Bhikku, was implicated in a sex scandal. Two women claimed to have had sex with the monk: one, a nun, on the deck of a ship off Scandinavia; the other, a harpist, in the back of a van in Europe. Phra Yantra dismissed the accusations saying "I think that normal hell is not enough for them. I think they should be punished in the deepest hell". Subsequent investigations cleared Phra Yantra, although his accusers maintain these were white-washes. The wider problem concerns how monk superstars deal with their fame and fortune. Phra Yantra travels abroad and has a coterie of women fans. So do other monks. Keeping the Buddhist precepts is far harder in 1990s Thailand, and many Thais lament the visible signs of worldly wealth that monks display. It is this gradual erosion of the ideals that monks should embrace rather than the odd lurid scandal which is the more important. Many monks come from poor backgrounds and few are well educated. The temptations are all too clear in a society where a newly wealthy laity see the lavish support of individual monks and their monasteries as a means to accumulate merit. Thais talk with distaste of *Buddhapanich* – commercialised Buddhism – where amulets are sold for US$20,000 and monks attain the status and trappings of rock stars.

Language and literature

Language

According to the Thai census, 97% of the population of Thailand speak Thai – the national language. However it would be more accurate to say that 97% of the population speak one of several related 'Tai' dialects. For example, in the Northeast people speak Lao or Isan, in the North, most converse in *Kham Muang* (literally, 'language of the principalities'), while in the South, they speak *Pak Tai* ('southern tongue'). Strictly-speaking, 'Thai', the language of officialdom and education, is Central Thai. To an extent, successive governments have been engaged in a policy of portraying the country as culturally homogenous and assuming that everyone who speaks one of a number of Tai dialects speaks Thai. However, over 50% of the country do not speak Central Thai as their first language.

The Thai language is an amalgam of Mon and Khmer, and the ancient Indian languages, Pali and Sanskrit. It has also been influenced by various Chinese dialects and by Malay. There remains strong academic disagreement as to whether it should be seen as primarily a language of the Sino-Tibetan group, or more closely linked to Austronesian languages. The Thai writing system was devised by King Ramkhamhaeng in 1283, who modelled it on an Indian system using Khmer characters. The modern Thai alphabet contains 44 consonants, 24 vowels and 4 diacritical tone marks. Words often show links with other languages, particularly technical words. For example *praisani*/post office (Sanskrit), *khipanawut*/guided missile (Pali) and *supermarket*/supermarket (English). There is also a royal court language (*rachasap*) with a specialised vocabulary, as well as a vocabularly to be used when talking to monks.

Literature

The first piece of Thai literature is recognized as being King Ramkhamhaeng's inscription No. 1 of 1292 (see page 77). The *Suphasit Phra Ruang* ('The maxims of King Ruang'), perhaps written by King Ramkhamhaeng himself, is regarded as the first piece of Thai poetry of the genre known as *suphasit*. It shows clear links with earlier Pali works and with Indian-Buddhist religious texts, and an adaptation of the original can be seen carved in marble at Wat Pho in Bangkok (see page 133).

Another important early piece of prose is the *Traiphum Phra Ruang* or the 'Three worlds of Phraruang' probably written by King Li Thai in the mid 14th century. The work investigates the 3

Buddhist realms – earth, heaven and hell – and also offers advice on how a *cakravartin* – or Universal Monarch – should govern.

The literary arts flourished during the Ayutthayan period, particular poetry. 5 forms of verse evolved during this period, and they are still in use today – *chan*, *kap*, *khlong*, *klon* and *rai*. The first 2 are Indian in origin, the last 3 are Thai. Each has strict rules of rhyme and structure.

The genre of poetry known as *nirat* reached its height during the reign of King Narai (1656-1688). These are long narrative poems, written in *khlong* form, usually describing a journey. They have proved useful to historians and other scholars in their attempts to reconstruct Thai life. The poem *Khlong Kamsuan Siprat* is regarded as the masterpiece of this genre. Unfortunately many of the manuscripts of these Ayutthayan works were lost when the Burmese sacked the city in 1767.

During the Rattanakosin period, focused on Bangkok/Thonburi, the first piece of Thai prose fiction was written, an historical romance written by Chao Phraya Phra Khlang. The first full version of the Ramakien was also produced in *klon* verse form (see page 134). The acknowledged poetic genius of the period was Sunthorn Phu (1786-1855) – who the Thais think of as their Shakespeare – and whose masterpiece is the 30,000 line romance *Phra Aphaimani* (see page 368).

The Revolution of 1932 led to a transformation in Thai literature. The first novel to be received with acclaim was Prince Akat Damkoeng's *Lakhon haeng chiwit* ('The circus of life') published in 1929. Sadly, this gifted novelist died at the age of 27. Two other talented novelists were the commoner Si Burapha, whose masterpiece is *Songkhram chiwit* ('War of life') (1932), and the female writer Dokmai Sot, whose publications include *Phu dii* ('The good person') (1937). The works of Dokmai Sot, like those of Prince Akat, deal with the theme of the clash of Thai and Western cultures. Their works are particularly pertinent today when many educated Thais are re-examining their cultural roots.

Since World War II, second rate love/romance writing has flourished. The plots vary only marginally from book to book: love triangles, jealousy, macho men, faithful women... This dismal outpouring is partly balanced by a handful of quality works. Notable are those of Kukrit Pramoj, a journalist and former Prime Minister, whose most famous and best work is *Si phaen din* ('The four reigns') (1953). This traces the history of a noble family from the late 19th century to the end of World War II.

During the political turmoil from the 1950s through to the present day, but particularly from 1973-1976, literature began to be used more explicitly as a tool of political commentary and criticism. *Phai daeng* ('Red bamboo') (1954) is a carefully constructed anti-communist novel by Kukrit Pramoj, while the poems of Angkhan Kanlayanaphong became favourites of the radical student movement of the 1970s. Many of the more radical novelists were gaoled during the 1950s, of whom the most talented was probably Si Burapha. He, and the other radical novelists' and poets' work represent a genre of socialist realism in which the country's afflictions are put down to capitalism and right wing politics. But perhaps the most successful of Thai novels are those that deal with the trials and tribulations of rural life: Kamphoon Boontawee's *Luuk Isan* ('Child of the Northeast') (1976) and Khammaan Khonkai's *Khru ban nok* ('The rural teacher') later made into the film *The teachers of Mad Dog Swamp*.

NB: Many of the better known Thai novels have been translated into English.*DK Books* sells the widest selection of Thai works in English (see relevant sections for addresses).

Dance, drama and music

The great Indian epic the Ramayana (in Thai known as the Ramakien, see page 134) has been an important influence on all Thai arts, but most clearly in dance and drama such as *nang* and *nang thalung* (shadow plays, see page 112), *khon* (masked dramas) and *lakhon* (classical dance dramas). Also important is the *likay* (folk drama).

Dance

Lakhon dance dramas are known to have been performed in the 17th century, and probably evolved from Javanese prototypes. They became very popular not just in the court but also in the countryside and among the common people. Consisting of 3 main forms, they draw upon the Jataka tales, the Ramakien, and upon local fables, legends and myths for their subject matter. Performers wear intricate costumes based on ancient dress, and character parts – such as demons and yogis – wear masks. In genuine lakhon all performers, bar clowns, are played by women. A chorus sings the parts, not the actors.

Drama

Khon masked drama evolved in the royal court of Siam, although its roots lie in folk dances of the countryside. Performers don elaborate jewelled costumes, men wearing masks and women crowns or gilded headdresses. Music accompanies the dance and words and songs are performed by an off-stage chorus. Many of the dances are interpretations of traditional myths, and performers are expected to begin their training at an early age.

The **ramwong** is a dance often performed at ceremonies and originates from the central region. The **fawn** is a similar Northern dance. Slow, graceful, synchronized dancing accompanied by drums and symbols, in which hand movements are used to evoke meaning, characterize the dance.

It is thought that **likay** evolved from Muslim Malay religious performances. It was adopted by the Thais and in time became primarily a comedy folk art enjoyed by common people, with singing and dancing. In recent years, likay artists have begun to incorporate political jibes into their repertoires. Cultured people in Bangkok used to look upon likay as rough and unsophisticated although in recent years it has gained greater recognition as an art form.

Nang shadow plays, with characters beautifully engraved on leather, are frequently performed at cremation ceremonies, particularly in the South (see page 466). There are usually 10 puppeteers in a nang troupe, who wear traditional costume and who are often made-up. The narrator (usually the oldest member of the troupe) offers some help with the story line, while a traditional phipat band provides musical accompaniment. Nang was probably introduced into Thailand from Java during the early Ayutthaya period. *Nang thalung* puppets are smaller, more finely carved, and usually with articulated arms (see page 112). In both cases, the figures 'perform' in front of, or behind, a screen, usually enacting stories from the Ramakien. Like likay, nang and nang thalung have, in the past, been looked down upon as rather crude, unsophisticated arts.

Unfortunately for those who are trying to preserve traditional Thai arts – among them the Thai Royal Family –

MUAY THAI: KICK BOXING

Along with Siamese cats and inaccurate films, Thailand is known in the West for *muay Thai* – literally Thai boxing – or 'kick boxing'. This art of self-defence is first mentioned in the Burmese chronicles of 1411. King Naresuan (1590-1605), one of Thailand's greatest monarchs, made muay Thai a compulsory element of military training and gradually it developed into a sport. Today it is Thailand's most popular sport and is one of the few ways that a poor country boy can turn his rags into riches. It is no coincidence that most of Thailand's best boxers have come from the harsh and impoverished Northeastern region which seems to turn out a never-ending stream of tough, determined young men.

A boy will begin training at the age of 6 or 7, he will be fighting by the age of 10, and competing in professional bouts at 16. Few boxers continue beyond the age of 25. In the countryside, boys herding buffalo will kick trees to hone their skills and learn to transcend pain, all with the intention of using their strength and agility to fight their way out of poverty. Trainers from Bangkok send scouts up-country to tour the provinces in search of boys with potential.

In muay Thai, any part of the body can be used to strike an opponent, except the head. Gloves were only introduced in the 1930s; before then, fists were wrapped in horse hide and studded with shell or glass fragments set in glue. Fatalities were common, and for a time in the 1920s muay Thai was officially banned. Today, fights are staged much like boxing in the West: they are held in a ring, with gloves, and consist of 5 three-minute rounds, with two minute rest periods between each round. Before beginning the boxers prostrate themselves on the canvas while an orchestra of drums and symbols raises the tension. The opponents *wai* to each corner before the music stops, and the fight begins. Punching is rare – far more effective are the kicks and viscious elbow stabs. The intensity of many contests make Western heavyweight boxing seem slow and ponderous.

they are gradually, but steadily, losing their popular appeal. Although tourists may expect and hope to witness a performance most Thais, both urban and rural, would rather watch the TV or go to the movies.

Music

Thai traditional music is a blending of musical elements from a number of cultures, namely Chinese, Indian and Khmer. This applies not just to the instruments, but also to the melodies. Although Thai music can therefore be seen to be derivative, it nonetheless developed into a distinctive form which is regarded as belonging to the 'high' musical cultures of Southeast Asia. In the past, talented young musicians would become attached to the king's court or that of a nobleman and there would receive training from established musicians. Musicians and composers independent of such patronage were rare, and public guilds seldom lasted very long.

With the ending of the absolute monarchy in 1932, the role of the nobility in supporting musicians began to die. Traditional music became viewed as 'unmodern' and performances were actively discouraged by the authorities. It has only been in about the last 2 decades that an interest in traditional Thai music has re-emerged. But because of the years of neglect, the pool of talented musicians is very small.

But although court music may have withered, folk music remained popular and vibrant throughout this period. Perhaps nowhere more so than in the Northeastern region of the country. Here *mor lam* singers are renowned, and in some cases they have become national celebrities. Accompanied by the haunting sound of the *khaen* (bamboo pipes) and singing 'songs from the ricefields' about rural poverty and unrequited love, they are among the most traditional of performers.

Textiles

Thai traditional textiles have experienced something of a rebirth since the end of World War II, with the support of the Royal Family, NGOs and the Jim Thompson Thai Silk Company. In 1947, Jim Thompson – an American resident in Bangkok – sent a sample of Thai silk to the editor of *Vogue* in New York. Then a near moribund industry, today it produces over 10 million metres of silk a year. In the past, cloth was made from silk, cotton or hemp. Because of a shortage of such natural yarns, it is common today to find cloth being woven from synthetic yarn. Likewise, chemical aniline dyes are used in place of natural animal and vegetable dyes although there has been a revival of interest in vegetable dyes (particularly on cotton) in recent years. Among the most distinctive of Thai textiles is *matmii* cloth, produced using the ikat dyeing technique (see below). The dyed yarn is then woven into cloth using plain weave, float weave, supplementary weft and tapestry weave techniques. In the North, hill peoples also produce allique'd cloth.

Clothing

The *pha sin* is an ankle length tubular piece of cloth made up of 3 pieces and worn by women. The waistband (*hua sin*) is usually plain, the main body of the skirt (known as the *pha sin*) plain or decorated, while the lower hem (*dtin sin*) may be intricately woven. Traditionally the pha sin was worn with a blouse or shawl (*pha sabai*), although it is common today to see women wearing T-shirts with the pha sin.

The *pha sarong* is the male equivalent of the pha sin and it is now a rare sight. As the name suggests, it is a tubular piece of cloth which is folded at the front and secured with a belt. It is worn with either a Western-style shirt or a *prarachatan* (a tight collared long sleeved shirt).

TEXTILES AND THE CYCLE OF LIFE

The cycle of life in Thailand is marked by the production, wearing and offering of different textiles. They are markers in the progression from birth to death. Yet, despite its centrality to life, weaving is a skill almost exclusively performed by women. Only male transvestites are allowed to cross this biologically determined divide. Indeed, weaving is a mark of womanhood. In the Northeastern region – where perhaps Thailand's finest textiles are produced – it is said:

"A good wife is like a ploughshare. If she is skilled at weaving, then her husband can wear fine clothes. A wife who talks harshly and is unskilled at her loom makes a family poor and shabby in dress."

A woman is only considered *suk* – or ripe – for marriage when she has mastered the skills of the loom; before then she is regarded as *dip* – or raw. An engaged girl often gives a *pha sin* to her mother-in-law – thereby demonstrating her suitability for marriage. She should also have produced a *pha sin* for herself and a *pha sabai* for her husband, a *pha hom* (blanket), *pha lop* (sheet) and *mawn* (pillow) for their bed, and a *pha sarong*. After the wedding ceremony, the wife changes into a wedding *pha sin*, while the groom dons clothes given to him by his parents-in-law. These clothes are known as *pha hawi haw*.

When a child is born to the couple, it is swaddled in clothes worn by the father (for a male child) or mother (for a female child). These are believed to offer protection to the new-born infant. For a male child, the most important transition after birth is his ordination into the monkhood. In the Northeast, the aspiring novice discards his old clothes for a silk *pha hang*, and then the *pha hang* for the white robes of the novice. When the young man then leaves his village for the first time, his mother will weave a silk *pha sarong* to confer protection against evil spirits. This may be inscribed with magical signs, and some are even believed to deflect bullets. Finally, at death, the lid of the coffin is draped with a *pha hang* for a man (often the same piece of cloth that the dead man wore at his ordination) and a *pha sin* for a woman.

Cloth

Matmii ikat (see page 282) woven cotton cloth is characteristic of the Northeastern region. Designs are invariably geometric and it is very unusual to find a piece which has not been dyed using chemicals. Designs are handed down by mothers to their daughters and encompass a broad range from simple *sai fon* ('falling rain') designs where random sections of weft are tied, to the more complex *mee gung* and *poom som*. The less common *pha kit* is a supplementary weft ikat, although the designs are similar to those found in matmii. The characteristic 'axe cushions' or *mawn kwan* of the Northeast are usually made from this cloth which is thick and loosely

woven. These cushions are traditionally given to monks (usually at the end of the Buddhist Rains Retreat) to rest upon. *Pha fai* is a simple cotton cloth, in blue or white and sometimes simply decorated, made for everyday use and also as part of the burial ceremony, when a white length of pha fai is draped over the coffin. Centres of weaving in the Northeast include: Khon Kaen, Udon Thani, Renu Nakhon (outside That Phanom), Surin, and Pak Thong Chai (outside Korat).

Except for the hilltribe textiles (see page 39), weaving in the North and Central regions is far less diverse than that of the Northeast. Indeed, most of the cloth that is hand woven is produced in

Lao (i.e. Northeastern) villages that have been relocated to this part of the country. Distinctive pha sin are woven by the Thai Lu of Phrae and Nan, featuring brightly coloured horizontal stripes interspersed with triangular designs. Centres of weaving in the North include: Pasang and San Kampaeng (both outside Chiang Mai), and Nan and Phrae.

The textiles of the South exhibit links with those of Malaysia and Sumatra. In general, the hand woven textile tradition is weak in this part of the country. *Pha yok* is similar to *songket* (a Malay cloth), consisting of cotton or silk interwoven with gold or silver yarns. *Han karok* is a technique in which 2-coloured twisted thread is woven. Centres of production in the South include villages around Trang and in the Lake Songkhla area.

RECOMMENDED READING: Conway, Susan (1992) *Thai textiles*, British Museum Press: London. A richly illustrated book with informative text, placing Thai textiles in the context of Thai society and history.

Crafts

Mother-of-pearl
The method used in Thailand differs from that in China and Vietnam. The 'pearl' is from the turban shell from which pieces are cut and sanded to a thickness of 1 mm. These are then glued to a wooden panel and the gaps between the design filled with layers of lac (a resin) before being highly polished. This art form reached its peak during the 17th and 18th centuries. Masterpieces include the doors at Wat Pho, Wat Phra Kaeo and Wat Benchamabophit (all in Bangkok) and the footprint of the Buddha at Wat Phra Singh in Chiang Mai. In Vietnam and China, the wood is chiseled-out and the mother-of-pearl cut to fit the incisions.

Nielloware
A dark amalgam of lead, copper and silver metals is rubbed into etched silver. The craft was introduced to Nakhon Si Thammarat (see page 461) from India and then spread N. It is used to decorate trays, betel boxes, vases, cigarette cases and other small objects.

Khon masks
The masks are of characters from the Ramakien and are made from plaster moulds. Layers of paper are pasted over the mould, glued, and then coated in lac. The masks are then painted and decorated.

Lacquerware
3 layers of lacquer from the sumac tree are brushed onto a wood or wicker base, and each layer is polished with charcoal. Then a fourth layer of lac is added, and once more highly polished with charcoal. After drying, the piece is inscribed with a sharp instrument and then soaked in a red dye for 2-3 days. Because this traditional method is so time consuming, artists today tend to paint the design on to the lacquer. The art dates from the middle of the Ayutthaya period, possibly only after Japanese artists visited the city. One of the finest examples is to be found in a pavilion at Bangkok's Suan Pakkard Palace (see page 153).

Kites
Kite-flying has been a popular pastime in Thailand certainly from the Sukhothai period (where it is described in the chronicles). During the Ayutthaya period an imperial edict forbade kite-flying over the Royal Palace, while La Loubère's journal (1688) records that it was a favourite sport of noblemen. Today it is most common to see competitions between 'chula' (formerly 'kula') and 'pukpao' at Sanaam Luang in Bangkok (see page 138). The chula kite is large – over 2 m in length – while the diamond shaped pukpao is far smaller and more agile. The frame is made from bamboo (*sisuk* variety) cut before the onset of the rains and, preferably, left to mature. The bamboo is then split and the paper skin attached according to a long-established system.

Puppets

Nang yai puppets, literally 'large skin', are carved from buffalo or cow hide and may be over 2 m in height. Though they can be skilfully decorated, nang yai are mechanically simple: there are no moving parts. Interestingly, some characters require particular types of hide. For example, a Rishi must be cut from the skin of a cow or bull which has been struck by lightning or died after a snakebite, or from a cow which has died calving. After curing and stretching the hide on a frame, the figure is carved out and then painted (if it is to be used for night performances, it is painted black).

Nang thalung are smaller than nang yai and are related to Javanese prototypes. They are more complex and have even stranger hide requirements than the nang yai: traditionally, key characters such as Rishi and Isavara need to be made from the soles of a dead (luckily) nang thalung puppet master. If master puppeteers are thin on the ground, then an animal which has died a violent death is acceptable. Incredibly, for the clown character, a small piece of skin from the sexual organ of a master puppeteer (again dead) should be attached to the lower lip of the puppet. One arm of the figure is usually articulated by a rod, enabling the puppet master to provide some additional expression to the character.

Modern Thailand

Politics

Bloodbath in Bangkok

In Feb 1991, **General Suchinda Kraprayoon** staged a bloodless coup d'état and ousted the democratically elected government of Prime Minister Chatichai Choonhavan. Suchinda claimed that he acted because of the extreme degree of corruption associated with Chatichai's administration. Most Thais took him at his word, happy that a manifestly corrupt government had been removed from power. Suchinda created an army dominated National Peacekeeping Council and asked the

---

THAILAND'S FLAG: NATION, RELIGION, MONARCHY

Thailand's flag was introduced in 1917 by Rama VI. It consists of horizontal stripes of red, white and blue. The two outer red stripes represent the Thai nation, the two white stripes, religion, and the inner blue band symbolizes the monarchy. The three stripes therefore represent the three pillars of society: nation, religion and monarchy. Thailand's athletes wear red, white and blue strip and the colours have become the Kingdom's unofficial national colours. Before 1917, Thailand's flag was a white elephant, symbolizing the monarchy, on a red background.

Motif of the former flag of Siam

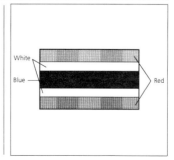

White / Blue / Red

civilian **Anand Panyarachun** to act as caretaker Prime Minister while a new constitution was being drawn-up and preparations made for elections. During 1991, Anand headed one of the most efficient and corruption-free administrations since 1932, introducing a raft of new bills that had been delayed under Chatichai's tenure. Despite army resistance to some of Anand's decisions, Suchinda did not interfere in the day-to-day running of the government.

But, while Anand was doing a fine job running the country in 1991, opposition politicians were becoming increasingly concerned about the army's intentions. Two former army generals, Chamlong Srimuang, the leader of Palang Dharma Party (see page 140), and Chaovalit Yongchaiyut, leader of the New Aspirations Party, formed the most vocal opposition to Suchinda's attempts – in their view – to cement the army's power by forging a pro-military constitution. In Nov, 100,000 people gathered in Bangkok to protest against the constitution which would allow an unelected person to become Prime Minister, and give the army the power to appoint 270 members of the Senate, the upper house. It is said Suchinda visited a Buddhist shrine in the southern Thai town of Nakhon Si Thammarat just after the rally to ask the guardian spirit's advice over the growing opposition. After setting off 5,000 firecrackers, he was told that unless he accepted the opposition's demands he would face a 'fateful event'.

The spirit's prediction turned out to be tragically correct. In the elections of Mar 1992, there was no clear winner. After much debate, a coalition of pro-military parties asked Narong Wongwan, the leader of the airforce-backed Sammakhi Tham Party, to become Prime Minister. This failed when it was alleged that Narong had been involved in drug trafficking, and that he had been denied a visa to visit the US in 1991. With no other obvious candidate, Suchinda – who had earlier made a public promise that he would not become Prime Minister – was offered the job. The unelected Suchinda tearfully agreed, and he became Premier on the 7th April.

Chamlong Srimuang took this as his cue to call his supporters onto the streets to resist what he viewed as the army's imposition of itself on the Thai people. In the elections, his Palang Dharma Party had won 32 out of the 35 seats in Bangkok – the political and economic heart of the country. On May 4th he announced he was going on hunger strike. Tens of thousands of people crowded into the streets around the Parliament buildings and then onto Sanaam Luang, near the Grand Palace. Suchinda tried to suppress coverage of the **demonstrations**, but failed. The ruling coalition agreed to a constitutional amendment that would ensure any future Prime Minister would have to be elected. Chamlong ended his fast on 9th May and asked his supporters to go home. The people of Thailand then waited for Suchinda to do as he promised. It quickly became clear that he had no intention of stepping down.

On Sunday 17th May, tens of thousands of demonstrators took to the streets once again to try and force Suchinda into honouring the agreement. Like the demonstration of 1973, the focus of discontent was the area around Sanaam Luang and the Democracy Monument in the heart of the capital. But unlike the events of almost two decades earlier, the demonstrators were not just young, radical students, but also members of the middle class with their mobile phones and designer jeans. Nonetheless, Suchinda acted just like his predecessor Prime Minister Thanom: he called on the army to clear the streets. Scores of people were killed as the army opened fire (after the confrontation, 52 bodies were recovered, although 163 people are still listed as

KING BHUMIBOL AND THE MONARCHY

Although Thailand has been a constitutional monarchy since the Revolution of 1932, King Bhumibol Adulyadej and the Royal Family have an influence that far exceeds their formal, constitutional powers. It seems that the leaders of the Revolution shyed away from emasculating the monarchy, and decided to keep the king at the centre of the Thai social and political universe. Nonetheless, the only truly active king since 1932 has been the present one, King Bhumibol, who acceded to the throne in 1945.

King Bhumibol Adulyadej – the name means Strength of the Land, Incomparable Power – has virtually single-handedly resurrected the Thai monarchy. The king was born in the US where his father was a doctor in Boston. He graduated in engineering from Lausanne, Switzerland and speaks English and French fluently. He is also a skilled jazz saxophonist and an accomplished yachtsman (he won a gold medal at the Asian Games).

After returning from his studies abroad to become King he entered the monkhood, and since then has continuously demonstrated his concern for the welfare of his people. The King and his Queen, Sirikit, travel the country over-seeing development projects which they finance, visiting remote villages, and taking a keen interest in the poor. The King has also largely managed to maintain his independence from the hurly-burly of Thai politics. When he has intervened, he has usually done so sensitively and with great effect. In October 1973, after the riots at Thammasat University, he requested that Prime Minister Thanom, along with his henchmen Praphat and Narong, leave the country to stem the tide of civil disorder. They obeyed. In a repeat of the events of 1973, in May 1992 the King called Prime Minister General Suchinda Kraprayoon to his palace where, recorded on television, he was publicly – though not overtly – humiliated for ordering the army to quell brutally demonstrations against his premiership. Three days later, Suchinda had resigned, and left the country.

The undoubted love and respect that virtually all Thais hold for their king raises the question of the future, and whether the monarchy can remain a stabilizing force. The suitability of his eldest son Crown Prince Vajiralongkorn has been questioned, while his eldest daughter Crown Princess Sirindhorn is respected and loved almost as much as the king himself. Who might accede is discussed, very privately, by all Thais. In Jan 1993, Vajiralongkorn – in an unprecedented move – lashed out at his critics. He was quoted in the *Bangkok Post* as saying: "[They say] I act as a powerful *chao poh* [Godfather] providing protection for sleazy business ... Do I look like a *chao poh* type? ... The money I spend is earned honestly. I do not want to touch money earned illegally or through the suffering of others." Whether this will scotch the rumours is yet to be seen. Some Thais worried about the succession are comforted by a legend that the Chakri Dynasty would only have nine monarchs: King Bhumibol is the ninth.

The respect that the Thais hold for the King and the Royal Family should be honoured by all visitors. Any open criticism should be avoided: *lèse majesté* is still an offence in Thailand. In cinemas, the national anthem is played before the film and the audience - including foreigners - is expected to stand. In towns in the countryside, at 0800 every morning the national anthem is relayed over P.A. systems, and pedestrians are again expected to stop what they are doing and stand to attention. It is in ways like this that the continuing influential role of the monarchy becomes clear.

missing by relatives). When demonstrators fled into the *Royal Hotel*, the army followed to drag them out and herd them off to gaol. Television audiences in the West were treated to pictures of a brutal, blood-soaked Land of Smiles.

Three days after the confrontation between the army and the demonstrators, **King Bhumibol** ordered both Suchinda and opposition leader Chamlong – who had to be released from gaol for the meeting – to his palace. There, television cameras were waiting to witness Suchinda's global, public humiliation. He and Chamlong prostrated themselves on the floor while the king lectured them, asking rhetorically: "What is the use of victory when the winner stands on wreckage?" Immediately afterwards, the army and the demonstrators withdrew from the streets. On Friday, Suchinda offered his resignation to the king and on Saturday, less than one week after the killing began, Suchinda Kraprayoon fled the country. In a televised address, Suchinda accepted responsibility for the deaths, but also managed to use his still considerable influence to secure an amnesty for himself and his men. The Editor of the Thai daily newspaper *The Nation* wrote just after the massacre: "Let us look at the man responsible for this unforgivable carnage. Gen. Suchinda Kraprayoon thought he was a man of his time – debonair, authoritative, capable. The medical college drop-out who found guns more to his liking, regrettably, only epitomized how woefully out of touch the Thai military was with the times."

Politics since the massacre of May 1992
After the riots of May 1992, and General Suchinda's (and by association, the army's) humiliating climb-down, Anand Panyarachun was appointed interim prime minister for a second spell. New elections were set for 13th September. The so-called Anand II government took action to curtail the powers of the armed forces and moved a number of high-ranking officers implicated in the brutal crack-down to inactive posts. The Thai media characterized the elections of September as a contest between 'angel' (pro-democracy) and 'devil' (pro-military) parties. However, despite public revulsion at the events of May – and to the surprise of many Westerners – the angel parties only secured a bare majority. The leader of the Democrat Party, Chuan Leekpai, was appointed 1992's fourth prime minister on 23rd September. Chuan, a mild-mannered Southerner, is viewed as 'clean' and honourable, but perhaps not sufficiently tough for the job ahead. Significantly, Chamlong Srimuang, who was the focus of the demonstrations, refused to accept a cabinet post – presumably because he wanted to make sure that he could police the actions of ministers and make sure they came up to his own high level of moral rectitude in public life.

Chuan's government began to take small steps to ensure that a repeat performance of May could not occur. However, the middle classes in Bangkok remain pessimistic about the prospects for true democracy. They note that the army's power remains almost as potent as before, and generals continue to warn that they may be forced to step in again should conditions demand it. It is notable for example, that attempts to have the amnesty of May revoked, failed and General Suchinda remains a free man. Justice, in the eyes of many Bangkokians, has simply not been done. Nonetheless, the new army commander General Wimol Wongwanich has gone some way to depoliticizing the army and has made it known that he and his fellow generals have 'learned lessons' from the May 1992 violence.

The ability of Thailand to confound observers was reflected in the criminal case brought against former Prime Minister Anand in March 1993 for malfeasance or official misconduct – with a maximum sentence of 5 years in prison. Regarded by many as having led the cleanest and most efficient administration in Thailand's history, Anand was brought to book for having interfered with the promotion process of the kingdom's notoriously factionalized judges. The case became a *cause célèbre* as admirers rallied round to defend Anand's reputation; this group became known as the FOA, or 'Friends of Anand' (presumably modelled on President Clinton's FOB – Friends of Bill). The contrast between Anand's predicament and that of General Suchinda – protected from prosecution by an amnesty – was all too clear to the average Thai on the street.

Although it is sometimes hard for foreigners to understand, the Thai army (see box) sees its role as 'protector' of the people against the excesses of corrupt civilian politicians, rather than the other way around. Politicians are seen to be irredeemably selfish, with an interest only in the size of their bank balances and there have been 18 military coups since 1932 as the army has been 'forced' to step in to 'protect the people'. There is no doubt that many rural Thais agree with this view – and for good reason – and army-backed political parties continue to garner millions of votes (with the help of billions of baht in bribes). There may be greater awareness of the dangers of excessive corruption, 'rent-seeking', patronage, cronyism and vote-buying, but the events since May show that the army climb-down hardly represents a watershed in the development of parliamentary democracy. Rather, it was just another step on a long – at time bloody – and tortuous road towards good, representative government. As one Thai academic was recently quoted in the *Financial Times* as saying, most rural MPs – whether of army or civilian persuasion – are simply "hoodlums in suits".

Despite the feeling that Chuan and his government is weak, he has survived a series of no-confidence votes in parliament. The opposition has argued that the government is ineffective in economic and foreign policy, but the tendency has been for the debates to degenerate into a series of personal attacks against individual ministers. In these rather tawdry affairs, the Prime Minister has managed to aquit himself rather effectively. After the corruption and violence of the late 1980s and early 1990s, the fact that Chuan is widely perceived to be personally honest (a characterisation which cannot be applied to every minister in his administration) is a dinstinct advantage. But even so many Thais view him as an ineffectual Prime Minister. Perhaps to

MORE GENERALS THAN TANKS

The army is one of Thailand's key institutions. It has been at the centre of political and economic power since the 'revolution' of 1932, mounting 18 coups since that date. There are currently 200,000 men in uniform. But, with the threat of internal insurrection from the CPT (Communist Party of Thailand) and the external threat from Vietnam now both virtually extinguished, it is becoming harder to justify such a large standing army, and the new commander General Wimol Wongwanich is in the process of slimming-down his forces. Most remarkable is the number of generals—somewhere between 700 and 1,000. This means that, in all likelihood, Thailand has more generals than it has tanks (720). Nearly half of the military's top brass have nothing to do, and the army is viewed as a job for life by those passing through the prestigious Chulachomklao Military Academy.

try and assuage this perception his government issued a 48-page booklet in late 1993 setting out their achievements – in itself, one might argue, a sign of insecurity.

In April 1994 **Chuan's administration faced its toughest test yet** when the opposition aligned itself with the Senate and managed to have a proposed new constitution sidelined in favour of a draft bill based on the pro-military 1978 constitution. The Senate saw its best interests lying with the opposition because the the government's new constitution envisaged a reduced Senate consisting of only 120 members, as against the existing 270. For the Senate, their action was clearly a desperate attempt at self-preservation; for the opposition it was, in the view of many, a 'cynical' ploy to bring down the coalition government. With Chuan's authority seriously dented there was talk of military intervention and the distinct possibility that the Prime Minister would be forced to dissolve parliament and call an election.

Two months later in June, Chalard Vorachat – one of the 'heroes' of the 1992 democracy demonstrations – began a hunger strike outside the Parliament buildings to call for further democratic reforms. Protected inside a steel cage to prevent the police from carrying him off and kept topped-up with a saline and glucose drip, he seemed to be demanding the impossible. But with the support of some sections of the media he may yet force further change from a jittery government.

At the end of 1993 in Chantaburi Province near the Cambodian border, the police uncovered a major cache of 1,500 tonnes of arms apparently sourced from China and destined for Khmers Rouges forces in Cambodia. Embarrassingly, the Thai army was implicated, controvening the 1991 Paris Peace Accord and the UN embargo of the Khmers Rouges. The discovery of the arms – which were later moved to a secret location – provided further proof for those observers who argue that despite the reforms introduced by Anand and then Chuan to reign in the army and limit its power, it remains a considerable force that acts according to its own perceived needs, and not those of the government and country. Chuan threatened to deal with anyone seen to be violating the UN embargo. So far they have done nothing to investigate the army's role in this little debacle. In April 1994, joint Cambodian Prime Minister Hun Sen openly accused the Thai army of supporting the Khmers Rouges, an accusation which the government and army angrily denied. The commander-in-chief of the Thai military General Wimol Wongwanich bluntly stated that Hun Sen was lying and threateningly stated that, if pushed to the limit, Thailand might have to respond to the accusations with "an eye for an eye...there are limits to our patience". Quite what he meant by this was not clear. What is clear is that given past collusion between the Thai army and the Khmers Rouges, protestations of innocence have a rather hollow ring.

In the first half of 1994 another scandal was revealed, this time among MPs rather than generals. It was revealed that opposition MP Thanong Siriprechapong had been charged in California with drug smuggling, where he is reportedly known as 'Thai Tony'. But Thanong appeared not to be the only one: reports filtered out that 17 current and former MPs were suspected by the US as involved in the drugs trade. As local commentators pointed out, this is almost to be expected. Becoming an MP is an expensive business and in the N and W the fastest way to riches is through drug trafficking. One MP said the parliament chamber 'smelt of marijuana' and demanded an election be called. PM Chuan responded that "the ones who caused to smell must be deodorised, not the entire house".

The bureaucracy

The Thai bureaucracy, like that in the other countries of Southeast Asia, is a many-headed hydra. Becoming a civil servant, or in Thai *kharatchakan* (literally 'servant of the crown') brings with it considerable prestige, a certain amount of power, a great deal of job security, and a limited salary. One way that bureaucrats have overcome the last of these is by *kin muang* – literally 'eating the country' – extracting from the land and its people far more than their own meagre salaries. Of course, there are also many committed government officials who act in what they perceive to be the best interests of the population whom they (in theory) serve. In spite of King Chulalongkorn's reforms of the civil service at the turn of the century, the relationship between bureaucrats and the people is still a 'top-down' one in which the official talks and the people listen. To a large extent, this is just a reflection of Thai social relations, and the pervasive superior-inferior/patron-client ties.

In general, petty officials are recruited locally. They will usually have been educated to secondary school level and have little chance of advancing to the higher echelons of the civil service. The more senior officials are university-educated and often have their roots (and hearts) in Bangkok. A challenge for the bureaucracy today is that Thailand's rapid economic growth has dramatically widened wage differentials between the public and private sectors. With a decline in the prestige associated with joining the civil service and becoming a *kharatchakan*, fewer talented young Thais are being enticed into the bureaucracy.

Education

Traditionally, young men gained a limited education when they entered the monkhood. A system of secular education was not introduced until the reign of King Chulalongkorn, who called on the expertise of many monks and employed them as teachers. When compulsory, universal primary school education was inaugurated in 1921 it was for a period of 4 years (to *bor sii*). Since 1978, all children have had to undergo 6 years of primary education (to *bor hok*). Primary school education is free but school uniforms and stationery must be paid for, and many farmers also complain when their children are not around to look after the buffalo and undertake other farm chores. Even a child of 6 is an economic resource in the countryside. Some Thais question whether the conservative, urban-orientated and Western-based curriculum is really relevant to those who spend their lives in agriculture and say a more vocational curriculum should be introduced. Nonetheless, the system as it currently stands has contributed towards the achievement of a literacy rate which exceeds 90%.

Secondary school education is divided into 2 periods of 3 years each: lower and upper secondary school. At both levels fees are levied. In 1988 while there were 7 million primary school pupils, there were only 0.5 million in upper secondary school, and a mere 166,000 at university. Most secondary school students live in urban areas. It is rare for a rural Thai to progress as far, and even rarer for them to gain entrance to higher education. Of Thailand's 14 institutes of higher education, 9 are located in Bangkok and they graduate 70% of students. The most prestigious is Chulalongkorn University, followed by the more radical Thammasat University. In 1988 Thailand's colleges of higher education produced nearly 64,000 students with Bachelor degrees. However, businessmen complain that the country trains too many students in the arts, and not enough in the sciences and engineering. There is already an estimated annual shortfall of 7,000 engineers in the country.

The press and media

Newspapers The first newspapers to

DISASTER AND DEATH

Thailand has an unenviable record for the scale of its disasters. Over the last few years there have been a succession of accidents that have led to major losses of life. Some commentators are beginning to ask at what cost Thailand's rapid economic growth has been attained.

1990, September	A lorry carrying gas cylinders collides with a tuk-tuk on Bangkok's expressway and bursts into flames.Death toll: 91.
1991, February	A lorry carrying dynamite explodes near Phangnga in the Southern region while onlookers gather around. Death toll: 171.
1992, March	A ferry transporting Buddhist pilgrims to Si Racha in the Eastern region sinks after colliding with an oil tanker. Death toll: 119.
1993, May	A fire at a toy factory outside Bangkok causes mayhem due to blocked escape exits. Death toll: 189.
1993, August	A hotel collapses in Korat, Northeast region. Death toll: 120.
1994, February	A ferry carrying Burmese workers back to Burma from Thailand capsizes. Death toll: about 200.

Thailand also scores highly in terms of traffic accidents and homicides. In 1987, 4,636 people died in traffic accidents and 5,229 were murdered (down from an horrific 10,661 in 1982) in Thailand. This translates into a homicide rate of 9.7/100,000; the figure for the US – in many people's mind the murder 'capital' of the world – is 8.6/100,000. It should be added that it is extremely rare for a tourist to be murdered.

appear in Thailand were published by American missionaries. The *Bangkok Recorder* (in Thai) appeared each month between 1844 and 1845, while the *Bangkok Daily Advertiser* (in English) appeared between 1868 and 1878. Today there are numerous daily and weekly publications serving a variety of markets. The widest-selling Thai newspapers are *Sayam Rat* and *Thai Rat*, the latter with a circulation of around 750,000 and a readership of as much as 10 times that. *Matichon*, with a far smaller circulation, is regarded as the leading 'serious' Thai language newspaper. Of the English language Press, the two most respected newspapers are the *Bangkok Post* and *The Nation*, both enjoying a high reputation for their reporting.

Newspapers are widely read in the cities, less so in the countryside, although many villages now have 'libraries' where magazines and newspapers are available. Except during periods of tension, such as following the coup d'état of February 1991 and the riots of May 1992, Thailand's press is probably the least controlled in Southeast Asia. Even during the recent riots, some newspapers indicated their views by running blank spaces where editorials would usually be placed, while others openly flouted Prime Minister Suchinda's restrictions. The only area where no hint of controversy is permitted is concerning the monarchy. Everyone and everything else is fair game, and the Thai newspapers make the British tabloids appear tame by comparison. The gory, annotated, photographs are the most visible example of this. But, investigative reporting does have its risks. Between 1979 and 1984, 47 journalists were murdered, largely because of the stories they were writing or researching. Few people have been charged with these murders – allegedly because the police themselves have been involved.

Radio and television Radio and television, by comparison, are tightly controlled by the government. Indeed, identical news broadcasts are transmitted on all Thailand's 300-odd radio stations simultaneously. The army and the government control the output from the TV stations, and if a Thai is looking for any semblance of an alternative perspective in a news item he or she will have to turn to the print media or to gossip and rumour. This was yet again reinforced during the riots of May 1992. Television programming is poor: inane game shows, soap operas and Chinese martial arts films top the billings. There is little that could be described as either morally or educationally uplifting.

Economy

Thailand has been touted as the next nation to join that exclusive club of Newly Industrializing Countries or NICs. Several years of high economic growth, a massive inflow of foreign investment from the late 1980s, perceived political stability, and a fiscally conservative government made Thailand the 'flavour of the month'. As if to give the Kingdom the international stamp of approval, the World Bank and International Monetary Fund held their conference in Bangkok in October 1991. Workers were also given a holiday to ease congestion in the capital. But this view of Thailand as an NIC overlooks a number of worrying facts. Most important, economic activity is highly concentrated – primarily in and around Bangkok. Wages in the capital are relatively high (in April 1993 the daily minimum wage was raised to ฿125 – US$5), and the city exudes wealth and sophistication. But in the countryside wages are stagnant – about ฿50 for a day's work in the fields – and poverty and malnutrition widespread. Non-agricultural incomes are 13 times higher than those of farmers and in recent years the gradual reduction in poverty has levelled off. Despite double digit growth rates, one in six households remain stubbornly mired in poverty. At the same time as the World Bank and the IMF was holding its glitzy conference in 1991, Thailand's NGOs were holding an alternative parallel conference designed to highlight the human and environmental costs of Thailand's 'development' (many activists in Thailand would be reluctant to use the word 'development' to describe a process of modernization that they would describe as mal-development').

Growth has also been based upon foreign technology and, often, capital. Thailand is not a Taiwan or South Korea with a creative, innovative, class of industrialists. Indeed, education – or rather the lack of it – is highlighted by most economists as one of the major constraints facing the kingdom as it continues down the path of 'development'. Only 2 in 10 workers have anything more than primary level education, and a mere fraction enter higher education. With only 29% of secondary school age

Region	REGIONAL ECONOMIES		
	Gross Regional Product (1991, bn baht)	Population (1992)	Monthly household income (1990, baht)
Bangkok	1,300	8.7	11,742
Central	566	10.0	5,827
South	207	7.4	5,153
North	255	11.7	4,719
Northeast	291	20.1	3,529

Sources: *National Statistical Office, 1993 and Far Eastern Economic Review, 1994*

children enrolled in full-time education, Thailand has the lowest enrolment rate among the ASEAN countries – even Indonesia, with a per capita income less than a half that of Thailand has nearly double the proportion registering in secondary schools. In the countryside, a derisory 10%-15% progress on from primary school. Without the skills that come from education, it is hard to see how the country can continue to entice foreign companies to invest. In short, there are fears that with wages rising, Thailand may lose its competitive edge. Some people see this scenario developing in the rising level of lay-offs in the textile sector. During the summer of 1993, 1,500 workers were sacked as companies moved their factories to Vietnam and Indonesia where wage levels are US$2 a day or less, as against Bangkok's US$5 a day. In Thailand, textile exports rose by only 3% in 1992; in Indonesia they increased by 50%. Although some people see this as an economic crisis in the making, other analysts are more sanguine and note that although textiles may be yesterday's industry so far as Thailand is concerned, electronics and other sectors are growing faster than ever.

Growth has also sometimes been at the expense of health, safety, the environment and workers' rights. On 10 May 1993 a fire at a toy factory outside Bangkok killed nearly 200 workers. By all accounts, fire precautions were minimal and most of the employees – largely women – were working for less than the minimum wage. There have also been other such disasters which have caused some people to question at what expense 'development' is being achieved (see page 119).

Thailand embarked on its current path to development in the late 1950s when General Sarit Thanarat became Prime Minister after a coup d'état and decided to abandon the preceding policy of economic nationalism. Government intervention in the economy was reduced, foreign investment welcomed, and a national development plan drawn up. Although it has taken a long time to reinvigorate the economy, and even today there is a sizeable public sector, this change of direction over 30 years ago paved the way for Thailand's current growth.

Economic development

Since the 1950s, there has seen a rapid expansion of the industrial and service sectors, and the relative decline of agriculture. Today, agriculture contributes just over 15% of GDP, while manufacturing alone contributes over a quarter. Rice, the main export for hundreds of years, is today exceeded in value terms by textiles, electronics, and tourism. Although the economy has diversified significantly, most Thais are still farmers. The slow growth of the agricultural sector compared with industry has meant that inequalities between town and country have widened. An average farm household in the Northeast earns less than ฿3,000 per month; in Bangkok, households can expect to have a monthly income of over ฿11,000. Nor are services such as schooling and health as widely accessible to rural Thais. This has engendered among many young rural Thais feelings of frustration: they are well aware of all the consumer goods that can be bought, but they are unable to afford them.

The discrepancy between rural and urban areas

This has led to a massive migration of men and women from the countryside to the towns and cities of Thailand, and especially to Bangkok. They work as tuk-tuk and saamlor drivers, labourers on building sites and in textile mills, and as prostitutes. Each month they send money back to their families, saving-up so they can afford to send their children to secondary school, buy a television, or extend their house

Whether the Thai economy can continue to absorb this army of 'surplus' labour will be a key challenge for the 1990s. **'Rural industrialization'** is one solution that is being tried. In effect, this means relocating industries such as textiles, shoe-making and gem cutting to rural areas, thereby employing people in the countryside and stemming the flow of migrants to Bangkok. There have been some notable successes: Northeast Textile in Nakhon Ratchasima, for example. On the face of it, it appears that everyone 'wins': rural people can live cheaply at home and benefit from wages that are not too much lower than in Bangkok; Bangkok does not suffer from the added congestion and infrastructural strain that each migrant creates; companies can save in lower wages, land and overhead costs; and the government can feel smug that it is helping to reduce poverty and under-production in the countryside. As Banjob Kaewsra, a 23-year old worker at Northeast Textile was quoted as saying in an article in the *Far Eastern Economic Review*, "Working here is better [than in Bangkok]. Wages aren't much lower and the cost of living is far less. Besides, its home." The trouble is that this all sounds rather familiar. Successive Thai governments have been trying to decentralize economic activity since the first Five Year Development Plan was introduced in 1961 and the yawning gap between Bangkok and the rest of the Kingdom has yawned wider ever since. But perhaps this is an idea whose time has come: Bangkok is ever more congested and the growing middle class now realise that there is a large section of the population who simply have not benefited from the Kingdom's rapid economic growth. In short, the mobile phone users are discovering a social conscience, and the government is beginning to sit up and take a serious look at the distribution of Thailand's wealth.

In his first major policy statement after being appointed prime minister in Sept 1992, Chuan promised to focus attention – and funds – on the plight of Thailand's rural population. Nonetheless, he is anxious not to undermine the country's reputation for fiscal prudence. Notably, three unelected bankers have been put in charge of the economy. Although all Thai cabinets contain ministers who owe their position to the 'debt' that the prime minister owes to them – rather than to any aptitude for the job – Chuan's is relatively clean. It certainly does not match former prime minister Chatichai's 'buffet cabinet' where there was enough money floating about to feed everyone.

Although Thailand's townspeople lead more comfortable lives than their country cousins, Thai farmers are relatively well-off, indeed rich, compared with those in India, Bangladesh or on Java. Thai farmers usually own their own land – although tenancy is a problem in some areas, especially in the Central region and parts of the North – nutrition is reasonable, and agricultural surpluses are the norm rather than the exception. Some farmers and intellectuals complain that the incorporation of rural Thailand into the national and international cash economies has meant that they have become vulnerable to fluctuations in the global market – and they plead for a return to a 'traditional' life. Most farmers however, have embraced the cash economy with alacrity and seem unimpressed by such protestations.

Social and economic change

This has been even more pronounced in urban Thailand. Here new activities, new classes, and new cultural forms have displaced 'tradition'. It is in the cities that Western consumer culture has made the greatest inroads, and it is here that politics and society are at their most vibrant and fast-changing. Unionized workers predominantly work in Bangkok; Marxist radicals, other opposition political groups, even environmentalists, are also Bangkok-based. To a rural Thai, venturing out of the countryside for the first time, Bangkok and the other cities of the kingdom must feel almost like alien worlds. As always in Thailand however, surface appearances can be deceptive: scratch the veneer of a Bangkok or a Thai urbanite, and not far below are the same elemental strands of a country dweller.

Paying the price of success: tourism in Thailand

For a few years Thailand was the place where everyone wanted to go and where every tour operator and hotel owner was making money. No more. In 1990, 5 million tourists visited the country, a dramatic increase from the numbers a decade earlier. But projections that arrivals would just keep on growing proved over-optimistic. Instead, arrivals stagnated. In 1991, 5.08 visitors came to the country; in 1992, 5.14 million, and in 1993, a rather more encouraging 5.76 million. Nonetheless, the stagnation of the industry was a shock for those who saw investing in tourist facilities as a sure thing. Hotel occupancy rates were 50% or less and hoteliers were slashing their room rates to encourage custom.

Why this should happen to a country with so much to offer is a lesson in the uncertainties of the tourist industry (see page 54). First of all there were domestic political problems that sullied the smiling face of Thailand. The *coup d'état* of 1991 and the widely reported massacre of demonstrators in 1992 (see page 112). On top of this, there was also the world recession – along with the Gulf War – which caused many potential long-haul holiday-makers in Europe and the U.S. to economise and go somewhere closer to home for their vacations. It is interesting that the only fast-growing market is for tourists from other countries in Asia – Taiwan, South Korea and China particularly.

Rather harder to pin down is Thailand's poor PR. It is said that the Kingdom is yesterday's destination. People have moved on to Indonesia, Vietnam and elsewhere. There seems to be a combination of factors here. Among 'travellers' or 'backpackers', Thailand is perceived to be spoilt. Among family holidaymakers, Thailand's AIDS crisis (see page 101) is a cause for concern. And among those looking for pristine beaches and a clean environment, over-development in places like Pattaya and Phuket is turning them away. All in all, the Tourist Authority of Thailand has an image problem that it is desperately trying to address. It has, for example, invented a new word – *wattanathammachaat*, or 'culture and nature' – to try and cash in on the eco-tourism bandwagon. The problem is that changing an impression is a long and arduous business. Just coining a few new words and introducing some slick advertising is unlikely to do the trick.

As this is a guidebook ostensibly trying to encourage people to visit Thailand (and Burma), it would seem appropriate to defend the Kingdom as a tourist destination. Like most images, those above do have a ring of truth. There can be no doubt that AIDS is a problem, that tourist facilities have been over-developed in some areas, and that environmental degradation is an issue of serious concern. But Thailand is a country the size of France and many towns do not see a tourist from one week to the next. Much of the Northeast is scarcely visited. The Northern towns of Nan, Phayao, Phrae and Pai are still charming. Islands in the South like Koh Lanta and Koh Tao are relatively undeveloped. And towns in the Central Plains like Suphanburi and Lopburi, and in the South like Phetburi are not on most people's itineraries. Indeed it is the word 'itinerary' which is part of the problem. With two or four weeks to spend in Thailand, many visitors will make a list of 'must do's'. This restricts 95% of travellers to just a handful of places, giving the impression that the whole country is over-crowded. Compared with most European destinations, the numbers of tourists visiting Thailand are still small.

THAILAND: FACT FILE

Geographic

Land area	513,115 sq km
Arable land as % of total	37%
Average annual rate of deforestation	2.5%
Highest mountain	2,298m (Chiang Mai)
Average rainfall in Bangkok	1,418mm
Average temperature in Bangkok	28.1°C

Economic

GNP/person (1991)	US$1,650
GDP/person (PPP*, 1991)	US$5,270
GNP growth (/capita 1980-1991)	5.9%
GNP growth 1991	7.9%
GNP growth 1992	7.4%
GNP growth 1993	7-8% (est.)
GNP (1991)	US$88.1 billion
% labour force in agriculture	67
Total debt (% GNP)	39%
Debt service ratio (% export)	13.1%
Military expenditure (% GDP)	3.5%

Social

Population	56.1 million
Population growth rate (1960-92)	2.4%
Adult literacy rate	93.8%
Mean years of schooling	3.9 years
Tertiary graduate as % of age group	5%
Population in absolute poverty	16.8 million
Rural population as % of total	77%
Growth of urban population (1960-92)	4.6%/year
Urban population in largest city (%)	58%
Televisions per 1,000 people	114

Health

Life expectancy at birth	68.7 years
Population with access to clean water	76%
Calorie intake as % of requirements	103%
Malnourished children under 5 years old	0.7 million
Contraceptive prevalence rate†	66%

*PPP = Purchasing Power Parity (based on what it costs to buy a similar basket of goods and services in different countries)

† % of women of childbearing age using contraception.

Source: World Bank (1993) *Human development report 1993*, OUP: New York.

BANGKOK

BANGKOK HIGHLIGHTS

Temples Bangkok's best known sight is the temple of *Wat Phra Kaeo*, situated within the grounds of the *Grand Palace* (page 135). Other notable temples include *Wat Pho* (page 133), *Wat Arun* (page 148), *Wat Suthat* (page 144) and *Wat Traimitr* (page 145).

Museums Bangkok's extensive *National Museum* houses the best collection in the country (page 139); other notable collections include those in *Jim Thompson's House* (page 153), the *Suan Pakkard Palace* (page 153) and *Vimanmek Palace* (page 151).

Markets The sprawling *Chatuchak Weekend market* (page 155), *Nakhon Kasem* or Thieves' market (page 145), *Pahurat Indian market* (page 144) and Chinatown's *Sampeng Lane* (page 145).

Boat trip On *Bangkok's canals* (page 146).

Excursions Day trips to the former capital and ruins of *Ayutthaya* (page 182), the *Bridge over the River Kwai* outside Kanchanaburi (page 382), the massive chedi at *Nakhon Pathom* (page 378), and the *floating market at Damnoen Saduak* (page 157).

CONTENTS

MAPS

Bangkok is not a city to be trifled with: a population of 11 million struggle to make their living in a conurbation with perhaps the worst traffic in the world; a level of pollution which causes children to lose four intelligence points by the time they are seven; and a climate which can take one's breath away. As journalist Hugo Gurdon wrote at the end of 1992: "One would have to describe Bangkok as unliveable were it not for the fact that more and more people live here". But, Bangkok is not just a perfect case study for academics studying the strains of rapid urban growth. There is charm and fun beneath the grime, and Bangkokians live life with a *joie de vivre*

BANGKOK CLIMATE

	Jan	Feb	Mar	Apr	May	Jun	Jul	Aug	Sep	Oct	Nov	Dec
Av Max (°C)	32	33	34	35	34	33	32	32	32	31	31	31
Av Min (°C)	20	22	24	25	25	24	24	24	24	24	22	20
Av Rain (mm)	8	20	36	58	198	160	160	175	305	206	66	5

Source: Pearce, E.A and Smith C.G. *The world weather guide*: Hutchinson, London

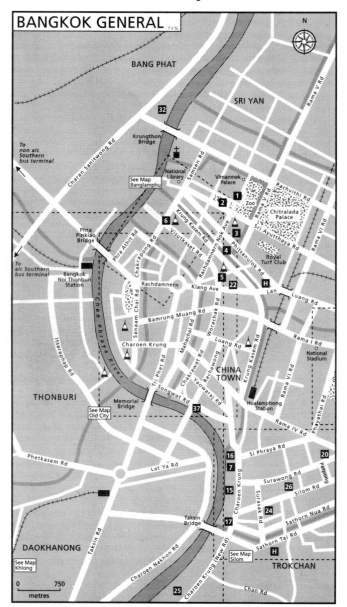

BANGKOK GENERAL

N

BANG PHAT

SRI YAN

Rama V Rd

Krungthon Bridge

Charan Sanitwong Rd

To non a/c Southern bus terminal

National Library

See Map Banglamphu

Samsen Rd

Vimanmek Palace

Rachvithi Rd

Zoo

Rama V Rd

Chitralada Palace

Sri Ayutthaya Rd

Rama VI Rd

Krung Kasem Rd

Visutkaset Rd

Rachdamnern Nok Ave

Phitsanulok Rd

Royal Turf Club

Phra Pinklao Bridge

Phra Athit Rd

Chakrapong Rd

To a/c Southern bus terminal

Bangkok Noi Thonburi Station

Rachdamnern

Sanaam Chai Rd

Rachdamnern

Klang Ave

Lan

Luang Rd

Rama I Rd

Bamrung Muang Rd

Itsaraphap Rd

Charoen Krung

Mahachai Rd

Worachak Rd

Luang Rd

Rachawong Rd

Krung Kasem Rd

National Stadium

THONBURI

Tri Phet Rd

Chakrawat Rd

CHINA TOWN

Rama VI Rd

Phayathai Rd

Songwat Rd

Yaowaraj Rd

Hualamphong Station

Memorial Bridge

Rama IV Rd

Phetkasem Rd

Lat Ya Rd

Si Phraya Rd

Surawong Rd

Silom Rd

Charoen Krung

Surasak Rd

Sathorn Nua Rd

Taksin Bridge

Sathorn Tai Rd

Taksin Rd

DAOKHANONG

See Map Khlong

See Map Silom

TROKCHAN

Charoen Nakhon Rd

Charoen Krung (New Rd)

Chan Rd

0   750
metres

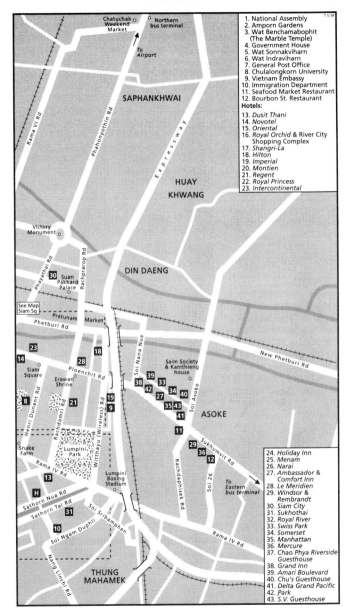

1. National Assembly
2. Amporn Gardens
3. Wat Benchamabophit (The Marble Temple)
4. Government House
5. Wat Sonnakviharn
6. Wat Indraviharn
7. General Post Office
8. Chulalongkorn University
9. Vietnam Embassy
10. Immigration Department
11. Seafood Market Restaurant
12. Bourbon St. Restaurant

Hotels:
13. *Dusit Thani*
14. *Novotel*
15. *Oriental*
16. *Royal Orchid & River City Shopping Complex*
17. *Shangri-La*
18. *Hilton*
19. *Imperial*
20. *Montien*
21. *Regent*
22. *Royal Princess*
23. *Intercontinental*

24. *Holiday Inn*
25. *Menam*
26. *Narai*
27. *Ambassador & Comfort Inn*
28. *Le Meridien*
29. *Windsor & Rembrandt*
30. *Siam City*
31. *Sukhothai*
32. *Royal River*
33. *Swiss Park*
34. *Somerset*
35. *Manhattan*
36. *Mercure*
37. *Chao Phya Riverside Guesthouse*
38. *Grand Inn*
39. *Amari Boulevard*
40. *Chu's Guesthouse*
41. *Delta Grand Pacific*
42. *Park*
43. *S.V. Guesthouse*

which belies the congestion. There are also numerous sights, including the spectacular Grand Palace, glittering wats (monasteries) and the breezy river, along with excellent food and good shopping.

The official name for Thailand's capital city begins Krungthep - phramaha - nakhonbawon - rathanakosin - mahinthara -yutthayaa - mahadilok - phiphobnobpharaat - raatchathaanii - buriiromudomsantisuk. It is not hard to see why Thais prefer the shortened version – Krungthep, or the 'City of Angels'. The name Bangkok is derived from 17th century Western maps, which referred to the city (or town as it then was) as Bancok, the 'village of the wild plum'. This name was only superseded by Krungthep in 1782, and so the Western name has deeper historical roots.

Thonburi

In 1767, Ayutthaya, then the capital of Siam, fell to the marauding Burmese for the second time and it was imperative that the remnants of the court and army find a more defensible site for a new capital. Taksin, the Lord of Tak, chose Thonburi, on the western banks of the Chao Phraya River, far from the Burmese and from Phitsanulok, where a rival to the throne had become ensconsed. In 3 years, Taksin had established a kingdom and crowned himself king. His reign was short-lived, however; the pressure of thwarting the Burmese over three arduous years caused him to go mad and in 1782 he was forced to abdicate. General Phraya Chakri was recalled from Cambodia and invited to accept the throne. This marked the beginning of the present Chakri Dynasty.

Bangkok: the new capital

In 1782, Chakri (now known as Rama I) moved his capital across the river to Bangkok (an even more defensible site) anticipating trouble from King Bodawpaya who had seized the throne of

Burma. The river that flows between Thonburi and Bangkok and on which many of the luxury hotels – such as *The Oriental* – are now located, is actually not a river at all, but a canal (or *khlong*). The canal was dug in the 16th century to reduce the distance between Ayutthaya and the sea by shortcutting a number of bends in the river. Since then, the canal has become the main channel of the Chao Phraya River. Its original course has shrunk in size, and is now represented by two khlongs, Bangkok Yai and Bangkok Noi.

This new capital of Siam grew in size and influence. Symbolically, many of the new buildings were constructed using bricks from the palaces and temples of the ruined former capital of Ayutthaya. But population growth was hardly spectacular – it appears that outbreaks of cholera sometimes reduced the population by a fifth or more in a matter of a few weeks. An almanac from 1820 records that "on the 7th month of the waxing moon, a little past 9 o'clock in the evening, a shining light was seen in the north-west and multitudes of people purged, vomited and died". In 1900 Bangkok had a population of approximately 200,000. By 1950 it had surpassed 1 million, and in 1990 it was, officially, 5,876,000. Most people believe that the official figure considerably understates the true population of the city – 11 million would be more realistic. By 2010, analysts believe Bangkok will have a population of 20 million. As the population of the city has expanded, so has the area that it encompasses: in 1900 it covered a mere 13.3 sq km; in 1958, 96.4 sq km; while today the Bangkok Metropolitan region extends over 1,600 sq km.

Bangkok dominates Thailand

In terms of size, Bangkok is at least 23 times larger than the country's second city, Chiang Mai – 40 times bigger, using the unofficial population estimates. It also dominates Thailand in cultural, political and economic terms. All Thai civil servants have the ambition of serving in Bangkok, while many regard a posting to the poor Northeast as (almost) the kiss of death. Most of the country's industry is located in and around the city (the area contributes 45% of national GDP), and Bangkok supports a far wider array of services than other towns in the country. Although the city contains only 10% of the kingdom's population, its colleges of higher education graduate 71% of degree students, it contains 83% of pharmacists, and has 69% of Thailand's telephone lines. It is because of Bangkok's dominance that people often, and inaccurately, say 'Bangkok is Thailand'.

Bangkok began life as a city of floating houses; in 1864 the French explorer Henri Mouhot wrote that "Bangkok is the Venice of the East [in the process making Bangkok one of several Asian cities to be landed with this sobriquet] and whether bent on business or pleasure you must go by water". In 1861, foreign consuls in Bangkok petitioned Rama IV and complained of ill-health due to their inability to go out riding in carriages or on horseback. The king complied with their request for roads and the first road was constructed running S in the 1860s – Charoen Krung (New Road). This did not initially alter Bangkok's watery character, for bridges to span the many canals were in limited supply. In addition, Charoen Krung was frequently under water during the monsoons. It was not until the late 19th century that King Chulalongkorn (Rama V) began to invest large sums of money in bridge and road building; notably, Rachdamnern Avenue ('the royal way for walking') and the Makawan Rungsun Bridge, which both link the Grand Palace with the new palace area of Dusit. This avenue was used at the end of the century for cycling (a royal craze at the time) and later for automobile processions which were announced in the newspapers.

In the rush to modernize, Bangkok may have buried its roots and in so doing, lost its charm. But beneath the patina of modern city life, Bangkok remains very much a Thai city, and has preserved a surprising amount of its past. Most obviously, a profusion of monasteries (wats) and palaces remain. In addition, not all the khlongs have been filled in, and by taking a long-tailed boat through Thonburi (see page 148) it is

RACING IN THE STREETS

In Bangkok, bored young men gain short-lived fame and money by racing through the darkened streets of the capital on motorcycles late at night on weekends. Gang members put their reputations on the line, and their lives, as they power down the wide and almost empty roads at over 160 kph. Large sums of money are gambled on the riders while 'rescue squads' wait to pick up the corpses that each night's racing produces. In Thai this dance with death is known as *sing* – from the English 'racing'. As journalist Gordon Fairclough explains: "Riders see themselves as members of an exclusive brotherhood, bound together by their willingness to risk death and dismemberment in the pursuit of thrills, notoriety and money". Although money is important, few of the riders are poor. Some even come from wealthy families. Critics of Thailand's climb into NIC-dom claim that the racing is a side-effect of the breakdown of traditional family life in the face of modernisation. The racers themselves tend not to engage in amateur sociology. They explain "It's fun. It's a high. We like the speed, and its better than taking drugs".

possible to gain an idea of what life must have been like in the 'Venice of the East'.

Flooding

Bangkok is built on unstable land, much of it below sea-level, and floods used to regularly afflict the capital. The most serious was in 1983 when 450 sq km of the city was submerged. Each year the Bangkok Metropolitan Authority announces a new flood prevention plan, and each year the city floods. The former populist Bangkok Governor, Chamlong Srimuang (see box), was perhaps the first politician seriously to address the problem of flooding. His blindingly obvious approach was to clear the many culverts of refuse, and some people believe that at last serious flooding is a thing of the past. This may be over-optimistic: like Venice, Bangkok is sinking by over 10 cm a year in some areas and it may be that the authorities are only delaying the inevitable.

First impressions

The immediate impression of the city to a first-time visitor is bedlam. The heat, noise, traffic, pollution – the general chaos – can be overwhelming. This was obviously the impression of Somerset Maugham, following his visit in 1930:

'I do not know why the insipid Eastern food sickened me. The heat of Bangkok was overwhelming. The wats oppressed me by their garish magnificence, making my head ache, and their fantastic ornaments filled me with malaise. All I saw looked too bright, the crowds in the street tired me, and the incessant din jangled my nerves. I felt very unwell...'

It is estimated that over 1 million Bangkokians live in slum or squatter communities, while average traffic speeds can be less than 10 km/hour. During peak periods the traffic congestion is such that 'gridlock' seems inevitable. The figures are sometimes hard to believe: US$500 million of petrol is consumed each year while cars wait at traffic lights; one day

in July 1992 it took 11 hours for some motorists to get home after a monsoon storm; and the number of cars on the capital's streets increases by 800 each day; while traffic speeds are snail pace – and expected to fall further. For those in Bangkok who are concerned about their city and the environment, the worst aspect is that things will undoubtedly get worse before they get any better – despite the plethora of road building programmes the car and truck population is growing faster than the roads to accommodate them. The government of former Prime Minister Anand did give the go-ahead to a number of important infrastructural projects, but many would say a decade too late. As one analyst recently said: "Bangkok is only just beginning to happen". Even editorial writers at the *Bangkok Post* who, one might imagine, are used to the traffic find it a constant topic for comment. At the end of 1993 it stated: "Bangkok's traffic congestion and pollution are just about the worst in the world – ever. Never in history have people had to live in the conditions we endure each day".

Solutions to Bangkok's **traffic problem** have been suggested, devised, contracts drawn-up, shelved, cancelled and then revived since the early 1980s. The process of finding a solution is almost as slow as the traffic itself. In addition to the failure to approach transport planning in a coordinated way, Bangkok has a number of characteristics which make it a special case. To begin with, Thailand was a city of canals; these have now been built over, but it means that the capital has a lower area of roads relative to its land area than any other capital – some 9% to New York's 24% and London's 22%. In addition, Bangkok is really Thailand's only city, making economic activity highly over-centralised. But there is more to it than just a series of historical accidents. Administration of roads is divided between numerous different agencies making coordination impossible. "It's like driving a bus with 16 hands on the wheel" one official is quoted as saying. The corruption that has accompanied many of the more grandiose projects, and the competition between various schemes – aerial railways, undergrounds, toll ways, free ways – has meant that none got off the ground until recently. Even when one project was finished – the 20 km-long, US$800 million Bangkok Expressway which was completed in March 1993 – it didn't open to traffic until September that year. The government, under pressure from the public, tried to get the consortium to lower the agreed toll of ฿30. They

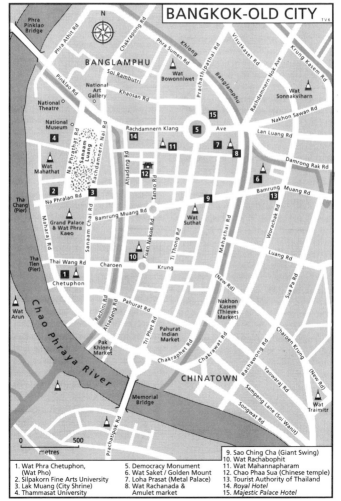

BANGKOK-OLD CITY

TV 6

1. Wat Phra Chetuphon, (Wat Pho)
2. Silpakorn Fine Arts University
3. Lak Muang (City Shrine)
4. Thammasat University
5. Democracy Monument
6. Wat Saket / Golden Mount
7. Loha Prasat (Metal Palace)
8. Wat Rachanada & Amulet market
9. Sao Ching Cha (Giant Swing)
10. Wat Rachabophit
11. Wat Mahannapharam
12. Chao Phaa Sua (Chinese temple)
13. Tourist Authority of Thailand
14. *Royal Hotel*
15. *Majestic Palace Hotel*

refused, saying it would make the venture commercially unviable, so the city authorities gained a court order and opened the road themselves whereup it promptly became jammed with traffic. Such actions on the part of the government threaten to scare away potential investors who require cast iron agreements if they are to undertake such BOT (Build, Operate, Transfer) projects. For commuters, the solution to the traffic problem is to transform their cars into mobile offices, to leave home at un-godly hours and, in some cases, to move elsewhere – like Chiang Mai (which, partly as a result, is experiencing its own traffic problems). Taxi drivers have taken up 'chicken footing' – skipping through hotel car parks to short-cut intersections.

With the traffic comes pollution. Traffic police stationed at busy intersections have 'respite booths' with oxygen tanks, face masks to protect them from the fumes, and regular health checks. Even so, directing traffic can, apparently, drive you mad. At the end of 1993, Lance Cpl Suradej Chumnet blew a fuse and switched all the traffic lights to green at one of Bangkok's busiest intersections. He then danced a jig amidst the chaos. A recent study found that 34% of police officers suffered from loss of hearing, and 23% had lung disease. Sitting in an open-sided *tuk-tuk* at traffic lights can seriously damage your health – or it seems as much with the fumes swirling around. It is for this reason that the *tuk-tuk* as a mode of transport in the capital is rapidly losing out to the air-conditioned taxi. There is no sewerage system and most water gets pumped straight into the *khlongs* (canals) and waterways where it poses a health hazard before emptying into the Chao Phraya river which, in its lower stretches, is biologically dead.

Despite the traffic conditions and pollution, Bangkok has a wealth of sights (even the traffic might be classified as a 'sight'): wats and palaces, markets and shopping, traditional dancing and Thai boxing, glorious food, tuk-tuks and water taxis. Ultimately, Bangkok and Bangkokians should win the affections of even the most demanding foreigner – although you may not be there long enough to get past the frustration phase. In Major Erik Seindenfaden's *Guide to Bangkok* published in 1928, the opening few sentences could be describing the city today:

'No other city in Southeastern Asia compares with Bangkok in the gripping and growing interest which leaves a permanent and fragrant impression on the mind of the visitor. It is difficult to set down in words, precisely whence comes the elusive fascination of Bangkok. With a wealth of imposing temples, beautiful palaces, other characteristic buildings and monuments, Bangkok offers a vista of fascinating views... In no other city is it possible to so often turn from the throng of the city street and find oneself, miraculously it would seem, in a little residential quarter... Even the most bitter misanthrope cannot but feel that in the very atmosphere of Bangkok, woven into all the stir and briskness of its daily life, is an impelling and pleasurable sense of more than mere contentment – of rare serenity and happiness everywhere.'

Places of interest

This section is divided into five main areas: the Old City, around the Grand Palace; the Golden Mount, to the east of the Old City; Chinatown, which lies to the south of the Golden Mount; the Dusit area, which is to the north and contains the present day parliament buildings and the King's residence; and Wat Arun and the khlongs, which are to the west, on the other bank of the Chao Phraya River in Thonburi. Other miscellaneous sights, not in these areas, are at the end of the section, under Other places of interest.

Getting around the sights

Buses, both a/c and non-a/c, travel to all city sights (see Local transport, page

178). A taxi or tuk-tuk for a centre of town trip should cost ฿40-100. If travelling by bus, a bus map is an invaluable aid. The express river taxi is a far more pleasant way to get around town and is also often quicker than going by road (see map page 147 for piers, and box page 146).

The Old City

The Old City contains the largest concentration of sights in Bangkok, and for visitors with only one day in the capital, this is the area to concentrate on. It is possible to walk around all the sights mentioned below quite easily in a single day. For the energetic, it would also be possible to visit the sights in and around the Golden Mount. If intending to walk around all the sights in the old city start from Wat Pho; if you have less time or less energy, begin with the Grand Palace.

Wat Phra Chetuphon

(Temple of the Reclining Buddha) or **Wat Pho**, as it is known to Westerners (a contraction of its original name Wat Po-

taram), has its entrance on Chetuphon Road on the south side of the complex. It is 200 years old and the largest wat in Bangkok, now most famous for its 46m long, 15m high gold-plated reclining Buddha, with beautiful mother-of-pearl soles (showing the 108 auspicious signs). The reclining Buddha is contained in a large viharn built during the reign of Rama III (1832).

The grounds of the wat contain more than 1,000 bronze images, rescued from the ruins of Ayutthaya and Sukhothai by Rama I's brother. The bot, or ubosoth, houses a bronze Ayutthayan Buddha in an attitude of meditation and the pedestal of this image contains the ashes of Rama I. Also notable is the 11-piece altar table set in front of the Buddha, and the magnificent mother-of-pearl inlaid doors which are possibly the best examples of this art from the Bangkok Period (depicting episodes from the Ramakien). The bot is enclosed by two galleries which house 394 seated bronze

WAT PHRA CHETUPHON (WAT PHO) ZT V6a

1 Sala kan parian or study hall
2 Viharn of the reclining Buddha
3 Enclosure of the royal chedis

4 Ubosoth (bot) or ordination hall
5 Cloister or phra rabieng

Source: adapted from a drawing by Kittisak Nualvilai based on aerial photographs and reproduced in Beek, Steve van and Tettoni, L. (1991) *The arts of Thailand*, Thames & Hudson: London

Buddha images. They were brought from the N during Rama I's reign and are of assorted periods and styles. Around the exterior base of the bot are marble reliefs telling the story of the Ramakien as adapted in the Thai poem the *Maxims of King Ruang* (formerly these reliefs were much copied by making rubbings onto rice paper). The 152 panels are the finest of their type in Bangkok. They recount only the second section of the Ramakien: the abduction and recovery of Ram's wife Seeda. The rather – to Western eyes – unsatisfactory conclusion to the story as told here has led some art historians to argue they were originally taken from Ayutthaya. Thai scholars argue otherwise.

THE THAI RAMAYANA: THE RAMAKIEN

The *Ramakien* – literally "The Story of Rama" – is an adaptation of the Indian Hindu classic, the Ramayana, which was written by the poet Valmiki about 2,000 years ago. This 48,000 line epic odyssey – often likened to the works of Homer – was introduced into mainland Southeast Asia in the early centuries of the first millennium. The heroes were simply transposed into a mythical, ancient, Southeast Asian landscape.

In Thailand, the Ramakien quickly became highly influential, as indicated by the name of the former capital of Siam, Ayutthaya. This is taken from the legendary hero's city of Ayodhia. Unfortunately, these early Thai translations of the Ramayana were destroyed following the sacking of Ayutthaya by the Burmese in 1767. The earliest extant version was written by King Taksin in about 1775, although Rama I's rather later rendering is usually regarded as the classic interpretation.

In many respects, King Chakri's version closely follows that of the original Indian story. It tells of the life of Ram (Rama), the King of Ayodhia. In the first part of the story, Ram renounces his throne following a long and convoluted court intrigue, and flees into exile. With his wife Seeda (Sita) and trusted companion Hanuman (the monkey god), they undertake a long and arduous journey. In the second part, his wife Seeda is abducted by the evil king Ravana, forcing Ram to

wage battle against the demons of Langka Island (Sri Lanka). He defeats the demons with the help of Hanuman and his monkey army, and recovers his wife. In the third and final part of the story – and here it diverges sharply from the Indian original – Seeda and Ram are reunited and reconciled with the help of the gods (in the Indian version there is no such reconciliation). Another difference to the Indian version is the significant role played by the Thai Hanuman – here an amorous adventurer who dominates much of the third part of the epic.

Hanuman
Adapted from Hallet, Holt (1890) *A thousand miles on an elephant in the Shan States*, William Blackwood: Edinburgh.

There are also numerous sub-plots which are original to the Ramakien, many building upon events in Thai history and local myth and folklore. In tone and issues of morality, the Thai version is less puritanical than the Indian original. There are also, of course, difference in dress, ecology, location and custom.

A particular feature of the wat are the 95 chedis of various sizes which are scattered across the 20-acre complex. To the left of the bot are 4 large chedis, memorials to the first 4 Bangkok kings. The library nearby is richly decorated with broken pieces of porcelain. The large top-hatted stone figures, the stone animals and the Chinese pagodas scattered throughout the compound came to Bangkok as ballast on the royal rice boats returning from China. Rama III wanted the wat to become known as a place of learning, a kind of exhibition of all the knowledge of the time and it is regarded as Thailand's first university. Admission: ฿10. Open: 0800-1700 Mon-Sun. **NB** from Tha Tien pier at the end of Thai Wang Road, close to Wat Pho, it is possible to get boats to Wat Arun (see page 146). Wat Pho is also probably Bangkok's most respected centre of traditional Thai massage (see page 172), and politicians, businessmen and mili-tary officers go there to seek relief from the tensions of modern life. For Westerners wishing to learn the art, special 30-hour courses can be taken for ฿3,000, stretching over either 15 days (2 hrs/day) or 10 days (3 hrs/day). The centre is located at the back of the Wat, on the opposite side from the entrance. A massage costs ฿150 for an hour.

Grand Palace and Wat Phra Kaeo

About 10-15 minutes walk from Wat Pho northwards along Sanaam Chai Road is the entrance to the **Grand Palace** and **Wat Phra Kaeo**. **NB** the main entrance is the Viseschaisri Gate on Na Phralan Road. The Grand Palace is situated on the banks of the Chao Phraya River and is the most spectacular – some might say 'gaudy' – collection of buildings in Bangkok. The complex covers an area of over 1.5 sq km and the architectural plan is almost identical to that of the Royal Palace in the former capital of Ayut-

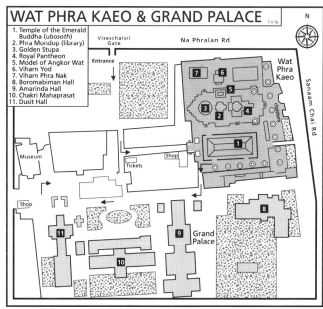

WAT PHRA KAEO & GRAND PALACE

1. Temple of the Emerald Buddha (*ubosoth*)
2. Phra Mondop (library)
3. Golden Stupa
4. Royal Pantheon
5. Model of Angkor Wat
6. Viharn Yod
7. Viharn Phra Nak
8. Boromabiman Hall
9. Amarinda Hall
10. Chakri Mahaprasat
11. Dusit Hall

THE EMERALD BUDDHA

Wat Phra Kaeo was specifically built to house the Emerald Buddha, the most venerated Buddha image in Thailand, carved from green jade (the emerald in the name referring only to its colour), a mere 75cm high, and seated in an attitude of meditation. It is believed to have been found in 1434 in Chiang Rai, and stylistically belongs to the Late Chiang Saen or Chiang Mai schools. Since then, it has been moved on a number of occasions – to Lampang, Chiang Mai and Laos (both Luang Prabang and Vientiane). It stayed in Vientiane for 214 years before being recaptured by the Thai army in 1778 and placed in Wat Phra Kaeo on 22nd March, 1784. The image wears seasonal costumes of gold and jewellery, one each for the hot, cool and the rainy seasons. The changing ceremony occurs 3 times a year in the presence of the King.

Buddha images are often thought to have personalities. The Phra Kaeo is no exception. It is said, for example, that such is the antipathy between the Phra Bang in Luang Prabang (Laos) and Phra Kaeo that they can never reside in the same town.

thaya. It was started in 1782 and was subsequently added to. Initially, the palace was the city, the seat of power, surrounded by high walls and built to be self-sufficient.

The buildings of greatest interest are clustered around **Wat Phra Kaeo**, or the 'Temple of the Emerald Buddha'. On entering the compound, the impression is one of glittering brilliance, as the outside is covered by a mosaic of coloured glass. The buildings were last restored for Bangkok's bicentenary in 1982 (the Wat Phra Kaeo Museum shows the methods used in the restoration process). Wat Phra Kaeo was built by Rama I in imitation of the royal chapel in Ayutthaya and was the first of the buildings within the Grand Palace complex to be constructed. While it was being erected the king lived in a small wooden building in one corner of the palace compound.

The ubosoth is raised on a marble platform with a frieze of gilded figures of garudas holding nagas running round the base. Bronze singhas act as door guardians. The door panels are of inlaid mother-of-pearl and date from Rama I's reign (late 18th century). Flanking the door posts are Chinese door guardians

riding on lions. Inside the temple, the Emerald Buddha (see box) sits high up, illuminated above a large golden altar. In addition, there are many other gilded Buddha images, mostly in the attitude of dispelling fear, and a series of mural paintings depicting the jataka stories. Those facing the Emerald Buddha show the enlightenment of the Buddha when he subdues the evil demon Mara. Mara is underneath, wringing out his hair, while on either side, the Buddha is surrounded by evil spirits. Those on one side have been subjugated; those on the other have not. The water from the wringing out of Mara's hair drowns the evil army, and the Buddha is shown 'touching ground' calling the earth goddess Thoranee up to witness his enlightenment. No photography is allowed inside the ubosoth.

Around the walls of the shaded cloister that encompasses Wat Phra Kaeo, is a continuous mural depicting the Ramakien – the Thai version of the Indian Ramayana. There are 178 sections in all, which were first painted during the reign of King Rama I but have since been restored on a number of occasions.

To the N of the ubosoth on a raised platform, are the **Royal Pantheon**, the

Phra Mondop (the library), 2 gilt stupas, a model of Angkor Wat and the Golden Stupa. At the entrance to the Royal Pantheon are gilded kinarees. The Royal Pantheon is only open to the public once a year on Chakri Day, 6 April (the anniversary of the founding of the present Royal Dynasty). On the same terrace there are 2 gilt stupas built by King Rama I in commemoration of his parents. The Mondop was also built by Rama I to house the first revised Buddhist scriptural canon. To the W of the mondop is the large Golden Stupa or chedi, with its circular base, in Ceylonese style. To the N of the mondop is a model of Angkor Wat constructed during the reign of King Mongkut (1851-1868) when Cambodia was under Thai suzerainty.

To the N again from the Royal Pantheon is the Supplementary Library and 2 viharns – Viharn Yod and Phra Nak. The former is encrusted in pieces of Chinese porcelain.

To the S of Wat Phra Kaeo are the buildings of the Grand Palace. These are interesting for the contrast that they make with those of Wat Phra Kaeo. Walk out through the cloisters. On your left can be seen Boromabiman Hall, which is French in style and was completed during the reign of Rama VI. His 3 successors lived here at one time or another. The Amarinda Hall has an impressive airy interior, with chunky pillars and gilded thrones. The Chakri Mahaprasart (the Palace Reception Hall) stands in front of a carefully manicured garden with topiary. It was built and lived in by Rama V shortly after he had returned from a trip to Java and Singapore in 1876, and it shows: the building is a rather unhappy amalgam of colonial and traditional Thai styles of architecture. Initially the intention was to top the structure with a Western dome, but the architects settled for a Thai-style roof. The building was completed in time for Bangkok's first centenary in 1882. King Chulalongkorn (Rama V) found the overcrowded Grand Palace oppressive and after a visit to Europe in 1897, built himself a new home at Vimanmek (see page 151) in the area to the N, known as Dusit. The present King Bhumibol lives in the Chitralada Palace, built by Rama VI, also in the Dusit area. The Grand Palace is now only used for state occasions. Next to the Chakri Mahaprasart is the raised Dusit Hall; a cool, airy building containing mother-of-pearl thrones. Near the Dusit Hall is a museum, which has information on the restoration of the Grand Palace, models of the Palace and many Buddha statues. There is a collection of old cannon, mainly supplied by London gun foundries. Close by is a small café selling refreshing coconut drinks. All labels in Thai, but there are free guided tours in English throughout the day. Admission: ฿100.

ADMISSION to the Grand Palace complex: ฿125, ticket office open 0830-1200, 1300-1530 Mon-Sun except Buddhist holidays when Wat Phra Kaeo is free but the rest of the palace is closed. The cost of the admission includes a free guidebook to the palace (with plan) as well as a ticket to the *Coin Pavilion*, with its collection of medals and 'honours' presented to members of the Royal Family and to the Vimanmek Palace in the Dusit area (see page 151). Decorum of dress is required (trousers can be hired for ฿10 near the entrance to the Grand Palace).

Immediately opposite the entrance to the Grand Palace is Silpakorn Fine Arts University. It contains an exhibition hall. Open: 0900-1900 Mon-Sun (see boards outside entrance for shows). Turn left outside the Grand Palace and a 5-minute walk leads to **Tha Chang pier and market**. The market sells fruit and food, cold drinks etc. There is also a small amulet (lucky charm) and second-hand section. From Tha Chang pier it is possible to get a boat to Wat Arun for about ฿150 return, or a water taxi (see page 148). To the north of the Grand Palace, across

Na Phralan Road, lies the large open space of the Pramane Ground (the Royal Cremation Ground) better known as **Sanaam Luang**. This area was originally used for the cremation of kings, queens and important princes. Later, foreigners began to use it as a race track and as a golf course. Today, Sanaam Luang is used for the annual **Royal Ploughing Ceremony**, held in May. This ancient Brahmanistic ritual, resurrected by Rama IV, signals the auspicious day on which farmers can begin to prepare their riceland, the time and date of the ceremony being set by Royal Astrologers. Bulls decorated with flowers pull a red and gold plough, while the selection of different lengths of cloth by the Ploughing Lord predicts whether the rains will be good or bad. Sanaam Luang is also used by the Thai public simply to stroll around – a popular pastime, particularly at weekends. **Kite-fighting** can be seen in the late afternoons between late-February and mid-April (the Kite Festival season). On Sundays, salesmen and women sell kites for ฿15-20 on Sanaam Luang.

In the SE corner of Sanaam Luang opposite the Grand Palace is Bangkok's **Lak Muang**, housing the City Pillar and horoscope, originally placed there by Rama I in 1782. The original shrine deteriorated due to lack of maintainance and Rama VI erected a new pillar, with the horoscope of the city inscribed in gold. It is protected by an elaborate pavilion with intricate gold-inlay doors, and is set below ground level. The shrine is believed to grant people's wishes, so it is a hive of activity all day. In a small pavilion to the left of the main entrance, Thai dancers are hired by supplicants to dance for the pleasure of the resident spirits – while providing a free spectacle for everyone else. Open: 24 hrs Mon-Sun. **NB:** there is no entrance charge to the Lak Muang compound; touts sometimes insist there is. Donations can be placed in the boxes within the shrine precincts. At the NE corner of Sanaam

KITE FIGHTING

Kite fighting is a sport which is taken very seriously – perhaps because they were used as weapons of war during the Sukhothai Period, as well as being used to ward off evil spirits during Brahmanic rites. King Rama V was an avid kite-flyer and allowed Sanaam Luang to be used for the sport from 1899. There are usually two teams, each with a different kind of kite: the 'chula' or male kite is the bigger of the two and sometimes requires a number of people to fly it. The 'pukpao' or female kite is smaller and more nimble and opposes the chula. The field is divided into two and the aim of the contest is to land the opposition in your half of the field. Attached to the chula kite are a number of hooks (*champa*) with which the kite-flyer grapples the pukpao and forces it to land in the opposite side of the field. The pukpao meanwhile has a loop with which the flyer lassoes the chula – which then crashes to the ground.

Luang, opposite the *Royal Hotel*, is a small statue of the **Goddess of the Earth** erected by King Chulalongkorn to provide drinking water for the public.

Wat Mahathat

North along Na Phrathat Road, on the river side of Sanaam Luang is **Wat Mahathat** (the Temple of the Great Relic), a temple famous as a meditation centre, which is tucked behind a façade of buildings and hard to find; walk under the archway marked 'Naradhip Centre for Research in Social Sciences' to reach the wat. For those interested in learning more about Buddhist meditation, contact monks in section five within the compound. The wat is a royal temple of the first grade and a number of Supreme Patriarchs of Bangkok have based themselves here.

The revision of the Tripitaka (the

Buddhist Canon) took place at the temple in 1788, and an examination system was established for monks and novices after a meeting at the wat in 1803. In 1801 the viharn was burnt down during an over-enthusiastic fireworks display. In 1824 the future Rama IV began his 24 years as a monk here, and it was again reconstructed between 1844 and 1851. Both viharn and bot, crammed in side-by-side, are undistinguished. Note that there are only 4 *bai sema* (boundary stones), and they are affixed to the walls of the building – presumably because there is so little room. The main Buddha images in the viharn and ordination hall are of brick and mortar. In the mondop are 28 bronze Buddha images, with another 108 in the gallery around the ordination hall. Most date from the Sukhothai Period. Open: 0900-1700 Mon-Sun.

Thammasat and National Museum
Attached to the wat is a fascinating daily market selling exotic herbal cures, amulets, clothes and food. It is worth a wander as few tourists venture into either the market or the wat. At weekends, the market spills out onto the surrounding streets (particularly Phra Chan Road) and amulet sellers line the pavement, their magical and holy talismen carefully displayed. Further north along Na Phrathat Road, is **Thammasat University**, the site of viciously suppressed student demonstrations in 1973 (see page 84). Sanaam Luang and Thammasat University remain a popular focus of discontent. Most recently, at the beginning of May 1992, massed demonstrations occurred here to demand the resignation of Prime Minister General Suchinda. The rally was led by former Bangkok Governor Chamlong Srimuang (see box, page 140).

Next to Thammasat lies the **National Museum**, reputedly the largest museum in Southeast Asia. It is an excellent place to view the full range of Thai art before visiting the ancient Thai capitals, Ayutthaya and Sukhothai.

Gallery No. 1, the gallery of Thai history, is interesting and informative, as well as being air-conditioned, so it is a good place to cool-off. The gallery clearly shows Kings Mongkut and Chulalongkorn's fascination with Western technology. The other 22 galleries and 19 rooms contain a vast assortment of arts and artefacts divided according to period and style. If you are interested in Thai art, the museum alone might take a day to browse around. A shortcoming for those with no background knowledge is the lack of information in some of the galleries and it is recommended that interested visitors buy the 'Guide to the National Museum, Bangkok' for ฿50 or join one of the tours. Admission: ฿20, together with a skimpy leaflet outlining the galleries. Open: 0900-1600, Wed-Sun, tickets on sale until 1530. For English, French, German, Spanish and Portuguese-speaking tour information call T 2241333. They are free, and start at 0930, lasting 2 hrs.

The Buddhaisawan Chapel, to the right of the ticket office for the National Museum, contains some of the finest Bangkok period murals in Thailand. The chapel was built in 1795 to house the famous Phra Sihing Buddha. Folklore has it that this image originated in Ceylon and when the boat carrying it to Thailand sank, it floated off on a plank to be washed ashore in Southern Thailand, near the town of Nakhon Si Thammarat. This, believe it or not, is probably untrue: the image is early Sukhothai in style (1250), admittedly showing Ceylonese influences, and almost certainly Northern Thai in origin. There are 2 other images that claim to be the magical Phra Buddha Sihing, one in Nakhon Si Thammarat (see page 464) and another in Chiang Mai (see page 233). The chapel's magnificent murals were painted between 1795 and 1797 and de-

CHAMLONG SRIMUANG: THE MR CLEAN OF THAI POLITICS

Chamlong Srimuang presents himself as a clean-living man of the people. He wears the rough, blue garb of the peasant – the *morhom* – eats one vegetarian meal a day, gives folksy speeches replete with home truths, sleeps on the floor, and has renounced all possessions. As a devout Buddhist, he also abstains from sexual relations with his wife, Sirilak, who shares his strong Buddhist beliefs. But Chamlong has not always led such a life. He rose to the rank of Major-General in the army, and was regarded as one of the most talented cadets in his intake to the Chulachomklao Military Academy, graduating at the top of his class. He took a MA at the US management training college in Monterey, California and saw active service in both Vietnam and Laos.

In retrospect, the signs of things to come were there all along: his fellow officers never quite regarded Chamlong as 'one of the boys', and in 1979 he and his wife joined the radical Santi Asoke Buddhist sect. In 1986 he abruptly resigned from the army and stood for election as Governor of Bangkok. His manifesto of clean and efficient administration struck a cord with the capital's growing middle class and he won the election – against the odds – with 49% of the vote. He then set about cleaning-up the capital in both an environmental and a moral sense. Four years later, despite other politicians doing their best to besmirch his image, he stood for a second term and raised his vote to 60%. His support broadened out to include Bangkok's important middle class. He is also said to be a favourite of the King. Certainly, he is a skilled manipulator of the media. It is said that he and a trusted adviser sat down with a large map of Bangkok when Chamlong was still governor of the capital, to work out the best locations for a series of flyovers. But his concern was to locate them where they would have the greatest impact on his image – not on congestion. Chamlong's courting of the media

pict stories from the Buddha's life. They are classical in style, without any sense of perspective, and the narrative of the Buddha's life begins to the right of the rear door behind the principal image, and progresses clockwise through 28 panels. German-speaking tours of the chapel are held on the third Tues of the month (0930).

Next to the National Museum is Thailand's **National Theatre**, a newish, large, Thai-style building on the corner of Na Phrathat and Phrapinklao Bridge roads. Thai classical drama and music are staged here on the last Friday of each month at 1730 as well as periodically on other days, T 2241342. Opposite the National Theatre is the **National Art Gallery** on Chao Fa Road. It exhibits traditional and contemporary work by Thai artists. Admission: ฿10. Open: Tues-Thurs, Sat and Sun 0900-1600.

The Golden Mount, Giant Swing and surrounding wats

The **Democracy Monument** is a 10-15 mins walk from the N side of Sanaam Luang, in the middle of Rachdamnern Klang Avenue. This rather stolid structure was completed in 1940 to commemorate the establishment of Siam as a constitutional monarchy. Its dimensions signify, in various ways, the date of the 'revolution' – the 24th June 1932. For example, the 75 buried cannon which surround the structure denote the Buddhist year (BE – or Buddhist Era) 2475 (1932 AD). In May 1992, the monument was the focus of the anti-Suchinda demonstrations, so brutally suppressed by the army. Scores of Thais died here, many others fleeing into the nearby *Royal Hotel*

mirrors that of his greatest rival – Samak, leader of the Bangkok-based Prachakorn Thai Party. Samak rose to fame on the back of a TV general knowledge quiz, *Tic Tac Toe*. In the quiz, contestants who answer the questions correctly are allowed to return the following week: Samak kept coming back for 18 months, after which he was a national celebrity and had a fast track into politics.

In March 1992, Chamlong stood for national election as the leader of the Phak Palang Dharma – or Buddhist Force Party (wags have rechristened the party the Palang Phak or Vegetable Force). His supporters see him as the Mahatma Gandhi of Thai politics, fighting a corrupt and degenerate system; his opponents, such as the former Prime Minister Kukrit Pramoj liken him to Ayatollah Khomeini.

In May 1992 he was the figurehead in the demonstrations against unelected prime minister General Suchinda Kraprayoon, which culminated in riots and the death of scores of demonstrators (**see page 112**). His hunger strike during the midst of the crisis brought him to international prominence.

Since then, although his party is a member of the ruling coalition, Chamlong himself has refused a cabinet post. He remains a maverick, on the outside of run-of-the-mill politics. He sees himself as the conscience of the government, making sure that cabinet ministers mirror his own high standards of moral rectitude in public life. But critics say they discern a tough operator beneath the surface. Political scientist Duncan McCargo has described him as "a Buddhist ascetic with authoritarian leanings". Following his party's disappointing performance in the Sept 1992 elections he retreated to manage a development project in Kanchanaburi province. At the beginning of 1994 he re-emerged on the political stage when he called for the election of provincial governors – they are currently appointed by the Interior Ministry. What Chamlong is trying to achieve is not clear; one thing is certain though – he has his eyes on the premiership.

(see page 112). From the Democracy Monument, across Mahachai Road, at the point where Rachdamnern Klang Avenue crosses Khlong Banglamphu can be seen the **Golden Mount** (also known as the Royal Mount), an impressive artificial hill nearly 80m high. The climb to the top is exhausting but worth it for the fabulous views of Bangkok. On the way up, the path passes holy trees, memorial plaques and Chinese shrines. The construction of the mount was begun during the reign of Rama III who intended to build the greatest chedi in his kingdom. The structure collapsed before completion, and Rama IV decided merely to pile up the rubble in a heap and place a far smaller golden chedi on its summit. The chedi contains a relic of the Buddha placed there by the present king after the structure had been most recently repaired in 1966. Admission: ฿5. Open: 0800-1800 Mon-Sun.

Wat Saket
This lies at the bottom of the mount, between it and Damrong Rak Road – the mount actually lies within the wat's compound. Saket means 'washing of hair' – Rama I is reputed to have stopped here and ceremoniously washed himself before being crowned King in Thonburi (see Festivals, November). The only building of real note is the *library* (*hor trai*) which is Ayutthayan in style. The door panels and lower windows are decorated with wood-carvings depicting everyday Ayutthayan life, while the window panels show Persian and French soldiers from Louis XIV's reign. Open: 0800-1800 Mon-Sun.

Also in the shadow of the Golden Mount but to the W and on the corner of Rachdamnern Klang Avenue and Mahachai Road lies Wat Rachanada and the Loha Prasat. Until 1989 these buildings were obscured by the Chalerm Thai movie theatre, a landmark which Bangkok's taxi and tuk-tuk drivers still refer to. In the place of the theatre there is now a neat garden, with an elaborate gilded **sala**, which is used to receive visiting dignitaries. Behind the garden

---

MAGIC DESIGNS AND TOKENS: TATTOOS AND AMULETS

Many, if not most, Thai men wear amulets or *khruang*. Some Thai women do so also. In the past tattooing was equally common, although today it is usually only in the countryside that males are extensively tattooed – sometimes from the ankle to the neck. Members of secret societies and criminal gangs use tattoos to indicate their allegiance and for the power they bestow. Amulets have histories: those believed to have great powers sell for tens of thousands of baht and there are several magazines devoted to amulet buying and collecting (available from most magazine stalls). Vendors keep amulets with their takings to protect against robbery, and insert them into food at the beginning of the day to ensure good sales. An amulet is only to be handled by the wearer – otherwise its power is dissipated, and might even be used against the owner.

Tattooing is primarily talismatic: magic designs, images of powerful wild beasts, texts reproduced in ancient Khmer script (*khom*) and religious motifs are believed to offer protection from harm and to give strength. They are even believed to deflect bullets, should the tattoo be sufficiently potent. The purpose of some tattoos is reflected in the use of 'invisible' ink made from sesame oil – the talismatic effects are independent of whether the tattoo can be seen. Most inks are commercial today (usually dark blue) although traditionally they were made from secret recipes incorporating such ingredients as the fat from the chin of a corpse (preferably seven corpses, taken during a full moon). Some Lao men, as a sign of their courage, would have themselves tattooed from the waist to just below the knees. The same is true of amulets. Amulets can be obtained from spirit doctors and monks and come in a variety of forms. Most common are amulets of a religious nature, known as *Phra khruang*. These are normally images of the Buddha or of a particularly revered monk. *Khruang rang* are usually made from tiger's teeth, buffalo horn or elephant tusk and protect the wearer in very specific ways – for example from drowning. *Khruang rang plu sek* meanwhile are magic formulas which are written down on an amulet, usually in old Khmer script, and then recited during an accident, attack or confrontation. The tattooist is not just a artist and technician. He, like the tattoos he creates, is a man of power. A master tattooist is highly respected and often given the title *ajarn* (teacher) or *mor phi* (spirit doctor). Monks can also become well-known for their tattoos. These are usually religious in tone, usually incorporating sentences from religious text. The tattoos are always beneficial or protective and always on the upper part of the body (the lower parts of the body are too lowly for a monk to tattoo).

Tattoos and amulets are not only used for protection, but also for attraction: men can have tattoos or amulets instilled with the power to attract women; women, alternatively, can buy amulets which protect them from the advances of men. *Khruang phlad khik* are phallic amulets, worn around the wrist or the waist – not around the neck. Not surprisingly, they are believed to ensure sexual prowess, as well as protection from such things as snake bites.

the strange looking **Loha Prasat** or-Metal Palace, with its 37 spires, is easily recognizable. This palace was built by Rama III in 1846, and is said to be modelled on the first Loha Prasat built in India 2,500 years ago. A second was constructed in Ceylon in 160 BC, although Bangkok's Loha Prasat is the only one still standing. The palace was built by Rama III as a memorial to his beloved niece Princess Soammanas Vadhanavadi. The 37 spires represent the 37 Dharma of the Bodhipakya. The building, which contains Buddha images and numerous meditation cells, has been closed to visitors for many years, although it is possible to walk around the outside.

Next to the Loha Prasat is the much more traditional **Wat Rachanada**. Wat Rachanada was built by Rama III for his niece who later became Rama IV's queen. The main Buddha image is made of copper mined in Nakhon Ratchasima province to the NE of Bangkok, and the ordination hall also has some fine doors. Open: 0600-1800 Mon-Sun. What makes the wat particularly worth visiting is the **Amulet market** (see page 142) to be found close by, between the Golden Mount and the wat. The sign, in English, below the covered part of the market reads 'Buddha and Antiques Centre'. The market also contains Buddha images and other religious artefacts and is open every day.

Wat Suthat

A 5 min walk S of Wat Rachanada, on Bamrung Muang Road, is the **Sao Ching Cha** or **Giant Swing**, consisting of two tall red pillars linked by an elaborate cross piece, set in the centre of a square. The Giant Swing was the original centre for a Brahmanic festival in honour of Siva. Young men, on a giant 'raft', would be swung high into the air to grab pouches of coins, hung from bamboo poles, between their teeth. Because the swinging was from E to W, it has been said that it symbolized the rising and setting of the sun. The festival was banned in the 1930s because of the injuries that occurred; prior to its

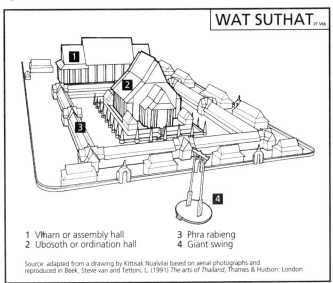

WAT SUTHAT zr V6b

1 Viharn or assembly hall
2 Ubosoth or ordination hall
3 Phra rabieng
4 Giant swing

Source: adapted from a drawing by Kittisak Nualvilai based on aerial photographs and reproduced in Beek, Steve van and Tettoni, L. (1991) *The arts of Thailand*, Thames & Hudson: London

banning, thousands would congregate around the Giant Swing for 2 days of dancing and music. The magnificent **Wat Suthat** faces the Giant Swing. The wat was begun by Rama I in 1807, and his intention was to build a temple that would equal the most glorious in Ayutthaya. The wat was not finished until the end of the reign of Rama III in 1851.

The viharn is in early-Bangkok style and is surrounded by Chinese pagodas. Its 6 pairs of doors, each made from a single piece of teak, are deeply carved with animals and celestial beings from the Himavanta forest. The central doors are said to have been carved by Rama II himself, and are considered some of the most important works of art of the period. Inside the viharn is the bronze Phra Sri Sakyamuni Buddha in an attitude of subduing Mara. This image was previously contained in Wat Mahathat in Sukhothai, established in 1362. Behind the Buddha is a very fine gilded stone carving from the Dvaravati Period (2nd-11th centuries AD), 2.5m in height and showing the miracle at Sravasti and the Buddha preaching in the Tavatimsa heaven.

The bot is the tallest in Bangkok and one of the largest in Thailand. The murals in the bot painted during the reign of Rama III are interesting in that they are traditional Thai in style, largely unaffected by Western artistic influences. They use flat colours and lack perspective. The bot also contains a particularly large cast Buddha image. Open: 0830-1800; the viharn is only open on weekends and Buddhist holidays 0900-1700.

Wat Rachabophit

The little visited Wat Rachabophit is close to the Ministry of the Interior on Rachabophit Road, a few minutes walk south of Wat Suthat down Ti Thong Road. It is recognizable by its distinctive doors carved in high relief with jaunty looking soldiers wearing European-style uniforms. The temple was started in 1869, took 20 years to complete, and is a rich blend of Western and Thai art forms (carried further in Wat Benchamabophit forty years later, see page 152). Wat Rachabophit is peculiar in that it follows the ancient temple plan of placing the Phra Chedi in the centre of the complex, surrounded by the other buildings. It later became the fashion to place the ordination hall at the centre.

The 43m high gilded chedi's most striking feature are the 5-coloured Chinese glass tiles which richly encrust the lower section. The ordination hall has 10 door panels and 28 window panels each decorated with gilded black lacquer on the inside and mother-of-pearl inlay on the outside showing the various royal insignia. They are felt to be among the masterpieces of the Rattanakosin Period (1782-present). The principal Buddha image in the ordination hall, in an attitude of meditation, sits on a base of Italian marble and is covered by the umbrella that protected the urn and ashes of Rama V. It also has a surprising interior – an oriental version of Italian Gothic, more like Versailles than Bangkok. Open: 0800-2000 Mon-Sun.

North of Wat Rachabophit, on Tanao Road is **Wat Mahannapharam**, in a large, tree-filled compound. A peaceful place to retreat to, it contains some good examples of high-walled, Bangkok Period architecture decorated with wood-carvings and mother-of-pearl inlay. Just S of here is the bustling **Chao Phaa Sua**, a Chinese temple with a fine tiled roof surmounted with mythological figures.

From Wat Rachabophit, it is only a short distance to the **Pahurat Indian Market** on Pahurat Road, where Indian, Malaysian and Thai textiles are sold. To get there, walk S on Ti Thong Road which quickly becomes Tri Phet Road. After a few blocks, Pahurat Road crosses Tri Phet Road. **Pak Khlong Market** is to be found a little further S on Tri Phet Road at the foot of the Memorial Bridge. It is a huge wholesale market for fresh produce, and a photographer's paradise.

It begins very early in the morning and has ended by 1000.

Chinatown and the Golden Buddha

Chinatown covers the area from Charoen Krung (or New Road) down to the river and leads on from Pahurat Road Market; cross over Chakraphet Road and immediately opposite is the entrance to Sampeng Lane. A trip through **Chinatown** can either begin with the Thieves Market to the NW, or at Wat Traimitr, the Golden Buddha, to the SE. An easy stroll between the two should not take more than 2 hrs. This part of Bangkok has a different atmosphere from elsewhere. Roads become narrower, buildings smaller, and there is a continuous bustle of activity. There remain some attractive, weathered examples of early 20th century shophouses. The industrious Sino-Thais of the area make everything from offertory candles and gold jewellery to metalwork, gravestones and light machinery.

Nakhon Kasem, or the Thieves Market, lies between Charoen Krung and Yaowaraj Road, to the E of the khlong that runs parallel to Mahachai Road. Its boundaries are marked by archways. As its name suggests, this market used to be the centre for the fencing of stolen goods. It is not quite so colourful today, but there remain a number of secondhand and antique shops which are worth a browse – such as the *Good Luck Antique Shop*. Amongst other things, musical instruments, brass ornaments, antique (and not so antique) coffee grinders are all on sale here.

Just to the SE of the Thieves Market are 2 interesting roads that run next to and parallel with one another: Yaowaraj Road and Sampeng Lane. **Yaowaraj Road**, a busy thoroughfare, is the centre of the country's gold trade. The trade is run by a cartel of 7 shops, the Gold Traders Association, and the price is

fixed by the government. The narrower, almost pedestrian **Sampeng Lane**, also called Soi Wanit, is just to the S of Yaowaraj Road. This road's history is shrouded in murder and intrigue. It used to be populated by prostitutes and opium addicts and was fought over by Chinese gangs. Today, it remains a commercial centre, but rather less illicit. It is still interesting (and cool, being shaded by awnings) to walk down, but there is not much to buy here – it is primarily a wholesale centre.

The most celebrated example of the goldsmiths' art in Thailand sits within **Wat Traimitr**, or the **Temple of the Golden Buddha**, which is located at the E edge of Chinatown, squashed between Charoen Krung, Yaowaraj Road and Traimitr Road (just to the S of Bangkok's Hualamphong railway station). The Golden Buddha is housed in a small, rather gaudy and unimpressive room. Although the leaflet offered to visitors says the 3m-high, 700 year-old image is 'unrivalled in beauty', be prepared to be disappointed. It is in fact rather featureless, showing the Buddha in an attitude of subduing Mara. What makes it special, drawing large numbers of visitors each day, is that it is made of 5.5 tonnes of solid gold. Apparently, when the East Asiatic Company was extending the port of Bangkok, they came across a huge stucco Buddha image which they obtained permission to move. However, whilst being moved by crane in 1957, it fell and the stucco cracked open to reveal a solid gold image. During the Ayutthayan Period it was the custom to cover valuable Buddha images in plaster to protect them from the Burmese, and this particular example stayed that way for several hundred years. In the grounds of the wat there is a school, crematorium, foodstalls and, inappropriately, a money changer. Admission: ฿10. Open: 0900-1700 Mon-Sun. Gold beaters can still be seen at work behind Suksaphan store.

Between the river and Soi Wanit 2

there is a warren of lanes, too small for traffic – this is the Chinatown of old. From here it is possible to thread your way through to the River City shopping complex which is air-conditioned and a good place to cool-off.

RECOMMENDED READING Visitors wishing to explore the wonders of Chinatown more thoroughly, should buy Nancy Chandler's *Map of Bangkok*, a lively, detailed map of all the shops, restaurants and out of the way wats and shrines. ฿40 from most bookstores.

Wat Arun and the khlongs

One of the most enjoyable ways to see Bangkok is by boat – and particularly by the fast and noisy **hang yaaws** (long-

THE CHAO PHRAYA RIVER EXPRESS

One of the most relaxing – and one of the cheapest – ways to see Bangkok is by taking the Chao Phraya River Express. These boats (or *rua duan*) link almost 40 piers (or *tha*) along the Chao Phraya River from Tha Wat Rajsingkorn in the S to Tha Nonthaburi in the N. The entire route entails a journey of about 1¼-1½ hr, and fares are ฿4, ฿6 or ฿8. Adjacent to many of the piers are excellent riverside restaurants. At peak periods, boats leave every 10 mins, off-peak about every 15-25 mins. Note that boats flying red or green pennants do not stop at every pier; they also exact a ฿1 surcharge. Also, boats will only stop if passengers wish to board or alight, so make your destination known.

Selected piers and places of interest, travelling upstream

Tha Orienten By the *Oriental Hotel*; access to *Silom Road*.

Tha River City In the shadow of the *Royal Orchid Hotel* and close to *River City* shopping centre.

Tha Ratchawong *Rabieng Ratchawong Restaurant*; access to *Chinatown* and *Sampeng Lane*.

Tha Saphan Phut Under the *Memorial Bridge* and close to *Pahurat Indian market*.

Tha Rachini *Pak Khlong Market*; just upstream, the *Catholic seminary* surrounded by high walls.

Tha Tien Close to *Wat Pho*; *Wat Arun* on the opposite bank; and just downstream from Wat Arun the *Vichaiprasit fort* headquarters of the Thai navy), lurking behind crenellated ramparts.

Tha Chang Just downstream is the *Grand Palace* peeking out above white-washed walls; *Wat Rakhang* with its white corn-cob prang lies opposite.

Tha Maharat *Lan The Restaurant*; access to *Wat Mahathat* and *Sanaam Luang*.

Tha Phra Arthit *Yen Jai Restaurant*; access to *Khaosan Road*.

Tha Visutkasat *Yok Yor Restaurant*; just upstream the elegant central *Bank of Thailand*.

Tha Thewes *Son Ngen Restaurant*; just upstream are *boatsheds* with royal barges; close to the *National Library*.

Tha Wat Chan just upstream is the *Singha Beer* Samoson brewery.

Tha Wat Khema *Wat Khema* in large, tree-filled compound.

Tha Wat Khian *Wat Kien*, semi-submerged.

Tha Nonthaburi last stop on the express boat route (see map, page 181).

tailed boats). You will know them when you see them; these powerful, lean machines roar around the river and the khlongs at break-neck speed, as though they are involved in a race to the death. There are innumerable tours around the khlongs of Thonburi taking in a number of sights which include the floating mar-

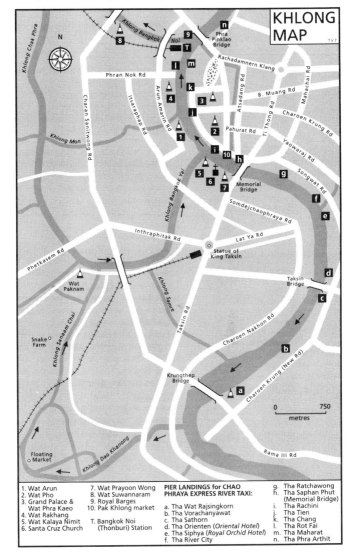

KHLONG MAP

TV 7

PIER LANDINGS for CHAO PHRAYA EXPRESS RIVER TAXI:

1. Wat Arun
2. Wat Pho
3. Grand Palace & Wat Phra Kaeo
4. Wat Rakhang
5. Wat Kalaya Nimit
6. Santa Cruz Church
7. Wat Prayoon Wong
8. Wat Suwannaram
9. Royal Barges
10. Pak Khlong market
T. Bangkok Noi (Thonburi) Station

a. Tha Wat Rajsingkorn
b. Tha Vorachanyawat
c. Tha Sathorn
d. Tha Orienten (*Oriental Hotel*)
e. Tha Siphya (*Royal Orchid Hotel*)
f. Tha River City
g. Tha Ratchawong
h. Tha Saphan Phut (Memorial Bridge)
i. Tha Rachini
j. Tha Tien
k. Tha Chang
l. Tha Rot Fai
m. Tha Maharat
n. Tha Phra Arthit

ket, snake farm and Wat Arun. Boats go from the various piers located along the E banks of the Chao Phraya River. The journey begins by travelling downstream along the Chao Phraya, before turning 'inland' after passing underneath the Krungthep Bridge. The route skirts past laden rice-barges, squatter communities on public land and houses overhanging the canals. This is a very popular route with tourists, and boats are intercepted by salesmen and women marketing everything from cold beer to straw hats. You may also get caught in a boat jam; traffic snarl-ups are not confined to the capital's roads. Nevertheless, the trip is a fascinating insight into what Bangkok must have been like when it was still the 'Venice of the East', and around every bend there seems to be yet another wat – some of them very beautiful. On private tours the first stop is usually the **Floating market** (*Talaat Nam*). This is now an artificial, ersatz gathering which exists purely for the tourist industry. It is worth only a brief visit. The nearest functioning floating market is at Damnoen Saduak (see excursions from Bangkok, page 157). The **Snake Farm** is the next stop where man fights snake in an epic battle of wills. Visitors can even pose with a python. The poisonous snakes are incited, to burst balloon with their fangs, 'proving' how dangerous they are. There is also a rather motley zoo with a collection of crocodiles and sad-looking animals in small cages. The other snake farm in Central Bangkok is (appropriately) attached to the Thai Red Cross and is more professional and cheaper (see page 155). Admission: ฿100, shows every 20 mins. Refreshments available. On leaving the snake farm, the boat will join up with Khlong Bangkok Yai at the site of the large **Wat Paknam**. Just before re-entering the Chao Phraya itself, the route passes by the impressive **Wat Kalaya Nimit**.

To the S of Wat Kalaya Nimit, on the Thonburi side of the river, is **Wat Prayoon Wong**, virtually in the shadow of Saphan Phut (a bridge). The wat is famous for its *Khao Tao* or turtle mountain. This is a concrete fantasyland of grottoes and peaks, with miniature chedis and viharns, all set around a pond teeming with turtles. These are released to gain merit and the animals clearly thrive in the murky water. To coin a phrase, rather grotty, but unusual. Also unusual is the large white chedi with its circular cloister surmounted with smaller chedis, and the viharn with a mondop at each corner, each containing an image of the Buddha. The bot adjacent to the viharn is attractively decayed with gold inlay doors and window shutters, and *bai sema* protected by large mondops. This wat is rarely visited by tourists. Khao Tao open: 0830-1730. Getting there: can be reached by taking a cross-river shuttle boat from Tha Saphan Phut (฿1). The large white chedi of Wat Prayoon Wong is clearly visible from the Bangkok side of the river. A short walk (5 mins) upstream from here is **Santa Cruz Church**, facing the river. The church, washed in pastel yellow with a domed tower, was built to serve the Portuguese community who lived in this part of Thonburi. Getting there: cross-river shuttles also stop at Tha Santa Cruz, running between here and Tha Rachini, close to the massive *Pak Khlong* fresh produce market.

Wat Arun

N on the Chao Phraya River is the famous Wat Arun, or the Temple of the Dawn, facing Wat Pho across the river. Wat Arun stands 81m high, making it the highest prang (tower) in Thailand. It was built in the early 19th century on the site of Wat Chaeng, the Royal Palace complex when Thonburi was briefly the capital of Thailand. The wat housed the Emerald Buddha before the image was transferred to Bangkok and it is said that King Taksin vowed to restore the wat after passing it one dawn. The prang is completely covered with pieces of Chinese porcelain and includes some delicate gold and black lacquered doors. The temple is really meant to be viewed from across the river; its scale and beauty can only be appreciated from a distance. Young, a European visitor to the capital, wrote in 1898: 'Thousands upon thousands of pieces of cheap china must have been smashed to bits in order to furnish sufficient material to decorate this curious structure....though the material is tawdry, the effect is indescribably wonderful'.

Energetic visitors can climb up to the halfway point and view the city. This is not recommended for people suffering from vertigo; the steps are very steep – be prepared for jelly-like legs after descending. Admission: ฿10. Open: 0830-1730 Mon-Sun. The men at the pier may demand ฿10 to help 'in the maintenance of the pier'. **NB** it is possible to get to Wat Arun by water-taxi from Tha Tien pier (at the end of Thai Wang Road near Wat Pho), or from Tha Chang (at the end of Na Phralan near Wat Phra Kaeo) (฿1). The best view of Wat Arun is in the evening from the Bangkok side of the river when the sun sets behind the prang.

After visiting Wat Arun, some tours

WAT ARUN, BANGKOK

then go further upstream to the mouth of Khlong Bangkok Noi where the **Royal Barges** are housed in a hangar-like boathouse. These ornately carved boats, winched out of the water in cradles, were used by the king at 'krathin' (see OK Phansa festival, page 513) to present robes to the monks in Wat Arun at the end of the rainy season. The ceremony ceased in 1967 but the Royal Thai Navy restored the barges for the revival of the spectacle, as part of the Chakri Dynasty's bicentennial celebrations in 1982. The oldest and most beautiful barge is the Sri Supannahong, built during the reign of Rama I (1782-1809) and repaired during that of Rama VI (1910-1925). It measures 45m long and 3m wide, weighs 15 tonnes and was created from a single piece of teak. It required a crew of 50 oarsmen, and 2 coxwains, along with such assorted crew members as a flagman, a rhythm-keeper and singer. Its gilded prow was carved in the form of a *hamsa* (or goose) and its stern, in the shape of a *naga*. Admission: ฿10. Open: 0830-1630 Mon-Sun (see Festivals, September, **page 160**).

Two additional rarely-visited wats, are Wat Suwannaram and Wat Rakhang. The royal **Wat Rakhang** is located just upstream from Wat Arun, almost opposite Tha Chang landing, and is identifiable from the river by the 2 plaster sailors standing to attention on either side of the jetty. The original wat on this site dates from the Ayutthaya Period: it has since been renovated on a number of occasions including during the reign of King Taksin and Rama I. The **Phra Prang** in the grounds of the wat is considered a fine, and particularly well-proportioned example of early Bangkok architecture (late 18th century). The ordination hall (not always open – the abbot may oblige if he is available) was built during the reign of Rama III and contains a fine gilded Buddha image in an attitude of meditation, over which is the nine-tiered umbrella used to shelter the urn of Rama I during the Royal Cremation. Also here is a fine mural recording the 10 previous lives of the Buddha (note the trip to hell) painted by Phra Wannavadvichitre, an eminent monk-artist of the time. The beautiful red-walled wooden **Tripitaka Hall** (originally a library built in the late 18th century) to the left of the viharn and bot when facing away from the river, was the residence of Rama I while he was a monk (before he became king) and Thonburi was still the capital of Siam. Consisting of 2 rooms, it is decorated with faded but nonetheless highly regarded murals of the Ramakien (painted by a monk-artist), black and gold chests, a portrait of the king, and some odd bits of old carved door. It is one of the most charming buildings in Bangkok. The hall is towards the back of the complex, behind the large white prang, it is in excellent condition, having been recently restored. Admission: ฿2. Open: 0500-2100 Mon-Sun (the river ferry stops at the wat).

Wat Suwannaram (see plan, page 91) is a short distance further on from the Royal Barges on Khlong Bangkok Noi, on the other side of the canal. The main buildings – which are particularly well proportioned – date from Rama I's reign (late 18th century), although the complex was later extensively renovated by Rama III. There was a wat on this site even prior to Rama I's reign, and the original name, Wat Thong (Golden Wat) remains in popular use. The ubosoth displays some fine wood-carving on the gable ends of the square pillared porches (Vishnu on his vehicle, Garuda), while the interior contains a series of murals, painted by 2 artists in professional competition with one another and commissioned by Rama III, and regarded by many as among the finest in Bangkok. The murals are in 2 'registers'; the murals on the long walls between the windows show the Ten Lives of the Buddha. The principal image in the bot is made of bronze and shows the Buddha calling the Earth Goddess to Witness. Sukhothai in style, it was presumably brought down from the old capital, probably in the first reign, although no records exist of its prior history. Next to the bot is the viharn abutted, unusually, by 2 cross halls at the front and rear. It was built during the reign of Rama IV. Wat Suwannaram is elegant and rarely visited and is a peaceful place to escape after the bustle of Wat Arun and the Floating Market.

Arranging a boat tour

Either book a tour at your hotel (see tours, page 158), or go to one of the piers and organize your own customized trip. The most frequented piers are located between the Oriental Hotel and the Grand Palace (see map, or ask at your hotel). The pier just to the south of the Royal Orchid Sheraton Hotel is recommended. Organizing your own trip gives greater freedom to stop and start when the mood takes you. It is best to go in the morning (0700). For the trip given above (excluding Wat Rakhang and Wat Suwannaram), the cost for a hang yaaw which can sit 10 people should be about ฿400-600 for the boat for a half-day. If visiting Rakhang and Suwannaram as well as the other sights, expect to pay about another ฿200-300 for the hire of a boat. Be sure to settle the route and cost before setting out.

The Dusit area

The Dusit area of Bangkok lies N of the Old City. The area is intersected by wide tree-lined avenues, and has an almost European flavour. The **Vimanmek Palace** lies off Rachvithi Road, just to the N of the National Assembly. Vimanmek is the largest golden teakwood mansion in the world. It was built by Rama V in 1901 and designed by one of his brothers. The palace makes an interesting contrast to Jim Thompson's House (see page 153) or Suan Pakkard (page 153). While Jim Thompson was enchanted by Thai arts, King Rama V was clearly taken with Western arts. It seems like a large Victorian hunting lodge – but raised off the ground – and is filled with china, silver and paintings from all over the world (as well as some gruesome hunting trophies). The photographs are fascinating – one shows the last time elephants were used in warfare in Thailand. Visitors are not free to wander, but must be shown around by one of the charming guides who demonstrate the continued deep reverence for King Rama V (tour approx 1hr). Admission: ฿50, ฿20 for children, tickets to the Grand Palace include entrance to Vimanmek Palace. Open: 0930-1600 (last tickets sold at 1500) Mon-Sun. Refreshments available. Buses do go past the palace, but from the centre of town it is easier to get a tuk-tuk or taxi (฿50-60).

From Vimanmek, it is a 10-15 minute walk to the Dusit Zoo, skirting around the **National Assembly** (which, before the 1932 coup was the Marble Throne Hall and is not open to visitors). The route is tree-lined, so it is possible to keep out of the sun or the rain. In the centre of the square in front of the National Assembly stands an equestrian statue of the venerated King Chulalongkorn. To the left lie the **Amporn Gardens**, the venue for royal social functions and fairs. Southwards from the square runs the impressive **Rachdamnern Nok Avenue**, a Siamese Champs Elysée. Enter the **Dusit Zoo** through Uthong Gate, just before the square. A pleasant walk through the zoo leads to the Chitralada Palace and Wat Benchamabophit. The zoo has a reasonable collection of animals from the region, some of which look rather the worse for wear. There is a children's playground, restaurants and pedal-boats can be hired on the lake. Admission: ฿10, ฿5 children. Open: 0800-1800 Mon-Sun.

From the Dusit Zoo's Suanchit Gate, a right turn down the tree-lined Rama

V Road leads to the present King Bhumibol's residence – **Chitralada Palace**. It was built by Rama VI and is not open to the public. Evidence of the King's forays into agricultural research may be visible. He has a great interest and concern for the development of the poorer, agricultural parts of his country, and invests large sums of his own money in royal projects. To the right of the intersection of Rama V and Sri Ayutthaya roads are the gold and ochre roofs of Wat Benchamabophit – about a 10 minute walk from the zoo.

Wat Benchamabophit

Or the **Marble Temple**, is the most modern of the royal temples and was only finished in 1911. It is of unusual architectural design (the architect was the king's half brother, Prince Naris), with carrara marble pillars, a marble courtyard and two large singhas guarding the entrance to the bot. Rama V was so pleased with the marble-faced ordination hall that he wrote to his brother: 'I never flatter anyone but I cannot help saying that you have captured my heart in accomplishing such beauty as this'. The interior is magnificently decorated with crossbeams of lacquer and gold, and in shallow niches in the walls are paintings of important stupas from all over the kingdom. The door panels are faced with bronze sculptures and the windows are of stained-glass, painted with angels. The cloisters around the assembly hall house 52 figures (both original and imitation) – a display of the evolution of the Buddha image in India, China and Japan. The Walking Buddha from the Sukhothai Period is particularly worth a look. The rear courtyard houses a large 80-year-old bodhi tree and a pond filled with turtles, released by people hoping to gain merit. The best time to visit this temple complex is early morning, when monks can be heard

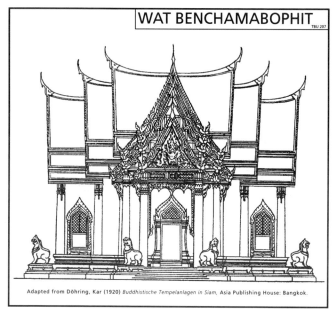

WAT BENCHAMABOPHIT

TBU 207

Adapted from Döhring, Kar (1920) *Buddhistische Tempelanlagen in Siam*, Asia Publishing House: Bangkok.

chanting inside the chapel. Admission: ฿10. Open: 0800-1700 Mon-Sun.

Government House is south of here on Nakhon Pathom Road. The building is a weird mixture of cathedral gothic and colonial Thai. It is only open on Wan Dek – a once yearly holiday for children held on the second Saturday in January. The little visited **Wat Sonnakviharn** is on Krung Kasem Road, located behind a car park and schoolyard. Enter by the doorway in the far right-hand corner of the schoolyard, or down Soi Sommanat. It is peaceful, unkempt, and rather beautiful, with fine gold lacquer doors, and a large gold tile-encrusted chedi. Open: Mon-Sun.

Other places of interest

In addition to the Vimanmek Palace, Bangkok also has a number of other beautiful Thai-style houses that are open to the public. **Suan Pakkard Palace** or Lettuce Garden Palace is at 352-354 Sri Ayutthaya Road, S of the Victory Monument. The 5 raised traditional Thai houses (domestic rather than royal) were built by Princess Chumbhot, a great-grand-daughter of King Rama IV. They contain her fine collection of antiquities, both historic and prehistoric (the latter are particularly rare). Like the artefacts in the National Museum, those in Suan Pakkard are also poorly labelled. The rear pavilion is particularly lovely, decorated in black and gold lacquerwork panels. Prince Chumbhot discovered this temple near Ayutthaya and reassembled and restored it there for his wife's 50th birthday. The grounds are very peaceful. Admission ฿80 – including a fan to ward off the heat. Open: 0900-1600, Mon-Sat. All receipts go to a fund for artists.

Jim Thompson's House is on the quiet Soi Kasemsan Song (2), opposite the National Stadium on Rama I Road. It is an assemblage of traditional teak Northern Thai houses, some more than 200 years old, transported here and re-

assembled (these houses were designed to be transportable, consisting of 5 parts – the floor, posts, roof, walls and decorative elements constructed without the use of nails). Jim Thompson arrived in Bangkok as an intelligence officer attached to the United States' O.S.S. (Office of Strategic Services) and then made his name by reinvigorating the Thai silk industry after World War II. He disappeared mysteriously in the Malaysian jungle on March 27th 1967, but his silk industry continues to thrive. (The *Jim Thompson Silk Company*, selling fine Thai silk, is at the NE end of Surawong Road. This shop is a tourist attraction in itself. Shoppers can buy high-quality bolts of silk and silk clothing here – anything from a pocket handkerchief to a silk suit. Prices are top of the scale.) Jim Thompson chose this site for his house partly because a collection of silk weavers lived nearby on Khlong Saensaep. The house contains an eclectic collection of antiques from Thailand and China, with work displayed as though it was still his home. Shoes must be removed before entering; walking barefoot around the house adds to the appreciation of the cool teak floorboards. Bustling Bangkok only intrudes in the form of the stench from the khlong that runs behind the house. Compulsory guided tours around the house. Admission: ฿100 (profits to charity). Open: 0900-1700, Mon-Sat. Getting there: bus along Rama I Rd, taxi or tuk-tuk.

A 10 min walk E along Rama I Road is the shopping area known as **Siam Square** (or Siam Sa-quare). This has the greatest concentration of fast food restaurants, boutiques and cinemas in the city. Needless to say, it is patronized by young Thais. The land on which this chequerboard of shops are built is owned by **Chulalongkorn University** – Bangkok's, and Thailand's, most prestigious. While Thammasat University on Sanaam Luang is known for its radical politics, Chulalongkorn is conserva-

BANGKOK: ANIMAL SUPERMARKET OF THE WORLD

Thailand has few laws restricting the import of endangered species of wildlife – either alive or dead – and the country acts as a collection point for animals from Burma, Cambodia and Laos, as well as further afield. Tiger skins and penises (the latter much prized by the Chinese), ivory, rhino horns and nails, cayman skins (from Latin America), live gibbons and tiger cubs, clouded leopard skins, hawksbill turtle shells, and rare palm cockatoos are all available in Bangkok, a city which has been called the 'wildlife supermarket of the world'. This is nothing particularly new: in 1833, government records show that 50-60 rhinoceros horns were exported, along with 26,000 pairs of deer's antler and 100,000 deer hides.

But pressure on Thailand's natural environment means that the scale of the threat is different. In 1991 the World Wide Fund for Nature labelled Thailand as "probably the worst country in the world for the illegal trade in endangered species". Before the Olympic Games in Seoul, South Korea, in 1988 it is said that 200 Malayan sun bears were smuggled from Thailand to Korea so that local athletes could consume their energy-enhancing gall bladders and meat. Even Korean tourists are able to dine on bear meat in restaurants in Bangkok – the animals are reportedly lowered alive in cages into vats of boiling water.

Critics claim that the Thai government flagrantly violates the rules of the Convention on International Trade in Endangered Species (CITES) – which it has officially acceded to – and ignores blatant trading in both live and dead endangered species. In recent years there has been increasing pressure from conservationists and from other governments to try and force the Thai authorities to clean-up their act. This, at last, appears to be having some success.

tive. Just S of Siam Square, on the campus itself (off Soi Chulalongkorn 12, behind the massive Mahboonkrong or MBK shopping centre; ask for 'sa-sin', the houses are nearby) is a collection of beautiful **traditional Thai houses**, newly built to help preserve Thai culture. Also on campus is the **Museum of Imaging Technology** with a few hands-on photographic displays. Occasional photographic exhibitions are also held here when it may be open other than on a Sat. Admission: ฿100. Open: 1000-1600 Sat. To get to the museum, enter the campus by the main entrance on the E side of Phaya Thai Road and walk along the S side of the playing field. Turn right after the Chemistry 2 building and then right again at the entrance to the Mathematics faculty. It is at the end of this walkway in the Dept of Photographic Science and Printing Technology.

E of Siam Square is the **Erawan Shrine** on the corner of Ploenchit and Rachdamri roads, at the Rachparasong intersection. This is Bangkok's most popular shrine, attracting not just Thais but also large numbers of other Asian visitors. The spirit of the shrine, the Hindu god Thao Maha Brahma, is reputed to grant people's wishes – it certainly has little artistic worth. In thanks, visitors offer garlands, wooden elephants and pay to have dances performed for them accompanied by the resident Thai orchestra. The popular *Thai Rath* newspaper reported in 1991 that some female devotees show their thanks by covorting naked at the shrine in the middle of the night. Others, rather more coy about exposing themselves in this way, have taken to giving the god pornographic videos instead. Although it is unlikely that visitors will be rewarded with the sight of naked bodies, the shrine is a hive of activity at most hours, incongruously set on a noisy, polluted intersection tucked into a corner, and in the shadow of the Sogo Department Store.

One other traditional house worth visiting is the home of the Siam Society, off Sukhumvit Road, at 131 Soi Asoke. The **Kamthieng House** is a 120-year-old N Thai house from Chiang Mai. It was donated to the society in 1963, transported to Bangkok and then reassembled a few years later. It now serves as an ethnological museum, devoted to preserving the traditional technologies and folk arts of Northern Thailand. It makes an interesting contrast to the fine arts displayed in Suan Pakkard Palace and Jim Thompson's house. The Siam Society houses a library, organizes lectures and tours and publishes books, magazines and pamphlets. Admission: ฿25, ฿10 for children. Open: 0900-1200, 1300-1700, Tues-Sat., T 2583491 for information on lectures.

Wat Indraviharn is rather isolated from the other sights, lying just off Visutkaset Road. It contains a 32m-high standing Buddha encrusted in gold tiles that can be seen from the entrance to the wat. The image is impressive only for its size. The topknot contains a relic of the Buddha brought from Ceylon. Few tourists. Open: Mon-Sun.

For those with a penchant for snakes, the **Snake Farm** of the Thai Red Cross is very central and easy to reach from Silom or Surawong roads. It was established in 1923, and raises snakes for serum production, which is distributed worldwide. The farm also has a collection of non-venomous snakes. During showtime (which lasts 30 minutes) various snakes are exhibited, and venom extracted. Visitors can fondle a python. The farm is well maintained and professional. Admission: ฿70. Open: 0830-1630 Mon-Fri (shows at 1100 and 1430), 0830-1200 Sat/Sun and holidays (show at 1100). The farm is within the Science Division of the Thai Red Cross Society at the corner of Rama IV and Henri Dunant roads.

Slightly further out of the centre of Bangkok is the **Chatuchak Weekend Market** which is off Phahonyothin Road, opposite the Northern bus terminal. Until 1982 this market was held at Sanaam Luang, but was moved because it had outgrown its original home and also because the authorities wanted to clean up the area for the Bangkok bicentenary celebrations. It is a huge conglomeration of 6,000 stallholders, selling virtually everything under the sun, and an estimated 100,000 people visit the market over a weekend. It is probably the best place to buy handicrafts and all things Thai in the whole Kingdom. There are antique stalls, basket stalls, textile sellers, shirt vendors, carvers, painters ... along with the usual array of fish sellers, vegetable hawkers, butchers and candle-stick makers. In

CHATUCHAK WEEKEND MARKET

1. Decorative Rocks, Cocks, & Bonsai
2. Agricultural Products & Clothing
3. Miscellaneous
4. Pets, Handicrafts
5. Pets
6. Clothing
7. Fresh & Dried Fruits
8. Plants, Clothing
9. Plants
10. Fresh & Dried Fruits, Ceramic Wares
11. Antiques
12. Buddha's Image, Plants & Books
13. Paintings, Plants

the last couple of years a number of bars and food stalls geared to tourists and Thai yuppies have also opened so it is possible to rest and recharge before foraging once more. Definitely worth a visit – and allocate half a day at least. In addition to the map below, Nancy Chandler's Map of Bangkok has an inset map of the market to help you get around. Believe it or not, the market is open on weekends, officially from 0900-1800 (although in fact it begins earlier). **Getting there:** a/c buses 2, 3, 10 and 13 go past the market, and non-a/c buses 8, 24, 26, 27, 29, 34, 39, 44, 59, and 96. Or take a taxi or tuk-tuk. Also here, in the N section of Chatuchak Park is the **Railway Museum** with a small collection of steam locomotives. Open: 0500-1200 Sun.

The **Science Museum and Planetarium** is just past Sukhumvit Soi 40, next to the Eastern bus terminal. It contains a planetarium, aeroplanes and other exhibits. Admission: ฿10. Open: 0900-2200 Wed-Sun. **Getting there:** bus (a/c 1, 8, 11, 13, non-a/c 2, 25, 38, 40, 48, 71, 119), taxi or tuk-tuk.

Excursions

Ancient City

(Muang Boran) lies 25 km SE of Bangkok in Samut Prakarn. It houses scaleddown constructions of Thailand's most famous wats and palaces (some of which can no longer be visited in their original locations) along with a handful of originals relocated here. Artisans maintain the buildings while helping to keep alive traditional crafts. The 50 ha site corresponds in shape to the map of Thailand, with the wats and palaces appropriately sited. Allocate a full day for a trip out to the Ancient City. Admission: ฿50. Open: 0830-1700, Mon-Sun. **Getting there:** there are 3 ways of getting to the Ancient City – either on the a/c city bus no 8 or 11, or non-a/c no 25 to Samut Prakarn

and then a short songthaew ride; or by bus from the Eastern bus terminal to Samut Prakarn; or on one of the innumerable organized tours (see tours, below).

Crocodile farm and zoo

This claims to be the world's oldest and largest crocodile farm. Founded in 1950 by a certain Mr Utai Youngprapakorn, it contains over 30,000 crocs of various species. The show includes the 'world famous' crocodile wrestling. Croc combat and elephant show-time is every hour between 0900 and 1600 Mon-Fri (no show at 1200), and every hour between 0900 and 1700 Sat/Sun and holidays. The farm also has a small zoo, train and playground. Admission: ฿120. Open: 0800-1900 (approx.) Mon-Sun, T 3870020/ 3871166. **Getting there:** a/c bus 8 or 11, or regular bus 25, 45, 102 or 119 along Sukhumvit Road; or a bus from the Eastern bus terminal to Samut Prakarn and then take a minibus to the crocodile farm; or a tour (see tours, below).

Watery excursions

Apart from the khlong trips outlined on page 146, there are other places to go on the river. The cheapest way to travel the river is by regular water taxi. There are 3 types (not including the *hang yaaws*):

First, the **Chao Phraya Express River Taxi** (*rua duan*) which runs on a regular route from Wat Rajsingkorn (near Krungthep Bridge, at the S end of Charoen Krung) northwards to Nonthaburi. Fares range from ฿4-16 and the service operates every 8-25 minutes depending on the time of day, 0600-1800 Mon-Sun (see map for stops). The boats are long and fast. There are also **ferries** which ply back and forth across the river, between Bangkok and Thonburi. The fare for these slower, chunkier boats is ฿1. Lastly, there are a number of other **boat services** linking Bangkok with stops along the khlongs which run off the main Chao Phraya River and into Thonburi. These are a good, cheap way of getting a glimpse of waterside life. Services from Tha Thien pier (by Wat Pho) to Khlong Mon, 0630-1800 Mon-Sun (every 30 mins) ฿4; from Memorial Bridge pier to Khlong Bang Waek, 0600-2130 Mon-Sun (every 15 mins) ฿10; from Tha Chang pier (by the Grand Palace) to Khoo Wiang floating market (market operates 0400-0700) and Khlong Bang Yai, 0615-2000 Mon-Sun (every 20 mins) ฿10; and from Nonthaburi's Phibun Pier (N of the city) to Khlong Om, 0400-2100 Mon-Sun (every 15 mins).

An interesting day trip by long-tailed boat takes visitors to a **traditional Thai house** 30 km from Bangkok, in Nonthaburi (see next entry). A day trip, including lunch costs ฿500. It is possible to stay here, as guests of the owner Mr Phaiboon (**A**), includes breakfast, fan rooms, outside bathrooms and no hot water. Call *Asian Overland Adventure*, T 2800740, F 2800741.

Nonthaburi

Nonthaburi is both a province and a provincial capital immediately to the N of Bangkok. Accessible by express river taxi from the city, the town has a provincial air that contrasts sharply with the overpowering capital: there are saamlors in the streets (now banished from Bangkok) and the pace of life is tangibly less frenetic. 30 mins walk away are rice fields and rural Thailand. A street market runs from the pier inland past the *sala klang* (provincial offices), selling clothes, sarong lengths, dried fish and unnecessary plastic objects. The buildings of the sala klang are early 19th century, wooden and decayed. Note the lamp posts with their durian accessories – Nonthaburi's durians are renowned across the kingdom. Walk through the sala klang compound (downriver) to reach an excellent riverside restaurant. Across the river and upstream (5 mins

by long-tailed boat) is Wat Chalem Phra Kiat, a refined wat built by Rama III as a tribute to his mother who is said to have lived in the vicinity. The gables of the bot are encrusted in ceramic tiles; the chedi behind the bot was built during the reign of Rama IV. Getting there: by express river taxi B6 (45 mins) to Tha Nonthaburi or by Bangkok city bus (nos 32, 64, 97 and 203).

Floating market at Damnoen Saduak

Ratchaburi Province, 109 km west of Bangkok. Sadly, it is becoming increasingly like the Floating Market in Thonburi, although it does still function as a legitimate market. Getting there: catch an early morning bus (no. 78) from the Southern bus terminal in Thonburi – aim to get to Damnoen Saduak between 0800-1000, as the market winds down after 1000, leaving only trinket stalls. The trip takes about 1½ hrs. A/c and non-a/c buses leave every 40 mins from 0600 (฿30-49) (T 4355031 for booking). The bus travels via Nakhon Pathom (where it is possible to stop on the way back and see the great chedi – see Nakhon Pathom page 379). Ask the conductor to drop you at Thanarat Bridge in Damnoen Saduak. Then either walk down the lane (1.5 km) that leads to the market and follows the canal, or take a river taxi for ฿10. There are a number of floating markets in the maze of khlongs – Ton Khem, Hia Kui and Khun Phithak – and it is best to hire a hang yaaw to explore the back-waters and roam around the markets, about ฿300/hr (agree the price before setting out). It is possible to combine a trip to Damnoen Saduak with a visit to the *Rose Garden* (see tours, page 158). Tour companies also visit the floating market.

Thai Human Imagery Museum

Situated 31 km out of Bangkok on Pinklao-Nakhon Chaisri highway, the museum is the Madame Tussauds of Bangkok. 'Breath-taking' sculptures include famous monks, Thai kings, and scenes from Thai life; the museum is probably more interesting to Thais than foreigners (T 01-2116261). Admission: ฿140. Open: 0900-1730 Mon-Fri, 0830-1800 Sat, Sun and holidays. Getting there: by bus from the Southern bus terminals (either a/c or non-a/c) towards Nakhon Pathom; ask to be let off at the museum.

Ayutthaya

The historic former capital of Siam lies 85 km north of the city and is one of the most interesting day excursions from Bangkok (see page 182). Getting there: regular buses from the Northern bus terminal throughout the day, or take a tour either by bus or by boat up the Chao Phraya River (see page 159).

Historic town of Nakhon Pathom

67 km from Bangkok (see page 378) and the renowned **Bridge over the River Kwai** in **Kanchanaburi** province (see page 382) can both be visited as day trips from Bangkok.

Phetburi

An ancient city 160 km S of Bangkok. It can just be visited in a day from the capital (see page 398). Getting there: by bus from the Southern bus terminal (2 hrs) or by train from Hualamphong station (2½ hrs).

Hua Hin

A beach resort 230 km S of Bangkok. It is accessible as a day tour by either bus from the Southern terminal 3½ hrs (฿41-74) or by train from Hualamphong station 3½-4 hrs (฿44-182) (see page 402).

Khao Yai National Park

This is Thailand's oldest national park and one of the most accessible, lying only 165 km NE of Bangkok, see page 301. Getting there: 3 hrs by car. Regular connections by bus from the Northern bus terminal to Pak Chong. From here there are regular buses into the park.

Tours

Bangkok has innumerable tour companies that can take visitors virtually anywhere. If there is not a tour to fit your bill – most run the same range of tours – many companies will organize one for you, for a price. Most top hotels have their own tour desk and it is probably easiest to book there (arrange to be picked up from your hotel as part of the deal). The tours given below are the most popular; prices per person are about ฿250-350 for a half day, ฿600 for a full day (incl lunch). A short list of companies is given at the end of the section; there are countless more.

Rose Garden

A Thai 'cultural village' spread over 15 ha of landscaped tropical grounds, 32 km W of Bangkok. Most people go for the cultural show – elephants at work, Thai classical dancing, Thai boxing, hilltribe dancing and a Buddhist ordination ceremony. The resort also has a hotel, restaurants, a swimming pool and tennis courts, as well as a golf course close by. Admission: ฿220. The cultural show is at 1500 Mon-Sun (Bangkok office: 195/15 Soi Chokchai Chongchamron Rama III Rd, T 2953261). Daily tour from Bangkok, half day (afternoons only).

Half day tours

Grand Palace Tour; Temple Tour to Wat Traimitr, Wat Pho and Wat Benjamabophit; Khlong Tour around khlongs and to Floating Market, Snake Farm and Wat Arun (mornings only); Old City Tour; Crocodile Farm Tour; Rice Barge and Khlong Tour (afternoons only); Damnoen Saduak Floating Market Tour.

Full day tours

Damnoen Saduak and Rose Garden; Thai Dinner and Classical Dance, eat in traditional Thai surrounding and consume toned-down Thai food, ฿250-300, 1900-2200. Pattaya, the infamous beach resort; River Kwai, a chance to see the famous Bridge over the River Kwai and war cemeteries, as well as the great chedi at Nakhon Pathom; Ayutthaya and Bang Pa-In. There are also boat tours to Ayutthaya and Bang Pa-In (see below).

Boat tours

The *Oriental Queen* sails up the Chao Phraya River daily from the *Oriental Hotel* to the old capital, Ayutthaya (see page 182), returning to Bangkok by a/c bus, ฿1,200, 0800-1700 with lunch (T 2360400); *Ayutthaya Princess* operates from the *Shangri-La Hotel* pier or the *Royal Sheraton* pier. The *Ayutthaya Princess* is a two-level vessel resembling a Royal Barge. Leaving at 0800 daily, there are daily cruises to Bang Pa-In, an a/c bus tour around Ayutthaya, returning to Bangkok by coach at 1730. You can also do the reverse: coach to Ayutthaya and then a boat back to Bangkok, arriving at 1730, ฿1,100, including buffet lunch on board. (Kian Gwan Building, 140 Wireless Rd, T 2559200.)

Mekhala is operated by the *Siam Exclusive Tours* on the same route. The difference is that *Mekhala* leaves Bangkok in the late evening and puts ashore for one night in Ayutthaya, supplying a romantic dinner on deck. The *Mekhala* is a converted rice barge accommodating 12-16 passengers in 6 a/c cabins with attached bathrooms. The barge arrives in Ayutthaya at Wat Kai Tia in the evening and departs the following morning for Bang Pa-In. To visit other sights, passengers are transferred to a long-tailed boat. An a/c minibus transports passengers back to Bangkok. The reverse, proceeding by road up to Ayutthaya/Bang Pa-In and returning on the rice barge, is also available ฿5,290 (single), ฿4,200 (twin). Book through travel agents or *Siam Exclusive Tours*, Bldg One, 7th Flr, 99 Witthayu Rd, T 2566153, F 2566665. Cheaper are the day boat tours to Bang Pa-In (see page 189) via Queen Sirikit's handicraft centre at Bang Sai and the stork sanctuary at Wat Phai Lom operated by the *Chao Phraya Express Boat Company*. Tours leave on Sat and Sun only from the Maharaj and Phra Athit piers at 0800 and 0805 respectively, returning 1530, ฿180 or ฿240, T 2815564.

Train tours

The State Railway of Thailand organise day trips to Nakhon Pathom (see page 378) and the Bridge over the River Kwai (see page 388) and to Ayutthaya (see page 182). Both trips run on weekends and holidays. The latter tour leaves Bangkok at 0630 and returns from Ayutthaya on the Chao Phraya River.

Dinner cruises

Chao Phraya, T 4335453; *Loy Nava*, T 4374932, ฿700. *Wanfah Cruise*, T 4335453, ฿650. *Ayutthaya Princess*, T 2559200 organizes Sunday dinner cruise for ฿850.

International

For tours to Vietnam, Laos, Cambodia and Burma, see page 177.

Festivals and major events

Jan: *Red Cross Fair* (moveable), held in Amporn Gardens next to the Parliament. Stalls, classical dancing, folk performances etc.

Feb: *Chinese New Year* (moveable), Chinatown closes down, but Chinese temples are packed. *Handicraft Fair* (mid-month), all the handicrafts are made by Thai prisoners.

Mar-Apr: *Kite Flying* (moveable, for one month), every afternoon/evening at Sanaam Luang there is kite fighting (see page 138). An *International Kite Festival* is held in late March at Sanaam Luang when kite fighting and demonstrations by kite-flyers from across the globe take place.

May: *Royal Ploughing Ceremony* (moveable), this celebrates the official start of the rice-planting season and is held at Sanaam Luang. It is an ancient Brahman ritual and is attended by the king (see page 138).

Sept: *Swan-boat races* (moveable), on the Chao Phraya River.

Nov: *Golden Mount Fair* (moveable), stalls and theatres set-up all around the Golden Mount and Wat Saket. Candles are carried in procession to the top of the mount. *Marathon* road race, fortunately at one of the coolest times of year.

Dec: *Trooping of the Colour* (moveable), the élite Royal Guards swear allegiance to the king and march past members of the Royal Family. It is held in the Royal Plaza near the equestrian statue of King Chulalongkorn.

Local information

● **Accommodation**

Price guide		
	US$	**Baht**
L	200+	5,000+
A+	100-200	2,500-5,000
A	50-100	1,250-2,500
B	25-50	625-1,250
C	15-25	375-625
D	8-15	200-375
E	4-8	100-200
F	<4	<100

Bangkok offers a vast range of accommodation at all levels of luxury. There are a number of hotel areas in the city, each with its own character and locational advantages. Accommodation has been divided into 5 such areas with a sixth – 'other' – for the handful situated elsewhere. A new type of hotel which has emerged in Bangkok in recent years is the 'boutique' hotel. These are small, with immaculate service, and represent an attempt to emulate the philosophy of 'small is beautiful'.

NB For business women travelling alone, the *Oriental*, *Dusit Theni* and *Amari Airport* hotels allocate a floor to women travellers, with all-female staff.

Many of the more expensive places to stay are on the **Chao Phraya River** with its views, good shopping and access to the old city. Running eastwards from the river are **Silom** and **Surawong** roads, in the heart of Bangkok's business district and close to many embassies. The bars of Patpong link the two roads. A more recently developed area is along **Sukhumvit Road** running east from Soi Nana Nua (Soi 3). The bulk of the accommodation here is in the **A-B** range, and within easy reach is a wide range of restaurants, 'girlie' bars, and reasonable shopping. But, the hotels are a long taxi or tuk-tuk ride from the sights of the old city and most of the places of interest to the tourist in Bangkok. In the vicinity of **Siam Square** are two deluxe hotels and several 'budget' class establishments (especially along Rama 1 Soi Kasemsan Nung). Siam Square is central, a good shopping area, with easy bus and taxi access to Silom and Sukhumvit roads and the sights of the old city. Guesthouses are to be found along and around **Khaosan Road** (an area known as Banglamphu); or just to the N, at the NW end of Sri Ayutthaya Rd there is a small cluster of rather friendly places. **Soi Ngam Duphli**, off Rama IV Rd, is the other big area for cheap places to stay. These hotel areas encompass about 90% of Bangkok's accommodation, although there are other places to stay scattered across the city; these are listed under **Other**.

● **Silom, Surawong and the River**

L *Dusit Thani*, 946 Rama IV Rd, T 2360450, F 2366400, a/c, restaurants, pool, when it was built it was the tallest building in Bangkok, refurbished, still excellent, though disappointing pool, rec; **L** *Evergreen Laurel Hotel*, 88 Sathorn Nua, T 2669988, F 2667222, a/c, restaurants, pool, one of the new 'boutique' hotels with only 130 rooms, all facilities and excellent service; **L** *Montien*, 54 Surawong Rd, T 2348060, F 2365219, a/c, restaurants, pool, one of the first high-rise hotels (opened 1967) with good location for business, shopping and bars, slick service, and continuing good reputation with loyal patrons; **L** *Oriental*, 48 Soi Oriental, Charoen Krung, T 2360400, F 2361939, a/c, restaurants, pool, one of the best hotels in the world, beautiful position overlooking the river, superb personal service despite size (400 rooms), Joseph Conrad, Somerset Maugham and Noel Coward all stayed here at one time, good shopping arcade, excellent programme of 'cultural' events,

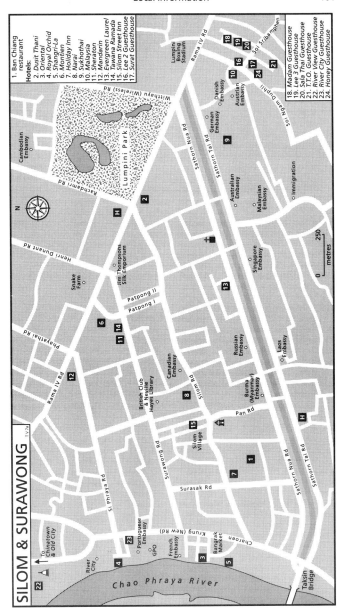

SILOM & SURAWONG

1. Ban Chiang restaurant

Hotels:
2. Dusit Thani
3. Oriental
4. Royal Orchid
5. Shangri-La
6. Montien
7. Holiday Inn
8. Narai
9. Sukhothai
10. Malaysia
11. Sheraton
12. Mandarin
13. Evergreen Laurel
14. Tawana Ramada
15. Silom Street Inn
16. Lee 2 Guesthouse
17. Surat Guesthouse
18. Madam Guesthouse
19. Lee 3 Guesthouse
20. Sala Thai Guesthouse
21. T.T.O. Guesthouse
22. River View Guesthouse
23. River City Guesthouse
24. Honey Guesthouse

and 6 excellent restaurants highly rec; **L** *Royal Orchid Sheraton*, 2 Captain Bush Lane, Si Phraya Rd, T 2345599, F 2368320, a/c, restaurants, pool, strong unpleasant smell of nearby khlong, lovely views over the river, close to River City shopping centre (good for antiques); **L** *Shangri-La*, 89 Soi Wat Suan Plu, Charoen Krung, T 2367777, F 2368579, a/c, restaurants, lovely pool, great location overlooking river, sometimes preferred to *Oriental*, recently upgraded and extended, rec; **L** *Sukhothai*, 13/3 Sathorn Tai Rd, T 2870222, F 2784980, a/c, restaurants (good Italian restaurant), pool, beautiful rooms and excellent service, rec; **L-A+** *Holiday Inn Crowne Plaza*, 981 Silom Rd, T 2384300, F 2385289, a/c, restaurants, pool, vast, pristine marble-filled hotel, all amenities, immensely comfortable, minimum atmosphere and character.

A+ *Menam*, 2074 Charoen Krung, T 2891148, F 2911048, a/c, restaurant, pool, good value for river-view rooms but inconvenient location, shuttle-boat makes sightseeing easier; **A+** *Monarch Lee Gardens*, 188 Silom Rd, T 2381991, F 2381999, a/c, restaurants, pool, opened 1992, stark and gleaming high-tech high-rise, all facilities, still trying hard to attract custom, discounts available; **A+** *Narai*, 222 Silom Rd, T 2370100, F 2367161, a/c, restaurant, pool, rather non-descript, with cold, marble-clad lobby; **A+** *Tarntawan Place*, 119/5-10 Surawong Rd, T 2382620, F 2383228, a/c, restaurant, pool, good service and rooms, rec; **A+** *Tawana Ramada*, 80 Surawong Rd, T 2360361, F 2363738, a/c, restaurant, pool, average hotel.

A *Mandarin*, 662 Rama IV Rd, T 2380230, F 2371620, a/c, restaurant, small pool, friendly atmosphere, comfortable rooms, popular nightclub; **A** *Manohra*, 412 Surawong Rd, T 2345070, F 2377662, a/c, coffee shop, small pool, unattractive rooms, mediocre service; **A** *Silom Plaza*, 320 Silom Rd, T 2368441, F 2367562, a/c, restaurant, small pool, caters mainly for East Asian tour groups, central but characterless, gently decaying; **A** *Silom Street Inn*, 284/11-13 Silom Rd, opposite the junction with Pan Rd (between sois 22 and 24), T 2384680, F 2384689, a/c, restaurant, pool, small new hotel, small, comfortable, 30 well-equipped rooms with CNN News, grubby rather seedy lobby, set back from road; **A** *Trinity Place*, 150 Silom Soi 5, T 2380052, F 2383984, a/c, restaurant, pool, attractive, small hotel.

B *Collins House (YMCA)*, 27 Sathorn Tai Rd, T 2872727, F 2871996, a/c, restaurant, large pool, clean, excellent value, friendly management; **B** *New Peninsula*, 295/3 Surawong Rd, T 2343910, a/c, restaurant, small pool, small rooms; **B** *River City Guesthouse*, 11/4 Charoen Krung Soi Rong Nam Khang 1, T 2351429, F 2373127, a/c, not very welcoming but rooms are a good size and clean, good bathrooms, short walk to River City and the river; **B** *Rose*, 118 Surawong Rd, T 2337695, a/c, restaurant, pool, opposite Patpong, favourite among single male visitors, but getting seedier by the month; **B** *Swan*, 31 Charoen Krung Soi 36, T 2348594, some a/c, great position, clean but scruffy rooms; **B** *Victory*, 322 Silom Rd, T 2339060, a/c, restaurant.

C *Chao Phya Riverside*, 1128 Songward Rd (opposite the Chinese school), T 2226344, some a/c, old style house overlooking river, clean rooms, atmospheric, unusual location; **C** *River View Guesthouse*, 768 Songwad Soi Panurangsri, T 2345429, F 2375428, some a/c, excellent hotel overlooking the river in Chinatown, rooms are large, clean, some with balconies, hw and friendly, professional management, Khun Phi Yai, the owner, is a pharmacist, so can even prescribe pills, highly rec.

● **Soi Ngam Duphli**

Soi Ngam Duphli is much the smaller of Bangkok's two centres of guesthouse accommodation. Locationally, the area is good for the shopping and bars of Silom Rd but inconvenient for most of the city's main places of interest in the old city. Guesthouses tend to be quieter and more refined than those of Khaosan Rd.

B *Malaysia*, 54 Rama IV Soi Ngam Duphli, T 2863582, F 2493120, a/c, restaurant, pool, once a Bangkok favourite for travellers.

C *T.T.O.*, 2/48 Soi Sribamphen, T 2866783, F 2871571, a/c, well-run and popular, homely atmosphere, rooms a little small; **C-D** *Honey*, 35/2-4 Soi Ngam Duphli, T 2863460, some a/c, large rooms, in a rather rambling block, clean and good value, service can be rather surly, no hot water.

D *Sala Thai Guesthouse*, 15 Soi Sribamphen, T 2871436, at end of peaceful, almost leafy, soi, clean rooms, family run, good food, but shared bathroom, rec; **D-E** *Anna*, 21/30 Soi Ngam Duphli, clean rooms, some with bathrooms; **D-E** *Home Sweet Home*, 27/7 Soi Sribamphen (opposite Boston Inn, down small soi, so relatively quiet, average rooms with attached bathrooms; **D-E** *Lee 3*, 13 Soi Saphan

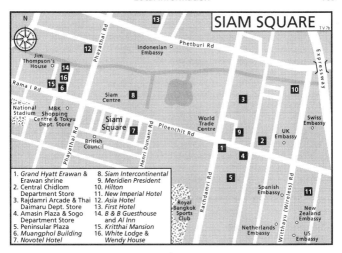

SIAM SQUARE T V 7b

1. Grand Hyatt Erawan & Erawan Shrine
2. Central Chidlom Department Store
3. Rajdamri Arcade & Thai Daimaru Dept. Store
4. Amasin Plaza & Sogo Department Store
5. Peninsular Plaza
6. Muangphol Building
7. Novotel Hotel
8. Siam Intercontinental
9. Meridien President
10. Hilton
11. New Imperial Hotel
12. Asia Hotel
13. First Hotel
14. B & B Guesthouse and Al Inn
15. Kritthai Mansion
16. White Lodge & Wendy House

Khu, T 2863042, some a/c, wooden house with character, down quiet soi, rooms are clean but with shared bathrooms, rec; **D-E** *Madam*, 11 Soi Saphan Khu, T 2869289, wooden house, friendly atmosphere, attached bathrooms, no hw, quiet, rec.

E *Lee 2*, 21/38-39 Soi Ngam Duphli, T 2862069, clean, friendly, rec; **E** *Lee 4*, 9 Soi Saphan Khu., T 2867874, spotless rooms and bathrooms, some with balconies and views over city, rec; **E** *Surat*, 2/18-20 Sribumphen Rd, T 2867919, some a/c, own bathroom, no hw, clean and well-run, rec.

● **Siam Square, Rama I Road and Phetburi Road**

L *Grand Hyatt Erawan*, 494 Rachdamri Rd, T 2541234, F 2535856, refurbished interior for much-loved old *Erawan Hotel*, towering structure behind with grandiose entrance and a plastic tree-filled atrium plus sumptious rooms and every facility; **L** *Hilton*, 2 Witthayu Rd, T 2530123, F 2536509, a/c, restaurants, attractive pool, set in lovely grounds, first class service; **L** *Imperial*, 6-10 Witthayu Rd, T 2540023, F 2533190, (on the edge of Siam Sq area), a/c, restaurants, pool, great facilities, lovely grounds, well-managed; **L** *Novotel*, Siam Sq Soi 6, T 2556888, F 2551824, a/c, restaurant, pool, undistinguished but commendably comfortable; **L** *Siam Intercontinental*, 967 Rama I Rd, T 2530355, F 2532275, a/c, restaurants, small pool, rela-

tively low-rise hotel, set in 26 acres of grounds, good sports facilities, excellent service.

A+ *Arnoma*, 99 Rachdamri Rd, T 2553411, F 2553456, a/c, several restaurants, pool, health club, business centre, 403 well-equipped rooms, though much like any others in this price bracket, good location for shopping and restaurants; **A+** *Le Meridien President*, 135/26 Gaysorn Rd, T 2530444, F 2537565, tranquil atmosphere, good service, excellent French food, a new sister hotel is being built next door – the luxury *President Tower*, due for completion in 1994, rec; **A+** *Regent Bangkok*, 155 Rachdamri Rd, T 2516127, F 2539195, a/c, restaurants (see Thai Restaurants, page 167), pool, excellent reputation amongst frequent visitors who insist on staying here, arguably the best range of cuisine in Bangkok; **A+** *Siam City*, 477 Sri Ayutthaya Rd, T 2470120, F 2470178, a/c, restaurants, pool, another new hotel, with all facilities, tastefully designed.

A *Asia*, 296 Phayathai Rd, T 2150808, F 2154360, a/c, restaurant, pool, ugly hotel situated on noisy thoroughfare.

B *Kritthai Mansion*, 931/1 Rama I Rd, T 2153042, a/c, restaurant, situated on noisy thoroughfare; **B** *Florida*, 43 Phayathai Rd, T 2453221, a/c, restaurant, pool; **B** *Prince*, 1537/1 New Phetburi Rd, T 2516171, a/c, restaurant, pool, all facilities but no character; **C** *A-1 Inn*, 25/13 Soi Kasemsan Nung (1), Rama I Rd,

T 2153029, a/c, well run, intimate hotel, rec.

C *Bed and Breakfast*, 36/42 Soi Kasemsan Nung (1), Rama 1 Rd, T 2153004, F 2152493, a/c, friendly efficient staff, clean but small rooms, good security, bright 'lobby', price includes breakfast, rec; **C** *Muangphol Building*, 931/9 Rama l Rd, T 2150033, F 2802540, a/c, pool, hot water, good sized rooms, reasonable rates; **C** *Wendy House*, 36/2 Soi Kasemsan Nung (1), Rama l Rd, T 2162436, F 2168053, a/c, spotless, but small rooms with eating area downstairs, hw; **C** *White Lodge*, 36/8 Soi Kasemsan Nung (1), Rama l Rd, T 2168867, F 2168228, a/c, hw, airy, light reasonably sized rooms, rec; **C-E** *Alternative Tour Guesthouse*, 14/1 Rachaprarop Soi Rachatapan, T 2452963, F 2467020, friendly, excellent source of information, attached to *Alternative Tour Company*, promoting culturally and environmentally sensitive tourism, clean.

● **Sukhumvit Road**

L *Imperial Queen's Park*, Sukhumvit Soi 22, T 2619000, F 2619530, massive new 37-storey hotel with a mind boggling 1,400 rooms. How service can, in any sense, be personal is hard to imagine, but all possible facilities, location is away from most sights and the main business district; **L** *Windsor Plaza Embassy Suites*, 8 Sukhumvit Soi 20, T 2580160, F 2581491, a/c, restaurants, pool, next door to the *Windsor Hotel*, 460 suites, health centre.

A+ *Delta Grand Pacific*, 259 Sukhumvit Rd, T 2544998, F 2552441, a/c, restaurants, pool, almost 400 rooms in this large high-rise hotel, all facilities but characterless for the price; **A+** *Hotel Mercure*, 12/3 Sukhumvit Soi 22, T 2597420, F 2582862, medium-sized hotel with 90 rooms, rather out of the way; **A+** *Rembrandt*, 15-15/1 Sukhumvit Soi 20, T 2617040, F 2617017, a/c, restaurants, pool, new hotel with lots of marble and limited ambience; **A+-A** *Somerset*, Sukhumvit Soi 15, T 2548500, F 2548534, a/c, restaurant, tiny enclosed pool, small hotel, rather ostentatious, rooms are non-descript but comfortable, baths are designed for people of small stature.

A *Amari Boulevard*, 2 Sukhumvit Soi 5, T 2552930, F 2552950, a/c, restauarant, pool; **A** *Ambassador*, 171 Sukhumvit Rd, T 2540444, F 2534123, a/c, restaurants, pool, large, impersonal rather characterless hotel, with great food hall (see restaurants); **A** *Comfort, The Promenade*, 18 Sukhumvit Soi 8, T 2534116, F 2547707, a/c, restaurant, small pool, fitness centre, rathe kitsch; **A** *Manhattan*, 13 Sukhumvit Soi 15, T 2550166,

F 2553481, a/c, restaurant, pool, recently renovated high-rise, lacks character but rooms are comfortable and competitively priced although some are rather shabby so ask to inspect; **A** *Park*, 6 Sukhumvit Soi 7, T 2554300, F 2554309, a/c, restaurant, excellent service, peaceful oasis; **A** *Swiss Park*, 155/23-24 Sukhumvit Soi 11, T 2540228, F 2540378, a/c, restaurant, pool, another overbearing neo-classical hotel; **A** *Tai-pan*, 25 Sukhumvit Soi 23, T 2609888, F 2597908, a/c, restaurant, pool, tasteful new hotel; **A** *Windsor*, 8 Sukhumvit Soi 20, T 2580160, F 2581491, a/c, restaurant, pool, tennis.

B *Bourbon Street*, 29/4-6 Sukhumvit Soi 22 (behind Washington Theatre), T 2590328, F 2594318, a/c, small number of rooms attached to this Cajun restaurant, well run and good value, rec; **B** *China*, 19/27-28 Sukhumvit Soi 19, T 2557571, F 2541333, a/c, restaurant, a small hotel masquerading as a large one, but rooms are up to the standard of more expensive places, so good value; **B** *Comfort*, 153/11-4 Sukhumvit Soi 11, T 2519250, F 2543562, a/c, restaurant, small hotel, friendly management, rec; **B** *Crown*, 503 Sukhumvit Soi 29, T 2580318, F 2584438, a/c, clean, good service; **B** *Grace*, 12 Nana North, Sukhumvit Soi 3, T 2530651, F 2530680, a/c, restaurant, pool, the sex hotel of Bangkok now trying to redeem itself; **B** *Grand*, 2/7-8 Sukhumvit Soi 3 (Nana Nua), T 2533380, F 2549020, a/c, restaurant, small hotel with friendly staff, good value; **B** *Mermaids Rest*, Sukhumvit Soi 8, a/c, restaurant, pool, rec; **B** *Nana*, 4 Sukhumvit Soi Nana Tai (Soi 4), T 2520121, F 2551769, a/c, restaurant, pool, refurbished, good value.

C *Atlanta*, 78 Sukhumvit Soi 2, T 2521650, a/c, restaurant, large pool, left-luggage facility, poste restante, daily video-shows, good tour company in foyer, rec; **C** *Golden Palace*, Sukhumvit Soi 1, T 2525115, a/c, restaurant, pool, rec.

D *Chu's*, 35 Sukhumvit Soi 19, T 2544683, restaurant, one of the cheapest in the area, good food, rec; **D** *Happy Inn*, 20/1 Sukhumvit Soi 4, T 2526508, some a/c, basic rooms, cheerful management; **D** *SV*, 19/35-36 Sukhumvit Soi 19, T 2544724, some a/c, another cheap hotel in this area, musty rooms, shared bathrooms and poor service; **D-E** *Disra House*, 593/28 Sukhumvit Soi 33-33/1, T 2585102, some a/c, friendly and well run place which comes highly recommended, rather out-of-the-way but good value a/c rooms.

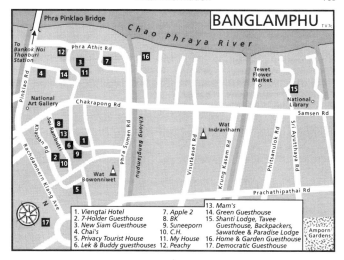

1. Viengtai Hotel
2. 7-Holder Guesthouse
3. New Siam Guesthouse
4. Chai's
5. Privacy Tourist House
6. Lek & Buddy guesthouses
7. Apple 2
8. BK
9. Suneeporn
10. C.H.
11. My House
12. Peachy
13. Mam's
14. Green Guesthouse
15. Shanti Lodge, Tavee
    Guesthouse, Backpackers,
    Sawatdee & Paradise Lodge
16. Home & Garden Guesthouse
17. Democratic Guesthouse

● Banglamphu (Khaosan Road) and surrounds

Khaosan Road lies NE of Sanaam Luang, just off Rachdamnern Klang Avenue, close to the Democracy Monument. It is continually expanding into new roads and sois, in particular the area W of Chakrapong Road. The sois off the main road are often quieter, such as Soi Chana Songkhran or Soi Rambutri. Note that rooms facing on Khaosan Rd tend to be very noisy.

A+ *Royal Princess*, 269 Lan Luang Rd, T 2813088, F 2801314, a/c, restaurants, pool, newish addition to Dusit chain of hotels, good facilities.

A *Majestic Palace*, 97 Rachdamnern Klang Ave (opposite Democracy Monument), T 2805610; F 2800965, a/c, restaurant, pool, old hotel given half-hearted face-lift, good location but rooms overpriced and limited facilities; **A** *Royal*, 2 Rachdamnern Klang Ave, T 2229111, F 2242083, a/c, restaurant, pool, old (by Bangkok standards) hotel which acted as a refuge for demonstrators during the 1991 riots, rooms are dated and featureless; **A** *Viengtai*, 42 Tanee Rd, Banglamphu, T 2815788, a/c, restaurant, pool, rooms are very good, clean relatively spacious, with all the advantages of this area in terms of proximity to the Old City.

C-D *7 Holder*, 216/2-3 Khaosan Rd, T 2813682, some a/c, clean, friendly; **C-**

D *New Siam*, Phra Athit 21 Soi Chana Songkram, T 2824554, F 2817461, some a/c, good restaurant, modern and clean, friendly helpful staff, airy rooms, but featureless block, tickets and tour information, fax facilities, lockers available, overpriced; **C-E** *Chart*, 58 Khaosan Rd, T 2803785, restaurant, some a/c, small but clean rooms, some have no windows; **C-E** *Green House*, 88/1 Khaosan Soi Rambutri, T 2820323, some a/c, ask for rooms away from street, rec.

D *Chai*, 49/4-8 Chao Fa Soi Rongmai, T 2814901, F 2818686, friendly atmosphere, clean and colourful with borgainvillea growing from the balconies and in the restaurant, last house down Soi Rambhtri, so away from the others; **D** *Pra Suri*, 85/1 Soi Pra Suri, 5 mins from Khaosan Rd, fan, restaurant, own bathrooms (no hot water), clean and quiet, very friendly and helpful family-run guesthouse, rec; **D-E** *BK*, 11/1 Chakrapong Soi Sulaow, T 2815278, some a/c, in busy area of Banglamphu, but guesthouse is set back from road, so not too noisy, clean but dark rooms, shared bathrooms, good information; **D-E** *Buddy*, 137/1 Khaosan Rd, T 2824351, off main street, some a/c, rooms are small and dingy but it remains popular, large open restaurant area bustles with people exchanging information; **D-E** *C.H.*, 216/1 Khaosan Rd, T 2822023, some a/c, good reputation, left luggage (฿5/day, ฿30/wk); **D-E** *Hello*, 63-65 Khaosan

Rd, T 2818579, some a/c, popular; **D-E** *Privacy Tourist House*, 69 Tanow Rd, T 2827028, popular, quiet, rec.

E *Apple 2*, 11 Phra Sumen Rd, T 2811219, old-time favourite; **E** *Arunothai (A.T.)*, 90/1, 5, 12 Khaosan Soi Rambutri, T 2826979, friendly owner; **E** *Bonny*, 132 Khaosan Rd, T 2819877, quiet, off main road; **E** *Chuanpis*, 86 Chakrapong Rd (nr intersection with Khaosan Rd, down small soi opposite Wat Chanasongkhram), popular, geared particularly to Israeli visitors, good food, average rooms, often full; **E** *Democratic*, 211/8 Rachdamnern Ave, T 2826035, F 2249149, set back, opposite the Democracy Monument, 4-storey concrete house with friendly management but small rooms and grubby stairwell; **E** *Dior*, 146-158 Khaosan Rd, T 2829142, small but clean rooms and bathrooms, quiet, as set back from road, 'family' atmosphere, rec; **E** *Emy*, 61 Chakrapong Soi Rambutri, T 2822737, friendly management; **E** *Home and Garden*, 16 Samphraya Rd (Samsen 3), T 2801475, away from main concentration of guesthouses, down quiet soi (quite difficult to find), good location for river taxi, rooms are small and basic but clean, well run and friendly, rec; **E** *Lek*, 90/9 Khaosan Soi Rambutri, T 2812775, popular; **E** *Mam's*, 119 Khaosan Rd, friendly, homely atmosphere, rec; **E** *Merry V*, 33-35 Phra Athit Soi Chana Songkram, T 2829267, some a/c, some rooms with balconies, lockers available; **E** *My House*, 37 Phra Athit Soi Chana Songkhram, T 2829263, post pick-up service, very popular; **E** *Nat*, 217 Khaosan Rd, brusque management but clean, larger than average rooms with fan, rec; **E** *P.S.*, 9 Phra Sumen Rd, T 2823932, spotlessly clean, rooms with no windows, but satellite TV and free tea and coffee, rec; **E** *Peachy*, 10 Phra Athit Rd, T 2816659, some a/c, clean rooms, pleasant restaurant area, rec; **E** *Rose Garden*, 28/6 Phra Athit Soi Trok Rongmai, T 2818366, friendly; **E** *Siam*, 76 Chakrapong Rd, T 2810930, rooms facing onto the street are noisy, small rooms but good clean bathrooms; **E** *Suneeporn*, 90/10 Khaosan Soi Rambutri, T 2826887, popular; **E** *Sweety*, 49 Thani Rd, clean, rec; **E-F** *Bangkok Youth Hostel*, 25/2 Phitsanulok Rd (off Samsen Rd), T 2820950, N of Khaosan Rd, away from the bustle, dorms available.

F *K.C.*, 60-64 Phra Sumen Rd Soi Khai Chae, T 2820618, friendly management, clean rooms, rec.

● **Sri Ayutthaya Road**

Sri Ayutthaya is emerging as an 'alternative' area for budget travellers. It is a central location with restaurants and foodstalls nearby, but does not suffer the over-crowding and sheer pandemonium of Khaosan Road.

D *Shanti Lodge*, 37 Sri Ayutthaya Rd, T 2812497, restaurant with extensive menu, very popular, rooms nicely done up, rec.

E *Backpackers Lodge*, 85 Sir Ayutthaya Rd, Soi 14, T 2823231, restaurant, rooms with fans, small patio, quiet and friendly, rec; **E** *Little Home*, 23/12 Sri Ayutthaya Rd, T 2821574, bit shabby, bigger garden and cheaper than *Backpackers*, but closer to main road; **E** *Paradise*, 57 Sri Ayutthaya Rd, T 2828673, some fans, small guesthouse, rooms with no outward-looking windows, friendly management; **E** *Sawatdee*, 71 Sri Ayutthaya Rd, T 2810757, Western menu, pokey rooms, popular with German travellers; **E** *Tavee*, 83 Sri Ayutthaya Rd, Soi 14, T 2801447, restaurant, fan, small garden, clean and pleasant, rec.

● **Others**

A+ *Central Plaza*, 1695 Phahonyothin Rd, T 5411234, F 5411087, a/c, restaurant, pool, out of town, close to w/e market, efficiently run, but inconveniently located.

A *Amari Airport*, 333 Chert Wudthakas Rd, T 5661020, F 5661941, a/c, restaurants, pool, connected to airport by foot-bridge; rooms look onto attractive gardens, useful hotel for transit passengers; **A** *Rama Gardens*, 9/9 Vibhavadi Rangsit Rd, Bangkaen (nr the airport), T 561002, F 5611025, a/c, restaurants, two attractive, large pools, out of town on road to airport, inconvenient for most, but spacious grounds with fitness centre, tennis, squash, golf, putting; **A** *Sunroute Bangkok*, 288 Rama IX Rd, T 2480011, F 2485990, a/c, restaurants, pool, part of a Japanese chain, markets itself as the 'route to satisfaction', located away from most sights and shopping; Dusit Riverside, over Sathorn Bridge in Thonburi (opening late 1992); **A-B** *Ramada Renaissance Bridgeview*, 3999 Rama III Rd, T 2923160, F 2923164, a/c, numerous restau-

Price guide		
	US$	**Baht**
♦♦♦♦	15+	375+
♦♦♦	5-15	125-375
♦♦	2-5	50-125
♦	under 2	under 50

rants, pools, tennis, squash, new 476 room high-rise overlooking Chao Phraya River, all facilities, poor location for sights, shopping and business.

● **Places to eat**

Bangkok has the largest and widest selection of restaurants in Thailand – everyone eats out, so the number of places is vast. Food is generally very good and cheap – this applies not just to Thai restaurants but also to places serving other Asian cuisines, and Western dishes. Roadside food is good value – many Thais eat on the street, businessmen and civil servants rubbing shoulders with factory workers and truck drivers. **NB**: most restaurants close between 2200 and 2230.

Thai: ◆◆◆◆*Bussaracum*, 35 Soi Phiphat off Convent Rd, T 2358915, changing menu, popular, rec; ◆◆◆*Ban Chiang*, 14 Srivdieng Rd, T 2367045, quite hard to find – ask for directions, old style Thai house, large menu of traditionally-prepared food; ◆◆◆*Ban Khun Phor*, 458/7-9 Siam Square Soi 8, T 2501252, good Thai food in stylish surroundings; ◆◆◆*Ban Krua*, 29/1 Saladaeng Soi 1, Silom Rd, simple decor, friendly atmosphere, a/c room or open-air garden, traditional Thai food; ◆◆◆*Banana Leaf*, Silom complex (basement floor), Silom Rd, T 3213124, excellent and very popular Thai restaurant with some unusual dishes, including *kai manaaw* (chicken in lime sauce), *nam tok muu* (spicy pork salad, Isan style) and fresh spring rolls 'Banana Leaf', booking recommended for lunch; 5 star *Dusit Thani Thai Restaurant*, 946 Rama IV Rd, beautiful surroundings – like an old Thai palace, exquisite Thai food, very expensive wines; ◆◆◆*Garden Restaurant*, 324/1 Phahonyothin Rd, open-air restaurant or the air-conditioned comfort of a wood panelled room, also serves Chinese, Japanese and International; ◆◆◆*Kaloang*, 2 Sri Ayutthaya Rd, T 2819228. Two dining areas, one on a pier, the other on a boat on the Chao Phraya River, attractive atmosphere, delicious food, rec.; ◆◆◆*Lemon Grass*, Sukhumvit Soi 24, T 2588637, Thai style house, rather dark interior, one step up from Cabbages and Condoms, rec; ◆◆◆*Moon Shadow*, 145 Gaysorn Rd, good seafood, choice of dining-rooms – a/c or open-air; ◆◆◆*Sarah Jane's*, 36/2 Soi Lang Suan, Ploenchit Rd, T 2526572, run by American lady, married to a Thai, best Thai salad in town and good duck, Isan food especially noteworthy, excellent value, rec; ◆◆◆*Seafood Market*, 388 Sukhumvit Rd (opposite Soi

Asoke), "if it swims we have it", choose your seafood from the 'supermarket' and then have it cooked to your own specifications before consuming the creatures either in the 'garden' or in the large, impersonal a/c dining room, very popular; ◆◆◆*Seven Seas*, Sukhumvit Soi 33, T 2597662, quirky 'nouvelle' Thai food, popular with young sophisticated and avant garde Thais; ◆◆◆*Side Walk*, 855/2 Silom Rd (opposite Central Dept Store), grilled specialities, also serves French, rec; 5 star [500฿+] *Spice Market*, Regent Hotel, 155 Rachdamri Rd, T 2516127, Westernized Thai, typical hotel decoration, arguably the citys best Thai food; ◆◆◆*Whole Earth*, 93/3 Ploenchit Soi Lang Suan, T 2525574, Thailand's best known vegetarian restaurant, live music, ask to sit at the back downstairs, or sit Thai-style upstairs; ◆◆◆◆*Ban Somrudee* 228/6-7 Siam Square Soi 2, T 2512085; ◆◆*Ban Bung*, 32/10 Mu 2 Intramara 45, Rachadapisek, well known garden restaurant of northern-style pavilions, row around the lake to build up an appetite; ◆◆*Ban Mai*, 121 Sukhumvit Soi 22, Sub-Soi 2, old Thai-style decorations in an attractive house with friendly atmosphere, good value; ◆◆*Cabbages and Condoms*, Sukhumvit Soi 12, Population Development Association (PDA) restaurant so all proceeds go to this charity, eat rice in the Condom Room, drink in the Vasectomy Room, good *tom yam kung* and honey-roast chicken, curries all rather similar, good value, rec; ◆◆*Isn't Classic*, 154 Silom Rd, excellent BBQ, king prawns and Isan specialities like spicy papaya salad (*somtam*); ◆◆*Princess Terrace*, Rama I Soi Kasemsan Nung (1), Thai and French food with BBQ specialities served in small restaurant with friendly service and open terrace down quiet lane, rec; ◆◆*Puang Kaew*, 108 Sukhumvit Soi 23. Large, unusual menu, also serves Chinese; ◆◆*Rung Pueng*, 37 Saladaeng, Soi 2, Silom Rd, traditional Thai food at reasonable prices; ◆◆*Sanuk Nuek*, 397/1 Sukhumvit Soi 55 (Soi Thonglor), small restaurant with unusual decorations, live folk music; ◆◆*September*, 120/1-2 Sukhumvit Soi 23, art nouveau setting, also serves Chinese and European, good value for money; ◆◆◆◆◆◆There are several excellent restaurants in *Silom Village*, a shopping mall, on Silom Rd [N side, opposite Pan Rd]. Huge range of food from hundreds of stalls, all cooked in front of you, rec; ◆◆◆◆*D'jit Pochana Oriental* (aka *Sala Rim Nom*), in Thonburi, directly opposite the *Oriental Hotel* (regular boat service from *Oriental* or *Royal Orchid Hotels*, free of charge), traditional Thai pavilion and excellent classic Thai cuisine; ♦♦♦–♦♦♦♦*Once Upon a Time*, 67 Soi Anumanrachaton, T 2338493, set in attractive traditional Thai house (between Silom and Surawong rds); ♦♦♦*Ban Thai*, Soi 32 or Ruen Thep, Silom Village, Silom Rd, with classical dancing and music; ♦♦♦*Tum Nak Thai*, 131 Rajdapisek Rd, 'largest' restaurant in the world, 3,000 seats, rather out of the way, classical dancing from 2000-2130; ♦♦*Suda*, 6-6/1 Sukhumvit Rd, Soi 14, rec; ♦♦*Wannakarm*, Sukhumvit Soi 23, T 2584241, well established, very Thai restaurant, grim decor, no English spoken, but rated food.

Foodstalls scattered across the city for a rice or noodle dish, where a meal will cost ฿15-30 instead of a minimum of ฿75 in the restaurants. For example, on the roads between Silom and Surawong Rd, or down Soi Somkid, next to Ploenchit Rd, or opposite on Soi Tonson.

Chinese: most Thai restaurants sell Chinese food, but there are also many dedicated Chinese establishments. **Siam Square** has a large number, particularly those specializing in shark's fin soup. For shark's fin try the *Scala Shark's Fin*, *Bangkok Shark's Fin*, and the *Penang Shark's Fin* all opposite the Scala Cinema, Siam Square Soi 1. ♦♦♦♦–♦♦♦*Kirin*, 226/1 Siam Square Soi 2, over 20 years old, traditional Chinese decor, good atmosphere; ♦♦♦*Art House*, 87 Sukhumvit Soi 55 (Soi Thonglor), country house with traditional Chinese furnishings, surrounded by gardens, particularly good seafood; ♦♦♦*Chinese Seafood Restaurant*, 33/1-5 16 Wall St Tower, Surawong Rd, Cantonese and Szechuan; ♦♦♦*Joo Long Lao*, 2/1 Sukhumvit Soi 2, spacious, with wide choice of dishes, rec; ♦♦♦*Lung Wah*, 848/13 Rama III Rd, large restaurant, with good reputation, serves shark's fin and other seafood, also serves Thai; ♦♦♦*Pata*, 26 Siam Square Soi 3; ♦♦♦*Shangarila*, 154/4-7 Silom Rd, bustling Shanghai restaurant with dim sum lunch; ♦♦*Tongkee*, 308-314 Sukhumvit Rd (opposite Soi 19), Kwangtung food, popular with Thais.

Other Asian cuisines: there are 4 or 5 **Indian** restaurants in a row on Sukhumvit Soi 11; ♦♦♦♦*Pho*, Soi Phetburi, off Phetburi Rd, just before central Chidlom Dept Store, best Vietnamese in town in modern trendy setting, advise non-smoking area; ♦♦♦♦*Rang Mahal*, *Rembrandt Hotel*, Sukhumvit Soi 18, T 2617100, best Indian food in town, very popular with the Indian community and spectacular views from the roof top position, so-

phisticated, elegant and...expensive; ♦♦♦*Akamon*, 233 Sukhumvit Soi 21, Japanese; ♦♦♦*Akbar*, 1/4 Sukhumvit Soi 3, Indian, Pakistani and Arabic; ♦♦♦*Bali*, 20/11 Ruamrudee Village, Soi Ruamrudee, Ploenchit Rd, only authentic Indonesian in Bangkok, friendly proprietress; ♦♦♦*China*, 231/3 Rachdamri Soi Sarasin, Bangkok's oldest Chinese restaurant, serving full range of Chinese cuisine; ♦♦♦*Himali Cha Cha*, 1229/11 Charoen Krung, good choice of Indian cuisine; ♦♦♦*Kobune*, 3rd Fl, Mahboonkhrong (MBK) Centre, Rama 1 Rd, Japanese, Sushi Bar or sunken tables, rec; ♦♦♦*Le Cam-Ly*, 2nd Fl, 1 Patpong Bldg, Surawong Rd, Vietnamese; ♦♦♦*Le Dalat*, Sukhumvit Soi 23, same management as Le Cam-Ly, reputed to serve the best Vietnamese food in Bangkok, arrive early or management may hassle; ♦♦♦*Mandalay*, 23/17 Ploenchit Soi Ruamrudee, authentic Burmese food, rec; ♦♦♦*Moghul Room*, 1/16 Sukhumvit Soi 11, wide choice of Indian and Muslim food; ♦♦♦*Mrs. Balbir's*, 155/18 Sukhumvit Soi 11, Indian; ♦♦♦*Otafuku*, 484 Siam Sq Soi 6, Henry Dunant Rd, Japanese, Sushi Bar or low tables; ♦♦*Ambassador Food Centre*, *Ambassador Hotel*, Sukhumvit Rd. A vast self-service, up-market hawkers' centre with a large selection of Asian foods at reasonable prices: Thai, Chinese, Japanese, Vietnamese etc, rec; ♦♦*Bangkok Brindawan*, 15 Sukhumvit Soi 35, South Indian, Sat lunch set-price buffet; ♦♦*Nawab*, 64/39 Soi Wat Suan Plu, Charoen Krung, North and South Indian dishes; ♦♦*New Korea*, 41/1 Soi Chuam Rewang, Sukhumvit Sois 15-19, excellent Korean food in small restaurant, rec; ♦♦♦*Pho*, Soi Phetburi, off Phetburi Rd, just before Central Chidlom Dept Store, best Vietnamese in town, in modern, trendy setting, non-smoking area advisable; ♦♦*Saigon-Rimsai*, 413/9 Sukhumvit Soi 55, Vietnamese and some Thai dishes, friendly atmosphere; ♦*Samrat*, 273-275 Chakraphet Rd, Pratuleck Lek, Indian and Pakistani food in restaurant down quiet lane off Chakraphet Rd, cheap and tasty, rec; ♦*Tamil Nadu*, 5/1 Silom Soi (Tambisa) 11, good, but limited menu.

International: ♦♦♦♦*Beccassine*, Sukhumvit, Soi Sawatdee, English and French home cooking, rec; ♦♦♦♦*Diva*, 49 Sukhumvit Soi 49, T 2587879, excellent French restaurant, with very good Italian dishes and crepe suzette which should not be missed, friendly service, attractive surroundings, good value, rec; ♦♦♦♦*Le Banyan*, 59 Sukhumvit Soi 8, T 2535556, excellent French food; ♦♦♦♦*La*

Grenouille, 220/4 Sukhumvit Soi 1, T 2539080, traditional French cuisine, French chef and manager, small restaurant makes booking essential, French wines and French atmosphere, rec; ◆◆◆◆*L'Hexagone*, 4 Sukhumvit Soi 55 (Soi Thonglor), French cuisine, in 'posh' surroundings; ◆◆◆◆*L'Opera*, 55 Sukhumvit Soi 39, T 2585606, Italian restaurant with Italian manager, conservatory, good food (excellent salted baked fish), professional service, lively atmosphere, popular, booking essential, rec; ◆◆◆◆*Neil's Tavern*, Soi Ruamrudee, T 2515644, best steak in town, popular with expats; ◆◆◆◆*Paesano*, 96/7 Soi Tonson (off Soi Langsuan), Ploenchit Rd, T 2522834, average Italian food, sometimes good, in friendly atmosphere, very popular with locals; ◆◆◆◆*Wit's Oyster Bar*, 20/10 Ruamrudee Village, T 2519455, Bangkok's first and only Oyster Bar, run by eccentric Thai, one of the few places where you can eat late, good salmon fishcakes, international cuisine; ◆◆◆*Bei Otto*, 1 Sukhumvit Soi 20, Thailand's best known German restaurant, large helpings; ◆◆◆*Bobby's Arms*, 2nd Fl, Car Park Bldg, Patpong 2 Rd, British pub food; ◆◆◆*Bourbon Street*, 29/4-6 Sukhumvit Soi 22 (behind Washington Theatre), Cajun specialities including gumbo, jambalaya and red fish, along with steaks and Mexican dishes, served in a/c restaurant with VDOs and central bar; ◆◆◆*Brussels Restaurant*, 23/4 Sukhumvit Soi 4, small and friendly, also serves Thai food; ◆◆◆*Chez Daniel Le Normand*, 1/9 Sukhumvit Soi 24, top class French restaurant; ◆◆◆*Classique Cuisine*, 122 Sukhumvit Soi 49, classic French cuisine; ◆◆◆*Den Hvide Svane*, Sukhumvit Soi 8, Scandinavian and Thai dishes, former are good, efficient and friendly service; ◆◆◆*Gino's*, 13 Sukhumvit Soi 15, Italian food in bright and airy surroundings, set lunch is good value; ◆◆◆*Gourmet Gallery*, 6/1 Soi Promsri 1 (between Sukhumvit Soi 39 and 40), interesting interior, with art work for sale, unusual menu of European and American food; ◆◆◆*Hard Rock Café*, 424/3-6 Siam Sq Soi 11, home-from-home for all burger-starved farangs, overpriced, videos, live music sometimes, and all the expected paraphernalia, a couple of Thai dishes have been included, large portions and good atmosphere. ◆◆◆*Haus Munchen*, Sukhumvit Soi 15, German food in quasi-Bavarian lodge, connoisseurs maintain cuisine is authentic enough; *La Brioche*, ground flr of Novotel Hotel, Siam Sq Soi 6, good range of French patisseries; ◆◆◆*Le Bordeaux*, 1/38 Sukhumvit Soi 39, range of

French dishes; ◆◆◆*Le Café Français*, 22 Sukhumvit Soi 24, French seafood; ◆◆◆*Le Café de Paris*, Patpong 2, traditional French food, rec; ◆◆◆*Le Metropolitain*, 135/6 Gaysorn Rd, family French food; ◆◆◆*Longhorn*, 120/9 Sukhumvit Soi 23, Cajun and Creole food; ◆◆◆*Restaurant Des Arts Nouveaux*, 127 Soi Charoensuk, Sukhumvit Soi 55, art nouveau interior, top class French cuisine; ◆◆◆*Ristorante Sorrento*, 66 North Sathorn Rd, excellent Italian food; ◆◆◆*Robertos 18*, 36 Sukhumvit, Soi 18, Italian; ◆◆◆*Senor Pico*, Rembrandt Hotel, 18 Sukhumvit Rd, Mexican, pseudo-Mexican decor, staff dressed Mexican style, large, rather uncosy restaurant, average cuisine; ◆◆◆*Stanley's French Restaurant*, 20/20-21 Ruamrudee Village, good French food, special Sunday brunch, closed Mondays; ◆◆◆*Sweet Basil*, 1 Silom Soi Srivieng (opposite Bangkok Christian College), Vietnamese; ◆◆◆*Tia Maria*, 14/18 Patpong Soi 1, best Mexican restaurant in Bangkok; ◆◆◆*Trattoria Da Roberto*, 37/9 Plaza Arcade, Patpong 2 Rd, authentic Italian setting; ◆◆*Caravan Coffee House*, Siam Sq Soi 5, large range of coffee or tea, food includes pizza, curry and some Thai food; ◆◆*Crazy Horse*, 5 Patpong 2 Rd, simple decor, but good French food, open until 0400; ◆◆*Harmonique*, 22 Charoen Krung, small elegant coffee shop with good music, fruit drinks and coffee.

Bakery: *Sweet Corner*, Siam Intercontinental Hotel, Rama I Rd, one of the best in Bangkok; *Jimmy*, 1270-2, near Oriental Lane, Charoen Krung, a/c, cakes and ice creams, very little else around here, so it's a good stopping place.

Afternoon tea: *The Authors Lounge*, Oriental Hotel; the *Bakery Shop*, Siam Intercontinental Hotel; *The Cup*, second floor of Peninsula Plaza, Rachdamri Rd; *The Regent Hotel* lobby (music accompaniment), Rachdamri Rd; the *Dusit Thani Hotel* library, Rama IV Rd.

Travellers' food available in the guesthouse/travellers' hotel areas (see above). *Hello* in Khaosan Rd has been recommended, the portions of food are a good size and they have a useful notice board for leaving messages. Nearly all the restaurants in Khaosan Rd show videos all afternoon and evening. If on a tight budget it is much more sensible to eat in Thai restaurants and stalls where it should be possible to have a good meal for ฿10-20.

● Fast Food

Bangkok now has a large number of Western

fast food outlets, such as *Pizza Hut*, *McDonalds*, *Kentucky Fried Chicken*, *Mister Donut*, *Dunkin' Donuts*, *Shakey's*, *Baskin Robbins* and *Burger King*. These are located in main shopping and tourist areas – Siam Square, Silom/Patpong roads, and Ploenchit Road.

● **Bars**

The greatest concentration of bars are in the two 'red light' districts of Bangkok – Patpong (between Silom and Surawong rds) and Soi Cowboy (Sukhumvit). Patpong was transformed from a street of 'tea houses' (brothels serving local clients) into a high-tech lane of go-go bars in 1969 when an American made a major investment. In fact there are two streets, side-by-side, Patpong 1 and Patpong 2. Patpong 1 is the larger and more active, with a host of stalls down the middle at night (see page 173); Patpong 2 supports cocktail bars and, appropriately, pharmacies and clinics for STDs, as well as a few go-go bars. The *Derby King* is one of the most popular with expats and serves what are reputed to be the best club sandwiches in Asia, if not the world. Soi Cowboy is named after the first bar here, the *Cowboy Bar*, established by a retired U.S. Airforce officer. Although some of the bars obviously also offer other forms of entertainment (something that quickly becomes blindingly obvious), there are, believe it or not, some excellent and very reasonably priced bars in these two areas. A small beer will cost ₿45-65, with good (if loud) music and perhaps videos thrown in for free. However, if opting for a bar with a 'show', be prepared to pay considerably more.

Warning Front men will assure customers that there is no entrance charge and a beer is only ₿60, but you can be certain that they will try to fleece you on the way out and can become aggressive if you refuse to pay. Even experienced Bangkok travellers find themselves in this predicament. Massages and more can also be obtained at many places in the Patpong and Soi Cowboy areas. **NB**: AIDS is a significant and growing problem in Thailand so it is strongly recommended that customers practice safe sex (see page 101).

A particularly civilized place to have a beer and watch the sun go down is on the verandah of the *Oriental Hotel*, by the banks of the Chao Phraya River. Expensive, but romantic. ✦✦✦*Basement Pub* (and restaurant), 946 Rama IV Rd. Live music. Also serves international food. Open 1800-2400. ✦✦✦*Black Scene*, 120/29-30 Sukhumvit Soi 23. Live jazz. Also serves Thai and French food. Open 1700-1300. *Bluebird*, Soi Cowboy, off Sukhumvit Soi 23. *Blue Sky*, Patpong 1 Rd, features a boxing ring in the centre of the bar where customers can drink and watch assorted types of contest; ✦✦✦*Bobby's Arms*, 2nd Floor, Car Park Bldg, Patpong 2 Rd. English pub and grill, with jazz on Sundays from 2000. Open 1100-0100. *Crazy Horse*, Patpong II Rd (go-go bar). *Gaslight*, Patpong 1 Rd, old time favourite among Patpong bars; *Gitanes*, 52 Soi Pasana 1, Sukhumvit Soi 63. Live music. Open 1800-0100. *King's Castle*, Patpong 1 Rd, another long-standing bar with core of regulars; *Royal Salute*, Patpong 2 Rd, cocktail bar where local farangs end their working days.

Hemingway Bar and Grill, 159/5-8 Sukhumvit Soi 55, live jazz and country music at the w/e, plus Thai and American food. Open 1800-0100. ✦✦*Old West Saloon*, 231/17 Rachdamri Soi Sarasin. Live country music, also serves international and Thai food. Open 1700-0100. ✦✦*Picasso Pub*, 1950-52 Ramkamhaeng Rd, Bangkapi. Live music, also serves Thai food. Open 1800-0300. ✦✦*Round Midnight*, 106/12 Soi Langsuan, live blues and jazz, some excellent bands play here, packed at weekends, good atmosphere and worth the trip. Also serves Thai and Italian food. Open 1700-0400. ✦✦*Trumpet Pub* (and restaurant), 7 Sukhumvit Soi 24. Live blues and jazz. Also serves Thai food. Open 1900-0200.

● **Airline offices**

For airport enquiries call, T 2860190. **Aeroflot**, Regent House, 183 Rachdamri Rd, T 2510617. **Air Canada**, 1053 Charoen Krung, T 2335900. **Air France**, Grd Flr, Charn Issara Tower, 942 Rama IV Rd, T 2339477. **Air India**, 16th Flr, Amarin Tower, 500 Ploenchit Rd, T 2569614. **Air Lanka**, Grd Flr, Charn Issara Tower, 942 Rama IV Rd, T 2369292. **Alitalia**, 8th Flr, Boonmitr Bldg, 138 Silom Rd, T 2334000. **American Airlines**, 518/5 Ploenchit Rd, T 2511393. **Bangkok Airways**, Queen Sirikit National Convention Centre, New Rajdapisek Rd, Klongtoey, T 2293434. **Bangladesh Biman**, Grd Flr, Chongkolnee Bldg, 56 Surawong Rd, T 2357643. **British Airways**, 2nd Flr, Charn Issara Tower, 942 Rama IV Rd, T 2360038. **Canadian Airlines**, 6th Flr, Maneeya Bldg, 518/5 Ploenchit Rd, T 2514521. **Cathay Pacific**, 5th Flr, Charn Issara Tower, 942 Rama IV Rd, T 2336105. **China Airlines**, 4th Flr, Peninsula Plaza, 153

Rachdamri Rd, T 2534241. **Continental Airlines**, C.P. Tower, 313 Silom Rd, T 2310113. **Delta Airlines**, 7th Flr, Patpong Bldg, Surawong Rd, T 2376838. **Egyptair**, C.P. Tower, 313 Silom Rd, T 2310503. **Finnair**, 6th Flr, Maneeya Bldg, 518 Ploenchit Rd, T 2515012. **Garuda**, 944/19 Rama IV Rd, T 2330981. **Gulf Air**, Grd Flr, Maneeya Bldg, 518 Ploenchit Rd, T 2547931. **Japan Airlines**, Wall Street Tower, 33 Surawong Rd, T 2332440. **KLM**, Patpong Bldg, 2 Surawong Rd, T 2355155. **Korean Air**, Grd Flr, Kong Bunma Bldg, (opp *Narai Hotel*), 699 Silom Rd, T 2340846. **Kuwait Airways**, 159 Rajdamri Rd, T 2515855. **Lufthansa**, Bank of America Bldg, 2/2 Witthayu Rd, T 2550370. **MAS**, 98-102 Surawong Rd, T 2364705. **Myanmar Airways**, Charn Issara Tower, 942 Rama IV Rd, T 2342985. **Pakistan International**, 52 Surawong Rd, T 2342961. **Philippine Airlines**, Chongkolnee Bldg, 56 Surawong Rd, T 2332350. **Qantas**, 11th Flr, Charn Issara Tower, 942 Rama IV Rd, T 2360102. **Royal Brunei**, 20th Flr, Charn Issara Tower, 942 Rama IV Rd, T 2340007. **Royal Nepal Airlines**, Sivadm Bldg, 1/4 Convent Rd, T 2333921. **Sabena**, CCT Bldg, 109 Surawong Rd, T 2332020. **SAS**, 412 Rama I Rd, T 2538333. **Saudi**, CCT Bldg, 109 Surawong Rd, T 2369395. **Singapore Airlines**, 12th Flr, Silom Centre, 2 Silom Rd, T 2360440. **Swissair**, 1 Silom Rd, T 2332935. **Thai**, 485 Silom Rd, T 2333810. **TWA**, 12th Flr, Charn Issara Tower, 942 Rama IV Rd, T 2337290. **Vietnam Airlines**, 584 Ploenchit Rd, T 2514242.

● **Banks & money changers**

There are countless exchange booths in all the tourist areas open 7 days a week, mostly 0800-1530, some from 0800-2100. Rates vary only marginally between banks, although if changing a large sum, it is worth shopping it around.

● **Embassies**

Australia, 37 Sathorn Tai Rd, T 2872680. **Brunei**, 154 Ekamai Soi 14, Sukhumvit 63, T 3916017, F 3815921. **Burma** (Myanmar), 132 Sathorn Nua Rd, T 2332237. **Canada**, 12th Flr, Boonmitr Bldg, 138 Silom Rd, T 2341561/8. **Czechoslovakia**, Robinson Bldg, 16th Flr, 99 Witthayu Rd, T 2556063. **Denmark**, 10 Sathorn Tai Soi Attakarnprasit, T 2132021. **Finland**, 16th Flr, Amarin Plaza, 500 Ploenchit Rd, T 2569306. **France**, 35 Customs House Lane, Charoen Krung, T 2340950. **Germany**, 9 Sathorn Tai Rd, T 2132331. **Indonesia**, 600-602 Phetburi Rd, T 2523135.

Greece, 79 Sukhumvit Soi 4, T 2542936, F 2542937. **Italy**, 399 Nang Linchi Rd, T 2872054. **Laos**, 193 Sathorn Tai Rd, T 2131203. **Malaysia**, 35 Sathorn Tai Rd, T 2861390. **Netherlands**, 106 Witthayu Rd, T 2547701. **New Zealand**, 93 Witthayu Rd, T 2518165. **Norway**, 1st Flr, Bank of America Bldg, Witthayu Rd, T 2530390. **Philippines**, 760 Sukhumvit Rd, T 2590139. **Singapore**, 129 Sathorn Tai Rd, T 2862111. **South Africa**, 6th Flr, Park Place, 231 Soi Sarasin, Rachdamri Rd, T 2538473. **Spain**, 93 Witthayu Rd, T 2526112. **Sweden**, 20th Flr, Pacific Place, 140 Sukhumvit Rd, T 2544954. **UK**, Wireless Rd, Bangkok 10500, T 2530191/9. **USA**, 95 Witthayu Rd, T 2525040. **Vietnam**, 83/1 Witthayu Rd, T 2517201.

● **Church Services**

Evangelical Church, Sukhumvit Soi 10 (0930 Sun service); the *International Church* (interdenominational), 67 Sukhumvit Soi 19 (0800 Sun service); *Baptist Church*, 2172/146 Phahonyothin Soi 36 (1800 Sun service); *Holy Redeemer*, 123/19 Wittayu Soi Ruam Rudee (Catholic, 5 services on Sun); *Christ Church*, 11 Convent Rd (Anglican – Episcopalian – Ecumenical) (3 Sun services at 0730, 1000 and 1800).

● **Entertainment**

Art Galleries: *The Artist's Gallery*, 60 Pan Rd, off Silom, selection of international works of art. *The Neilson Hays Library*, 195 Surawong Rd, has a changing programme of exhibitions.

Buddhism: the headquarters of the World Fellowship of Buddhists is at 33 Sukhumvit Rd (between Soi 1 and Soi 3). Meditation classes are held in English on Wed at 1700-2000; lectures on Buddhism are held on the first Wed of each month at 1800-2000.

Classical Music: at the Goethe Institute 18/1 Sathorn Tai Soi Attakarnprasit; check newspapers for programme.

Cinemas: most cinemas have daily showings at 1200, 1400, 1700, 1915 and 2115, with a 1300 matinee on weekends and holidays. Cinemas with English soundtracks include *Central Theatre 2*, T 5411065, *Lido*, T 2526729, *Pantip*, T 2512390, *Pata*, T 4230568, *Mackenna*, T 2517163, *Washington 1*, T 2582045, *Washington 2*, T 2582008, *Scala*, T 2512861, *Villa*, T 2589291. *The Alliance Française*, 29 Sathorn Tai Rd, T 2132122 shows French films. Remember to stand for the National Anthem,

TRADITIONAL THAI MASSAGE

While a little less arousing than the Patpong-style massage, the traditional Thai massage or *nuat boroan* is probably more relaxing, using methods similar to those of Shiatsu, reflexology and osteopathic manipulation. It aims to release blocked channels of energy and soothe tired muscles. A full massage should last 1-2 hrs and cost ฿150/hr. The thumbs are used to apply pressure on 'lines' of muscles, so both relaxing and invigorating the muscles. Headaches, ankle and knee pains, neck and back problems can all be alleviated through this ancient art. Centres of massage can be found in most Thai towns - wats and tourist offices are the best sources of information on where to go. In Bangkok, Wat Pho is the best known centre (see page 133).

which is played before every performance. Details of showings from English language newspapers.

Cultural centres: British Council, 428 Siam Square Soi 8, T 2526136, for films, books and other Anglocentric entertainment; Check in 'What's On' section of Sunday Bangkok Post for programme of events; **Alliance Française**, 29 Sathorn Tai Rd; **Goethe Institute**, 18/1 Sathorn Tai Soi Attakarnprasit; **Siam Society**, 131 Soi 21 (Asoke) Sukhumvit, T 2583494, open Tues-Sat. Promotes Thai culture and organises trips within (and beyond) Thailand.

Discos: *Dianas*, 3rd Flr, Oriental Plaza, Charoen Krung Soi 38; *Grand Palace*, 19th Flr, Rajapark Bldg, Sukhumvit Soi Asoke, 2100-0200.

Fortune Tellers: there are up to ten soothsayers in the *Montien Hotel* lobby, Surawong Rd, on a regular basis.

Health Club: *Phillip Wain International*, 8th Fl, Pacific Place, 140 Sukhumvit Rd, T 2542544. Open Mon-Sat 0700-2200.

Music (see also **Bars**, page 170, for more places with live music): *Brown Sugar*, 231/20 Sarasin Rd (opposite Lumpini Park). *Round Midnight*, 106/12 Soi Langsuan, jazz and blues bands from 2030-0400. *Blue Moon*,

145 Gaysorn Rd. 1830-0500 for country, rhythm, jazz and blues – particularly Fri and Sun for jazz.

Magic Land, 72 Phahonyothin Rd. Amusement park with ferris wheel, roller coaster, etc. Admission: ฿40 adults, ฿30 children. Open: 1000-1800 Mon-Sun. **Getting there**: near *Central Plaza Hotel* – ask for 'Daen Neramit'.

Safari World: 300 acre complex in Minburi, 9 km from the city centre, with animals and amusement park (T 5107295). **Getting there**: bus no 26 from the Victory Monument to Minburi where a minibus service runs to the park.

Siam Park City: water world, theme park, zoo, botanical gardens and fair all rolled into one, 101 Sukhapibarn 2 Rd, Bangkapi, T 5171032, 30 mins E of town, or 1 hr by bus 26 or 27 from Victory Monument. Admission: ฿200. Open: 1000-1800 Mon-Fri, 0900-1900 Sat-Sun.

Thai Cookery Course: the *Oriental Hotel* organises a 5 day course, with different areas of cuisine covered each day, 0900-1200. ฿2,500/class or ฿11,000 for 5 classes.

Thai Performing Arts: classical dancing and music is often performed at restaurants after a 'traditional' Thai meal has been served. Many tour companies or travel agents organize these 'cultural evenings'. *National Theatre*, Na Phrathat Rd, (T 2214885 for programme). Thai classical dramas, dancing and music on the last Friday of each month at 1730 and periodically on other days. *Thailand Cultural Centre*, Rachdaphisek Rd, Huai Khwang, T 2470028 for programme of events. *College of Dramatic Arts*, near National Theatre, T 2241391. *Baan Thai Restaurant*, 7 Sukhumvit Soi 32, T 2585403, 2100-2145. *Chao Phraya Restaurant*, Pinklao Bridge, Arun Amarin Rd, T 4742389; *Maneeya's Lotus Room*, Ploenchit Rd, T 2526312, 2015-2100; *Piman Restaurant*, 46 Sukhumvit Soi 49, T 2587866, 2045-2130; *Ruen Thep*, Silom Village Trade Centre, T 2339447, 2020-2120; *D'jit Pochana Coka Sala Rim Nam*, the *Oriental Hotel's* Thai restaurant, on the Thonburi side of the Chao Phraya River shuttle boat from the *Oriental*, Charoen Nakhon Rd, T 4376221; *Suwannahong Restaurant*, Sri Ayutthaya Rd, T 2454448, 2015-2115; *Tum-Nak-Thai Restaurant*, 131 Rachdaphisek Rd, T 2773828 2030-2130.

Thai Traditional Massage: see box.

● **Hospitals & medical services**
Bangkok Adventist Hospital, 430 Phitsanulok Rd, Dusit, T 2811422/2821100; *Bangkok Nursing Home*, 9 Convent Rd, T 2332610; *St. Louis Hospital*, 215 Sathorn Tai Rd, T 2120033. **Health Clinics**: *Dental Polyclinic*, New Phetburi Rd, T 3145070; *Dental Hospital*, 88/88 Sukhumvit 49, T 2605000, F 2605026, good, but expensive; *Clinic Banglamphu*, 187 Chakrapong Rd, T 2827479.

● **Immigration**
Sathorn Tai Soi Suanphlu, T 2873101.

● **Library**
National Library, Samsen Rd, close to Sri Ayutthaya Rd; *Neilson Hays Library*, 195 Surawong Rd, T 2331731, next door to British Club, in attractive old Thai house, English language books available but subscription fee needed.

● **Post & telecommunications**
Central GPO (*Praysani Klang* for taxi drivers): Charoen Krung, opposite the *Ramada Hotel*. Open 0800-2000 Mon-Fri and 0800-1300 weekend and holidays. The money and postal order service is open 0800-1700, Mon-Fri, 0800-1200 Sat. Closed on Sun and holidays. 24 hr telegram and telephone service (phone rates are reduced 2100-0700) and a packing service. **Post Office**: Tani Rd, closest for Khaosan Rd.

Area code: 662.

● **Shopping**
See also page 496. Most shops do not open until 1000-1100. Nancy Chandler's *Map of Bangkok* is the best shopping guide. Bangkok still stocks a wonderful range of goods, but do not expect to pick up a bargain – prices are high. Stallholders are out for all they can get – so bargain hard here. Most department stores are now fixed price. There is no real centre in Bangkok and as a result there are a number of major shopping areas:

1. Sukhumvit: Sukhumvit Road, and the sois to the N are lined with shops and stalls, especially around the *Ambassador* and *Landmark* hotels. Many tailors and made-to-measure shoe shops are to be found in this area.

2. Central: 2 areas close to each other centred on Rama I and Ploenchit roads. At the intersection of Phayathai and Rama I roads there is Siam Square (for teenage trendy Western clothing, bags, belts, jewellery, bookshops, some antique shops and American fast food chains) and the massive – and highly popular – Mah Boonkhrong Centre (MBK), with countless small shops and stalls and the Tokyu Department Store. *Peninsular Plaza*, between the *Hyatt Erawan* and *Regent* hotels is considered the smartest shopping plaza in Bangkok. For those looking for fashion clothes and accessories, this is probably the best area. A short distance to the E, centred on Ploenchit/Rachprarop roads, are more shopping arcades and large department stores, including the World Trade Centre, Thai Daimaru, Robinsons and Central Chidlom. N along Rachprasong Road, crossing over Khlong Saensap, at the intersection with Phetburi Road is the Pratunam market, good for fabrics and clothing.

3. Patpong/Silom – Patpong is more of a night market (opening at 2100), the streets are packed with stalls selling the usual array of stall goods which seem to stay the same from year to year (fake designer clothing, watches, bags etc.). **NB** Bargain hard. The E end of Silom has a scattering of similar stalls open during the day time, and *Robinsons Department Store*. Surawong Rd (at the other end of Patpong) has Thai silk, antiques and a few handicraft shops.

4. West Silom/Charoen Krung (New Rd): antiques, jewellery, silk, stamps, coins and bronzeware. Stalls set up here at 2100. A 15 min walk N along Charoen Krung (close to the *Orchid Sheraton Hotel*) is the River City Shopping Plaza, specializing in art and antiques.

5. Banglamphu/Khaosan Road: vast variety of low-priced goods, such as ready-made clothes, shoes, bags, jewellery and cassette tapes.

6. Lardphrao-Phahonyothin: some distance N of town, not far from the Weekend Market (see page 155) is the huge Central Plaza shopping complex. It houses a branch of the Central Department Store and has many boutiques and gift shops.

Department Stores: *Central* is the largest chain of department stores in Bangkok, with a range of Thai and imported goods at fixed prices; credit cards are accepted. Main shops on Silom Rd, Ploenchit Rd (Chidlom Branch), and in the Central Plaza, just N of the Northern bus terminal. Other department stores include *Thai Daimaru* on Rachdamri and Sukhumvit (opposite Soi 71), *Robinson's* on corner of Silom and Rama IV roads, Sukhumvit (near Soi 19) and Rachdamri roads, *Tokyu* in MBK Tower on Rama I Road, *Sogo* in the Amarin Plaza on Ploenchit Road, and *Zen*, World Trade Centre, corner of Rama I and Rajdamri roads.

Supermarkets: *Central Department Store*

(see above), *Robinsons* – open until midnight (see above), *Villa Supermarket*, between Sois 33 and 35, Sukhumvit Rd – for everything you are unable to find anywhere else, *Isetan*, (World Trade Centre), Rachdamri Rd.

Markets The markets in Bangkok are an excellent place to browse, take photographs and pick up bargains. The largest is the *Weekend Market* at Chatuchak Park (see page 155). The *Tewes Market*, near the National Library, is a photographers dream; a daily market, selling flowers and plants. *Pratunam Market* is spread over a large area around Rachprarop Rd, and is famous for clothing and fabric. *Nakhon Kasem* known as the *Thieves Market*, in the heart of Chinatown, houses a number of 'antique' shops selling brassware, old electric fans and woodcarvings (tough bargaining recommended, and don't expect everything to be genuine – see page 145). Close by are the wholesale stalls of *Sampeng Lane* (see page 145) and the *Pahurat Cloth Market* (see page 144). *Bangrak Market*, S of the General Post Office, near the river and the *Shangri-La Hotel*, sells exotic fruit, clothing and flowers. *Pak Khlong Market* is a wholesale market selling fresh produce, orchids and cut flowers and is situated near the Memorial Bridge (see page 144). *Phahonyothin Market* is Bangkok's newest, opposite the Northern bus terminal, and sells potted plants and orchids.

Specialist Shops Antiques: Chinese porcelain, old Thai paintings, Burmese tapestries, wooden figures, hilltribe art, Thai ceramics and Buddhist art. Be careful of fakes – go to the well-known shops only. Even they, however, have been known to sell fake Khmer sculpture which even the experts find difficult to tell apart from the real thing. Permission to take antiques out of the country must be obtained from the *Fine Arts Department* on Na Phrathat Rd, T 2214817. Shops will often arrange export licences for their customers. Buddha images may not be taken out of the country – although many are. A large number of the more expensive antique shops are concentrated in *River City*, a shopping complex next to the *Royal Orchid Sheraton Hotel* and an excellent place to start. More shops can be found in the Gaysorn area. *NeOld*, 149 Surawong Rd has a good selection of new and old objects, but it's pricey. *Peng Seng*, 942/1-3 Rama IV Rd, on the corner of Surawong Rd, has an excellent selection of antiques. *Thai House Antiques*, 720/6 Sukhumvit (near Soi 28). *L'Arcadia*, 12/2 Sukhumvit Soi 23, Burmese antiques, beds, ceramics, carvings, doors, expensive but good quality. *Jim Thompson's*, Surawang Rd, for a range of antiques, wooden artefacts, furnishings and carpets.

NB: some of the more unscrupulous shops have allegedly 'obtained' works of art from Burma and Cambodia; customers can choose their piece from a brochure, and then it is 'removed' from the appropriate monument. Whether it is real or fake, this is NOT to be encouraged. Report offending shops to the *Fine Arts Department* or the Tourist Police. For the serious, see Brown, Robin (1989) *Guide to buying antiques and arts and crafts in Thailand*, Times Books: Singapore.

Books: *Asia Books* has the most extensive stock of books in Bangkok. They can be found at 221 Sukhumvit Rd, between Sois 15 and 17; 2nd floor Peninsula Plaza, Rachdamri Rd; Ground floor and 3rd floors, Landmark Plaza. Patpong has two book stores – *The Bookseller* (81, Patpong I) and *Bangkok Christian Bookstore*. *Chulalongkorn University Book Centre*, in University compound (ask for '*suun nang suu Chula*') for academic, business and travel books. *DK (Duang Kamol) Books* in Siam Square (with other branches on Surawong Rd, near the corner of Patpong, and on the 3rd floor of the Mahboonkhrong Centre) is the best source of locally published books in English. *Elite Used Books*, 593/5 Sukhumvit Rd, near Villa Supermarket. Good range of secondhand books in several languages. *White Lotus*, 26 Soi Attakarnprasit, Sathorn Tai Rd, collectors books on Southeast Asia. *Kinokuniya*, 6th floor, Isetan Dept Store, World Trade Centre, Rachdamri Rd, selection of English language books. *Dokya*, 258/8-10 Soi Siam Sq 3. Books are also sold in the Central Department Stores, 1027 Ploenchit Rd, 1691 Pahonyothin Rd, and 306 Silom Rd.

Bronzeware: Thai or the less elaborate Western designs are available in Bangkok. There are a number of shops along Charoen Krung, N from Silom Road, e.g. Siam Bronze Factory at No.1250.

Celadon: distinctive ceramic ware, originally produced during the Sukhothai Period (from the late 13th century), and recently revived (see page 208). *Thai Celadon House*, 8/8 Rachdapisek Rd, Sukhumvit Rd (Soi 16), also sells seconds, or from *Narayana Phand*, Rach-

BUYING GEMS AND JEWELLERY

More people lose their money through gem and jewellery scams in Thailand than in any other way (60% of complaints to the TAT involve gem scams). **DO NOT** fall for any story about gem sales, special holidays, tax breaks – no matter how convincing. **NEVER** buy gems from people on the street (or beach) and try not to be taken to a shop by an intermediary. **ANY** unsolicited approach is likely to be a scam. The problem is perceived to be so serious that in some countries, Thai embassies are handing out warning leaflets with visas. For more background to Thailand and Burma's gems see page 372.

Rules of thumb to avoid being cheated

● Choose a specialist store in a relatively prestigious part of town (the TAT will informally recommend stores).

● Note that no stores are authorized by the TAT or by the Thai government; if they claim as much they are lying.

● It is advisable to buy from shops who are members of the Thai Gem and Jewellery Traders Association.

● Avoid touts.

● Never be rushed into a purchase.

● Do not believe stories about vast profits from re-selling gems at home. They are lies.

● Do not agree to have items mailed ("for safety").

● If buying a valuable gem, a certificate of identification is a good insurance policy. The Department of Mineral Resources (Rama VI Rd, T 2461694) and the Asian Institute of Gemological Sciences (484 Rachadapisek Rd, T 5132112) will both examine stones and give such certificates.

● Compare prices; competition is stiff among the reputable shops; be suspicious of 'bargain' prices.

● Ask for a receipt detailing the stone and recording the price.

For more information (and background reading on Thailand) the '*Buyer's Guide to Thai Gems and Jewellery*', by John Hoskin can be bought at Asia Books.

---

damri Rd.

Designer ware: clothing, watches, leather goods etc, all convincing imitations, can be bought for very reasonable prices from the many roadside stalls along Sukhumvit and Silom roads, Siam Square and in other tourist areas. Times Square, on Sukhumvit 14 has several 'designer clothing' shops.

Dolls: there is a Thai doll factory on Soi Ratchataphan (Soi Mo Leng) off Rachprarop Rd in Pratunam. The factory sells dolls to visitors and also has a display. Open: 0800-1700 Mon-Sat (T 2453008).

Furniture: between Soi 43 and Soi 45, Sukhumvit Rd, is an area where rattan furniture is sold. *Rattan House*, 795-797 Sukhumvit Rd (between Soi 43 and 45); *Corner 43*, 487/1-2 Sukhumvit Rd (between Soi 25-27).

Gold: this is considerably cheaper than in USA or Europe; there is a concentration of shops along Yaowaraj Road (Chinatown), mostly selling the yellow 'Asian' gold.

Handicrafts: the *State Handicraft Centre*, (*Narayana Phand*), 127 Rachdamri Rd, just N of Gaysorn, is a good place to view the range of goods made around the country. *House of Handicrafts*, *Regent Hotel*, 155 Rajdamri Rd; *House of Handicrafts*, 3rd floor, Amarin Plaza, 496-502 Ploenchit Rd.

Jewellery: Thailand has become the world's largest gem cutting centre and it is an excellent place to buy both gems and jewellery. The best buy of the native precious stones is the sapphire. Modern jewellery is well designed and of a high quality. Always insist on a certificate of authenticity and a receipt. *Ban Mo*, on

Pahurat Road, north of Memorial Bridge is the centre of the gem business although there are shops in all the tourist areas particularly on Silom Rd near the intersection with Surasak Rd, e.g. *Mr Ho's*, 987 Silom Rd, *Uthai Gems*, 28/7 Soi Ruam Rudi, off Ploenchit Rd, just east of Witthayu Rd are rec. For western designs, *Living Extra* and *Yves Joaillier* are to be found on the 3rd floor of the Charn Issara Tower, 942 Rama IV Rd. Dedicated gem buildings are now under construction, e.g. *Gems Tower* opposite Oriental Lane (completion due March 1993), while the Jewellery Trade Centre is under construction on the corner of Silom Rd and Surasak Rd, next door to the *Holiday Inn Crowne Plaza*. This is due to be finished August 1995 and will be an important gem centre and diamond house. (T 2373600 for information.)

Pottery: there are several pottery 'factories' on the LHS of the road on the way to the Rose Garden, near Samut Sakhon (see page 158).

Shoes: The *Siam Bootery* is a chain of shops for handmade footwear.

Silk: beware of 'bargains', as the silk may have been interwoven with rayon. It is best to stick to the well-known shops unless you know what you are doing. Silk varies greatly in quality. Generally, the heavier the weight the more expensive the fabric. There are a number of specialist silk shops at the top of Surawong Road (near Rama IV), including the famous *Jim Thompson's* (which is expensive, but has the best selection). Open: 0900-2100 Mon-Sun. For average quality, expect to pay between ฿300-600/metre. There are also a number of shops along the bottom half of Silom Road (towards Charoen Krung). *Home Made (HM) Thai Silk*, 45 Sukhumvit Soi 35 (silk made on premises), good quality matmii silk (see page 331). *Khompastr*, 52/10 Surawong Rd, near *Montien Hotel*, distinctive screen-printed fabric from Hua Hin.

Spectacles: glasses and contact lenses are a good buy in Bangkok and can be made-up in 24 hours. Opticians are to be found throughout the city.

Tailoring services: Bangkok's tailors are skilled at copying anything; either from fashion magazines or from a piece of your own clothing. Always request a fitting, ask to see a finished garment, ask for a price in writing and pay as small a deposit as possible. Tailors are concentrated along Silom, Sukhumvit and Ploenchit roads and Gaysorn Square. Indian tailors appear to offer the quickest service.

Macways, 392/13 Soi 5 Siam Square and *N and Y Boutique*, 11 Chartered Bank Lane (Oriental Avenue), near the *Oriental Hotel* (for ladies tailored clothes) have both been recommended.

Textiles: *Prayer Textile Gallery*, 197 Phayathai Rd, good range and excellent quality traditional and Laotian textiles.

● **Sports**

Facilities for sports such as badminton, squash or tennis are either available at the 4 to 5-star hotels or are listed in Bangkok's Yellow Pages.

Bowling: *P.S. Bowl*, 1191 Ramkamhaeng Rd, Huamark, 1030-0100 Mon-Thur, 1030-0200 Fri, Sat, Sun.

Diving: *Dive Master*, 110/63 Ladprao Soi 18, T 5121664, F 5124889, organise dive trips, NAVI and PADI courses and sell (or rent) diving equipment.

Golf: *Royal Thai Army*, 459 Ram Inthra Rd, Bangkhen, T 5211530, 25 mins from city centre; *Krungthep Sports Golf Club*, 516 Krungthep Kritha Rd, Huamark, Bangkapi, T 3740491, 30 mins from city centre; *Railway Training Centre Golf Club*, Vibhavadi Rangsit Rd, Bangkhen, T 2710130, 15 mins from city centre; *Royal Thai Airforce Golf Club*, Vibhavadi Rangsit Rd, Bangkhen, T 5236103; *UNICO Golf Course*, 47 Mu 7, Krungthep Kritha Rd, Phra Khanong, T 3779038, 20 mins from city centre. Each has an 18-hole course and clubs can usually be hired for about ฿250. Green fees are usually double at weekends. Phone to check availability. Other courses, rather further afield include: *Navatanee*, 22 Mu 1 Sukhaphiban 2 Rd, Bangkapi, T 3746127. *Rose Garden*, 4/8 Sukhumvit Soi 3, T 2953261, 45 mins from the city centre (green fees ฿300 weekdays, ฿600 weekends, club hire ฿200); *Royal Dusit*, Phitsanulok Rd, T 2814320 (green fees ฿320, weekdays ฿500 weekends, club hire ฿200). *Muang-Ake*, 34 Mu 7, Phahonyothin Rd, Amphoe Muang, Pathum Thani, T 5339336, 40 mins from city centre (green fees ฿300 weekdays, ฿600 weekends, club hire ฿300). Phone to check regulations for temporary membership. There are also a number of golf practice ranges off New Phetburi and Sukhumvit rds. Check the Yellow Pages for details.

Horse racing: at the *Royal Turf Club* and *Royal Sports Club* at the weekends, each card usually consists of 10 races. Check newspapers for details.

TOUR COMPANIES SPECIALIZING IN INDOCHINA AND BURMA

Bangkok is the world's centre for tour companies specializing in Indochina and Burma. Many of the cheaper outfits serving the backpacking market are concentrated in the Khaosan Rd area (Banglamphu); these will arrange independent visas as well as tours. The more expensive companies will usually only book tours (visa included). The cost of visas as of 1994 was approximately: ฿1,300-1,500 Vietnam (1 month, 5-7 days to arrange); ฿2,300-2,500 Laos (1 month, 5 days to arrange); ฿1,200-1,300 Cambodia (1 month, 2 days to arrange); ฿500-600 (2 weeks, 2 days to arrange) Burma.

Kite flying: kites are sold at Sanaam Luang for ฿15-20 on Sundays and public holidays during the 'season' (**see page 138**).

Spectator sports: Sanaam Luang, near the Grand Palace, is a good place to sample traditional Thai sports. From late Feb to the middle of Apr there is a traditional Thai Sports Fair held here. It is possible to watch **kite-fighting**, and **takraw** (the only Thai ball game, a takraw ball is made of rattan, 5"-6" in diameter. Players hit the ball over a net to an opposing team, using their feet, head, knees and elbows), **Thai chess**, **krabi** and **krabong** (a swordfighting contest).

Swimming: *NTT Sports Club*, 612/26 Soi Lao Lada, Phra Pinklao Bridge Rd. Large pool open to public with sports centre, just north of Sanaam Luang, on the river (฿100).

Tennis: courts in many hotels. Public courts available at *Central Tennis Club*, Sathorn Tai Soi Attakarnprasit, T 2867202, ฿50-90/hr.

Thai boxing: is both a sport and a means of self-defence and was first developed during the Ayutthaya Period, 1350-1767. It differs from Western boxing in that contestants are allowed to use almost any part of their body. Traditional music is played during bouts (see box, page 108). There are two boxing stadiums in Bangkok – Lumpini (T 2514303) and Rachdamnern Stadium (T 2814205). At Lumpini, boxing nights are Tue, Fri and Sat, ฿258 for a ringside seat; at Rachdamnern Stadium, Mon, Wed, Thur and Sun at 1800 (T 2814205).

● **Tour companies & travel agents**
Travel agents abound in the tourist and hotel areas of the city – Khaosan Rd/Banglamphu, Sukhumvit, Soi Ngam Duphli, and Silom (several down Pan Rd, a soi opposite Silom Village). All major hotels will have their own in-house agent. Most will book airline, bus and train tickets, arrange tours, and book hotel rooms.

Because there are so many to choose from, it is worth shopping around for the best deal. For those wishing to travel to Vietnam, Laos, Cambodia and Burma, specialist agents are recommended as they are usually able to arrange visas – for a fee. These agents are marked (I and B) in the listing below. *Alternative Tour*, 14/1 Soi Rajatapan, Rajaprarop Rd, T 2452963, F 2467020, offer excellent 'alternative' tours of the country, enabling visitors to see the 'real' Thailand, not just tourist sights; *Asian Holiday Tour*, 294/8 Phayathai Rd, T 2155749; *Asian Lines Travel* (I and B), 755 Silom Rd, T 2331510, F 2334885; *Banglamphu Tour Service* (I and B), 17 Khaosan Rd, T 2813122, F 2803642; *Dee Jai Tours*, 2nd flr, 491/29 Silom Plaza Bldg, Silom Rd, T 2341685, F 2374231; *Diethelm Travel* (I and B), Kian Gwan Bldg II, 140/1, Witthayu Rd, T 2559150, F 2560248; *Dior Tours* (I and B), 146-158 Khaosan Rd, T 2829142; *East-West* (I and B), 46/1 Sukhumvit Soi Nana Nua, T 2530681; *Exotissimo* (I and B), 21/17 Sukhumvit Soi 4, T 2535240, F 2547683 and 755 Silom Rd, T 2359196, F 2834885; *Fortune Tours*, 9 Captain Bush Lane, Charoen Krung 30, T 2371050; *Guest House and Tour* (I and B), 46/1 Khaosan Rd, T 2823849, F 2812348; *MK Ways* (I and B), 18/4 Sathorn Tai Soi 3 (Saint Louis), T 2122532, F 2545583; *Pawana Tour and Travel* (I and B), 72/2 Khaosan Rd, T 2678018, F 2800370; *Siam Wings*, 173/1-3 Surawong Rd, T 2534757, F 2366808; *Skyline Travel Service* (I and B), 491/39-40 Silom Plaza (2nd Flr), Silom Rd, T 2331864, F 2366585; *Thai Travel Service*, 119/4 Surawong Rd, T 2349360; *Top Thailand Tour* (I and B), 61 Khaosan Rd, T 2802251, F 2823337; *Tour East* (I and B), Rajapark Bldg, 10th flr, 163 Asoke Rd, T 2593160, F 2583236; *Transindo* (I and B), Thasos Bldg (9th Flr), 1675 Chan Rd, T 2873241, F 2873246; *Vista Travel* (I and B), 244/4

Khaosan Rd, T 2800348; *Western Union*, branch in the foyer of *Atlanta Hotel*, 78 Sukhumvit Soi 2, T 2552151, good all round service.

● **Tourist offices**

Tourist Authority of Thailand (TAT), 372 Bamrung Muang Rd, T 2260075. Open: Mon-Sun, 0830-1630. There is also a counter at Don Muang airport (in the Arrivals Hall, T 5238972) and offices at 1 Napralarn Rd, T 2260056, and the Chatuchak Weekend Market (Kampaeng Phet Rd). The main office is very helpful and provides a great deal of information for independent travellers – certainly worth a visit.

● **Tourist Police**

509 Worachak Rd, T 2216206-10.

● **Transport**

Local Bus: this is the cheapest way to get around town. A bus map marking the routes is indispensable. The *Bangkok Thailand* map and *Latest tours guide to Bangkok and Thailand* both cost ฿35; available from most bookshops as well as many hotel and travel agents/ tour companies. Major bus stops also have maps of routes and instructions in English displayed. Standard non-a/c buses cost ฿2.50-6. A/c buses cost ฿6-16 depending on distance. Travelling all the way from Silom Road to the airport by a/c bus, for example, costs ฿14; most inner city journeys cost ฿6.

Car hire: approximate cost, ฿1000-1200/day, ฿6,000-8,000/week; Hertz and Avis charge more than the local firms, but have better insurance cover. **Not** recommended for use in Bangkok. **Avis**, 2/12 Witthayu Rd, T 2555300. **Central Car Rent**, 115/5 Soi Ton-Son, Ploenchit Rd, T 2512778. **Dollar Car Rent**, 272 Si Phraya Rd, T 2330848. **Grand Car Rent**, 233-5 Asoke-Din Daeng Rd, T 2482991. **Hertz**, 420 Sukhumvit Soi 71, T 3900341. **Highway Car Rent**, 1018/5 Rama IV Rd, T 2357746. **Inter Car Rent**, 45 Sukhumvit Rd, T 2529223. **Silver International**, 102 Esso Gas station, 22 Sukhumvit Rd, T 2596867. **SMT Rent-a-Car**, 931/11 Rama I Rd, T 2168020, F 2168039.

Express boats: travel between Nonthaburi in the N and Wat Rajsingkorn (near Krungthep bridge) in the S. Fares are calculated by zone and range from ฿6-14. At peak hours boats leave every 10 mins, off-peak about 15-25 mins (see map, page 147 for piers, and page 156). The journey from one end of the route to the other takes 75 mins. Note that boats

---

BANGKOK'S PUBLIC TRANSPORT	
taxis	45,000
tuk tuks	7,405
motorcycle taxis	120,000
llegal taxis	6,000

flying red or green pennants do not stop at all piers (they also exact a ฿1 express surcharge). Also, boats will only stop if passengers wish to board or alight, so make your destination known.

Ferries: small ferries take passengers across the Chao Phraya River, ฿1 (see map on page 147 for piers).

Khlong or long-tailed boats: can be rented for ฿150-200/hr, or more (**see page 151**.)

Motorcycle taxi: a relatively new innovation in Bangkok (and now present in other towns in Thailand) they are the fastest, and most terrifying, way to get from A to B. Riders wear numbered vests and tend to congregate in particular areas; agree a fare, hop on the back, and hope for the best. Their 'devil may care' attitude has made them bitter enemies of many other road users. Expect to pay ฿10-20.

Taxi: most taxis are metered (they must have a/c to register). There are a number of unmarked, unofficial taxis which are to be found around the tourist sites. Fares start at ฿35 and it should cost ฿40-100 for most trips in the city. Sometimes taxis refuse to use the meter – insist they do so, otherwise they'll rip you off.

Tuk-tuk: the formerly ubiquitous motorized saamlor is rapidly becoming a piece of history in Bangkok, although they can still always be found near tourist sites. Best for short journeys: they are uncomfortable and, being open to the elements, you are likely to be asphyxiated by car fumes. Bargaining is essential and the fare must be negotiated before boarding, most journeys cost at least ฿40. Both tuk-tuk and taxi drivers may try to take you to restaurants or shops – do not be persuaded; they are often mediocre places charging high prices.

Long distance Bangkok lies at the heart of Thailand's transport network. Virtually all trains and buses end up here and it is possible to reach anywhere in the country from the capital.

Bangkok is also a regional transport hub, and there are flights to most international destinations. For international transportation, see page 492.

Air: *Don Muang Airport* is 25 km N of the city. Regular connections on Thai to many of the provincial capitals (see route map, page 502). For airport details see page 493. There are a number of Thai offices in Bangkok, Head Office for domestic flights is 89 Vibhavadi Rangsit Rd, T 5130121, but this is inconveniently located north of town. Two more central offices are at 6 Lan Luang Rd and 485 Silom Rd. Tickets can also be bought at most travel agents. **Bangkok Airways** flies to Koh Samui, Hua Hin, Phuket and Mae Hong Son.

Train: Bangkok has 2 main railway stations. The primary station, catering for most destinations, is Hualamphong, Rama IV Rd, T 2237010/2237020; condensed railway timetables in English can be picked up from the information counter in the main concourse. Trains to Nakhon Pathom and Kanchanaburi leave from the Bangkok Noi or Thonburi station on the other side of the Chao Phraya River. Sample destinations and fares: **Chiang Mai** (751 km) ฿537-121. **Ayutthaya** (71 km) ฿15-60. **Khon Kaen** (450 km) ฿77-333. **Kanchanaburi** (133 km) ฿28-111. **Phetburi** (167 km) ฿34-138. **Hat Yai** (945 km) ฿149-664. **See page 504** for route map and page 503 for more information on Thailand's railways.

Road Bus: there are 3 bus stations in Bangkok.

The **Northern bus terminal** or *Mor Chit*, Phahonyothin Rd, T 2794484-7, serves all destinations in the N and NE. There are two **Southern bus terminals**. A/c buses leave from the terminals on Charansanitwong Rd (T 4351199) near the Thonburi (Bangkok Noi) railway station. Non-a/c buses leave from a new terminal on Phra Pinklao Rd (T 4345557) near the intersection with route 338. Both terminals serve destinations in the W as well as the S. The **Eastern bus terminal**, Sukhumvit Rd (Soi Ekamai), between Soi 40 and Soi 42, T 3912504 serves Pattaya and other destinations in the Eastern region. Buses leave for most major destinations throughout the day, and often well into the night. There are overnight buses on the longer routes – Chiang Mai, Hat Yai, Chiang Rai, Phuket, Ubon Ratchathani. Even the smallest provincial towns such as Mahasarakham have deluxe a/c buses connecting them with Bangkok. Note that in addition to the government-operated buses there are many private companies which run 'tour' buses to most of the major tourist destinations. Tickets bought through travel agents will normally be for these private tour buses, which leave from offices all over the city. Shop around as prices may vary. Note that although fares are usually slightly higher, passengers may be picked-up from their hotel/guesthouse therefore saving on the ride (and inconvenience) of getting out to the bus terminal, e.g. private overnight buses to Chiang Mai leave every evening at 1800 from Khaosan Rd (฿50-220).

THE CENTRAL PLAINS

CONTENTS

MAPS

The Central Plains region encompasses the fertile and productive valley of the Chao Phraya River where much of Thailand's rice is grown. Scenically, the area is rather monotonous. The valley is too wide (200 km in the south, 60 km in the north) and the gradient too shallow to be noticeable. Historically and economically though, the Central Plains has been of crucial significance. The region has, in effect, supported the Thai state, producing the rice surplus that provided much of the country's exports until the 1950s.

85 km N of Bangkok is the former capital of Siam, Ayutthaya, resplendent with ruined wats. Further N still is the ancient Khmer city of Lopburi, while to the W of Ayutthaya is the small, but attractive, town of Suphanburi. Continuing N either on route 32 from Ayutthaya or route 311 from Lopburi, the road reaches the large city of Nakhon Sawan, marking the division between the Central Plains region and the Lower North.

At the edges of the flood plain, the land becomes more upland in character and is too dry to cultivate wet rice. It is planted instead with dry land crops such as maize and cassava. Beyond these marginal uplands are mountains: to the E, the Phetchabun range of hills, and to the W the Tenasserim range. The latter were heavily forested until relatively recently, and are still inhabited by hilltribes. Today, the forested area has been much reduced. Logging companies, often linked to the Thai Army, have responded to the lack of trees in Thailand by turning their attention to Burma, transporting timber across the border through such towns as Mae Sot.

But the key to Thailand's wealth before World War II was the flood plain of the Chao Phraya. The Chao Phraya River proper begins at the town of Nakhon Sawan, 240 km N of Bangkok where the Ping, Wang, Nan and Yom rivers all finally converge. Nakhon Sawan is often regarded as the dividing point between the Upper and Lower Central Plains.

The history of Thailand, for over 700 years, has been focused on the Central Region. It contains the ruins of the 2 former capitals of Siam – Sukhothai and Ayutthaya – as well as the ruins of the less well known city of Si Satchanalai. Thai cultural traditions are dominated by those of the Central Plains. Any visitors wishing to immerse themselves in Thailand's past should spend some time travelling up through the Central region, rather than rushing through, straight to the North.

Although Bangkok is treated in this book, and by the Thai authorities, as a separate region, it is geographically part of the Central Plains. The logic of the city's location was the same as that for the earlier capitals of Ayutthaya and

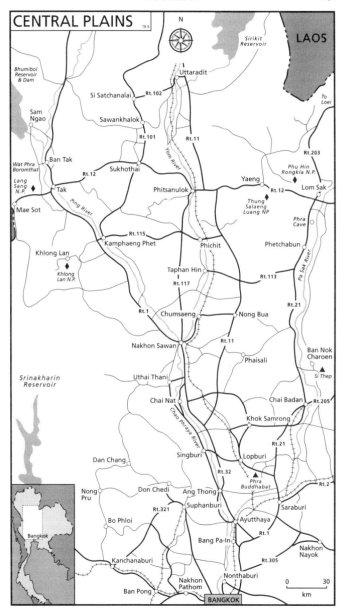

CENTRAL PLAINS

	Bangkok	Ayutthaya	Ang Thong	Nakhon Sawan	Kamphaeng Phet	Tak	Lampang	Lamphun	Chiang Mai	Mae Hong Son	Phayao	Chiang Rai	Nan	Phrae	Uttaradit	Sukhothai	Phitsanulok
Ayutthaya	76																
Ang Thong	105	31															
Nakhon Sawan	240	172	141														
Kamphaeng Phet	358	289	258	117													
Tak	426	357	326	185	68												
Lampang	599	531	500	359	241	174											
Lamphun	670	602	571	428	316	244	71										
Chiang Mai	696	623	592	449	337	265	92	21									
Mae Hong Son	924	856	825	683	569	480	412	342	349								
Phayao	691	620	589	448	382	304	131	201	222	543							
Chiang Rai	785	714	683	542	477	398	225	295	182	634	94						
Nan	668	597	566	425	359	362	227	297	318	639	176	270					
Phrae	551	479	448	307	241	244	109	180	201	521	141	235	118				
Uttaradit	491	419	388	247	177	179	140	210	231	552	214	308	191	74			
Sukhothai	427	358	327	188	77	79	207	277	296	578	337	400	282	165	100		
Phitsanulok	377	301	270	129	103	138	244	312	333	637	319	413	295	178	118	59	
Lopburi	153	96	67	130	247	315	489	558	579	814	578	672	554	437	377	316	259

North and Central Thailand, distances between provincial capitals (Km)

Sukhothai – at the centre of rice production and trade. And although rice may have been eclipsed as the kingdom's principal export, the Central Plains, with Bangkok now as its economic hub, still dominates the country.

AYUTTHAYA

Ayutthaya was founded in 1350 by a Prince of Uthong on the site of an ancient Indianized settlement. It is said that the Prince and his court were forced to leave Uthong following an outbreak of cholera, and after a brief interlude at the nearby Wat Panancherng, founded the city of Ayutthaya. The Royal Chronicles of Ayutthaya record: "In 712, a Year of the Tiger, second of the decade, on Friday, the sixth day of the waxing moon of the fifth month, at three *nalika* and nine *bat* after the break of dawn, the capital city of Ayutthaya was first established (i.e. Friday 4th March, 1351, at about 0900)". Another account reports that it was not until the surrounding marsh was drained that the town was freed from epidemics and could prosper.

History

Ayutthaya's name derives from 'Ayodhya', a sacred town in the Indian epic, the Ramayana. It became one of the most prosperous kingdoms in the Southeast Asian region and by 1378 the King of Sukhothai had been forced to swear his allegiance and submit to the suzerainty of Ayutthaya. Ultimately stretched from Angkor (Cambodia) in the E, to Pegu (Burma) in the W. In 1500 it was reported that the kingdom was exporting 30 junk loads (10,000 tonnes) of rice to Malacca each year. Ayutthaya was also an important source of animal skins, ivory, resins and other forest products.

The city is situated on an island at the confluence of 3 rivers – the Chao Phraya, Pa Sak and Lopburi. Its strong defensive position proved a distinct advantage as Ayutthaya was invaded by the Burmese alone on no less than 24 occasions. Given that the Ayutthayan Period lasted for over 400 years from 1350 to 1767, the town exudes history. One of Ayutthaya's most famous kings was Trailokant (1448-1488), a model of the benevolent monarch. He is best known for his love of justice and his administrative and legislative reforms. This may seem surprising in view of some of the less than enlightened legal practices employed later in the Ayutthayan Period. A plaintiff and defendant might, for example, have to plunge their hands into molten tin, or their heads into water, to see which party was the guilty one.

A succession struggle in the mid-16th century heralded the beginning of 20 years of intermittent warfare with the Burmese, who managed to seize and occupy Ayutthaya. This led to the emergence of another Thai hero, King Naresuan (1590-1605), who recaptured the city and led his country back to independence. Under King Narai (1656-1688), Ayutthaya became a rich, cosmopolitan trading post. Merchants came to the city from Portugal, Spain, Holland, China, Arabia, Persia, Malaya, India and Japan. In its heyday, Ayutthaya was said to have 40 different nationalities living in and around the city walls, and in the 16th century it supported a population larger than London at that time.

The city was strongly fortified, with ramparts 20m high and 5m thick, and was protected on all sides by waterways: rivers on 3 sides, and a linking canal on the fourth. Accounts by foreign visitors clearly record their awe at the size and magnificence of the city which, with its temples (over 400 – many gilded or decorated in mosaic) and canals was an Oriental Venice. The cosmopolitan atmosphere was evident on the waterways where royal barges rubbed shoulders with Chinese junks, Arab dhows and ocean-going schooners. Jean de Lacombe, a French visitor of the 17th century wrote of the house of Juric that "the richness of its materials, transcend every other building of the World, renders it a Dwelling worthy of an Emperor of the whole World". While Glanius, in 1682, described the city as being so gilded that in the sunshine the light reflected from the spires "disturbed the eyes". Visitors found endless sources of amusement in the city. There were elephant jousts, elephant and tiger fights, Thai boxing (*muay Thai*), masked plays, and puppet theatre. It was said that the King of Ayutthaya was so wealthy that even the elephants were fed from vessels of gold.

One European became particularly influential: King Narai's Greek foreign affairs officer (and later Prime Minister), Constantine Phaulcon. It was at this time the word 'farang' – to describe any white foreigner – entered the Thai vocabulary, derived from 'ferenghi', the Indian for 'French'. In 1688, Narai was taken ill and at the same time, the French – who Phaulcon had been encouraging – became a serious threat, gaining control of a fortress in Bangkok. An anti-French lobby arrested the by now very unpopular Phaulcon and had him executed for suspected designs on the throne. The French troops were expelled and for the next century Europeans were kept at arms length. It was not until the 19th century that they regained influence in the Thai court.

In the mid-18th century, the kingdom was again invaded by the Burmese, reputedly for the 24th time. In 1767 they were finally successful in vanquishing the defenders. The city was sacked, its defences destroyed and, unable to consolidate their position, the Burmese left for home, taking with them large numbers of prisoners and leaving the city in ruins. The population was reduced from one million to 10,000 (many inhabitants were marched to Burma). Ayutthaya never recovered from this final attack, and the magnificent temples were left to deteriorate.

The modern town of Ayutthaya is concentrated in the E quarter of the old walled city, and beyond the walls to the E. Much of the rest of the old city is green and open, interspersed with abandoned wats and new government buildings.

NB: Ayutthaya is one of the most popular day tours from Bangkok (see page 158) but

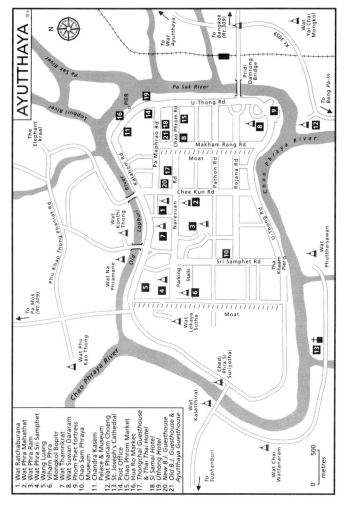

AYUTTHAYA

1. Wat Ratchaburana
2. Wat Phra Mahathat
3. Wat Phra Ram
4. Wat Phra Sri Samphet
5. Wang Luang
6. Viharn Phra Mongkol Bopitr
7. Wat Thammikrat
8. Wat Suwan Dararam
9. Phom Phet Fortress
10. Chao Sam Phraya Museum
11. Chandra Kasem Palace & Museum
12. Wat Phanam Choeng
13. St. Joseph's Cathedral
14. Post Office
15. Chao Phrom Market
16. Hua Ro Market
17. Thongchai Guesthouse
18. Si Samai Hotel
19. U-thong Hotel
20. New B.J. Guesthouse
21. Old B.J. Guesthouse & Ayutthaya Guesthouse

for those with an imagination and an interest in ruins, there is more than enough to occupy a whole day. The day tour allows about 2 hrs; a frustratingly short time for a superficial glance at this ancient capital. Ignore tour operators who maintain there is no accommodation here – it is perfectly adequate.

The sheer size of the site means that the considerable numbers of tourists are easily dispersed among the ruins, leaving the visitor to wander in complete tranquility along shady brick-paved walkways, among chedis built of a mellow red brick, which stand amongst trees reminiscent of the olive and cork trees of Southern France.

Away from the vendors stalls, the quietness comes as a stark contrast to the high-pressure bustle of Bangkok.

Places of interest

The easiest way to visit the central ruins is by saamlor; the area is too large to walk around comfortably. The route below takes in the most important wats. Ayutthaya's other fine ruins are described in the second half of this section. For Ayutthayan style, see page 96.

Wat Ratchaburana was built by King Boromraja II in 1424 on the cremation site of his two brothers (Princes Ai and Yo) who were killed while contesting the throne. The Khmer-style prang (which has been partially restored) still stands amidst the ruins of the wat. Remains of figures supporting the structure surround the prang along with some stucco work, garuda figures, and poorly restored standing Buddha images in the niches. Half-way up the prang, steep stairs lead downwards into the bowels of the structure where disappointing murals can just be discerned in the dim light. Some of the most important treasures yet found in Ayutthaya were discovered here when the site was excavated in 1958: bronze Buddha images, precious stones and golden royal regalia belonging, it is assumed, to the 2 brothers. Much of the viharn to the E

of the prang remains intact, giving an idea of how the compound must have looked. Scattered remains of countless Buddha images litter the grounds. Admission: ฿20.

Wat Phra Mahathat lies across the road from Wat Ratchaburana, on the opposite corner of Chee Kun and Naresuan roads. It was founded in 1384, making it one of the earliest prangs in Ayutthaya, and was the largest of all Ayutthaya's temples, built to house holy relics of the Buddha (hence its name). It is said that King Boromraja I (1370-1388) was meditating one dawn when he saw a glow emanating from the earth; he took this to mean that a relic of the Buddha lay under the soil and ordered a wat to be founded. Only the large base remains of the original Khmer-style prang, which was an impressive 50m high, built of laterite and brick. When the Fine Arts Department excavated the site in 1956 they found a number of gold Buddha images as well as relics of the Buddha inside a gold casket (now exhibited in the National Museum, Bangkok). The prang is surrounded by walls, which are in turn surrounded by smaller prangs and chedis, some of which are rather precariously supported. Like Wat Ratchaburana, remnants of Buddha torsos and heads are scattered in the grounds. Admission: ฿20.

Travelling W on Naresuan Road, to the S is another of the older wats, **Wat Phra Ram**, begun in 1369 by King Ramesuan (1369-1370), the son of Ayutthaya's founder. The entrance to the compound is through tall archways, designed to be high enough for elephants to pass under. The slender prang has been partially restored, but there are still some original stucco nagas and garudas, as well as standing Buddha images in the niches.

Wat Phra Sri Samphet lies within the extensive grounds of Wang Luang (the Royal Palace) and was the largest and most beautiful wat in Ayutthaya –

the equivalent of Wat Phra Kaeo in Bangkok. It was built in 1491, and subsequently extended during the reigns of several kings. The wat was only used on royal religious occasions and unlike most wats it had no quarters for monks. Three – highly regarded – restored Ceylonese-style chedis dominate the compound. They contain the ashes of King Trailokant (1448-1488) and his 2 sons (who were also kings of Ayutthaya). There are no prangs here; the 3 central chedis are surrounded by alternate smaller chedis and viharns. Remains of walls and leaning pillars give an impression of the vastness of the wat. In 1500 it is alleged that a 16m standing Buddha was cast by King Ramathipodi II (1491-1529) and covered in 340 kg of gold leaf. The image's name – Phra Sri Samphet – later became the name of the wat. When the Burmese invaded the city in 1767 the image was set on fire in order to release the gold, in the process destroying both it and the temple. A model of this Buddha can be seen in Wat Pho in Bangkok (see page 133). Admission: ฿20.

Looking N from Wat Phra Sri Samphet, one can see the extensive foundations of **Wang Luang**. The palace was constructed by King Trailokant and was only one of 3 palaces used by the Ayutthayan kings. It originally consisted of 5 main buildings, although the Burmese did such an effective demolition job that today only the foundations remain. This was aided by the fact that the palace was built of wood – only religious buildings and monuments were allowed to be built of brick or stone. Within the palace's double walls were stables to house 100 elephants and the extent of the foundations gives some idea of how impressive the palace must have been. Admission: ฿20.

S of Wat Phra Sri Samphet stands the **Viharn Phra Mongkol Bopitr**. This is a 'new' viharn built in 1956 and modelled on the 15th century original which was razed by the Burmese. It houses one of the largest bronze Buddhas in the world:

nearly 12.5m high, seated in an attitude of subduing Mara. This black image is made of sheets of copper-bronze, fastened onto a core of brick and plaster. It probably dates from the 16th century as it is early-Ayutthayan in style (it was certainly mentioned in a royal order of 1603). Until 1956, when it was restored, the image had been left exposed to the elements and was badly damaged. The Buddha sits on a raised platform and stares imperiously down on the many pilgrims who pay homage by sticking copious amounts of gold leaf to its base.

Other places of interest

Taking the road W beside the Viharn Phra Mongkol Bopitr, cross over the moat and a winding road leads to the small **Wat Lokaya Sutha**, of which little remains except a large white reclining Buddha (which faces a row of foodstalls) and a small prang. Travel back past Wang Luang to the main road, turn E and after 250m the road crosses the Old Lopburi River. From the bridge one can see **Wat Na Phramane**, a restored wat which dates from 1503 and is one of the most complete examples of Ayutthayan architecture. A treaty to end one of the many wars with Burma was signed here in 1549. Over 2 centuries later in 1767, the Burmese used the position to attack the city once again and it is said that the King of Burma suffered a mortal blow from a cannon which backfired during the initial bombardment. Perhaps because of this cruel twist of fate, the Burmese left the wat intact. Even without the helping hands of the Burmese, the wat still fell into disrepair and was not restored until 1838. The lovely early Ayutthayan bot is the largest in the city and contains an impressive crowned bronze Buddha image in an attitude of subduing Mara. Unusually, the Buddha is dressed – in king's dress of the Ayutthayan Period. The ceiling is painted with red and gold stars. Next to the bot is the beautiful **Viharn Noi** ('little' viharn) which houses a small green stone Buddha image, seated in the 'European manner' and dating from the Dvaravati Period. It was found in the ruins of Wat Mahathat but is believed to have come from Nakhon Pathom. Some people even maintain that it originally came from Ceylon some 1300 years ago, although this is unlikely. This bot antedates the rest of the complex, having been built by Rama III (1824-1851) specifically to house the Dvaravati Buddha. **NB:** the image can not always be viewed. Admission: ฿10.

A short distance to the E of Wat Na Phramane, across a small tributary of the Old Lopburi River, are the ruins of **Wat Konthi Thong**. S over the bridge again and a short distance E along Kalahom Road is **Wat Thamrikrat**, with lions surrounding an overgrown chedi.

Set apart from the other wats is the little visited **Wat Suwan Dararam**. To get there, take Uthong Road, S of Pridi Damrong Bridge and just before the remnants of **Phom Phet fortress** turn down a narrow lane. The wat was built towards the end of the Ayutthayan Period by the father of the founder of the current Chakri Dynasty. When Rama I ascended to the throne in Bangkok he had the temple restored and then renamed it Suwan Dararam in honour of his parents. It is still in use today. The bot dips towards the centre, a feature of the architecture of the period and contains a series of vivid murals depicting the Jataka stories, images of heaven and hell and, facing the main Buddha image, the Buddha subduing Mara with the earth goddess as his witness. The principal image is an enlarged stone copy of the Emerald Buddha in Bangkok. The viharn is also notable for its fine murals. Painted in 1931, they show episodes from the life of King Naresuan (1590-1605). As at Wat Na Pramane however, the buildings are not always open – ask one of the monks if you can see the murals.

The **Chao Sam Phraya Museum** located on Rojana Road was opened in 1961 (votive tablets excavated from Wat Ratchaburana were auctioned off to raise funds for its construction) and it houses many of Ayutthaya's relics, in particular the Mongkol Buddha. Admission: ฿10. Open: 0900-1200, 1300-1600 Wed-Sun.

The extensive **waterways** of Ayutthaya (over 50 km of them) are a pleasant way to see some of the less accessible sights. Long-tailed boats can be taken from the landing pier opposite Chandra Kasem Palace in the NE corner of the town. During the dry season, it is not possible to circle the entire island; the Old Lopburi River becomes unnavigable. The usual route goes S down the Pa Sak River and round as far as Wat Chai Wattanaram, on the Chao Phraya River. **NB:** all the wats described below can also be reached by road.

The **Chandra Kasem Palace** was built by the 17th King of Ayutthaya, Maha Thammaraj (1569-1590), for his son Prince Naresuan. Like most other buildings, the palace was destroyed by the Burmese. It was later restored by King Mongkut in the 19th century for use as one of his provincial residences. Within the palace is Ayutthaya's second, and smaller, **museum**. It offers more interesting surroundings than the Chao Sam Phraya Museum but an inferior collection. Buddha heads, torsos and other works of art line the walls of the palace grounds – sadly enclosed by thick wire mesh. Admission: ฿10. Open: 0900-1200, 1300-1600 Wed-Sun.

Wat Phanam Choeng lies close to the junction of the Pa Sak and Chao Phraya rivers and is the first wat to be reached by boat, travelling clockwise from the Chandra Kasem pier. It is a restored wat, which cannot be accurately dated. However, the 19m high seated Buddha image in the viharn (immediately behind the bot) is mentioned in a chronicle as having been made in 1324 – some 26 years before Ayutthaya became the capital. It is likely that the wat was founded at the same time, making it the oldest in Ayutthaya. The Buddha sits in an attitude of subduing Mara and is made of brick and plaster and is gilded. It sits crammed into the viharn, dark, somnolent and atmospheric. Unusually in Thailand, behind the image, the wall is pockmarked with tiny niches, each containing a small Buddha. The principle image was popular with Chinese traders, who would pray before it, before embarking on long journeys. It is still worshipped by people from all over the country and is popularly known as 'Luangpor To'. Judging from the Chinese characters that adorn the entrance, it is still popular with the Chinese community. This image is said to have wept tears when Ayutthaya was sacked by the Burmese in 1767.

Wat Phutthaisawan, an active wat, contains within its compound a partially overgrown prang. A ferry carries passengers over to the monastery from the Tha Khaam pier immediately opposite. It can also be reached by road. Travelling further W along the Chao Phraya, the handsome restored **Catholic Cathedral of St. Joseph** comes into view. It was built to serve the large European community living in Ayutthaya during its heyday as a trading centre.

Turning N, **Wat Chai Wattanaram** occupies a magnificent position on the W bank of the Chao Phraya River, to the W of the city. Constructed in 1630, it is a large complex, and the latest to be 'restored'. A decapitated Buddha sits overlooking the river in front of the ruins, while the large central prang is surrounded by 2 rows of smaller chedis and prang-like chedis. The wat was built by King Prasat Thong (1630-1656) and he initially planned to build a monument of Angkor-esque proportions. He later adopted a less ambitious plan. Sadly, the fine stucco work depicting scenes from the lives of the Buddha has all but disappeared – although there is the possibility that the Fine Arts Department may try to recreate the originals. This wat was particularly badly damaged during the Burmese assault on the city in 1767. A row of headless Buddhas and Buddha remnants sit on raised plinths around the walls. Admission: ฿20. N of here is **Wat Kasatthirat**. This wat represents the end of a river tour unless the Old Lopburi River is navigable in which case Wat Na Phramane (see page 186) and Wat Konthi Thong can also be reached returning, full circle, to the Chandra Kasem pier.

Two active wats are to be found SE of the town, along route 3059 (which goes on to the Summer Palace at Bang Pa-In, see page 189). The first is **Wat Yai Chai Mongkol**, also known as Wat Chao Phraya Thai, or simply Wat Yai ('big' wat). It was built by King Uthong (aka King Ramathibodi I) in 1357 for a group of monks who had studied, and been ordained, in Ceylon. The imposing 72m high chedi was built in the Ceylonese style (now with a rather alarming tilt) to celebrate the victory of King Naresuan over the Prince of Burma in 1592 in singlehanded elephant combat. It was at this time that the wat received its current name – previously it has been known as Wat Pa Keo. The wat remained unused from the fall of Ayutthaya until 1957 when a group of monks took up residence and began to restore it. Admission: ฿10. The second active wat is the above mentioned Wat Phanam Choeng.

4 km N of Ayutthaya off the road to Pa Mok is **Wat Phu Kao Thong**, or the Golden Mount Chedi. The principal chedi was built by the Burmese King Burengnong after he had conquered Ayutthaya in 1549, and at 80m high it dominates the surrounding countryside. The wat is rather older, having been founded by King Uthong's son in 1387. After King Naresuan regained Ayutthaya's independence in 1584, the chedi was remodelled in Ayutthayan style. As a result, the bottom portion of the chedi

up to the balustrade is Mon in style and the upper storeys are Thai. In 1956 a 2500 gm gold ball was mounted on top of the chedi to mark 2500 years of Buddhism. Only a few people will bother to make the journey by tuk-tuk to this wat which is artistically inferior to those within the city walls.

NE of the city, on the banks of the Old Lopburi River, are the only remaining **Elephant kraals** in Thailand. They were built in the reign of King Maha Chakrapat in 1580 to capture wild elephants. The kraals are square-shaped enclosures with double walls. The inner walls are made of massive teak posts fixed firmly to the ground at close intervals. The outer are made of earth, faced with brick and are 3m high. The kraals have 2 entrances: one to allow the decoy elephant to lure the herd into the enclosure, and the other to lead them out again, to be trained for war or work. The outer wall on the W side is slightly wider to provide a platform from which the king, seated in a pavilion, could watch the elephant round-up. The last round-up of wild elephants occurred in May 1903, to entertain royal guests during King Chulalongkorn's reign. The kraal has been extensively restored and is rather clinical as a result. **Getting there**: take a saamlor from Chee Kun Road northwards over the Old Lopburi River to reach the kraal. If coming from Wat Phu Kao Thong, cross the Pa Mok highway and drive for 3.5 km.

Excursions

Bang Pa-In, 20 km down river, makes a pleasant contrast to the ruins of Ayutthaya. It became the summer residence of the Ayutthayan kings of the 17th century. King Prasat Thong (1630-1656) started the trend of retiring here during the hot season, and he built both a palace and a temple – Wat Chumphon Nikayaram (an example of the third period of Ayutthayan architecture) – on an island in the middle of the Chao Phraya River. The palace is in turn located in the middle of a lake that the king had created on the island. It is said that his fondness for Bang Pa-In was because he was born on the island.

After the capital of Thailand was moved to Bangkok, Bang Pa-In was abandoned and left to degenerate. It was not until Rama IV stopped here on a journey to Ayutthaya that a restoration programme was begun and both he and his son, King Chulalongkorn (Rama V), visited Bang Pa-In regularly. King Chulalongkorn also had a number of new halls built in the period 1872-1889, and today the only original (although much restored) buildings that remain are those of **Wat Chumphon Nikayaram**, outside the palace walls, near the bridge and close to the railway station. All the other buildings at Bang Pa-In date from the late 19th and 20th centuries and are a strange mixture of Oriental, Italian and Victorian styles. Restoration is currently in progress throughout the site.

The description below follows the suggested 'official' route, passing through immaculately kept gardens. Considerable restoration work is currently under way throughout the site. The **Varophat Phiman Hall** is essentially Corinthian in style and was built by Chulalongkorn in 1876 as his private residence. From there, a covered bridge leads to the inner palace. Immediately on the right, the **Thewarat Khanlai Gate** (not really a gate at all but a pavilion) overlooks the much photographed **Isawan Thipaya-at Hall** in the middle of the lake. It is modelled on the Aphorn Phimok Hall in the Grand Palace, Bangkok. Facing the gate and bridge is the **Phra Thinang Uthayan Phumisathian**, painted a two-tone green. Designed to resemble a Swiss chalet, it looks more like a New England country house. Behind the 'chalet', the **Vehat Chamroon Hall**, built in 1889, is Chinese in style and was a gift from Chinese traders to King Chulalongkorn. It is the only

BY RIVER TO BANGKOK

The 4 hr river trip from Bang Pa-In back to Bangkok is quite an event in itself. If you make for an outside seat in the bows, the boat's own speed provides a pleasant cool breeze and you can enjoy looking at the activities on the river banks and on the water. The Chao Phraya River is extensively used as a commercial highway. The tug-boats, pulling long strings of dumpy black barges, are as different as they could be from their work-a-day sisters in Europe or America. Their steeply raked decks sweep down almost to water-level at the stern, whilst an awning stretching from the brightly painted little wheelhouse in the bows to the stern provides shade. Midships, their huge diesel engines effortlessly growl their loads towards their destinations.

On the banks, houses on stilts nestle among the trees, each with its own jetty and some sort of boat. As Bangkok approaches, the river becomes much busier, bustling with ferries, rice barges with their distinctively rounded wooden hulls, little canoes selling food and vegetables and the fast *hang yaaws*, their drivers revving their noisy engines without mercy and rushing about in clouds of spray. The tour boats get back to Bangkok's *Oriental Hotel* pier in the early evening, when Wat Arun's towering prang is a splendid sight against the setting sun. Kenneth Graham would be pleased to see that in Thailand there appears to be a whole nation of 'Ratties' and that here too there is simply nothing finer than "messing about in boats".

building open to the public and contains some interesting Chinese artefacts and furniture (much of which looks excruciatingly uncomfortable). In front of the Vehat Chamroon Hall stands the **Hor Vithun Thasna**, a tall observation tower. Another bridge leads to memorials; the second commemorates Queen Sunanda, Rama V's half sister and favourite wife who drowned here; it is said her servants watched her drown because of the law that forbade a commoner from touching royalty. S of the palace, over the Chao Phraya River is the gothic-style **Wat Nivet Thamaprawat** built in 1878 and resembling a Christian church. Admission to Bang Pa-In complex: ฿50 (guidebook included). Open: 0830-1730 Mon-Sun. Currency exchange facilities available. **Getting there:** boats can be hired from the pier opposite the Chandra Kasem Palace in Ayutthaya – ฿250-300, 1 way, ฿400, return (3 hrs). There is a regular minibus service from Ayutthaya's Chao Prom Market, 50 mins (฿30). Regular bus connections from

Bangkok's Northern terminal, 1 hr (non-a/c ฿13) or by boat (see Bangkok tours, **page 158**). Regular train connections from Hualamphong to Bang Pa-In, 1¼ hrs (฿12-49).

Wat Khun Inthapramun lies 7 km N of Ang Thong (a town 40 km north of Ayutthaya), just short of the district town of Pho Thong. Turn left at a red sign in Thai, identifiable by the reclining Buddha above the lettering. 2 km along the road is the wat, which has a single claim to fame: it contains the largest reclining Buddha in Thailand – 50m in length, 11m high, and dating from the Sukhothai Period. The image is contained within a ruined viharn for which funds are currently being sought for renovation. The wat is named after a tax collector, Khun Inthapramun, who spent the king's revenue lengthening the original image and was promptly flogged to death by his king. So much for religious devotion. It is said that during the reign of Rama V, the image spoke; muffled sounds were heard coming from the Buddha, so the abbot enquired 'Are you not well, Sir?', to which the image responded 'Thank you, I am quite well...but trouble is on its way; within two months, there will be a bad outbreak of cholera'. The abbot asked what measures should be taken and the Buddha is said to have provided a herbal remedy which proved effective. Getting there: buses to Ang Thong from Chao Phrom Road and then a local bus to Pho Thong; ask to be let off at the wat.

Wat Phra Phuttha Saiyat Pa Mok (or simply Wat Pa Mok) is located 12 km N of town in Amphoe (district) Pa Mok. Of note in the wat is a 22.5m long reclining Buddha which, it is said, King Narai visited while he was leading his troops to fight King Maha Uparacha of Burma. If so, it must be several hundred years old. The image is contained within a fine viharn and approached, unusually, along a long covered walkway. Getting there: songthaews from Chao Phrom Road to Pa Mok and ask for directions.

Festivals
Nov: *Loi Krathong*, festival of lights (see page 513).

Tours
See Bangkok section, page 158.

Local information
● **Accommodation**
B *Ayutthaya Grand*, 55/5 Rojana Rd, T 244483, F 244492, B 5111029, a/c, restaurant, pool, all facilities; **B** *Uthong Inn*, 210 Rojana Rd, Amphoe Phra Nakhon Si, T 42618, inconvenient location E of town, some a/c, otherwise comfortable.

C *Si Samai*, 12 Chao Phrom Rd, T 245228, some a/c, clean, good location, but even the more expensive a/c rooms have no hot water, seems to have lost custom to the 2 *B.J.* Guesthouses; **C-E** *Thongchai Guesthouse*, off Chee Kun Rd, T 252083, some a/c, good value.

D *Uthong*, 86 Uthong Rd, T 251136, some a/c, large clean rooms, central; **D-E** *Cathay*, 36/5-6 Uthong Rd, T 251562, very average; **D-E** *Thai Thai*, 13/1 Naresuan Rd, T 251505, some a/c, no hot water, good location, good sized, clean rooms.

E-F *Ayutthaya Guesthouse*, T 251468, very popular with good food and shared facilities; **E-F** *Old B.J. Guesthouse*, T 251526, shared bathrooms, good food, very friendly management, bicycles for hire (฿50/day), rec; **E-F** *New B.J.Guesthouse*, 19/29 Naresuan Rd, T 251512, restaurant, friendly, clean, very popular, rec.

● **Places to eat**
♦♦*Thai Bin La*, corner Naresuan and Chee Kun rds; ♦♦*Phae Kung Kao*, 4 Uthong Rd, floating restaurant to the S of Pridi Damrong bridge; ♦♦*Ruen Pai*, floating restaurant north of Pridi Damrong bridge; ♦♦*O's*, 66/6 Uthong Rd (opposite Wat Thamrikrat), also serves seafood; *Saikon* and *Ruanaroprong*, near the S junction of Chee Kun and Uthong rds, both overlook the river; ♦♦*Som's*, 9/7 Chee Kun Rd; ♦♦*Wa Kawai*, 50/3-5 Uthong Rd, overlooks the river.

Foodstalls: there is a night market with cheap foodstalls in the parking area in front of Chandra Kasem Palace; stalls are also concentrated at the W end of Chao Phrom Rd and in the market at the NE corner of the city on Uthong Rd.

● **Banks & money changers**
Thai Military, Chao Phrom Rd; **Thai Farmers**, Chao Phrom Rd; **Siam City**, Uthong Rd (close to *Uthong Hotel*); **Bangkok**, Uthong Rd (next to *Cathay Hotel*).

● **Post and telecommunications**
Area code: 035. **Post Office**: Uthong Rd (south from the Chandra Kasem Palace).

● **Tourist offices**
TAT (temporary office), Si Sanphet Rd, T 246076, F 246078. Areas of responsibility are Ayutthaya, Ang Thong, Suphanburi and Nonthaburi.

● **Transport**
85 km N of Bangkok.

Local Bicycles: can be hired from many guesthouses (e.g. *Old B.J.'s*); expect to pay about ฿50/day. **Long-tailed boats**: can be hired at the jetty opposite Chandra Kasem Palace in the NE corner of town. Expect to pay ฿250 for an hour's journey (boats can take 8 people). The *B.J. Guesthouse* also arrange boats. **Saamlors**: around town should not cost more than ฿10-20; they can also be hired by the hour. **Songthaews**: from the train station into town cost ฿5. They can also be chartered for ฿250-300/day.

Train: the station is just over the river, off Rojana Rd. Regular connections with Bangkok's Hualamphong station 1½ hrs (฿15-60), and with all stops N to Chiang Mai 12 hrs. It is possible to catch a train from Don Muang Airport, making it unnecessary to enter Bangkok.

Road Bus: station is on Chao Phrom Rd, almost opposite the *Si Samai Hotel*. Regular a/c and non-a/c connections with Bangkok's Northern bus terminal 1½ hrs (฿17-36) and stops N including Phitsanulok, Chiang Mai and Sukhothai (5 hrs). Note that non-a/c buses are often full because Ayutthaya is only a stop N from Bangkok.

Boat: (see Bangkok Tours, page 158) from Tha Tien pier in Bangkok daily at 1000. Private boats can also be hired from the pier opposite Chandra Kasem Palace in Ayutthaya.

AROUND AYUTTHAYA

Lopburi

The historic town of Lopburi has been seemingly caught between competing powers for over 1000 years. The discovery of neolithic and bronze age remains indicate that the site on the left bank of the Lopburi River was in use in prehistoric times. The town became a major centre during the Dvaravati Period (6th-11th century), when it was known as Lavo (the original settlers were the 'Lavah', related to the Mon). In 950 it fell to the expanding Khmers who made it a provincial capital: in Thailand, the Khmer period of art and architecture is known as 'Lopburi' because of their artistic impact evident in the town and surrounding area (see page 88). By the 14th century, Khmer influence had waned and the Thais reclaimed Lopburi. In 1350 King Uthong of Ayutthaya gave his son – Prince Ramesuan – governorship of the town, indicating its continued importance. It fell into obscurity during the 16th century, but was resuscitated when King Narai (1656-1688) restored the city with the assistance of European architects. With Narai's death in Lopburi, the town entered another period of obscurity but was again restored to glory during Rama IV's reign. Today, Lopburi is a major military base, with the new town located to the E of the railway line. Most of the historic sights are to the W. It is more convenient for sightseeing to be based in the old city; all the sights here are within walking distance of one another.

Places of interest

When King Narai declared Lopburi his second capital in the 17th century, he set about restoring the town with the help of Italian and French architects. He built the **Narai Ratchaniwet Palace** (also known as the Lopburi Palace, or King Narai's Palace) between 1665 and 1677, which became his 'summer' retreat (he lived here for more than 6 months each year). Surrounded by massive walls, the main gate is on Sorasak Road, opposite the *Asia Lopburi Hotel*. The well-kept palace grounds are divided into 3 sections: an outer, a middle, and an inner courtyard.

The outer courtyard, now in ruins, contained the 'functional' buildings: a *tank* to supply water to the palace (transported down terracotta pipes from a lake some distance away), storage warehouses for hides and spices and elephant and horse stables. There was also a **Banquet Hall** for royal visitors, and on the S wall, an audience hall – **Tuk Phrachao Hao**. It was here that those plotting against King Narai, while he was seriously ill, are reputed to have met to discuss their plans. The niches that line the inner side of the walls by the main gates would have contained oil lamps, lit during festivals and important functions.

An archway leads to the middle courtyard. On the left are the tall ruins of the **Dusitsawan Thanya Mahaprasat Hall**, built in 1685 for audiences with visiting dignitaries. When the French ambassador Chevalier de Chaumont was received here, his account records that the hall was lined with French mir-

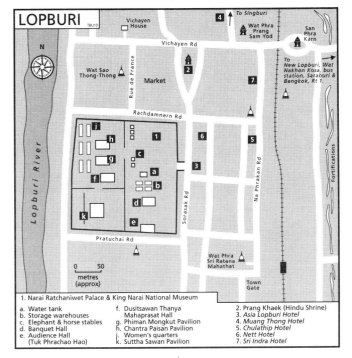

LOPBURI TBU10

Vichayen House
To Singburi
Wat Phra Prang Sam Yod
San Phra Karn
Vichayen Rd
Wat Sao Thong-Thong
Rue de France
Market
To New Lopburi, Wat Nakhon Kosa, bus station, Saraburi & Bangkok, Rt 1.
Rachdamnern Rd
Lopburi River
Na Phrakan Rd
Sorasak Rd
Fortifications
Pratuchai Rd
Wat Phra Sri Ratana Mahathat
Town Gate

0   50
metres
(approx)

1. Narai Ratchaniwet Palace & King Narai National Museum

a. Water tank
b. Storage warehouses
c. Elephant & horse stables
d. Banquet Hall
e. Audience Hall (Tuk Phrachao Hao)
f. Dusitsawan Thanya Mahaprasat Hall
g. Phiman Mongkut Pavilion
h. Chantra Paisan Pavilion
j. Women's quarters
k. Suttha Sawan Pavilion

2. Prang Khaek (Hindu Shrine)
3. Asia Lopburi Hotel
4. Muang Thong Hotel
5. Chulathip Hotel
6. Nett Hotel
7. Sri Indra Hotel

rors. The front portion of the hall is French in style, the rear Thai. The king would have received visitors from the window throne in the centre of the hall. Next to this is the **Phiman Mongkut Pavilion**, now the **King Narai Museum**. It was built in 1863 by King Rama IV for his own use and is in colonial style. It is made up of several buildings all connected with each other and acts as the museum, housing a fine collection spanning all periods of Thai art but concentrating, not surprisingly, on Lopburi Period sculpture. Some of the Buddha images are exquisite. To the north, the **Chantra Paisan Pavilion**, looking like a wat, was one of the first structures built by King Narai and served as his audience hall until the Suttha Sawan Pavilion was completed. Restored by King Mongkut in 1863, the pavilion houses more artefacts, notably, a collection of Thai cabinets. Behind these buildings were the **Women's Quarters**, again built by Rama IV. One of them has been turned into a **Farmer's Museum** displaying traditional Central Plains farming technology and other implements used in rural life – for pottery and iron production, weaving and fishing. The other buildings in the Women's Quarters are in the process of being restored.

The inner courtyard contains the ruins of King Narai's own residence – the **Suttha Sawan Pavilion**. It is isolated from the rest of the complex and was surrounded by gardens, ponds (where the king took his bath under huge canopies) and fountains. King Narai died in this pavilion on 11th July 1688 while his opponents plotted against him. It is said that to protect those who had remained loyal, he dedicated the building and its grounds as a monastery, and ordained those who had remained with him as monks. As a result, when King Mongkut began to renovate the palace in the 19th century he had to deconsecrate the 'temple' before starting work. After King Narai's death the palace was used for his successor's (one of his regimental commanders) coronation ceremony and was then abandoned until the mid-19th century, when Rama IV ordered a restoration programme. Admission: ¢10. Open: 0830-1200, 1300-1630 Wed-Sun.

Wat Phra Prang Sam Yod (Wat of Three Prangs), is a very good example of Khmer provincial art. It is a laterite and sandstone shrine whose 3 spires originally represented the 3 Hindu deities: Brahma, Vishnu and Siva. Another interpretation has it that because the Khmer king of the time, Jayavarman VII (1181-1217) was a strict Mahayana Buddhist, the 3 prangs symbolize the Buddha (the central tower), Bodhisattva Avalokitasvara or the future Buddha (the S tower) and Prajnaparamita, the Mahayana Goddess of Wisdom (the N tower). Depending on one's viewpoint, either King Narai converted it to a Buddhist temple in the 17th century, or it was always Buddhist. Whatever the case, it still reflects the syncretic religions of the time. The S prang has remnants of some fine stucco friezes and naga heads; also note how the stone door frames are carved to resemble their wooden antecedents. Unfortunately, monkeys over-run the enclosure. The wat lies N of Vichayen Road, next to the railway line. Nearby, on the other side of the railway track is the Brahmanic shrine **San Phra Karn** constructed in 1951. The shrine contains a stone statue of Vishnu with a Buddha's head. Up some steps behind the shrine is a guardian house, probably built by King Narai, containing a strange assortment of Buddhist and Hindu images. It lies on top of the remains of a Khmer laterite struc-

---

CONSTANTINE PHAULCON – GREEK ADVENTURER, SIAMESE MINISTER, CATHOLIC ZEALOT

Constantine Phaulcon (1647-1688) was a Greek adventurer who became, for a short time, the most influential man in Siam barring the king. He arrived in Ayutthaya in 1678 with the English East India Company, learnt Thai and became an interpreter in the court. By 1682 he had worked his way up through the bureaucracy to become the Mahatthai – the most senior position. But it was also at this time that, in retrospect, he sealed his fate. Phaulcon acted as interpreter for a French mission led by Mgr. Pallu. An avid Catholic having recently been converted by Jesuit priests, Phaulcon was enthralled by the idea of converting King Narai and his subjects to Christianity. He discussed with the king – who was his most trusted adviser – the superiority of Catholicism versus Buddhism, and seemed to be representing the interests of the French in negotiations, rather than those of Siam. Phaulcon made many enemies among powerful Siamese, who doubted his integrity and his intentions. By 1688, Phaulcon's activities were becoming increasingly unacceptable, and he was also linked by association with the excesses of French and British troops, with the proselytizing of priests, and with the effect that foreign traders were having upon local businessmen. A plot was hatched to kill the foreigner on the king's death. In March 1688, when the king fell seriously ill, Phra Phetracha – a claimant for the throne – had Phaulcon arrested, tried and convicted for treason, and then executed on June 5.

ture. Monkeys are obviously a problem here, as the entire shrine has been enclosed in a cage, in order to keep them at bay. The shrine is interesting for its activity rather than for any artistic merit.

W along Vichayen Road, is the Khmer **Prang Khaek**. Built in the late 8th century, this, like Prang Sam Yod, was also originally a Hindu shrine. The 3 brick spires represent the oldest Khmer prangs found in the Central region of Thailand. It was restored by King Narai in the 17th century, but today lies in ruins.

Further W along Vichayen Road are the remains of **Vichayen House**, better known as **Constantine Phaulcon's House**, the highly influential adviser to King Narai. The house, European in style, was initially constructed for Chevalier de Chaumont, the first French ambassador to Thailand who lived here in 1685. Later, it was used by the Greek Prime Minister, Phaulcon, as his residence. On entering the gates, his residence lay on the left-hand side, a Roman Catholic Chapel was straight ahead and a reception hall to the right. Admission: ฿20.

Opposite the railway station is the entrance to **Wat Phra Sri Ratana Mahathat** with 2 claims to fame: it is the oldest wat in Lopburi and also houses the tallest prang. The prang, slender and elegant (rather than squat like those of the NE), is of laterite, faced in places, with the last fragments of what must have been fine stucco-work. Dating it has presented something of a problem. Originally it was thought to be contemporary with Angkor Wat in Cambodia (i.e. 12th century). Now, it is considered to date from the 14th century, and to belong to the Uthong School, when the Thais had captured the town from the Khmers. Indeed, it may represent the first example of a 'Tai' as opposed to a Khmer prang, symbolizing the eclipse of the Khmers in the region. The problem is that numerous (and on-going) restorations

have tended to obscure the origins of the buildings. In front of the prang is a viharn dating from King Narai's reign with traditional Thai style doors and gothic windows. Admission: ฿20.

NW of the palace is **Wat Sao Thong-Thong**, on France Road (Rue de France in Roman characters). There is nothing much here except a viharn built by Narai in Western style, as a church for the Christian envoys. Within the viharn (now Buddhist) is a large seated Buddha, while along the walls are niches containing more assorted Buddha images.

Excursions

Wat Phra Buddhabat lies 24 km S of the old city in the town of Phra Buddhabat. The wat is founded on the site of a large and revered footprint of the Buddha. The habit of modelling footprints of the Buddha with the 108 auspicious signs and the Wheel of Law seems to have begun in the 14th century. As Steve van Beek and Luca Tettoni write in *The arts of Thailand*: "Little did [the Sukhothai artists] know what they had begun because today, nearly every hill of any size is topped by a small shrine whose object of veneration is a Buddha Footprint, usually of gargantuan dimensions". The most renowned is that at Wat Phra Buddhabat. A short stairway, flanked by 2 well-wrought many-headed nagas, leads up to a cluster of shrines, salas, chedis and pavilions set at different levels. The ornate tile-encrusted mondop, built to cover the footprint, was constructed during Rama I's reign. It has 4 pairs of exquisite mother-of-pearl doors. The footprint itself, which is a natural impression made in the limestone rock (depending on one's beliefs), was first discovered in the reign of King Song Tham (1610-1628). It is 150 cm long, edged in gold, and set down below floor level. The print must be special: pilgrims not only rub gold leaf onto it but also rain down coins and banknotes – hence the protective grill. It is said that

King Song Tham ordered officials to search for the footprint having been told by Ceylonese monks that one might be found in Thailand. A hunter stumbled across it while trailing a wounded deer, and the site was declared a shrine. Behind the mondop, there is a viharn with two large Buddha images, unusually back-to-back: a large seated Ayutthayan Buddha in front, and a reclining Buddha behind. A large annual festival is held here (see below, Festivals). **Getting there**: take Route 1 S and after 23 km turn onto Route 310. Catch a Saraburi bus from the bus station; passengers are let off on the main road, so either walk the 1 km to the shrine or take a saamlor.

Si Thep is a little visited historical park 80 km NE of Lopburi, 8 km off Route 21. It is a former city which predates Lopburi and which has, in turn, been Hindu and then Buddhist. During the 6th-8th centuries it was part of the Mon Dvaravati Kingdom, before being incorporated into the Khmer Empire in the 10th century. The city forms 2 distinct sections: an inner, earlier city designed by Dvaravati architects, and a later, outer city which envelopes the inner and which was designed by Khmer planners. In all, it measures 4 km by 1.5 km, making it one of the largest archaeological sites in Thailand. Work on excavating and renovating the temples is still at an early stage, and many are still choked with vegetation. The earlier Mon Period produced some superb sculpture: the 8th century sandstone Vishnus are particularly sensitively carved and are regarded by some art historians as being among the finest pieces produced in Southeast Asia. The later Khmer pieces are derivative, and though fine, are not regarded as highly as similar works from other sites in the Northeast of Thailand. So far, only 1 Buddha image has been unearthed. **Getting there**: take a bus N towards Phetchabun on Route 21 and get off 5 km or so after the town of Si Thep. The ruins lie 8 km off the main road, not far from the village of Ban Nok Charoen. It should be possible either to take a motorcycle taxi or a local songthaew (ask for *muang boraan Si Thep* or *muang kao Si Thep*).

Festivals

Feb: *King Narai Reign Festival* (15-17th) processions, stalls and traditional dancing, centred around King Narai's Palace; **Mar**: *Phra Bhuddhabat fair and festival* (moveable) at Wat Phra Bhuddhabat draws large crowds; folk music and handicraft market.

Local information
● Accommodation

B *Lopburi Inn*, 28/9 Narai Maharat Rd, T 412300, F 411892, a/c, best in town, but over 4 km from old city and the sights.

D *Asia Lopburi*, 1/7-8 Sorasak Rd, T 411892, a/c, restaurant, clean, friendly, hot water, very central for sights, rec; **D-E** *Muang Thong*, 1/5-7 Prang Sam Yod Rd, T 411036, some a/c, on a busy road; **D-E** *Sri Indra*, 3-5 Na Phrakan Rd, T 411261, some a/c, very average, good location.

E *Chulathip*, 17-18 Na Phrakan Rd, T 411672, good position; **E** *Nett*, 17/1-2 Rachdamnern Soi 2, T 411738, clean, the best of the cheaper hotels.

● Places to eat
The orchards around Lopburi are reputed to produce the finest *noi naa* or custard apples in Thailand. A local speciality is coconut jelly, served with ice. The jelly is a mixture of coconut and glycerine. Lopburi has a good selection of Chinese-Thai restaurants, especially along Na Phrakan Road, e.g. next to *Asia Lopburi Hotel* on Sorasak Road, friendly, good food. The *market* between Rachdamnern Road and Rue de France provides the usual range of stall foods, as do the stalls along Sorasak Road. *Ice-cream parlour*, N end of Sorasak Rd also serves Thai food, middle. ◆*Suk Si*, 28 Rachdamnern Rd, Thai, Chinese.

● Banks & money changers
Krung Thai, 74 Vichayen Rd; **Thai Military**, corner of Sorasak and Rachdamnern rds.

● Post & telecommunications
Post Office: on road to Singburi, not far from Prang Sam Yod. **Area code**: 036.

● **Tourist offices**

TAT (temporary office), HM The Queen's Celebration Building, Narai Maharat Rd, T 422768, F 422769. Areas of responsibility are Lopburi, Nakhon Sawan, Uthai Thani and Singburi.

● **Transport**

155 km from Bangkok, 75 km from Ayutthaya.

Train: regular connections with Bangkok's Hualamphong station 2¾ hrs (฿28-111) and with Ayutthaya 1 hr.

Road Bus: the bus station for both a/c and non-a/c is in the new town, 2 km from the old town, close to the roundabout where Routes 311 and 3016 cross (Wongwian Sra Kaeo). Regular connections with Bangkok's Northern bus terminal 2-3 hrs (฿32-72) and with Ayutthaya 1 hr. Buses from Kanchanaburi via Suphanburi and Singburi 6 hrs.

Suphanburi

This historic town was founded in the latter part of the 9th century, and became an important centre during the Dvaravati Period, when it was known as Phanchumburi. However, different kings seem to have been unsure as to exactly where the town should be positioned; it has switched from one bank of the Tha Jeen River to the other on a number of occasions. It was not until Rama VI came to the throne that its final location on the E bank of the river was arrived at.

Places of interest

Not many visitors make it here but there are a couple of interesting wats to visit and Suphanburi might make a good stop-over. The town has a well-kept air, with manicured central reservations on the main roads and scattered ruined chedis. It also boasts a smart new hotel, the *Kalapruek*, presumably built to accommodate visitors to the Don Chedi Fair (see Festivals below).

Take a saamlor or tuk-tuk to visit the sights. **Wat Phra Rup** is an active wat which lies across the river on Malimaen Road and left down Khunchang Road. The viharn to the right as you enter the compound houses a striking large reclining Buddha – Phra Phut Sai Yaat.

On the upper floor of one of the buildings to the left of the central bot is a beautiful carved wooden footprint of the Buddha. Both date from the late Uthong Period (14th century). The carving is kept in a locked room which will be willingly opened, upon request.

Returning to Malimaen Road, the prang of **Wat Phra Sri Ratana Mahathat** can be clearly seen on the other side of the road. The road leading to the wat is marked with a fish sign. The wat was built between the late 14th and early 15th century and features a large Khmer prang containing relics of the Buddha. Some of the original stucco remains. Close to the prang is a ruined bot with a seated Buddha. Some renovations took place during the second half of the Ayutthaya Period.

Continuing down Malimaen Road, towards Kanchanaburi, about 3 km from town, is **Wat Palelai**, also known as Wat Pa ('Forest' wat). It dates from the Uthong Period. The Viharn Luang Phor Tor (meaning 'Viharn of the Immense Buddha Image') contains a large seated Buddha (in the unusual attitude of a wandering forest monk) believed to possess great powers. It would appear to be an important pilgrimage place for Thais, as the Buddha image (and 2 other seated Buddha images in the side aisles) are plastered in gold leaf. Good foodstalls in the compound.

Festivals

Jan: *Don Chedi Fair* (23rd-31st) held at Don Chedi, 32 km N of town on Route 322. In 1582, King Naresuan of Ayutthaya won an elephant duel against the Burmese Crown Prince and liberated the Thai Kingdom. A memorial was constructed to commemorate the event, in 1951 a Ceylonese-style pagoda was constructed over the original structure. The fair is the Memorial Day of King Naresuan. Usual festivities.

Local information
● **Accommodation**

B-C *Kalapruek*, 135/1 Prachatipatai Rd,

T 522555, a/c, best in town.

D-E *KAT*, 433 Phra Phan-va-sar, T 521619, some a/c, clean, friendly.

● **Transport**
170 km N of Bangkok, 95 km from Singburi. **Road Bus**: regular connections with Bangkok's Northern bus terminal 1½ hrs (฿47-60), Kanchanaburi (฿21), Singburi and Lopburi.

Nakhon Sawan

Nakhon Sawan, or Paknam Pho ('river mouth') is a major commercial centre 241 km N of Bangkok. It is regarded as the 'gateway' to the N but is rarely visited by tourists. The town is situated at the confluence of 4 rivers – the Ping, Wang, Yom and Nan. It became an important centre for the teak trade, as rafts travelling down from the N were broken up into smaller rafts for the journey S. As Thailand's teak forests were decimated, so this activity declined until finally, in early 1989, the Thai government announced a ban on all logging in the kingdom. Now the town's ties with water are bound up with irrigation: close by is one of the major diversion dams which help to control flooding and the supply of water for rice cultivation in the Central Plains.

Places of interest

Wat Chomkiri Nagaproth stands on a hill just before Dejativong Bridge, with a good view over the city. The wat dates from the Sukhothai Period (although extensive renovation has succeeded in obliterating this fact). It contains a fine seated Buddha image from the Ayutthaya Period and a footprint of the Buddha.

Excursions

Bung Boraphet is an area of swampland covering over 22,000 ha about 10 km from the city. It is famous for the *sua* fish which abound in the swamp and which are regarded as a delicacy. There is also an aquarium here. **Getting there**: by chartered car or by boat from the landing behind the city market (40 mins).

Festivals

Feb: *Dragon and Lion Parade* (moveable), associated with Chinese New Year which (due to Nakhon Sawan's large ethnic Chinese population) is celebrated more enthusiastically and colourfully here than in almost any other town in Thailand. Lion dances, music, parades of virgins...the hotels are usually booked up in this week; **Nov/Dec**: (12th lunar month) Celebrations are held at *Wat Chomkiri Nagaproth*.

Local information
● **Accommodation**

A-A+ *Nakhon Sawan Thani*, B 2384790, new luxury hotel scheduled to open October 1995, judging by other hotels in the Thani group, it will be the most luxurious in town.

B *Piman*, 605/244 Asia Rd, T 222473, a/c, restaurant, pool, comfortable but dull hotel with good facilities including nightclub and ballroom dancing.

C *Irawan*, 1-5 Matuli Rd, T 221889, a/c.

E *Sri Phitak*, 109/5 Matuli Rd, T 221076.

● **Transport**
241 km N of Bangkok. **Train**: regular connections with Bangkok's Hualamphong station 4 hrs (฿48-97).

Road Bus: regular connections with Bangkok's Northern bus terminal (฿47-87). Also buses from Ayutthaya and other towns on route running N towards Chiang Mai.

ROUTES NORTH TO SI SATCHANALAI

From Nakhon Sawan Route 117 runs N to Phitsanulok (where buses link up with the Northeast). From here it is 50 km W to Sukhothai town and its historical sights. Continuing N from Sukhothai, Route 101 passes through the ancient city of Si Satchanalai before reaching the Northern region, and the beautiful towns of Lampang, Lamphun and Chiang Mai. Alternatively, route 11 to the E of Phitsanulok and the Yom River passes close by the provincial capital of Uttaradit, and from there into the Northern region.

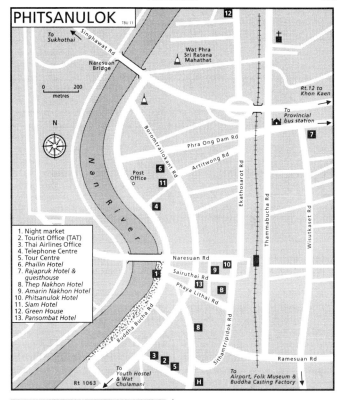

PHITSANULOK TBU 11

To Sukhothai

Singhawat Rd

Naresuan Bridge

Wat Phra Sri Ratana Mahathat

Rt.12 to Khon Kaen

To Provincial bus station

0   200
metres

N

N a n   R i v e r

Boromtrailokant Rd

Phra Ong Dam Rd

Artitwong Rd

Ekathosarot Rd

Thammabucha Rd

Wisutkaset Rd

Post Office

Naresuan Rd

Sairuthai Rd

Phaya Lithai Rd

Sithamtripidok Rd

Ramesuan Rd

Buddha Bucha Rd

To Youth Hostel & Wat Chulamani

Rt 1063

To Airport, Folk Museum & Buddha Casting Factory

1. Night market
2. Tourist Office (TAT)
3. Thai Airlines Office
4. Telephone Centre
5. Tour Centre
6. Phailin Hotel
7. Rajapruk Hotel & guesthouse
8. Thep Nakhon Hotel
9. Amarin Nakhon Hotel
10. Phitsanulok Hotel
11. Siam Hotel
12. Green House
13. Pansombat Hotel

Phitsanulok

Phitsanulok was the birthplace of one of the heroes of Thai history: King Naresuan the Great of Ayutthaya (reigned 1590-1605) (there is a shrine to the king on the W side of the river facing Wat Mahathat). However, shortly after his birth the young Naresuan was bundled off to Burma as a guarantee of his father's – King Thammaracha – good behaviour. He did not return to Phitsanulok until he was 16, when he was awarded the principality to govern by his father. Here he developed his military and political skills which were to stand him in good stead when he assumed the throne of Ayutthaya 19 years later in 1590 (see box). For the short period of 25 years, during the reign of King Boromtrailokant (1448-1488) of Ayutthaya, Phitsanulok was actually the capital of Siam.

Today, Phitsanulok is merely a large, bustling and largely characterless town linking the Central Plains with the North and Northeast. But, it does have some places of interest including the magnificent Wat Phra Sri Ratana Mahathat and has a collection of comfortable Western-style hotels, making it a convenient base from which to visit the historic cities of Sukhothai and Si Satchanalai.

KING NARESUAN THE GREAT OF AYUTTHAYA

King Naresuan of Ayutthaya (1590-1605) was one of Thailand's great kings, and one of only five who have posthumously been awarded the sobriquet 'the Great'. In 1569 the Burmese had taken Ayutthaya and placed a puppet monarch on the throne. The great kingdom appeared to be on the wane. But Naresuan, who in David Wyatt's words was "one of those rare figures in Siamese history who, by virtue of dynamic leadership, personal courage, and decisive character, succeed in herculean tasks that have daunted others before them", proceeded to challenge the Burmese. He confronted their forces in 1585, 1585-86 and in 1586-87, defeating armies that grew larger by turn. Finally, at the beginning of 1593, the decisive battle occurred at Nong Sarai, to the north-west of Suphanburi. The Burmese had assembled an army of monumental proportions. During the initial skirmish, Naresuan saw the Burmese crown prince mounted on his war elephant and, according to the chronicles, shouted across the battle field: "Come forth and let us fight an elephant duel for the honour of our kingdoms". When the Burmese prince lunged with his lance, Naresuan ducked beneath the blow to rake, and kill, his opponent with his sword. The battle was won and Ayutthaya was once again in a position to flourish.

Places of interest

At first glance, Phitsanulok appears an ugly modern town; most of the old wooden buildings which graced the city were destroyed in a disastrous fire in the 1960's, and their replacements are uninspired to say the very least. However, the town is attractively positioned on the banks of the River Nan, with houseboats lining the steep banks. It is also home to one of the most important shrines in Thailand – **Wat Phra Sri Ratana Mahathat**, or simply Wat Yai (meaning 'big' wat). The monastery was built in the reign of King Phya Li Thai of Sukhothai, in 1357 and is to be found on the E bank of the River Nan, close to the Naresuan Bridge.

The bot contains one of the most highly regarded and venerated Buddha images in Thailand – the *Phra Buddha Chinaraj*. The image is cast in bronze in an attitude of subduing Mara. In the early 17th century, King Eka Thossarot is said to have given some gold to the wat so that it could be beaten into sheets and used to plate the Buddha. The image is a superlative example of late Sukhothai style – corpulent body, rounded face,

serene, almost grave expression, and fingers all the same length (see section on Sukhothai style, page 91). The head is covered in tight spiralled curls and is surrounded by a flame-like ketumala. The whole effect is accentuated by lighting from below and a dark backdrop. This Buddha is said to have wept tears of blood when the city was captured by the Ayutthayan army in the early 14th century. The 3-tiered bot in which the image is contained is also impressive. It has a low sweeping roof supported by black and gold pillars, which accentuates the massive gilded bronze Buddha image seated at the end of the nave. The entrance is through inlaid mother-of-pearl doors, made in 1756 in the reign of King Boromkot to replace the original ones of carved wood (**NB**: this is a very sacred site and visitors wearing shorts or revealing clothing will not be admitted). The 36m high prang in the centre of the complex was rebuilt in the popular Ayutthayan style when King Boromtrailokant visited Phitsanulok. Stairs lead up to a niche containing relics of the Buddha. Also in the wat compound is the **Buddha Chinnarat**

National Museum with a small collection of Sukhothai Buddhas and assorted ceramics. Admission: ฿5. Open: 0900-1600 Wed-Sun.

The excellent TAT Office in Phitsanulok, in some might say a futile attempt to lure more people to the city, are promoting walking tours of the capital. One of the sights being promoted is the **Folk Museum** on Wisutkaset Road which exhibits items from everyday rural life, in particular agricultural implements and tools; nothing special. Open: 0830-1200, 1300-1630 Mon-Sun. Across the street, and run by the same man, is a **factory casting Buddha images**. These are produced using the lost wax method and range in size from diminutive to monstrous. It is usually possible to see at least some of the production processes. The door is always shut; open it and go in, open: 0800-1700. The **riverside night market**, S of the new bridge, is open from 1800 to midnight and is a great bustle of activity, colour and smell. Stalls include food of every variety and a range of goods including handicrafts, amulets, clothes and other trinkets.

THE 'LOST WAX' PROCESS

A core of clay is moulded into the desired form and then covered in beeswax and shellac. Details are engraved into the beeswax. The waxed core is then coated with a watery mixture of clay and cow's dung, and built up into a thick layer of clay. This is then fired in a kiln, the wax running out through vents cut into the clay. Molten bronze is poured into the mould where it fills the void left by the wax and after cooling the mould is broken to reveal the image.

Excursions

Wat Chulamani, 5 km to the S of Phitsanulok on Route 1063, was probably the original town centre. During the Khmer period it was known as Muang Song Kwae ('Two River Town'), as it lies between the Nan and the Kwae Noi. It was built by King Boromtrailokant (1448-1488). The wat compound houses the remains of an ornate Khmer-style prang and bot, some monastery walls, and Buddha images housed under a make-shift shelter. Disappointing for those who have just experienced the wonders of the ancient city of Sukhothai. Getting there: buses leave from the City bus centre near the railway station on Ekathosarot Road every 10 mins, 20 min journey (฿3).

Phu Hin Rongkla National Park is situated 120 km from Phitsanulok, off route 2113, which links Phitsanulok with Loei. It covers 5,000 sq km over 3 provinces – Phitsanulok, Phetchabun and Loei. The park, which has been partly deforested, was a stronghold of the Communist Party of Thailand (CPT) until the early 1980s and hundreds of disaffected students fled here following the Thammasat University massacre of 1976. The government encouraged farmers to settle in the park to deny the guerillas refuge; now that the CPT has been vanquished, the same farmers have been told they are illegal squatters and must move. So much for helping in the fight against Communism. The buildings used by the CPT for training and indoctrination (3 km SW of the park headquarters) have been preserved and in some cases rebuilt, and have now become sights of historical interest to the Thais – particularly those former students and their families who joined the movement after the student demonstrations of 1973-76. The base supported a political and military school, with printing press and communications centre, a small hospital, cafeteria and air raid shelter. Rising to 1780m, the park has a diverse flora ranging from dry dipterocarp forest at low altitudes to pine forest on the upper slopes and including numerous orchids and lichins. Wildlife, though it has suffered from hunting, includes small populations of tiger, bear, sambar deer and hornbills. **Accommodation**: bungalows are available at park headquarters (book in advance B 5790529) and there is a camping ground (tents for hire, ฿40), 2 restaurants (take own food if self-catering) and money changer. **Getting there**: catch a bus towards Loei and get off at Nakhon Thai 3 hrs (฿28) and then a songthaew to the park (฿10-20). If travelling by car or motorcycle, drive to Ban Yaeng at the 68 km marker and turn left towards Nakhon Thai; turn right after another 24 km at Ban Nong Krathao. The headquarters are 28 km along this road.

Tours

Piti Tour and Phitsanulok Tour Centre organize city tours and tours to Sukhothai and Si Satchanalai by private car.

Festivals

Jan/Feb: *Phra Buddha Chinarat* (moveable) a 6 day fair which honours the Phra Buddha Chinarat, held at Wat Phra Sri Ratana Mahathat, with entertainment and stalls selling local products; **Oct**: *Boat Races* (first weekend) on the stretch of the Nan overlooked by Wat Mahathat.

Local information
● Accommodation

A *Phailin*, 38 Boromtrailokant Rd, T 252411, B 2157110, a/c, restaurant, best hotel in town, professionally managed, with clean, well-equipped rooms, more to farang's decorative tastes than most; **A-B** *Rajapruk*, 99/9 Phra Ong Dam Rd, T 258788, F 251395, B 2514612, a/c, restaurant, pool, ugly hotel with an almost Soviet or E European flavour, cluttered and impersonal.

B *Thep Nakhon*, 43/1 Sithamtripidok Rd, T 258507, F 251897, B 3982087, a/c, large hotel, Asian in atmosphere, comfortable but unrefined.

C *Nanchao*, 242 Boromtrailokant Rd, T 252510, a/c, comfortable modern hotel with reasonable rates, rec; **C-D** *Amarin Nakhon*, 3/1 Chaophraya Rd, T 258588, F 258945, a/c, restaurant, 'Thai businessman's hotel'.

D *Rajapruk Guesthouse*, Phra Ong Dam Rd (behind the *Rajapruk Hotel* above a row of

garages), T 258477, some a/c, large, clean rooms, if rather featureless and a little worn; **E-D** *Phitsanulok*, 82 Naresuan Rd, T 258425. Several near the railway station: **D** *Siam*, 4/8 Artitwong Rd, T 258844, some a/c.

E *Green House*, 11/12 Ekathosarot Rd, T 252803, formerly No 4 Guesthouse, best travellers' place in town, N of centre, clean, good information; **E** *Pansombat*, 4/1 Sairuthai Rd, T 258179, rather dirty Chinese-style hotel, no hot water; **D-F** *Youth Hostel*, 38 Sanambin Rd, T 242060, SE of the railway, attractive wooden building, clean large rooms, helpful owner, bicycles for rent.

● Places to eat

Phitsanulok has two specialities for which it is known across Thailand: excellent *kluay thaak* or sweet bananas, and its *thao mai luai* or morning glory, these are flashfried in a wok with a great burst of flame and then tossed onto the plate. 'Flying Vegetable' artistes can be seen at work in the night market and at one or two restaurants. Several houseboat restaurants are to be found along Buddha Bucha Rd, near Naresuan Bridge.

Thai: ♦*Poon Sri*, Phaya Lithai Rd, rec; ♦♦♦*Song Khwae Houseboat*, Buddha Bucha Rd, also serves Chinese food; ♦♦*Sor Lert Rod*, 4/5 Boromtrailokant Rd, near *Phailin Hotel*, rec; ♦♦*Tiparot*, 9 Soi Lue Thai Rd, also serves Chinese food; ♦♦*Viroys*, 99/18-19 Phra Ong Dam Rd, excellent Chinese food with morning glory frying for the uninitiated; ♦♦-♦♦♦*Bi Bi's Pub*, Sithamtripidok Rd, European steaks, grills and a few Thai dishes.

Foodstalls: the riverside night market is open from 1800 to midnight, excellent stalls selling Thai and Chinese food. Thai sweets (deserts) like *khao niaw sangkayaa* (sticky rice and custard) can be bought from the foodstalls on Phaya Lithai Rd in the evening.

Bakery: *K.T.*, Phaya Lithai Rd, excellent range of cakes and pastries.

● Bars

Bi Bi's Pub, Sithamtripidok Rd (down soi near *Thep Nakhon Hotel*), cocktails and a wide range of drinks in an a/c 'chalet'; *Thip Beer House* (opposite *Phailin Hotel*), Boromtrailokant Rd, ice-cold beer in open bar.

● Airline offices

Thai Airways, 209/26-28 Boromtrailokant Rd, T 258020.

● **Banks & money changers**
Bangkok, 35 Naresuan Rd; **Krung Thai**, 31/1 Naresuan Rd; **Thai Farmers**, 144/1 Boromtrailokant Rd.

● **Hospital & medical services**
Hospital: Sithamtripidok Rd, T 258812.

● **Post & telecommunications**
Post Office and Telephone Centre: Buddha Bucha Rd. **Area code**: 055.

● **Shopping**
Antiques and handicrafts: *Mondok Thai*, 10 Sithamtripidok Rd; *Hat Tim*, 1/1 Sithamtripidok Rd. The *night market* on Buddha Bucha Rd, on the river, sells everything from handicrafts, clothes and toys to amulets (see page 142) – something Phitsanulok has a reputation for. The *Topland Arcade* is a large a/c shopping centre on Boromtrailokant Rd.

● **Tour companies & travel agents**
Piti Tour, 43/11 Boromtrailokant Rd; *Phitsanulok Tour Centre*, 55/45 Surasri Trade Center, Boromtrailokant Rd, T 242206.

● **Tourist Police**
Boromtrailokant Rd, next to TAT office, T 251179.

● **Tourist office**
TAT, 209/7-8 Surasi Shopping Centre, Boromtrailokant Rd, T 252742. Areas of responsibility are Phitsanulok and Sukhothai.

● **Transport**
498 km N of Bangkok.

Local Songthaews, tuk-tuks, saamlors and buses (฿3) around town.

Air: airport is just out of town on Sanambin Rd, T 258029. Thai Airways have daily connections with Bangkok. Connections with Loei (3/week), Tak (4/week), Lampang (4/week), Chiang Mai (daily), Mae Hong Son (3/week), Mae Sot (4/week) and Nan (3/week). From the airport, take a songthaew into town or buses run to/from the City bus centre near the railway station every 10 mins (฿3).

Train: swiss 'chalet' style station, with steam locomotive parked outside, is on Ekathosarot Rd, T 258005. Regular connections with Bangkok's Hualamphong station 6 hrs (฿69-292). Lopburi 5 hrs (฿49-204), Ayutthaya 7 hrs (฿58-245). Also with Uttaradit, Nakhon Sawan, Lampang 4-5 hrs (฿48-200) and Chiang Mai 6-7 hrs (฿65-276). For those travelling straight on to Sukhothai, take a tuk-tuk the 4 km to the bus station on the road E (Route 12) to Lom Sak.

Road Bus: terminal on the road E to Lom Sak (Route 12) 2 km out of town (T 242430). Phitsanulok is a transport hub, linking N, NE and Central Plains, so buses go almost everywhere. Bus no 7 leaves the local bus station for the bus terminal every 10 mins (30 mins journey). Regular connections with Bangkok (from the Northern bus terminal), 7 hrs (฿150-250), Kamphaeng Phet 3 hrs (฿27), Uttaradit 2 hrs (฿27), Nan 5 hrs (via Uttaradit), Phrae 2 hrs, Udorn (via Loei), Sukhothai, Pattaya, Tak 3 hrs (฿36-51), Mae Sot 5 hrs (฿50), Nakhon Sawan 2 hrs (฿28), Chiang Mai 5½ hrs (฿86-155), Lampang 4 hrs (฿63), Khon Kaen 5 hrs (฿92-129). Also buses to Korat, Udon Thani and Chiang Rai. Private a/c and VIP tour buses leave from 3 offices in the centre of town.

Sukhothai

History
King Intradit ('Glorious Sun-King') founded the Sukhothai Kingdom in 1240, having successfully driven off the Khmers following a single-handed elephant duel with the Khmer commander. Sukhothai, meaning 'dawn of happiness', became the **first capital of Siam** and the following 200 years (until the early 15th century) is considered the pinnacle of Thai civilization. There were 9 kings of the Sukhothai Dynasty, the most famous being King Intradit's third son, Ramkhamhaeng, whose reign is disputed but believed to have been 1275-1317. He was the first ruler to leave accounts of the state inscribed in stone stelae (now displayed in the National Museum in Bangkok). These provide a wealth of information on conquests, taxation and political philosophy. Realizing the importance of a national language as a unifying force, the King created the Thai script, derived from Mon and Khmer, and the inscription No. 1 of 1292 is regarded by many as the first work of Thai literature (see page 77).

King Ramkhamhaeng vastly expanded his kingdom, which at its peak encompassed much of present-day Thailand, except the northern kingdom of Lanna Thai, Lopburi and the Khorat

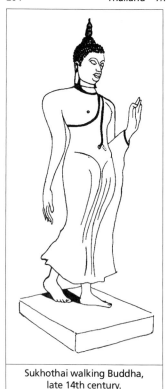

Sukhothai walking Buddha,
late 14th century.

Plateau (which were still controlled by the waning Khmer Empire). The Sukhothai Kingdom also extended S down the Malay Peninsula and W into Lower Burma.

Ramkhamhaeng is commonly portrayed as an absolute monarch but one who governed his people with justice and magnanimity. If anyone wanted to lodge a complaint, they would ring a bell at the gate and he would grant them an audience. Naturally, the inscriptions on which much of our knowledge of Sukhothai and King Ramkhamhaeng is based are rather fanciful. Even so, his reign was a brilliant one. King Ramkhamhaeng was responsible for the intro-

duction of Theravada Buddhism, when he brought Ceylonese monks to his kingdom – partly intended to displace the influence of the Khmers. He displayed considerable diplomatic powers and cultivated good relations with his northern neighbours in order to form an alliance against the Khmers. In addition, he opened relations with China, establishing both economic and cultural links. The fine pottery produced at Sukhothai and Si Satchanalai is thought by some scholars to have developed only after the arrival of expert Chinese potters with their knowledge of advanced glazing techniques (see page 208).

If historical records are to be believed (and the story sounds ominously apocryphal), his closest brush with death came when he was foolish enough to fall in love with the wife of the King of Phayao whom he was visiting. Princess Ua Chiengsaen returned his affection, but when her husband discovered the affair, he arrested Ramkhamhaeng. The love-stricken King was about to be put to death when Phya Mengrai, the great king of Chiang Mai, called on them to resolve their differences. Ramkhamhaeng apologized and was ordered to pay 999,000 cowrie shells in penance. Then the 3 kings went to the River Ping and swore perpetual friendship by drinking a cup of water mixed with blood from their fingers.

The Sukhothai Period saw a flowering not just of ceramic arts, but of art in general (see page 91). The Buddha images are regarded as the most beautiful and original to have ever been produced in Thailand. And the walking Buddha image carved in the round is perhaps the greatest innovation of the artists of the period. There had previously been walking Buddhas in bas-relief, but never free-standing. The style is graceful and languid, with an expression of bliss and an enigmatic smile. It was not to last: by the second half of the 14th century, the smile had become a smirk and the gen-

SUKHOTHAI: A 'GOLDEN AGE' OR MOTHER OF INVENTION?

At the beginning of March 1989, several hundred people – mostly scholars – assembled at the Bangkok Bank's headquarters on Silom Road to debate an issue that threatened to undermine the very identity of the Thai people. Some archaeologists had begun to argue that the famous inscription no. 1 on which the interpretation of King Ramkhamhaeng's reign is based (see page 77), is a forgery. They maintained that the then Prince Mongkut's remarkably timely 'discovery' of the inscription in 1833 served Siam's political purposes – it showed to the expansionist British and French that the country was a 'civilized' kingdom that could govern itself without outside interference. Along with certain literary and artistic anomalies, this led some commentators to maintain that King Mongkut created King Ramkhamhaeng – or at least his popular image – to protect his kingdom from the colonial powers.

Before Mongkut stumbled upon inscription no. 1, knowledge of Sukhothai's history was based upon myth and legend. The great king Phra Ruang – who was believed to have hatched from the egg of a *naga* (serpent) and to be so powerful that he could make trees flower – was clearly the stuff of imagination. And some scholars also argued the same was true of King Ramkhamhaeng. Since the meeting of 1989, academic opinion has swung back to viewing Mongkut's discovery as genuine. However, this does not detract from the fact that inscription no. 1 – and the other inscriptions – are fanciful portrayals of history carved to serve the interests of an élite, not to reflect 'reality'. As Betty Gosling writes in *Sukhothai: its history, culture and art* (1991) "...the controversy emphasizes the need to consider Sukhothai inscriptions...not in the golden afterglow of Thai mythology, but in the harsh daylight of objective research".

eral expression degenerated into one of haughtiness.

King Ramkhamhaeng's son, Lo Thai (1327-1346) was an ineffectual leader, overshadowed even in death by his father, and much of the territories gained by the previous reign were lost. By the sixth reign of the Sukhothai Dynasty, the kingdom was in decline and by the seventh, Sukhothai paid homage to Ayutthaya. In 1438 Ayutthaya officially incorporated Sukhothai into its realm and the first Thai kingdom had succumbed to its younger and more vigorous neighbour.

Places of interest

The ancient city of Sukhothai is 12 km outside the modern, and unattractive, town which was rebuilt after being destroyed by a fire in the late 1950s. The old city and its surroundings are a national historical park covering 640 ha which was officially opened in 1988, after a decade of restoration work. A total of 192 wats were restored. It is very well-cared for, with lotus ponds, flowering trees and manicured lawns and has become a haven for bird life. The old city is 1.8 km long and 1.4 km wide, and originally it was encompassed by triple earthen ramparts and two moats, pierced by four gates. Within the city there are 21 historical sites, outside the walls are another 70 or so places of historical interest. At one time the city may have been home to as many as 300,000 people, with an efficient funnel system to bring water from the mountains into the city and a network of roads. It was an urban centre to rival any in Europe at the time. Within the city are monuments of many different styles – as if the architects were attempting to imbue the centre with the magical power of other

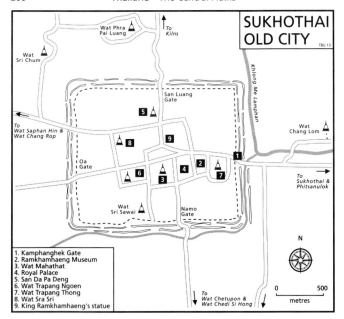

SUKHOTHAI OLD CITY

TBU 13

1. Kamphanghek Gate
2. Ramkhamhaeng Museum
3. Wat Mahathat
4. Royal Palace
5. San Da Pa Deng
6. Wat Trapang Ngoen
7. Wat Trapang Thong
8. Wat Sra Sri
9. King Ramkhamhaeng's statue

Buddhist sites: there are Mon chedis, Khmer prangs and Sri Lankan chedis as well as monuments of clearly Sukhothai inspiration.

The Ramkhamhaeng National Museum is situated just inside the **Kamphang-hek** (Broken Wall) **Gate** – the entrance gate – and is a good place to begin a tour of the site (bicycles and motorbikes can be hired close by). The museum contains a copy of Ramkhamhaeng's stela and some wonderful Buddha images along with explanatory information. It also houses a range of household goods which give some indication of the sophistication of Sukhothai society. Admission: ฿10. Open: 0900-1200, 1300-1600 Wed-Sun (closed public holidays).

The centre of the Sukhothai Kingdom was **Wat Mahathat** and the royal palace (the earliest example of a royal palace in Thailand), to be found W of the museum. This was both the religious and the political centre of the Kingdom and represents the first truly 'Sukhothai' monument. The complex was begun by King Intradit, expanded by King Ramkhamhaeng and finally completed by King Lo Thai in 1345, or thereabouts. In total, the shrine contains nearly 200 chedis (containing the ashes of the Sukhothai royal family), 10 viharns and a plethora of other structures.

The principal building is the central sanctuary, which has a large lotus-bud chedi at its core. King Lo Thai is said to have rebuilt the sanctuary in the 1340s to house the hair and neckbone relics of the Buddha which had been brought back from Ceylon. The central tower, is surrounded by 4 smaller chedis in Srivijaya-Ceylonese style, alternating with 4 Khmer prangs. The entire ensemble is raised up on a 2-tiered base with a stucco frieze of walking monks in relief (rather poorly restored and probably later in date). They are shown walking clockwise around the monument; pilgrims to the wat would have circumambulated in the same fashion (known as pradaksina).

The Khmer prangs would originally have had stucco decorations on their superstructure, depicting mythical animals and spirits. Most have long since eroded away. However, on the pediments of the E prang can be seen 2 scenes from the life of the Buddha: his birth and his death (there were 12 such scenes). Such decoration was not designed just to beautify the monument; most pilgrims would have been illiterate and the panels would also have helped to guide and educate the worshipper. In its original form, the wat was encrusted in stucco decoration and then covered in gold leaf. The central summit of the wat represented the mythical Mount Meru, and the whole sanctuary was in effect a magic diagram.

"Mount Meru was located in the centre of the universe and...Kailsa was on its summit. Gods dwelt at the highest levels, the many mythical creatures and earth spirits inhabited the terraced slopes. Around Mount Meru rose the lesser pinnacles arranged in six and seven concentric rings. At their feet lay the continents and islands which in turn were surrounded by vast oceans whose far boundaries were demarcated by a wall of rock" (Stratton & Scott, 1981: 54-5).

Some original Buddha images still sit among the ruins. Particularly unusual are the 2 monumental standing Buddhas, in an attitude of forgiveness, either side of the central sanctuary, enclosed by brick walls, with their heads protruding over the top.

The **Royal Palace** or **Phra Ruang Palace** is found just to the east of Wat Mahathat. Little remains of the original structure. It was here that King Mongkut, while he was still the Crown Prince, found the famous inscription No.1 of King Ramkhamhaeng in 1833.

To the N of Wat Mahathat is **San Da Pa Deng**, the oldest existing structure from the Sukhothai era. It is a small Khmer laterite prang built during the first half of the 12th century.

Wat Trapang Ngoen and Wat Trapang Thong flank Wat Mahathat and the Royal Palace. **Wat Trapang Ngoen** (Wat Silver Pond) lies to the W and contains a large lotus-bud chedi similar in style to that at Wat Mahathat. The difference here is that the Buddha images found in the niches towards the summit of the chedi are all in the walking attitude. **Wat Trapang Thong** lies to the E of Wat Mahathat and the Royal Palace. Particularly fine are the stucco reliefs, of which perhaps the most beautiful is that on the S side of the mondop. It shows the Buddha descending from the Tavatimsa Heaven with the attendant Brahma on his left and Indra on his right. Although Hindu gods, Brahma and Indra are said to have converted to Buddhism. Being deities themselves, they too have divinities in attendance. The Buddha is protected by 2 parasols, above which are more deities. Particularly striking is the simplicity of the Buddha's flowing, monastic robes, and the elaborate garments of the other deities and divinities. The sculpture is considered the finest piece of stucco work from the Sukhothai Period.

Wat Sra Sri, to the N of Wat Trapang Ngoen, is a popular photo-spot, as the bot is reflected in a pond. A Ceylonese-style chedi dominates the complex, which also contains a fine, large seated Buddha image enclosed by columns. To the E of here is a **statue of King Ramkhamhaeng** seated on a copy of the stone throne (the Phra Thaen Manang Silabat) that was found on the site of the Royal Palace and which is now in the Wat Phra Kaeo Museum in Bangkok. The statue was erected in 1969 and the high relief carvings depict famous episodes from the life of the illustrious king.

To the SW of Wat Mahathat is **Wat Sri Sawai**, enclosed within laterite walls. It was built during the time that Sukhothai was under Khmer domination. The prang is in the 3-tower style, with the largest central prang (rather badly restored) being 20m tall. The stucco decoration was added to the towers in the 15th century, as were their upper brick portions. The lower laterite levels are the original sections, built under Khmer influence. It must originally have been a Hindu shrine, as carvings of Vishnu and other Hindu divinities have been found on the site. Only later was it converted into a Buddhist shrine.

A 2 km ride to the S of the city is **Wat Chetupon** built in the late 13th or perhaps early 14th century. It is not a very exciting wat but the journey there gives one an idea of the scale of the whole site and the road passes through an attractive village. Slate slabs run round the viharn while the bridges across the moat are also of slate. On the 4 walls of the mondop are two stucco images of the Buddha in high relief, walking and standing. E of Wat Chetupon is **Wat Chedi Si Hong**, with small but interesting stucco figures of elephant heads and human figures in bas relief.

Take the NW gate out of the city to visit the impressive **Wat Sri Chum**. A large mondop with a narrow vaulted entrance, encloses an enormous brick and stucco seated Buddha image; possibly the *Phra Atchana* mentioned in the stele of Ramkhamhaeng. It was probably built during the 7th reign of the Sukhothai Kingdom (mid-14th century) and is said to have caused a Burmese army to flee in terror such is the power of its withering gaze. The large Buddha seems almost suffocated by the surrounding walls which must have been added at a later stage. There is a stairway in the mondop which leads up to a space behind the head of the image (closed since 1988). Here there are line carvings recounting the jataka tales,

CERAMICS OF SUKHOTHAI AND SI SATCHANALAI

Popular history has it that the technology of ceramics production was introduced into Thailand after King Ramkhamhaeng visited the Yuan court of China in 1292, and requested that a group of Chinese potters accompany him back to his kingdom. This is almost certainly false. It seems far more likely that Chinese potters arrived in Thailand spontaneously, trying to escape from the wars and instability of Southern Sung China (late 13th century). Their skills recognized, they would have been welcomed by the Thais. There was probably already a primitive ceramics industry in Thailand; the Chinese were able to build upon this and immeasurably improve the quality and range of output, incorporating their own designs and techniques.

Important centres of production included Pha Yang and Ko-noi just outside the walls of Si Satchanalai (where Sawankhalok ware was produced) and Sukhothai. The best work was produced at Pa Yang, with the best known being the wonderful Sawankhalok celadons, and probably the finest the incised brown and pearl wares. Celadon refers to the colour of the glaze which ranges from blue-green to grey. Some connoisseurs regard the celadon produced at Si Satchanalai during the 14th and 15th centuries as being almost as fine in quality as that of the famous Longquan kilns in China's Zhejiang province.

The terminology for the different wares is somewhat confusing. Sukhothai ware should refer to all products of the kingdom; foreigners often use it to mean only those wares from Old Sukhothai town. Sawankhalok is ware from the kilns in the vicinity of Si Satchanalai.

covering the slate slab ceiling. Each slab depicts one story, skilfully carved with free-flowing lines – which originally would have been enlivened with paint. These are the finest and earliest (c.1350) to be found in Thailand (there are examples from Wat Sri Chum in the National Museum, Bangkok). What is surprising is that they should be positioned in such a dark and inaccessible place. It is thought that they were designed to instruct pilgrims, but they could hardly do so in this location. Some scholars maintain that they were originally produced for Wat Mahathat and were only later moved to Wat Sri Chum for safe-keeping. The image here is said to have talked on a number of occasions – although the back stairs provide a useful hiding place for someone to play a practical joke.

E of Wat Sri Chum is **Wat Phra Pai Luang**, primarily interesting for the remains of 3 laterite prangs. It was built during the reign of King Jayavarman VII (a Khmer king who ruled 1181-1217). Its Khmer inspiration is clearly evident in the square base and indented tiers. Only the N prang retains some of the original fine stucco-work with naga-makara arches bordering the pediment. To the E of the prang is a later stupa with niches on all 4 sides containing damaged Buddha images. Further E still is a ruined mondop with the remains of large stucco Buddha images, standing, walking and reclining. In total Wat Phra Pai Luang contains over 30 stupas of assorted styles. It is thought that not only was it originally a Hindu shrine but that it was also the site of an earlier Khmer town.

To visit **Wat Saphan Hin**, take the NW road 3 km beyond the city walls (rather than the longer, rougher route from Oa Gate). A large standing Buddha image (in an attitude of forgiveness) stands on a hill here (possibly the *Phra Attharot* image referred to in the inscriptions). The name of the wat means 'stone bridge', a reference to the steep slate path leading to the wat, which is still in place. **Wat Chang Rop**, a little to the S of Wat Saphan Hin, has a chedi with caryatid base of Ceylonese derivation.

N of this wat are ruins of 14th-15th century **kilns**, where Chinese-inspired ceramics were made. Although the raw materials were of poor quality, and the firing techniques primitive, the pottery produced is very appealing. Free-flowing and uninhibited in style, the decorations are based upon T'zu Chou and Annamese prototypes. The more famous Sawankhalok wares were produced at Si Satchanalai. To the E of the city is **Wat Chang Lom** (founded by Ramkhamhaeng), with a large chedi surrounded by caryatids, similar to Wat Chang Rop.

ADMISSION TO HISTORICAL PARK: ฿20/person, ฿30/car,bus, ฿20/bike plus ฿20 extra for some of the outer wats (Wat Sri Chum, Wat Chang Lom). Open: 0600-1800 Mon-Sun. Food and souvenir stalls are to be found just N of Wat Trapang Ngoen.

GETTING AROUND THE RUINS: If arriving by public bus, either hire a bicycle (฿15-20/day) or moped (฿100/day) from the entrance gate close to the museum, or take the trolley bus which tours the major sights (฿20). Getting there: there are a number of ways of getting to the Old City. Cheapest is to catch one of the quaint buses that run from the stop near the Tirat Cinema and police box on Charodwithithong Rd on the western side of the bridge in the new town, leaving every 10 mins 0600-1730 (฿5). Tuk-tuks should take visitors to the Park for about ฿50. Alternatively either go on a tour (see below), hire a motorbike (฿120), or charter a tuk-tuk for the trip there and back along with trips around the site (฿150 for 3 hrs).

Excursions
Si Satchanalai: see page 211.

Tours
Many hotels and guesthouses arrange tours to Sukhothai and Si Satchanalai, e.g. *Chinawat Hotel*, *Sky House*, *Sawatipong Hotel* and *No. 4* (฿100-300 for Sukhothai, ฿200-350 for Si Satchanalai).

Festivals

Oct/Nov: *Loi Krathong and Candle festival* (moveable), candles are lit, there are firework displays, folk dancing and a sound and light show at the Old City. Sukhothai is reputed to be the 'home' of this most beautiful of Thai festivals. It is said that one of the king's mistresses carved the first *krathong* from a piece of fruit and floated it down the river to her king. Today the festival symbolizes the floating away of the previous year's sins, although traditionally it was linked to the gift of water. The Thai word for irrigation, *chonprathaan*, literally means the 'gift of water' and the festival comes at the end of the rainy season, when the rice is maturing in the paddy fields. Krathongs used to be made from leaves; now, polystyrene is used, and the boats are laden with candles, sticks of incense and other gifts for Mae Khong Kha, the Goddess of Water.

Local information

● Accommodation in the Old City

C *The Old Sukhothai Cultural Centre* (aka Thai Village House), next to Wat Chang Lom is the only place to stay in Old Sukhothai itself, advance booking is needed between Oct and Apr, T 612275, F 612583, restaurant, attractive teak bungalows, rec. The *Nam Kang Garden Restaurant* is a good outdoor restaurant here.

A+-B *Paylin*, Jarodwithithong Rd, a short distance from the Old City on the road leading to Sukhothai new town, T 613310, F 613317, BT 2157119, BF 2155640, a/c, restaurants, pool, rates negotiable.

E *Suwan Guesthouse*, near the entrance to the park, at the bend in the main road, but set 50m back, attractive teak house with small rooms, good base if Old Sukhothai is the main reason to be here.

● Accommodation in Modern Sukhothai Town

A-C *Rachthani*, 229 Charodwithithong Rd, T 611031, F 612878, W of the bridge, a/c, restaurant, popular with tour groups.

B *Northern Palace*, 43 Singhawat Rd, T 611193, F 612038, a/c, restaurant, pool, best in town, runs tours (for guests only) to Sukhothai and Si Satchanalai, ฿200 and ฿350 respectively; **B-E** *River View*, 92/1 Nikhon Kasem Rd, T 611656, F 613373, some a/c, restaurant, good range of rooms available.

C-D *Chinnawat*, 1-3 Nikhon Kasem Rd, T 611385, some a/c, restaurant, friendly, lots of information but shabby; **C-F** *Sky*, 28-30 Prasert Pong Rd, T 612236, F 611212, W of the bridge, some a/c, hot water, bicycles and motorbikes available, well run, good information, rec (a new *Sky 2* guesthouse, under the same management, has recently opened, also rec).

D *Sawatdipong*, 56/2-5 Singhawat Rd, T 611567, F 612268, some a/c and hot water; **D-E** *Sukhothai*, 15/5 Singhawat Rd, T 611133, F 612028, some a/c, restaurant, central, rather noisy.

E *No. 4*, 62/16 Vichian Chamnong Rd, T 611315, clean; **F** *No. 4*, 170 Rachthani Rd, T 611315, attractive teak house by the river, clean and peaceful, rooms available in the main house or in new bungalow set near a pond (mosquitoes a problem), English speaking, lots of information, very popular, rec; **F** *No 4*, 234/6 Charodwithithong Rd, T 611315, Soi Panitsan, the third of the 'No 4s', only 5 rooms, English speaking, friendly owners; **F** *Yupa*, 44 Pravet Nakhon Rd, T 612578, on the W bank of the river, good views, friendly owners.

● Places to eat

Thai: *Chinnawat*, 1-3 Nikhon Kasem Rd, good bakery, fruit and noodles; *Dream Café 1*, Nikhon Kasem Rd (next to *Chinnawat Hotel*), also serves International; *Dream Café 2*, near *Sawatdipong Hotel*, Singhawat Rd, also serves International; *Leaf Bakery*, 23/6 Singhawat Rd; *Rainbow Café*, off Nikhon Kasem Rd (nr. night market), also serves International; ♦♦*Sukhothai Coca*, 56/2-5 Singhawat Rd (*Sawatdipong Hotel*). **Chinese**: *Kho Joeng Hong*, Nikhon Kasem Rd (closed by 2000), budget.

Foodstalls: ♦the night market, off Nikhon Kasem Road, opposite the cinema, for good stalls.

● Banks & money changers

Bangkok, 49 Singhawat Rd; Bangkok Bank of Commerce, 15 Singhawat Rd; Thai Farmers, 134 Charoen Withi Rd.

● Shopping

Cultural Centre, near the Historical Park offers antiques, weaving and handicrafts such as Sawankhalok pottery. *Phra Mae Ya Shrine*

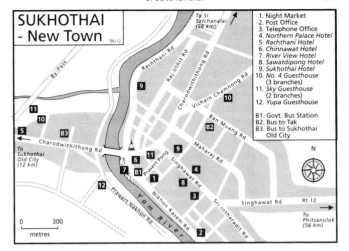

SUKHOTHAI
- New Town TBU 12

1. Night Market
2. Post Office
3. Telephone Office
4. Northern Palace Hotel
5. Rachthani Hotel
6. Chinnawat Hotel
7. River View Hotel
8. Sawatdipong Hotel
9. Sukhothai Hotel
10. No. 4 Guesthouse (3 branches)
11. Sky Guesthouse (2 branches)
12. Yupa Guesthouse

B1. Govt. Bus Station
B2. Bus to Tak
B3. Bus to Sukhothai Old City

shop, in front of the Municipal Hall for antiques and local cloth. *Hat Sieo village*, near Si Satchanalai is noted for its weaving.

● **Hospital & medical services**
Hospital: Charodwithithong Rd, T 611782.

● **Police**
Nikhon Kasem Rd, T 611010.

● **Post & telecommunications**
Post Office: Nikhon Kasem Rd. **Area code**: 055.

● **Tour companies & travel agents**
Sky, 28-30 Prasert Pong Rd, T 612236.

● **Transport**
466 km from Bangkok, 56 km from Phitsanulok.

Local (For transport to the Old City see above).
Bicycle hire: ฿20/day at the restaurants on the road opposite the museum (Old City) or from *Sawatdipong Hotel* or *Sky Tour*. **Motorbike hire**: ฿120-130/day (*Sky Tour, Sawatdipong Hotel, Chinnawat Hotel*). **Tuk-tuks**: for town trips and for excursions further afield.

Air: Bangkok Airways are planning to open a route from Bangkok to Sukhothai.

Road Bus: for Bangkok, Chiang Mai and Khon Kaen the station is at 9 Prasert Pong Rd. For Tak, buses leave from Ban Muang Rd, and for Phitsanulok from Singhawat Rd. Regular connections with Bangkok's Northern bus terminal 7-8 hrs (฿84-190), Chiang Mai via Lampang 4 1/2 hrs (฿72-100), Khon Kaen, Phitsanulok, Nakhon Sawan, Chiang Rai, Uttaradit, Nan, Phrae and Tak.

Private bus companies: *Win-Tour* are on Charodwithithong Rd, T 611039 and operate buses to many of the destinations noted above.

Si Satchanalai

Referred to by Thais as Si Sat, this is the twin city to Sukhothai and lies to the N, on the west bank of the Yom River. During the fourth reign of Sukhothai it became the seat of the king's son, and the 2 cities were linked by a road, the Phra Ruang Highway. Si Satchanalai was probably built on the site of a Khmer town called Chaliang. It was bounded by a moat 10m wide and by town walls that stood 3 rows deep on 3 sides and a single row deep on the E side (which was protected by the river). 6 gates pierce these walls. The city was rediscovered by a retired British Consular official called Reginald le May, whose particular love became Si Satchanalai. It remained relatively undiscovered by tourists until 1987, when a grant was provided to prepare the town for Visit Thailand Year. The sight has been 'cleaned up', rather

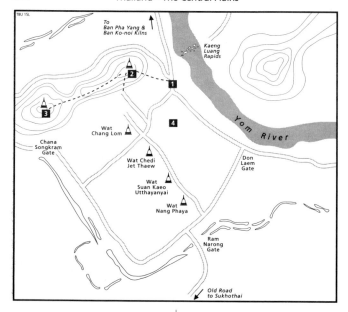

as Sukhothai has been, and in the process has lost some of its charm – at least to romantic Westerners brought up on images of vegetation-choked lost cities. Even so, Si Satchanalai makes a fascinating side trip from Sukhothai. There is no modern town here; the whole area has become a 'Historical Park', with an admission fee of ฿20/person, ฿30 for a car, ฿20 for a motorbike or bicycle. The most regal way to visit the sights is by elephant; an elephant 'rank' is to be found by Wat Chang Lom, ฿5.

Places of interest

Si Satchanalai is littered with monuments, only the major ones are mentioned below. **Wat Chang Lom**, probably the finest wat in the park, lies in the heart of the old city and is the most sacred wat in Si Satchanalai. It lies in front of the gates to the park and is specifically mentioned in Ramkhamhaeng's inscriptions. The principle chedi was built by the King between 1285 and 1291 to contain sacred relics of the Buddha. The Ceylonese-style chedi is the earliest example of its kind in Thailand and became the prototype for many others (like the wat of the same name in Sukhothai). It is made of laterite and stucco and sits on a 2-storey square base. On the lowest tier are the remains of 39 standing elephant caryatids (probably post-dating the chedi) separated by columns, which would have been supports for lanterns. Stairs take the pilgrim from the lower, earthly levels, upwards towards the more spiritual realm of the Buddha. Here, on the second tier, 20 niches contain stucco seated Buddha images, portrayed in quiet meditation (all now mutilated). Above the second tier is an octagonal plinth, 4 circular mouldings, the smooth bell-shaped stupa, and finally an honorific umbrella spire towering into the heavens both physically and symbolically. The chedi is enclosed by 50m long

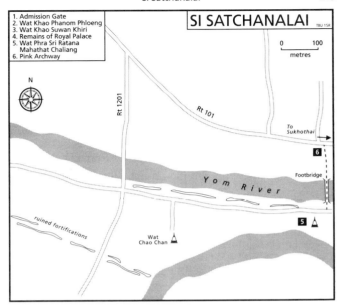

1. Admission Gate
2. Wat Khao Phanom Phloeng
3. Wat Khao Suwan Khiri
4. Remains of Royal Palace
5. Wat Phra Sri Ratana Mahathat Chaliang
6. Pink Archway

SI SATCHANALAI TBU 15R

0   100
metres

N

Rt 1201

Rt 101

To Sukhothai

6

Footbridge

Yom River

ruined fortifications

Wat Chao Chan

5

laterite walls, and in front of it are the ruins of a large viharn, together with another smaller stupa and viharn.

Wat Chedi Jet Thaew (S of Wat Chang Lom) stands within a ditch and 2 rows of laterite walls pierced by 4 gates. The wat contains the remnants of 7 rows of lotus-bud chedis – some 34 in total – which house the ashes of members of the Si Satchanalai ruling family. The largest stands on a square base, and was probably built by King Li Thai (1347-1368). The mondop tower (14th century) displays a fusion of stylistic elements: the corbelled archway of overlapping blocks was a technique used by both Khmer and Sukhothai architects, above this are niches holding Buddha images which are then crowned by a Ceylonese bell and umbrella spire. Other noteworthy elements are the Burmese-style stucco decorations on a chedi in the NE corner, and a Srivijaya-style Buddha (sadly, it has been unsympathetically restored)

sitting under a naga on the N side. A number of the chedis display remnants of fine naga-makara arches: 5-headed nagas issue forth from the makaras which form the double curve of the arch.

S of here is **Wat Suan Kaeo Utthay-anyai** and the southernmost wat within the walls, **Wat Nang Phaya** (Temple of the Queen). The latter is enclosed by single walls of laterite, with 4 gateways. A Ceylonese-style chedi dominates the compound. The fine stucco floral motifs (now protected by a shed) on the W wall of the large laterite viharn are early Ayutthayan in style (15th century).

Wat Khao Phanom Phloeng lies on a 20m high hillock on the N side of the town and is reached by a laterite staircase. It comprises a Ceylonese-style chedi, a large seated Buddha and some stone columns. To the W and linked by a path and staircase, on a higher hillock, are the remains of **Wat Khao Suwan Khiri**.

To the SE, 2 km outside the Si Satchanalai city walls, is the area known as Chaliang. Positioned on the banks of the Yom River is **Wat Phra Sri Ratana Mahathat Chaliang** (or **Wat Phra Prang**), an impressive laterite prang originally built in the mid 15th century and then rather badly restored in the reign of King Boromkot (1733-1758). In front of the prang are the ruins of a viharn which houses a large seated Sukhothai Buddha image, with long, graceful fingers 'touching ground'. Even more beautiful is the smaller walking Buddha of brick and stucco to the left. It is thought to be one of the finest from the Sukhothai Period displaying that enigmatic 'Sukhothai smile' (see illustration, page 204). The wat also contains a number of other interesting Buddha images. **Wat Chao Chan**, 500m W of Wat Phra Prang, contains a prang built in the time of the Khmer King Jayavarman Vll (1181-1217).

N of the city, at Ban Pha Yang and Ban Ko-noi, remains of **ceramic kilns** have been discovered, dating from the 1350s. The pottery produced from here is known as 'Sawankhalok', after the early Ayutthaya name for the district (there is a town of the same name to the south). The kilns at **Ban Pha Yang** lie 500m N of the old city walls, and so far 21 kilns have been found, all of the closed kiln variety. It is thought that they produced architectural and high quality ceramics (see page 208).

Local information
● **Accommodation**
Wang Yom, off route 101 to Sawankhalok, T (055) 611179, restaurant, lovely gardens and position; **C** for hut, **A** for a/c Thai cottage (incl breakfast).

● **Transport**
54 km N of Sukhothai.

Local Si Satchanalai is more compact than Sukhothai Old City and the main monuments can be seen on foot. But to reach Chaliang and the sights outside the city walls it is best to hire a **bicycle** (฿20/day) from the shop, 1 km down

Route 1201 towards the site, or at the pink archway that leads to Chaliang.

Road Bus: regular connections from 0600-1800 with Sukhothai from the bus stop near the Sukhothai hotel, 1 hr (฿18). Ask to be dropped off at the *muang kao* (old city). For Chaliang, get off at the pink archway on Route 101, 2 km before Route 1201, which leads to a suspension footbridge crossing the Yom River to Chaliang.

Motorbike: for hire in Sukhothai (see above).

Uttaradit

Uttaradit is a dusty provincial capital; most people's only contact with the town is during a brief stop at the bus terminal. The area in the vicinity of Uttaradit seems to have been at the very edge of the Khmer sphere of influence during the 13th century. Later, it lay at the heart of King Ramkhamhaeng's emerging kingdom of Sukhothai. When Sukhothai began to collapse with Ramkhamhaeng's death in 1317 so Uttaradit again came to mark the northern frontier of Sukhothai.

In the centre of the town is **Wat Tha Thanon** which contains a revered Chiang Saen-period seated image of the Buddha cast in bronze.

Excursions
Wat Phra Boromthat, also known as Wat That Thung Yang, is a wat with ancient origins although many of the structures have had to be re-built. It lies 5 km west of town near Thung Yang market. Getting there: by local bus.

Wat Phra Yun Buddhabat Yukhon is a hill top wat 6 km from the city. Its unusual architecture dates from the Chiang Saen period.

Sirikit Dam lies 58km from town. Like the other dams that control the waters of the tributaries of the Chao Phraya River north of its confluence at Nakhon Sawan, the Sirikit was built to improve flood control and generate power. It is named after the Queen of Thailand. Getting there: by bus.

Festivals

Sept: the *Langsat Fair*, a fruit for which Uttaradit is well known in Thailand, is held early in the month in the grounds of Wat Mae Plu School.

Local information

● **Accommodation**

A-B *Seeharaj*, 163 Borom Art Rd, T 411106, a/c, pool, large hotel with 124 rooms and surprisingly plush for a place like Uttaradit.

C-D *Wiwat*, 159 Borom Art Rd, T 411779, 80 rooms, some a/c.

D-E *Numchai*, 213/3-4 Borom Art Rd, T 411253, 50 basic rooms.

E-F *Heaven*, 185/1 Chonpratan-Sirikit Rd, T 412866, 15 very basic rooms.

● **Useful Addresses**
Area code: 055.

● **Transport**
481 km from Bangkok.

Train: connections with Bangkok's Hualamphong station, 9 hrs (฿82-356) and stations north to Chiang Mai, 5 hrs.

Road Bus: bus connections with Bangkok's Northern bus terminal, 7 hrs (a/c ฿208) and with other towns in the Central Plains and the North. Some buses also leave here and travel up to the Khorat Plateau and the Northeast.

ROUTES NORTH TO MAE SOT

A second, less frequently used, route from Nakhon Sawan northwards runs up Route 1 to the historical city of Kamphaeng Phet and on to Tak. From Tak it is possible to travel west to the border town of Mae Sot with trekking and views over to Burma. Travelling north from Tak, the route passes from the Central to the Northern region, and thence to Lampang, Lamphun and Chiang Mai.

Kamphaeng Phet

Kamphaeng Phet (or 'Diamond Wall') acted, as its name suggests, as a garrison town for the capital, Sukhothai, 80 km to the N. It was built by King Li Thai (1347-1368) on the banks of the River Ping in his attempts to consolidate the Sukhothai Kingdom at a time when surrounding states were growing in influence. Although King Li Thai does not have the reputation of his illustrious predecessor King Ramkhamhaeng, he was by all accounts a skilful and scholarly man. He entered the monkhood in 1362, legitimizing Theravada Buddhism as the 'state' religion. He wrote the *Traiphum* (*The Three Worlds*), a Buddhist treatise, and it was also during his reign that Sukhothai sculpture arguably attained its purest form. Evidence of this flowering of art is to be seen in and around Kamphaeng Phet.

Modern Kamphaeng Phet is sleepy and easy-going – traffic still seems to move in an entirely random fashion. With a proportion of its older, wooden, shuttered and tiled buildings still surviving, the town retains a modicum of 'character' – something which cannot be said for many Thai towns.

Places of interest

The 6m high defensive walls still stand – earthen ramparts topped with laterite – beyond which is a moat to further deter attackers. Within the walls – an area of 0.5 km by 2.5 km – lie 2 old wats, Wat Phra Kaeo and Wat Phra That as well as the **Provincial Museum**. The museum contains, in the entrance hall, what is commonly regarded as one of the finest bronzes of Siva in Thailand. Cast in 1510, in the Khmer 'Bayon' style, its head and hands were removed by an over-zealous German visitor in 1886. Fortunately, he was intercepted, and his limbs and head (the statue's, not the German's) were re-united with the torso. The museum contains some good examples of Buddha images found in the locality. Admission: ฿5. Open: 0900-1200, 1300-1600 Wed-Sun.

From the museum, walk W to **Wat Phrathat**. Not much remains except a chedi and a well-weathered seated Buddha (of laterite) sitting in the viharn.

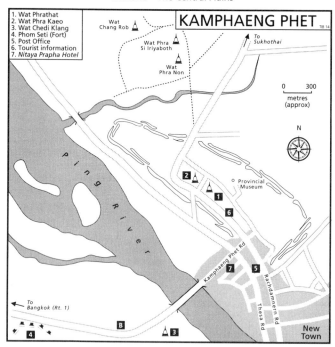

1. Wat Phrathat
2. Wat Phra Kaeo
3. Wat Chedi Klang
4. Phom Seti (Fort)
5. Post Office
6. Tourist information
7. Nitaya Prapha Hotel

KAMPHAENG PHET

Wat Chang Rob

Wat Phra Si Iriyaboth

Wat Phra Non

To Sukhothai

0   300
metres (approx)

N

Provincial Museum

Kamphaeng Phet Rd

Rachdamnern Rd

Thesa Rd

To Bangkok (Rt. 1)

Ping River

New Town

Immediately N, **Wat Phra Kaeo** was probably the largest and most important wat in Kamphaeng Phet. It was initially built during the Sukhothai Period and then extensively re-modelled in the Ayutthaya Period. The wat is surrounded by laterite walls, with a central Ceylonese-style chedi, resting on a square base. The bottom tier of niches once contained 32 singha, whilst the niches above held 16 Buddha images, none of which is intact. Two weathered Buddha images sit facing the chedi, as well as much later images of a reclining Buddha and two seated Buddhas. Admission: ฿20 (retain tickets for admission to the other sections of the historical park outside the city walls).

Most of the more interesting ruins lie outside the ramparts, to the N of town, and it is necessary to have transport (i.e.

a saamlor) to get to them. The first wat of significance to be reached is **Wat Phra Non**, surrounded by laterite walls, with not much remaining; the viharn, with its massive columns, would have contained a reclining Buddha. To the W of the viharn is a large square-based and 8-sided laterite stupa. Most of the images and other ornamentation have been pillaged through the years.

N from here, there is the slightly better preserved **Wat Phra Si Iriyaboth**. This wat derives its name from the large Buddha images that were to be found in the mondop at the end of the viharn. The name of the wat literally means 'four postures' – standing, reclining, sitting and walking. They were all in high stucco relief, one on each side of the mondop. The impressive standing image is the only one in reasonable repair and is a good example of Sukhothai sculpture, dating from the 14th-15th century. The remains of the walking image give the impression of grace, so typical of the Sukhothai Period.

A little over 500m to the NW of Wat Phra Si Iriyaboth is **Wat Chang Rob** (the Shrine of the Elephants). This consists of a huge Ceylonese-style laterite chedi (or what is left of it) with its base surrounded by 68 elephant caryatids (also of Ceylonese influence). Only one row of elephants, on the S side, are preserved. Numerous other ruins of wats are scattered around the town, some in thick undergrowth, others amidst paddy fields – particularly to the NE and SW. Only the most interesting have been described above.

On the right-hand side of the approach road to Kamphaeng Phet (Route 1) are the remains of a laterite fort, **Phom Seti**, which pre-dates the existing town. The fort was built to replace an earlier settlement called Chakangrao. Just before the bridge, on the right-hand side, is the unusually-shaped, square, restored chedi of **Wat Chedi Klang**, also built before Kamphaeng Phet was established by King Li Thai.

Festivals

Sept/Oct: *Kluai Khai (Banana) Festival* (moveable), Kamphaeng province produces ฿160 million of bananas annually. This annual event honours the fruit and features an entirely innocent Miss Banana Pageant.

Local information
● Accommodation

Most hotels are situated in the new town. **C** *Chakungrao*, 123/1 Thesa Rd, T 711315, F 711326, B 2795322, a/c, restaurant, tennis court, good value, comfortable, rec; **C** *Phet*, 99 Wichit Soi 3, T 712810, F 712917, B 2701520, a/c, small pool, good value, comfortable, rec.

D *Kor Chokchai*, 7-31 Rachdamnern Soi 6, T 711247, some a/c, clean; **D** *Nawarat*, 2 Thesa Soi Prapan, T 711106, F 711961, a/c, restaurant, clean and comfortable; **D-E** *Rach-*

damnern, 114 Rachdamnern Rd, T 711029, some a/c.

E *Nitaya Prapha*, 118/1 Thesa Rd, T 711381, best position for getting to ruins, old wooden building.

● Places to eat

Thai: *Kitti Pochana 2*, Wichit Rd; *Kor Kaew*, Rachdamnern Soi 6 (attached to the *Kor Chokchai Hotel*), also serves Chinese; ♦♦*Maalay*, 77 Thesa Rd – look out for the rice baskets hanging outside, Isan (NE) food; ♦♦*Yaat Phet*, Thesa Rd (corner of Soi 10).

● Banks & money changers

Thai Farmers, 233 Charoensuk Rd.

● Post & telecommunications

Post Office: corner of Thesa Rd and Thesa 1 Soi 3. **Area code**: 055.

● Shopping

Fruit: one of Kamphaeng Phet's claims to fame is its bananas and especially its *Kluai khai*, sweet banana, of which some ฿160 million worth is said to be sold annually. **Hammocks**: between Nakhon Sawan and Khampaeng Phet, on Route 1, is one of the best places to buy hammocks in Thailand. Made out of kenaf (*bor kaew*), an inferior jute substitute, they are sold at roadside stalls ฿50-150. *Great Department Store*, Charoensuk Rd (opposite the *Phet Hotel*).

● Tourist offices

Tourist Information Office, Thesa Rd (near Soi 13). Hardly deserves such a title – no maps, no help, in short, no information. Open: 0800-2000.

● Transport

358 km from Bangkok, 114 km NW of Nakhon Sawan.

Local Saamlor: can be hired for a tour of the ruins.

Road Bus: terminal is 1½ km from the bridge, some way out of town. Regular connections with Bangkok's Northern bus terminal 5 hrs (฿69-155) and with Phitsanulok, Chiang Mai, Tak, Nan, Phrae and Chiang Rai.

Tak

Tak, sprawling along the E bank of the Ping River, was once a junction in the river trade but is now better known as a smuggling centre: drugs, teak and gems from Burma are exchanged for guns and consumer goods from Thailand. The Phahonyothin Highway is often lined with logging lorries carrying timber from Burma – a trade which has the political and commercial support of the Thai Army. Still small and distinctly provincial, Tak has managed (so far) to retain some of its traditional architecture – attractive wooden houses with tiled roofs are scattered amongst the ubiquitous concrete shophouses. Like a number of other areas in the more peripheral areas of Thailand, Christian missionaries have been active in Tak province and there is a large Catholic Church on the Phahonyothin Highway.

Places of interest

Official 'sights' in Tak are pretty few and far between. To the N of town, on the other side of Route 12 to Sukhothai, is a **statue of King Taksin**, one of the heroes and father figures of the Thai nation. He is depicted seated with a sword across his lap. In addition to the road bridge across the Ping to the S of town, there is also a long, slender and rather unusual **suspension bridge** for motorcycles and pedestrians N of the *Viang Tak 2 Hotel*. As in any other town, Tak has its share of markets and wats. There is a large **general market** between Jompon and Rimping roads, and a smaller **food market** opposite the *Viang Tak Hotel* on Mahatthai Bamrung Rd. The wats in Tak are undistinguished although Wat Phra Boromthat 36 km to the NW is worth a detour (see Excursions).

Excursions

Lang Sang National Park is 13 km SW of Tak, 1 km off Route 105 to Mae Sot. It covers just over 100 sq km and supports small populations of leopard, various deer, and bear – much of the wildlife has been denuded through years of hunting (usually illegal). There are a number of trails leading to waterfalls, together with a hilltribe centre. Limited accommodation is available in the park and camping is permitted. Admission: ฿3, ฿20 (car).

Wat Phra Boromthat is 36 km from Tak, some way off Route 1 NW towards Thoen and Lampang. Although it is rather difficult to get to, the journey is worth the effort, not least because it is via **Ban Tak**, an attractive village of wooden houses situated on the banks of the Ping River, as yet untouched by the concrete mixer. Wat Phra Boromthat itself is set on a hill, about 5 km from Ban Tak, with views over paddy fields. The chedi is Burmese in style and there is an attractive old viharn in the compound, with rustic carvings on the window shutters and doors. On the other side of the road from the wat is **Chedi Yuttha Hatti (Wat Prathat)**, a lotus-shaped chedi said to have been built as a memorial to King Ramkhamhaeng's victory in elephant combat over King Khun Sam Chon, ruler of Mae Sot. Getting there: take a bus N on Route 1 to the district town of Ban Tak, then another (infrequent) bus going towards Sam Ngao (on Route 1107). The bus crosses the Ping River then turns N on Route 1107. Get off at the junction with Route 1175 (after about 5 km) and walk the final kilometre up the hill to the wat.

Bhumibol Dam (*Khuan Bhumipon*), named after the present King of Thailand, represents the first of Thailand's multi-purpose dams and was officially opened in May 1964. The operations area below the dam is immaculately maintained with gardens, an information centre (where visitors must collect a pass to visit the dam), shops, some guesthouse accommodation (B 4244021) and homes for the engineers. This impressive dam is over 150m high and holds back a reservoir 100 km long with, apparently, a capacity of 12,200 million cubic metres of water. *Long-tailed boats* take day-trippers across the reservoir, and stalls at the top of the dam sell dried fish and other delicacies. Open: 0700-1730. Getting there: take a bus N up Route 1 to the turn off for the dam (43 km from Tak), then another bus to the dam (a further 17 km away). Ask for '*Khuan Bhumipon*'.

Mae Sot can also be visited as a day trip from Tak (see page 219). There are regular buses, journey time about 2 hrs.

Local information
● **Accommodation**

B-C *Viang Tak*, 25/3 Mahatthai Bamrung Rd, T 511910, F 512169, B 5121544, a/c, restaurant, night-club, good value.

C *Viang Tak 2*, Chumphon Rd, T 512686, F 512169, B 5121544, a/c, overlooking the Ping River, good value, rec.

E *Tak*, 18/10 Mahatthai Bamrung Rd, T 513422, some character – wooden floors, no hot water, but clean.

F *Mae Ping*, 231/4-6 Mahatthai Bamrung Rd, T 511918.

● **Places to eat**
There are a number of large 'garden' restaurants along Phahonyothin Rd, e.g. *Jintanaa*. Stall food from the market on Mahatthai Bamrung Rd.

● **Airline offices**
Thai, 485 Taksin Rd, T 512164.

● **Banks & money changers**
Krung Thai, Taksin Rd (corner of Soi 9). **Siam City**, 125 Mahatthai Bamrung Rd. **Thai Military**, 77/2 Mahatthai Bamrung Rd.

● **Post & telecommunications**
Post Office: off Mahatthai Bamrung Rd in the north of town. **Area code**: 055.

● **Tourist office**
TAT, Mahadthaibamroong Rd, T 514341. Areas of responsibility are Tak, Pichit and Kamphaeng Phet.

● **Transport**
65 km N of Kamphaeng Phet and 423 km from Bangkok.

Local Tuk-tuks.

Air: airport is 14 km out of town off Route 12 E towards Sukhothai. 4 connections a week with Bangkok (via Phitsanulok), Chiang Mai and Mae Sot.

Road Bus: non-a/c buses leave from the station near crossroads of Phahonyothin Rd and Route 12 (to Sukhothai). Regular connections with Bangkok's Northern bus terminal 6 hrs (฿80-180). Connections with Kamphaeng Phet and Sukhothai.

Mae Sot

Mae Sot lies 5 km from the Burmese border, near the end of Route 105 which, from Tak, swoops its way through hills and forest to Mae Sot and the Moei River valley. The town has developed into a locally important trading centre and just about every ethnic group can be seen wandering the streets: Tais, Chinese, Burmese, Karen, Meo (Hmong) and other hilltribes. Although Mae Sot has 'quietened-down' over the last few years, it still has a reputation as being one of the more lawless towns in Thailand. With a flourishing, and sometimes illicit, trade in drugs, teak and gems, this is perhaps unsurprising. The importance of teak has grown since the Thai government imposed a ban on all logging in Thailand, and companies have turned instead to concessions in E Burma, close to Mae Sot, to secure their wood. Whether the army and police force are protecting the forests or are making a tidy profit out of the industry is never quite clear. At the beginning of 1992, Burmese Army incursions into Thailand near Mae Sot pursuing Karen rebels led to a diplomatic incident, and once again underscored Mae Sot's reputation as a slightly 'dangerous' frontier town.

The authorities in Mae Sot are now attempting to diversify the town's economy and build a reputation as a tourist destination and trekking centre. They have been fairly successful in this regard and there is now a modern, Western-style hotel on the outskirts of the town – the *Mae Sot Hills*. Even so, there still appear to be more darkened windowed Mercedes and BMWs plying the road from Mae Sot to Tak than along most other stretches of highway in Thailand.

Excursions
Burmese border lies 5 km W of Mae Sot, and runs down the middle of the Moei River. There is talk of building a bridge across the river, directly linking Mae Sot with the Burmese town of Myawady.

There is a busy market selling Burmese goods here (hats, blankets, gems), with gun-toting Thai rangers, powder-covered Burmese girls, and a few restaurants. A fire in 1993 destroyed a large section of the market. It can also be enjoyable watching the long-tailed boats negotiating the fast-flowing river and there are tantalizing views into Burma. But really, the goods are all rather shoddy and far better markets can be found all over Thailand – but then they don't have the kudos of being on the Burmese border. **Getting there**: regular songthaews leave from the W end of Prasat Withi Rd, near the department store (฿7).

Trekking

(See page 275) This is gradually expanding in the Mae Sot area as travellers make their way to the W of Thailand, rather than to the more established trekking centres of the North; it remains relatively 'under-trekked' in comparison to the Chiang Mai/Chiang Rai areas. Treks tend to either go S to Umphang or N towards Mae Sariang and incorporate visits to caves, waterfalls, hilltribe villages, and Karen refugee camps. The usual array of raft trips and elephant rides are available in addition to straight forward trekking. Approximate rate: ฿1,600 for a 3 day/2 night trek, ฿2,700 for 4 days/3 nights, dependent upon whether raft trips and elephant rides are part of the deal.

Tours

Day tours of local sights (฿800) are arranged by the *Mae Sot Travel Centre* (also provide maps of town and surrounding area). *Mae Sot Guesthouse* specializes in treks to Umphang.

Local information
● **Accommodation**
A-B *Mae Sot Hills*, 100 Asia Rd, T 532601, F 532600, a/c, restaurant, pool, tennis courts, on the outskirts of town.

B *Monkrating Resort*, 14/21 Asia Rd, T 531409, F 532279, B 5125156, restaurant; **B** *Pornthep*, 25/4 Prasart Withi Rd, T 532590,

F 532596, a/c, restaurant.
C-D *Siam*, 185 Prasat Withi Rd, T 531176, some a/c.
D *First*, 444 Sawat Withi Rd, T 531770, some a/c, large, clean rooms; **D-F** *Mae Sot Guesthouse*, 216 Intharakit Rd, T 63110, teak house, set back from road, 50m from wat, quiet, small simple rooms in main house, bigger rooms with hot water and a/c in stone bungalow, clean, organize trekking tours, rec (dormitory beds available), good source of information, they collect unwanted clothing to distribute to Burmese refugees in the area.

E *No 4 Guesthouse*, 736 Intharakit Rd, large building set back from road, very popular; **F** *Mae Moei*, Intharakit Rd, rather unfriendly; **F** *Cathriya*, 766 Intharakit Rd, basic; *Mae Sot House*, 14/21 Asia Rd, T 531409, clean and well-run (dormitory beds available).

● **Resort**
A-C *Thaweechailand*, 9 km outside Mae Sot on the road to Tak, T 531287, restaurant.

● **Places to eat**
Canton (*Kwangtung*), 2/1 Soi Sriphanich, best Chinese; ♦*Fah Fah*, Tang Kim Chiang Rd, bakery/Thai; ♦*Pim Hut*, Tang Kim Chiang Rd, European, Thai and Chinese dishes and ice-cream; ♦♦*Neung Nut*, Intharakit Rd, garden restaurant; *Kao Pochana*, 36/7 Prasat Withithong Rd.

Foodstalls: along Prasat Withi Rd.

● **Airline offices**
Thai, 76/1 Prasat Withi Rd, T 531730.

● **Banks & money changers**
Siam Commercial, 544/1-5 Intharakit Rd. Thai Farmers, 84/9 Prasat Withi Rd. **Thai Military**, 179/7 Prasat Withi Rd.

● **Post & telecommunications**
Post Office: next to *Mae Moei Hotel* on Intharakit Rd. **Area code**: 055. **Overseas telephone service**: on Intharakit Rd.

● **Shopping**
Burmese goods: on sale in the market on the Moei River and in the market behind the *Siam Hotel*. **Gems**: a good buy – most of the jewellery shops are concentrated on Prasat Withi Rd around the *Siam Hotel*. **Department Store**: 100/3-7 Prasat Withi Rd.

● **Sport**
Swimming: *Mae Sot Hills Hotel* has a pool open to non-residents for ฿25.

● **Tour companies & travel agents**
Mae Sot Travel Centre, 14/21 Asia Rd, T 531409.

● **Transport**
87 km W of Tak, and 510 km from Bangkok.

Local Saamlors, tuk-tuks. **Motorbike hire**: Prasat Withi Rd (close to the Bangkok Bank).

Air: airport 1½ km out of town on Route 105 to Burmese border. 4 connections a week on Thai with Tak, Chiang Mai and Phitsanulok.

Bangkok Airways are planning to begin a service with Bangkok.

Road Bus: regular bus and minibus connections with Tak 2 hrs (ϕ25) and with Bangkok's Northern bus terminal 10 hrs (ϕ225). Connections with Sukhothai and Phitsanulok. The road N to Mae Sariang is good until the last stretch, but still negotiable by car. Songthaews make the journey to Mae Sariang, departing 4 times a day, 5 hrs (ϕ150).

THE NORTHERN REGION

To the north of the Central Plains is the Northern region, best known for the hilltribes who inhabit the mountainous areas that fringe its borders. Those looking for an energetic outdoor holiday, with trekking, perhaps a raft trip and visits to hilltribe communities, should head for this part of the kingdom. The North also contains many sights of historical importance, perhaps the most notable being in and around the towns of Lampang (see page 223), Lamphun (see page 227) and Chiang Mai (see page 229).

The North is more geographically fragmented than the Central Plains, as valleys and rivers become narrower and the mountains more impressive. The ancient Tai states that developed in this part of Thailand – dating back to the 13th century – were constrained by the topography of the area. Although they constructed monuments of considerable artistic merit, and were locally powerful, they never managed to extend territorially to the same extent as the kingdoms of the Central region. In the mountains that divided one valley from another, hilltribe peoples, each with their own distinctive culture (see page 275) maintained an existence through shifting cultivation (see page 29). They only came into contact with the settled agriculturalists of the plains intermittently for trade purposes. Thus the North came to consist of 2 quite separate and distinctive groups: the lowlanders or *Khon muang*, and the hill peoples or *Chao Khao*.

Like other more remote regions of Thailand, the mountains and forests of the North became a haven for the guerillas of the Communist Party of Thailand (CPT). The cadres of the CPT played upon the dissatisfactions of the alienated hilltribes, and garnered considerable support during the 1970s and early 1980s. The area also became a centre for heroin poppy production (see page 279) and large expanses of land on the margins of the region were controlled by opium warlords such as Khun Sa. Although these areas may *de jure* have been governed by the Thai authorities, *de facto* they were under the control of others.

Today the situation is much changed. Opium production has been largely displaced and pushed into Burma and Laos, and the CPT vanquished. Tourism is flourishing, agriculture increasingly commercialized, and there has been some limited industrialization. Pressure of people on land resources has led to increasing tenancy and there is now a large army of landless peasants – probably numbering close to 1 million. Some continue to live in the countryside, working on the land of others. Still more have migrated to urban areas – particularly Bangkok – to secure work.

The hilltribes have also been increasingly incorporated into the Thai state. Improvements in communications have drawn the highlanders into the cash economy, while the dominance of the lowlanders is causing a process of cultural as well as economic and political integration to take place. Some argue that this 'forced assimilation' of the hilltribes is destroying their identity, producing cultural cripples (see page 275).

Future possibilities There is talk of linking Thailand, Burma and China. The Thai railway which currently ends in Chiang Mai might be extended to join up with the Chinese track to Kunming. More likely, flights may soon be introduced from Chiang Mai and/or Chiang Rai to Jinghong in Xishuangbanna, Yunnan, where the culture is also 'Tai' (also see page 262).

LAMPANG TO CHIANG MAI

From the ancient town of Lampang, Route 11 runs north-westwards to Lamphun (77 km) and from there to Chiang Mai (another 26 km), the unofficial capital of the North. Close to Lampang is arguably the most beautiful wat in Thailand: Wat Lampang Luang. Lamphun, the former capital of the Mon Kingdom of Haripunjaya, features highly unusual stepped chedis, to be seen nowhere else in the country. The walled city of Chiang Mai is the tourist centre of the North with multitudes of hotels, restaurants and trekking companies, beautiful wats, and the centre of

handicraft production and Northern culture.

Lampang

Lampang is one of Thailand's most attractive provincial capitals, having retained a number of its old wooden buildings. Horse-drawn carriages – the town's symbol – are still used as taxis rather than the frenetic tuk-tuk. Established in the 7th century Dvaravati Period, Lampang became a prosperous trading centre with a wealth of ornate and well-endowed wats. The influence of the Burmese is clearly reflected in the architecture of some of the more important wats. It is easiest to visit the wats by saamlor or horse-drawn carriage.

Places of interest

Wat Phra Kaeo Don Tao and its 'sister' Wat Chadaram can be found on Phra Kaeo Road, N across the Rachada Phisek Bridge. Wat Phra Kaeo housed the Emerald Buddha now in Wat Phra Kaeo, Bangkok, for 32 years. The ceilings and columns of the 18th century viharn are carved in wood and are intricately inlaid with porcelain and enamel. In the compound, there is also a Burmese-style chapel (probably late 18th century) and a golden chedi. Admission: ฿10. Next door, **Wat Chadaram** is less highly regarded although it contains possibly the most attractive building in the whole complex: a small, intimate, well proportioned, wooden viharn.

Wat Chedi Sao (the 'temple of the 20 chedis') is 3 km NE of the town, 1 km off the Lampang-Jae Hom road at Ban Wang Moh. A principal white chedi surrounded by smaller acolytes stand amongst the rice fields together with a strange assortment of concrete animals and monks. Get there by saamlor or carriage or take a songthaew towards Jae Hom from Boonyawat Road.

The beautiful **Wat Sri Chum**, on Tippowan Road (also known as Sri Chum Road) was constructed 200 years ago and

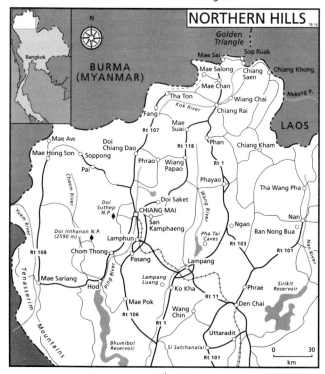

is registered with the Fine Arts Department as a 'national treasure'. The monastery is regarded as one of the finest Burmese-style wats in Thailand. Tragically, the richly carved and painted viharn, one of the finest structures in the compound, was destroyed by fire in 1993. The compound exudes an ambience of peaceful meditation, although sadly the wat is in urgent need of funds to complete the restoration of its delicate buildings and, possibly, to rebuild the razed viharn. Admission: ฿10. Open: 0700-1830. **Wat Rong Muang** is also S of the river and can be found close to the intersection of Wangkhwa and Thakrawnoi roads. Yellow and faded red, built of wood and corrugated iron, it rises up in tiers almost like a fantasy building.

In addition to its wats, Lampang also has a number of interesting secular buildings. The old wooden **railway station** is a charming point of arrival and departure, while the streets off Boonyawat Road contain a number of traditional Northern-style wooden houses.

Excursions

Wat Phra That Lampang Luang is a magnificent wat which lies some 25 km SW of Lampang off Route 1 and is one of the finest and most beautiful wats in Thailand. It stands on a slight hill, surrounded by a mellow brick wall (all that remains of the original fortressed city which was sited here more than 1,000 years ago). Originally this wat was an ancient *wiang* – a fortified site, protected by walls, moats and ramparts – and was

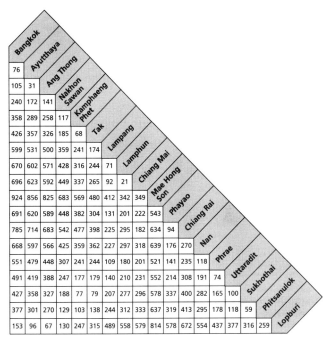

	Bangkok	Ayutthaya	Ang Thong	Nakhon Sawan	Kamphaeng Phet	Tak	Lampang	Lamphun	Chiang Mai	Mae Hong Son	Phayao	Chiang Rai	Nan	Phrae	Uttaradit	Sukhothai	Phitsanulok
Ayutthaya	76																
Ang Thong	105	31															
Nakhon Sawan	240	172	141														
Kamphaeng Phet	358	289	258	117													
Tak	426	357	326	185	68												
Lampang	599	531	500	359	241	174											
Lamphun	670	602	571	428	316	244	71										
Chiang Mai	696	623	592	449	337	265	92	21									
Mae Hong Son	924	856	825	683	569	480	412	342	349								
Phayao	691	620	589	448	382	304	131	201	222	543							
Chiang Rai	785	714	683	542	477	398	225	295	182	634	94						
Nan	668	597	566	425	359	362	227	297	318	639	176	270					
Phrae	551	479	448	307	241	244	109	180	201	521	141	235	118				
Uttaradit	491	419	388	247	177	179	140	210	231	552	214	308	191	74			
Sukhothai	427	358	327	188	77	79	207	277	296	578	337	400	282	165	100		
Phitsanulok	377	301	270	129	103	138	244	312	333	637	319	413	295	178	118	59	
Lopburi	153	96	67	130	247	315	489	558	579	814	578	672	554	437	377	316	259

North and Central Thailand, distances between provincial capitals (Km)

one of a series of such fortresses linked with Lampang. The wat is approached by a staircase flanked by guardian lions and nagas, and is entered through an archway of intricate stone carving, built around the late 15th century. The large central viharn (**Viharn Luang**) also dates from the late 15th century and is open on all 4 sides. It houses a *ku* – a brick, stucco and gilded pyramid peculiar to Northern wats – containing a Buddha image, a collection of thrones, and some lively murals from the early 19th century or possibly even the 18th century. These are now faded and deteriorated but among the scenes that can be discerned are farmers ploughing, women weaving, houses and temples, fruit pickers, and tattooed men. The building, with its intricate woodcarving and some fine pattern work on the pillars and ceiling, is dazzling. Behind the viharn is the **principal chedi**, 45m high and containing a hair of the Buddha. Made of beaten copper and brass plates over a brick core, it is typically Lanna Thai in style and was erected in the late 15th century. The **Buddha Viharn** to the left of the chedi is thought to date from the 13th century. Beautifully carved and painted, it contains a seated Buddha image. To the right of the main viharn are 2 more small, but equally beautiful, viharns: the **Viharn Nam Tam**, is thought to date from the early 16th century, and may be the oldest wooden building in Thailand.

Outside the walls, through the southern doorway, is an enormous and ancient **bodhi tree** supported by a veritable army

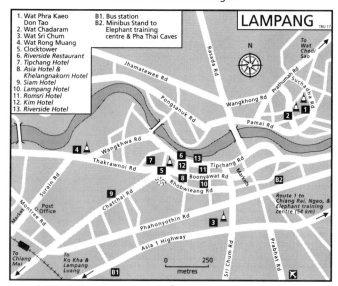

1. Wat Phra Kaeo Don Tao
2. Wat Chadaram
3. Wat Sri Chum
4. Wat Rong Muang
5. Clocktower
6. *Riverside Restaurant*
7. *Tipchang Hotel*
8. *Asia Hotel & Khelangnakorn Hotel*
9. *Siam Hotel*
10. *Lampang Hotel*
11. *Romsri Hotel*
12. *Kim Hotel*
13. *Riverside Hotel*

B1. Bus station
B2. Minibus Stand to Elephant training centre & Pha Thai Caves

LAMPANG TBU 17

of crutches. Close by is a small, musty and rather unexciting **museum**. Next to this is a fine raised **scripture library** and a viharn within which is another revered Emerald Buddha rumoured to have been made from the same block of jasper as the famous Emerald Buddha in Bangkok. It dates from the Chiang Saen Period (1057-1757) and shows the Buddha meditating. Obscured by two rows of steel bars, the image does not begin to compare with the wat buildings in terms of beauty. It can only be viewed 0900-1200, 1300-1700. Admission to the wat: by donation. **Getting there**: by songthaew to Ko Kha and then by motorbike taxi the last 4 km to the wat. Songthaews for Ko Kha run along Phahonyothin Road. Alternatively, charter a songthaew from Lampang (฿150).

Excursions

Young elephant training centre lies 38 km NW of town near Thung Kwian on the road to Chiang Mai (highway 11). Approximately a dozen elephants are trained each year for forest work and there are about 100 animals here in total. Calves are 3 to 5 years old when they arrive and they undergo a five-year training. Admission: ฿50. 'Taught' between 0900 and 1100 daily, except public and Buddhist holidays and the dry season from Mar to May, T 227051. Rather less crowded than the training centres nearer Chiang Mai, the shows are more authentic and put the elephants through their paces, stacking, carrying and pulling logs. The most highly prized elephants of all are 'white' elephants – in fact, they are a pale pink. These animals are considered so holy that they used to be fed off gold platters. Rama IV wrote a treatise on their characteristics of which one was the possession of a 'beautiful snore'. **Getting there**: by early morning bus towards Chiang Mai; get off at the 37 km marker (ask for '*suan pa chang Thung Kwian*'). **NB**: the camp has recently moved from its previous location on the Lampang-Ngao highway.

Pha Thai caves are some of the most spectacular caves in Thailand, found on the road to Ngao. These are associated with a wat and are located about 20 km before Ngao. **Getting there**: take a bus on from Ban Pang La towards Ngao.

Festivals

Feb: *Luang Wiang Lakon* (moveable), 5 important Buddha images are carried through the streets in procession. Traditional dancing and a sound and light show at Wat Lampang Luang.

Local information
● Accommodation

A *Wieng Lakorn*, a new 100-room hotel due to open in 1994; **A-B** *Lampang River Lodge*, 330 Moo 11 Tambon Chompoo, T 5100173, 6 km S of Lampang on banks of Wang River, a/c, restaurant, individual Thai-style bungalows on stilts, a new hotel in an attractive position.

B-C *Tipchang Lampang*, 54/22 Thakrawnoi Rd, T 226501, F 225362, B 5140173, a/c, restaurant, dirty pool, 'best' hotel in town, rather tacky, unfriendly staff, overpriced.

C *Asia Lampang*, 229 Boonyawat Rd, T 217844, a/c, restaurant, large, non-descript rooms but good value, rec; **C-D** *Khelangnak-orn*, 719-720 Suan Dok Rd, T 217137, some a/c, restaurant, comfortable rooms.

D *Kim*, 168 Boonyawat Rd, T 217721, some a/c; **D** *Riverside*, own bathroom, right on the river, recently opened wooden house; **D** *Siam*, 260/29 Chatchai Rd, T 217472, some a/c; **D-E** *Lampang*, 696 Suan Dok Rd, T 217311, F 227313, some a/c, friendly, best in this range, rec; **D-E** *Romsiri*, 142 Boonyawat Rd, T 217054, some a/c.

E-F *Ruangsak*, 271 Tipchang Rd, T 217841.

● Places to eat

◆◆*Riverside* (*Baan Rim Nam*), 328 Tipchang Rd. Wooden house overlooking the river, wonderful atmosphere, good Thai and international food, rec. Thai. **Foodstalls**: near the railway station.

● Airline offices

Thai, 314 Sanambin Rd, T 217078.

● Banks & money changers

Thai Farmers, 284/8 Chatchai Rd; Siam Commercial, Chatchai Rd; Thai Military, 173-175 Chatchai Rd.

● Post & telecommunications

Post Office: Surain Rd (opposite the railway station). **Area code**: 054.

● Shopping

Lampang is famous for its ceramics, there are more than 50 factories in and around the town, a number are to be found to the W of town along Phahonyothin Rd (e.g. *Chao Lampang* and *Ceramic Art* at 246/1) and Route 1 towards Ko Kha (e.g. *Art Lampang*).

● Tourist offices

There is an information counter at the bus station. Friendly, helpful people but limited command of English.

● Transport

604 km N of Bangkok, 93 km S of Chiang Mai.

Local transport Horse-drawn carriages: ฿50-80 for a tour around town (depending upon route) or ฿100/hr. **Saamlors**: to hire for ฿50/hr.

Air: airport is on the S edge of town, off Prabhat Rd. Daily flights to Bangkok via Phitsanulok.

Train: station is on W side of town, at the end of Surain Rd. Regular connections with Bangkok's Hualamphong station 12 hrs (฿106-463) and Chiang Mai 2 hrs (฿23-48).

Road Bus: station is on Route 1, just E of the railway line (15 min walk to centre of town), left luggage at bus station, ฿5. Regular connections with Bangkok's Northern bus terminal 9 hrs (฿140-262), Chiang Mai 2 hrs (฿29), Chiang Rai, Sukhothai, Tak and Phitsanulok. Buses from Chiang Mai leave from the Old Chiang Mai-Lamphun Rd, near the tourist office.

Taxi: taxis from Chiang Mai leave from the corner of Chang Klan and Tha Phae rds.

Lamphun

Lamphun is perhaps Thailand's oldest preserved town and is easily reached from Chiang Mai. The city is situated on the banks of the Ping River and was formerly the capital of the Haripunjaya Kingdom founded in 660 AD by Queen Chama Devi. It became a powerful centre of the Mon culture which resisted the advances of the Kingdom of Lanna until King Mengrai succeeded in taking the city in 1281. In so doing he brought to an end the Chama Devi Dynasty and the last vestige of the once powerful Mons.

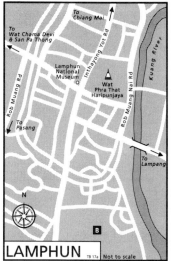

LAMPHUN   TB 17a   Not to scale

The Haripunjaya Kingdom was perhaps the most fervently Buddhist of all – unlike other areas, no images of Hindu gods have been found here. The town is also famous for its longans, so much so that in August there is a **Longan Fair** with a contest to judge the best fruit and another to select the year's Miss Lamyai (longan).

Places of interest

Wat Phra That Haripunjaya is a famous and venerated place of Buddhist teaching. It is best entered from the riverside where singhas (guardian lions) flank the entrance. Within the wat compound are an assortment of buildings from different eras. The 50m tall *central chedi* with its gold 9-tiered honorific umbrella (weighing, apparently, 6,498.75 gm) was started in 897 AD. Also notable is the rare 5-stepped *pyramid chedi* (similar to that at Wat Chama Devi – see below), pierced by niches which originally housed standing Buddha images of decreasing size. Most have long since disappeared. The *ubosoth* has fine gilded doors. A gigantic bronze *gong* is housed to the right of the entrance and an ancient raised *library* is on the left. The wat has a small *museum* open: 0900-1200, 1300-1600 Wed-Sun. During the sixth lunar month a festival and fair are held at the wat on full moon day. Leaving the wat by the back entrance and almost opposite on Inthayongyot Rd is the **Haripunjaya** or **Lamphun National Museum**. Housed in a modern building, it contains a modest collection of Buddhas and other artefacts from the area. Admission: ฿10. Open: 0900-1200, 1300-1600 Wed-Sun.

Wat Chama Devi, better known as **Wat Kukut**, lies 1½ km W of town on Chama Devi Road. It is said that Princess Chama Devi selected the spot by having an archer shoot an arrow to the N from town: he must have been a very strong man. The wat was originally founded in 755AD by the Khmers. Although many of the wat buildings are unspectacular, this wat is of great architectural significance as it contains the prototype for the rare stepped-pyramid chedi. Built in 1218, this square based chedi of brick and stucco has 5 tiers of niches. Each contains a standing Buddha of great beauty in an attitude of dispelling fear, diminishing in size upwards, and thereby giving an illusion of height. The style of the Buddha images is noticeably Dvaravati, with their rather attractive wider faces and elongated ears. Originally the top of the chedi was encased in gold, but this was subsequently removed and the wat became known as Wat Kukut or Wat 'without top'. The chedi contains the ashes of Queen Chama Devi. It is similar in style to Satmahal at Polannaruwa in Sri Lanka. Next to it, in the shadow of the viharn, is the smaller – and also unusual – Ratana Chedi with an octagonal base and standing Buddhas in each layer of niches. It was constructed in the 12th century.

Excursions

Cotton weaving centre of **Pasang** lies 12 km SW from Lamphun on Route 106. The market here sells batiks, silk, woodcarvings and other local crafts as well as cotton cloth. **Getting there**: regular songthaews from Lamphun.

Festivals

Aug: *Lamyai festival* (moveable), parades, elephant shows, beauty pageant and a competition to judge the sweetest and juiciest lamyai (or longan) fruit.

Local information
● Accommodation

There are no up-market hotels in Lamphun; most people use Chiang Mai as a base and visit here only as a day trip. However, a new 70-room hotel is under construction and is scheduled to open in 1993/4. **D-E** *Sri Lamphun*, 51/2 Inthayongyot Rd, T 511176, just S of Wat Phra That Haripunjaya, rooms are grubby.

● Hospitals & medical services
Lamphun Hospital: Rimping Rd, T 511233.

● Post & telecommunications
Post Office: Inthayongyot Rd. **Area code**: 053.

● Transport
26 km from Chiang Mai, 77 km from Lampang, 668 km from Bangkok.

Train: the station is just under 2 km N of the city, Charoenrat Rd. 5 connections 1 day with Bangkok (฿118-520) and with Chiang Mai.

Road Bus: the terminal is 500m S of Wat Haripunjaya on Inthayongyot Rd. 2 a/c and 3 non-a/c departures/day from Bangkok's Northern bus terminal 10 hrs (฿155-292); regular connections with Chiang Mai (from the Old Lamphun-Chiang Mai Rd, just over the Nawarat Bridge and near the TAT office) and from Lampang.

CHIANG MAI

History

Around 1290 King Mengrai succeeded in annexing Haripunjaya (Lamphun), the last of the Mon kingdoms. Up until that point, the capital of his kingdom had been Chiang Rai but with the defeat of Lamphun he decided to move his capital S to a more central location. In 1296 he chose a site on the banks of the Ping River and called his new capital, Nopburi Sri Nakawan Ping Chiang Mai, later shortened to Chiang Mai or 'New City'. It is said that he chose the site after seeing 1 big mouse and 4 small mice scurry down a hole beneath a holy Bodhi tree (*Ficus religiosa* – the tree under which the Buddha attained enlightenment). This he took to be a good omen, and with his friends King Ramkhamhaeng of Sukhothai and King Ngarm Muang of Phayao who agreed with the portents, he made this the heart of his Kingdom of Lanna or a 'million rice fields'. Through his reign, Mengrai succeeded in expanding his kingdom enormously: in 1259 he became King of Chiang Saen; from there he extended the areas under his control to Fang and Chiang Rai; and then, finally, to Haripunjaya. The land in itself was unimportant; King Mengrai was concerned with the control of people, and he spent much of his reign founding new towns which he would settle with people who would then owe him allegiance.

Like his friend King Ramkhamhaeng, Mengrai was a great patron of

CLIMATE: CHIANG MAI												
	Jan	Feb	Mar	Apr	May	Jun	Jul	Aug	Sep	Oct	Nov	Dec
Av Max (°C)	29	32	34	36	34	32	31	31	31	31	30	28
Av Min (°C)	13	14	17	22	23	23	23	23	23	21	19	15
Av Rain (mm)	0	10	8	36	122	112	213	193	249	94	31	13

Source: Pearce, E.A and Smith C.G. *The world weather guide*: Hutchinson, London

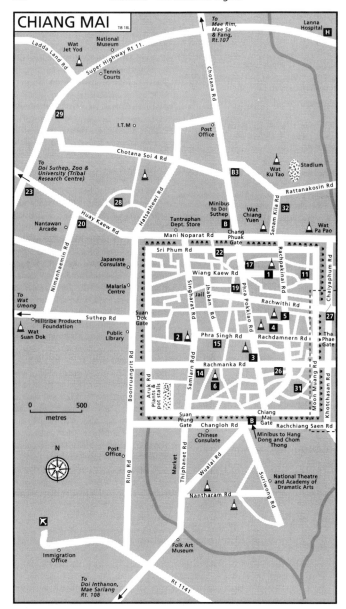

CHIANG MAI

TI8 18L

To
Mae Rim,
Mae Sa
& Fang,
Rt.107

Lanna
Hospital **H**

Ladda Land Rd

Wat
Jet Yod

National
Museum

Super Highway Rt 11.

Tennis
Courts

Chotana Rd

29

I.T.M

Post
Office

Chotana Soi 4 Rd

B3

Wat
Ku Tao

Stadium

To
Doi Suthep, Zoo &
University (Tribal
Research Centre)

23

Hatsathewi Rd

Rattanakosin Rd

28

Sanam Kila Rd

32

Huay Kaew Rd

20

Nantawan
Arcade

Tantraphan
Dept. Store

Minibus
to Doi
Suthep

B

Wat
Chiang Yuen

Wat
Pa Pao

Nimanhaemin Rd

Mani Noparat Rd

Chang
Phuak
Gate

Japanese
Consulate

Sri Phum Rd

22

Rachpakinai Rd

17

1

11

Chaiyaphum Rd

Malaria
Centre

Wiang Kaew Rd

19

Phra Pokklao Rd

Rachwithi Rd

Singharat Rd

Jhaban Rd

Jail

4

5

To
Wat
Umong

Suthep Rd

Suan
Dok
Gate

27

Tha
Phae
Gate

Wat
Suan Dok

Hilltribe Products
Foundation

Public
Library

2

Phra Singh Rd

Rachdamnern Rd

15

3

Boonruangrit Rd

Samlarn Rd

Rachmanka Rd

Moon Muang Rd

14

26

Khotchasan Rd

6

31

0   500

metres

Aruk Rd
Plants &
pot stalls

Suan
Prung
Gate

Chiang
Mai
Gate

B

N

Changloh Rd

Rachchiang Saen Rd

Post
Office

Chinese
Consulate

Minibus to Hang
Dong and Chom
Thong

Ring Rd

Thiphanet Rd

Market

Wualai Rd

Suriwong Rd

National Theatre
and Academy of
Dramatic Arts

Nantharam Rd

Immigration
Office

Folk Art
Museum

To
Doi Inthanon,
Mae Sariang
Rt. 108

Rt 1141

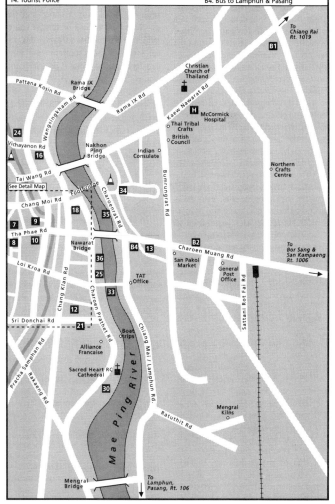

1. Wat Chiang Man
2. Wat Phra Singh
3. Wat Chedi Luang
4. Wat Duang Dii
5. Wat Umong
6. Wat Mengrai
7. Wat Chedowan
8. Wat Mahawan
9. Wat Saen Fang
10. Wat Bupharam
11. Somphet Market
12. Anusarn Market
13. Dechanukrau boxing ring
14. Tourist Police

15. Main Police Station
16. US Consulate
17. Thai Airlines Office
18. Mae Ping Post Office
19. Sripoom Post Office
20. *Chiang Mai Orchid Hotel*
21. *Chiang Mai Plaza Hotel*
22. *Mountain View Guesthouse*
23. *Rincome Hotel*
24. *President Hotel*
25. *Diamond Riverside Hotel*
26. *Anodard Hotel*
27. *Darets Guesthouse*

28. *YMCA*
29. *Holiday Inn Green Hills Hotel*
30. *Once upon a Time Hotel*
31. *Thailand Guesthouse*
32. *SSS Guesthouse*
33. Bridge for motorbikes & bicycles
34. *Bain Garden Restaurant*
35. *The Riverside Restaurant*
36. *River View Lodge*
B1. Long distance bus station
B2. Buses to Bor Sang & San Kampaeng
B3. Chang Puak bus station; Bus & Minibus to Mae Rim & Chiang Dao
B4. Bus to Lamphun & Pasang

TIB 18R

Theravada Buddhism. He brought monks from Ceylon to unify the country through promoting this religion of both King and commoner. From Mengrai's reign up until the 15th century, Chiang Mai flourished. Towards the end of the 15th century, during the reign of King Tiloka (1442-1488), relations with up-and-coming Ayutthaya became strained. The 2 kingdoms engaged in a series of wars with few gains on either side, although many stories recount the bravery and cunning of each side's warriors. Muen Loknakorn, one of Tiloka's most skilful commanders, is said to have defeated the Ayutthayan army on one occasion by creeping into their camp at night, and cutting the tails off their elephants. With the elephants careering around the camp in pain, the Ayutthayans thought they were being attacked, and fled in confusion.

Although relations between Chiang Mai and Ayutthaya were fractious, it was actually the Burmese who eventually captured the city of Chiang Mai in 1556. King Bayinnaung, who had unified all of Burma, took Chiang Mai after a battle of 3 days and the city remained under Burmese regency for the next 220 years. There was constant conflict during these years and by the time the Burmese succeeded in overthrowing Ayutthaya in 1767, the city of Chiang Mai was decimated and depopulated. In 1775, General Taksin united the Kingdom of Thailand and a semi-autonomous prince of the Lampang Dynasty was appointed to rule the North. It was not until 1938 that Chiang Mai lost its semi-independence and came under direct rule from Bangkok.

Today, Chiang Mai is the second largest city in Thailand with a population of 250,000, a thriving commercial centre as well as a favourite tourist destination. The TAT estimates that 12% of Thailand's tourists travel to Chiang Mai. Its attractions to the visitor are obvious: the city has a rich and colourful history, still evident in the architecture of the city which includes over 300 wats; it is manageable and 'user friendly' (unlike Bangkok); it has perhaps the greatest concentration of handicraft industries in the country; and it is also an excellent base from which to go trekking and visit the famous hilltribe villages in the surrounding highlands. Chiang Mai has developed into a major tourist centre with a good infrastructure including excellent hotels and restaurants in all price categories. In so doing it may have lost some of its charm. Bangkok's problems of traffic congestion, pollution and frantic property development have arrived in Chiang Mai – albeit on a smaller scale. This is rather ironic in that part of the cause is people escaping congestion, pollution and development in Bangkok – and in so doing bringing the problems with them. Various tax breaks have attracted more than 80 companies to Chiang Mai and the surrounding area.

In 1995 Chiang Mai plans to host the South-East Asian Games; in 1996, the city celebrates its 700th anniversary. All this attention may do more harm than good – at least as far as tourists and locals looking for a respite from Bangkok. Nonetheless, Reginald Le May's observations of 1938 are not entirely redundant:

"Chiangmai possesses a singular beauty. I was stationed there in 1913, and again in 1915, and completely succumbed to its charms; and when I visited it afresh in 1927, after twelve years' absence, I found it more enchanting than ever, with its brick-red palace-fort surrounded by a lotus-filled moat dating from about 1350, its shady avenues, its broad flowing river, and its innumerable temples each within its leafy garden, where the tiled roofs and stately stupas, the swept courtyards, the green mango trees and the heavenly blue sky above all combined to induce a feeling of such peace and happiness as it would be hard to match elsewhere."

Places of interest

Chiang Mai is centred on a square moat and defensive wall built during the 19th century although their origins lie in the late 13th century. The four corner bastions are reasonably preserved (although parts of the wall have been rather insensitively rebuilt) and are a useful reference point when roaming the city. Much of the rest of the towns walls were demolished during World War II and the bricks used for road construction. Not surprisingly, given Chiang Mai's turbulent history, many of the more important and interesting wats are located within the city walls.

Wat Chiang Man, situated in the NE of the walled town, is on Rachpakinai Road within a peaceful compound. The wat is the oldest in the city and was built by King Mengrai soon after he had chosen the site for his new capital in 1296. It is said that he resided here while waiting for his new city to be constructed. The wat is Northern Thai in style, most clearly evident in the gilded woodcarving and fretwork which decorate the various pavilions. The gold-topped chedi *Chang Lom* is supported by rows of elephants, similar to those of the 2 chedis of the same name at Si Satchanalai and Sukhothai. Two ancient Buddha images are contained behind bars within the viharn on the right-hand side as you enter the compound. One is the tiny crystal Buddha, *Phra Sae Tang Tamani* (standing 10 cm high). This image, possibly originally from Lopburi, is thought to have been brought to Chiang Mai from Lamphun by King Mengrai in 1281, where it had already resided for 600 years. The second is the stone Buddha, *Phra Sila* (literally, 'Stone Buddha'), in bas-relief, believed to have originated in India or Ceylon about 2500 years ago. It is supposed to have been made by Ajatacatru at Rajagriha in India, after the death of the Buddha and contains his relics. From India it was taken to Ceylon, and from there was brought by monks to Chiang Mai after first residing at both Sukhothai and Lampang. The image is carved in a dark stone, later gilded over, and shows the Buddha taming the wild elephant Nalagiri, sent to kill him by Ajatacatru. Both the Phra Sae Tang Tamani and the Phra Sila are believed to have the power to bring rain and are paraded through the streets of Chiang Mai and drenched in water during the Songkran Festival in April at the end of the dry season.

Wat Phra Singh, the 'Temple of the Lion Buddha', is arguably Chiang Mai's most important and certainly its largest wat. It is situated in the W quarter of the old city and is impressively positioned at the end of Phra Singh Road. The wat was founded in 1345 and contains a number of beautiful buildings decorated with fine woodcarving. Towards the back of the compound is the intimate *Lai Kham Viharn*, which houses the venerated Phra Buddha Singh image. It was built between 1385 and 1400 and the walls are decorated with early 18th century murals. Two walls are painted in the more rustic Lanna Thai style, and depict women weaving and the traditional costumes of the North. Another two walls are printed in central Thai style: here there are Burmese noblemen, central Thai princes, court scenes and battles. The two sets of murals make a fascinating contrast. The former concentrate on the lives of ordinary people; the latter on the élites. The *Phra Buddha Sihing* is yet another image with a colourful and rather doubtful provenance. It is said to have come from Ceylon by a rather roundabout route (see page 463), but as art historians point out, is Sukhothai in style. The head, which was stolen in 1922, is a copy. Among the other buildings in the wat is an attractive *raised library* (*hor trai*), with intricate carved wood decorations, inset with mother-of-pearl.

Wat Chedi Luang, on Phra Pokklao Road, to the east of Wat Phra Singh, is a 500-year-old ruined chedi which once stood some 90m high. Built initially in 1401 and then substantially enlarged between 1475 and 1478 by King Tiloka, the chedi was partially destroyed during an earthquake in 1545 and never rebuilt. Now the Fine Arts Department, after an interlude of a mere 450 years, are attempting to restore it. Judging by the remains, it must have been an impressive monument, especially as the entire chedi was encased in metal plates, covered with gold leaf. The wat has 2 particular claims to fame: during the 15th century, the E niche of the chedi housed the famous Emerald Buddha, now in Bangkok, and second, King Mengrai is believed to have been killed by a bolt of lightning in the temple compound. The airy viharn still contains a mid-15th century standing Buddha, along with a series of framed paintings depicting some of the jataka stories. Chiang Mai's rather uninteresting **Lak Muang**, or city pillar, is to be found within the compound.

Also within the city walls, just N of the intersection of Rachdamnern and Phra Pokklao roads, is a haven of peace at **Wat Duang Dii**. The compound contains 3 Northern Thai wooden temple buildings with fine woodcarving and attractively weathered doors. Note the small, almost Chinese-pagoda roofed, structure to the left of the gate with its meticulous stucco work. Behind the viharn and bot is a square-based chedi with elephants at each corner, and topped with copper plate. Close by is the less attractive **Wat Umong** with a pair of formerly stucco-clad chedis, now weathered down to brick. **Wat Mengrai**, is situated in the S quarter of the city.

Outside the walls, **Wat Suan Dok** (or **Wat Bupharam**), lies to the W of town on Suthep Road. Originally built in the 14th century but subsequently much restored and enlarged, the wat contains the ashes of Chiang Mai's royal family housed in many white, variously-shaped, mini-chedis. Not content with just 1 relic, the large central chedi is said

to house 8 relics of the Lord Buddha. On the sides of its base are 4 finely moulded brick and stucco naga slipways and gates. The large, open-walled viharn which confronts the visitor on entering the complex displays some good wood-carving on its exterior walls. The 2 large Buddha images, seated back-to-back at one end of the building, are inferior. Behind the viharn is the bot which houses a 6m gilded bronze Buddha image in the Chiang Saen style, seated in an attitude of subduing Mara. The walls are decorated with lively, if rather too gaudy for Western tastes, scenes from the jataka stories. The wat is also a centre of Thai traditional massage – ask one of the monks for information.

Continuing W on Suthep Rd, is the turn-off for **Wat Umong**, about 1 km off the road down a narrow lane. The wat was founded in 1371 by King Ku Na (1355-1385) who promoted the establishment of a new, ascetic school of forest dwelling monks. In 1369 he brought a leading Sukhothai monk to Chiang Mai – the Venerable Sumana – and built Wat Umong for him and his followers. Sumana studied here until his death in 1389. The wat features a statue of the fasting Buddha, reduced to skin and bones. Also here is a garden and lake as well as the tunnels after which the wat is named. Vivid, almost lurid, murals decorate one building and the wat is a centre for meditation. To get there take a songthaew or bus (nos 1 and 4) along Suthep Rd and ask to be let off at the turning for Wat Umong.

The beautiful **Wat Jet Yod** (literally, '7 spires'), is just off the 'superhighway' at the intersection with Ladda Land Road, NW of the city and close to the National Museum. It was begun in 1453 and contains a highly unusual square chedi with 7 spires. These represent the 7 weeks the Buddha resided in the gardens at Bodhgaya, after his enlightenment under the Bodhi tree. According to the chronicles the structure is a copy of the 13th century Mahabodhi temple in Pagan, Burma, which itself was a copy of the famous temple at Bodhgaya in Bihar (although it is hard to see the resemblance). On the faces of the chedi are an assortment of superbly modelled, stucco figures in bas relief, while at one end is a 'walk-in' niche containing a large Buddha image, dating from 1455, in an attitude of subduing Mara. The stucco work represents the 70 celestial deities and are among the finest works from the Lanna School of art. They are wonderfully modelled, flying, their expressions serene. At the back of the compound is the small **Phra Chedi** and associated bot, both raised off the ground on a small brick platform. Next to this is a much larger chedi with 4 niches containing images of the Buddha subduing Mara. Unfortunately, the wat was ransacked by the Burmese in 1566 and its buildings were badly damaged. The stucco facing of the original structures has in large part disappeared, leaving only attractively weathered brick. A new, gaudy, gold and red viharn rather detracts from the 'lost city' atmosphere of the compound.

The National Museum lies just to the east of Wat Jet Yod on Highway 11. It is a cool relief from 'Wat spotting' and has a fine collection of Buddha images and Sawankhalok china downstairs, as well as some impressive ethnological exhibits upstairs. Admission: ฿10. Open: 0900-1600 Wed-Sun.

Wat Ku Tao, to the N of the city off Chotana Road, dates from 1613. It is situated in a leafy compound and has an unusual chedi, shaped like a pile of inverted alms bowls.

Given that Chiang Mai has over 300 wats, there are a great many to choose from. Others worth a fleeting visit for those not yet 'watted out' include: **Wat Chiang Yeun** and **Wat Pa Pao** just outside the N walls of the city; and **Wat Chedowan**, **Wat Mahawan**, **Wat Saen Fang** and **Wat Bupharam** – all on Tha Phae Road – between the E walls of the city and the Ping River. **Wat Mahawan** displays some accomplished woodcarving on its viharn, washed in a delicate yellow, while the white stupa is guarded by a fearsome array of singhas – mythical lions – some with bodies hanging from their gaping jaws. **Wat Bupheram** has two, fine old viharns (viharn yai [big] and lek [small]), a new and rather gaudy raised viharn, a small bot and a white stupa. Of the viharns, the finest is the viharn lek, built about 300 years ago in Lanna Thai style. The small 'nave' is crowded with Buddha images and features Chinese plates, adhered to the wooden ceiling. The façade of the viharn – which is in need of funds for renovation – has some fine woodcarving. Also impressive are the carved doors of the viharn yai: note the carving of the Buddha subduing the wild elephant Nalagiri, sent to attack him.

The **Folk Art Museum** (or Lanna Folk Museum) is just south of the junction of Thiphanet and Wualai roads and is housed in a traditional Northern Thai house (130 years old) with a modest collection of kitchenware, betel nut and tobacco holders, ceramics etc. Admission: ฿20. Open: 1000-1600 Fri-Wed. The **Tribal Research Centre** on Chiang Mai University's campus is worth visiting for those intending to go trekking (see page 239).

The **Night Market** dominates the W side of Chang Klan Road; it consists of a number of purpose built buildings with hundreds of stalls selling a huge array of tribal goods as well as clothing, jewellery, tapes etc. (see page 245). For a completely different atmosphere, walk through Chiang Mai's 'Chinatown' which lies to the N of Tha Phae Rd, between the moat and the river. True to form, this area buzzes with business activity. Small workshops run by entrepreneurial Sino-Thais jostle between excellent small restaurants serving reasonably priced Thai and Chinese food. Few tourists explore this area.

The **Chiang Mai Zoo and Botanical Gardens** are to be found at the end of Huay Kaew Road, W of town at the foot of Doi Suthep. The animals here are better cared for than in many SE Asian zoos, although that may not be saying a great deal. The zoo occupies an attractive position on a hillside overlooking the Chiang Mai Valley, and covers 85 ha of parkland. Admission: ฿10. Open: 0800-1700 Mon-Sun. Getting there: No. 3 bus from Chang Puak Gate, or songthaew.

Excursions

Doi Suthep is a hill overlooking the town, 16 km to the NW. A steep winding road climbs 1000m to the base of a 300 step naga staircase which in turn leads up to **Wat Phrathat** (usually known by visitors simply as Doi Suthep), a very popular pilgrimage spot for Thais, perched on the hillside, and offering spectacular views of the city and plain below. Avoid the climb by taking the cable car which has a suggested ฿5 donation charge. A white elephant is alleged to have collapsed here, after King Kuena (1367-1385) gave it the task of finding a propitious site for a shrine to house a holy relic of the Lord Buddha. A chedi was built to house the relic, which was embellished and extended 2 centuries later.

The 24m high chedi, recently replated, is topped with a 5-tiered honorific parasol. There are a number of Buddha images in both Sukhothai and Chiang Saen styles arrayed in the gallery surrounding the chedi. The whole compound is surrounded by bells (which visitors can ring) and meditation instruction is available at the wat. Getting there: minibus from Mani Noparat Road, by Chang Puak Gate (฿50 return), or take bus No. 3 to the zoo and then change onto a minibus. A taxi should cost about ฿200 return, a songthaew ฿30 up and ฿20 down again. The temple is closed after 1630.

Phu Ping Palace, 5 km past Wat Phrathat, is the winter residence of the King. The immaculate gardens are open 0830-1630 Fri-Sun and public holidays when the Royal Family is not in residence. Getting there: the Doi Suthep minibus continues on to the Phu Ping Palace.

Doi Pui, 4 km past Phu Ping Palace, down a deteriorating track, is a rather commercialized Meo village. Nonetheless, it is worth a visit for those unable to get to other, more traditional, villages. There are 2 second-rate museum huts, one focusing on opium production, the other on the different hilltribes. On the hillside above the village is a rather unexpected English flower garden (in full bloom in Jan). Getting there: charter a songthaew or take a minibus from Mani Noparat Rd, by Chang Puak Gate, and then charter a songthaew from Doi Suthep.

Wiang Kum Kam is a ruined former city 5 km S of Chiang Mai. A *wiang* is a fortified site, and Wiang Kum Kam was an outlier of the Mon Haripunjaya Kingdom which had its capital at Lamphun. The city was established by the Mons in the 12th or 13th centuries and was not abandoned until the 18th century. Today, archaeologists are gradually beginning to uncover the site which covers an area of about 9 sq km and contains the remains of at least 20 wats. The most complete monument is **Wat Kan Thom** (in Thai, Wat Chang Kham); also notable is the chedi of Si Liam which takes the form of a stepped pyramid – a unique Mon architectural style. However the most important archaeological discovery has been a series of inscriptions which seem to indicate that King Ramkhamhaeng was not the 'inventor' of the Thai script, but rather made adaptations to a script that was already in use. It is best-known for its paper umbrellas, made by hand and then printed. The shaft is made from local softwood, the ribs from bamboo, and the covering from oiled rice paper. Getting there: accessible by bicycle or motorbike, or by tuk-tuk. Take route 106 S

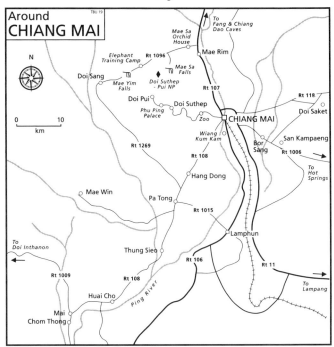

Around CHIANG MAI

TBU 19

N

To Fang & Chiang Dao Caves

Mae Sa Orchid House

Mae Rim

Rt 1096

Elephant Training Camp

Mae Sa Falls

Doi Sang

Mae Yim Falls

Doi Suthep - Pui NP

Rt 107

Rt 118

Doi Pui

Doi Suthep

Doi Saket

Phu Ping Palace

Zoo

CHIANG MAI

0   10

km

Wiang Kum Kam

San Kampaeng

Bor Sang

Rt 1006

Rt 1269

Rt 108

To Hot Springs

Hang Dong

Mae Win

Pa Tong

Rt 1015

Lamphun

To Doi Inthanon

Thung Sieo

Rt 106

Rt 11

To Lampang

Rt 1009

Rt 108

Huai Cho

Ping River

Mai Chom Thong

---

towards Lamphun; the ruins are signposted off to the right about 3 km from Chiang Mai, from where it is another 2 km.

Bor Sang, the Umbrella Village, lies due E of the city. This 15 km stretch of road, from Chiang Mai to San Kampaeng, has become a ribbon development of numerous 'workshops' and showrooms. It is worth heading out here if you are looking for things to buy (see shopping). It is best known for its paper umbrellas, made by hand and then painted. The shaft is made from local softwood, the ribs from bamboo, and the covering from oiled rice paper. *Getting there*: take a bus from the N side of Charoen Muang Road, just E of Nawarat Bridge.

Mae Sa Valley orientated E-W, lies off Route 107, N of town. It has a number of attractions along with a selection of 'back-to-nature' resorts (popular with Thais). The **Sai Nam Phung Orchid and Butterfly Farm** (among others) is a kilometre off Route 1096, about 4 km from the intersection with Route 107. It has the best selection of orchids in the area as well as a small butterfly enclosure (unusual jewellery for sale). Admission: ฿10. Open: 0700-1700. A short distance further on is a **Snake Farm** (shows 0700-1415, ฿80), and then the **Maesa House**, a small private museum displaying assorted prehistoric artefacts, musical instruments, Sukhothai ceramics, and World War II relics. Admission: ฿30. Open 0800-1700, Mon-Sat. The **Mae Sa Waterfall** is located in the **Doi Suthep-Pui National Park**, a kilometre off Route 1096 and about 3 km on from Maesa House. The waterfall is in fact a succession of minifalls – relatively peaceful, with a visitors' centre and a number of stalls. Special parking for 'Royal' cars. Admission: ฿3/person, ฿20/car. Open: 0800-1800, Mon-Sun. Most popular of all in the valley is the **Elephant Training Camp**, 3 km further on from the waterfall. Visitors can watch elephants bathing, dragging logs and perform other feats – are the mahouts really necessary, or could the pachyderms do it by themselves? At the end of the show visitors can indulge in an elephant ride. There is a daily show. Admission: ฿40, 0940-1100. Continuing further on along Route 1096 there are, in turn, the **Mae Yim Falls** (17 km), **Doi Sang** – a Meo tribal village (25 km), and the **Nang Koi Falls** (34 km). Accommodation: **B** *Samoeng Resort*, rt 1096, T 487072, F 487075, restaurant, pool, jacuzzi, hot water. Getting there: a half to one day trip from Chiang Mai on a chartered songthaew, or hired motorbike or car. Alternatively take a public bus/songthaew to Mae Rim from the Chang Puak bus station and then catch a songthaew on. The valley lies 16 km N of town on Route 107, and then W on Route 1096. Route 1096 links up with Route 1269 and emerges again at the town of Hang Dong, a 'basket village', 15 km south of Chiang Mai. The entire circular route is some 110 km.

Chiang Dao Caves lie 78 km N of Chiang Mai on Route 107 (almost 6 km off the main road – turn left in the town of Chiang Dao, just after the 72 km marker). The caves penetrate deep into the limestone hills which represent the E extension of the Himalayas and are associated with a wat, **Wat Chiang Dao**. They are amongst the most extensive in Thailand and are a popular pilgrimage spot for monks. The caverns contain an assortment of Buddha and hermit images as well as some impressive natural rock formations. Guides with kerosene lamps show visitors around, although it is only possible to explore a small part of the system. Admission: ฿5. Getting

there: catch a bus to Fang from the Chang Puak bus station on Chotana Road and get off at Chiang Dao. Songthaews take visitors the final 6 km from the main road to the caves.

Lamphun, a historic city, lies 26 km S of Chiang Mai (see page 227). Getting there: buses leave regularly from the Old Lamphun-Chiang Mai Road, just over the Nawarat Bridge and near the TAT office. The route is along a beautiful 15 km avenue of massive *yang khao* trees (*Dipterocarpus alatus*). The latex from these trees is used for waterproofing and as a fuel for torches (it is flammable).

Lampang lies 93 km S of Chiang Mai and is easily visited on a day trip (see page 223). Outside Lampang is the incomparable **Wat Phra That Lampang Luang** (see page 224). The **Young Elephant Training Centre** en route to Lampang is also worth a visit (see page 226). Getting there: by bus from Nawarat Bridge or from the Arcade terminal.

Cotton weaving centre of Pasang is 12 km SW of Lamphun. Getting there: regular songthaews from Lamphun and from Chiang Mai (same stop as for Lamphun).

Hang Dong, **Chom Thong** and the **Doi Inthanon National Park** (see page 249). Getting there: buses, minibuses and *songthaews* for Hang Dong and Chom Thong leave from around the Chiang Mai Gate. From Hang Dong there are songthaews to Doi Inthanon.

Trekking

(See Hilltribes and trekking, page 275.) There are scores of trekking companies in Chiang Mai. Competition is stiff, and most provide roughly the same assortment of treks, ranging from 1 night to over a week. Treks can also incorporate raft trips and elephant rides. Motorcycle trekking is also becoming popular, although it is environmentally destructive bringing noise to otherwise quiet areas and promoting soil erosion. Some companies, in order to convince potential customers that they will be pioneers, offer a money-back guarantee should they come into contact with other trekkers. The TAT office distributes a list of recommended trekking operators and a leaflet on what to look out for when choosing your trip. The **Tribal Research Institute**, situated at the back of the Chiang Mai University campus on Huay Kaew Road provides information on the various hilltribes, maps of the trekking areas, and a library of books on these fascinating people. Open: 0900-1600 Mon-Fri. There is a small ethnographic museum attached to the centre, open: 0830-1200, 1300-1630 Mon-Fri. An informative book on the hilltribes can be bought here for ฿35.

Choosing a guide When choosing a guide for the trip, ensure that he can speak the hilltribe dialect as well as good English (or French, German etc). **NB**: many of the best guides are freelance, and others move from company to company. Avoid companies who do not register with the Tourist Police before departure. You can check on a company's reputation by contacting the police department. **Beware of leaving valuables** in guesthouses in Chiang Mai; however reliable the owner may appear, it is always safer to deposit valuables such as passport, jewellery and money in a bank (banks on Tha Phae Road have safety deposits and charge about ฿200/month). Insects: remember to take protection against mosquitoes; long trousers and long-sleeved shirts are essential for the night-time. Prices for treks start at about ฿700-900 for a single night, and increase by ฿200 for each additional night. Elephant treks are more expensive. Nonetheless, it is possible to book a 3 day/4 night trek, with rafting and an elephant ride for about ฿1,500 per person. There are scores of trekking companies in Chiang Mai (a list can be obtained from the TAT office). Guesthouses also often provide a trek-

king service (e.g. *Chiang Mai Souvenir Guesthouse, Lek House*). Many of the companies are concentrated along Tha Phae, Chaiyaphum, Moon Muang and Kotchasan roads (see Tour companies list and travel agents).

Tours

A range of day tours run from Chiang Mai to such sights as Wat Phrathat Doi Suthep, the Phu Ping Palace and a Meo village (฿250); the Mae Sa Valley to visit a waterfall, orchid farm and elephants at work (฿450); Doi Inthanon National Park (฿850); Bor Sang (the Umbrella village) and San Kampaeng (฿100); Chiang Rai and the Golden Triangle (฿900), even the Sukhothai historical park over 200 km S (฿1,500). A ride on an elephant, some bamboo rafting and a visit to an orchid farm cost about ฿600. Tour operators are to be found concentrated along Tha Phae, Chang Klan and Moon Muang roads. See Tour companies and travel agents for listings. A notable operator is *Chiang Mai Green Tour and Trekking*, which tries to provide eco-friendly and culturally-sensitive tours. However, they also run motorbike treks which can hardly be said to be the former. Many of the larger tour companies and travel agents will also arrange visas and tours to Burma, Cambodia, Laos and Vietnam. Visas cost ฿1,500 for Vietnam and Cambodia, ฿2,500 for Laos.

Festivals

Jan: *Chiang Mai Winter Fair* (moveable), a 10-day festival held late Dec/early Jan, based in the Municipal Stadium. Exhibitions, Miss Beauty Contest, musical performances; *Bor Sang Umbrella Fair* (outside Chiang Mai, mid-month) celebrates traditional skill of umbrella making, and features contests, exhibitions and stalls selling umbrellas and other handicrafts. Miss Bor Sang, a beauty contest, is also held.

Feb: *Flower Festival* (1st Fri, Sat and Sun) floral floats, flower displays, handicraft sales and beauty contests.

Apr: *Songkran* (13th-16th public holiday) traditional Thai New Year celebrated with more enthusiasm in Chiang Mai than elsewhere. Boisterous water-throwing, particularly directed at farangs; expect to be soaked to the skin for the entire four days. Given that it is the hottest time of year, no bad thing – unless you are going out for a business lunch or dinner (leave your camera in your hotel).

Nov: *Yi Peng Loi Krathong* (mid-month) the ritual of the lighted balloon. Colourful balloons are launched into the sky, in order to banish troubles. In the evenings, homes and shops are lit up with lanterns, and balloons are floated on the rivers.

Local information

● **Accommodation**

Price guide

	US$	Baht
L	200+	5,000+
A+	100-200	2,500-5,000
A	50-100	1,250-2,500
B	25-50	625-1,250
C	15-25	375-625
D	8-15	200-375
E	4-8	100-200
F	<4	<100

Chiang Mai has a vast range of accommodation to choose from, mostly concentrated to the east of the old walled city. There are over 150 guesthouses and some 80 hotels, so below is only a selection. Stiff competition, a proliferation of new hotels and a stagnant industry mean room rates are slashed in many instances. It is rare for visitors to have to pay the set room rate.

A+-A *Amari Rincome*, 301 Huay Kaew Rd, T 221044, F 221915, W of town, a/c, restaurant, pool, popular with tour groups, a little frayed at the edges, set price buffet lunch, out of town centre but with friendly staff and 14 apartments that can be rented on a monthly basis; **A+-A** *Chiang Mai Orchid*, 100-102 Huay Kaew Rd, T 222099, F 221625, W of town, a/c, restaurants, large pool, large but attractive hotel recently expanded, health club, efficient service, rec; **A+-A** *Chiang Inn*, 100 Chang Klan Rd, T 270070, F 274299, a/c, restaurant (rec, particularly good Western breakfasts), pool, one of Chiang Mai's older first class hotels, but kept up-to-date and pristine, very

central in the heart of the night market area; **A+-A** *Novotel Suriwongse*, 110 Chang Klan Rd, T 270051, F 270064, a/c, good restaurants, pool, all facilities, the slightly frayed exterior betrays a renovated interior, central, rec although some rooms look out directly onto neighbouring blocks.

A *Duangtawan*, 132 Loi Kroa Rd, T 270384, F 275304, a/c, restaurants, pool, new high rise hotel with 554 rooms, luxurious but rather sterile and indistinguishable, all facilities, convenient for Night Market, no charge for children under 12; **A** *Holiday Inn Green Hills*, 24 Chiang Mai – Lampang Super Highway, T 220100, F 221602, a/c, 4 restaurants, pool, tennis, golf, business centre, new hotel on W side of town; **A** *Mae Ping*, 153 Sri Donchai Rd, T 270160, F 251069, a/c, restaurant, large ugly tower block in big plot, Chinese in character, popular with Asian tourists; **A** *Royal Princess*, 112 Chang Klan Rd, T 281033, F 281044, a/c, restaurant, pool, part of the Dusit chain of hotels, central, quite noisy (on the main road), 200 rooms with excellent service, rec; **A** *Chiang Mai Plaza*, 92 Sri Donchai Rd, T 270040, F 272230, a/c, restaurant, pool, large, impersonal but central to night market and restaurants; **A+-B** *Chiang Mai President*, 226 Vichayanon Rd, T 251025, a/c, restaurant, pool, good value; **A-C** *Once Upon a Time*, 385/2 Charoen Prathet Rd, T 274932, F 2338493, some a/c, restaurant, traditional northern Thai wooden house on the river, rooms with four poster beds and mosquito nets, very romantic, highly rec (**NB**: the hotel was closed in 1993 during a change of ownership; latest reports are that it has now reopened, but whether standards have been maintained is not clear).

C *Chatree*, 11/10 Suriwong Rd, T 279179, F 279085, some a/c, coffee shop, good pool, good rates, hot water, popular with long-term visitors during the winter, relaxed atmosphere; **C** *Gap House*, 3 Soi 4 Rachdamnern Rd, restaurant, incl breakfast, central location, attractive rooms, good value, rec; **C** *Lai Thai*, 111/4-5 Khotchasan Rd, T 271725, F 272724, some a/c, restaurant, good clean pool, free baby cots, spotless rooms, cross between a N Thai house and Swiss chalet, popular and well-run, good facilities, attractive surroundings, tours, trekking and motorbike rental; **rec**; **C** *Montri*, 2-6 Rachdamnern Rd, T 211070, F 217416, some a/c, restaurant, clean, good central position near Tha Phae Gate, large rooms sparsely furnished, the restaurant here (*J.J.'s*) is one of Chiang Mai's more popular places – but rooms tend to be very noisy due to hotel's position on an intersection; **C** *Riverfront Resort*, 43/3 Chang Klan Rd, T 275125, F 282988, some a/c, restaurant, Lanna Thai house on the banks of the Ping River, live Northern Thai music in restaurant at night; **C-D** *Anodard*, 57 Rachmanka Rd, T 211055, restaurant, pool; **C-E** *Alternative Tour Guesthouse*, 39 Jah Bon Rd, T 221704, clean, good source of information, part of Alternative Tour Company.

D *La Villa*, 145 Rachdamnern Rd, T 277403, F 277403, some a/c.

E *Chiang Mai Garden Guesthouse*, 82-86 Rachmanka Rd, T 278881, very clean large rooms with bathroom, rec; **E** *Chiang Mai Tour & Guesthouse*, 31 Phra Pokklao Soi 3, T 278455, own bathroom, hot shower and Asian loo, restaurant, videos, tours and treks arranged, pleasant staff but not much atmosphere.

● **Area around Moon Muang Rd**

C *Top North*, 15 Soi 2 Moon Muang Rd, T 278900, F 278485, some a/c, pool, modern concrete block, well-run but rather sterile, check rooms as cleanliness varies, pool usually crowded, popular but needs to improve, over-priced; **C-E** *Thailand*, 38/1 Moon Muang Soi 2, some a/c, bright and airy rooms in otherwise featureless block, own bathroom, hot water, rec.

D-E *North Star House*, 38 Moon Muang Soi 2, T 213190, a/c, hot water, rather prison-like dark rooms, but popular with access to pool for small charge.

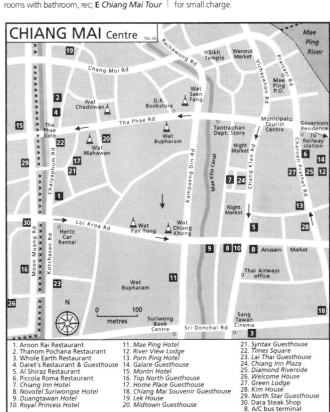

CHIANG MAI Centre

1. Aroon Rai Restaurant
2. Thanom Pochana Restaurant
3. Whole Earth Restaurant
4. Daret's Restaurant & Guesthouse
5. Al Shiraz Restaurant
6. Piccola Roma Restaurant
7. Chiang Inn Hotel
8. Novotel Suriwongse Hotel
9. Duangtawan Hotel
10. Royal Princess Hotel
11. Mae Ping Hotel
12. River View Lodge
13. Porn Ping Hotel
14. Galare Guesthouse
15. Montri Hotel
16. Top North Guesthouse
17. Home Place Guesthouse
18. Chiang Mai Souvenir Guesthouse
19. Lek House
20. Midtown Guesthouse
21. Syntax Guesthouse
22. Times Square
23. Lai Thai Guesthouse
24. Chiang Inn Plaza
25. Diamond Riverside
26. Welcome House
27. Green Lodge
28. Kim House
29. North Star Guesthouse
30. Dara Steak Shop
B. A/C bus terminal

E *Kent*, 5 Rachmanka Soi 1, T 217578, clean; **E** *Kritsada House*, 50-50/1 Moon Muang Soi 2, T 217762, some hot water, rec; **E** *Libra*, 28 Moon Muang Soi 9, T 210687, clean rooms, friendly owners; **E** *NAT*, 7 Phra Pokklao Soi 6, T 277878, hot water; **E** *Panda*, Moon Muang Soi 2, clean, friendly, rec; **E** *Rose*, 87 Rachmanka Rd, T 278324; **E** *Welcome House*, 48/4 Moon Muang Soi 2, T 278447, own bathroom, rec; **E-F** *Sai Tam*, 21 Moon Muang Soi 2, T 211575; **E-F** *SSS*, 48/3 Sanam Kila Rd, T 217424, restaurant, very basic but clean, friendly staff, good atmosphere, tours and treks organized, great place to meet other travellers, highly rec; **F** *Gemini*, 22 Rachdamnern Rd, T 210578; **F** *Kamol*, 1 Moon Muang Rd; **F** *Pete's*, 46/3 Moon Muang Soi 9, T 210617, basic but adequate; **F** *Rose Garden*, 25/2 Rachwithi Soi 1, T 217929, quiet, garden location within city walls, hot water; **F** *Somwang*, 2/2 Rachmanka Soi 2, T 210505; **F** *Toy*, 45/1 Moon Muang Soi 1, rooms are dark and dingy, but with attached bathroom, well priced; **F** *Weekender*, 129/1-4 Rachwithi Rd, T 211761, rec.

● **Outside eastern city wall**

C-D *Home Place*, 9 Tha Phae Soi 6, T 273493, F 273494, some a/c, clean, quiet, very good service, helpful advice, clean rooms, central location, rec.

D *Chiang Mai Inn*, 15/1 Soi 2 Chaiyaphum Rd, T 251401, some a/c, friendly guesthouse, good place for travellers information on treks, etc; **D-E** *Sarah's*, 20 Tha Phae Soi 4, T 279423, run by an English woman married to a Burmese; **E** *Chiang Mai Souvenir*, 118 Charoen Prathet Soi Anusarn, T 282335, good sized rooms but shared bathrooms, in converted private house with large leafy garden and peaceful atmosphere, good trekking, rec.

E *Daret's*, 4/5 Chaiyaphum Rd, T 235440, popular restaurant, good source of information, although standards have declined, rooms can be grubby, check out time 1000, rather detached service, good trekking centre, motorbikes and bicycles for hire; **E** *Lek House*, 22 Chaiyaphum Rd, T 252686, quiet compound down narrow soi, rooms are good on the upper floor, slightly murky below, small bathrooms in need of upkeep, but good information and peaceful atmosphere, rec; **E** *Living House*, 4 Tha Phae Soi 5, fan, hot water, rooms with bathrooms, clean and quiet, rec; **E** *Midtown*, 7 Tha Phae Soi 4, T 273191, clean, plain rooms with hot water, centrally located down soi near Wat Mahawan, rather listless service; **E** *Renait Minicourt*, 56

Chaiyaphum Rd, T 251294, F 251120, restaurant, bare rooms, attached bathrooms, hot water, rooftop garden, French speaking; **E** *Syntax*, 2/2 Tha Phae Soi 6, T 276011, unfriendly and overpriced for shared bathrooms; **E** *Times Square*, 2/10 Tha Phae Soi 6, T 282448, clean, but rooms are small and pokey, and rather overpriced, although it benefits from an attractive breezy rooftop garden.

F *Chang Moi*, 29 Chang Moi Kao Rd, T 251839.

● **On the W bank of the river, off Charoen Prathet Rd**

A *Diamond Riverside*, 33/10 Charoen Prathet Rd, T 270081, F 271482, a/c, restaurant, pool, large high rise hotel, river views from rather spartan rooms, riverside pool and verandah, discounts available, good value, rec; **A** *River View Lodge*, 25 Soi 2 Charoen Prathet Rd, T 271109, F 279019, a/c, restaurant, pool, small, quiet, riverside hotel with large, rather plain rooms, some with wonderful views, attractive verandah and pool overlooking the Mae Ping, breakfast included, run by very friendly Thai family, who have good English, rec; **A+-B** *Porn Ping*, 46-48 Charoen Prathet Rd, T 270100, F 270119, a/c, restaurant, pool, tallest hotel in town, friendly staff, good location for shopping.

C *Galare*, 7 Soi 2 Charoen Prathet Rd, T 273885, F 279088, some a/c, small hotel in leafy compound, lovely position on the river, large, clean rooms, efficient service, rec; **C** *Green Lodge*, 60 Charoen Prathet Rd, T 279188, F 279188, some a/c, clean rooms with attached bathrooms in small, but featureless hotel on busy road; **C** *Kim House*, 62 Charoen Prathet Rd, T 282441, some a/c, small hotel down small, secluded soi, with clean rooms and welcoming atmosphere, rec.

D *Chiang Mai*, 91 Charoen Prathet Rd, T 236501, some a/c, restaurant, overlooking river, rec; **D** *Ratana*, 3/5 Charoen Prathet Rd, T 252716, some a/c, clean.

● **On the E bank of the river**

E *Hollanda Montri*, 265 Charoenrat Rd, T 242450, a/c, hot water, coffee shop, same Dutch management as *The Riverside* restaurant; **E** *Je T'aime*, 247-9 Charoenrat Rd, T 241912; **E** *Mee's*, 193/1 Charoenrat Rd, T 243534; **E-F** *SSS*, 48/3 Sanam Kila Rd, T 217424, restaurant, very basic but clean, friendly staff, good atmosphere, tours and treks organized, great place to meet other travellers, rec.

Price guide	US$	Baht
◆◆◆◆	15+	375+
◆◆◆	5-15	125-375
◆◆	2-5	50-125
◆	under 2	under 50

● **Places to eat**

For listing of where to have a Northern Kantoke meal plus cultural show, see Entertainment. Some of the best Thai food, particularly sea-food, is served from numerous small and large restaurants, and countless stalls, in the *Anusarn market* area. The best place to see what is on offer in a small area; food available all day but best at night when there is a cacophony of talking, frying and chopping.

Thai: ◆◆*Aroon Rai*, 43-45 Kotchasan Rd, very big restaurant, good value Thai food, N Thai specialities, popular, rec; ◆*Chang Moi*, Boon-ruangrit Rd, just N of Malaria Centre, excellent *kuay tiaw* (noodle soup); rec; ◆◆*Galae*, 65 Suthep Rd, in the foothills of Doi Suthep on the edge of a reservoir, Thai and N Thai dishes; ◆◆◆-◆◆◆◆*The Gallery*, 25-29 Charoen Rat Rd, T 248601, quiet and refined Thai restaurant with river view, superb food, highly rec for a special night out (must book); ◆◆*Honey BBQ Chicken*, Charoen Prathet Rd, northeastern food, excellent 'Chiang Mai' chicken, open-air restaurant, popular with locals; ◆*Indigo*, junction of highways 106 and the Superhighway S of town, rec; ◆◆*Kai Thong*, 67 Kotchasan Rd, 'jungle' food, novelty value only; *Krua Thai*, S side of town, on Route 106, nr junction with super highway; ◆◆*Lanna Himping*, 28/1 Wangsingkham Rd, especially good seafood, rec; ◆*Mangsawirat*, 9/1 Laruk Rd, vegetarian; ◆*Doi House*, 250 Tha Phae Rd Soi 2, cheap noodle and rice house; ◆*Dara Steak Shop*, 1 Rachmanka Rd, good breakfast stop – yoghurts and lassis.

◆◆*Nang Nuan Seafood*, 27/2-5 Kuan Klang Rd, on the Ping River, also serves Chinese and International food, popular with tour groups; ◆◆◆*New Krua Thai*, 87/2 Oom Muang Rd, also serves Chinese, open-air, good sea-food; ◆◆*Mai Thai*, corner of Charoen Prathet and Anusarn rds, Thai food and some western dishes in attractive wooden, Thai house with garden; ◆◆◆*Riverside*, 9-11 Charoen Rat Rd, T 243239, also serves International food, very popular restaurant overlooking the Ping River, live music, good service, good value for money, booking advised, rec.

◆◆*Ruanthai*, Charoen Prathet Rd; *Ta-Krite*, Samlarn Soi 1, just to the south of Wat Phra Singh, clean, relaxed, rec; ◆*Thanom Pochana*, Chai-yaphum Rd, clean, 'dress appropriate', full of locals, overpriced; ◆◆◆*Whole Earth*, 88 Sri Don-chai Rd, also serves Indian, traditional house, situated in lovely garden, very civilized, with unobtrusive live Thai classical music, rec.

Other Asian cuisines: ◆◆*Al Shiraz*, 123 Chang Klan Rd, popular Indian, food moderate but friendly and homely atmosphere; ◆◆◆◆*Jasmine*, *Royal Princess Hotel*, Chang Klan Rd, excellent Chinese food (*dimsum* at lunchtime); *Koto*, Aruk Rd (on the inside of the moat, W side – behind the pottery stalls), Japanese. ◆◆◆◆*White Orchid*, in the *Diamond Hotel*, 33/10 Charoen Prathet Rd, Chinese, on the banks of the Ping River, also serves seafood and Thai food, rec.

International: ◆◆◆*Alt Heidelberg*, 96/17 Huay Kaew Rd, best German food in town, also serves other International food; ◆◆◆*Babylon*, 100/63 Huay Kaew Rd, good pizzas, rec; ◆◆◆*Bacco*, 158 Tha Phae Rd, opposite Tan-traphan Dept Store, recently opened Italian res-taurant in old teak house; *Ban Rai Steak House*, Wiang Kaew Rd, English, open air, rec; ◆*Daret's*, 4/5 Chaiyaphum Rd, good travellers' food and fruit shakes, very popular but rather smug, slow service; ◆◆◆*German Beer Garden*, 48 Charoen Prathet Rd (opposite *Diamond Riverside Hotel*), German specials served in roadside 'garden', good BBQ; ◆◆◆*Hard Rock Café*, 6 Kotchasan Soi 1, burgers, fries etc but not the original —good music, reasonable food; ◆◆*Haus Munchen*, Loi Kroa Rd (near Chang Klan Rd), popular German restaurant; ◆◆◆*Hungry Horse*, Loi Kroa Rd (near Chang Klan Rd), pizza, pastas and steaks, generous servings; *J.J.Bakery* (*Mon-tri Hotel*), Tha Phae Gate and in the *Chiang Inn Plaza*, Chang Klan Rd, good breakfasts and sand-wiches, very popular; ◆◆◆◆*La Grillade*, *Chiang Inn Hotel*, Chang Klan Rd, menu includes good French dishes; ◆◆◆*La Villa*, Rachdamnern Rd, Italian, mostly pizza, slow service.

◆◆◆*Le Chalet*, Charoen Prathet Rd, French, nice building, rec; ◆◆◆◆*Le Coq d'Or*, 68/1 Koh Klang Rd, a long established international restau-rant set in gardens S of town, refined, prices to match; ◆◆*Le Croissant*, Tha Phae Rd, good travellers' food and fruit shakes; *Lek House*, 22 Chaiyaphum Rd, yoghurts, fruit shakes, steaks; ◆◆◆*Papillon*, 12/1 Sattani Rot Fai Rd, next to railway station, French, rec; ◆◆◆*Pic-cola Roma*, 3/2-3 Charoen Prathet Rd, good Italian food made by an Italian chef; ◆◆*Pizza Hut*,

Chang Klan Rd (near night market); ♦♦*Pizza Peacock*, 138 Tha Phae Rd, fondu, kebabs, pizza and some Thai dishes; ♦*Tha Phae Café*, 79/81 Tha Phae Rd; ♦*Thai-German Dairy Products*, Rachdamnern Rd, delicious yoghurt and muesli, rec; *Thai-German Dairy*, Huay Kaew Rd (opposite the zoo), sells good yoghurt and cheeses.

Fast Food: *Burger King, Pizza Hut, Svenson's Icecream* and *Mister Donut* have opened outlets in the new, vast, *Chiang Inn Plaza*, near the night market on Chang Klan Rd.

Foodstalls: *Anusarn Market* (SE of the Night Market) stalls mostly at night but also smaller number throughout the day, cheap (฿10-15 single dish meals), lively and fun, rec; stalls along Chang Klan Rd sell delicious pancakes ฿3-7; *Somphet market* on Moon Muang Rd for takeaway curries, fresh fish, meat and fruit.

● **Bars**
Many of the bars are concentrated around the SE wall of the city. *Black Cat*, 25 Moon Muang Rd, open: 1300-0100, happy hour: 1700-1900; *Baritone*, Kad Suan Kaew Shopping Mall, Huay Kaew Rd, live jazz, happy hours until 1900; *Byblos*, *Rincome Hotel*, Huay Kaew Rd; *Early Times*, Kotchasan Rd, open-air and live heavy metal music; *Nina Pub*, 95/25 Nantawan Arcade, Nimanhemin Rd; *Playboy Bunny Club*, The Riverside, 63 Charoenrat Rd; *The Pub*, 88 Huay Kaew Rd, quasi-English replica, food (♦♦♦)overpriced and still relaxing in the after-glow of an 8-year-old review in *Newsweek*; Amarit beer on draught is the main attraction, run by a charming Thai woman with excellent English, only worth a visit if you're after the company of other 'farangs'; *Your Place Bar*, NE corner of the moat.

● **Airline offices**
Cathay Pacific, Rachawong Rd; **Japan Airlines**, 62/6 Charoen Prathet Rd; **Thai**, 240 Phra Pokklao Rd, T 210042.

● **Banks & money changers**
Several banks on Tha Phae Rd and plenty of exchange services along Chang Klan and Tha Phae roads. *SK Money Changer*, 73/8 Charoen Prathet Rd (between *Diamond Riverside Hotel* and *Anusarn Market*), open: Mon-Sun 0900-2100. Most banks offer a safety deposit service (useful for leaving valuables when embarking on a trek), expect to pay about ฿200/month.

● **Churches**
Christian Church of Thailand: Kaew Nawarat Rd, English service on Sun 1700. *Seven Foun-*

tains Catholic Chapel: 97 Huay Kaew Rd, English service on Sun 0930.

● **Embassies and consulates**
British, Canal Rd, T 276006; **French Honorary Consulate**, 138 Charoen Prathet Rd, T 281466; **India**, 113 Bumrungrat Rd, T 243066; **Japanese**, 12/1 Boonruangrit Rd, T 221451; **U.S.A.**, 387 Vichayanon Rd, T 252629.

● **Entertainment**
Alliance Française, 138 Charoen Prathet Rd, T 275277 presents French cultural (and some Northern Thai) activities.

British Council: 198 Bumrungrat Rd.

Cinema: *Sang Tawan*, corner of Chang Klan and Sri Donchai rds.

Cultural shows: *Khun Kaew Palace*, 252 Phra Pokklao Rd (N end), T 214315, admission: ฿180 (book in advance), open: 1900-2200 Mon-Sun; *Old Chiang Mai Cultural Centre*, 185/3 Wualai Rd, T 275097, admission: ฿180 (book in advance), Khantoke dinner, followed by hilltribe show, Mon-Sun 1900-2200; the *Diamond Riverside Hotel* on Charoen Prathet Rd and the *Galare Food Centre* in the Night Bazaar, Chang Klan Rd, also organize Kantoke dinners, 1900. ฿180.

Disco: *Porn Ping Hotel*, Charoen Prathet Rd, *Chiang Mai Orchid Hotel*, Huay Kaew Rd.

Library: 21/1 Rachmanka Rd, *Soi 2*. Open: 0800-1700 Mon-Sat. Advice on routes, books on Thailand and novels available.

Kantoke Dinners: (Northern food served on low tables to diners who sit uncomfortably on the floor), to the accompaniment of rather tacky music.

Music: *Early Times*, Kotchasan Rd, open-air and live heavy metal music; *Baritone*, 96 Praisani Rd, live jazz from 2100.

Thai boxing: *Dechanukrau boxing ring*, S of San Pakoi market, on Bumrungrat Rd. Matches every w/e at 2000 (฿20/70).

Traditional Thai Massage: (see page 172), there are a number in town; *Baan Nit*, Soi 2 Chaiyaphum Rd, ฿100/hr, welcoming atmosphere, professional, coffee and snacks available, rec; *ITM (Institute of Thai Massage)*, 5 Santisuk I Rd, T 215108, 5-10 day courses in basic Thai massage, 0900-1600; *Rinkaew Povech*, 183/4 Wualai Rd, T 234565; *Samun Phrai*, 62 Charoen Prathet Rd (near *Kim House*), open 0830-2100, also herbal sauna, rec. Courses in traditional Thai massage can be taken at the

Moh Shivagakomarpaj Foundation, Old Chiang Mai Traditional Hospital, 78/1 Soi Moh Shivagakomarpaj (opposite Old Chiang Mai Cultural Centre, Chiang Mai-Hod Rd), T 275085. Courses last 11 days (fee ฿2,270) and run from the beginning and middle of each month.

● **Hospitals & medical services**
McCormick Hospital, Kaew Nawarat Rd, T 240823 is recommended. English speaking doctors, Mon-Fri 1700-2000.

● **Immigration:**
Fang Rd, just before the airport, T 277510 (visa extensions possible, see page 488).

● **Police**
Main Police Station: corner of Phra Singh and Jhaban rds. **Malaria Centre**: Boonruangrit Rd, N of Suan Dok Gate. **Tourist Police**: corner of Samlarn and Rachmanka rds and next to the TAT office on the Chiang Mai-Lamphon Rd, T 248974.

● **Post & telecommunications**
General Post Office: Charoen Muang Rd (W of the railway station), telegram counter open daily 24 hrs, T 241056. Other Post Offices include **Mae Ping Post Office** on Praisani Rd, with telephone service opposite, **Sriphum Post Office** on Phra Pokklao Rd, **Night Bazaar Post Office**, in the basement of the bazaar, Chang Klan Rd, open until 2300. Post Office at the airport offers telegram and international telephone services. Many travel agents in town offer overseas call service. **Area code**: 053.

● **Shipping and Packing Companies**
Packers available around the Post Offices; shippers along Wualai Rd, many S from the Superhighway.

● **Shopping**
The **Night Markets**, situated on the W and E sides of Chang Klan Rd, are now a major tourist attraction in Chiang Mai and consist of 2 or 3-storey purpose-built buildings containing countless stalls. The set up is no longer a ramshackle affair and many would say the whole area has been rather sanitized. However, it is an excellent place to browse and, along with a wide range of tribal handicrafts, it is possible to buy T-shirts, watches, cheap tapes, leather goods, children's clothes and Burmese 'antiques'. Beware of wood carved products which may well be made of polymer resin. In addition, there are some better quality shops selling jewellery, antiques and silks (both ready-made and lengths) on the first floor of the Viang Ping Building. Most stalls and shops open at about 1800 and close around 2300. **Warorot Market**, N of Tha Phae Rd for clothing, fabric, sportswear, hilltribe handicrafts. Open 0700-1600. **Fruit stalls and market** on both sides of moat north of Tha Phae Gate. Some tuk-tuk drivers are subsidised by factories, so will take you to see silver, silk, enamel factories for about ฿20 each, with no obligation to buy.

Antiques: beware of fakes. There are a number of shops in Tha Phae Rd and opposite the *Rincome Hotel* in the Nantawan Arcade; *Oriental Spirit*, 28 Rachmanka Rd; *Antique House*, 71 Charoen Parthet Rd; *Oriental Style*, 36 Charoenrat Rd, rec; *Banmai*, 37/5 Charoenmuang Rd (see below for suppliers outside Chiang Mai).

Books and Maps: *Nancy Chandler* and *DK Maps* are both good sources of information on Chiang Mai; *D.K. Bookstore*, 234 Tha Phae Rd; *Suriwong Book Centre*, 54/1-5 Sri Donchai Rd (most extensive collection of books in English on Thailand in Chiang Mai); *Book Exchange*, 21/1 Soi 2 Rachmanka, books bought and sold, guidebooks and maps available.

Ceramics: 6 km north of Chiang Mai on the Mae Rim Rd, factory producing Thai Celadon, modelled on Sawankhalok pottery; *Mengrai Kilns*, 31/1 Ratuthit Rd, 2 km SE of Nawarat Bridge. Open: 0800-1700 Mon-Sun; *Suan Buak Haad* in the SW corner of the city on Aruk Rd has a good selection of rustic pottery, large tongs and baskets; *Naiyana*, 283-286 Chang Moi Rd for large pottery tongs.

Clothing: huge assortment of T-shirts, cotton clothing and tribal clothing in the 3 Night Markets on Chang Klan Rd.

Handicrafts: Chiang Mai is the centre for hilltribe handicrafts. There is a bewildering array of goods, much of which is of poor quality. Bargain for everything. See Hilltribe section on page 283 for more detailed information on the various styles of clothing; *Co-op Handicraft*, next to *Thai Farmer's Bank* on Tha Phae Rd; *Hilltribe Products Foundation*, next to *Wat Suan Dok* on Suthep Rd; *Thai Tribal Crafts*, 208 Bumrungrat Rd, near McCormick Hospital – run by Karen and Lahu church organizations on a non-profit basis, good selection, quality and prices.

Honey: good range of local honeys from *Bees Knees*, 17 Chang Klan Rd.

Jewellery: *Shiraz Co*, 170 Tha Phae Rd.

Lacework: *Sarapee Handmade Lace*, 2 Rachwithi Rd, claims to be the only workshop in SE Asia using silk thread.

Lacquerware: *Vichaikul*, near *Wat Nantharam*; *Masusook Antiques*, 263/2-3 Tha Phae Rd.

Paper: *Mountain Products*, 252 Nimanhaemin Rd Soi 6, for Sa Paper, a local handmade paper, made from the bark of the Sa tree.

Silverwork: Hilltribe jewellery particularly. Wualai Rd to the S of the city, and the roads roundabout have the biggest concentration of shops; *Charoen Panich*, 244-248 Tha Phae Rd has a selection; *Siam Silver Ware*, 5 Wualai Soi 3; *Sipsong Panna*, 95/19 Nimanhaemin Rd, opposite *Rincome Hotel*, selection of Thai, Lao and Burmese silverware; *Narinthip Tour*, 59/3 Loi Kroa Rd, for silver and hilltribe silver; *Tada Silverware* on Huay Kaew Rd.

Supermarkets/Department stores: *Tantraphan* have 3 stores on Tha Phae Rd, on the N side of the city, on Mani Noparat Rd and the Tantraphan Airport Plaza, at the intersection of Hang Dong Rd and the Ring Rd, good selection of Western food, clothing and household goods. *Rimping Superstore*, Lamphun Rd and 171 Chotana Rd, *7 Eleven stores* on Huay Kaew, Chotana and Chang Klan rds.

Tailors: *Far Mee*, 66 Square U Pakut, Tha Phae Rd; many of the stalls in and around Warorot Market will make up clothes.

Terracotta: Plaques, murals, statues, pots at *Ban Phor Liang Meun*, 36 Phra Pokklao Rd, a factory showroom.

Textiles: *Pothong House*, 4 Moon Muang Soi 5 for Khmer, Lao and hilltribe fabrics; *Chataporn*, 194 Tha Phae Rd, for silks, cotton and made-up garments; *Shinawatra Silk*, 14/4-8 Huay Kaew Rd (see below for suppliers outside Chiang Mai); *Studio Naenna*, 188 Soi 19 Nimanhaemin Rd, handwoven cloth, made up; *Le Bombyx*, 3 km out of town on the San Kampaeng Rd, ready to wear and made to measure silk and cotton clothing.

Woodcarving: *Banyen*, 201/1 Wualai Rd, just to the S of the Superhighway on road 108. Craftsmen can be seen at work at *Chiang Mai Carving Centre*, Rachchiangsaen Rd and at Singharat Rd. Wholesale furniture suppliers can be found off the roads to Hang Dong.

Outside Chiang Mai Travelling E on Route 1006, towards San Kampaeng, there is a ribbon of shops, (often with factories and display rooms

attached) selling umbrellas (at Bor Sang), jewellery, handicrafts, lacquerware, woodcarvings, 'antiques', cotton and silk (at San Kampaeng, 15 km), ceramics. The Umbrella Fair, in January, has a colourful display of every size and shape of umbrella. **Getting there**: bus from N side of Charoen Muang Rd (∅4).

Hang Dong is a basket area S of town on Route 108. **Getting there**: buses leave from Chiang Mai Gate.

Pasang is a cotton-weavers village, 36 km S of the city on Route 108. **Getting there**: buses leave from E side of Charoen Rat Rd, near the TAT office, ∅5.

● **Sports**

Fitness Park: *Huay Kaew Fitness Park* is on Huay Kaew Rd at the bottom of Doi Suthep near the zoo.

Go-kart racing: *Chiang Mai Speedway*, 8 km out of town on route 108, racing every Sat and Sun afternoons, open Mon-Sun; *Chiang Mai Gokart*, San Kampaeng Rd, near Bor Sang intersection.

Golf: *Lanna Public Golf Course*, Chotana Rd (at Nong Bua, 4 km N of the city). Green fee ∅400, ∅600 at weekends, club hire ∅250. Open: 0600-1800. There is also a driving range here. *Gymkhana Club*, Chiangmai-Lamphun Rd; *Driving range* opposite *Banyen*, where Route 108 meets the superhighway; *Mae Sa Resort*, km 3, Mae Sa Waterfall Rd, T 222203; *Green Valley Golf Club*, green fees ∅1,000, ∅1,500 weekends.

Horse Racing: Next to the *Lanna Public Golf Course*, Chotana Rd (4 km N of the city), races every Sun from 1200-1730. **Horse Riding**: *Lanna Sports Centre*, Chotana Rd (N of town).

Squash: *Gymkana Club*, Chiang Mai-Lamphun Rd, every Thurs 1730.

Swimming: *Rincome Hotel*, Huay Kaew Rd, ∅40; *Top North Guesthouse*, 15 Moon Muang Rd Soi 2, ∅50; *Anodard Hotel*, 57 Rachmanka Rd.

Tennis: *Rincome Hotel*, Huay Kaew Rd. *Anantasiri Courts*, Superhighway, (near the National Museum). *Kaeo Kasem Courts*, Canal Rd (off Huay Kaew Rd), not far from the strawberry fields.

Yoga: *Khun Wai*, Huay Kaew Rd, Mon-Sat 0800-1800, ∅100/hr.

● **Tour companies & travel agents**

There are numerous travel agents along Tha Phae, Chang Klan and Moon Muang (in the vicinity of Tha Phae Gate) roads, most of whom will offer tours and treks over the North. They will also book air, train and bus tickets out of Chiang Mai. **NB** The TAT recommend that services should only be bought from companies that register with the tourist Business and Guide Registration Office; they provide a list of all such companies. *Accord Tour and Trekking*, 422 Tha Phae Rd, T 235396; *Chiang Mai Air International*, 2/2 Chaiyaphum Rd, Tha Phae Gate, T 234655, F 252386; *Chiang Mai Green Tour and Trekking*, 29/31 Chiang Mai-Lamphun Rd (nr TAT office), T 241272; *New Way*, 9 Tha Phae Rd Soi 6, T 273494, F 273494; *Paradise*, 32-46 Chang Klan Rd, T 274336; *Skybird*, 92/3 Sri Donchai Rd, T 249991; *Sompet*, 129/1-4 Moon Muang Rd, T 213516, rec; *Songserm*, 8 Chaiyaphum Rd (close to Tha Phae Gate); *Freebird Trekking*, Moon Muang Soi 2 (at the *Panda Guesthouse*), rec; *Galare Travel Service*, 54-56 Tha Phae Rd, T 236237; *Inthanon Tour*, 100/19 Huay Kaew Rd, T 212373; *Maimai's Tribal Tours* at Pete's Guesthouse, 46/3 Moon Muang Soi 9 Rd, T 210617. Tours to Pai area rec. *North Star*, 242 Tha Phae Rd, T 235065 rec; *Summit Tours and Trekking*, 28 Tha Phae Rd, T 233351, rec.

● **Tourist offices**

TAT, 105/1 Chiang Mai-Lamphun Rd, T 248604, F 248605 (open 0830-1630 Mon-Sun). Helpful and informative, with a good range of maps and leaflets, including information on guesthouses and guidelines for trekking. Areas of responsibility are Chiang Mai, Lamphun, Lampang and Mae Hong Son. **Chiang Mai Municipal Tourist Information Centre** corner of Tha Phae and Charoen Prathet rds. The only one of its type in Thailand, good maps and some other handouts, but not yet up to TAT standard. Open: Mon-Fri 0830-1200, 1300-1630.

● **Transport**

697 km from Bangkok.

Local Bicycle hire: from Chang Phuak Gate and at the S end of Moon Muang Rd, ฿22/day, or on Nakhon Ping Bridge, plus some guesthouses.

Bus: ฿3-5 (the latter is for a/c) anywhere in town (the bus routes are given in Nancy Chandler's Map of Chiang Mai).

Car or jeep hire: starts at ฿800-1500/day, ฿6000/week. *Hertz* and *Avis* are slightly more expensive, but are more reliable. **Hertz**, 90 Sri Donchai Rd (main office – next to *Chiang Mai Plaza Hotel*), T 279474, 12/3 Loi Kroa Rd, T 279473, *Novotel Suriwongse Hotel*, T 270058 and *Chiang Mai*

Plaza, T 270040; **Avis**, 14/14 Huay Kaew Rd (opposite *Chiang Mai Orchid Hotel*), T 21316, *Royal Princess Hotel*, T 281033 or the airport, T 222013. **North Wheels** 127/2 Moon Muang Rd, T 216189, seems reliable. There are plenty of others, but check insurance cover and the car before setting off. It is even possible to hire a self-drive tuk-tuk from *PC Service*, 56 Chaiyaphum Rd.

Motorbike hire: at the S end of Moon Muang Rd and at guesthouses. ฿150-300/day. Insurance sometimes available, e.g. *Ladda Motorcycle Rental*, Moon Muang Soi 2 (at the *Panda Guest House*); *P.O.P.*, 51 Kotchasan Rd, T 276014, ฿250 for 24 hrs (plus optional ฿50 insurance).

Sii-lor ('four wheels'): these converted red pick-ups are known as songthaews ('two rows') in most other towns, but in Chiang Mai they are usually referred to as sii-lors. They are the most common means of transport around town. Travelling on regular routes costs ฿5, ฿10 if you want them to take you somewhere off their route. Before boarding, tell the driver where you want to go and he will either say 'yes' or, if it's not on his route, he will quote you a price for the trip. Use landmarks (such as hotels, bridges, gates etc) rather than street names as a guide for where you want to go. **Tuk-tuk**: minimum ฿10/trip, ฿30 for longer journeys; **Saamlor**: ฿5-10 within city, ฿20 for longer distances.

Air: the airport is 3 km SW of town. It contains a bank, post office, tourist information counter, and snack bar. Regular connections on *Thai* with Bangkok, 1 hr. Connections on *Thai* with Chiang Rai 40 mins, Mae Hong Son 30 mins, Nan 45 mins, Mae Sot 50 mins, Phuket 2 hrs, Phitsanulok 35 mins, Khon Kaen 1 hr 25 mins and Tak 1 hr 40 mins. Bangkok Airways also operate a service to Bangkok. **International air connections**: with Hong Kong, Pagan and Mandalay in Burma (Myanmer), and Kunming in S China.

    Transport to town Thai Airways operate a 'limousine' service to all hotels, ฿100/person and a shuttle bus service between the airport and their office in town (but you can get off anywhere in town), ฿40.

Train: station is in the E of the town, on Charoen Muang Rd, across the Ping River, T for same day booking and T 242094 for advanced booking (recommended). Left luggage 0600-1800, ฿5/bag for first 5 days, ฿10/bag from then on. Regular connections with Bangkok's Hualamphong station and towns along the route, 11-15 hrs. The overnight express train leaves Bangkok at 1800 (13½ hrs), the Special express leaves at 1940 (12 hrs).

Road Bus: the long distance bus station or Bor Kor Sor (BKS) is at the Chiang Mai Arcade, on the corner of the super highway and Kaew Nawarat rds, NE of town, T 242664. Most companies will provide a transfer service to the station: pick-up points are Anusarn Market, Narawat Bridge, Sang Tawan Cinema and Chiang Inn Hotel Lane. Tuk-tuks and siilors wait at the station to take passengers into town. Regular connections with Bangkok's Northern bus terminal 9-12 hrs (non-a/c ฿190, a/c ฿237-304, VIP ฿470), Phitsanulok 6 hrs, Sukhothai 5 hrs, Chiang Rai 3-4 hrs (non-a/c ฿57, a/c ฿79-102), Mae Sariang 4-5 hrs, Mae Hong Son 8-9 hrs (non-a/c ฿115, a/c ฿206), Pai 4 hrs, Nan 7 hrs and other Northern towns. A number of tour companies organize coaches to the capital; these are concentrated in the Anusarn market area and usually provide transport to the Arcade terminal, from where the buses depart. Buses to closer destinations (such as Mae Rim, Phrao, Chiang Dao, Fang, Thaton, Bor Sang, San Kampeang, Lamphun and Pasang) go from Chotana Rd, N of Chang Puak Gate.

THE WESTERN LOOP: MAE SARIANG, MAE HONG SON & PAI

Some of the most spectacular scenery in Thailand lies to the west of Chiang Mai where the Tenasserim range divides Burma from Thailand. Travelling southwest from Chiang Mai on Route 108, the road passes close to Doi Inthanon, one of the country's most famous peaks and national parks, and passes through Chom Thong (50 km). From here the road follows narrow river valleys before reaching Mae Sariang not far from the Burmese border, a good trekking point, and 188 km from Chiang Mai. The hill town of Mae Hong Son, with its Burmese-style wats, is 160 km due north of Mae Sariang and is another popular trekking centre. Until recently the northern section of this loop was almost impassable during the rainy season. Today it is much improved and Pai is accessible from both east and west. From Pai the road returns to Chiang Mai through the Mae Sa Valley and south along Route 107, a total of 140 km.

Chom Thong

This featureless roadside town is a necessary stopping-off point for trips on public transport to Doi Inthanon. It is notable only for the historic **Wat Phrathat Si Chom Thong** (situated on the left-hand side of the main road from Chiang Mai). This impressive wat has a gilded Burmese chedi, dated 1451, and a Burmese-style bot and viharn built in 1516. Both are of great beauty, and the raised bot (on the left as you enter the complex) exhibits some fine woodcarving. The ancient viharn is cluttered with Buddha images. A smaller white chedi is faced with 4 standing Buddhas, and there is also an impressive assorted collection of miniature Buddha images.

• **Transport** 58 km from Chiang Mai on the Chiang Mai-Hod highway (Route 108). **By bus**:

regular connections with Chiang Mai from the Chiang Mai Gate.

Doi Inthanon and the National Park

Located off Route 108, on Route 1009, Doi Inthanon is Thailand's highest peak at 2595m (see map, page 171). The mountain is a National Park and the winding route to the top is stunning, with terraced rice fields, cultivated valleys and a few hilltribe villages. The park covers 482 sq km and is one of the most visited in Thailand. Although the drive to the top is dramatic, the park's flora and fauna can only really be appreciated by taking one of the hiking trails off the main road. The flora ranges from dry deciduous forest on the lower slopes, to moist evergreen between 1000-1800m, to 'cloud' forest and a sphagnum (moss) bog towards the summit. There are even some relict pines. Once the habitat of bears and tigers, the wildlife has been severely depleted through over-hunting. However, it is still occasionally possible to see flying squirrel, red-toothed shrew, Chinese pangolin and Pere David's vole, as well as an abundance of butterflies and moths.

Just beneath the summit, in a spectacular position, are a pair of bronze and gold-tiled chedis, one dedicated to the King in 1989, and the other dedicated to Queen Sirikit at the end of 1992 and opened at the beginning of 1993. Both chedis contain intricate symbolism and have been built to reaffirm the unity of the Thai nation. The ashes of Chiang Mai's last king, Inthawichayanon, are contained in a small white chedi on the summit itself – the ultimate reflection of the idea that no one should be higher than the king, in life or in death. Disappointingly, the views from this point are obscured by trees. The radar station on the peak must not be photographed. Close by is a small wat, and next to that a shrine dedicated to 2 pilots whose plane crashed into the peak. There are

a number of **waterfalls** on the slopes: the **Mae Klang Falls** (near the 8 km marker and not far from the visitors centre), **Wachiratan Falls** (26 km down from summit and near the 21 km marker) and **Siriphum Falls** (3-4 km off the road near the 31 km marker and not far from the Park Headquarters), as well as the large **Borichinda Cave** (a 2 km hike off the main road near the visitors centre at the 9 km marker). But, the **Mae Ya Falls**, in the S of the park are the most spectacular, plunging more than 250 m (they lie 15 km from park H.Q. and are accessible from Chom Thong town). Ask for details at the Visitor's Centre a few kilometres on from the park's entrance checkpoint. The best time to visit the mountain is between Nov and Feb when it is most likely to be clear. Admission to the park: ฿20 for car, ฿5 for motorbike, ฿50 for songthaew and minibus. Open: 0600-1800.

● **Accommodation** There are bungalows (**A-C**, sleeping 4-30 people) at the 31 km outstation on the route up the mountain. To book, phone B 5790529 or write to the Superintendent, Doi Inthanon National Park, Chom Thong District, Chiang Mai 50160. Advance reservation recommended. There is a camping ground at the 31 km mark (฿5/person). Small tents (฿50/night) and blankets are available for hire.

● **Places to eat** A small 'Park Shop' at the 31 km mark will serve meals. There are no stalls on the summit although a new restaurant opened near the chedis, near the summit, in 1993.

● **Transport** 105 km from Chiang Mai. Take a yellow songthaew for the 58 km from Chiang Mai Gate to Chom Thong (฿10). From Chom Thong market, take another yellow songthaew to the Mae Klang Falls (฿5) or the Wachiratan Falls (฿10). To reach Mae Ya Falls and Doi Inthanon summit a songthaew must be chartered (this will seat 10 people); ฿350 and ฿500 respectively. 1¼ hrs to the summit from Chom Thong.

Mae Sariang

Mae Sariang is a good departure point for trekking. The road from Chom

Thong runs up the Ping valley, before turning W to follow the Chaem River, climbing steadily through beautiful dipterocarp forest, the Op Luang National Park (17 km from Hod), and into the mountains of Western Thailand. Mae Sariang is a small market town on the banks of the Yuam River. There is little to draw people here, except as a stopping-off point for Mae Hong Son or as a starting point for trekking. There are a handful of unremarkable wats; **Wat Utthayarom**, known locally as Wat Chom Soong, is Burmese in style but also displays two Mon-inspired white chedis. Other monasteries include **Wat Sri Bunruang** (in town) and **Wat Joom Thong** (on a hill overlooking town). The latter has a large and recently constructed white seated Buddha image surveying the valley below.

Trekking (See Hilltribes and trekking, page 275.) The owners of the *Riverside Guesthouse* organize treks to the Burmese border. Chan trekking company operates through the *Roj Thip Restaurant* at 661 Wiang Mai Rd.

● **Accommodation C-D** *Kamolsorn*, 283 Mae Sariang Rd, T 681204, some a/c, hot water, rec; **C-D** *Mitraree*, 158 Mae Sariang Rd, T 681110, some a/c, hot water; **C-D** *New Mitraree Guesthouse*, 34 Wiang Mai Rd, T 681109, some a/c, hot water, featureless, lovely views from the balcony over rice-fields; **E** *Mae Sariang Guesthouse*, 1 Laeng Phanit (opposite Wat Utthayarom); **E** *Riverside*, 85/1 Laeng Phanit Rd, T 681188, own bathroom, hot water, rec; **E** *See View* (no sea), 70 Wiang Mai Rd (across river), T 681154, friendly, hot water, with good sized rooms in stone bungalows, smaller wooded rooms also available, with shared facilities, rec; **E** *Sakamit Guesthouse*, Wiang Mai Rd (near the Shell station), very little custom – a poor sign; *Mae Sariang Resort* (2.5 km out of town on road to Chiang Mai, 1 km off main road on the river), attractive setting.

● **Places to eat** *Bakery House*, 187 Wiang Mai Rd, good breakfasts, excellent pancakes, rec; *Inthira*, Wiang Mai Rd, Chinese; *Lobby Café*, Wiang Mai Rd; *Roj Thip*, 661 Wiang Mai Rd; ◆–◆◆*Bamboo*, Wiang Mai Rd (near crossroads with Mae Sariang Rd), good Thai food; ◆◆*Ruan Phrae*, down Soi to Wat Sri Bunruang, off Wiang Mai Rd, Thai and Chinese, rec.

● **Banks & money changers** Thai Farmers, 150/1 Wiang Mai Rd.

● **Useful addresses** Post Office (and overseas telephone): 31/1 Wiang Mai Rd. **Area code**: 053.

● **Transport** 188 km from Chiang Mai. **By bus**: station is close to *Riverside Guesthouse*, next to Wat Jong Sung. Regular connections with Chiang Mai 4 hrs, Mae Hong Son 4$\frac{1}{2}$ hrs and one connection a day with Bangkok. The road S to Mae Sot, following the Burmese border, is much improved and the only rough stretch is immediately to the S of Mae Sariang. Songthaews depart 4 times a day for Mae Sot, 5 hrs (฿150).

Mae Hong Son

Mae Hong Son lies in a forested valley, surrounded by mountains and lives up to its claim to being the 'Switzerland of Thailand'. It is about as far removed from 'Tailand' as you are likely to get, with only 2% of the population here being ethnic Tais. The great majority belong to one or other of the various hilltribes; mostly Karen, but also Lisu, Hmong and Lahu. During the winter months, the temperatures can get as low as 2°C, so you will need to take a sweater. It is also often misty. An excellent centre for trekking, the town is changing rapidly (some would say *has* changed) from a backpackers' hideaway to a 'tour' centre, with the construction of two major hotels: the *Holiday Inn* and the *Tara*.

Towards the end of 1992, Burmese forces occupied the Thai village of Huay Pleung to the NW of Mae Hong Son. The Burmese have been fighting Karenni rebels who killed 50 Burmese troops in a skirmish at the beginning of Sept. They perceive the rebels to have received support from the Thai authorities. Journalist Bertil Lintner reported that the Burmese refer to Thai troops as *yeme* or 'female soldiers' and quoted a

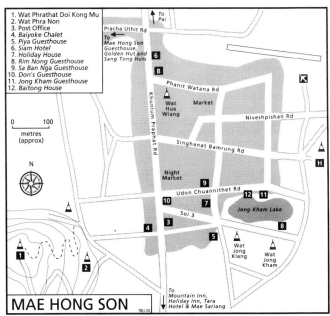

1. Wat Phrathat Doi Kong Mu
2. Wat Phra Non
3. Post Office
4. Baiyoke Chalet
5. Piya Guesthouse
6. Siam Hotel
7. Holiday House
8. Rim Nong Guesthouse
9. Sa Ban Nga Guesthouse
10. Don's Guesthouse
11. Jong Kham Guesthouse
12. Baitong House

MAE HONG SON

TBU 20

source in Mae Hong Son as saying that the "Thais, for their part, mention the Burmese army in a whisper, as if they were talking about a ghost or an evil spirit".

Places of interest

Most postcards of the town picture the lake, with **Wat Jong Klang**, a Burmese wat, in the background. It is particularly beautiful in the early morning, when mist rises off the lake. Wat Jong Klang started life as a rest pavilion for monks on pilgrimage, with a wat being built by the Shans living in the area between 1867 and 1871. The monastery contains some 50 carved Burmese wooden dolls (or *tukata*) depicting characters from the *Jataka* stories (ask to see them) as well as a series of mediocre painted glass panels on the same theme. Next door, in the same compound, is **Wat Jong Kham**, a Tibetan structure with a large seated Buddha. **Wat Hua Wiang**, next to the

market, contains an important Burmese-style brass Buddha image – the *Phra Chao Phla La Khaeng*, in an attitude of subduing Mara. It is said that the image was cast in 9 pieces in Burma and transported to Mae Hong Son along the Pai River.

Doi Kong Mu, the hill overlooking the town, provides superb views of the valley (on a good day) and is home to a Burmese-style wat – **Wat Phrathat Doi Kong Mu**, known locally as Wat Plai Doi. The *wat* was constructed by the first King of Mae Hong Son in the mid-19th century. A path from the town winds its way up the hill, or alternatively go by tuk-tuk. At the foot of Doi Kung Mu Hill is **Wat Phra Non** which contains a 12m long Burmese-style reclining Buddha.

Excursions

Mae Aw is a Hmong and KMT (Kuomintang – the remnants of Chiang Kai Shek's army) village in the mountains to the N of Mae Hong Son, on the border with Burma. There are stunning views over Burma. **Getting there:** by songthaew (2 hrs) (from Singhanat Bamrung Rd at about 0800), or arrange a trek.

Trekking

(See Hilltribes and trekking, page 275). Most guesthouses will organize treks, ranging from trips down the Salween River to the Burmese border, to Mae Sot, elephant treks, and rafting on the Pai River. Treks can be organized from one day to a week, and the average price is ฿250/day. *Nam Rim Tours* organise a 7 day

trek to Chiang Mai. The *Piya Guesthouse, Holiday House, Rose Garden* and the *Jungle King* as well as the *Rim Nong Restaurant* all organize treks (see Accommodation or Restaurants for addresses).

Tours

There are assorted day tours to such sights as Pha Sua Waterfall, Pang Tong Summer Palace, the KMT village of Mae Aw (see excursions), Fish Cave and Tam Nam Lot (Water Cave). Tour companies include: *Nam Rim Tours*, 5/2 Khunlum Praphat Rd T 611174 (opposite the Post Office), rec; *Rim Nong Restaurant* (on S

THE SELLING OF THE PADAUNG OR 'LONG-NECKED KAREN'

The Padaung, a Burmese people from the state of Kayah, are better known as the 'Long-Necked Karen' or, derogatorily, as the 'giraffe people'. Forced out of Myanmar (Burma) during their long struggle for autonomy, they have become refugees in Thailand and objects of tourist fascination. Their eponymous name says it all: women Padaung 'lengthen' their necks using brass rings which they add from birth. An adult Padaung can have a neck 30 cm long, and be weighed down with 5 kg of brass.

Why the Padaung should do this, in one sense, is clear: it is regarded as beautiful. But their explanations of how the custom arose in the first place take several forms. Some Padaung maintain that women began to add rings to their necks to protect themselves from tiger attack. Another explanation is that they were designed to disfigure the body so that Padaung women would not be taken to the Burmese court as concubines or prostitutes. A third reason relates to the myth of the origins of the Padaung people. It is said that they arose after a dragon had been impregnated by the wind, and that the lengthening of the neck is designed to mimic the dragon's long, and beautiful neck.

Sadly, Thai entrepreneurs in allegiance with the army and Karen rebels have exploited the Padaung's refugee status (they have few rights in Thailand), their relative naiveté regarding matters commercial, and their only asset from a tourist perspective – their long necks. Most tourists who take tours to the two refugee camps (paying 250 baht to enter the villages) in Mae Hong Son Province leave disgusted at the 'selling' of these people. John Davies, a Chiang Mai resident who runs culturally-sensitive tours to the hill peoples observes: "It's a freak show brought into Thailand for commercial gain – tourism at its worst". And yet even he caved into the demands of *Asia Voyages* who insisted that the Padaung be included in his tour if they were to feed their clients into his operation. The tourist dollar speaks. But the hard fact is that the Padaung have little else to sell. One women, Ba Nang, is paid 1,000 baht a month simply to pose for photographs. Does she like it in Thailand? "I love Thailand. Here it's easy to find food; easy living and no problems." Like so many other indigenous peoples in Southeast Asia, the Padaung find themselves caught in a web of poverty, oppression, exploitation and powerlessness.

side of the lake); and *Jungle King* (to the N of the lake).

Festivals

Apr: *Poi Sang Long* (moveable, beginning of month). 10-16 year old boys are ordained into the monkhood. Beforehand, they are dressed up as princes (the historic Buddha was a prince) and on the following day there is a colourful procession through town starting from Wat Kham Ko. **Oct**: *Tak Bak Devo* (moveable). Celebrates the Buddha's descent from the Tavatimsa heaven. Festivities centre on the hill-top Wat Phrathat Doi Kong Mu.

Local information

● **Accommodation**

Most of the more expensive hotels are located at the S end of town, off the map. **A** *Holiday Inn*, 114/5-7 Khunlum Praphat Rd, T 611390, F 611524, B 2542614, a/c, several restaurants, pool, large hotel outside town good facilities including tennis courts; **A** *Mae Hong Son Tara*, 149 Moo 8, Tambon Pang Moo, T 611473, F 611252, a/c, restaurant, pool, situated out of town in extensive attractive gardens, raised balcony restaurant, 104 rooms, with satellite TV, well run.

B *Mae Hong Son Resort*, 24 Ban Huay Dua (3 km from town off route to Mae Sariang – turn right after the police station), T 611504, a/c, restaurant; **B** *Baiyoke Chalet*, 90 Khunlum Praphat Rd, T 611486, F 611533, a/c, restaurant, hot water, clean and friendly; **B** *Saammok Villas*, 28/1 Tambon Tapon Daeng, T 611478 (3 km from town off route to Mae Sariang – turn right after the police station), a/c, restaurant, pool.

C *Mountain Inn*, 112 Khunlum Praphat Rd, T 611309, F 612248, a/c, restaurant, rather motel-esque, once clean, but apparently gone downhill, overpriced; **C** *Panorama*, Khunlum Praphat Rd, some a/c, clean, bright rooms, friendly management.

D *Piya Guesthouse*, 1 Soi 3 Khunlum Praphat Rd, T 611260, fan, hot water, rec; **D** *Siam*, 23 Khunlum Praphat Rd, T 611148, some a/c.

● **Guesthouses**

Most guesthouses are concentrated around the lake or on Pracha Uthit Rd (opposite the bus station). **D** *Golden Hut*, Pracha Uthit Rd, stone bungalows and huts with hot water; **D-E** *Sang Tong Huts*, Pracha Uthit Rd, huts, some with hot water baths.

E *Holiday House*, 21 Pradit Jong Kham Rd, hot water, lakeside position, friendly and professionally managed, rec; **E** *Jong Kham*, lakeside, bungalows and some cheaper rooms in the main house; **E** *Mae Hong Son Guesthouse*, Pracha Uthit Rd, near *Dio Kong Mu*, simple huts; **E** *Rim Nong*, 4/1 Chamnansatid Rd, restaurant lakeside position, dormitory accommodation available; **E** *Sa Ban Nga House*, 14 Udon Chuannithet Rd, some rooms with hot water, friendly, clean and well-run.

F *Baitong*, lakeside location, clean and well-run; **F** *Don's Guesthouse*, 77/1 Khunlum Praphat Rd, T 611362; **F** *Jungle King*, 19 Pradit Jong Kham Rd; **F** *Johnnie Guesthouse*, friendly and welcoming atmosphere, treks arranged; **F** *Rose Garden*, lakeside.

● **Places to eat**

The largest concentration of restaurants is on Khunlum Praphat Rd. The cheapest (and best?) place to eat is in the night market, also on Khunlum Praphat Rd. Service can be slow. ◆◆*Cheers*, 37 Udon Chuannithet Rd, overlooking lake, Thai, rec; ◆◆*Bamboo*, Khunlum Praphat Rd (next to *Good Luck*), very good Thai, Chinese and international food; ◆◆*Good Luck*, Khunlum Praphat Rd, popular international vegetarian food, good value; ◆◆*Khaimuk*, 71 Singhanat Bamrung Rd, good Thai food; ◆◆◆*Mountain Inn Hotel*, 122 Khunlum Praphat Rd, Thai; ◆*Rim Nong*, on S side of the lake, Thai; *Phuekhun*, Khunlum Praphat Rd, International; *Sunny's Coffeeshop*, Khunlum Praphat Rd, International.

● **Airline offices**

Thai, Singhanat Bamrung Rd, T 611297.

● **Banks & money changers**

Bangkok, Khunlum Praphat Rd (0830-1900); Krung Thai, Singhanat Bamrung Rd; Thai Farmers, 76 Khunlum Praphat Rd. **NB** It is difficult to change money in Mae Hong Son on Sundays and public holidays, unless you are staying at the *Holiday Inn* or *Tara*.

● **Best time to visit**

Between Nov and Mar when the mist is at bay. But the nights are cold, so take a sweater and blanket.

● **Entertainment**

Disco: at the *Holiday Inn*. Traditional massage and herbal steam bath is a Mae Hong Son speciality; particularly welcome for those just back from strenuous treks. Available at several places around town, e.g. *Piya Guesthouse* (฿200/hr) or on Pracha Uthit Rd.

● **Hospital & medical services**
Hospital: at the E end of Singhanat Bamrung Rd. **Clinic**: Khunlum Praphat Rd.

● **Immigration**
Khunlum Praphat Rd (opposite the bus station).

● **Post & telecommunications**
Post Office: S end of town, corner of Khunlum Praphat Rd and Soi 3, open 7 days a week for telephone. **Area code**: 053.

● **Shopping**
Handicrafts: *Thai Handicraft Centre*, Khunlum Praphat Rd; *Chokeadradet*, 645 Khunlum Praphat Rd for antiques, tribal handicrafts and junk. Rec.

● **Sport**
Fitness Park: around the lake.

● **Tour companies & travel agents**
Several along Khunlum Praphet Rd.

● **Tourist offices**
Tourist Information booth (poor) at the Night Market.

● **Tourist Police**
Khunlum Praphat Rd, next to the Night Market.

● **Transport**
360 km from Chiang Mai (274 km on northern route). 170 km from Mae Sariang.

Local Bicycle hire: from *Jungle King*, ฿25/day. **Motorbike and jeep hire**: *Khuntu Trading*, 48 Khunlum Praphat Rd charge ฿150/day for motorbikes. Many other places rent out motorbikes.

Air: airport is to the N of town on Niveshpishan Rd. Regular daily connections on Thai with Chiang Mai 35 mins (฿330) and Bangkok, 2 hrs 10 mins; Bangkok Airways also operate a daily service with Bangkok, 1 hr 50 mins.

Road Bus: station on Khunlum Praphat Rd. 2 routes from Chiang Mai: the northern, more gruelling route via Pai (see below), (a/c ฿175) or the route described above, from the S (฿115-206). Regular connections with Bangkok, 12½ hrs (฿241-442).

Road to Pai

The road has recently been upgraded and it is a stunning journey with magnificent views. The road winds through beautiful cultivated valleys and forest. 18 km out of Mae Hong Son is **Tham Pla** (or Fish Cave). 2 hours NW of Pai is the **Shan** village of **Soppong**, a prosperous centre serving the needs of the surrounding hill-tribe communities. (There are two guest-houses close to Soppong (5 km), run by an Australian who has married a Thai. One is called *Cave Lodge*, rec.)

Pai

This small town lies in an upland valley. It has a charming, unspoilt atmosphere and is a good alternative base for hill-tribe visits. **Wat Klang** and **Wat Luang** are Burmese in style.

Excursions
Lisu, **Shan**, **Red Lahu** and **Kuomintang-Chinese** villages are all in the vicinity. There are also easy and attractive walks through the surrounding country-side.

Trekking
(See Hilltribes and trekking, page 275.) Most guesthouses run treks. *Charlie's* (who offer 'no elephants, no rafting, no mercy'), *Pai Trekking* and *Duang* all pool customers. They offer very good, simple, but genuine treks. Average price is ฿300/day. 1-4 day treks available.

Local information
● **Accommodation**
C (for a) *Pai Mountain Lodge*, 7 km NW of town, T 699068, for those wanting to 'get away from it all'.

D *Rim Pai Cottages*, 17 Moo 3, Wiang Tai, T 699133, price includes breakfast, best accommodation in Pai, hot water, tree-house available, nice position on river, rec; **D** *Pai in the Sky*, 150 Wiang Tai, restaurant, helpful owner, with lots of trekking information, clean, bare rooms.

E *Duang*, 5 Rung Siyanon Rd, T 699101, opposite bus station, very clean and quiet, family run guesthouse, trekking organised, will change cash, rec; **E** *Nunyas*, Rung-Siyanon Rd, T 699051, hot water, garden, newish; **E** *Pai Villa*, 89/3 Banu Pakham Wiang Tai, bathroom, nice position on river, rec.

F *Big*, Rungsiyanon Rd; **E-F** *Charlie's*, 9 Rungsiyanon Rd (next to Krung Thai Bank), nice garden, rec; **F** *Happy Rabbit*, restaurant, opposite *Pai in the Sky*.

● **Places to eat**
♦*Pai in the Sky*, 150 Wiang Tai. Thai and International, rec; ♦♦*Home Style*, near the clinic, excellent travellers food, good value.

● **Banks & money changers**
Krungthai, Rungsiyanon Rd.

● **Entertainment**
Traditional massage: opposite the *Rim Pai Cottages*.

● **Useful addresses**
Area code: 053. **Clinic**: open 1730-2030.

● **Transport to & from Pai**
140 km from Chiang Mai.

Local Bicycle hire: ฿30/day next to Wat Klang and at *Northern Green* bike shop, near the bus station. **Motorbike hire**: ฿150/day (same place as bikes).

Road Bus: regular connections with Chiang Mai, 8 hrs (฿85-90) and Mae Hong Son, 4 hrs (฿90). **4-wheel pick-up**: regular morning connections with Mae Hong Son, via Soppong.

NORTH TO KOK RIVER

Route 107 runs north from Chiang Mai to the former strategic town of Fang (152 km). From here a road winds eastwards over the mountains towards Chiang Rai; during 1993 it was being improved and may soon have a public bus service. Few people stop in Fang; most merely pass through en route to Tha Ton where boats and rafts can be hired to travel down the Kok River to Chiang Rai.

Fang

Fang was founded by King Mengrai in the 13th century although its strategic location at the head of a valley means it has probably been an important trading and exchange settlement for considerably longer than 7 centuries. The government has had some success in encouraging the predominantly Yao hilltribes to switch from opium production to other cash crops such as cabbages and potatoes – so-called crop substitu-

tion programmes. The valley land surrounding Fang is particularly fertile and is used for rice, fruit and vegetable cultivation. The Fang Oil Refinery not far from the town on Route 109 also provides employment.

Fang is visited by a handful of tourists as a trekking base. More often visitors merely pass through Fang en route to Tha Ton where boats leave for the journey down the Kok River to Chiang Rai (see below).

Excursions

Chiang Dao Caves is a large cave complex, 90 km S of Fang off Route 107 towards Chiang Mai (see page 238). Getting there: take a bus to Chiang Mai and get off at the town of Chiang Dao. Songthaews take passengers the final 6 km to the caves.

Hot Springs (*bor nam rawn*) can be found 12 km W of Fang near Ban Muang Chom. Getting there: turn left shortly after leaving the town on the road N to Tha Ton.

Trekking

(See Hilltribes and trekking, page 275.) The wife of the owner of the *Crocodile Dundee Guesthouse* organizes the best treks in town. The *Dew Guesthouse* also provides a trekking service.

Local information
● **Accommodation**
D-E *Chok Thani*, 425 Chotana Rd, T 451252, some a/c, 'best' in town but not very pleasant, just off the main road.

E *Crocodile Dundee Guesthouse*, 9 Mu 9 Tambon Vieng (1 km from the bus station on the main road back towards Chiang Mai), T 451293, F 451187, the best place in town – clean wooden rooms, hot water, owners with good English and advice, rec; **E** *Uang Kham* (Ueng Khum), 227 Tha Phae Rd Soi 3, T 451268, clean bungalows, hot water, rec; **E-F** *Thip Dararat*, 43 Tha Phae Rd, T 451633, the more expensive rooms have hot water, dingy.

F *Dew Guesthouse*, Tha Phae Rd Soi 3 (not far from the Ueng Khum), rather disorganized.

● **Places to eat**
JJ's Bakery (opposite Wat Chedi Ngam, on the main road) cakes, Thai and international; *Muang Fang* (on the main road, next to the Bangkok Bank), Thai.

● **Banks & money changers**
A number on the main road.

● **Post & telecommunications**
Post Office: past the bus station, not far from the Bangkok Bank on the main road.

● **Transport**
152 km from Chiang Mai.

Road Bus: station is on the main road in the centre of town. Regular connections with Chiang Mai from the Chang Puak bus station on Chotana Rd, 3 hrs.

    Songthaew: regular connections with Tha Ton 40 mins (₿7). There are 2 routes to Chiang Rai: either take the songthaew from Fang to Mae Suai, 40 mins (₿30), then catch a bus to Chiang Rai (95 km). Alternatively, take a songthaew from Tha Ton up to Doi Mae Salong (₿50), then to Mae Chan (₿30), then on to Chiang Rai 114 km (₿15). **NB:** Route 109 from Chiang Rai via Mae Suai (120 km) and the Fang Oil Refinery is being improved and may have a songthaew/bus service sometime in 1993.

Tha Ton

Tha Ton lies on the Mae Kok, and is a good starting point for trips on the Kok River to Chiang Rai, and for treks to the various hilltribe villages in the area. **Wat Tha Ton** overlooks the river, not far from the bridge.

    The **boat trip to Chiang Rai** takes 4-5 hrs on a *long-tailed boat*, which is noisy and uncomfortable (₿170). A more relaxing form of transport is a gentle drift (at least in the dry season) on a bamboo raft (contact *Thaton House, Thip's Traveller's House* or one of the other guesthouses). Most guesthouses will combine the raft trip with a trek and/or elephant ride in various combinations. The rafts dock at the *Dusit Island Resort* in Chiang Rai. The regular long-tail boat leaves at 1230 although they can be chartered at any time (max. 8 passengers, ₿1700).

Trekking
(See Hilltribes and trekking, page 275.) The regular boat down the Kok River stops at riverside villages from where it is possible to trek to hilltribe communities, for instance, Tahamakeng 1 hr from Tha Ton (Lahu and Lisu villages within easy reach), Ban Mai 45 mins on from Tahamakeng (Lahu, Karen and Akha villages), and Mae Salak further on still (Lahu, Lisu and Yao villages). Most guesthouses in Tha Ton will help you to organize these trekking or raft/boat trips. **Warning** in the past trekkers have been robbed, but the TAT office in Chiang Rai inform us that there are now police checkpoints along the route, making it safer.

Local information
● **Accommodation**
B *Mae Kok River Lodge*, opposite riverbank to town, T 222172, a/c, restaurant, pool, attractive gardens, when business is poor they offer special 'Traveller Offer' bringing rates down to our 'D' category.

E-F *Thip's Travellers House*, now at 2 sites, the newer is near the bridge, the older is 50 m upstream, both have restaurants; **F** *Thaton House*, 344 Mu 3 Ban Tha Ton (50m from the bus station, not far from the bridge), rec; *Siam Kok* (close to the pier).

● **Places to eat**
There are a number of attractive riverside restaurants.

● **Transport**
23 km from Fang. **Road Bus**: connections with Chiang Mai 4 hrs, or a minibus to Fang which connects with more frequent buses to Chiang Mai 40 mins (₿7).

Boat: to Chiang Rai, departs at 1230 and takes 4-5 hrs (₿170).

CHIANG RAI, MEKONG & GOLDEN TRIANGLE

Chiang Rai is the largest town in the far north of Thailand and a popular tourist centre. Route 118 is the most direct road from Chiang Mai (180 km), although buses from Bangkok and the South travel up Route 1 and through the town of Phayao. Chiang Rai has become Thailand's second-largest trekking centre, and is used as a base to explore the towns of the Golden Triangle and settlements on the Mekong River. Chiang Saen, 60 km NE of Chiang Rai, was the capital of the Chiang Saen Kingdom and is situated on the banks of the Mekong. Travelling downstream for 70 km the road reaches the small outpost of Chiang Khong. Meanwhile, 11 km upstream from Chiang Saen is Sop Ruak, at the apex of the Golden Triangle and a quickly expanding tourist centre. Mae Sai, upstream still further and 61 km north of Chiang Rai is Thailand's most northerly town and a busy border trading-post with Burma. A new road runs off route 110 to the hill town of Mae Salong, from where a poor track continues W to Tha Ton.

Phayao

Phayao is a relatively quiet, and rarely visited town on the route up to Chiang Rai. It is attractively set on a lake and makes a worthwhile alternative place to stay on the route N to Chiang Rai. Phayao became a provincial capital when a province of the same name was created in 1977 and still seems to be coming to terms with its new-found importance. Historically, the town appears to have been an important defensive site for many years – perhaps as far back as the bronze age. **Wat Si Khom Kham**, located on the N banks of Phayao Lake, dates from the 12th century. The viharn contains an important 17m high Buddha image made in the 16th century. However, in recent years its origins have been obscured through an enthusiastic re-building programme. There is now a fantasyland of concrete animals and ogres to compliment the more usual wat inhabitants. A festival is held here each May. Another 12th century wat in the town is **Wat Luang Raja Santham**.

● **Accommodation B** *Phayao Hotel*, 445 Phahonyothin Rd, T 481970, F 481973, a/c, large, comfortable hotel, best in town; **D** *Than Thong*, 55-57 Donsanam Rd, T 431302, F 481256, some a/c, clean rooms, good value; **D** *Watthana*, 69 Donsanam Rd, T 431203, some a/c; **E** *Chalermsak*, 915 Phahonyothin Rd, T 431063.

● **Places to eat** Restaurants can be found on Chai Kwan Rd and Phahonyothin Rd. *Ying Prom*, 225-229 Phahonyothin Rd.

● **Useful addresses** Area code: 054.

● **Transport** 747 km from Bangkok, 142 km from Lampang, 93 km from Chiang Rai. **By bus**: connections with Chiang Mai (3 hrs) and Chiang Rai and with Bangkok's Northern bus terminal 10 hrs (a/c ฿171).

Chiang Rai

Chiang Rai is the capital of Thailand's most northerly province. The city was founded in 1268 by King Mengrai, who later moved his capital here. The city became one of the key *muang* or city states within the Lanna Kingdom's sphere of control – until Lanna began to disintegrate in the 16th century. Although it is now Thailand's most northerly town, at the time of its foundation Chiang Rai represented the most southerly bulwark against the Mons. It was later conquered by the Burmese and only became part of Thailand again in 1786.

Given the town's ancient roots, it is rather disappointingly short of sights of historical interest, with ugly shophouse architecture predominating. Even the local TAT office admits that the town itself has little to offer in the way of 'sights'. However, accommodation is of a high standard and Chiang Rai makes a good base for trekking and visiting the towns and countryside to the N.

Places of interest

The city's finest monastery is **Wat Phra Kaeo**, at the N end of Trairat Rd. The wat was probably founded in the 13th century when it was known as Wat Pa-

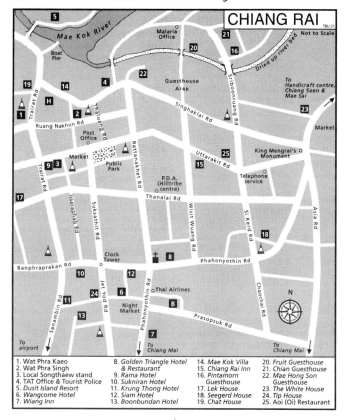

CHIANG RAI TBU 21

Not to Scale

Mae Kok River

Malaria Office

Boat Pier

Guesthouse Area

Trairat Rd

Ruang Nakhon Rd

Thalung Rd

Post Office

Singhaklai Rd

Sriboonruang Rd

Dried up river bed

To Handicraft centre, Chiang Saen & Mae Sai

Market

Market

Public Park

Rattanakhet Rd

Uttarakit Rd

King Mengrai's Monument

P.D.A. (Hilltribe centre)

Trairat Rd

Issaraphab Rd

Suksathit Rd

Thanalai Rd

Wisit Wuang Rd

Telephone service

Si Kerd Rd

Asia Rd

Clock Tower

Banphraprakan Rd

Phahonyothin Rd

Chachai Rd

Sanambin Rd

Jet Yod Rd

Thai Airlines

Phahonyothin Rd

N

Night Market

Prasopsuk Rd

To airport

To Chiang Mai

To Chiang Mai

1. Wat Phra Kaeo	8. Golden Triangle Hotel & Restaurant
2. Wat Phra Singh	9. Rama Hotel
3. Local Songthaew stand	10. Sukniran Hotel
4. TAT Office & Tourist Police	11. Krung Thong Hotel
5. Dusit Island Resort	12. Siam Hotel
6. Wangcome Hotel	13. Boonbundan Hotel
7. Wiang Inn	
14. Mae Kok Villa	20. Fruit Guesthouse
15. Chiang Rai Inn	21. Chian Guesthouse
16. Pintamorn Guesthouse	22. Mae Hong Son Guesthouse
17. Lek House	23. The White House
18. Seegerd House	24. Tip House
19. Chat House	25. Aoi (Oi) Restaurant

year. In 1434 however – or as local legend would have it – the stupa was struck by lightning to reveal the famous Emerald Buddha or *Phra Kaeo*, now in residence in Bangkok's Temple of the Emerald Buddha (see page 135). Following this momentous discovery, the wat was re-named Wat Phra Kaeo and was elevated to the status of a royal wat in 1987. The finest structure here is the bot, built in Chiangsaen style and featuring accomplished woodcarving, a pair of fine nagas flanking the entrance way and inside, a highly regarded 13th century image of the Buddha calling the earth goddess to

witness, in Indian Pala style. Also in the bot, protected by a gold mondop, is a copy of the Emerald Buddha, presented to the monastery by a wealthy Chinese in 1991.

Above Wat Phra Kaeo, perched at the top of a small hill, is **Wat Ngam Muang**, unremarkable save for the views it offers of the city and surrounding countryside. However, historically, it is important, as the stupa here contains the ashes of the great King Mengrai (?-1317). The edifice is currently being renovated and will have a statue of the king placed in front of his *ku*. Further NW still is **Wat**

Doi Thong, again, and as its name indicates, built at the top of a small hill. The wat contains the city pillar *(lak muang)*. **Wat Phra Singh** (dating from 1385) is an important teaching monastery on Singhaklai Rd, in the N of town. Note the finely wrought animal medallions below the windows of the bot – rats, elephants, tigers, snakes and other beasts and the gaudy but vivacious murals that decorate the interior. Also unusual is the Bodhi tree, surrounded by images of the Buddha in each of the principal mudras. In the E of town, at the so-called *haa yaek* (five-way junction) on Phahonyothin Rd, is the new **statue of King Mengrai**, Chiang Rai's most illustrious king.

The Population and Development Association's (PDA) **Hill Tribe Education Center** at 620/25 Thanalai Rd is one of the more interesting attractions in the town, with a small informative hilltribe museum and an audiovisual presentation on hilltribe life, 1300-1330 Mon-Fri (or on request, for a small fee, in English, Thai, French or Japanese). The PDA, better known for its family planning work, is attempting to provide hilltribe communities with additional income-earning opportunities, as the pressures of commercial life increase.

Excursions

The towns of **Chiang Saen** (ancient capital of the kingdom of the same name), **Sop Ruak** (the Golden Triangle) and **Mae Sai** (border town with Burma) can all be visited as a day trip from Chiang Rai (see below).

Ban Du is a paper-making village 8 km N of Chiang Rai, off route 110. Paper is produced from the bark of the *sa* tree which is stripped off, air dried, soaked in water, boiled in caustic soda, and finally beaten before being made into paper. **Getting there**: by songthaew or bus travelling N on Route 110 (towards Mae Sai), or by tuk-tuk.

Trekking

(See Hilltribes and trekking, page 275.) A 2 day/1 night raft trip should cost about ฿800-1,100/person, 4 day/3 night trek about ฿1,500-2,000. Most treks are cheaper if organized through guesthouses. The usual range of elephant rides and boat trips as part of a trek are also offered. Before embarking on a trek, it is worthwhile visiting the Hilltribe Education Center (see above). Tribes in the area include Karen, Lisu, Lahu and Akha. Trekking companies are concentrated around the *Wangcome Hotel* plaza area; most guesthouses also offer trekking services, for listing, see below. The TAT office produces a list of companies with average prices and other useful advice.

Tours

Day tours to visit hilltribe villages, Sop Ruak and the Golden Triangle, Mae Sai, Mae Salong, and Chiang Saen are organized by most of the tour/trekking companies listed below (฿600). Tours which include an elephant ride and boat trip plus visits to hilltribe villages cost about ฿700.

Local information
● **Accommodation**

Most of the guesthouses are to be found on the 'island' between the 2 branches of the Kok River. **A+** *Dusit Island Resort*, 1129 Kraisorasit Rd, T 715777, F 715801, a/c, restaurant, pool, lavish hotel, just out of town on an 'island' in the river, best in Chiang Rai, with every facility.

A *Inn Come*, 172/6 Ratbumrung Rd, T 717850, F 717855, a/c, restaurant; **A** *Little Duck*, 4 Phahonyothin Rd, 2 km S of town, T 715621, F 715639, a/c, restaurant, pool, large, rather impersonal but professionally run hotel with all amenities; **A** *Mae Kok*, Chiang Rai-Thaton Rd, T 715858, a/c, restaurant, pool; **A** *Rim Kok Resort*, 6 Mu 4 Chiang Rai-Thaton Rd, T 716445, F 715859, B 2790102, a/c, restaurant, pool, lavish, N of the river on the edge of town; **A** *Wangcome*, 869/90 Premwipak Rd, T 711800, F 712973, a/c, restaurant, pool, very central, rather ugly high-rise block, with uninteresting rooms; **A** *Wiang Inn*, 893 Phahonyothin Rd, T 71153,

F 711877, a/c, restaurant, pool, the original 'luxury' hotel in town, renovated in 1992/93 and still holding its own against the competition, attractive rooms, rec.

B *Chiang Rai Inn*, 661 Uttarakit Rd, T 712673, F 711488, a/c, new hotel in modern interpretation of N Thai architecture, large, spotless rooms, immaculate bathrooms, hot water, rather clinical but comfortable, discounts available, good value; **B** *Golden Triangle*, 590 Phahonyothin Rd, T 711339, F 713963, a/c, restaurant, attractive grounds, popular and peaceful, well-run, rec; **B** *Prima*, Seegerd Rd, T 716306, a/c, restaurant; **B-C** *Rama*, 331/4 Trairat Rd, T 711344, a/c, dark and dingy but good rooms.

C *Sukniran*, 424/1 Banphaprakan Rd, T 712036, some a/c, good position close to clock tower, airy lobby and rooms facing a courtyard away from the main road, so not too noisy; **C** *YMCA*, 70 Phahonyothin Rd, T 713785, F 714336, a/c, pool, clean and well kept, but some distance out of town towards Mae Sai past the handicraft centre; **C-E** *Boonbundan Guesthouse*, 1005/13 Chet Yod Rd, T 717040, F 712914, some a/c, outdoor eating area, quiet leafy compound near centre of town, professionally managed, good range of services, clean room with hot water, wide range of rates, rec.

D *Krung Thong*, 412 Sanambin Rd, T 711033, a/c, clean; **D-E** *Koh Loy Riverhouse*, 485 Tanam Rd, T 715084, 'A' frame bungalows overlooking what is left of the Mae Kok's original channel, plain and rather overpriced, but quiet and peaceful, hw; **D-F** *Mae Kok Villa* (Chiang Rai Youth Hostel), 445 Singhaklai Rd, T 711786, this former secondary school makes for an unusual hotel, elegant though rather ramshackle wooden building, containing dorms, while the bungalows in the big, leafy, riverside compound are large, if slightly murky, more expensive rooms with hw (10% discount for ISIC card holders); **D-F** *Pintamorn Guesthouse*, 199/1-3 Mu 21 Singhaklai Rd, T 714161, some a/c, run by a Hawaiian, who has given the guesthouse a distinctly 'Western' feel, with Indian murals and posters of James Dean, rooms are clean and of a good size, hot water.

E *Chian House*, 172 Sriboonruang Rd (on the island), T 713388, pool, the cheapest place with a pool in town (fed by ground water), clean and friendly, if a bit concrete, more expensive rooms are a good size with hw; **E** *Mae Hong Son*, 126 Singhaklai Rd, traditional house, quiet, clean, good source of information, rec; **E** *Porn's House*, 503 Ratanaket Rd, large clean rooms, friendly; **E** *Siam*, 531/6-8 Banphaprakan Rd, T 711077, usual ugly Chinese-style hotel on main road, fan, hw; **E** *Star*, 594/2 Phahonyothin Rd, T 715190, hot water, rec; **E** *Tip House*, 1017/2 Chet Yod Rd, T 716672, central location, but set off main road, single storey bungalow rooms, attached bathrooms with hot water, clean; **E-F** *Chat House*, 3/2 Trairat Soi Songkaew (nr Wat Phra Kaeo), T 711481, in a quiet, leafy compound, rooms are clean but a little worn, trekking and motorbike hire available, hot water, dorm beds, rec; **E-F** *Kok River Hut*, 339-339/1 Phahonyothin Soi Hom Nuan, T 713821, on river, many services; **E-F** *The White House*, 789 Phahonyothin Rd, T 713427, set back off Chiang Rai's main road, leafy compound, large but bare and rather cold rooms, clean, some with hw.

F *Fruit*, on the island, popular, rec; **F** *Head*, 279 Soi 2 Rachayota Rd, good range of services; **F** *Lek House*, 95 Thanalai Rd, T 713337; **F** *Moon*, 345 Kohloy Rd, T 716092 (on the island), quiet, clean, hot water, rec; **F** *Si Kerd House*, 717/1 Si Kerd Rd, T 712804, friendly, good information, organize trekking, rec.

● **Places to eat**

The greatest variety of restaurants are to be found in the streets around the *Wangcome Hotel*, from Mexican to French to cheap Thai and Chinese. **Thai**: ♦*Aoi (Oi)*, Uttarakit Rd (nr *Chiangrai Inn Hotel*), clean, serving excellent local and other Thai dishes; ♦♦*Big 7*, 160 Kwae Wai Rd, near Mae Kok River, traditional style Thai food, rec; ♦♦♦*Chiangrai Island Restaurant*, 1129/1 Kraisorasit Rd (part of the Dusit Island Resort), N Thai specialities, also serves international; ♦♦*Golden Triangle Café*, 590 Phahonyothin Rd, also serves international, rec; *Muang Man Café and cocktail lounge*, opposite Caltex station on Phahonyothin Rd, also serves International; *Phetburi*, Banphraprakan Rd, opposite *Sukniran Hotel*, large selection of curries, eat in or take-away, ฿15/dish; ♦*Phor Krua* (the cook), 1023/4 Chet Yod Rd (behind *Wangcome Hotel*), excellent N Thai and other Thai food, rec; *Ratburi*, Banphraprakan Rd, opposite *Sukniran Hotel*, large selection of curries, eat in or take-away, ฿15/dish; ♦♦*Tha Rua*, by boat pier. At present overlooking mudbanks, due to development of Dusit Resort.

International: *Country Road Restaurant and Pub*, corner of Chaochai and Phahonyothin rds; *Frenchy Bar and Restaurant*, 1015 M.4 Chet Yod Rd, French; ♦♦♦*La Cantina*, Soi Punyodyana (nr *Wangcome Hotel*), Italian, with unusual regional dishes; *Haw Naliga*, 401/1-2 Banphraprakan Rd (W of *Ratburi* and *Phetburi* restaurants), country setting, rec; ♦♦*Tio Pepe*, Soi Punyodyana (nr *Wangcome Hotel*), Mexican food and cold beer.

● **Airline offices**
Thai, 870 Phahonyothin Rd, T 711179.

● **Banks & money changers**
Profusion of exchange booths and banks on Thanalai and Phahonyothin rds.

● **Hospitals & medical services**
Overbrook opposite *Chat House*, Trairat Rd, T 311366. *Provincial*: on Sanambin Rd.

● **Post & telecommunications**
Post Office: on Uttarakit Rd at the N end of Suksathit Rd. **Area code**: 053.

● **Sports**
The *Pintamorn Sportsclub* at 115/1-8 Wat Sriboonruang Rd has a sauna (฿50), exercise room (฿50) and pool table.

● **Shopping**
Hilltribe goods, silver, textiles, woodcarvings: many shops in town around the *Wangcome Hotel* plaza area and on Phahonyothin Rd; Hilltribe Education Center at 620/25 Thanalai Rd sells genuine hilltribe textiles and other goods, all profits being returned to the communities. **Handicraft centres** out of town (e.g. *Chiang Rai Handicrafts Centre* 3 km out on road to Chiang Saen). *Chiang Rai Silverware*, 869/145 Premawaphat Rd. For more unusual woodcarvings and silverware, try *Silver Birch*, 891 Phahonyothin Rd, nr *Wiang Inn*, more expensive but finely crafted. *Ego*, 869/81-82 (adjacent *Wangcome Hotel*), for Burmese and hilltribe antiques, beads, jewellery, carvings, textiles, reasonable prices, rec. **Night market**: Phahonyothin Rd, selling range of T-shirts etc. **Department store**: corner of Banphraprakan and Sanambin rds.

● **Tour and trekking companies and travel agents**
A number along Phahonyothin and Premwipak rds (a soi off Phahonyothin, nr the *Wangcome Hotel*). *Chiangrai Travel and Tour*, 869/95 Premwipak Rd, T 713314, F 713967; *Far-East North Tours*, 873/8 Phahonyothin Rd, T 713615, rec; *Golden Triangle Tours*, 590 Phahonyothin Rd, T 711339 (attached to the *Golden Triangle Hotel*), rec; *Maesalong Tour*, 882/4 Phahonyothin Rd, T 712515. *Oasis Tour and Trek*, 869/96 Premwipak Rd, T 713535; *PDA*, 620/25 Thanalai Rd, T 713410. Primarily a charity, working to improve the lot of the hilltribes, but they will organize treks, with guides who speak the dialect. Advanced notice is recommended; *P.D. Tour*, 834/6 Phahonyothin Rd, T 711893; *Poy Siam Travel*, 541 Phahonyothin Rd, T 716206; *Universe Travel*, 110 Trairat Rd, T 713225. Guesthouses which organize treks include (see Accommodation for full address): *Boonbundan*, *Chat House*, *Chian House*, *Head*, *Koh Loy River House*, *Mae Hong Son* (rec), *Moon* (rec), *Mae Kok Villa*, *Pintamorn*, *The White House*.

● **Tourist offices**
TAT, 448/16 Singhaklai Rd (nr the river, opposite Wat Phra Singh), T 717433, F 717434, well run office which opened in 1992, useful town maps and information on trekking and accommodation. Areas of responsibility are Chiang Rai, Phayao, Uttaradit, Phrae and Nan.

● **Tourist Police**
Singhaklai Rd (below the TAT office, opposite Wat Phra Singh), T 711786.

● **Transport**
197 km (new route) 334 km (old route) from Chiang Mai. @IS = **Local Bicycles**: ฿20-40/day, hired from guesthouses.
Car hire: *Chiang Rai Ekkachai*, 733/7 Phahonyothin Rd and from many companies around the *Wangcome Hotel*.
Jeep hire: ฿1,000/day from many guesthouses e.g. *Head Guesthouse*, *See Gerd House*, *Mae Hong Son Guesthouse*, *Moon Guesthouse* and from some tour companies (e.g. *P.D.Tours*).
Motorbike hire: ฿150-200/day, from most guesthouses.
Saamlors, tuk-tuks and songthaews for longer trips. The local songthaew stand is nr the morning market on Uttarakit Rd.

Air: the new international airport is 8 km N of the city. Regular connections with Chiang Mai 40 mins and Bangkok 1 hr 25 mins. The runway has been lengthened to take wide-bodied jets like the B-747 so direct flights from other Asian destinations may commence soon.

Road Bus: Central bus station is just off Phahonyothin Rd, in the centre of town (but over 1 km from the main concentration of guesthouses). Regular connections with Chiang Saen every 15 mins, 1 hr 30 mins (฿17) and

Mae Sai every 15 mins, 1 hr 40 mins (฿17), Chiang Mai Phayao 1 hr 40 mins, Phrae 4 hrs, Nan 6 hrs, Chiang Kham 2 hrs, Chiang Khong 3 hrs, Lampang 5 hrs, Phitsanulok (via Sukhothai) 6 hrs, Khon Kaen 12 hrs, Nakhon Ratchasima 13 hrs, Bangkok 12 hrs (฿189 non-a/c, ฿364 a/c, ฿525 VIP) and Pattaya. From Chiang Mai, buses taking the old route (*sai kao*) leave from the Old Lamphun Rd, near the Narawat Bridge; those on the new route (*sai mai*) leave from the Arcade bus station, NE of the city on the 'Superhighway'. The old route goes via Lampang and Phayao 6 hrs (฿59 non-a/c, ฿83 a/c); the new route takes Route 1019, via Doi Saket and Wiang Papao (hot springs) 4 hrs (฿57 non-a/c, ฿102 a/c).

Boat: long-tailed boats leave from the pier at the N end of Trairat Rd to Tha Ton daily at 1030 (฿170). Boats can be chartered for ฿300/hr or for ฿1700 to Tha Ton, ฿500 to Rim Kok, ฿1500 to Chiang Khong. A boat takes a max of 8 passengers, the pier is open 0700-1600, daily (see page 256).

Chiang Saen

Chiang Saen is an ancient capital on the banks of the Mekong River, the last village before the famed 'Golden Triangle'. It was probably established during the early years of this millennium and became the capital of the Chiang Saen Kingdom, founded in 1328 by King Saen Phu, the grandson of King Mengrai. Captured in the 16th century by the Burmese, the town became a Burmese stronghold in their constant wars with the Thais. It was not recaptured until Rama I sent an army here in 1803. Fearing that the Burmese might use the town to mount raids against his kingdom in the future, Rama I ordered it to be destroyed. Chiang Saen remained deserted for 100 years.

Today, with the impressive town ramparts still very much in evidence, it is a charming one-street market town. Quiet, with wooden shophouses and a scattering of ruins lying haphazardly and untended amidst the undergrowth, it has so far managed to escape the uncontrolled tourist development evident in other towns in Northern Thailand.

However plans are afoot to link Chiang Saen, by ship, with Yunnan in China. In Sept 1992 a 120-tonne ship with 60 Chinese delegates aboard made the 385 km trip down the Mekong River, possibly presaging the inauguration of a scheduled service soon.

Places of interest

Entering the town from Chiang Rai, the ruins of **Wat Phrathat Chedi Luang** can be seen on the right-hand side shortly after passing through the city's ancient ramparts. Built by King Saen Phu in 1331, this wat was established as the main monastery in the city. The chedi is 60m tall, sitting on an octagonal base, with a bell-shaped summit. Next door is the **Chiang Saen National Museum**, containing some typical Chiang Saen style Buddha figures: oval-faced and slender-bodied, they are regarded as among the first true 'Thai' works of art. The museum also has a modest collection of prehistoric artefacts and hilltribe tools and clothing. Admission: ฿5. Open: 0900-1200, 1300-1600 Wed-Sun.

W of the town, just outside the city ramparts, is the beautiful **Wat Pa Sak** or the 'Forest of Teak Wat' – so-called because of a wall of teak planted around the wat. The monastery was founded in 1295 during the reign of Ramkhamhaeng of Sukhothai and actually predates the town. The unusual pyramid-shaped chedi is the main building of interest here. Art historians see a combination of influences in the chedi: Pagan (Burma), Dvaravati, Sukhothai, even Srivijaya. The niches along the base contain alternating Devatas (heavenly beings) and standing Buddha images – poorly restored. Much of the fine stucco work, save for fragments of nagas and garudas, has disappeared (some can be seen in the Chiang Saen Museum). Admission: ฿20.

2½ km N of Wat Pa Sak, following the ramparts and on a hill, is **Wat Phrathat Chom Kitti**, which may date from as

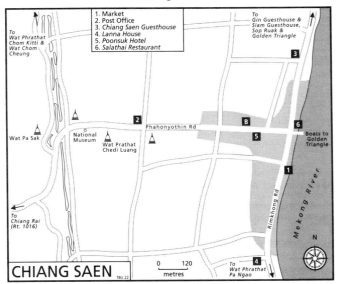

1. Market
2. Post Office
3. Chiang Saen Guesthouse
4. Lanna House
5. Poonsuk Hotel
6. Salathai Restaurant

To Wat Phrathat Chom Kitti & Wat Chom Cheung

To Gin Guesthouse & Siam Guesthouse, Sop Ruak & Golden Triangle

Wat Pa Sak

National Museum

Wat Prathat Chedi Luang

Phahonyothin Rd

To Chiang Rai (Rt. 1016)

Boats to Golden Triangle

Mekong River

Rimkhong Rd

To Wat Phrathat Pa Ngao

CHIANG SAEN TBU 22

0   120
metres

early as the 10th century. A golden topped stupa is being restored but there is little else save for the views of the river and surrounding countryside. **Wat Chom Cheung**, a small ruined chedi, lies close by on the same hill.

The **market**, strung-out along the riverbank, sells plenty of unnecessary plastic objects and is a good place to watch hilltribe people (Karen and Lua among others) browsing through the goods.

Excursions

Wat Phrathat Pa Ngao lies 4 km from Chiang Saen along the road which follows the Mekong downstream. Perched on a hill, it provides excellent views of the river and countryside. For **Sop Ruak** and the **Golden Triangle** take the same road upstream, 11 km from town (see below). **Getting there**: by songthaew or by long-tailed boat. Boats can be hired from the jetty below the Salathai Restaurant and will also take passengers to **riverside villages**. Bargain hard.

Trekking

(See Hilltribes and Trekking, page 275.) *Chiang Saen Tour*, Phahonyothin Rd (next to the *Poonsuk Hotel*), rather disorganized, but runs treks to Mae Salong.

Tours

Chiang Saen Tour (next to the *Poonsuk Hotel*) offers day tours to Mae Salong, the refugee camp and Mae Sai for ฿400.

In mid-1994, MP World Trading Co are due to begin operating four boats which will cruise up the Mekong River to China's Sipsong Panna Province. They are building an hotel on the banks of the Mekong in Sipsong Panna to accommodate passengers. The journey up-river will take 8-10 hrs, downriver about 6-8 hrs. Permission for the enterprise has been gained from the three relevant governments: Thailand, China and Laos. It is anticipated that boats will leave from Chiang Saen.

Local information
● **Accommodation**

D *Gin's House*, Rimkhong Rd (N of town, just outside the old city walls, on river side of the

road), restaurant, bikes and motorbikes for rent.
E-F *Lanna House*, 39 Rimkhong Rd (S of Salathai Restaurant) run down but quite popular.
F *Chiang Saen*, Rimkhong Rd (N of Salathai Restaurant), restaurant for Thai food and breakfast, private bathroom, nice position, clean, rec; **F** *Poonsuk*, 95 Phahonyothin Rd (close to the bus stop on the main road); **F** *Siam*, 234 Rimkhong Rd, clean, rec.

● **Places to eat**
There are a number of cheap *kuaytiaw* stalls along the riverbank. Further out of town towards Sop Ruak and the Golden Triangle are better riverside restaurants selling good Thai food, e.g. *Rim Khong* (3 km) and the *Mekong River Banks* (4 km). Restaurants in town include: **♦***Salathai*, Rimkhong Rd (at the end of the main road, above the jetty). Thai; *Popeye*, Phahonyothin Rd (next to the *Poonsuk*).

● **Banks & money changers**
Siam Commercial, 116 Phahonyothin Rd.

● **Post & telecommunications**
Post Office: Phahonyothin Rd. **Area code**: 053.

● **Transport**
32 km from Mae Chan, 60 km from Chiang Rai.

Local Long-tailed boats: from the jetty below the Salathai Restaurant can be chartered for trips to the Golden Triangle, ฿300/boat.
    Motorbike hire: from some guesthouses (e.g. *Siam* ฿150/day), but are in short supply.
    Motorized saamlors: by the bus-stop for trips around the sights.

Road Bus: regular connections with Chiang Rai 1 hr 20 mins (฿17) and Mae Sai 1 hr (฿30).

Chiang Khong

Chiang Khong is a border settlement situated on the south bank of the Mekong River. For such a small town, it has had a relatively high profile in Thai history. In the 1260s, King Mengrai extended control over the area and Chiang Khong became one of the Lanna Thai Kingdom's major principalities. Later the town was captured by the Burmese. Today, Chiang Khong owes its continued existence to legal and illicit trade with Laos: gems, agricultural products and livestock from Laos are traded for

consumer goods and other luxuries. Thais and Laos make the crossing to trade but foreigners, for the time being at least, are not allowed to venture into Laos. There is not much here, although its position on the Mekong and the relaxed atmosphere makes it an attractive spot to unwind. **Wat Luang**, in the centre of town, dates from the 13th century. Like Nong Khai and the other towns that line the Mekong in the Northeastern region, the rare – and delicious – *pla buk* catfish is caught here (see page 342).

Trekking (See Hilltribes and trekking, page 275.) There are hilltribe villages within reach of Chiang Khong, but the trekking industry here is relatively undeveloped. Ask at the guesthouses to see if a guide is available.

● **Accommodation C-D** *Fang Khong*, 63 Mu 2, Sai Klang Rd (centre of town), T 791063, some a/c, hot water **D** *Wiang Kaew*, Sai Klang Rd, T 791140, well run and comfortable, wooden house in attractive garden compound with views over the river, rec; **E** *Ban Tammila*, 8/1 Sai Klang Rd (N end of town), T 791234, bungalows with river views, more superior than most in this price range, rec.

● **Useful addresses** Area code: 053.

● **Transport** 137 km from Chiang Rai, 70 km from Chiang Saen. **Boat**: boats can be chartered to make the journey to/from Chiang Saen (about ฿150/head). **Bus**: hourly connections with Chiang Rai 3 hrs (฿31). **Songthaew**: daily connections with Chiang Saen.

Sop Ruak

This small 'village', 11 km N of Chiang Saen at the apex of the Golden Triangle, where Burma, Laos and Thailand meet, has become a busy tourist spot – on the basis (largely unwarranted) of its association with drugs, intrigue and violence. A multitude of stalls line the road, selling hilltribe handicrafts, and Burmese and Laotian goods. Two first class hotels have been built to exploit the romance of the place. The 'Golden Triangle Paradise Resort' is still under construction on 32 ha of leased Burmese land and will include a casino. This has required fancy footwork on the part both of the Thais and Burmese. In Thailand, gambling is illegal yet because the resort will not be on Thai soil, the government can turn a blind eye to the development. Equally, the Burmese, having leased the land out for 30 years can claim that it is no business of theirs, and therefore remain ideologically unsullied. A cunning way of exploiting the Thai, and especially the Sino-Thai, love of gambling. There are fears, however, that the casino will become a drug money laundering centre.

Excursions Wanglao lies 4 km W, towards Mae Sai, past *Le Meridien Baanboran Hotel*, and is a rice-farming community which has a number of handicraft stalls. *Songthaews* run through here, on the (longer) back route to Mae Sai.

● **Tours** Boat trips to the border and to hill-tribe communities.

● **Trekking** (See Hilltribes and trekking, page 275.) *Jungle Flower*, next to *Golden Triangle Hotel*. Boat trips to Laos. 3 day trek for 3 people, ฿5,500 (elephant rides, hilltribe villages etc).

● **Accommodation** There are a number of new hotels around Sop Ruak. **A+-A** *Delta Golden Triangle*, 222 Golden Triangle, T 777031, F 777005, B 2607791, a/c, restaurant, pool, a rather monstrous hotel for a small village, overlooking the river with plush rooms; **A+** *Le Meridien Baanboran*, N of Sop Ruak, T 716678, F 716702, B 2548147, a/c, restaurant, pool, 'traditional' architecture taken to the limit, good service, wonderful evening views, rather too new and pristine for this timeless area of Thailand; **F** *Northern Villa*, N of town, T 712212, good restaurant, hot water, nice position.

Quite a few guesthouses along the river road; **E** *Bua*, S of the village; **F** *Golden Hut*, N of the village; **F** *Golden Triangle Guesthouse*, near the landing-pier; **F** *Phukham*, opposite Bua; **F** *Poppy*, N of the village, close to the *Delta Golden Triangle*.

● **Banks & money changers** Mobile currency exchange.

● **Tour companies & travel agents** *Dits Travel*, *Baanboran Hotel*, T 716678, F 716680.

● **Transport** 11 km from Chiang Saen. **Local Boat hire**: from the pier, for trips to Chiang Saen for ฿300/boat. **Car hire**: from *Golden Triangle Hotel* (Avis). **Motorcycle hire**: from *Jungle Flower Trekking*, near the *Golden Triangle Hotel*. **Road Bus**: one a day from Chiang Saen. **Minibus**: from the Salathai Restaurant, Chiang Saen. **Songthaew**: from Mae Sai, 40 mins, (฿25) or from Chiang Saen, 10 mins, (฿10). **Boat**: from the Salathai Restaurant, Chiang Saen (฿300/boat).

Mae Sai

Mae Sai marks Thailand's northernmost point. The town is a busy trading centre with Burma and has a rather clandestine and frenetic frontier atmosphere. The area around the bridge is the centre of activity, with stalls and shops selling gems and Burmese and Chinese goods. There are also an abundance of Burmese hawkers (selling Burmese coins and postage stamps) and beggars.

The town of Mae Sai is rather drab but the movement of myriad peoples across the border makes this an interesting place to visit. **Wat Phrathat Doi Wao** sits on a hill overlooking the town, off Phahonyothin Road, not far from the *Top North Hotel*.

Excursions The border with Burma has recently opened to allow tourists, as well as Burmese and Thais to cross the bridge that spans the River Sai and leads to the Burmese village of Tachilek. Here, foreigners are free to roam for the day but not to stay overnight (border fee US$5). The Burmese will also allow tour groups of at least 10 people (not more than 50) to travel the 167 km (8-10 hrs) to Chiang Tung (Kengtung). They charge a border fee of US$18 and a transportation fee of US$10 at Tachilek (the trip into Burma does not count as an exit/re-entry for single entry Thai visas). Accommodation in Chiang Tung is said to be restricted, expensive (**B**) and poor. The 'visa' is for a 3 night 2 day visit only. Note that petrol is not available in this part of Burma (only diesel), so if driving independently, bring sufficient for the trip. Note that the above regulations may be subject to sudden change (border open 0600-1800 Mon-Sun). Dits Travel organize tours to Burma, see page 265 for address.

Luang Cave (Tham Luang) is an impressive cave 3 km off Route 110 to Chiang Rai, 7 km from town, with large caverns and natural rock formations. Getting there: by regular songthaew to turn-off; ask for *Tham loo-ang*.

Doi Tung is a hill village almost 50 km S of Mae Sai. Travel S on Route 110 from Mae Sai for 22 km to Huai Klai and then turn off on to Route 1149. The road snakes its way past Akha, Lahu and KMT villages and former poppy fields before reaching *Wat Phrathat Doi Tung*, a total of 24 km from the main road. The twin chedis are said to contain the left collarbone of the Buddha and the views from the wat are breathtaking. It is easiest to explore the area by rented motorbike. However, buses will drop passengers off at Ban Huai Khrai from where infrequent songthaews run to Doi Tung. The *Khwan Guesthouse* is 2 km along Route 1149 while the *Akha Guesthouse* (in the Akha village of Ban Pakha) is 7 km along the road for visitors who wish to stay overnight. Both are good sources of information on the surrounding area. **Caution**: this was a violent area until recently, with drug dealers, opium poppy cultivators, and drug suppression units battling for control. Now largely 'pacified', visitors should still be careful. Getting there: take a bus heading for Chiang Rai and ask to be let off in Huai Klai village. From there, a minibus can be chartered for ฿350.

● **Trekking** (See Hilltribes and trekking, page 275.) Not many people trek from here; however, the *Mae Sai Plaza Guesthouse*, *Mae Sai Riverside* and the *Northern Guesthouse* all organize treks for about ฿300/day.

● **Accommodation A** *Wang Thong*, 299 Phahonyothin Rd, T 731248, F 731249, a/c, restaurant, pool, large new hotel; **C-D** *Thai Thong*, Phahonyothin Rd, some a/c; **C-D** *Top North*, 306 Phahonyothin Rd, T 731955, some a/c; **D** *Mae Sai Riverside*, Sawlomchong Rd (at end of road), hot water, opened 1991; **E** *Mae Sai*, 125/5 Phahonyothin Rd, T 731462, some a/c; **E** *Mae Sai Plaza Guesthouse*, 386/3 Sawlomchong Rd, T 732230, good position overlooking river, private bathroom and hot water, very popular, with good source of local information, rec; **E** *Northern Guesthouse*, 402 Tumphachom Rd, T 731537, clean and quiet, hot water; **F** *Chad's House*, 52/1 Phahonyothin Rd (1.5 km from the bridge back towards Mae Chan and Chiang Rai).

● **Places to eat** Number of riverside restaurants. *Rabiang Kaew*, Phahonyothin Rd (nr *Top North Hotel*). Thai, with N Thai specialities; *Mae Sai Complex*, overlooking river, E of bridge.

● **Banks & money changers** Thai Farmers, 122/1 Phahonyothin Rd; **Krung Thai**, Phahonyothin Rd; **Bangkok**, Phahonyothin Rd.

● **Post & telecommunications** Post Office: Phahonyothin Rd (2 km from bridge towards Mae Chan).

● **Shopping** Gems: *Mandalay Shop*, 381/1-4 Phahonyothin Rd for Burmese jade, sapphires and rubies (see page 372).

● **Transport** 34 km from Mae Chan, 61 km from Chiang Rai, 906 km from Bangkok. **Local** Motorbike hire: from *Northern* and *Mae Sai Plaza Guesthouses*, ฿150-250/day. **Road Bus**: regular connections with Bangkok's Northern bus terminal 13 hrs 30 mins (฿169-305), Chiang Mai 4¼-5 hrs (฿59-104), Chiang Rai 1 hr 20 mins (฿14). Songthaew: connections with Chiang Saen and Golden Triangle ฿25-30.

Mae Salong (Santikhiri)

Mae Salong is situated at an altitude of over 1,200m close to the border with Burma. After the Communist victory in China in 1949, remnants of the nationalist KMT (Kuomintang) sought refuge here and developed it as a base from which they would mount an invasion of China. This wish has since faded into fantasy and the Thai authorities have attempted to integrate the exiled Chinese into the Thai mainstream. A paved road was recently completed and the town is now easily accessible.

Despite the attempts to Thai-ify Mae Salong, it still feels like a little corner of China. Chinese herbs and vegetables are grown in the surrounding countryside and sold at the morning market, many of the inhabitants still speak Chinese, Yunnanese food is sold on the streets, and there are glimpses of China around every corner. It is also an alternative place to trek from.

Excursions Pha Dua is a Yao village 15 km from Mae Salong. It was founded by Yao tribespeople escaping from the Communist Pathet Lao Laos 45 years ago and during the 1960s it became a centre for the trade in opium. With the opium trade curtailed by the government, the inhabitants have turned to food crops, such as cabbages and strawberries, and to tourism, to earn a living. Handicrafts from Burma, Nan (in the eastern highlands) – even Nepal – are sold from small stalls while women and children parade the streets in their traditional indigo costumes. Getting there: on a tour or by songthaew.

● **Trekking** (See Hilltribes and trekking, page 275.) Treks to Akha, Hmong, Shan and other hilltribe villages are arranged by the *Mae Salong Guest House* and the *Shin Sane Guest House*, among others.

● **Accommodation A-B** *Mae Salong Resort*, T 765014, very comfortable resort in forest surroundings, but expensive; **B** *Mae Salong Villa*, T 765114, hot water, good views, some bungalows and better value than the Mae Salong Resort; **D** *Mae Salong Guest House*, T 711264, some rooms with hot water, clean, friendly and well-run, organize treks; **F** *Shin Sane*, basic rooms in wooden house; **F** *Rainbow*, basic.

● **Places to eat** Mae Salong is a good place to eat Yunnanese (S. Chinese) food – either from street-side stalls or at more expensive restaurants (like that at the *Mae Salong Resort*).

● **Post & telecommunications** Area code: 053.

● **Transport** 68 km from Chiang Rai. **Songthaew**: regular connections with Chiang Rai 1½ hrs; also morning songthaew connections along a rough road with Tha Ton 2 hrs (during the rainy season the road is sometimes closed).

EASTERN HIGHLANDS OF THE NORTH

This is the least travelled of the main routes in the North. From Phrae, Route 101 runs north-eastwards towards the border with Laos, and terminates at Nan, 340 km from Chiang Mai. This part of Thailand contains some of the finest stands of forest in the country.

Phrae

Phrae is an attractive provincial capital that lies off the main tourist trail. The town is situated in a narrow rice valley on the banks of the Mae Yom River, flanked by mountains to the E and W. During the months of the cold season between Dec and Feb it becomes distinctly chilly at night and in the early morning, and the locals wrap themselves in sweaters and coats whilst waiting for the sun to take the chill out of the day.

History

Phrae was founded in the 12th century – when it was known as Wiang Kosai or Silk Cloth City – and is one of the oldest cities in Thailand. It still has its own 'royal' family and was an independent Thai *muang* (city state) until the early 16th century, when it was captured by an army from Ayutthaya. When Ayutthaya's power began to wane in the 18th century, Phrae – like many other northern principalities – came under the sway of the Burmese. It was finally incorporated into the Siamese state in the 19th century.

Phrae's ancient roots can still be seen in the city walls and moat which separate the old city from the new commer-

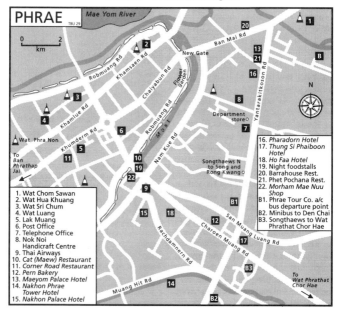

PHRAE

TBU 29

Mae Yom River

0 2
km

Robmuang Rd
Khamsaen Rd
Khamlue Rd
Chaiyabun Rd
Khumderm Rd
Robmuang Rd
Nam Kue Rd
Moat
Rachdamnern Rd
Muang Hit Rd
Yantarakitkoson Rd
Charoen Muang Rd
San Muang Luang Rd

New Gate
Ban Mai Rd
Flower Garden
Department store

To Ban Phrathap Jai

Songthaews N to Song and Rong Kwang

To Wat Phrathat Chor Hae

N

1. Wat Chom Sawan
2. Wat Hua Khuang
3. Wat Sri Chum
4. Wat Luang
5. Lak Muang
6. Post Office
7. Telephone Office
8. Nok Noi Handicraft Centre
9. Thai Airways
10. Cat (Maew) Restaurant
11. Corner Road Restaurant
12. Pern Bakery
13. Maeyom Palace Hotel
14. Nakhon Phrae Tower Hotel
15. Nakhon Palace Hotel

16. Pharadorn Hotel
17. Thung Si Phaiboon Hotel
18. Ho Faa Hotel
19. Night foodstalls
20. Barrahouse Rest.
21. Phet Pochana Rest.
22. Morham Mae Nuu Shop
B1. Phrae Tour Co. a/c bus departure point
B2. Minibus to Den Chai
B3. Songthaews to Wat Phrathat Chor Hae

cial centre. On Charoen Muang Road, there are also a handful of attractive wooden Chinese shophouses – although the scourge of uncontrolled redevelopment is gradually gnawing away at the remnants of old Phrae. Although Phrae may have ancient roots, the province is best known in Thailand for the quality of its *morhom* – the rough blue garb of the Thai farmer. The morhom has been popularized by the charismatic populist politician Chamlong Srimuang (see page 140) and it has now become something of a fashion statement among the young of Bangkok (see Shopping, below).

Places of interest

The Burmese-style **Wat Chom Sawan** is on the edge of town, about 1 km NE of the centre, on the road to Nan. It is one of the most beautiful monasteries in this part of Thailand, and was commissioned by Rama V (1868-1910) and designed by a Burmese architect. Like most Burmese wats, the bot (ordination hall) and viharn (assembly hall) are consolidated in one elaborate, multi-roofed towering structure with verandahs and side rooms. It has survived relatively unscathed: the wooden roof tiles have not been replaced by corrugated iron, and the rich original interior decoration of mirror tiles upon a deep red ground is also intact. Ask one of the monks to point out the rare Buddhist texts carved on sheets of ivory, and the bamboo and gold Buddha 'basket'. There is also a less remarkable collection of amulets, coins and betel boxes. At the front of the compound is a Burmese-style chedi, surrounded by 13 acolyte chedis. Built of brick and stucco, it has been allowed to gently weather into a mellow state of decrepid elegance. Near the chedi and along the E wall of the compound are some rather unfortunate caged boar, and rather more fortunate caged birds. Admission: by donation.

Wat Hua Khuang, within the city walls at the N edge of town, is notable only for its large, abandoned brick chedi.

Not far away at the N extension of Charoen Muang Rd (and also within the city walls) is **Wat Sri Chum**. The interiors of the bot and viharn here are stark and rather beautiful with seated and standing Buddha images in extremely high relief. Above the seated image, angels, again in relief, shower flowers down upon the Buddha.

Wat Luang is a few minutes walk from Wat Sri Chum, near the city wall and moat. The wat was founded in the 12th century at about the same time as the city, although continuous renovation and expansion has tended to obscure its ancient origins. Particularly beautiful, however, is the Lanna Thai-style chedi, with its (admittedly rather crude) elephant caryatids and honorific umbrellas. The wat also supports an impressive museum which the monks are happy to show visitors. In its varied collection (unfortunately with very little explanatory information in English) are valuable Buddha images, swords, coins, burial caskets, Buddhist texts, old photographs (one of a decapitation), betel boxes and jewellery. An old northern house with all the accessories of traditional life is also part of the collection. Admission: by donation. Finally, the wat is also notable for its fine well pavilion on the W wall and the individual monks kutis, or cells, like small bungalows, along the S wall.

Ban Phrathap Jai is in the W suburbs of town. The tourist authorities are promoting this 'house' (in fact it was constructed in 1972 out of 9 old teak houses) as one of the biggest teak Thai-style mansions in the country: it is disappointing in its ersatz atmosphere and crudity. The house is situated in a 'garden' of concrete animals and is really just a reason to attract visitors to the shops here, selling woodcarvings, 'antiques' and clothing. Admission: ฿20. Open: 0800-1700 Mon-Sun. Get there by saamlor (not more than ฿10) or walk the 2 km from the city centre.

Excursions

Wat Phrathat Chor Hae is a hilltop wat 8 km SE of town. It probably dates from the 12th-13th century and the 28 m-high chedi is said to contain a hair of the Lord Buddha brought here by the Indian Emperor Asoka. The chedi is surrounded by a small cloister and linked to this is an ornate, high ceilinged, viharn with bold murals depicting episodes from the Buddha's life. The name of the wat is the same as that of a particularly fine cloth woven by the people of the area, and in which the chedi is shrouded each year. Also here at the foot of the hill are a number of souvenir stalls and a small, rather sad, wildlife park (the Suan Sat Chor Hae) (open: 0700-1700 Mon-Sun). Getting there: by songthaew from Charoen Muang Rd, near the intersection with Yantarakitkoson Rd, ฿6. **NB**: there are few return songthaews in the afternoon so it is best to make the trip in the morning.

Muang Phi, or the City of Ghosts, is marketed as Thailand's Grand Canyon – which does little justice to the real thing. It is an area of strange eroded rock formations about 15 km NE of town. Turn right after 9 km off Route 101 to Nan, and onto Route 1134; the turning for the canyon is 6 km along Route 1134 and lies about 2 km off the road. Getting there: easiest by chartered songthaew, as the area lies off the main highway (about ฿200). Alternatively take a bus towards Nan and get off at the intersection with Route 1134. Occasional songthaews travel this road.

Tours and trekking

(See Hilltribes and trekking, page 275.) Phrae has not built up much of a trekking infrastructure yet, although the elusive Mlabri tribe are accessible from town (see box, page 286). Ask at the *Mae Yom Palace Hotel* for information or travel to Nan where facilities are better developed (see below).

Local information
● Accommodation
B *Maeyom Palace*, 181/6 Yantarakitkoson Rd, T 521028, F 522904, a/c, restaurant, pool, best hotel in town, situated 1 km from the town centre, large rooms and professional service, organizes tours to hilltribe villages and home industries, discounts available, bikes for hire; **B** *Nakhon Phrae Tower*, 3 Muang Hit Rd, T 521321, F 521937, monstrous hotel, opened Dec 1992, towers over the city, good rooms but no pool (as yet) and little 'northern' ambience.

C *Nakhon Palace*, 118 Rachdamnern Rd, T 511122, some a/c, ugly hotel sprawling across both sides of the street, average rooms, central.

D *Pharadorn*, 177 Yantarakitkoson Rd, T 511177, some a/c, restaurant, large concrete barn, but rooms are spacious, clean and well maintained, a/c rooms benefit from carpets and hot water, good value, rec; **D-E** *Thung Si Phaiboon*, Yantarakitkoson Rd (near intersection with Charoen Muang Rd), T 511011, some a/c, large characterless rooms, Asian squat toilets, rooms arranged in a 'U' around a courtyard, visitors sleeping in rooms on the street may be woken up by an early morning market.

E *Ho Faa*, Charoen Muang Rd, T 511140, small, Chinese hotel near centre of town, only average.

● Places to eat
Thai: ♦*Phet Pochana*, Yantarakitkoson Rd (next to the *Maeyom Palace Hotel*), open air restaurant, also serves Chinese dishes; ♦*Arun Chai*, Charoen Muang Rd (opposite *Ho Faa Hotel*), good food; ♦*Barrahouse*, 45 Ban Mai Rd (1 km from town on road to Nan), friendly owners, good food, clean and welcoming, coffee and ice-cream along with usual Thai/Chinese dishes; *Ban Rai*, Yantarakitkoson Rd, large outdoor garden restaurant, 2 km out of town on road S; ♦*Corner Road*, corner of Lak Muang and Khumderm rds, also serves ice-cream, clean, friendly and pleasant atmosphere; ♦♦♦*Krua Yom Hom* (*Maeyom Palace Hotel*), Yantarakitkoson Rd, expensive Thai, Chinese and European food, but live band and seafood BBQ in evening on terrace makes it

worth it; ♦*Luuk Kaew*, Yantarakitkoson Rd (opposite *Maeyom Palace Hotel*), excellent Thai and Chinese food, succulent satay, highly rec; ♦*Cat* (*Maew*) 83 Charoen Muang Rd (nr intersection with Rob Muang Rd), good food in pleasant restaurant, rec.

Bakery: *Pern Bakery*, 347 Charoen Muang Rd. Cakes, pastries, coffee and ice-cream.

● Bars
Several on Rachdamnern Rd.

● Airline office
Thai, Rachdamnern Rd, T 511123.

● Banks & money changers
Several on Charoen Muang Rd.

● Entertainment
Traditional Thai massage: *Maeyom Palace Hotel*, Yantarakitkoson Rd.

● Sports
Golf: small 9 hole course 2 km SE of town, near the airport. Open to non-members; it is said there are clubs for hire. **Swimming:** at the *Maeyom Palace Hotel*.

● Shopping
Antiques: *Ban Phrathap Jai* (see Places of interest).

Clothing: Phrae is a centre of *morhom* production – the traditional blue garb of the Northern farmer. A simple tunic costs ฿60-100. Available all over town but recommended is *Morhom Mae Nuu*, 60-62 Charoen Muang Rd. Another centre of production is the village of *Tung Hong*, 3 km NE of town, on route 101 to Nan. **Getting there:** by songthaew from the bus station on Tantharakitkoson Rd.

Handicrafts: *Nok Noi Handicraft Centre*, 6/3 Yantarakitkoson Trok [Soi] 2. Woodcarvings, some clothing, baskets, hats. *Ban Phrathap Jai house*.

Supermarket: *Yong Wattana*, Yantarakitkoson Rd.

● Post & telecommunications
Area code: 054. **Post Office:** Charoen Muang Rd (in the old city), with telephone, telex and telegram facilities. **Telephone:** 163/2 Yantarakitkoson Rd.

● Transport to & from Phrae
627 km from Bangkok, 116 km from Nan.

Local transport Songthaew: is the main form of local transport. Songthaews running N to Song and Rong Kwang leave from outside the Piriyalai School on Yantarakitkoson Rd;

those running S to Den Chai (for the nearest train station) depart from Yantarakitkoson Rd near the intersection with Muang Hit Rd (by the petrol station).

Air: the airport is 2 km SE of town. Daily connections with Bangkok, 1 hr 20 mins and Nan, 30 mins.

Train: the nearest train station to Phrae is at Den Chai, 24 km SW of town. Connections S to Bangkok 8¹/₂ hrs (ø60-389) and N to Chiang Mai (4¹/₂ hrs).

Road Bus: the terminal is 1 km NE of the city centre off Yantarakitkoson Rd, opposite the *Maeyom Palace Hotel*. Regular connections with Bangkok's Northern bus terminal 8¹/₄ hrs (ø128) Nan 2¹/₂ hrs (ø33), Uttaradit, Chiang Mai and other towns in the N. A/c tour buses for Bangkok leave from *Phrae Tour's* offices at 141/6 Yantarakitkoson Rd at 2030 and 2100 (ø238).

Nan

Nan occupies a small valley in the far eastern highlands of the N – about 50 km from the border with Laos. It is thought the earliest settlers in the area came from the court of Laos in 1282. They established a town 70 km north of Nan, and from that point the Nan valley became an important centre. However, if local legend is to be believed, the Buddha himself was trekking here, picking out auspicious sites for wats, over 2,500 years ago. The 13th century inscriptions of King Ramkhamhaeng of Sukhothai named Nan as one of the *muang* whose 'submission he received', although it would probably be more accurate to view the royal house of Nan ruling largely free from interference until the 15th century, when Lanna established suzerainty over Nan. Even then, the turbulent politics of the area with the Burmese, Lao, Siamese and the partially independent muang of the area all vying with one another, coupled with Nan's remote location, afforded it considerable independence.

Nan, is a province to be explored for its natural beauty, with teak forests (or today, rather, teak plantations), fertile valleys chequered with paddy fields, hilltribes, and fast-running rivers. It was not until 1931 that the central authorities managed to overcome the area's inaccessibility and bring it under Bangkok's direct control. Even since then, there have been periods – most recently in the 1970s when Communist insurgency was a problem – when the army and the police have treated the province virtually as a no-go area. It still exudes an atmosphere of other-worldliness and isolation.

Places of interest

The **National Museum** on Phakong Road, once the home of the Nan royal family, houses an impressive collection, including beautiful wood and bronze Buddha images, house models, ethnographic pieces, dioramas, ceramics, textiles, jewellery and musical instruments. The main exhibit is on the 2nd floor: it is a 97 cm-long black elephant tusk which once belonged to the Nan royal family, and is reputed to have magical powers. Protected within a steel cage, it is clearly regarded as the most valuable exhibit here, but pales into mediocrity next to the beautiful Buddha images and other works of art. All exhibits are well displayed and explained – it is an excellent museum, well worth visiting. Admission: ø10. Open: 0900-1200, 1300-1600, Wed-Sun.

Wat Phumin is a 5 minute walk from the National Museum on Phakong Road, and is one of Nan's artistic treasures. It was built in 1596 but has since been restored on numerous occasions – most extensively between 1865 and 1873. The unusual cruciform bot cum viharn (although it is surrounded by *bai sema*, the structure is both bot and viharn rolled into one) is supported by the coils of two magnificent nagas (mythical serpents). The head forms the buttress of the N entrance and the tail, the S. Inside there are some of the finest murals to be found in the N. Painted in

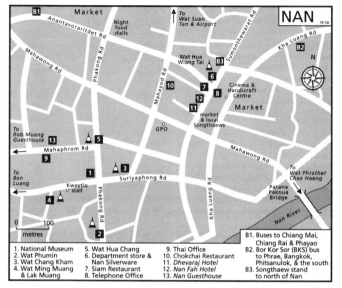

NAN TB 58

1. National Museum
2. Wat Phumin
3. Wat Chang Kham
4. Wat Ming Muang & Lak Muang
5. Wat Hua Chang
6. Department store & Nan Silverware
7. Siam Restaurant
8. Telephone Office
9. Thai Office
10. Chokchai Restaurant
11. *Dhevaraj Hotel*
12. *Nan Fah Hotel*
13. *Nan Guesthouse*

B1. Buses to Chiang Mai, Chiang Rai & Phayao
B2. Bor Kor Sor (BKS) bus to Phrae, Bangkok, Phitsanulok, & the south
B3. Songthaew stand to north of Nan

the middle of the 19th century, they depict a handful of the jataka tales, but also illustrate aspects of northern Thai life: hunting, weaving, lovers, musicians, elephants and courtiers along with bearded Europeans and steamships, the curses of hell, elephants, people being boiled alive, lovers, courtiers, Indian emissaries (or traders?) offering gifts of books, people with over large testicles, starving men – a myriad of activity. Note the two life-size murals of a Burmese couple, both wearing lungyi (the Burmese Sarong) – he has red circles and dancing monkeys tattooed on his chest to ward off evil. The naive style of the murals – large areas of empty space, figures of various sizes – distinguish them from the more sophisticated art of Bangkok. Four Sukhothai-style gilded stucco Buddhas each in an attitude of vanquishing Mara face outwards towards the cardinal points. The carved doors of the building, with animals, birds and flowers, are also particularly fine.

Wat Chang Kham, next to the Sala Klang (provincial offices), features a chedi supported by elephant buttresses (caryatids), similar in inspiration to those at Si Satchanalai, Kamphaeng Phet and Sukhothai. The viharn was built in 1547 and contains three Sukhothai-style Buddha images, two walking and one standing. Also note the accomplished woodcarving on the façades of both the bot and the viharn, and the guardian singhas at the entrances to both. **Wat Phya Phu** built in 1427 – since much restored – contains some examples of the post-classic Sukhothai Buddha image. The bronze walking Buddha, for example, dated to 1426, shows the stylized features and the asymmetrical posture of the classic Sukhothai image, yet the robe is rigid, the face rounder. Many art historians regard such images as inferior, lacking the "grandeur and exultation of the classic Buddha image" (Stratton and Scott, 1981: 81).

Wat Ming Muang on Suriyaphong Rd contains the city of Nan's *lak muang* or city pillar, liberally draped in garlands. **Wat Hua Chang**, on the corner of Phakong and Mahaphrom rds features an elegant 2-storey stone and wood tripitaka or scripture library, a square based ched with four Buddhas in raised niches each in the attitude of vanquishing Mara and a fine bot (with *bai sema*). **Wat Hua Wiang Tai** is on Sumonthewarat Rd, just N of Anantavoraritdet Rd. It is very gaudy, with nagas running along the top of the surrounding wall and bright vivacious murals painted on the exterior of the viharn. Other wats in the area include **Wat Suan Tan** in Tambon Nai Wiang which has a prang, unusual for the area, and a 15th century bronze Buddha image named Phra Chao Thong Thit. A fireworks display takes place at the wat during Songkran.

Excursions

Wat Phrathat Chae Haeng, 3 km SE of town, was built in 1355. The 55m-high, gold-sheeted chedi is Lao in style, and the bot has an interesting multi-tiered roof (a fair with fireworks and processions is held here on the full moon day of the first lunar month). Also notable are the fine pair of nagas that form the balustrade of the approach stairway to the monastery. **Getting there**: a 30 minute walk across the Nan River and then E, or rent a bicycle/motorbike.

Sao Din in Amphoe Na Noi lies to the S of Nan, off Route 1026. It is a heavily eroded canyon – almost prehistoric in atmosphere – with tall earth pillars and deeply eroded earth. **Getting there**: either catch a local bus to Amphoe Na Noi and then charter a motorcycle taxi, or charter a songthaew from town.

Tha Wang Pha, an amphoe (district) capital 40 km to the N of Nan on Route 1080, is rather easier to get to. The town is famous for its Thai Lue weaving, much of which is produced in surrounding villages and then brought here for marketing. The Thai Lue were forced out of Yunnan in southern China by King Rama I (1782-1809). At the conclusion of the Thai-Burmese wars, they were settled in Nan province and turned to farming, and are now peacefully assimilated into the Thai population. But the Thai Lu have not lost all their cultural distinctiveness: they are skilled weavers and the women still wear a tubular *pha sin* of bright horizontal stripes and a short black jacket decorated with multicoloured embroidered stripes and silver jewellery. Thai Lue textiles and jewellery are available in town. En route to Tha Wang Pha, about 35 km N of Nan is the turn-off for **Ban Nong Bua** and the fine **Wat Nong Bua**. The monastery is Thai Lue in design and features fine murals executed by the same artists who decorated Wat Phumin in Nan (see above). Thai Lue textiles are also available in the small town. **Getting there**: by regular local bus or songthaew from the stand on Sumonthewarat Rd, just N of Anantavoraritdet Rd. For Ban Nong Bua get off at the fork before The Wang Pha and walk about 2 km (tell the conductor where you are going).

Doi Phu Khao National Park, 40 km N of Nan, a good day trip by motorbike.

Tours

The best tour company in town is the *Phu Travel Service* (see tour companies below). Mr Phu rents out bicycles and motorbikes and arranges tours to see the elusive Mlabri tribe (see box, page 286), the Doi Phu Khao National Park, provincial sites and boat tours up the Nan River. Prices from about ฿400/day. The *Dhevaraj* and *Nan Fah* hotels and the *Rop Muang Guesthouse* also organize tours.

Trekking

(See Hilltribes and trekking, page 275) *Phu Travel Service*. (see Tour companies below) organize treks into the surrounding area, including to see the Mlabri people (see box, page 286).

Festivals

Mid Oct-mid Nov: *Boat races*, at the end

of the Buddhist Lent. These races are thought to have first started about a century ago, when they were part of the Songkran celebrations. Now they are associated with the robe giving ceremony, kathin. These distinctive boats are hollowed out logs, painted in bright designs. There is a lively fair in the weeks before (and during) the races.

Local information
● Accommodation
B-C *Dhevaraj*, 466 Sumonthewarat Rd, T 710094, some a/c, restaurant, best in town but rather overpriced – really just an average hotel with pretensions, rooms are set around a courtyard, are clean, with hot water and satellite tv.

C *Nan Fah*, 438-440 Sumonthewarat Rd, T 772640, some a/c, known as the 'wooden hotel', it has some character, rooms are clean and airy, bathrooms have hot water and Western toilets, gift shop and tours arranged.

F *Nan Guesthouse*, 57/16 Mahaphrom Rd, T 771849, clean and attractive, quiet location, not always very efficient, one visitor complained that food was sporadic and that it was run by children who spoke no English, rents out bicycles, some dorm beds; **F** *Rob Muang Guesthouse*, 3/1 Rob Muang Rd, T 772559, friendly guesthouse with clean rooms plus dorm beds, not just a farang place, it is also popular with Thais, the owner will help organize treks and tours, bicycles and motorbikes for rent, rec.

● Places to eat
◆◆*Siam*, Sumonthewarat Rd (near the *Nan Fah Hotel*), despite its dingy appearance, this is possibly the best restaurant in Nan, freshly cooked Thai and Chinese dishes, generous portions, efficient service – very well patronized by locals; ◆*Chokchai*, Mahayod Rd, good food in friendly surroundings; ◆*No name*, 38/1 Suriyaphong Rd (next to Wat Ming Muang), excellent spicy *kwaytio khao soi* (egg noodles in curry broth).

● Airline offices
Thai, 34 Mahaphrom Rd, T 710377.

● Banks & money changers
Thai Farmers and Bangkok on Sumonthewarat Rd.

● Post & telecommunications
Area code: 054. **Post Office**: Mahawong Rd (with telephone, fax, telegram facilities). **Telephone centre**: 345/7 Sumonthewarat Rd.

● Shopping
Department store: *Nara Department store*, Sumonthewarat Rd (N of intersection with Anantaroraritdet Rd).

Jewellery: *Nan Silverware*, corner of Sumonthewarat and Anantaroraritdet rds for locally produced jewellery.

Handicrafts: *Ban Fai*, Kha Luang Rd. Basketry, textiles and woodcarving. There is also a shop in the *Nan Fah Hotel*, Sumonthewarat Rd selling various handicrafts (textiles, silverwork and woodcarving) at reasonable prices, rec.

● Tour companies & travel agents
Phu Travel Service, 453/4 Sumonthewarat Rd, T 710636.

● Transport
749 km from Bangkok, 340 km from Chiang Mai, 116 km from Phrae.

Local Saamlors and songthaews. **Bicycles and motorbike hire**: from *Phu Travel Service* and from the *Nan* and *Rob Muang* guesthouses.

Air: the airport is on the N edge of town (5 km from the centre). Connections with Bangkok (daily) 2 hrs 10 mins, Chiang Mai (3/week) 45 mins, Phitsanulok (3/week) 55 mins and Phrae (daily) 30 mins.

Road Bus: Nan has 2 bus terminals. Buses for towns to the N and W including Chiang Rai, Chiang Mai 9 hrs (∲70), Lamphun, Lampang, Phayao, Phrae and Den Chai, leave from the station off Anantavoraritdet Rd about 1 km W of the town centre. Buses serving destinations to the S, including Bangkok's northern bus terminal 12 hrs (∲155-289), Phitsanulok, Uttaradit, Nakhon Sawan, Kamphaeng Phet and Sukhothai leave from the BKS terminal 0.5 km to the N of the city centre on Kha Luang Rd. VIP and a/c buses serve all major destinations. **NB**: buses running N to Chiang Rai take 2 routes; either the shorter trip W and NW on Routes 1091 and 1251 to Phayao and then N to Chiang Rai, or by first running S to Phrae and then N to Phayao and Chiang Rai.

HILLTRIBES AND TREKKING

A visit to a hilltribe village is one of the main reasons why people travel to the North of Thailand. The hilltribe population (*Chao Khao* in Thai – literally 'Mountain People'), numbers about 550,000, or approximately 1% of the total population of the country. However, these 0.5 million people are far from homogenous: each hilltribe, and there are nine recognised by the government, has a different language, dress, religion, artistic heritage and culture. They meet their subsistence needs in different ways and often occupy different ecological niches. In some respects they are as far removed from one another as they are from the lowland Thais. As their name suggests, the hilltribes occupy the highland areas that fringe the Northern region, with the largest populations in the provinces of Chiang Mai (143,000), Chiang Rai (98,000), Mae Hong Son (83,000), and Tak (69,000). Although this guide follows the tradition of using the term 'hilltribe' to describe these diverse peoples, it is in many regards an unfortunate one. They are not tribes in the anthropological sense, derived as it is from the study of the peoples of Africa. And the word 'tribe' has unfortunate, and inaccurate, connotations of 'primitive' and 'savage'.

Cultural extinction?

Much of the concern that has been focused upon the hilltribes dwells on their increasingly untenable position in a country where they occupy a distinctly subordinate position. Over a number of years, the Thai government has tried culturally and economically to assimilate the hilltribes into the Thai state (read, Tai state). Projects have attempted to settle them in *nikhom* (resettlement villages) and to "instil a strong sense of Thai citizenship, obligation and faith in the institutions of Nation, Religion and Monarchy..." (Thai Army document). This desire on the part of the government is understandable, when one considers that the hilltribes occupy strategically sensitive border areas.

THE HILLTRIBES OF THAILAND				
Tribe	Population in Thailand	**Origins**	**Date of arrival**	**Location in Thailand (province)**
Karen (Yang/Kariang)	270,000	Burma	C18th	Mae Hong Son
Hmong (Meo)	82,000	China	late C19th	Chiang Rai Nan
Lahu (Mussur)	60,000	Yunnan (China)	late C19th	Chiang Mai Chiang Rai
Mien (Yao)	36,000	South China	mid C19th	Chiang Rai Nan
Akha (Kaw)	33,000	Yunnan (China)	early C20th	Chiang Rai
Lisu (Lisaw)	25,000	Salween (China)	early C20th	Chiang Mai
Other tribal groups				
Htin	29,000	—	—	—
Lua	8,000	—	—	—
Khamu	7,000	—	—	—
Mlabri	138	—	—	—

There are a number of factors that have lent weight to this policy of resettlement and integration: the former strength of the Communist Party of Thailand, the narcotics problem (it has been estimated that as recently as 30 years ago 45% of hilltribe households were engaged in the cultivation of the poppy), the more recent concern with the preservation of Thailand's few remaining forests, as well as the simple demographic reality that Thailand's population is growing. However, in many respects the most significant process encouraging change has been the commercialization of life among the

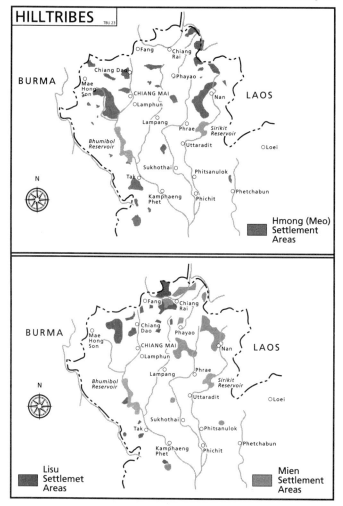

HILLTRIBES TBU 23

Hmong (Meo) Settlement Areas

Lisu Settlemet Areas

Mien Settlement Areas

THE HILLTRIBE CALENDAR

	Karen	Hmong	Mien (Yao)	Akha	Lisu	Lahu
Jan	village ceremony	new year festival	embroidering	weaving	new year festival	scoring poppies
Feb	site selection	scoring poppies	scoring poppies	clearing fields	2nd new year festival	new year festival
Mar	clearing field	clearing field	clearing field	burning field	clearing field	burning field
Apr	burning field	burning field	burning field	rice spirit ceremony	burning field	field spirit house
May	rice planting	rice planting	rice and maize planting	rice planting	rice dibbling	rice planting
Jun	field spirit offering	weeding	weeding	weeding	weeding	weeding
Jul	field spirit offering	weeding	weeding	weeding	weeding	weeding
Aug	weeding	weeding	harvesting	swinging ceremony	soul calling ceremony	weeding
Sep	rat trapping	poppy seeding	poppy seeding	maize harvest	maize harvest	-
Oct	rice harvest	thinning poppy field	rice harvest	rice harvest	poppy seeding	field spirit offering
Nov	rice harvest	rice harvest	rice harvest	rice harvest	rice harvest	rice harvest
Dec	rice threshing	new year festival	rice threshing	new year festival	rice threshing	field spirit offering

Source: Tribal Research Institute, Chiang Mai University

hilltribes: as they have been inexorably drawn into the market economy, so their traditional subsistence systems and ethics have become increasingly obsolete. This process is voluntary, spontaneous and profound.

Although tourists may feel that they are somehow more culturally aware and sensitive than the next man or woman and therefore can watch and not influence, this is of course untrue. As people, and especially monetized Westerners, push their way into the last remaining remote areas of the North in an endless quest for the 'real thing', they are helping to erode that for which they search. Not that the hilltribes could ever remain, or ever have been, isolated. There has always been contact and trade between the hilltribes and the lowland peoples. Their 'Westernization' or 'Thai-ization' is popularly seen as a 'bad thing'. This says more about our romantic image of the Rousseau-esque tribal peoples of the world than it does about the realities of life in the mountains. Certainly, it is impossible selectively to develop the hilltribe communities. If they are to have the benefits of schooling and medical care, then they must also receive – or to come into contact with – all those other, and perhaps less desirable, facets of modern Thai life. And if culture is functional, as anthropologists would have us believe, then in so doing they are experiencing a process of cultural erosion. To dramatize slightly, they are on the road to cultural extinction.

Hilltribe economy and culture

Traditionally, most of the hilltribes practised slash and burn agriculture (see page 29), also known as swiddening or shifting cultivation. They would burn a small area of forest, cultivate it for a few years by planting rice, corn and other crops, and then, when the soil was exhausted, abandon the land until the vegetation had regenerated to replenish the soil. Some groups merely shifted fields in a 10-15 year rotation; others not only shifted fields but also their villages, relocating in a fresh area of forest when the land had become depleted of nutrients. To obtain salt, metal implements and other goods which could not be made or found in the hills, the tribal peoples would trade forest products such as resins and animal skins with the settled lowland Thais. This simplified picture of the hilltribe economy is being gradually eroded for a variety of reasons, the most significant being that today there is simply not enough land available in most areas to practice such an extensive system of agriculture.

The Karen (or Kariang, Yang)

Origins

The Karen, also known as the Kariang or Yang, are found along the Thai-Burmese border, concentrated in the Mae Hong Son region. They are the largest tribal group in Thailand, numbering about 270,000. Their origins are in Burma, where today many more are fighting a long-term and low-intensity war against the Burmese authorities for greater autonomy. The Karen started to infiltrate into Thailand in the 18th century and moved into areas occupied by the Lawa, possibly the oldest established tribe in Thailand. The evidence of this contact between the two groups can still be seen in the dress, ornamentation and implements of the Karen.

Economy and society

The Karen are divided into two main sub-groups, the Sgaw and the Pwo. The Pwo make up about 20% of the total population and the Sgaw the remaining 80%. Most Karen live in mountain villages and practice shifting cultivation of the rotating field type (i.e. they move their fields, but not their villages). They prevent soil erosion on the steep slopes by taking care to maintain belts of forest

growth between 'swiddens' or fields, by leaving saplings and tree roots to help bind the soil, and by not turning the soil before planting. When a community grows so large that the distance to the outer fields becomes excessive, a group of villagers establish a satellite village beyond the boundaries of the mother village. However, with the pressure on land and the incentive to commercialize production this traditional pioneering strategy is often no longer possible. Karen are being forced to try and increase yields by developing irrigation, and some Karen have moved down into the valleys and taken-up settled agriculture, imitating the methods of the lowland Thais.

Karen houses are built on stilts out of bamboo, with thatched roofs. Animals are kept under the house at night for protection against wild animals and rustlers. Most houses have only one room and a spacious verandah. A household usually consists of a husband and wife plus their unmarried children. Should a man's wife die, he is not permitted to remarry until his children have left the home, as this would cause conflict with the spirits. Indeed, much of Karen life is dictated by the spirits. The most important is the 'Lord of Land and Water' who controls the productivity of the land and calls upon the rice spirit to grow. Also important is the matrilineal ancestor guardian spirit (*bga*).

The priest is the most revered individual in the village: he is the ritual leader and it is he who sets dates for the annual ceremonies. The post is an ancestral one and only changes when the priest dies – at which time the village must change location as well (although the distance may only be nominal). As the Karen have been incorporated into the Thai state, so increasing numbers have turned to Buddhism. The role of European missionaries in the highland areas also means that there are significant numbers of Christian Karen. A cen-

PAPAVER SOMNIFERUM: THE OPIUM OF THE PEOPLE

The hilltribes of Northern Thailand, and the very name the Golden Triangle, is synonymous in many people's minds with the cultivation of the opium poppy (*Papaver somniferum* L.). It is a favourite cash crop of the Lahu, Lisu, Mien and Hmong (the Karen and Akha only rarely grow it). The attractions of cultivating the poppy are clear: it is profitable, can be grown at high altitudes (above 1500 m), has low bulk (important when there is no transport) and does not rot. This explains why, although cultivation has been banned in Thailand since 1959, it has only been since the 1980s that the Thai government, with US assistance, has significantly reduced the area cultivated. Today, most opium is grown in Burma and Laos, not in Thailand – although most is traded through the kingdom.

The opium poppy is usually grown as part of a rotation, alternating with maize. It is sown in Sept/Oct (the end of the wet season) and 'harvesting' stretches from the beginning of Jan through to the end of Mar. Harvesting occurs after the petals have dropped off the seed heads. The 'pod' is then carefully scoured with a sharp knife, from top to bottom, allowing the sap to ooze through and oxidize on the surface of the pod. The next day, the brown gum is scraped off, rolled into balls, and wrapped in banana leaves. It is now ready for sale to the buyers who travel the hills.

Though a profitable crop, opium production has not benefited the hilltribes. In the government's eyes it has made them latent criminals, and opium addiction is widespread – among the Hmong it is thought to be about 30% of the population. Efforts to change the ways of the hilltribes have focused upon crop substitution programmes (encouraging farmers to cultivate crops such as cabbages) and simple intimidation.

---

tral Karen myth tells of a younger 'white brother' from across the water who would arrive with the skills of writing given to him by God. This no doubt helped the missionaries enormously when they arrived, pasty-faced and clutching bibles. In most cases however, while converting to Buddhism or Christianity, the Karen have at the same time maintained a healthy belief in their traditional spirits.

Material culture

The Karen are prolific weavers. Weaving is done on simple back-strap looms and many Karen still spin their own thread. The upper garments worn by men, women and children are all made in the same way: two strips of material are folded in half, the fold running along the shoulder. They are then sewn together along the centre of the garment and down the sides, leaving holes for the head and arms. The stitching is not merely functional, it is an integral part of the design. Until girls marry, they wear only this garment, full length to just below their knees, and made of white cotton. The Sgaw embroider a band of red or pink around their waists, the Pwo embroider red diamond patterns along the lower edge. Married women wear this garment as an overblouse and they also wear a sarong. The over-blouse is considerably more elaborate than that of the girls: Job's-tear seeds (seeds from a grass) are woven into the design, or a pattern is woven around the border. Pwo women tend to embroider all over the blouse.

The sarong is made up of two strips of material, sewn horizontally and stitched together to make a tubular skirt. They are held up with a cord or metal belt and are worn knee or ankle-length, longer for formal occasions. The colour is predominantly red. The men's shirts are usually hip length, with elaborate embroidery. They wear sarongs or Thai peasant-style pants.

The Sgaw women and girls wear multiple strands of small beads, which hang from mid-chest to waist length, normally red, white or yellow. The Pwo wear them around their neck and to mid-chest length and they are mostly black. Their necklaces are made from old 'bullet coins', strung on braided red thread. Pwo women wear lots of bracelets of silver, copper, brass or aluminium. Sgaw are more moderate in their use of jewellery. All Karen wear silver cup-shaped earrings, which often have coloured tufts of wool attached.

The Hmong (or Meo)

Origins

The Hmong, also known as the Meo, are the second largest tribal group in Thailand, numbering about 82,000. Although their origins are rather hazy, the Hmong themselves claim that they have their roots in the icy north. They had arrived in Laos by 1850 and by the end of the 19th century had migrated into the provinces of Chiang Rai and Nan. Today they are scattered right across the Northern region and have spread over a larger area than any other tribe apart from the Karen.

Economy and society

There are two sub-groups of the Hmong, the Blue and the White Hmong. The Hmong value their independence, and tend to live at high altitudes, away from other tribes. This independence, and their association with poppy cultivation, has meant that of all the hilltribes it is the Hmong who have been most severely persecuted by the Thai authorities. They are perceived to be a threat to the security of the state, a tribe that needs to be controlled and carefully watched. Like most hilltribes, they prac-

tice shifting cultivation, moving their villages when the surrounding land has been exhausted. The process of moving is stretched out over 2 seasons: an advance party finds a suitable site, builds temporary shelters, clears the land and plants rice, and only after the harvest do the rest of the inhabitants follow on.

Hmong villages tend not to be fenced, while their houses are built of wood or bamboo at ground level. Each house has a main living area, and 2 or 3 sleeping rooms. The extended family is headed by the oldest male: he settles family disputes and has supreme authority over family affairs. Like the Karen, the Hmong too are spirit worshippers and believe in household spirits. Every house has an altar, where protection for the household is sought. Despite 20th century pressures (particularly scarcity of land), they maintain a strong sense of identity. The children may be educated in Thai schools but they invariably return to farming alongside their parents.

Material culture

The Hmong are the only tribe in Thailand who make batik: indigo-dyed batik makes up the main panel of their skirts, with appliqué and embroidery added to it. The women also wear black leggings from their knees to their ankles, black jackets (with embroidery), and a black panel or 'apron', held in place with a cummerbund. Even the smallest children wear clothes of intricate design with exquisite needlework. Today much of the cloth is purchased from the market or from traders; traditionally it would have been woven by hand on a foot-treddle/back-strap loom.

The White Hmong tend to wear less elaborate clothing from day to day, saving it for special occasions only. Hmong men wear loose-fitting black trousers, black jackets (sometimes embroidered), and coloured or embroidered sashes.

The Hmong particularly value silver jewellery: it signifies wealth and a good life. Men, women and children wear silver – tiers of neck rings, heavy silver chains with lock-shaped pendants, earrings and pointed rings on every finger. All the family jewellery is brought out at New Year and is an impressive sight, symbolizing the wealth of the family.

Even though the Hmong are perhaps the most independent of all the hilltribes, they too are being drawn into the 'modern' world. Some still grow the poppy at higher elevations, but the general shortage of land is forcing them to descend to lower altitudes, to take up irrigated rice farming, to grow cash

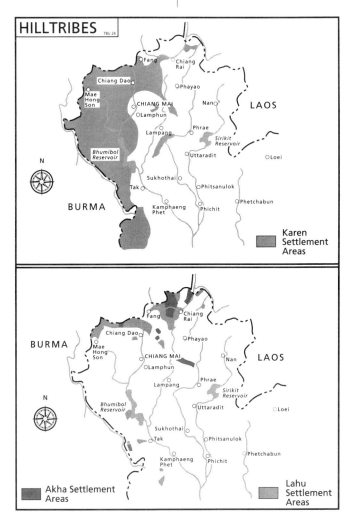

crops, and to mix with the lowland Thais. This has led to conflicts between the Hmong and the lowlanders as they compete for the same resources – previously they would have been occupying quite different ecological niches.

The Lahu (or Mussur)

Origins

The Lahu in Thailand are found along the Burmese border and number about 60,000. They originated in Yunnan (S. China) and migrated from Burma into Thailand at the end of the 19th century. Today the majority of Thai Lahu are found in the provinces of Chiang Mai and Chiang Rai. There are a number of Lahu sub-groups, each with slightly different traditions and clothing. The 2 dominant groups are the Black Lahu and the Yellow Lahu, which themselves are sub-divided.

Economy and society

Traditionally the Lahu lived at relatively high elevations, 1200m or higher. Pres-

---

IKAT PRODUCTION

Ikat is a technique of patterning cloth characteristic of Southeast Asia and is produced from the hills of Burma to the islands of Eastern Indonesia. The word comes from the Malay word *mengikat* which means to bind or tie. Very simply, either the warp or the weft, and in one case both, are tied with material or fibre so that they resist the action of the dye. Hence the technique's name - resist dyeing. By dyeing, retieing and dyeing again through a number of cycles it is possible to build up complex patterns. Ikat is distinguishable by the bleeding of the dye which inevitably occurs no matter how carefully the threads are tied; this gives the finished cloth a blurred finish. The earliest ikats so far found date from the 14th-15th centuries.

To prepare the cloth for dyeing, the warp or weft is strung tight on a frame. Individual threads, or groups of threads are then tied together with fibre and leaves. In some areas wax is then smeared on top to help in the resist process. The main colour is usually dyed first, secondary colours later. With complex patterns (which are done from memory, plans are only required for new designs) and using natural dyes, it may take up to 6 months to produce a piece of cloth. Prices are correspondingly high – in Eastern Indonesia for example, top grade cloths can easily exceed 1,000,000Rp (US$500), and ritual cloths considerable more than this. Today, the pressures of the market place mean that it is more likely that cloth is produced using chemical dyes (which need only one short soaking, not multiple long ones as with some natural dyes), and design motifs have generally become larger and less complex. Traditionally, warp ikat used cotton (rarely silk) and weft ikat, silk. Silk in many areas has given way to cotton, and cotton sometimes to synthetic yarns. Double ikat, where incredibly both the warp *and* the weft are tied-dyed, is produced in only one spot in Southeast Asia: a village in eastern Bali.

Warp Ikat:	Weft Ikat:
Sumatra (Bataks)	Sulawesi (Bugis)
Borneo (Dayaks)	North-east Java
Sulawesi (Toraja)	East Sumatra
East Nusa Tenggara (Savu, Flores, Sumba, Rote)	Bali
	Burma (Shans)
Double Ikat:	Thailand
East Bali	Laos
	Cambodia

sure on land and commercialization has encouraged most of these groups to move down the slopes, and most of these have now taken up irrigated rice farming in the small, high valleys which dissect the Northern region of Thailand.

Villages are about 30 houses strong, with about 6 people in each house. Their houses are built on stilts and consist of the main living area, a bedroom, a spirit altar, and a fireplace. Houses are usually built of wood or bamboo, and thatch. The men are less dominant in the family hierarchy than in other tribes: they help around the home and share in the care of their chil-

dren and livestock, as well as gathering water and firewood (the very epitome of a liberated male). A typical household is nuclear rather than extended, consisting of a man, his wife, and their unmarried children. It is also not unusual for a married daughter and her husband and children to live in the household.

The Lahu believe in spirits, in the soul and in a God. Missionary work by Christians, and also by Buddhists, means that many Lahu villages are now ostensibly Christian or Buddhist. It is estimated for example, that one-third of all Lahu live within Christian com-

A THAI HILLTRIBE CLOTHING PRIMER

Karen are among the best and most prolific of hilltribe weavers. Their traditional striped warp ikat, dyed in soft hues, is characteristically inter-sewn with job's seeds. Girls wear creamy white smocks with red stitching, whilst women wear coloured smocks and strings of beads. Their tunics are made up of two lengths of cloth, worn vertically, sewn together down the centre and sides, leaving a hole for the neck and the arms.

Hmong (Meo) produce exquisite embroidery made up of appliquéd layers of fabric of geometric shapes worn by men, women and children. Some of the patternwork on their pleated skirts is achieved by batik (the only hilltribe to do this). Jackets are of black velvet or satinized cotton, with embroidered lapels. They wear black or white leggings and sashes to hold up their skirts. Hand weaving is a dying art among the Hmong.

Lahu (Mussur) groups traditionally wore a diverse array of clothing. All embroider, but many have now abandoned the use of traditional dress. Another common feature is the shoulder bag – primarily red in the case of the Lahu Nyi (the 'Red' Lahu), black among the Lahu Sheh Leh (and often tassled), black with patchwork for the Lahu Na, and often striped in the case of the Lahu Shi.

Mien (Yao) embroidery is distinguished by cross-stitching on indigo fabric, worn as baggy trousers and turbans. They are one of the easiest of the hilltribes to identify because of their distinctive red-collared jackets. Virtually none of the cloth is hand woven – it is bought and then sometimes re-dyed before being decorated.

Akha are most easily distinguished by their elaborate head-dresses, made up of silver beads, coins and buttons. Akha cloth is limited to plain weave, dyed with indigo (after weaving) – and still often made from home-grown cotton. This is then decorated with embroidery, shells, buttons, silver, and seeds. Akha patchwork is highly intricate work involving the assembly of tiny pieces of cloth.

Lisu wear very brightly coloured clothing and (at festivals) lots of jewellery. Particularly notable are the green and blue kaftans with red sleeves, worn with baggy Chinese trousers and black turbans. Lisu weaving has virtually died out.

munities. But this does not mean that they have rejected their traditional beliefs: they have adopted new religions while at the same time maintaining their animistic ones.

Material culture

Because each Lahu group has distinct clothing and ornamentation, it is difficult to characterize a 'general' dress for the tribe as a whole. To simplify, Lahu dress is predominantly black or blue with border designs of embroidery or appliqué. Some wear short jackets and sarongs, others wear longer jackets and leggings. Most of their cloth is now bought and machine-made; traditionally it would have been hand-woven. The jackets are held together with large, often elaborate, silver buckles. All Lahu make caps for their children and the cloth shoulder bag is also a characteristic Lahu accessory.

Ornamentation is similarly varied. The Lahu Nyi women wear wide silver bracelets, neck rings and earrings. The Lahu Sheh Leh wear large numbers of small white beads around their necks and silver bracelets. The Lahu Na wear engraved and moulded silver bracelets, and on special occasions heavy silver chains, bells and pendants. The Lahu Shi wear red and white beads around their necks and heavy silver earrings.

The Mien (or Yao)

Origins

The Mien or Yao, are unique among the hilltribes in that they have a tradition of writing based on Chinese characters. Mien legend has it that they came from 'across the sea' during the 14th century, although it is generally thought that their roots are in S China where they originated about 2,000 years ago. They first migrated into Thailand from Laos in the middle of the 19th century, and they currently number about 36,000, mostly in the provinces of Chiang Rai and Nan, close to the Laotian border.

Economy and society

The Mien village is not enclosed and is usually found on sloping ground. The houses are large, wooden affairs, as they need to accommodate an extended family of sometimes 20 or more members. They are built on the ground, not on stilts, and have 1 large living area and 4 or more bedrooms. As with other tribes, the construction of the house must be undertaken carefully. The house needs to be orientated appropriately, so that the spirits are not disturbed, and the ancestral altar installed on an auspicious day.

The Mien combine 2 religious beliefs: on the one hand they recognize and pay their dues to spirits and ancestors (informing them of family developments), on the other, they follow Taoism as it was practiced in China in the 13th and 14th centuries. The Taoist rituals are expensive, and the Mien appear to spend a great deal of their lives struggling to save enough money to afford the various ceremonies, such as weddings, merit-making and death ceremonies. The Mien economy is based upon the shifting cultivation of dry rice, corn, and small quantities of opium poppy.

Material culture

The Mien women dress distinctively, with black turbans and red-ruffed tunics, making them easy to distinguish from the other hilltribes. All their clothes are made of black or indigo-dyed homespun cotton, which is then embroidered using distinctive cross-stitching. Their trousers are the most elaborate garments. Unusually, they sew from the back of the cloth and cannot see the pattern they are making. The children wear embroidered caps with red pompoms on the top and by the ears. The men's dress is a simple indigo-dyed jacket and trousers, with little embroidery.

The Akha (or Kaw)

Origins

The Akha, or Kaw, number about 33,000 in Thailand and are found in a relatively small area of the north near Chiang Rai. They have their origins in Yunnan, southern China, and from there spread into Burma (where there are nearly 200,000), and rather later into Thailand. The first Akha village was not established in Thailand until the very beginning of the 20th century. They prefer to live along ridges, at about 1000m.

Economy and society

The Akha are shifting cultivators, growing primarily dry rice on mountainsides but also a wide variety of vegetables. The cultivation of rice is bound up with myths and rituals: the rice plant is regarded as a sentient being, and the selection of the swidden, its clearance, the planting of the rice seed, the care of the growing plants, and finally the harvest of the rice, must all be done according to the Akha Way. Any offence to the rice soul must be rectified by ceremonies.

Akha villages are identified by their gates, a village swing and high-roofed houses on posts. They have no word for religion but believe in the 'Akha Way'. They are able to recite the names of all their male ancestors (60 names or more) and they keep an ancestral altar in their homes, at which food is offered up at important times in the year such as New Year, during the village swing ceremony, and after the rice harvest.

At the upper and lower ends of the village are gates which are renewed every year. Visitors should walk through them in order to rid themselves of the spirit of the jungle. The gates are sacred, and must not be defiled. Visitors must not touch the gates and should avoid going through them if they do not intend to enter a house in the village. A pair of wooden male and female carved figures are placed inside the entrance to signify that this is the realm of human beings. The two most important Akha festivals are the 4-day Swinging Ceremony celebrated during Aug, and New Year when festivities also extend over 4 days.

Material culture

Akha clothing is made of homespun blue-black cloth, which is appliquéd for decoration. Particularly characteristic of the Akha is their head-dress, which is adorned with jewellery. The basic clothing of an Akha woman is a head-dress, a jacket, a short skirt worn on their hips, with a sash and leggings worn from the ankle to below the knee. They wear their jewellery as an integral part of their clothing, mostly sewn to their head-dresses. Girls wear similar clothing to the women, except that they sport caps rather than the elaborate head-dress of the mature women. The change from girl's clothes to women's clothes occurs through 4 stages during adolescence. Unmarried girls can be identified by the small gourds tied to their waist and head-dress.

Men's clothing is much less elaborate. They wear loose-fitting Chinese-style black pants, and a black jacket which may be embroidered. Both men and women use cloth shoulder bags.

Today the Akha are finding it increasingly difficult to follow the 'Akha Way'. Their complex rituals set them apart from both the lowland Thais and from the other hilltribes. There is no land, no game, and the modern world has little use or time for their ways. The conflicts and pressures which the Akha currently face, and their inability to reconcile the old with the new, is claimed by some to explain why the incidence of opium addiction among the Akha is so high.

The Lisu (or Lisaw)

Origins

The Lisu number some 25,000 in Thailand, and live in the mountainous region NW of Chiang Mai. They probably originated in China, at the headwaters of the Salween River, and did not begin to settle in Thailand until the beginning of the 20th century.

THE MLABRI: THE SPIRITS OF THE YELLOW LEAVES

The elusive Mlabri 'tribe' represent one of the few remaining groups of hunter gatherers in Southeast Asia. They are also known as the Phi Tong Luang or 'Spirits of the Yellow Leaves' because when their shelters of rattan and banana leaves turn yellow they take this as a sign from the spirits that it is time to move on. The destruction of Thailand's forests, even in this relatively inaccessible corner of the Kingdom, means that the Mlabri have been forced to lead more sedentary lives, turning to settled agriculture in place of hunting and gathering. There are probably only a hundred Mlabri living in Thailand today – in 1974, the ethnographer Gordon Young estimated that the population was a mere 50. Currently, it is thought that there are 138 Mlabri living in Thailand.

Traditionally the Mlabri hunted using spears, but when stalking larger game, rather than throwing the weapon, they would brace it against the ground and allow the charging animal to impale itself on the point. In this way, the Mlabri were able to kill the great saladang wild buffalo (*Bos gaurus*), as well as bears and tigers. Smaller game was more common however, and this was supplemented with tubers, nuts, honey and other forest products to provide a balanced diet. Many of the Mlabri's traditions are already on the verge of extinction. Hunting and gathering is no longer a tenable livelihood in Thailand's denuded forests, the work of American missionaries has led to their conversion to Christianity, and disease and inter-marriage with other tribes is reducing their number. Perhaps this is no bad thing: as recently as the 1980s, a Mlabri was displayed in a cage in a Bangkok department store. Today, the problem is that the few Mlabri still alive, finding their forests impoverished, have been forced to become cheap labourers for groups such as the Hmong.

Economy and society

The Lisu grow rice and vegetables for subsistence and opium for sale. Rice is grown at lower altitudes and the opium poppy at over 1500m. Villages are located so that the inhabitants can maintain some independence from the Thai authorities. At the same time they need to be relatively close to a market so that they can trade.

Lisu houses may be built either on the ground or raised above it: the former are more popular at higher altitudes as they are said to be warmer. The floors and walls are made from wood and bamboo, and the roof is thatched. The house is divided into a bedroom, a large living area, and also contains a guest platform. Within each house there will also be a fireplace and an ancestral altar.

Each village has a 'village guardian spirit shrine' which is located above the village, in a roofed pavilion which women are forbidden to enter. Local disputes are settled by a headman, and kinship is based upon patrilineal clans. As well as the village guardian, the Lisu worship Wu Sa, the creator, and a multitude of spirits of the forest, ancestors, trees, the sun, moon, and everyday objects. Coupled with this, the Lisu fear possession by weretigers (*phi pheu*) and vampires (*phu seu*).

Material culture

Lisu clothing is some of the most brightly coloured, and most distinctive, of all the hilltribes. They make up their clothes from machine-made cloth. The women wear long tunics – often bright blue, with red sleeves and pattern-work around the yoke – black knee-length pants and red leggings. A wide black sash is wound tightly round the waist. Looped around this at the back is a pair

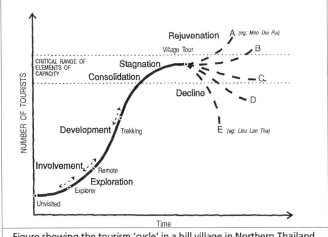

Figure showing the tourism 'cycle' in a hill village in Northern Thailand.
Adapted from: Dearden, Philip (1991)

of tassels consisting of many tightly woven threads, with pompoms attached to the ends (sometimes as many as 500 strands in a pair of tassels). Turbans, again with coloured tassels attached, are worn for special occasions. The man's attire is simpler; a black jacket, blue or green trousers and black leggings.

The most important ceremony is New Year (celebrated on the same day as the Chinese), when the villagers dress up in all their finery and partake in a series of rituals. At this time, the women wear copious amounts of silver jewellery: tunics with rows of silver buttons sewn onto them, and abundant heavy necklaces.

Seeing the hilltribes and organizing a trek

There are a variety of ways to see the hilltribes, ranging from an easy visit of a single day, to a strenuous trek of a week. Although many will tell you that it is not possible to experience the 'real thing' unless you opt for the most exhausting and adventurous programme on offer,

every encounter between a foreigner and a hilltribe community is artificial. As the Heisenberg principle has it, just by being there a visitor has a profound affect.

If you do not want to live rough, to spend 5 days tramping around the forests, or to spend your money on visiting the hilltribes, then opt for a **half day or day trip** by taxi, bus or hired motorcycle. The major towns of the North all have hilltribe communities within easy reach. On arrival you will probably be hounded by handicraft salespeople, you may well have to pay for any photographs that you take, but at least you will get a taste of a hilltribe village and their traditional costumes. You can also leave smug with the knowledge that you have not contributed much to the process of cultural erosion.

Longer trips can either take the form of a 2 or 3 day excursion by bus, raft, boat and foot, or a trek of up to a week or more. The **excursions** are usually more comfortable, more highly organized, and do not venture far into the wilds of the

VISITING THE HILLTRIBES: HOUSE RULES

Etiquette and customs vary between the hilltribes. However, the following are general rules of good behaviour that should be adhered to whenever possible.

1. Dress modestly and avoid undressing/changing in public.
2. Ask permission before photographing anyone (old people and pregnant women often object to having their photograph taken). Be aware that hill people are unlikely to pose out of the kindness of their hearts – don't begrudge them the money; for many, tourism is their livelihood.
3. Ask permission before entering a house.
4. Do not touch or photograph village shrines.
5. Do not smoke opium.
6. Avoid sitting or stepping on door sills.
7. Avoid excessive displays of wealth and be sensitive when giving gifts (for children, pens are better than sweets).
8. Avoid introducing Western medicines.

North. They are easily booked through one of the many companies in Chiang Mai, Chiang Rai, Mae Hong Son and the other trekking towns of the region. **Trekking** into the hills is undoubtedly the best way to see the hilltribes however. To keep the adventure of trekking alive (or perhaps, the myth of adventure) most companies now promote 'non-touristic' trekking – if that is not a contradiction in terms. They guarantee a trek will not meet another trekking party. It is most important to try and get a knowledgeable guide who speaks good English as well as the language(s) of the tribe(s) that are to be visited. He is your link with the hilltribes: he will warn you what not to do, tell you of their customs, rituals, economy and religion, and ensure your safety. Ask other tourists who have recently returned from treks about their experiences: a personal recommendation is hard to beat and they will also have the most up-to-date information. Sometimes an even better alternative is to hire a **private guide** although this is obviously more expensive. A final way to see the people of the hills is simply to **set off on your own** either on foot or motorbike. This can be very rewarding – and is becoming increasingly popular – but it does have its risks: parts of the

North are still fairly lawless and every year there are reports of hold-ups, even murders, of tourists. Remember, it's a jungle out there: take care preparing your trip and let someone know your schedule and itinerary. It is also easy to get lost, and unless you go prepared with the appropriate books, maps and other information it is unlikely that you will gain much of an insight into hilltribe life. Most hilltribe villages will offer a place to sleep – usually in the headman's house; expect to pay about ฿50. If you are intending to venture out on your own, it is a good idea to visit the Hilltribe Research Center at Chiang Mai University before you leave, and to get a map of the hilltribe areas (available from *D.K. Books*, 234 Tha Phae Rd, Chiang Mai).

Practicalities of trekking

When to trek The best time to trek is during the cool, dry season between Oct and Feb. In Mar and Apr, although it is still dry, temperatures can be uncomfortably high and the vegetation is parched. During the wet season paths are muddy and walking can be difficult.

What to take Leave valuables behind in a bank safe deposit box. **NB:** Trekkers who leave their credit cards for

TREKKING AREAS OF THE NORTH		
Centres	**Trekking areas**	**Tribes**
Around Chiang Mai	North, west and south-west of the city. Rafting on the Mae Tang.	Lisu, Akha, Karen, Lahu, Hmong and Shan.
Around Chiang Rai	Mainly along or near the Kok River and to the north in the vicinity of the Golden Triangle. Rafting on the Kok River.	Karen, Lisu, Akha, Hmong, Yao and Lahu.
Around Mae Hong Son	Most treks either run south to Mae Sariang or north and east to Pai. Rafting on the Pai River.	Karen, Lisu, Shan, Kaya, Hmong, Red Lahu and 'long-necked Karen' – more properly known as Padong, as well as KMT villages.
Eastern Highlands	West of Nan	Hmong, Karen, Yao, Akha, Lahu and the Mlabri or Yellow Leaves people.

safekeeping in their guesthouses have sometimes found that a large bill awaits them on their return home. A safe deposit box hired at a bank is the safest way to leave your valuables.

Choosing a trekking company In Chiang Mai there are over 100 trekking companies, and many more in other trekking centres of the North. Check that the company is registered with the police and that they notify the Tourist Police before departure (as they are required to do). Shop around to get an idea of prices and try to get a personal recommendation from another tourist. Note that the best guides may move between companies or work for more than one.

Trekking companies should advise on what to take and many provide rucksacks, sleeping bags, first aid kits and food. However the following is a check list of items that might be useful:

● good walking shoes

● bed sheet (blanket/sleeping bag in the cold season Nov-Feb)

● raincoat (July-Oct)

● insect repellent

● toiletries (soap, toothpaste, toilet paper)

● small first aid kit (including antiseptic, plasters, diarrhoea pills, salt tablets)

● sun protection (sun cream/sun hat)

● photocopy of passport if venturing into border area.

Health precautions
By living in hilltribe villages, even if for only a few days, the health hazard is amplified significantly. Innoculation against hepatitis (gamma globulin) and protection against malaria are both strongly recommended. Particular dietary care should be exercised: do not drink unboiled or untreated water, and avoid uncooked vegetables. Although the hilltribe population may look healthy, remember that the incidence of parasitic infection in most communities is not far off 100%.

The cost of a trek
It does not take long to work out the going price for a trek – just ask around. For a basic walking trek, costs are ฿250-500/day, the cheaper end of the range relating to trekking companies that specialize in the backpacking market; if rafting and elephant rides are also included, the cost rises to ฿500-1,000/day.

Opium smoking
For some, one of the attractions of trekking is the chance to smoke opium. It

should be remembered that opium smoking as well as opium cultivation are illegal in Thailand. It is also not unusual for first-time users to experience adverse physical and psychological side-effects. **NB:** police regularly stop and search tourists who are motorcycle trekking. Be careful not to carry any illicit substances.

Trekking areas

The main trekking centres are Chiang Mai, Chiang Rai and Mae Hong Son. There are also companies in Mae Sot, Mae Sariang, Pai, Fang, Tha Ton, Chiang Saen, Sop Ruak, Mae Sai and Nan, and also in a handful of other places.

Books

McKinnon, John and Vienne, Bernard (1989) *Hill tribes today: problems in change*, White-Lotus/Orstom: Bangkok. Lewis, Paul and Lewis, Elaine (1984) *Peoples of the Golden Triangle: six tribes in Thailand*, Thames and Hudson: London. Tapp, Nicholas (1986) *The Hmong of Thailand: opium people of the Golden Triangle*, report No. 4, Anti-slavery Society: London. Tapp, Nicholas (1989) *Sovereignty and rebellion: the White Hmong of Northern Thailand*, Oxford University Press: Singapore. Ada Guntamala and Kornvika Puapratum (1992) *Trekking through Northern Thailand*, Silkworm Books: Chiang Mai. **Maps** *Guide Map of Chiang Rai*, Bangkok Guides: Bangkok. *The Mae Kok River*, Chang Puak: Bangkok; the Thai government also publishes 1:250,000 topographic sheet maps of every province, especially useful if venturing out without a guide.

THE NORTHEASTERN REGION

CONTENTS

MAPS

The Northeastern region of Thailand, also known as the Isan region, is a massive sandstone plateau that undulates gently at between 100m and 200m above sea-level. It covers 170,000 sq km, or one third of the total land area of the Kingdom of Thailand and also supports about a third of the total population, some 20 million people. Considering its size, the Northeast is surprisingly coherent from a geographical point of view: to the north and east it is bordered by the Mekong River which forms the boundary between Thailand and Laos; and to the South and West by two ranges of mountains – the Phnom Dangrek and Phetchabun hills respectively.

These geographical features, and in particular the mountains to the S and W, have effectively isolated the Northeast from the rest of the country. This is clearly reflected in the poem *Nirat Nongkhai* written during a military campaign of the 1870s, in which it took two months, 170 elephants, 500 oxen and many horses to proceed up the forested trail from Bangkok to Korat (Nakhon Ratchasima), on the SW edge of the region. With his men dying all around him from malaria and food poisoning, and finding it difficult to procure supplies, the army's commander managed to miss the vital battle and returned to Bangkok having never confronted the enemy.

From books, and from talking to people in Bangkok, it is easy to reach the conclusion that the Isan region has always been a marginal area. The environment is the harshest of anywhere in Thailand with sparse and intermittent rainfall, and the soils are some of the poorest in all Southeast Asia. W.A. Graham, a European visitor to Isan at the beginning of the 20th century wrote that the Northeast was, in his opinion, "one of the most miserable [regions] imaginable".

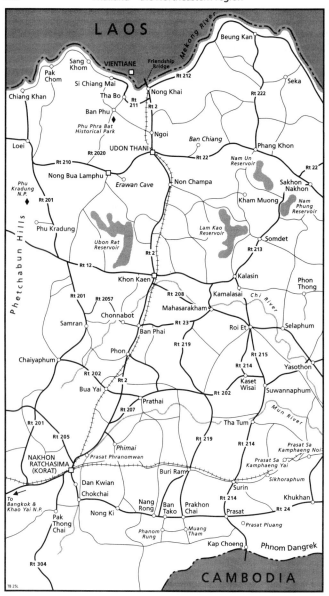

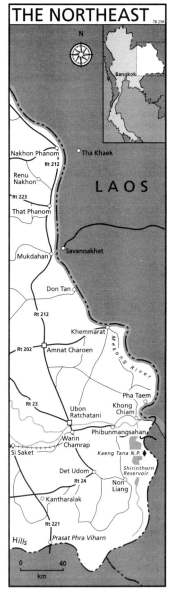

THE NORTHEAST

TB 25A

N

Bangkok

LAOS

Nakhon Phanom
Rt 212
Tha Khaek

Renu
Nakhon
Rt 223
That Phanom

Savannakhet

Mukdahan

Don Tan

Rt 212

Khemmarat
Rt 202
Amnat Charoen

Pha Taem
Rt 23
Ubon
Ratchatani
Khong
Chiam
Phibunmangsahan
Warin
Chamrap
Si Saket
Kaeng Tana N.P.

Shirinthorn
Reservoir

Det Udom
Rt 24
Non
Liang

Kanthalarak

Rt 221

Hills

Prasat Phra Viharn

Mekong River

0   40
km

Warrington-Smyth at the end of the 19th century expressed similar sentiments when he wrote on leaving the region that he and his companions were "thankful to wipe the whole Khorat plateau from our memories". The inhabitants of the area are distinct from the rest of the country. They are Lao rather than Thai, and are culturally more closely affiliated with the people of Laos. They speak a dialect of Thai, Isan or Lao, dress differently, and eat different food. This distinctiveness, coupled with the poverty of the area, played a part in making the Northeast one of the strongholds of the Communist Party of Thailand. Francis Cripps, who worked as a school teacher in Mahasarakham, writes:

"'Mahasarakham?' they asked. 'Where is that?...Oh! In the northeast?' They looked at me with pity. Communist infiltrators, drought, hard, unpalatable glutinous rice – these were the hazards of life on the neglected...north-eastern plateau" (1965:15).

Most of the population of the Northeast are farmers. They grow glutinous or 'sticky' rice (*khaaw niaw*) to meet their subsistence needs, and increasingly an assortment of upland cash crops such as cassava and kenaf (an inferior jute substitute) to earn an income. They have also traditionally migrated to Bangkok during the dry season to find work to boost their meagre incomes. Today, many thousands make the trip to the capital to work as tuk-tuk drivers, poultry slaughterers, and servants. Some villages become so depopulated that they seem to consist of only the very old and the very young. Despite this migration, average incomes are only a third of those in other parts of Thailand, and the average wage for an agricultural labourer performing a back-breaking task such as transplanting rice is only ฿50/day; in Bangkok the official minimum wage is now ฿125/day.

With the heat, the poverty, the perceived threat of Communism, and the general backwardness of the Northeast, most other Thais steer well clear of the area. But, historically, the Khorat Plateau has played a very important role in the development not just of Thailand, but arguably of the whole of Southeast Asia. At Ban Chiang, a village to the E of Udon Thani, some of the world's earliest evidence of agriculture has been uncovered, dating back 5,000-7,000 years (see page 333). Later, the Khorat Plateau formed an integral part of the magnificent Khmer Empire based at Angkor which flourished during the 12th-13th centuries. The still impressive ruins at Phimai, Phanom Rung, and Muang Tham among other sites clearly show that the Northeast has not always been devoid of 'civilized' life, whatever those in Bangkok might like to think.

Very few visitors to Thailand (less than 1%) take the trouble to visit the Northeast, and those that do invariably merely visit Korat and the Khmer town of Phimai. This is understandable, in that tourist facilities are the least developed of any region in the country. But the people of the Khorat Plateau do have a charm lacking in the rest of Thailand. They are more laid back, more passive, more understanding. Even the countryside, so harsh at the end of the dry season in Apr and May when the heat is like a furnace, has its attractions: the neat mini-valleys with their chequer boards of paddy fields, the few remaining stands of dry dipterocarp savanna forest,

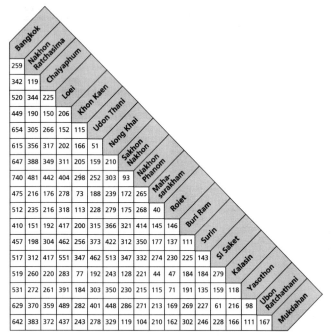

	Bangkok	Nakhon Ratchasima	Chaiyaphum	Loei	Khon Kaen	Udon Thani	Nong Khai	Sakhon Nakhon	Nakhon Phanom	Maha-sarakham	Roiet	Buri Ram	Surin	Si Saket	Kalasin	Yasothon	Ubon Ratchathani
Nakhon Ratchasima	259																
Chaiyaphum	342	119															
Loei	520	344	225														
Khon Kaen	449	190	150	206													
Udon Thani	654	305	266	152	115												
Nong Khai	615	356	317	202	166	51											
Sakhon Nakhon	647	388	349	311	205	159	210										
Nakhon Phanom	740	481	442	404	298	252	303	93									
Maha-sarakham	475	216	176	278	73	188	239	172	265								
Roiet	512	235	216	318	113	228	279	175	268	40							
Buri Ram	410	151	192	417	200	315	366	321	414	145	146						
Surin	457	198	304	462	256	373	422	312	350	177	137	111					
Si Saket	517	312	417	551	347	462	513	347	332	274	230	225	143				
Kalasin	519	260	220	283	77	192	243	128	221	44	47	184	184	279			
Yasothon	531	272	261	391	184	303	350	230	215	115	71	191	135	159	118		
Ubon Ratchathani	629	370	359	489	282	401	448	286	271	213	169	269	227	61	216	98	
Mukdahan	642	383	372	437	243	278	329	119	104	210	162	302	246	228	166	111	167

Northeast Thailand: Distances by road between provincial capitals (Km)

the 1500m mountain Phu Kradung, the Mekong River and the area's tradition of fine cotton and silk weaving.

The region consists of 19 provinces, the two newest being created in 1993 when two districts were upgraded to provincial status: Amnat Charoen (previously part of Ubon Ratchathani) and Nong Bua Lamphu (previously part of Udon Thani). Travelling around the Northeast is relatively easy. During the Vietnam War the Thai government, with financial support from the US, built an impressive network of roads, in an attempt to keep the resurgence of Communism at bay. The opening of the Friendship Bridge in early 1994, the first bridge across the Mekong, linking Nong Khai in the Northeast with Viantiane, the capital of Laos, may presage greater tourist activity in this part of the country (and greater business activity). As Laos tentatively opens its doors to tourists, so the attraction of using the Northeast as a stepping stone to Laos will increase. Already international hotel chains have opened hotels in Nong Khai.

The minor Khmer sites of the Northeast

Prasat Khao Noi

A small prasat in Prachinburi province, recently restored by the Fine Arts Department. The prasat consists of three prangs of which the central example has been extensively restored. The carving here is very early - probably dating from the middle of the 7th century (although the central prang is 11th century). The lintels have been removed and placed in the Prachinburi Museum.

Prasat Phum Phen

Situated in the Sangkha District of Surin Province, it is relatively well preserved for a prasat that dates from the 7th century, making it one of the oldest in Thailand. The square floor plan indicates that the prasat was probably built on to an earlier structure. Red paint has been found on some of the walls, indicating that the interior was probably painted. The finest lintels discovered here are on show at the National Museum in Bangkok.

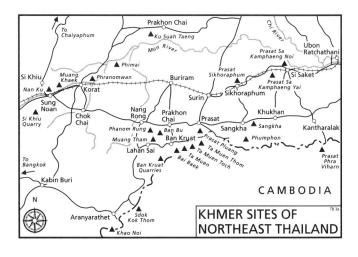

KHMER SITES OF NORTHEAST THAILAND

Prasat Nern Kuu and Prasat Muang Khaek

Both these shrines are located in Song Nern District, Nakhon Ratchasima Province, 30km to the W of Korat City. Both were built in the 10th century and are thought to have been religious centres linked to the ancient city of Khorakhapura. Prasat Nern Kuu consists of a small square stella enclosed within a wall. Prasat Muang Khaek was probably built around 940 AD. The main sandstone prang stands on a high brick base and is stylistically similar to the temple of the Chola period in India.

Prasat Sadok Kok Thom

Located 33km N of Aranyaprathet in Prachin Buri Province, it dates from the 11th century reign of Udayadityavarman and like other Khmer sites was 'caught up' in the Cambodian civil war. It only became open to Thai visitors in 1990. One gopura is in good condition, and there is also a collapsed prang and enclosing walls. An inscription found here has been highly important in reconstructing the life of Jayavarman II.

Prasat Narai Jeng Weng

This small prasat is to be found in Muang District, Sakhon Nakhon Province. Over the entrance to the porch on the E side is a carving of Indra riding Airavata.

Prasat Yai He Nga

Dates from the 12th century and is situated in Sangkhla District, Surin Province. Unusually, it consists of two prangs (three would be usual), with the main prang, for whatever reason, left unbuilt. It is in use by Buddhist monks.

Prang Ku Suan Taeng

This comprises three prangs built during the 12th century and located in the Puthai Song District of Buriram Province. The corbelled ceiling within the main, central prang is still in an excellent state of repair.

Prasat Ta Muan Toch

Dates from the reign of Jayavarman VII and is situated in Ta Muan District, Surin Province. An inscription indicates that this prasat was built as a religious edifice attached to a hospital. The hospital was one of 102 built on Jayavarman VII's orders. Other inscriptions from the site list the nurses and doctors employed here and some of the drugs that they dispensed.

Prasat Ta Muan and Prasat Ban Bu

These were both built under the orders of Jayavarman VII as resting places for travellers making the journey between Phimai and Angkor. The buildings at Ta Muan are better preserved that at Ban Bu.

Other Khmer sites noted in individual entries: Prasat Phranomwan, Prasat Pluang, Prasat Phra Viharn, Prasat Na Kamphaeng Noi, Prasat Na Kamphaeng Yai, Prasat Sikhoraphum, Phnom Rung, Muang Tam, Phimai.

NOTE: the above is only intended as a guide for those who wish to see some of the sites which are infrequently visited. The information has been gleaned mainly from secondary sources.

PRINCIPAL SOURCE: most of the information above is a summary condensed from Smitthi Siribhadra and Elizabeth Moore's *Palaces of the gods: Khmer art and architecture in Thailand*, River Books: Bangkok.

NAKHON RATCHASIMA (KORAT)

Most visitors to the Northeastern region travel only as far as Nakhon Ratchasima, or Korat, 256 km from Bangkok. This is the largest town in the area and the main base for visiting the magnificent Khmer monuments of Phimai, Phanom Rung and Muang Tham. From Korat, Route 226 runs eastwards towards Ubon Ratchathani (311 km), and Route 2 northwards to Khon Kaen (189 km) and

Nong Khai (another 172 km).

Nakhon Ratchasima (Korat)

The Friendship Highway (Route 2), built with American Aid during the Vietnam War, links Saraburi with Nakhon Ratchasima or Korat, the provincial capital of the province of the same name. Korat is an important and relatively prosperous commercial centre with more than its fair share of Thai yuppies, and is (possibly) the largest town in the Northeast. People say that it is not really an Isan town at all, located as it is on the borders between the Central Plains and the Khorat Plateau. During the Vietnamese War, Korat was an important US airbase and warplanes set out to bomb the routes that supplied the Communist Vietcong fighting in South Vietnam.

The city was established when the older settlements of Sema and Khorakpura were merged under King Narai in the 17th century. Today, the older part of the town lies to the W while the newer section is within the moat, to the E. Korat is usually only considered as a convenient jumping-off point for visits to the Khmer ruins of Phimai, Phnom Rung and Muang Tham. However, it does have some sights of interest.

Places of interest

The remains of the town walls, and the moat that still embraces the city, date from the 8th-10th centuries. More obvious are the town gates which have been rebuilt and make useful points of reference while exploring this large and rapidly expanding city. **Mahawirawong Museum**, in the grounds of Wat Sutchinda just outside the city moat, on Rachdamnern Road, houses a small collection of Khmer art poorly displayed and labelled. Admission: ฿10. Open: 0900-1600 Wed-Sun. The **Thao Suranari Shrine** is in the centre of town, by the Chumphon Gate. This bronze monument erected in 1934 commemorates the revered wife of a provincial governor – popularly known as Khunying Mo – who in 1826 saved the town from an invading Lao army. As a result, she has become something of a regional heroine; local people come to pay their respects, wrap the statue in ribbons and rub gold leaf onto elephant statues given as gifts for wishes granted. Most evenings, traditional Isan (Northeastern) folk songs are performed at the shrine and in late March/early April a 10 daylong festival honours the heroine (see festivals).

Wat Sala Loi, just outside the NE corner of the city moat, is a modern wat, with an ubosoth resembling a Chinese junk. It was built in 1973 and is meant to symbolize a boat taking the faithful to nirvana. It is one of the few modern wats with any originality of design in Thailand: the great majority repeat the same visual themes. Getting there: walk or take bus No. 5.

A new **night market** is to be found on Manat Road, between Chumphon and Mahatthai roads (set up jointly by the Governor, the city authorities, the police and the TAT). There are lots of foodstalls here, as well as some clothes and handicraft stalls. The market is open every day from 1800. The **general market** is opposite Wat Sakae, on Suranari Road.

Excursions

Phimai See page 303. Getting there: regular departures from the terminal off Suranari Rd, ฿14 (1½ hr). The last bus from Phimai back to Korat leaves at 1800.

Prasat Phranomwan is a smaller, inferior version of Phimai which can be found about a third of the way between Korat and Phimai next to a new monastery. This structure began life as a Hindu temple, and was only later converted for use as a Buddhist wat. The central prang and adjoining pavilion are enclosed within a galleried wall. When it was built is not certain: the carving on the lintels is early 11th century in style, yet the

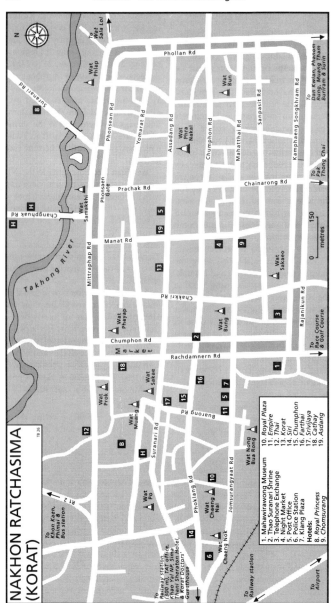

NAKHON RATCHASIMA (KORAT)

To Non Sung station
(30km), TAT office,
Khao Yai NP, Sima
Thani Sheraton Hotel,
& Korat Doctor's
Guesthouse

To
Khon Kaen,
Phimai &
Bus station
Rt 2

To Railway station

To
Airport

To
Dan Kwian, Phanom
Rung, Muang Tham
Buriram & Surin

To
Pak
Thong Chai

To
Race Course
& Golf Course

To
Wat
Sala Loi

Roads:
Suranari Rd
Phollan Rd
Phonsean Rd
Yomarat Rd
Assadang Rd
Chumphon Rd
Sanpasit Rd
Kamphaeng Songkhram Rd
Mahatthai Rd
Changphuak Rd
Prachak Rd
Chainarong Rd
Mittraphap Rd
Manat Rd
Chakkri Rd
Rajanikun Rd
Chumphon Rd
Rachdamnern Rd
Buarong Rd
Suranari Rd
Phoklang Rd
Jomsurangyaat Rd
Chaeng Nok

Wats:
Wat Phlap
Wat Bun
Wat Phra Nakai
Wat Samakkhi
Wat Phayap
Wat Sakaeo
Wat Bung
Wat Prok
Wat Sakae
Wat Muang
Wat Po
Wat Cheang Nai
Wat Nong Bua Rong

Phonsaen Gate

Market

metres
0   150

Hotels:
8. Royal Princess
9. Chomsurang
10. Royal Plaza
11. Empire
12. Thai
13. Korat
14. Siri
15. Chumphon
16. Farthai
17. Srivijaya
18. Galaxy
19. Asdang

1. Mahawirawong Museum
2. Thao Suranari Shrine
3. Telephone Exchange
4. Night Market
5. Post Office
6. Police Station
7. Klang Plaza

inscriptions refer to the Khmer King Yasovarman who ruled in 889. There are also art historians who believe that it was built largely during the early 10th century by another Cambodian king, Suryavarman I. The site is undergoing limited renovation, but the quality and the quantity of the carving does not begin to compare with either Phimai or Phanom Rung. Most of the lintels have been removed to museums; only the one over the N entrance to the main sanctuary remains. Buddhas (added at a later date) occupy the dilapidated niches. Originally, a wide moat surrounded the shrine, and to the E there is still a large baray or reservoir – both of which had cosmological significance in creating a model of the Hindu universe. **Getting there:** direct buses leave from Phonsaen Gate at 0700, 1000 and 1200 (฿5). Buses running towards Phimai pass the turn-off for Phranomwan; ask to be let off at Ban Saen Muang and either walk the 4 km to the monument or catch one of the irregular local songthaews. If driving, note that it is not yet signposted from Korat, although there is a sign if driving from the opposite direction (ie from Phimai). About 15 km from Korat driving N on Route 2, after crossing the flyover over the railway line and not far past the Korat A & M Institute of Technology, turn right. Drive 4 km through the villages of Saen Muang and Nong Bua to the site.

Ban Prasat is a prehistoric site dating back about 5,000 years. The dig has been converted into an open air museum, much like Ban Chiang outside Udon Thani (see page 334). Indeed, there seem to be close cultural links between Ban Prasat and Ban Chiang. Similar high quality, red slipped and burnished trumpet rimmed pots have been discovered at both sites. Rice was eaten as the subsistence crop, domestic animals raised, and the technology of bronze casting understood. The unearthing of sea shell ornaments also indicates communication with the coast. The examination of skeletons unearthed at the site reveals a high infant mortality rate, and a relatively short lifespan – only 34-36 years. **Getting there:** by bus towards Phimai. The site is 2 km off the main road and 45 km from Korat city, on the left-hand side, before the turning for Phimai. Ask for Ban Prasat.

Phanom Rung lies 112 km SE of Korat, 64 km S of Buri Ram, and is the finest Khmer temple in Thailand – giving a hint of what the less accessible Angkor Wat in Cambodia must be like. Indeed, it is thought to have been a stopping-off point on the road from Angkor to Phimai. Similar in layout to Phimai, both monuments are believed to have been the prototype for Angkor Wat.

Phanom Rung was built in sandstone and laterite over a period of 200 years between the 10th and early 13th centuries. It stands majestically at the top of Rainbow Hill, an inactive volcano overlooking the Thai-Cambodian border. The name Phanom Rung means 'Large Hill'. It was built on a grand scale – the approach is along a 160m avenue of pink sandstone pillars (*nang riang*). A monumental staircase on 5 levels is reached via a 5-headed naga bridge. Some of the nagas are particularly finely carved and well preserved and this 'bridge' is one of Thailand's Khmer treasures. The style indicates a date of the 12th century and their detail is superb: crowned heads studded with jewels, carefully carved scales and backbones, and magnificent rearing bodies. The naga bridge represented a symbolic division between the worlds of mortals and gods. From here the pilgrim climbed upwards to the sanctuary itself, a divine place of beauty and power.

Inscriptions found at Phanom Rung indicate that this area was controlled by a king who ruled autonomously from Angkor – King Narendraditya. The King was a relative of King Suryavarman II (1112-1152) who occupied the throne at Angkor. Suryavarman used relatives such as Narendraditya to extend his influences into Northeast Thailand. After bringing the area under his control, it seems that Narendraditya retired from the cut and thrust of kingship to become an ascetic. Or at least that is what the inscriptions would have us to believe. The King's son Hiranya took his place on the throne.

The central Hindu sanctuary (the **Prasat Phanom Rung**) is of typical Khmer design, being symmetrical, of cruciform plan, with 4 gopuras leading to antechambers. It was probably built between 1050 and 1150, most likely by the Khmer King Suryavarman II. The outstanding stone carvings on the central prang illustrate scenes from the Ramayana, the Puranas and the Mahabharata. The Reclining Vishnu Lintel on the main, E porch was discovered in the Art Institute of Chicago in 1973 and after repeated requests from the Fine Arts Department in Bangkok, it was returned to Thailand in 1988. It can now be seen in its original position. The pediment of this same eastern face portrays Siva cavorting in his dance of creation and destruction. The central hall of the shrine would probably have had a wooden floor – visitors now have to step down below ground level. The quality of the carving at Phanom Rung is regarded by some as being the finest of the Angkor period. Lunet de Lajonquiere who first surveyed the site in 1907 wrote that "in plan, execution and decoration it is among the most perfect of its kind".

The oldest structures within the walls are the 2 brick *prasat* to the NE of the central building, believed to have been built between 900 and 960 AD. The site was abandoned in the 13th century and was not acknowledged as a historical site by the Fine Arts Department until 1935. Renovation began in 1972, and was finally completed in 1988. It is now a national historical park. Admission: ฿20. Open:

0730-1800 Mon-Sun. The Busabong Festival is held here every Apr.

Getting there: Catch a bus towards Surin along Route 24 and get off at Ban Tako, 14 km beyond the district town of Nang Rong. In Nang Rong it is possible to stay at *Honey Inn*, 8/1 Soi Srikoon. The *Honey* is run by Mr Phaisan, a teacher, who will also help arrange tours in the area. From Ban Tako either take a motorcycle taxi (which wait at the intersection) to the site and back again (difficult to negotiate below ฿180) or a songthaew to Ban Dorn Nong Haen (฿5-10), and from there to the foot of the hill (some songthaews go straight to the foot of the hill). From here it is possible to walk. Alternatively, a bus from Ban Tako goes 6 km in the right direction (฿8) and a chartered songthaew for 4 people should cost about ฿200 with a 2 hr stop at the ruins. From Phanom Rung it is a short trip – 8 km – on to Muang Tham (see below), so it is worth paying a little extra if chartering a motorcycle taxi. An easier way to see the monument, and the others in the area, is simply to join a tour (see tours below). The route to the site is well signposted.

Muang Tham or 'Temple of the Lower City', is found 8 km from Phanom Rung and was built on a smaller, more intimate scale. This 10th-11th century Khmer palace was completed by King Jayavarman V, although the absence of inscriptions makes exact dating impossible. It is thought to have been the palace of the regional governor of the area. It is surrounded by colossal laterite walls pierced by 4 gopuras, at the 4 points of the compass. 3 still retain their sculpted lintels. The carving of foliage and nagas across sandstone blocks shows that the structure was built before any carving was undertaken. Only after the blocks had been put in place were artists set to work. Nagas decorate the 'L' shaped ponds which lie within the walls and surround the central courtyard and its 5 brick chedis, 4 of which have been rebuilt. These probably symbolize the 5-peaked Mount Meru. The nagas here are stylistically different from those at Phanom Rung: they are smooth-headed rather than adorned with crowns, leading art historians to conclude that this prasat is earlier in date by some 100-200 years. Many regard these nagas as unparalleled in their beauty. Lotuses are carved on some of their chests, jewels stream for their mouths, garlands adorn them. The carving here also indicates that artists were allowed considerable freedom. The same figures are portrayed in very different ways on different lintels – for example the rishis. Until 1990 Muang Tham had a wonderfully dilapidated air – sandstone bas-relief lintels lay scattered alongside unworked blocks of stone. It is undergoing restoration by the Fine Arts Department. Admission: ¢20. Open: 0730-1800 Mon-Sun. **Getting there:** catch a Surin bus to Prakhon Chai on Route 24. From there songthaews leave for Muang Tham. If the trip is to be combined with a visit to Phanom Rung, it is necessary to charter a motorcycle taxi, or hitch from Phanom Rung – there is no public transport yet (see Phanom Rung, above, for details).

Ban Dan Kwian, 15 km to the SE of Korat on Route 224, is a pottery centre. Rust-coloured clay from the local river is used to make beautiful vases, pots, wind chimes, fish and other objects. Countless stalls and shops line the main road. Unfortunately, most are too big to transport home. There is also an exhibition of Asian carts and a tourist information centre (on the right hand side on entering the village from Korat). **Getting there:** take a bus towards Chokchai from the S gate on Kamphaeng Songkhram and Chainarong roads, ¢6 (30 mins).

Pak Thong Chai, 30 km S on Route 304, and 2 km off the main road, is a silk-weaving village with cloth for sale. It has become rather commercialized in recent

years; a weaving centre has opened and cloth is now relatively expensive. 4 km from Pak Thong Chai is Wat Na Phrathat notable both for its rare early Rattanakosin murals in the *bot* (ordination hall), and the fine woodcarving over the doorway to the *hor trai* or scripture library. **Getting to Pak Thong Chai:** buses leave from the bus station in Korat every 30 mins, ¢10 (1 hr).

Khao Yai National Park was the first park to be founded in Thailand, in 1962, and is one of the country's finest. It covers an area of 2000 sq km and encompasses the limestone Dangrek mountain range, a large area of rainforest, waterfalls and a good selection of wildlife. Short trails are marked in the park; for longer hikes, a guide is usually needed. The tourist office and visitor's centre at Khao Yai provide maps and organize guides. *Kong Kaeo Waterfall* is a short walk from the visitor's centre. 6 km E is the *Haew Suwat Waterfall* (3-4 hr walk). Waterfalls are at their best between Jun and Nov, wildlife is best seen during Apr and May, although Aug and Sept are good months to see the hornbills. Night time is good for animal observation, when you might be able to see sambar and barking deer, porcupine, gibbon, pig-tailed macaques, mongoose, civet cats and elephants. Unfortunately because of the park's easy accessibility from Bangkok, it is over-run with visitors. In late 1992, for a time, the authorities actually forbade visitors to stay overnight, such was the pressure on wildlife. Even so, the week and nighttime car 'safaris' are so numerous that vehicles are virtually bumper-to-bumper searching out the animals. Accommodation: **A** *Juldis Khao Yai Resort*, Thannarat Rd, Km 17 Pak Chong, T 2352414, B 2552480, a/c, restaurant, pool, tennis courts and golf available at this new resort. **Getting there:** the park turning is at the 165 km marker on Route 2. 4 buses leave Korat for Pak Chong in the morning (¢20). From Bangkok, take a bus or train to Pak Chong. The bus from here to Khao Yai leaves at 1700 and costs ฿20 (the bus stop is near Ratchasima Transport Co.).

Tours

The most convenient way to visit Phanom Rung and Muang Tham is to go on a tour. A day tour, taking in the above plus the pottery and silk villages, minimum 2 people, costs ฿850 with *United Eastern Tour*, they organize tours to Phimai, Phranomwan and Khao Yai National Park.

Festivals

Mar-Apr: *Tao Suranari Fair* (end of month) a 10 day fair commemorating the local heroine. Exhibitions, parades, bazaars etc.

Local information
● Accommodation

As an important commercial centre, Korat has a good stock of hotels – some 25 in total. Most, though, are geared to Thais, not farangs. **A+** *Royal Princess Korat*, B 2813088, new 200-room hotel due to open in 1994, should be the best in the city with pool and tennis courts, situated N of town across the Takhong River off Suranari Rd and about 2 km from the town centre; **A-A+** *Sheraton Sima Thani*, Mittraphap Rd, T 213100, F 213121, B 2345599, a/c, restaurants, pool, health club, newest and best in town with over 130 rooms but not central, W of town next to the TAT office.

B *Chomsurang*, 2701/2 Mahatthai Rd, T 257088, F 252897, a/c, restaurant, pool, overpriced but comfortable with good facilities; **B** *Royal Plaza*, 547 Jomsurangyaat Rd, T 354127, F 257434, a/c, restaurant, pool, large, featureless block, no windows in lower-priced rooms, the new extension may improve it; **B-C** *Siri*, 167-8 Phoklang Rd, T 242831, some a/c, centrally located, bare but clean rooms.

C *Anachak (Empire)*, 62/1 Jomsurangyaat Rd, T 243825, a/c, restaurant, average; **C** *Sirivijaya*, 9-11 Buarong Rd, T 242194, some a/c, restaurant, good location; **C** *Sri-patana*, 346 Suranari Rd, T 242944, a/c, restaurant, pool, comfortable but characterless; **C** *Thai*, 646-650 Mittraphap Rd, T 241613, a/c, clean rooms, ugly hotel; **C-D** *Korat*, 191 Assadang Rd, T 242260, some a/c, average.

D *Chumphon*, 124 Phoklang Rd, T 242453, some a/c; **D** *Farthai*, 35-39 Phoklang Rd, T 242533, some a/c, must have been built by a prison architect, but rooms OK and central; **D-E** *Raschasima*, 294-296 Chumphon Rd, T 242837, some a/c, 72 bare rooms.

E *Asdang*, 315 Assadang Rd, T 242514, some a/c, 40 rooms in medium-sized Chinese-style hotel; **E** *Cathay*, 3692/5-6 Rachdamnern Rd, T 242889, 49 very plain rooms, many poorly maintained; **E-F** *Korat Doctor's Guesthouse*, 78 Suebsiri Rd Soi 4, T 255846, some a/c, hot water, mosquitoes can be a problem, rooms do not always have nets or fan, clean, very good value and good source of information, quiet and welcoming with homely atmosphere, car rental available, rec (W of centre, towards TAT, bus no. 1 runs past the street leading to the guesthouse, Mukamontri Rd, the guesthouse is on the left hand side).

● Places to eat

Restaurants Thai/Chinese: Good Thai and Chinese food to be found by the W gates, near the Thao Suranari Shrine e.g. ◆◆◆*The Emperor* (in the *Sheraton Sima Thani*), Mittraphap Rd, best Chinese restaurant in town – prices to match; ◆◆*The Great Wall*, ◆◆*Green House Garden*, 50-52 Jomsurangyaat Rd (next to the Post Office) away from the road in a sheltered 'garden'; *Phokaphan*, Washara Sarit Rd, rec; ◆◆*Spider*, Chumphon Rd, regular Thai dishes and some Isan food, good portions, also serves International food; ◆◆*SPK* (*Suan Phak*), 196 Chumphon Rd, hangout for the Korat trendies, but good food, also serves cakes, rec; *Thale Thai*, Mahatthai Rd, opposite the *Chomsurang Hotel*, also serves seafood.

Bakery: *Ploi Bakery*, Chumphon Rd (near the Thao Surinari Shrine), also serves Thai food.

Night market: the new night market on Manat Road, open from 1800, has a good range of cheap Thai/Chinese cafés and excellent foodstalls. A number of bars and restaurants are to be found on Jomsurangyaat Road. Good *kiaytiaw* restaurant, close to the corner of Buarong and Jomsurangyaat roads.

● Airline offices

Thai, 14 Manat Rd, T 257211.

● Banks & money changers

On Mittraphap and Chumphon rds. **Bangkok**, Jomsurangyaat Rd, close to the Post Office.

● Entertainment

Turkish Baths: Korat has a reputation for its

Turkish Baths. Ask at the TAT office for the latest recommendations or try: **Chao Phraya** on Jomsurangyaat Road or the **Osaka** at the intersection of Suranari and Phoklang roads.

● **Police**

Sanpasit Rd, T 242010. **Tourist police**: T 213333.

● **Post & telecommunications**

Post Office: main branch on Assadang Rd, between Prachak and Manat rds, also one at 48 Jomsurangyaat Rd. **Area code**: 044.

● **Shopping**

Books: *DK Books*, Chumphon Rd (E of *lak muang*).

Matmii (hand-woven cloth): Korat is the centre for matmii, both silk and cotton (see matmii box, page 331). There are a number of shops around the central square. *Thusnee Thai Silk*, 680 Rachdamnern Rd (opposite the Thao Suranari Shrine.) *Today Silk*, Rachdamnern Rd. *Klang Plaza Department Store*, Assadang Rd.

● **Sport**

Swimming: The *Sripatana Hotel* on Suranari Rd charges ₿20/day for use of their swimming pool; the *Thep Nakhon* on Mittraphap Rd, ₿60. **Tennis**: Thot-saporn Court, 1658 Mittraphap Rd, T 251819, open: 0900-2000 Mon-Sun, ₿25/hr.

● **Hospitals & medical services**

Maharaj Hospital, near the bus station on Suranari Rd, T 254990.

● **Tour companies & travel agents**

United Eastern, 2098-2100 Mittraphap Rd, next to TAT office, T 258713; *Prayurakit*, 40-44 Suranari Rd, T 252114; *Hill Top Tour*, 516/4 Friendship Rd, Pak Chong, Korat, T 311671 for organized tours of Khao Yai National Park.

● **Tourist offices**

TAT, 2102-2104 Mittraphap Rd (on W edge of town – inconveniently located – although town bus no. 2 runs out here), T 213666 (open 0830-1630 Mon-Sun). Areas of responsibility are Korat, Busi Ram, Susiu and Chaiyaphum.

● **Transport to & from Korat**

256 km from Bangkok. It is possible to travel from Korat to Pattaya and the E coast, avoiding the capital, by taking routes 304, 33 and 317.

Local Tuk-tuks and saamlors. **Bus**: the TAT office supplies a map with bus routes marked. **Motorcycles**: can be hired from Virojyarnyon,

554-556 Phoklang Rd, ₿150-200/day.

Air: the airport is 5 km S of town on route 304. Regular connections with Bangkok (daily) 30 mins (₿650) and Ubon Ratchatani (1/week) 45 mins.

Train: the station is on Mukamontri Rd, in the W of town (T 242044). Regular connections with Bangkok's Hualamphong station 5-6 hrs (₿50-207).

Road Bus: a/c and non-a/c buses leave from the new terminal 2 km NW of town on Route 2 to Khon Kaen. Regular connections with Bangkok's Northern bus terminal 4-5 hrs (a/c ₿115, non-a/c ₿64), other Northeastern towns, with Chiang Mai, Chiang Rai, Phitsanulok and with Chantaburi. There are also bus connections with the E coast, including Pattaya.

Phimai

The ancient town of **Phimai**, NE of Korat, lies on the Mun River, a tributary of the Mekong and one of the Northeast's major waterways. The town itself is small, rather charming, with only 2 hotels, and has one major attraction to offer the visitor: the magnificent Khmer sanctuary of Phimai, around which the new town has grown. The site was important even prior to the arrival of the Khmers: excavations have revealed burnished blackware pottery, from as early as 500 AD. The Mun River and one of its minor tributaries formed a natural defensive position and the site also benefited from an extensive area of rich alluvium suitable for agriculture. These twin advantages of security and nutrition meant that this areas was probably occupied almost continuously for over seven centuries up to the establishment of the Khmer sanctuary for which Phimai is known. Dating from the reign of the Cambodian King Jayavarman VII (1181-1201), Phimai was built at the W edge of his Khmer kingdom, on a Hindu site. A road ran the 240 km from his capital at Angkor to Phimai, via Muang Tham and Phanom Rung. Unlike other Khmer monuments which face E, Phimai faces SE – probably so that it would face Angkor, although some scholars have postulated it was due to the influence of Funan, also to the S. The Chinese, who controlled maritime trade at the time, also had a custom of southern orientation.

The original complex lay within a walled rectangle 1000m by 560m, set on an artificial island. There are 4 gopuras, which have been placed in such a way that their entrances coincide with the sanctuary entrances. The S gate, *Pratu Chai* or 'Victory Gate' faces SE and was built wide enough to accommodate an elephant. Shortly before the gate is the *Khlang Ngoen*, or Treasury, where important pilgrims were lodged. The discovery of grindstones here has also led some authorities to maintain it was used as a grain storehouse – possibly to prepare ritual offerings. From this gate, walking towards the central prang along a raised path (the ponds would have been full), are 2 rest pavilions built by Jayavarman VII. Within the compound are 3 prangs: the largest, *Prang Prathan*, is made of white sandstone; those on either side are of laterite (*Prang Phromathat*) and red sandstone (*Prang Hin Daeng*). The Prang Phromathat originally held a statue of Jayavarman VII. The central, and largest, prang is a major departure for Khmer architecture. Though similar to Phnom Rung in plan, the elegant curving prang was something new entirely. It later probably became the model for the famous towers at Angkor.

Another unusual feature of Phimai is the predominance of Buddhist motifs in the carvings that adorn the temple. The lintel over the S gateway to the main sanctuary shows the Buddha meditating under a protective naga, the naga's coiled body lifting the Buddha above the swirling flood waters. Another scene, magnificently carved on the corridor leading into the S antechamber depicts the Buddha vanquishing the evil forces of Mara. On the W side of the building is a lintel showing the Buddha preach-

ing – both hands raised. The inspiration here seems to be Mon.

To the right of the gateway into the walled compound is a 'homeless lintels' park (leading one to speculate whether the Fine Arts Department have reassembled the stones in the right order) where the artistry of the Khmers can be examined at close quarters. The temple was dedicated to Mahayana Buddhism, yet Hindu motifs are clearly discernible. Indeed, the main entrance-way shows Siva dancing. On the lintel over the E porch of the main, central prang, is a carving showing the final victory of Krishna over the evil Kamsa. The carvings at Phimai are spectacular in their verve and skill. As Elizabeth Moore and Smitthi Siribhadra write:

"The confidence and prosperity of Khmer culture reached its height during the 12th and 13th centuries. This is reflected at Phimai in the tensioned human figures; men and women who move amongst the riotous vegetation to fill the lintels surface."

Of particular interest to art historians is the design of the gateways with their petal-like decorations, similar to those at

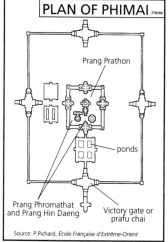

PLAN OF PHIMAI

Prang Prathon

ponds

Prang Phromathat and Prang Hin Daeng

Victory gate or prafu chai

Source: P.Pichard, École Française d'Extrême-Orient

Angkor itself. As Phimai predates Angkor, there is speculation that it served as the prototype for Angkor Wat. The site has been restored by the Fine Arts Department and was officially opened in 1989. Admission: ฿20. Open: 0730-1800 Mon-Sun. An open-air **museum** on the edge of the town, just before the bridge, displays carved lintels and statues found in the area. Open: 0830-1630 Wed-Sun. Guidebook available, ฿60.

On Route 206, just over the bridge which marks the edge of Phimai town, is Thailand's largest **banyan tree** at Sai

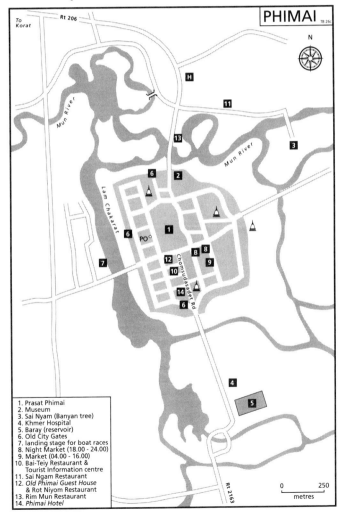

PHIMAI

1. Prasat Phimai
2. Museum
3. Sai Nyam (Banyan tree)
4. Khmer Hospital
5. Baray (reservoir)
6. Old City Gates
7. landing stage for boat races
8. Night Market (18.00 - 24.00)
9. Market (04.00 - 16.00)
10. Bai-Teiy Restaurant &
    Tourist Information centre
11. Sai Ngam Restaurant
12. *Old Phimai Guest House*
    & Rot Niyom Restaurant
13. Rim Mun Restaurant
14. *Phimai Hotel*

Ngam. A good place for lunch – there are many foodstalls here. Walk the 2 km or catch a saamlor from Phimai (฿40 return).

Festivals

Nov: *Phimai Boat-races* (2nd weekend) held on the Phlaimat River, competition of decorated boats, various stalls.

Local information

● **Accommodation**

D-F *Phimai Hotel*, 305/1-2 Haruthairom Rd, T 471689, some a/c, comfortable but plain rooms.

E *Old Phimai Guesthouse*, dorm (F), just off Chomsudasadet Rd, T 471918, friendly, informative owner, attractive rooms, atmospheric, a much nicer place to stay than any in Korat (at the price), rec.

● **Places to eat**

The best food at night is served at the night market near the SE corner of the prasat, open 1800-2400. Good Isan food is also available at the *Rot Niyom* off Chomsudasadet Rd, and the *Rim Mun Restaurant* overlooking the river to the N. *Sai Ngam* is a 'garden restaurant' further N still.

● **Banks & money changers**

Currency exchange service opposite the entrance to the Phimai Historical Park.

● **Tourist information**

The *Baia Teiy Restaurant*, off Chomsudasadet Rd, acts as an informal tourist information centre.

● **Transport**

54 km from Korat.

Local Bicycle hire: ฿25/day from the *Old Phimai Guesthouse* and from the *Bai Teiy Restaurant*.

Road Bus: regular connections with Korat's main bus station on Suranari Rd 1½ hrs, last bus leaves Korat at 2000 and leaves Phimai at 1800. 1 bus a day (and 2 night buses) to Bangkok at 1030 (6½ hrs).

THE ROUTE EAST: SURIN TO UBON

From Korat, Route 226 runs eastwards across the Tung Kula Rong Hai or the 'Weeping Plain'. This area came under the sway of the great Khmer Empire, and a number of towns can be used as bases to visit the lesser known Khmer monuments found here: Buri Ram, Surin and Si Saket in particular. Surin, 260 km from Korat is famous for its yearly elephant round-up; Route 226 eventually reaches the city of Ubon Ratchathani, 311 km from Korat, and a former US Airforce base. 103 km North-West of Ubon is the town of Yasothon, renowned in Thailand for holding the most spectacular *ngarn bang fai* or rocket festival in the Kingdom.

Buri Ram

The province of Buri Ram contains the magnificent Khmer sanctuary of Phanom Rung (see Excursions), and yet few people stay in the capital, preferring instead to travel from the larger city of Korat.

A new **Isan Cultural Centre** to preserve and develop the Northeast's distinctive Isan culture has been opened at the Buri Ram teacher's college on Jira Rd. The Centre, housed in a new building designed to look like a Khmer prasat, supports a museum containing artefacts found in the province and beyond (for example some Ban Chiang pottery), and also stages dance, music and drama performances, and exhibitions of folk art. So far the collection is small and most is labelled only in Thai. Opening hours are sporadic. The town's **fresh market** is off Soonthonthep Rd, not far N of Buri Ram's largest wat, the peaceful but otherwise plain **Wat Klang**.

Excursions

Phanom Rung, one of the finest Khmer sanctuaries in Thailand, is within easy reach of Buri Ram, 64 km S of the city (see page 299). Getting there: by bus from the station off Thani Rd towards Prakhon Chai. Get off at Ban Tako, before Prakhon Chai and then see details on page 300.

Muang Tham, 60 km S of Buri Ram is

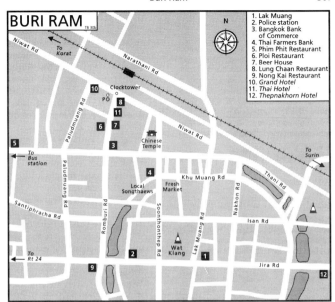

BURI RAM TB 30b

N

1. Lak Muang
2. Police station
3. Bangkok Bank of Commerce
4. Thai Farmers Bank
5. Phim Phit Restaurant
6. Ploi Restaurant
7. Beer House
8. Lung Chaan Restaurant
9. Nong Kai Restaurant
10. Grand Hotel
11. Thai Hotel
12. Thepnakhorn Hotel

also easily accessible and a visit here can be combined with one to Phanom Rung (see page 300). **Getting there**: take a bus from the station off Thani Rd to Prakhon Chai; from there songthaews leave from Muang Tam.

Khao Krudung is a 300m volcanic cinder cone 8 km SE of town. The hill, rising up from the surrounding rice plain, is a holy place and is crowned by a white 20m-high statue of the Buddha. The views from the summit are best at sunset (although public transport is limited in the afternoon). **Getting there**: by songthaew in the morning from the station near the market, off Sriphet Rd.

Festivals

Nov: *annual boat races at Satuk*, 40 km N of Buri Ram. The races take place on the Mun River, with contestants coming from all over Thailand to compete. The event opens with an elephant parade and festivities, beauty pageants and dancing fill the evenings. **Dec**: *kite festi-*

val is held early in the month at Huai Chorakee Mak Reservoir just S of Buri Ram. Processions of vehicles decorated with kites and a beauty pageant.

Local information
● **Accommodation**

B-C *Thepnakom Hotel*, 139 Jira Rd (on edge of town, off route 219), T 613400, F 613400; **B-D** *Buri Ram*, 148 Niwat Rd, T 612504, F 612147, some a/c, 81 rooms in this plain hotel.

C-D *Grand*, 137 Niwat Rd, T 611179, some a/c, plain slab of a hotel with bare rooms, close to the railway station, a/c rooms with hot water; **C-D** *Thai*, 38/1 Romburi Rd, T 611112, F 612461, some a/c, the best of the hotels in the town centre, although that is not saying much, all rooms with hot water, clean but plain and immemorable.

E *Pracha Samakhi Hotel*, 147/9 Suthornthep Rd, T 611198, 18 very basic rooms.

● **Places to eat**

Buri Ram is famous for its fiery papaya *pok pok* salad, similar to the more widely available Isan dish, *somtam*. ♦♦♦*Phim Phit*, Thani Rd, a/c seafood restaurant selling fresh water and sea water fish, crabs and prawns, the fresh water fish is excellent; **✦✦Beer House**, Romburi Rd, open air bar and restaurant specialising in ice cold beer and chargrilled seafood, rec; **✦✦Ploi**, Romburi Rd, ice creams, cakes and coffee in a/c coffee shop; **✦Lung Chaan Restaurant**, Romburi Rd (near *Thai Hotel*), excellent cheap Thai/Chinese food with superb *kwaytio* and other simple dishes; **✦Nong Kai Restaurant**, Romburi Rd (S end), pleasant shady open air noodle house with excellent noodle soup specialities.

● **Banks & money changers**
Bangkok Bank of Commerce, corner of Thani and Romburi Rds; **Thai Farmers**, 132 Soonthouthep Rd.

● **Shopping**
Handicrafts: Buri Ram is known for silk and cotton cloth woven in Amphoe (district) Phuttaisong and Amphoe Napho. Cloth available from shops on Romburi and Thani rds. Distinctive Isan crafts including *matmii* ikat cloth and woven baskets.

● **Post & telecommunications**
Post Office: intersection of Romburi and Niwat rds, by the railway station. **Area code**: 044.

● **Transport**
410 km from Bangkok.

Local Pink town buses criss-cross the town. The terminal for local songthaew's is near the market off Sriphet Rd.

Train: the station is at the end of Romburi Rd, near the centre of town, connections with Bangkok's Hualamphong station and all stops between Bangkok and Ubon Ratchathani.

Road Bus: the station is on the E side of town off Bulamduan and Thani rds. Regular a/c, 6½ hrs (฿139-179) and non-a/c, 6½ hrs (฿79) connections with Bangkok's Northern bus terminal and with Pattaya, Chantaburi and Trat, as well as many towns in the Northeast including Khon Kaen, Mahasarakham, Ubon, Si Saket and Surin.

Surin

Surin is a silk-producing town best known for its **Elephant round-up** in the third week of Nov. The forested Thai/Cambodian border has long been the domain of a tribe of elephant catchers called the Suay. At the beginning of this century there were 100,000 domesticated elephants in Thailand and the Suay were much in demand looking after the working population and catching wild elephants. With the advent of other forms of transport the need for elephants declined, and today there are only about 4,000 working elephants. Contact the TAT in Bangkok for full information on the festival.

During the festival, 40,000 people come to watch the Suay practise their skills with at least 200 elephants. They take part in parades and mock battles, there are also demonstrations of Thai dance and an unusual game of soccer played by elephants and their mahouts. For the rest of the year Surin becomes a backwater: the only reason to stay here is to visit the numerous Khmer temples that are to be found in this S portion of the Northeast.

Wooden shophouses are still to be found scattered around town. The shophouse – shop cum garage on the ground floor, residential on the first floor – is the most popular type of building in Thailand, and in many other parts of Southeast Asia. It is highly flexible and economical, as it combines home and business in one structure. Even buildings constructed today follow the shophouse format. One area where these traditional shophouses can be found is in Surin's small **Chinatown** off Thetsabarn 1 Rd. There is also a small Chinese temple here: **Mun Borisurin Samatkhi Kuson**. A bustling morning **market** can be found between Thetsabarn and Krungsi-Nai roads and a very small museum at the S edge of town on Chitbamrung Road (open 0830-1630 Mon-Fri).

Excursions
Ban Tha Klang is a settlement of Suay – the 'tribe' who tame and train elephants – 58 km N of town. Out of the official Elephant round-up festival period, it is sometimes possible to see

To Bangkok

N

To Ubon Ratchathani

S. Nikhomrat Rd   Surin Phakdii Rd

Thetsabarn 1 Rd

Krungsi Nai Rd

Chinatown

Tat Mai Lang Rd

Sirirat Rd

Thetsabarn 3 Rd

Lak Muang Rd

To Golf driving range

Wat Nong Bua

Chitbamrung Rd

Thetsabarn 2 Rd

Moonsart Rd

Thetsabarn 1 Rd

Wat Klang

Wat Burapharam

Thonsarn Rd

Wat Sala Loi

Bungalow Rurrong Rd

To Race track & Airport

Thetsabarn 2 Rd

Lak Muang Rd Rt 2077

Canal

1. Surin Plaza
2. Silk, Silver & Handicrafts shop
3. Phetkasem Department Store
4. Morning market &
   local songthaews
5. Post office
6. Telephone office
7. Wai Waam Steakhouse
8. Phailin Restaurant
9. Samrap Ton Khruang
   Restaurant
10. Country Road
    Restaurant & Bar

Hotels:
11. Piroms Guesthouse
12. Amarin
13. Ron's Guesthouse
14. Tharin
15. Memorial

B1. Bus station
B2. A/c tour buses
    to Bangkok

training in progress here. Getting there: by hourly bus from the terminal in town, 2 hrs.

Prasat Sikhoraphum (aka Prasat Ban Ra-ngaeng) can be found at the 34 km marker from Surin to Si Saket (Route 226). 4 small prangs sit on a laterite base, surrounding a larger central prang. A Khmer temple dating from the 12th century, Sikhoraphum began life as a Hindu shrine. Later, during the 16th century, it was converted into a Lao Buddhist temple – which explains its hybrid architecture. Sadly, the Fine Arts Department seems to be renovating the complex in a rather heavy-handed manner. Even so, the central prang retains some beautiful carvings on the lintels (dancing Siva) and door jambs (door guardians and floral designs). The layout of the temple is unusual: four brick towers surrounded by a moat enclose a central, taller, prang.

This is reminiscent of Pre Rup and Angkor Wat in Cambodia. Admission: ฿20. Getting there: by local bus going to Si Saket.

Prasat Sa Kamphaeng Noi, another Khmer site, lies E of Sikoraphum, 94 km from Surin on Route 2084 and 9 km before Si Saket. The ruins are in the compound of an active wat and consist of the remains of a Khmer stupa and library, surrounded by a laterite wall. Stylistically, it belongs to Jayavarman VII's reign (12th century), and it is thought that it may have been a healing house (*arokhaya sala*). It has been postulated that Jayavarman VII's building programme was so extensive that many structures were technically poorly built – explaining why some have collapsed. Prasat Sa Kamphaeng Noi falls into this category and there is a visible difference in the quality of the stonework and masonry between here and the sister sanctuary of Prasat Sa Kamphaeng Yai (see below). The hospital is built of laterite and sandstone (for the *gopuras*) and there is a ritual laterite-lined bathing pool just outside the sanctuary. Also here, built on the Khmer *baray* (reservoir), is a modern naga bridge leading to a sala. It is not worth a major detour, but could be included in a tour of the Khmer temples of the area. Getting there: by local bus running to Si Saket; get off at the 94 km marker, 9 km from Si Saket.

Prasat Sa Kamphaeng Yai are more extensive Khmer ruins than Noi (above), and are also to be found in the compound of a wat. The discovery of artefacts – such as an accomplished bronze guardian figure – indicate that this was an important site. They lie 500m off Route 226, just after crossing the railway line at the 74 km marker. This shrine is said to have been built in the 11th century as a sanctuary probably dedicated to Siva, but was converted into a Buddhist temple in the 13th century. As a consequence, the fine carvings on the sandstone lintels and pediments show a mixture of religious subjects. An enormous gallery of laterite blocks, with a passageway and pierced by gopuras at the four cardinal points, surrounds the central stupas. The 'windows' in the gallery are stylistically similar to those at Phanom Rung and Prasat Phra Viharn, supporting the view that it was built in the early 11th century. These retain some beautiful carvings but have been rather unsympathetically restored, using modern angular bricks, which fail to blend in with the original laterite. The style of carving varies over the temple, indicating a long-term sequence of construction. Getting there: local bus going to Si Saket.

Prasat Pluang is a well-restored, neat prasat 30 km south of Surin. Leave Surin on Route 214, and 2 km beyond the town of Prasat, after crossing Route 24, turn left. The monument is 500m off the main road and is signposted. The prasat is raised up

on a high laterite base. It is built in Baphuon style, and was probably constructed during the latter part of the 11th century. Excavations by the Fine Arts Fine Department, which began in the 1970s, indicate that the temple was never completed. Two unfinished naga cornices were unearthed during excavations. Fine carvings adorn 3 of its 4 faces. On the E pediment Krishna lifts the Wathana bull by the horns. Admission: ฿20. Open: 0730-1800 Mon-Sun. Getting there: catch a bus to Prasat. From the market place in Prasat take a songthaew to Pluang village.

Prasat Ta Muan Thon is to be found in Kab Choeng District, Surin Province about 60 km due south of town on the Thai-Cambodian border. The site has only recently been opened to visitors – its position on the border made if of strategic value to the warring factions in Cambodia. Built in the 11th century during the reign of Khmer King Jayavarman VII it is situated on the road that linked Angkor in Cambodia with Phimai. This was once a fine and extensive temple, although it has been extensively damaged in recent years – largely during a period of occupation by Khmers Rouges troops. There is an impressive 30m-long staircase leading down into Cambodian territory, a central sanctuary, and associated minor prangs and buildings. This was clearly a major site, although archaeological work will need to continue for several more years before an idea of its extent is appreciated. Getting there: not currently possible on public transport. However, the site is close to Phnom Rung and Muang ham and could be included in a tour of these better known Khmer sites.

Prasat Phra Viharn is a long excursion from Surin, but possible in a day on public transport. See page 315 for details on the site. Getting there: catch an early train or bus to Si Saket. From the bus station in Si Saket take a local bus to Kantharalak, and make it known you wish to go to Prasat Phra Viharn. The bus will stop at the Kantharalak before continuing on towards Phum Saron. The driver should drop you off at the intersection a few kilometres before reaching Phum Saron. From here it is necessary to hitch or take a motorcycle taxi. Alternatively go on a tour (see Tours) or hire a car or songthaew.

Two silk-weaving villages lie within easy reach of Surin. Matmii silk and cotton ikat is made (see page 331) at **Khawao Sinrin**, 14 km N of town on route 214 and at **Chanrom**, 9 km to the E on route 2077. Villagers at Ban Khawao Sinrin also make silverware. Getting there: songthaews run to both villages from the market area off Thetsabarn 3 Rd (by the clock tower), but only in the mornings. However songthaews can be hired for the journey.

Tours
The Phetkasem Hotel organizes day trips and overnight tours to the Khmer monuments of the area as well as to local silk weaving and Suay elephant training villages. *Mr Pirom* (see hotels) organizes highly recommended tours to the temples at weekends.

Festivals
Nov: *Elephant Round-up* (third week), see above.

Local information
● **Accommodation**
NB: during the Round-up, hotels in Surin become booked up and rates accordingly. **A** *Tarin*, 60 Sirirat Rd, T 514281, F 511580, a/c, restaurant, pool, snooker and night clubs, opened 1991, best in town, large high rise hotel with over 200 rooms, one of the most comfortable places to stay in the NE and professionally run by Kiwi manager, close to bus station on NE side of town.

B-C *Phetkasem*, 104 Chitbamrung Rd, T 511274, F 514041, a/c, restaurant, pool, 5 storey hotel with 162 rooms, small rather grubby pool which is more like a theatre, rooms are good value, but now a little dated and frayed around the edges.

C-D *New Hotel*, 6-8 Tanasarn Rd, T 511341,

F 511971, some a/c, large hotel with worn and dirty prison-like corridors, but rooms and suprisingly clean, no hot water and bolshy management, close to train station, hardly 'new'.

D-E *Amarin*, 103 Thetsabarn 1 Rd, T 511112, large, basic hotel, friendly but no hot water, no character, rooms can be grubby; **D-E** *Saeng Thong*, 155-161 Tanasarn Rd, T 512099, some a/c.

E-F *Krungsi*, 185 Krungsi-Nai Rd, T 513137; **E-F** *Ron's Guesthouse*, 165/1 Sirirat Rd, T 515721, F 515721, new guesthouse with just 3 rooms, run by a retired Texan who also owns the *Country Roads Restaurant* opposite, and his Thai wife, wooden shophouse on edge of town not far from bus station, clean rooms, shared bathroom, hot water, Ron is an excellent source of information and help; **E-F** *Thanachai*, 14 Thetsabarn 1 Rd, T 511002; **E-F** *Pirom's Guesthouse*, 242 Krungsi-Nai Rd, basic rooms in a wooden house backing onto a small lake but Mr Pirom is a mine of information and very friendly, and the guesthouse is clean and well-run, Mr Pirom will organise trips to Khmer sites and elsewhere at the weekends, rec.

● **Places to eat**
Foodstalls around the train station in the evenings. ◆◆*Country Roads Restaurant and Bar*, 165/1 Sirirat Rd, a retired Texan runs this attractive open air place with his Thai wife, good food (simple Thai dishes, burgers, etc), music, cold beers, local farangs assemble here to exchange gossip, the best place for a long evening drinking and chatting; ◆◆*Samrap Ton Khruang*, Tat Mai Lang Rd, good Thai and Lao food, and mediocre European, in sophisticated a/c restaurant, attractive decor and well-run, good value for the ambience, rec; ◆◆*Wai Waan*, Sanit Nikhom Rd, steaks, pizzas and burgers in dark a/c bar-like atmosphere, also some average Thai food available; ◆*Phailin Restaurant*, 174 Tonasarn Rd, open air restaurant with excellent cheap Thai and Lao food.

● **Banks & money changers**
Thai Farmers, 353 Tanasarn Rd.

● **Post & telecommunications**
Post Office: corner of Tanasarn and Thetsabarn 1 rds. **Area code**: 045.

● **Shopping**
Silk: Surin province is one of the centres of silk production in the Northeast with villages in the area producing fine *matmii* silk and cotton ikat

cloth (see page 331). See **Excursions** for details on how to visit silk-weaving villages. There are a number of shops on Chitbamrung Rd near the bus station, e.g. *Surinat*, 361-363 Chitbamrung Rd and *Nong Ying* (close to *Phetkasem Hotel*). In the same area are numerous tailors. There are also two shops selling silk and cotton cloth near the *Phetkasem Hotel*, *Net Craft* and *Mai Surin*.

Silverware: silverware is also a traditional product of the area and many shops selling cloth also have small displays of local silverware. *Phetkasem Department Store*, Thetsabarn 1 Rd. *Surin Plaza*, large new a/c department store with restaurant and coffee bar and wide array of expensive imported goods.

● **Sports**
Bowling: *Phetkasem Bowl*, near the *Phetkasem Hotel*, 104 Chitbamrung Rd. **Golf**: the *Rim Khong* golf driving range is 2 km W of town on route 226 towards Burram, just before the intersection with route 214.

● **Useful addresses**
Hospital: T 511757. **Police**: Lak Muang Rd, T 511007.

● **Transport**
454 km from Bangkok, 260 km from Korat.

Local Bicycles: for hire from *Pirom's Guesthouse* (see **Accommodation**), ฿30/day. **Songthaews**: to surrounding villages leave from the market area off Thetsabarn 3 Rd (near the clock tower), mostly in the morning. Drivers will also charter their vehicles out – expect to pay about ฿500/day. Vehicles can be rented through the *Tarin Hotel*.

Train: the station is at the N end of Tanasarn Rd with, appropriately, a statue of 3 elephants outside. Regular connections with Bangkok's Hualamphong station 8 hrs (฿73-312) and stops en route between Ubon and Bangkok. The overnight a/c express leaves Bangkok at 2100 and arrives in Surin at 0400. **NB**: tickets must be booked 2 weeks in advance for travel during Nov when the Elephant Round-up is under way. TAT organize a special train during this period.

Road Bus: the station is off Chitbamrung Rd. Regular a/c and non-a/c connections with Bangkok's Northern bus terminal 6-7 hrs (a/c ฿152-195, non-a/c ฿108). Special a/c buses are laid on by tour companies and major hotels for the Elephant Round-up. Regular connections with Korat, Ubon and from other Northeastern towns and also with Chiang Mai. A/c tour buses to Bangkok leave from the offices of Kitikarn Ratchasima near the Surin Plaza.

Si Saket

Si Saket is a good base from which to visit the lesser-known Khmer sites in the Lower Northeast (see page 295). The town is a small provincial capital with little to recommend it. There is a daily **market** off Khukhun Rd, down Chaisawat Rd.

Excursions
Wat Prasat Sa Kamphaeng Noi (see page 309) is just over 8 km W of Si Saket on route 2084. Getting there: take a local bus from the *bor kor sor* station towards Surin and get off just after the 8 km marker; the site is signposted.

Wat Prasat Sa Kamphaeng Yai (see page 310) is located in Ban (village) Sa Kamphaeng Yai on route 226 about 40 km from Si Saket. Getting there: take a local bus running towards Surin.

Prasat Sikhoraphum (see page 309) is located on route 266, 34 km before reaching Surin and 69 km from Si Saket. Getting there: take a local bus running towards Surin.

Prasat Phra Viharn lies just over the border in Cambodia and is also accessible as a day trip from Si Saket on public transport. See page 315 for details on the site. Getting there: from the bus station, take an early local bus to Kantharalak, and make it known you wish to go to Prasat Phra Viharn. The bus will stop at Kantharalak before continuing on towards Phum Saron. The driver should drop you off at the intersection a few kilometres before reaching Phum Saron. From here it is necessary to hitch or take a motorcycle taxi. Alternatively hire a car for the day (ask at the *Kessiri Hotel*).

Local information
● **Accommodation**
B *Kessiri Hotel*, 1102-5 Khukhan Rd,

T 614007, F 612144, a/c restaurant, pool, new hotel which soft-opened in 1994, surprisingly luxurious for a small town with 11th floor roof top pool and Thai restaurant, satellite TV, coffee shop with starched linen, marble foyer, but already showing signs of shabbiness.

C-E *Phromphiman*, 849/1 Lak Muang Rd, T 611141, some a/c, not far from the railway line on the W side of town, unremarkable, comfortable enough.

E *Thai Soem Thai*, Si Saket Rd, T 611458, 32 fan rooms in this featureless hotel patronised mostly by truckers and travelling salesmen.

● **Banks & money changers**
Thai Farmers, 1492/4 Khukhun Rd.

● **Telecommunications**
Area code: 045.

● **Transport**
571 km from Bangkok.

Train: the station is in the centre of town on Kaanrotfai Rd. Regular connections with Bangkok's Hualamphong station (₿87-376) and stations en route between Bangkok and Ubon.

Road Bus: the terminal (*bor kor sor*) is on the S side of town off Khukhun Rd. Regular connections with Bangkok's Northern bus terminal, 8-9 hrs (a/c ₿245; non-a/c ₿107-131) and with other Northeastern centres.

Ubon Ratchathani

The 'Royal City of the Lotus' is an important provincial capital on the Mun River. Like a number of other towns in the Northeast, Ubon was a US Airforce base during the Vietnam War and as a result houses a good selection of Western-style hotels as well as bars and massage parlours. The money that filtered into the town during the war meant that it became one of the richest in the region: this can still be seen reflected in the impressive, although slowly decaying, public buildings. Like Udon Thani, there is still a small community of ex-GIs who have married local women and are living out their days in this corner of Thailand. With Bangkok and surrounds booming, some of the wealth is filtering back to the Northeast and can be seen in cities like Ubon: extravagant parties,

Mercedes cars and lavish restaurants.

Places of interest
There is a good archaeological, historical and cultural **museum** (the Ubon branch of the National Museum in Bangkok) on Khuan Thani Road housed in a *panya*-style building erected in 1918. The collection includes prehistoric artefacts collected in the province as well as pieces from the historic period including Khmer artefacts, and cultural pieces such as local textiles and musical instruments. Open: 0900-1600 Wed-Sun.

Wat Phrathat Nong Bua is 500m to the left off Chayangkun Road travelling N to Nakhon Phanom, not far past the army base. It is a large white angular chedi which is said to be a copy of the Mahabodhi stupa in Bodhgaya, India. It is certainly unusual in the Thai context. Jataka reliefs and cloaked standing Buddhas in various stances are depicted on the outside of the chedi. Take town bus No. 2 or 3 or go by tuk-tuk.

Wat Thungsrimuang, on Luang Road and named after the field (or *thung*) by the provincial hall, is a short walk from the TAT office. The wat is notable for its red-stained wooden *hor trai* (or library) on stilts, in the middle of a stagnant pond. The library contains Buddhist texts and rare examples of Isan literature, but is usually locked. The monastery was built during the reign of Rama III (1824-1851) and there is a fine late Ayutthayan-style bot, graciously decaying. The bot features murals depicting Northeastern country life and episodes from the life of the Buddha, but is usually firmly locked. The viharn, built more recently, contains garish and rather crude murals – and is usually open. Such is life. **Wat Subatanaram**, at the W end of Phromathep Road, is pleasantly situated overlooking the Mun River. It was built in 1853 and supports monks of the Dharmayuthi sect. It is significant for its collection of lintels which surround the bot, commemorat-

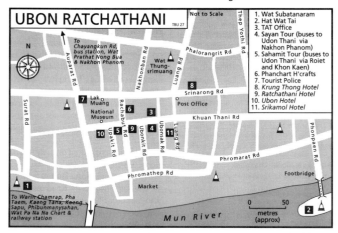

UBON RATCHATHANI   TBU 27   Not to Scale

1. Wat Subatanaram
2. Hat Wat Tai
3. TAT Office
4. Sayan Tour (buses to Udon Thani via Nakhon Phanom)
5. Sahamit Tour (buses to Udon Thani via Roiet and Khon Kaen)
6. Phanchart H'crafts
7. Tourist Police
8. Krung Thong Hotel
9. Ratchathani Hotel
10. Ubon Hotel
11. Srikamol Hotel

ing the dead. One of the sandstone lintels is Khmer and is said to date from the 7th century. Also here is a massive, suspended wooden gong, said to be the largest in the country.

Hat Wat Tai is a large sandbank in the middle of the Mun River, linked by a rope footbridge to Phonpaen Road. The residents of Ubon come here for picnics. Foodstalls and swimming. Take bus No. 1, then walk S along Phonpaen Road.

There is a bustling **fruit and vegetable market** between the river and Phromathep Road, E of the bridge. Crossing over the bridge, the town of **Warin Chamrap** has a number of old, attractively decayed wooden colonial-style buildings of wood or brick and stucco.

Excursions
Kaeng Sapu are a series of rapids on the Mun River 1 km outside the district town of Phibunmangsahan and about 45 km from Ubon, They do not compare with the rapids at Kaeng Tana National Park (see below) but are much easier to reach. Inner tubes can be hired to float down river and there is a small market with foodstalls and poor quality handicrafts. **Wat Sarakaew** is close by with a viharn showing some colonial influences. **Getting there**: take town bus Nos 1, 3 or 6 to Warin Chamrap. From here buses run to Phibunmangsahan. The rapids are 1 km from town; either walk or take a saamlor.

Pha Taem is a sandstone cliff overlooking the Mekong River in Khong Chiam district 98 km from Ubon (along route 2112 and then onto route 2368). The Mekong at this point cuts through a wide and deep gorge and the views from the cliff top across the river to Laos are spectacular. Ochre prehistoric paintings, about 3,000 years old, of figures, turtles, elephants, fish and geometric forms stretch for some 400m along a cliff set high above the Mekong. A trail leads down and then along the face of the cliff past three groups of paintings now protected (or, as the sign puts it, "decidedly fenced") by rather unsightly barbed wire. Two viewing towers allow the images to be viewed at eye level. 2 km before the turn off for Pha Taem is **Sao Chaliang** an area of strange, heavily eroded sandstone rock formations. **Getting there**: rather difficult to reach on public transport. First take an Ubon town bus to Warin Chamrap (No. 1, 3 or 6), and from there

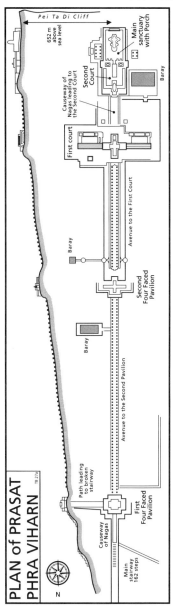

PLAN of PRASAT PHRA VIHARN

Pei Ta Di Cliff

652 m above sea level

Main sanctuary with Porch

Baray

Second Court

Causeway of Nagas leading to the Second Court

First court

Avenue to the First Court

Baray

Avenue to the Second Pavilion

Second Four Faced Pavilion

Baray

Path leading to broken stairway

First Four Faced Pavilion

Causeway of Nagas

Main stairway 162 steps

N

to Khong Chiam via Phibun Mangsahan (where accommodation is available, see below). There are also some direct buses to Khong Chiam from Ubon. From Khong Chiam charter a tuk-tuk for the last 20 km to the cliff (฿150 return). *Chongmek Travellers* and *Takerng Tour* organize boat trips there (see Tours) or hire a motorbike or car (see Local transport).

Kaeng Tana National Park, on the Mun River, lies about 75 km to the E of Ubon, off Route 217 where the park office is located. Alternatively the park can be reached via route 2222 which affords excellent views of the Kaeng Tana – a series of rapids. The rapids are 2 km off route 2222. The park covers 8,000 ha and was gazetted in 1981. The Kaeng Tana – the Tana rapids – after which the park is named, are found at a point where the Mun River squeezes through a rocky outcrop before flowing into the Mekong. In the dry season the rocks present an almost lunar landscape of giant ossified bones, jumbled together into a heap of eroded boulders. It is possible to chicken leap across the river to midstream. The controversial Pak Mun Dam, completed in 1994 and designed to generate hydropower and irrigate land can be seen from the rapids. During the dry season it is possible to swim here although the current is usually too strong for safe bathing in the wet season. **Accommodation**: bungalow accommodation available. **Getting there**: easiest on a tour (see Tours) or by private car/motorcycle (see Local transport). There is no easy way to reach the rapids on public transport. However, the nearest town is Khong Chiam. To get to Khong Chiam take town bus Nos 1, 3 or 6 to Warin Chamrap. From Warin, buses run to Khong Chiam, and from there motorcycle taxis may be available to Kaeng Tana. Accommodation is available in Khong Chiam (see page 318).

Prasat Phra Viharn ('Holy Monastery'), known in Cambodian as *Preah Vihear*, lies S of Ubon, perched on a 500m-high escarpment at the end of Route 221. This magnificent Khmer sanctuary lies on the Cambodian and there has been some discussion as to which side of the border it belongs: 30 years ago the international court in The Hague ruled that it lay inside Cambodian territory. At the beginning of 1992 it 'opened' to visitors for the first time for years. The Thai army has cleared a path through the mines and barbed wire to the Cambodian border. Nonetheless, it is best to check with the TAT office in Ubon, Korat or in Bangkok before making the 150 km journey from Ubon (or from Surin or Si Saket which are also a day's drive away). As Prasat Phra Viharn becomes more accessible, it is sure to become a required stop on any tour of the Northeast's Khmer heritage.

Built about 100 years before Angkor, it occupies one of the most spectacular positions of any monument in Southeast Asia, at the top of a steep escarpment and overlooking the Khmers Rouges-controlled jungle of Cambodia. A hill-top location – whenever possible – was deemed important for all Khmer sanctuaries. In the case of Prasat Phra Viharn it was especially important as this shrine was dedicated to Siva – the god whose abode was Mount Kailasa. The temple is orientated N-S along the escarpment, with a sheer drop on one side of 500m to the Cambodian jungle below. In total, the walkways, courtyards and gates stretch 850m along the escarpment, climbing 120m in the process. In places the stairs are cut from the rock itself; elsewhere they have been assembled from rock quarried and then carted to the site. Nagas carved from sandstone line the route upwards; stylistically they belong to the 11th century. In total, there are five *gopuras* or gateways, numbered I to V from the sanctuary outwards. Multiple nagas, kalas and kirtamukhas decorate these gateways and the balustrades, pediments and pillars that link them. At the final gateway, Gopura I, the pathway enters into a courtyard with a ruined prang within. The courtyard was encircled by a gallery, still intact on the east and west sides. Doors from here lead to two annexes – probably used for ritual purposes.

When Prasat Phra Viharn was built is not certain. Much seems to be linked to King Suryavarman I (1002-1050), and it has been hypothesised that this was his personal temple. But there are also inscriptions from the reign of King Suryavarman II (1113-1150) and he certainly seems to have commissioned parts of the second courtyard (between Gopuras I and II). With the death of Suryavarman II, Prasat Phra Viharn appears to have been abandoned, and fell into disrepair. As Smitthi Siribhadra and Elizabeth Moore observe in their book *Palaces of the gods*, it is difficult to imagine today the life and colour that filled Prasat Phra Viharn and the other Khmer temples. "Ritual feasts and offering included peacock feather fans with gold handles, rings with nine jewels, and golden bowls. The life of the court was filled with colour and music, for the temple also required offerings of dancers, flower receptacles, sacred cloths, incense and candles." Open 0800-1600 Mon-Sun. Entrance: ฿200. A stone stairway leads upwards through several sanctuaries to a shrine dedicated to Siva on the summit. The carvings are finely executed and particularly well preserved. **NB**: the site was closed in April 1994 due to fighting between the Khmers Rouges and forces of the State of Cambodia; check with the TAT office in Ubon, Korat or in Bangkok before embarking. Getting there is difficult: it is quickest to catch a bus towards Kantharalak, half way along Route 221 to the site, getting off at Phum Saron (tell the driver where you are going. From here it is necessary to hitch or take a motorcycle taxi. There are occasional songthaews travelling the road, but they don't always go the whole way. Alternatively, take a tour (see below) or hire a motorbike or car (see Local transport).

Wat Pa Na Na Chart is a forest wat 14

km from Ubon on route 226 towards Surin. The wat is a popular meditation retreat for *farangs* (foreigners) interested in Buddhism. **Getting there:** by local bus running towards Surin from the station in Warin Chamrap to the S of town, over the Mun River. Get to Warin Chamrap by town bus 1, 2 or 6.

Tours

Takerng Tour organize tours to the Kaeng Tana Rapids and Pha Taem (approx. ฿1000/person). *Chongmek Travellers* organize tours along the Mekong River, taking in a Blu village and the Pha Taem cave paintings, with a night in a fishing village. ฿1340/person, minimum 3 people for trip. Tours to Prasat Phra Viharn are also now available from companies in Ubon. In addition, the State Railways of Thailand offer a weekend trip to Prasat Phra Viharn leaving at 0925 on Sat and returning 0535 on Mon, including accommodation in Ubon and all transport, ฿2,650/person, T 2256964 or visit the advance booking office at Hualamphong Station, Bangkok.

Festivals

Jul: *Candle Festival* (moveable, for 5 days from the first day of the Buddhist Lent or *Khao Phansa*). Enormous sculpted beeswax candles are made by villagers from all over the province and are ceremoniously paraded through the streets before being presented to the monks. The festival seems to have been introduced during the reign of Rama I. The Buddha is said to have remarked that the monk Anurudha, in one of his previous lives, led his people out of darkness using a candle – the festival celebrates the feat and is also associated with learning and enlightenment. Candles are given to the monks so that they have light to read the sacred texts during the Buddhist Lent.

Local information
● Accommodation

20-30% discounts off the quoted rate available at many hotels. A new hotel, the *Tohsang Ubon* to the S of town will open soon,

T 245531, F 244814 for details. **A-B** *Pathumrat*, 337 Chayangkun Rd, T 241501, F 242313, N of town centre, near the market bus station, a/c, restaurant, pool, built during the Vietnam war to meet US military demand, it still exudes 70s kitsch, some rooms have been modernised but the *hong kao* – old rooms – have character and atmosphere, best run hotel in town; **A-B** *Regent Palace*, 265-71 Chayangkun Rd, T 255529, F 241804, a/c, restaurant, newest hotel in town but poorly maintained rooms are already looking worn and jaded.

B *Srikamol*, 26 Ubonsak Rd, T 255804, F 243792, a/c, restaurant, ugly towerblock, featureless rooms.

C-D *Racha*, 149/21 Chayangkun Rd, T 254155, some a/c, hot water in a/c rooms, plain and basic; **C-D** *Ratchathani*, 229 Khuan Thani Rd, T 244388, F 243561, some a/c, featureless block in the centre of town near the TAT office, all rooms with TV and hot water, clean and generally well-run, rooms are competitively priced; **D** *Badin*, 14 Palochai Rd, T 255777.

D *Krung Thong*, 24 Srinarong Rd, T 241609, a/c, restaurant; **D** *Pathumrat Guesthouse*, 337 Chayangkun (attached to the more lavish *Pathumrat*), a/c, stuck away round the back of the hotel, clean, dark rooms; **D-E** *Suriyat*, 47/1-4 Suriyat Rd, T 241144, some a/c, grubby.

E *Tokyo*, 178 Upparat Rd, T 241739, some a/c, small rooms.

F *Homsa-ard*, 30 Suriyat Rd, Sa-ard means 'clean' but it isn't.

● Places to eat

◆◆◆-◆◆◆◆*Hong Fah Restaurant*, Chayangkun Rd (opposite the bus station), expensive but excellent Chinese food in sophisticated a/c restaurant; ◆◆◆-◆◆◆◆*Seafood Garden*, Chayangkun Rd (about 1 km N of the bus station on the opposite side of the road), large seafood restaurant, BBQ fish and prawn specialities, a/c room but tables on open air by far the best in the evening; ◆◆-◆◆◆*Antaman Seafood*, Suppasit Rd (opposite the Caltex garage, not far from Wat Jaeng), BBQ seafood including *gung pao* (prawns), *maengda* (horseshoe crabs), sea and riverfish and crabs; ◆◆*Indochina Restaurant*, Suppasit Rd (not far from Wat Jaeng), Vietnamese food in basic restaurant, good value; ◆◆*Phon*, Yutthaphan Rd, opposite fire station, Thai and Chinese, rec; ◆◆*S and P Bakery Shoppe*, 207 Chayangkun Rd, pastries, ice cream and pizzas in pristine a/c western-style surroundings, a little piece of Bangkok in Ubon; ◆-◆◆*No name res-*

taurant, Suppasit Rd (not far from Wat Jaeng), a rather grubby looking place serving delicious *muhan* or BBQ suckling pig. 3 chinese restaurants on Khuan Thani Rd, close to *Ratchathani Hotel* e.g. *Rim Mun 2*, rec.

● **Bars**
10 Pub, Khuan Thani Rd, opposite National Museum; *Ziggy Pub*, Upakit Rd.

● **Airline offices**
Thai, 292/9 Chayangkun Rd, T 254431.

● **Banks & money changers**
Bangkok, 88 Chayangkun Rd; Thai Farmers, 356/9 Phromathep Rd; Siam Commercial, Chayangkun Rd; Thai Military, 130 Chayangkun Rd.

● **Sports**
Golf course at the airport.

● **Shopping**
 Baskets: on Luang Rd, near the intersection with Khuan Thai Rd is a short strip of shops specialising in basketwork. **Department Store**: *Ubon Plaza*, Uparat Rd, a/c department store and supermarket selling all necessities; *Ying Yong Department Store*, 143 Chayangkun Rd. **Handicrafts**: *Phanchart*, 158 Rachabut Rd – selection of antiques and northeastern handicrafts including an excellent range of matmii silk (see page 331). **Silk**: *Ketkaew*, 132 Rachabut Rd.

● **Post & telecommunications**
Post Office: corner of Srinarong and Luang Rd. **Area code**: 045.

● **Tour companies & travel agents**
Chongmek Travellers, Srikamol Hotel, 26 Ubonsak Rd, T 255804; *Takerng Tour*, 425 Phromathep Rd, T 255777.

● **Tourist offices**
TAT, 264/1 Khuan Thani Rd, T 243770. Provides a map of Ubon with bus routes and other handouts. Areas of responsibility are Ubon Ratchathani, Si Saket and Yasothon.

● **Tourist police**
Corner of Srinarong and Uparat Rds, T 243770.

● **Useful addresses**
Immigration: Phibun Mangsahan Rd, T 441108. **Hospital**: Samphasit Rd, T 254906.

● **Transport**
629 km from Bangkok, 311 km from Korat, 270 km from Nakhon Phanom, 167 km from Mukdahan, 99 km from Yasothon.

Local Car and motorbike hire: drivers of cars often wait on Rachabut Rd and near the TAT office. A car and driver for the day, including petrol, will cost about ฿800. *Watana*, 39/8 Suriyat Rd (฿250 for a motorbike, ฿1,000-1,200 for a car). **Town buses**: town buses follow 13 routes across town; pick up a list from the TAT office (fare ฿2).

Air: airport on the N side of town. Regular daily connections with Bangkok 1 hr (฿1,345).

Train: the station is S of the river along the road towards Warin Chamrap. Regular connections with Bangkok's Hualamphong station 10 hrs (฿95-416), and all stations in between.

Road Bus: BKS station for non-a/c buses is some distance N of town not far from Wat Nong Bua, at the end of Chayangkun Rd. Get there by town bus 2 or 3. The station for a/c and non-a/c buses to Bangkok is at the back of the market on Chayangkun Rd, S of the *Prathurat Hotel*. Regular connections with Bangkok's Northern bus terminal 8 hrs (a/c ฿287, 10.30 hrs,; VIP ฿400; non-a/c ฿161), Nakhon Phanom 5½-7 hrs, and less frequently with other Northeastern towns; a/c and non-a/c tour buses to Bangkok also leave from Khuan Thani Rd, opposite the TAT Office; *Sahamit Tour* on Khuan Thani Rd near the National Museum, run buses to Udon Thani via Mukdahan, That Phanom and Nakhon Phanom; *Chayan Tour* near the *Ratchathani Hotel*, run buses to Udon Thani via Yasothon, Roiet, Mahasarakhan and Khon Kaen.

Khong Chiam

Kong Chiam is an attractive district town at Thailand's eastern-most point and situated on the Mekong River – close to the confluence of the Mun and Mekong, the so called two coloured river or Maenam Song Sii. There is accommodation here and some excellent restaurants. Inner tubes can be hired to swim in the Mekong and it makes an alternative and much quieter place to stay than Ubon. Khong Chiam can also be used as a base to visit the other sights in this Eastern-most area of Thailand (see Excursions, below).

Excursions
Pha Taem, **Kaeng Sapu** and **Kaeng Tana National Park** are all far closer to Khong

Chiam than Ubon (see Excursions, Ubon). Reaching them, though, can be difficult as public transport is limited.

Local information
● Accommodation

C *Wooden Chalets*, Santirat Rd, T 351101, 2 beautiful wooden chalets with lovely gardens and large balcony overlooking the Mekong, romantic and a good place to stay in the winter, but can be noisy; **C-E** *Khong Chiam Guesthouse*, some a/c, private bathrooms, good source of information, motorcycle for hire.

E *Pio Guesthouse*, Kaew Pradit Rd, well managed guesthouse on edge of town with good information and mini-market geared to farang tastes close by.

F *Apple Guesthouse*, Kaew Pradit Rd, T 351160, new, clean with attached shower, good cheap restaurant, motorbikes for hire (β150/day), very helpful and friendly owners.

● Places to eat

✦✦*Araya*, Santirat Rd, overlooking the Mekong, a beautiful and breezy place to eat with Mekong river fish specialities including *yisok*.

● Banks & money changers

Krung Thai Bank, Santirat Rd (exchange facilities available).

● Transport

Road Bus: catch town bus 1, 3 or 6 from Ubon Ratchathani to Warin Chamrap; and from there to Khong Chiam via Phibunmangsahan. There are also a/c bus connections with Bangkok's Northern bus terminal.

Yasothon

Yasothon is a small provincial capital NW of Ubon. Even by the standards of most of the North East, Thailand's tourist boom is a mere whisper in the wind. There are no remotely international hotels, nor even any traveller's guesthouses. All the more reason, some would say, the travel here. There is really only one reason to visit the town: to see the famous **rocket festival** – or *bun bang fai* – which is held in its most extravagant form outside the *Sala Changwat*

YASOTHON

To Roi Et

Chi River

To Ban Sri Thaan

1. Wat That or Wat Mahathat
2. Market
3. Isan Handicrafts
4. Thai Military Bank
5. Siam Commercial Bank
6. Thai Farmers Bank
7. Yot Nakhon Hotel

B1. Bus station
B2. a/c buses to Bangkok

Uthairamrit Rd
Withdamrong Rd
Soi Thetsabarn 3
Warrirat(chadei) Rd
Jaengsanit Rd
Nakhon Prathum Rd
Damrong Wimonkhun Rd
Rathkhet Rd
Srisunthon Rd
Sri Worarat Rd
Jomphonburi Rd
Khuan Thani Rd

(Provincial Office) on the edge of town on the road N towards Roiet (route 23). Once a region-wide festival, Yasothon has made it its own (see box).

In the centre of Yasothon, on Withdamrong Rd, is a daily **market** which, though not geared to tourists, does sell functional handicrafts: Isan pillows and cushions, and baskets and woven sticky rice containers. **Wat Mahathat,** just off the main road, is said to date from the foundation of the city. Its ancient roots are barely discernable amidst the new construction.

Excursions

Ban Sri Thaan lies 20 km SE of town off route 202 towards Amphoe Amnaat Jeroen. The village is famous for its *mon*

BUN BANG FAI: THE NORTHEAST'S SKY ROCKET FESTIVAL

Perhaps the Northeast's best known festival is the *bun bang fai* or skyrocket festival. This is celebrated across the region between May and June – the end of the dry season – though most fervently in the town of Yasothon over the second weekend of May. The festival was originally linked to animist beliefs, but through time it also became closely associated with Buddhism. The climax of the festival involves the firing of massive rockets into the air to ensure bountiful rain by propiating the rain god Vassakarn (or, as some people maintain, Phya Thaen), who also has a penchant for fire. The rockets can be 4m or more long and contain as much as 500 kg of gunpowder. As well as these *bang jut* rockets, there are also *bang eh* – rockets which are heavily and extravagently decorated and which are not fired, and just for show. Traditionally the rockets were made of bamboo; now steel and plastic storm pipes are used such is the size of *bang jut*. Specialist rocket-makers commissioned months before hand have taken over from the amateurs of the past. The rockets are mounted on a bamboo scaffold and fired into the air with much cheering and shouting – and exchanging of money as gambling has become part and parcel of the event. In 1992 there were 60 rockets fired, about a third to a half of which worked. The rocket which reaches the greatest height wins. The festival is preceded by a procession of monks, dancing troupes and musicians. There is even a beauty contest – *Thida bang fai ko,* or the Sparkling daughters of the skyrockets.

But like many festivals in Thailand, *bun bang fai* has been co-opted by the state and made a national event. In Yasothon, the provincial governor is closely involved in the celebrations, as are various government offices and army leaders. This means that it has been sanitised and made an official 'spectacle', for both tourists and Thais. Though it is still possible to see traditional *bang fai* in villages in the Northeast, they too are changing or disappearing as the Yasothon event becomes definitive.

In the past, *bun bang fai* were local festivals when neighbouring villages would take it in turns to bear the cost. The rockets were made by Buddhist monks who were the only people with the time and knowledge to build the gunpowder-packed rockets. It was far more lewd and wild than today. Men wearing phallic symbols would parade through the village, drunken groups would dance wildly imitating sexual intercourse, and young men and women would take the opportunity to meet and court. At the same time, young boys would be ordained and monks blessed. The governor of Yasothon has banned the use of phallic symbols – regarding them as unfitting for a national event – although he has had a more difficult time trying to outlaw drunkenness.

khit or traditional Isan axe pillows. These brightly coloured triangular cushions are made of cotton and stuffed with kapok. Getting there: take route 202 SE of town towards Amphoe Amnaat Jeroen. Between the 18 and 19 km markers (before Bon Pa Tew), turn right towards Ban Sri Thaan, It is a further 3 km along the track. Buses from the station in town will drop people at the turn-off. Motorcycle/saamlors wait to take ferry visitors the last 3 km to the village.

Festivals
May: *Bun bang fai (skyrocket) festival*, celebrated most fervently here in Yasothon (see box).

Local information
● **Accommodation**
C-D *Yot Nakhon*, 143 Uthairamrit Rd, T 711481, F 711476, some a/c, large, featureless but comfortable enough, with, so it is claimed, a 24-hr coffee shop, a/c rooms have TVs but no hot water.

D-F *Surawit Watthana*, 128/1 Jaeng Sanit Rd, T 711690.

● **Banks & money changers**
Thai Farmers Bank, 289 Jaeng Sanit Rd.

● **Shopping**
Handicrafts: Baskets from the market in the centre of town. Near the market on the main road, Jaeng Sanit Rd, is a handicraft shop selling axe pillows, Northeasten textiles and some baskets. Yasothon is renowned in Thailand for the quality of its triangular, colourful, axe cushions or *mon khit*. Most famous for making them is Ban Sri Thaan, 20 km away (see Excursions).

● **Transport**
103 km from Ubon. **Road Bus**: the bus station is at the NE edge of town, an easy walk from the centre. Non-a/c buses to Ubon, Udorn, Roiet, Mahasarakham and Khon Kaen as well as with Bangkok's Northern bus terminal, 10 hrs (฿99). A/c buses leave from offices close to the station for Bangkok, 10 hrs (฿179) and Ubon.

THE HEARTLAND OF THE KHORAT PLATEAU

Three provinces straddle the Chi River and lie in the middle of the Khorat Plateau: Mahasarakham, Roiet and Kalasin. These are farming provinces off the tourist trail. They are *en route* to nowhere yet encapsulate the culture and economy of the Northeast. They are centres of Northeastern culture and came under the influence of the great Khmer empire – probably marking its most northerly extent in this part of Thailand. The roads are good, and accommodation adequate.

Mahasarakham

Mahasarakham, known locally as Sarakham, is a quiet provincial capital situated right in centre of the Khorat Plateau. There is a university here – really a teacher training college (Srinakharinwirot Mahasarakham) and the town is known as a centre for Northeastern handicrafts and music, with the university and a new research institute – the **Research Institute of Northeastern Art and Culture** – acting as a focus for their development. The institute has a small permanent exhibition of textiles, basketry and other handicrafts and sells a number of publications – mostly in Thai. It is located behind the main lecture building of the university. Ask for *Satapun Wichai Isan*. The university is 2 km W of town on the road to Khon Kaen. Ask for *mor saw war*. **Wat Mahachai** on Soi Atasaanwiset houses a collection of regional literature and works of art in the Northern Culture Museum which is situated in the wat compound. The museum is often locked; such is the level of visitor demand. The wat is otherwise unremarkable.

There is a **daily fresh market** on the corner of Nakhon Sawan and Worayut rds, in the centre of town. Also with the usual array of goods and foods, forest products like the *maeng da* beetle are also sold (see page 70). A night market operates every evening on Nakwichai Rd – the best place to eat (see **Places to eat**).

Excursions

Tambon Kwao, 5 km E of Mahasarakham off route 208 towards Roiet, is a centre of pottery production. The turn-off for the village is 4 km along route 208, and then 1 km down a laterite track. Getting there: take one of the regular local buses from the station on Somtawin Rd.

Prang Ku is a late Khmer site 12 km from town on the road to Roiet. The site was a 'hospital' – a place of healing – at the Northern edge of the Khmer empire. The prang is in a poor state of repair, with no decoration or carving, and rather rudimentarily reconstructed. Nearby is a large *baray* or reservoir. The site is also used to stage a small *bun bang fai* festival in May (the scaffold for the rockets is on the shores of the baray – see page 320).

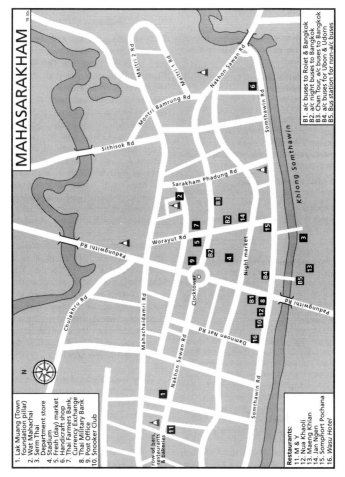

MAHASARAKHAM

B1. a/c buses to Roiet & Bangkok
B2. a/c night buses to Bangkok
B3. Chan Tour, a/c buses to Bangkok
B4. a/c buses for Ubon & Udorn
B5. Bus station for non-a/c buses

1. Lak Muang (Town foundation pillar)
2. Wat Mahachai
3. Serm Thai
4. Department store
5. Stadium
6. Fresh (day) market
7. Handicraft shop
8. Thai Farmers Bank, Currency Exchange
9. Thai Military Bank
10. Post Office
10. Snooker Club

Restaurants:
11. M & Y
12. Nua Khaoli
13. Maeng Khian
14. Jae Ngen
15. Somport Pochana
16. Wasu Hotel

Getting there: take a bus from the station on Somtawin Rd running SE towards Roiet (route 208) and get off just past the 12 km marker. The prang is signposted and lies 1½ km off the main road on the left hand side.

Festivals

Feb: *Bun Boek Fa and Red Cross Fair* (moveable) week-long festival held in the grounds of the *Sala Changwat*, the provincial offices, on Nakhan Sawan Rd in the centre of town. Dances, beauty contest, silk weaving and local produce on sale. **May**: *Bun bang fai* (moveable) Northeast skyrocket festival (see page 320). A small example is held at Prang Ku, 12 km from town (see Excursions).

Local information

● **Accommodation**

C *Wasu Hotel*, 1096/4 Damnoen Rd, T 723075, F 721290, some a/c, restaurant, plain concrete hotel with nearly 100 equally plain and uninspired rooms, but clean enough, restaurant has live music in the evening as Thai female crooners belt out badly performed songs for the benefit of Thai male visitors – an education in coffee shop culture if not in music, the 'no guns' notice on the door may worry some visitors.

E *Bua Daeng Bungalow*, 648/11 Chuthangkun Rd; **E** *Pattana Hotel*, 1227/4-8 Somtawin Rd, T 711473, very grubby and barrack-like hotel close to the bus station, mostly used by bus and truck drivers; **E** *Suthorn Hotel*, 1157/1 Worayut Rd, T 711201, some a/c, small hotel in town centre with 30 rooms, a/c rooms have attached bathrooms, basic.

● **Places to eat**

◆◆–◆◆◆*M and Y*, Nakhon Sawan Rd (about 1 km from town centre), seafood restaurant, tables in garden, excellent char-grilled prawns, rec; ◆◆*Nua Khaoli*, Somtawin Rd (near intersection with Padungwithi Rd), cook-your-own on hot plates at each table, good food, clean and fun, rec; ◆–◆◆*Maeng Khian*, behind the bus station (*bor kor sor*), a/c restaurant in ranch house style with live music, Thai food, with good Isan specialities; ◆*Jan Ngen*, Warayut Rd (corner with Nakwichai Rd), wide selection of Thai dishes, a/c room; ◆*Somphort Pochana*, Somtawin Rd (near intersection with Warayut Rd), good Chinese and Thai dishes, excellent

value. There is a row of good restaurants, bars and bakeries on Nakhon Sawan Rd about 1 km from the town centre near the turn-off for Kalasin; they mainly meet student demand from Mahasarakham University.

Night Food Market or *Talaat tor rung*, on Nakwichai Rd, best place to eat in the evenings (0600-2100), selling Isan specialities like *kai yang* (BBQ chicken), *somtam* (hot papaya salad) and *laap* (minced meat with herbs) as well as rice and noodle dishes.

● **Banks & money changers**

Thai Farmers Bank, Worayut Rd; **Thai Military Bank**, Padongwithi Rd. (Both with currency exchange.)

● **Post & telecommunications**

Post Office: facing the clock tower on Nakhon Sawan Rd. **Area code**: 043.

● **Shopping**

Handicrafts: small shop on Somtawin Rd, selling local baskets, pottery, etc (see map for location). **Newspapers**: English language newspapers available from the stall in the market area on Nakhonsawan Rd. *Serm Thai*, Khlong Som Tha Rd (next to bus station), a/c department store with food centre.

● **Transport**

475 km from Bangkok.

Road Bus: the bus station for non-a/c buses is just S of the town centre on Somtawin Rd. Non-a/c buses leave regularly for Bangkok's Northern bus terminal, 7 hrs (฿113) and other Northeastern towns. A/c buses leave from various offices around town for Bangkok, 7 hrs (฿203), Ubon, Udon and elsewhere (see map).

Roiet

Roiet is the capital of a province encompassing one of the poorest agricultural areas in Thailand. The Tung Kula Rong Hai is a large, dry, salty and infertile plain which covers much of the province, as well as parts of Mahasarakham, Buri Ram and Surin. The name means the 'Weeping Plain of the Kula' (the Kula being a group of nomadic agriculturalists). Millions of baht has been invested in projects to improve the land and productivity of agriculture. Although there have been some successes, the incidence of circular migration – the

THE STORY OF QUAN AM

Quan Am was turned onto the streets by her husband for some unspecified wrong doing and, dressed as monk, took refuge in a monastery. There, a woman accused her of fathering, and then abandoning, her child. Accepting the blame (why, no one knows), she was again turned out onto the streets, only to return to the monastery much later when she was on the point of death – to confess her true identity. When the Emperor of China heard the tale, she made Quan Am the Guardian Spirit of Mother and Child, and couples without a son now pray to her. Quan Am's husband is sometimes depicted as a parakeet, with the Goddess usually holding her adopted son in one arm and standing on a lotus leaf (the symbol of purity).

movement of young men and women to Bangkok and elsewhere in a seasonal search for work – illustrates the inability of the land to support a population with rapidly rising needs and expectations.

Roiet is built around a lake – the **Bung Phlan Chai**. The island in the centre, linked by footbridges, contains the town's *lak muang* or foundation pillar, protected by a sala. Also here is a large Sukhothai-style walking Buddha. This, and the moat which surrounds the city on three sides along with well-stocked gardens makes Roiet seem better planned, and more airy than most other Thai towns. Paddle boats can be hired on the lake, and locals picnic here in the cool season.

Wat Klang Ming Muang is in the NE quarter of the city on Charoenphanit Rd. The monastery is thought to pre-date the founding of the city and the bot, with its fine sweeping gables, was probably built in the Ayutthaya period (18th century). On the outside of the bot are a series of murals telling the life of the Buddha and the gathering of the 12 disciples or *devata*. In some areas rather badly decayed (they were last renovated in 1941), they are nonetheless bright and energetic. **Wat Phung Phralaan Chai** at the SW corner of the lake is also ancient but vigorous re-building has obliterated the old – excepting the *bai sema* or boundary stones which surround the new *bot*. The concrete high relief moral-

ity tales which surround the 3-storeyed, moated *mondop* are enjoyable. But Roiet's most obvious 'sight' (if size is anything to go by) is the massive 59m **standing Buddha of Wat Buraphaphiram** on the E side of town near Rop Muang Rd. The Buddha is known as Phra Phutta Ratana Mongkhon Maha.

On Ploenchit Rd is the **Mun Nithi Roiet Chinese Temple**. In classic Chinese style, the ground floor is a trading business; the temple is on the first floor. Three altars face the room. To the left, one dedicated to the corpulent 'laughing' Buddha; in the centre, to the historic Buddha and various future Buddhas (or Bodhisattras); to the right, to Kuan Yin or Quan Am the Chinese Goddess of Mercy (see box). The pagoda pragmatically combines Theravada and Mahayana Buddhism (see page 39) and Daoism and Confucianism. Despite Thailand's large Chinese population – 15% or so – it is relatively rare to see Chinese pagodas/temples. This is partly because the Chinese have assimilated so seamlessly and become good Theravada Buddhists. Another reason is a wish to blend in, to reduce any chance of persecution. At times of economic nationalism – 'Thailand for the Thais' – the Chinese have been discriminated against. Another, smaller, Chinese pagoda is the **Sala Chao Roiet** on Phadungphanit Rd, not far from the lake.

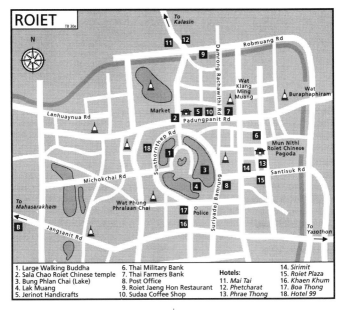

ROIET
TB 30e

To Kalasin

Robmuang Rd

Damrong Rachawithi Rd

Wat Klang Ming Muang

Wat Buraphaphiram

Lanhuaynua Rd

Market

Padungpanit Rd

Mun Nithi Roiet Chinese Pagoda

Sunthornthep Rd

Suriyadej Ramnarong Rd

Santisuk Rd

Michokchai Rd

To Mahasarakham

Wat Phung Phralaan Chai

Police

To Yasothon

Jangsanit Rd

		Hotels:	
1. Large Walking Buddha	6. Thai Military Bank		14. *Sirimit*
2. Sala Chao Roiet Chinese temple	7. Thai Farmers Bank		15. *Roiet Plaza*
3. Bung Phlan Chai (Lake)	8. Post Office	11. *Mai Tai*	16. *Khaen Khum*
4. Lak Muang	9. Roiet Jaeng Hon Restaurant	12. *Phetcharat*	17. *Boa Thong*
5. Jerinot Handicrafts	10. Sudaa Coffee Shop	13. *Phrae Thong*	18. *Hotel 99*

The **market** on and between Phadungphanit and Hai Sok rds sells Isan handicrafts and fresh foods, including insects. On the roadside, women market the ingredients for betel 'nut' (see page 34).

Excursions

Roiet reservoir is 3 km from town and is a popular day's outing for locals at the weekend. *Getting there*: by saamlor.

Prasat Ku or **Prasat Nong Ku** is a Khmer sanctuary tower about 10 km E of town. Few visitors come here and it has only recently begun to be excavated and researched. The site consists of a 3-tiered central prang, walled, with door niches and balustrade and dates from the 11th century. Some carved lintels have been found and are on display, although there is talk of removing them to a museum. The prasat is in the grounds of Wat Sri Ratanaram. *Getting there*: take a bus from the station on Jaeng Sanit Rd towards Yasothon (route 23). Get off at about the 8 km marker – Prasat Ku is off to the right, about 1 km.

Ku Kasingh is a second Khmer temple, rather more difficult to get to from Roiet. The site consists of 3 prasat raised on a single sandstone plinth. The whole is surrounded by walls and a moat and is undergoing renovation by the Thai Fine Arts Department. From the style of carving of the lintels, and the layout of the temple, it is thought to date from the 11th century – the Baphuon period. *Getting there*: the site is at Ban (village) Ku Kasingh in Amphoe (district) Kaset Wisai, almost into Surin province. Take route 215 and then 214 S towards Sawannaphum and Surin – buses leave for Surin from the station on Jaeng Sanit Rd. The track to Ban Ku Kasingh and the Prasat are about 20 km S of Suwannaphum, on the right hand side.

Ku Phra Kona, a third Khmer sanctuary, is not far N of Ku Kasingh. Like Ku Kasingh it consists of 3 prangs, one of which has been re-modelled (in 1928) into a tiered 'stupa' rather like Wat Phrathat Haripunjaya in Lamphun. A *baray* or reservoir 300m from the site was probably linked by a naga bridge. The sanctuary is Baphuon in style and probably dates from the mid 11th century. **Getting there**: take route 215 and then 214 S towards Suwannaphum and Surin – buses leave for Surin from the station on Jaeng Sanit Rd. Ku Phra Kona is at Ban Ku, about 12 km S of Suwannaphum.

Festivals

May: *Bun bang fai (skyrocket) festival* celebrated most fervently in Yasothon (see page 320), but a more traditional example is held in the district town of Suwannaphum, S of Roiet. Get there by regular bus from the station on Jaeng Sanit Rd.

Local information
● **Accommodation**

The Dusit group's **A** *Roiet Thani Hotel* is due to open at the end of 1994. **A-B** *Mai Thai*, 99 Haisok Rd, T 511136, F 512277, a/c, most lavish hotel at N edge of town with over 100 rooms, large coffee shop and illusions of grandeur, rooms are good value with hot water baths, TVs and some with views.

B-D *Phetcharat Hotel*, 66-80 Haisok Rd, T 511741, F 514078, N edge of town, a/c, restaurant, 3-storey hotel, good value a/c rooms, clean but bland.

D *Bungalow 99*, 102 Pracha-Thammarak Rd, T 511035, some a/c, looks new and inviting but rooms are disappointing, a/c rooms have hot water, all with small balconies, poorly maintained; **D** *Khaen Khum*, 50-62 Rathakitkhaikhlaa, T 511508, some a/c, well managed and maintained, the best of the Chinese-style hotels in Roiet, a/c rooms have hot water; **D-E** *Bua Thong*, 40-46 Rathakitkhaikhlaa, T 511142, some a/c, best rooms on top floor where windows allow a breeze in, squat loos, no hot water, no frills but friendly; **D-E** *Phrae Thong*, 29 Ploenchit Rd, T 511127, some a/c, not very well maintained, squat loos, no hot water, but a/c rooms are cheap.

● **Places to eat**

Excellent evening food market by the Post Office, from dusk until 2100, best choice of food in town including Isan specialities.

♦♦*Roiet Jaeng Hon*, Rop Muang Rd, Thai dishes served at restaurant facing the moat; ♦*Sudaa*, 399 Phadungphanit, bakery and coffee shop.

● **Banks & money changers**

Thai Farmers Bank, 431 Phadungphanit Rd; **Thai Military Bank**, Ploenchit Rd (near intersection with Sukkasem Rd).

● **Shopping**

Department Store: Roiet Plaza, intersection of Santisuk and Ploenchit rds (near the Chinese temple). **Handicrafts**: Roiet is a centre for production of silk and cotton ikat cloth. It is sold by the *phun* and can range from ฿100/phun for simple cotton cloth to ฿3,000 for a piece of finest quality silk. Go to *Jerinot*, 383 Phadungphanit Rd to see a wide selection and to gauge prices. Also sold here and in market stalls are axe cushions, baskets, *khaens* (a Northeastern flute) and other handicrafts.

● **Post & telecommunications**

Post Office: Suriyadejbamrung Rd (at intersection with Santisuk Rd). **Telephone**: overseas calls can be made from the Post Office. **Area code**: 043.

● **Tranport**

512 km from Bangkok.

Road Bus: the bus station is to the W of town, off Jaeng Sanit Rd (route 23 towards Mahasarakham). Non-a/c buses to Bangkok, 8 hrs (฿122), Kalasin, Khon Kaen, Ubon, Udorn, Nong khai, Mahasarakham, Buriram, Surin and Korat. A/c bus connections with Bangkok's Northern terminal, 8 hrs (฿220, VIP bus ฿340).

Kalasin

Kalasin is one of Thailand's smallest provinces and was once only an *amphoe*, or district. It still hardly exudes the ambience of even a Northeastern provincial capital. Although it may be a backwater today, the discovery of the Dvaravati site of Muang Fa Daed nearby (see Excursions, below) indicates that, like other parts of the Northeast, this was a centre of activity in the early centuries of the first millennium AD.

There are not many, if any, notable 'sights' in Kalasin. But it is a quiet, rather charming provincial capital. In the centre of town on Kalasin Road is a

KALASIN TB 30d

1. Statue of Thao Somphamit
2. Krung Thai Bank
3. Siam Commercial Bank
4. Daily Fresh Market
5. Cinema
6. Post Office
7. English newspapers
8. Sairung Ice Cream Parlour / coffee shop
9. Restaurant

Hotels:
10. Saeng Thong
11. Saithong
12. Kalasin Plaza
13. Suphak
14. Sai Thong Bungalow
15. Phaiboon
16. Songthaews to local villages

bronze statue of Thao Somphamit, who founded the city, he holds a kettle and clutches his sword. At the Southern end of Somphamit Rd, not far from the bus station, is a row of **travelling cinema companies.** They take films to out-of-the-way towns, bringing with them generators and a screen to enlighten villagers with the latest Kung Fu release. The spread of electricity and the television means the companies – like travelling dance troupes – are struggling for business. On the Eastern edge of town, at the end of Kalasin Rd is a vibrant **open market** where villagers come to sell live fish, fruit and vegetables and to buy clothes and other necessities.

Wat Klang, a large teaching wat on Kalasin Rd, enshrines an impressive black Buddha image cast in bronze. During periods of drought, the image is carried in procession through the town to divine rain. Unfortunately it is kept in the *bot* which is usually locked. But the new rather gaudy *bot* does have some high relief concrete panels around it. These depict scenes from Northeastern country life – transplanting rice, spinning silk, playing the *khaen* and pounding rice. At the far end from the entrance on Kalasin Rd, young chicks cry out *mae phom* (my mother!) as their mother's head is chopped off in a demeritous fashion. Also at Wat Klang is a footprint of the Buddha, again reputed to have considerable magical powers.

Wat Sribamruang, at the N edge of town off Somphamit Rd, is more interesting. It contains a number of beautiful *baisema* or boundary stones from Muang Fa Daed (see below Excursions).

Excursions

Muang Fa Daed is an ancient double-moated town, probably established in the 8th century AD, and one of the most important archaeological sites in the

Northeast. Beautiful carved sandstone *bai sema* or boundary stones have been unearthed (some of which can be seen at Wat Sribamruang in Kalasin town, see above), along with clay and one bronze, pipes. The place is probably only of interest to budding archaeologists, as getting there is difficult. **Getting there:** the site is 19 km from Kalasin town. Take route 214 S towards Roiet for 13 km. Turn right at the Kamalasai School intersection and travel for another 6 km to the site. It is possible to take a bus to the intersection and then hire a motorised *saalmor*. Ask for *muang boraan* (ancient town), Muang Fa Daed.

Ban Phon is a specialist weaving village 70 km NE of Kalasin town. The Phu Thai people, a distinct cultural group within Isan, weave finely patterned silk cloth known as *phrae wa*. Their work is supported by the Queen Sirikit foundation. Cloth can be bought and the production process observed at the village. **Getting there:** catch a bus running towards the district town of Kham Muong from the station on Khaengsamrong Rd. The bus passes the turn off for the village. Ask for Ban Phon.

Festivals

May: *Bun bang far (skyrocket) festival* this festival, for which the Northeast is renowed, is usually associated with Yasothon (see page 320) but a more traditional example is held annually at the district town of Kamalasai, 13 km S of Kalasin town. Get there by regular bus from the station on Khaengsamrong Rd.

Local information
● **Accommodation**
A-B *New Hotel*, under construction due for completion end of 1994, 1½ km out of town, over the Lam Pao river, 150+ rooms, a/c, restaurant, pool, will be best in town, on open field site.

C-D *Suphak*, 81/7 Saenha Rd, T 811315, some a/c, restaurant, 52 rooms, coffee shop, plain rooms, some with hot water showers, echoing hallways, pre-dates the era of imaginative design in Thailand.

D-E *Phaiboon*, 125/1-2 Somphamit Rd, T 811661, F 813346, some a/c, hot water, rather plain barrack-like hotel in centre of town, OK for a stop-over; **D-E** *Saithong Bungalow*, Somphamit Rd, T 813348, F 813346, some a/c, completed early in 1994, these clean rooms have hot water and pristine bathrooms, TVs in the a/c rooms, central location.

E-F *Saithong Hotel*, Phirom Rd, fan rooms, run down and dirty; **F** *Saengthong*, 100-102 Kalasin Rd, T 811555, grotty hotel with shared facilities.

● **Places to eat**
♦♦*Sairung*, Onrotpheton, a/c ice cream parlour and coffee shop.

● **Banks & money changers**
Krung Thai, intersection of Somphamit and Kalasin rds.

● **Post & telecommunications**
Post Office: Kalasin Rd (near the statue of Thao Somphamit). **Area code**: 043.

● **Shopping**
Kalasin Plaza, Thetsabaan 23 Rd (set back), a/c shopping plaza. *English language newspapers* for sale on Thetsabaan 23 Rd, near Kalasin Plaza.

● **Transport**
519 km from Bangkok. **Road Bus**: the bus terminal for a/c and non-a/c buses is on the SW edge of town, just off Khaengsamrong Rd. Regular connections with Bangkok's Northern bus terminal, 8 hrs (a/c ฿221, non-a/c ฿123) and with other Northeastern centres.

NORTH FROM KORAT TO UDON THANI

From Korat Route 2 runs north across the gently undulating plateau of the Isan region. West of here, near the Phetchabun mountains, is the sleepy town of Chaiyaphum. Khon Kaen, 189 km from Korat is one of the largest cities in the Northeast. Route 12 winds westwards from here through the Phetchabun range of hills to Phitsanulok – where it links up with the Central Plains and the North – a nerve tingling journey along mountain roads. 117 km further north from Khon Kaen is Udon Thani, the site of a former US base and close to

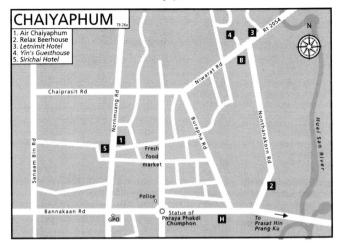

CHAIYAPHUM TB 26a

1. Air Chaiyaphum
2. Relax Beerhouse
3. Letnimit Hotel
4. Yin's Guesthouse
5. Sirichai Hotel

Chaiprasit Rd

Normmuang Rd

Niwarat Rd

Rt 2054

Burapha Rd

Nonthanakorn Rd

Sanaam Bin Rd

Fresh food market

Police

Bannakaan Rd

GPO

Statue of Phraya Phakdi Chumphon

To Prasat Hin Prang Ku

Huai Sao River

the important archaeological site of Ban Chiang. Continuing north for another 55 km the road reaches Nong Khai.

Chaiyaphum

Chaiyaphum is a small provincial capital off the main tourist routes and with little obvious to attract the visitor. But those who truly want to avoid other tourists and sample provincial Northeastern Thai life might find this small corner of Thailand entertaining.

Places of interest

In the centre of town at Chaiyaphum's traffic circle is a statue of the founder of the city – **Phraya Phakdi Chumphon**. Rather more interesting is **Prasat Hin Prang Ku** or simply **Prang Ku**, a 12th century Khmer sanctuary tower 2 km E of the town centre on Bannakaan Rd. Built of laterite blocks, it scarcely matches the Khmer monuments to be found elsewhere on the Khorat Plateau. What little carving there is – kala heads, a few lintels – is rather crude and provincial. Within the prang is a Dvaravati Buddha, highly revered by the townspeople. The statue is ritually bathed on the day of the full moon in April. Get

there by saamlor, bicycle, or walk.

Chaiyaphum lies on the margins of the Khorat Plateau and the land around here is often planted to kenaf, an inferior jute substitute that is used to make rope and gunny bags. It is harvested during the winter months, and bundles of the fibre can be seen soaking in the ponds that often line the main roads. The stalks are retted to remove the green part of the plant, leaving only the fibre. Unfortunately this process also pollutes and deoxygenates the water, making the ponds and creeks useless for fish raising.

Excursions

Ban Khwao is a village well known for the quality of its silk. Like Surin, Chaiyaphum and the surrounding area is a centre for silk production and weaving. Guesthouses will help arrange tours to silk weaving villages. Alternatively, simply catch a songthaew from Nornmuang Rd (near the intersection with Tantawan Rd) close to the centre of town, to Ban Khwao, 14 km W of Chaiyaphum (on route 225).

Local information
● **Accommodation**
C-D *Letnimit*, 14 Niwarat Rd, T 811522,

F 822335, a/c, dull hotel opposite the bus station with equally dull rooms, interesting for the insight it offers into the Thai travelling businessman; **C-D** *Sirichai*, Nornmuang Rd, T 812848, some a/c, dull Sino-Thai hotel in the centre of town.

E *Yin's Guesthouse*, off Niwarat Rd (directly opposite the bus station, 150m down a dirt track and facing a small lake), partitioned rooms in raised wooden house, basic but friendly, run by a Norwegian and his Thai wife, bicycles lent gratis.

● **Places to eat**
The best food in town is to be had at the night market in Taksin Rd. *Relax Beerhouse*, Nonthanakorn Rd (near the intersection with Bannakaan Rd), ice cold beer, relaxing as the name suggests.

● **Banks & money changers**
Banks with exchange facilities are located on Uthittham Rd (eg **Krung Thai**) and Hot Thai Rd (eg **Thai Farmers**).

● **Post & telecommunications**
Post Office: intersection of Bannakaan Rd and Nornmuang Rd (telephone and fax facilities available). **Area code**: 044.

● **Transport**
330 km from Bangkok. **Road Bus**: the BKS is on the NE edge of town about 1 km from the centre. Regular bus connections with Bangkok's Northern bus terminal, 7 hrs (฿147 a/c, ฿65 non-a/c) and with Phitsanulok, Chiang Mai and with towns in the Northeast. A/c buses (VIP and standard) to Bangkok leave from the offices of *Air Chaiyaphum* at 202/8-9 Nornmuang Rd, just to the N of the *Sirichai Hotel* in the town centre.

Khon Kaen

Khon Kaen is a large commercial centre with, at least superficially, little charm. It supports the largest university in the Northeastern region and is an important administrative centre. Selected by the government as a 'growth pole' during the 1960s to help facilitate the development of the region, it was also home to

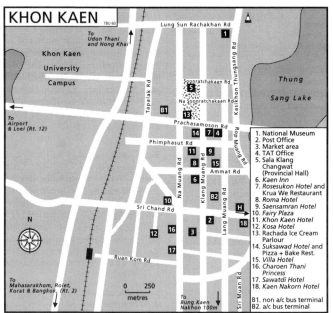

KHON KAEN TBU 60

To Udon Thani and Nong Khai

Khon Kaen University Campus

Thung Sang Lake

To Airport & Loei (Rt. 12)

Lung Sun Rachakhan Rd

Tapalak Rd
Soonratchakaan Rd
Na Soonratchakaan Rd
Kasikhon Thungsang Rd
Prachasamoson Rd
Phimphasut Rd
Na Muang Rd
Klang Muang Rd
Ammat Rd
Rop Muang Rd
Sri Chand Rd
Lang Muang Rd
Ruan Kom Rd
Sri Muan Rd

To Mahasarakhom, Roiet, Korat & Bangkok, (Rt. 2)

To Bung Kaen Nakhon 100m

0   250
metres

1. National Museum
2. Post Office
3. Market area
4. TAT Office
5. Sala Klang Changwat (Provincial Hall)
6. *Kaen Inn*
7. *Rosesukon Hotel* and *Krua We Restaurant*
8. *Roma Hotel*
9. *Saensamran Hotel*
10. *Fairy Plaza*
11. *Khon Kaen Hotel*
12. *Kosa Hotel*
13. *Rachada Ice Cream Parlour*
14. *Suksawad Hotel* and *Pizza + Bake Rest.*
15. *Villa Hotel*
16. *Charoen Thani Princess*
17. *Sawatdi Hotel*
18. *Kaen Nakorn Hotel*

B1. non a/c bus terminal
B2. a/c bus terminal

a US Airforce base during the Vietnam War. Partly in consequence, it has a good selection of hotels (more since built), cinemas, restaurants and bars. It is also growing and developing fast, with new hotels, cinemas, restaurants, shopping plazas and karaoke bars opening each year.

Because Khon Kaen is one of the principal transport hubs of the Northeast, tourists may find that they need to spend a night here en route elsewhere. There is little reason to spend more time than that and the town is not yet geared to tourist visitors. Most foreigners who come here are on business. But, Khon Kaen does support an excellent branch of the **National Museum** at the intersection of Kasikhon Thungsang and Lungsun Rachakhan roads (at the NE edge of the city). It contains among other things, a good collection of Ban Chiang artefacts and beautiful Dvaravati boundary stones. Admission: ฿10. Open: 0900-1200, 1300-1600 Wed-Sun. **Bung Kaen Nakhon** at the Southern edge of the city is used by local residents and a recreation spot for picnics.

Excursions

Chonnabot is both a small town and a district near Khon Kaen. The villages here are well-known for the quality and variety of their matmii silk and cotton cloth. Much is sent to Bangkok for sale (for example at Chatuchak weekend market), but it is best bought here where it can also be seen being made. Note that

---

MATMII: QUEEN OF CLOTHS

Matmii cloth is perhaps the Northeast's most distinctive and best-known handicraft. Some would say, work of art. It is a form of ikat, with the characteristic blurring of colours that is an inevitable product of the tie-dyeing process (**see page 282**).

Matmii can be made of either silk or cotton yarn. It is the silk cloths which are inevitably the finest and most expensive. The geometric designs are usually based on nature – snakes, flowers and birds – although these have become so abstracted in most cases as to be almost unrecognisable. However, cloths from Laos (or those made in Thailand but imitating Lao designs) do sometimes clearly depict elephants, geese and other animals. Designs are handed down from mother to daughter and range from the simple *sai fon* (falling rain) design where random sections of weft are tied, to the more complex *mee gung* and *poon som*. The less common *pha kit* is a supplementary weft ikat, although the designs are similar to those of matmii. Natural dyes derived from roots, insects and earths are very rarely used today; almost all cloth is dyed using chemical dyes which are cheaper, fix more easily and provide a wider range of colours to the weaver. There is, however, a movement to rediscover some of these natural dyes and promote their use again.

The resuscitation of the matmii weaving industry in the Northeast is closely associated with the work of Queen Sirikit. Until the mid-1970s, matmii production was in decline as cheaper and more colourful machine-made textiles – often made from synthetic yarn – became popular. But now wearing shirts and skirts made from matmii has become *de rigueur* in Bangkok and tourist demand has also boosted the industry.

Buying matmii: matmii is usually sold by the *phun*, a length. A sarong length is usually two *phun*. Prices vary according to whether the cloth is silk or cotton and the complexity of the design. A simple cotton matmii may cost only ฿150/*phun*; the finest silk ฿3,000 or more.

cloth is bought by the *phun*. A normal sarong length will be about 2 *phun*, so prices will rarely relate to the whole piece of cloth. Chonnabot town, the capital of the district lies 12 km off Route 2 travelling S towards Korat (turn-off near Km 399 marker onto route 2057). **Getting there**: take a local bus from the station on Prachasamoson Rd.

Festivals

Late Nov to early Dec: *Silk Fair and Phuk Siao (friendship) Festival* (moveable). Wide variety of silks on sale and production processes demonstrated. People tie threads around each other's wrists to symbolize their friendship, known as *phuk siao* (*siao* means 'friend' in Lao). Folk culture performances. The festival is centred on the Sala Klang Changwat or Provincial Hall on the N side of town.

Local information
● Accommodation

As one of the Northeast's main commercial centres, Khon Kaen is well provided for with good and mid-range hotels. But there are no guesthouses to compare with those in other tourist areas, only cheap hotels. Yet another multi-storey luxury hotel is due to open in 1995. **A** *Charoen Thani Princess*, 260 Sri Chand Rd, T 220400, F 220488, a/c, restaurant, pool, newest and most expensive hotel in Khon Kaen with 320 rooms in gleaming high rise block, a little piece of Bangkok in Khon Kaen, bar the chairs in the lobby, central location and good rates available.

B *Kaen Inn*, 56 Klang Muang Rd, T 237744, F 239457, a/c, restaurant, new hotel, well run but rather characterless with all 'business' facilities; **B** *Khon Kaen*, 43/2 Phimphasut Rd, T 237711, F 242458, a/c, restaurant, geared to Thai businessmen with bars and massage parlours, comfortable – no more; **B** *Kosa*, 250-252 Srichand Rd, T 225014, F 225013, a/c, restaurant, pool, the original 'Western' hotel, comfortable rooms, massage parlour, live music in the restaurant, rec; **B** *Rosesukon*, 1/10 Klang Muang Rd, T 237797, F 238579, a/c, comfortable modern hotel lacking in any character barring the novel notion of placing slices of lemon in the men's urinals as an environmentally friendly form of air freshener.

C *Roma*, 50/2 Klang Muang Rd, T 236276, some a/c, the poor cousin to the *Khon Kaen*, bare functional rooms in bare functional block

which looks as though it has been made out of lego – but reasonable for a/c and hot water.

D *Kaen Nakorn*, 690 Srichand Rd, T 224268, a/c, clean; **D** *Villa*, 79/1 Klang Muang Rd, T 236640, a/c, massage parlour attached and certain amount of 'short term' business, but reasonably clean; **D-E** *Sawatdi*, 177-9 Na Muang Rd, T 221600.

E *Saensamran*, 55-59 Klang Muang Rd, T 239611, friendly and the best cheap hotel to stay (the choice is very thin), but rooms are dark and dingy on the ground floor; **E** *Si Nakhon*, 86/5 Samakkhi Rd; **E** *Suksawad*, 2/2 Klang Muang Rd, wooden building down soi off main road, so relatively quiet, rooms are shabby but clean, tendency to be rather unfriendly, attached bathrooms.

● Places to eat

Usual array of foodstalls to be found on the streets. The best selection of cheaper Chinese/Thai restaurants is on the stretch of Klang Muang Rd between the *Kaen Inn* and *Suksawad* hotels. **◆◆***Best Place*, Klang Muang Rd (near *Kaen Inn*), rather sanitised a/c restaurant, serving pizzas, burgers and other similar dishes; **◆◆***Diamond Garden* (Beer Garden), Srichand Rd (near the Fairy Plaza), Thai; **◆◆***Krua We*, 1/1 Klang Muang Rd, good Vietnamese food in attractive wooden house, rec; **◆◆***Parrot*, 175 Srichand Rd, International; **◆◆***Pizza and Bake*, Klang Muang Rd, pizzas, burgers and various Thai dishes, good place for breakfast and Western food if needed; **◆***Nong Lek*, 54/1-3 Klang Muang Rd, well patronized Chinese restaurant, specialities include *khaaw na pet* (rice and duck) and seafood dishes, rec; **◆***Rachadaa*, corner of Na Muang and Prachasamoson Rds, ice creams served at tables set in a small garden; *Sweet Home*, 79 Fairy Plaza, Srichand Rd. Ice Cream and bakery.

● Airline offices

Thai, 183/6 Maliwan Rd, T 236523.

● Banks & money changers

Bangkok, Srichand Rd (near the *Kosa Hotel*); Siam Commercial, 491 Srichand Rd; Krung Thai, 457-461 Srichand Rd; Thai Farmers, 145 Prachasamoson Rd.

● Entertainment

Along with the high density of karaoke bars and massage parlours, there is also a cinema on Srichand Rd not far from the *Kosa Hotel*, which has a room where the soundtrack of English language films is piped.

● **Hospital & medical services**
Srichand Rd, T 236005.

● **Police**
Klang Muang Rd, T 211162 (near Post Office).

● **Post & telecommunications**
Post Office: Klang Muang Rd (near the inter-section with Srichand Rd). **Area code**: 043.

● **Shopping**
There is a general market area opposite the bus station on Prachasamosorn Road, and a larger market on Klang Muang Road. Villagers hawk textiles on the street. **Silk**: good quality matmii silk and other traditional cloth can be found in Khon Kaen. *Prathamakant*, 79/2-3 Ruanrom Rd, silk, cotton and handicrafts. *DK Books* have a branch at the Fairy Plaza, Srichand Rd. *Cheret*, 54/2-24 Klang Muang Rd and *Heng Hguan Hiang*, 54/1-2 Klang Muang Rd (near intersec-tion with Srichand Rd) both sell textiles, axe-pil-lows, Isan food and other handicrafts. Other local products include spicy pork sausages which can be seen hanging in many shops.

● **Travel agents**
Northeast Travel Service, 87/56 Klang Muang Rd, T 244792, F 243238, at the a/c bus terminal.

● **Tourist offices**
TAT, Prachasamoson Rd (near the *Rosesukon Hotel*), T 244498, F 244497. New and helpful branch of the TAT with good maps and details on accommodation and attractions in and around Khon Kaen. Areas of responsibility are Khon Kaen, Mahasarakham, Roiet and Kalasin.

● **Transport**
450 km from Bangkok, 189 km from Korat, 207 km from Loei and 117 km from Udon.

Local Saamlors and tuk tuts. But the cheapest way around town is by songthaew. These coloured converted pick-ups run along 12 routes, fare ฿3. A list of the routes and stops can be picked up from the TAT office.

Air: airport is 2 km off Route 12 to Phitsanulok, 6 km from town. Regular daily connections with Bangkok 55 mins and Chiang Mai (2/week) 1 hr 25 mins.

Train: station on Station Rd in the SW quarter of town. Regular connections with Bangkok's Hualamphong station 8 hrs (฿77-333), Korat and other stops on route N to Nong Khai.

Road Bus: the vast non-a/c bus station is on Prachasamoson Rd; a/c buses leave from the terminal just off Klang Muang Rd. Regular connections with Bangkok's Northern bus ter-minal (a/c ฿193, 7 hrs; VIP ฿295; non-a/c ฿107). Buses, both a/c and non-a/c, run to most other Northeastern towns and to Chiang Mai and Chiang Rai and to Rayong (for Pattaya).

West from the Northeast to Phitsanulok

The route passes through the Petchabun Mountains, descending (sometimes in hair-raising fashion) from the harsh ter-rain of the Northeast to the more fertile rice plains of the North. The land before the turn-off for Lom Sak (200 km from Khon Kaen and 100 km from Phitsanu-lok and the usual bus route to Loei) is surely some of the most depressing in Thailand – at least for anyone with an environmental conscience. The forest has been decimated and all that remains is a wasteland of bare treetrunks and grassland. The area was a stronghold of the CPT until the early 1980s and has since been declared a national park – the Phu Hin Rongkla National Park (see page 201). It was partly in order to de-prive the Communist rebels of a safe haven that the government allowed, some would say encouraged, the defor-estation of the area.

Udon Thani

Udon is a busy town with seemingly the greatest concentration of pedal saamlors in Thailand. This makes for hazardous driving. The N quarter of the town con-tains government offices, with large, tree-filled compounds. Elsewhere the atmosphere is frenetic (or as close to frenetic as it is possible to get in this part of Thailand). The neatly kept palm-fringed roundabouts provide a tropical Riviera feel amidst the bustle.

Like Khon Kaen, Udon was a boom town during the Vietnam War, so it re-tains reminders of that time, with mas-sage parlours, bars, coffee shops and fully air-conditioned hotels. It is said that about 60 former US servicemen have married Thais and settled here.

There is even an Udon branch of the US Veterans of Foreign Wars Association, along with a relay station of VoA (Voice of America) so the US-Udon link lives on. Most tourists only stay here because of its proximity to the outstanding prehistoric site at Ban Chiang.

Excursions

Ban Chiang lies 50 km E of Udon, and represents one of the most important archaeological sites to be uncovered in Southeast Asia since World War II. The site was accidentally discovered by an American anthropology student, Stephen Young, in 1966. While walking in the village fields he fell over the root of a kapok tree and into history: all around him, protruding from the ground, were potsherds. Appreciating that his find might be significant, he sent the potsherds for analysis to the Fine Arts Department in Bangkok and then later to the University of Pennsylvania. Rumours of his finds spread and much of the area was then ransacked by the villagers, who sold the pieces they unearthed to collectors in Bangkok and abroad. Organized excavations only really commenced during the 1970's, when a Thai archaeologist, Pisit Charoenwongsa, and Chester Gorman, from Pennsylvania, arrived to investigate the site (Gorman tragically died of cancer at the age of only 43 in 1981). Even though their task was compromised by the random digging of villagers and others, they still managed to unearth 18 tonnes of material in two years including 5,000 bags of sherds and 123 burials.

The site spans a time period of over 5,000 years. Perhaps the greatest discovery is the bronzeware which has been dated to 3600 BC, thus pre-dating bronzeware found in the Middle East by 500 years. This shattered the belief that bronze metallurgy had developed in the Tigris and Euphrates basin about 3000 BC, and from there diffused to other parts of the world. The finds also indicated to archaeologists that they had been wrong about the relationship between China and Thailand; the oldest known bronzes from China only go back to 2000 BC, so bronze technology may well have gone from Thailand to China instead of vice versa, as had been previously believed. The site at Ban Chiang also provides evidence of an early development of agriculture. Again, it had previously been thought that settled agriculture evolved far later in Southeast Asia (which was regarded as a cultural backwater) than in China and the Middle East. Such a perspective can no longer be sustained following the excavations at Ban Chiang and elsewhere in the Northeast (e.g. Non Nok Tha and Ban Na Di).

Nevertheless, there is still heated debate among archaeologists about the dating and interpretation of many of the finds. In addition, despite these dramatic discoveries little is known of the agricultural society which inhabited the site, and which produced beautiful pots of burnt ochre 'swirl' design, sophisticated metalwork and jewellery. It was obviously not a hostile society, as the vast majority of the bronze artefacts discovered have been bangles, bracelets and anklets. The large number of infant burials (in jars) has also led archaeologists to speculate that the inhabitants led a precarious existence – and possibly practised infanticide to stabilize population against food supply.

There are 2 burial pits at *Wat Pho Si Nai*, on the edge of the village of Ban Chiang. They have been left open for visitors to gain an idea of the process of excavation and the distribution of the finds – the first 'on site' museum in Thailand. At the other side of the village is a new, and excellent, orthodox *museum*. The Ban Chiang story is retold with clarity, displaying excellent models and many of the finds (the exhibition was put together with the help of the Smithsonian, Washington DC and toured the US between 1982 and 1986). Admission: ¢10. Open:

0830-1700 Wed-Sun. To cash in on the visitors to the site (tour buses now come here) the villagers of Ban Chiang, prevented from selling artefacts openly, market a range of handicrafts instead in shops around the museum.

Getting there: Ban Chiang is 56 km E of Udon Thani; after 50 km turn left onto Route 2225 (signposted to the Ban Chiang Museum). The village is another 6 km along this road. Buses run direct to the village from the Udon bus station. Alternatively take a bus going along Route 22 to Sakhon Nakhon and ask to be let off at Ban Chiang (just after the 50 km marker). Tuk-tuk drivers hang around the junction to take visitors to the site: ฿10 one-way.

Erawan Cave (Tham Erawan, 'Elephant Cave') is found 40 km W of Udon, about 2 km off Route 210 on the left-hand side of the road. The cave (as usual, linked to a wat) is larger and more impressive than the usual selection of holes in the ground that pass as caves in Thailand. **Getting there:** by bus en route to Loei.

Phu Phra Bat Historical Park 60 km north of the Erawan Caves, this sight has been almost continuously inhabited since prehistoric times (see page 343).

Local information
● **Accommodation**
B *Charoen*, 549 Pho Sri Rd, T 248155, F 246126, a/c, restaurant, pool, Western-style, comfortable, good value, with newly opened wing offering high level of comfort – at a higher price, rec.

C *Charoensri Palace*, 60 Pho Sri Rd, T 242611, F 222601, a/c, restaurant; **C** *Udon*, 81-89 Mak Khaeng Rd, T 248160, F 242782, central with 90 rooms, noisy and a little dishevelled, but friendly; **C-E** *Chaiyaphon*, 209-211 Mak Khaeng Rd, T 221913, some a/c.

D-E *King*, 57 Pho Sri Rd, T 221634, some a/c; **D-E** *Paradise*, 44/29 Pho Sri Rd, T 221956, some a/c; **D-E** *Sawaddiphap*, 264/3 Prachak Rd; **D-E** *Thailand*, 4/1-6 Surakhon Rd, T 221951, some a/c.

E-F *Srisawat*, 123 Prachak Rd, rather seedy place with just 28 rooms, and noisy; **E-F** *Suk-*

somjai, 226 Pho Sri Rd, T 221821.

● **Places to eat**
Fresh-baked 'baguettes' are available in Udon Thani; the bakeries here are some of the best in the country. Local specialities include shredded pork or *muu yong* and preserved meats. *Kluai Mai*, 58 Mak Khaeng Rd, Thai; *Seun Hia*, 54 Mak Khaeng Rd, Chinese; ♦♦*Charoen Hotel*, 549 Pho Sri Rd, expat hang out with surprisingly good Thai food, Thai and International; *Chao Wang*, 1 Udon Thani Rd; *Thanoo Thong*, 5 Mukkhamontri Rd.

● **Airline offices**
Thai, 60 Mak Khaeng Rd, T 246697.

● **Banks & money changers**
Bangkok Bank, Pho Sri Rd; **Krung Thai**, 216 Mak Khaeng Rd; **Thai Farmers**, 236 Pho Sri Rd.

● **Hospital & medical services**
Pho Niyom Rd, T 222572.

● **Immigration**
Pho Sri Rd, T 222889.

● **Police**
Sisuk Rd, T 222285.

● **Post & telecommunications**
Post Office: Wattana Rd (near the Provincial Governor's Office). **Area code**: 042.

● **Travel agents**
Kannika Tour, 36/9 Srisatha Rd, T 241378, F 241378 (tours in the Northeast and to Laos, Cambodia and Vietnam); *Toy Ting*, 55/1-5 Thahaan Rd, T 244771.

● **Tourist offices**
TAT (temporary office), c/o Provisional Education Office, Phosi Rd, T 241968. Areas of responsibility are Udon Thani, Nong Khai and Loei.

● **Transport**
560 km from Bangkok, 117 km from Khon Kaen, 306 km from Korat.

Local Car rental: *VIP Car Rent*, 824 Pho Sri Rd, T 223758; *Parada Car Rent*, 78/1 Mak Khaeng Rd, T 244147.

Air: airport 2 km out of town off Route 2 S to Khon Kaen. Regular daily connections with Bangkok 1 hr and Sakhon Nakhon (4/week), ½ hr.

Train: station is off Lang Sathanirotfai Rd. Regular connections with Bangkok's Hualamphong station 10 hrs (฿95-413) and all stops en route – Ayutthaya, Saraburi, Korat, Khon

Kaen and on to Nong Khai.

Road Bus: Udon has 2 bus stations; BKS '2' is on the N edge of town about 2 km from the centre; buses also stop, however, at the more central BKS '1' on Sai Uthit Rd, just off Pho Sri Rd. Passengers can get to/from BKS 2 by yellow town buses which run into the centre. Regular connections with Bangkok's Northern bus terminal 11-12 hrs (a/c ฿241, non-a/c ฿134) and with Nong Khai, Khon Kaen, Korat, Loei and other Northeastern towns as well as with Phitsanulok where there are bus connections to other Central Plains and Northern region destinations.

THE NORTHERN MEKONG RIVER ROUTE

The Mekong River forms the border between Thailand and Laos for several hundred kilometres in the Northeastern region. The Mekong River route begins for many at Loei, a provincial capital 50 km S of the Mekong and within easy reach of a number of fine national parks in the Phetchabun hills, including the popular Phu Kradung National Park. The riverside town of Chiang Khan provides a peaceful base with atmospheric accommodation. Travelling downstream, the beautiful river road passes through, in turn, Pak Chom (41 km from Chiang Khan), Sang Khom (another 63 km) and Si Chiangmai (a further 39 km) before reaching the provincial capital of Nong Khai (in total, 200 km from Chiang Khan). Nong Khai, with ferry access to Laos and the capital Viantiane, has become increasingly popular and two large hotels have recently opened. The town is one of the most attractive in the region, with French-style colonial architecture.

Loei

Loei – or Muang Loei as it is known – is a frontier settlement with dusty streets and seedy-looking shophouses, situated on the Loei River. Most tourists visit Loei either as a stop-off on the way to Chiang Khan (see below) or to sample the remarkable scenery of the area – there are no city

'sights' as such. Of all the provinces of the Northeast, Loei has managed to preserve the greatest proportion of its forests and the surrounding area was a haven for guerillas of the Communist Party of Thailand until the early 1980s. There are a number of national parks in the province, of which the most famous is the **Phu Kradung National Park** (see below). Also accessible is the **Phu Hin Rongkla National Park**, an area formerly used as a sanctuary by the CPT, and the **Phu Reua National Park**.

Excursions

Phu Kradung National Park is named after Phu Kradung or 'Bell Mountain', the highest point in the province of Loei at 1571m. The mountain is in fact a plateau which lies at between 1200m and 1500m. There are 3 explanations as to the origin of the mountain's name: one, and the most logical, is that it merely refers to the shape of the peak. The second, that it refers to the wild bulls (*krating*; the popular stimulant drink 'krating daeng' means 'red bull') that used to inhabit the area. And the third, and the more pleasing, is that on Buddhist holy days the noise of a bell can be heard issuing from the mountain. It is one of the coolest areas in Thailand; temperatures sometimes fall to near freezing-point from Nov to Jan, so come prepared. Loei, not coincidentally, is one of the centres for the production and sale of heavy cotton quilts. The park covers 348 sq km and supports a range of vegetation types: tropical evergreen forest, savanna forest, and even some trees typical of temperate locations (e.g. oak and beech). Mammals found in the park include wild pig, Asian wild dog and the white-handed gibbon, along with less frequently seen elephants, Asiatic black bears and sambar barking deer. There are at least 130 species of bird in the park. Residents include the brown hornbill, maroon oriole, large scimitar babbler and the snowy-browed flycatcher. There are nearly 50 km of marked trails for the keen trekker and naturalist and the park is one of the most beautiful in all Thailand. The park station at Sithan (at the foot of the mountain) has an Information Centre, restaurants and porters. Tents can be hired (฿50) and camping is permitted at the summit (฿5). Trekking maps are available, and it is a strenuous 6 km hike up to the plateau itself (where the Park HQ is situated and there is some basic accommodation (**E**), B 2713737, and stalls selling food and basic necessities). Porters will carry luggage for ฿5/kg. It is a very popular spot with Thais so can be quite crowded at the weekends during the dry season, especially from Dec to mid-Jan. The park lies 82 km S of Loei, 8 km off route 201 on route 2019. Getting there: bus from Loei to Phu Kradung town 1½ hrs (the Khon Kaen bus, leaving every 30 mins); from here there are motorcycles, songthaews and tuk-tuks to cover the final 8 km to the park office. From the S, catch a bus via Chumphae to Pa Nok Kao. From there, local buses leave for Phu Kradung town (8 km) and then motorcycles or charter cars are available for the trip to the park. Admission to park: ฿25. Gates open: 0700-1500 Mon-Sun. **NB**: the park is closed during the rainy season from June to Aug. Best time to visit: Feb to Apr to see wild flowers, Nov to Dec to see the waterfalls at their best.

Phu Hin Rongkla National Park lies about 150 km SW of Loei on route 2113 to Phitsanulok. It was used as a base by the CPT in the 1970s and early 1980s and has become a sight, of sorts, as a result (see page 201 for more details). Getting there: catch one of the regular buses towards Phitsanulok via Nakhon Thai, and get off at Nakhon Thai (note that a/c buses usually go via Lom Sak and not via Nakhon Thai). From there, songthaews run to the Park.

Tham Paa Phu, a Buddhist meditation cave, is 11 km from town on the road to Tha Li. Kutis are arranged along a steep cliff – a peaceful place. Getting there: by bus towards Tha Li (฿5) or by tuk tuk (฿50).

Erawan Caves are located 54 km E of Loei, 2 km off route 210 running towards Udon Thani (see Excursions Udon Thani, page 335). Getting there: by bus en route to Udon.

Tha Li and Chiang Khan are on the frontier with Laos, about 50 km N of Loei. For travellers searching for a 'Wild Northeast' atmosphere (or as close as it is possible to get these days), both towns are worth visiting (see below for information on Chiang Khan). Tha Li is a small settlement, where goods smuggled in from Laos can be bought. Getting there: by songthaew from Loei.

Phu Reua National Park, literally 'Boat Mountain' National Park, lies 1.5 km outside the district town of Phu Rua, 50 km SW of Loei. The highest point here approaches 1,500m and temperatures can fall to below freezing. Accommodation: there are bungalows at the visitors' centre and a camping ground part way up the mountain. In addition, there are two 'back to nature' resorts, 2 km N of Phu Rua town, on the road to Loei. The *Phu Rua Resort*, T 899048 and the *Phu Rua Chalet*, T 812048. Getting there: regular buses from Loei to Nakhon Thai (route 203), 1 hr. The turn off for the park is at the 48 km mark. A laterite road leads for 4 km to the park entrance.

Festivals
Feb: *Cotton Blossom Fair* (moveable: early in the month), marks the end of the cool season. Cotton is in full bloom at this time. Cotton Blossom Beauty Queen contest, processions, floats, local folk dancing and handicraft stalls. **June**: *Phi Ta Khon* (moveable: early in the month), similar to Halloween, originates from an obscure Buddhist legend. Locals dress in strange costumes and run around town evoking the spirits.

Local information
● Accommodation
There is little to choose between the 3 main hotels, just 5 mins apart on foot. **C-D** *King*, 11/9-12 Chumsai Rd, T 811701, some a/c, restaurant, characterless but clean and well-managed – staff wear purple uniforms; **C-E** *Phu Luang*, 55 Charoenrat Rd, T 811532, some a/c, comfortable bare rooms, hot water, TV, undistinguished Thai hotel, but OK as a base.

D *Thai Udom*, 122/1 Charoenrat Rd, T 811763, some a/c, a little shabby but clean, hot water in all rooms from 1800, good showers.

E-F *Muang Loei Guesthouse*, 103/72 Soi A.D., 50m off Ruamchai Rd, down unmarked soi (200m from bus station, before Thai Military Bank), some dorm beds, clean, professional management, good source of information, delicious mini-baguettes trucked in from Udon every morning, bicycle (฿30) or motorbike (฿100-200) hire, rec; **E-F** *Sarai Thong*, 26/5 Ruamjit Rd, T 811582.

F *Muang Loei Guesthouse*, 3,16/9 Ruam Pattana (off Ruamchai Rd), bare, simple rooms, average; **F** *Pin Can Saw Guesthouse*, 35/10 Soi Saeng Sawang.

● Places to eat
♦*Savita bakery*, 139 Charoenrat Rd, good breakfasts and Thai food – efficient, with cakes, coffee, ice-cream plus all the usual dishes served by staff dressed in red football shirts and baseball jackets; ♦*Tong-O*, 64 Charoenrat Rd, (opposite *Phu Luang Hotel*), a/c restaurant and bar ('beer house'), open 1600-0200, large menu of Thai dishes; ♦♦*King Hotel Coffee Shop*, 11/9-12 Chumsai Rd, good for ice-cream sundaes in a/c splendour; ♦*Nang Nuan*, 68 Sathorn Chiang Khan Rd, attractive, well run outdoor restaurant with *nua yaang* speciality – cook-it-yourself BBQ, rec; ♦*Luuk Chao Bu*, Sathorn Chiang Khan (near the clocktower), good Thai dishes with generous portions.

● Airline offices
Thai, 191/1 Charoenrat Rd, T 812344.

● Banks & money changers
Thai Farmers, Ruamchai Rd; Siam Commercial, 3/8 Ruamchai Rd – both banks have exchange facilities.

● Hospital & medical services
Loei-Chiang Khan Rd, T 811806.

● Police
Phiphatmongkhon Rd, T 811254.

● Post & telecommunications
Post Office: Charoenrat Rd (S end) (telephone here). **Area code**: 042.

● Sports
Swimming: Muang Loei Land Swimming Pool, open 1000-2000 Mon-Sun, get there by tuk-tuk (฿15) or by town bus/songthaew (฿3)

● Shopping
Loei is known for its warm quilts, available in many shops around town.

● Transport
558 km from Bangkok, 150 km from Udon Thani, 206 km from Khon Kaen, 287 km from Phitsanulok, 50 km from Chiang Khan.

Local transport Bicycle hire: from *Muang Loei Guesthouse*, Ruamchai Rd, ฿30/day; **Motorbike hire**: from *Muang Loei Guesthouse*, ฿100-200/day. **Motorized saamlor**: ฿5-10 around town; Songthaews for out of town trips.

Air: the airport is 5 km S of town. Connections on Thai with Bangkok via Phitsanulok on Mon, Wed and Sat. Bangkok Airways are also planning to open a route with Bangkok.

Road Bus: the bus terminal (BKS) is about 1 km W of the town centre on Ruamchai Rd; the local equivalent of the tuk-tuk will transport passengers into town for ฿5, or take a blue songthaew for ฿3. Regular connections with Bangkok's Northern bus terminal 10 hrs (a/c ฿279, VIP ฿340, non-a/c ฿134-155) and with Udon Thani 4 hrs and Khon Kaen. Connections with Phitsanulok 4 hrs, and from there on to Chiang Mai and other destinations in the N and central regions. Note that some buses travel via Lom Sak to Phitsanulok and others via Nathon Thai. There are also regular connections with Chiang Khan 1 hr (฿14) and from there along the Mekong River route downstream (E).

Chiang Khan

Chiang Khan is a place to visit for people who enjoy slow, lazy days watching a river – in this case the mighty Mekong – drifting by. There are no bars or discos here, few obvious sights, and accommodation, though characterful, is basic. The town marks the beginning (or end) of the Mekong River route. Chiang Khan is strung out for 2 km along the river and consists of just two parallel streets, linked by some 20 sois (lanes). The riverfront road (Chai Khong Road) is quieter with much of the original wooden shophouse architecture still standing; the inland road is the relatively busy route 2186, linking Loei and Nong Khai.

Wat Tha Khok at the E edge of town near Soi 20 overlooks the Mekong but displays little of artistic merit, bar the slightly unusual viharn. On the W edge of town is **Wat Sri Khun Muang**. It is notable for its Lao-style chedi and the gaudy, vibrant murals on the exterior of the viharn.

Excursions

One of the most worthwhile things to do from Chiang Khan is simply to hire a bicycle or motorbike and journey

---

THE MEKONG: GREAT RIVER OF SOUTHEAST ASIA

The Mekong River is one of the 12 great rivers of the world. It stretches 4,500 km from its source on the Tibet Plateau in China to its mouth (or mouths) in the Mekong Delta of Vietnam. Each year, the river empties 475 billion m^3 of water into the South China Sea. Along its course it flows through Burma, Laos, Thailand, Cambodia and Vietnam – all of the countries that constitute mainland Southeast Asia – as well as China. In both a symbolic and a physical sense then, it links the region. Bringing fertile silt to the land along its banks, but particularly to the Mekong Delta, the river contributes to Southeast Asia's agricultural wealth. In former times: a tributary of the Mekong which drains the Tonle Sap (the Great Lake of Angkor and Cambodia), provided the rice surplus on which that fabulous empire was founded. The Tonle Sap acts like a great regulator, storing water in time of flood and then releasing it when levels recede again.

The first European to explore the Mekong River was the French naval officer Francis Garnier. His Mekong Expedition (1866-1868), followed the great river upstream from its delta in Cochin China, and in the process discovered the lost ruins of Angkor, tropical jungles, tribal groups, and much else besides. Of the 9,960 km that the expedition covered, 5,060 km were 'discovered' for the first time. The motivation for the trip was to find a southern route into the Heavenly Kingdom – China. In this they failed. The river is navigable only as far as the Lao-Cambodian border where the Khone rapids make it impassable. Nonetheless, the report of the expedition is one of the finest of its genre.

Today the Mekong itself is perceived as a source of potential economic wealth – not just as a path to riches. The Mekong Secretariat was established in 1957 to harness the waters of the river for hydropower and irrigation. The Secretariat devised a grandiose plan incorporating a succession of seven huge dams which would store 142 billion m^3 of water, irrigate 4.3 million hectares of riceland, and generate 24,200MW of power. But the Vietnam War intervened to disrupt construction. Only Laos' Nam Ngum Dam on a tributary of the Mekong was ever built – and even though this generates only 150MW of power, electricity exports to Thailand are one of Laos' largest export earners. Now that the countries of mainland Southeast Asia are on friendly terms once more, the Secretariat and its scheme have been given a new lease of life. But in the intervening years, fears about the environmental consequences of big dams have raised new questions. The Mekong Secretariat has moderated its plans and is now looking at less ambitious, and less contentious, ways to harness the Mekong River.

through the surrounding countryside, sampling local life, stopping at villages en route. The best route runs upstream, crossing the Loei River and running W.

Kaeng Ku Kou, a series of rapids, lie 4 km downstream from Chiang Khan. There is a small park here where vendours sell spicy Isan food and it is easy enough to while away an afternoon. Most hotels/guesthouses will arrange boat trips to the rapids, ฿150-250 for the 2 hr journey, depending on the number of people.

Local information

● Accommodation

Chiang Khan has a good selection of atmospheric guesthouses; hardly luxurious but they make a change from the usual dull Thai hotels. **D** *Nam*, 112 Chai Khong Rd (near Soi 4), T 821295, F 821342, some a/c, elegant, French-style colonial house with wonderful teak floors and attractive riverside verandah with views along the Mekong.

E *Sook Somboon*, 243/3 Chai Khong Rd (opposite Soi 8), T 821064, wooden hotel overlooking the Mekong, attractive verandah restaurant built over the river, rooms with attached bathrooms are a little disappointing in comparison to the restaurant, overpriced; **E-F** *Chiang Khan*, 282 Chai Khong Rd, T 821023, opposite end of town from the Loei bus stop, rather run down, although riverside position helps.

F *Poonsawat*, 251/2 Chai Khong Rd Soi 9, T 821114, attractive wooden hotel, clean rooms, friendly management, shared bathrooms, small book collection to help while away the hours, rec; **F** *Zen*, 126/1 Chai Khong Rd Soi 12, T 821110, traditional, stilted village house converted into atmospheric guesthouse, friendly, with an enthusiastic band of supporters, rooms however are rather small and box-like, small library of books available.

● Places to eat

Isan food is excellent in Chiang Khan; a local speciality is live shrimps, fished straight from the Mekong River, served squirming in a spicy marinade. There are several riverside restaurants – the best places to eat, with views over the Mekong to Laos. ♦*Prachamit*, 263/2 Si Chiang Khan Rd (near Soi 9), frequented by locals, no riverside position but good food; ♦*Mekong Riverside*, Chai Khong Rd (opposite Soi 10), quiet verandah, views over the Mekong, good food, especially fish dishes; ♦*Rabiang Rim Khong*, Chai Khong Road (opposite Soi 10), small restaurant overlooking Mekong, good food, generous portions; ♦*Sook Somboon Hotel*, 243/3 Chai Khong Rd, wonderful position overhanging the Mekong, excellent fish dishes, including succulent sweet and sour fish; ♦*No Name*, Chai Khong Soi 9 (opposite *Poonsawat Hotel*), very popular restaurant serving large portions of freshly wokked rice and noodle dishes.

● Banks & money changers

Thai Farmers (exchange facilities), 444 Si Chiang Khan Rd.

● Entertainment

Massage: of the medicinal form, although more often than not given by untrained masseuses trying to earn a few extra baht.

● Shopping

Thai Samakkhi, 356 Chai Khong Rd (near Soi 12), handicrafts, including local textiles; *Suankaan Phaap*, 101/1 Chai Khong Rd (between Sois 12 and 13). **Textiles**: *Niyom Thai*, 246 Chai Khong Rd (near Soi 13). There are also several shops near the Thai Farmers Bank on Si Chiang Khan Rd. **Newspapers**: day-old Bangkok Posts available from *Prachamit Restaurant*.

● Post & telecommunications

Post Office: Chai Khong Rd (E edge of town). **Area code**: 042.

● Transport

50 km from Loei, 41 km from Pak Chom, 103 km from Sang Khom.

Local Bicycle hire: from most guesthouses (฿30/day). **Local tuk-tuks**: for charter (฿5-10 around town). **Motorbike hire**: from *Zen Guesthouse* (฿200/day).

Road Bus: buses from Loei stop at the W end of town; it is a 10 min walk to the main area of hotels and guesthouses, or take a tuk-tuk (฿5). Regular bus (in fact converted truck) connections with Loei 1 hr (฿14) and E towards Pak Chom, Sang Khom, Si Chiangmai and on to Nong Khai. A/c bus connections with Bangkok from the station on Soi 9 (inland from Si Chiang Khan Rd).

Pak Chom

Pak Chom figured briefly in world affairs when it became the service centre for the huge Ban Winai Hmong refugee camp. The Hmong (see page 280) fought for the Royalists against the Communist Pathet Lao in Laos's civil war and when the latter were finally victorious in 1975, hundreds of thousands fled across the border to Thailand to escape political persecution. Now, with warming relations between Laos and Thailand, the refugees are returning to their homes on the other side of the Mekong and the refugee camp will soon be history. One of the best accounts of this brief slice of history is Lynellyn D Long's *Ban Vinai: the refugee camp* (Columbia University Press: New York) which traces the lives of three refugee families. As a French Jesuit priest who worked at the camp explained to the author: "Before they had a life revolving around the seasons... Here they cannot really work... Here people make only dreams". This could be the epitaph for all. Other than this tenuous link with recent events, Pak Chom has little to offer the traveller.

● **Accommodation** **F** *Pak Chom Guesthouse*, W edge of town, basic.

● **Transport** 41 km from Chiang Khan, 63 km from Sang Khom. **Bus**: connections with Chiang Khan 1 hr and Loei to the W and with Sang Khom (45 mins), Si Chiangmai and Nong Khai to the E.

Sang Khom

Sang Khom is little more than a village, but with four riverside guesthouses and attractive surrounding countryside, it has become a refuge for people wishing to escape from the stresses of life and the more popular tourist routes. As one visitor recently put it, "the only thing to worry about is finding something to worry about".

2 km West of Sang Khom on the road to Pak Chom is **Wat Hai Sok**, beautifully positioned overlooking the Mekong. The bananas grown in the countryside around the town are highly regarded and are cured, sweetened and then sold across the country as *kluay khai*.

Excursions

Guesthouses arrange **boat and fishing trips** on the Mekong (฿50-60/person). Inner tubes are also available from guesthouses to languidly float down the Mekong (out of the rainy season). Guesthouses have suggested itineraries for those intending to explore the surrounding **countryside**; best by bicycle or motorcycle.

Local information
● **Accommodation**

In 1992 the Mekong was so swollen with monsoon rains that two of the guesthouses lost bungalows as the bank collapsed; as the owners wryly say, their huts are now in Vietnam. There is little to choose between the 4 guesthouses in Sang Khom. **F** *Bovy*, Rim Khong Rd. Overlooking the river, 1 km W of the town 'centre'; **F** *DD*, 190 Rim Khong Rd, T 441021, simple bamboo huts on the river bank, good source of information, professional; **F** *TXK*, Rim Khong Rd, basic bamboo huts overlooking the river, only a handful although 'Mama', the maternal owner, has big plans; **F** *River Huts*, Rim Khong Rd, well-run by a farang with small library and good information.

● **Entertainment**

Massage: Thai traditional massage at the *DD Guesthouse* (฿60/hr) by experienced male masseuse and at *River Huts*. Also herbal sauna at *DD* and *River Huts*.

● **Post & telecommunications**

Telephone: international telephone calls can be made from *DD Guesthouse*.

● **Transport to & from Sang Khom**

104 km from Chiang Khan, 40 km from Si Chiangmai, 96 km from Nong Khai.

Local Bicycle hire: ฿30/day. **Motorcycle hire**: ฿150-200/day, both from the *DD* and *River Huts* guesthouses; the best way to explore the backroads.

Bus: connections W to Loei via Chiang Khan and E to Nong Khai via Si Chiangmai.

Si Chiangmai

Si Chiangmai is a small, rather dusty town, best known as a centre of spring roll wrapper production. These are made from rice flour and can be seen drying on racks in the sun in villages all around the town. The main road is noisy and unattractive, but the riverside road is quiet and peaceful with restaurants built over the Mekong. The town's proximity to Laos is seen reflected in the baguettes which are freshly baked each day.

● **Accommodation E-F** *Tim I* and *Tim II*, some dorm beds, attractive, quiet huts on the riverfront, Swiss management, good source of information, motorcycles, bicycles and boats for hire, best in town.

● **Transport 40 km from Sang Khom. Bus:** regular connections with Nong Khai 45 mins and Udon Thani. Less regular connections W along the river road to Loei via Sang Khom and Chiang Khan.

Nong Khai

Nong Khai is situated at the end of Route 2, the Friendship Highway, and on the banks of the mighty Mekong River which forms the border between Thailand and Laos. It is also a railhead, lying at the end of the line NE from Bangkok. From here, while supping on a cold beer, you can look across to Tha Dua in Laos and imagine the enormous and rare *pla buk* catfish (*Pangasianodon gigas*), weighing up to 340 kg, foraging on the river bed. The fish was first described by Western science in 1930, al-

though Thai and Lao villagers and fishermen were, of course, well aware of its existence way before then. The *pla buk* is unusual for a catfish in that it is vegetarian. It is also becoming increasingly rare – despite attempts at breeding and re-stocking – and fewer are reported to be making the journey up-river to China's Lake Tali to spawn.

Nong Khai is fast loosing its provincial flavour as neighbouring Laos opens up – with some trepidation – to tourists and investors. The Australian-financed Friendship Bridge at Tambon Meechai 2 km from town, the first bridge across the lower reaches of the Mekong River, was officially opened on 8th April 1994. To cope with the expected surge in arrivals, three major new hotels have opened, the *Nong Khai Holiday Inn*, the *Nong Khai Grand Thani* and the *Jommanee*. Check with the Lao Embassy in Bangkok for visas and whether the border is open (see page 344).

The influence of the French presence in Indochina can be seen reflected in the **architecture** of Meechai Road which runs parallel with the river. In addition to the rather dubious excitement of being on the frontier with Laos – not too

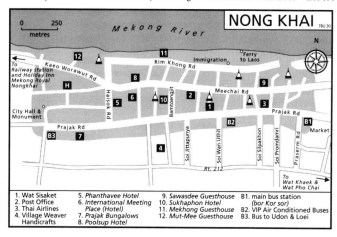

NONG KHAI TBU 30

Mekong River

1. Wat Sisaket	5. *Phanthavee Hotel*	9. *Sawasdee Guesthouse*	B1. main bus station
2. Post Office	6. *International Meeting*	10. *Sukhaphon Hotel*	(bor Kor sor)
3. Thai Airlines	*Place (Hotel)*	11. *Mekhong Guesthouse*	B2. VIP Air Conditioned Buses
4. Village Weaver	7. *Prajak Bungalows*	12. *Mut-Mee Guesthouse*	B3. Bus to Udon & Loei
Handicrafts	8. *Poolsup Hotel*		

BRIDGING THE MEKONG

In April 1994, King Bhumibol of Thailand and the President of Laos, accompanied by Prime Minister Chuan Leekpai of Thailand and Australia's Prime Minister Keating opened the first bridge to span the lower reaches of the Mekong River, linking Nong Khai in Northeast Thailand with Vientiane in Laos. The bridge has been a long time in coming. It was first mooted in the 1950s, but war in Indochina and hostility between Laos and Thailand scuppered plans until the late 1980s. Then, with the cold war ending and growing rapprochement between the countries of Indochina and Asean, the bridge, as they say, became an idea whose time had come

The 1.2 km-long Friendship Bridge has been financed with US$30 million of aid from Australia. For land-locked Laos, it offers an easier route to Thailand and through Thailand to the sea. For Thailand, it offers an entree into one of the least developed countries in the world, rich in natural resources and potential. While for Australia, it demonstrated the country's Asian credentials. The Thais would like to build one, and maybe two, further bridges, possible at Mukdahan and Nakhon Pathom. The government of Laos is rather more circumspect, worrying that bridges not only bolster trade, but also bring consumerism, crime, prostitution and environmental degradation.

far away at Ban Rom Klao the Thai and Lao armies fought a vicious minor battle during the late 1980s – Nong Khai is also a charming, quiet and laidback riverside town: the sort of place where jaded travellers get 'stuck' for several days doing nothing but enjoying the romantic atmosphere of the place. Should that be too sedentary, there are a number of (admittedly largely unremarkable) wats to visit. Notable is the important teaching wat, **Wat Sisaket** and, towards the E of town past the bus station, **Wat Pho Chai** with its Lao-style viharn and venerated solid gold Buddha, looted from Vientiane by the future Rama I. On the riverfront road, Rim Khong Rd, there is a daily **market** where goods from Laos and beyond are on sale. Nong Khai also happens to be the logical place to start or end a tour of the Thai towns which line the Mekong River.

Excursions

Wat Phrathat Bang Phuan is 22 km SW of Nong Khai. Travel S down Route 2 towards Udon and turn right after 12 km onto Route 211 towards Si Chiang Mai. The wat is another 10 km along this road and is well signposted now that it has become a national historical sight. The wat contains an Indian-style stupa, similar (it is presumed) to the original Phra Pathom Chedi in Nakhon Pathom. Its exact date of construction is unknown, but it is believed to date from the early centuries AD. A newer chedi was built on the sight in 1559, which toppled over in 1970. In 1978 it was restored. As a result, the unrestored Lao chedis in this same compound are now of greater historical interest. The site is really only worth visiting en route to/from Udon or Nong Khai, and it doesn't begin to compare with other historical sights in the Northeast. Getting there: songthaew or bus running towards Si Chiang Mai, or catch a bus going South on Route 2 and get off at the junction with Route 211; then catch a bus or songthaew W from here.

Phu Phra Bat Historical Park encompasses an area of 650 ha in the Phu Phan hills and has been a site of almost continuous human habitation since prehistoric times. It was clearly felt to be endowed with considerable religious significance. There are prehistoric cave paintings, Dvaravati boundary stones (7th-10th centuries), Lopburi Bodhisattvas (10th-13th centuries), Lang Chan Buddha images (14th-18th centuries), and a stupa built in 1920 to shelter a Buddha footprint. The terrain consists of rocky outcrops, bare sandy soil, and savanna forest, and it is easy to imagine why people for thousands of years have regarded the area as a magical place. The problem is that it is difficult to get to except by private car or motorcycle. But it is worth it for the peace. Open: 0830-1700 Mon-Sun. The park is just about equidistant from Nong Khai and Udon Thani – almost 70 km. Getting there: catch a songthaew or bus to Ban Phu, the town where Routes 2020 and 2021 meet. From there (it is signposted), the park is another 12 km by songthaew towards Ban Tiu, with a 30 min walk at the end (quicker to take a motorcycle taxi from here).

Wat Phutthamamakasama-khom or, rather more simply, **Wat Khaek** ('Indian' Wat) was established in the late 1970s and lies 4.5 km E of Nong Khai on Route 212 to Beung Kan. The wat promotes a strange mixture of Buddhist and Hindu beliefs, and is dominated by a vast array of strange brick and cement statues. Some are clearly of Buddhist and Hindu inspiration; others are rather harder to interpret: a life-size elephant being attacked by a large pack of dogs for example. This represents a Thai proverb; a man who is confident he has done no wrong need not worry about malicious rumour "as an elephant does not care about barking dogs". The figures are arranged in a garden and music blares out from an equally large concrete encrusted PA system. Very weird to the uninitiated (there is a similar wat and collection of statues outside Vientiane in Laos). Even tour buses visit the wat, so well-known has its strange brand of Buddhism become. Getting there: songthaew heading towards Beung Kan (Route 212) or by tuk-tuk. Turn right after the 4 km marker, just past the St Paul Nongkhai School (signpost to Sala

Kaeou), and it is 500m off the main road.

Tours to Laos

Several companies and guesthouses organize visas for Laos, but note that passports still have to be couriered to Bangkok for stamping so it takes a minimum of 4 working days to secure your visa. The *International Meeting Place* will arrange a one month business visa for ฿2,500, allowing more freedom to travel than a tourist visa (but still not easy). Agents that will arrange visas include: *Pam Tour*, 1121/1 Haisok Rd; *International Meeting Place*, 1117 Soi Chuanjit, F 412644; *Udom Rot Restaurant*, 193 Rim Kong Rd (see also page 177).

Festivals

Mar: *Nong Khai Show* (2nd week); **May**: *Rocket Festival*, or *ngarn bang fai* (2nd week) (see page 319); **Jul**: *Candle Festival* (the beginning of the Buddhist Lent or Phansa) (see page 317); **Oct**: *Boat races* on the Mekong (moveable). Naga-prowed canoes with up to 40 oarsmen race along the river with a great deal of cheering and drinking from the onlookers that line the bank.

Local information
● **Accommodation**

With the opening of the new bridge, large hotels have opened in Nong Khai providing (almost) Bangkok-level opulence. Also, guesthouses in Nong Khai are of a high standard. **A+** *Holiday Inn Mekong Royal Nongkhai*, 222 Jomanee Rd (W of railway station, out of town), T 420024, F 421280, B 2713125, a/c, restaurant, pool, tennis, on the outskirts of town, 8-storeyed block with nearly 200 rooms overlooking Mekong with all facilities, best in town.

A *Nongkhai Grand Thani*, 589 Muu 5 Nong Khai Poanpisai Rd, T 420033, F 420044, B 2376809, 2 km E of town on Route 212, a/c, restaurant, pool, disco, 'luxury' hotel opened 1992, high-rise block on edge of town, all facilities.

C-E *Phanthavee* (and across the road the *Phanthavee Bungalows*), 1241 Haisok Rd, T 411569, some a/c, management is brusque and unfriendly; rooms are clean but otherwise unremarkable.

D-E *Prajak Bungalows*, 1178 Prajak Rd, T 411116; **D-F** *Pongwichit*, 1244/1-2 Bamtoengjit Rd, T 411583, some a/c.

E *International Meeting Place*,1117 Soi Chuanjit, F 412644, run by a convivial Australian, clean rooms in attractive wooden house, beer (ice cold) available in industrial quantities, rec; **E** *Poolsup*, 843 Meechai Rd, T 411031, Chinese style hotel with perhaps the most hideous chair in the world in the 'foyer'; but don't be put off, the rooms are OK and the proprietress is charming – try her cool rainwater; **E** *Vientiane Guesthouse*, Meechai Rd Soi Wat Naak, near the Post Office, T 411393, clean wooden rooms, quiet, rec. **E-F** *Sawasdee Guesthouse*, 402 Meechai Rd, T 412602, F420259, some a/c, old wooden house with inner courtyard, clean rooms and immaculate bathrooms, help-yourself coffee, friendly, good source of information, fan, hot water; **E-F** *Sukhaphon*, 823 Bamtoengjit Rd, T 411894, old wooden hotel.

F *Mekhong Guesthouse*, 519 Rim Khong, T 412320, clean wooden rooms, on the river with a good verandah and information, rec; **F** *Mut-Mee Guesthouse*, 1111/4 Kaeo Worawut Rd, good restaurant, large rooms, nice garden by the river with hammocks, very friendly management, information on Laos, rec.

● **Places to eat**

Thai: ♦♦*Banya Pochona*, 295 Rim Khong Rd, Chinese, Thai and Laos food, fish dishes particularly good, ฿20-40 for simple dishes, ฿150 for elaborate meal; ♦♦*Indochine*, 189/1 Meechai Rd, also serves Vietnamese, rec; ♦♦*Khun Daeng*, 521 Rim Khong Rd (just W from Udom Rot and the Immigration office), views over the Mekong River, seafood and Isan specialities; ♦♦*Udom Rot*, 193 Rim Khong Rd, views over the Mekong River, Thai, seafood. ♦*Open air café* at intersection of Meechai and Haisok Rd.

● **Bars**

Arthit's Pub, Prajak Rd, a little further on from the **Thai** office (live music).

● **Airline offices**

Thai, 453 Prachak Rd, T 411530.

● **Banks & money changers**

Bangkok, 374 Sisaket Rd; **Krung Thai**, 102 Meechai Rd; **Thai Farmers**, 929 Meechai Rd.

● **Hospital & medical services**

Meechai Rd, T 411504.

● **Immigration**

Sisaket Rd, T 411154.

● **Police**

Meechai Rd, T 411020.

● **Post & telecommunications**

Area code: 042. **Post Office**: Meechai Rd (opposite Soi Prisnee).

● **Shopping**

The best area to browse is down Rim Khong Road which (as the name suggests) runs along the river bank. Here Northeastern and Lao handicrafts are sold together with Chinese, Soviet and East European goods. It is possible to come away with a (former) Soviet military watch, an Isan 'axe' pillow, and 'French' sandalwood soap made in Laos. For better quality handicrafts visit *Village Weaver Handicrafts* on Prajak Road, a short distance on from the bus station, or at their showroom on Soi Jittapunya.

Books excellent bookshop and book exchange near the *Mut-Mee Guesthouse*.

● **Tour companies & travel agents**

With the opening of the Friendship Bridge to Laos in April 1994, tour operators have multiplied and there are now more than 10. *Udorn Business Travel* (Nongkhai branch), 447/10 Haisok Rd, T 411393 (will arrange tours to Laos along with necessary visas).

● **Transport**

620 km from Bangkok, 55 km from Udon Thani, 204 km from Loei.

Local transport Bicycle hire: from *Mut-Mee Guesthouse* ฿40/day; **Motorcycle hire**: from the *International Meeting Place*, 1117 Soi Chuanjit (฿200/day).

Train: station is 3 km from town, W on Kaeo Worawut Rd. Regular connections with Bangkok's Hualamphong station 11 hrs (฿103-450) and all stops NE – Ayutthaya, Saraburi, Korat, Khon Kaen and Udon.

Road Bus: BKS is on the E side of town on Praserm Rd, off Prajak Rd. Regular connections with Bangkok's Northern bus terminal 9-10 hrs (a/c ฿263, VIP ฿405, non-a/c ฿146) and Khon Kaen, Udon Thani and other Northeastern towns. Note that tuk-tuk drivers have taken to hounding farangs and charging exorbitant rates. Don't pay more than ฿10. VIP buses for Bangkok leave from 745 Prajak Rd. A/c buses from the corner of Haisok and Prajak rds. A/c buses also depart from the BKS station. **NB**: there are lots of sharks about.

International connections with Laos The Friendship Bridge over the Mekong River at Tambon Meechai 2 km from town opened in 1994 and now offers the first road link across the Mekong. The Bridge is open from 0800-1800 Mon-Sun. Tourists must obtain a visa from travel agents in Bangkok (there are several near the Lao Embassy at 193 Sathorn Tai Rd). Visas can be applied for in Nong Khai through agents, but passports are then sent to Bangkok for processing.

THE SOUTHERN MEKONG RIVER ROUTE

From Nong Khai, Route 212 follows the Mekong River eastwards and then south-eastwards to the riverside town of Beung Kan (137 km), and from there to the provincial capital of Nakhon Phanom (another 175 km). An alternative route from Udon Thani (via Ban Chiang) would pass close to the provincial capital of Sakhon Nakhon. Continuing southwards from Nakhon Phanom on the river road for another 50 km, Route 212 reaches That Phanom – the site of one of the most revered chedis in Thailand: Wat That Phanom. This area is also a centre of traditional textile production, particularly around the town of Renu Nakhon 15 km north of That Phanom. From That Phanom, Route 212 links up with the newly created provincial capital of Mukdahan (50 km south from That Phanom) and then, cutting away from the Mekong, with Ubon Ratchathani, a total of 267 km from Nakhon Phanom.

Beung Kan

A much more scenic and adventurous way to reach Nakhon Phanom is by taking the river road, Route 212, E from Nong Khai. This road follows the Mekong for nearly 320 km. The only logical place to break the journey is in the small and largely forgettable district town of Beung Kan, 137 km from Nong Khai and 175 km from Nakhon Phanom.

● **Accommodation** Basic accommodation only. **F** *Chanthra*, Chansin Rd; **F** *Neramit*, Prasatchai Rd; **F** *Samanmit*, Prasatchai Rd; **F** *Santisuk*, Prasatchai Rd.

● **Transport** 137 km from Nong Khai, 175 km from Nakhon Phanom. **Bus**: regular connections with Nong Khai and Nakhon Phanom.

Nakhon Phanom

Nakhon Phanom is an unexciting ramshackle place. Should the world be about to end, Nakhon Phanom would be among the last places to know. It does, however, have one plus point: it is situated on the Mekong River with the mountains of Laos as a backdrop. Like Nong Khai, sipping a beer or eating catfish curry overlooking the river does have a strange romantic appeal. But, most people only visit Nakhon Phanom en route to Phra That Phanom Chedi which is 50 km to the S and is the Northeast's most revered religious building (see That Phanom, below). Nakhon Phanom is the closest town with adequate hotels to the wat. Nakhon Phanom's limited sights include **Wat Sri Thep** on Srithep Road and **Wat Mahathat** (with a lotus-bud chedi), at the S end of Sunthon Vichit Road. Or simply wander along the river front past handicraft shops and a Chinese temple. There is a morning market on the river.

Excursions

Wat That Phanom (see page 349) lies 50 km S of town. **Getting there**: regular buses from the station near the market (฿20).

Renu Nakhon (see page 349) is a weaving centre 6.5 km off the main highway (Route 212), on the way to That Phanom. **Getting there**: by bus from the station near the market.

Wat Phrathat Narai Chengweng (Phrathat Naweng) is a Khmer prang dating from the 11th or 12th century. In spite of being reconstructed in what appears to be a remarkably haphazard fashion (surely the Khmers, master builders,

NAKHON PHANOM
TB 30a
Not to Scale

N

LAOS

Langsalanlang Rd

Aphibarn Bancha Rd

Sunthorn Vichit Rd

Rachathun Rd

Fuang Nakhon Rd

Poankaew Rd

To Airport & Sakhon Nakhon

Clocktower

Pier

Pier

M e k o n g   R i v e r

Thutsanapathun Rd

Wat Sri Thep

Wat Phosri

To That Phanom & Mukdahan

LAOS

1. Post Office
2. Police
3. Immigration Office
4. Telephone Office
5. TAT Office
6. *Mae Nam Khong Grand View* Hotel
7. *Nakhon Phanom* Hotel
8. *First* Hotel
9. *River Inn*
10. *Srithep* Hotel

would have cut stone that fitted?) this small sanctuary is very satisfying. Lying in a peaceful wat compound, it displays finely carved lintels: the E lintel (above the entrance to the sanctuary) shows Siva dancing; the N face, Vishnu reclining on a naga. The wat is 88 km W of Nakhon Phanom on Route 22, at the junction with Route 223 (it is signposted). Walk through a green archway, and the wat is 500m along a dirt track. **Getting there**: take a bus travelling towards Sakhon Nakhon from the bus station near the market.

Phrathat Choeng Chum in the provincial capital of Sakhon Nakhon is an important pilgrimage place for Thais. See page 331.

Festivals

Oct: *Ok Phansa* (9-13th, end of Buddhist Lent) four day celebrations with *long-boat races*, and the launching of illuminated boats onto the Mekong.

Local information

● **Accommodation**

A-B *Nam Khong Grand View*, 527 Sunthorn Vichit Rd, T 513564, F 511071, a/c, restaurant, pool, new hotel with 114 rooms, best in town.

B-C *Nakhon Phanom*, 403 Aphibarn Bancha Rd, T 511455, F 511071, a/c, restaurant, pool, rather shabby, best rooms in the new wing.

C-D *River Inn*, 137 Sunthorn Vichit Rd, T 511305, some a/c, restaurant, nice position overlooking river, but overpriced and shabby, noisy rooms on the road side; **C-D** *Sri Thep*, 708/11 Srithep Rd, T 511437, F 511346, some a/c, nothing special.

D-E *First*, 370 Srithep Rd, T 511253, some a/c; **D-E** *Lucky*, 131 Aphibarn Bancha Rd, T 511274.

E *Chakkawan*, 676/12-13 Aphibarn Bancha Rd, T 511298.

● **Places to eat**
Ban Suan, 405 Sunthorn Vichit Rd; *Golden Giant Catfish*, Sunthorn Vichit Rd; *NKP Bakery*, by *Nakhon Phanom Hotel*; *Sri Nakhon*, 544/4 Thamrong Prasit Rd.

● **Banks & money changers**
Bangkok, Srithep Rd; *Thai Farmers*, 439 Aphibarn Bancha Rd.

● **Hospitals & medical services**
Sunthorn Vichit Rd, T 511422.

● **Immigration**
Sunthorn Vichit Rd, T 51147.

● **Police**
Sunthorn Vichit Rd (N end) 3.

● **Post & telecommunications**
Post Office: Sunthorn Vichit Rd (N end). **Telephone Office**: off Fuang Nakhon Rd. **Area code**: 042.

● **Shopping**
Souvenir and handicraft shops on the riverfront (Sunthorn Vichit Rd) e.g. *Tida*.

● **Sport**
Snooker: *Nakhon Phanom Hotel*, Aphibarn Bancha Rd.

● **Tourist offices**
TAT (temporary office), c/o 2/16 Salaklang Rd, T 513490, F 513492. Areas of responsibility are Nakhon Phanom, Sakhon Nakhon and Mukdahan.

● **Transport**
735 km from Bangkok, 242 km from Udon and 296 km from Nong Khai.

Road Bus: the station is near the market, opposite the *Nakhon Phanom Hotel*. Regular connections with Khon Kaen, Ubon, Bangkok, 13 hrs (a/c ฿130, VIP ฿480, non-a/c ฿172) and Nong Khai via Sakhon Nakhon. If you wish to take the more interesting route which follows the Mekong, then take a bus to Beung Kan and change. Tour buses running S to Ubon leave twice a day at 0700 and 1400 near the *Windsor Hotel*, 4½ hrs.

Sakhon Nakhon

Sakhon Nakhon is an ancient town and was one of the Khmer empires' more important provincial centres in the Northeast. It supports the second most sacred Lao-style stupa in Thailand – the **Phrathat Choeng Chum** (the most sacred is That Phanom). This 24m-tall, white, angular, lotus bud chedi has become an important pilgrimage spot for Thais. The chedi is built over a laterite Khmer prang dating from the 11th or 12th century. Another important religious site in town is **Wat Pa Suthawat**, opposite the town hall. This is important not for any artistic merit but because one of Thailand's most revered monks lived and died here – Phra Acaan Man Bhuritatto better known as Luang Pho Man (1871-1949). A chapel in his memory has been constructed and his (few) possessions kept on display.

The **Phu Thai** ethnic group inhabit the area around Sakhon Nakhon, and the Wax Castle festival is associated with them (see below). The 32 sq km **Nong Han Lake** is close to town. Boats can be hired to visit the islands of the lake, and it is a popular place at weekends.

Excursions
Phrathat Narai Chengweng is another important chedi, situated 5 km from town in the village of Ban Thai. It is made of laterite and is Khom in style. Getting there: by songthaew or local bus.

Festivals
Oct: *Wax Castle Ceremony*, celebrated at *Ok Phansa* (the end of the Buddhist lent), when elaborate and intricately detailed models of wats are moulded out of bees-wax in order to gain merit. Images of the Buddha are placed inside these temporary edifices and they are paraded through town accompanied by Northeastern music, singing and dancing. *Boat races* take place at Nong Han Lake at the same time.

Local information
● **Accommodation**
The Dusit group of hotels is planning to open the *Srisakol Thani Hotel* at the beginning of 1995. It will become the only international hotel in town. **C** *Dusit*, 1782-4 Yuwa Phattana Rd, T 711198 F 713115, some a/c, swimming pool, not an up-country equivalent of the Dusit Thani in Bangkok, 102 rather average rooms; **C** *Imperial*, 1892 Suk Khasem Rd, T 713320, some a/c,

180 rooms and a snooker parlour.

D-E *Somkiat*, 1348/4 Kamchatphai, T 711740, some a/c, a central block with 22 additional bungalows.

E *Araya*, 1432 Prempreeda Rd, T 711224, some a/c, 50 simple rooms.

● **Transport**
647 km from Bangkok. **Road Bus**: regular connections with Bangkok's Northern bus terminal, 11 hrs (a/c ฿271, VIP ฿420, non-a/c ฿150) and with other Northeastern centres.

That Phanom

The small town of That Phanom is a quaint riverside settlement with one attraction: **Wat That Phanom**, the most revered temple in the Northeast and the second most revered by the people of Laos (the most revered being That Luang in Vientiane). The wat is dominated by an impressive 52m white and gold Lao-style chedi. Around its square base the chedi is decorated with carved brick slabs telling the stories of the 5 state rulers who are said to have built the original stupa in the 9th century. Since then it has been restored no less than 7 times, most recently in 1977 by the Thai Fine Arts Department. This final restoration followed the chedi's collapse after heavy rains in 1975. A legend said that should the chedi fall, then so too would the country of Laos – shortly afterwards the Communist Pathet Lao took Luang Prabang and Vientiane, and ousted the American-backed government. The chedi is surrounded by seated Buddha images that the many hundreds of pilgrims have covered in gold leaf. During festivals and religious holidays the wat is seething with people making offerings of flowers and incense.

On Mon and Thurs a 'Lao' market is held upstream from town when hoards of Laotians cross the Mekong to market their wares. They arrive laden with pigs, wild forest products, and herbal remedies, returning home with cash and Thai consumer goods. The market winds down soon after mid-day.

Being so close to Laos is tantalizing: but although Laos and Thais spend the day being ferried back and forth across the river for ฿10, *farangs* are still not allowed to make the crossing.

Excursions
Renu Nakhon, a traditional weaving and embroidery centre, is almost 15 km NW of That Phanom. Travel 8 km N on Route 212, and then left onto Route 2031 for another 6.5 km (currently an unmade-up road being improved). On market days (Wed) and fair days the central wat of the village is home to hundreds of stalls selling a wide selection of local and Lao textiles (cotton and silk) as well as made-up garments and Isan axe pillows. Outside the wat compound, there are permanent shops selling a similar selection of cloth and local handicrafts throughout the week. Cloth is sold by the *phun* and there are about 2 *phun* in a sarong length. Prices quoted therefore do not usually relate to the piece. For simple cotton cloth expect to pay ฿100-200/*phun*. For the best silk up to ฿3,000. **Getting there**: by bus from That Phanom (or Nakhon Phanom) to Renu Nakhon.

Festivals
Jan/Feb: *Phra That Phanom Chedi Homage-paying Fair* (full moon) – the Northeast's largest temple fair when thousands of pilgrims converge on the wat and walk around the chedi in homage. Dancing, bands and other entertainments – perhaps the most vivid display of Northeastern regional identity. The entire town is engulfed by market stalls, selling a vast array of goods for the week of the festival, day and night.

Local information
● **Accommodation**
When the fair is on, it is difficult to find a room. No up-market hotels here, so to be comfortable visitors will need to stay in Nakhon Phanom. **F** *E-sarn Guesthouse*, 29/18 Mu 14 Soi Pherpushanee (W of bus terminal on inner, river street), rooms in traditional country

house, in peaceful leafy compound; **F** _Niyana's Guesthouse_, 65 Rim Khong Soi Withisaorachon, restaurant, in peaceful position on the riverbank nr the pier, upstream from town, large rooms with fans and nets, helpful and friendly owner, tours and motorbikes for rent; **E-F** _Saengthong_, 34 Phanom Phanarak Rd, small hotel with just 17 rooms, shabby but has character, rec.

● **Places to eat**

Foodstalls and restaurants can be found on the riverfront and along Rachdamnern Rd – try the _Thatuenom Pochana_ or _Somkhane_, both fish restaurants close to the triumphal arch.

● **Banks & money changers**

Thai Military, on the main road into town (Route 212), N of Wat That Phanom.

● **Useful addresses**

Immigration: Rachdamnern Rd, by the river, T 541090. **Post Office**: N of the Thai Military Bank.

● **Transport**

50 km from Nakhon Phanom.

Road Bus: regular connections with Nakhon Phanom and Ubon Ratchatani.

Mukdahan

Mukdahan is the capital of Thailand's newest province created in 1982. The town's greatest claim to fame is as the hometown of one of Thailand's best-known leaders – Field Marshal Sarit Thanarat (see page 84). Although Mukdahan is changing fast as one of the gateways to an emerging Laos, until recently many of the villages roundabouts were cut off from the outside world during the wet season. There are still a few old-style wooden houses – but they are fast disappearing.

The town is situated on the Mekong River, and lies directly opposite the important Lao town of Savannakhet. It is like a quiet version of Nong Khai. For the best views of the river and surrounding countryside, climb **Phu Manorom**, a small hill 5 km S of town. Take route 2034 S towards Don Tan and after 2 km turn right. The summit is another 3 km from the turn-off.

Because of its location, Mukdahan has become an important trading centre with goods from Laos – gems, timber, cattle and agricultural commodities – being exchanged for Thai consumer goods. There is a Lao and Thai **market**, held daily, along the river road running S from **Wat Si Mongkhon Tai** which is situated opposite the pier where boats from Laos land. It is best to get to the market in the morning. Along with Thai consumer goods, Lao silk and cotton cloth (see Shopping, below), good French bread, china, 'axe' cushions and baskets are also sold. Near the pier and opposite Wat Si Mongkhon Tai is a Bodhi tree (_Ficus religiosa_). Traditional soothsayer often offer their advice here. The pier and riverside road is a good place to watch Mukdahan life go – slowly – by.

Wat Sri Sumong on Samran Chai Khong Rd, the river road, is interesting for the colonial architectural elements reflected in the bot or ordination hall: the arches over the windows and the verandah. Between the bot and the more orthodox viharn is a small example of the distinctive Lao, lotus bud chedi. A little further N on the river road, **Wat Yod Kaew Sriwichai** also has Lao lotus bud chedis and a large, gold Buddha in the mudra of spinning the Wheel of Law.

Excursions

Phu Pha Thoep National Park (also known as Mukdahan National Park) lies 15 km S of Mukdahan, off route 2034. The park was gazetted in 1984 and covers a modest 54 sq km. The principal forest type here is dry dipterocarp savanna forest and there are a succession of oddly-shaped rock outcrops easily accessible from park headquarters. The environment almost feels prehistoric, and fossils and finger paintings have been found amidst the boulders. Cut into the cliff face which rises above the headquarters is a cave packed with Buddha images deposited here by villagers.

MUKDAHAN TB 30†

N

Phithak Santirat Rd

Soi Kaew Mongkhon

Pier for boats to Laos

Mekong River

Song Nang Rd

Police & a/c buses

Muang Mai Rd

Soi Phitak Phanomkhet

← To Bus station (1.5 km)

Samut Sakdarak Rd

Wat Yod Kaew Sriwichai

Soi Janthep

Soi Damrong Mukda

Wat Sri Sumong

Soi Sri Sumong

Samut Sakdarak Rd

Soi Sri Worabut

To Indo-China Intercontinental Hotel (500 m) & Phu Manorani

1. Tour companies to Laos & Cambodia
2. Lao handicrafts shop
3. Sa-aat Antiques
4. Immigration office
5. Post Office
6. Thai Farmers Bank
7. Bangkok Bank of Commerce
8. Bangkok Bank

Restaurants:
9. Phit Bakery
10. Enjoy
11. No name restaurant in wooden house
12. Phai Rim Khong
13. Sukhawadi
14. River View
15. Sala Foremost
16. *Mukdahan Hotel*
17. *Hong Kong Hotel*
18. *Hua Nam Hotel*

Tours

There are four small tour offices opposite Wat Si Mongkhon Tai, at the N end of Samran Chai Khong Rd – *TAR Tour*, *Mukdahan Tour (Thailand)*, *Sompong Tour* and *Sakonpasa Department Store*. They are mainly oriented towards Thai tourists travelling to Laos and Vietnam. However they will organise tours for foreigners *but only if they already have a visa* for the country concerned. Day tours to Laos cost ฿370-470, a 4 day/3 night tour to Vietnam ฿18,000, and a 3 day/2 night tour to Laos ฿12,500.

Local information
● **Accommodation**

A *Indochina Intercontinental*, Samut Sakdarak Rd, T 611893, 1 km S of town centre, a/c, restaurant, new hotel opening mid-1994, will be best in town with 154 rooms.

B-C *Mukdahan*, 8/8 Samut Sakdarak Rd, T 611619, ½ km S of the town centre, some a/c, 4-storey hotel, quite new but already frayed at the edges, a/c rooms have hot water and TV but no ambience, coffee shop with live music.

C-E *Hua Nam*, 36 Samut Sakdarak Rd, T 611137, some a/c, central location on corner with Song Nang Sathit Rd, looks from the outside like a regular Chinese-style hotel, but rooms are large, clean and well maintained, a/c rooms with TVs and hot water, set around courtyard so relatively quiet despite central crossroads location, rec.

D-E *Hong Kong*, 161/1-2 Phithak Santirat Rd, T 611123, some a/c, Chinese-style hotel, quite well maintained, a/c rooms have hot water, central; **D-E** *Sansuk Bungalow*, 2 Phithak Santirat Rd, T 611294, some a/c, near the centre of town, clean rooms with friendly management, the best of the cheaper accommodation.

● **Places to eat**

The best places to eat are along the river. Tables are set out on the pavement overlooking the Mekong and Laos. In the evening, with fairy light lit trees, and a gentle breeze, there can be few more attractive places to eat and drink. Riverside restaurants include the *River View*, *Sukhawadi* and *Phai Rim Khong*. ♦♦-♦♦♦*Enjoy Restaurant*, 7/1 Samut Sakdarak Rd, bright and cheerful restaurant with Lao speci-

Accommodation: no bungalows, but camping is permitted. Getting there: catch a songthaew travelling S towards Don Tan; the turning for the park is between the 14 and 15 km markers and it is a 2 km walk from there to the park headquarters.

Wat Phu Daan Tae contains a massive sitting Buddha made of brick and concrete, surrounded by acolytes. It can be seen clearly from route 212, running S towards Ubon, about 50 km from town. Getting there: only worth stopping for the seriously committed. Take a bus running S towards Ubon.

alities, a few Vietnamese dishes and river fish and prawns; ♦♦*Phai Rim Khong* (*Riverside*), Samran Chai Khong Rd, a riverside restaurant to the S of town, serving good Thai dishes in attractive location with good views; ♦♦*River View*, Samran Chai Khong Rd, chalet-style restaurant with tables overlooking Mekong, average Thai and Lao food, spectacular setting; ♦♦*Sukhawadi*, Samran Chai Khong, Mekong fish is best, but other Thai dishes available, great position on the river; ♦*Foremost*, 74/1 Samut Sakdarak Rd, breakfast, ice cream and coffee in a/c room; ♦*Night market*, Song Nang Sathit Rd (W end near the bus station). The best place for cheap Isan dishes and also for Vietnamese stall food. ♦*No Name Restaurant*, Phithak Santirat Rd (on roundabout), excellent cheap Thai dishes served from old wooden house; ♦*Phit Bakery*, 709 Phithak Santirat, good breakfasts, coffee, cakes and ice creams, friendly, rec.

● **Banks & money changers**

Bangkok Bank, Song Nang Sathit Rd; **Thai Farmers Bank**, Song Nang Sathit Rd.

● **Immigration**

Samran Chai Khong Rd, T 611074.

● **Shopping**

Handicrafts: Mukdahan is a good place to buy Lao/Isan handicrafts like baskets, axe cushions and textiles. Cloth is usually sold by the *phun*; a sarong length is normally 2 *phun*, so when asking the price do not be surprised if the whole piece costs twice (or more) than the amount quoted. Cotton cloth is normally

₿100/*phun*; silk costs several times more. The textiles with the elephant motif are distinctively Lao, although much of the cloth is now woven in Thailand, especially around Nong Khai. Textiles and other handicrafts can be bought in the daily riverside market (see Places of interest, above). There are also permanent shops on Samut Sakdarak Rd. **Antiques**: *Sa-aat*, 77 Samut Sakdarak Rd, small collection of antiques for sale including Chinese ceramics, old irons, Buddhist alms bowls and amulets.

● **Post & telecommunications**

Post Office: Phithak Santirat Rd (on the roundabout). **Area code**: 042.

● **Transport**

50 km S of That Phanom, 170 km N of Ubon.

Road Bus: the bus terminal (*bor kor sor*) for non-a/c and *some* a/c buses is at the W end of Song Nang Sathit Rd, about 2 km from the town centre (a ₿10 motor saamlor ride). Buses from here to Ubon, Nakhon Phanom and That Phanom, and some other NE towns, as well as Bangkok. A/c tour buses leave from close to Bangkok Bank on Song Nang Sathit Rd. Connections with Bangkok's northern bus terminal 12 hrs (a/c ₿287, VIP ₿445, non-a/c ₿158), N to That Phanom and Nakhon Phanom 2 hrs, and S to Ubon Ratchathani 3 hrs. Tour buses leave from *Sahamit Tours*, offices on Samut Sakdarak Rd, also close to the town centre.

International connections to Laos Ferries to Laos leave from the pier near Wat Si Mongkhon Tai. But as yet, foreigners are only permitted if they already have a visa.

THE EASTERN REGION

CONTENTS

MAPS

The Eastern region is sandwiched between the Gulf of Thailand to the south and the Damrek range of mountains to the north. It covers 37,507 sq km and stretches 400 km from Bangkok, south-eastwards to Trat on the Cambodian border. It is similar to the Western region, in that it is small in area, without any focal city, and lacking a characteristic regional culture. It is also akin to the West in that, at least until not very long ago, the East was a region of fruit trees, gem mining and forests – a relatively quiet and traditional area. It also had a flourishing fishing industry exploiting the waters of the Gulf of Thailand and serving the Bangkok market.

Although these activities have been overshadowed by recent developments, there are still orchards between Rayong and Chantaburi, a multitude of fishing communities along the Gulf coast, and a major centre for gem mining at Chantaburi, where many of Thailand's finest sapphires come.

However, the East has been transformed since the 1960s. Illegal loggers have largely cleared the area of trees, and landless families from other parts of the Kingdom – with the encouragement and support of Chinese middlemen – have moved in to plant the land to upland crops such as cassava and maize. As the forests were being replaced by crops, the beaches of the eastern Gulf were witnessing an extraordinary growth in tourism. This was focused on the famous (to some infamous) beach resort of Pattaya, about 150 km from Bangkok. Beginning as a resort for small numbers of Thais and *farangs* who wished to escape from the capital for weekend breaks, Pattaya developed into one of the key destinations for American GIs on leave during the Vietnam War. With the end of that war, Pattaya adroitly switched its attention to the international tourist market, attracting increasing numbers of men (and a few women). A Tourist Authority of Thailand survey revealed that over one-fifth of all tourists to Thailand visited the area of Pattaya and Chonburi. Assuming the survey is accurate (never a sensible assumption to make in Thailand), this would mean that in 1989 nearly a million tourists visited this resort – the Thai equivalent of the Costa del Sol.

Although tourism is important to the economy of the East – and there is still room for further expansion – in recent years this has been superceded by its role as an overspill area for Bangkok. As Bangkok's infrastructure came under ever greater pressure, the government began looking for ways to ease the strain on the capital. In the early 1980s, it came up with the much vaunted Eastern Seaboard Development Project, a massive scheme to develop roads, ports, rail links, pipelines and gas separation plants concentrated along a corridor between the towns of Chonburi and Rayong. The project has suffered interminable delays and scandals – with much land speculation, corruption, murder and intrigue – but it is now 'on stream'. On the 1¾ hour drive from Bangkok the transformation of the region is evident.

CHONBURI TO PATTAYA

Route 3 from Bangkok follows Thailand's eastern seaboard to the Cambodian border. The first 130 km (on the new Highway 34) is a ribbon of development – effectively Bangkok's industrial overspill. Companies have moved here to escape the high land prices and congestion of the capital. As a result former sleepy towns like Chonburi and Si Racha have been engulfed. 147 km from Bangkok is the renowned beach resort of Pattaya, brash and brazen. Past Pattaya, Route 3 swings eastwards and passes through the town of Rayong (70

km from Pattaya), and then Ban Phe, where boats leave for the island of Koh Samet. Continuing on Route 3, Chantaburi is 109 km from Rayong, and Trat another 70 km on from here. Both towns are highly regarded for their fruit and gems. From the port of Laem Ngop, 17 km from Trat, boats leave for Koh Chang.

Chonburi

Chonburi is the first significant town travelling SE from Bangkok along Route 3. It is an important commercial centre with oyster farms and fruit processing and canning plants serving the sugarcane, cassava and coconut farms and plantations of the area. It also has a reputation as a battlefield for the Chinese mafia. There is not much of interest for the tourist in this dusty town. The

oldest and most important wat in the province is **Wat Intharam**, which is near the old market. The wat, dating from the Ayutthaya Period, is unusual in that it has not been extensively restored. The bot contains an excellent series of formally structured murals with no sense of perspective dating from the late 18th century. Near the centre of town is **Wat Dhamma Nimitr**, which contains a 37-m high image of the Buddha in a boat and covered in gold mosaic. Not only is this Buddha image the largest in the region, it is also one of the few in the country with a maritime theme.

● **Festivals** Oct: *Buffalo Races* (moveable). Races and contests between buffalo and man.

● **Accommodation B-C** *Sukjai Bungalow*, 17/32 Phayasatya Rd, T 282255, some a/c; *Likhit*, 781 Chetchamnong Rd, T 273810, F 273811, some a/c, restaurant.

● **Transport** 80 km from Bangkok, 67 km from Pattaya. **Road Bus**: regular connections with Bangkok's Eastern bus terminal (฿20-37), Pattaya and other eastern destinations.

Bang Saen

Bang Saen is a beach resort popular with middle-class Thais. It is crowded at the weekends but practically deserted during the week. The town is clearly attempting to become another Pattaya, although it is difficult to see how it will succeed. That said, it does have a Hotels and Tourism Training Institute, so it should provide skilled services – and the town is surprisingly clean. On Monkey Hill there is the **shrine of Chao Mae Khao Sammuk**, a Chinese girl who drowned herself in the 18th century after her parents refused to allow her to marry the man she loved. Now a Goddess, many Sino-Thais visit the shrine to improve their luck. The oyster beds for which the town is known can be seen from the hill. There is usually a welcome onshore breeze on the sandy palm-fringed beach. The **Ocean World Amusement Park** is on the Beach Road,

T 383096. Admission: ฿150 adults, ฿100 children. Open: Mon-Sun. There is a **Marine Science Museum** in Srinakarinwirot University.

● **Accommodation A-C** *Bang Saen Beach Resort*, 55-150 Beach Rd, T 381675, B 2536385, a/c, restaurant, pool, close to the action; **A-C** *Bang Saen Villa*, T 282088, F 383333, a/c, restaurant, pool; **C-D** *Saen Sabai Bungalow*, 153 Beach Rd, T 381063, a/c, restaurant.

● **Places to eat** Good seafood.

● **Banks & money changers** Siam Commercial, 53/1 Bang Saen Rd.

● **Post & telecommunications Area code**: 039.

● **Transport** 18 km S of Chonburi, 98 km from Bangkok. **Road Bus**: regular connections with Bangkok's Eastern Bus terminal (1½ hrs) and with Chonburi and Pattaya.

Si Racha

Si Racha is the home of a locally famous hot chilli sauce (*nam prik Si Racha*), usually eaten with seafood, for which the town also has a reputation. The town has a profusion of seafood restaurants, the most enjoyable of which are built on jetties which protrude out to sea. Westerners usually visit Si Racha in order to reach the island of Koh Si Chang (see below), but the town does have character and is worth more than a cursory wander.

A short distance to the N of town is a small, gaudy but nevertheless enjoyable **Sino-Thai wat** built on a rocky islet – Koh Loi – connected to the mainland by a long causeway. The monastery commemorates a monk who spent many years on the rock and it boasts a Buddha's footprint as well as an image of the Chinese Goddess of Mercy, Kuan Yin (see Quan Am box, page 324). On Choemchomphon Road, the waterfront road, and almost opposite Soi 16, the **Jaw Phor Samut Dam Chinese temple** said to be 100 years old. Up the road towards the clock-tower at the southern end is a large covered **market**. However, perhaps the most enjoyable feature of Si Racha (and of Koh Si Chang) are the overpowered, chariot-like **motorized saamlors**. Purring along, with deep bucket seats and massive engines, the machines seem like outrageous modernized rickshaws. They cannot be a terribly efficient form of transport and it probably will not be long before they are elbowed-out by the ubiquitous tuk-tuk – unless their macho appeal helps them to survive.

Now that the Eastern Seaboard, and in particular the length of coast between Chonburi and Rayong, has been chosen as the overspill area for Bangkok's industry there has been an upsurge in activity around Si Racha. **Laem Chabang**, just the other side of Khao Nam Sap, a modest hill 10 km to the S of town, is being developed into a major deep-water port and can be seen from the road to Pattaya. Even closer to Si Racha, just a few km S, is the Thai Oil refinery. So far, Si Racha has maintained its poise amidst all the activity.

● **Accommodation** Like its restaurants, all the hotels mentioned below are also built over the sea – which makes a pleasant change from the usual featureless budget accommodation available in Thai towns. **B-C** *Grand Bungalow*, 9 Choemchomphon Rd, T 312537, S end; **C-E** *Srivichai*, Choemchomphon Rd Soi 8, T 311212, wooden hotel, friendly, rec; **D-F** *Bungalow Sri Wattana*, Choemchomphon Rd Soi 8, T 311037, wooden hotel, friendly, rec; **D-E** *Samchai*, Choemchomphon Rd Soi 10, T 311134, some a/c, wooden hotel, clean rooms, good atmosphere, rec.

● **Places to eat** Seafood and Thai: *Si Racha Seafood*, Choemchomphon Rd (near the bus stop); *Cherinot*, Choemchomphon Rd Soi 14 (pier), also serves Chinese; *Jaw Sii*, 98 Choemchomphon Rd, also serves Chinese; *Hua Huat*, 102 Choemchomphon Rd, also serves Chinese.

● **Banks & money changers** Bangkok Bank of Commerce, Surasak Rd.

● **Transport** 24 km S of Chonburi, 29 km N of Pattaya, 105 km from Bangkok. **Road Bus:** regular connections with Bangkok's Eastern bus terminal (non a/c ₿26) as well as with Pattaya and Chonburi.

Koh Si Chang

Koh Si Chang is a modest sized island about 40 mins ferry-ride from Si Racha. Although it is quite feasible to visit the island as a day trip, there are hotels and camping facilities for those who might wish to stay longer. Koh Si Chang used to be the trans-shipment point for both cargo and passenger vessels before the Chao Phraya River was dredged sufficiently to allow ships to reach Bangkok. Even though many vessels now by-pass Si Racha, the surrounding water is still choc-a-bloc with ships at anchor, their cargoes being unloaded into smaller lighters and barges.

Places of interest

At the N edge of the town, set high up on a hill (a tiring walk to the top), there is a **Chinese temple – Chaw Por Khaw Yai**. With an assortment of variously decorated shrines and caves, and with views of the island and town, it makes a good first stop after docking at the jetty beneath the temple. A particular favourite with the Chinese at Chinese New Year, it is said that during the festivities, over 5,000 people visit the shrine each evening.

On the W side of the island is **Khaw Khad**, a popular seaside fishing spot for Bangkokians. Not far away to the S, and overlooking the town, is a **Buddhist retreat** set among limestone caves (unlit). A large yellow seated Buddha image looks out over the bay. On the E coast, S of the retreat, are the **ruins of a palace** built by Rama V. It was abandoned in 1893 when the French took control of the island during their confrontation with the Thais regarding each country's respective rights of suzerainty over Laos. Not much remains – in fact, most of the structure was dismantled and rebuilt in Bangkok. Rather eerie stairways, balustrades and an empty reservoir remain scattered across the rocky, frangipani-covered hillside – as if the palace had been vaporized. The only building of any size remaining is **Wat Atsadangnimit**, which is still revered. Open: 0800-1800.

The island also has a number of **beaches** and reasonable swimming and snorkelling. The quietest beach with the best coral is **Tham Phang** on the W side of the island (฿80 by tuk-tuk); easier to reach are **Tha Wang** (next to the palace) and **Hat Sai Kaew** (over the hill from the palace). At weekends the island becomes crowded with Thai day-trippers; it is more relaxed during the week.

Local information

● **Accommodation**

C *Benz*, T 216091, some a/c, unusual stone bungalows; **C** *Champ*, T 216105, some a/c, restaurant; **C-D** *Tew Phai*, T 216084, some a/c, good restaurant, welcoming management and usually busy with activity, the best of the cheaper places to stay.

D *Green House*, T 216024, simple rooms at the edge of the town.

● **Camping**

This is possible, but bring your own equipment; at weekends Thais from the mainland camp in large numbers.

● **Banks & money changers**

Thai Farmers, 9-9/1-2 Coast Rd.

● **Post & telecommunications**

Area code: 038.

● **Transport**

Local There are a number of the massive motorized **saamlors** that are also found in Si Racha and Chonburi. Given that the roads (in reality, paths) only allow the drivers to attain a speed of about 30 km/hr, they must be among the most overpowered taxis in the world. A tour of all the sights should not be more than ฿100 – and in chariot-like splendour (the owner of No. 38, Nerng, speaks reasonable English).

Sea Boat: regular daytime ferry service from Jermjomphon Rd Soi 14 in Si Racha 0900-1700 outward, 0630-1630 return, 40 mins (฿20). At low water the boats run from Koh Loi causeway which runs out to the wat on the N side of Si Racha.

PATTAYA

Pattaya or 'South-west wind' is argued by some to be Thailand's premier beach resort. Only 20 years ago, it was a little-known coastal village frequented by fishermen, farmers and a handful of Thai and *farang* weekenders. It began to metamorphose when the US navy set up shop at the nearby port of Sattahip (40 km further down the coast) and American sailors began to demand something more than just sand and sea. As the war in Vietnam escalated, so the influx of GIs on 'rest and recreation' also grew and Pattaya responded enthusiastically (not by chance, Pattaya was selected as an R & R destination for the UN forces in Cambodia bringing the town the title 'city of peace'). Today, it provides over 20,000 hotel rooms and supplies everything you could ever need from a beach holiday – except peace and quiet. Given its origins in the Vietnam War, it is hardly surprising that Pattaya's stock in trade is entertainment for unaccompanied men who arrive in droves; many of them on package tours. At any one time, about 4,000 girls are touting for work around the many bars and restaurants of Pattaya.

In 1990 2.7 million people are said to have visited Pattaya. This has inevitably led to environmental problems. Lack of treatment of polluted water has meant that the beaches are not as clean as they once were. However, in 1992, the government intends to spend US$42 million in an effort to clean up Pattaya's act and Pattaya is already Thailand's first provincial city to have a water treatment plant. Indeed, Pattaya is going out of its way to play down its go-go bar image and promote a 'family' resort profile. This is deemed to be good for business, and perhaps the only way that occupancy rates can be maintained when the sex industry in Thailand is coming under such scrutiny, both for health and social reasons. It was no coincidence that an international conference on 'sustainable tourism' was held in Jomtien, outside Pattaya, in March 1993. The conference produced the so-called Pattaya Protocol—a series of guidelines on how to promote culturally and environmentally sensitive tourism.

The busiest and noisiest area is at the S end of town (South Pattaya or 'The Village') where there must be one of the

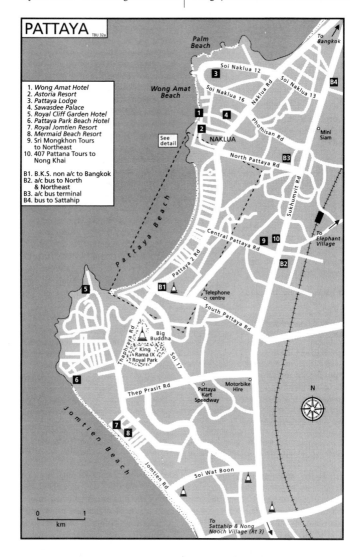

PATTAYA TBU 32a

1. Wong Amat Hotel
2. Astoria Resort
3. Pattaya Lodge
4. Sawasdee Palace
5. Royal Cliff Garden Hotel
6. Pattaya Park Beach Hotel
7. Royal Jomtien Resort
8. Mermaid Beach Resort
9. Sri Mongkhon Tours to Northeast
10. 407 Pattana Tours to Nong Khai

B1. B.K.S. non a/c to Bangkok
B2. a/c bus to North & Northeast
B3. a/c bus terminal
B4. bus to Sattahip

highest concentration of bars, discos, massage parlours, prostitutes and transvestites of any place in the world. Many people find this aspect of Pattaya repugnant. However, there is no pretence here – either on the part of the hosts or their guests. This is a beach resort of the most lurid kind. **Warning**: it is worth bearing in mind that whatever people might tell you, Thailand *does* have an **AIDS** problem, the most serious in Asia (see page 101).

Pattaya may be infamous in the West as a city of sin, but there is more to the resort than this popular perception might indicate. It is also a haven for watersports lovers: there is sailing, parasailing, windsurfing, ski-boating, snorkelling, deep-sea fishing and scuba diving. And for the non-beach lover, there are trips to sapphire mines, orchid farms and elephant kraals as well as tennis, golf (the Siam Country Club has the best course in Thailand), bowling and a multitude of other sports. Pattaya is also remarkably good value. It is probably this, coupled with the range of activities and services on offer (and Pattaya's accessibility) which explains why – despite the bad press – the resort has so many repeat guests (25-50%).

The town itself is simple to get around. It consists of one long straight seafront road running the length of the beach (Pattaya Beach Road), together with another parallel road just inland (Pattaya 2 Road). Linking the 2 there are innumerable 'sois' (lanes) packed with bars, restaurants and hotels. The greatest concentration of restaurants and bars is at the S end of town.

S of Pattaya Bay, past the Big Buddha on the hill, is the quieter **Jomtien Beach**, which is becoming more popular by the month. Here there are more hotels, restaurants and sports facilities as well as a cleaner, shadier beach.

Excursions

Mini Siam is a cultural and historical park where Thailand's most famous 'sights' are recreated in quarter-sized models. Getting there: by tour or by songthaew; the park lies 3 km N of Pattaya Beach, on the Sukhumvit highway (Route 3) running to Bangkok. Open: 0700-2200.

Khao Khieo 'Open Zoo' is a 500 ha forested area supporting 130 species of bird and 38 mammal (including a few leopards); there is also a wildlife education centre with museum, and the requisite waterfall (*Chanta Then*). There is no overnight accommodation. Admission: adults ฿10, children ฿5, ฿10 for a car. Getting there: 30 km N on Route 3, turn inland near Bang Saen on Route 3144. The park lies close to Bang Phra Golf Course.

Elephant Village near the Siam Country Club. Admission: ฿250, show at 1430. Contact *Tropicana Hotel* for booking, T 428645-8, Ext Elephant Village Counter or T 249174.

Nong Nooch Orchid Wonderland is a 200 ha park containing immaculate gardens with lakes (and boating), an orchid farm, family zoo, Thai handicraft demonstrations and a twice-daily (1000-1130 and 1500-1630) 'cultural spectacular' with Thai dancing, Thai boxing and an elephant show. It is similar to the 'Rose Garden' complex outside Bangkok and is rather artificial, though it serves a purpose for tourists visiting nowhere but Pattaya and is popular with children. Accommodation is available in traditional Thai cottages and there are a number of restaurants. It is located 18 km S on Route 3. Admission: ฿20, ฿150 for the cultural show, or take a tour from Pattaya for ฿250. Open: 0900-1800 Mon-Sun.

Bang Saray is a fishing village 20 km S of Pattaya on Route 3, with seafood restaurants (notably the *Ruan Talay*) and a good base for game-fishing trips, which can be arranged at the Fisherman's Inn, Fisherman's Lodge, or the Sea Sand

Club; a chartered boat costs about ฿2500. Accommodation: **B** *Fisherman's Lodge*, T 436069, a/c, restaurant; **B** *Fisherman's Inn*, T 436095, a/c, restaurant, pool, spacious grounds; **C** *Bang Saray Villa*, T 437919, a/c, restaurant, pool. The Sea Sand Club has facilities for windsurfing. Getting there: by bus from Pattaya.

Offshore Islands When Pattaya gets too much, many people retire to one of the offshore islands for rest and recreation of a different kind. The largest island (and the only one with accommodation) is **Koh Larn**, with good snorkelling and scuba diving waters surrounding it. Glass-bottomed boats are available for touring the reef, as is the full array of watersports. The island even has an 18-hole golf course. Accommodation: *Koh Larn Resort*; its office is at 183 Soi Post Office, T 428422. **B** for bungalows, which includes the boat fare and transfer to the bungalows. Getting there: the Resort office will organize boats, or tickets can be purchased from the booth next to the Sailing Club. Boats depart at 0930 and 1130, returning at 1600, 45 mins (฿100). Boats can be chartered for ฿1500/day. A shared sailing junk ฿250 (inclusive of lunch and coral reef viewing), or a chartered sailing junk costs ฿3,000/day. 'Tours' to Koh Larn, have watersports organized by the travel agent.

Further afield are the islands of **Koh Lin**, **Koh Sak** and **Koh Phai**, where there is better coral but fewer facilities. Only charter-boats visit these islands, for double the price of Koh Larn.

Tours
There are countless tours organized by the many travel agents in town: the standard long-distance trips are to Koh Samet, the sapphire mines near Chantaburi, Ayutthaya and Bang Pa-In, Bangkok, the floating market, Kanchanaburi and the River Kwai Bridge (2 days). There are also local tours to Nong Nooch village, the Elephant Village and Khao Khieo open zoo, among others. Prices for day tours (meal included) range from ฿600-1,200.

Festivals
Apr: *Annual Pattaya Festival* celebrates nothing in particular but is a good excuse for a jamboree.

Local information
● **Accommodation**
Pattaya has the biggest selection of hotels in Thailand outside Bangkok (over 300 places to stay at the last count), although there is little left here for the budget traveller, with rooms from ฿350 upwards. There are 3 distinct areas of accommodation. At the N end of the beach is the area of Naklua. This is the quieter end of town. Pattaya beach is busier and gets noisier and more active from N to S. On round the headland is Jomtien beach, with a better beach but less nightlife. All accommodation in our 'A' range has a/c, restaurant, pool, and prices are exclusive of tax. A continuing room glut means reduced rates (up to 50% even in peak season) should be offered except at weekends and high season.

Naklua: **A+** *Central Wong Amat*, Soi Naklua 18, T 426990, B 5471234.

A *Woodlands Resort*, 164/1 Pattaya-Naklua Rd, T 421707, F 425663, on the edge of Pattaya and Naklua, this hotel has tried to recreate a colonial lodge-type atmosphere – only partially successfully, but it is quiet, leafy and airy with attractive rooms and pool and landscaped gardens.

B *Astoria*, Naklua Rd, T 427061, F 427070, a/c, pool; **B** *Garden Lodge*, Naklua Rd, T 429109, F 421221, a/c, pool, bungalow rooms looking onto mature gardens, quiet and excellent value, rec; **B** *Gardenia* , nr. N Pattaya Rd, T 426356, F 426358, a/c, pool; **B** *Loma*, Soi Naklua 18, T 427461, F 421501, a/c, restaurant, pool; **B** *Sea View Resort*, Soi Naklua 18, T 424825, a/c, restaurant, pool.

C *A.A. Villa*, Soi Naklua 12, T 225515; **C** *Marina Inn*, Soi Naklua 12, T 225134; **C** *Sawasdee Place*, Naklua Rd (nr Soi 16), T 225651, F 225616, a/c, pool, rec; **C** *Sea Lodge*, Naklua Rd, T 425128, F 425129, a/c, pool.

Pattaya Beach: **L-A+** *Royal Cliff Beach*, 353 Moo 12 Cliff Rd, S Pattaya, T 250421, F 250511, a/c, restaurants, pool, every imaginable facility in this almost 1,000 room hotel; **L-A** *Royal Garden*, 218 Moo 10, Pattaya 2 Rd,

PATTAYA BEACH

TBU 32

1. TAT Office
   & Tourist Police
2. Post Office
3. Immigration Office
4. Bowling Alley
5. Wat Chai Mongkhon
6. Thai Limousine service
7. International clinic
8. *Dusit Resort*
9. *Montien Hotel*
10. *Merlin Hotel*
11. *Amari Orchid Resort*
12. *Regent Marina Hotel*
13. *Novotel Tropicana Hotel*
14. *Royal Cruise Hotel*
15. *Palm Lodge Hotel*
16. *Bay Breeze Hotel*
17. *Beach View Hotel*
18. *Palm Garden Hotel*
19. *Nautical Inn*
20. *Ocean View Hotel*
21. *A.A. Pattaya Hotel*
22. *ANZAC Hotel*
23. *BJ's Guesthouse*
24. *Chris' Guesthouse*
25. *Diana Inn*
26. *Honey Inn*
27. *Royal Night Hotel*
28. *Thai Palace Hotel*
29. *Golden Guesthouse*
30. *Sawasdee Mansion*
    & Guesthouse
31. *Orchid Lodge Hotel*
32. Orient Express Restaurant
33. Grand Sole Restaurant
34. Oslo Restaurant
35. Tiffanys
36. Pattaya Palladium
37. Alcazar Cabaret
38. D.K. Books

B. Non a/c bus station
   to Bangkok

T 428126, F 429929, a/c, restaurants, pool, tennis, new 4-storey shopping mall.

A+ Nova Lodge, Beach Rd (N end), T 420016, F 429959, large pool and gardens, tennis, simple (given the rates) rooms with balconies, central position; **A+ Dusit Resort**, 240 Beach Rd (N end), T 425611, F 428239, health club, tennis, squash courts, watersports, shopping arcade, disco, excellent hotel with good service and all facilities; **A+ Golden Beach**, Pattaya 2 Rd, opp. Soi 9, T 422331; **A+ Montien**, Beach Rd, T 428155, B 2337060, central location, extensive mature gardens, still excellent hotel, despite its age and size; **A+-A Siam Bayview**, 310/2 Moo 10 Pattaya 2 Rd, T 423871, F 423879, B 2211004, a/c, restaurant, pool, night club.

A Amari Orchid Resort, Beach Rd, N Pattaya, T 428161, F 428165, large hotel on extensive plot of land at N end of beach, quiet, away from bars and discos, peaceful; **A Merlin Pattaya** (formerly Ramada), Pattaya Beach Rd (nr Central Pattaya Rd), T 428755, F 421673, B 2557611, one of Pattaya's original high-rise hotels with 360 rooms in 3 wings, a large compound, equally large pool, but rather impersonal; **A Tropicana**, 98 Pattaya 2 Rd, T 428645, F 423031, B 2162278, almost 200 rooms in this low rise hotel which occupies a large plot in the centre of town, rooms are unimaginative and the hotel rather impersonal, competitive rates; **A Baiyoke**, 557 Pratumnak Rd, S Pattaya, T 423300, F 426124, B 2550155; **A Regent Marina**, 463/31 N Pattaya Beach Rd, T 429977, F 423296, B 3902511, situated in quiet N end of town, well designed with excellent music bar – the Laser Pub; **A Royal Cruise**, 499 Beach Rd, nr Soi 2, T 424242, F 424242, novel design – the hotel looks like a cruise liner (the 'first cruise on land', as they bill it) – rooms (or 'cabins') are average however, though rates are good and it offers a wide range of facilities including sauna, gym, jacuzzi.

B A.A. Pattaya, 182-182/2 Beach Rd, Soi 13, T 428656, F 429057, a/c, pool, new hotel (1992), in midst of bar-land, attractive 4th floor pool, well equipped rooms and excellent rates as it struggles to attract custom, rec; **B Bay Breeze**, 503/2 Pattaya 2 Rd (nr Soi 10), T 428384, F 429137, a/c, restaurant, pool, new hotel in centre of town, away from beach but rooms are large and well equipped, rather featureless but good value; **B Beach View**, 389 Beach Rd, nr Soi 2, T 422660, F 422664,

a/c, restaurant, pool, one of Pattaya's older hotels, rooms are dated and the pool is small, but room rates are keenly priced; **B Diamond Beach**, Beach Rd, Soi 14, T 429885, a/c, restaurant, pool; **B Grand**, 103 Mu 10, Soi 14, T 428249, a/c, friendly, good service; **B Ma Maison**, Soi 13 Beach Rd, T 429318, a/c, pool; **B Nautical Inn**, Soi 11 Beach Rd, T 429890, F 428116, a/c, restaurant, pool, older and now rather dated, low-rise hotel on large plot of land in the centre of town, large rooms are a little run down, but has more character than most, with distinct seaside atmosphere; **B Ocean View**, Pattaya Beach Rd (nr Soi 9), T 428084, F 424123, a/c, restaurant, pool, built over 20 years ago, which means rooms are a good size – if a touch dated and seedy – and the hotel benefits from a big compound in a prime position, good value; **B Palm Garden**, Pattaya 2 Rd (N end), T 429386, F 429188, a/c, restaurant, pool, rooms and corridors are rather dingy, but large compound, clean and well-maintained, good pool and excellent value; **B-C Palm Lodge**, N. Pattaya Beach Rd (nr Soi 6), T 428779, small hotel catering mainly for single male visitors, small pool, central, good room rates.

The bulk of the cheaper accommodation is at the S end of the beach and is in our 'C' range; non a/c rooms are cheaper. **C ANZAC**, 325 Pattayaaland 1, T 427822, F 427823, a/c, restaurant, homely atmosphere, well run; **C B.J.**, 405 Beach Rd (N end), T 421148, a/c, good value rooms in a small guesthouse above a restaurant; **C B.R.**, Soi 12 Beach Rd, T 426449, a/c; **C Caesar Palace**, Pattaya 2 Rd opp. Soi 8, T 428607, a/c, restaurant, pool; **C Charming Inn**, Beach Rd, nr Soi 3, T 428895, a/c; **C Chris**, Soi 12, Beach Rd, T 429586, F 422140, a/c, near centre of town down quiet soi in secluded compound, large, clean rooms, Australian-run, friendly, rec; **C Diana Inn**, 216/6-9 Pattaya 2 Rd, between sois 11 and 12, T 429675, F 424566, a/c, restaurant, pool, on busy road but rooms have good facilities for price, modern, well-run, friendly; **C Die Post-Stuben**, Soi Post Office, T 426049, a/c; **C Honey Inn**, 529/2 Pattaya 2 Rd, Soi 10, T 428117, a/c, restaurant, pool, large, clean rooms, small pool, frequented largely by single men – not a family hotel, but good value nonetheless, down quiet soi, away from beach; **C Thai Palace**, 212 Pattaya 2 Rd, T 423062, F 427698, a/c, restaurant, small pool, central, rooms arranged around a courtyard, clean and competitively priced; **C-D Royal Night Hotel-bungalow**, 362/9 Pattaya Beach Soi 5, T 428038, quiet hotel half way down Soi 5, small shaded pool, good rooms, hot water, popular.

D *Moonlight*, Pattayaland 1, T 429645, a/c; **D** *K.P.*, Soi Yamato, T 422390, a/c; **D** *Malibu*, Soi Post Office, T 428667; **D** *Nags Head*, 485 Pattaya 2 Rd, nr Soi Post Office, a/c; **D** *Nipa House*, Soi Yamato, T 425851, some a/c; **D** *Porn*, Soi Yamato, T 429625, some a/c; **D** *Sawasdee Mansion and Guesthouse*, 502/1 Pattaya 2 Rd Soi 10, T 425360, some a/c, one of the cheapest places in town, clean.

Jomtien: **L-A** *Asia*, 325 Cliff Rd, T 250602, F 250496, B 2150808, health club, tennis, golf, all facilities.

A *Ambassador City*, 21/10 Sukhumvit Rd, Km 55, Jomtien Beach, T 255501, F 255731, B 2550444, enormous; **A** *Pattaya Park*, 345 Jomtien Beach Rd, (N end), T 251201, F 251209, B 5110717; **A** *Royal Jomtien*, 408 Moo 12 Jomtien Beach, T 231350, F 231369, B 2541865, a/c, restaurant, pool, tennis, unexciting high-rise; **A** *Sugar Hut*, 391/18 Thaphraya Rd, on the way to Jomtien Beach, T 251686, F 251689, a/c, restaurant, 2 pools, overgrown gardens with rabbits and peacocks. Thai-style bungalows ('single' is adequate for 2 people), not on the beach, but very attractive grounds, rec.

B *Island View*, Cliff Rd, T 250813, F 250818, B 2498941, a/c, restaurant, pool; **B** *Mermaid's Beach Resort*, 75/102 Moo 12 Nong Prue, Jomtien Beach Rd, T 428755, F 421673, a/c, restaurant, pool; **B** *Sea Breeze*, Jomtien Beach, T 231056, F 231059, a/c, restaurant, pool.

● **Places to eat**

Pattaya has the greatest choice of international cuisine outside Bangkok. This ranges from excellent 5-star restaurants, to European fast-food chains, to foodstalls on the beach or down the sois.

Seafood: The best seafood is on Jomtien beach or at the S end of Pattaya beach. ♦♦♦*Lobster Pot*, 228 Beach Rd, South Pattaya, on a pier over the water, known for very fresh seafood; ♦♦*Nang Nual*, 214/10 Beach Rd, S Pattaya, on the waterfront, rec (another *Nang Nual* restaurant is in Jomtien); *Seafood Palace*, on the pier, S end of Beach Rd.

Thai: *Benjarong*, Royal Wing, *Royal Cliff Beach Hotel*; *Deeprom*, 503 Moo 9 Central Pattaya Rd, rec; *Kruatalay*, Pattaya Park, Jomtien beach, plus seafood; ♦♦♦*PIC Kitchen*, Soi 5, 4 traditional Thai pavilions, Thai classical dancing, rec; ♦♦*Ruen Thai*, Pattaya 2 Rd, opp.

Soi Post Office, rec; ♦♦♦*Somsak*, 436/24 Soi 1, N Pattaya, rec.

Other Asian Cuisine: ♦♦♦*Akamon*, 468/19 Pattaya 2 Rd, best known Japanese restaurant in town; ♦♦♦*Alibaba*, 1/15-16 Central Pattaya Rd, Indian; ♦♦♦*Arirang*, Soi 5 Beach Rd, Korean; ♦♦♦*Empress*, Dusit Resort, large Chinese restaurant overlooking Pattaya Bay, good dim sum lunches; ♦♦*Café India*, 183/9 Soi Post Office; ♦♦♦*Koreano*, Soi 1 Beach Rd, Korean; *Mai Kai Supper Club*, Beach Rd, Polynesian, Haitian band; ♦♦♦*Narissa*, Siam Bayview, N Pattaya, Chinese, speciality Peking Duck; *Thang Long*, Soi 3 Beach Rd, Vietnamese; ♦♦♦*White Orchid*, 110/3 S Pattaya Rd, good Chinese food; ♦♦♦*Yamato*, Pattaya Beach Soi 13, sushi bar (฿100) and sukiyaki, sashimi and tempura, all excellent.

International: ♦♦♦*Alt Heidelberg*, 273 Beach Rd, roadside bistro, open 0900-0200, German cook and owner, German sausages, draught beer; ♦*Amsterdam*, Regent Marina Complex, Thai/German/English/breakfast; *Aussie Ken's Toast Shop*, 205/31 Pattaya 2 Rd, fish and chips, sandwiches, cheap beer; *Bella Napoli*, Naklua Rd, Italian; ♦♦*Blue Parrot*, Pattayaland 2 Rd, Mexican; ♦♦*Buccaneer*, Beach Rd, seafood and steaks in rooftop restaurant above the *Nipa Lodge*; ♦♦♦*Dolf Riks*, Regent Marina Complex, speciality Indonesian, some international, one of the original Pattaya restaurants; ♦♦*Dream Bakery*, 485/3 Pattaya 2 Rd, English breakfasts, Thai; ♦♦♦*El Toro Steakhouse*, 215 Pattaya 2 Rd, top quality steaks. ♦♦♦*Green Bottle*, Pattaya 2 Rd (between Sois 10 & 11), Ersatz English pub with exposed 'beams', grills, seafood; ♦*Ice Café Berlin*, Pattaya 2 Rd, German; ♦♦*Italiano Espresso*, 325/1 Beach Rd, S Pattaya, traditional Italian food, and Thai dishes; ♦♦♦*La Gritta*, Beach Rd (N end past Soi 1), some people maintain this restaurant serves the best Italian in town, pizzas, pasta dishes and seafood specialities; ♦♦♦*Noble House*, Pattaya Beach Rd (nr Soi 10), Italian, seafood and German dishes, good German breakfasts with fresh coffee; ♦♦♦*Orient Express*, Beach Rd (just N of Central Pattaya Rd), 2 'Orient Express' coaches converted into dining cars serving average European food in novel surroundings; ♦♦*Oslo*, 325/14 Pattayaland Soi 2, S Pattaya. Scandinavian style restaurant, with Scandinavian buffet and individual dishes; ♦♦♦*Papa's*, 219 Soi Yamato, range of international food including fondue, steaks and seafood; *Pattaya Princess*, floating restaurant, pier at S end of Beach Rd; ♦♦♦*Peppermill*, 16 Beach Rd, nr Soi Post Office, first class French food; ♦♦♦*Savai Swiss*, Pattaya 2 Rd, Soi 6, Swiss style, with international food; ♦♦*Zum Wiener Schnitzel*, 98/7 Beach Rd, traditional German and some Thai food, large helpings.

● Bars
The majority of Pattaya's bars are concentrated at the S end of the beach, between Beach Road and Pattaya 2 Road and there are hundreds to choose from. They are mostly open-air, lined with stools. The men-only bars are around Pattayaland Soi 3, and the Karaoke bars are along Pattaya 2 Road.

● Airline offices
Thai, *Royal Cliff Hotel*, Cliff Rd.

● Banks & money changers
There are countless exchange facilities both on the beach road and on the many sois running E-W, many stay open until 2200.

● Entertainment
Pattaya comes to life as dusk approaches – it is a beach version of Bangkok's Patpong. Music blares out from the many bars, discos and massage parlours which are mainly concentrated in South Pattaya, referred to as 'The Strip'.

Traditional Thai dance: *PIC Kitchen*, Soi 5, Wed 1930, ฿100; *Ruen Thai*, Pattaya 2 Rd, opp. Soi P.O, rec. ฿120. **Cabaret shows**: *Alcazar* and *Tiffanys*, both on Pattaya 2 Rd are the two biggest establishments in town. There is also *Simon's*, on Pattayaland Soi 2 (all transvestite shows).

Disco: average admission ฿250, a selection are – *Disco Duck*, Pattaya Resort Hotel; *Marina Disco*, Regent Marina Hotel; *Captain's Club*, Dusit Resort; *Green House*, Pattaya 2 Rd; *Pattaya Palladium*, Pattaya 2 Rd, N end, the largest disco in SE Asia.

● Hospitals & medical services
Pattaya International Clinic, Soi 4, Beach Rd, T 428374, *Pattaya Memorial Hospital*, 328/1 Central Pattaya Rd, T 429422, 24 hr service.

● Post & telecommunications
Post Office: Soi Post Office. **Telephone exchange service**: South Pattaya Rd, open 24 hrs. **Safety deposit**: overseas service on Soi Post Office, ฿200/month. **Area code**: 038.

● Shopping
There are hundreds of market stalls and small shops on Pattaya 2 Rd selling jewellery, fashion ware, handicrafts, leather goods, silk, fake watches etc. In addition, several new shopping plazas are being constructed. The *Diamond Beach Hotel* and *Royal Garden Resort* are both building new malls, as is *Central Department Store* and *Mike's*.

Books: *DK Books*, Pattaya Beach Rd, Soi Post Office, best selection of books in Pattaya.

Department stores: *Mike's*, Beach Rd; *Booneua Shopping Plaza*, South Pattaya Rd.

Gemstones/jewellery: *World Gems*, Beach Rd; *Best Gems*, South Pattaya Rd; *Pattaya Lapidary*, Beach Rd.

Handicrafts: *Northern Thai Handicrafts*, 215 Pattaya 2 Rd; *Shinawatra*, Pattaya 2 Rd; Nong Nooch Village Pharmacists: plenty of drug stores on South Pattaya Rd.

Silk: *Dada Thai Silk* (plus tailoring), 345 Beach Rd (south end); *Shinawatra Thai Silk*, 78/13 Pattaya 2 Rd; *Fantasia*, (hand wrapped silk flowers), *Booneua Shopping Plaza*, South Pattaya Rd.

Supermarkets: plenty to choose from for Western food and pharmacy. **Tailors**: *Royal Garden Boutique*, Royal Garden Hotel, Pattaya Beach Rd.; *Princess Fashion*, Complex Hotel, 235/5 Beach Rd, S Pattaya; *Marco Custom Tailors*, opposite Montien Pattaya, 75/5-6 Pattaya 2 Rd.

● Sport
Badminton: Soi 17. Open 24 hrs a day. ฿60/hr, racquet hire ฿5-10, shuttlecock ฿16.

Bowling: there are 4 bowling alleys in Pattaya. Pattaya Bowl (rec), Pattaya 2 Rd, N Pattaya, a/c, 20 lanes, Open: 1000-0200 Mon-Sun. ฿30 until 1700, ฿35 until 0200, ฿40 on w/ends.

Bungee jumping: near Jomtien Beach, Kiwi Thai Bungee jump is said to be the highest in the world, T 427555. Open: 1400-2100, Mon-Sun.

Diving: there are an abundance of dive shops, offering a range of services – dives from the offshore islands, instruction and equipment hire. A recommended and established centre is *Seafari* on Beach Rd, run by an American couple. Cost for a days diving to the near islands is ฿700 (group rate), to the outer islands and a wreck dive, ฿1000. A day's introductory instruction costs ฿2000, and a 4 day course, about ฿9000. *Stevens Dive Shop*, on Beach Rd, T 428392 has similar rates. Other dive shops include *Mermaid's Dive School* on Soi Mermaid, Jomtien Beach, T 232219 and *Dave's*

Divers Den, Pattaya-Naklua Rd, T 221860 (NAUI).

Fishing: at Panarak Park, en route to the Siam Country Club, freshwater lake. Hourly fee: ₿25, bait and rod hire: ₿40.

Fitness: Pattaya Fitness Centre is near the Regent Marina Complex, N Pattaya, with weight-lifting facilities, gym and sauna. Open: 0800-2000 Mon-Sun. There is a fitness park on the road over the hill to Jomtien.

Game-fishing: there are 4 or 5 game fishing operators in Pattaya (approx price ₿4-6,000 for a day's boat charter, usually with food and drink provided; prices vary according to size and type of vessel). Fish commonly caught in local waters include shark, king mackerel, garoupa and marlin. Martin Henniker, at *Jenny's Hotel*, Soi Pattayaland 1 is recommended. *The Fisherman's Club*, Soi Yodsak (Soi 6) takes groups of 4-10 anglers and offer 3 different packages (including an overnight trip). The *Dusit Resort* organize angling contests. Angling equipment is available from Alan Ross at the *Pattaya Sports Supply* shop, opposite the *Regent Marina Hotel* (N Pattaya). For larger boat expeditions (30 or so anglers), expect to pay about ₿800, organized by Dieter at Deutsches Haus, Soi 4.

Golf: there are now 9 courses within 50 km of Pattaya. *Siam Country Club* is the closest to town, 20 mins from Pattaya, T 428002; green fees ₿750. Restaurant and swimming pool available. *Royal Thai Navy Course*, near Sattahip, 35 mins from town, T 428422, green fees ₿250, slow and uneven greens but characterful. Two other courses are the *Bangpra International* (one of the oldest courses in Thailand, accommodation and restaurant available) and the *Panya Resort* (45 mins from town, large clubhouse with restaurant), both near Chonburi. Outings organized by *Cherry Tree Golf Tours* from the Red Lion Pub, South Pattaya, T 422385 or by Mike Smith at *Caesars Bar*, Beach Rd – he's chairman of *Pattaya Sports Club*. 9-hole course behind the *Asia Pattaya Hotel*, green fees ₿50. Mini golf course, Naklua Rd, 500m N of *Dusit Resort*, ₿20. *Green Way Driving Range*, Sukhumvit Highway, 2 km S of S Pattaya. *Aussie Ken's*, Pattaya 2 Rd, computer golf simulator for up to 4 players.

Go-Kart: *Pattaya Kart Speedway*, Thepprasit Rd, Jomtien beach, T 422044, 80cc karts for children, 120cc for adults, ₿50-200 for 10 mins. Open: 1000-1800, Mon-Sun.

Jetboats: for rent, about ₿800/hr.

Motor racing: at *Bira International Circuit*, Km 14, Route 36. Races held at w/ends.

Parasailing: near *Montien*, *Royal Cliff*, *Asia Pattaya* and *Wong Amat* hotels, ₿300 for 5 min flight.

Riding: Reo Ranch, 5 km from Sukhumvit Rd, towards Siam Country Club, T 421188, ₿300-400/hr for experienced riders.

Running: *Hash House Harriers* meet every Mon at 1600 at the *Wild Chicken Bar*, Soi Post Office.

Sailing: lasers for ₿300/hr, Hobie Cats and Prindles for ₿500-600/hr. Rental areas – *Wong Amat Hotel* for N Pattaya, *Ocean View* for Central and *Surf House* for Jomtien.

Snooker: *Pattaya Bowl*, Pattaya 2 Rd, N Pattaya, ₿100/hr. Open: 1000-0200 Mon-Sun. Above Mike's Department Store, Beach Rd, is a small club with 5 tables, ₿100/hr, rec.

Shooting: *Tiffany's*, Pattaya 2 Rd, ₿120, with additional expense for bullets and target. Open: 0900-2100 Mon-Sun.

Snorkelling: day trips to the offshore islands can be organized through the dive shops, about ₿500.

Speedboats: for rent, about ₿600/hr.

Squash: Cherry Tree on the Siam Country Club road, T 423686.

Swimming: there are now designated swimming 'zones' on Pattaya and Jomtien beaches.

Tennis: many hotels have courts. Instruction is often available, ₿100-150/hr.

Water scooters: on the beach. ₿300/hr.

Water skiing: the water off Pattaya Beach is not particularly good for this, as it is rarely calm. However, an artificial freshwater lake has been created for waterskiers at Lake Land, T 232690, S of Pattaya on Sukhumvit Rd, ₿300 for 2 hrs. Restaurant by the lake.

Water World: at *Pattaya Park Beach Resort*, between Pattaya and Jomtien beach. Admission: ₿50 for adults, ₿30 for children.

Windsurfing: many different schools. Best time to windsurf is from Oct to Jun, about ₿300/hr.

● **Tourist office**
TAT, 382/1 Beach Road, T 428750, F 429113, with helpful staff and lots of information. Areas of responsibility are Pattaya and Samut Prakan.

● **Tourist Police**
T 429371 or T 1699 24 hr service and **Sea**

Rescue: T 433752 are to be found on Beach Rd, next to the TAT office.

● **Tour companies & travel agents**

For cheap airfare and tours to Indochina, the best informed travel agent is *Exotissimo*, 183/19 Soi Post Office, T 422788. Other travel agents include: *Alymear*, 159/18 Naklua Rd, T 424401; *Ben Adisti*, 78/128 Jomtien Beach Rd, T 231601; *Fly Bangkok*, 219/19 Soi Yamato, T 424223; *Lee Tours*, 183 Soi Post Office, T 429738; *Malibu Travel*, 183 Soi Post Office, T 423180; *Sanren Trading*, Beach Rd, close to Soi 4, T 425919.

● **Transport**

147 km S of Bangkok.

Local Songthaews: are in abundance along Beach Road (for travelling S) and on Pattaya 2 Rd (for travelling N), ฿5 for short trips, ฿10 between Naklua and Pattaya beach, ฿30 to Jomtien. **Motorbike/jeep/car hire**: along Beach Rd (bargaining required), Jeeps ฿500-700/day, motorbikes ฿200/day. Avis at *Dusit Resort* (T 429901) and the *Royal Cliff Beach Resort* (T 250421). **Boat charter**: from along Beach Rd. ฿700-1500/day (seats 12 people).

Air Bangkok Airways operate daily flights from Bangkok and Chiang Mai to 'Pattaya'; and from Pattaya to Phuket. In fact the Pattaya Airport is at U-Tapao, 40 km to the S, so it is hardly worthwhile. Minibuses to U-Tapao leave from the *Hotel Sole* on Pattaya 2 Rd, 2 hrs before departure (฿150). **International connections with Hong Kong and Singapore**: there is, as yet, no Bangkok Airways office in Pattaya; book through a travel agent. Buses to Bangkok's Don Muang airport leave every 2 hrs from 0700-1700 (฿130).

Train The station is off the Sukhumvit Highway, 200m N of the intersection with Central Pattaya Rd. There is a limited train service between Pattaya and Bangkok. The Bangkok-Pattaya train leaves at 0700, and the Pattaya-Bangkok at 1330, 3½ hrs (฿30).

Road Bus: a/c buses (including buses from Don Muang Airport) stop at the a/c bus terminal on N Pattaya Rd, near to the intersection with the Sukhumvit Highway. Songthaews take passengers to S Pattaya, past most of the Pattaya beach hotels (฿10) and to Jomtien beach (฿20). Regular connections with Bangkok's Eastern bus terminal on Sukhumvit Soi Ekamai (Soi 63) 1¾-2½ hrs (฿37-66) (0540-2100) or less frequent connections from the Northern bus terminal in Bangkok (Mor Chit).

Hotels and travel agencies in Bangkok also run tour bus services to Pattaya. Non a/c buses to Bangkok leave from the BKS stop in front of Wat Chai Mongkhon, near the intersection of Pattaya 2 and S Pattaya rds. The main BKS terminal (non a/c) for buses to other Eastern region destinations (e.g. Rayong, Sattahip, Si Racha) and beyond, is in Jomtien, near the intersection of Beach Rd and Chaiyapruk Rd. If staying in Pattaya City, it is possible to stand on the Sukhumvit Highway and wave down the appropriate bus. Tour buses to the N (Chiang Mai, Mae Hong Son, Mae Sai, Phitsanulok etc) leave from the station on the Sukhumvit Highway, near the intersection with Central Pattaya Rd. Nearby, buses also leave for Ubon (*Sri Mongkhon Tour*) and Nong Khai (*407 Pattana Tour*), both in the NE. **Limousine service**: *Thai* operates a service from Don Muang airport, Bangkok to Pattaya. T 423140 for bookings from Pattaya.

Sea Boat: a daily ferry service is due to begin operating in the middle of 1993 linking Pattaya with Cha-am in the South. Ask at the TAT office for latest details.

PATTAYA TO KOH SAMET

Sattahip

Sattahip is 20 km S of Pattaya and, like Pattaya, was also frequented by the US military. Now the port of Sattahip is the headquarters of the Thai navy which itself uses it as a vacation spot; many of the beautiful beaches are reserved for the military. It has recently been developed into an important commercial deep-sea port to take some of the pressure off Bangkok's stretched port facilities. The town has little to offer tourists: a modern and rather garish wat, a bustling market, and a few restaurants.

Samaesan

Samaesan is a small, quiet and unspoilt fishing village, 52 km S of Pattaya. Offshore there are a number of beautiful islands: **Koh Ai Raet**, **Koh Samaesan**, **Koh Kham**, **Koh Chuang** and **Koh Chan**. It is possible to hire boats to visit the islands – enquiries can be made at the Lam Samaesan Seafood Restaurant (about ฿300). There is basic accommodation available in Samaesan.

Rayong

Rayong is famous, at least in the Thai context, for its *nam pla* (fish sauce) – made from a decomposed silver fish. This is usually mixed with chillies to produce the fiery *nam pla prik*. For most Thais: no *nam pla*, no eat and in Thai elections it is not uncommon to find voters being 'bought' with free bottles of the watery sauce. The area also has many orchards and it has a good reputation for fruit, as well as sea cucumbers. But the town does not have much to offer, except a few beaches, a 12m-long reclining Buddha at **Wat Pa Pradu** which, unusually, reclines to its left and dates from the Ayutthaya period. Also worth visiting is **Wat Khot Thimtharaam** on Thimtharaam Road. The monastery was built in 1464 and features some interesting murals. Most people merely pass through Rayong on their way to the island of Koh Samet. Accommodation is poor, and the town is unattractive.

● **Festivals** May: *Fruit Fair* (moveable) local fruits, handicrafts on sale.

● **Accommodation A** *Sinsiam Resort*, 235 Laem Mae-Pim, T 2117026, B 4373648, a/c, restaurant, pool; **B-E** *Otani*, 69 Sukhumvit Rd, T 611112, some a/c, large rooms but dirty; **C** *Rayong*, 65/1-3 Sukhumvit Rd, T 611073, a/c, ugly.

● **Banks & money changers** Thai Farmers, Sukhumvit Rd.

● **Tourist offices** TAT, 153/4 Sukhumvit Rd, T 655420. Areas of responsibility are Rayong and Chanthaburi.

● **Transport** 221 km from Bangkok, 70 km from Pattaya. **Local Car hire:** *Rayong Mahanakorn Co*, 74/3 Ratbamrang Rd, opposite Manora Massage Parlour, ฿1,200/day. **Road Bus:** regular connections with Bangkok's Eastern bus terminal (฿38-80), Pattaya and other E coast towns.

Ban Phe

Once a small fishing village with a national reputation for its fish sauce, Ban Phe has become a way station for visitors heading for Koh Samet. It has many food and handicraft stalls, but few foreign tourists bother to stay any longer than it takes to catch the boat. In the vicinity of the village are a number of mediocre beaches lined with bungalows and resorts – **Hat Ban Phe**, **Hat Mae Ram Phung** (to the W), **Laem Mae Phim**, **Suan Son** and **Wang Kaew** (all to the E) which are largely frequented by Thai tourists.

● **Accommodation** Resort and bungalow developments line the 25 km of coast E and W of Ban Phe. In Ban Phe, try: **D** *Nual Napu*, T 651668, some a/c (E of the market, close to the pier for Koh Samet).

Outside Ban Phe: A+ *Rayong Resort*, Laem Tarn, Ban Phe, T 651000, F 651007, a/c, restaurant, pool, 167-room resort, on a cape with private beach, average rooms for the price; **B** *Diamond Phe*, 286/12 Ban Phe Rd, T 615826, a/c, E of Ban Phe near the pier for Koh Samet, plain and rather kitsch but comfortable and convenient.

● **Banks & money changers** Krung Thai, a short distance W of the pier (if going to Samet it is a good idea to change money here as the rates are better than on the island).

● **Post & telecommunications Area code:** 038.

● **Transport** 20 km SE of Rayong, 223 km from Bangkok. **Road Bus:** regular connections direct from Bangkok's Eastern bus terminal (a/c ฿80) and from Pattaya, 1 hr. Or via Rayong (฿38-80), and then a songthaew to Ban Phe (฿10).

Koh Samet

Koh Samet is a 6 km-long lozenge-shaped island which used to be known as Koh Keo Pisadan. Until the early 1980s it was home to a small community of fishermen and was visited by a few intrepid travellers. The famous 19th century Thai romantic poet Sunthorn Phu retired to this beautiful island and,

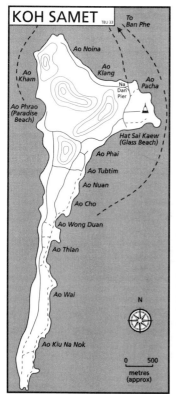

KOH SAMET TBU 33

To Ban Phe

Ao Noina

Ao Kham

Ao Klang

Na Dan Pier

Ao Pacha

Ao Phrao (Paradise Beach)

Hat Sai Kaew (Glass Beach)

Ao Phai

Ao Tubtim

Ao Nuan

Ao Cho

Ao Wong Duan

Ao Thian

Ao Wai

Ao Kiu Na Nok

N

0   500
metres
(approx)

inspired, proceeded to write his finest work, the epic *Phra Aphaimani*. The poem recounts the story of a prince, banished by his father to live with a sea-dwelling, broken-hearted giantess. Escaping to Koh Samet with the help of a mermaid, the prince kills the pursuing giant with his magic flute and marries the mermaid. It is unlikely Sunthorn Phu would find the necessary quiet today: over the past decade, Koh Samet has become increasingly popular with young Thai holiday-makers and with foreign visitors. Because of its relative proximity to Bangkok (Ban Phe is only 223 km from the capital), it is particu-

larly popular with Thais at the weekend and during public holidays, when it is best to avoid the island.

In 1981 Samet became part of the Koh Samet National Park which also includes the neighbouring Kuti and Thalu islands as well as 100 sq km of surrounding sea (hence the admission fee of ฿50, ฿25 for children). The park authorities have ostensibly insisted that all accommodation remains limited to bungalows set back behind the tree line of the beach. This is difficult to reconcile with the scale and pattern of development that has occurred. The park authorities have threatened to shut the island down on the basis that every bungalow owner is breaking the law; it was actually closed to tourists in May 1990 following a raid by police chief Pratin Santiprabob during which he arrested 45 resort operators. After a protest from bungalow owners, business was resumed – but only on the condition that they pay monthly fines to the Forestry Department. Next to each of the park offices is a sign that reads, rather forbiddingly:

'Small bungalow operators on Samet Island are now charged for forest encroachment. The accommodations are seized as evidences for legal pending and the operations should be closed down. So all visitors should refrain from staying in bungalows or any premise. Anyone found violating this order i.e. staying in bungalow will be prosecuted under the Act of National Parks (2504 BE) with the penalty of one month's imprisonment or ฿1,000 fine or both'.

Fortunately TAT assures tourists that they will not be imprisoned although they do recommend that people only visit the island as a day trip. The rubbish created by tourism is becoming an environmental threat on the island. However hard the park authorities and TAT may try to protect Samet, they seem to be fighting a losing battle. People are still staying on the island in their thousands and yet more bungalows are being built. At the end of 1992, the Park

authorities banned overnight stays for a second time and arrivals plummeted by 70%. Overnight stays have now resumed again, but there is still considerable pressure from environmentalists to reduce the number of bungalows and to ban motorbikes, songthaews and charter boats. But many bungalow operators were living on the island prior to 1981 when it was declared a national park. As the owner of the *Wong Duan Resort* recently said: "It is unfair. We fight, work hard, pay taxes and invest a lot of money ... the Forestry Department never invested anything. Now they are the owners and we are the encroachers."

Samet is a comparatively dry island (1,350 mm/yr – Chantaburi 50 km away has rainfall of 3,164 mm/yr) and therefore a good place to visit during the rainy season. However, between May and Oct there can be strong winds, and the seas are rough. The island's limited supply of fresh water was a constraint to tourist expansion for a number of years. Now it is shipped in and most of the bungalows have a reasonable supply. Malaria is particularly prevalent, so take all precautions – such as wearing long-sleeved shirts and trousers after sunset.

Most visitors land at the main **Na Dan Pier** in the NE of the island. Along the beach here there is a collection of featureless bungalows. Unless you want to watch the boats come in (there is little else to do), head for one of the other bays.

Hat Sai Kaew (Glass Beach) is a 10 minute walk from Na Dan Pier. This was once a beautiful spot, but it has been disfigured by uncontrolled development. Shophouses, discos, bars and travel agents line the path from Na Dan to Hat Sai Kaew. The beach does, however, have a sandy bottom which makes it an excellent place to swim (especially for children). 1 km SW from Hat Sai Kaew, is **Ao Phai**, which is less developed and more peaceful. The bungalows here cater for *farang* rather than for Thai visitors. 2½ km from Ao Phai, past the

smaller **Ao Tubtim**, **Ao Nuan** and **Ao Cho**, is **Ao Wong Duan**. This crescent-shaped bay has a number of more up-market resort developments. Consequently there is also a wider range of facilities: water-skiing, diving, boat trips, and windsurfing. Continuing S from Ao Wong Duan is **Ao Thian**, **Ao Wai** and **Ao Kiu Na Nok**, each with a single group of bungalows. These are the most peaceful locations on Koh Samet, and the island's finest coral is also found off the southern tip of the island.

Ao Phrao (2 km from Sai Kaew) or Paradise Beach is the only beach to have been developed (so far) on the W side of the island. Isolated from the other beaches, with 3 sets of bungalows, and with the best sunsets, it is possibly the most peaceful and romantic spot on Samet. Its sandy bottom also makes it excellent for swimming.

Excursions
Hire a fishing boat (or go on a tour), take a picnic, and explore the **Kuti** and **Thalu islands**.

Tours
Small operators on many of the beaches organize boat trips to outlying islands such as Koh Kuti and Koh Thalu for fishing, diving and snorkelling: *Delfimarin* are at Ao Wong Duan; *Nop's Tours* are at Ao Phai.

Local information
● **Accommodation**
Koh Samet mostly offers bungalow accommodation, although there are an increasing number of more sophisticated 'resorts' – mostly at Ao Wong Duan. Only a selection of the bungalows is given below (at last count there were a total of 42 developments). The best source of information on whether standards are being maintained is recent visitors – ask those leaving the island.

Hat Sai Kaew (10 bungalow developments): **C-E** *White Sand*, T 2127249, restaurant (good seafood), rather industrial in size; bungalows 6 deep on the beach, 90 in all; **E** *Sai Kaew*, well-spaced and positioned, rec; **E** *Sea View*.

Ao Phai (6 bungalow developments): **B-D** *Ao Phai Hut*, T 2112967, good position, rec; **C-E** *Silver Sand*, T 21160; **D-E** *Naga*, home made bread, good food, library, relaxed, rec; **D-E** *Seabreeze*, organize boat and fishing trips, friendly, with good range of facilities; **E** *Odd's Little Hut*, rec.

Ao Wong Duan (5 bungalow developments): **B** *Wong Duan Resort*, T 3210731, B 2500424, a/c, pool, most expensive on Samet; **B-D** *Malibu Garden Resort*, T 3210345, restaurant, more sophisticated than most.

Ao Kiu Na Nok: A-B *Ao Kiu Na Nok Villas*, some a/c and hot water, remote and quiet.

Ao Phrao (3 bungalow developments): **B-C** *Ao Phrao*; **C-E** *S.K. Hut*, T 2126663, quiet, rec.

● **Camping**
Because the island is a national park, it is permissible to camp on any of the beaches. The best area is on the W coast, which means a walk on one of the many trails of not more than 3 km.

● **Banks & money changers**
The island has no banks, so for the best rates, change money on the mainland. However, a number of the bungalows and travel agents do offer a money changing service.

● **Police**
Hat Sai Kaew.

● **Post & telecommunications**
Post Office: between Hat Sai Kaew and Ao Phai (Poste Restante). Open: 0830-1500 Mon-Fri, 0830-1200 Sat. **Telephone office**: between Hat Sai Kaew and Na Dan (for overseas calls).

● **Sports**
The major beaches offer sailing, windsurfing (฿150/hr), scuba-diving, snorkelling, and water-skiing (฿400/15 mins). Ao Wong Duan has the best selection of water sports. The best snorkelling is to be found at Ao Wai, Ao Kiu Na Nok and Ao Phrao.

● **Travel agents**
Citizen Travel, Hat Sai Kaew; *Citizen Travel 2*, Ao Phai; *C.P. Travel Service*, Hat Sai Kaew.

● **Transport**
Local Songthaews: are the main form of public transport, bouncing along the tracks that crisscross the island. Rates range from ฿5-20. **Motorcycles**: can be hired although they are expensive (฿80-100/hr, ฿500/day) and they dis-

turb the peace (or what is left of it). The rental companies explain that because the roads are so bad their machines have a very short life expectancy. As Koh Samet is only 6 km long and 3 km wide, walking is always a possibility.

Road & Sea Regular connections with Bangkok's Eastern bus terminal and from Pattaya to Ban Phe, or to Rayong and then a songthaew. There are regular boats from Ban Phe Pier throughout the day departing when full, 30-40 mins (฿30). Most boats dock at Na Dan or Ao Wong Duan. Some will also drop passengers off at Ao Phrao. Boats visit the S beaches of Ao Thian, Ao Wai and Ao Kiu Na Nok less frequently – enquire before departure. Travel agents on Khaosan Rd, Bangkok, also arrange transport to Samet.

CHANTABURI

Chantaburi or the 'City of the Moon' has built its wealth and reputation on its rubies and sapphires – and especially the famous 'red' sapphire or *Thapthim Siam* (see box).

Many of the gem mines were developed during the 19th century by Shan people from Burma, who are regarded as being among the best miners in the world. Muang Chan – as it is locally known – also has a large Chinese and Vietnamese population, which is reflected in the general atmosphere of the town: narrower streets, shuttered wooden shophouses, Chinese temples and an air of industriousness. The active French-style **Catholic Cathedral** of the Immaculate Conception was built in 1880 and is the largest church in Thailand. Architecturally uninspiring (coloured beige and grey), it is significant merely for its presence. The Cathedral was built to serve the large number of Vietnamese Catholics who fled their homeland and settled here. On weekdays at 1600, children disgorge from the school near the Cathedral and an array of foodstalls miraculously appears in the compound, selling mouthwatering-looking snacks. The footbridge near the compound leads into the old part of town; the most interesting street-architecture in

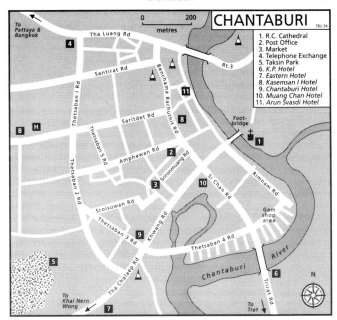

CHANTABURI TBU 34

1. R.C. Cathedral
2. Post Office
3. Market
4. Telephone Exchange
5. Taksin Park
6. K.P. Hotel
7. Eastern Hotel
8. Kasemsan I Hotel
9. Chantaburi Hotel
10. Muang Chan Hotel
11. Arun Svasdi Hotel

the town is to be found in the road parallel to the river, westwards towards the main bridge. The Vietnamese part of town lies to the N of the cathedral, on the opposite side of the river.

It is Chantaburi's gems which attract most people's attention, but in addition, the province is highly regarded as a source of some of the best durians in Thailand, which flourish in the lush climate. The finest can cost several hundred baht (over a week's wages for an agricultural labourer), a fact which can seem astonishing to visitors who regard the fruit as repulsive ('carrion in custard' as one Englishman is said to have remarked) (see page 17).

Excursions

Khai Nern Wong – a ruined fort – lies 4.5 km SE of town off Tha Chalaep Road. Take the turning towards Tha Mai, and walk or drive for another 200m. The fort is not as well preserved as the

official tourist literature suggests. King Taksin retreated here after Ayutthaya fell to the Burmese in 1767. With his army consisting mainly of Chinese, it is thought Taksin decided to flee to the region of his kingdom with the largest number of Chinese settlers. Consequently, he proceeded from Chonburi to Rayong and finally to Chantaburi. Even so, he had to wage a battle against the ruler of Chantaburi in June 1767 to secure his position.

Khao Ploi Waen is a small hill 4 km past the fort. There is an active wat at the bottom of the hill and a Ceylonese-style chedi on the top, built during the reign of King Rama IV. It is a steep climb up steps to the top of the hill, where there are good views of the surrounding countryside with its orchards. The hill is pockmarked with gem mines, although they are all now abandoned and the vegetation has made a good job of covering-up the evidence.

Nam Tok Plui is a waterfall located within the 16,800 ha Khao Sa Bap National Park, gazetted in 1975. It is to be found off Route 3, S towards Trat. After about 14 km, at Ban Plui, a left turn is signposted to the waterfall (there is a large, rather grand, Chinese temple close to the turn-off). Facing the waterfall are two chedis, the Alongkon Chedi and one commissioned by Rama V as a memorial to Princess Sunantha Kumareeratana in 1876. Park bungalow accommodation available, T 5790529. **Getting there:** by minibus from the municipal market.

THE TEARS OF THE GODS: RUBIES AND SAPPHIRES

Major deposits of two of the world's most precious stones are found distributed right across mainland Southeast Asia: rubies and sapphires are mined in Thailand, Burma, Vietnam, Cambodia and Laos. The finest of all come from Burma, and especially from the renowned Mogok Stone Tract, which supports a town of 100,000 almost entirely upon the proceeds of the gem industry. Here peerless examples are unearthed, including the rare 'pigeon's blood' ruby. One Thai trader was recently reported saying that "Asking to see the pigeon's blood is like asking to see the face of God".

Although the Burmese government tries to keep a tight grip on the industry, many of the gems pass into the hands of Thai gem dealers, often with the connivance of the Thai army. Corruption, violence, murder, arson and blackmail are all part and parcel of the trade. Currently, thousands of Thais are mining gems in Khmer Rouge controlled territory in Cambodia (especially around Pailin) – with the protection of the vilified Khmer Rouge and the support of the Thai Army. Through fair means and foul, Bangkok has become the centre of the world's gem business and Thailand is the largest exporter of cut stones – indeed, it has a virtual monopoly of the sapphire trade. Thai buyers conclude deals with mines in Australia, Kenya, Sri Lanka, the USA – across the globe – and have a stranglehold on the business. Those who try to buck the system and bypass Bangkok risk having a contract taken out on their lives.

Rubies and sapphires are different colours of corundum, the crystalline form of aluminium oxide. Small quantities of various trace elements give the gems their colour; in the case of rubies, chromium and for blue sapphires, titanium. Sapphires are also found in a spectrum of other colours including green and yellow. Rubies are among the rarest of gems, and command prices four times higher than equivalent diamonds. The Burmese call the ruby *ma naw ma ya* or 'desire-fulfilling stones'.

The colour of sapphires can be changed through heat treatment (the most advanced form is called diffusion treatment) to 1500-1600°C (sapphires melt at 2050°C). For example, relatively valueless colourless geuda sapphires from Sri Lanka, turn a brilliant blue or yellow after heating. The technique is an ancient one: Pliny the Elder described the heating of agate by Romans nearly 2,000 years ago, while the Arabs had developed heat treatment into almost a science by the 13th century. Today, almost all sapphires and rubies are heat treated. The most valued colour for sapphires is cornflower blue – dark, almost black, sapphires command a lower price. The value of a stone is based on the four 'C's: Colour, Clarity, Cut and Carat (1 carat = 200mg). Note that almost all stones are heat treated to improve their colour. For information on buying gems in Thailand, see page 175.

Oasis Sea World is 25 km S of town off route 3 near the small town of Laem Sing. The station covers 11 ha and was established to breed two species of dolphin – the humpbacked and Irrawaddy. Dolphin shows are performed at regular intervals through the day. Open: Mon-Sun 0800-1700. Admission: ฿40 (adults), ฿20 (children). For information T (039) 312567.

Nam Tok Krating, another waterfall, can be found within the Kitchakut National Park (along with a few bat-filled caves), and is about 25 km NW of town. The water is believed to have healing powers.

Bo Rai is a gem mining area near the Cambodian border, with a gem market (see page 374).

Festivals

June: *Fruit fair* (moveable), celebrating local fruits such as durian, jackfruit, pomelo and rambutan; cultural shows, handicraft exhibitions.

Local information
● **Accommodation**
The *Modern House Princess*, a 150-room hotel built by the Princess Group is due to open in late 1994 and should become the most expensive hotel in town. **B-C** *K.P.*, 43/151-152 Trirat Rd, T 311756, a/c, more individual than most Thai hotels, rec.

C *Eastern*, 899 Tha Chalaep Rd, T 12218, a/c, restaurant, overpriced, boring rooms, very slow lifts; **C-D** *Chanta Nimit*, 116-118 Rimnam Rd, T 312388, some a/c, very average, slightly out of town.

D *Kasemsan Nung (I)*, 98/1 Benchama Rachuthit Rd, T 312340, some a/c, large, clean rooms in big hotel, well-run, but some rooms can be noisy; **D-E** *Chantaburi*, 42/6 Tha Chalaep Rd, T 311300, some a/c, just about the only thing going for it is that it is central; **D-E** *Muang Chan*, 257-259 Si Chan Rd, T 312909.

E *Arun Svasdi*, 239 Sukha Phiban Rd, T 311082, situated in the most attractive part of town, small but clean rooms with homely atmosphere; **E** *S. Sukchai*, 28 Tha Chalaep Rd, T 311292, basic but relatively clean, central; **E** *Sai Samphan*, 1/3 Tha Chalaep Rd, T 311389.

● **Places to eat**
Most restaurants are on Tha Chalaep Road. Where the road runs along the eastern side of King Taksin Lake, there is a profusion of pubs, bars and ice-cream parlours – this is where the Chantaburi yuppies hang-out.

● **Banks & money changers**
Thai Farmers, 103 Sirong Muang Rd; **Bangkok**, 50 Tha Chalaep Rd.

● **Post & telecommunications**
Post Office: at the intersection of Amphawan and Si Chan roads. **Area code**: 039.

● **Shopping**
Gems and jewellery: Si Chan Rd, or 'Gem Street' has the best selection of jewellery shops and gem stores, however you are unlikely to pick up a bargain.

Rattan and basketwork: Chantaburi is regarded as one of the centres of fine rattan work in Thailand. Available from numerous shops in town.

● **Transport**
330 km from Bangkok. If coming from the Northeast, it is possible to avoid the capital by taking routes 304, 33 and 317 S from Korat. The road descends from the Khorat plateau and follows the Thai/Cambodian border, through frequent checkpoints, S to Chantaburi.

Road Bus: regular connections with Bangkok's Eastern bus terminal (฿56-103). Also buses from Pattaya, Rayong, Ban Phe and other E seaboard towns.

CHANTABURI TO KOH CHANG

Trat

Trat is the provincial capital and the closest Thai town of any size to Cambodia. Like Chantaburi, it is a gem centre (see box, page 177). As the prospects of lasting peace in Cambodia get ever-so-slowly brighter, and as the government in Cambodia opts for Gorbachev style policies of *perestroika*, so Chinese businessmen in Trat are getting increasingly excited about business prospects across the border.

Most people visit Trat en route to

beautiful Koh Chang. There is little to keep visitors in the town any longer than they need to catch a bus or boat onwards. However, if your boat/bus connection means that you are stranded here, then there is a bustling **covered market** (attractively known in official literature as the 'Municipal Shopping Mall') in the centre of town on Sukhumvit Road. It offers a good selection of food and drink stalls. There is also an active **night market** N of the shopping mall on Sukhumvit Road. **Wat Buppharam**, also known as **Wat Plai Klong** dates from the late Ayutthaya Period. It is notable for its wooden viharn and monk's *kutis*, and is 2 km W of town, down the road opposite the shopping mall.

Excursions

Bo Rai on the Cambodian border, has a selection of gem markets. **Hung Tung Market** operates in the morning between 0700 and 1000; **Khlong Yor Market** between 1300 and 1500. Getting there: songthaews leave from outside the market.

An even better source of gems is over the border, in Cambodia: since 1991, thousands of Thais, after being taxed US$60 each by the Khmer Rouge, have been penetrating the Cambodian jungles in search of their fortunes. One was quoted as saying, 'Over that mountain, a few days' walk away, you just stick your hands in the ground and the dirt is filled with precious stones'. Under pressure from the UN and the international community, the Thai government has tried – or at least given the impression of trying – to stop the flow of gems, so that the flow of funds to the Khmer Rouge also stops. In this they have been only partially successful. Tourists are not advised to try their luck.

Khlong Yai is the southernmost town on this E arm of Thailand and an important fishing port. The trip there is worthwhile for the dramatic scenery, and the port itself is pretty and bustling. Getting

there: by songthaew from the back of the municipal market (₿25) or shared taxi from the front of the market (₿35 each).

Festivals

Jun: *Rakham Fruit Fair* celebrates Trat's reputation as a fruit growing centre.

Local information

● **Accommodation**

B-E *Muang Trat*, 4 Sukhumvit Rd, T 511091, some a/c, restaurant, clean rooms.

C-E *Thai Rungrot*, 296 Sukhumvit Rd, T 511141, some a/c, north of town, to the right of Sukhumvit Rd.

D-F *Tung Nguan Seng*, 66-77 Sukhumvit Rd, T 511028.

F *Foremost Guesthouse*, 49 Thoncharoen Rd, by the canal, last turn on the left off Sukhumvit Rd, towards Laem Ngop, T 511923, clean and friendly with lots of local information, rec.

● **Banks & money changers**

Siam Commercial, Sukhumvit Rd; Thai Farmers, 63 Sukhumvit Rd; Thai Military, Sukhumvit Rd.

● **Post & telecommunications**

Area code: 039.

● **Tourist offices**

Tourist information office on Soi Sukhumvit, not far from the market; helpful and informative.

● **Transport**

400 km from Bangkok.

Local Motorbike hire: from Soi Sukhumvit, just S of the municipal market.

Road Bus: a/c station is on Sukhumvit Rd, just N of the night market. Non a/c buses leave from Wi Wattana Rd, N, off Sukhumvit Rd. Regular connections with Bangkok's Eastern bus terminal 5½ hrs (₿87-140), with Pattaya 3½ hrs (₿100), with Chantaburi 1 hr 40 mins (₿18). **By songthaew**: to Laem Ngop from outside the municipal market on Sukhumvit Rd (₿10). **By shared taxi**: to Chantaburi 50 mins (₿30 each).

Sea Boat: from near the *Foremost Guesthouse*, boats leave very irregularly to Koh Kut.

Laem Ngop

This sleepy fishing village – in fact the district capital – has a long pier lined with boats, along with good seafood and a relaxed atmosphere. But this is unlikely to last: Laem Ngop is poised to explode into life as Koh Chang – an offshore island – becomes Thailand's next island beach resort (see below). At the time of writing, the town had a handful of guesthouses and some restaurants by the pier. There is a small tourist information centre in the Amphoe (district) Office, offering information on bungalows on Koh Chang and the other islands in the National Marine Park. The headquarters for the park are at Laem Ngop.

● **Accommodation** There are a number of guesthouses on the main road into the village. **E-F** at places such as *Chut Kaew, Captain Daniel's, Laem Ngop Inn* and the *Isan Guesthouse*.

● **Banks & money changers** Mobile exchange service at the pier. 0900-1600.

● **Travel agents** *A.D. Tour*, by the pier, T 2128014.

● **Tourist offices** TAT, 100 Mu 1 Trat, Laem Ngop Rd, T 597255. Areas of responsibility are Trat and the islands.

● **Transport** 17 km from Trat. **Road Songthaew**: from the stand outside the shopping mall in Trat. 30 mins.

Koh Chang

This – as yet – unspoilt island is Thailand's second largest and is part of a Marine National Park which also includes another 50-odd islands and islets. Despite the 'protection' that its Park status should offer, Koh Chang is developing rapidly, with resorts and bungalows springing-up virtually overnight along its shores. It is a matter of conjecture as to how long the island will remain uspoilt. Given the changes that have occurred elsewhere – Phuket, Samui and Samet – it is easy to be pessimistic about the environmental future of Koh Chang.

Koh Chang is surrounded by deep blue water – of the Hollywood movie variety – and the best beaches are on the W or seaward side of the island – **Sai Khao** (white sand), **Khlong Phrao** and **Bang Bao**. These can be reached on foot (a good 40 mins from Khlong Son), although motorcycle and jeep taxis are now available. There are plans to build a paved road around the island which will no doubt accelerate the pace of development. The rugged mountainous interior is largely covered with virgin rainforest. Koh Chang is famed for its wild boar and the **Ma Yom Waterfall** – which is on the E side of the island. King Chulalongkorn (Rama V) visited this waterfall on no less than 6 occasions at the end of the 19th century, so even given the Thai predilection for waterfalls of any size, it counts as an impressive one. To prove the point, the king carved his initials (or had them carved) on a stone to mark one of his visits.

NB: Travellers have reported that mosquitoes and sandflies are a problem on Koh Chang and surrounding islands, so nets and insect repellent are essential.

BEST TIME TO VISIT: Nov to May.

Other nearby islands

There are many other smaller islands near Koh Chang, which are likewise gradually being developed. These are mostly off the south coast, and are the best areas for snorkelling and diving. The next largest island, **Koh Kut** has lovely beaches, the exclusive *Koh Kut Island Resort* (**A+**) and just a handful of bungalows (**F**); boats leave from Koh Chang 2-3 times a week. Food is limited (some recent visitors recommend taking your own) but the beaches are wonderful. There is a good waterfall and the coral is said to be good. However, mosquitoes are bad. The tiny island of **Koh Kham** has 2 bungalows (**F**), tents and the *Koh Kham Resort* (**E**). Boats leave from Laem Ngop, 3½ hrs (฿150). **Koh Rang** is well known for its swallows nests and turtle eggs, as well as good coral and rock formations for divers.

Other islands with bungalows are

Koh Phrao, **Koh Ngam**, **Koh Whai**, **Koh Lao Ya** (with accommodation at the **A** *Lao Ya Resort*, T 512552, a/c, hot water, half board compulsory, excellent restaurant; the ultimate place for 'getting away from it all'; **Koh Khlum** and **Koh Maak** (**A-B** *Koh Maak Resort*, reservations from Bangkok on T 3196714 or from Trat on T 3270220).

Local information
● Accommodation

Rapid development means that the list below may date quickly. The best source of informa-tion is travellers returning from the island. Check the guest book at the *Foremost Guesthouse* in Trat. Almost all the accommodation is simple A-frames, with wood-slat walls, thatched roofs, communal showers and no protection against mosquitoes – although some establishments will provide netting. Down the W coast from Ao Khlong Son:

Ao Khlong Son: **E** *Khlong Son*; *Mannee*, rather run down but friendly and enthusiastic management; *Manop*.

Ao Sai Khao: **B-E** *Haad Sai Khao* (*White Sand Beach Resort*), secluded location, good bungalows and professional management; **E-**

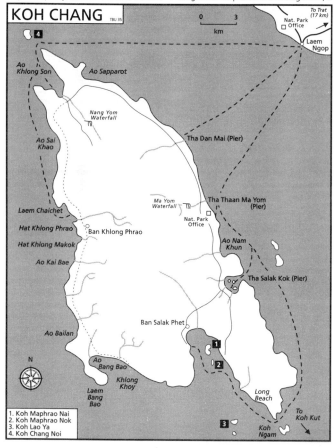

KOH CHANG TBU 35

0   3
km

To Trat (17 km)

Nat. Park Office

Laem Ngop

Ao Khlong Son

Ao Sapparot

Nang Yom Waterfall

Ao Sai Khao

Tha Dan Mai (Pier)

Ma Yom Waterfall

Tha Thaan Ma Yom (Pier)

Nat. Park Office

Laem Chaichet

Hat Khlong Phrao

Ban Khlong Phrao

Ao Nam Khun

Hat Khlong Makok

Ao Kai Bae

Tha Salak Kok (Pier)

Ban Salak Phet

Ao Bailan

N

Ao Bang Bao

Khlong Khoy

Long Beach

Laem Bang Bao

To Koh Kut

Koh Ngam

1. Koh Maphrao Nai
2. Koh Maphrao Nok
3. Koh Lao Ya
4. Koh Chang Noi

F *Coconut* (with pet sloth), S of Ao Khlong Son with own beach, quiet and secluded.

Hat Khlong Phrao: **A** *Hat Khlong Phrao*, a/c, restaurant, best on island, some bungalows, plus a 2-storey block, beautiful beach, good for swimming; **A** *Koh Chang Resort*, a/c, expensive and well appointed bungalows, reservations at 1091/179-181 Metro Trade Centre, New Phetburi Rd, B 2770482, F 2761233, or 12-3 M1 Laem Ngop, T 512818; **E** *PSS*, on mouth of Khlong Phrao, good food, restaurant, rec; **E-F** *Chokdee*.

Ao Kai Bae: **B-D** *Sea View*; **D-E** *Kai Bae Hut*; **F** *Porn*.

Ao Bang Bao: **D** *Sunset*, T 2128014, mosquito nets provided, camping available in the grounds; **E** *Bang Bao Beach Resort*, only average.

Tha Thaan Ma Yom: **E-F** *National Park*, bungalows, not recommended.

● **Places to eat**
Guesthouses tend to serve an unchanging array of Thai and travellers' fare; restaurants and bars are appearing gradually and the gastronomy should improve. Grilled seafood is the best bet. *JJ Sabai Land* is on Khlong Phrao beach, Thai and Western food available. There is also a shop for fruit shakes here.

● **Banks & money changers**
There are no banks, and rates are poor at the guesthouses that change money.

● **Post & telecommunications**
There is a telephone (overseas calls possible), money exchange, stamps and letterbox and general grocery store at the southern end of Sai Khao beach.

● **Tourist office**
There is an information centre on Sai Khao beach where boat trips, fishing and snorkelling can all be arranged.

● **Transport**
To get to Koh Chang, take a bus to Trat (see Trat section), a songthaew to Laem Ngop and then a boat to the island.

Local No cars, but there are motorbike and jeep **taxis**. **Motorbike hire**: from many of the guesthouses, but because the tracks are so rough they have a short working life and rates are consequently high – ฿100-400/day.

Sea Boat: boats leave daily for the various beaches from the pier at Laem Ngop (฿30-100). Boats to Khlong Son Beach take 1 hr, to Thaan Ma Yom Pier 50 mins, to Dan Mai Pier 35 mins. During peak season (Nov-May) there are two departures daily to the main W coast beaches; one a day to the E coast beaches. Outward boats tend to leave between 1200 and 1500; return boats in the morning, between 0600 and 0900. Between June and Oct boats are more irregular and some routes do not operate. **NB**: it is only possible to reach Koh Chang in a day from Bangkok by taking an early morning bus (first a/c bus 0700, non-a/c 0420).

THE WESTERN REGION

CONTENTS

The Western region stretches from the outskirts of Bangkok westwards to the frontier with Burma and includes the historic city of Nakhon Pathom (with its imposing chedi) and Kanchanaburi. The total distance from Bangkok to Saam Ong (the Three Pagodas Pass), deep in the mountains that skirt the border between Thailand and Burma, is 370 km. Although Kanchanaburi is only 128 km from Bangkok, until quite recently the land beyond the town was forested and lawless. Guerillas of the Communist Party of Thailand found sanctuary in the hills, and large expanses of the Western region were no-go areas for the Thai authorities. This has now changed, and the region is quickly being opened up for agriculture and tourism.

For foreign visitors, perhaps the most evocative name and sight is the 'Bridge over the River Kwai'. This railway bridge, built by allied POWs during World War II at great human cost, lies on the outskirts of the town of Kanchanaburi. The line was constructed under the orders of the Japanese to link Thailand with Burma and it is still possible to cross the bridge by train. However, the Western region has more to offer than just a 1940s vintage railway bridge. The town of Nakhon Pathom 56 km from Bangkok contains the largest chedi in Thailand – the 127m-tall Phra Pathom Chedi. The town itself is one of the oldest in Thailand, dating back to the early centuries of the Christian era and it later became one of the centres of the Dvaravati Kingdom. Further W, in the valleys that surround Kanchanaburi, a Danish POW working on the River Kwai Bridge found significant 4,000 year old neolithic remains at Ban Kao. Close by are the ruins of the ancient Khmer city of Muang Singh. But, the main reason why visitors take the trouble to travel W is to marvel at the scenery of the (fast disappearing) wilderness area beyond Kanchanaburi. This is especially true of the increasing numbers of Thai tourists aiming to escape from the pollution, noise and stress of Bangkok.

NAKHON PATHOM

Route 323 runs west from Bangkok towards the Burmese border and the mountains of the Tenasserim range. Only 67 km from Bangkok is Nakhon Pathom – easily accessible as a day trip from the capital. The city may be the most ancient in Thailand, and at its heart is the largest chedi in the kingdom. Continuing north-west on Route 323 for another 55 km, the road reaches the provincial capital of Kanchanaburi, site of the infamous Bridge over the River Kwai. The road from Bangkok to Kanchanaburi is not an attractive one; it is built up almost all the way. From here the road works upwards through secondary, degraded forest towards Burma. Saam Ong (or Three Pagodas Pass), 240 km from Kanchanaburi, marks the border.

History

Nakhon Pathom is one of the oldest

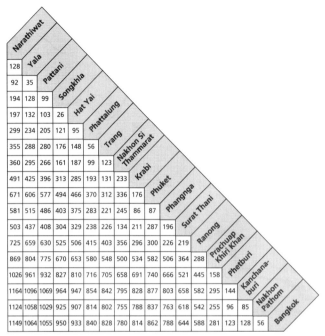

South and West Thailand, distances between provincial capitals (Km)

cities in Thailand (though there is little left to show for it). Some scholars believe that the great Indian Emperor Asoka dispatched 2 missionaries here from India in the 3rd century BC to expound the teachings of Buddhism. It later became the centre of the Dvaravati Kingdom (from the 6th-11th centuries) (see page 73). The **Phra Pathom Chedi** is the largest in Thailand and dominates the heart of the town. The existing chedi was begun in 1853 at the instigation of King Mongkut (who visited its ruined predecessor while still a monk) and took 17 years to complete. The bell-shaped structure stands 127m-high, encasing a much older, smaller Mon shrine (4th century). This was added to in the Khmer period and subsequently sacked by the Burmese in 1057. A 19m-high copy of the original can be seen on the outer platform to the east of the chedi. The new structure collapsed in a rainstorm and the present chedi was finally completed by King Chulalongkorn. The Thai habit of rebuilding over collapsed chedis is because though the site remains holy irrespective of the condition of the monument, it is only by the act of building – of creating something new – that a monarch or benefactor accumulates religious merit.

The Phra Pathom Chedi is encrusted in gold and ochre tiles, supported by 2 ballustrades, and surrounded by a circular gallery. The inner walls of the gallery are inscribed in Pali with Buddhist teachings. The outer walls house 66

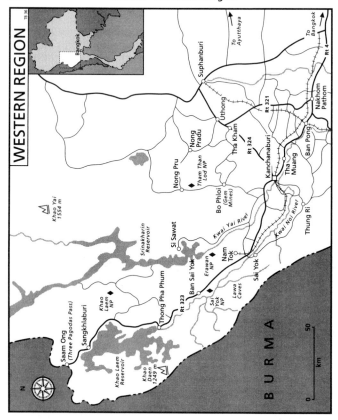

Buddha images in different positions. In addition to the chedi, the temple complex houses 4 viharns located at the cardinal points, and a bot to the S of the great stupa. The inner chamber of the E viharn, or **Viharn Luang**, displays a painting of the stupa depicting the original within it. The walls are covered with murals showing creatures and hermits paying homage to the chedi. The main entrance to the monastery is to the N, and the **Northern Viharn** contains a large standing Buddha which towers over visitors as they walk up the stairs towards the chedi. This image is known as **Phra Ruang Rojanarit**; it is a restored image, found by King Rama VI at Si Satchanalai while he was still a prince. At the base of the statue lie the ashes of the great king. The inner chamber of the Northern Viharn contains an image of the Buddha receiving gifts of a beehive and a jug of water from an elephant and a monkey. The bot was built during King Rama VII's reign and contains a Dvaravati-style Buddha image made of white stone, seated in a preaching position. Admission: ฿10. Open: 0600-1800 Mon-Sun.

The Phra Pathom Chedi **National**

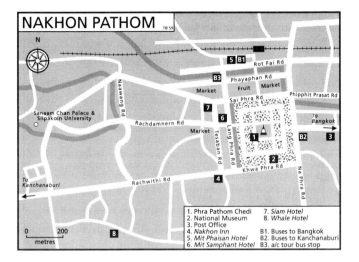

NAKHON PATHOM

N

To Bangkok

To Kanchanaburi

Sanaam Chan Palace & Silpakoin University

Naawang Rd
Rachdamnern Rd
Tesaban Rd
Lang Phra Rd
Rachwithi Rd
Khwa Phra Rd
Na Phra Rd
Rot Fai Rd
Phayaphan Rd
Sai Phra Rd
Phipphit Prasat Rd

Market
Fruit Market
Market

0   200   metres

1. Phra Pathom Chedi
2. National Museum
3. Post Office
4. *Nakhon Inn*
5. *Mit Phaisan Hotel*
6. *Mit Samphant Hotel*
7. *Siam Hotel*
8. *Whale Hotel*
B1. Buses to Bangkok
B2. Buses to Kanchanaburi
B3. a/c tour bus stop

Museum can be found just outside the S walls of the chedi and contains a good collection of Dvaravati sculpture and other works of art. Admission: ฿5. Open: 0900-1200, 1300-1600 Wed-Sun. A second **museum** can be found near the E viharn; its collection is a hotch-potch of poorly displayed artefacts and momentoes including coins, shells, statues and amulets. Open: 0900-1200, 1300-1600 Wed-Sun. A bustling **fruit market**, the Talaat Bon, is within easy walking distance to the N of the chedi. A speciality here is *khaaw lam* – sticky rice and bean cooked in bamboo.

Sanaam Chan Palace, is to be found in a peaceful, leafy park about 10 minutes saamlor ride west from the great chedi. The park is surrounded by a canal and contains a small zoo and playground. The palace was built by Rama VI, and is now used for government offices. It is of interest principally for its unusual interpretation of English Tudor, including a beamed and enclosed

bridge crossing the moat. The park is surrounded by houses similar in style to those found in some of the colonial hill resorts of Southeast Asia.

Excursions

Floating market at **Damnoen Saduak** can be visited at the same time as a visit to Nakhon Pathom. Getting there: take a bus from the S side of the chedi, on Lung Phra Rd (see page 157 for details).

Festivals

Sept: *Food and Fruit Fair* (1st-7th), array of fruits grown in province, Thai and Chinese food preparation, floats and entertainment; **Nov**: a *fair* lights up the spire of Phra Pathom Chedi.

Local information
● **Accommodation**

There are no attractive places to stay here – it's better not to stop a night. **A+-A** *Rose Garden Country Resort*, 32 km marker Phetkasem highway, Sampran, T 321684, B 2532276, a/c, cultural centre with traditional dancing etc, rather artificial – some way out of Nakhon Pathom.

C *Nakhon Inn*, 55 Rachwithi Rd, T 251152,

a/c, coffee shop, looks like *Whale Hotel*, but is in a better state of repair, best in town; **C Whale**, 151/79 Rachwithi Rd, T 251020, a/c, large and characterless, grim exterior, run down.

D Mit Phaisan, 120/30 Phayaphan Rd, T 243122, some a/c/some hot water, same management as *Mit Samphant* but slightly better rooms.

E Mit Samphant, 2/11 Lang Phra Rd, T 252010, basic, no windows, no expense lavished on decor, entrance through electrical shop, or in the side street; **E Siam**, 2/1-8 Rachdamnern Rd, T 252230, some a/c, basic, prison-like corridors, no hot water, clean sheets.

● **Banks & money changers**
First Bangkok City, Sai Phra Rd (N of the chedi and fruit market); **Siam City**, Sai Phra Rd (N of the chedi and fruit market).

● **Post & telecommunications**
Post Office: Tesaban Rd (running E from the chedi). **Area code**: 034.

● **Transport**
67 km from Bangkok.

Train The station is to the N of the fruit market, an easy walk to/from the chedi. Regular connections with Hualamphong station, Bangkok 1 hr. Connections on to Kanchanaburi, 0918 or 1451 from Nakhon Pathom. Connections to S destinations: Phetburi, Hua Hin and Surat Thani.

Road Bus: a/c buses stop to the N of the fruit market, an easy walk to the chedi. Regular a/c and non-a/c connections (every 15 mins) with Bangkok's Southern bus terminal 1 hr (a/c ₿22). Connections with Kanchanaburi.

KANCHANABURI

Famous for its proximity to the **Bridge over the River Kwai** and close to the Thai/Burmese border, this is an area of great natural beauty and is a good jumping-off point for visits to national parks, trips on the River Kwai or excursions to one of a number of waterfalls and caves. The province's wealth is derived from gems mined at the Bo-Phloi mines, teak trading with Burma, sugarcane plantations and tourism. It was from here that the Japanese set allied prisoners-of-war

to work on the construction of the notorious 'death railway' linking Thailand with Burma during World War II (see box).

The province of Kanchanaburi is becoming increasingly popular with Thai tourists trying to 'get away from it all' and commune with nature. This is reflected in the large number of 'resorts' and 'jungle lodges' that have been developed in recent years, which are dotted across the countryside, promising peace and tranquility. The Bangkok equivalent of the yuppie can be seen frequenting the many floating restaurants and discos found along the river.

Kanchanaburi itself was only established in the 1830s, although the ruins of Muang Singh (see Excursions, below) over 40 km to the W date from the Khmer period. On entering the town (called Muang Kan by most locals), visitors may notice the fish-shaped street signs. The fish in question is the *yisok*, a small fresh-water fish found in the rivers of the province; it is the symbol of Kanchanaburi. Another slice of Thai fauna for which this area of Thailand is known is Kitti's hog-nosed bat. This bat – the smallest in the world, with a body the size of a bumblebee – was discovered in 1973 by Dr Kitti Thonglongya in limestone caves near the Rive Kwai Bridge.

Places of interest

The **JEATH War Museum** (the letters denoting the countries involved) can be found by the river, at the end of Wisuttharangsi Road, where there is a reconstruction of a POW camp and other war memorabilia. The most interesting element of the display are the photographs of life and work on the railway. The museum was established in 1977 and is run by the monks of Wat Chanasongkhram. As the museum's brochure explains, it has been constructed 'not for the maintenance of hatred among human beings...but to warn and teach us the lesson

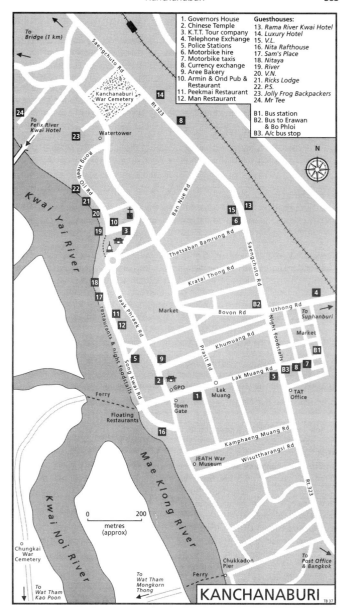

1. Governors House
2. Chinese Temple
3. K.T.T. Tour company
4. Telephone Exchange
5. Police Stations
6. Motorbike hire
7. Motorbike taxis
8. Currency exchange
9. Aree Bakery
10. Armin & Ond Pub & Restaurant
11. Peekmai Restaurant
12. Man Restaurant

Guesthouses:
13. *Rama River Kwai Hotel*
14. *Luxury Hotel*
15. *V.L.*
16. *Nita Rafthouse*
17. *Sam's Place*
18. *Nitaya*
19. *River*
20. *V.N.*
21. *Ricks Lodge*
22. *P.S.*
23. *Jolly Frog Backpackers*
24. *Mr Tee*

B1. Bus station
B2. Bus to Erawan & Bo Phloi
B3. A/c bus stop

KANCHANABURI

THE DEATH RAILWAY

The construction of the bridge over the River Kwai and the associated Death Railway is one the more infamous episodes of the Second World War in Southeast Asia. For the Japanese high command, the logic of building a rail link between Siam and Burma was clear. They lacked the merchant fleet to carry supplies to and from their fast expanding empire, and it would cut almost 2,000 km off the journey from Japan to Rangoon. It was perceived to be crucial to the Japanese war effort. The problem was that the Japanese lacked the labour to construct the line through some of the wettest and most inhospitable land in the region. They estimated that given their resources it would take 5-6 years to finish. The solution to their dilemma was simple: to employ some of the 300,000 POWs who had so far been captured, most of whom were being unproductively incarcerated on Singapore.

Work began in June 1942. The Japanese engineer Fatamatsu chose a route which ran along the river valley of the Kwai Noi, a decision which has since been much criticized because of the harshness of the terrain. But the river was a useful artery of communication, and this allowed construction to begin simultaneously in a number of places – a crucial factor when speed was of the essence. Most of the materials were locally sourced – there was simply not the fleet capacity to import materials and equipment from Japan. As a result, no less than 680 of the 688 bridges built were constructed of timber. Rails were pillaged from secondary tracks in Burma and Malaya, and bamboo and softwoods were extensively used in construction. In all, over 3 million cubic metres of rock were shifted, 15 km of bridges built and 415 km of track laid. The workforce at its peak numbered 61,000 Allied POWs and an estimated 250,000 Asians. Work was hard; a prisoner, Naylor wrote:

We started work the day after we arrived, carrying huge baulks of timber. It was the heaviest work I have ever known; the Japs drove us on and by nightfall I was so tired and sore that I could not eat my dinner and just crawled on to the bed and fell asleep. The next day was spent carrying stretchers of earth, also heavy work and incredibly monotonous. The hours were 8.30 am to 7.30 pm with an hour for lunch.

The Japanese, but particularly the Korean overseers, adopted a harsh code of

of how terrible war is'. Admission: ฿20 (no photographs). Open: 0830-1800 Mon-Sun.

The **Kanchanaburi War Cemetery** (Don Rak) is about 1.5 km from the centre of town on Saengchuto Road, travelling NW. It is immaculately maintained by the Commonwealth Cemeteries Commission. Open: 0800-1700 Mon-Sun, you can always look over the gates. To get there, walk, hire a bicycle or take a *saamlor*. The **Chungkai (UK) War Cemetery** is 2 km S of town. Small, peaceful and well kept. Get there by boat from in front of the town gates,

or by tuk-tuk or bicycle. The **Bridge over the River Kwai** (pronounced Kway in Thai, not Kwai) is 3-4 km N of the town, again on Saengchuto Road. Architecturally unexciting, it is of purely historical interest. The central span was destroyed by Allied bombing towards the end of the war, and has been rebuilt in a different style. Visitors can walk over the bridge, visit a **World War II Museum** and **Art Gallery** (admission ฿30) or browse in the many souvenir stalls. There is an old locomotive here and several restaurants along the riverbank (and on the river). The whole area is

discipline – face-slapping, blows with rifle butts, standing erect for hours on end, and solitary confinement for weeks in small cells made of mud and bamboo. The poor diet meant that the men were able to work at only half-pace, although it is interesting that the Australians who were both bigger and in better condition before they arrived, were usually allotted to do the heavier work. By 1943, some of the men were in an appalling state. In Colonel Toosey's report of October 1945 he wrote:

On one occasion a party of 60, mostly stretcher cases, were dumped off a train in a paddy field some 2 miles from the Camp in the pouring rain at 0300 hrs. ... As a typical example I can remember one man who was so thin that he could be lifted easily in one arm. His hair was growing down his back and was full of maggots; his clothing consisted of a ragged pair of shorts soaked with dysentery excreta; he was lousy and covered with flies all the time. He was so weak that he was unable to lift his head to brush away the flies which were clustered on his eyes and on the sore places of his body. I forced the Japanese Staff to come and look at these parties, which could be smelt for some hundreds of yards, but with the exception of the Camp Comdt. they showed no signs of sympathy, and sometimes merely laughed. (Quoted in Davies,1991:116).

The railway was finished in late 1943, the line from Nong Pladuk being linked with that from Burma on 17th October. For the POWs it was not the end however. Even after the Japanese capitulated on 10th August 1945, the men had to wait for some while before they were liberated. During this period of limbo, Allied officers were worried most about venereal disease, and Colonel Toosey radioed to Delhi for 10,000 condoms to be dropped by air – an incredible thought given the physical condition of the former POWs. In all, 16,000 allied prisoners lost their lives and Kanchanaburi contains the graves of 7,000 of the victims in two war cemeteries. Less well known, 75,000 Asian forced labourers also died constructing the railway. Their sufferings are not celebrated.

Numerous books have been written about the Death Railway and the Bridge over the River Kwai including: Coast, J (1946) *Railway of death*, Commodore: London; Davies, P (1991) *The man behind the bridge: Colonel Toosey and the River Kwai*, Athlone: London; Hardie, R. (1983) *The Burma-Siam railway: the secret diary of Dr. Robert Hardie 1942-1945*, Imperial War Museum: London; Gordon, E. (1963) *Miracle on the River Kwai*, Collins: London; Kinvig, C. (1973) *Death railway*, Pan: London.

quite a mess at the moment, as a building programme is under way. Boats can be rented at the bridge. Getting there: take a saamlor, or hire a bicycle.

Muang Kan's **lak muang** (city pillar), encrusted in gold leaf and draped with flowers can be seen in the middle of Lak Muang Road. Close by are the gates to Kanchanaburi town. Walking through the gates and turning right (N) is the old and most attractive part of town with wooden shophouses.

Excursions
Wat Tham Kao Poon is 5 km SW of town, a few km on from the Chungkai Cemetery. It is rather a gaudy temple with caves attached. Follow the arrows through the cave system. The tunnel is narrow in places, and large individuals may find it a squeeze. The kitsch lighting is almost worth the visit in itself. There is a large Buddha image at the bottom of the system (and smaller ones elsewhere), as well as cells (*kutis*) in which monks can meditate. Intrepid explorers will find they emerge at the back of the hill. No entrance fee to the caves but visitors are encouraged to make a contribution to the maintenance of the monastery (฿10-20). Getting there: hire

a bicycle or tuk-tuk or charter a boat from in front of the town gates.

Wat Tham Mongkorn Thong nestles in foothills, 5½ km S of town. An unimpressive wat with a complex of unimpressive limestone caves attached. These are reached by walking up a long flight of stairs with dragons forming the balustrades. Inside, there are yet more meditation cells (there must be a great number of hermits in Kanchanaburi), bats and bat-like smells (not recommended for the squeamish). The caves are narrow in places and visitors may have to crawl on their hands and knees. The exit is up a short steel ladder at the end of the cave system half way up the hill. Visitors are expected to make a small contribution before entering the caves. Getting there: rather difficult to reach by public transport; occasional buses from the bus station, or cross the river by ferryboat at Chukkadon Pier, or charter a tuk-tuk or songthaew.

The **77 km train ride** on the **Death Railway** from Kanchanaburi NW to the small town of Nam Tok is scenically very dramatic. The train stops at the ancient Khmer site of Muang Singh en route (see below). Getting there: 3 trains each way daily, leaving Kanchanaburi at 0600, 1030 and 1628, approx 2 hrs (฿17).

Wat Tham Sua and **Wat Tham Kao Noi** lie 20 km SE of Kanchanaburi. The main temple is a strange, pagoda-like affair perched on a hilly outcrop, and can be seen from afar. At the base of the hill is a Chinese temple and a short walk further is the steep dragon-lined staircase that leads up the hill to the wat itself. The pagoda is a weird amalgam of Chinese and Thai, new and old (it contains modern steel windows topped with fluorescent lights). The view of the surrounding area is worth the climb. The wat also has a series of caves. The Vajiralongkorn Dam is not far away. Getting there: by hired motorbike or chartered tuk-tuk/songthaew.

Phu Phra caves and **Wat Tham Kun Phaen** are about 20 km N of town just off Route 323 to Sangkhlaburi. The wat and its associated caves nestles in foothills which rise up towards Burma. Back on Route 323 is the **Kanchanaburi Cultural Centre**, with a collection of handicrafts, artefacts and historical exhibits. Getting there: by bus 8203 (tell the bus conductor where you want to get off) or hire a motorbike or songthaew/tuk-tuk.

Ban Kao is a neolithic site (2000 BC) 35 km from Kanchanaburi discovered by one of the Danish POW's working on the death railway. It was not until 1961 that a Thai-Danish archaeological team confirmed the find and its significance. A small archaeological museum near to the site houses many of the bones and artefacts. Open: 0900-1600 Wed-Sun. For non-archaeologists the museum is not particularly exciting, but it is en route to Muang Singh Historical Park, 8 km away. Getting there: hire a tuk-tuk/songthaew or a motorbike.

Muang Singh Historical Park (City of Lions) is an ancient Khmer town on the banks of the Kwai Noi River about 45 km W of Kanchanaburi town. The site covers several square kilometres but the main, central prang and associated buildings are concentrated over a small area. The city is built of deep red laterite and reached its apogee during the 12th-13th centuries when it flourished as a trading node linking Siam with the Indian Ocean. The city represents an artistic and strategic outlier of the great Cambodian Empire (perhaps the furthest W) and it is mentioned in inscriptions from the reign of the Khmer King Jayavarman VII. The moat and original outer walls can still be seen and some archaeologists have postulated that the remains provide evidence that an advanced system of water control was in use. It is not as complete or impressive as other archaeological sites in Thailand but is peaceful and interesting to wander around. On the inside of the N wall of the major shrine is a carving of a 4-armed figure – probably Avalokitesvara Bodhisattva (the future Buddha). The discovery of a 1.6m high stone statue of a Bodhisattva (now on display in the National Museum in Bangkok) indicates that the building was used as a Mahayana Buddhist shrine. Much of the stucco decoration that once covered the buildings has disappeared and no inscriptions have been discovered. Admission: ฿20. Open: Mon-Sun. Restaurants and refreshments available close to the central ruins. Getting there: hire a tuk-tuk/songthaew or motorbike or take the train (see local transport below for details), or hitch a lift.

Khao Phang or **Sai Yok Noi waterfall** lies 60 km NW of Kanchanaburi on Route 323. The falls are only impressive in the wet season (July-Sept) although the pools provide refreshing swimming year round. Close by are the **Vang Ba Dalh** caves. Getting there: take bus 8203 from Kanchanaburi town 1 hr (฿18). It is 1 km to the falls and 2 km to the caves (the sign for the falls is in Thai only, so follow signs to the cave which are in English).

Sai Yok National Park lies 104 km NW of Kanchanaburi. Tigers and elephants still inhabit this wild region of stunning scenery, which stretches all the way to the Burmese border. The park's main attraction is the **Sai Yok Yai waterfall**. Also near Sai Yok Yai are the **Daowadung Caves** (30 mins N by boat from the falls and then a 3 km walk). Best time to visit: May to Dec. Accommodation: some park bungalows available and camping facilities. Getting there: boats can be hired from Pak Saeng pier in Tambon Tha Saaw, about 50 km N of Kanchanaburi town. A boat (max. 10 people) to the park (including the Lawa caves and Sai Yok Yai waterfall) should cost about ฿1200/boat (seating 10-12 people) (or go on a tour) and the trip will take 2½ hrs upstream and 1½ hrs down.

Erawan National Park is an area of great natural beauty, with some impressive waterfalls. Best time to visit is during the rainy season – the falls are not nearly as dramatic during the dry season. It is a 10 min walk from the bus station to the park gates, another 15 mins to the 'reception centre', and then a further 10 mins to the first of the series of 7 falls that constitute the **Erawan Falls**. The walk to the falls is through forest, and the pools make a refreshing dip. The first of the falls is most popular with swimmers and picnickers. Level 3 is very beautiful, level 7 is well worth the steep climb. The impressive **Phrathat Caves** are located about 10 km NW of headquarters, a good hike or easy drive. Ask at reception for directions. En route to Erawan the road passes the **Tha Thungna Dam**. This whole area has been at the centre of an intense environmental controversy over the construction of a third dam upriver from the Srinakharin Dam (which is just above the Erawan Falls). The proposed Nam Choan Dam would have flooded large areas of the Thung Yai and Huai Kha Khaeng wildlife sanctuaries, and destroyed rare stands of riverine tropical forest. The fact that public pressure ensured that the plans were shelved in 1989 represents the first significant victory for environmentalists in Thailand, and they are now a political force to be reckoned with. In 1992 the two sanctuaries were declared Southeast Asia's first Natural World Heritage Site by UNESCO, vindicating the environmentalists' stand. Admission to the park: ฿3 for adults, ฿1 for children. Open: 0600-1800 Mon-Sun. Accommodation: bungalows and dormitories (F) as well as restaurants and assorted stalls. Getting there: regular buses (8170) from Kanchanaburi from 0800 (65 km), 1½-2 hrs (฿21). **NB:** the last bus back to Kanchanaburi leaves Erawan at 1600.

Bo Phloi, 50 km N of town, lies at the centre of one of Thailand's main gem-mining areas, with some 8 open-cast mines extracting sapphires, onyx and semi-precious stones and a number of polishing plants (see page 372). Displays of local production techniques are given. Getting there: bus 325 from Kanchanaburi bus station, 1½ hrs (฿14).

Tours

Raft and boat trips, and motorized raft restaurants and discos are now very popular. Raft trips are not very easily organized oneself, and it is probably better to go through a tour operator. The *River Kwai Village Hotel* organizes river tours to the Lawa Caves and Sai Yok Yai Falls. *The BT Travel Co. Ltd* organizes raft trips to the Chungkai Cemetery together with fishing and swimming on the River Kwai Noi for ฿190/person. They also arrange a/c minibus tours to Muang Singh Historical Park, Ban Kao, Sai Yok Noi and elsewhere. The most comprehensive tour costs ฿290/person. Inquiries about tours can be made at the TAT office. Hotels and guesthouses in Kanchanaburi are also a good source of information on tours and side trips. *K.T.T.* (Kanchanaburi Trekking Tour Company), organise jungle treks, elephant rides, raft trips, visits to waterfalls and caves (฿600/day). Some overnight trips. In Bangkok virtually every hotel or tour office will be able to offer a day tour (or longer) to Kanchanaburi and surrounding sights. A day-long tour should cost about ฿600/person (see Tours, Bangkok, page 159).

The State Railways of Thailand offer a worthwhile all-day tour from Bangkok to Kanchanaburi on weekends and holidays. The train leaves Thonburi station at 0615, stopping at Nakhon Pathom (40 minute stop), the River Kwai Bridge (30 minute stop), and arrives at Nam Tok at 1130. A minibus service (฿2) then goes to Khao Pang/Sai Yok Noi waterfall, the last bus leaving the falls for Nam Tok station at 1410. The train then leaves Nam Tok at 1430, arriving Kanchanaburi 1605 (45 minute stop to visit the POW cemetery) and returning to Bangkok at 1930 (฿75).

The State Railways also offer a number of other tours with overnight stays, rafting and fishing. For details on all tours contact the Railway Advance Book Office at Hualamphong Station in Bangkok, T 2256964. Advance booking recommended. A shorter train trip can be organised from Kanchanaburi to Nam Tok, leaving daily at 1030. Contact the *Train Travel Tour Company*, T 561052 or Kanchanaburi Train Station, T 511285.

Festivals

Nov/Dec: *River Kwai Bridge Week* (moveable). The festival starts on the evening of the first day, with a religious ceremony conducted by dozens of monks and then a procession from the City Pillar Shrine to the bridge. The 45 minute *son et lumière* to commemorate the destruction of the original bridge by allied bombs in 1945 is very realistic. Other events include long boat races, exhibitions, steam train rides, cultural shows.

Local information
● Accommodation

A+ *Felix River Kwai Hotel*, 9/1 Moo 3 Thamakhom, T 515061, F 515086, B 2553410, a/c, restaurant, large pool, new hotel N of bridge on W bank of Kwai Yai River, all facilities, rather rambling and large but most luxurious available.

A-B *River Kwai*, 284/3-16 Saengchuto Rd, T 511184, F 511269, a/c, restaurant, pool, large unappealing hotel, has had a face-lift but will become tatty again, big discounts available during the week, popular tour group hotel, large massage parlour next door.

D *Rick's Lodge*, 48/5 Rong Heeb Oil 2 Rd, T 514831, F 514831, restaurant with Thai and European food, A frame huts, with beds on top and sitting-room and bathroom below, 11 rooms, some with river views, organises treks and tours, rec; **D-E** *Luxury*, 284/1-5 Saengchuto Rd, T 511169, some a/c; **D-E** *Prasopsuk*, 677 Saengchuto Rd, T 511777, a/c; **D-E** *River Guesthouse*, 42 Rong Heeb Oil Rd, T 512491, restaurant (with 'honesty system'), more expensive rooms have own shower and fan, very popular travellers hangout, basic huts on the waterfront, videos nightly; **D-E** *Sam's Place*, 7/3 Song Kwai Rd, T 513971, restaurant, rooms with shower, attractively designed, tours organised, very basic plumbing arrangements, floating restaurant next door has rather noisy crooners late into the night, rec; **D-E** *V.L.*, 18/11 Saengchuto Rd, T 513546, some a/c, small restaurant, 3 storey block, clean, large rooms with baths.

E *Jolly Frog Backpackers*, 28 Mae Nam Kwai Rd, T 514579, large restaurant with expensive Thai and European menu, popular place, well set up for travellers, quite civilised with attractive garden over-looking river, standard rooms, looking onto garden, English and German speaking management, canoe for rent; **E** *Mr Tee*, 12 Soi Laos, River Kwai Rd, restaurant, fan, some rooms with shower, average rooms, but attractive quiet location, N of town, on the river, good value, rec; **E** *Nita Rafthouse*, 27/1 Phakphrak Rd, T 514521, restaurant, small basic rooms (some **F**), but very friendly owner with good English, boats, motorbike and bike for hire, videos at night, rec: **E** *Nitaya Rafthouse*, Song Kwai Rd (N end), T 513341, restaurant, basic rooms, not very good English; **E** *P.S. Guesthouse*, Rong Heeb Oil 3 Rd, T 513039, restaurant, some rooms with bathrooms, some tours, cleaner than many, quietest along this strip; **E** *V.N. Guesthouse*, 44 Rong Heeb Oil 2 Rd, T 514082, restaurant, some rooms with shower, not such a good outlook, not much charm, standard rooms.

● **Resorts**
There are a large number of 'back to nature' resorts around Kanchanaburi. The following are in the vicinity of the town; most cater for Thai tourists. **A** *Home Phu Toey*, B 2803488, near Sai Yok Waterfall, just N of Lawa Caves, a/c, restaurant, lake for swimming, accommodation in Thai-style huts, very attractive location, overnight trip from Bangkok includes food, travel and tour of area; **A** *Kwai Noi Island Resort*, 144/4 Mu 4, Tha Maka Village (about 20 km outside Kanchanaburi), T 513359, B 5135399; **A** *River Kwai Village*, B 2517552, 70 km NW of town, near Nam Tok, a/c, restaurant, pool, hotel and raft accommodation in remote setting.

B *Kasem Island Resort*, 27 Chaichumphon Rd, T 513359, B 2556303, on an island on the Mae Klong, restaurant, attractive, clean rafts; **B** *River Kwai Jungle House*, 96/1 Mu 3, Amphoe Sai Yok (40 km from Kanchanaburi, nr Muang Singh Historical Park), T 561052, B 2333762, rattan bungalows float on the river; **B** *River Kwai Rafts*, beyond the Kwai Bridge, B 2453069, restaurant, rooms on floating bamboo rafts; **B** *River Kwai Village Hotel*, Sai Yok, T 2517552, 70 km N of Kanchanaburi, bungalows, long tailed boat excursions. Several bungalows at Sai Yok include: **National Park bungalows**, B 5794842, ฿500-1,000/bungalow.

C *Saiyok Valley Resort*, T 5389934.

● **Places to eat**
Most restaurants are to be found along Song Kwai Rd. Almost all restaurants cater for Thai tourists and therefore have accompanying 'crooners' (Thai singers). **♦♦***Baan Nua*, **♦♦***Mae Nam*, and **♦♦***Ruan Ploi* are all floating restaurants on the banks of the River Kwai. **♦♦***Armin & Ond*, Rong Heeb Oil Rd, Thai and European food, garden, travellers' hangout; **♦♦***Man*, Song Kwai Rd, popular with locals, extensive menu, spicy salads, popular; **♦♦***New Isan*, 292/1-2 Saengchuto Rd, popular with locals and tourists, rec; **♦♦***Peekmai*, Song Kwai Rd, NE Thai food, extensive menu, crooners can be a little off-putting; **♦♦***Saiyoke*, near River Kwai Bridge and **♦♦***Solo*, near River Kwai Bridge, both are large restaurants, catering for tour groups, extensive Thai menus, not much English spoken; **♦***Jukkru*, Song Kwai Rd, large selection, lots of fish; **♦***No 1 Coffeeshop*, Rong Heeb Oil Rd, next to *Rick's Lodge*, small café on the road selling coffees and European food, English speaking.

Foodstalls open up along the river in the evening and there is also an excellent night market with a great range of food available in the vicinity of the bus station (rec). *Aree Bakery*, Baak Phraek Rd, delicious ice-creams and breakfasts. *Sii Fa Bakery*, by bus terminal, good range of pastries.

● **Bars**
Along the riverfront, several karaoke joints. Cocktails at *Armin & Ond*, opposite *River Guesthouse*, N of town.

● **Banks & money changers**
A number near the bus station and the market Bangkok, 2 Uthong Rd; Thai Farmers, 160/80-2 Saengchuto Rd; Thai Military, 160/34 Saengchuto Rd.

● **Hospitals & medical services**
There is a hospital on Saengchuto Rd, close to Saengchuto Soi 20.

● **Police**
Corner of Saengchuto and Lak Muang rds.

● **Post & telecommunications**

Post Office: Saengchuto Rd (not far from Sathani Rot Fai Rd) – some distance out of town towards Bangkok). **Area code**: 034.

● **Shopping**

Souvenir shops found near the bridge. Usual array of handicrafts. Bargain for purchases.

Gemstones: blue sapphires, onyx and topaz are all mined at Bo Phloi, 50 km from Kanchanaburi. Good prices for them at shops near the bridge or in the market area of town. Baak Phraek Rd is a pleasant road to walk down, with several clothes shops, tailors, kitchen and basketware shops.

● **Sports**

Fishing: on the Kwai River, Khao Laem and Srinakharin reservoirs. Travel agents will help organize expeditions.

● **Tour companies & travel agents**

B.T. Travel, Saengchuto Rd (behind TAT), T 511967; *K.T.T.* (Kanchanaburi Trekking Tour Company), corner of Rong Heeb Oil 2 Rd, T 9228589, branch at *Nitaya Rafthouse*, N end of Song Kwai Rd; *T.C.S.*, 286/165 Saengchuto Rd, T 515266; *R.S.P. Travel Centre*, Saengchuto Rd, T 512280; *River Kwai Village Hotel*, booking office in Bangkok, 1054/4 New Phetburi Rd, T 2517552; *Silver Star Tours*, 812 Saengchuto Rd, T 511445.

● **Tourist offices**

TAT, Saengchuto Rd, T 511200 (walk S, towards Bangkok, from the market and bus station). A good first stop as they supply up-to-date information on accommodation. Areas of responsibility are Kanchanaburi, Nakhon Pathom, Samut Sakhon and Samut Songkhram.

● **Transport**

122 km NW of Bangkok.

Local Songthaews/tuk-tuks: most useful for out-of-town trips. Charter one at the bus station. To Wat Tham Kao Poon, Ban Kao and then to the Khmer ruins at Muang Singh Historical Park (100 km in total) about 3½ hrs (approx ฿200). **Saamlor**: charter for 2-3 hrs should cost about ฿100, for a trip to the Kwai bridge, JEATH museum and the cemetery. **Bicycles**: a good way to get around town and out to the bridge. Hire in town for ฿20/day (there is a shop on Baak Phraek Rd just N of the town gates) or ask at guesthouses. **Motorbikes/scooters**: can be hired on Saengchuto Rd (e.g. next to *V.L. Guesthouse* at 18/11) or

near the TAT office or on Song Kwai Rd (next door to *Peekmai Restaurant*, 0800-1900, closed Sun), ฿150-500/day. **Jeeps**: can be hired on Saengchuto Rd, beside TAT office and on Song Kwai Rd. **Boat**: for hire along riverfront for trips upriver, or from the guesthouses.

Train The station is 2 km NW of town on Saengchuto Rd, not far from the cemetery (T 511285). Regular connections with Nakhon Pathom and on to Hualampong Station. W/e and holidays, special service (see tours). There is a left luggage office at the station.

Road Bus: non-a/c buses leave from the station in the market area, behind Saengchuto Rd. A/c buses leave from the corner of Saengchuto Rd, opposite Lak Muang Rd. Regular connections with Bangkok's Southern bus terminal, (a/c bus No 81), 2 hrs (฿62), or non-a/c bus 3-4 hrs. Also connections with Nakhon Pathom (฿20) from where there are buses to the floating market at Damnoen Saduak (see page 157).

SANGKHLABURI AND SAAM ONG (THREE PAGODAS PASS)

The route to Sangkhlaburi (or 'Sangkhla', as it is known) and Saam Ong follows the valley of the Kwai Noi with the scenery becoming increasingly rugged towards Sangkhlaburi.

The road passes through remnant forests and cultivated land revealing deep red tropical soils planted to upland crops such as cassava, tamarind, mango and cotton. There is accommodation at **B-C** *Thong Pha Phum*, T 599058, at the S edge of the Khao Laem reservoir, if people want to stop half way. From here N, the road becomes increasingly windy, and the landscape more mountainous and densely forested. The last 40 km before Sangkhlaburi the road skirts the shore of the reservoir; a strange landscape of submerged (now dead) trees and what appear to be raft-houses. This upland area is home to several different ethnic groups: Karen, Mon and Burmese, as well as Thais. Sangkhlaburi is positioned on the edge of the huge Khao

Laem reservoir, which was created in 1983. The village is a centre for wood and drugs smuggling and other illicit trading. It is interesting for its diverse nationalities: Karen, Mon, Burmese, Indians, Pakistanis and Chinese. The **morning market** here provides a range of textiles and various Burmese goods. A 400m **wooden bridge** across the lake is said to be the longest in Thailand. It was largely built by the Mon people. It leads to a **Mon village** (Waeng Kha) which is interesting to walk around. The 5,000 inhabitants (approximately) are displaced Burmese who cannot get a Thai passport and can only work around Sangkhla. From 1948 onwards, refugees have fled Burma for the relative safety of Thailand. Most of them will never be allowed a visa or resident's permit. In 1982, the old town of Sangkhlaburi was flooded by the dam and these refugees were again left with nothing (no homes and no land). The abbot of the flooded Wat Sam Prasop was able to acquire land

for a new wat and helped 500 households to re-establish themselves. However, these people are not wanted by the Thai government, and there have been several raids by the army to catch Mon people without identity cards. At present, they are protected by the abbot, but he is now 84 years old, so their future is uncertain. The attraction of Saam Ong, which lies 20 km on from Sangkhlaburi is its position on the border with Burma. This was the traditional invasion route for Burmese soldiers during the Ayutthayan Period (see pages 78 and 183). Although there is really nothing much to see here, the town does exude an illicit air and is a major smuggling point between Burma and Thailand. Relations between Thailand and Burma deteriorated markedly at the end of 1992 after Burmese troops occupied hill 491 on Thai territory. A serious conflict was only averted by the timely intervention of Thai King Bhumibol. The number of refugees who have been forced to settle

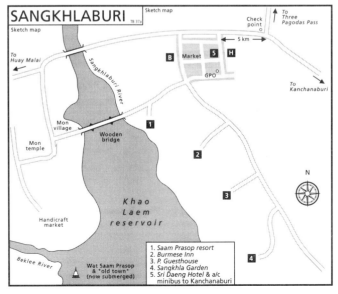

SANGKHLABURI TB 37a

Sketch map

To Huay Malai

Sangkhlaburi River

Mon village

Mon temple

Handicraft market

Beklee River

Wooden bridge

Khao Laem reservoir

Wat Saam Prasop & "old town" (now submerged)

Sketch map

Check point

To Three Pagodas Pass

5 km

B   Market   5   H

GPO

To Kanchanaburi

N

1. Saam Prasop resort
2. Burmese Inn
3. P. Guesthouse
4. Sangkhla Garden
5. Sri Daeng Hotel & a/c minibus to Kanchanaburi

1   2   3   4

in the area bears testament to the continuing harshness of the Burmese regime (see page 543).

Excursions

Wat Wang Wiwekaram is situated across the lake from Sangkhlaburi on a hill. It was built in 1982 to replace the old temple (Wat Sam Prasop) which was buried by the reservoir and is revered by the Mons, Karens and Burmese as well as by the Thais of the area. The wat is dominated by a chedi said to be modelled on the Mahabodhi stupa in Bodhgaya, India and there are good views from the summit. The eastern part of the wat has a Burmese handicraft market, which is very busy at the weekends. Sarongs, silk, cloth, lacquerware, silver jewellery are all for sale. Avoid the 'gems', they are almost certainly synthetic.

Saam Ong, or Three Pagodas Pass, is an unexciting spot; there is a tacky market in a rather makeshift shelter, selling a few Burmese goods (teak, umghi, seed pearls) and a lot of Chinese imports. Avoid the 'gems', they will be fake. **NB**: There is a Tourist Police office at the pass if you encounter problems. The pagodas themselves are truly unremarkable. At the border, posters declare 'Love your Motherland' and 'Respect the Law': visitors can pay ฿130 or US$3 immigration fee to enter Burma and the village of **Payathonzu** (meaning Three Pagodas), which is more market than village.

On the border lies the remains of the Burmese/Thai/Japanese railway. Motorbike taxis can transport you to the market area of the village (฿10 from the songthaew drop-off point). The market here is marginally more interesting than at Saam Ong, with a range of handicrafts, jewellery, Burmese blankets, and an alarming amount of teak furniture.

Beyond the village, there is another border post, beyond which visitors are forbidden to go. Sometimes this area opens up to tourists. Burmese restrictions may vary between 2-20 km. **NB**: It is inadvisable to cross the border anywhere other than at a checkpoint. Similarly, do not go beyond Payathonzu without permission of the SLORC (Burmese army). *Getting there*: songthaews leave every 40 minutes from the bus station, 30 mins (฿30).

The **Kroeng Tho waterfall**, 12 km beyond the border (into Burma) is one of the best in the area, but is rarely accessible to tourists. It is similar to the Erawan Falls (see page 387), with impressive cascades. After a 40 mins walk alongside the river and the cascades (there are no trails), you reach the concrete walls of a reservoir, built by the Japanese during World War II. *Getting there*: songthaews leave every 40 minutes from the bus station, 30 mins (฿30).

Ban Songkaria is a Mon village, 6 km N from the turn off to Three Pagodas Pass. It was once the HQ for the Mon army. The airstrip on the right-hand side of the road (opposite the village) was originally used by the Thai Air Force. There has been talk of flights to Kanchanaburi and Bangkok.

Thung Yai Wildlife Sanctuary The entrance to Thung Yai lies 15 km NE of Sangkhla, in the Karen village of Ban Sane Pong. Within the Park, is the **Takien Thong Waterfall**, with big pools for swimming. The falls lie 26 km from Sangkhla N of Ban Sane Pong, but only accessible by taking the main road N for 13 km from the turn off to Three Pagodas Pass, and then a right turn down a dirt road for 9 km, which is possible to drive down on motorbikes during the dry season. During the rainy season (June-Oct) the whole area is less accessible.

Wang Bandan Cave lies 18 km N from the turn off to Three Pagodas Pass, 2 km down a track to the right of the road. Monks still live in the cave, but it is only a question of time before they flee from the tourists. The entrance and exit are different. There is no entrance fee, but the monks may try to charge ฿50 to guide visitors through the cave.

Tours

P. Guesthouse and *Burmese Inn* both organize trips around Sangkhlaburi. Trips include visits to Karen village by boat, a 2 hr elephant ride through the jungle, swimming and lunch and bamboo white-water rafting. The *Burmese Inn* may be able to organize a visit to a Karen camp. **NB**: Malaria is common in this area, particularly in the jungle, so take precautions and try to avoid being bitten.

Local information

● **Accommodation**

A *Runtee Palace*, raft hotel, 1½ hrs boat trip S from Sangkhla; **A-C** *Three Pagodas Resort*, 1½ km before pass on right-hand side, T 4124159, restaurant, overpriced weekend resort for Thais.

C *Sam Prasop Resort*, overlooking lake, by the wooden bridge, T 595050, a/c, restaurant, individual bungalows, small rooms with bathroom, no English spoken; **C** *Sangkhla Garden*, overlooking lake, T 595096, a/c, restaurant, geared for Thai tourists; **C-D** *Sri Daeng*, in town, T 595026, a/c and hot water, unattractive rooms and location.

E *Burmese Inn*, 52/3 Tambon Nong Loo,

T 595146, restaurant, fan available, outside mandis, not as nice a position as *P. Guesthouse*, rooms quite basic, friendly European owner (speaks English and German) who will organise tours, boat and jeep available for hire, rec.

F *P. Guesthouse*, T 595140, good restaurant (with honesty system), very basic huts with wafer thin walls, mattresses on the floor, mandis outside, attractive position overlooking lake, well set up for travellers, helpful owner will organise tours and trekking (see above), motorbikes (฿150/day) and mountain bikes (฿50/day), motorbike taxis to town, boat for hire ฿10 for 2 hrs, massage ฿80/hr, car available. Construction is underway for a new restaurant, ultimately, more upmarket bungalows, rec.

● **Post & telecommunications**

Post office: in town (see map). **Area code**: 034.

● **Transport**

240 km from Kanchanaburi, 335 km from Bangkok.

Local Motorbike taxis: ฿10 to almost everywhere. They are to be found in town, by the bridge, or can be hailed along the road.

Road Bus: regular connections on non-a/c bus with Kanchanaburi, 5-6 hrs (฿70). **A/c minibus**: hourly connections with Kanchanaburi, 3 hrs (฿100).

SOUTHERN THAILAND

Many Southerners (or the 'Thai Pak Tai') are Muslim. They speak a dialect which has more in common with Malay than with Thai and they wear sarongs. Historically, they have identified – culturally and sometimes politically – with Malaysia.

The Malays of Southern Thailand do not have much in common with, or much regard for, Central Thai bureaucracy and the far S has had its share of banditry and separatist rebellion: first from the Malay-speaking Muslims – who have always felt a bit uncomfortable in the land of Buddhism and Bangkok bureaucrats – and then from the Communists (of both the Thai and Malaysian variety). All of these insurrections are in terminal decline: the Thai Communists had their heyday in the 1970's, while the Communist Party of Malaya, which was based in the jungle around Betong, finally capitulated to the authorities in 1990. But there remains a feeling of alienation and separateness which even the King has been unable to dispel. Today, Islamic revivalism gives the Thai government more cause for concern. The King recently built a palace at Narathiwat (almost the southernmost town) in an attempt to stave off feelings of isolation, but nevertheless Southern Thais still believe they are discriminated against by the dominant Central Thais.

The South is rich in natural resources; tin is mined throughout its 14 provinces, and is refined in Phuket's huge smelter. The tropical climate, with no appreciable dry season, has proved a suitable environment for the cultivation of plantation crops such as rubber and coconut and land planted to rubber far exceeds that planted to rice. Finally, the rich tropical seas and long coastline on both the Gulf of Thailand and the An-

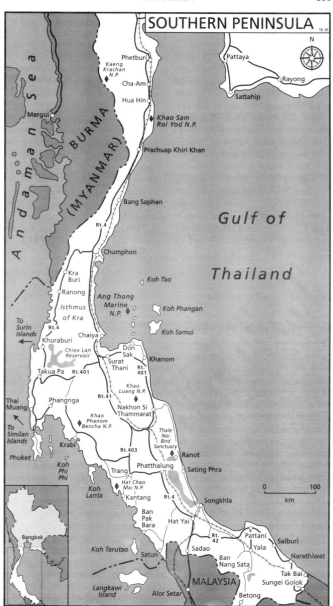

SOUTHERN PENINSULA

TB 38

N

Andaman Sea

BURMA (MYANMAR)

Mergui

Phetburi

Kaeng Krachan N.P.

Cha-Am

Hua Hin

Khao Sam Roi Yod N.P.

Prachuap Khiri Khan

Pattaya

Rayong

Sattahip

Bang Saphan

Gulf of

Thailand

Rt.4

Chumphon

Kra Buri

Koh Tao

Ranong

Isthmus of Kra

Ang Thong Marine N.P.

Koh Phangan

To Surin Islands

Rt.4

Khuraburi

Chaiya

Koh Samui

Chieo Lan Reservoir

Don Sak

Takua Pa

Rt.401

Surat Thani

Khanom

Rt.401

Phangnga

Rt.41

Khao Luang N.P.

Thai Muang

Khao Phanom Bencha N.P.

Nakhon Si Thammarat

To Similan Islands

Krabi

Rt.403

Thale Noi Bird Sanctuary

Phuket

Ranot

Koh Phi Phi

Trang

Phatthalung

Sating Phra

Koh Lanta

Hat Chao Mai N.P.

Kantang

Rt.4

Songkhla

0   100

km

Ban Pak Bara

Hat Yai

Rt. 42

Pattani

Saiburi

Koh Tarutao

Satun

Sadao

Ban Nang Sata

Yala

Narathiwat

Bangkok

Langkawi Island

Alor Setar

MALAYSIA

Betong

Tak Bai

Sungei Golok

daman Sea support a thriving fishing industry; more than 12,000 fishing vessels registered in the South brought in 407,000 tonnes of fish in 1989. These natural advantages have helped to provide the people of the South with the highest standard of living in Thailand. An unskilled rubber tapper can earn ฿200 a day. By comparison, the minimum wage in Bangkok is ฿125 while a farm labourer in the Northeast could not hope to earn much more than ฿30-40 a day. There is also the added attraction of Malaysia nearby: many thousands of Southern Thais travel across the border to work on the rice farms and plantations, earning the equivalent of up to ฿400 a day. A proposal to build an economic corridor between Krabi and the E coast of the peninsula (south of Surat Thani), including new port facilities and an oil refinery, may further boost the South's economic potential.

Journeying S down the peninsula, the countryside becomes increasingly 'Malay'; the vegetation is more tropical and rice paddys are supplanted by rubber plantations. Villages are dominated by mosques rather than Buddhist wats and the *pha sin* is replaced by the sarong. Even the cuisine of the South is distinct from that of Central Thailand. Specialities include southern rice noodles, kor lae chicken and preserved fish kidney curry. Most visitors remember only the region's famed seafood.

The Gulf of Thailand and the Andaman Sea are to Thailand what the

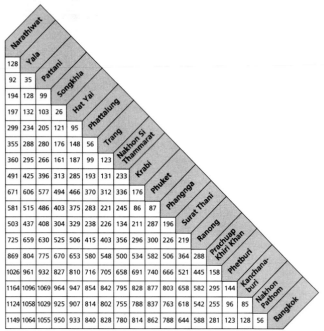

South and West Thailand, distances between provincial capitals (Km)

Mediterranean is to Europe: travel N for a cultural holiday, but go S for white, sandy beaches. In 1990 about 1.2 million tourists visited the South. The most popular holiday destinations are Phuket Island on the Andaman Sea, 862 km from Bangkok (which can now be reached directly from Europe by air) and the smaller Koh Samui (*koh* means 'island') in the Gulf of Thailand and more than 600 km from Bangkok.

A brief history of the South

Until the 13th century the South was orientated politically, culturally, artistically and economically towards the Malay Peninsula, China and India – not towards the Thai 'mainland'. The geographical features of the area – two coastlines, small pockets of agricultural land, and the dividing range of mountains – encouraged the evolution of autonomous political units. Historians have gleaned most of their knowledge of the South from the accounts of Chinese traders. It seems that the various peninsula states depended upon trade with China; luxury items such as precious stones, rhinoceros horn, perfumes, spices, cardamom and ivory were carried by Indian, Arab, Chinese and Persian traders to the rich markets of the Middle Kingdom (China). Before the 13th century, the region had been in the Indian sphere of influence from 3rd-5th century, the Mon from the 5th-8th century, the Srivijayan from the 8th-10th century and the Khmer from the 10th-13th century.

The earliest of these periods corresponds with the spread of Indian civilization to Southeast Asia. Indian traders, with their superior ships and navigational skills, controlled the trade to China and settled in large numbers along the Malay Peninsula. Culture and art took its inspiration from Indian prototypes and a number of Indian-style sculptures, both Hindu and Buddhist, have been unearthed in the region.

By the 5th century, local entrepreneurs were cashing in on the trade with China, ushering in the Mon and Peninsula Period (5th-8th century). As the economic influence of Indian traders declined, so too did the cultural and artistic influence of the Indian subcontinent, although Sanskrit remained the language of the elite. Artists in the South, though still influenced by India, began to develop local styles. Towards the 7th century and into the 8th, Mon influences became increasingly important. A Chinese ambassador's account of the period records that envoys were welcomed by elephants bearing canopies of peacock feathers and surrounded by men and women blowing conch shells and beating drums. The king, seated on a 3-tiered throne, faced a golden ox with incense burning on either side. The ox, representing the bull Nandi, and the king, presumably analogous to Siva, illustrates that the Brahmanic influence was still strong. The kingdoms of this time were wealthy, colourful and exotic.

During the 8th century, as the Srivijayan Empire extended its control over the peninsula, so the artistic focus of the South shifted once more: this time southwards, to Sumatra and Java. Again however, the art and architecture of this Srivijayan Period (8th-10th century) does not slavishly reproduce imported motifs. The artists working in towns like Chaiya incorporated their own stylistic innovations.

Finally, between the 11th and the 13th century, Khmer influence – so strong in Central and Northeastern Thailand – also began to supplant Srivijayan influence in the South. Khmer became the language of diplomacy, and Khmer inscriptions and artistic styles began to make an impact in the region.

Given this wealth of influences it is not surprising that the art and architecture of the South, though not nearly as prodigious as that of the Central and Northern regions, is at least as varied.

The town of Chaiya alone has 6 styles assigned to it dating from the 5th to the 13th centuries.

It was not until the latter part of the 13th century, that the Peninsula states began to be influenced by the new, powerful and vibrant Tai kingdom of Sukhothai. The inscriptions of King Ramkhamhaeng (late 13th century) list under 'the places whose submission he received', the southern towns of Phetburi and Nakhon Si Thammarat. However, 'receiving submission' is very different from direct and firm control, and the principalities of the South were allowed a fair degree of autonomy, until the administrative reforms of the 19th century. The South's history of independence from the central Thai state is part of the reason why separatist movements managed to gain support here.

SOUTHERN PENINSULA PHETBURI - CHUMPHON

At its narrowest, this part of Thailand is only 20 km wide and only one road, the busy Route 4, links Bangkok with the South. The historic town of Phetburi, with perhaps the best preserved Ayutthayan wats in Thailand, is 160 km south of Bangkok and can be visited as a day trip from the capital. Another 70 km south is Hua Hin, Thailand's original and premier beach resort until it was eclipsed by Phuket and Pattaya. The route south is environmentally depressing: the forest has been almost totally extirpated, leaving only scrubland or degraded secondary forest.

Phetburi

Phetburi (or Phetchaburi) is an historic provincial capital on the banks of the Phetburi River. The town is one of the oldest in Thailand. Initially, its wealth and influence was based upon the working of the coastal salt pans found in the vicinity of the town, and which Thai chronicles record as being exploited as early as the 12th century. By the 16th century, Phetburi was supplying salt to most of Siam and the Malay Peninsula. It became particularly important during the Ayutthaya Period and because the town was not sacked by the Burmese (as Ayutthaya was in 1767) its fine examples of Ayutthayan art and architecture are in good condition (see Ayutthayan style, page 96). Later, during the 19th century, Phetburi became a popular retreat for the Thai royal family, and they built a palace here. Because of its royal connections, Phetburi was *the* town to visit and to be seen in. Today, Phetburi is famous for its paid assassins who usually carry out their work from the backs of motorcycles with large calibre pistols. Each time there is a national election, 15-20 politicians and their canvassers (so-called *hua khanen*) are killed. As in Chonburi, Thailand's other capital of crime, the police seem strangely unable to charge anyone.

As Phetburi is only 160 km S of Bangkok (2 hrs by bus) it can be seen in a day from the capital. It has poor accommodation, so for those wishing to spend more time viewing the town's wats, it is probably best to stay at Hua Hin, Cha-am, Nakhon Pathom or at the *Rose Garden Hotel* (see page 381).

Places of interest

Phetburi is littered with wats – below is a selection of some of the more interesting examples. Although it is possible to walk around these monasteries in half a day, travelling by saamlor is much less exhausting. Note that often the ordination halls (or bots) are locked; occasionally, if the abbot can be found, he may be persuaded to open them up.

Wat Phra Sri Ratana Mahathat is situated in the heart of the town on Damnoenkasem Road and can be seen from a distance. It is dominated by five, much restored, Khmer-style white prangs, probably dating from the Ayut-

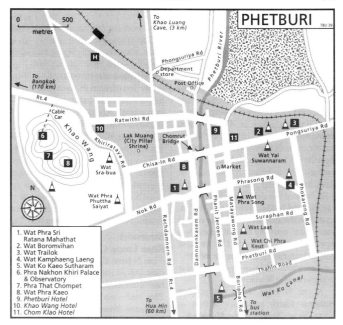

PHETBURI TBU 39

0   500
metres

To
Khao Luang
Cave, (3 km)

Phongsuriya Rd

Department
store

Post Office

To
Bangkok
(170 km)

Rt.4

Cable
Car

Khao Wang

Ratwithi Rd

Khirirataya Rd

Lak Muang
(City Pillar
Shrine)

Chomrut
Bridge

Wat
Sra-bua

Chisa-In Rd

Wat Phra
Phuttha
Saiyat

Nok Rd

Rachdamern Rd

Rt.4

To
Hua Hin
(60 km)

Pongsuriya Rd

Wat Yai
Suwannaram

Phrasong Rd

Market

Wat
Phra Song

Phanit Jeroen Rd

Matayawong Rd

Suraphan Rd

Wat Laat

Wat Chi Phra
Keut

Phetburi Rd

Thahin Road

Phokarong Rd

Boriphat Rd

Wat Ko Canal

To
bus
station

1. Wat Phra Sri
   Ratana Mahathat
2. Wat Boromvihan
3. Wat Trailok
4. Wat Kamphaeng Laeng
5. Wat Ko Kaeo Sutharam
6. Phra Nakhon Khiri Palace
   & Observatory
7. Phra That Chompet
8. Wat Phra Kaeo
9. Phetburi Hotel
10. Khao Wang Hotel
11. Chom Klao Hotel

thaya Period. The largest is 42m-high. Inside the bot, richly decorated with murals, are 3 highly regarded Buddha images, ranged one in front of the other: Luangpor Mahathat, Luangpor Ban Laem and Luangpor Lhao Takrao. The principal image depicts the crowned Buddha. The complex makes an attractive cluster of buildings. Musicians and dancers are paid by those who want to give thanks for wishes granted.

Across Chomrut Bridge and E along Pongsuriya Road is **Wat Yai Suwannaram**, on the right-hand side, within a spacious compound with a large pond. The wat was built during the Ayutthaya Period and then extensively restored in the reign of Rama V. The bot contains some particularly fine Ayutthayan murals showing celestial beings and, facing the principal Buddha image, Mara tempting the Buddha. Note the 6-toed bronze Buddha image on the rear wall

which is thought to be pre-Ayutthayan in date. Behind the bot is a large teak pavilion *(sala kan parian)* with 3 doorways at the front and 2 at the back. The front door panels have fine coloured glass insets, while the (sword?) mark on the right-hand panel is said to have been made by a Burmese warrior en route to attack Ayutthaya. The wat also houses an elegant old wooden library. **Wat Boromvihan** and **Wat Trailok** are next to one another on the opposite side of the road, and a short distance to the E of Suwannaram. They are distinctive only for their wooden dormitories (or *kuti*) on stilts.

S down Phokarong Road, and W a short distance along Phrasong Road, is **Wat Kamphaeng Laeng**. The 5 Khmer laterite prangs (one in very poor condition) – reminiscent of those in the Northeast – have been dated to the 12th century. Little of the original stucco work remains, but they are nonetheless rather pleasing. Surrounded by thick laterite walls, the wat may have originally been a Hindu temple – a statue of a Hindu goddess was found here in 1956.

W back towards the centre of town, and S down Matayawong Road are, in turn, **Wat Phra Song**, **Wat Laat** and **Wat Chi Phra Keut**, all on the left-hand side of the road. Just before reaching a bridge over Wat Ko Canal, is **Wat Ko Kaeo Sutharam**. The bot contains early 18th century murals showing scenes from the Buddha's life and from Buddhist cosmology. The fact that the mural of the Buddha subduing Mara is on the rear wall, behind the principal Buddha image, has led to speculation that the entrance to the building was relocated at some time, possibly to gain access to a newly constructed road. The wat also houses interesting quarters for monks – long wooden buildings on stilts, similar to those at Wat Boromvihan.

At the W edge of the city is **Phra Nakhon Khiri**, popularly known as Khao Wang ('Palace on the Mountain'), a palace built in 1858 during the reign of Rama IV and perched on the top of a 95m-high hill. The palace represents an amalgam of Thai, Western and Chinese artistic styles. The hill complex is dotted with frangipani trees with 3 areas of architectural interest on the 3 peaks. On the W rise is the royal palace itself. This has recently been restored and is now a well-maintained museum, containing an eclectic mixture of artefacts collected by Ramas IV and V who regularly stayed here. The airy building, with good views over the surrounding plain, has a Mediterranean feel to it. Admission: ฿10. Open: 0900-1600 Wed-Sun. Also on this peak is the Hor Chatchavan Viangchai, an observatory tower which Rama IV used to further his astronomical studies. On the central rise of the hill is the Phra That Chomphet, a white stupa erected by Rama IV. On the E rise sits **Wat Maha Samanaram**. Within the bot there are mural paintings by Khrua In Khong,

quite a well known Thai painter. The wat dates from the Ayutthayan Period. A cable car takes visitors up the W side of Khao Wang for ฿25. Open: 0800-1730 Mon-Fri, 0800-1800 Sat and Sun.

Wat Sra-bua at the foot of Khao Wang is late Ayutthayan in style. The bot exhibits some fine gables, pedestal and stucco work. Also at the foot of the hill, slightly S from Wat Sra-bua is the poorly maintained **Wat Phra Phuttha Saiyat**. Within the corrugated iron-roofed viharn is a notable 43m-long brick and plaster reclining Buddha dating from the mid-18th century. The image is unusual both in the moulding of the pillow, and in the manner in which the arm protrudes into the body of the building.

Excursions

Khao Luang Cave is on Route 3173, 3 km N from Phetburi. It offers stalactites, stupas and multitudes of second-rate Buddha images in various poses. This cave was frequently visited by European visitors to Phetburi in the 19th century. Mary Lovina Court (1886), an early example of the inquisitive but destructive Western tourist wrote: "At the mouth of the cave we found some curious rocks, and succeeded in breaking off several good specimens". She was also enchanted by the caves themselves in which, she records, there "are the greatest wonders". Mary Court ended her sojourn telling some Buddhist visitors about "the better God than the idols by which they had knelt". On the right hand side, at the entrance to the cave is a monastery called **Wat Bun Thawi**, with attractive carved wooden door panels. Getting there: by saamlor.

Kaeng Krachan National Park (see page 403) lies around 50 km SW of town. Getting there: buses from Phetburi run past the turn-off for Kaeng Krachan Dam (Route 3175). From here, there are occasional minibuses which take visitors to the dam and the park headquarters (another 8 km) or hitch a lift.

Festivals
Feb: *Phra Nakhon Khiri Fair* (moveable) *son et lumière* show.

Local information
● **Accommodation**
A-B *Regent*, recently opened, best hotel in town, comfortable, good facilities.

D *Khao Wang*, 174/1-3 Ratwithi Rd, T 425167, some a/c; **D** *Phetkasem*, 86/1 Phetkasem Rd, T 425581, some a/c; **D-E** *Chom Klao*, 1/3 Pongsuriya Rd, T 425398.

E *Phetburi*, 39 Pongsuriya Rd, T 425315; **E** *Rattana Phakdi*, Chisa-In Rd, T 425041; **E** *Sriphet*, 73/4 Phetkasem Rd, T 425965.

● **Places to eat**
Phetburi is well-known for its desserts, including *khanom mo kaeng* (a hard custard made of mung bean, egg, coconut and sugar, baked over an open fire), *khao kriap* (a pastry with sesame, coconut and sugar) and excellent *kluai khai* (sweet bananas). There are several good Thai restaurants along Phet Kasem Rd, including the *Ban Khanom Thai* (literally, the 'Thai Sweet House', at no. 130) and *Rotthip* (no. 45/22). Both ♦-♦♦.

● **Post & telecommunications**
Area code: 032.

● **Transport**
160 km S of Bangkok.

Local Saamlors: can be hired for about ฿50/hr.

Train The station is 1.5 km NW of town. Regular connections with Bangkok's Hualamphong station 2½ hrs, via Nakhon Pathom. Trains to Bangkok mostly leave Phetburi in the morning (฿34-138). Trains to Hua Hin, Surat Thani and S destinations.

Road Bus: regular a/c connections with Bangkok's Southern bus terminal near the Thonburi train station 2 hrs (฿65); non-a/c buses from the new terminal on Phra Pinklao Rd 2 hrs (฿35). Also connections with Cha-am, Hua Hin and other S destinations.

Cha-am

Cha-am is reputed to have been a stopping place for King Naresuan's troops when they were travelling south. The name 'Cha-am' may have derived from the Thai word 'cha-an', meaning to clean the saddle. Cha-am is a beach resort with no town to speak of, some excellent hotels and a sizeable building programme of new hotels and condominiums for wealthy Bangkokians. It does not have the charm of Hua Hin nor the facilities of Pattaya or Phuket, but it is easily accessible from Bangkok.

Excursions
Maruekkhathayawan Palace, designed by an Italian and built by Rama VI in 1924, is situated about 2 km S of town. The palace is made of teak and is under renovation – it has been for 20 years. Admission: by donation. Open: 0800-1600 Mon-Sun. **Getting there**: by saamlor, or catch a bus heading for Hua Hin and walk 2 km from the turn-off.

Local information
● **Accommodation**
L-A+ *Dusit Resort and Polo Club*, 1349 Phetkasem Rd, T 520009, F 520296, B 2384790, a/c, restaurant, pool, large, stylish hotel block, with horse-riding and polo 'motifs' throughout. Superb facilities include range of watersports, fitness centre, tennis courts, horse-riding and an enormous swimming pool, Thai arts and crafts demonstrations.

A+ *Cha-am Lagoon Resort*, Klongtien Rd, T 471327, B 2586589, a/c, restaurant, pool; **A+** *Golden Sand*, 853 Phetkasem Rd, T471985, F 471984, B 2598977, a/c, restaurant, pool, high-rise block with views onto the sea. Facilities include tennis, squash, watersports, fitness centre; **A+-A** *Beach Garden*, 249/21 Phetkasem Rd, T 471350, F 471291, B 2336886, a/c, restaurant, pool, right on the beach, 3 storey block and some cottage accommodation, facilities include watersports, tennis, fishing and a mini-golf course; **A+-A** *Regent*, 849/21 Phetkasem Rd, T 471480, F 471492, B 2510305, a/c, restaurants, pools, hotel and cottage accommodation on a 300 acre site, and every conceivable facility; **A+-A** *Methavalai*, 220 Ruamchit Rd, T 471145, F 471590, B 2151316, a/c, not on the beach, some bungalows with several bedrooms – ideal for families.

A *Kaenchan*, 241/3 Ruamchit Rd, T 471314, F 471531, some a/c, small pool on the rooftop, range of accommodation; **A-C** *Santisuk*, 263/3 Ruamchit Rd, T 471212, B 2511847, range of accommodation, some a/c.

B-C *Rung Aran Bungalow*, 236/26 Ruamchit Rd, T 471226, a/c; **B-D** *Cha-am Villa*, 24/1 Ruamchit Rd, T 471241, F 471079, a/c.

C *Golden Villa*, 248/13 Ruamchit Rd, T 471881, a/c; **C-D** *Pratarnchoke House*, 240/3 Ruamchit Rd, T 471215.

● **Places to eat**
Between the *Beach Garden* and the *Regent* there are several restaurants, notably ◆◆*'Family Shop'*, on the beach, good barbecued fish. Plenty of seafood restaurants along Ruamchit Rd.

● **Post & telecommunications**
Area code: 032.

● **Tourist office**
TAT, 500/51 Phetkasem Rd, T 471005. Areas of responsibility are Cha-am and Prachuap Khiri Khan.

● **Transport**
25 km N of Hua Hin.

Road Bus: regular connections with Bangkok's Southern bus terminal 2½ hrs (฿82), Phetburi, Hua Hin and S destinations.

Sea Boat: a daily ferry service is due to begin operating in the middle of 1993 linking Cha-am with Pattaya. Ask at the TAT office for latest details.

Hua Hin

Thailand's first beach resort, **Hua Hin** has had an almost continuous royal connection since the late 19th century. In 1868, King Mongkut journeyed to Hua Hin to observe a total eclipse of the sun. In 1910, Prince Chakrabongse, brother of Rama VI, visited Hua Hin on a hunting trip and was so enchanted by the area that he built himself a villa. The first of the royal palaces was built by Prince Naris, son of Rama V – Saen Samran House. In the early 1920's, King Vajiravudh (Rama VI) – no doubt influenced by his brother Chakrabongse – began work on a teakwood palace, 'Deer Park'. The final stamp of royal approval came in the late 1920's, when King Phrajadipok (Rama VII) built another palace, which he named **Klai Kangwon**, literally 'Far From Worries' (not open to the public except when a permit has

been obtained from the Royal Household in advance). It was designed by one of Prince Naris' sons. The name could not have been more inappropriate: the king was staying at Klai Kangwon in 1932 when he was dislodged from the throne by a coup d'état, see page 82.

Early guidebooks, reminiscent of English seaside towns, named the resort Hua Hin-on-Sea. *Hua* (head) *Hin* (rock) refers to a stone outcrop at the end of the fine white sand beach. The resort has a very different atmosphere to Pattaya, having promoted itself as the 'Queen of Tranquility'. There are no massage parlours and few bars blaring out Western music; this is a resort for those in search of early nights. Until the 1980s, it was a forgotten backwater of an earlier, and less frenetic, tourist era. Recently revived, it is undergoing rapid change. Condominiums are springing up along the coast to cater for wealthy holidaymakers from Bangkok. In addition, three new golf-courses are being constructed to serve Thailand's growing army of golfers – as well as avid Japanese players.

Places of interest
The famous **Railway Hotel** was built in 1923 by a Thai prince, Purachatra, who headed the State Railways of Thailand. It became Thailand's premier seaside hotel, but by the 1960s had fallen into rather glorious disrepair. It experienced a short burst of stardom when the building played the role of the Phnom Penh Hotel in the film the 'Killing Fields', but it still seemed destined to rot into oblivion. Saved by privatization, it was renovated and substantially expanded in 1986 and is now an excellent 5-star hotel. Unfortunately, it has been renamed, and goes under the unromantic name of the Sofitel Central. At the other end of Damnoenkasem Road from the Railway Hotel, on the other side of the main highway, is the **Railway Station** itself. The station has a rather quaint Royal

HUA HIN TBU 40

0 ___ 100
metres
(approx)

To Bangkok
(230 km)

To Nongphlab Village

Damrongrat Rd

Rt 4

Srasong Rd

Phetkasem Rd

Chomsin Rd

Seafood Restaurants

Night Market

Naebkhaehat Rd

Dechanuchit Rd

Night Market

Dechanuchit Rd

Poonsuk Rd

Amnuaysin Rd

Naresdamri Rd

Guesthouse Area

Damnoenkasem Rd

Post Office

Tourist Stalls

Tourist Stalls

Fishing Pier

Gulf of Thailand

N

1. Hotel Sofitel (Railway Hotel)
2. Klai Kangwon Palace
3. Golf Course
4. TAT Office
5. Police Station
6. Telephone Office
7. Melia Hua Hin Hotel
8. Ban Boosarin Hotel
9. Jed Pee Nong Hotel
10. Siriphetkasem Hotel (Pran Tour)
11. Thanan Chai Hotel

To Khao Takiab (80 km), Khao Krilas (9 km) & Prachuap Khiri Khan

Waiting Room on the platform.

Khao Takiab (or Chopstick Hill), S of town is a dirty, unremarkable hill with a large standing Buddha facing the sea. As Hua Hin expands, so this area is also developing. At present, it resembles a building site. Nearby is **Khao Krilat**, a rock covered in assorted shrines, stupas, ponds, salas and Buddha images. To get there, take a local bus from Dechanuchit Road (฿2).

Excursions

Kaeng Krachan National Park, 63 km NW of Hua Hin, is Thailand's largest protected area. It supports a wealth of large mammal species – elephant, tiger, leopard, gibbon, the Malayan pangolin – and birds, in particular, hornbills, minivets, pheasants and bee-eaters. Endangered species include the woolynecked stork and the plain-pouched hornbill. Extensive trails lead through undisturbed forest and past a succession of waterfalls (the best being Pa La-U), to hot springs and a Karen village. Guides are advisable and cost ฿100/day. Phanoen Thung Mountain offers superb views of the surrounding countryside (warm clothes are needed for the chilly mornings). It is a 6 hr hike to the summit. En route to Pa La-U, 27 km from Hua Hin and close to Nongphlab village, are 3 caves: **Dao**, **Lablae** and **Kailon**, which contain the usual array of stalactites and stalagmites. Guides with lanterns will take visitors through the caves for ฿30. Boat trips can be made on the reservoir. **Accommodation:** bungalows are available at headquarters (฿300-1000/bungalow), camping is also allowed; Thai food available. **Getting there:** take a minibus from the station on Srasong Road to the village of Fa Prathan, 53 km (฿15). For the caves, take the same bus but get off at Nongphlab village (฿10) and ask at the police station for directions – the caves are a 45 min to 1 hour walk away. Tours are also available (see below).

Khao Sam Roi Yod National Park (Mountain of Three Hundred Peaks), lies about 45 km S of Hua Hin, E off Route 4. It occupies an area of limestone hills surrounded by salt-water flats, and borders the Gulf of Thailand. A haven for water birds, the area has been extensively developed (and exploited) as a centre of prawn and fish farming limiting the marshland available to the waterbirds who breed here. The plains of Sam Roi Yod were also used as the location for Pol Pot's Killing Fields in the film of the same name. The park has the advantage of being relatively small – it covers just 98 sq km – with readily accessible sights: wildlife (including the rare and shy serow), forest walks, caves (Phraya Nakhon, close to Ban Bang Pu beach, with two large sinkholes where the roof collapsed a century ago, and a pavilion which was built in 1896 for the visit of King Rama V and Sai cave, which contains impressive stalactites and stalagmites and 'petrified waterfall', created from dripping water) and quiet beaches. (Bird life includes painted storks, herons, egrets and many different waders.) Boats can be hired from local fishermen, organised at Park headquarters, to visit caves and beaches (฿200-700). Boat trips usually sight schools of dolphin. The biggest challenge facing the park – which supports a remarkable range of habitats for such a small area – is encroachment by private shrimp ponds. The park now distributes a very useful guide with comprehensive details on fauna and flora and other natural sights in the park. Available at the park HQ. Accommodation: **B-D** bungalows (for reservations, telephone B 5614292), either for hire in their entirety or per couple (฿100/night) and a camping ground, although the tents for hire are now very worn and not really

suitable for use. Bungalows are available at both the park HQ and at Laem Sala Beach. **NB**: take mosquito repellent. Getting there: by bus from Hua Hin to Pranburi (there are also trains to Pranburi, as well as trains and buses from Bangkok). From Pranburi it is necessary to charter a songthaew (฿250) or take a motorcycle taxi (฿150) to the park HQ. **NB**: be sure you are taken to Khao Sam Roi Yod *National Park*, and not Khao Sam Roi Yod *village*. For Laem Sala Beach (located within the park), there are regular songthaews from Pranburi market to Bang Pu village between 0600 and 1600.

Tours

Companies run day tours to the Sam Roi Yod and Kaeng Krachan National Parks, and to the Pa La-U waterfall, all at ฿600, including lunch (see above).

Local information
● **Accommodation**

A+ *Royal Garden Resort*, 107/1 Phetkasem Rd, T 511881, F 512422, B 2518659, a/c, restaurant, pool, to complement the even larger 'L' shaped block, good sports facilities including tennis, fitness centre, watersports. There's also a mini-zoo and shopping arcade, rec; **A+** *Royal Garden Tower*, 43/1 Phetkasem Rd, T 512412, F 512417, B 2558822, a/c, suites only; **A+** *Royal Garden Village*, 45 Phetkasem Rd, T 520250, F 520259, B 2518659, a/c, restaurant, pool, teak pavilions set around a pool, good sports facilities, no beach to speak of; **A+-A** *Sofitel Central* (previously, the *Railway Hotel*), 1 Damnoenkasem Rd, T 512021, F 511014, B 2330256, a/c, restaurant, pool, Hua Hin's orginal premier hotel, with the building of another wing, has become almost too large, but still maintains excellent service, attractive rooms and good position, rec; **A+-A** *City Beach Resort*, 16 Damnoenkasem Rd, T 511940, F 512488, a/c, restaurant, pool, central, ugly; **A+-A** *Melia Hua Hin*, 33 Naresdamri Rd, T 512879, F 511135, BT 2710205, BF 2700596, a/c, restaurants, pool with water slide and jacuzzi, new ugly high-rise hotel with all facilities, all rooms have sea views; **A+-A** *Sailom*, 29 Phetkasem Rd, T 511890, B 2580652, a/c, restaurant, pool.

A *Sport Villa*, 10/95 Phetkasem Rd,

T 511453, a/c, restaurant, large pool, sauna, 3 km S of town; **A-B** *Hua Hin Highland Resort*, 4/15 Ban Samophrong, T 2112579, B 2800750, a/c, N of town, popular with golfers.

B *Hua Hin Palace*, 55/6 Phetkasem Rd, T 511151, a/c; **B** *Chanchai*, 117/1-18 Phetkasem Rd, T 511461, a/c; **B** *Khao Takiab Resort*, 1/2-5 Khao Takiab Village, S of town, some a/c; **B** *Sirin*, Damnoenkasem Rd, T 511150, a/c. **B** *Ban Boosarin*, 8/8 Poonsuk Rd, T 512089, a/c, rec; **B-C** *Fresh Inn*, 132 Naresdamri Rd, T 511389, some a/c, restaurant; **B-D** *Thanan Chai*, 11 Damrongrat Rd, T 511755, some a/c, N of centre, but quite good value.

C *Hua Hin*, 5/1 Soi Binthabat, Poonsuk Rd, T 511653, a/c, restaurant; **C** *Jed Pee Nong*, 13/7 Damnoenkasem Rd, T 512381, some a/c, popular; **C** *Parichart*, Naresdamri Rd, some a/c, clean, friendly, rec.

● **Guesthouses**
These are concentrated around Naresdamri Road, one road in from the beach; some residents rent out rooms in their private houses. **D** *Chatchai*, 59/1-3 Phetkasem Rd, T 511034; **D** *Kanokporn*, Damnoenkasem Rd, rec.

E *Europa*, 158 Naresdamri Rd, restaurant; **E** *Naresdamri*, 174 Naresdamri Rd.

● **Places to eat**
Try the central market for breakfast. Good seafood widely available particularly at northern end of Naresdamri Rd. **Seafood**: *Charlie's Seafood*, Naresdamri Rd, also serves Thai; *Charoen Pochana*, Naresdamri Rd, also serves Thai; *Europa*, Naresdamri Rd, also serves International and Thai; ✦✦✦*Meekaruna*, 26/1 Naresdamri Rd, small pavilion, rec; ✦✦✦*Seangthai*, Naresdamri Rd, also serves Thai, large open-air restaurant on the seafront; *Supharos*, 69/2-3 Phetkasem Rd, also serves Chinese; ✦✦✦*Tappikaew House*, 7 Naebkaehat Rd, attractive Thai restaurant, indoor and outdoor eating by the sea; *Tharachan*, Phetkasem Rd, also serves Thai. Chinese restaurants are to be found around the junction of Phetkasem and Naebkhaehat rds.

International: *Beer Garden*, Naresdamri Rd, also serves Thai; *La Villa*, Poonsuk Rd, Italian; ✦✦*Lo Stivale*, 132 Naresdamri Rd, Italian, rec.

● **Banks & money changers**
There are a number of currency exchange booths along Phetkasem Road.

● **Hospitals & medical services**
511-743 Phetkasem Rd, T 511743 (4 km downtown).

● **Police Station**
Damnoenkasem Rd, T 511027.

● **Post & telecommunications**
Post Office: 21 Damnoenkasem Rd. **Overseas Telephone Office**: Damnoenkasem Rd. **Area code**: 032.

● **Sports**
Golf: *Royal Hua Hin Golf Course*, designed in 1926 by a Scottish engineer working on the Royal Siamese Railway, is the oldest in Thailand and recently upgraded. Open to the public: 0600-1800, Mon-Sun, green fees: ฿250 at the weekend and ฿150 during the week (per 9 holes). Caddys available: ฿100. **Minigolf**: Phetkasem Rd, T 511585 (S of town), open 0900-2300 Mon-Sun ฿60-100/person. 3 more golf courses are under construction.

Watersports and **horse riding**: along the beach.

Snooker: parlours in town.

● **Shopping**
The most distinctive buy is a locally produced printed cotton called *pha Khommaphat*.

Night market: on Dechanuchit Rd, close to the bus station. Open: dusk-2200.

Seashell souvenirs: to be avoided.

Shopping centre: 1/9 Srasong Rd.

● **Tour companies & travel agents**
Concentrated on Damnoenkasem and Phetkasem rds. *Western Tours Hua Hin*, 11 Damnoenkasem Rd, T 512560; *Pran Tour*, 1st flr, *Siriphetkasem Hotel*, Srasong Rd, T 511654; *Hua Hin Travel*, The Royal Garden Resort.

● **Tourist offices**
Municipality Tourist Office, 114 Phetkasem Rd, T 512120. Open: Mon-Sun 0830-1630.

● **Transport**
230 km S of Bangkok, it is presently a 3 hour drive from Bangkok, along a hazardous 2 lane highway (particularly bad over the last 80 km from Phetburi), jammed with *siplors* (10-wheel trucks).

Local Bus: station on Dechanuchit Rd. Buses to Khao Krilas or Khao Takiab every 20 mins, ฿5. **Saamlor**: ฿10-20 around town, ฿80 for a sightseeing tour. **Taxis**: run prescribed routes for set fares, taxi stand on Phetkasem Rd, opposite *Chatchai Hotel*. Taxis can be hired for the day for ฿300 plus petrol. Motorcycle taxis (identified by 'taxi' sign) will take you wherever you want to go. **Car rental**: jeeps ฿800-1,000/day (on Damnoenkasem and Phetkasem rds). **Motorbike rental**: ฿200/day upwards (on Damnoenkasem and Phetkasem rds). **Bicycle rental**: ฿30-50/day (on Damnoenkasem and Phetkasem roads).

Air Bangkok Airways (T 5352498) run twice daily connections with Bangkok 35 mins (฿750). Yellowbirds run seaplanes to/from Cha-am twice daily, for details, T 2756257.

Train The station is on Damnoenkasem Rd, T 511073. Regular connections with Bangkok's Hualamphong station (same train as to Phetburi) 3½-4 hrs (฿44-182). Day excursions run on weekends, leaving Hualamphong at 0615, arriving Hua Hin at 1130, departing from Hua Hin at 1630, arriving Bangkok 2030. Regular connections with Phetburi 1 hr (฿13-52).

Road Bus: station is on Srasong Rd, next to the Chatchai market, T 511654. Regular a/c connections with Bangkok's Southern bus terminal near the Thonburi train station 3½ hrs (฿92); non-a/c buses leave from the new terminal on Phra Pinklao Rd 3½ hrs (฿63). Also connections with Phetburi, Cha-am and other southern destinations. **Taxi**: 3 hrs from Bangkok, about ฿1,500.

Prachuap Khiri Khan

Prachuap Khiri Khan is a small and peaceful resort with a long crescent-shaped beach. The town is more popular with Thais than with *farangs* and it has a reputation for good seafood. An exhausting climb up **Khao Chong Krachok**, the 'Mountain with the Mirror' (past armies of preening monkeys), is rewarded with fine views of the surrounding countryside and bay. At the summit there is an unremarkable shrine containing yet another footprint of the Buddha. There is a good **night market** at the corner of Phitakchat and Kong-Kiat rds.

Excursions
Ao Manao is an attractive beach 5 km S of town.

Huai Yang Waterfall is 28 km S of Prachuap, and 7 km off the main road (turn-

ing W at Ban Huai Yaang). Not worth visiting in the dry season, it merely illustrates the Thai penchant for waterfalls (and caves) of all sorts.

Tours
Informal tours can be organised with *Pinit*, who can often be found on the beach. He has motorbikes and will take you to wats, caves, waterfalls, or nearby islands.

Local information
● **Accommodation**
On weekends, accommodation is hard to find, with the influx of Thais. **B-C** *Hat Thong*, 7 Susuk Rd, T 611960, F 611033, a/c, comfortable, overlooking the sea, best in town; **B-C** *Rimhab Rest*, 35 Suanson R. D. Moung, T 601626, bungalows close to the coast.

D *Kings*, 800/3 Phithakchat Rd, T 611170, a/c; **E-F** *Inthira*, Kong-Kiat Rd.

E *Yutichai*, 35 Kong-Kiat Rd.

● **Places to eat**
Seafood restaurants along the seafront and by the pier. ♦♦*Plern Samud* (next to the *Hat Thong Hotel*), rec.

● **Shopping**
Prachuap is best known for its printed cotton, known as *pha khommaphat*.

● **Post & telecommunications**
Post Office: around the corner from *Hat Thong Hotel*.

● **Tourist office**
On Sarathip Rd.

● **Transport**
323 km from Bangkok, 93 km S of Hua Hin.

Local Motorized saamlor: Prachuap has its own distinctive form of tuk-tuk – motorcycles with sidecars and benchseats.

Train The station is on the W side of town, regular connections with Bangkok's Hualamphong station 5 hrs (฿58-245), Hua Hin and destinations S.

Road Bus: the station is on Phithakchat Rd, regular a/c connections with Bangkok's Southern bus terminal near the Thonburi train station 5 hrs (฿130); non-a/c buses leave from the new terminal on Phra Pinklao Rd 5 hrs (฿58).

Chumphon

Considered the 'gateway to the south', this is where the southern highway divides, one route running W and then S on Route 4 to Ranong, Phuket and the Andaman Sea side of the Peninsula; the other, S on Route 41 to Surat Thani, Koh Samui, Nakhon Si Thammarat and the waters of the Gulf of Thailand. At the end of 1988, Typhoon Gay tore its way through Chumphon province, causing extensive flooding and the death of more than 300 villagers. The positive side of the disaster was that it led to a ban on all logging in Thailand; deforestation was perceived to be to blame for the severe flooding.

Chumphon is 8 km off Route 4/41. There is not much to see, but there are some good beaches nearby.

Excursions

Paknam Chumphon lies 11 km SE of Chumphon (on Route 4901), on the coast, at the mouth of the Chumphon River. This is a big fishing village with boats for hire to the nearby islands where swiftlets build their nests for the Chinese speciality, bird's nest soup – *yanwo*, in Chinese (see page 433). Many concessionaires are accompanied by bodyguards; visitors should seek permission before venturing to the nest sites. Islands include Koh Phrao, Koh Lanka Chiu and Koh Rang Nok. Getting there: songthaews from opposite the morning market on the southern side of town.

Local information

● Accommodation

A-B *Pornsawan Home and Beach Resort*, Pharadon Phap Beach, on the Chumphon estuary, T 521031, F 521529, a/c, restaurant, pool, tennis.

B *Janson Chumphon*, off 188-65 Saladaeng Rd, T 502502, F 502503, a/c, restaurant, pool, newest in town, clean but dull; **B-C** *Chumphon Cabana*, Thung Wua Laen Beach (16 km N of town), T 501990, restaurant, overlooks the beach, boats for hire for scuba-diving.

C *Pharadorn Inn*, 180/12 Pharadorn Rd, T 511598, some a/c, restaurant, pool; **C** *Tha Taphao*, 66/1 Tha Taphao Rd, T 511479, F 502479, some a/c, restaurant, rather scruffy.

D *Suriwong*, 125/27-29 Saladaeng Rd, T 511203, some a/c, well-run.

● Places to eat

There are two *night markets* on Kam Luang Chumphon Rd and on Tha Taphao Rd. There are also several restaurants on Tha Taphao and Sala Daeng rds.

● Post & telecommunications

Post Office: Paraminthara Mankha Rd. **Area code**: 077.

● Transport

500 km S of Bangkok, 121 km N of Rayong.

Train Station at W end of Kram Luang Chumphon Rd. Regular connections with Bangkok's Hualamphong station 7½ hrs (∅102-656) and all S destinations.

Road Bus: terminal on Tha Taphao Rd, not far from the night market. Regular a/c connections with Bangkok's Southern bus terminal near the Thonburi train station 7 hrs (∅280); non-a/c buses leave from the new terminal on Phra Pinklao Rd 7 hrs (∅157). Also connections with all S destinations.

WEST COAST: CHUMPHON TO PHUKET

Just to the west of Chumphon the highway divides. Route 4 runs down the east coast of the peninsula, usually out of sight of the Andaman Sea. Ranong is about 130 km south of Chumphon and is famous for its hot springs. At this point the Kra Isthmus is at its narrowest. 120 km south from Ranong is an area called Khao Lak, an undeveloped beach which is rapidly growing in popularity. Another 80 km south, and you reach Phuket Island and province; the largest beach resort in the South. After Phuket, Route 4 skirts north-eastwards to Phangnga (100 km from Phuket) and then south to Krabi (another 85 km). Krabi is the main departure point for the islands of Koh Lanta and Koh Phi

Phi, and also has a number of good beaches close by. From Krabi, Route 4037 links up with Surat Thani and the east coast, although Route 4 continues southwards to Trang, 317 km from Phuket. Boats for islands in the Andaman Sea leave from Pakmeng, Trang's port.

Ranong

Ranong province is the first southern province bordering the Indian Ocean and Thailand's rainiest (often in excess of 5,000 mm/year), thinnest and least populated. Kra Buri, 58 km N of Ranong, is the point where the Kra Isthmus is also at its narrowest, and there has been debate for centuries about the benefits of digging a canal across the Isthmus, so linking the Gulf of Thailand with the Andaman Sea. The project is currently out of favour.

The name Ranong is derived from *rae* (tin) *nong* (rich), and the town was established in the late 18th century by a family from Hokkien, China. Large numbers of Chinese labourers came to the town to work in the tin mines on which its prosperity was based and even today Ranong has a predominantly Sino-Thai population. In town there are a number of attractive 19th century Chinese-style houses.

Places of interest

Ranong is one of the few towns in the area with reasonable hotels and is often used as a stopping-off point for those travelling overland from Bangkok to Phuket. The town contains **geo-thermal mineral water springs** (65°C) at **Wat Tapotharam**, 2 km E of the town and behind the *Janson Thara Hotel*. The hot water bubbles up into concrete tubs (named *bor mae, bor por* and *bor luuk saaw* – mother, father and daughter pools respectively) – not too hot to touch, but hot enough to cook an egg in. The springs also provide the *Janson Thara Hotel* with thermal water for hot baths

and a giant jacuzzi. There is a small park with a cable bridge over the river, a number of bathing pools (sometimes empty of water), and a second-rate animal-garden. The wat is rather dull, containing a footprint of the Buddha. Getting there: by songthaew along Route 2; ask for '*bor naam rawn*' (hot water well).

Excursions

Port of Ranong lies 3 km from town. Each morning the dock seethes with activity as Thai and Burmese fishing boats unload their catches. Boats can be hired at a pontoon next to the dock, to tour the bustling harbour and look across the Kra River estuary to the Burmese border (approximately ฿300). **NB:** border officials can be touchy, carry your passport with you. Ranong is an important point of contact between Burma and Thailand. Not only is there considerable trade, but many Burmese, in search of higher wages, cross the estuary to work.

Surin and **Similan Islands** can be reached from Ranong Port, see page 426.

Local information
● **Accommodation**
A new 151-room hotel is under construction by the Amari group and is schedule for completion in mid-1995. It should become the best hotel in town. **B** *Janson Thara*, 2/10 Phetkasem Rd, Bang Rin, T 811510, F 821821, B 4242050, a/c, restaurant, pool, international style hotel, the bath-water comes straight from the thermal springs, check-in before 1600 to enjoy the thermal baths in the hotel; **B** *Janson Thara Resort*, (out of town) Paknam Ranong, T 821611, B 4242050, a/c, restaurant, pool, overlooks Kra River estuary.

D-E *Asia*, 39/9 Ruang Rat Rd, T 811113, some a/c, clean.

E *Sin Ranong*, 26/23-4 Ruangrat Rd, T 811454.

● **Transport**
600 km S of Bangkok, 304 km N of Phuket.

Road Bus: buses stop at *Rueng Rat Hotel*, Ruengrat Rd; the terminal is on the edge of town, near the *Janson Thara Hotel*. Regular a/c and non-a/c connections with Bangkok's Southern bus terminal near the Thonburi railway station (฿110-385). Also connections with Chumphon, Surat Thani and Phuket. For private coach companies T 2816939 or 2817011.

Khao Lak

Khao Lak is a relatively recent discovery for visitors to Thailand, popular with Germans. It is a tiny coastal village, with one village shop, roughly midway between Takua Pa (30 km N) and Thai Muang (30 km S), 80 km N of Phuket on the Andaman Sea coast. The beach remains unspoilt, with little development (as yet). Its popularity lies in the fact that it is 'off the beaten track' and is the closest departure point for the Similan Islands (see page 426).

Excursions

Waterfalls, there are several along the coast, two of the best are **Chongfah** (5 km N) and **Lumpee** (20 km S). Getting there: the easiest way is by hired motorbike, ฿200/day (see Local transport).

Coral reef, an interesting half day trip is to a local reef, 45 minutes by long-tail boat. Charges are about ฿300 for snorkelling equipment and ฿1,000 for diving, which includes equipment and two dives.

Turtle Beach, at Thai Muang National Park, is a 20 km-long stretch of beach where turtles, including the giant leatherback, come ashore at night to nest from November to February (entrance fee ฿20). Young turtles can be seen hatching from March to July.

Tours

Tours to the **Similan Islands** (see page 426) are organised by *Poseidon Bungalows* and by *Khao Lak Bungalows*. A three day trip costs ฿2,800, including transport, accommodation and all food. They will also organise diving trips. *Poseidon Bungalows* will shortly be organising 5 day trips to the **Surin Islands** (see page 426). The *Thai Dive Company*, T (076) 571434, have an office in Thai Muang and will organize transport from Phuket. This is a British managed company, with a friendly and professional manner. They are well equipped and supply excellent food. A 3 day dive costs ฿9,200, 2 days, ฿6,900. There is a 25% discount for non-divers. *Garden Beach Resort* organize snorkelling and fishing trips (฿300/day including meals) and trips to waterfalls (฿250-450/day). Peter and Mani, of the *Khao Lak Restaurant* organize walking jungle trips (฿450/day, including food), boat tours around Phangnga Bay, diving to Similan and Surin.

Local information
● **Accommodation**

B-E *Khao Lak Bungalows*, the most northerly set of bungalows on Khao Lak beach, next door to the *Garden Beach Resort*, T 7231197, small beachfront restaurant, traditional Thai style bungalows, eight small rooms at the lower price, some luxury bungalows, 7 family apartments, the owners, Gerd and Noi, organise exotic trips (quite expensive), such as a cave tour to the Khao Soc National Park and snorkelling/diving trips to the Similan Islands.

C-D *Garden Beach Resort*, a few minutes walk N of *Nang Thong Bay Resort*, T 7231179, extensive menu at beachfront restaurant, mainly Thai food, but a few European favourites, all rooms have fans and attached bathroom, Nom, who runs the bungalows, has good English, and is helpful, onward bus and air tickets bookable here (see **Tours**); **C-E** *Nang Thong Bay Resort*, Km 60 Hat Nang Thong, T 7231181, large, 2 storey restaurant with extensive menu serving European and Thai food (rec), good value breakfasts, all rooms with bathrooms and fans, a more up-market resort on the beach, the manageress Yoy speaks excellent English and is very helpful, this is the only place in Khao Lak where you can change money, onward bus tickets can be booked from here, rec; **C-E** *Poseidon Bungalows*, 1/6 Tambon Lam Kaen, Mu 2, Amphoe Thai Muang, T 7231418, 5 km S of main Khao Lak area, range of rooms, some with bathrooms and beachfronts, restaurant built out over the sea on stilts, Thai and European food, the bungalows are situated in a sheltered bay, surrounded by jungle and rubber plantations, the owners are very friendly and are a mine of local information, they can organise day trips to local places of interest, boat trips and snorkelling, secluded beach.

D-E Khao Lak Resort, Km 58 Si Takua Pa Rd, T 721061, coming from the S, through Khao Lak National Park, this is the first set of bungalows, some rooms have attached bathrooms, others are very basic, unattractive resort, fallen into disrepair, only open in high season.

A new set of bungalows is being built which will be operating next season, and they will be run under the same management as *Nang Thong Bay*. These are situated between *Khao Lak Resort* and *Nang Thong Bay Resort*. There will be 40 double rooms and a restaurant, probably run at the same high standards at *Nang Thong*. The name has not yet been decided, but will contain Nang Thong in the title.

● **Places to eat**
Several good restaurants attached to the bungalows, see above. A row of **foodstalls** can be found next to the Information Stand, on the beach. ◆*Khao Lak Restaurant*, on the main road, Thai, International and American breakfast (see **Tours**). Tiny bar/snack shop on the beach run by Thai fishermen – no English spoken.

● **Bars**
Gypsy Bar, beneath the restaurant at the *Khao Lak Bungalows*, the only place in the area to get a late night drink. Open in the high season only.

● **Banks & money changers**
At *Nang Thong Resort*.

● **Post & telecommunications**
The nearest **Post Office** is at Lam Kaen, a small village 5 km S of Khao Lak. Banks, shops and post offices can also be found in Takua Pa and Thai Muang, both 30 km north and south of Khao Lak respectively. **Area code**: 076.

● **Sport**
Sea Dragon Dive Centre (T 7231418), situated on the main road, just N of *Poseidon Bungalows*. They offer a full range of PADI courses (from ฿5,900 for a 4 day certificate course), and a one day fun course, with one dive (฿1,200) and diving trips to Similan Islands (3 day trip costs ฿6,800 (฿3,000 for snorkellers), including diving equipment, food and accommodation, twice-weekly departures during the season). They plan to organise budget diving trips to the Surin Islands soon, including Richlieu Rock, which is famous for its frequent

sightings of whale sharks. Call in for latest information on the Similans   tea and coffee are free. All equipment can be hired or purchased from the centre. Massage parlour on the beach.

● **Tourist information**
There is a small information stand on the beach, between *Nang Thong Bay Resort* and *Garden Beach Resort*, staffed by people with an extensive knowledge of the area. They will organise tours to any of the places mentioned in the excursion section above. Open 0900-1100, 1600-1800.

● **Transport**
80 km N of Phuket.

Local Motorbikes: for hire from *Nang Thong Resort* and from *Garden Beach Resort* and from *Khao Lak Restaurant*, ฿200/day. **Jeeps**: for hire from *Nang Thong Resort* and from *Garden Beach Resort*, ฿800/day.

Road Bus: some a/c and non-a/c connections with the Southern Bus terminal in Bangkok. Departs 1900, about 13 hrs (฿310). From Krabi and Phangnga, take a bus towards Phuket and change at Kochloi to a bus running N towards Takua Pa and Ranong. From Phuket take a local bus to Takua Pa or an a/c bus towards Ranong. There is no actual sign on the roadside, but there are signs for the guesthouses. It is a 5 minute walk from the road through a rubber plantation to the beach. Many buses now travel on a new road which bypasses Khao Lak and goes straight to Phang Nga town, and then on to Phuket. Check that your bus passes through Khao Lak/Takua Pa/Ranong. Different bus companies have different routes.

PHUKET ISLAND, KOH SIMILAN & KOH SURIN

Phuket lies on the W coast of the Kra Isthmus in the warm Andaman Sea and is connected to the mainland by the 700m-long Sarasin causeway. The name Phuket is derived from the Malay word *bukit*, meaning hill, and it is Thailand's only island to have provincial status. Known as the 'Pearl of Thailand' because of its shape, it measures 21 km at its widest point, and is 48 km long. With a land area of 550 sq km, it is about the same size as Singapore – making it Thai-

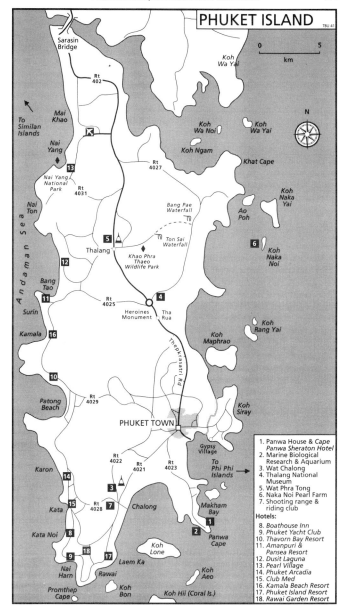

PHUKET ISLAND

TBU 41

1. Panwa House & Cape Panwa Sheraton Hotel
2. Marine Biological Research & Aquarium
3. Wat Chalong
4. Thalang National Museum
5. Wat Phra Tong
6. Naka Noi Pearl Farm
7. Shooting range & riding club

Hotels:

8. Boathouse Inn
9. Phuket Yacht Club
10. Thavorn Bay Resort
11. Amanpuri & Pansea Resort
12. Dusit Laguna
13. Pearl Village
14. Phuket Arcadia
15. Club Med
16. Kamala Beach Resort
17. Phuket Island Resort
18. Rawai Garden Resort

land's largest island. Phuket was first 'discovered' by Arab and Indian navigators around the end of the 9th century, although it is said to have been marked on charts as far back as the 1st century. The first Europeans (Dutch pearl traders) arrived in the 16th century. **Phuket Town**, the island's capital in the SE, was built in the middle of the last century to replace Thalang, which had been destroyed by the Burmese in 1800.

The province derives much of its wealth from tin production. Phuket was first mentioned as a major source of tin in the mid-16th century (when it was known as Junkceylon). Modern tin-mining methods were introduced by the Englishman Captain Edward Miles in 1907, with elephants living on the island transporting the ore from the mines to be smelted. Such was the wealth generated that Phuket Town was probably the first place in all Thailand to have paved roads and cars, around 1910. Today, Phuket remains the centre of tin production in Thailand. Rubber (which accounts for 29% of the land area), coconut, seafood and tourism all contribute to the island's wealth; its people are among the wealthiest in Thailand, a fact reflected in the richly endowed temples. The population of Phuket has risen from 6,000 in the early 1900s, to 140,000, with five times that number of visitors every year.

Phuket offers little in the way of sights of historical interest, but much of natural beauty, although the wild elephants, rhinos and tigers which once roamed the island have long since been killed. There are national parks, long sandy beaches (particularly on the W coast), good snorkelling and diving, peaceful coconut groves and rubber plantations, and some traditional villages. Phuket seems big enough to absorb large numbers of tourists and still maintain a semblance of 'tradition' in some areas.

Places of interest

There are a handful of historical and cultural sights. S of Phuket Town, down Sakdidej Road which becomes Route 4129, in the grounds of the *Cape Panwa Sheraton Hotel*, is **Panwa House**, a fine example of Sino-Portuguese architecture. At the tip of Panwa Cape is the **Marine Biological Research Centre and Aquarium**. The air-conditioned aquarium is well laid out, with a good collection of salt and fresh water fish, lobsters, molluscs and turtles. Admission: ฿10. Open: 1000-1600 Mon-Sun. There are regular buses between Phuket town and the Aquarium. It is possible to charter long-tailed boats from here to **Koh Hii** (฿600) and **Koh Mai Ton** (฿1200) or to go fishing (฿1200).

6 km south of Phuket Town, just N of Chalong Junction, is the ostentatious **Wat Chalong**, best-known for its gold-leaf encrusted statues of the previous abbots, Luang Pho Chaem and Luang Pho Chuang. The former was highly respected for his medical skills, which proved to be particularly valuable when Phuket's Chinese miners revolted in 1876. The halving of the international price of tin coupled with Bangkok's attempt to extract excessive taxes from the province raised the ire of the Chinese. 2,000 gathered around the governor's house, and when they failed to take the building turned their attention to the less well defended villages. The spree of killing and looting was only finally brought to an end at Wat Chalong.

12 km N from Phuket Town on Route 402, towards the airport, is the village of **Tha Rua**. At the crossroads there is a statue of two female warriors: **Muk** and **Chan**. These sisters helped to repel an army of Burmese invaders in 1785 by dressing up all the women of the town as men, so fooling the Burmese. Rama I awarded them titles for their deeds, and they are celebrated in bronze, swords drawn. The statue was erected in 1966 and Thais rub gold-leaf on its base as a

sign of respect and to gain merit. The **Thalang National Museum** is just E of this crossroads on Route 4027. It has a well-presented collection, displaying various facets of Phuket's history and culture. Admission: by donation. Open: 0900-1600 Wed-Sat.

Continuing N on Route 402, just beyond the district town of Thalang, is **Wat Phra Tong**, surrounded by life-sized concrete animals. The wat contains a buried Buddha image, with just its head protruding from the ground, covered in gold-leaf. Legend has it that shortly after a boy had tethered his buffalo to a post, they both fell mysteriously ill. On excavating the post, villagers discovered this golden Buddha. It is believed that anyone trying to disinter the image will meet with a disaster – Burmese invaders attempted to do so in 1785 and they were attacked by a swarm of hornets.

Khao Phra Thaeo Wildlife Park lies 20 km from Phuket Town. Turn E off the main road in Thalang and follow signs for Ton Sai Waterfall. This beautiful, peaceful road winds through stands of rubber trees and degraded forest. The park supports wild boar and monkeys and represents the last remnant of the island's natural forest ecosystem. The **Ton Sai Waterfall** is located within the park, but is really only worth a visit during the rainy season. There are bungalows and a lakeside restaurant here, and a number of hiking routes. Visitors can swim in the upper pool. Open: 0600-1800.

The road E from the waterfall becomes rough and can only be negotiated on foot or by motorbike. This track leads to **Bang Pae Waterfall**. Alternatively, the falls can be approached from the other direction, by turning off Route 4027 and driving 1 km along a dirt track. There is a beautiful lake, refreshment stands, forest trails, and bathing pools. Open: 0600-1800. Also off Route 4027, at **Ao Poh**, there is a long wooden jetty where boat tours leave for Naka Noi Island and Pearl Farm – Thailand's largest (see below).

Most people do not go to Phuket for history or culture. They go for **beaches**, and in this respect the island is hard to beat. Its size, and the length of its beaches means that it is still possible to find a peaceful spot to sunbathe. The best beaches are on the W coast, although the resort of Patong is far from peaceful. The E coast is rocky and fringed with mangroves and the beaches are poor for swimming. Details on the various beaches are given after the section on Phuket Town. There are now some excellent luxury hotels on Phuket; the island is no longer a haven for backpackers – most have moved on to cheaper locations such as Phi Phi, Samui and Lanta. That said, it is still possible (just) to stay relatively cheaply on Phuket.

Tour by motorbike or jeep

In order to explore some of the sights mentioned above, it is best to hire a motorbike or jeep for the day. A suggested route might run N from Phuket Town or east from Patong to Tha Rua, the Heroines Monument and the National Museum at Thalang. Take a side trip to Ton Sai Waterfall and the National Park, then continue N on Route 402, before turning left for Nai Yang Beach and National Park. Crossing Route 402, drive E through rubber plantations, taking in Bang Pae Waterfall, before returning to the main road at the Heroine's Monument. A half to one day trip.

Excursions

Koh Yao Noi and **Koh Yao Yai** are two largish islands to the E of Phuket Island. They remain untouched by the tourist industry and hold a scattering of fishing villages. Getting there: boat from E coast of Phuket (about ฿30).

Tours

Full-day tours to **Phi Phi islands** are organized by *Aloha Tour*, *Cruise Centre*, *Pee Pee Hydrocraft* (฿750), *Silver Queen*, and *Songserm Travel* (who operate a large catamaran called the *King Cruiser*). Day trips to Phi Phi are also available on the

Andaman Queen, T 215261, leaving at 0830 (฿750-950).

Similan Islands (see page 426). Full-day tours leave from Chalong or Patong beaches. *Phuket Travel and Tour Co* and *Songserm Travel*, organize tours for about ฿1,500, which includes a tour of the reef in a glass-bottomed boat, lunch, and dinner on the boat back to Phuket. Many other tour companies in Phuket Town and on Patong Beach organize similar tours.

Phangnga Bay (see page 428). A day trip costs about ฿650.

Coral Island (Koh Hii) Full-day tours include swimming, snorkelling and fishing. Boats leave from Makham Bay.

Naka Noi Island and the Pearl Farm Boats leave from Ao Poh, in the NE of the island, for the 15 mins trip. Tours, including admission to the Pearl Farm and a 'demonstration,' cost ฿350. Private boats can be chartered through the *Ao Poh Centre*, T 212901. Pearl Farm open: Mon-Sun 0900-1530, show at 1100. Accommodation available at bungalow resort. **NB**: ensure your visit is to Naka Noi, rather than Naka Yai, where the 'Pearl Farm' seems to be a fake.

Tour by glass-bottomed boat 2-hour cruises in the Andaman Sea, ฿300 (or on a chartered basis for ฿5,000/2 hrs).

Yacht charter from Nov-May, boats can be chartered to sail the waters around Phuket. *Thai Yachting Co*, B1-2 Patong View Plaza, 94 Thaweewong Rd, T 321301, F 321541, B 2516755, depending on the number of people in the party, a week's trip costs about US$2000, including meals, professional crew, transfers, fishing and snorkelling equipment; *South East Asia Yacht Charter*, PO Box 15, Patong Beach, T 321292, 4-7 day diving tours to Similan and Surin Islands, PADI diving courses also available.

Swimming

Swimming and snorkelling are safe from November to April when the sea is calm. But during the monsoon between May and Oct, there can be strong surf and undertows – especially after storms. Swimmers should check the beaches for red flags, which indicate whether conditions are dangerous.

Diving in Phuket

The warm, clear water off Phuket is rich in marine life, and affords excellent diving opportunities. Dive centres will normally offer introductory courses for those who have never dived before, leading to one of the internationally recognized certificates (such as PADI). For those with diving experience there are a range of tours from single day, 2-dive outings, to one week expeditions to offshore islands such as the Similan and Surin Islands. Prices vary, but a day-trip to Phi Phi with 2 dives should cost about ฿2,100/person, and to the Similans about ฿2,700/person. 4 days and 3 nights, around ฿10,250 (8 dives) and 5 days and 4 nights about ฿12,750 (10 dives). Snorkelling is good on the outer islands; the waters around Phuket Island itself are mediocre. It is best to catch one of the boat tours to Phi Phi Island for the day and snorkel on either side of the land bridge that separates the 2 halves of Phi Phi Don (see page 434). But even here, development has reduced the clarity of the waters. For the best snorkelling and diving it is necessary to go to the Similan Islands.

Diving centres The greatest concentration of diving companies is to be found along Patong Beach Road, on Kata and Karon beaches, at Ao Chalong and in Phuket Town. Phuket Town: *Phuket Aquatic Safaris*, 62/9 Rasada Centre, Rasada Rd, T 216562; *Andaman Sea Diving*, 3rd Flr, Tian Sin Bldg, 54 Phuket Rd, T 215766. Patong, all on the Beach Road: *Ocean Divers*, *Patong Beach Hotel*, T 321166; *Andaman Divers*, T 321155; *Santana*, T 321360; *Fantasea Divers*, T 321309; *South East Asia*, T 321292.

Kata/Karon: *Siam Diving Centre*, Kata-Karon Beach, T 381608; *Marina Cottage*, Kata Beach, T 381625; *Phuket International Diving Centre (PIDC)*, Le Meridien, Karon Noi Beach, T 321480.

Festivals

Jul: *Marathon* (2nd week). **Oct**: *Chinese Vegetarian festival* or *Ngan Kin Jeh* (moveable), lasts 9 days and marks the beginning of Taoist lent. No meat is eaten, alcohol consumed nor sex indulged in (in order to cleanse the soul) and men pierce their cheeks or tongues with long spears and other sharp objects and walk over hot coals and (supposedly) feel no pain. On the 8th day there is a procession through town. The festival is celebrated elsewhere, but most enthusiastically in Phuket, and especially at Wat Jui Tui on Ranong Rd in Phuket Town. **Dec**: *King's Cup Regatta* (2nd week). Yacht competition in the Andaman Sea, off Phuket.

Local information

● **Accommodation**

This is arranged by beach, with an additional section on hotels in Phuket Town. **NB:** during the low season (Jun to Oct) room rates may be as much as half the high-season price. All rates quoted are high-season. It is highly recommended to book hotel rooms during high-season (particularly at Christmas and New Year).

● **Transport**

890 km S of Bangkok.

Local Bus: for Patong, Kamala, Surin, Makham Bay, Nai Yang, Kata, Karon and Chalong buses leave every 30 mins between 0800 and 1600 from the market on Ranong Rd in Phuket Town; for Nai Harn and Rawai, they leave from Bangkok Rd, close to the Fountain Circle, in Phuket Town (฿10-20). **Small minibuses**: can be chartered for journeys around the island. Karon to town – ฿120, town to airport – ฿150, Patong to town – ฿100. **Car hire**: jeeps can be hired from small outfits along most beaches, expect to pay ฿550-1,200/day, depending on age of car etc. **Avis** has an office opposite Phuket airport, T 311358 and desks at various hotels including *Le Meridien*, the *Holiday Inn*, the *Phuket Cabana* (all on Patong Beach), the *Dusit Laguna* (on Bang Tao Beach) and the *Metropole* (in Phuket Town) (฿990-1200/day,

฿6,000-7800/week). **Hertz** has a desk at the airport, T 311162, and at the *Patong Merlin* and *Tara Patong*; prices are similar to Avis. There are other local companies down Rasada Road in Phuket Town (see Phuket Town). **Motorbike hire**: As above, ฿250-350/day. **Long-tailed boat**: these can be hired to visit reefs and the more isolated coves, ฿600-1200/day.

Air The airport is to the N of the island, 28 km from Phuket Town. For flight reservations, T 211195 (domestic) and T 212855 (international) on Phuket, and T 2800070 in Bangkok. Regular domestic connections on Thai and Bangkok Airways with Bangkok, 1 hr 15 mins (฿1,620), with Chiang Mai (4/week) 2 hrs, Hat Yai (daily) 55 mins, Nakhon Si Thammarat (3/week) 1 hr 40 mins, Surat Thani (daily) 35 mins and Trang (2/week) 40 mins. Bangkok Airways also run twice daily connections with Koh Samui 50 mins (฿1210). **International connections** with Hong Kong, Malaysia and Singapore. Airlines include ANA, Bangkok Airways, Dragonair, MAS, Qantas, Thai and Tradewinds. *Airport facilities*: café, left luggage (open 0800-2030, ฿20/day), Thai reconfirmation desk, **Hertz** car rental, currency exchange, and hotel information. *Transport to town*: **Thai** run a minibus service into town for ฿50 (from Phuket Town to the airport, the minibus leaves from the Thai office, 78 Ranong Rd) or a limousine service for ฿250. There is also a bus to Patong, Kata and Karon beaches for ฿80, or to Ranong Rd in Phuket Town (฿15).

Train There is no rail service to Phuket. However, some visitors take the train to Phun Phin, outside Surat Thani (usually the overnight train), where buses wait to take passengers on to Phuket 6 hrs (see page 445).

Road Bus: station is on Phangnga Road, T 211480. Regular a/c connections with Bangkok's Southern bus terminal near the Thonburi train station 14 hrs (฿450); non-a/c buses leave from the new terminal on Phra Pinklao Rd 14 hrs (฿201). Private a/c buses also ply this route. Regular morning connections with Hat Yai 8 hrs (฿92-145), Trang 6 hrs (฿62), Surat Thani 6 hrs (฿61). Regular connections with Krabi 4 hrs (฿38). **By taxi**: taxis will leave when they are full (usually with 5 passengers). For Surat Thani, they leave from the coffee shop opposite the Pearl Cinema on Phangnga Road (฿150/person).

Phuket Town

Phuket Town is interesting for its **Sino-Portuguese architecture** (similar to that of Penang and Macao), dating back 100-130 years. Wealthy Chinese tin barons built spacious colonial-style residences set in large grounds to celebrate their success. The best examples are along Thalang, Yaowarat, Ranong and Damrong roads and include the Chartered Bank (the first foreign bank to establish offices in Thailand), the Thai Airways office on Ranong Road opposite the market, and the Sala Phuket on Damrong Road. There is some talk of renovation, in an attempt to preserve these deteriorating buildings. There are **night markets** on Ong Sim Phai and Tilok Uthit 1 roads.

Khao Rang, a hill overlooking Phuket Town, can either be reached by foot (a longish climb) or by songthaew or tuk-tuk. It is a public park, with fitness track, and affords a good view of the island and countryside to the SW. Other views of the island are obscured by trees (chartered tuk-tuk ฿50 round trip).

Koh Sire/Siray – or Sire Island – is connected to Phuket by a short bridge. There is not much to see here; fishing boats unload their catches (turn right immediately after crossing the bridge) and there is a village of sea gypsies (or *chao talay*) and fishermen who embrace animist beliefs. They are thought to be descended from Andaman/Nicobar islanders to the W of Phuket (chartered tuk-tuk ฿60 round-trip).

Saphan Hin, a small promontory to the S of town, is a place where Thais congregate in the evening. With the on-shore breeze, array of street sellers, and a wonderful spirit house, it is worth the trip. It is just a shame the beach is like a rubbish tip.

The **Crocodile Farm and Elephant Land** (open zoo, snake farm, aquarium and aviary) is on Chana Charoen Road. Daily shows at 1100 and 1530. Admission: ฿200. Open: 0900-1800 Mon-Sun.

The **Snake Farm** is on Thepkrasatri Road, just N of the turn-off to Patong. Snake shows from 1100-2400. Snake-leather goods for sale.

Tours

Travel agents in town will organize full or half-day tours to Phangnga Bay, Phi Phi Island, Coral Island, the pearl farm, or scuba-diving around Phuket Town.

Local information
● **Accommodation**

Hotels in town are rather uninspired; most people avoid staying here and head straight for the beaches. **A+-A** *Metropole*, 1 Montri Rd, T 215050, F 215990, a/c, restaurant, ostentatious Chinese-style hotel with pretensions of grandeur; **A+-B** *City*, Thepkrasatri Rd, T 216910, F 213554, B 2535768, a/c, restaurant, pool; **A+-B** *Pearl*, 42 Montri Rd, T 211044, F 212911, B 2601022, a/c, restaurant, pool, small attractive garden, clean rooms; **A+-B** *Phuket Merlin*, 158/1 Yaowarat Rd, T 212866, F 216429, B 2532536, a/c, restaurant, pool, clean, comfortable high rise block, free shuttle bus to Patong Beach throughout the day.

A-B *Daeng Plaza*, Phuket Rd, T 213951, F 213884, a/c, restaurant.

B-C *Rongrawee Mansion*, 222/18 Yaowarat Rd Soi 3, T 213275, F 212195, a/c, restaurant; **B-C** *Thavorn*, 74 Rasada Rd, T 211333, F 2450189, a/c, restaurant, pool, central and dull but good value.

C *Siri*, 231 Yaowarat Rd, T 211307; **C-D** *Downtown Inn*, 56/16-19 Ranong Rd, T 216884, a/c; **C-D** *Imperial*, Phuket Rd, T 212311, a/c.

D *Montri*, 12/6 Montri Rd, T 212936; **D-E** *On On*, 19 Phangnga Rd, T 211154, some a/c, attractive old style hotel but rather shabby rooms.

E *J&P*, 43/4 Suthat Rd, T 216065, clean, rec; **E** *Koh Sawan*, 19/8 Poonphol Rd, T 211867, a/c, restaurant, pool; **E** *Siam*, 13-15 Phuket Rd, T 212328, noisy location but clean rooms.

F *Charoensuk*, 136 Thalang Rd, T 211203, a/c, restaurant; **F** *Laemthong*, 13 Soi Romanee, Thalang Rd, T 212310, very basic.

● **Places to eat**

Thai: ✦✦✦*Krua-Thai*, 62/7 Rasada Centre, clean restaurant with well-presented food, rec; ✦✦✦*Lucky Seafood*, 66/1 Phuket Rd, Saphan

Hin, seafood, large restaurant with Chinese/Thai food, not central; ✦*Mae Porn*, 50-52 Phangnga Rd, grubby restaurant but good food, a/c room available, rec. ✦✦✦*Phuket Seafood*, 66/2 Phuket Rd Saphan Hin, seafood, large, Chinese/Thai restaurant, not central. ✦✦*Phuket View*, Khao Rang, seafood, good position on Rang Hill with views overlooking Phuket Town, average food. *Tunk-Kao*, Khao Rang, seafood, good views.

Other Asian cuisines: *Erawan*, 41/34 Montri Rd, seafood, Chinese; ✦✦✦*Lai-An*, 58 Rasada Rd, Chinese, rec; ✦✦*Kaw Yam and Bakery*, 11/1 Thung Kha Rd; *Omar E Khyam*, 54/1 Montri Rd, Indian.

International: ✦*Kanda Bakery*, 31-33 Rasada Rd, spotlessly clean, serves breakfast, rec; ✦✦*Le Café*, Rasada Centre, elegant café serving burgers, steaks, sandwiches, cappucino and milkshakes; *Le Glacier*, 43/3

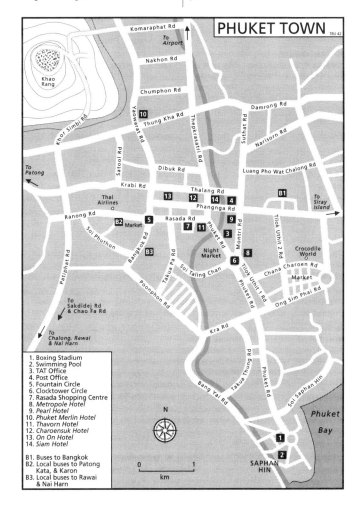

PHUKET TOWN TBU 42

1. Boxing Stadium
2. Swimming Pool
3. TAT Office
4. Post Office
5. Fountain Circle
6. Clocktower Circle
7. Rasada Shopping Centre
8. Metropole Hotel
9. Pearl Hotel
10. Phuket Merlin Hotel
11. Thavorn Hotel
12. Charoensuk Hotel
13. On On Hotel
14. Siam Hotel

B1: Buses to Bangkok
B2: Local buses to Patong Kata, & Karon
B3: Local buses to Rawai & Nai Harn

0   1
km

Rasada Centre, ice-creams; *Suthep Roast Chicken*, 480 Phuket Rd.

● **Airline offices**
Bangkok Airways, 158/2-3 Yaowarat Rd, T 212341; **Dragonair**, 37/52 Montri Rd, (from Hong Kong); **Malaysia Airlines**, *Merlin Hotel*, T 216675; **Thai**, 41/33 Montri Rd, T 212400; **Thai** (domestic), 78 Ranong Rd, T 211195; **Tradewinds**, 95/20 Phuket Rd, T 213891 (from Singapore).

● **Banks & money changers**
Several along Rasada, Phuket, Phangnga and Thepkrasatri rds.

● **Entertainment**
Cinema: 4 cinemas renting headphones with English dialogue. *The Pearl* is on corner of Montri and Phangnga rds, 3 shows daily at 1230, 1900 and 2130. Some shows with the English soundtrack (ask at ticket office).

Cultural Shows: *Orchid Garden and Thai Village*, 2 km off Thepkrasatri Rd, T 214860. Sword fighting, Thai boxing, Thai Classical dancing, folk dances, almost one hectare of orchid gardens, handicraft centre and elephants. Admission: ฿190. Open: 1000-2200.

Discos: most discos run from 2100-0200. *Marina Club* at the *Phuket Merlin*, 158/1 Yaowarat Rd; *The Wave* at the *Pearl Hotel*, Montri Rd; *Diamond Club* at the *Thavorn Hotel*, Rasada Rd (cover charge ฿50 for women, ฿70 for men).

Thai Boxing: every Fri at 2000 (tickets available from 1600). The stadium is on South Phuket Rd (Saphan Hin). Admission: ฿60-150.

● **Hospitals & medical services**
Wachira, Yaowarat Rd, T 211114; *Mission*, 4/1 Thepkasatri Rd, T 211173.

● **Post & telecommunications**
Post Office: Montri Rd. **Telephone centre**: 122/2 Phangnga Rd, open 24 hrs. **Area code**: 076; directory assistance: 13; overseas phone service: 100; **Long distance, telephone and fax centre**: Phangnga Rd.

● **Shopping**
Most souvenirs found here can be bought more cheaply elsewhere in Thailand, and if travelling back to Bangkok, it is best to wait. Best buys are pearls and gold jewellery.

Antiques: *Ban Boran Antiques*, 114 Rasada Rd.

Books: *Seng Ho Phuket Co*, 2/14-16 Montri Rd.

Department store: *Rasada Centre*, or *Ocean Shopping Mall*, opposite the *Metropole Hotel*.

Handicrafts: *Cheewa Thai Crafts Centre*, 250/1 Thepkrasatri Rd. *Native Handicraft Centre*, 9 Thepkrasatri Rd, just past the turn-off to Patong Beach. *Dam Dam*, Rasada Rd (near the fountain circle), interesting selection.

Jewellery: Montri and Rasada Rds.

Pearls: *Pearl Centre*, 83 Ranong Rd. *Mook Manee*, 53 Phuket Rd. *Phuket Pearl*, 51-7 Rasada Rd.

Pewterware: *Phuket Pewter Centre*, 52 Phuket Rd.

Silk: *Shinawatra Thai Silk*, Thepkrasatri Rd, just N of turn-off to Patong Beach. Hand-weaving demonstrations, huge range of silk products, tailor-made clothes, leather goods, 'antiques', pots.

● **Sports**
Bowling: *Pearl*, behind Pearl theatre, Phangnga Rd.

Diving: see page 414.

Jogging: Fitness Park on Khao Rang.

Game Fishing: *Phuket Tourist Centre*, 125/7 Phangnga Rd, T 211849. *Andaman Queen Tour*, 44 Phuket Rd, T 211276, F 215261.

Golf: see page 421.

Shooting range: indoor and outdoor, snooker club and restaurant, at 82/2 Patak Rd (W of Chalong 5-way intersection). Open: Mon-Sun 0900-1800.

Snooker: *Nimit Snooker Club*, 53/57 Nimit 1 Rd, T 213202. Open: 0900-late, VIP table ฿120/hr, standard ฿50/hr.

● **Tour companies & travel agents**
There are several around Rasada Road and the Rasada centre, and along Phuket Road: *Dits Travel*, 11 Sakdidej Rd, T 212848, F 213934; *Songserm Travel*, 64/2 Rasada Centre, Rasada Rd, T 214272; *Silver Queen*, 1/10 Thung Kha Rd, T 214056, they also have a desk at the *Patong Merlin Hotel*; *Aloha Tour*, Chalong Bay, T 216726; *Cruise Centre*, Rawai Beach, T 381793; *Pee Pee Hydrocraft*, Makham Bay, T 211530.

● **Tourist offices**
TAT, 73-75 Phuket Rd, T 212213, F 213582. Good source of information, with an up-to-date hotel price list. Areas of responsibility are

Phuket and Phangnga.

● **Tourist Police**
Emergency call, T 212213 (till 1630), then Police on T 212115.

● **Useful addresses**
American Express agent: *Sea Tour*, 95/4 Phuket Rd, T 216979. **Christian Church**: Chao Fa Rd, Sunday service at 1030. **Immigration office**: South Phuket Rd (close to Saphan Hin), T 212108. **24 hr petrol station**: Esso, Thepkasatri Rd.

● **Transport**
Local Tuk-Tuk: ฿7 within town, ฿10 from town to suburbs. **Car hire**: *Pure Car Rent*, 75 Rasada Rd, T 211002 ฿900/day. *Phuket Horizon Car Rent*, 108/1 Rasada Rd, T 211151 ฿950/day. **Motorbike hire**: from the same places.

The Beaches

The beach areas listed below begin with the principal resort of Patong, followed by the beaches S of Patong from Karon and anti-clockwise to Chalong. Finally, there is a section on the less-visited beaches of the W coast, N of Patong.

Patong Beach

The most-developed beach on Phuket is the 3 km-long **Patong**, 15 km due W of Phuket Town. It began to metamorphose from a hippy paradise into a commercial centre during the 1970s. It is the Pattaya of the S, with a mass of neon signs advertising the many hotels, massage parlours, restaurants, straight bars, gay bars, nightclubs, supermarkets and discos. Looking down the main drag, Patong could be anywhere: south of France, the west coast of the US....there is little sense of 'Thai-ness' here. The cheap accommodation has now been almost entirely displaced to remoter parts of the island. Sadly, there is little indication that any thought has been given to the overall planning of the area: individual hotels and restaurants can be excellent, but the whole ensemble lacks coherence or any architectural merit. Developers bypass planning restrictions by offering 'gifts' to the appropriate officials. One thing cannot be denied though: Patong generates a great deal of foreign exchange.

Patong Beach offers the widest selection of watersports on Phuket and in spite of the hotel development, it is still possible to snorkel on the reef at the S end of the bay. Patong could not, in any sense, be described as peaceful, but it is the best place to stay if you are looking for an active nightlife. The beach is also safe for children, as the seabed shelves gently and the water is generally calm.

Tours
Between Nov and Apr, express boats leave Patong for day trips to the Similan Islands (see page 426). *Thai Tour Patong Beach*, T 213275, organize two-hour tours in a glass-bottomed boat to view the coral reef. Daily departures from Patong Beach at 1000, 1200, 1400 and 1600 (฿300).

● **Accommodation**
There are dozens of hotels on Patong Beach Rd (also known as Thaweewong Rd). The following is only a small selection. **A+** *Club Andaman*, 77/1 Patong Beach Rd, T 340530, F 340527, B 2701627, a/c, restaurant, pool, large new block and some older thatched cottages, set in large spacious grounds, fitness centre, tennis courts, watersports, children's games room; **A+** *Amari Coral Beach*, 104 Trai Trang Rd, T 340106, F 340115, B 2526087, on secluded promontory at S end of beach, a/c, restaurant, pool, fitness centre, tennis courts, private beach; **A+-A** *Diamond Cliff Resort*, 61/9 Kalim Beach, T 340501, F 340507, a/c, restaurant, pool, N end of Patong, large impressive resort on side of hill but no beach immediately in front of hotel, tennis courts, mini-golf, health club; **A+-A** *Holiday Inn*, 86/11 Patong Beach Rd, T 340608, F 340435, B 2340847, a/c, restaurants, pool, ugly concrete hotel block on the beach, popular with tour groups, tennis, watersports, gym, golf driving range, diving centre, mini zoo; **A+-A** *Merlin*, 99/2 Patong Beach Rd, T 340037, F 340394, B 2532641, a/c, restaurant, pool, S end, attractively laid out with well-designed, spacious rooms, nice garden, watersports, fitness club.

A *Patong Beach Bungalows*, 96/1 Patong Beach Rd, T 340117, a/c, restaurant, pool; **A** *Patong Beach*, 94 Patong Beach Rd, T 340611, F 340541, B 2330420, middle of beach, a/c, restaurant, pool, health club; **A** *Phuket Cabana*, 94 Patong Beach Rd, T 342100, F 340178, centre of beach, a/c, restaurant, pool, wooden Thai-style cabins rather close together but hotel is in a good location by the beach; **A-B** *Holiday Resort*, Patong Beach Rd, T 340119, F 340101, S end, a/c, restaurant, pool; **A-B** *Neptuna*, 82/49-50 Rat Uthit Rd, T 321188.

B *Beau Rivage*, 77/15-17 Rat Uthit Rd, T 340850, a/c; **B** *K Hotel*, 82/47 Rat Uthit Rd, T 340507, some a/c, pool, quiet; **B** *Patong Villa*, 85/3 Patong Beach Rd, T 340132, centre of beach, restaurant, pool.

C *Capricorn*, 82/29 Rat Uthit Rd, T 340390, private bathroom; **C** *Odins*, 78/59-68 Rat Uthit Rd, clean; **C** *Paradise*, 93 Patong Beach Rd, T 340172, S end, a/c; **C-E** *Shamrock Park Inn*, Rat Uthit Rd.

D *Ban Koson*, 81/3 Patong Beach Rd, T 340135, Near Soi Post Office; **D** *Club Oasis*, 86/4 Patong Beach Rd, T 340258, near Soi Post Office; **D** *Golden Field*, Patong Beach Rd, T 340375; **D** *Jeep I*, 81/7 Bangla Rd, T 340264, huts in a grassy compound; **D** *Jeep II*, 38/8 Rat Uthit Rd, T 340100, centre of beach; **D** *Royal Palms*, 86/4 Patong Beach Rd, T 340141, near Soi Post Office; **D** *White*, 81/4 Rat Uthit Rd, quiet, nice garden, rec.

● **Places to eat**

As with accommodation, there is a huge selection of restaurants selling all types of food; seafood is recommended.

Thai: ♦♦♦♦*Baan Rim Pa*, 100/7 Kalim Beach Rd, open terrace, on cliff overlooking bay, great position but expensive; *Krua Thai*, 99/61 Rat Uthit Rd (S end); ♦♦♦*Malee's Seafood*, 94/4 Patong Beach Rd, also serves Chinese and International dishes, outdoor verandah; *No.4 Seafood*, Bangla Rd, seafood; ♦♦♦*Patong Seafood*, 98/2 Patong Beach Rd, seafood, basic but good.

Indian: *Kashmir*, 83-50 Patong Beach Rd; ♦♦♦*Shalimar*, 89/59 Soi Post Office, seafood specialities.

International: *Babylon*, 93/12 Bangla Rd, Italian; ♦♦♦*Buffalo Steak House*, 94/25-26 Soi Patong Resort, off Bangla Rd; ♦♦*Doolie's Place*, 82/51 Soi Bangla, garden and unattractive minizoo, steaks, pizzas; *Expat Rock 'n' Roll*, burgers;

♦♦*Lai Mai*, 86/15 Patong Beach Rd, great Western breakfasts; *Mon Bijou*, 72/5 Rat Uthit Rd, German; *Vecchio Venezia*, Bangla Rd, pizza.

● **Bars**

Bars in Patong are concentrated along Rat Uthit Rd and Soi Bangla. *Black and White*, 70/123 Paradise Complex; *Bounty Bar*, Bangla Rd; *Captain Hook's*, 70/142 Paradise Complex; *Maxims*, Rat Uthit Rd; *Oasis*, off Bangla Rd; *Stardust a go-go*, Soi Sunset.

● **Banks & money changers**

Banks and currency exchange booths are concentrated on Patong Beach Rd (Thaweewong Rd).

● **Entertainment**

Cultural shows: a Thai-style house on the hill before Patong Beach provides Thai boxing,

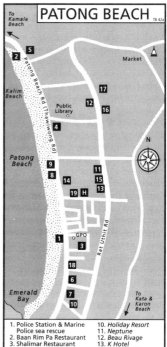

PATONG BEACH TB 42a

1. Police Station & Marine Police sea rescue
2. Baan Rim Pa Restaurant
3. Shalimar Restaurant
4. Club Andaman
5. Diamond Cliff Resort
6. Holiday Inn
7. Merlin
8. Patong Beach Bungalow
9. Phuket Cabana
10. Holiday Resort
11. Neptune
12. Beau Rivage
13. K Hotel
14. Patong Villa
15. Capricorn
16. Odins
17. Shamrock Park Inn
18. Club Oasis
19. Jeep

classical dance, sword fighting. Two shows a night, with Thai dinner, T 7230841.

Discos: *Banana* at *Patong Beach Hotel*, *Deep Sea Video Theque* at *Phuket Arcadia Hotel* and at *Le Crocodile*.

Music: *Le Crocodile*, just off Bangla Rd, and at many of the bars. Also the usual assortment of massage parlours, straight and gay bars, and revues.

● **Hospitals & medical services**
Kathu hospital on Rat Uthit Rd.

● **Post & telecommunications**
Post Office: Patong Beach Rd (the beachfront road) near Soi Permpong Pattana (aka Soi Post Office). **Area code**: 076.

● **Shopping**
Night Plaza – a vast purpose-built building behind the *Holiday Inn* selling handicrafts, clothing, jewellery, cassette tapes etc.

● **Sports**
Bungee jumping: *Tarzan's Jungle Jump*, near intersection on the townside of the bottom of the hill in Patong.

Diving: centres are concentrated along Patong Beach Rd. Trips range from one day tours to Phi Phi Island, to week-long expeditions to the Similan Islands National Park and the Surin Islands. See general diving section on page 414 for listings.

Fitness: the Fitness Club Centre with aerobics, sauna and body building is in the *Holiday Inn* on Patong Beach. Open: 0900-2100 Mon-Sat, 1200-2100 Sun. Daily, weekly and monthly membership is available.

Game Fishing: quite a few operators along Patong Beach Road. Expect to pay about ฿1500-2000/day. Go-Kart racing: track at bottom of hill leading to Patong.

Go-Kart racing: track at bottom of hill leading to Patong.

Golf: Phuket Golf and Country Club, on main road between Phuket Town and Patong, T 213383, 18-hole, ฿150. Open: 0800-1800. Caddy ฿100.

Mini Golf: Pirate's Cove, behind *Holiday Inn*, two 18 hole courses.

A wide range of **watersports**: windsurfing, waterskiing, sailing, diving, snorkelling, deepsea fishing. Ask at your hotel or at one of the sports shops along Patong Beach Rd.

● **Tourist Police**
Turn left at S end of beach, behind the *Holiday Resort*; local police station, T 212115.

● **Travel agents**
Magnum Travel, Patong Beach Rd, T 381840; *Travel Company*, 89/71 Patong Beach Rd, T 321292.

● **Transport**
15 km W of town.

Local Jeeps and motorcycles: can be hired from outlets along the beach. **Avis** has desks at the *Holiday Inn* (T 340608) and *Phuket Cabana Hotel* (T 340138), **Hertz** is at the *Merlin* (T 340037) and *Thara* (T 340520).

Road Songthaews/minibuses: from Ranong Rd, by the market in Phuket Town (฿10). **Chartered tuk-tuk**: ฿100 one way, ฿140 round trip.

Karon and Kata beaches

The horseshoe-shaped **Karon and Kata beaches** S of Patong are divided by a narrow rocky outcrop. Karon started tourist life as a haven for backpackers; it is now well-developed, with a range of hotels and bungalows and a wide selection of restaurants.

Kata consists of 2 beaches: Kata Yai (Big Kata) and Kata Noi (Little Kata), divided by a cliff. Kata Noi is dominated by the *Kata Thani Hotel*, although there are a few bungalows here. The snorkelling is good around Koh Pu, the island in the middle of the bay, and at the S end of Kata Noi. Kata Yai is a sprawling mass of development: hotels, souvenir shops and roadside restaurants abound. It has no real charm – although it does provide excellent facilities for the holiday-maker. Karon is similar in style but it has an even less attractive beach with no trees to provide shade.

Local information
● **Accommodation on Karon**
A+ *Arcadia*, T 381039, F 381136, B 2547901, centre of beach, a/c, restaurant, pool, modern, over-bearing high-rise, all rooms overlook the sea, health club, tennis, watersports, beach disappointing; **A+** *Le Meridien*, T 340480, F 340479, B 2548147, a/c, restaurants, pool, nightclub, fitness centre,

tennis, watersports, very private and secluded with massive landscaped pool to complement the even larger 'L' shaped block, good sports facilities; **A++-A** *Islandia Park Resort*, T 381492, F 381491, B 5123798, a/c, restaurant, pool, high-rise block, all rooms facing sea, new and plush (for how long?).

A *Karon Beach Resort*, T 381527, F 381529, a/c, restaurant, pool right on the beach at the S end of the bay, slightly frayed interior, all rooms with balconies overlooking beach; **A** *Karon Villa Royal Wing*, T 381139, F 3811122, B 2516628, centre of beach, a/c, restaurant, pool; **A** *Phuket Island View*, T 381633, S end of beach, a/c, restaurant, pool; **A** *Sand Resort*, T 212901, a/c, restaurant, simple bungalows, clean, small rooms; **A** *Thavorn Palm Beach*, T 381034, F 381555, B 2453193, a/c, restaurant, 4 pools, centre of beach; **A-B** *Karon Inn*, T 381521, a/c, restaurant, centre of beach.

B *Golden Sand*, T 381494; **B** *Kampong Karon*, T 212901; **B** *Marina Cottage*, PO Box 143, S end of beach, T 381625, F 381516, a/c, two good restaurants, beautiful secluded pool, individual cottages in beautiful grounds, no private beach, *Marina Divers* here, tours and boat trips organised, rec.; **B-C** *Green Valley*, T 381468, a/c, restaurant.

C *Phuket Ocean Resort 1*, N end of beach area, not on beach, T 381599; **C-E** *My Friend*, N end of beach, simple huts within easy reach of the beach.

D *Happy Hut*, 121/2 Kata-Karon Beach, small, clean and green; **D** *Karon Sea View* (next to *Sand Resort*), good value chalets.

E-F *Dream Hut*, N end of beach, basic, clean, very small chalets, not on beach.

● **Accommodation on Kata**
(all with restaurant, pool and a/c) **L-A+** *Boathouse Inn*, T 330015, F 330561, S end of beach, several restaurants (good seafood), pool, attractive high-end choice, big hotel, but retains the feel of a small hotel, very well run, large central jacuzzi.

A+ *Club Med*, T 381139, F 381122, B 2539780, centre of beach, looking rather threadbare, superb sports activities, large piece of private beach, excellent for children. The Club Med is currently in conflict with the provincial governor over plans to upgrade a road in front of the resort and are threatening to withdraw from Thailand; **A+** *Kata Beach Resort*, T 381530, F 381534, S end, very flash

KARON & KATA BEACHES
Not to scale

To Patong

1. Arcadia
2. Le Meridien
3. Islendia Park Resort
4. Karon Beach Resort
5. Karon Villa
6. Phuket Island View
7. Sand Resort
8. Thavorn Palm Beach

N

Karon Beach

Kata Beach

Post Office

To Phuket town & shooting range

Kata Noi Beach

To Nai Harn Beach

9. Marina Cottage
10. Green Valley
11. Phuket Ocean Resort
12. My Friend
13. Happy Hut
14. Karon Sea View
15. Boathouse Inn
16. Club Med
17. Kata Beach Resort
18. Kata Thani
19. Kata Delight
20. Chao Khuan
21. Kata Garden Resort
22. Friendship
23. Cool Breeze
24. Fantasy Hill

new resort, watersports, good for children.

A *Amari Kata Thani*, Kata Noi Beach, T 330124, F 330426, BT 2514727, BF 2555707, a/c, restaurants, unexciting pools, large average hotel, popular with package holidays, but lovely beach; **A** *Hayashi Thai House*, T 381710, away from beach; **A** *Kata Delight*, T 381481, S end, a/c, restaurant; **A** *Kata Inn*, T 214828, a/c. **A-B** *Chao Khuan*, T 381403, between Kata Noi and

Kata, a/c, restaurant; **A** *Mansion*, T 381565, a/c, restaurant, quiet area of beach.

B-C *Kata Garden Resort*, T 381627, F 381466, some a/c, clean; **B-C** *Kata Guesthouse*, T 381627, S end.

C *Rose Inn*, T 214839, N end; **C-D** *Friendship*, Kata Noi.

D *Kata Tropicana*, T 211606, simple chalets, friendly and clean, rec.

E *Cool Breeze*, Kata Noi; **E** *Fantasy Hill*, between Karon and Kata, rather noisy; **E** *Kata Noi Bay Inn*, Kata Noi.

● **Places to eat**

Ruan Thep, S end of beach, Thai. **International**: *Co Co Cabana*, pizza, N end of Karon; *Maxim*, seafood, S end of Karon; ♦♦*Swiss Bakery*, Western Inn, rec; *Gustos* and ♦♦*No 2* near Kata Thani Hotel.

● **Sports**

Diving: *Siam Diving Centre* S end of Karon Beach, T 381608 – organize diving expeditions to the Similan Islands; *Marina Divers*, T 330272, F 330516, PADI certified courses, very professional set up, rec; and *PIDC Divers* at *Le Meridien Hotel*, T 321479.

Horse riding: next to shooting range, T 381667, ฿600/hr. Open: 0700-1200, 1300-1830.

Shooting range: Phuket Shooting Range, 82/2 Patak Rd, T 381667, off Route 4028 between Kata and Chalong. Open: 0930-1800 Mon-Sun.

● **Transport**

20 km from Phuket Town.

Road Songthaews: to both Karon and Kata leave regularly from the Ranong Rd Market, Phuket Town (฿10).

Nai Harn and Promthep Cape

Nai Harn, 18 km SW of Phuket Town, is one of the island's most beautiful locations, with spectacular sunsets. It is now possible to stay here in luxury at the *Phuket Yacht Club* (built, illegally, on protected land). During the monsoon season between May and Oct, the surf and currents can be particularly vicious and care should be taken when swimming. From Nai Harn it is possible to walk to **Promthep Cape**, the best place to view the sunset. Walk out to the cape itself or simply look down on the surrounding sea and coastline from the road, for a spectacular view. Near the highest point there is a shrine covered in gold leaf and surrounded by wooden elephants.

Local information

● **Accommodation**

L *Phuket Yacht Club*, T 381156, F 381164, BT 2544264, BF 2545365, part of Mandarin Hotel group, a/c, restaurants, pool, lovely position on hill, overlooking Nai Harn and Promthep Cape, well-run luxurious hotel, each room has a large secluded balcony with good west-facing views, massive bathrooms, excellent food, fitness club, tennis courts, lovely beach, the hotel was built contravening environmental laws but as money can move mountains in Thailand, little could or can be done.

A+-C *Jungle Beach*, T 214291, F 381108, some a/c, pool, remote, attractive position.

D *Ao Saen*; **D** *Nai Harn Ya Noi*.

E *Jongdee*; **E** *Nai Harn bungalow*; **E** *Sunset*, basic, but wonderful view.

● **Places to eat**

The Moorings, good seafood, great views at sunset, secluded restaurant, access through Phuket Yacht Club car park, rec.

● **Sports**

Waterskiing, **windsurfing**, **mini-golf**, **herbal sauna**.

Riding: *Crazy Horse Club*, rides on the beach or along mountain trails (฿300/hr).

Rawai

To the N of Promthep Cape, up the E side of the island the first beach is **Rawai**, 14 km from Phuket Town. This crescent-shaped beach is now relatively developed although not to the same degree, nor in the same style, as Patong or Karon. It is patronized by Thai tourists rather than foreigners and as a result has a quite different atmosphere. There is a small market selling assorted handicrafts and various snacks. The bay is sheltered from the monsoon and it is safe to swim throughout the year. But the beach is rather dirty and it is rocky. At Rawai there is a 'sea gypsy' tribal village, **Chao Le**.

Local information
● Accommodation
A+ *Phuket Island Resort*, T 381010, F 381018, B 2525320, a/c, restaurant, pool, luxurious hotel with almost every conceivable facility.

B *Atlas Resort*, T 381279.

C *Rawai Resort*, T 381298, a/c, restaurant.

D *Rawai Garden Resort*, T 381292, restaurant.

E *Pornmae*, T 381300.

● Sport
Diving: equipment can be hired from the *Phuket Island Resort*.

Laem Ka and Chalong beaches

The next beaches up the E coast are **Laem Ka Beach** and **Chalong**. Ao Chalong is 1 km off the main road. There is not much here for the sun and sea-worshipper and the beach is rather dirty. Offshore tin-dredging is said to have ruined the beach. Boats can be caught to the offshore islands for game fishing, snorkelling and scuba diving from Chalong's long pier, and there is a small collection of good seafood restaurants. The rest of the east coast has not been developed for tourists as the coast is rocky.

Tours *Aloha Tours* (T 381220) and the *Chalong Bay Boat Centre* (T 381852) both on Wisit Rd. *Ao Chalong* arrange trips to Phi Phi, Coral, and Raja Islands and fishing and diving expeditions.

Local information
● Accommodation
C *Laem Ka Beach Inn*, T 381305, restaurant.

D *Ao Chalong*, T 381190, restaurant.

● Places to eat
♦♦♦*Kan Eang Seafood*, on the beach, excellent selection of seafood, rec; *Ruan Thai Seafood*.

● Sport
Golf: 18-hole mini-golf course (open 1000-2300) left of the narrow road to Ao Chalong from the main road. Sailing centre and dive shop (see dive section, page 414).

Koh Lone, Koh Maiton and Cape Panwa

The Marine Research Centre and aquarium are to be found on this remote point (see page 412), as well as Panwa House, in the grounds of the only significant hotel here – the *Cape Panwa Sheraton*. Boat trips to nearby islands leave from the cape.

Local information
● Accommodation on Koh Lone
B *Lone Pavilion*, T 381374 a/c, restaurant.

C *Lone Island Resort*, T 211253.

● Accommodation on Koh Maiton
L *The Maiton Resort*, PO Box 376, T 214954, F 214959, a/c, restaurants, pool, individual Thai pavilions with wooden floors and separate sitting-room, good sports facilities and beautiful white-sand beaches.

● Accommodation on Cape Panwa
A+-A *Cape Panwa Sheraton*, T 391123, F 391210, beautifully secluded, some bungalows for families, tennis courts, fitness centre, electric train down to the private beach, coral reef 40m off-shore, rec. A small island off the cape is home to one hotel, the **A** *Tapao Yai Island Resort*, T 391217, all facilities.

North from Patong

Travelling N from Patong, there remain some beautiful unspoilt beaches. This part of Phuket's shoreline has virtually no cheap accommodation but a number of exclusive hotels.

● **Accommodation** **A** *Thavorn Bay Resort*, between Kamala and Patong beaches, on the Kao Phanthurat Pass, T 340486.

Kamala Beach

10 km N of Patong and the road there is still unsurfaced. The beach itself is rather bare, with little shade, but the village has a nice atmosphere, with its own post office, telephone service, police station, health centre and a number of good seafood restaurants.

● **Accommodation on Kamala** **L** *Kamala Bay Terrace Resort*, 16/12 Moo 6, Tambon Kamala, T 723-0263, F 723-0223, a/c, restaurant, pool, built on hillside overlooking the sea, quieter location than most, but rooms unremarkable for the price. **A** *Kamala Beach Resort*, T 212775, F 211841, a/c, restaurant, pool, family run and good value for money, price includes breakfast and dinner, rec.

● **Places to eat** ◆◆◆*Fisherman's Tavern*, good French and Thai food.

Surin Beach

Lined with casuarina trees and is patronized mostly by Thais. The seabed shelves away steeply from the shoreline and swimming can be dangerous. Small golfcourse here.

Pansea Beach is a tiny beach just N of Surin with two exclusive hotels on it: L *Amanpuri Resort*, 118/1 Pansea Beach, T 324333, F 324100, B 2870226, a/c, restaurant, pool, more expensive rooms are beautifully designed Thai pavilions, with every detail in place. Superb facilities include private yacht, watersports, tennis and squash courts, fitness centre, private beach, library, undoubtedly the best on Phuket but not recommended for small children, because of many steps around the resort; **L-A+** *Pansea Resort*, T 324017, F 324252, B 2374792, N end of the beach, a/c, restaurant, pool, exclusive resort with range of traditional Thai cottages to sleep from 2-10 people, superb facilities, including all watersports, cinema, library, games room, secluded beach.

● **Places to eat** The Thai restaurant (◆◆◆◆) at the *Amanpuri* is considered the best on the island, at least 48 hrs advanced booking needed during peak season (T 324394), rec.

Bang Tao

Bang Tao is a quiet beach with a few bungalows, undergoing further developments. The southern end of the beach is unattractive.

● **Accommodation** **L-A+** *Sheraton Grande Laguna*, Northern most resort, T 324101, F 324108, B 2345599, a/c, 5 restaurants, large pool with jacuzzis and waterfall, brand new hotel, with accommodation out on stilts on the lagoon, tennis courts, golf, health centre – in short, all facilities; **A+** *Dusit Laguna*, T 324320, F 311174, B 2384790, a/c, restaurant, pool, built on its own island, flanked by lagoons, excellent facilities include a large pool, tennis courts, watersports and good facilities for children.

A *Lanna Resort*, T 212553, F 222502, 4 bungalows sleeping 2 to 6 people each, Thai style, 10 mins from beach, no a/c, but secluded with space, rather overpriced; **A** *Royal Park Travelodge Resort*, Southern most resort on the beach, T 324021, F 324243, B 5411524, a/c, several restaurants, pool, large 3-storey hotel, with watersports, tennis, fitness room, gift shops.

B-D *Bang Tao Lagoon Bungalows* (N end), T 7230664, F 381395; **B-C** *Bang Tao Cottages* (S end).

● **Sport Golf**: *Banyan Tree Golf Centre*, north of *Sheraton Grande Laguna* Beach Hotel.

Nai Ton

Between Bang Tao and Nai Yang is the isolated beach of Nai Ton currently consisting of one drinks stall, where deckchairs and umbrellas can be hired. However, the track leading to it is in the process of being improved and doubtless, the beach will soon be developed. South of Nai Ton is an exquisite cove, most easily accessible by boat.

Nai Yang

Nai Yang is the northern-most beach and part of the **Nai Yang National Park**. It is close to the airport and 37 km from Phuket Town (entrance ฿5 for car). The park encompasses Nai Yang and Mai Khao beaches, which together measure 9 km, making it the longest stretch of beach on the island. The area was declared a national park in 1981 to protect the turtles which lay their eggs here from Nov to Mar. Eggs are collected by the Fisheries Department and young turtles are released on 13th Apr each year, on 'Turtle Release Festival Day'. The N end of the beach (where there is good snorkelling on the reef) is peaceful and secluded, with the only accommodation being in the National Park bungalows. The Visitors Centre is open from 0830-1630 Mon-Sat. Further S, there is more activity, with a range of luxury hotels and bungalows.

● **Accommodation A+** *Crown Nai Yang Suite Hotel*, T 320320, F 327323, a/c, restaurant, pool; **A+** *Pearl Village*, T 327006, F 327338, B 2601027, a/c, restaurant, attractive pool, well run, friendly management, beautiful gardens, facilities include tennis courts, horse riding, elephant riding, good for families, rec.

B-D *National Park bungalows*, T 21201.

● **Camping** Available in the National Park (฿60).

● **Places to eat** Several seafood places, for example, *Nai Yang Seafood*.

● **Banks & money changers** Mobile exchange van.

● **Transport** 30 km from Phuket Town. **Road Bus**: from the market on Ranong Rd in Phuket Town.

Koh Similan

The **Similan Islands National Park** consists of 9 islands, imaginatively named *Koh* (meaning island) *1*, through to *Koh 9*. They lie 80 km NW of Phuket and are some of the most beautiful, unspoilt tropical idylls to be found in SE Asia. Koh 4 is the central island and houses the park office and some dormitory and camping accommodation. Koh 9 is the most popular diving location. At the end of Mar/beginning of Apr, underwater visibility is not good, but this is the best time to see manta rays and whale sharks. The water surrounding the archipelago supports a wealth of marine life and is considered one the best diving locations in the world as well as a good place for anglers. **Best time to visit**: Dec to Apr; the west monsoon makes the islands virtually inaccessible during the rest of the year.

Tours

See page 414. Most dive companies in Phuket offer tours to the Similan Islands (see page 414). Hotels in Khao Lak (see page 410), organize boat and dive trips to Similan.

Local information
● **Accommodation**

Bungalows and camping facilities (bring your own tent, ฿20) are available on Koh 4 (**E-F**). There are also some bungalows and a restaurant on Koh 8. Reservations can be made at the Similan National Park Office, Thai Muang.

● **Useful addresses**

For information on weather conditions T 2580437.

● **Transport**
40 km off shore.

Sea Boat: boats leave from Ao Chalong, Phuket 6-10 hrs. Vessels also depart from Thap Lamu pier, 20 km N of Thai Muang, 3-5 hrs. Finally, boats leave from Ranong, a busy deepsea fishing port. Although it is possible to visit the Similan Islands independently, it can be an expensive and/or time-consuming business; it is far easier to book onto a tour (see above).

Koh Surin

5 islands make up this Marine National Park, just S of the Burmese border, and 53 km off the mainland. The two main islands are **Koh Surin Tai** and **Koh Surin Nua** (South and North Surin respectively), separated by a narrow strait which can be waded at low tide. Both islands are hilly, with few inhabitants; a small community of Chao Le fishermen live on Koh Surin Tai. The diving and snorkelling is good here and the coral reefs are said to be the most diverse in Thailand. However, overfishing has led some people to maintain that diving is now better around the Similan Islands. Novices will still find the experience both exhilarating and enchanting. The National Park office is at Ao Mae Yai, on the SW side of Koh Surin Nua. **Best time to visit**: Dec to Mar. **NB**: Koh Surin Tai may close to visitors during the full moon each March, when the Chao Le hold an important festival.

Local information
● **Accommodation**

At **Ao Mai Yai**, SW side of Koh Surin Nua,

3 dormitories, ฿1500 (for whole dormitory), T (076) 411545 for details. There is also a bungalow that sleeps 6, ฿600.

● **Camping**
On S side of island, there is a campground, ฿80 for a tent for two people.

● **Places to eat**
Food is supplied at the bungalow, ฿250/day for 3 set meals.

● **Useful addresses**
For information on weather conditions T 2580437.

● **Transport**
Local Long-tail boats: can be hired, ฿400 for 4 hrs.

Sea Boats: leave from Patong or Rawai on Phuket (10 hrs), from Ranong (through the *Jansom Thara Hotel*) or from the pier at Ban Hin Lat, 1 km W of Khuraburi 4-5 hrs (฿500).

PHUKET TO PHATTALUNG

The drive to Phangnga from Phuket passes through impressive limestone scenery. En route, it is possible to watch rubber being processed by smallholders. Not long ago, over-mature rubber trees (those more than 25 years old) were cut down and processed into charcoal. Today, due to the efforts of an enterprising Taiwanese businessman, a rubber-wood furniture industry has developed. As the road nears Phangnga, there are a number of roads down to the coast, from where tours to Phangnga Bay depart. At these junctions, men frantically beckon potential customers.

Phangnga

Phangnga itself is a bit of a one-horse town, though spectacularly located in the midst of limestone crags. Due to the limestone geology, there are a number of caves in the vicinity. Just at the outskirts of town on Route 4 towards Phuket, on the left-hand side, are the **Sinakharin Gardens**, visible from the road. Within the gardens is **Tham Luu Sii**, a watery,

sun-filled cave which would be beautiful if it were not for the concrete pathways. At the entrance to the cave sits Luu Sii, the cave guardian, under an umbrella. **Tham Phung Chang** is a little closer into town on the other side of the road, set behind provincial government buildings. There is a spring and Buddha images in this unremarkable cave, and a small pool where local boys swim.

Excursions
Phangnga Bay is best known as the location for the James Bond movie *The Man with the Golden Gun*. Limestone rocks tower out of the sea (some as high as 100m) and boats can be hired to tour the area from Tha Don, the Phangnga customs pier (see Tours, below). **Getting there**: take a songthaew to the pier (฿10) from Phangnga town. 7 km along Route 4 there is a turning to the left (Route 4144 – signposted Phangnga Bay and the Ao Phangnga National Park Headquarters), and the pier is another 3 km down this road. Long-tailed boats can be chartered from the pier for a trip around the sights of Phangnga Bay for about ฿350-450 (see below for details). **Accommodation**: bungalows are available at the headquarters of the National Park (which incorporates the Bay).

Tham Suwan Kuha is 12 km from Phangnga on Route 4 to Phuket. A turning to the right leads to this airy cave temple. It is popular with Thais and is full of Buddha images, the largest of which is a poorly-proportioned reclining Buddha. Stairs lead up to a series of tunnels, containing some impressive natural rock formations. King Chulalongkorn visited the cave in 1890 and his initials are carved into the rock. The cave is associated with a wat, Wat Suwan Kuha or Wat Tham. Admission: ฿10. Getting there: take a bus travelling SW along Route 4 towards Phuket.

Wat Tham Khao Thao is 12 km from Phangnga on Route 4152 to Krabi, on the left-hand side of the road, under a cliff

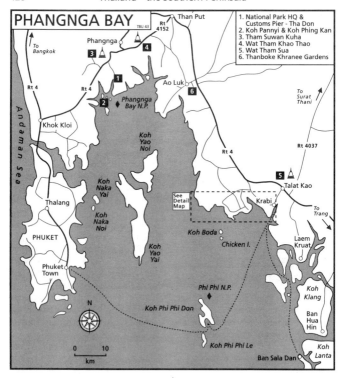

PHANGNGA BAY

1. National Park HQ & Customs Pier - Tha Don
2. Koh Pannyi & Koh Phing Kan
3. Tham Suwan Kuha
4. Wat Tham Khao Thao
5. Wat Tham Sua
6. Thanboke Khranee Gardens

wall. There are views of the surrounding plain which can be seen from a stairway being built up the cliff-face. **Getting there**: take a bus along Route 4152 towards Krabi.

Tours

The standard tour of **Phangnga Bay** winds through mangrove swamps and nipa palm, past striking limestone cliffs, before arriving at **Tham Lod** – not really a cave at all, but a tunnel, cut into the limestone through which boats can pass. From Tham Lod, the route skirts past the Muslim fishing village of **Koh Pannyi** with its turquoise green mosque (and seafood restaurants), and then reaches the 'highlight' of the trip: **James Bond Island**, or **Koh Phing Kan**.

Greatly over-rated, the 'famous' overhanging rock, like a chisel, seems much smaller than it should be, and the beach and cave are littered with trinket-stalls and other tourists. Close to Koh Pannyi are some **ancient cave paintings** of dolphins and other creatures. Tours can be booked at the *Ratanapung* and *Thaweesuk hotels*. Day trip 0830-1430 (฿100); overnight with seafood dinner, 0830-0900 the next day (฿250).

Local information
● **Accommodation**

A *Phangnga Bay Resort*, 20 Thadon Rd (out of town, near the customs pier), T 411067, F 412057, B 2162882, a/c, restaurant, pool, mostly tour groups, modern, overpriced.

B *Phangnga Valley Resort*, 5/5 Phetkasem Rd, T 411201, F 411201, restaurant, just before town, lovely setting, 15 bungalows; **B** *Sun Splendour Lodge*, 40 Mu 7, Bangsak, T 421580.

D *Lak Muang 2*, 540 Phetkasem Rd, T 411218, F 411500, a/c, restaurant, pool, good value, but featureless, rec.

E *Lak Muang 1*, 1/2 Phetkasem Rd, T 411125, F 411512, some a/c, restaurant.

F *Ratanaphong*, 111 Phetkasem Rd, T 411247, in town centre, but friendly with clean, though unremarkable, rooms, rec; **F** *Thaweesuk*, 79 Phetkasem Rd, T 411686, large clean rooms, breezy rooftop restaurant, welcoming and good information, rec.

● **Places to eat**
Cafés on Phetkasem Road, near the market, sell the usual array of Thai dishes; including excellent *khaaw man kai* (chicken and rice).

● **Banks & money changers**
Mostly on the main street, Phetkasem Rd.

● **Post & telecommunications**
Post Office: on Phetkasem Rd, 2 km from centre on main road entering town from Phuket. **Area code**: 076.

● **Transport**
100 km from Phuket, 879 km from Bangkok.

Local Motorbikes: can be hired from the *Thaweesuk Hotel*.

Road Bus: buses from Bangkok's Southern bus terminal near the Thonburi railway station twice a day, 15 hrs (฿184-346); T 434119 for a/c bus information and T 4345557 for non-a/c bus information. Regular connections with Phuket's bus terminal on Phangnga Rd, near Theprakasitri Rd, 1¾ hrs (฿22). From Krabi, a local bus takes 1½ hrs (฿25).

Krabi

From Phangnga to Krabi, the road passes mangrove swamps and nipa palm, more dramatic karst formations and impressive stands of tropical forest.

Krabi is a provincial capital, situated on the banks of the Krabi River, close to where it empties into the Andaman Sea. The town is visited by tourists largely because it is a jumping-off point to the **Phi Phi Islands** (see page 433), although there are also some good beaches and cheap accommodation nearby (see below). There is a **general market** on Srisawat and Sukhon roads, and a **night market** close to the Chao Fah Pier.

Excursions
Wat Tham Sua or the Tiger Cave Temple, is 3 km NE of town just past Talat Kao down a track on the left and has dozens of kutis (monastic cells) set into the limestone cliff. Walk behind the ridge where the bot is situated to find a network of limestone caves, which eventually lead back to the entrance. Getting there: take a songthaew N to Talat Kao, and then a bus or songthaew E along Route 4 (ask to be let off at Wat Tham Sua). Walk to the cave from the main road.

Susaan Hoi literally 'shell cemetery', is 17 km from Krabi, near the village of Laem Pho (not far from Ao Nang Beach). Great slabs of what looks like concrete are littered along the shoreline but which on closer inspection turn out to be countless fossilized freshwater shells, laid-down 75 million years ago. It is one of only three such cemeteries in the world; the others are in the USA and Japan. Time your visit to coincide with low tide when more of the pavement is exposed. Accommodation: *Rock Cottages*, T 612728. Getting there: songthaews from the riverside in Krabi.

Thanboke Khranee Garden is a beautiful, cool and peaceful forest grove with emerald rock pools, streams and walkways. Swimming is permitted in the upper pool. Getting there: take Route 4 back towards Phangnga; turn left down Route 4039 for Ao Luk, after 45 km. 2 km down this road there is a sign for the gardens, to the left. By public transport, take a songthaew from Krabi to Ao Luk, and then walk or catch a local songthaew.

Ao Nang and **Nopparat Thara Beaches** See page 432 for details.

Festivals
Boat races on the river, very noisy.

Tours
Most tour companies operate daily and

overnight tours around Phangnga Bay (see page 428), often incorporating a visit to Wat Tham Suwan Kuha and other local sights. Expect to pay about ฿250 (lunch included). *Phi Phi Marine Travel* offer a 2-3 hr round-trip to the Phi Phi Islands every Sat, Sun and holidays, departing from Chao Fah Pier. Cost: ฿200.

Local information
● Accommodation
Hotels and guesthouses in Krabi are very ordinary. **A-B** *Tongsai Village*, c/o Phi Phi Marine Travel Co Ltd, T 611496, F 612251.

B-D *Vieng Thong*, 155 Uttarakit Rd, T 611288, some a/c; **B-D** *Thai*, 7 Issara Rd, T 611122, some a/c.

C-D *Chao Fah Valley Resort*, 50 Chao Fah Rd, T 612499, some a/c, quiet wood and rattan bungalows in attractive garden, rec.

D *Naowarat*, 403 Uttarakit Rd, T 611581, some a/c; **D** *KR Mansion*, 52/1 Chao Fah Rd, T 612761, F 612545, some a/c, well priced restaurant, clean, bright and airy rooms, friendly staff, though rather pushy with their overpriced tours and tickets.

E *New Hotel*, 9-11 Phattana Rd, T 611541, some a/c.

F *Cha*, Chao Fah Rd, T 611141, restaurant, basic huts set in garden compound, motorbike and jeep hire; **F** *Jungle Tours & Guesthouse*, Uttarakit Rd, restaurant with good basic meals, shared bathroom facilities, tiny, dark rooms but comfy beds and very friendly family owners, tickets and tours sold; **F** *Kanab Naam*, 59 Uttarakit Rd, T 612552, rec; *Thammachart*, 13 Khong Kha Rd, T 612536, rec.

● Places to eat
Thai: *Kotung*, Prachachuan Rd, good seafood; *Rimnan Seafood*, Phattana Rd, rec; *Rean Pare*, Uttarakit Rd (floating restaurant), attractive location but overpriced food; *Thammachart*, 13 Khong Kha Rd, rec. **International**: *Pizza House*, 83 Uttarakit Rd; ✦*Kwun Coffee Corner*, 75 Uttarakit Rd, fresh coffee, sandwiches, milk shakes, ice-creams, cheap Thai food, rec. **Foodstalls**: there is a Night Market around the pier.

● Bars
Toyama, 228 Uttarakit Rd (on the hill).

● Banks & money changers
Several on Uttarakit Rd. Siam bank exchange seems to have the best rates, open daily.

● Immigration office
Next to the Post Office on Uttarakit Rd.

● Shopping
Books: 91 Uttarakit Rd. Book exchange on Khong Kha Rd. Tacky souvenirs from Uttarakit Rd.

● Sports
Gamefishing: *Phi Phi Marine Travel Co* can arrange expeditions to catch marlin, sailfish, barracuda and tuna.

● Post & telecommunications
Post Office: Uttarakit Rd (half way up the hill, not far from the Customs Pier). It has a poste restante counter and international telephone. **Area code**: 075.

● Tour companies & travel agents
Concentrated on Uttarakit and Ruen-Ruedee roads and close to the Chao Fah Pier. Guesthouses often double-up as tour companies and travel agents. *K.P.B.*, 42-44 Prachachuan Rd, T 612788; *Leebi Travel*, 3-7 Issara Rd, T 611150; *Mermaid Tour*, 1/1 Chao Fah Rd, T 611949, opposite pier; *P.P. Family Co*, 35 Prachachuan Rd, T 611717, cheap tickets, rec; *Seaside*, 10 Ruen-Ruedee Rd, T 612351; *Songserm Travel*, Vieng Thong Hotel, 155 Uttarakit Rd, T 611188; *Emerald Tour*, 2/1 Khong Kha Rd, T 612258; *Krabi Sea Tour*,

KRABI TBU 44

0 ___ 400
metres

1. Chao Fah Pier
2. Night Market
3. Food Stalls
4. Chao Fah Valley Resort
5. Thai Hotel
6. Vieng Thong Hotel
7. New Hotel
8. Cha Guesthouse
9. Thammachart Guesthouse
10. KR Mansion
11. Kwun Coffee Corner
B1. Minibus to Ao Nang
B2. Minibus to Talat Kao
B3. Minibus to Nopparat Thara Beach

71/1 Uttarakit Rd, T 611308; *Thammachart Tour*, 13 Khong Kha Rd, T 612536; *Phi Phi Marine Travel*, 201/1-4 Uttarakit Rd, T 611496.

● **Tourist information**

Good maps of Krabi and the surrounding area can be obtained from the stationers opposite the Post Office on Uttarakit Road (∅50).

● **Transport**

85 km from Phangnga, 180 km from Phuket and 867 km from Bangkok.

Local Motorbike hire: many of the guesthouses and tour companies hire-out scooters and motorbikes, ∅300-500/day; for example, *Cha Guesthouse* and *Mermaid Tour*. **Songthaews**: drive through town, stopping at various places such as Phattana Rd, in front of *Travel & Tour*, for Ao Phra Nang; and in front of the foodstalls on Uttarakit Rd for Noppharat Thara Beach.

Air Regular connections with Phuket, and from there take a bus to Krabi.

Train Some people take the train (usually the overnight sleeper) to Phun Phiu (Surat Thani) where the train is met by buses for the 3 hr journey to Krabi. Buses drop travellers at the tourist office in Krabi, where booking for the islands can be made. Alternatively travel to Trang or Nakhon Si Thammarat.

Road Bus: station is 4 km out of town, in Talat Kao, close to the intersection of Uttarakit Rd and Route 4 (take a minibus there from Uttarakit Rd for ∅3). 5 evening a/c connections daily with Bangkok's Southern bus terminal, 16 hrs (∅370), 2 VIP buses leave in the evening (∅440); non-a/c buses leave from the new terminal on Phra Pinklao Rd 16 hrs (∅195). Regular connections with Phuket (leaving Phuket at 1050, 1250 and 1430), 4 hrs (∅35-102), 2 morning buses to Koh Samui, via Surat Thani, 7 hrs (∅100, inclusive of ferry) or 6 hrs by *Songserm Travel* (∅200 inclusive of boat), regular connections with Surat Thani 3 hrs (∅50) and Trang (∅30), a/c minibuses to Hat Yai (∅150). Tickets and information available from travel agents. **Taxi**: to Trang 2 hrs (∅150). **International connections to Malaysia and Singapore** by a/c minibus to Singapore (∅650), Kuala Lumpur (∅440) and Penang (∅385).

Train & Road Combination tickets from Bangkok via Surat Thani (∅625). Travel agents will book tickets.

Sea Boat: every Tues and Thurs at 0830 express boats from Makham Bay, Phuket 3½ hrs (∅400), stopping at Phi Phi, 1½ hrs (∅240) en route. To Phuket, the boat leaves at 1300 on Tues and Thurs.

Ao Nang and Nopparat Thara

The beaches at Ao Nang and Nopparat Thara lie 18 km and 22 km respectively to the W of Krabi town. The road there winds for 15 km past limestone cliffs, a large reclining Buddha and forest. **Ao Nang** provides a range of accommodation and facilities including diving, windsurfing, fishing and tours to the surrounding islands. It is still relatively quiet, with a peaceful atmosphere, sandy, gently shelving beach, calm waters, and beautiful – and dramatic –

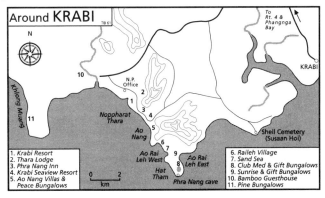

Around **KRABI**

1. Krabi Resort
2. Thara Lodge
3. Phra Nang Inn
4. Krabi Seaview Resort
5. Ao Nang Villas & Peace Bungalows
6. Raileh Village
7. Sand Sea
8. Club Med & Gift Bungalows
9. Sunrise & Gift Bungalows
10. Bamboo Guesthouse
11. Pine Bungalows

limestone scenery. The surrounding beaches, coves, caves and grottoes provide good trekking and boat trip destinations. Note that between May and Oct the monsoon makes swimming risky and many bungalows shut down for the season. Excellent seafood available here.

3 km N of Ao Nang, **Nopparat Thara Beach** is a long sandy beach, popular with Thai picnickers and is part of the Phi Phi Islands National Park. At low tide it is possible to walk out to some of the islands in the bay.

Phra Nang is the peninsular to the S of Ao Nang. There are no roads on Phra Nang, which makes it a beautifully secluded place to stay. The point consists of Rai Leh West and Hat Tham on the W side and Rai Leh East on the E. The beaches here are beautiful clean white sand, with clear blue water. The limestone rock formations are spectacular, and there are interesting caves with stalagmites and stalacmites to explore. At the Southern extremity of the bay is a mountain cave dedicated to the goddess of the area – Phra Nang. There's a walkway from Rai Leh East through to Hat Tham (partly because of the construction of the new Club Med). On the walkway, there is a sign to an inland lagoon, about a tough 15 minute climb (good views from the top).

There is no accommodation or restaurants on Hat Tham. On Rai Leh East and West there are a few bars but no shops. The bungalows sell most essentials. All the bungalows have restaurants serving delicious seafood.

Excursions

Shell cemetery or *Susaan Hoi* lies 5 km E of Ao Nang (see page 429).

Koh Boda is 30 mins by boat from Ao Phra Nang (฿50). It is a haven for snorkellers, with wonderfully clear water. Round-trip excursions last 5 hrs (฿300). There are bungalows available on the island for ฿350, book through the *Krabi Resort* (T 611389 or B 2518094). The

bungalows are a good size, restaurant, 'Western' loos, not particularly friendly staff. Camping on the island (฿50). The nearby **Koh Gai** is also a 30 min boat trip from Ao Phra Nang.

Koh Phi Phi is accessible as a day trip from Ao Nang (see page 433). Arrange a ticket for the boat trip through your guesthouse. The boat departs from Ao Nang at 0830 returning at 1500 (฿250).

Local information
● **Accommodation**

Ao Nang: **A** *Ao Nang Villa*, (Krabi T 612431), a/c, restaurant; **A** *Krabi Resort* (office in Krabi at 53-57 Phattana Rd, T 612160, B 2089165), at N end, a/c, restaurant overlooking the sea, nice pool, some bungalows, rec; **B** *Peace*, T 611944, a/c.

B *Phra Nang Inn*, PO Box 25, T 612173, a/c, restaurant, small pool, good views, unexciting rooms; **B-C** *Krabi Seaview Resort* (office in Krabi at 171-173 Uttarakit Rd, T 611648), a/c, set back from the beach and the road.

C *Ao Nang Thara*, T 7230517, F 3916245, between Ao Nang and Nopparat Thara, good restaurant, own bathroom, wonderful views overlooking both beaches, water garden, clean, friendly management, rec.

D *Phra Nang Place*, Laem Nang, T 512172, F 612251, on private plantation, catch a boat from Ao Nang or Krabi, restaurant, quiet location and well designed; **D** *Starlight*, restaurant, grass huts, primitive bathrooms, Asian loos, mosquito nets, no electricity during the day.

Nopparat Thara: **C-B** The headquarters of the *Nopparat Thara and Phi Phi Islands National Park* has some bungalows and camping facilities.

D *Emerald Bungalow*, catch a boat from Nopparat Thara pier across the estuary, westwards. .

F *Bamboo*, on round the coast from Noppharat Thara over the river, restaurant, shared facilities, very basic, friendly staff, rec, to get there, take a bus from Krabi to the National Park office, the staff from Bamboo will pick you up from here (5 min boat trip over river).

Khlong Muang: **E** *Pine Bungalow*, (Krabi T 612192), basic grass huts with mosquito nets, friendly staff, Asian loos, cold water, boat trips to nearby islands arranged, dirt road all the way there, rec.

Rai Leh West: this is a beautiful beach, but huts have been bunched together tightly here, making for overcrowded conditions and very basic (but not cheap) accommodation. To get there, take a boat from Ao Nang. Boats to Phi Phi stop at Rai Leh West. **B-D** *Sand Sea*, T 611944, range of accommodation, good restaurant, rec.

C-D *Rai Leh Village Bungalows*, T 612728 ext 27, good restaurant on the beach, range of accommodation.

D *Sunrise Bay*, restaurant, own bathrooms; **D** *Rai Leh Bay Bungalows*, T 611789, restaurant, good size bungalows with bathroom.

E *Gift Bungalow*, T 612458, rec; **E-F** *Joy*, N of Rai Leh East.

Rai Leh East: dominated by *Club Med*.

Phra Nang headland: **L+** *Dusit Rayavadee*, 67 Moo 5 Susaan Hoi Rd, T (B) 2380032.

● **Places to eat**
Many of the guesthouses sell good seafood. There is also a strip of restaurants at the N end of Ao Nang, selling excellent (but quite expensive) seafood. Good seafood on Rai Leh West.

● **Banks & money changers**
Exchange booths along Ao Nang beachfront, the exchange rate is bad here – it's best to change money before leaving Krabi.

● **Police station**
Half way along the beach road.

● **Sports**
Watersports, fishing and diving: *Marine Sports Centre*. A dive school at Rai Leh East provides 4 days diving for ฿6500 (T 7220115), friendly staff.

● **Travel agents**
Ao Nang Ban Lae Travel (close to *Krabi Resort*).

● **Transport**
20 km from Krabi.

Local Jeeps: (฿800-1,200/day) and **motorbikes**: (฿250/day) for hire from travel agents or guesthouses.

Road Songthaew: regular connections with Krabi 30 min (฿30). From Phattana Rd, in front of *Travel & Tour*, for Ao Nang; and in front of the foodstalls on Uttarakit Rd for Nopparat Thara Beach (฿20-30).

Sea Boat: to Phra Nang and Ao Rai Leh from Krabi waterfront, near the floating restaurant; departures throughout the day 45 mins. Express boats take 1½ hrs from Pio Nang and Phi Phi (฿150).

Koh Phi Phi

Koh Phi Phi consists of two beautiful islands – **Phi Phi Le** and **Phi Phi Don**. All accommodation is on the larger Phi Phi Don. Shaped like an anvil and fringed by sheer limestone cliffs and golden beaches, it offers good swimming, snorkelling and diving. The western arm has no tourist accommodation on it. Boats dock at the 'neck' – **Ton Sai Bay** – near the village of the same name. Formerly, a quiet Muslim fishing community, it is

---

BIRD'S NEST SOUP

The tiny nests of the brown-rumped swift (*Collocalia esculenta*), also known as the edible-nest swiftlet or sea swallow, are collected for bird's nest soup, a Chinese delicacy, throughout Southeast Asia. The semi-oval nests are made of silk-like strands of saliva secreted by the birds which, when cooked in broth, softens and becomes a little like noodles. Like so many Chinese delicacies, the nests are believed to have aphrodisiac qualities, and the soup has even been suggested as a cure for AIDS. The red nests are the most highly valued, and the Vietnamese Emperor Minh Mang (1820-1840) is said to have owed his extraordinary vitality to his inordinate consumption of bird's nest soup. This may explain why restaurants serving it in Southern Thailand are usually also associated with a plethora of massage parlours. Collecting the nests is a precarious business and is only officially allowed twice a year – between Feb and Apr and in Sept. The collectors climb flimsy bamboo poles into total darkness, with candles strapped to their heads. In Hong Kong a kilo of nests may sell for US$2,000 and nest-concessions in Thailand are vigorously protected.

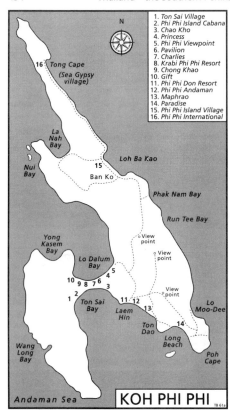

List of locations (map key):

1. Ton Sai Village
2. Phi Phi Island Cabana
3. Chao Kho
4. Princess
5. Phi Phi Viewpoint
6. Pavilion
7. Charlies
8. Krabi Phi Phi Resort
9. Chong Khao
10. Gift
11. Phi Phi Don Resort
12. Phi Phi Andaman
13. Maphrao
14. Paradise
15. Phi Phi Island Village
16. Phi Phi International

KOH PHI PHI

Phi Phi Le is a National Park, entirely girdled by sheer cliffs, where swiftlets nest (see box). It is not possible to stay on Phi Phi Le but it can be visited by boat. Most boat excursions include a visit to the **Viking Cave**, which contains prehistoric paintings of what look like Viking longboats, and the cliffs where birds' nests are harvested for bird's nest soup (see box).

Excursions

Hire a long-tailed boat from the village, or from your resort to take a trip around the island. Boats seat 8 people, half-day trip, ฿500/boat.

It is possible to climb to one of the **viewpoints** on the island by walking E from the village. The ascent takes about 30 mins. A walk to Long Beach along the beach, or on the track, takes about 20 mins.

Phi Phi Le: there are regular trips to see the cliff formations, the Viking Cave, Lo Samah Bay and Maya Bay (about ฿140/person).

Local information
● **Accommodation**

Hotels and bungalows are poor value for money in comparison to other beach resorts in Thailand. Most accommodation is clustered on the central 'neck' of the anvil, close to Ton Sai village, on both the N and S shores. Rooms get very booked up during peak season at Christmas and New Year.

Ton Sai Bay: **A** *Ton Sai Village*, contact *Phi Phi Marine Travel*, 201 Uttarakit Rd, Krabi, T 611496, F 612196, B 2557600, a/c, best hotel on this side of the island, but still overpriced;

now almost entirely geared to the demands of tourists with restaurants, dive schools, tour companies, currency exchanges, laundry services and souvenir shops. Unfortunately, the island is too small to absorb the number of visitors that now flock here; evident in the piles of rubbish and the worrying statistic that 80% of the fresh water wells are contaminated with faeces. The best snorkelling on the island is at **Hat Yao** (Long Beach). **NB**: it is possible to travel to Koh Phi Phi all year round but during the rainy season (Oct-May), the boat trip can be very rough and not for the faint-hearted.

A-B *Phi Phi Island Cabana* (contact *Phi Phi Marine Travel*, 201 Uttarakit Rd, Krabi, T 611496, F 612196, B 2557600), some a/c, small, dark rooms, overpriced.

B-C *Phi Phi Don Resort*, stone bungalows on the beach, newer ones built behind.

D *Chao Kho*, small bungalows.

Lo Dalum Bay: facing N, this beach is clean and relatively quiet. **A** *Phi Phi Princess*, T 612188, F 7230495, a/c, restaurant, satellite TV, individual bungalows, rather close together.

B *Phi Phi Pavilion*, next to *Charlies*, T 611295, F 611578, price includes breakfast; **B** *Phi Phi Viewpoint*, T 722011, built attractively on the side of the hill, big wooden bungalows with good views, rec; **B-C** *Charlies*, T 7230495, restaurant is expensive, overpriced, some with bathroom, cheaper huts packed close together.

D-E *Chong Khao*, noisy location next to the generator; **D-E** *Gift*, noisy location next to the generator.

East from Ton Sai Bay, there are the following beaches: **Laem Hin**: **C-E** *Phi Phi Andaman*, large number of small huts, own bathrooms.

D *Bay View Resort*, restaurant, private bathroom; **D** *Gipsys Village* (behind *Phi Phi Don Resort*), big stone bungalows, quieter and cleaner than most here, rec.

Ton Dao Beach: **D-E** *Maprao*, restaurant, quiet, private beach.

F *Waikiki*, basic huts, private cove before Long Beach.

Long Beach (Hat Yao): good for snorkelling. **C-D** *Paradise*, T 7230484, quiet, best beach on the island, large number of bungalows with own bathrooms, big restaurant, videos, boats to Ton Sai, rec.

On the E coast: Lo Ba Kao Beach: **A** *Phi Phi Island Village*, T 2111907 or B 2770704, set alone to the N of the island, some a/c overpriced.

Laem Tong: **A+-B** *Phi Phi International* T 611741 or B 2500768, to the N of the island, good diving and snorkelling.

● **Places to eat**
There are about 5 good seafood restaurants in the village, all with similar menus. All display (and barbecue) their catch on the street. **✦✦***Mama Resto*, French. Friendly, popular and excellent food, rec; **✦✦***Patcharee Seafood*, rec; **✦✦***Captain's*, good Thai food and Western breakfasts; **✦✦***Pizza House*, Italian. French bakery sells delicious croissants.

● **Bars**
A number of bars are to be found on the track from Ton Sai to the northern shore. Many show latest video releases.

● **Entertainment**
Boxing: 'stadium' occasionally holds fights on national holidays.

Secondhand books: for sale or to rent on track from Ton Sai to the northern shore.

Thai massage: ฿100/hr (many masseurs are untrained).

Videos: at bungalows.

● **Post & telecommunications**
Stamps: can be bought, and letters can be posted in the postboxes in the village. **Area code**: 075.

● **Rescue unit and first aid**
Next to *Phi Phi Andaman*.

● **Sport**
Diving: there are a number of dive schools on the island. *S.S.I. (Scuba School International)*, which offers a five day certificate course, has been recommended, alternatively, book up with one of the many dive centres on Phuket.

Game fishing: can be organized in the village.

Paddle boats: for rent for ฿50/hr from the northern shore.

Snorkelling: Snorkels and fins can be hired from most bungalows or in the village.

Waterskiing: off the north shore.

● **Travel agents**
There are several agents in Ton Sai, all charging similar prices and able to organise all sorts of tickets.

● **Transport**
Phi Phi lies between Krabi and Phuket and can be reached from both.

Sea Boat: connections with the Chao Fah Pier in Krabi at 0900 and 1300, 1½ hrs (฿125-200). Boats to Krabi from Phi Phi leave around 0900 and 1430. Connections with Ao Nang 2 hrs (฿135-150), Koh Lanta 1½-2 hrs (฿180-250) and Koh Tarutao. Connections with Phuket from Patong, Siray and Chalong (*Aloha Tours*, T 381215) 1½-2½ hrs (฿180-250). The '*King Cruiser*', run by Ferryline and Songserm (Rasada Centre, Phuket Town, T 214272) make two trips a day from Makham Bay 1½ hrs (฿80), from Tien Sin (on the *Andaman Queen*, T 215261) at about 0830, 1 hr 20 mins (฿250-350).

Koh Lanta

'Koh Lanta' is actually a group of islands, the three largest of which are Koh Lanta Yai, Koh Lanta Noi and Koh Klang. It is one of the more recent areas to be invaded by tourists. It is about the same size as Koh Samui and so far it has 19 bungalow resorts (about 500 rooms), mostly along the west coast of Koh Lanta Yai and most of which are owned by locals. Over 100,000 tourists visited Koh Lanta last year and this year about 120,000 are expected. Land prices are already high as a result of frenetic speculation, with 1 *rai* (0.4 acre, 0.15 ha) worth ฿1-2 million. But locals are being encouraged not to sell their land to speculators. The people of Lanta are very conscious of the mistakes made on Phi Phi and Phuket and they are striving to maintain the peaceful atmosphere. However, they have asked for a paved road to replace the dirt track which circles the island, apart from the Southern tip where the National Park is. Rubbish collection is to be improved and electricity and phone links will be extended. Koh Lanta has been designated a 'site of natural beauty' and the area is now a National Park. Fishing, rubber and tourism are the main industries.

There is nothing to do on Lanta except lap up the sun, snorkel in the beautiful water surrounding the islands and sample the seafood. **Kaw Kwang (Deer Neck) Beach** is a long crescent of sand on the NW edge of Koh Lanta Yai, with safe swimming and good coral and fish for snorkellers.

Tours

All bungalows offer day trips to Trang's Andaman Islands (see page 440), ฿350/person or ฿600/boat. A ferry leaves Sala Dan at 0830 for the day-trip to Phi Phi, ฿240/person. Fishing trips are organized by *La Creperie*, ฿450/day, ฿1200 for 2 days (which includes camping on a deserted island with food provided).

Local information
● **Accommodation**

All guesthouses are scattered down the west coast of Koh Lanta Yai. All guesthouses offer free pick-up from the pier at Sala Dan, except *Lanta Paradise*, who charge ฿25 each way. **C** *Lanta Charlie Beach Resort*, T 7230876, huge, modern, dirty, electricity, lively resort (disco and bar); **C-E** *Kaw Kwang Beach Bungalow*, restaurant, lovely beach.

D *Deer Neck Cabanas*, T 7230623, friendly management but swampy beach, bungalows rec; **D** *Lanta Paradise*, T 7230530, not such a pleasant beach to the S, all with bathrooms and electricity; **D** *Lanta Villa*, Lo Bara Beach, just to S of *Deer Neck Cabanas*, T 611944, own bathroom, electricity; **D** *Relax Bay Tropicana*, Phra-Ae Beach, restaurant; **D-E** *Golden Bay*, Kaw Kwang Beach, clean, own bathroom, electricity; **D-F** *Kaw Kwang*, Kaw Kwang Beach, safe swimming, own bathroom, convenient location, rec; **D-F** *Lanta Sea House*, shared bathroom.

E *Lanta Palm Beach*, T 7230528, huts rather close together, some electricity, all with bathrooms, tents ฿30; **E** *Seasun*, T 7230497, pretty cove, not such good snorkelling, Muslim owners, electricity, all with bathrooms; **E-F** *Lanta Garden*, Kaw Kwang Beach, most basic on the island, small huts, no facilities.

F *Lanta Marina Huts*, restaurant, lovely beach S of Kaw Kwang, only resort on it, 'A' frames and tents (฿30), electricity in restaurant only, good fish on menu, rec.

● **Places to eat**

All the guesthouses provide restaurants with similar menus; Thai and European food with lots of seafood and fruit. *Lanta Marina Huts*, good fish. In Sala Dan there are some small cafés. Three restaurants overlook the bay between Lanta Yai and Lanta Noi (rather windy): *Seaview 1* (aka 'Monkey in the Back'), slow service, good seafood, no electricity, cheap; *Seaview 2*, larger menu, Thai and seafood, friendly, cheap; *La Creperie*, French food.

● **Bars**
Lanta Charlie.

● **Banks & money changers**
No official exchanges, but most bungalows will change money for you – often at a poor rate of exchange.

● **Entertainment**
Disco: *Lanta Charlie*.

Thai Folk Music: *Lanta Charlie*.

● **Hospitals & medical services**
Hospital: Lanta Pier. **Health Centre**: in Sala Dan.

● **Police**
Sala Dan.

● **Post & telecommunications**
Post Office: Lanta Pier.

● **Sports**
Pool Tables: in Sala Dan, opposite Sea View 1.

Snorkelling: known locally as 'snorking'. Most guesthouses hire out equipment at about ฿30/day, although the quality is varied.

● **Travel agents**
Makaira Tour Centre, 18 Moo 1 Sala Dan.

● **Transport**
Local Pick-up trucks: some ply the island, ฿100 to end of the island, others serve individual bungalows only. **Long-tailed boats**: bungalows rent these for ฿600/day. **Motorbikes**: from bungalows for ฿300/day or ฿50/hr. **Mountain bikes**: from bungalows for ฿130/day.

Sea Boat: Lanta Pier is in Sala Dan. Regular connections with Chao Fah Pier in Krabi, 2-3 boats a day. 2 hrs to Sala Dan, via Koh Jam (฿150). The boat leaves Sala Dan for Krabi at 0730 and 0830. Alternatively, from Krabi – take a taxi from in front of *New Hotel* to Bo Muang Pier, about 80 km away in Amphoe Klong Thom, daily departures, 45 mins (฿50). To Phi Phi, ฿240 return. There are also boat connections with Ban Hua Hin, on S tip of Koh Klang or from Bo Muang, E of Koh Lanta on the coast. Songthaews from Krabi go to Ban Hua Hin (฿25) and Bo Muang (daily at 1100). The boat to Koh Lanta takes 45 mins.

Koh Jam

One bungalow operation on this tiny island **E** *Joy Bungalow*, T 7230502, 30 bungalows; the ultimate in escapism, at least for the present.

● **Transport By boat**: the boat from Krabi to Koh Lanta goes via Koh Jam (see above). There are also connections with Koh Phi Phi and with Laem Kruat, on the mainland.

Koh Bubu

Koh Bubu is a tiny island in the Lanta group E of Koh Lanta Yai. There is one bungalow establishment here, with 13 bungalows (D-E), restaurant and little else except sea and solitude.

● **Transport Road & Sea** Regular vans from Krabi at 1030 to Bo Muang village pier, then by boat to Samsan Pier on E coast of Lanta Yai (฿100), and finally on to Bubu by chartered long-tailed boat (฿150-200), contact *Thammachart*, Khong Kha Rd, Krabi. There is a free ferry service from Lanta Pier to Bubu (one a day).

Trang

Trang is an important port and commercial centre but is a rather nondescript Chinese town. In the years to come Trang will become an increasingly important jumping-off point for people heading to the exotic, coral islands just off the coast.

The town was established as a trading centre in the 1st century A.D., and flourished between the 7th and 12th centuries. Its importance rested on its role as a relay point for communications between the east coast of Thailand and Palembang (Srivijaya) in Sumatra. It was then known as Krung Thani and later as Trangkhapura, the 'City of Waves'. The name was shortened in the 19th century to Trang. During the Ayutthaya Period, the town was located at the mouth of the river and was a popular port of entry for Western visitors continuing north to Ayutthaya. Later, during King Mongkut's reign, the town was moved inland because of frequent flooding.

The arrival of the Teochew (Chinese) community in the latter half of the 19th century was a boon to the local economy which, until the introduction of rubber from Malaysia, was reliant on tin mining. Trang's rubber plantations were the first in Thailand (the first tree was planted just south of the city) and its former ruler, Phraya Rasdanupradit Mahitsara Phakdi, is credited with encouraging the spread of its cultivation. He also built the twisting road from Trang across the Banthat Range to Phat-

TRANG TBU 57

To Nakhon Si Thammarat & buses to Bangkok

To Pattalung & Hat Yai

Not to Scale

Khlong Huay Yang

Utmalaat Rd

Huay Yod Rd

Visetkul Rd

Kao Rd

Rachdamnern Rd

Saingaam Rd

Rachdamnern Rd

Phraram VI Rd

Kantang Rd

Talad Rd

Visetkul Soi 1

Rusda Rd

To Satun

Visetkul Rd

N

1. Taklang & Municipal Market
2. Clock Tower
3. Taxis to Katang, Chao Mai &
   Khao Chong Forest Park
4. Taxis to Krabi
5. Post Office
6. *Thumrin Hotel*
7. *Trang Hotel*
8. *Wattana Hotel*
9. *Koteng Hotel*
10. *Queens Hotel*
11. *Plaza Hotel*

talung. There is a statue of him 1 km out
of town on the Phattalung road. Rubber
small-holdings and plantations are still
the biggest money-earner in the region.

Trang has retained the atmosphere of
a Chinese immigrant community with
some good Chinese restaurants and several Chinese shrines. The **Kwan Tee
Hun shrine**, dedicated to a bearded war
god, is in Ban Bang Rok, 3 km north of
Trang on route 4.

Excursions
Beaches around Trang Trang's embry-
onic tourism industry has so far escaped
the hard sell of Phuket and Pattaya –
excellent news for nature-lovers, reef-di-
vers and explorers. The strip of coast
running south from Pakmeng (38 km
west from Trang) round to Kantang,
boasts some of the South's best beaches.

Best time to visit: Jan-April; out of the
monsoon.

Pakmeng and Chang Lang beaches are
the most accessible – 40 km west of Trang
town. To the north, down the road from
Sikao is **Hua Hin**, which also has a good
beach and is famed for its *hoi tapao* –
sweet-fleshed oysters. Unfortunately the
oyster season climaxes in November –
the peak of the wet season. Hua Hin Bay
is dotted with limestone outcrop islets.
Other beaches to the S include: *Hat San*,
Hat Yong Ling, Hat Yao and *Hat Chao Mai*.
Accommodation: in the fishing village of
Chao Mai (F). There are also impressive
caves near the village, known for their
layered curtain stalactites. The beaches
and many of the offshore islands fall
under the jurisdiction of the 230 sq km
Hat Chao Mai National Park. Accommo-

dation available at park headquarters (6 km outside Chao Mai); 3 guesthouses, accommodating 5 people each, ฿120/head. Further south of Kantang, in Amphoe Palien, is *Hat Samran*. Getting there: taxis to Pakmeng, Chao Mai, Katang and Palien leave from outside Trang's Diamond Department Store, near the railway station.

Khao Chong Forest Park 20 km from town, off the Trang-Phattalung road, supports one of the few remaining areas of tropical forest in the area and has two waterfalls (*Nam Tok Ton Yai* and *Nam Tok Ton Noi*), where government resthouses are available. Getting there: taxis leave from outside the Diamond Department Store, near the railway station (฿100).

Andaman Islands See page 440.

Tours

Trang Travel, for trips to the Andaman Islands. The company runs a boat and offers day-long excursions for a minimum of four, visiting islands and reefs on request, for ฿500-600 (including lunch).

Festivals

Oct: *Vegetarian Festival* (moveable). Nine day-long festival in which a strict vegetarian diet is observed to purify the body. Mediums pierce their cheeks and tongues with spears and walk on hot coals. On the sixth day a procession makes its way around town, in which everyone dresses in traditional costumes. The same event occurs in Phuket.

Local information
● Accommodation
Most of Trang's hotels are on Phraram VI Rd, between the clock tower and the railway station. **B** *Thumrin*, Thumrin Sq, T 211011, F 218057, B 4370136, a/c, restaurant, most upmarket in Trang; **B-C** *Trang*, 134 Visetkul Rd (clocktower intersection), T 218157, some a/c, restaurant, large rooms.

C-D *Wattana*, 127/3-4 Phraram VI Rd, T 218184, some a/c, restaurant.

D *Koteng*, 77-79 Phraram VI Rd, T 218622, some a/c, restaurant, friendly owners;

D *Queen's*, Visetkul Rd, T 218229, some a/c, restaurant; **D-E** *Plaza*, Visetkul Rd Soi 1, T 218720, some a/c.

E *Maitri*, 4-8 Sathani Rd, T 218103, shared bathroom.

● Places to eat
Trang's barbecued pork is delicious, it is made from a traditional recipe and is the speciality of several Chinese restaurants. **Thai**: ✦*Sritrang Bakery*, Phattalung Rd. Deserts are a speciality; ✦*Trokpla Seafood*, Trokpla Soi, Rama VI Rd.

Chinese: ✦*Jan Jan*, Thaklang Rd. Barbecued pork; ✦*Ko Choi*, Wienkapang Rd. Also serves Thai; ✦*Ko Lan*, Huai Yod Rd. Trang-style barbecued pork; ✦*Koyao*, Huai Yod Rd. Vast menu; ✦✦*Thumrin Coffee Shop*, 99 Thumrin Sq, extensive menu.

International: ✦*Hoa*, at the front of Diamond Department Store. Coffee shop and bar. ✦*Queen's Hotel restaurant*, Visetkul Rd, good American breakfast; ✦*Sin Oh Cha*, next to railway station (opposite Diamond Department Store). Coffee shop.

Foodstalls: 2 night markets offer good food, one is on Visetkul Rd, N of clocktower, the other is in the square in front of the railway station.

● Airline offices
Thai, 199 Visetkul Rd (not in the centre of town), T 218066.

● Banks & money changers
Banks are clustered along Phraram VI Rd.

● Post & telecommunications
General Post Office and Telegraph Office: Jermpanya Rd. **Area code**: 075.

● Shopping
Best buys include locally woven cotton and wickerwork.

Markets: Thaklang and Municipal Markets are next door to each other in the centre of town, off Rachdamnern Rd; they are a good place to browse for local goods.

● Sports
Diving: *Rainbow Divers*, 63/6 Soi 2, Visetkul Rd, T 218820, offer courses and trips to a reef.

Snorkelling: equipment for hire from *Trang Travel*, Thumrin Sq.

● Tour companies & travel agents
Trang Travel, Thumrin Sq, T 219598/9, F 218057.

● **Transport**

828 km from Bangkok, 317 km from Phuket, 163 km from Hat Yai.

Local Motorbike hire: at corner of Municipal market on Rachdamnern Rd, ฿200/day.

Air The airport is 7 km from town. Daily connections on Thai with Bangkok 2 hrs 10 mins, and connections with Nakhon Si Thammarat (4/week) 30 mins, Phuket (2/week) 40 mins and Surat Thani (3/week) 30 mins. Bangkok Airways also operate daily connections with Bangkok.

Train The station is at the end of Phraram VI Rd. Overnight connections with Bangkok 15½ hrs (฿282). Regular connections with Kantang (the main port for Trang).

Road Bus: most buses leave from the railway station, but those to Bangkok leave from Huai Yod Rd (1 km from railway station). Buses to Satun leave from Jermpanya Rd. Overnight connections with Bangkok 12 hrs (฿314-445) and regular connections with Satun (฿32), Hat Yai (฿35), Phuket (฿62), Krabi (฿30), Phattalung (฿15) and Nakhon Si Thammarat (฿30). **Taxi**: to Nakhon Si Thammarat and Surat Thani leave from Huai Yod Rd (near junction with Rachdamnern Rd), taxis to Krabi leave from the railway station, taxis to Phattalung and Hat Yai leave from Phattalung Rd (opposite the police station), and to Satun they leave from Jermpanya Rd. Phuket (฿150), Krabi (฿50), Nakhon Si Thammarat (฿60), Hat Yai (฿50), Satun (฿50), Phattalung (฿30).

Trang's Andaman Islands

Trang's Andaman Islands number 47 in total, spread out to the South of Koh Lanta. Few tourists – relatively speaking – visit the islands, although their beauty, rich bird life, and the clear waters that surround them make future development highly likely.

Although **Koh Hai (Ngai)** forms the southernmost part of Krabi province, and is most easily reached from Pakmeng in Trang province, 16 km away, it is also possible to get there from Koh Phi Phi and Koh Lanta. This 5 sq km island is cloaked in jungle and fringed with glorious beaches. A coral reef sweeps down the east side, ending in two big rocks, between which rips a strong current – but the coral around these rocks is magnificent. Koh Hai is used as the jumping-off point for trips to the other islands.

Koh Chuak and **Koh Waen** (between Koh Hai and Koh Mook) are also snorkellers' havens – the latter is the best reef for seafan corals.

On the western side of **Koh Mook** is the **Emerald Cave** or **Tham Morakot** – known locally as Tham Nam – which can only be entered by boat (or fearless swimmers) at low tide, through a narrow opening. After the blackness of the 80m-long passage it opens into daylight again at a circular pool of emerald water ringed with powdery white sand and a backdrop of precipitous cliffs. **Be warned:** you can only leave the pool at low tide. The island's W coast has white beaches backed by high cliffs where swallows nest. There are also beautiful beaches on the east coast facing the craggy mainland, and between the two – or so the local fishermen maintain – lives a colony of mermaids.

Koh Kradan, part of which falls within the bounds of the Chao Mai National Park, is regarded as the most beautiful of Trang's islands, with splendid beaches and fine coral, particularly on the east side. Two Japanese warships sunk during World War II lie off the shore and are popular dive spots. The areas not encompassed by the National Park are a mixture of rubber smallholdings and coconut groves.

Koh Talibong (Libong), which is part of the Petra Islands group to the south, is renowned for its oysters and birdlife. The Juhoi Cape and the eastern third of the island is a major stopping-off point for migratory birds, and in March and April the island is an ornithologists' El Dorado. Typical visitors, on their way back to northern latitudes, include brown-headed gulls, crab plovers, four species of terns, waders, curlews, godwits, redshanks, greenshanks, reef egrets and black-necked storks.

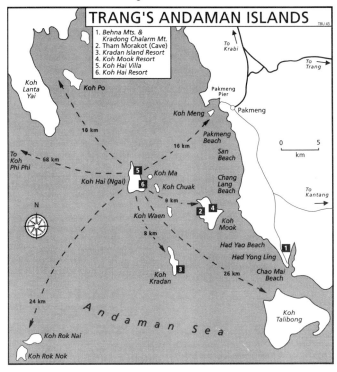

TRANG'S ANDAMAN ISLANDS

TBU 45

1. Behna Mts. &
   Kradong Chalarm Mt.
2. Tham Morakot (Cave)
3. Kradan Island Resort
4. Koh Mook Resort
5. Koh Hai Villa
6. Koh Hai Resort

From October to March the island is famed for its unique Hoi Chakteen oysters. The rare manatee (*Manatus Senegalensis*) and the green turtle also inhabit the waters off the island. The best coral reef is off the south-west coast, directly opposite the *Libong Beach Resort*. Snorkelling equipment is available from the resort who also provide fishing gear. Libong's main town is Ban Hin Kao, where the daily ferry from Kantang docks. Motorcycle taxis take visitors along rough trails to the island's beaches and villages. There is one hotel on the island (see Accommodation) and no nightlife. The population is almost exclusively Muslim, and alcohol is not widely available.

Koh Sukorn (Muu), Koh Petra, Koh Lao Lieng (Nua and **Tai)** are also part of the Petra Islands group, off Palien, 47 km south of Trang and can be reached from there or Kantang. **Koh Sukorn** (locally known as Koh Muu – or Pig Island) is, rather ironically, inhabited by Muslims. Apart from its golden powder-sand beaches, its main claim to fame are the mouth-watering water melons that are grown here (March/April).

Koh Petra and **Koh Lao Lieng** have sheer cliffs which are the domain of the birds nest collectors who risk life and limb for swiftlet saliva (see page 433). The islands have excellent sandy beaches on their east coasts and impressive reefs which are exposed at low tide. Dolphins can often be seen offshore.

Local information

● Accommodation

Koh Hai: *B Koh Hai Resort*, SE corner of the island, with its own magnificent private beach. More upmarket than *Koh Hai Villa*, chalets have fans and private balconies. They can be booked through the Trang office, 205 Sam-Yaek Mohwith, T 210317 or B 3166108, F 3167916.

D *Koh Hai Villa* is half way up the east side of the island, facing the reef, T 218674, 15 grass-roofed chalets equipped with mosquito nets, restaurant, tents also available (฿150). *Trang Travel*, opposite the *Thumrin Hotel* in Trang, must be notified prior to departure.

Koh Mook: **D-E** *Koh Mook Resort*, only accommodation on the island opened for business in 1991, fantastic views, some rooms with attached bath. Can be booked through Trang office, Tipayarat Vitaya School, T 219499.

Koh Kradan: **B-C** *Kradan Island Resort*, only accommodation on the island, restaurant. Rather expensive for the quality of accommodation provided although tents are available for ฿150. Can be booked through Trang office, 25/36 Sathani Rd (next to railway station) T 211391 or B 3920635. They also run a daily boat service to the island (฿240 return).

Koh Talibong (Libong): **C** *Libong Beach Resort*, Ban Lan Khao, large open-fronted restaurant with about 15 basic bungalows set in a coconut grove facing onto a sandy beach, 5 km from the main town Ban Hin Khao, opened in 1993. The Conservation of Wildlife Committee on Libong Island also have a free guesthouse at Laem Juhol on the E coast. The guesthouse must be booked in advance, and food is not available. Letters can be addressed to the secretary at the Libong Regional Department, P.O. Box 5, Kantang, Trang 92110 (T 075-251932).

● Places to eat

Hotels run their own restaurants.

● Best time to visit

Jan-April. The weather is unsuitable for island-hopping from May-Dec and although it is still possible to charter boats out of season, it can be expensive and risky: the water is cloudy and you may be stranded by a squall.

● Transport

Sea Boat: boats leave from Pakmeng, about 25 km W of Trang. Taxis leave from the Diamond Department Store near the railway station in Trang to Pakmeng (฿10). Boats from Pakmeng to Koh Hai 45 mins (฿100 one way, ฿700 day return); to Koh Mook 1 hr (฿100 one way, ฿700 day return); to Koh Kradan 1½ hrs (฿150 one way, ฿900 day return). *Kradan Island Resort* operates a hovercraft which takes a maximum of 5 people (฿600 return).

For Koh Talibong (Libong), it is cheaper and faster to take a taxi the 24 km from Trang to Kantang (฿10). From there a ferry leaves daily at 12.40 for Koh Talibong's 'capital' of Ban Hin Khao. From there motorcycles take visitors the 5 km to the only hotel, the *Libong Beach Resort*. *Trang Travel*, opposite the *Thumrin Hotel* in Trang, also operates a boat which can be chartered to any of the islands. For those with less time on their hands, they offer day excursions (see Tours, Trang).

The islands can be reached from several small ports and fishing villages along the Trang coast, the main ones being Pakmeng and Kantang (24 km from Trang) (both ฿10 taxi ride from Trang), Chao Mai and Palien. It is also possible to charter boats with the Muslim fishermen who live on the islands.

THE EAST COAST: CHUMPHON TO PHATTALUNG

Just west of Chumphon the road south divides; Route 4 runs down the west coast of the peninsula, while Route 41 skirts inland down the east coast. Surat Thani, over 200 km south of Chumphon, is the departure point for Koh Samui and other islands in the Gulf of Thailand. About 50 km north of Surat Thani is the important historic town of Chaiya. Taking Route 41 south, is Nakhon Si Thammarat (180 km) another historic town associated with the Sumatran-based Srivijayan Empire. From here Route 403 traverses the peninsula to Trang, while Route 41 links up with Phattalung, nearly 900 km south of Bangkok.

Surat Thani

Surat Thani or 'City of the Good People' is a provincial capital and the jumping-off point for Koh Samui. During the

1970s, the Communist Party of Thailand was active in the area, the guerrillas being disillusioned ethnic Tais, not Malays as further south. Although the town has an interesting river front worth a visit, its main purpose serves as a transportation hub; either to Koh Samui, Koh Phangan or Koh Tao, or south to Krabi. **Suan Sattarana Park** lies S of town, on the river. Boats can be hired for trips on the river (฿200 for up to 6 people). The better journey is upstream. There is a big **Chinese temple** and an attractive old viharn in the compound of **Wat Sai**, both on Thi Lek Road, near the *Seree Hotel*. The town brightens up considerably during the *Chak Phra Festival* in September or October (see below).

Excursions

Chaiya lies 594 km S of Bangkok and 50 km N of Surat Thani on Route 41. The city was an important outpost of the Sumatran-based Srivijayan Empire and dates from the late 7th century – making it one of the most ancient settlements in Thailand. Given the quantity of antiquities found in the area, some scholars have suggested that Chaiya may have been the capital of Srivijaya, rather than Palembang (Sumatra) as usually thought. Recent excavations in Sumatra however, seem to have confirmed Palembang as the capital. The Mahayana Buddhist empire of Srivijaya dominated Sumatra, the Malay Peninsula, and parts of Thailand and Java between the 7th and 13th centuries. It had cultural and commercial links with Dvaravati, Cambodia, north and south India and particularly Java. The syncretic art of this civilization clearly reveals these links. Many of the artefacts found in the area are now exhibited in the National Museum in Bangkok.

2 km outside Chaiya, 1 km from the Chaiya railway station, stands **Wat Phra Boromthat Chaiya**, one of the most revered temples in Thailand. Within the wat compound, the central chedi is strongly reminiscent of the 8th century candis of Central Java, square in plan with four porches and rising in tiers topped with miniature chedis. The chedi is constructed of brick and vege-

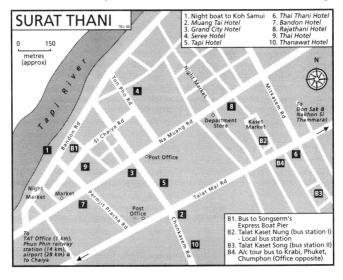

SURAT THANI TBU 46

0   150
metres (approx)

1. Night boat to Koh Samui
2. Muang Tai Hotel
3. Grand City Hotel
4. Seree Hotel
5. Tapi Hotel
6. Thai Thani Hotel
7. Bandon Hotel
8. Rajathani Hotel
9. Thai Hotel
10. Thanawat Hotel

Tapi River
Ton Pho Rd
Si Chaiya Rd
Bandon Rd
Night Market
Na Muang Rd
Mitkasem Rd
Post Office
Permjit Pracha Rd
Chonkasem Rd
Talat Mai Rd
Post Office
Night Market
Market
Department Store
Kaset Market

To Don Sak & Nakhon Si Thammarat

To TAT Office (1 km), Phun Phin railway station (14 km), airport (28 km) & to Chaiya

B1. Bus to Songserm's Express Boat Pier
B2. Talat Kaset Nung (bus station I) - Local bus station
B3. Talat Kaset Song (bus station II)
B4. A/c tour bus to Krabi, Phuket, Chumphon (Office opposite)

table mortar and is thought to be 1200 years old. Even though it was extensively restored in 1901 and again in 1930, its Srivijayan origins are still evident. A small museum nearby exhibits relics found in the vicinity which have not been 'acquired' by the National Museum in Bangkok. Another architectural link with Srivijaya can be seen at **Wat Kaeo**, which contains a recently restored sanctuary reminiscent of Cham structures of the 9th century (Hoa-lai type, south Vietnam), but again with Javanese overtones (with particular links to Candi Kalasan on the Prambanan Plain). Just outside Chaiya is the village of Poomriang, where visitors can watch silk being woven. Accommodation: E *Udornlarb*, large clean rooms. Getting there: trains from Surat Thani's Phun Phin station northwards stop at Chaiya (40 mins). Regular buses from Surat Thani to Chaiya from Talat Kaset Nung (1). Regular songthaews ('taxis') from close to Talat Kaset Song (2) (฿30).

Wat Suan Mok lies 50 km N of Surat Thani on Route 41 and is a popular forest wat (*wat pa*) which has become an international Buddhist retreat. The abbot is the nationally renowned Ajarn Poh who is assisted by a number of foreigners. Ten day *anapanasati* meditation courses are held here beginning on the first day of each month; pick up a leaflet from Surat Thani's TAT office or telephone Khun Supit on B 4682857. Enrolment onto the course takes place on the last day of the month, on a first-come first-served basis and the full course costs ฿600 including tasty rice and vegetable meals. Getting there: by bus from Talat Kaset Nung (1); the road passes the wat (1 hr).

Monkey training centre is S of Surat Thani on Route 401, towards Nakhon Si Thammarat, 2 km off the main road. The only monkey capable of being trained to pick coconuts is the pig-tailed macaque (or *ling kung* in Thai). The male is usually trained, as the female is smaller and not so

strong; strength is needed to break off the stem of the coconut. The training can start when the animals are 8 months old. The course lasts 3-5 months, and when fully trained, the monkeys can pick as many as 800 coconuts in a day and will work for 12-15 years. Getting there: take a songthaew or bus from Surat Thani heading towards Nakhon Si Thammarat, on Talat Mai Road, which becomes Route 401. The turning to the centre is on the right-hand side, just over the Thathong Bridge, past a wat and school. The centre is 2 km down this road. **NB**: there were rumours that the centre was due to close down; check at the TAT office before leaving.

Festivals

Aug: *Rambutan Fair* (moveable). **Oct-Nov**: *Chak Phra Festival* (moveable) marks the end of the 3 month Buddhist Rains Retreat and the return to earth of the Buddha. Processions of Buddha images and boat races on the Tapi River, in long boats manned by up to 50 oarsmen. Gifts are offered to monks as this is also *kathin*, celebrated across Buddhist Thailand.

Local information
● **Accommodation**

Surat Thani must surely have the most confusing hotel names in all of Thailand: **B** *Wang Tai*, 1 Talat Mai Rd, T 283020, F 281007, B 2537947, a/c, restaurant, pool, top hotel in town (SW of town centre).

C *Siam Thani*, 180 Surat-Phun Phin Rd, T 273081, F 282169, a/c, restaurant, pool, tennis; **C** *Siam Thara*, 1/144 Donnok Rd, T 273740, F 282169, a/c, restaurant; **C-D** *Lamphoo Bungalow*, Tapi River Island, T 272495, some a/c, restaurant, for a change of scene, this accommodation is a little more unusual; **C-D** *Muang Tai*, 390-392 Talat Mai Rd, T 272559, some a/c; **C-D** *Tapi*, 100 Chonkasem Rd, T 272575, some a/c; **C-D** *Thairungruang*, T 273249, F 286353, some a/c, characterless but clean and functional.

D *Rajathani*, 293/96-99 Talat Kaset, T 272972; **D** *Seree*, 2/2-5 Ton Pho Rd, T 272279, some a/c, clean; **D** *Thai*, 24/4-6 Si Chaiya Rd, average rooms, Thai toilet; **D** *Thanawat*, 261/19 Chonkasem Rd, T 272473; **D-E** *Thai Thani*, 442/306-8 Talat Mai Rd, T 273521.

E *Bandon*, Na Muang Rd, clean small rooms, Thai toilet, cheaper and better than *Surat*; **E** *Grand City*, 428/6-10 Na Muang Rd, T 272560, some a/c, rather small, scruffy rooms, friendly; **E** *Surat*, 496 Na Muang Rd, T 272505.

● **Places to eat**
♦*J Home*, near corner of Chonkasem and Na Muang rds, a/c café, English menus; ♦*Malisas*, in the Night Market, for coffee, beer, icecream; ♦♦*Suan Isaan*, near Donnok Rd, in a small soi, large traditional Thai house, Northeastern Thai food, menu in Thai but excellent food, rec; ♦♦*Kampan*, Pakdee Rd, Thai.

Foodstalls: on Ton Pho Rd (delicious mussel omelettes near to intersection with Na Muang Rd). Plentiful supply of fruit and kanom stalls along the waterfront. Market next to the local bus terminal (Talat Kaset 1). Good **Night Market** on Na Muang Rd and road down to Si Chaiya Rd from Na Muang Rd. **Breakfast**: Good European breakfast in little café opposite the pier.

● **Airline offices**
Thai, 3/27-28 Karunrat Rd, T 273710.

● **Banks & money changers**
Several currency exchanges on Na Muang and Chonkasem rds. An exchange van operates from 0630-1800 across the street from the Koh Samui/Koh Phangan boat pier.

● **Hospitals & medical services**
Bandon Hospital, Na Muang Rd.

● **Post & telecommunications**
Main Post Office: near corner of Talat Mai and Chonkasem rds. **Branch Post Office**: on corner of Na Muang and Chonkasem rds (check letters are franked in your presence). **Telephone service**: for overseas calls on Don Nok Rd. **Area code**: 077.

● **Shopping**
Department Stores: *Jula Department Store*, Vithi That Rd. *Sahathai Department Store*, Na Muang Rd.

Jewellery: at shops near corner of Chonkasem and Na Muang rds.

● **Sports**
Massage: available at the *Seree Hotel* (β80/hr).

Swimming: non-residents can use the pools at the *Wang Tai* or the *Siam Thani Hotel*.

● **Tour companies & travel agents**
Phantip, 442/24-25 Talat Mai Rd, T 272230, opposite *Thai Thani Hotel*. *Songserm Travel Centre Co Ltd*, opposite night boat pier, T 285124; *Samui Tour*, 326/12 Talat Mai Rd, T 282352; *Samui Ferry Co*, T 423026. *Ferry Phangan Co*, 10 Chonkasem Rd, T 286461. Other agents organizing bus transport are to be found on Bandon, Chonkasem and Na Muang rds.

● **Tourist office**
TAT, 5 Talat Mai Rd, T 288818, F 282828, near *Wang Tai Hotel*, SW of town centre. Open: 0830-1630 Mon-Sun. Good source of information for less frequented sights in the province. Areas of responsibility are Surat Thani, Chumphon and Ranong.

● **Tourist Police**
Na Muang Rd, T 272095.

Transpor
644 km S of Bangkok.

Local Songthaews: known as 'taxis'. Suzuki vans, bus. **Motorbike hire**: shop next to *Samui Tours* on Talat Mai Rd (β350-750/day).

Air The airport is 27 km S of town on Phetkasem Rd, T 200605. Regular twice daily connections with Bangkok 1 hr (β1710), Trang (3/week) 30 mins (β495), Nakhon Si Thammarat (3/week) 30 mins (β340), Phuket (daily) 30 mins (β475).

Train The station is at Phun Phin, 14 km W of Surat Thani (T 311213) local buses go into town stopping at the Talat Kaset Nung (1) terminal (β6). Regular connections with Hualamphong station, Bangkok 11-13 hrs (β127-524). The 1830 train is the most convenient for catching a ferry to Koh Samui. Trains out of Phun Phin are often full: advance booking can be made at *Phantip* travel agency on Talat Mai Rd. *Songserm Travel Service*, Koh Samui also arrange reservations. Regular connections with Hua Hin, Trang, Yala, Hat Yai and Sungei Golok. Buses meet the train for the transfer to the various ferry terminals for Koh Samui, Phangan and Tao (see page 449). An international express leaves for Butterworth at 0155 (11 hrs) from where it continues on to Kuala Lumpur and Singapore.

Road Bus: the two stations in Surat Thani are within easy walking distance of one another – Talat Kaset Nung (1) is for local buses (e.g. Krabi) and Talat Kaset Song (2) for longer distance journeys. Regular a/c connections with Southern bus terminal in Thonburi (Bangkok), 11 hrs (฿222-440); non-a/c connections with the new terminal on Phra Pinklao Rd 11 hrs (฿150). Also buses to Narathiwat 6 hrs (฿127), Trang 3 hrs (฿50), Phuket 6 hrs (฿77-139), Nakhon Si Thammarat 2½ hrs (฿30-40), Krabi 3½ hrs (฿50-80) and Hat Yai 5 hrs (฿85-120) and on to Kuala Lumpur and Singapore. Note that the border at Sungei Golok closes at 1700; not all buses (and despite protestations to the contrary) make it there before then so be prepared to spend a night in Sungei Golok. **Private tour companies** run bus services to/from Bangkok 10 hrs (฿285-440) and Krabi 3-4 hrs (฿80) (see travel agents for listing). The advantage of taking a tour bus from here to Krabi is that they go all the way into Krabi town, to the Chao Fah Pier, rather than stopping at the bus station, out of town. Tour buses to Bangkok go from opposite the Phangan Ferry Office on Chonkasem Rd. **Taxi**: terminal next to bus termi-nal. Taxis to Trang 3 hrs (฿110), Nakhon 2 hrs (฿60), Krabi 2 hrs (฿150), Hat Yai 3½ hrs (฿150), Phuket 4 hrs (฿150), Phangnga 4 hrs (฿150).

Sea Hovercraft: a service leaves from Tha Thong Pier, 5 km from Surat Thani at 0730 and 1030, 1½ hrs (฿350), it docks at Na Thon Pier, Koh Samui.

KOH SAMUI

Koh Samui is the third largest of Thailand's islands, after Phuket and Koh Chang. Over the last decade tourism has exploded and now that it is accessible by air, the island is making the transition from a backpackers haven to a sophisticated beach resort. Unlike Phuket, it does still cater for the budget traveller, with a great variety of bungalows scat-

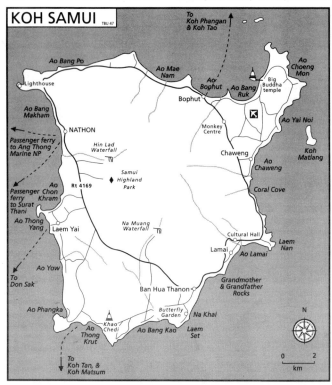

tered around its shores.

Koh Samui is the largest in an archipelago of 80 islands, 6 of which are inhabited. It is 25 km long and 21 km wide. About 35,000 people live here, many of whom are fishermen-turned hoteliers. The number of annual visitors is many times this figure. Apart from tourism, the mainstay of the economy is coconuts; 2 million are exported to Bangkok each month. Monkeys are taught to scale the trees and pluck down the ripe nuts; even this traditional industry has cashed-in on tourism – visitors can watch the monkeys at work and also visit the coconut fibre factory, about 5 km from the Hin Lad waterfall. (A monkey training centre has been established outside Surat Thani, see page 444.)

The island's main attractions are its wonderful beaches; most people head straight there, where they remain until they leave. However, if boredom sets in, there are motorbikes or jeeps for hire to explore inland. Two-thirds of the island is forested and hilly with some impressive (in the wet season) waterfalls – **Hin Lad waterfall** and wat are 3 km S of Nathon and can be reached from the town on foot, or by road 1 km off Route 4169. **Na Muang waterfall**, in the centre of the island has a 30m drop (and a good pool for swimming). Songthaews leave for the waterfall from Nathon. The sign to **Samui Highland Park** is just before the 3 km marker, S of Nathon. From here, it is a 2 hour climb to the highest ridge, through rubber plantations (the route can be confusing, so ask directions). There are good views of the S and W coasts from the top. The **Temple of the Big Buddha** sits on an island linked to the mainland by a short causeway, near Bophut Beach. This unremarkable, rather featureless modern seated image is 12m high. There is a **Monkey Centre** just S of Bophut, which holds several monkey and elephant shows daily. There is a **Cultural Hall** and small museum near Ban Lamai and a group of phallic rock formations, known as **Grandfather and Grandmother Rocks** (or, less obtusely, the **Genital Rocks**) at the S end of Lamai Beach. The **Samui Butterfly Garden** is near Laem Set. It features a large screened garden, a bee farm, a hillside observatory, observation platforms for views of the coast, an insect museum, a glass-bottomed boat for viewing a coral reef and a restaurant. Admission: ฿50 (adult), ฿20 (child). Open: 0830-1800.

BEST TIME TO VISIT between Feb and Jul when the sea is calm. May to Oct can be wet, while Oct to Jan is often windy.

The following sections have been organized by beach, beginning at Nathon (the largest town) and working clockwise around the island.

Local information
● Accommodation

In 1992, there were over 300 registered bungalows and hotels providing over 6,000 rooms (with yet more under construction); the choice is overwhelming. For nightlife, the 2 most popular beaches are still Lamai and Chaweng, both on the E side of the island. They also have the longest stretches of uninterrupted beach, with good swimming and watersports. Mae Nam and Bophut, on the N shore, are also becoming popular, with good watersports. For a quieter scene, there are some remote bungalows down the W shore, although it is best to hire a vehicle, as many of them are off the main road. Some of these bungalows have their own generators, so electricity may only be available in the evenings. The advantage of staying on this side of the island is to see the spectacular sunsets. The list of places to stay is not comprehensive; bungalows survive on reputation and it is often best to stay somewhere which has been personally recommended.

NB: accommodation prices tend to soar during the peak months. Bargain during the off-season; a reduction of up to 50% is possible.

● Post & telecommunications

Telephone calls are much cheaper if made at the Post Office. High street 'booths' are 3-4 times more expensive.

● **Transport**

84 km NE of Surat Thani. The easiest way to get to Koh Samui is by air. The overland journey can be rather arduous, with an overnight bus (or train) to Surat Thani, another bus to the ferry and then the crossing to the island, but is considerably cheaper. It is possible to buy 'combination' bus/ferry tickets from any travel agent in Khaosan Rd (Bangkok), prices vary so it's worth shopping around, they should cost about ฿260.

Air The airport is in the north-east of the island. *Airport facilities*: hotel reservation, re-confirmation of flights, restaurant. *Transport to town or beach*: a/c minibus costs ฿60, private car costs ฿250. Regular connections with Bangkok on **Bangkok Airways**, 1 hr 10 mins (฿2080, plus ฿100 airport tax). **Bangkok Airways** also fly to Phuket twice a day, 50 mins (฿1210), T 2534014 (Bangkok) and T 272610 (Koh Samui) for reservations. **Thai** flies to Surat Thani, 1 hr (฿1710, plus ฿20 airport tax) with a connecting limousine/boat service for ฿150.

Train From Bangkok's Hualamphong station to Phun Phin, outside Surat Thani, 10-12 hrs (฿107-470). The State Railway runs a rail/bus/ferry service from Bangkok to Koh Samui 16 hrs (฿182-549). Note that it is not necessary to buy a combination ticket; buses from all the ferry companies meet trains to transfer passengers to the various ferry terminals.

Road Bus: to Surat Thani, from Bangkok's Southern bus terminal, a/c buses leave between 2000 and 2200, 12 hrs (฿222-350). See page 445 for further details.

Sea Boat: the listings below may seem confusing, but because of the number of tourists visiting Koh Samui, the transport system is well organized and it is difficult to go wrong. The options are:

1. *Songserm Travel* run 3 **express boats** daily during the peak season (Nov-May), leaving Surat Thani 0730, 1200 and 1400, and leaving Koh Samui at 0730, 1230 and 1500, 2 hrs (฿145). These boats usually dock at Tha Thong Pier, 6 km E of Surat Thani and at Nathon Pier, on Koh Samui. To reach Tha Thong Pier, take a bus from Ban Don Rd, on the riverfront in Surat Thani. On leaving Koh Samui, a/c buses meet the 0730 express boat for transfers to Phuket (฿150), Krabi (฿150), Hat Yai (฿150) and Penang (฿380). T 2529654 (Bangkok) for more information.

2. **The Island Jet** leaves daily at 0830 from a pier about 4 km from Ban Don at Paknam Tapee, 1¹⁄₂ hrs (฿175). Tickets can be purchased from the Ferry Phangan office on the corner of Bandon and Chonkasem rds in Surat Thani, T 421221 (Koh Samui), T 286461 (Surat Thani), T 2544215 (Bangkok) for reservations.

3. **The slow overnight boat** leaves from the pier in Surat Thani (otherwise known as Ban Don) at 2300, 6-7 hrs (฿50-80) and docks at the pier in Nathon.

4. **The vehicle and passenger ferry** leaves from Don Sak, 60 km from Surat. Travellers arriving by train at Phun Phin will be transferred to Don Sak. Buses from Surat Thani to Don Sak leave 1¹⁄₂ hrs before ferry departs either from *Samui Tour*, Talat Mai Rd or from *Phuntip Tour*, Talat Kaset I. The ferry docks at Tong Yang, S of Nathon. 5 ferries leave Samui and Surat Thani daily, 1¹⁄₂ hrs (฿40/person). T 282352 in Surat Thani for more information. Songthaews run from Tong Yang to Nathon and the beaches (฿15-20).

Nathon

Nathon is Koh Samui's capital, where the ferry docks. It is a town geared to tourists, with travel agents, exchange booths, clothes stalls, bars, and restaurants supplying travellers' food. Nathon consists of 3 roads running parallel to the seafront, with 2 main roads at either end linking them together.

Tours

Day trips to **Ang Thong National Marine Park** for snorkelling, fishing and diving leave Nathon at 0830 and return at 1700 (฿300). There are also day tours around the island (฿380, including lunch). Book with *Samui Holiday Tour*, 112/2 Chonvithi Rd, T 421043 or at *Highway Travel Booking*, 11/11 Taweraj Pakdi Rd, T 421285 (opposite the pier). *Songserm* organize day tours to Koh Phangan, 2 to 3 boats each day, 30 mins (฿60).

Excursions

Ang Thong (or 'Golden Basin') **Marine National Park** is made up of 40 islands lying NW of Koh Samui, featuring limestone massifs, tropical rainforests and beaches. Particular features are **Mae Koh** (a beautiful beach) and **Thale Nai** (an emerald saltwater lake), both on **Koh Mae Koh and Koh Sam Sao**, which has a coral reef and a huge rock arch as well as a hill providing good views of the surrounding islands. The area is the major spawning ground of the short-bodied mackerel, a popular eating fish in Thailand. Good snorkelling, swimming and walking. The park's headquarters are on Koh Wua Talap. Best time to visit: Feb to May. Accommodation: available on Koh Wua Talap (T 286025 or B 5790529), 5 guesthouses sleep 10-20 people each, ฿600-1,000/guesthouse, tents available for rent (฿50). Getting there: daily tour from Nathon pier, leaving at about 0800 (฿240). It is possible to leave the tour, stay on Koh Wua Talap and rejoin it several days later at no extra charge (make sure you tell the ferry driver which day you want to be picked up). The boat returns to Nathon at about 1700.

Koh Phangan Passenger boats travel from Big Buddha, at the N of the island, to Koh Phangan, leaving at about 0930, 40 mins (see page 456).

Local information
● Accommodation
Few people stay in Nathon, for obvious reasons. **C-D** *Seaside Palace*, seafront road, T 421079, F 421080, a/c, clean, adequate and well maintained rooms, hot water.

● Places to eat
Thai: **♦♦**good noodle and rice restaurant almost opposite the pier.

International: *Bird in the Hand*, N end of town, on E/W road; *El Pirata*, near *Bird in the Hand*, Spanish; **♦♦***Fountain*, Anthgong Rd, Italian proprietor (and food), rec; *Golden Lion*, opposite *El Pirata*, European/seafood; **♦***New York Deli and Grill*, nr market at southern end of main rd, pizza, seafood, pasta, breakfast, rather dirty; **♦***R.T. Bakery*, corner of main rd and Watana Rd, excellent breakfasts, rolls and croissant; **♦♦***Sunset House*, S end of town overlooking the sea. Good Thai and International food; **♦♦***Tang*, near market at S end of main rd, pizza, pasta, sandwiches.

● Bars
Eden, main rd. Open 1600-0300. There are a number of other bars near the *Bird in the Hand* restaurant, at N end of town.

● Airline offices
Bangkok Airways, southern end of seafront road, T 421489.

● Banks & money changers
Exchange booths along the seafront and main roads. Open: 0830-1700 or 1800 Mon-Sun.

● Entertainment
Tattoo artist: on S E/W road.

Thai Boxing: at N end of town.

Thai traditional massage: at N end of seafront road.

● Hospitals & medical services
Hospital: 3 km S of town, 1 km off Route 4169. **Clinic & dentist**: on main road in town.

● Post & telecommunications
Post Office: to the north of the pier, international telephone and poste restante service. **Area code**: 077.

● Shopping
The main road has a number of beachware clothing, jewellery and tape shops, second-hand bookshops and supermarkets. The covered market at the N end sells the usual stall goods.

Gifts: *Blue Samui*, S end of Angthong Rd.

Handicrafts: *Outlook*, main E/W road to the S of town.

Shoemaker: on the main E/W road to the S of town.

Silk and jewellery shop: on the seafront road.

Supermarket: *Giant*, sells English, German and French newspapers as well as good range of European food.

T-shirt shop: next to *Blue Samui* on Angthong Rd, for the best designs in town, if not on the island.

● Sports
Scuba diving: there are a number of different dive schools on the island. *Swiss Dive Centre* (41 Na-Amphur Rd), *Matlang Divers* (67 Watana Rd), *Koh Samui Divers* (64 Nathon Pier) and *Pro Divers* all have shops in town, as well as having small offices on the various beaches. Most of the schools have English-speaking instructors. A 5 day PADI course should cost about ฿7,000-8,000. A one-day trip for those with certification, including 2 dives and food, costs about ฿1200-1800, depending on the dive destination. A trip to one of the islands, 2 nights/3 days, for about

6 dives, will cost around ฿4,000. The best time for diving is April and the best water is to be found around Koh Tao, Tan, Matsum and the Marine Park. Visibility is obviously variable, depending on the weather. Most of the schools also organize advanced open-water courses, rescue and first aid.

● **Tour companies & travel agents**

There are many travel agents cluttered along the seafront (particularly around the pier) and main roads, providing air/train/bus bookings and reconfirmation of flights. For example, *Songserm*, 64/1-2 Nathon Pier, Chonvithi Rd, T 421228 seems efficient; they organize joint train and express boat tickets from Bangkok, via Surat Thani and on to Koh Phangan.

● **Tourist police**

3 km S of town T 421245, just past turning to Hin Lad waterfall.

● **Useful addresses**

Catholic church services: 0830 and 1830. **Immigration office**: on main road next to the police station. A 2-month tourist visa can be extended here by 30 days for ฿550.

● **Transport**

Local Motorbike and jeep hire: cheaper from the town than on the beaches. Jeep hire is ฿600-900/day without insurance. **Songthaews**: the most common form of transport, songthaews visit all the island's beaches during daylight hours. Their final destination is usually written on the front of the vehicle and they stop anywhere (to Lamai, ฿20 and to Chaweng ฿25). **Motorbike taxis**: available from the port. **Hitching**: is quite easy.

Bang Po

C-D *Sunbeam*, only bungalow here, quiet location, clean, friendly, private beach, some private bathrooms, rec.

Mae Nam

A quiet, clean beach, good for swimming and a good atmosphere.

Local information
● **Accommodation**

L *Santiburi*, 12/12 Moo 1 Tambon Maenam, T 425031, F 425040, (BT 2360450, BF 2366400), (part of the Dusit group of hotels), a/c, restaurant, pool, superb new resort of beautifully furnished Thai-style villas and suites, watersports, tennis and squash courts.

A+ *Seafan*, T 421350, F 421350, B 2553542, a/c, pool, restaurant, overpriced but lovely wooden bungalows on stilts, whirlpool, attractive gardens, watersports facilities.

A *Chaiya Rai*, T 425290, F 425290, a/c, restaurant, pool, price includes breakfast, excellent service, large, clean and well maintained bungalows, rec.

D *Co-Co Palm*, quiet, nice garden, rec; **D** *Mae Nam Resort*; **D** *Naplarn*, off beach, big, clean rooms, own bathroom, rec; **D** *Rainbow*, bungalows close together, some private bathrooms; **D-E** *Home Bay*, quiet, rather scruffy, some private bathrooms; **D-E** *Tokoh*, average rooms, nice beach.

E *O.K. Village*, off the beach, restaurant, own bathroom, rec; **E** *Shady Shacks*, restaurant, recently refurbished, clean, some private bathrooms, friendly, good value.

● **Transport**

Local Motorbike hire: on the beach.

Bophut

Bophut beach is growing in popularity and now has currency exchanges, bookshops, restaurants and good watersports facilities. A daily passenger boat leaves here for Koh Phangan (Hat Rin), at 1030 and 1530, 50 mins (฿50), see page 456. For those in need of some night life, there is a nightly taxi service from the various hotels into Chaweng and Lamai, leaving Bophut at 2000 and returning 0300-0400 (฿50).

Excursions

Bophut Guesthouse offers fishing, snorkelling and sightseeing charters.

Local information
● **Accommodation**

L *Euphoria*, T 286948, F 286949, B 2557901, a/c, restaurant, pool, large new hotel with 3-storey accommodation, tennis courts, putting green, watersports.

A *Samui Palm Beach*, T 421358, B 2542905, a/c, restaurant, pool, attractive bungalows facing the sea, some cheaper accommodation with no sea view; **A-C** *Sandy Resort*, T 421353, F 421354, B 3146690, some a/c, 2 storey apartment block and some bungalows, hot water; **A-C** *Smile*, T 421361, some a/c, pool, small bungalows, nice beach, no hot water; **A-D** *Ziggy Stardust*, hot water, fan, restaurant (expensive), best place on Bophut, attractively laid out, traditional Thai bungalows, friendly staff (German spoken), snorkelling can be arranged, rec.

B-D *New Boon*, T 421362, some a/c, new but already scruffy, no hot water; **B-D** *World*, T 421356, F 421355, B 5876564, some a/c, hot water, restaurant, pool.

D-E *Boon*, tiny huts, calm, popular (watersports available); **D-E** *Peace*, T 421357, restaurant, numerous bungalows, windsurfing facilities; **D-F** *Calm Beach Resort*, run down but quiet, no mosquito nets for cheapest bungalows.

E-F *Oasis*, near pier for boats to Hat Rin (Koh Phangan), rooms in private house.

● **Places to eat**
Magic, good food, friendly, rec.

● **Sports**
Go Kart Track: Open 1000-1800.

Fishing: organized by *Bophut Guesthouse*.

Snorkelling: organized by *Bophut Guesthouse*.

Watersports facilities: include windsurfing and waterskiing (฿150), sailing (฿300) and jetskis (฿350-800).

Big Buddha or Bang Ruk

A small bay which has become increasingly popular, despite being near the road. Accommodation is rather cramped, as the bungalows are squashed between the beach and the road. However, the beach is quiet and palm-fringed and the water is good in summer, but gets choppy in winter when it is unsuitable for swimming.

Local information
● **Accommodation**
A-B *Farn Bay Resort*, T 273920, F 286276, some a/c, restaurant, pool, videos, overpriced, breakfast included, hot water; *L.A. Resort*, some a/c; **A-B** *Nara Lodge*, T 421364, B 2482094, a/c, restaurant, pool, tennis court, videos, some hot water, motel-style accommodation, US manager, popular with families.

D *Big Buddha Bungalows*, restaurant, large, comfortable rooms, good value; **D** *Champ Bungalows*, some a/c, friendly, diving school.

E *Sunset Song*, T 421363, average rooms,

private bathroom.

● **Places to eat**
Crowded House, good food, pool table, video and bar.

● **Sports**
Diving: *Swiss Dive Resort*.

Sailing, fishing and snorkelling: organized by *Asian Yacht Charter*.

Choeng Mon

At the north-easternmost part of the island, this attractive bay has a good beach for swimming, especially for children. A number of large hotels have recently been built here.

Local information
● **Accommodation**
A+ *Imperial Tongsai*, T 425015, F 425462, B 2619000, a/c, restaurant, pool, large hotel built on hillside overlooking its own private bay, hotel and cottage accommodation, watersports, tennis courts; **A+** *Boat House* (Imperial Group), T 425041, F 425460, B 2619000, a/c, restaurant, pool, converted rice barges make for unusual accommodation (some standard rooms too), watersports available, boat-shaped pool.

A *Sun Sand*, T 421024, F 421322, a/c, restaurant, on hill with lovely views but steep climb down to beach.

B-E *Chat Kaeo*, some a/c, restaurant, not very attractive rooms; **B-F** *Choengmon*, some a/c, quiet, some hot water, rec.

C *P.S. Villas*, T 286956, clean, good value bungalows.

● **Transport**
Local Car hire: Avis, *Imperial Tongsai*, T 425015.

Chaweng

This is the biggest beach on the island, split into 3 areas – north, central and Chaweng Noi. **Chaweng Noi** is to the S, round a headland and has 3 of the most expensive hotels on the island. **Central Chaweng** is a glorious sweep of sand with lovely water for swimming and a proliferation of bungalows, restaurants and bars. There is no real village atmosphere but it does have the most extensive tourist infrastructure on the island, with watersports facilities, travel agencies, supermarkets and a strip of rather scruffy Pattaya-like bars, discos, clubs and restaurants. Some areas of the beach are crowded (in particular the N end) but it is large enough to find a quiet spot. The beach appears to be less clean to the N.

Local information
● **Accommodation**

A+ *Blue Lagoon* (N end), T 421401, B 2533915, a/c, restaurant, good pool, well designed accommodation; **A+** *Imperial* (S end), T 422020, F 422396, B 2619000, a/c, restaurant, attractive, large, saltwater and freshwater pools, watersports, the original 5-star hotel on the island; **A+** *Samui Yacht Club*, T 421378, F 421378, B 3196042, S end of beach, just before headland, a/c, restaurant, pool, traditional-style thatched attractive bungalows set in coconut plantation, fitness centre, private beach; **A+** *Victoria*, T 286943, F 421421, B 4245392, a/c, restaurant, pool, S end, 2/3 storey 'Victorian' building.

A *Amari Palm Reef* (N end), T 422015, F 422394, a/c, restaurant, interesting pool, Thai-style, 2-storey bungalows rather close together; **A** *Chaweng Cabana*, T 421377, F 421378, a/c, rather cramped; **A** *Chaweng Cove*, T 286957, B 5100950, a/c, restaurant, hot water, lovely gardens; **A** *Chaweng Regent*, 155/4 Chaweng Beach, T 422008, F 422222, a/c, good restaurant (seafood speciality, Thai and European), rather unexciting pool, new resort with individual bungalows, well laid out; **A** *Chaweng Resort*, T 421378, F 421378, a/c, restaurant, pool, attractive gardens, hot water, rec; **A** *Coral Bay Resort*, T 286902, F 286902, B 2337711, N of Chaweng Beach (Yai Noi Bay), a/c, restaurant, pool, hot water, poor beach, overpriced; **A** *Pansea*, T 421384, F 421385, B 2356075, a/c, restaurant, set in spacious grounds, no pool but free watersports; **A** *Princess Village*, T 421382, F 421382, B 2340983, N end of beach, a/c, lovely restaurant on seafront, beautifully presented Ayutthayan-style wooden houses on stilts, run by a European, rec; **A** *Regent*, T 286910, F 286910, B 4184066, a/c, restaurant, pool, health club, gym, all facilities, price includes breakfast; **A** *Tropicana Beach Resort*, T 421408, F 421408, B 3187058, restaurant, pool; **A** *Villa Flora*, T 281535, B 2517646, a/c, restaurant, 2 pools; **A** *Vil-

lage*, T 421382, B 2340982, some a/c, restaurant, Thai-style bungalows, simpler version of *Princess Village*; **A** *White House*, T 421382, B 2340983, some a/c, restaurant, thatched cottages, ideal for families; **A-B** *Chaweng Guesthouse*, T 421375, F 421162, B 2351017, some a/c; **A-D** *Munchies*, some a/c. Unfriendly, bungalows close together.

B *Arabian*, T 421379, some private bathrooms; **B** *Central Bay*, T 272222, a/c, hot water; **B** *Chaba*, T 421380, B 2368044, a/c, restaurant, hot water; **B** *JR*, restaurant, bungalows close together; **B** *Matlang Resort*, T 272222, some a/c, restaurant; **B** *The Island*, PO Box 52, F 421178, a/c, restaurant, N end of beach, some a/c, good restaurant, bathrooms, individual huts right on the beach, attractive garden, run by farang, bar open after 2200, ideal for 'trendy backpackers'; **B-C** *Cabana*, T 421405, some a/c, N end of beach, well laid out; **B-C** *Chaweng Buri Resort*, T 422465, F 422377, a/c, individual bungalows, minimally furnished; **B-C** *Chaweng Gardens*, T 422265, F 422265, some a/c, bungalows close together but well designed.

C-D *Joy*, T 421376, rather scruffy; **D** *Best*, popular, rather anti-social management; **D** *Lucky Mother* (N end), friendly, clean, excellent food, some private bathrooms, rec.

D *Seaside*, some private bathrooms; **D** *Coral Park*, private bathrooms, rec.

E *Charlies'*, basic but clean and very popular, some bathrooms; **E** *Spa Resort*, a sort of down-market health resort which comes much recommended, run by an American and his Thai wife, with sauna, steam room and excellent bungalows with attached bathrooms.

● **Places to eat**
♦♦♦ *Eden*, attractive thatched pavilions, excellent seafood.

● **Bars**
Bananas, *Reggae* (large bar, videos and disco, opens late), *Mao*, *Green Mango* and *Eden* are all on the road parallel to the beach.

● **Banks & money changers**
On road parallel to beach.

● **Churches**
Catholic Church: on main road. Service at 1030.

● **Entertainment**
Disco: *Black Cat* and *Green Mango* are both on the road parallel to the beach.

● **Hospitals & medical services**
Clinic: one on road into Chaweng from Route 4169, one near the *Thai Restaurant.*

● **Sports**
Bungee jumping.

Diving: *Koh Samui Divers* (T 421465) are to be found on the beach; *Matlang Divers* are at Matlang Resort.

Snorkelling: masks and fins can be hired from most bungalows. The water is best at Coral Cove, between Chaweng and Lamai or at Yai Noi, N of Chaweng.

Speedboats: can be rented for ฿1200/hr.

Watersports: include windsurfing, catamaran sailing (฿400/hr), waterskiing (฿200/session), jetskis (฿400/hr), jet scooters (฿400/hr), parasailing (฿400/10 min fly). Chaweng Cabana has good watersports.

● **Shopping**
Along the road parallel to the beach, there are beachware, cassette-tape and jewellery shops.

● **Travel agents**
Dits Travel, Chaweng Beach, T 422494. There are a number of booking agencies on the road parallel to the beach.

● **Transport**
Local Minibus: an a/c minibus leaves for the airport from the N end of the beach road 6 times a day (฿40). **Car hire**: Avis, *Imperial Hotel*, T 422020.

Between Chaweng and Lamai

There is no beach along this stretch of coast but some snorkelling off the rocky shore. D-F *Coral Cove Resort*; *Silver Beach.*

Laem Nan headland

Several bungalows including: A-C *Royal Blue Lagoon*, T 272222 ext 991, a/c, restaurant, pool, lovely gardens, natural lagoon surrounded by coral makes good swimming, some recent visitors have complained of rather surly management.

Lamai

Koh Samui's 'second' beach is 5 km long and has a large assortment of accommodation. Rates are similar to Chaweng,

but the supporting 'tourist village' has developed rapidly and is somewhat dishevelled looking. However, the beach itself is still nice. The renowned 'grandfather' and 'grandmother' rocks are to be found here.

Tours
Companies along the main road parallel to the beach, for trips around the islands, fishing and snorkelling.

Local information
● **Accommodation**
A *Pavilion* (N end), T 421420, F 421420, B 2373125, a/c, restaurant, pool, some attractive octagonal thatched wooden cottages, some not so attractive 2-storey blocks, jacuzzi; **A** *Samui Laguna Resort*, T 2722222 x223, B 2525244, a/c, restaurant, pool, 3 storeys; **A-C** *Aloha* T 421418, F 421419, some a/c, restaurant, attached bathroom, pleasant garden; **A-C** *Golden Sand* T 421430, pool, hot water; **A-D** *Rose Garden* (N end) T 421410, some a/c, popular, some hot water, rec; **A-D** *Weekender*, T 421427, F 421429, some a/c, restaurant, pool, tennis courts, friendly, rec.

B *Casanovas*, T 421425, B 2820452, a/c, restaurant, pool, fairly new accommodation; **B** *Sand Sea Resort* (N end) T 421415, some a/c, restaurant, small pool; **B-C** *Best*, T 421416, some a/c, average rooms, unattractive location; **B-C** *Lamai Inn 99*, T 421427, F 421427, some a/c, restaurant, average rooms.

C *Golden Sea Breeze*, rather shabby, attached bathroom; **C-E** *Coconut Beach*, shabby, some attached bathrooms; **C-E** *Rocky* (S end), secluded beach, nice huts and garden, rec.

D *Marina I and II*, T 421426, popular, attached bathroom; **D** *Mira Mare* (N end), restaurant, average rooms, attached bathroom; **D** *Sea Garden*, average rooms; **D** *Somthong*, average rooms.

E *Animal House*, average rooms, attached bathroom; **E** *Whitesand*, large, clean bungalows on beachfront, attached bathroom.

● **Places to eat**
International cuisine is widely available along the road parallel to the beach in restaurants such as *Il Tempo, Papas, Rimklong, L'Auberge, Toms Bakery.*

● **Bars**
Most are located down the sois which link the main road and the beach.

● **Banks & money changers**
Currency exchanges are to be found along the main road parallel to the beach.

● **Entertainment**
Buffalo fighting: in the stadium at the N end (ask at hotel for date of next fight).

Disco: *Flamingo, Mix* (large dancefloor), and *Time Spaceadrome*.

Herbal steam centre: next to the *Weekender Villa* at the N end.

Massage: on the beach.

Thai boxing: Classes available.

Videos: at many of the bungalows.

● **Hospitals & medical services**
Muang Thai Clinic: near *Flamingo* disco, T 272222 x959, 24 hr service, or by *Best Resort*.

● **Post & telecommunications**
Post Office: S end of main road.

● **Shopping**
Jewellery, beachware and clothing boutiques along the main road.

● **Sports**
Diving: *Matlang Divers* are based at *Aloha*; *Swiss Dive Centre* are at *Weekender*; *Pro Divers* is run by a Swede – Svensk Talande (with good English), who is based at *Rocky Bungalows*, T 017250448.

Snooker club.

Watersports: waterskiing (฿300), jetskiis, windsurfing, parasailing (฿500), snorkelling at southern end of the beach.

● **Travel agents**
Companies along the main road organize ticket reservations.

● **Transport**
Local Songthaews: to Nathon (฿15). **Jeep and motorbike hire**: widely available.

The south coast

The small beaches that line the south coast from Ban Hua Thanon W to Thong Krut are quieter and less developed, with only a handful of hotels and bungalows.

Ban Hua Thanon (a village) F *Natta Guesthouse*, on the main road.

Na Khai A *Samui Orchid*, T 421079, F 421080, a/c, restaurant, large pool, some older bungalows and a new 3-floor 'apartment' block; B *Hilton Garden Resort*, T 421056, F 2482961, B 2457669, a/c, restaurant, large pool, fitness centre, snooker.

Laem Set A+-A *Laem Set Inn* (110 Mu 2, Hua Thanon), T 424393, F 424394, an exclusive, secluded resort on the next headland, run by an Englishman, lovely pool but beach only good for swimming from Oct to April. From Apr to Oct the reef offshore is exposed but this makes some good snorkelling, food rec, no a/c or screens in double bungalows but all beds have mosquito nets. Screened rooms for family bungalows and the suites. Attractive houses, rec.

Bang Kao A quiet but not very attractive

LAEM SET INN
"IDYLLIC..." (VOGUE)
SEE AD PAGE 447

beach. D *Waikiki*, average rooms; E *River Garden*, attached bathroom.

Thong Krut E *Thong Krut bungalow*, rather close to the road but very quiet, friendly and unspoilt, rec. Ferries go from Thong Krut to Koh Tan and Koh Matsum and there are several tour companies here who organize fishing and snorkelling trips.

The west coast

Like the south coast, the western coastline south of Nathon is undeveloped, with secluded coves and beautiful sunsets. Phangka, near the south-west tip of the island has good snorkelling in the quiet waters of a small bay; Thong Yang, further N, is an isolated strip of beach, relatively untouched by the frantic developments underway elsewhere. The vehicle ferry from Don Sak, on the mainland, docks here. Chon Khram is the last bay before Nathon.

Phangka

● **Accommodation** F *Gems House*, clean, attached bathroom, rec; **D-E** *Sea Gull*, some attached bathrooms; **D-E** *Pearl Bay*, some attached bathrooms; **E** *Emerald Cove*, clean, attached bathrooms, rec; **D** *Coco Cabana*, T 421465, N of Phangka, just before vehicle ferry, friendly, quiet, some bathrooms.

Chon Khram

● **Accommodation** **D-E** *Lipa Lodge*, friendly; **B-E** *International*, T 423366, some a/c, range of bungalows, some hot water.

KOH PHANGAN

Koh Phangan is Koh Samui's younger sister: it is smaller than Samui, stretching 15 km N to S and 10 km E to W, and is at an earlier 'stage' in the tourist development cycle. Bungalows are generally basic and tourist facilities less extensive. Fishing and coconut production remain the mainstays of the economy and villages still have a traditional air. However, the pace of development is

accelerating. The number of bungalows increased from a mere 8 in 1983 to 23 by 1986, while between 1989 and 1990 the number rose from 94 to 146. In 1993, the 5-storey *Phangan Central Hotel* opened in Thong Sala: shades of things to come. Though still relatively unspoilt, more and more travellers are passing Koh Phangan by and continuing on to the next and more remote island of Koh Tao (see below). Although there are no hotels yet on Phangan, there is talk in town of 'big' Bangkok money being attracted by the tourist potential. These tropical islands that fringe the coast are liable to change more rapidly than any other tourist destination in Thailand.

The main village of Koh Phangan is the port of **Thong Sala** where most boats from Koh Samui, Surat Thani, and Koh Tao dock. Thong Sala has a branch of the Siam City Bank, telephone and fax facilities, a post office and telegraph service (*poste restante*), travel and tour agents, a small supermarket, dive shops, photo processing, motorbike hire, and a second-hand bookstore. The greatest concentration of bungalows is at **Hat Rin** on the southern 'foot' of the island.

Places of interest

Koh Phangan offers 'natural' sights such as waterfalls, forests, coral, and viewpoints but little of historical or cultural interest. The best way to explore the island is on foot, following one of the many tracks that link the various villages and beaches, which cannot be negotiated by songthaew or (sometimes) by motorbike. Roads are unpaved and poor, although improvement work is underway. Even the longest hike is an easy day's walk. It is a good idea to buy one of the maps of the island available in town (in Surat Thani and Koh Samui).

Phaeng waterfall is to be found in the interior of the island, about 4.5 km from Thong Sala and 2 km from the village of Maduawan. The walk E to Hat Sadet runs parallel to a river along which are

3 waterfalls and the initials of several Thai kings who visited here, including King Chulalongkorn (Rama V) and the present King Bhumibol (Rama IX). Other waterfalls include **Ta Luang** and **Wung Sigh** in the NW corner, **Paradise** in the N (and near the *Paradise Resort*), and **Thaan Prawes** and **Wung Thong** in the NE corner. The highest point is **Khao Ra** (627m). A path runs to the summit although visitors have reported that the trail is indistinct and a guide is necessary. Outside Ban Tai, on the coast and to the east of Thong Sala, is **Wat Khao Tum** and the **Vipassana Meditation Centre.** There are views from the hill-top wat to samui and the Ang Thong Islands. Ten day meditation courses are held every month with 20 day courses and 3-month retreats also available (all in English). All-in fees are ฿900 for 10 days, ฿2,000 for 20 days. Write to: Wat Khao Tum, Phangan, Surat Thani, Thailand, for more information. It is possible to walk on a trail from Hat Rin up the E coast to Hat Sadet and then on to Thong Nai Pan, where 4 wheel drive vehicles offer a daily service to Thong

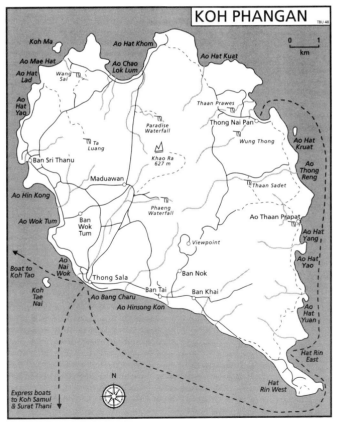

Sala, depending on the weather (฿60).

Except for Hat Rin, the beaches are uncrowded although not as beautiful as those on Koh Samui. The water is good for snorkelling.

Excursions

Boats leave from Thong Sala for Ang Thong Marine National Park (see page 450).

Local information
● **Accommodation**

There are no big hotels and most bungalows are still without fans and private bathrooms. In general, expect to pay in our F range for a hut with shared bathroom, D-E for a bungalow with private bathroom. The higher of the price ranges given for most of the accommodation indicates an attached bathroom. Hat Rin is more expensive than other beaches. During the high season (Dec-Feb and Jul-Sept), prices are 50% higher than in the low season: bargain if bungalows seem empty. The bungalows are listed below in order, running anti-clockwise round the island from the capital, Thong Sala.

Thong Sala: **B-C** *Phangan Central Hotel*, opened in 1993, the 5-storey hotel offers a/c rooms with TVs and fridges.

C-D *Buakhao Inn*, recently opened with a/c rooms.

E *Shady Nook*, clean, comfortable. Useful if taking the early morning ferry.

From Thong Sala to Ban Tai: Bang Charu and Hinsong Kon: this stretch of beach is unpopular with visitors due to its proximity to Thong Sala and as a result accommodation is good value. The beach shelves gently and is good for children, but the water is a little murky. Bungalows are well spread out and quiet: **E-F** *Petchr Cottage*; **E-F** *Phangan Villa*; **F** *Moonlight*, basic; **F** *Sundance*, basic; **D-E** *Charm Beach Resort*, range of accommodation, compound dirty, basic; **F** *First Bay Resort*, good value; **E-F** *Bunbandan*, secluded, peaceful, rec.

From Ban Tai to Ban Khai and the end of the road: some snorkelling, good swimming, generally quiet and secluded. **F** *S.P. Bungalows* (formerly Birdsville), secluded, popular and good value, little dirty, near a Chinese temple; **E-F** *The Pink One*; **E-F** *Triangle Lodge*, F 421263, clean and well-run, rec; **E** *Mac Bay Resort*, slightly better than most, well run, clean, rec; **F** *Jub Bungalow*, good, friendly, secluded, rec; **F** *Lee's*

Garden, quiet, well-run, rec; **F** *Banja Beach*, friendly, good food, rec; **F** *Thong Yang*, friendly, good food, rec.

Hat Rin

Hat Rin is at the south-eastern tip of Koh Phangan. The best, and most popular beaches are to be found here, with some good snorkelling. It also has the greatest concentration of bungalows which are packed close together (except on the hillsides). It is THE place for parties, noise and activity. Boats from the Big Buddha (Koh Samui) land at Hat Rin. A road from Thong Sala to Hat Rin is under construction, boats run from both Thong Sala and Ban Khai to Hat Rin. A boat leaves Hat Rin about 1030, 45 mins (฿40), where it meets up with boats to Koh Samui and Surat Thani. The 'East' beach is more attractive – it is cleaned every morning and there are waves. The 'West' beach is dirtier and is almost non-existent at high tide; accommodation is slightly cheaper here. The two beaches are only 10 mins walk apart and are both wonderfully quiet until about 1300, as most people are sleeping off the night's excesses.

Hat Rin 'West': **E** *Hatrin Village*, fan, own shower and toilet, electricity, hammocks, rec; **E-F** *Bird*; **E-F** *Palm Beach*, popular; **D** *Friendly*, clean, higher standard than most; **E-F** *Family House*, basic.

Hat Rin 'East': **D-E** *Paradise*, large complex of 50 bungalows, some better equipped with bathrooms; **E** *Sea Garden*; **D-E** *Seaview*, restaurant (with videos), bungalows right on the beach, with balcony and hammock, mosquito nets, own clean bathroom, not too noisy this end, highly rec; **D-F** *Serenity Hill*, N end of beach, quieter than most.

Thong Nai Pan is a quiet bay with a good beach and excellent snorkelling; it was Rama V's favourite beach on the island: **A-D** *Panviman Resort*, T 377048, the most exclusive and expensive accommodation on Phangan, the hotel is built on a cliff overlooking the bay; it has been continually upgraded so that from being a budget bungalow operation a few years ago, it is now a 'luxury' development with stone-built villas with a/c, plus a few of the original wooden bungalows; **E-F** *White Sand*, good food and very popular with visitors, rec; **F** *Chanchit Dreamland*, basic; **F** *Nice Beach*, 6 bungalows, basic, good food.

Hat Kuat lies 5 km NW of Thong Nai Pan, it is even more isolated, with a beautiful beach and basic but generally well-run bungalows: **F** *Bottle Beach*; **F** *OD Bungalows*, N end, bungalows built perched on boulders, with bamboo walkways, superb views and sunsets, basic.

Chao Lok Lum is a deep, sheltered bay on Koh Phangan's N coast. It is gradually developing into a quiet, comparatively refined, beach resort area. The *NAS German Diving School* is based here (T 283718): **E** *Chaoloklum Resort*; **E** *Paradise*, inland from the coast, very friendly with swimming at a nearby waterfall, rec.

Hat Yaaw is an attractive beach on the W coast with good swimming and snorkelling. 20 mins by songthaew from Thong Sala. Bungalows are spread-out and quiet: **F** *Silver Beach*, good swimming, comfortable and clean basic bungalows, rec; **F** *Blue Coral*, basic; **E-F** *Had Yao*, excellent food, clean and friendly, rec; **F** *Ibiza*, clean spacious bungalows, popular, rec; **D-F** *Sandy Bay*, good food and very popular, rec.

Ban Sri Thanu is a long but rather narrow beach, swimming conditions here are average. 15 mins by songthaew from Thong Sala. It is a quiet place to stay: **E** *Great Bay Resort*, rather characterless; **D-F** *Seetanu*, big bungalows, good location and facilities, rec; **E** *Nantakarn Resort*, T 7250225, on the headland (Laem Sri Thanu), built close together and rather characterless; **F** *Laem Son*, near Laem Son Lake (fresh water swimming), poor beach, basic; **F** *Sea View Rainbow*, basic but clean; **D-F** *Loy Fa*, on a headland, bungalows are spacious, no beach – poor swimming.

Ban Wok Tum N of Thong Sala and S of Ban Sri Thanu; the beaches here are average and swimming is poor because the seabed shelves gently. Accommodation is good value: **E** *Siripun*, S of Wok Tum, popular bungalows, fans, swimming ok; **F** *Kiet*, excellent food, average bungalows but good value on beach, Italian managed; **F** *OK*, friendly, short distance off the beach; **F** *Chuenjit Garden*, positioned above the beach, good food; **E-F** *Lipstick*, N of Wok Tum, quiet location, rocky swimming, some fans in rooms; **F** *Cookies*, basic; **E-F** *Cham*.

● **Places to eat**
Most visitors eat at their bungalows and some serve excellent, and cheap, seafood. Most of

the cheaper bungalows serve standard meals of rice and noodles. However there are also increasing numbers of restaurants and cafés in virtually every village and hamlet. Word-of-mouth recommendations are the best guide; new ones are opening all the time, and old ones deteriorate; ♦*Mr Chin* at Thong Sala Pier sells good food.

● **Bars**
In Hat Rin and Thong Sala. Night life starts around 2200.

● **Banks & money changers**
Siam City Bank (currency exchange centre), Thong Sala.

● **Entertainment**
Thai boxing: at Thong Sala. Boxers from Bangkok and elsewhere, fights every 2-3 weeks, especially on holidays. ฿50 and ฿100 tickets.

Traditional massage: at most beaches (฿60-80/hr).

Videos: at some of the bars or guesthouses.

● **Hospitals & medical services**
3.5 km from town towards Ban Hin Kong (north).

● **Post & telecommunications**
International telephone and fax service: Thong Sala. **Area code**: 077.

● **Sports**
Diving and **Fishing**: *Ang Thong Island Tours*, Thong Sala. *NAS German Diving School*, T 283718, Chao Lok Lum. They also organise snorkelling trips. Expect to pay ฿1,500 for a days diving.

● **Tour companies & travel agents**
Songserm Travel Co, 35/1 Talat Thong Sala, T 272222. *Mr Chin*, Thong Sala Pier, T 377010, F 377039.

● **Transport**
12 km N of Koh Samui.

Local Boat: long-tailed boats take passengers from Thong Sala to Hat Rin, Thong Nai Pan, Mae Hat and between the beaches. Depending on the trip, expect to pay about ฿70/person from Thong Sala to Thong Nai Pan. Boat charter is about ฿300-฿500. **Songthaews** and **motorcycle taxis**: can reach most destinations with the notable exception of Hat Rin (฿30-40). **Motorcycle hire**: in Thong Sala and from the more popular beaches. Some of the guesthouses also hire out motorbikes. Expect to pay ₿150/day upwards. **Walking**: is the best way to see the island.

Train The State Railways of Thailand run a train/bus/ferry service to Koh Phangan from Bangkok's Hualamphong Station (₿459-489).

Sea Boat: All boats dock at the pier at Thong Sala.

1. **The Island Jet** is the quickest boat to Koh Phangan. It leaves from the terminal at Paknam Tapee, about 4 km from Surat Thani, T 286461 (Surat Thani), T 287033 (Koh Phangan) for reservations. One crossing daily, leaving Surat Thani 0830 and Koh Phangan 1130, 2 hrs (₿180). It also travels to Koh Samui, 30 mins (₿65).

2. **A ferry** leaves daily from Don Sak Pier, Surat Thani, at 0915, 3¾ hrs (₿105-125). Buses leave Surat Thani at 0745. Contact Ferry Phangan, on corner of Bandon and Chonkasem rds in Surat Thani, T 286461, or in Thong Sala, Phangan, T 377028.

3. **An express boat** leaves twice a day from Don Sak Pier, Surat Thani, at 0730 and 1330 (and from Phangan at 0615 and 1300), 3¼ hrs (₿145). Buses from Surat Thani, from the airport, and from Phun Phin Railway Station connect with these boats.

4. **A night boat** leaves from the pier at Bandon, Surat Thani at 2300 (and from Phangan at 2100), 6 hrs (₿70-90).

From Koh Samui, express boats leave from Nathon at 1000 and 1600 (and from Phangan to Samui at 0615 and 1300), 45 mins (₿60). A boat also leaves from near the Big Buddha, on Samui and lands at Hat Rin E or W, 45 mins (₿50). *Songserm* ferries also link Koh Phangan with Koh Tao, departing daily at 1230 (leaving Koh Tao at 0900) 2½ hrs (₿150).

Koh Tao

4 km wide and 8 km long, Koh Tao – or Turtle Island – has some of the best diving and snorkelling in the Gulf of Thailand. It is one step more remote than Koh Phangan, with just a scattering of basic bungalows.

Koh Tao is a rugged island, with not many beaches. Its main income is coconuts, but tourism is likely to eclipse that shortly. On the western shore, Hat Sai Ri is a sweeping crescent of beach lined with coconut palms. South of here is Koh Tao's 'capital': Ban Mae Hat. Boats from Koh Phangan dock at the village which

also supports a scattering of restaurants, dive shops, a pharmacy, a grocery and postal and currency exchange facilities. Off the island's north-west coast is Koh Nang Yuan (see Excursions, below). The east coast is made up of a series of small, secluded coves, some of which have bungalows. The snorkelling is best off the east coast, especially around Mamuang and Laem Thian. Paths criss-cross the island, linking the beaches, coves and villages.

Although Koh Tao is still relatively unspoilt, the speed of development is very rapid. Speculators and developers see Koh Tao as another Koh Samui and have begun to buy up the best beach sites – there are already nearly 40 bungalow developments.

Excursions

Koh Nang Yuan lies off the NW coast of Koh Tao and is surrounded by crystal clear water. Once a detention centre for political prisoners, the three islands that make up this mini-archipelago are surrounded by wonderful coral and are linked by sandbars at low tide. There is one bungalow complex, the *Nang Yuan* with the best accommodation on Koh Tao (**C-D**), and on excellent seafood restaurant and diving school. Getting there: daily boat at 1030 and 1630 (₿15) from Ban Hat Sai Ri. Round-the-island day long boat trip, with snorkelling, ₿100.

BEST TIME TO VISIT Between June and Aug the south-west monsoon lashes Koh Tao, and some bungalows shut down for the season. Dec to Jan is the high season; bungalows are often full during these peak months.

Local information
● **Accommodation**

There have been reports of tourists being forcibly evicted from their bungalows because they have not spent enough money in the restaurant attached. Enquire before checking-in whether there is a minimum expenditure required. Most bungalow accommodation is in our **E-F** categories, with shared bathrooms and no electricity. There is only one up-market development on Koh Nang Yuan although more

KOH TAO TBU 62

rise; F *Diamond*; F *Laem Thian*.

Ao Ta Note (E coast): F *Ta Note Bay*, professionally run, rec.

Ao Leuk (E coast): F *Ao Leuk Resort*; F *Kiet*, on the headland, popular.

Ao Chalok Ban Kao (S coast): E *Viewpoint*, bungalows overlook the sea, own bathroom with western loo, very clean and cosy, with a balcony, restaurant with trust system of payment, very friendly young Thais run it. Longboat trip round island and to Koh Nang Yuan (Ø80), highly rec.

    F *Laem Khlong*; F *Koh Tao Cottages*, T 286062, F 286062; F *Ta Toh Lagoon*.

Ao Thian OK (S coast): E *Rocky Bungalows*, only bungalows in bay, mosquito nets provided, basic but friendly, reasonably priced food.

● **Banks & money changers**
Facilities available in Ban Mae Hat, but rates are poor.

● **Sports**
Diving: *Koh Samui Divers* (T 421316) have a dive centre, clubhouse and some bungalows. Book from Koh Samui or on Koh Tao to join a dive group. There are now lots of dive schools on the island. Rates are about Ø6,500 for an 'open water' course. Masks and fins can be hired from most guesthouses, Ø50/day.

● **Transport**
59 km N of Koh Samui, 47 km N of Koh Phangan.

Sea Boat: Boats to Koh Phangan go on to Koh Tao. *Songserm* run one a day leaving Koh Phangan at 1230, 2½ hrs (Ø150). Boats leave from Bophut beach on Koh Samui 3 mornings a week, 4½ hrs (Ø120, tickets available from *Koh Tao Travel*, Bophut). Boats to/from Chumphon's Paknam dock run nightly (at 2400, from Chumphon) and at 1000 from Koh Tao, subject to weather conditions 5-6 hrs (Ø200). Nightboat from Surat Thani, every night 2300, Ø200. Minibuses then take passengers on to Bangkok if desired.

are sure to follow. Most bungalows are concentrated on the western and southern shores of the island. More secluded accommodation can be found on the east coast. Because bungalows change so rapidly, it is best to rely on reports from travellers who have recently stayed on the island. Bungalow owners meet the ferry in an attempt to attract business, most then take passengers by longboat to their establishments.

Around Ban Mae Hat (W coast): F *Coral Beach*; F *Khao*; F *Neptune*, attractive position; F *Saithong*, popular but reports of deteriorating service; *Char*, good location facing small beach, well run, rec.

Hat Sai Ri (W coast): D *Crystal Bungalows*, stone bungalows, more sophisticated than others on beach.

    E *Queen*, bungalows with attached bathrooms.

    F *Sai Ri Cottages*, simple huts with good food; F *O-Chai*, basic bungalows, homely atmosphere; F *Mahana Bay*, facing Koh Nang Yuan; F *CFT*; *Dam*, basic bungalows.

Ao Mamuang (N coast): F *Mango Bay*, secluded; F *Coral Cove*, peaceful and well managed, rec.

Ao Hinwong (E coast): F *Sahat*, secluded bay, very peaceful, rec.

Ao Mao and Laem Thian (E coast): F *Sun-*

<h1 style="text-align:center">SOUTH
TO PHATTALUNG</h1>

Nakhon Si Thammarat

Nakhon Si Thammarat ('the Glorious City of the Dead' or Nagara Sri Dhammaraja, 'the City of the Sacred Dharma Kings'), has masqueraded under many

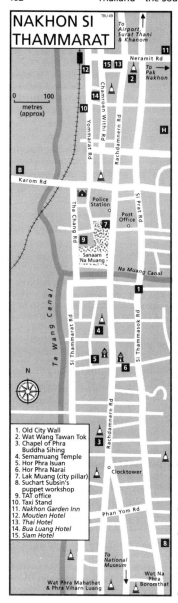

NAKHON SI THAMMARAT

TBU 49

To Airport, Surat Thani & Khanom

Neramit Rd

To Pak Nakhon

0   100
metres
(approx)

Chamroen Withi Rd

Yommarat Rd

Rachadamnern Rd

Karom Rd

Tha Chang Rd

Police Station

Si Prat Rd

Post Office

Sanaam Na Muang

Na Muang Canal

Ta Wang Canal

Si Thammarat Rd

Si Thammasok Rd

N

Rachadamnern Rd

Clocktower

Phan Yom Rd

To National Museum

Wat Phra Mahathat & Phra Viharn Luang

Wat Na Phra Boromthat

1. Old City Wall
2. Wat Wang Tawan Tok
3. Chapel of Phra Buddha Sihing
4. Semamuang Temple
5. Hor Phra Isuan
6. Hor Phra Narai
7. Lak Muang (city pillar)
8. Suchart Subsin's puppet workshop
9. TAT office
10. Taxi Stand
11. *Nakhon Garden Inn*
12. *Moutien Hotel*
13. *Thai Hotel*
14. *Bua Luang Hotel*
15. *Siam Hotel*

different aliases: Marco Polo referred to it as Lo-Kag, the Portuguese called it Ligor – thought to have been its original name – while to the Chinese it was Tung Ma-ling. Today, it is the second biggest city in the South and most people know it simply as Nakhon.

Nakhon has links with both the Dvaravati and Srivijayan empires. Archaeological artefacts from the area indicate that the province figured prominently as a centre of both Hinduism and Mahayana Buddhism from the 3rd century. There has been some discussion whether the distinctive art produced here should warrant a separate label (the School of Nakhon Si Thammarat) or whether it was merely an outlier, albeit an innovative one, of Srivijaya. Buddhist priests from Nakhon are supposed to have propagated religion throughout the country perhaps even influencing the development of Buddhism in Sukhothai. The city is surrounded by rich agricultural land, and has been a rice exporter for centuries.

Nakhon was at its most powerful and important during King Thammasokarat's reign in the 13th century, when it was busily trading with South India and Ceylon. But as Sukhothai and then Ayutthaya grew in influence, the city went into a gradual decline. During the 17th century, King Narai's principal concubine banished the bright young poet, Si Phrat, to Nakhon. Here he continued to compose risqué rhymes about the women of the governor's court. His youthful impertinence lost him his head.

Nakhon used to have the dubious honour of being regarded as one of the crime capitals of Thailand – a position it had held, apparently, since the 13th century. Locals maintain that the city has now cleaned up its act and Nakhon is probably best-known today for its prawn farms and nielloware industry (see page 111). The shop where the industry started some 50 years ago still stands on Sitama Road and production techniques are demonstrated on Si Thammasok I Rd. Elsewhere, other than in a few handicraft shops on Tha Chang Road, nielloware is a rather illusive commodity, although the National Museum has some examples on display.

Places of interest

A 2.2 km-long wall formerly enclosed the old city and its wats – only a couple of fragments of this remain (the most impressive section is opposite the town jail on Rachdamnern Road). **Wat Phra Mahathat**, 2 km S of town on Rachdamnern Road, is the oldest temple in town and the biggest in South Thailand – as well as being one of the region's most important. The wat dates from 757 AD, and was originally a Srivijayan Mahayana Buddhist shrine. The 77m-high stupa, *Phra Boromathat* – a copy of the Mahathupa in Ceylon – was built early in the 13th century to hold relics of the Buddha from Ceylon. However, the wat underwent extensive restoration in the Ayutthayan Period and endured further alterations in 1990. The chedi's square base, its voluptuous body and towering spire are all Ceylonese-inspired. Below the spire is a small square platform decorated with murals. The spire itself is said to be topped with 962 kg of gold, while the base is surrounded by small stupas. The covered cloisters at its base contain many recently-restored Buddha images. Also here is the *Vihara Bodhi Langka*, a jumbled treasure-trove of a museum. It contains a large collection of archaeological artefacts, donated jewellery, bodhi trees, Buddhas, and a collection of 6th-13th century Dvaravati sculpture – some of the latter are particularly fine. The mural at the bottom of the stairs tells the story of the early life of the Buddha. While the doorway at the top is decorated with figures of Vishnu and Phrom dating from the Sukhothai Period. Admission: ฿5. The cloisters are open 0830-1200 and 1300-1630 Mon-Sun.

The nearby **Phra Viharn Luang** (to the left of the main entrance to the stupa) is an impressive building – with an intricately painted and decorated ceiling – dating from the 18th century.

The **Nakhon Si Thammarat National Museum**, also on Rachdamnern Road, beyond the wats, is one of the town's most worthwhile sights. The impressive collection includes many interesting Indian-influenced pieces as well as rare pieces from the Dvaravati and later Ayutthaya Periods. Some exhibits are labelled in English. The section on art in South Thailand explains and charts the development of the unusual local Phra Phutthasihing (or Buddha Sihing) style of Buddha image, which was popular locally in the 16th century. Also in this section is the oldest Vishnu statue in Southeast Asian art (holding a conch shell on his hip) dating from the 5th century. The museum has sections on folk arts and crafts and local everyday implements. To the right of the entrance hall, in the prehistory section, stand 2 large Dongson bronze kettle drums – 2 of only 12 found in the country. The one decorated with 4 ornamental frogs is the biggest ever found in Thailand. Admission: ฿10. Open: 0900-1200, 1300-1600 Wed-Sun.

Back in the centre of town is **Wat Wang Tawan Tok**, across Rachdamnern Road from the bookshop. It has, at the far side of its sprawling compound, a southern Thai-style wooden house, built between 1888 and 1901. Unfortunately the intervening decades have taken their toll. Originally the house (which is really 3 houses in one) was constructed without nails – it has since been poorly repaired using them. The door panels, window frames and gables, all rather weather-beaten now, were once intricately carved.

The **Chapel of Phra Buddha Sihing**, sandwiched between 2 large provincial office buildings just before Rachdamnern Road splits in 2, may contain one of Thailand's most important Buddha images. During the 13th century an image, magically created, was shipped to Thailand from Ceylon (hence the name – Sihing for the Sinhalese people). The Nakhon statue, like the other 2 images that claim to be the Phra Buddha Sihing (one in Bangkok, see page 136 and one in Chiang Mai, page 233), is not Ceylonese in style at all: it conforms with the Thai style of the peninsular.

There are 2 13th-14th century Hindu temples in the city, along Rachdamnern Road. The first is **Hor Phra Isuan,** next to the Semamuang Temple, housing an image of Siva, the destroyer. Opposite is **Hor Phra Narai** which once contained images of Vishnu, now in the city museum.

Excursions

Beaches around Nakhon are unattractive, with filthy water. But 80 km N, near Khanom district, there are some secluded stretches of shoreline: **Khanom beach** (2 km from the village), and **Nai Phlao beach** nearby. Accommodation: B *Khanab Nam Diamond Cliff Resort,* T 529144, a/c, restaurant, pool; B-C *Nai Phlao Bay Resort,* T 529039, a/c, restaurant, rec; B-C *Supar Villa,* T 529237, a/c, restaurant, probably the best deal on the beach, rec. Getting there: regular buses from Nakhon (฿20), a/c micro buses (฿60). The beaches are situated about 8 km off the main road; turn at the 80 km marker.

Khao Luang National Park lies less than 10 km west of Nakhon and is named after Khao Luang, a peak of 1835m – the highest in the South. Within the boundaries of the mountainous, 570 sq km national park are 3 waterfalls. **Karom Waterfall** lies 30 km from Nakhon, off Route 4015, there is a Visitors Centre here. Also here are cool forest trails and fast-flowing streams. The park is said to support small populations of tiger, leopard and elephant, although many naturalists believe they are on the verge of extinction here. To get there, take a bus to Lansaka (then walk 3 km to falls) or charter a minibus direct. **Phrom Lok Waterfall** is about 25 km from Nakhon, off

Route 4132. To get there, take a minibus from Nakhon and motorbike taxis can be hired for ฿10 for the last 8 km trip to the falls. However, the most spectacular of the waterfalls is **Krung Ching** – 'waterfall of a hundred thousand raindrops' – 70 km out of town, and a 4 km walk from the park's accommodation. The 1835m climb up **Khao Luang** starts from Kiriwong Village, 23 km from Nakhon, off Route 4015. The mountain is the highest in S Thailand and part of the Nakhon Si Thammarat range, running from Koh Samui south through Surat Thani to Satun. The scenic village, surrounded by forest, was partially destroyed by mudslides in 1988 – an event which led to the introduction of a nationwide logging ban at the beginning of 1989. The climb takes 3 days and is very steep in parts, with over 60 degree slopes. There is no accommodation, so it is necessary to carry your own equipment and food. Dr Buncha Pongpanit, the owner of *Saun Sangsan Nakhon Bookstore,* Rachdamnern Road (close to Bovern Bazaar) will sometimes organize climbs for tourists. Getting there: Mazda songthaews leave Nakhon for Kiriwong every 15 minutes or so (฿15).

Khao Wang Thong Cave is one of the less publicized sights in the Nakhon area. It lies 100 km N of town, 11 km off Route 4142. The cave is on the S side of the middle peak of 3 limestone mountains near Ban Khao Wang Thong in Khanom district. Villagers and a group of Nakhon conservationists saved the cave from a dolomite mining company in 1990. The entrance is past the cave keeper's house, 15 minutes' walk uphill from the village. A few tight squeezes and a short ladder climb are rewarded by some of Thailand's most spectacular cave formations. Its 4 spacious chambers – one of which has been dubbed 'the throne hall' – are sumptuously decorated with gleaming white curtain stalactites. It is presently maintained by groups of local villagers and plans are afoot to install a lighting system. Until then, it is advisable to bring a strong flashlight. Getting there: by chartered songthaew, around ฿800/day.

Festivals

Feb: *Hae Pha Khun That* (20th-29th) 3 day event when homage is paid to locally enshrined relics of the Buddha; **Oct**: *Tenth Lunar Month Festival* (moveable). A 10-day celebration, the climax of which is the colourful procession down Rachdamnern Road to Wat Phra Mahathat; *Chak Phra Pak Tai* (moveable) centred around Wat Mahathat, includes performances of nang thalung (shadow-plays) and lakhon (classical dance). This is a southern Thai festival also held in Songkhla and Surat Thani.

Local information

● Accommodation

B-D *Thaksin*, 1584/23 Si Prat Rd, T 342790, a/c.

C *Nakhon Garden Inn*, 1/4 Pak Nakhon Rd, T 344831, a/c, restaurant, vying with the *Thai Hotel* for Nakhon's number one slot, rec; **C-D** *Monthien*, 1509/40 Yommarat Rd, T 341908, some a/c, rec; **C-E** *Thai*, 1375 Rachdamnern Rd, T 341509, some a/c, restaurant, best hotel in a rather mediocre bunch, rec.

D-E *Bua Luang*, 1487/19 Sai Luang Muang, Chamroen Withi Rd, T 341518, F 342977, some a/c, large clean rooms, popular with businessmen; **D-E** *Siam*, 1403/17 Chamroen Withi Rd, T 356090; **D-E** *Yaowarat*, 1475 Yommarat Rd, T 356089.

● Places to eat

Prawns are Nakhon's speciality – farms abound in the area. Good seafood (including saltwater prawns) at reasonable prices is served in most of the town's restaurants.

Thai: **♦♦***Dang Ah*, 74 Rachdamnern Rd, excellent sea-fresh tandoori prawns, also serves Chinese, rec; **♦***Lakorn*, at the back of Bovorn Bazaar off Rachdamnern Rd, only restaurant in Nakhon with an Indian rubber tree growing through the middle of it, pleasant eating spot, with open verandahs, no menu in English, but good variety of standard dishes; **♦♦***Pak Nakhon*, 10 km out of town on Pak Nakhon Rd, highly rec. for seafood, also serves Chinese; **♦***Yellow Curry House*, 1467 Yommarat Rd, cheap and cheerful, rec. by locals.

International: **♦***D.D. Cocktail Lounge*, Rachdamnern Rd, American breakfasts, ice-cream and Irish coffee; **♦***Hao Coffee Shop*, in Bovorn Bazaar, off Rachdamnern Rd, attempt at creating some ambience: charmingly decorated with antiques and assorted oddities; *Ligos*, on corner of Rachdamnern Rd and Bovorn Bazaar, and a branch in the alleyway opposite the front entrance of the *Thai Hotel*, good selection of pastries and doughnuts, cheap.

● Foodstalls

Nam Cha Rim Tang is a stall at the entrance to Bovorn Bazaar, which sets up in the early evening and produces exceedingly good banana rotis. Lining Rachdamnern Rd, along the wall of the playing fields for nearly a km (up to *Dang Ah* restaurant) there are countless stalls selling *som tam*, a chilli-hot papaya salad.

● Airline offices

Thai, 1612 Rachdamnern Rd, T 342491 and T 343874.

● Banks & money changers

Bangkok, 1747 Rachdamnern Rd; **Bank of Ayudhya**, 1366/1-3 Rachdamnern Rd; **Thai Farmers**, 1360 Rachdamnern Rd; **Siam Commercial**, 1166 Rachdamnern Rd.

● Entertainment

Shadow plays: most of the plays relate tales from the Ramakien (see page 134) and the jataka tales. Narrators sing in ear-piercing falsetto accompanied by a band comprised of *tab* (drums), *pi* (flute), *mong* (bass gong), *saw* (fiddle) and *ching* (miniature cymbals). There are 2 sizes of puppets. *Nang yai* (large puppets) which may be 2m tall, and *nang lek* (small puppets) (see page 108). Shows and demonstrations of how the puppets are made can be seen at the workshop of Suchart Subsin, 110/18 Si Thammasok Soi 3 (take the road opposite Wat Phra Mahathat, turn left – there's a small pond at the top of the soi where Suchart Subsin is signposted – and walk 50m). This group have undertaken several royal performances. Shows cost ฿50 but are free if you buy ฿250 worth of puppets.

● Post & telecommunications

Post Office: Rachdamnern Rd (opposite the police station). **Area code**: 075.

● Sports

Thai Boxing: every Sun 2100 in the stadium, Rachdamnern Rd. ฿40.

● Shopping

Nakhon is the centre of the S Thai handicrafts industry. Nielloware, *yan liphao* basketry (woven from strands of vine of the same name), shadow puppets, Thai silk brocades and *pak yok* weaving are local specialities.

Books: *Saun Sangsan Nakhon Bookstore*, Rachdamnern Rd close to Bovorn Bazaar has a small selection of English books plus articles on the surrounding area.

Handicrafts: shops on Tha Chang Rd, notably the *Thai Handicraft Centre*, *Nabin House* and *Manat Shop*. Odds and ends can also be picked up in the market in front of Wat Phra Mahathat.

Nielloware: original shop on Chakrapetch Rd. A few handicraft shops on Tha Chang Rd also sell it.

Shadow puppets: from the craftsmen at *Suchart House*, Si Thammasok Rd, Soi 3 (see above) and stalls around Wat Phra Mahathat.

Yan liphao: best at *Tha Rua Village*, 10 km out of town on Route 408 or shops on Tha Chang Rd.

● **Tourist offices**

TAT, Sanam Na Muang, Rachdamnern Rd, T 346516, open 0830-1630, Mon-Sun.

● **Transport**

800 km S of Bangkok.

Local Songthaew: from one end of town to the other (฿3-4).

Air Airport lies N of town. Connections with Bangkok (4/week) 1 hr 55 mins, Phuket (3/week) 1 hr 40 mins, Surat Thani (3/week) 35 mins and Trang (4/week) 30 mins.

Train Station on Yommarat Rd. Overnight connections with Bangkok. Most southbound trains stop at the junction of Khao Chum Thong, 30 km W of Nakhon, from where one must take a bus or taxi. 2 trains go into Nakhon itself, the Rapid No. 47, which leaves Bangkok's Hualamphong station at 1730 and arrives at Nakhon the next day at 0835, and the Express No. 15, which leaves Bangkok at 1920 and arrives at 1000 (฿133-590).

Road Bus: buses leave from W of the mosque. Overnight connections with Bangkok's southern bus terminal 12 hrs (฿182-420). Regular connections with Krabi 4 hrs (฿50), Surat Thani 2½ hrs (฿60) and with other southern towns.

Phattalung

The 'town of the hollow hill,' is so named because of the cave systems in its limestone hills (Khao Hua Taek to the W and Khao Ok Thalu to the E). But Phattalung's main claim to fame is as the place where *nang thalung*, Thai shadowplays, originated; records mention them as far back as the 15th century. *Nang* means leather and *thalung* probably derives from Phattalung. That said, nang thalung was not definitely 'invented' in Thailand: it is thought to have reached Siam from Java (where wayang kulit have been shadow dancing for centuries) possibly via Cambodia. The more popular Thai *khon* dances developed from it, supplanting the nang thalung everywhere except in the south. Performances of this traditional form of theatre can still be seen in Phattalung (only during festivals) and in Nakhon Si Thammarat. Performances begin around midnight – emphasizing the artform's links with the spirit world – and end at about 0400.

Wat Kuhasawan, to the W side of town on the road to Tha Miram, is associated with a large cave, **Tham Kuhasawan**, containing countless Buddha images. Steps lead around the cave to the top of the mountain, from where there is a good view of the surrounding countryside. On the second set of steps is a statue to commemorate a hermit who lived in the cave. **Tham Malai Cave** is 3 km N of Phattalung – take a boat from behind the railway station to get there.

Excursions

Wat Wang is 6 km E of the town, on the road to Lam Pam, and is thought to be several hundred years old. The original chedi lies in front of the wat, while the closed bot contains unrestored murals dating back 200 years. Getting there: motorbike taxis (฿20 return) from outside the post office.

Lam Pam is the nearest 'coastal' village, situated on the **Thale Sap Songkhla** an unspectacular and highly toxic inland sea – swimming is not advisable (see page 471). But from the beach stalls at sunset (which serve simple seafood), it is peaceful, verging on the picturesque. Accommodation: **D** *Lam Pam Resort*, T 611486, good restaurant, chalets, near the lake, are very clean and have mosquito screens, no hot water or fans, raft trips on the lake. Getting there: songthaew or motorbike taxis (₿25-30 return) from outside the post office.

The **Thale Noi Waterbird Sanctuary** is 36 km NE of Phattalung at the northernmost end of the Thale Sap Songkhla, where the water is fresh (towards its southern end it is saline). The sanctuary supports nearly 200 species of bird (100 of which are waterfowl) and becomes an ornithological paradise between Jan and Apr when the migrants stop here. The best way to see the birdlife (jacanas, crakes, egrets, teal...) is by hiring a boat to venture along the waterways (₿150/hr). Accommodation: **D** Forestry Department bungalow on the lake. Getting there: bus from Poh-Saat Rd, 1 hr (₿10).

Local information
● **Accommodation**
If you have to stay in Phattalung, it would be worth staying at the *Lam Pam Resort* at the coastal village of Lam Pam (see Excursions, above), which is easily reached from town. **C-E** *Ho Fah*, 28-30 Khuha-Sawan Rd, T 611645, dismal.

D-E *Thai*, 14-14/1-5 Dissara-Sakharin Rd, T 611636, sad but true: the 'best' hotel in town.

● **Places to eat**
Thai: ✦*Klert Beer*, 6/4 Dissara-Sakharin, just down from *Thai Hotel*, Phattalung's best attempt at ambience, simple but good menu – including seafood.

Out of town: ✦*Lam Pam Resort*, Lam Pam, good menu with lots of seafood.

● **Banks & money changers**
Thai Farmers, Ramet Rd (main road through town).

● **Post & telecommunications**
Post Office: off Ramet Rd, not far from the railway station. **Area code**: 074.

● **Transport**
888 km from Bangkok, 110 km from Hat Yai.
Local Motorbike taxis (₿5) and **songthaews**

from Ramet Rd, next to the post office.
Train Station between the canal and Nivat Rd. Overnight connections with Bangkok, 15 hrs (₿137-611) and regular connections with all stops on Bangkok-Butterworth route, Sungei Golok 5 hrs, Hat Yai 1 hr 20 mins, Yala 3 hrs 20 mins and Surat Thani 4 hrs.

Road Bus: buses leave from between the market place and the railway station. Overnight connections with Bangkok 12 hrs (₿200-376); also connections with Nakhon Si Thammarat 1½ hrs and Hat Yai 1½ hrs. **Taxi**: leave from Phracha Bamrung Rd at the crossroads close to the *Thai Hotel*. To Trang and Nakhon Si Thammarat.

THE SOUTHERN PROVINCES

The largest towns in the South are the twin settlements of Hat Yai and Songkhla, 950 km south of Bangkok. Both are vibrant commercial and tourist centres primarily geared to visitors from Malaysia: few Western tourists stop here. From this southern conurbation, Route 42 links up with Pattani (103 km) and Narathiwat (197 km), both Thai towns with distinct 'Malay' overtones. S of Pattani is Yala (35 km), while W of Songkhla on Route 4 and Route 406 is Satun (125 km). The islands of the Turatao National Park can be reached from Ban Pak Bara, N of Satun.

Hat Yai

Hat Yai is a thriving commercial and shopping centre and one of Thailand's largest cities. Being only 50 km from the border, Malaysians stream into Hat Yai, boosting an already healthy local economy, the key elements of which are the 'barbershop' and ancient massage industries. For all its sins, Hat Yai is the unofficial capital of the South and the local tourist office is doing its best to change the city's image to a more wholesome one. In this it may be fighting a losing battle.

During 1993 and 1994 Hat Yai gained a reputation of an even more unsavoury hue: as a centre for bombing and arson. Between Aug 1993 and June 1994, over 30 such cases were reported. The question which has not yet been adequately answered is, who is responsible? Initially, everyone assumed it must be Muslim separatists. But by the middle of 1994 some local people were beginning to suggest that it was part of a Bangkok plot to destabilise the elected Chuan government.

Hat Yai's paucity of anything culturally interesting is exemplified by **Wat Hat Yai Nai**, which, for the town's top sight, is mediocre. The wat is 3 km west of Hat Yai, off Phetkasem Road (before U-Taphao Bridge), and houses the world's third longest reclining Buddha (35m tip to toe) – *Phra Phuttahat-mongkol*. This spectacularly hideous statue now resides in a massive new concrete viharn. It is occasionally possible to climb inside the Buddha for an inspection of his lungs, but the temple authorities now seem to have restricted access to this breath-taking pleasure. At the exit to the compound, next to a merry-go-round of 10 rotating monks, a

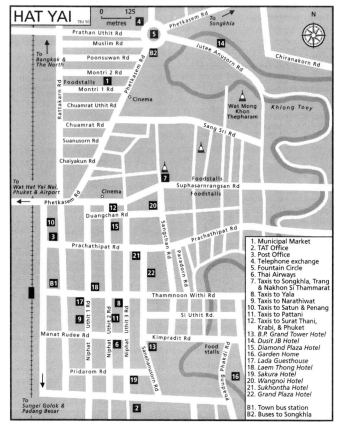

HAT YAI

0   125
metres

1. Municipal Market
2. TAT Office
3. Post Office
4. Telephone exchange
5. Fountain Circle
6. Thai Airways
7. Taxis to Songkhla, Trang & Nakhon Si Thammarat
8. Taxis to Yala
9. Taxis to Narathiwat
10. Taxis to Satun & Penang
11. Taxis to Pattani
12. Taxis to Surat Thani, Krabi, & Phuket
13. B.P. Grand Tower Hotel
14. Dusit JB Hotel
15. Diamond Plaza Hotel
16. Garden Home
17. Lada Guesthouse
18. Laem Thong Hotel
19. Sakura Hotel
20. Wangnoi Hotel
21. Sukhontha Hotel
22. Grand Plaza Hotel

B1. Town bus station
B2. Buses to Songkhla

banner reads: 'May the triple gems always be with you'.

Excursions

Ton Nga Chang are cascades which lie 24 km W of town along route 4, best seen from Oct to Dec. *Getting there:* take a bus from the market (₿15).

Tham Khao Rup Chang 10 km from Padang Besar (on the Thai/Malaysian border) consists of 3 large caverns featuring stalactites and stalagmites.

Tours

Agents operate tours of the area, mainly to Songkhla and surrounding sights.

Local information
● Accommodation

Hat Yai has a huge collection of hotels, and there are new ones springing up all the time. Recently built establishments tend to be much cleaner, and are often good value for money. The town's hotel industry has a symbiotic relationship with its booming 'hairdressing' industry. For those venturing into barbershop country in pursuit of a room for the night, there is a general rule of thumb: if a TV costs an extra ₿100, it's likely there are pornographic films on the in-house video. The distinction between 'Thai Traditional Massage' (ubiquitous throughout Thailand) and 'Ancient Massage' (ubiquitous throughout Hat Yai and the South) should also be noted. Ancient masseuses usually belong to the oldest profession. Many of them are located around Tanrattanakorn and Phaduangpakdi rds. Hotels with clocks showing Malaysian or Singapore time in the lobbies cater for Malaysian and Singaporean clientele. Not far away, on the other side of the fetid khlong however, is Boss Square around which there are a number of smart, clean hotels and restaurants.

L-B *BP Grand Tower*, 74 Sanehanusorn Rd, T 239051, F 239767, a/c, restaurant, pool, a large new top-of-the-range addition to Hat Yai's hotels.

A *Dusit JB*, 99 Jutee-Anusorn Rd, T 234300, F 234328, a/c, restaurant, pool, the Ritz of Hat Yai, but not central; **A-B** *Daiichi*, 29 Chaiyakun Uthit 4 Rd, T 230724, F 231315, a/c, restaurant, enormous, glitzy hotel, catering for conventions, small but smart rooms, reasonable value for money; **A-B** *Grand Plaza*, 24/1 Sanehanusorn Rd, T 234340, F 230050, a/c,

restaurant, pool, better than many in town.

B *Diamond Plaza*, 62 Niphat Uthit 3 Rd, T 230130, F 239824, a/c, restaurant (see Restaurants), this plush, tastefully appointed international class hotel, with its polite staff is completely out of place in Hat Yai, and good value, rec; **B** *Florida*, 8 Sripoovanart Rd, T 234555, F 234553, a/c, restaurant.

C *Garden Home*, 51/2 Hoi Mook Rd, T 234444, 232283, a/c, restaurant (sometimes), plush and well looked-after modern hotel, built around waterfall garden, rooms at the front have small balconies, all are well-appointed and excellent value for money, rec; **C** *Lada Guesthouse*, 13-15 Thammnoon Withi Rd, T 243770, a/c, convenient for station and very clean, good value; **C** *Rajthani*, 1 Thammnoon Withi Rd, T 231020, a/c, restaurant, Station hotel, so convenient for transit stop-overs although rooms are average; **C** *Sakura*, 185/1 Niphat Uthit 3 Rd, T 246688, F 235936, a/c, restaurant, clean, reasonable and very popular; **C-D** *Laem Thong*, 46 Thammnoon Withi Rd, T 244433, F 237574, a/c, clean old Chinese hotel, fan rooms are particularly good value, rec; **C-D** *Louise Guesthouse*, 21-23 Thammnoon Withi Rd, T 220966, F 232259, a/c, convenient for station, rec.

D-E *Wangnoi*, 114/1 Sangchan Rd, T 245729, a/c, clean, good value, but short on windows.

● Places to eat

Thai: ♦♦*Jay Lek*, 190 Niphat Uthit 2, some Chinese dishes; ♦*Mag Mai*, 27/1 Niyomrat Rd; ♦♦*Pee Lik 59*, across from *Sakura Hotel* on junction of Niyomrat Rd and Niphat Uthit 3 Rd, barbequed seafood in a large (and very popular) open-air restaurant, rec; ♦♦*Isan Garden*, Padungpakdee Rd (opposite *Ambassador Hotel*), Isan food in open-air restaurant next to the stinking khlong.

International: ♦♦♦*Diamond Plaza Hotel*, 62 Niphat Uthit 3 Rd, extensive international menu, with good selection of Thai seafood, in a classy atmosphere, rec; ♦♦*Fern*, off Chaiyakun Uthit 1 (down soi next to *Merlin Hotel*), also serves Thai and Chinese cuisine, with good seafood menu, rec; ♦*Joyce Bakery and Beer House*, Niphat Uthit 3, friendly, large menu; ♦*Nakhon Ni*, 167 Niphat Uthit 2, good breakfasts, salads and pizza as well as a good selection of Thai food; ♦*Boat*, 190/11 Niphat Uthit 3, cakes, ice-creams and soft drinks;

♦♦*Sometime*, *Hat Yai Garden Home Hotel*, 51/2 Hoi Mook Rd, reasonably priced menu with a good selection of seafood.

Foodstalls: Suphasarnrangsan Rd, Chee Kim Yong Complex, Hat Yai municipal market.

● **Bars**

Post Laserdisc, Thammnoon Withi Rd, music/video bar; *Lipstick Cocktail Lounge*, Royal, 106 Prachathipat Rd.

● **Airline offices**

Thai, 166/4 Niphat Uthit 2 Rd, T 245851; MAS, *Lee Garden Hotel*, Thammnoon Withi Rd, T 243729.

● **Banks & money changers**

Thai Farmers, 188 Phetkasem Rd; Bangkok, 37 Niphat Uthit 2 Rd, open until 1900 or 2000. Large hotels have money changers.

● **Consulates**

American, Sadao Rd, T 311589; Malaysian, 4 Sukhum Rd, T 311062.

● **Entertainment**

Bull fighting: on 1st Sat of every month, 100-1500, contact TAT for information.

Cinema: with English-speaking soundproofrooms – *Siam* on Phetkasem Rd, *Coliseum* on Prachathipat Rd, *Chalerm Thai* on Suphasarnrangsan Rd and *Hat Yai Rama* on Phetkasem Rd.

Disco: *New York Club*, Manhattan Palace, 29 Lamai Songkroh 4 Rd. *Royal*, 106 Prachathipat Rd.

Nightclubs: in many of the major hotels, such as the *Nora*, *Lee Gardens*, *Emperor*, *Kosit*. There are karaoke bars on every street and 'sexy shows' in several hotels and hairdressing outlets.

● **Hospitals & medical services**

Rattakarn Rd, T 243875.

● **Immigration**

Nasathanee Rd

● **Police**

T 243021/243333. **Tourist Police**: 1/1 Soi 2, Niphat Uthit 3, T 246733.

● **Post & telecommunications**

Post Office: Niphat Songkroh Rd and Rattakarn Rd. **Telephone centre**: Phangnga Rd. **Area code**: 074.

● **Shopping**

The principal shopping areas are concentrated around Niphat Uthit 1, 2 and 3 rds, Sane-hanusorn Rd and the Plaza Market. The narrow sois between these roads are packed with stalls.

Books: *Praevittaya Bookshop*, 124/1 Niphat Uthit 3. Regional and international English-language magazines available; *DK Books*, Thammnoon Withi Rd, W end, for English-language books.

● **Sport**

Bowling: *Sukhontha Bowl*, *Sukhontha Hotel*, Prachathipat Rd.

Bullfights: held twice a month, on the first and second Sats of the month. On the first Sat they are held in an arena next to the *Nora Hotel* off Thammnoon Withi Rd, and on the second Sat at the Hat Yai arena on Route 4, near the airport. Matches (and gambling) take place continuously from 1030 to 1800. Admission: ฿10-30.

Golf: *Kho Hong Golf Course*, 4 km NE of town on Route 407, nine holes. Green fees: ฿100.

Thai Boxing: competitions held every Saturday from 1400-1700 in the Television Stadium. Admission: ฿5.

Swimming: *Phasawang Big Splash*, in front of *Sincere Hotel*, 33/1 Phasawang 5 Rd (NE of town, off Phetkasem Rd). A 15m slide in a blue lagoon – well, almost.

● **Tour companies & travel agents**

Arch, 9 Jutee Uthit 2 Rd, T 233058; *Bhuket*, 24/1 Niyomrat Rd, T 233934; *Golden*, *Dusit JB Hotel*, T 234673; *Hat Yai Swanthai Tour*, 108 Thammnoon Withi Rd, T 246706; *Sabai*, 121 Niphat Uthit 2 Rd, T 243758; *Saeng*, 1 Si Uthit Rd, T 233566; *Sakura*, 79/12 Thammnoon Withi Rd, T 244654; *Songkhla*, 218-220 Niphat Uthit 3 Rd, T 246282; *Southern Paradise*, Dusit JB Hotel, T 234200; *Thaveechart*, 160 Thammnoon Withi Rd, T 245572.

● **Tourist offices**

TAT, 1/1 Soi 2, Niphat Uthit 3 Rd, T 243747, F 245986. Areas of responsibility are Songkhla, Hat Yai and Satul.

● **Transport**

933 km from Bangkok, 480 km from Phuket, 209 km from Nakhon Si Thammarat, 290 km from Sungei Golok.

Local Tuk-tuks and **songthaews** around town cost ฿4-10, bargain for longer distances. **Car hire**: Hat Yai Car Rent, 189 Thammnoon Withi

Rd (opposite *Nora Hotel*), T 234591; **Avis Rent-A-Car**, Grd floor, *Dusit JB Hotel*, 99 Jutee-Anusorn Rd, T 234300; **Jutee Car Rent**, 59/2 Jutee-Anusorn Rd, T 239447. Cheapest car rental in town with prices starting at around ฿1,200.

Air Airport (T 244145, 244521) is 12 km W of town. *Transport to town*: Thai Airways bus or songthaew (฿40). Regular daily connections with Bangkok 1 hr 25 mins, Phuket 40 mins, Pattani (2/week) 25 mins, and Narathiwat (3/week) 40 mins.

Train Station on Ratakan Rd. Overnight connections with Bangkok, 16-19 hrs (฿149-664). Regular connections with Phattalung, Yala, Sungei Golok and Surat Thani.

Road Bus: a/c buses leave from the station on Shotikul Rd. All non-a/c buses leave from the Municipal Market on Montri 1 Rd. Buses to Songkhla leave from Phetkasem Rd by the clock tower. Overnight connections with Bangkok 14 hrs (฿227-428). Also regular connections with Phuket 6 hrs (฿122-197), Krabi 4 hrs (฿91-167), Koh Samui (฿200, including ferry), Nakhon Si Thammarat 2 hrs (฿53-82), Satun 1 hr (฿27-35), Sungei Golok 4 hrs (฿96), Surat Thani 4 hrs (฿84-120), Songkhla 30 mins (฿8). **Taxi**: see map for positions of taxi ranks.

● **Transport to Malaysia and Singapore**
Air Daily connections with Singapore (1 hr 20 mins) and Penang (40 mins) on MAS.

Train Daily connections with Padang Besar (on the Malaysian border), Butterworth, 4 hrs, Kuala Lumpur and Singapore.

Road Bus: there are several travel agencies on Niphat Uthit 2 Rd offering packages by bus S to Butterworth and Singapore, most going via Padang Besar. For long distance journeys S it is better to take the bus to Padang Besar, 1 hr and change on to the train S down the W coast of Peninsular Malaysia and on to Singapore (see above). But there are through buses to Butterworth (for Penang), Kuala Lumpur 13 hrs and Singapore 17 hrs. There are also Malaysian shared taxis from Padang Besar. **Taxi**: to Penang leave from the railway station (฿220).

Agents include: *Asia Tours*, 85 Niphat Uthit 2 Rd, T 232147; *Magic Tour*, 93/1 Niphat Uthit 2 Rd, (*Cathay Hotel*), T 234535.

Songkhla

Songkhla, known historically as Singora, is situated on a spit of land between the Gulf of Thailand and the mouth of a huge lake – the **Thale Sap Songkhla**. This is Thailand's largest – and probably most polluted – body of inland water – 80 km long and 20 km wide. Although it is a freshwater lake, the water is quite salty closer to the Gulf. The lake used to be a fertile fishing ground but catches are now small due to extensive dumping of effluent.

The city's early history is as murky as its lake, but like Nakhon Si Thammarat, it was incorporated into the Srivijayan Empire (8th-13th century). Unfortunately, little remains of this period apart from a number of small Srivijayan bronze images unearthed at nearby Sating Phra. Songkhla was mentioned in 1769 when a Chinese merchant, Yienghoa, petitioned the king for licences to collect bird's nests from Koh Siand and Koh Ha in the E of the province. The present city was built in 1836 by Phraya Vichian Khiri, the governor of Songkhla during the reign of Rama III. Later, Chinese immigrants flooded into south Thailand hoping to make their fortunes from tin mining. Their descendants settled in Songkhla, and the town retains its Chinese atmosphere. Songkhla is the provincial capital, although its sister city Hat Yai is the main commercial centre. There is a sizeable expatriate population here, mainly oil-workers servicing the offshore platforms in the gulf.

Although the port is unsuitable for big ships and has gone into decline, the waterfront on the inland sea side still bustles with activity as fishermen unload their catch in the early morning and evenings. Fish – fresh, frozen, fermented and sun-dried – is one of Songkhla's major exports. The fish-packing factories along the road to Hat Yai bear malodorous witness to the scale of the fish industry. The town itself is a mixture of Chinese, Malay and Thai styles. The town's oldest thoroughfare is Nakhon Nai Road where many old Chinese shophouses still stand.

The town is surrounded on 3 sides by

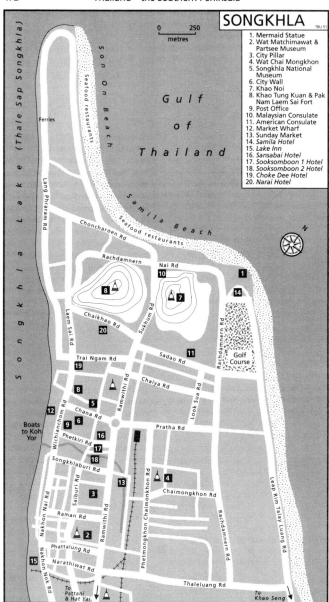

SONGKHLA TBU 51

1. Mermaid Statue
2. Wat Matchimawat & Partsee Museum
3. City Pillar
4. Wat Chai Mongkhon
5. Songkhla National Museum
6. City Wall
7. Khao Noi
8. Khao Tung Kuan & Pak Nam Laem Sai Fort
9. Post Office
10. Malaysian Consulate
11. American Consulate
12. Market Wharf
13. Sunday Market
14. *Samila Hotel*
15. *Lake Inn*
16. *Sansabai Hotel*
17. *Sooksomboon 1 Hotel*
18. *Sooksomboon 2 Hotel*
19. *Choke Dee Hotel*
20. *Narai Hotel*

water, but swimming is only possible (or advisable) on the seaward side. The focal point of the main beach, Laem Samila (or Samila Beach), is a pouting bronze mermaid, opposite the *Samila Hotel*. Further up the peninsula is Son On Beach, lined with seafood restaurants. The two offshore islands, Koh Nu and Koh Maew (Mouse and Cat Island respectively) are both uninhabited.

Places of interest

Wat Matchimawat (also called **Wat Klang**), in the centre of town on Saiburi Road, is 400 years old and the largest temple in Songkhla. The **Partsee Museum** within the complex has a chaotic display of disparate items: from human skulls to Buddha statues, stuffed snakes and coins. Nothing is labelled and the museum is badly lit. Open: 0900-1700 Wed-Sun. The bot is said to contain some interesting 19th century frescoes, representing the arrival of European navigators in the South China Sea, although it is usually locked. On Nang Ngam Road, not far from Wat Matchimawat stands the **city pillar** (*lak muang*).

The other main wat in Songkhla is **Wat Chai Mongkhon**, known for its Buddha relic from Ceylon, which is buried somewhere in the main pagoda.

The **Songkhla National Museum** is housed in an 1870's Sino-Thai style building, built as a private residence for the influential Phraya Sunthranuraksa family. Phraya Sunthranuraksa was governor of Nakhon Si Thammarat province in the latter years of the 19th century. After decades of neglect, the building was renovated in 1977 and converted into a museum. It is situated between Rong Muang and Chana roads. On the ground floor there is a good prehistory section including a collection of primitive jewellery. Archaeological investigations have shown the Songkhla area to have been a thriving commercial centre for centuries and some of the 8th and 9th century finds are exhibited in

the museum along with Tang Dynasty ceramics from the 7th to 10th centuries. Upstairs is a large collection of southern religious art, as well as furniture (including King Mongkut's bed) and various household items. Admission: ฿10. Open: 0900-1200, 1300-1600 Wed-Sun.

Opposite the museum on Chana Road are some remains of the **city wall**, built in 1839 by Phraya Vichian Khiri, then governor of Songkhla.

The N end of the peninsula is dominated by 2 hills. On the top of **Khao Noi** there is an old chedi and a small topiary garden affording panoramic views of the town. **Khao Tung Kuan**, to the W of Khao Noi, is littered with shrines which were restored during the reign of Rama IV. The chedi at the top of the hill was built by King Mongkut in 1866. **Pak Nam Laem Sai Fort** is on the side of the hill, on Laem Sai Road. It dates from the early 19th century.

Excursions

Folklore Museum (also known as the *Khatichon Wittaya Museum*) is found within the Institute of S Thai Studies, 4 km SW of town on Hat Yai-Songkhla road (Saiburi Road). It has exhibitions on southern arts and culture: shadow plays, traditional medicines and ancient beads. Open: 0830-1630 Mon-Fri.

National Institute of Coastal Aquaculture lies 3 km S of town, in Khao Seng. It was set up as an information and development centre for the coastal fisheries. It is possible to visit the laboratories and hatcheries as well as the fish museum (T 311895 to arrange visit). Khao Seng itself is a muslim fishing village, known for its hand painted boats (*kor lae*). Getting there: songthaew (฿10).

Boat trips on the Thale Sap Songkhla leave from the Market Wharf. A boat taxi across the lake costs ฿1, and to hire a boat costs around ฿100. Koh Yor is one of the main islands on the inland sea and is worth visiting to see the cotton-weaving industry there (*phaa kaw yor*). The cotton is good quality and is woven on traditional looms. There are also two wats on the island, Khao Bo and Thai Yaw. Koh Si Ko further N, is famous for its bird's nests. **Getting there**: boat taxis are available from the Songkhla inlet, near Khlong Kwang (฿10). The island can also be reached by taxi via Tinsulanond Bridge.

Khu Khut Waterfowl Park 30 km N of Songkhla, near Sating Phra has a huge migratory bird population between Dec and Apr; over 140 species have been recorded. The best time to visit is early in the morning. Accommodation: **E** *Kukon Guesthouse*. **Getting there**: boats can be hired from Khu Khut village (฿100-200). Regular buses from Songkhla to Sating Phra (฿6), motorbike taxis from there (฿5).

Wat Pakho is about 10 km N of Khu Khut (half way between Sating Phra and Ranot) on the lake. It is better known for its legend than its architecture, although it has a reclining Buddha and some murals. The story: once upon a time Luang Pho Thuat, an abbot, was kidnapped by pirates while crossing the lake. Their boat ran into a violent squall and the abbot and his captors, stranded mid-journey, ran out of food and fresh water. The venerated Luang Pho Thuat saved the day by turning the saltwater lake into drinking water. The pirates were so impressed that, duly quenched, they released him. A statue of the holy man stands in the complex. **Getting there**: same buses as to Khu Khut Waterfowl Park (฿12).

Chana, 33 km S of Songkhla, stages singing competitions for its captive dove population between Jan and Jul. The competitions are taken very seriously and good avine singers sell for large sums. Dove cages are hung from 8m-high poles and their singing judged for pitch, melody and volume. **Getting there**: bus 1881 (฿9).

Festivals
Sept-Oct: *Chinese Lunar Festival* (moveable), Thais of Chinese origin make offerings to the moon or Queen of the Heavens. Festivities include lion and dragon dances, lantern processions, folk entertainment.

Local information
● **Accommodation**
A *Hat Kaeo Resort*, 5 km N of town, towards Khu Khut Waterfowl Park, on the Sathingphra Strait, T 331059, F 331058, a/c, restaurant, pool, situated on a lagoon, rooms and bungalows available; **A-B** *Samila*, 1 Rachdamnern Rd, T 311310, F 322448, a/c, restaurant, spectacularly unattractive building, obviously Russian-inspired, most rooms have a balcony and views out to sea, business hotel.

C *Lake Inn*, 301-303 Nakhon Nok Rd, T 314823, F 314843, a/c, restaurant, refurbished in 1991 and well-appointed, the more expensive front rooms (rec) have great views of the lake, looking out over the wharf where the fishing boats put in; **C-D** *Queen*, 20 Saiburi Rd, T 311138, F 313252, a/c, cheaper rooms have no windows; **C-D** *Sansabai*, 1 Phetkiri Rd, T 311106, some a/c, clean, but over-priced; **C-E** *Sooksomboon 1*, 40 Phetkiri Rd, T 311049, some a/c, new rooms more expensive.

D *Chan*, 469 Saiburi Rd, T 311903, some a/c, restaurant, S of town; **D** *Sooksomboon 2*, 14-18 Saiburi Rd, T 311149, a/c, restaurant, old hotel with some fan-cooled rooms, and a plush new annex, excellent value, with spotless, spacious, very comfortable rooms, rec.

E *Choke Dee*, 14/19 Wichianchom Rd, T 311158, a/c, restaurant, refurbished in 1991 and well-appointed, the more expensive front rooms (rec.) have great views of the lake, looking out over the wharf where the fishing boats put in; **E** *Narai*, 14 Chaikhao Rd, T 311078, rooms basic but clean, only a few rooms with attached bath, small, friendly, family run hotel although a bit out of town; *Pavilion*, 17/1 Pratha Rd, burnt down, but a new one is being erected, price unknown.

● **Places to eat**
Thai and Chinese: A number of shops along Nang Ngam Rd. ♦*Ban Mo*, Songkraburi Rd. **Seafood**: a string of restaurants on Son On Beach all offer excellent fresh seafood. ♦♦*Mark*, one of the first you come to, rec. Also a group of seafood restaurants on Samila Beach, outside the entrance to the *Samila Hotel*.

Foodstalls: Several small stalls on Samila Beach.

● **Bars**
Laguna Terrace, *Lake Inn*, 301 Nakhon Nok Rd. Roof top bar, good views.

● **Banks & money changers**
Bangkok, **Thai Farmers** and **Bank of Ayutthaya** all on Wichianchom Rd, near the market. **Thai Military** on corner of Nakhon Nok and Ramwithi rds.

● **Embassies & consulates**
American Consulate, Sadao Rd, T 311589. **Malaysian Consulate**, 4 Sukhum Rd, T 311062.

● **Hospitals & medical services**
161 Ramwithi Rd, T 311494.

● **Post & telecommunications**
Post Office: opposite the market on Wichianchom Rd, nearby telephone office for international calls. **Area code**: 074.

● **Sport**
Golf: *Songkhla Golf Course*, nine-hole beachside course next to the *Samila Hotel*. Clubs for hire. Green fees, ฿100.

Watersports: *Watersports Centre* on Samila Beach, near the golf course, hires out rowing boats, paddle boats, speedboats and jetskis.

● **Shopping**
The main shopping areas are along Nakhon Nai and Nang Ngam roads.

Markets: Central Market, on Nakhon Nai Rd, opposite the Post Office. Sunday market near the main bus and taxi stand.

Textiles: Songkhla is known for *phaa kaw yor* woven cotton, made on Koh Yaw in the middle of the lake. Available in shops along Nang Ngam and Nakhon Nai roads.

● **Tour companies & travel agents**
Piya Tours, 51 Plata Rd, T 313770.

● **Transport**
950 km S of Bangkok, 30 km from Hat Yai.

Local Songthaews: ฿5 around town. There are always several around the bus station.

Air Nearest airport at Hat Yai (see page 470).

Train Nearest station is at Hat Yai (see page 471).

Road Bus: buses leave from Wichianchom Rd. Overnight connections with Bangkok, 13 hrs (฿224-425). Regular connections with Hat Yai 40 mins (฿9), Nakhon Si Thammarat, 2½ hrs (฿53-76). **Taxi**: long distance taxis leave from Wichianchom Rd, Hat Yai.

Sea Boat: ferries across the lake leave from Lang Phraram Rd, N of town. There is a boat which travels to Bangkok, 14 hrs (฿425).

Pattani

Pattani province, once a semi-autonomous Malay-speaking sultanate, is the heartland of Muslim South Thailand – although there are a lot of Thai-speaking Muslims here too. Unlike the Chinese, the Malays of South Thailand are not recent immigrants. Their descendants settled on the lower Kra Isthmus centuries ago, yet they have never willingly assimilated into modern Thailand. Few have found their way into local or central government and school children prefer to drop out after primary education rather than continue their studies in the Thai medium.

In the early 1970s a separatist group, the United Pattani Freedom Movement (bankrolled by Colonel Gadaffi), sprang up in defiance of heavy-handed Thai bureaucracy. A decade later their rebellion had all but died out, but the seeds

PATTANI

1. Market
2. Harbour
3. Taxis to Hat Yai & Songkhla
4. Chong Ar & Palace Hotels
5. Thai An Hotel
6. Thai Hua Hotel

To Harbour
To Yala, Matsayit Kreu Se & Narathiwat
Taxi Rank
Post Office
Matsayit Klang Mosque
To Songkhla & Hat Yai
To My Gardens Hotel
To Narathiwat & Sungei Golok

Pattani River
Pattani Phirom Rd
Decha Rd
Rudi Rd
Prida Rd
Makrut Rd
Pipit Rd
Udomvithi Rd
Yarang Rd

0   500
metres

of alienation remain today. In recent years the King has tried to make Muslims feel more a part of the Thai nation – by presenting awards for Koranic studies and meeting with Muslim leaders. However, Malay Muslims remain unenthusiastic celebrants of water festivals and other Buddhist holidays which dominate the Thai calendar.

Pattani is strongly Muslim and the big mosque, **Matsayit Klang**, is its only place of interest. It is on Yarang Road, 200m from the bus stop. Pattani is a very picturesque town though, particularly along the river, where the **harbour** is choked with gaily painted fishing vessels.

Excursions

Beaches There are several beaches not far from town, Rachadapisek, 13 km to the N and Thachii and Panare to the S.

Matsayit Kreu Se is the oldest mosque in the area. It lies 8 km E of Pattani, on Route 42 in the village of Ban Kreu Se. The mosque was built in 1578 by Lim To Khieng, a Chinese immigrant who married a local Pattani woman and converted to Islam. His betrothal was not received enthusiastically by his family, and on hearing the news his sister travelled from China to dissuade him and encourage him to return to the fold. He agreed to go back to China as soon as he had finished the construction of Matsayit Kreu Se, but the cunning Mr Lim saw to it that the mosque was never completed. Its brick walls and arches are still standing in a well-tended garden and the mosque is in use today. Locals say that after 400 years, plans are afoot to finish its construction, but would-be contractors risk being struck by lightning: this is said to be the fate awaiting those who try. Though the story is quaint the mosque is unremarkable. **Getting there**: bus to Narathiwat (฿12).

Festivals

Mar: *Chao Mae Lim Kornaeo* (2nd weekend) fire walking festival.

Local information

● Accommodation

B-D *My Gardens*, 8/28 Charoenpradit Rd, W of town, T 348933, some a/c, restaurant, best hotel in town.

C *Leela Resort*, 52 km S of Pattani (10 km from Chana), T 7120144, some a/c.

D-E *Chong Ar* and *Palace*, 190 Prida Rd, T 349039, some a/c, basic.

E *Thai An*, 67 Pattani Phirom Rd, T 348267, basic; **E** *Thai Hua*, 91 Pattani Phirom Rd, T 349104.

● Places to eat

Thai: ♦*Black Coffee*, on the roundabout by the clocktower, good selection of coffees, menu in Thai; ♦♦*Diana* (opposite *My Gardens Hotel*), opens 1800, seafood speciality; ♦♦*River*, Rong-Ang Rd (road straight down from clocktower to the river), set on a bend in the river; very picturesque, excellent Thai menu, rec. by locals.

Chinese: ♦♦*Chong Ar*, 190 Prida Rd, large selection; *Pornthip*, 9/38 Watanatham Rd, T 348123, large fancy restaurant with a huge menu with all the expensive specialities, prices quoted are for parties of 6-10, so no need to panic, open: 1000-0200. ♦♦*Pailin* (*My Gardens Hotel* restaurant), also serves seafood.

● Airline offices

Thai, 9 Prida Rd, T 394149.

● Entertainment

Black Coffee, by the clocktower, band in the evenings. *Pornthip*, live Chinese pop band.

● Post & telecommunications

Post Office: Pipit Rd (not far from the bridge). **Area code**: 073.

● Transport

1,149 km from Bangkok, 109 km from Hat Yai.

Local Songthaews: ฿5 around town.

Air Connections twice a week with Bangkok, via Hat Yai.

Road Bus: buses leave from the intersection of Rudi/Ramkomud/Yarang rds. Overnight connections with Bangkok's Southern bus terminal on Pinklao-Nakhon Chaisi Rd, 15 hrs (฿246-464). Regular connections with Narathiwat (฿30) and Hat Yai (฿43). **Taxis**: most taxis leave from stands near the bus stops on Yarang Rd, taxis to Hat Yai leave from near the bridge.

Narathiwat

Narathiwat is an Islamic stronghold and has one of the biggest mosques in South Thailand. There is also a **Muslim fishing village** beyond the market to the N of the town, where they still use the brightly painted *kor lae* – traditional fishing boats with curved bows and tails. Today the kor lae is an endangered species: diesel-powered Darwinism dictates that long-tails do it better. Across the bridge from the Muslim village is a pleasant beach area, rather like Samila Beach at Songkhla. North of the fishing village is a long sandy beach where there are several small outdoor restaurants serving seafood.

NARATHIWAT TBU 52

1. Thai Airways
2. Night Market
3. Motorbike taxis
4. Pacific Hotel
5. Tanyong Hotel
6. Rex Hotel
7. Yaowarat Hotel
8. Narathiwat Hotel
9. Bang Nara Hotel

Food stalls

0   75
metres
(approx)

Muslim
Fishing
Village

To
Airport

Market

Pichit Bamrung Rd

Puphapakdi Rd

Sophaphisai Rd

Chamroonnara Rd

Bang Nara River

Clock
Tower

N

Warakhamphiphit Rd

To
Taksin Palace
& Tak Bai
(30 km)

To
Pattani

In September 1993, guerrillas of the Pattani United Liberation Organisation ambushed a train in Narathiwat province, killing one Thai student and injuring 9 other passengers. The event showed that although the CPT might be moribund, there are still dissatisfied extremist elements in the South fighting for separatism, 1993 also saw arson attacks on a number of schools in the area, making the period one of the most 'active' for a number of years.

Excursions

Wat Khao Kong is 6 km SW of town and holds a 25m-high seated golden Buddha image (Phra Buddha Taksin Ming Mongkol), located on a small hill. It is more than 15m from knee to knee and decorated with gold mosaic tiles. Getting there: songthaew (฿5).

Taksin Palace is the Royal Summer Palace on Manao Bay, 8 km S of Narathiwat, off the main Narathiwat-Tak Bai Road. The palace is worth a visit for its beautifully kept gardens right on the coast. The palace itself is modern and not of great interest. Open: 0800-1200, 1300-1630 Mon-Sun, except when the King or Queen are in residence (usually between Aug and Sept). Getting there: songthaew (฿8).

Beaches There are several good beaches and a handful of resorts between Narathiwat and Tak Bai – such as **Panon Resort**, 3 km from Taksin Palace (signposted off the main road). Few Westerners stop off in these places – they are mostly used by Malaysians. The beaches are deserted and safe for swimming, although it's not the cleanest stretch of sand in Thailand. Accommodation: **D** *Panon Resort*, a/c, restaurant, concrete bungalows and chalets, cheaper motel-style rooms a bit like factory units. Getting there: songthaew (฿10).

Festivals

May: *Jao Mae To-Mo Fair*. **Sept**: *Narathiwat Fair* (3rd week), Kor lae boat racing takes place on the Bang Nara River. Dove cooing contests and sale of local produce.

Local information
● Accommodation

Not a very high standard. Most of the hotels are strung out along and just off Pichit Bamrung Rd. A 151-room hotel is under construction by the Princess group of hotels. It is scheduled to open in mid-1995 and will become the best hotel in the city. **B** *Tanyong*, 16/1 Sophaphisai Rd, T 511477, F 511834, a/c, restaurant, once the best hotel in town, the Tanyong hasn't yet adjusted to the idea of competition, clean but over-priced.

C *Pacific*, 42/1-2 Warakhamphiphit Rd, T 511076, a/c, restaurant, well appointed and very good value, rec.

D-E *Rex*, 6/1-2 Chamroonnara Rd, T 511134, F 511190, a/c, restaurant; **D-E** *Yaowarat*, 131 Pichit Bamrung Rd, T 512058/9, F 511320, a/c, clean, basic.

E *Narathiwat*, 341 Pupha Pakdi Rd, T 511063, attractive wooden building on waterfront; **E-F** *Bang Nara*, 274 Pupha Pakdi Rd, T 511036, clean and large rooms.

● Places to eat

Thai: ✦*Boonthong*, 55 Sophapisai Rd; ✦*Run Thai*, Satilraya Rd.

Seafood: Line of scruffy seafood stalls along the beach just to the N of town. ✦✦*Bang Nara*, Tak Bai Rd (by the bridge), a little out of town, but excellent seafood and views over the mosquito-infested river; ✦*Nasir*, Pichit Bamrung Rd, also serves Thai and Malay food.

International: *Tanyong Hotel*, 16/1 Sophapisai Rd, set meal rates, huge restaurant, band at night; ✦*Smerp*, opposite *Yaowarat* on Chamroonnara, Foremost ice-creams and cold drinks; ✦✦*Nida Foodland*, Sophapisai Rd, Chinese; ✦✦*Rimnam*, 3 km down Tak Bai Rd, T 511559, the town's most sophisticated restaurant patronized by the high society of Narathiwat, it's a longish hike out of town on the road S, but worth the trouble, seafood and curries.

● Airline offices

Thai, 322-324 Phuphapakdi Rd, T 511161.

● Banks & money changers

Thai Farmers, Phuphapakdi Rd, beyond Thai Airlines office.

● Post & telecommunications

Area code: 073.

● Transport

1315 km from Bangkok.

Local Songthaews. Motorbike taxis: from opposite the market.

Air Airport N of town. Connections with Bangkok (3/week) via Hat Yai.

Road Bus: buses leave from near the Muslim fishing village and from Pichit Bamrung Rd. Overnight connections with Bangkok 17 hrs (฿267-516). Regular connections with Hat Yai, Pattani, Yala and Sungei Golok. **Taxi**: from Pichit Bamrung Rd.

Tak Bai

Tak Bai is the first village on the road south from Narathiwat; its major attraction is **Wat Chonthala Singh**, the last bastion of Thai Buddhist culture before the Malaysian border. When Malaya's British colonial administration laid claim to the former Thai provinces that are now the states of Perlis and Kedah (to the W) at the beginning of the century, they had their eyes on Narathiwat too. Rama V defiantly built this strategically important wat to stake Siam's territorial claim to the area.

Within its sprawling compound are a collection of sadly dilapidated wooden buildings in the beautiful and distinctive southern style. The monks, workmen and everyone else in and around the wat enclave speak Thai – nearly everyone else in Tak Bai speaks Malay. The wat is signposted off the road in Tak Bai (to get there, go straight through the market and turn left) and sits in a picturesque spot on the riverbank.

2 km down the road from Tak Bai is the small port town of **Ta Ba**, where passenger and car ferries ply the river to and from Malaysia. Ta Ba has an exciting, colourful **market**, with what must be some of the juiciest, tastiest fruit in Southeast Asia – particularly during the mango and durian seasons.

Local information
● Accommodation

All the hotels are on the road to Narathiwat, about 1 km from the port of Ta Ba.

C *Taba Plaza*, 7/20 Takbai-Taba Rd, T 581234, a/c, restaurant; **C-D** *Masaya Resort*, 58/7

Muangmai Rd, T 581125, some a/c, restaurant, clean and best of the 3.

D *Pornphet*, 58/22 Takbai Rd, T 581331, some a/c, restaurant.

● **Banks & money changers**
Bank next to the *Taba Plaza Hotel* with exchange facilities.

● **Travel agent**
Taba Tours, Takbai-Taba Rd (next to *Taba Plaza Hotel*); express bus and train tickets (from Sungei Golok).

● **Transport**
33 km from Narathiwat.

Road Bus: buses leave from pier by Ta Ba market and pick up passengers in Tak Bai. Regular connections with Narathiwat and Sungei Golok. **Taxi**: from pier by Ta Ba market.

● **Transport to Malaysia**
Ta Ba is a little-used but speedy crossing-point between Thailand and Malaysia, as taxi and bus stands on both sides are adjacent to the ferry. The disadvantage is that Ta Ba is not well connected with other towns in Thailand, although it is easy enough to get to Sungei Golok (just 32 km to the W) for the train N.

Sea Boat: the border is open 0700-1600 Mon-Sun (Thai time). Passenger ferry crossing from next to Ta Ba market and bus stop. If crossing with a car it is necessary to go through the customs section in a large compound next door. Regular crossings from Ta Ba to Pengkalan Kubor, Malaysia (β30 or M$3). On the Malaysian side, there are regular buses from Pengkalan Kubor to Kota Bahru (M$1.20).

Yala

Yala is the capital of the only landlocked province on the Kra Isthmus. The town is predominantly Muslim and has one of the biggest mosques in Thailand. **Chuang Phuak Park**, to the N of the railway station, is a popular spot with locals, offering a large man-made lake with boats for hire.

Excursions
Bang Lang Dam lies 12 km off the Yala-Betong road, 10 km S of Ban Nang Sata. The road twists up through the hills to two small villages, Ban Santi 1 and 2 on the far side of the lake. There

1. Wat Phutaphoom
2. Thai Airways
3. Market
4. Taxis to Betong, Hat Yai & Songkhla
5. Taxis to Pattani
6. Yala Rama Hotel
7. Merry Hotel
8. Sri Yala Hotel
9. Thepwimarn Hotel

B1. Buses to Pattani
B2. Buses to all other destinations

is a very picturesque drive overlooking the lake, which is dotted with tiny islands. **Bang Lang National Park** is another 3 km further down the Yala-Betong road. Accommodation: **E** Bungalows by the lake, run by the electricity generating authority, T 213699, reservations essential as it is a popular venue for conferences; the road to the bungalows is to the right up a very steep hill just after the entrance barrier, restaurant, pool and tennis courts. **Getting there**: songthaew from the railway station (β20).

Wat Khupha (Wat Naa Tham) – one of the most important monuments in the South – is signposted off the Yala-Hat Yai road, 8 km NW of town. A small museum by the entrance to the cave temple exhibits some of the Srivijayan finds from the area: votive tablets, manuscripts and small bronze figures. Wat Khupha was assumed by archaeologists to have been an important religious centre in the south during the Srivijaya Period from the 7th to 13th century. The 25m reclining Buddha is in the main cave sanctuary of this pleasant cave temple. Its sprawling interior is dramatically lit by shafts of light. The statue has been restored and is believed to have an older Bodhisattva figure inside. The original image dates from 757AD, and was commissioned by the Srivijayan King of Palembang (Sumatra). There are a couple of other cave temples to explore nearby – take the path along the bottom of the rock face. The caves are huge and well illuminated but not especially interesting. There are several other caves in the area. Getting there: songthaew from the railway station (฿2).

Festivals

Mar: *Dove competition* (1st weekend), and ASEAN competition, with exhibitions. **May/Jun**: *Yala city pillar* celebrations (moveable) in honour of the town's guardian spirit, Jao Paw Lak Muang. Traditional Southern Thai entertainment such as shadow puppet performances.

Local information
● Accommodation

B-C *Yala Rama*, 21 Sribamrung Rd, T 212563, F 214532, a/c, restaurant, best in town.

D-E *Merry*, 25-27 Phuthumvithi Rd, T 212693, some a/c, largish rooms; **D-E** *Sri Yala*, 16-22 Chaicharat Rd, T 212170, some a/c, restaurant, second best in town; **D-E** *Thepwimarn*, 31-37 Sribamrung Rd, T 212400, some a/c, restaurant, basic.

● Places to eat

♦♦*Wild West*, Rotfai Rd (next to the bus station), Thai; **♦***Sriyala*, 16 Chaicharat Rd, large international menu; **♦♦***Yala Rama Coffee Shop*, 21 Sribamrung Rd, reasonable Thai buffet and international food.

● Entertainment

Wild West, Rotfai Rd. Folk music in the evenings.

● Post & telecommunications
Area code: 073.

● Transport

1153 km from Bangkok, 178 km from Hat Yai.

Train Station on NE side of town. Overnight connections with Bangkok (฿165-738) and other stops N. Also regular connections with Hat Yai and Sungei Golok.

Road Bus: Pattani buses leave from Pattani Rd on the far side of the railway track. Buses to all other destinations leave from the station next to the railway station, just up from the *Yala Rama Hotel*. Regular connections with Bangkok 16 hrs (฿244-460), Hat Yai last bus 1400, Songkhla, Pattani, Sungei Golok. Betong buses (mini Mercedes) leave mornings only. No buses to Narathiwat. **Taxi**: from along the road in front of the railway station.

Betong

After the magnificent mountain drive from Yala which winds up through dramatic limestone hills, Betong is a disappointing, ugly town, full of barbershops, massage parlours and hotels catering for Malaysians on cross-border weekends and 'business trips'. It is, however, an interesting border crossing-point.

Until 1990, when Chin Peng's Communist Party of Malaya came out of the jungle and the rebels laid down their arms, Betong's forested hills concealed his HQ and acted as the base for guerillas heading S down the peninsula. Joint Malaysian-Thai army patrols regularly mounted search and destroy missions against the CPM base, known ominously as 'Target One'. The Communists made this as difficult as possible by seeding trails with anti-personnel mines, which they are now being made to clear in joint Thai-Malaysian-CPM operations. Now that this subversive excitement is history, Betong's only claim to fame – other than its sex industry – is an enormous postbox which is said to be the biggest in the world.

Excursions

Betong Hot Springs are situated 10 km from town; drive 3 km and then turn right onto a dirt track for a further 7 km. The big steaming pool is rather dirty,

PITYAMIT ONE: FROM GUERRILLA CAMP TO HOLIDAY CAMP

The Malayan Emergency was one of the few insurgencies which the communists lost. But their shelling, ambushes, bombings and assassinations cost the lives of more than 10,000 soldiers and civilians over 40 years. The Emergency started just after the Second World War. At its peak, tens of thousands of Commonwealth troops were pitted against an estimated 3,500 communists – most of whom were Chinese – in the Malayan jungle. Newly independent Malaysia pronounced the Emergency officially over in 1960. They had the communists on the run. The guerrillas fled across Malaysia's jungled frontier into South Thailand – but once ensconsed there, they held out for another 30 years against both the Malaysian and Thai armies.

Most of their secret camps were never found. The communists had laced the border itself with booby trap devices and regularly launched attacks and ambushes across the border. The people on the frontline of the war were the residents of the Malaysian border town of Pengkalan Hulu (formerly Keroh), which means 'forward base'. Many attrocities were committed in and around the town, which was still under curfew until well into the 1980s. The communists also made themselves unpopular in Thailand, where they demanded protection money from local businesses around Betong. They never surrendered, but finally, in 1989, they reached what was known as "an honourable settlement" with the Malaysian and Thai governments, bringing to an end one of the world's longest-running insurgencies. Realizing that most of the former guerrillas would be unwilling to return to their homeland, King Bhumipol of Thailand offered them land around their former camps and built them houses. One of those camps, Pityamit I, has now opened to the public for the first time. Like others in the vicinity, nobody knew it was there until very recently.

Having laid down their Kalashnikovs, former revolutionaries now take tourists round their old jungle stronghold. Some sell herbal medicine and soft drinks to the tourists; others have become vegetable farmers at the Highland Friendship Cooperative (the camp's new name). The trees which once afforded them thick cover from helicopter gunships have been chopped down and the steep hillsides have been planted out. About 1,200 former fighters have now settled into their new lives but few have any regrets about their old ones as members of the Communist Party of Malaya's pro-Moscow splinter group. "Money is important", one of them told a visiting journalist. "Without it you can't do anything." They are happy to regail tourists with tales of the jungle. Some have been living in it since 1948. Although they admit that communism world-wide appears to have failed, they urge those who are prepared to listen not to jump to hasty conclusions. "Our generation shouldn't be the ones to jump to that conclusion," they say. "That should be up to our sons and grandsons."

About 100 former communists have returned to booming modern Malaysia. They are in detention under the country's Internal Security Act in Taiping, where in the words of their comrades across the border, they are being "rehabilitated" and "brain-washed". In Kuala Lumpur, few people stop to think of the Emergency years; they seem like ancient history now because things have moved so fast. But if it's all be partially forgotten, the communists themselves have not been forgiven as the scars still run deep. Now, however, Malaysia has new problems to attend to. In an article contributed to the *International Herald Tribune* newspaper in 1993, Malaysia's deputy Prime Minister, Anwar Ibrahim, wrote: "Religious fundamentalism is potentially as threatening to global peace and stabilty as was communism – if not more so, since it appeals to sentiments and traditions with a far longer history than Marxism-Leninism."

although the smaller pool is cleaner. The springs are in a pleasant setting surrounded by hills. There are several stalls catering mainly for elderly Chinese tour groups hoping for a cure or second lease of life. Getting there: hire a saamlor from Betong (฿100 upwards).

Highland Friendship Village (Pityamit One) is 10 km up the road from the hot springs and is a former jungle base camp belonging to the Marxist-Leninist faction of the Communist Party of Malaya, which fought the Malaysian and Thai armies from here for nearly 30 years (see box). Even the intelligence services of both armies were unaware of the existence of the camp until after the communists laid down their arms in 1989. At the entrance, there is now a 4m-high statue of four white doves in the middle of a fountain. (This is the emblem of the village – the former guerrillas themselves refer to them as "peace pigeons"; literature from one Betong hotel misguidedly refers to the statue as "a seagull memorial"). The camp's residents sell souvenirs to tourists and host guided tours of the old jungle camp itself, which is a 10 min walk up the hillside to the right of the main entrance. Exhibits are carefully labelled; they include uniforms and other regalia and memorabilia of the former People's Liberation Army of Malaya. Camp facilities are on show – including the kitchen area which had an ingenious flue, constructed so as to suck up the smoke and embers and release them on the other side of the hill enabling the camp's location to remain a secret. The pride of the camp, however, is its network of subterranean tunnels in which the comrades once sheltered from Malaysian mortars and Thai patrols. They took 50 cadres three months to dig, working round the clock in shifts. 10m underground there are eating and sleeping areas and a radio communications room. Other nearby camps had similar tunnel systems, but they have not yet been opened to the public as their environs are still strewn with boobytraps. Accommodation: *Friendship Resort,* Pityamit One, fan, food available at hot springs, clean little white rooms in two modern bungalows on hillside overlooking village, modestly furnished but pleasant, pleasant alternative to staying in Betong. Getting there: as with hot springs, hire saamlor/taxi from Betong (฿150-200).

Ban Sakai is home to a community of formerly semi-nomadic Sakai 'aboriginals'. Turn left near a bridge off the main Betong-Yala road between the km 66 and km 67 markers. The road follows the river up the valley for 4 km; Ban Sakai is signposted from the main village. In Malaysia, the Sakai are called *orang asli* (indigenous man); the Thais are less polite, referring to them as *ngao* – or 'rambutans', as the fruit has a not dissimilar hairstyle. This is one of the few remaining groups of Sakai in Thailand, although they are largely settled now. Most work as tappers in the local rubber holdings. Getting there: take Yala buses and walk 4 km from the main road.

Local information
● Accommodation

Although most of Betong's hotels cater for the sex industry, a number of new, more sophisticated hotels have recently opened, the best of which is the *Merlin*. Prices are mainly quoted in Malaysian ringgit. **B** *Merlin*, 33 Chayachaowalit Rd, T 230222, F 231357, a/c, restaurant, pool, superb value for money, very high standard of rooms with wide range of facilities including fitness centre, snooker club, sauna and disco, rec; **B** *Penthouse Resort*, 68/1 Rattanasatien Rd, T 230644, F 230879, a/c, restaurant, smaller rooms than *Merlin*, but well-kept in lush garden surrounds, good range of facilities.

C-D *Cathay*, 17-21 Chantarothai Rd, T 230999, a/c, restaurant, formerly top hotel in town, newly spruced-up to keep pace with recent arrivals, reasonably clean, spacious rooms, facilities include barber shop and disco, ticketing agent; **C-D** *Khong Kha*, 1 Thammwithi Rd, T 230441, some a/c, restaurant, poor.

D *Fortuna*, 50-58 Pakdidamrong Rd, T 231180, a/c, restaurant, reasonable value, best of lower bracket; **D-E** *Thai*, 25 Rattanakit Rd, T 230074, some a/c, restaurant, 'short stay' hotel.

E *Sri Betong 2*, 16/3-5 Chayachawalit Rd, T 230355, dark and dingy.

● **Places to eat**

Chinese: Several restaurants around town, ♦*New Restaurant*, on the road in front of the clock tower, is the best, standard Chinese fare, serves dim sum for breakfast. Plenty more restaurants along Sukhayang Rd.

Malay and Chinese stalls behind the *Cathay Hotel*.

● **Banks & money changers**

Thai Farmers and Thai Military opposite Esso station.

● **Post & telecommunications**

Area code: 073.

● **Transport**

Road Bus: daily connection with Yala (₿31) from the road in front of the clocktower. **Taxi**: to Yala, 4 hrs from the road in front of the clocktower.

● **Transport to Malaysia**

The border post is 8 km out of town but it is only a short stroll across to Malaysia and there are plenty of taxis waiting the other side. It is marked by an old boundary stone emblazoned with a quaint colonial map of Malaya.

Road Taxi: from Betong to the border post (₿80 for the whole taxi) or saamlor (₿10). From the Malaysian side of the border post to Keroh (M$1). From Keroh to Sungai Petani (M$25).

Sungei Golok

This border town is the jumping-off point for the E coast of Malaysia and is another unattractive Southern Thai town catering for Malaysian 'business travellers'. The border crossing connects with Rantau Panjang.

Local information
● **Accommodation**

Most of the hotels are around Charoenkhet Rd. Many are used by Malaysians on short stays and the quality of accommodation is uniformly poor. Hotels accept Thai baht or Malaysian ringgit.

B *Genting*, 141 Asia 18 Rd, T 613231, F 611259, a/c, restaurant, good sized pool, featureless block; **B** *Grand Garden*, 66 Soi 3 Prachawiwat Rd, T 611219, F 613500, a/c, restaurant, small pool with waterfall, featureless rooms; **B** *Marina*, 173 Charoenkhet Soi 3, T 613881, F 613385, a/c, restaurant, pool; **B-C** *Tara Regent*, 45 Charoenkhet Soi Phuthon, T 611801, F 613385, some a/c, restaurant; **B-D** *Merlin*, 40 Charoenkhet Rd, T 611003, a/c.

C *Intertower*, 160-166 Prachawiwat Rd, T 611700, F 613400, a/c, restaurant.

D-E *An An*, 183 Prachawiwat Rd, T 611058, some a/c; **D-E** *Savoy*, 8/2 Charoenkhet Rd, T 611093, some a/c.

● **Post & telecommunications**

Area code: 073.

● **Shopping**

Malaysian batik is available in shops all around town.

● **Tourist office**

Tourist centre service (temporary office), Asia 18 Rd, next to immigration post on the bridge, T 612126, F 615230. Areas of responsibility are Narathiwat, Yala and Pattani.

● **Transport**

1,220 km from Bangkok.

Local Motorcycle taxi: from town over the border (₿10).

Train Station on Asia 18 Rd (the road to the border). Overnight connections with Bangkok (₿180-808). Connections to Yala, Hat Yai, Phattalung, Nakhon Si Thammarat.

Road Bus: station on Bussayapan Rd (near *An An Hotel*). Overnight connections with Bangkok 18 hrs (₿282-533). Regular connections with Surat Thani 10 hrs, Hat Yai 4 hrs (₿60), Narathiwat 1 hr. **Taxi**: Tak Bai, Narathiwat, Pattani, Yala, Hat Yai.

● **Transport to Malaysia**

Border open 0500-1700 Mon-Sun, Thai time. This is the main crossing-point on the E side of the peninsula, as Sungei Golok is well connected with other towns by train and bus. But the bus stop and railway station in Sungei Golok are at least 1 km from Golok Bridge (the crossing-point), so it is necessary to hire a motorbike or trishaw to go from the railway station or bus stop across the bridge.

Road Bus: Rantau Panjang's bus stand is 1 km from Golok Bridge. Regular connections with

Kota Bahru. **Taxi**: taxi stand in Rantau Panjang is opposite Golok Bridge. Taxis to almost anywhere in Malaysia. Per seat: Kota Bahru (M$3.50), Kuala Lumpur (M$43), Butterworth (M$30) and Alor Star (M$35).

Satun

Surrounded by mountains, Satun is cut off from the Malaysian Peninsula and the eastern side of the Kra Isthmus.

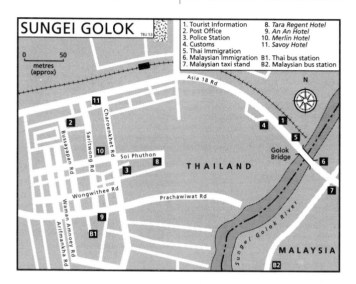

SUNGEI GOLOK TBU 53

1. Tourist Information
2. Post Office
3. Police Station
4. Customs
5. Thai Immigration
6. Malaysian Immigration
7. Malaysian taxi stand
8. Tara Regent Hotel
9. An An Hotel
10. Merlin Hotel
11. Savoy Hotel
B1. Thai bus station
B2. Malaysian bus station

0   50
metres (approx)

Asia 18 Rd

Charoenkhet Rd
Bussayapan Rd
Saritvong Rd
Soi Phuthon
Wongwithee Rd
Waman Amnoey Rd
Arilmankha Rd
Prachawiwat Rd

THAILAND

Golok Bridge

Sungei Golok River

MALAYSIA

CROSSING THE BORDER: THAILAND & MALAYSIA

By train The train between Bangkok and Kuala Lumpur and Singapore crosses the Thai-Malaysia border just after the border town of **Padang Besar**. There is also a line which runs through the eastern border town of **Sungei Golok**.

By road (running from E to W): **1. Tak Bai** is on the Thai peninsula's E coast; just to the S is the border town of Ta Ba. Ferries run from Ta Ba, across the border, to Pengkalan Kubor. Taxis and buses wait at both ferry jetties to take passengers to Sungei Golok (Thailand) or Kota Bahru (Malaysia). Border open: 0700-1600 (**see page 479**). **2. Sungei Golok** is the main eastern crossing point; buses and trains stop 1 km N of the border, taxis wait just S, but it is another 1 km walk to Rantau Panjang (Malaysia) and the bus station. Bus connections from Rantau Panjang to Kota Bahru and taxis to almost anywhere in Malaysia; buses, trains and taxis from Sungei Golok to Bangkok and most southern Thai towns. Border open: 0500-1700 (**see page 483**). **3. Betong** is 8 km N of the border; and the Malaysian town of Keroh a few kilometres S. Taxis wait on either side to take passengers to these two towns, where there are buses to Narathiwat (Thailand) and Sungai Petani (Malaysia) (**see page 483**). **4. Satun** is 8 km N of Ban Pak Bara on the peninsula's west coast. Daily ferries from Ban Pak Bara to the Malaysian island of Langkawi (**see page 485**).

There is not much to see in Satun, but it is a jumping-off point for Koh Turatao and the Adang-Rawi Islands (see below) as well as Pulau Langkawi, Malaysia. It is mainly a Malay-Muslim area, similar to Yala, Pattani and Narathiwat.

Excursions

Thaleban National Park lies 40 km from Satun, bordering Malaysia, with a freshwater lake, waterfalls and caves. The park has a large bird population: hawks, hornbills, falcons and many migratory birds. Animal residents include Dusky Leaf Monkeys, White-handed Gibbon, Lesser Mousedeer, wild boar and, it is said, the Sumatran Rhinoceros. There is some cabin and dormitory accommodation at the Park HQ, and a restaurant.

Tours

Charan Tour, runs boat tours every day to the islands between Oct and May. Lunch and snorkelling equipment are provided.

Local information
● Accommodation
A-C *Wangmai*, 43 Satunthani Rd, T 711607, a/c, restaurant, Satun's best.

D *Satunthani*, 90 Satunthani Rd, T 711010, a/c, restaurant.

● Places to eat
Smile, round the corner from *Wangmai Hotel* on Satuntanee Phiman, fastfood, budget; *The Baker's*, on Satuntanee Phiman, the main street into town, pastries, ice-cream and soft drinks, budget; ♦*Kualuang*, Satuntanee Phiman, best in a group of small Thai restaurants.

● Banks & money changers
Thai Military, Buriwanit Rd (across from Hat Yai taxi rank on Buriwanit Rd); Thai Farmers, opposite the market.

● Post & telecommunications
Area code: 074.

● Tour companies & travel agents
Charan Tour, 19/6 Satunthani Rd, T 711453, F 711982; *Satun Travel Ferry Service* (part of *Charan Tour*), Satunthani Rd, opposite *Wangmai Hotel*.

● Transport
1,065 km from Bangkok.

Local Motorbike taxis: from outside Thai Farmers Bank, near the market and from outside *Satunthani Hotel* on Satunthani Rd.

Road Bus: overnight connections with Bangkok 15 hrs (฿223-427). Regular connections with Hat Yai and Trang from outside the wat. **Taxi**: Hat Yai from Bureevanith Rd, Trang from taxi rank next to Chinese temple.

● Transport to Malaysia
Sea Boat: ferries leave from Ban Pak Bara, 8 km N of Satun. Buses to Ban Pak Bara leave from the market, songthaew. There are buses direct from Hat Yai to Ban Pak Bara during the tourist season. Daily ferries to Langkawi (฿150). Tickets can be purchased in advance from *Charan Tour*.

Turatao National Park and the Adang-Rawi Archipelago

Turatao was Thailand's first marine national park, created in 1974. It is made up of 61 islands, the main ones being Turatao, Adang, Rawi, Lipe, Klang, Dong and Lek. The park is divided into 2 main areas: the Turatao Archipelago and the Adang-Rawi Archipelago.

The mountainous island of **Turatao** is the largest of the islands. Its highest point is 708m. To Bu cliff, just behind the park headquarters on Ao Phante, has good views and is the spot for sunset romantics. The main beaches are Ao Moh Lai, Hin Ngam, Ao Phante, Ao Chak and Ao Son, mostly on the W of the island. The prison at Ao Talo U-Dang, in the S, was once used as a concentration camp for Thailand's political prisoners; the graveyard, charcoal furnaces and a fish fermentation plant still remain. The other main camp was at Ao Talo Wao on the E side of the island and was used for high security criminals. A road, built by inmates, connects the two camps. It is said that high class political prisoners were segregated from the lowlier criminals, and the latter had to wait upon the former.

Coconut plantations still exist on Tu-

TURATAO NP & THE ADANG-RAWI ARCHIPELAGO

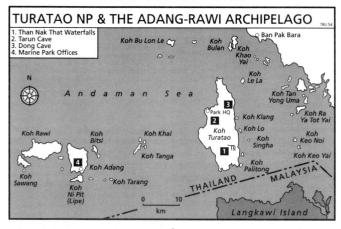

1. Than Nak That Waterfalls
2. Tarun Cave
3. Dong Cave
4. Marine Park Offices

ratao but the forests have barely been touched, providing a natural habitat for lemur, wild boar, macaques and mouse deer. There are said to be crocodiles in Khlong Phante and there is a large cave on the Choraka (crocodile) water system known as Crocodile Cave (bring a flashlight). There are also a huge variety of birds on the islands, including colonies of swiftlets found in the numerous limestone caves – mainly on Koh Lo Tong (to the S of Turatao) and Koh Ta Kieng (to the NE). Many of the islands' caves have been used by pirates for centuries but some are still unexplored. Large tracts of mangrove forest are found here, especially along Khlong Phante Malacca on Turatao. The islands are also known for their trilobite fossils, 4 to 5 million years old, found not just on Turatao but all over the national park.

Turatao is just 4.8 km N of Malaysia's *Langkawi Island*, which, in contrast is already a leading tourism destination. Both the Malaysian and Thai islands were traditionally pirates' lairs and Turatao and Langkawi were said to be cursed and hidden from the outside world for 7 generations.

Adang and **Rawi** are the main islands in the archipelago of the same name;

they lie 43 km W of Turatao with rugged granite hills (rising as high as 703m). Koh Adang is almost entirely forested. The main beaches on Adang are Khai, Laem Son, Ao Lo Lae Lae and Lo Lipa, and Sai Khao on Rawi. **Koh Lipe** is the flattest island in the group and has the largest settlement in the archipelago, of Chao Le fisherpeople, who were the original inhabitants of the islands. They have their own unique culture, language and peculiar architectural style. The Chao Le hold a traditional ceremony called *pla juk* twice a year. A miniature boat is built out of *rakam* and *teenped* wood by the villagers. Once the boat is completed, offerings are placed in it, and the Chao Le dance until dawn and then launch the boat out to sea, loaded with the village's communal bad luck. The prisoners originally incarcerated on Turatao have been moved to Koh Lipe where they now complete their sentences. **Koh Hin Ngam** is SW of Adang and is known for its strange-shaped stones found on the beaches. **Koh Khai** has white powdery sand beaches and some excellent diving.

Koh Bulan and **Koh Bulan-Le** have developed into quiet beach resorts with simple bungalow accommodation. The islands are inhabited by Sea Gypsies or *Chao Ley* who meet their needs through fishing. News that a company has purchased 70 *rai* (about 40 acres) of land indicates possible future tourist development. Koh Bulan is visited once a day by boat from Ban Pak Bara (฿80); Koh Bulan-Le can only be reached by long-tail boat from Koh Bulan.

Despite dynamite-fishing in some areas, the island waters still have reasonable coral, and provide some of the best dive sites in Thailand – particularly around the natural stone arch on Koh Khai. Adang Island has magnificent coral reefs. Whales, dolphins and turtles are common here.

BEST TIME TO VISIT Nov to April, coolest months are Nov and Dec. Park is closed May-Oct.

Tours
For tours to Turatao, see Satun, page 485.

Local information
● **Accommodation**
Turatao: Book through the National Parks office in Bangkok T 5790529 or T (074) 711383. There is also a National Parks office at Ban Pak Bara pier. Accommodation is on the north and west of Turatao. *Tabag Bungalows*, on N tip of Turatao, 2 rooms **B**, 1 room **C** – rooms accommodate 4 people; **D** *Bamboo house*; **F**/person '*Longhouse*' dormitory. Hired tent ฿60, own tent ฿10.

Adang: *Bamboo longhouse* with 10 rooms, each accommodating 4 people at **F**/person.

● **Camping**
Charan Tours can organize tent hire (see page 485). **Turatao**: Best spots for camping are on Ao Jak and Ao San.

● **Places to eat**
Hotels all run restaurants.

Koh Lipe: Food and drink are sold in the *Chao Le*.

● **Sport**
Snorkelling: equipment for hire on Adang. Some of the best spots for coral in the park are: NW of Koh Rang Nok, NW of Turatao, SE of Koh Rawi and around Mu Ko Klang between Turatao and Adang.

● **Transport**
Turatao lies 31 km off the coast, Adang is 80 km off the coast.

Local Boats: for hire from Turatao and Adang. ฿350 to go between the two islands. ฿200 to Crocodile Cave from Turatao.

Sea Boat: from Ban Pak Bara, 62 km N of Satun. Boats to Turatao at 1030 and 1400 from Nov-May, 2 hrs (฿70 one way). Return from Turatao at 0900 and 1400. The sea is usually too rough from May to Oct, although boats can be chartered at the discretion of their captains throughout the year (฿500 plus). Boats to Adang and Rawi are less frequent but can also be chartered from Turatao.

● **To get to Ban Pak Bara**
Road Bus: from the market in Satun (฿20), or from in front of Plaza Market, Hat Yai at 0745 during the tourist season. Buses from Ban Pak Bara to Satun connect with ferries. **Taxi**: to Langu (from Satun) (฿20) and then a songthaew to Ban Pak Bara (฿8).

INFORMATION FOR VISITORS

CONTENTS

Before you go

Entry requirements

● **Visas**

All tourists must possess passports valid for at least 6 months longer than their intended stay in Thailand. No visa is required for tourists arriving by air, holding a confirmed onward air ticket and who intend to stay for up to 15 days (not extendable). Tourists are fined ฿100/day each day they exceed the 15 day limit. The same applies to tourists who arrive via the Thai-Malaysian border by sea, rail or road. This applies to nationals of the following countries: Argentina, Australia, Austria, Belgium, Brazil, Brunei, Burma, Canada, Denmark, Fiji, Finland, France, Germany, Greece, Hong Kong, Iceland, Indonesia, Ireland, Italy, Japan, Jordan, Kenya, Luxembourg, Malaysia, Mexico, Netherlands, Norway, Papua New Guinea, Philippines, Portugal, Republic of Korea, Senegal, Singapore, Spain, South Africa, Sweden, Switzerland, Turkey, UK, USA, Vanuatu, Western Samoa. Malaysian nationals arriving by road from Malaysia do not need evidence of onward journey. Nationals from New Zealand, Sweden, Denmark, Norway and Finland do not require a visa for visits of up to three months.

Tourist visas These are valid for 60 days from date of entry (single entry), transit visas for 30 days (single entry). **Visa extensions** are obtainable from the Immigration Department in Bangkok (see below) for ฿500. The process used to be interminable, but the system is now much improved and relatively painless. Extensions can also be issued in other towns, such as Koh Samui (see page 451) and Chiang Mai (page 245). Applicants must bring two photocopies of their passport ID page and the page on which their tourist visa is stamped, together with three passport photographs. It may be easier to leave the country and then re-enter having obtained a new tourist visa. Visas are issued by all Thai embassies and consulates.

90-day non-immigrant visas These are also issued and can be obtained in the applicant's home country (about US$30). A letter from the applicant's company or organization guaranteeing their repatriation should be submitted at the same time.

In the UK there is now a visa information line, operating 24 hrs a day, T 0891 600 150.

● **Immigration Department**
Soi Suan Phlu, Sathorn Thai Road, Bangkok 10120, T 2864231.

● **Vaccinations**
No vaccinations required, unless coming from an infected area (if visitors have been in a yellow fever infected area in the 10 days before arrival, and do not have a vaccination certificate, they will be vaccinated and kept in quarantine for 6 days, or deported. See health section below for details.

● **Representation overseas**
Australia, 111 Empire Circuit, Yarralumla, Canberra, A.C.T. 2600, T (06) 2731149, 2732937; **Austria**, Weimarer Strasse 68, 1180

Vienna, T (0222) 3103423; **Belgium**, Square du Val de la Cambre 2, 1050 Brussels, T 2 6406810; **Canada**, 180 Island Park Drive, Ottawa, Ontario, K1Y 0A2, T (613) 722 4444; **Denmark**, Norgesmindevej 18, 2900 Hellerup, Copenhagen, T (31) 6250101; **France**, 8 Rue Greuze, 75116 Paris, T 47043222; **Germany**, Uberstrasse 65, 5300 Bonn 2, T (0228) 355065; **Greece**, 23 Taigetou Street, PO Box 65215, Paleo Psychico 15452, Athens, T 6717969; **Italy**, Via Nomentana, 132, 00162 Rome, T (396) 8320729; **Japan**, 3-14-6, Kami-Osaki, Shinagawa-ku, Tokyo 141, T (03) 3441-1386; **Laos**, Route Phonekheng, PO Box 128, Vientiane, T 2508; **Malaysia**, 206 Jalan Ampang, 50450 Kuala Lumpur, T (03) 2488222; **Myanmar**, 91, Pyay Road, Rangoon, T 21713; **Nepal**, Jyoti Kendra Building, Thapathali, PO Box 3333, Kathmandu, T 213910; **Netherlands**, 1 Buitenrustweg, 2517 KD, The Hague, T (070) 3452088; **New Zealand**, 2 Cook Street, PO Box 17-226, Karori, T 768618; **Norway**, Munkedamsveien 59B, 0270 Oslo 2, T (02) 832517-8; **Portugal**, Avenida Almirante Gago Coutinho 68A, 1700 Lisbon, T 805350; **Spain**, Calle del Segre, 29, 20 A, 28002 Madrid, T (341) 5632903; **Sweden**, Sandhamnsgatan 36 (5th Floor), PO Box 27065, 10251 Stockholm, T (08) 6672160; **Switzerland**, Eigerstrasse 60 (3rd Floor), 3007 Bern, T (031) 462281; **UK**, 29-30 Queens Gate, London, SW7 5JB, T 071 589 0173 (there are also consulates in Birmingham, Glasgow, Liverpool, Cardiff and Hull); **USA**, 2300 Kalorama Road N.W., Washington, D.C. 20008, T (202) 4837200.

● **Tourist information**

The Tourist Authority of Thailand (TAT) is Thailand's very efficient tourism organization. The head office moved in 1993 to 372 Bamrung Muang Rd, Bangkok, T 2260060, F 2246221. Local offices are found in most major tourist destinations in the country and their addresses are listed in the appropriate sections. TAT offices are a useful source of local information, often providing maps of the town, listings of hotels/guesthouses and information on local tourist attractions. Opening hours: 0830-1630 Mon-Sun.

Overseas offices are: *Australia*, 12th Floor, Royal Exchange Bldg, 56 Pitt Street, Sydney, T 02 247-7549, F 02 251-2465; *France*, 90 Avenue des Champs Elysées, 75008 Paris, T 4562-8656, F 01 4563-7888; *Germany*, Bethmann Str. 58/IV, D-6000 Frankfurt/Main 1,

T 069 295-704, F 069 281-468; *Hong Kong*, Room 401 Fairmont House, 8 Cotton Tree Drive, Central, Hong Kong, T 868-0732, F 868-4584; *Italy*, Via Barberini 50, 00187 Roma, T 06 474-7410, F 06 474-7660; *Japan*, Hiranomachi Yachiyo Bldg 5F, 1-8-13 Hiranomachi Chuo-ku, Osaka 541, T 06 231-4434, F 06 231-4337, and Hibiya Mitsui Bldg., 1-2 Yurakucho 1-Chome, Chiyoda-ku, Tokyo 100, T 03 580-6776-7, F 03 508-7808; *Malaysia*, c/o Royal Thai Embassy, 206 Jalan Ampang, Kuala Lumpur, T 242601, F 093 248918; *Singapore*, c/o Royal Thai Embassy, 370 Orchard Rd, Singapore, T 737 3060, F 732 2458; *UK*, 49 Albemarle Street, London W1X 3FE, T 071-499 7679, F 071-629-5519; *USA*, 5 World Trade Center, Suite No. 2449, New York N.Y. 10048, T 212 432-0433, F 212 912-0920 and 3440 Wilshire Blvd., Suite 1101, Los Angeles, CA 90010, T 213 382-2353, F 213 380-6476.

● **Specialist tour operators**

UK: *Abercrombie & Kent Travel*, Sloane Square House, Holbein Place, London SW1W 8NS, T 071 730 9600, F 071 730 9376; *All Season Tours*, 5 Cavendish Court, Sylvester Rd, Wembley, Middlesex HA0 3AE, T 081 900 0227/0238, F 081 903 0491; *Asian Affair Holidays*, 143/147 Regent St, London W1R 7LB, T 071 439 2601, F 071 287 2677; *Asia Voyages*, 230 Station Rd, Addlestone, Surrey KT15 2PH, T 0932 820050, F 0932 820633; *Eastravel*, 79 Norwich Rd, Ipswich, Suffolk 1P1 2PR, T 0473 214 305, F 0473 232 740; *Encounter Overland Ltd*, 267 Old Brompton Rd, London SW5, T 071 370 6845, F 071 244 9737; *Explore Worldwide*, 1 Frederick St, Aldershot, Hants GU11 1LQ, T 0252 319 448/9, F 0252 343 170; *Exodus Expeditions*, 9 Weir Rd, London SW12 0LT, T 081 675 5550, F 081 673 0779; *Far East Travel Centre*, 33 Maddox St, London W1R 9LD, T 071 414 8844, F 071 414 8848; *Far East Travel Centre*, 23 John Dalton St, Manchester M2 6FW, T 061 833 0784, F 061 835 2405; *Guerba Expeditions Ltd*, 101 Eden Vale Rd, Westbury, Wiltshire BA13 3QX, T 0373 858 956, F 0373 858 351; *Hayes & Jarvis Travel*, 152 King St, Hayes House, London W6 0QU, T 081 748 0088, F 081 741 0299; *Magic of the Orient*, 2 Kingsland Court, Three Bridges, Crawley, West Sussex RH10 1HL, T 0293 537 700, F 0293 537 888; *Oriental Magic Holidays*, Gold Medal House, Metropolitan Drive, Preston New Road, Blackpool FY3 9LT, T 0253 791 100, F 0253 791 333; *Page & Moy*, 136-140

London Rd, Leicester LE2 1EN, T 0533 524 462, F 0533 549 949; *Premier Faraway Holidays*, Westbrook, Milton Rd, Cambridge CB4 1YQ, T 0223 65626, F 0223 324373; *Saga Holidays*, Saga Building, Middleburg Square, Folkestone, Kent CT20 1AZ, T 0303 711502 (Ext 1513), F 0303 220391; *Simply Tropix*, Suite 23, Alice Court, 116 Putney Bridge Rd, London SW15 2NQ, T 081 875 1777, F 081 875 9111; *Scotia Air Holidays*, 57 Bothwell St, Glasgow G2 6RF, T 041 440 1094, F 041 440 0330; *Thai Adventures*, PO Box 82, Victoria St, Alderney, Channel Islands, T 0481 823 417, F 0481 823 495; *Tana Specialist Travel*, 2 Ely St, Stratford upon Avon, Warwickshire CV37 6LW, T 0789 414 200, F 0789 414 420; *The Imaginative Traveller*, 14 Barley Mow Passage, Chiswick, London W4 4PH, T 081 742 3113, F 081 742 3045; *The Orchid Travel Company*, 14 Gildredge Rd, Eastbourne, East Sussex BN21 4RL, T 0323 412441, F 0323 411913; *Thai My Way*, Misbourne House, Amersham Rd, Chalfont St Giles, Buckinghamshire HP8 4RY, T 0494 873 022, F 0494 452 611; *Twohig Travel*, 8 Burgh Quay, Dublin, Ireland, T 010 35316 772 666, F 010 35316 772 691; *Tradewinds Faraway Holidays*, Concord House, Forest St, Chester CH1 1QR, T 0800 585 976, F 0244 310 255; *Travel Bag*, 12 High St, Alton, Hampshire GU34 1BN, T 0420 887 24, F 0420 821 33. **Special interest tours**: *Fairway International Travel Ltd*, 3 Crown Yard, Southgate, Elland, West Yorkshire HX5 0DQ, T 0422 378 141, F 0422 310 716. **Birdwatching**: *Ornitholidays*, 1 Victoria Drive, Bognor Regis, West Sussex PO21 2PW, T 0243 821 2301, F 0243 829 574. **Walking**: *Ramblers Holidays*, PO Box 43, Welwyn Garden City, Herts AL8 6PQ, T 0707 331 133, F 0707 333 276. **Cruise**: *Princess Cruises*, 77 New Oxford St, London WC1A 1PP, T 071 831 1881, F 071 240 2805; *Ocean Cruise Lines UK Ltd*, 10 Frederick Close, Stanhope Place, London W2 2HD, T 071 723 5557, F 071 262 2361.

France: *Aeromarine*, 22 rue Royer-Collard, 75005 Paris, T 43 29 30 22, F 47 20 68 92; *Asia*, 35 rue Galande, 75005 Paris, T 44 41 50 00, F 44 41 50 09; *Asie Tours*, 23 rue Linnois, 75015 Paris, T 44 37 21 00, F 44 37 21 09; *Aux 4 Coins du Monde*, 1 rue Aubert-Dubayet, 38000 Grenoble, T 16 76 43 16 47, F 16 76 50 38 91; *Club Mediterranée*, Place de la Bourse, 75002 Paris, T 42 61 85 00, Tx 210078; *Voyages Dépêche*, 42 bis rue d'Alsace Lorraine, 31000 Toulouse, T 16 61 23

40 15; *Quest Voyages*, 50 avenue de Gaulle, 72000 Le Mans, T 16 43 24 83 80, Tx 720450; *Provaleur*, 85-87 rue de Sèze, 69006 Lyon, T 16 78 65 65 65, F 16 78 52 56 29; *Sud-Ouest Voyages*, 61 rue Sainte Catherine, 33000 Bordeaux, T 16 56 48 21 39, F 16 56 43 25 93; *Terrien*, 1 allée de Turenne, 44003 Nantes, T 16 40 47 91 83; *Est Voyages*, 5 bis avenue Foch, 54000 Nancy, T 16 83 59 80 54; *Les Voyagistes Réunis*, 10 bd de Magenta, 75010 Paris, T 42 41 60 00, Tx 240050; *Nord-Sud Voyages*, 60 rue du Molinel, 59000 Lille, T 16 20 06 50 70; *Voyages Pour Tous*, 40 rue de Marseille, 33000 Bordeaux, T 16 57 81 12 00, F 16 56 01 20 36; *Jet Tours*, 23 rue Raspail, 94200 Ivry, T 45 15 70 00, F 45 15 75 59; *Kuoni*, 95 rue d'Amsterdam, 75008 Paris, T 42 85 71 22, F 40 23 06 26; *Nouvelles Frontières*, 87 Bd de Grenelle, 75738 Paris Cédex 15, T 45 68 70 00, F 40 44 59 94; *Orients*, 29 rue des Boulangers, 75005 Paris, T 46 34 29 00, Tx 201368; *Rev'asie/Mondial Tour*, 390 rue d'Estienne d'Orves. 92700 Colombes, T 46 49 41 00, F 47 84 77 81; *Fram*, 1 rue Lapcyrouse, 31008 Toulouse-Cédex, T 16 62 15 16 17, F 16 62 15 17 17, Paris T 40 26 30 31.

Germany: *Abenteuer & Exotik Fernreisen*, Alte Rabenstr. 24b, Hamburg T 040-454404, F 040-453355; *Biblische Reisen*, Silberburgstr. 121 Stuttgart, T 0711-619250, F 0711-6192544; *Hauser Exkursionen*, Marienstr. 17, Munich, T 089-23500645, F 089-2913714; *CSV-Morgenstern Reisen Gmbh*, Alt-Sossenheim 47, Frankfurt am Main, T 069-346010, F 069-345195; *TVI Studienreisen*, Karl-Wiechert-Allee 23, Hannover, T 0511-5670, F 0511-5671301; *ASEAN Dreams*, Humboldstr. 123, Koblenz, T 0261-701041, F 0261-702123; *ASEAN Tours & Travel*, Graf-Adolf-Str. 57, Düsseldorf, T 0211-938010, F 0211-9380188; *Asien Reisen*, Europaplatz 20, Stuttgart, T 0711-7156091, F 0711-7157082; *Contours Golfreisen*, Pettenkoferstr. 24, Munich, T 089-530346, F 089-537044, golf specialist; *B.T.T.S. Tauchresien Gmbh*, Dalbergstr. 8, Frankfurt, T 069-333153, F 069-303094, diving specialist; *Reiservice für Traveller*, Wanderbeker Chaussee 7, Hamburg, T 040-257596, F 040-2500092, diving specialist.

When to go

● **Best time to visit**
(See page 64 for more details) Nov to Feb when

the rains have ended and temperatures are at their lowest. Although the rainy season brings thoughts of torrential day-long tropical rain to many people, this is rarely the case: heavy showers interspersed with clear skies is a more accurate description, and it is perfectly sensible to visit Thailand during the monsoon. Hours of daily sun average 5-6 hr even during rainy season. Visitors will also benefit from lower hotel room rates.

Health

See page 19, main health section, details on health and health care.

Vaccinations: no vaccinations are required, but cholera immunization and a tetanus booster are advisable. A gamma globulin injection (against hepatitis) is also recommended. There is a vaccination clinic in the Science Division of the Thai Red Cross Society, at the corner of Rama IV and Henri Dunant rds, Bangkok, T 2520161.

Malaria: anti-malarial tablets are essential outside Bangkok, Chiang Mai, Phuket and Pattaya. Be sure to ask your doctor to recommend the appropriate type(s) – some particularly resistant strains are prevalent in Thailand and most are now resistant to Chloroquine. Mosquito coils, electronic mosquito 'Vape-mats', repellents and nets are all worthwhile. Despite anti-malarial drugs, it is worth taking all possible precautions to avoid being bitten by mosquitoes – most bites occur between dawn and dusk, when protective clothing such as long-sleeved shirts and trousers should be worn. In general, the risk of malaria increases in direct proportion to the adventurousness of travel. In urban areas and main tourist areas there is little danger.

Heat exhaustion and dehydration : Thailand is hot and can be exhausting, so take care to avoid over-exertion. By perspiring profusely, loss of body fluids and salts can cause nausea, headaches and dizziness. This can be partially prevented by taking salt and by drinking lots of water. Sachets of electrolyte salts which can be dissolved in water are widely available in Thailand.

● Medical facilities

For full listing of hospitals, check the Yellow Pages, or listings under Useful addresses in each town. Hospitals in Bangkok and Chiang Mai are of a reasonable (Western) standard.

● Food and water

Tap water is not recommended for drinking. Cut fruit or uncooked vegetables from roadside stalls may not always be clean.

● Travelling with children

(For more information and a check-list, see the general introduction.) Disposable nappies are now widely available in Thailand, although they are expensive. Powdered milks and a good range of powdered foods are on sale in most supermarkets. Bottled water is available everywhere. Fruit is a good source of nutrition and is also widely available. Anti-malarials are recommended (quarter to half dosage) if travelling outside the main cities and tourist destinations.

Money

● ATMs (cash dispensers)

American Express can be used at Bangkok Bank, JCB at Siam Commercial Bank, Master Card at Siam Commercial, Visa at Bangkok Bank.

● Credit cards

Major credit cards such as American Express, Visa, Diners Club, Carte Blanche, Master Charge/Access are accepted in leading hotels, restaurants, department stores and several large stores for tourists. Visitors may have some problems upcountry where the use of credit cards is less common. **Notification of credit card loss**: American Express, IBM Bldg, Phahonyothin Rd, T 2730022; Diners Club, Dusit Thani Bldg, Rama IV Rd, T 2332645, 2335775; JCB T 2561361, 2561351; Visa and Master Card, Thai Farmers Bank Bldg, Phahonyothin Rd, T 2701801-10.

● Cost of living

Visitors staying in first class hotels and eating in hotel restaurants will probably spend a minimum of ฿1500/day. Tourists staying in cheaper air-conditioned accommodation, and eating in local restaurants will probably spend about ฿500-750/day. A backpacker, staying in fan-cooled guesthouses and eating cheaply, might expect to be able to live on ฿200/day. In Bangkok, expect to pay 20-30% more.

● Currency

The unit of Thai currency is the **baht** (฿), which is divided into 100 **satang**. Notes in circulation include ฿10 (brown), ฿20 (green), ฿50 (blue), ฿100 (red), ฿500 (purple) and new ฿1000. ฿1 and ฿5 notes are also legal tender, although they are never seen. Coins include 5 satang, 10 satang, 25 satang and 50 satang, and ฿1, ฿5, and ฿10. **NB:** there are different sized ฿1 and ฿5 coins, which can be confusing.

● **Exchange rates**

The exchange rate can be found in the daily newspapers. It is best to change money at banks or money changers which give better rates than hotels. First class hotels have 24 hour money changers. There is a charge of ฿10/cheque when changing travellers' cheques (passport required). Indonesian Rupiah and Nepalese Rupees cannot be exchanged for Thai currency.

Getting there

Air

The majority of visitors arrive in Thailand through Bangkok's Don Muang airport. There are also international flights to Chiang Mai in the N and to Phuket in the S (see below). More than 35 airlines and charter companies fly to Bangkok. Thai International is the national airline.

● **From Europe**

Approx. time from London to Bangkok (non-stop): 12 hours. There are direct flights from most major cities in Europe. From **London** Heathrow airlines include Qantas, British Airways, and Thai Airways. Philippine Airlines flies from Gatwick. There are flights from **Zurich**, **Paris**, **Rome**, **Athens** and **Copenhagen**.

● **From the USA and Canada**

Approx. time from Los Angeles: 21 hours. Northwest Airlines has flights from **San Francisco** and **Los Angeles**. Air Canada flies from **Vancouver**.

● **From Australasia**

There are flights from **Sydney** and **Melbourne** (approx. 9 hours) daily with Qantas. Thai Airways fly from Sydney. There is also a choice of other flights with British Airways, Alitalia, Lufthansa, and Lauda Air which are less frequent. There are flights from **Perth** with Thai Airways, Qantas or British Airways. From **Auckland** Air New Zealand and Thai Airways and British Airways.

● **From South Asia**

Thai Airways and Air India fly from **Delhi**. Both Air Lanka and Thai Airways fly from **Colombo**. From **Dhaka** there are flights with Biman Bangladesh Airlines or Thai Airways. PIA flies from **Karachi**, as do Thai Airways and Air France. Balkan flies from **Male**. Royal Nepal Airlines and Thai Airways fly from **Kathmandu**.

● **From the Far East**

Numerous airlines fly from **Hong Kong**, **Tokyo** and **Manila**.

● **From the Middle East**

From **Bahrain** Gulf Air, Egyptair from **Cairo**.

It is possible to fly direct to **Chiang Mai** and to **Phuket** from Frankfurt on Condor, Vienna on Lauda Air, Zurich on Ball Air, Amsterdam on Martin Air, Singapore on Tradewinds, Hong Kong on Dragonair, Taipei on China Airlines.

Train

Regular rail services link Singapore and Bangkok, via Kuala Lumpur, Butterworth and the major southern Thai towns. Express a/c trains take two days from Singapore, 34 hours from Kuala Lumpur, 24 hours from Butterworth (opposite Penang). The *Magic Arrow Express* leaves Singapore on Sun, Tues and Thurs, Bangkok-Singapore (฿899-1,965), Bangkok-Kuala Lumpur (฿659-1,432) and to Ipoh (฿530-1,145). An additional train from Butterworth departs at 1340, arriving Bangkok 0835 the next day. The train from Bangkok to Butterworth departs 1515, arriving Butterworth 1225 (฿457-1,147). All tickets should be booked in advance. The most luxurious way to journey by train to Thailand is aboard the *Eastern & Oriental (E&O) Express*. The a/c train of 22 carriages including a salon car, dining car, bar and observation deck and carrying just 132 passengers runs once a week from Singapore to Bangkok and back. Luxurious carriages, fine wines and food designed for European rather than Asian sensibilities make this not just a mode of transport but an experience. The journey takes 43 hrs with stops in Kuala Lumpur, Butterworth and Padang Besar. But such luxury is expensive: US$1,130-2,950. For information call Bangkok 2514862; London (071) 9286000; US (800) 5242420; Singapore (065) 2272068.

There are currently no other rail services available out of Thailand to Burma, Vietnam, Cambodia or Laos. There is talk of the railway to Phnom Penh via Battambang being reactivated, should political conditions improve.

Road

The main road access is to and from Malaysia. The principal land border crossings into Malaysia are near Betong in Yala Province and from

Sungei Golok in Narathiwat Province (see page 484). In April 1994 the Friendship Bridge linking Nong Khai with Laos opened – and became the first bridge across the Mekong River. To cross into Laos here foreigners need to obtain a visa in Bangkok – although a consulate is due to open in Nong Khai. In 1992, an overland crossing to Burma opened at Mae Sai in the N, but only for forays into the immediate vicinity. The border at Saam Ong in the W can also be crossed by foreigners, but again only for day trips into Burma.

Sea

No regular, scheduled cruise liners sail to Thailand any longer but it is sometimes possible to enter Thailand on a freighter, arriving at Khlong Toey Port. For information on how to book a berth on a cargo ship, see page 11. The *Bangkok Post* publishes a weekly shipping post with details on ships leaving the kingdom.

There are frequent passenger ferries from Pak Bara, near Satun, in Southern Thailand to Perlis and Langkawi Island, both in Malaysia (see page 485). The passenger and car ferries at Ta Ba, near the town of Tak Bai, south of Narathiwat, make for a fast border crossing to Pengkalan Kubor in Malaysia (see page 479). An alternative is to hitch a lift on a yacht from Phuket (Thailand) or from Penang (Malaysia). Check at the respective yacht clubs for information.

Customs

● Duty free allowance

250 gr of cigars or cigarettes (or 200 cigarettes) and 1 litre of wine or spirits. One still camera with five rolls of film or one movie camera with 3 rolls of 8mm or 16mm film.

● Currency regulations

Non-residents can bring in up to ฿2,000/person and unlimited foreign currency although amounts exceeding US$10,000 must be declared. Maximum amount permitted to take out of the country is ฿50,000/person.

● Prohibited items

All narcotics; obscene literature, pornography; fire arms (except with a permit from the Police Department or local registration office).

Some species of plants and animals are prohibited, for more information contact the Royal Forestry Department, Phahonyothin Rd, Bangkok, T 5792776. Permission of entry for animals by air is obtainable at the airport. An application must be made to the Department of Livestock Development, Bangkok, T 2515136 for entry by sea. Vaccination certificates are required; dogs and cats need rabies certificates.

● Export restrictions

No Buddha or Bodhisattva images or fragments should be taken out of Thailand, except for worshipping by Buddhists, for cultural exchanges or for research. However, obviously many people do – you only have to look in the antique shops to see the abundance for sale. A licence should be obtained from the Department of Fine Arts, Na Prathat Rd, Bangkok, T 2241370, from Chiang Mai National Museum, T 221308 or from the Songkhla National Museum, Songkhla, T 311728. Five days notice is needed; take two passport photographs of the object and photocopies of your passport.

When you arrive

● Airport information

Don Muang airport lies 25 km N of Bangkok. Facilities include: banks and currency exchange, post office, left luggage (฿20/item/day – max. 4 months), hotel booking agency, airport information, airport clinic, lost and found baggage service, duty-free shops, restaurants and bars. **NB**: food is expensive here – cheap food is available across the footbridge at the railway station. The *Airport Hotel* is linked to the international terminal by a walkway. It provides a 'ministay' service for passengers who wish to 'freshen-up' and take a room for up to three hours between 0800 and 1800 (฿400 T 5661020/1). **International flight information**: T 5351254 for departures, T 5351301 for arrivals. **Domestic flight information**: T 5351253. The domestic terminal has a hotel booking counter, post office, restaurant and bookshop. A free shuttle bus between the International and Domestic terminals is available every 30 minutes.

Transport to town By taxi: official taxi booking service in the arrivals hall, ฿230 to the centre of town. **Warning**: there have been cases of visitors being robbed in unofficial taxis. The sedan service into town costs ฿400-500. Cars are newer, more comfortable and better maintained than the average city taxi. It takes 30 minutes to 1 hour to central Bangkok, depending on the time of day and the state of the traffic. The new elevated expressway reduces journey time to 20 mins – ask the taxi driver to take this route if your destination is in the Sukhumvit Rd area of town (฿30 surcharge). But the elevated Don Muang expressway which (should) whisk people right into the centre of town down Phahonyothin Rd is still under construction and is not due to be completed until early 1995, possibly later. Note that there have been some complaints about taxi drivers at the domestic terminal forming a cartel, refusing to use their meters and charging a fixed rate considerably above the meter rate.

By bus: cheapest and slowest way into town, 1¹/₂-3 hrs (depending on time of day) (฿7-15). The bus stop is 50m N of the arrivals hall. Buses are crowded during rush-hours and there is little room for luggage. Bus 59 goes to Khaosan Road, bus 29 goes to Bangkok's Hualamphong railway station, via the Northern bus terminal and Siam Square. A/c bus 10 goes to Samsen Road and Silom Road via the Northern bus terminal, a/c bus 4 goes to Silom Road, a/c bus 13 goes to Sukhumvit Road and the Eastern bus terminal, a/c bus 29 goes to the Northern bus terminal, Siam Square and Hualamphong railway station. **By minibus**: ฿100 to major hotels, ฿60 shuttle bus to the *Asia Hotel* on Phayathai Road. ฿50-80 to Khaosan Rd, depending on the time of day. Direct buses to Pattaya at 0900, 1200 and 1700, ฿180. **By train**: the station is on the other side of the north-south highway from the airport. Regular trains to Bangkok's Hualamphong station, ฿5. The State Railways of Thailand runs an 'Airport Express' 5 times a day, with a/c shuttle bus from Don Muang station to airport terminal, 35 mins (฿100). **Hotel pick-up services**: many of the more expensive hotels operate airport pick-up services if informed of your arrival ahead of time. **By ferry**: a civilized way to avoid the traffic. If booked at the *Oriental*, *Shangri-la* or *Sheraton* Hotels it is possible to get a minibus from the airport to the ferry terminal on the river. Then take the hour long river crossing by long-tailed boat to the appropriate hotel.

● **Airport tax**

Payable on departure – ฿200 for international flights, ฿20 for domestic flights. **Tax clearance**: any foreign visitor who has derived income while staying in Thailand must pay income tax. In addition, all travellers who have stayed in Thailand for 90 days or more in any one calendar year must obtain a tax clearance certificate. To avoid delay at the airport, contact the Revenue Department, T 2829899.

● **Clothing**

In towns and at religious sights, it is courteous to avoid wearing shorts and singlets. Visitors who are inappropriately dressed may not be allowed into temples. Thais always look neat and clean. *Mai rieb-roi* means 'not neat' and is considered a great insult. Beach resorts are a law unto themselves – casual clothes are the norm, although nudity is still very much frowned upon by Thais. In the most expensive restaurants in Bangkok diners may well be expected to wear a jacket and tie.

● **Conduct**

Thais are generally very understanding of the foibles and habits of foreigners (*farangs*) and will forgive and forget most indiscretions. However, there are a number of 'dos and don'ts' which are worth observing:

Bargaining This is common, except in the large department stores (although they may give a discount on expensive items of jewellery or furniture) and on items like soap, books and most necessities. Expect to pay anything from 25-75% less than the asking price, depending on the bargainer's skill and the shopkeeper's mood. Bargaining is viewed as a game, so enter into it with good humour.

Common greeting *Wai*: hands are held together as if in prayer, and the higher the wai, the more respectful the greeting. By watching Thai's wai it is possible to ascertain their relative seniority. Again, foreigners are not expected to conform to this custom – a simple wai at chest to chin height is all that is required. When *farangs* and Thais do business it is common to shake hands.

Observant visitors will quickly notice that men and women rarely show open, public signs of affection. It is not uncommon however to see men holding hands – this is invariably a sign of simple friendship, nothing more. That said, in Bangkok traditional customs have broken down and in areas such as Siam Square it is common to see young lovers, hand-in-hand.

Heads, heart and feet More generally, try not to openly point your feet at anyone – feet are viewed as spiritually the lowest part of the body. At the same time, never touch anyone's head which is the holiest, as well as the highest, part. Among Thais, the personal characteristic of *jai yen* is very highly regarded; literally, this means to have a 'cool heart'. It embodies calmness, having an even temper and not displaying emotion. Although foreigners generally receive special dispensation, and are not expected to conform to Thai customs (all *farang* are thought to have 'hot hearts'), it is important to try and keep calm in any disagreement – losing one's temper leads to loss of face and subsequent loss of respect. An associated personal characteristic which Thais try to develop is *kreng jai*; this embodies being understanding of other people's needs, desires and feelings – in short, not imposing oneself.

A quality of *sanuk*, which can be roughly translated as 'fun' or *joie de vivre*, is important to Thais. Activities are undertaken because they are sanuk, others avoided because they are *mai sanuk* ('not fun'). Perhaps it is because of this apparent love of life that so many visitors returning from Thailand remark on how Thais always appear happy and smiling. However, it is worth bearing in mind that the interplay of *jai yen* and *kreng jai* means that everything may not be quite as it appears.

The monarchy Never criticize any member of the royal family or the institution itself (see page 114). The monarchy is held in very high esteem and *lèse majesté* remains an imprisonable offence. In cinemas, the National Anthem is played before the show and the audience is expected to stand. At other events, take your lead from the crowd as to how to behave. A dying custom, but one which is still adhered to in smaller towns, is that everybody stops in their tracks at 0800, when the **National Anthem** is relayed by loudspeaker.

Monastery (*wat*) **etiquette** Remove shoes on entering, do not climb over Buddha images or have pictures taken in front of one. Wear modest clothing – women should not expose their shoulders or wear dresses that are too short (see below, clothing). Females should never hand anything directly to monks, or venture into the monks' quarters.

Smoking Prohibited on domestic flights, public buses and in cinemas.

Further reading A useful book delving deeper into the do's and don'ts of living in Thailand is Robert and Nanthapa Cooper's *Culture shock: Thailand*, Time Books International: Singapore (1990). It is available from most bookshops.

● **Emergencies**
Police 191, 123; **Tourist Police** 195; **Fire** 199; **Ambulance** 2522171-5. **Tourist Police head**

office: Section 4, sub-division 8, Crime Suppression Division, Vorachak Rd, Bangkok, T 2257758. **Tourist Assistance Centre**, Rachdamnern Nok Ave, Bangkok, T 2828129.

● **Hours of business**
Banks: 0830-1530 Mon-Fri. **Currency exchange services**: 0830-2200 Mon-Sun in Bangkok and Pattaya, 0830-1930 in Phuket and 0830-1630 Mon-Fri in other towns. **Government offices**: 0830-1200, 1300-1630 Mon-Fri. **Tourist offices**: 0830-1630 Mon-Sun. **Shops**: 0830-1700, larger shops: 1000-1900 or 2100.

● **Official time**
7 hours ahead of GMT.

● **Safety**
The Communist Party of Thailand (CPT) which was influential in parts of the South, North and Northeast during the late 1970s and early 1980s is virtually moribund and does not pose a threat to visitors. However, there have been some worrying attacks on tourists and a handful of murders, most recently in May 1993 when a tourist on Koh Samui tried to resist a group of thieves. It must be emphasized that these are very few and far between. Most have occurred when visitors have become involved in local conflicts, or when they have tried to outwit thieves. Robbery is much more common; it ranges from simple pick-pocketing, to the drugging (and subsequent robbing) of bus and train passengers. As in all countries, watchfulness and simple common sense should be employed. Women travelling alone should be especially careful. Always lock hotel rooms and place valuables in a safe deposit if available (or if not, take them with you).

Travel throughout almost all of the country is safe. Special care should be taken along the Thai/Cambodian border which is sensitive and should be avoided at night. Perhaps the greatest danger is from the traffic itself. Thai drivers have a 'devil may care' attitude towards the highway code, and there are many quite horrific accidents. Be very careful crossing the road – just because there is a pedestrian crossing, do not expect drivers to stop. Be particularly wary when driving or riding a motorcycle (see page 506). The above warnings should not be made too much of: Thailand in the main is a safe and wonderful country to travel through and the great majority of visitors have no bad experiences. If you do suffer some mishap, report the incident to the police: there are now special tourist police to deal with such complaints in tourist centres (see Emergencies below for telephone numbers).

● **Shopping**

Bangkok and Chiang Mai are the shopping 'centres' of Thailand. Many people now prefer Chiang Mai, as the shops are concentrated in a smaller area and there is a good range of quality things to buy, especially handicrafts. It is difficult to find bargains in Bangkok any longer. The department stores and shopping malls contain high-price, high-quality merchandise (all at a fixed price), much of which is imported. The market and roadside stalls continue to stock fake designer labels, but customers need to bargain *ruthlessly*. The widest selection of **Thai silk** is available in Bangkok, although cheaper silk as well as good quality cotton can be obtained in the Northeast (the traditional centre of silk weaving). **Tailor-made clothing** is available (suits, shirts and dresses), although designs are sometimes rather out-dated; it might be better for the tailor to copy an article of your own clothing (see page 176). However, things change and there are now some top designers in Bangkok. **Leather goods** include custom-made crocodile skin shoes and boots (for those who aren't squeamish, after seeing the brutes in one of the crocodile farms).

Bangkok is also a good place to buy **jewellery** – gold, sapphires and rubies – and the same applies to **antiques**, bronzeware and celadon (see page 208). **NB**: See section on safety – regarding tricksters, below. Handicrafts are best purchased upcountry, for example in Chiang Mai. In general, Bangkok has by far the best selection of goods, and by shopping around, visitors will probably be able to get just as good a price as they would upcountry.

Competition Between shopkeepers competition is fierce. Do not be persuaded into buying something before having a chance to price it elsewhere – Thais can be enormously persuasive. **NB:** Also, watch out for guarantees of authenticity – fake antiques abound, and even professionals find it difficult to know a 1990 Khmer sculpture from a 10th century one.

● **Tipping**

Generally unnecessary. A 10% service charge is now expected on room, food and drinks bills in the smarter hotels as well as a tip for any personal service. Increasingly, the more expensive restaurants add a 10% service charge; others expect a small tip.

● **Tricksters**

Tricksters, rip-off artists, fraudsters, less than honest salesmen – call them what you will – are likely to be far more of a problem than simple theft. People may well approach you in the street offering incredible one-off bargains, and giving what might seem to be very plausible reasons for your sudden good fortune. Be wary in all such cases and do not be pressed into making a hasty decision. Unfortunately, more often than not, the salesman is trying to pull a fast one. Favourite 'bargains' are precious stones, whose authenticity is 'demonstrated' before your very eyes. Although many Thais do like to talk to *farangs* and practice their English, in tourist areas there are also those who offer their friendship for pecuniary rather than linguistic reasons. Sad as it is to say so, it is probably a good idea to be suspicious.

● **Voltage**

220 volts (50 cycles) throughout Thailand. Most first and tourist class hotels have outlets for shavers and hair dryers. Adaptors are recommended, as almost all sockets are two pronged.

● **Weights and measures**

Thailand uses the metric system, although there are some traditional measures still in use, in particular the *rai*, which equals 0.16 hectares. There are four *ngaan* in a *rai*. Other local measures include the *krasorp* (sack) which equals 25 kg and the *tang* which is 10-11 kg. However, for most purchases (e.g. fruit) the kilogram is now the norm.

Where to stay

As a premier tourist destination and one of the world's fastest-growing economies, Thailand has a large selection of hotels – including some of the very best in the world. However, outside the tourist centres, there is still an absence of adequate 'Western style' accommodation. Most 'Thai' hotels are distinctly lacking in character and are poorly maintained. Due to the popularity of the country with backpackers, there are also a large number of small guesthouses, geared to Westerners serving Western food and catering to the foibles of foreigners.

● **Accommodation**

Hotels are listed under eight categories,

according to the *average* price of a double/twin room for one night. It should be noted that many hotels will have a range of rooms, some with air-conditioning (a/c) and attached bathroom facilities, others with just a fan and shared facilities. Prices can therefore vary a great deal. If a hotel entry lists 'some a/c', then these rooms are likely to be in the upper part of the range, perhaps even in the next range. Unlike, say, Indonesia, few hotels in Thailand provide breakfast in the price of the room. A service charge of 10% and government tax of 11% will usually be added to the bill in the more expensive hotels (categories B-L). Ask whether the quoted price includes tax when checking-in. Prices in Bangkok are inflated. **NB**: during the off-season, hotels in tourist destinations may halve their room rates so it is always worthwhile bargaining or asking whether there is a 'special' price. Given the fierce competition among hotels (because of a stagnation in the tourist industry), it is even worth trying during the peak season. Over-building has meant that there is a glut of rooms in some towns and hotels are desperate for business.

Hotel Classification

L: ฿5,000+ luxury and **A+:** ฿2,500-5,000 **International**: the entire range of business services (fax, translation, seminar rooms etc), sports facilities (gym, swimming pool etc), Asian and Western restaurants, bars, and discotheques.

A: ฿1,250-2,500 **First class**: usually offer comprehensive business, sports and recreational facilities, with a range of restaurants and bars.

B: ฿625-1,250 **Tourist class**: these will probably have a swimming pool and all rooms will have air-conditioning and an attached bathroom. Other services include one or more restaurants and 24-hour coffee shop/room service. Some may have televisions in the rooms showing cable films.

C: ฿375-625 **Economy**: rooms should be air-conditioned and have attached bathrooms with hot water. A restaurant and room service will probably be available. Sports facilities are unlikely.

D: ฿200-375 **Budget**: rooms are unlikely to be air-conditioned although they should have an attached bathroom. Toilets may be either Western-style or of the 'squat' Asian variety, depending on whether the town is on the tourist route. Toilet paper should be provided. Many in this price range, out of tourist areas, are 'Thai' hotels. Bed linen and towels are usually provided, and there may be a restaurant.

E: ฿100-200 **Guesthouse**: fan-cooled rooms, in some cases with shared bathroom facilities. Toilets are likely to be of the 'squat' Asian variety, with no toilet paper provided. Bed linen should be provided, although towels may not. Rooms are small, facilities few. Guesthouses popular with foreigners may be excellent sources of information and also sometimes offer cheap tours and services such as bicycle and motorcycle hire. Places in this category vary a great deal, and can change very rapidly. One year's best bargain becomes the following year's health hazard. Other travellers are the best source of up-to-the-minute reviews on whether standards have plummeted.

F: under ฿100 **Guesthouse**: fan-cooled rooms, usually with shared bathroom facilities. Toilets are likely to be of the 'squat' Asian variety with no toilet paper provided. Some of these guesthouses can be filthy, vermin-infested, places. At the same time others are superb value. As in the category above, standards change very fast and other travellers are the best source of information.

Food and drink

Food

Thai cuisine is an intermingling of Tai (see page 76), Chinese, and to a lesser extent, Indian cuisines. This helps to explain why restaurants produce dishes which must be some of the (spicy) hottest in the world, as well as some which are rather bland. *Laap* (raw – now more frequently cooked – chopped beef mixed with rice, herbs and spices) is a traditional 'Tai' dish; *pla priaw waan* (whole fish with soy and ginger) is Chinese in origin; while *gaeng mussaman* (beef 'Muslim' curry) was brought to Thailand by Muslim immigrants. Even *satay*, paraded by most restaurants as a Thai dish, has been introduced from Malaysia and Indonesia (who themselves adopted it from Arab traders during the Middle Ages).

Despite these various influences, Thai cooking is distinctive. Thais have managed to combine the best of each tradition, adapting elements to fit their own preferences. Remarkably, considering how ubiquitous it is in Thai cooking, the chilli pepper is a New World fruit and was not introduced into Thailand until the late 16th century (along with the pineapple and papaya).

When a Thai asks another Thai whether he has eaten he will ask, literally, whether he has 'eaten rice' (*kin khaaw*). Similarly, the accompanying dishes are referred to as food 'with the rice'. A Thai meal is based around rice, and many wealthy Bangkokians own farms up-country where they cultivate their favourite variety. A meal usually consists (along with the rice) of a soup like *tom yam kung* (prawn soup), *kaeng* (a curry) and *krueng kieng* (a number of side dishes). Generally, Thai food is chilli-hot, and aromatic herbs and grasses (like lemon grass) are used to give a distinctive flavour. *Nam pla* (fish sauce) and *nam prik* (nam pla, chillies, garlic, sugar, shrimps and lime juice) are two condiments that are taken with almost all meals. Food is eaten with a spoon and fork, and dishes are usually served all at once; it is unimportant to a Thai that food be hot. Try the open-air foodstalls to be found in every town which are frequented by middle-class Thais as well as the poor and where a meal costs only ฿15-20. Many small restaurants have no menus. Away from the main tourist spots, 'Western' breakfasts are commonly unavailable, so be prepared to eat Thai-style (noodle or rice soup or fried rice). Finally, due to Thai-

land's large Chinese population (or at least Thais with Chinese roots), there are also many Chinese-style restaurants whose cuisine is variously 'Thai-ified'. A popular innovation over the last 5 years or so has been the *suan a-haan* or garden restaurant. These are often on the edge of towns, with tables set in gardens, sometimes with bamboo furniture and ponds.

Cuisine

It is impossible even to begin to provide a comprehensive list of Thai dishes. However (and at the risk of offending connoisseurs by omitting their favourites) popular dishes include:

● **Soups (***gaeng chud***)**
Tom yam kung – hot and sour prawn soup
Tom ka kai – chicken in coconut milk with laos (*ka*, or laos, is an exotic spice)
Khaaw tom – rice soup with egg and pork (a common breakfast dish). It is said that the soup can cure fevers and other illnesses. Probably best for a hangover.
Kwaytio – Chinese noodle soup served with a variety of additional ingredients, often available from roadside stalls and from smaller restaurants – mostly served up until lunchtime.

● **Rice and noodle-based dishes**
Single-dish meals served at roadside stalls and in many restaurants (especially cheaper ones).
Khaaw phat kai/mu/kung – fried rice with chicken/pork/prawn
Khaaw man kai – rice with chicken
Khaaw mu daeng – rice with red pork
Khaaw soi – a form of *Kwaytio*, with egg noodles in a curry broth
Phak sii-u – wide noodles, fried with egg,

vegetables and meat/prawns
Phat thai – Thai fried noodles
Mee krop – Thai crisp-fried noodles

● **Curries (***gaeng***)**

Gaeng phet kai/nua – chicken/beef curry
Gaeng khiaw waan kai/nua/phet/pla – green chicken/beef/duck/fish curry (the colour is due to the large number of whole green chillies pounded to make the paste that forms the base of this very hot curry)
Gaeng mussaman – Muslim beef curry

● **Meat dishes**

Laap – chopped (once raw, now more frequently cooked) meat with herbs and spices
Kai/nua phat prik – fried chicken/beef with chillies
Nua priaw waan – sweet and sour beef

THAI FOOD GLOSSARY

a-haan	food	mekong	Thai whisky
ba-mii	egg noodles	mit	knife
bia	beer	muu	pork
chaa	tea	nam chaa	tea
check bin/bill	cheque	nam kheng	ice
chorn	spoon	nam kuat	bottled water
jaan	plate	nam manaaw soda	lime soda
gaeng	curry	nam plaa	fish sauce
gaeng chud	soup	nam plaa prik	fish sauce with chilli
kaafae (ron)	coffee (hot)		
kaew	glass	nam plaaw	plain water
kai	chicken	nam som	orange juice
kap klaem	snacks to be eaten when drinking	nam taan	sugar
		nam tom	boiled water
kwaytio	noodle soup, white noodles	nom	milk
		nua	meat (usually beef)
khaaw niaw	sticky rice		
khaaw tom	rice gruel	phak	vegetables
khaaw/khao	rice	phat	to stir fry
khai	egg	phet	hot (chilli)
khai dao	fried egg	phon lamai	fruit
khanom	sweet, dessert or cake	pla	fish
		priaw	sour
khanom cake	cake	priaw waan	sweet and sour
khanom pang	bread	prik	hot chilli
khanom pang ping	toast	raan a-haan	restaurant
		ratnaa	in gravy
khing	ginger	rawn	hot (temperature)
khuan	scramble	sa-te	satay
khuat	bottle	sorm	fork
kin	to eat	talaat	market
kleua	salt	thao mai luai	morning glory
krueng kieng	side dishes	thua	nut/bean
kung	crab	tom	to boil
lao	liquor	tort	to deep fry
man	root vegetable	waan	sweet
man farang	potatoes	yam	salad
manaaw	lemon	yen	cold

Mu waan – sweet pork
Kai/mu/nua phat kapow – fried meat with basil and chillies
Kai tort – Thai fried chicken
Kai tua – chicken in peanut sauce
Kai yang – garlic chicken
Priao wan – sweet and sour pork with vegetables

● **Seafood**
Pla priaw waan – whole fried fish with ginger sauce
Pla too tort – Thai fried fish
Haw mok – steamed fish curry
Pla nerng – steamed fish
Thotman plaa – fried curried fish cakes

● **Salads (***yam***)**
Yam nua – Thai beef salad
Som tam – green papaya salad with tomatoes, chillies, garlic, chopped dried shrimps and lemon (can be extremely hot)

● **Vegetables**
Phak phat ruam mit – mixed fried vegetables

● **Sweets (***kanom***)**
Khaaw niaw sankhayaa – sticky rice and custard
Khaaw niaw mamuang – sticky rice and mango (a seasonal favourite)
Kluay buat chee – bananas in coconut milk
Kanom mo kaeng – baked custard squares
Kluay tort – Thai fried bananas
Leenchee loi mek – chilled lychis in custard

● **Fruits (see page 17)**
Chomphu – rose apple
Khanun – jackfruit. Season: Jan-Jun
Kluay – banana. Season: year round
Lamyai – longan; thin brown shell with translucent fruit similar to lychee. Season: Jun-Aug
Linchi – lychee. Season: Apr-Jun
Lamut – sapodilla
Makham wan – tamarind. Season: Dec-Feb
Malakho – papaya. Season: year round
Manaaw – lime. Season: year round
Mang khud – mangosteen. Season: Apr-Sept
Maprao – coconut. Season: year round
Majeung – star apple
Mamuang – mango. Season: Mar-June
Ngo – rambutan. Season: May-Sept
Noi na – custard (or sugar) apple. Season: June-Sept
Sapparot – pineapple. Season: Apr-June, Dec-Jan
Som – orange. Season: year round
Som o – pomelo. Season: Aug-Nov
Taeng mo – watermelon. Season: Oct-Mar
Thurian – durian. Season: May-Aug.

Cookery courses

For those interested in taking a course in Thai cookery, contact: UFM Food Centre Co Ltd., 593/29-39 Sukhumvit Soi 33/1, T 2590620; the Thai Cooking School at the *Oriental Hotel*, 48 Oriental Avenue, T 4376211; Modern Housewife Centre, 45/6-7 Setsiri Rd, T 2792831.

Tourist centres also provide good European, American and Japanese food at reasonable prices. Bangkok boasts some superb restaurants. Less expensive Western fastfood restaurants can also be found – McDonalds, Pizza Hut, Kentucky Fried Chicken and others.

Drink

● **Drinking water**
Water in smaller restaurants can be risky, so many people recommend that visitors drink bottled water (widely available) or **hot tea**.

● **Soft drinks**
Coffee is also now consumed throughout Thailand (usually served with coffeemate or *creamer*). In stalls and restaurants, coffee come with a glass of Chinese tea. Soft drinks are widely available. Many roadside stalls prepare **fresh fruit juices** in liquidizers (*bun*) while hotels produce all the usual cocktails.

● **Alcohol**
Spirits Major brands of spirits are served in most hotels and bars, although not always off the tourist path. The most popular spirit among Thais is *Mekhong* – **local cane whisky** – which can be drunk straight or with mixers such as Coca-Cola. It can seem rather sweet to the Western palate but it is the cheapest form of alcohol.

Beer drinking is spreading fast. In 1987, beer consumption was 98 million litres; in 1992, 330 million litres.

The most popular local beer is *Singha* beer brewed by Boon Rowd. The company commands 89% of the beer market. It is said that the beer's distinctive taste is due to the formaldehyde that it contains. When the company removed the chemical (it was no longer needed as bottling technology had been improved) there was such an outcry from Thais that they quickly reincorporated it. Whether or not the story is true, an evening drinking *Singha* can result in quite a hangover. It's alcohol content of 6% must be partly to blame. Among expatriates, the most popular Thai beer is the more expensive *Kloster* brand (similar to a light German beer) with an alcohol content of 5.7%. *Singha* introduced a light beer called *Singha Gold* a few years ago which is quite similar to *Kloster*. *Amarit* is a third, rather less widely available, brand but popular with foreigners and brewed by the same company who produce *Kloster*. Between them, *Kloster* and *Amarit* control about 10% of the market. The newest 'local' beer to enter the fray is *Carlsberg*. They have built a brewery N of Bangkok and done their homework. The beer is sweeter and lighter than *Singha* and *Kloster* but still strong with an alcohol content of 6%. Whether it can make inroads into the established brands' market is to be seen. Beer is relatively expensive in Thai terms as it is heavily taxed by the government. But it is a high status drink, so as Thais become wealthier, more are turning to beer in preference to traditional, local whiskies. In a café expect to pay ฿30-50 for a small beer, in a coffee shop or bar ฿40-65, and in a hotel bar or restaurant, more than ฿60.

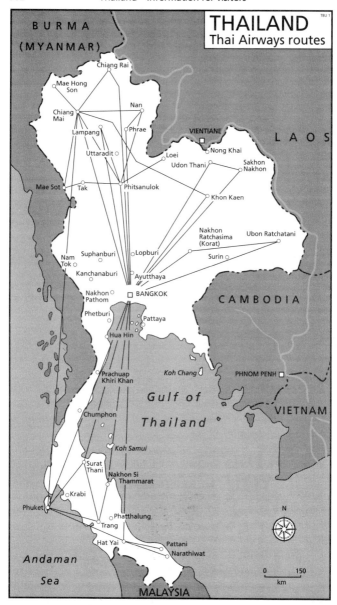

THAILAND
Thai Airways routes

BURMA (MYANMAR)

LAOS

CAMBODIA

VIETNAM

MALAYSIA

Gulf of Thailand

Andaman Sea

Chiang Rai
Mae Hong Son
Nan
Chiang Mai
Lampang
Phrae
VIENTIANE
Uttaradit
Loei
Nong Khai
Sakhon Nakhon
Udon Thani
Mae Sot
Tak
Phitsanulok
Khon Kaen
Nakhon Ratchasima (Korat)
Ubon Ratchatani
Nam Tok
Suphanburi
Lopburi
Surin
Kanchanaburi
Ayutthaya
Nakhon Pathom
BANGKOK
Phetburi
Pattaya
Hua Hin
Koh Chang
PHNOM PENH
Prachuap Khiri Khan
Chumphon
Koh Samui
Surat Thani
Nakhon Si Thammarat
Krabi
Phatthalung
Phuket
Trang
Hat Yai
Pattani
Narathiwat

N

0   150
km

Getting around

Air

Thai flies to 9 destinations in the North – Chiang Mai, Chiang Rai, Lampang, Mae Hong Son, Mae Sot, Nan, Phitsanulok, Phrae and Tak; 6 in the North East – Khon Kaen, Loei, Nakhon Ratchasima, Sakhon Nakhon, Ubon Ratchathani and Udon Thani; and 7 in the South – Hat Yai, Nakhon Si Thammarat, Narathiwat, Pattani, Phuket, Surat Thani and Trang. Thai sell a *Discover Thailand's Natural Heritage* ticket; US$239 buys 4 coupons, with US$50 for each additional coupon to a maximum of 8 coupons. The ticket is only worthwhile if travelling on longer legs, e.g. North to South. Full payment and reservation for the first sector must be made prior to arrival in Thailand, and the trip must begin in Bangkok. **Head office for Thai** is 89 Vibhavadi Rangsit Rd, T 5130121 or book flights through one of the local offices or a travel agent displaying the Thai logo. **Bangkok Airways** (see next page), flies from Bangkok to Koh Samui, Hua Hin, Mae Hong Son, Chiang Mai, Pattaya, Trang and from Koh Samui to Phuket; prices are competitive. **Yellowbirds** have recently begun a service to Hua Hin and Krabi.

Train

The State Railway of Thailand is efficient, clean and comfortable, with four main routes to the North, Northeast, East and South. It is safer than bus travel but can take longer. The choice is 1st class a/c compartments, 2nd class sleepers, 2nd class a/c sit-ups with reclining chairs and 3rd class sit-ups. Travelling 3rd class is often the cheapest way to travel long distance. 1st and 2nd class is more expensive than the bus but infinitely more comfortable. Express trains are known as *rot duan*, special express trains as *rot duan phiset* and rapid trains as *rot raew*. Express and rapid trains are faster as they make fewer stops; there is a surcharge for the service. Reservations for sleepers should be made in advance at Bangkok's Hualamphong station. It is advisable to book the bottom sleeper, as lights are bright on top (in 2nd class compartments). It still may be difficult to get a seat at certain times of year, such as during festivals (like Songkran in April). It is possible to pick up timetables at Hualamphong station (from the information booth in the main concourse): there are two types – the 'condensed' timetable (by region) showing all rapid routes and complete, separate timetables for all classes. Some travel agencies book tickets. The advance booking office is at Hualamphong

THAI AIRWAYS: SAMPLE DOMESTIC ROUTES AND FARES		
Route	**Hours**	**Fare (baht)***
Bangkok to:		
Chiang Mai	1 hr 5 mins	1,950
Hat Yai	1 hr 25 mins	2,580
Khon Kaen	55 mins	1,320
Korat	40 mins	540
Nakhon Si Thammarat	1 hr 55 mins	1,770
Surat Thani	1 hr 5 mins	2,010
Ubon Ratchathani	1 hr 5 mins	1,345
Chiang Mai to:		
Chiang Rai	40 mins	420
Mae Hong Son	40 mins	345
Nan	45 mins	510
Tak	1 hr 40 mins	765

* early 1994 fares quoted, one way (return fares are double)

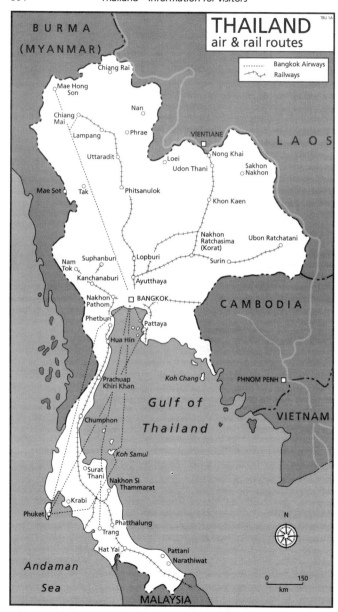

THAILAND
air & rail routes

TBU 1A

- - - - Bangkok Airways
—⌣— Railways

BURMA
(MYANMAR)

Chiang Rai

Mae Hong
Son

Nan

Chiang
Mai

Lampang

Phrae

VIENTIANE

LAOS

Uttaradit

Loei

Nong Khai

Udon Thani

Sakhon
Nakhon

Mae Sot

Tak

Phitsanulok

Khon Kaen

Nakhon
Ratchasima
(Korat)

Ubon Ratchatani

Nam
Tok

Suphanburi

Lopburi

Surin

Kanchanaburi

Ayutthaya

Nakhon
Pathom

BANGKOK

CAMBODIA

Phetburi

Pattaya

Hua Hin

Koh Chang

PHNOM PENH

Prachuap
Khiri Khan

Gulf

VIETNAM

Chumphon

of

Thailand

Koh Samui

Surat
Thani

Nakhon Si
Thammarat

Krabi

Phuket

Phatthalung

Trang

Hat Yai

Pattani

Narathiwat

Andaman

Sea

N

0   150
km

MALAYSIA

station, T 2233762. A queue-by-ticket arrangement works efficiently, and travellers do not have to wait long. If you change a reservation the charge is ฿10. If travelling north or south during the day, it is a good idea to get a seat on the side of the carriage out of the sun.

A 'bullet train' may soon transport visitors along the eastern seaboard to Pattaya.

● **Tourist passes**
A 20-day rail pass costs ฿1100 for adults, ฿550 for children (blue pass), valid on all trains, 2nd and 3rd class, supplementary charges NOT included. A red pass includes supplementary charges, ฿2000 for adults, ฿1000 for children. For further details visit the Advance Booking Office at Hualamphong station in Bangkok.

Boat

The waterways of Thailand are extensive. However, most people limit their water travel to trips around Bangkok (see page 146) or to Ayutthaya (page 187). *Hang-yaaws* (long-tailed boats) are the most common form of water-travel – they are motorised, noisy, fast, and entertaining.

● **Cruise holidays**
The following tour operators can organize cruise holidays: *Siam Cruise*, 33/10-11 Sukhumvit Soi Chaiyod (Soi 11), T 2554563; *Seatran Travel*, 1091/157 Metro Shopping Arcade, Phetburi Rd, T 2535307; *Songserm Travel Centre*, 121/7 Soi Chalermla, Phayathai Rd, T 2500768; *Phuket Travel and Tour*, 1091/159

STATE RAILWAYS OF THAILAND: SAMPLE ROUTES AND FARES

Route		Fare (baht)*		
	Hours	**1st Class**	**2nd Class**	**3rd Class**
Bangkok north to:				
Ayutthaya	1 hr 35 min	60	31	15
Phitsanulok	5-6 hrs	292	143	69
Lamphun	13 hrs	520	247	118
Chiang Mai	11-13 hrs	537	255	121
Bangkok north-east to:				
Korat	5 hrs	207	104	50
Ubon Ratchathani	10 hrs	416	200	95
Khon Kaen	8 hrs	333	162	77
Nong Khai	10½ hrs	450	215	103
Bangkok south to:				
Nakhon Pathom	1½ hrs	54	28	14
Kanchanaburi	2½ hrs	111	57	28
Hua Hin	4 hrs 10 min	182	92	44
Surat Thani	11 hrs	470	224	107
Trang	15 hrs	597	282	135
Hat Yai	16 hrs	664	313	149
Butterworth (Malaysia)	21 hrs	1,015	457	-

* early 1994 fares quoted. Supplementary charges not included: ฿30 for express train, ฿20 for rapid train, ฿50 for special express, ฿50 for a/c, ฿70-250 for a berth depending on class.

Metro Shopping Arcade, Phetburi Rd, T 2535510; *Thai Yachting*, 7th Floor, Rachdamri Arcade, Rachdamri Rd, T 2531733; *Asia Voyage*, Grd Floor, Charn Issara Tower, 942/38 Rama IV Rd, T 2354100; *Yacht Charter*, 61/3 Mahadlek Luang 3, Rachdamri Rd, T 2519668.

Bus

Private and state-run buses leave Bangkok for every town in Thailand; it is an extensive network and an inexpensive way to travel. The government bus company is called *Bor Kor Sor* (an abbreviation of *Borisat Khon Song*), and every town in Thailand will have a BKS terminal. There are small stop-in-every-town local buses plus the faster long distance buses (*rot duan* – express – or *rot air* – a/c). Standard a/c buses come in two grades: *chan nung* (first class) and *chan song* (second class). *Chan song* have more seats and less elbow and leg room. The local buses are slower and cramped but are a great experience for those wishing to sample local life. The seats at the very back are reserved for monks (why, is a mystery), so be ready to move if necessary. For longer/overnight jour-neys a/c deluxe (sometimes known as *rot tour*) or VIP buses provide stewardess service, with food and drink supplied en route, and more leg room (plus constant Thai music or videos). Many fares include meals at roadside restaurants, so keep hold of your ticket. **NB**: the overnight a/c buses are very cold and it is a good idea to take a few extra layers of clothing.

● **Private tour buses**
Many tour companies operate bus services in Thailand; travel agents in Bangkok will supply information. These buses are normally more comfortable than the state buses but are more expensive. Overnight trips usually involve a meal stop (included in price of ticket) and stewardess service for drinks and snacks. They often leave from outside the company office which may not be located at the central bus station.

Car hire

There are two schools of thought on car hire in Thailand: one, that under no circumstances should *farangs* (foreigners) drive themselves;

OF HELMETS AND HAIR-DOS

In an act which many Thais thought long overdue, the government announced in 1992 that it was introducing a new law making the wearing of helmets by Thailand's one million motorcyclists compulsory. As the number of young Thais killed in motorcycle accidents has escalated to monumental proportions, it seemed only sensible. In typical Thai style however, opponents of the law managed to have a muddled, half-law introduced.

Motorcycle taxi drivers argued that the law would wreck their livelihoods as women passengers will not wear helmets other people had donned, adding that it would also ruin their own hairstyles, while dangerously obstructing their vision. They also maintained that there were not sufficient helmets on sale to meet the demand – even though they could be seen on roadside stalls across the capital. A third strand of the argument is that poor Thais are unable to afford the outlay, even though Indonesia with a per capita income a quarter that of Thailand's has successfully introduced such a statute. In December 1992 the authorities caved-in: it was decided that the law would only apply in Bangkok, and then on only 240 main roads in the capital – as if people are not killed outside the capital nor on its minor *sois* (lanes). The head of one of Bangkok's more prestigious universities – Mahidol – voiced his outrage and the government's inability to stand up to pressure groups, however forceful the argument might be in terms of public health.

By 1994 there were signs around Bangkok indicating where helmets had to be worn. Fortunately, the hassle of taking a helmet off means that most motorcyclists wear them continuously on their bikes. Upcountry, helmets are still thin on the ground, although even there they are beginning to have an impact.

and second, that hiring a car is one of the best ways of seeing the country and reaching the more inaccessible sights. Increasing numbers of people *are* hiring their own cars and inter- nationally respected car hire firms are expanding their operations (such as Hertz and Avis). Roads and service stations are generally excellent. Driving is on the left-hand side of the road.

BUSES OF THAILAND: SAMPLE ROUTES AND FARES

Route	Distance	Approx hrs by a/c bus*	VIP+	Fare** a/c	Non-a/c
Bangkok north to:					
Ayutthaya	75 km	1.30	-	36	22
Phitsanulok	368 km	5.30	230	161	88/95
Lampang	610 km	9	-	262	140
Chiang Mai	713 km	9.45	470	304	161
Chiang Rai	849 km	11.50	525	364	182
Mae Hong Son	928 km	12.35	-	442	241
Nan	677 km	10.30	330	289	170
Bangkok north-east to:					
Korat	256 km	4-5	-	115	64
Surin	451 km	6.40	-	195	108
Ubon Ratchathani	679 km	10	400	290	161
Khon Kaen	444 km	7	295	193	107
Nong Khai	614 km	9	405	263	146
Bangkok south to:					
Nakhon Pathom	56 km	1	-	22	16
Hua Hin	201 km	3½	-	92	63
Surat Thani	668 km	11	350	285	151
Phuket	891 km	14	450	368	201
Krabi	867 km	14	440	368	195
Trang	862 km	14	400	366	194
Songkhla	1,004 km	16	500	425	224
Sungai Kolok	1,266 km	18	-	533	282
Bangkok east to:					
Chonburi	80 km	-	-	40	26
Pattaya	136 km	-	-	66	37
Dan Phe	196 km	-	-	90	50
Chantaburi	239 km	-	-	108	48
Trat	317 km	-	-	140	78

* slower by non-a/c bus
** early 1994 fares quoted; note that fares may have increased.
+VIP coaches have fewer seats (just 8 rows) and seats that can recline further; VIP coaches are not available on all routes and most travel only on over-night journeys.

However, there are a few points that should be kept in mind: accidents in Thailand are often horrific. Towards the end of 1990 a gas tanker collided with a tuk-tuk on the Bangkok expressway, exploded, and killed more than 60 people, with many others horrendously burned. If involved in an accident, and they occur with great frequency, you – as a foreigner – are likely to be found the guilty party and expected to meet the costs. **Ensure that the cost of hire includes insurance cover.** On the road, size wins: buses and *siplors* (ten-wheel trucks) may well overtake, despite the approach of an oncoming vehicle; it's best to pull over. Driving at night has its own risks; long-distance bus and truck drivers frequently take stimulants to keep awake and it is not unknown for vehicles to travel without lights in the middle of the road.

The average cost of hiring a car from a reputable firm is ฿1,000/day, ฿6,000/week, or ฿20,000/month. Some rentals come with insurance automatically included; for others it must be specifically requested and a surcharge is added. An international drivers' licence, or a UK, US, French, German, Australian, New Zealand, Singapore or Hong Kong licence is required. The lower age limit is 20 years (more for some firms). Addresses of car hire firms are included in the sections on the main tourist destinations. If the mere thought of competing with Thai drivers is terrifying, an option is to hire a chauffeur along with the car. For this service an extra ฿300-500/day is usually charged.

Other land transport

Towns in Thailand will often have their own distinctive forms of transport for hire. In Chonburi and Si Racha chariot-like seats have been attached to large motorbikes; in Lampang, horse-drawn carts are used and in Prachuap Kiri Khan there are motorbikes with side-cars.

● Bicycle touring

This is becoming increasingly popular. It is a good way to see the country and to meet the people (although most Thais will think you mad). It is safest and most relaxing to route as much of the trip as possible off the main highways, where cars and ten-wheeled trucks sometimes like to drive on the hard shoulder.

● Hitchhiking

Thai people rarely hitchhike and tourists who try could find themselves waiting a long time at the roadside. It is sometimes possible to wave down vehicles at the more popular beach resorts.

● Motorbike taxi

These are becoming increasingly popular, and are the cheapest, quickest and most dangerous way to get from 'A' to 'B'. Riders wear coloured vests (sometimes numbered) and tend to congregate at important intersections or outside, for example, shopping centres. Agree a price before boarding – expect to pay ฿10-20.

● Motorbike hire

Mostly confined to holiday resorts and prices vary from place to place. ฿200-300/day is usual for a 100-150 cc machine. Often licences do not have to be shown and insurance will not be available. Off the main roads and in quieter areas it can be an enjoyable and cheap way to see the country. Borrow a helmet if at all possible and expect anything larger than you to ignore your presence on the road. Be extremely wary. Thousands of Thais are killed in motorcycle accidents each year and large numbers of tourists also suffer injuries. Riding in shorts and flip-flops is dangerous. Some travellers are now not just hiring motorbikes to explore a local area, but are touring the entire country by motorcycle. It is the cheapest way to be independent of public transport, but the risks rise accordingly.

● Saamlor ('three wheels')

These come in the form of pedal or motorized machines. Saamlor drivers abound and will descend on travellers in any town. Fares should be bargained and agreed before setting off. Drivers are a useful source of local information and will know most places of interest, plus hotels and restaurants (and sometimes their prices). In Bangkok, and now in some other large towns, the saamlor is a motorized, gas powered, scooter known affectionately as the **tuk-tuk** (because of the noise that they make). Pedal-powered saamlors were outlawed in Bangkok a few years ago and they are now gradually being replaced by the noisier motorized version throughout the country. Always bargain and agree a price before setting out on a journey. It will not take long to discover what is a reasonable price, but don't expect to pay the same as a Thai.

● Songthaew ('two rows')

Songthaews are pick-up trucks fitted with two benches and can be found in many up-country towns. They normally run fixed routes, with set fares, but can often be hired and used as a taxi service (agree a price before setting out). To stop a songathaew use the electric buzzers often provided or tap the side of the vehicle with a coin.

● **Taxi**
Standard taxis can be found in some Thai towns. This is the most expensive form of public motorized transport, and many now have the added luxury of air-conditioning. In Bangkok almost all taxis have meters. If un-metered, agree a price before setting off, and always bargain. In the south of Thailand, long-distance share taxis are common.

Communications

● **Language**
The Thai language is tonal and, strictly-speaking, monosyllabic. There are five tones: high, low, rising, falling and mid tone. These are used to distinguish between words which would otherwise be identical. For example: *mai* (low tone, new), *mai* (rising, silk), *mai* (midtone, burn), *mai* (high tone, question indicator), and *mai* (falling tone, negative indicator). Not surprisingly, many visitors find it hard to hear the different tones, and it is difficult to make much progress during a short visit (unlike, say, with Malaysian or Indonesian). The tonal nature of the language also explains why so much of Thai humour is based around homonyms – and especially when farangs say what they do not mean. Although tones make Thai a challenge for foreign visitors, other aspects of the language are easier to grasp: there are no marked plurals in nouns, no marked tenses in verbs, no definite or indefinite articles, and no affixes or suffixes.

Visitors may well experience two oddities of the Thai language being reflected in the way that Thais speak English. An 'l' or 'r' at the end of a word in Thai becomes an 'n', while an 's' becomes a 't'. So some Thais refer to the 'Shell' Oil Company as 'Shen', a name like 'Les' becomes 'Let', while 'cheque bill' becomes 'cheque bin'. It is also impossible to have two consonants after one another in Thai. If it occurs, a Thai will automatically insert a vowel (even though it is not written). So the soft drink 'Sprite' becomes 'Sa-prite', and the English word 'start', 'sa-tart'.

In general, English is reasonably widely spoken on the tourist trail, and visitors should be able to find someone to help. English is taught to all school children, and competence in English is regarded as a very useful qualification. Off the tourist trail making yourself understood becomes more difficult.

Despite Thai being a difficult language to pick up, it is worth trying to learn a few words, even if your visit to Thailand is short. Thais generally feel honoured that a *farang* is bothering to learn their language, and will be patient and helpful. If they laugh at some of your pronunciations do not be put off – it is not meant to be critical.

● **Postal services**
Local postal charges: ฿1 (postcard) and ฿2 (letter, 20 g). **International postal charges**: Europe and Australasia – ฿8 (postcard), ฿12.50

consonant 'y'   consonant 'b'

tone marks

consonant 's'   vowels

USEFUL THAI WORDS & PHRASES

Thai is a tonal language with five tones: mid tone (no mark), high tone (´), low tone (ˋ), falling tone (^) and rising tone (ˇ). Tones are used to distinguish between words which are otherwise the same. For example, 'see' pronounced with a low tone means 'four'; with a rising tone, it means 'colour'. Thai is not written in roman script but using an alphabet derived from Khmer. The romanisation given below is only intended to help in pronouncing Thai words. There is no accepted method of Romanisation and some of the sounds in Thai cannot be accurately reproduced using Roman script.

Polite particles: at the end of sentences males use the polite particle 'krúp', and females, 'kâ' or ká.

Learning Thai: the list of words and phrases below is only very rudimentary. For anyone serious about learning Thai it is best to buy a dedicated Thai language text book or to enrol on a Thai course. Recommended among the various 'teach yourself Thai' books is: Somsong Buasai and David Smyth's (1990) *Thai in a Week*, Hodder & Stoughton: London. A useful mini-dictionary is the Hugo *Thai phrase book* (1990). For those interested in learning to read and write Thai, the best 'teach yourself' course is the *Linguaphone* course.

Useful words and phrases

Yes/no	*chái/mâi chái,* or:
	krúp (kâ)/mâi krúp (kâ)
Thank you/no thank you	*kòrp-kOOn/mâi ao kòrp-kOOn*
Hello, good morning, goodbye	*sa-wùt dee krúp (kâ)*
What is your name? My name is...	*Koon chêu a-rai krúp (kâ)*
Excuse me, sorry!	*kŏr-tôht krúp (kâ)*
Can/do you speak English?	*KOON pôot pah-săh ung-grìt*
a little, a bit	*nít-nòy*
Where's the...	*yòo têe-năi...*
How much is...	*tâo-rài...*
It doesn't matter, never mind,	*mâi bpen rai*
that's all right	
Pardon?	*a-rai ná?*
I don't understand	*pŏm (chún) mâi kao jái*
How are you? Not very well	*sa-bai dee mái? Mâi sa-bai*

The hotel

What is the charge each night?	*kâh hôrng wun la tâo-rài?*
Is the room air conditioned?	*hôrng dtit air rěu bplào?*
Can I see the room first please?	*kŏr doo hôrng gòrn dâi mái?*
Does the room have hot water?	*hôrng mii náhm rórn mái?*
Does the room have a bathroom?	*hôrng mii hôrng náhm mái?*
Can I have the bill please?	*kŏr bin nòy dâi mái?*

Travel

Where is the train station?	*sa-tăhn-nee rót fai yòo têe-năi?*
Where is the bus station?	*sa-tăhn-nee rót may yòo têe-năi?*
How much to go to...?	*bpai...tâo-rài?*
That's expensive	*pairng bpai nòy*
Will you go for...*baht*?	*...baht bpai mái?*
What time does the	*rót may/rót fai bpai...òrk gèe*
bus/train leave for...?	*mohng?*
Is it far?	*glai mái?*
Turn left/turn right	*lée-o sái / lée-o kwăh*
Go straight on	*ler-ee bpai èek*

It's straight ahead	*yòo dtrong nâh*

Restaurants

Can I see a menu?	*kǒr doo may-noo nòy?*
Can I have...?/ I would like...?	*Kǒr...?*
Is it very (hot) spicy?	*pèt mâhk mái?*
I am thirsty	*pǒm (chún) hěw náhm*
I am hungry	*pǒm (chún) hěw*
Breakfast	*ah-hǎhn cháo*
lunch	*ah-hǎhn glanhg wun*

Time & days

in the morning	*dtorn cháo*	Monday	*wun jun*
in the afternoon	*dtorn bài*	Tuesday	*wun ung-kahn*
in the evening	*dtorn yen*	Wednesday	*wun pÓOt*
today	*wun née*	Thursday	*wun pá-réu-hùt*
tomorrow	*prÔOng née*	Friday	*wun sÔOk*
yesterday	*mêu-a wahn née*	Saturday	*wun sǎo*
		Sunday	*wun ah-tít*

Numbers

1	*nèung*	9	*gâo*	100	*(nèung) róy*
2	*sǒrng*	10	*sìp*	101	*(nèung) róy-nèung*
3	*sǎhm*	11	*sìp-et*	150	*(nèung) róy-hâh-sìp*
4	*sèe*	12	*sìp-sǒrng...etc*	200	*sǒrng róy...etc*
5	*hâa*	20	*yêe-sìp*	1,000	*(nèung) pun*
6	*hòk*	21	*yêe-sìp-et*	10,000	*mèun*
7	*jèt*	22	*yêe-sìp-sǒrng...etc*	100,000	*sǎirn*
8	*bpàirt*	30	*sǎhm-sìp*	1,000,000	*láhn*

Basic vocabulary

airport	*sa-nǎhm bin*	hotel	*rôhng rairm*
bank	*ta-nah-kahn*	island	*gòr*
bathroom	*hôrng náhm*	market	*dta-làht*
beach	*hàht*	medicine	*yah*
beautiful	*sǒo-ay*	open	*bpèrt*
big	*yài*	police	*dtum-ròo-ut*
boat	*reu-a*	police station	*sa-tǎh-nee*
bus	*rót may*		*dtum-ròo-ut*
bus station	*sa-tǎh-nee rót may*	post office	*bprai-sa-nee*
buy	*séu*	restaurant	*ráhn ah-hǎhn*
chemist	*ráhn kai yah*	road	*thanon*
clean	*sa-àht*	room	*hôrng*
closed	*bpìt*	shop	*ráhn*
cold	*yen*	sick (ill)	*mâi sa-bai*
day	*wun*	silk	*mǎi*
delicious	*a-ròy*	small	*lék*
dirty	*sòk-ga-bpròk*	stop	*yÒOt*
doctor	*mǒr*	taxi	*táirk-sêe*
eat	*gin (kâo)*	that	*nún*
embassy	*sa-tǎhn tôot*	this	*née*
excellent	*yêe-um*	ticket	*dtǒo-a*
expensive	*pairng*	toilet	*hôrng náhm*
food	*ah-hǎhn*	town	*meu-ung*
fruit	*pǒn-la-mái*	train station	*sa-tǎh-nee rót fai*
hospital	*rohng pa-yah-bahn*	very	*mâhk*
hot (temp)	*rórn*	water	*náhm*
hot (spicy)	*pèt*	what	*a-rai*

(letter, 10 g); US – ₿9 (postcard), ₿14.50 (letter, 10 g). Airletters cost ₿8.50. Poste Restante: correspondents should write the family name in capital letters and underline it, to avoid confusion.

Outside Bangkok, most post offices are open from 0800-1630 Mon-Fri and only the larger ones will be open on Saturdays.

Fax services: now widely available in most towns. Postal and telex/fax services are available in most large hotels.

● **Telephone services**
From Bangkok there is direct dialling to most countries. Outside Bangkok, it is best to go to a local telephone exchange for 'phoning outside the country.

Codes: local area codes vary according to province, they are listed under "**Post & telecommunications**" in each town; the code can also be found at the front of the telephone directory. **Directory inquiries**: domestic long distance including Malaysia and Vientiane (Laos) – 101, Greater Bangkok BMA – 183, international calls T 2350030-5, although hotel operators will invariably help make the call if asked. **Callboxes** cost ₿1, some boxes take the old coin, some take the new. All telephone numbers marked in the text with a prefix 'B' mean that they are Bangkok numbers.

Entertainment

● **Newspapers**
There are three major English language daily papers – the *Bangkok Post*, the *Nation Review* and the *Bangkok World* (an evening paper). The first two provide good international news coverage. There are a number of Thai language dailies and weeklys as well as Chinese language newspapers. The Thai media is one of the least controlled in Southeast Asia (although controls were imposed following the coup at the beginning of 1991 and during the demonstrations of May 1992), and the local newspapers are sometimes scandalously colourful, with gruesome annotated pictures of traffic accidents and murder victims. International newspapers and magazines are readily available in Bangkok, Chiang Mai, Pattaya and Phuket, although they are more difficult to come by upcountry.

● **Television and radio**
Five TV channels, with English language sound track available on FM. Channel 3 – 105.5 MHz,

Channel 7 – 103.5 MHz, Channel 9 – 107 MHz and Channel 11 – 88 MHz. The *Bangkok Post* stars programmes where English soundtrack is available on FM. Shortwave radio can receive the BBC World Service, Voice of America, Radio Moscow and other foreign broadcasts, see page 18.

Holidays and festivals

Festivals with month only are moveable; a booklet of holidays and festivals is available from most TAT offices.

Jan: *New Year's Day* (1st: public holiday).

Feb: *Magha Puja* (full-moon: public holiday) Buddhist holy day, celebrates the occasion when the Buddha's disciples miraculously gathered together to hear him preach. Culminates in a candle-lit procession around the temple *bot* (or ordination hall). The faithful make offerings and gain merit. ***Chinese New Year*** (moveable, end of Jan/beginning of Feb) celebrated by Thailand's large Chinese population. The festival extends over 15 days; spirits are appeased, and offerings are made to the ancestors and to the spirits. Good wishes and lucky money are exchanged, and Chinese-run shops and businesses shut down.

Apr: *Chakri Day* (6th: public holiday) commemorates the founding of the present Chakri Dynasty. *Songkran* (moveable: public holiday) marks the beginning of the Buddhist New Year. The festival is particularly big in the north (Chiang Mai, Lampang, Lamphun and Chiang Rai). It is a 3 to 5 day celebration, with parades, dancing and folk entertainment. Traditionally, the first day represents the last chance for a 'spring clean'. Rubbish is burnt, in the belief that old and dirty things will cause misfortune in the coming year. The wat is the focal point of celebrations. Revered Buddha images are carried through the streets, accompanied by singers and dancers. The second day is the main water-throwing day. The water-throwing practice was originally an act of homage to ancestors and family elders. Young people pay respect by pouring scented water over the elders heads. The older generation sprinkle water over Buddha images. Gifts are given. This uninhibited water-throwing continues for all 3 days (although it is now banned in Bangkok). On the third day birds, fish and turtles are all released, to gain merit and in remembrance of departed souls.

May: *Coronation Day* (5th: public holiday) commemorates the present King Bhumibol's crowning in 1950. *Ploughing Ceremony* (moveable: public holiday) performed by the King at Sanaam Luang near the Grand Palace in Bangkok. Brahmanic in origin, it traditionally marks the auspicious date when farmers could begin preparing their riceland. Impressive bulls decorated with flowers pull a sacred gold plough.

June: *Visakha Puja* (full-moon: public holiday) holiest of all Buddhist days, it marks the Buddha's birth, enlightenment and death. Candle-lit processions are held at most temples.

Aug: *The Queen's Birthday* (12th: public holiday). *Asalha Puja and Khao Phansa* (full-moon: public holiday) – commemorates the Buddha's first sermon to his disciples and marks the beginning of the Buddhist Lent. Monks reside in their monasteries for the three month Buddhist Rains Retreat to study and meditate, and young men temporarily become monks. Ordination ceremonies all over the country and villagers give white cotton robes to the monks to wear during the Lent ritual bathing.

Oct: *Ok Phansa* (three lunar months after Asalha Puja) marks the end of the Buddhist Lent and the beginning of Krathin, when gifts – usually a new set of cotton robes – are offered to the monks. Particularly venerated monks are sometimes given silk robes as a sign of respect and esteem. Krathin itself is celebrated over two days. It marks the end of the monks' retreat and the re-entry of novices into secular society. Processions and fairs are held all over the country; villagers wear their best clothes and food, money, pillows and bed linen are offered to the monks of the local wat. *Chulalongkorn Day* (23rd: public holiday) honours King Chulalongkorn (1868-1910), perhaps Thailand's most beloved and revered king.

Nov: *Loi Krathong* (full-moon) a *krathong* is a small model boat made to contain a candle, incense and flowers. The festival comes at the end of the rainy season and honours the goddess of water. The little boats are pushed out onto canals, lakes and rivers. Sadly, few krathongs are now made of leaves: polystyrene has taken over and the morning after Loi Krathong lakes and river banks are littered with the wrecks of the night's festivities. **NB**: the 'quaint' candles in flower pots sold in many shops at this time, are in fact large firecrackers.

Dec: *The King's Birthday* (5th: public holiday). Flags and portraits of the King are erected all over Bangkok, especially down Rachdamnern Avenue and around the Grand Palace.

Constitution Day (10th: public holiday). *New Year's Eve* (31st: public holiday).

NB: regional and local festivals are noted in appropriate sections.

Further reading

Fickle, Dorothy (1989) *Images of the Buddha in Thailand*, OUP: Singapore. Grey, Anthony (1990) *The Bangkok secret*, Pan: London. Novel of intrigue based around the murder/assassination of King Ananda; banned in Thailand. Ekachai, Sanitsuda (1990) *Behind the smile: voices of Thailand*, Thai Development Support Committee: Bangkok. Vignettes of Thai life and the strains of development by a *Bangkok Post* journalist; interesting and informative. Keyes, Charles, F. (1987) *Thailand: Buddhist kingdom as modern nation-state*, Westview Press: Boulder, Colorado. Good, clearly written background to Thailand. Kruger, Rayne (1964) *The devil's discus*, Cassell: London. Best investigation into the death of King Ananda; banned in Thailand. Labbe, A.J. (1985) *Ban Chiang, art and prehistory of Northeast Thailand*, Bowers Museum: Santa Ana, Calif. Leonowens, Anna [1870] (1988) *The English governess at the Siamese court*, Oxford University Press: Singapore. The book on which the play and film *The King and I* was based starring Yul Brynner. A travesty of history but entertaining nonetheless and now re-printed. Manich Jumsai (1972) *Popular history of Thailand*, Chalermit: Bangkok. Maugham, Somerset (1930) *The gentlemen in the parlour: a record of a journey from Rangoon to Haiphong*, Heinemann: London. Ringis, Rita (1990) *Thai temples and temple murals*, OUP: Singapore. Shearer, Alistair (1989) *Thailand: the lotus kingdom*, John Murray: London. Good background to culture and history of Thailand, rather derivative but entertaining. Smitthi Siribhadra and Moore, Elizabeth (1991) *Palaces of the gods: Khmer art and architecture in Thailand*, River Books: Bangkok. Expensive but nicely illustrated coffee table book covering the Khmer monuments of Thailand, text by an art historian at London's School of Oriental and African Studies. Stratton, Carol and Scott, Miriam M. (1981) *The art of Sukhothai: Thailand's golden age*, Oxford University Press: Kuala Lumpur. Tapp, Nicholas (1989) *Sovereignty and rebellion: the White Hmong of Northern Thailand*, Oxford University Press: Singapore. Scholarly study of the tensions under which the Hmong are forced to live their lives. Terwiel, B.J. (1983) *A history of modern Thailand, 1767-1942*, University of Queensland Press: St Lucia, Queensland. Van Beek, S. and Tettoni, L.I. (1991) *The arts of Thailand*, Thames & Hudson: London (revised). Glossy coffee table book with good photographs and informative text. Warren, William (1970) *The legendary American: the remarkable career and strange disappearance of Jim Thompson*, Houghton Mifflin: Boston. West, Richard (1991) *Thailand: the last domino*, Michael Joseph: London. An 'alternative' travel book which provides considerable historical and cultural background; entertaining and interesting, very occasionally inaccurate. Wright, Joseph (1991) *The balancing act: a history of modern Thailand*, Pacific Rim Press: Oakland. Most detailed modern history (to 1991) but not as scholarly as Wyatt's volume. Wyatt, David K. (1982) *Thailand: a short history*, Yale University Press: New Haven. Simply, the best history of Thailand from the beginning of recorded Thai history to the 1980s.

Acknowledgements

Chris Hawes, Canada; Sonya Engelen, Sydney; Martin Hartnett, London. English Department, Surat Thani Teachers College; Lucas Cardholm, Lund; L Matzig, Diethelm Travel; Sarah Posner, Thai Airways, London; Silachai Surai, at Chiang Rai TAT; Nittaya Puengprayoon at Pattaya TAT; Chamnan Muangtim at Nakhon Si Thammarat TAT; Wiboon Nimitrwanich at Phitsanulok TAT; Porntip Pattanakul at Hat Yai TAT; Chattan Kunjara Na Ayudhya at Bangkok TAT; Jakarin Phudpong at Surat Thani TAT; Naowarat Pongpakdee at Nakhon Ratchasima TAT; Phuket TAT; Chiang Mai TAT; Russell Murdoch and Elaine Kovacs, Dorset, UK; Pierre-Yves Atlan, Paris; Sally Burbage, UK; Jake Reimann, UK; Ulli Link, Germany; Volker Maisenbacher, Germany; Nittaya Puengprayoon, Pattaya TAT office; Wichukorn Kularbsri, Sungei Golok TAT office; Chamnan Muangtim, Nakhon Si Thammarat TAT office; Chaing Rai TAT office; Pongsan Pitakmahaketu, Kanchanaburi TAT office; Cath Stewart, London; RD Tucker, Holland; Joel and Lesley Winston, Saudi Arabia; Yongyod Thangtrakul, Chiang Mai TAT office; Clare Barry, London; Armin Hermann, Saugkhlaburi, Thailand; Virachai Plasai, Thai Embassy, UK; Robert Taylor, UK; A van Elzakker and M van der Plas, Holland; Jim Enright, Khao Sam Roi Yod National Park, Thailand; Kevin Savage, St Albans.

BURMA (MYANMAR)

INTRODUCTION

In 1989 the military government changed Burma's name to Myanmar. The political implications of the change were not immense: it was as if Germany had suddenly announced that the world should call it Deutschland. In tourist brochures, Burma sells itself as *Shwe Pyidaw* – 'The Golden Land' – another old Burmese name for the country. Apart from its thousands of glittering pagodas, the name reflects Burma's wealth of natural resources, from teak and oil to jade and rubies, huge fish stocks in the Andaman Sea and some of the richest farmland in Asia, in the Irrawaddy delta area. But there is tragic irony in all this, for over the past 3 decades, Burma's old dictator, Ne Win, has transformed 'The Golden Land' from one of the richest economies in Asia into one of the 10 poorest countries in the world. Despite its potential, and the fact that more than 3/4 of the population is literate, Burma has been reduced to a state of abject poverty. It has become, in UN parlance, a Least Developed Nation. Burma was once a leading rice exporter, but now one tenth of its children, under the age of 3, suffer from severe malnutrition. Lack of medicine for readily curable diseases results in the unnecessary deaths of 175,000 children under the age of 5 each year – an infant mortality rate of 10%. These days, 80% of primary school children fail to complete 5 years of education.

CONTENTS

MAPS

Burma was one of Britain's most profitable colonies – but it was exploited by the colonial government. Kyaw Nyein, deputy prime minister in the late 1950s, described Burma under colonial rule: "The country presented a picture of a social pyramid which had the millions of poor, ignorant, exploited Burmese at its base, and a few outsiders, British, Indians and Chinese, at its apex." Hopes that this situation could be reversed were vested in national hero Aung San (see page 529). But tragically, Aung San was assassinated less than 6 months before independence in 1947. Since then Burma's social fabric and economy have disintegrated. Today, instead of a few outsiders at the apex, a corrupt, incompetent and

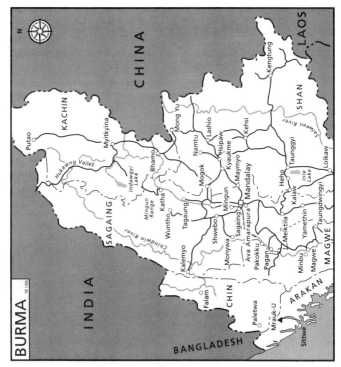

repressive military élite sits at the top, maintaining opulent lifestyles at the expense of the majority. In the way people associate the name Cambodia more with the Khmer Rouge Killing Fields than with the glories of Angkor Wat, Burma has become known more for its tyrannical government and its brutal suppression of dissent than for its historical, artistic and cultural heritage.

Following Ne Win's military coup d'état in 1962, Burma turned its back on the outside world. Inside the country, the government remained deeply unpopular and economic stagnation and deterioration led to years of sporadic protests, culminating in the mass-demonstrations of 1988. The military junta – the State Law and Order Restoration Council, or the SLORC – tried to rectify the situation by adopting an 'open door' policy. It courted foreign investors in a desperate bid to earn hard currency and plundered the country's natural resources in the process. The SLORC also held a general election in 1990 in which they were overwhelmingly voted out of power – a vote which they have studiously chosen to ignore. More than US$1 billion a year is spent on defence; the army rules by fear and continues to wage war on minorities.

But tyranny is not new to Burma: since the 9th century, its enthralling history has been a blood-curdling tale of warring kingdoms and violent

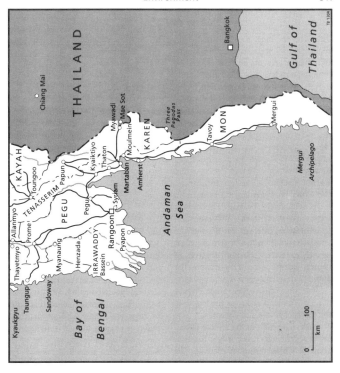

dynastic infighting. In contrast, the gentility and warmth of the Burmese people has always left a lasting impression on visitors. In the mid-19th century, the colonial Chief Commissioner to Burma, Lieutenant General Albert Fytche, said: "No European has ever been into free and kindly intercourse with [the Burmese] without being struck with their virtues". For the time being, however, they remain under a virtueless government. As opposition leaders like Aung San Suu Kyi have been silenced, many Burmese believe the only hope for the future is within the ranks of the military elite itself. A foreign diplomat in Rangoon says: "The only way things will change will be on the SLORC's terms. They can't afford to give up too much, but there are people within the SLORC who would like to see the back of brutal military dictatorship".

Environment

Land

Burma covers a land area of 676,552 sq km and stretches for over 1,930 km from the inaccessible N Himalayan region to the S tip of the Tenasserim region, which extends down the Kra Isthmus and faces the Andaman Sea. It is about the size of the United Kingdom and France combined and twice the size of Vietnam. Burma borders India and Bangladesh to the NW and W, China and Laos to the

NE and Thailand to the E and SE. It is shaped like a rhomboid – vaguely like a kite, with the long, narrow Tenasserim region as its jungled and mountainous tail. Its borders do not correspond to ethnic boundaries – they are mainly defined by mountain ranges which surround Burma on 3 sides and form a great horseshoe enclosing the Irrawaddy, Chindwin and Sittang river systems. Burma's mountains pose great obstacles to commerce and transportation, impeding E-W communication. Even during British colonial times, when Burma was part of the Indian Empire, the links between Burma and India were exclusively by sea. The mountains also prevent the SW monsoon from blowing into central Burma: the annual rainfall on the W Arakan coast usually exceeds 5,000 mm, whereas in central Burma – the Dry Zone – the annual rainfall may be as low as 640 mm.

The huge and rugged Shan Plateau borders Thailand and runs the length of the states of Karen and Tenasserim. The N borders are high in the remote Himalayan region, which is partly a continuation of China's Yunnan plateau. The Burmese, Chinese and Indian frontiers meet next to Burma's highest peak, the Hkakobo Razi (5,881m), which overlooks E Tibet. The N border with China runs for 2,185 km and the Kachin Hills has long been a disputed area. The Bangladesh and Indian borders follow the natural barrier formed by the Chin, Patkai, Manipur and Naga hills. These are actually substantial mountains, rather than hills, and the frontier line runs from mountaintop to mountaintop.

There are several crossing points from Thailand into Burma – the best known being the Three Pagodas Pass – SE of Amherst (in Karen State) and NW of Kanchanaburi in Thailand. Further W, on the W side of the Sittang River, is the volcanic Pegu Yoma (Pegu Range) which stretches to the N and culminates – just to the SE of Pagan – at Mount Popa

(see page 613). The Pegu Yoma's southernmost hill is crowned with the magnificent Shwedagon Pagoda. This range runs lengthwise down the centre of Burma, between the E and W ranges.

Two river valleys dominate the central plain of Burma both running N-S: the Irrawaddy to the W, and the smaller Sittang to the E. The Irrawaddy is Burma's main communications artery and was known as the 'Road to Mandalay' by British colonialists – giving rise to Rudyard Kipling's famous lines:

"On the road to Mandalay,
  Where the flyin'-fishes play,
  An' the dawn comes up like thunder
  outer China 'crost the Bay!"

The Irrawaddy flows over 2,000 km from the Kachin Hills in the N to the Andaman Sea. The river effectively divides Burma in 2 and is only bridged at Ava (just outside Mandalay) but is navigable for 1,450 km – even in the dry season. The Irrawaddy originates in E Tibet and flows S through the state of Kachin. It is joined by the river Chindwin SW of Mandalay. Before it reaches the sea it divides into the sprawling delta region, one of the richest farming areas in the world. The central plain is divided into Upper Burma – the area surrounding Mandalay, Prome and Toungoo – and Lower Burma, focusing on Rangoon. Central Burma is seismologically unstable; a severe earthquake in Jul 1975 caused serious damage to the ancient capital of Pagan. The Pegu Yoma, running between the 2 rivers, is heavily forested and until recently there were no roads running E-W linking the 2 river-valleys. The Sittang River, to the E of the Irrawaddy basin, has a tidal bore which is a notorious hazard to shipping. Further E, the Salween River is only navigable close to its mouth.

Climate

The Tropic of Cancer crosses the country 160 km N of Mandalay. Burma is usually classified as having a tropical monsoon climate, although roughly half the coun-

BURMESE NAMES – CHANGING PLACES

The Burmese government has reverted to calling the country and the main cities by their original Burmese names, which can cause confusion. The decision to change Burma to Myanmar, which followed consultations between General Ne Win and his astrologers, was announced on 27 May 1989. The old dictator's lucky number is 9 - hence the 27th (2+7=9). The change befuddled Burma-watchers, but Bangkok-based journalist Bertil Lintner believes it was done "in order to protect Burma's indigenous character... when foreign capital and outside influences were entering the country..." Ne Win has always tried to keep one step ahead of fate. The "Burmanization" is inconsequential - in Burmese, Burma has always been Myanmar. The decision to change town names was announced on 18 Jun (1+8=9). The former names and the new names are listed below:

Burma	*Myanmar*	Pegu	*Bago*
Pagan	*Bagan*	Prome	*Pyay or Pyi*
Rangoon	*Yangon*	Irrawaddy	*Ayeyarwady*
Akyap	*Sittwe*	Salween	*Thaniwin*
Bassein	*Pathein*	Sittang	*Sittoung*
Moulmein	*Mawlamyine*		

try lies outside the tropical zone. Its climate is similar to India's – cool from Oct to the end of Feb (21-28°C), hot from the beginning of Mar to the beginning of Jun (temperatures can reach 45°C in central Burma) and rainy from Jun to the end of Sept. The NE monsoon, from the dry uplands of the Yunnan Plateau, blows from Nov to Mar bringing a long, dry season. From May to Oct the prevailing wind shifts and the SW monsoon dominates, bringing rain from the Bay of Bengal.

Regions facing the prevailing winds – particularly Arakan and Tenasserim, which are both backed by steep mountain ranges – receive some of the heaviest rainfall in the world. Sittwe (Akyab) in Arakan receives an average of 5,180 mm of rain a year, of which 4,980 mm falls during the 6 months of the SW monsoon. The mountain areas – particularly the Shan Plateau – are cool and comparatively dry. One traveller during the British colonial era described them as a 'tropical Scotland'. There is an arid belt in the heart of the country around Pagan. This Dry Zone is in the rain-shadow of the SW monsoon and some parts of the central lowlands receive as little as 640 mm of rain a year.

Flora and fauna

Burma's natural vegetation varies according to regional rainfall patterns. But on the whole Burma is densely forested with conifers, teak, and tropical forest. The Irrawaddy delta area used to be thickly forested but has been cleared over the past century for agriculture. The forests have also been destroyed by shifting cultivation (see page 29) and, increasingly, by logging – mainly by Thai timber companies (see page 562). But Burma's forests still account for about ¾ of the world's teak reserves. In the Dry Zone of central Burma (around Pagan), cacti and acacia trees are a common sight. Burma's flora has not been as thoroughly studied as other areas of Southeast Asia but is known for its diversity; there are thought to be over a thousand varieties of orchid, for example.

Burma still has a large population of wildlife, including elephants, tigers, leopards, the mithan (a type of wild buffalo), the endangered Sumatran rhinoceros, wild boar, monkeys, flying squirrels, porcupines, civet cats, red and black deer, black bears and the Malayan sun bear. Burma is home to some 1000 species of birds, 40 of which are under worldwide threat of extinction. There are also 52 varieties of poisonous snake – Burma has the highest death rate from snakebites in the world. The most highly infested areas are the Dry Zone (snakes live in many of Pagan's ruined temples) and the Irrawaddy delta. The deadliest snakes are Russel's viper and the Asiatic king cobra. The animal most Westerners associate with Burma is the Burmese cat. It is actually from Thailand and was the result of a lengthy period of experimental cross-breeding with Siamese cats.

History

Burma's early history is practically uncharted but by the 8th century the Mons – who probably originated in Central Asia – occupied the lower portions of the Irrawaddy basin, while the Burmans had established themselves on the upper reaches of the Irrawaddy. Burma's subsequent violent history largely concerns the struggle between these 2 predominant racial groups. Kings fought wars in order to carry off slaves from the kingdoms they conquered; it was important to have a large labour force to build temples and pagodas and to grow rice.

The Glass Palace Chronicle of the Kings of Burma (a 19th century historical mythology) claims that the Burmese kings were descendants of the Buddha's family but historians have found no evidence of any ruler before the 11th century King Anawrahta of Pagan. From the 10th century on, the Burmans were the largest group; they were also the most important in terms of their historical, cultural and political contribution to Burma's heritage. Between the 11th and 19th centuries, the Burmans succeeded in uniting the country under one monarch on 3 separate occasions. When each of these empires fragmented, Burma became a muddle of quarrelling races. In the 19th century, the Burmese frequently clashed with the British and were defeated in 1885, resulting in the capture and exile of the last king.

Early history

There are traces of some form of settlement in Burma as far back as 2,500-2,000 BC. The Pyus were the first settlers and occupied the upper Irrawaddy River. The early Pyu city of Sri Kshetra, near present day Prome (see page 586), was enclosed in a massive wall and was possibly even bigger than the later Burmese cities of Pagan and Mandalay. When the Pyu capital was captured and the people enslaved by the neighbouring power in Yunnan, the Burmese moved into the power vacuum in the Irrawaddy area. The Burmese came to dominate both the Pyu and the Mon.

The Mons settled in the lower Irrawaddy delta region around Thaton and were the first people to establish Buddhism in Burma. Little is known about the earliest phases of Mon art – although their artistic and architectural skills were obviously coveted and their works have been unearthed not just in Burma, but also in Thailand and Cambodia. The great King Anawrahta brought Mon craftsmen to Pagan where their temple and stupa designs characterized the first recognizable architectural 'period' – the Mon Period. The last group to migrate from China were the Tai, who fled the Mongul invasions from the 9th-11th centuries and settled in the hills on the present Thai-Burma border.

The First Burmese Empire

Pagan was the first established centre of Burma; it was founded in 849 at a strategic location on the banks of the Irrawaddy. It was also close to the mystical Mount Popa, the most significant centre of *nat* (spirit) worship in Burma, which pre-dated the arrival of Buddhism (see page 544). In 1044 King Anawrahta seized the throne at Pagan.

Twelve years later, he was converted to Theravada Buddhism by **Shin Arahan**, a missionary-monk from the Mon court at Thaton; he immediately set about building the Shwezigon temple (see page 608). In 1057 Anawrahta declared war on the Mons to capture the Tripitaka, the Buddhist scriptures, which the Mon King Manuha refused to give up. Anawrahta besieged the Mon capital of Pegu for months until Manuha surrendered and the city was destroyed. Anawrahta returned to Pagan with the Mon royal family, 32 white elephants (each of which was laden with the sacred books of the Tripitaka) and Thaton's remaining 30,000 inhabitants – including craftsmen and builders. The Mon king was dedicated to the Shwezigon as a pagoda slave. But despite their inglorious defeat, the sophisticated Mons proceeded to dominate Pagan's cultural life for the next century – many of the thousands of pagodas at Pagan are Mon in style and the Burmans evolved their script from Mon.

Anawrahta also succeeded in breaking the power of the Shan states – the S ones came under Burmese suzerainty – and he brought Arakan into his dominion. Despite his war-like tendencies, Anawrahta is said to have been a very religious man. He is believed to have dispatched a ship laden with treasure to Bodhgaya in India, where the Buddha gained enlightenment, to pay for the restoration of the Mahabodhi temple. Anawrahta was killed by a wild buffalo in 1077, but by then he had already put in place the foundation of the First Burmese Empire. During his son, King Sawlu's, reign (1077-1084), the kingdom continued to expand. It grew even bigger under **King Kyanzittha's** reign (1084-1113), when parts of the S Tenasserim region came under the control of Pagan. Kyanzittha began the construction of the Ananda pagoda – the most famous temple on the Pagan Plain. The 12th century was Pagan's Golden Age, when

it was known – rather optimistically – as 'the city of 4 million pagodas'. The Pagan civilization is believed to have been supported by rice cultivation, made possible by a highly developed system of irrigation canals.

In 1248 **King Narathihapati** came to the throne; he is reputed to have been a hedonist who enjoyed a luxurious lifestyle. He completed the lavish Mingalazedi pagoda at Pagan in 1274 – but appears to have gone bankrupt in the process. Pagan's economy fell apart and no more pagodas were built. In 1287 **Kublai Khan** led a Mongul invasion which captured the city and brought the First Burmese Empire to an undignified end. The king fled to Bassein earning the title Tarakpyenrin (meaning the 'king who fled from the Chinese'), leaving the Monguls in his beautiful royal capital. The Mongul military campaign against the Burman kingdom of Pagan was recorded in the diary of Venetian merchant Marco Polo when he visited the Imperial Court of China 5 years later. After 5 months' exile in Bassein, the Burmese king tried to return to Pagan but made it only as far as Prome, where his eldest son was a governor. He murdered his father by forcing poison down his throat and then battled with his 2 brothers for the throne. He succeeded – but was deposed in 1298, marking the end of the Anawrahta Dynasty.

The kingdom broke into a number of smaller states. From 1298-1364 the Shans established power in Upper Burma, with their capital at Ava (founded 1364/5), near modern Mandalay. From 1364-1554, the Shans dominated the Irrawaddy rice growing area and expanded into what is now Kachin state and along the Chindwin River. The Shans did not manage to amalgamate into a single powerful empire – but remained split into small kingdoms, frequently feuding against one another. Only the W kingdom of Arakan remained completely independent and spread N into Chittagong (in present-day Bangla-

---

PHILIP DE BRITO – KING OF THIEVES

In 1603 the Portuguese adventurer Philip de Brito y Nicote, a former ship's cabin-boy, declared himself King of Lower Burma, with his capital at Syriam. He had the backing of the Portuguese Viceroy of Goa (having married his daughter), the friendship of the Mons, the acceptance of the Arakanese, and was tolerated by the Burmans. However, he quickly undid his feats of diplomacy by compelling about 100,000 Mons to convert to Christianity, plundering relic chambers throughout Lower Burma and stealing the 32-tonne bell which the Mon King Dhammazedi had donated to Rangoon's Shwedagon in the 15th century. Having overstepped the mark once too often, De Brito was damned by Burma's monks and then attacked by the Burman King Anaukhpetlun, Bayinnaung's grandson, whose troops besieged Syriam for a month. De Brito was captured by the Burmans and impaled on a stake. He was allowed to choose where, but ignored advice to have it run through his vital organs. As a result, it took him 3 days to die. All the leading Portuguese were executed and the remainder were employed as palace servants at Ava.

---

desh). The Arakanese capital was at Wethali until 1433 when they moved it to Mrauk U (Myohaung).

Meanwhile, the Mons, who had been under Burman subjugation for 2½ centuries, formed their own kingdom in Lower Burma. King Wareru – son-in-law of King Ramkhamhaeng, ruler of the Thai kingdom of Sukhothai – re-established Mon dominance, based first at Martaban. In 1385, Razadarit succeeded to the Mon throne and ruled Lower Burma from Pegu. The Mon kingdom prospered as a trading centre, exporting rice to India and Malaysia. Queen Shinsawbu (1453-1472) raised the height of the Shwedagon pagoda in Rangoon. The queen went so far as to donate her own weight in gold to gild the outside.

The Second Burmese Empire

Many Burmans fled S from Shan domination and established a centre around Toungoo and the Burmese and the Shan kingdoms remained in a permanent state of war. The kingdom survived, sandwiched between the Shans to the N and the Mons to the S. When King Minkyino came to the throne in 1486 there was a revival of the Burman national spirit and the Toungoo Dynasty

was founded. In 1530, the 16-year-old Tabengshweti succeeded his father and decided to re-unite Burma. He captured the Mon port of Bassein in 1535 and then went on to attack Pegu. He stormed the city 3 times, succeeding in 1539. With Bassein and Pegu under his belt, he then captured Prome and was recognized as the undisputed king of Lower Burma.

Meanwhile, to the N, the Shan King of Ava was gaining notoriety for persecuting monks and plundering pagodas. Kings who engaged in such activities never lasted long in Burma, and, sure enough, his actions prompted a conspiracy to overthrow him. When he was successfully ousted, the Shans united and took Prome and then beseiged the strongly fortified capital of Arakan, Myohaung. While besieging the city the Shans heard word of a Siamese invasion from the E. The Shans had expanded their empire too quickly and were unable to control such a vast swathe of territory. As the Shan kingdom began to disintegrate, Bayinnaung (Burman King Tabengshweti's brother-in-law) inherited the throne in 1550 and re-established Burman control over Lower Burma. He attacked Pegu 3 years later and the Mons fled to Prome; Bayin-

BURMESE KINGS: RULES OF SUCCESSION

As there was no rule of ascendancy in Burma, it was fairly usual for a new Burmese king to execute all his rivals to secure his claim to the throne. The only rule seems to have been that no royal blood could be spilt on Burmese soil; over the years, a number of innovative techniques were masterminded by which kings disposed of their relatives. Burning them alive and drowning were quite popular – Bodawpaya, when he came to the throne, got rid of all his relations, including their children and servants, by setting them alight. One of the more blood-thirsty royal purges was carried out by King Thibaw, Burma's last king, who outraged British Victorian society with his 'savagery' when it was discovered how he had dispensed with rival heirs. He had them all tied up in blood-red velvet sacks and beaten to death during a *pwe* (festival) which lasted 3 days and conveniently drowned the cries of his victims. The British had no idea that this barbaric behaviour was standard practice and the London press told the world about the horrors of the Burmese court and the inhumanity of King Thibaw.

naung then targeted Prome and the city was starved into surrender in 1552. Bayinnaung crowned his successes with the capture of Ava in 1555. In doing so, he destroyed the power of the Shan states and laid the foundations of the Second Burmese Empire. But Bayinnaung was not content to stop there and turned his attention to neighbouring Siam. First, he captured Chiang Mai, then set his sights on Ayutthaya. The King of Ayutthaya was known to have 4 white elephants which Bayinnaung coveted – white elephants had great religious significance as they were (and are) believed to symbolize an earlier incarnation of the Buddha. On the pretext of a manufactured border dispute, King Bayinnaung launched a successful attack on the Siamese capital in 1564.

The Siamese king, queen and youngest son were taken prisoner and the heir to the throne was left to govern as a tributary king. In Burma, the deposed king of Ayutthaya became a monk and his younger son died. King Bayinnaung, in a compassionate moment, then allowed his widow and children to return home to Ayutthaya – a move which proved to be a tactical error as their return prompted the tributary king to re-assert his independence. Bayinnaung was furious and launched a fresh Burmese inva-

sion of Siam. He left with 200,000 troops, many of whom died during the subsequent 7-month siege of Ayutthaya. The Burmese finally captured the city however and the belligerent King Bayinnaung went on to attack Vientiane in Laos. But King Razagyri of Arakan took advantage of the depleted Burman army and attacked Toungoo, taking the white elephants as booty. From then on the King of Arakan had the title 'Lord of the White Elephant'.

For all his warmongering, Bayinnaung seems to have been a model Buddhist: he forbade the sacrificing of slaves, horses and elephants and sent brooms of his own hair (and that of his wives) to sweep the Temple of the Sacred Tooth in Kandy, Ceylon. He eventually died in 1581, apparently leaving 97 children, and was succeeded by the eldest, Nandanaung, who ruled from 1581-1599. King Nandanaung did not have his father's force of character, military skills or administrative ability. In 18 years, he lost nearly everything his father had fought for and the empire broke up again due to internal feuding. In 1636 the capital was moved to Ava, but by then the empire was in decline. The Mons were once again becoming increasingly assertive; they re-established their kingdom in the S, with Pegu as the capital. Ava was recaptured by the Mons in 1752, with the help of French arms. Nandanaung was taken captive back to Pegu and the Second Burmese Empire floundered and the Toungoo Dynasty dissolved. The Mons then shifted their capital to Ava.

The Third Burmese Empire

The Mon conquest of Ava was short-lived. The Southerners were unpopular and within a year of taking the city, they had a revolt on their hands. Alaungpaya, a local official from the nearby town of Shwebo, refused to swear allegiance to the Mons and with the help of a large following he recaptured Ava in 1753. Within 4 years, Pegu had also fallen to Alaungpaya's forces; the Mon fled to the small town of Dagon, to the SW. Three years later, Alaungpaya sacked the town, renaming it *Yangon* – 'the end of war'. But it was not the end of war, having conquered the Mons, Alaungpaya attacked Ayutthaya in 1760. He was fatally wounded in the process. But in his few short years as King of Burma, he had founded the Konbaung Dynasty, and with it, the Third (and final) Burmese Empire. The dynasty lasted for over a century (1752-1865), during which time the capital – which was first at Shwebo – shifted between Ava (1765-1783, 1823-1837) and Amarapura (1783-1823, 1837-1857) before moving to Mandalay in 1857.

Alaungpaya's second son, Hsinbyushin, came to the throne after a short reign by his elder brother, Naungdawgyi (1760-1763). He continued his father's expansionist policy and finally took Ayutthaya in 1767, after 7 years of fighting. He returned to Ava with Siamese artists, dancers, musicians and craftsmen who gave fresh cultural impetus to Burma. The Mons had been crushed and the Shan *sawbwas* (feudal lords) were made to pay tribute to the Burmese. The kingdom's NE borders came under threat from the Chinese – they invaded 4 times between 1765 and 1769 but were repulsed on each occasion. In 1769 King Hsinbyushin forced them to make peace and the 2 sides signed a treaty. Europeans began to set up trading posts in the Irrawaddy delta region at this time; the French struck deals with the Mon while the English made agreements with the Burmese.

Bodawpaya, Alaungpaya's 5th son, came to the throne in 1782. He founded Amarapura, moving his capital from Ava. Bodawpaya conquered Arakan in 1784 and recovered all the Burman treasures taken by the Arakanese 2 centuries before, including the Mahamuni image (see page 627). Burmese control over Arakan resulted in protracted wrangles with the British, who by then were firmly ensconsed in Bengal. Relations with the British deteriorated further when Bodawpaya pursued Arakanese rebels seeking refuge, across the border – this was not to be the last time refugees flooded over the border (see page 543). Conflict ensued; the British wanted a demarcated border while the Burmese were content to have a zone of overlapping influence. To add to their annoyance, British merchants complained about being badly treated by the king's officials in Rangoon. The British decided enough was enough and diplomatic relations were severed in 1811.

Bodawpaya turned his attention to the administration of his empire. He investigated the existing tax systems and revoked exemptions for religious establishments which incurred the wrath of the monkhood – as did his claim to be a Bodhisattva. Bodawpaya died in 1819 at the age of 75 and was succeeded by King Bagyidaw. The Maharajah of Manipur (a princely state in the W hills to the S of Nagaland) who previously paid tribute to the Burmese crown, did not attend Bagyidaw's coronation. This resulted in the subsequent punitative expedition that took the Burmese into British India.

The expansion of the British into Burma

This intrusion was used by the British as a pretext for launching the **First Anglo-Burmese War**. The British took Rangoon in 1824 and then advanced on Ava. In 1826, the Burmese agreed to the British peace terms and the Treaty of Yandabo was signed. This ceded the Arakan and Tenasserim regions to the British – which were ruled from Calcutta, headquarters of the British East India Company. Manipur also became part of British India.

But the peace treaty did little to ease relations between the British and Burmese. The Burmese kings felt insulted at having to deal with the viceroy of India instead of British royalty. In 1837 King Bagyidaw's brother, **Tharrawaddy**, seized the throne and had the queen, her brother, Bagyidaw's only son, his family and ministers all executed. He made no attempt to improve relations with Britain, and neither did his successor to the Lion Throne, **Pagan Min**, who became king in 1846. He executed thousands – some history books say as many as 6,000 – of his wealthier and more influential subjects on trumped-up charges. During his reign, relations with the British became increasingly strained. In 1852, the **Second Anglo-Burmese War** broke out after 2 British shipmasters complained about unfair treatment. They had been imprisoned having been charged with murder and were forced to pay a large 'ransom' for their release. British military action was short and sharp and within a year they announced their annexation of Lower Burma. Early in 1853, hostilities ceased, leaving the British in full control of trade on the Irrawaddy.

The same year – to the great relief of both the Burmese and the British – Pagan Min was succeeded by his younger brother, the progressive **Mindon Min**, who ruled from 1853-1878. The new king moved the capital to Amarapura and then to his new city of Mandalay. The move was designed to fulfil a prophesy of the Buddha that a great city would one day be built on the site. Court astrologers also calculated that Mandalay was the centre of the universe – not Amarapura. King Mindon attempted to bring Burma into greater contact with the outside world: he improved the administrative structure of the state, introducing a new income tax; he built new roads and commissioned a telegraph system; he set up modern factories using European machinery and European managers. He also sent some of his sons to study with an Anglican missionary and did all he could to repair relations with Britain. A commercial treaty was signed with the British, who sent a Resident to Mandalay. King Mindon hosted the Fifth Great Buddhist Synod in 1872 at Mandalay. In these ways he gained the respect of the British and the admiration of his own people.

The Burmese found the foreign presence in Mandalay hard to tolerate and with the death of Mindon, the atmosphere thickened. King Mindon died before he could name a successor, and **Thibaw**, a lesser prince, was manoeuvred onto the throne by one of King Mindon's queens and her daughter, Supayalat. (In his poem *The Road to Mandalay*, Rudyard Kipling remarks that the British soldiers referred to her as 'Soupplate'.) In true Burmese style, the new King Thibaw proceeded, under Supayalat's direction, to massacre all likely contenders to the throne. His inhumanity outraged British public opinion. London was becoming increasingly worried by French intentions to build a railway between Mandalay and the French colonial port of Haiphong in Annam (N Vietnam). When Thibaw provoked a dispute with a British timber company, the British had the pretext they needed to invade Upper Burma. In 1886 they took Mandalay and imposed

WHITE ELEPHANTS AND THEATRE AT THE ROYAL COURT

The British were amazed at life in the Burmese court: the strict rules of protocol prompted much debate, particularly 'the shoe question'. They were indignant at having to remove their shoes on entering pagodas and while having an audience with the king. Amused by the ritual quandary surrounding the decision of which umbrella the king should use, but the British were more bemused by the status accorded the white elephant. The 'Lord White Elephant' – or *Sinbyudaw* – commanded social status second only to the king in the hierarchy of the royal court. Sinbyudaw were treated with reverence and had white parasols held over them wherever they went. Young white elephants were even suckled by women in the royal court who considered it a great honour to feed the elephant with their own milk. The elephants were ritually washed, perfumed and entertained by court performers. In reality albino elephants are a pinky pale grey. The Sinbyudaw gave rise to the English term – 'a white elephant' – which originally meant a rare or very valuable possession, the upkeep of which was very expensive. In time, it came to mean an elaborate venture which proves useless and unwanted.

colonial rule throughout Burma; Thibaw and Supayalat were deposed and exiled to Madras in S India. Supayalat was eventually buried at the foot of the Shwedagon pagoda in Rangoon (the stupa can be seen today on Shwedagon Road), as the British feared nationalist rebellion if the funeral took place in Mandalay.

British colonial rule

Burma was known as 'Further India' and was run on the principle of 'divide and rule'. The colonial administration relied heavily on Indian bureaucrats and by 1930 – to the resentment of the Burmese – Indian immigrants comprised $\frac{1}{2}$ the population of Rangoon. The British permitted the country's many racial minorities to exercise limited autonomy. Burma was divided into 2 regions: Burma proper, where Burmans were in a majority – which included Arakan and Tenasserim – and the hill areas, inhabited by other minorities. The Burmese heartland was administered by direct rule. The hill areas – which included the Shan states, the Karen states, and the tribal groups in the Kachin, Chin and Naga hills – retained their traditional leadership, although they were under British supervision. These policies gave rise to tensions that continue to plague today's government.

The colonial government built roads and railways, and river steamers, belonging to the Irrawaddy Flotilla Company, operated between Rangoon and Mandalay. The British brought electricity to Rangoon, improved urban sanitation, built hospitals and redesigned the capital on a grid system.

While the British set about building and modernizing, they benefited greatly from an economic boom in the Irrawaddy delta region. When they first arrived in Burma, much of the delta was swampland. But under the British, Burmese farmers began to settle in the delta and clear land for rice cultivation. In 1855, paddy fields covered 400,000 ha; by 1873 the forests had been cleared sufficiently to double the productive area. Land under rice cultivation increased by another 400,000 ha roughly every 7 years, reaching 4 million ha in 1930. Population in the area – which was about 1.5 million in the mid-19th century – increased more than 5-fold.

Initially the rice paddys were farmed by Burmese smallholders but as rice prices rose, larger holdings were bought up and large tracts of land cleared by pioneers from central Burma. The agricultural economy in the delta region was dependent on complex credit facilities, run by Indian Chettiars – S Indian money-lenders – who extended credit to farmers at much lower rates than Burmese money-lenders. The Chettiars grew into a very prosperous community. Land rents had risen dramatically during the boom years and when the world economic depression set in in the 1930s, rice prices slumped and small-holders went bust. Between 1930 and 1935, the amount of land owned by the Chettiars trebled in size due to foreclosures, leaving them with well over a $\frac{1}{4}$ of the delta's prime land. The agrarian crisis triggered anti-Indian riots, which started in Rangoon in May 1930 and then spread to the countryside.

From the beginning of the colonial period, the British stressed the benefits of education, and formal Western-style schooling replaced the traditional monastic education system. Rangoon University was founded in 1920 and a new urban élite evolved. They attempted to bridge the gap between old and new Burma by calling for the reform of traditional Buddhist beliefs and practices. In 1906, the Young Men's Buddhist Association (YMBA) was established in an effort to assert Burmese cultural identity and remain distinct from their colonizers. In 1916, the YMBA objected to the fact that Europeans persisted in wearing shoes inside religious buildings, which was considered disdainful. After demonstrations in over 50 towns, the government ruled that abbots should have the right to determine how visitors should dress in their monasteries – a ruling hailed as a victory for the YMBA.

Following the introduction of greater self-government in India and the spread of Marxism, the YMBA renamed itself the General Council of Burmese Associations and demanded more autonomy

for Burma. A strike was organized at Rangoon University the year it was founded, and this spread across the country as schools were boycotted. The most serious uprising was initiated by a monk called Saya San; it represented the first concerted effort to expel the British by force. From 1930-1932, during what became known as the Saya San Rebellion, 3,000 of his men were massacred and 9,000 taken prisoner, while the government suffered casualties of only 138. Saya San was hanged in 1937. The underground nationalist movement also gained momentum in the 1930s and at the University of Rangoon the All-Burma Student Movement emerged. The colonial regime was clearly shaken by the extent of the unrest and the level of violence and in 1935 the Government of Burma Act finally granted Burma autonomy. In 1936, the groups' leaders – Thakin Aung San and Thakin Nu – led another strike at the university. They called themselves Thakin as it was previously an honorific only used to address Europeans. In 1937 Burma was formally separated from British India. It received its own constitution, an elected legislature and 4 popular governments served until the Japanese occupation.

World War II and independence

Japan invaded Burma in 1942, helped by the new Burmese Independence Army (BIA) – a band of men secretly trained by the Japanese before the war and led by Aung San, who had emerged as one of the outstanding leaders during the student riots in Rangoon. The BIA grew in number from 30 to 23,000 as Japan advanced through Lower Burma. The Burmese saw the Japanese occupation as a way to expel the British colonialists and to gain independence. The British were quickly overwhelmed by the rapid advance of the Japanese 15th Army and retreated, still fighting, to India. Their 'scorched earth' policy – which involved torching everything of

THE BURMA ROAD

Mandalay was the gateway to the Burma Road, a strategic highway built between 1937 and 1939 to link the W interior of China with the sea. It ran for 1,200 km from Lashio (NE of Mandalay) to Kunming in China's Yunnan Province and was the chief supply route for Chiang Kai-shek's Chinese nationalist forces (the Kuomintang – or KMT) in the run-up to and during World War II. The Burma Road carried munitions from India to KMT forces, who spearheaded the resistance to the Japanese occupation of China. Having occupied Rangoon in Mar 1942, the Japanese 15th Army pushed N in 3 columns, smashing through Allied defences and driving the KMT north, through the Shan states to the Yunnan border. The Japanese troops were supported by Thai forces: Bangkok forged an alliance with Tokyo in the hope that it could lay claim to the Shan states. The E column of the 15th Army finally cut the Burma Road on 30 Apr 1942. (Chiang Kai-shek entered into an alliance with the Chinese Communists against the Japanese.) The Burma Road was recaptured in 1945 and is now a principal overland drugs trail from the Golden Triangle (see page 556). Traffickers take consignments of raw opium on mule-trains up to the heroin refineries that in recent years have been mushrooming along the Yunnan border. The road is being improved to bear the greatly increased border trade between China and Burma. Teak, jade, heroin, cigarettes, gems and food goes out to China; pots, pans, beer, car parts, mechanical goods, carpets and clothes come back in.

value and sabotaging the infrastructure they had built up over decades – left total devastation in their wake. Fierce warfare erupted between the British and the Japanese and BIA, in which casualties were high – as many as 27,000 may have died. Many of the British and Allied troops who died – some hand-to-hand combat – are buried at the Htaukkyan cemetery near Rangoon (see page 580).

The war produced many heroes. Stilwell, an American, having retreated through the jungle into India with 114 men, retraced his steps (through Assam, across the Chindwin River to Myitkyina and helped recapture Rangoon in May 1945. Wingate, a British war-hero, successfully penetrated the Japanese lines. His men were known as the Chindits – after the mythological Chinthes, the undefeatable temple lions. Chennault was another hero, who led the airborne division – nicknamed 'the Flying Tigers' – who were feared by the Japanese. US ground forces in Burma were known as 'Merrill's Marauders' and consisted of

about 3,000 men, of which many were killed. The outstanding hero in Burma, was General William Slim, head of the 14th Army, which killed all but a few thousand of the 200,000 Japanese in Burma.

The 800 km-long Ledo Road – from Assam to Mong Yo, where it joins the Burma Road – was built during the war by 35,000 Burmese and several thousand engineers, as a supply route to China. Many died during the construction process; the Ledo Road ran through jungle and mountainous terrain and became known as 'the man-a-mile road'. Until it was completed, supplies were flown in over the 'hump' – the high Himalayan peaks – one of the most hazardous air routes of the war. Many planes were shot down and more than 1,000 airmen were killed.

Under Japanese occupation, Burma was declared independent, with Aung San as Minister of Defence and General Ne Win as Chief-of-Staff of the newly formed Burma National Army (BNA).

BOGYOKE AUNG SAN – YOUNG BLOOD

Burma's national hero and most famous martyr, whose portrait was held aloft in the pro-democracy demonstrations of 1988, was born in Natmauk, central Burma in 1915. At Rangoon University he read English, modern history and political science and became involved in politics. He emerged as a leader of the Burmese student movement and at one stage was suspended from the university for provocative articles which were published in the university magazine. He was a leading light of the All-Burma Student Movement and as an organizer of the 1936 student strike, he gained notoriety with the British colonial regime. He was arrested in 1939, the year he became secretary of the Communist Party of Burma. The following year he fled to Japan and received military training from the Japanese. His group of 'Thirty Comrades' founded the Burma National Army (BNA) which fought alongside the Japanese 15th Army for much of World War II.

The BNA gained prestige in Burma by taking over day-to-day administration of the country – particularly in rural areas – during the Japanese occupation. Bogyoke (General) Aung San became defence minister of the Japanese-backed 'puppet' administration. In 1943 Burma was granted nominal independence by the Japanese, but by then, Aung San and his colleagues had turned against their erstwhile supporters, and had formed the Anti-Facist People's Freedom League, which established contacts with the British army in India. In the dying months of the war, Aung San switched allegiance to the Allies and his forces joined British troops in recapturing Rangoon and driving the Japanese out.

The British wanted to treat Aung San as a collaborator but Admiral Lord Louis Mountbatten – the Supreme Commander of Allied Forces in Southeast Asia – stepped in, believing the 30-year-old Aung San to be the one man who could bridge the warring political and ethnic factions in Burma. The following year, Aung San negotiated a deal by which Burma would be granted independence, with British Prime Minister Clement Atlee. In 1947, 3 months before his party swept the polls, he signed an agreement with ethnic minority leaders. All seemed set for Aung San to emerge as the leader of an independent, united Burma. These hopes were shattered on 19 Jul 1947.

The fateful event is described by Burma-specialist Bertil Lintner: "...two military jeeps sped down the streets of Rangoon. They stopped outside what was then the Secretariat in Dalhousie Street [now Maha Bandoola Street]. Some young men in uniform, armed with sub-machine guns, jumped out and rushed into the old, colonial red-brick building. On reaching the room where Aung San was holding a cabinet meeting... they pointed their guns at the assembled ministers, shouting: "Remain seated! Don't move!" Aung San rose to his feet – and the men opened fire. The shooting continued for about 30 seconds, and then the uniformed men left the building, jumped into their jeeps outside and sped off... It was 10.37 am." Later the same day, U Saw, a right-wing politician who had been a rival for the premiership, was arrested and charged; the following May, he was convicted and hanged. Aung San left a widow and 3 children; 2 boys (one of whom drowned) and a daughter, Suu Kyi. Forty-one years later, Suu Kyi brought the Aung San name back to the forefront of Burmese politics by stepping into her father's shoes (see page 550).

GENERAL NE WIN – THE MAN WHO WOULD BE KING

Burma's old military dictator, Ne Win, has been at the helm of Burma's brutal, corrupt and incompetent military regime since his coup d'état in 1962. Today he is the most feared man in the country; Burmese do not mention him by name – they call him 'Number One'. He is believed to have amassed a sizeable personal fortune which is held in foreign banks. It was Ne Win who created Military Intelligence (MI) which over the years has built up a network of spies throughout Burma (see page 553). Unsurprisingly, however, he is said to be paranoid about his personal security – he reportedly keeps a revolver on his desk and on the rare occasions he ventures out in public, he is surrounded by bodyguards.

Ironically, Ne Win is not a Burman. The man who expelled foreign nationals from Burma is himself half-Chinese and was called Shu Maung before he settled on what he thought was an appropriate Burmese name: Ne Win means 'Brilliant as the Sun'. In the early 1940s he became one of nationalist leader Aung San's 'Thirty Comrades' who led the Burma National Army during World War II. They received their military training from the Japanese Imperial Army before the war, and in the days running up to the Japanese invasion of Burma, gathered in Bangkok where they pledged undying allegiance, drinking each other's blood from a communal cup.

Before the war Shu Maung studied medicine at Judson College, Rangoon, but failed to complete the course and became involved in politics through his uncle, who was a member of the pre-war Thakin Party. Following Aung San's assassination in 1947, Bogyoke (General) Ne Win headed the army and 10 years after independence, when Prime Minister U Nu's elected government was threatening to fall apart, he was invited to form a caretaker government. This evidently gave the general a taste for power, for on 2 Mar 1962 he led a successful coup, after which he headed the Revolutionary Council and presided over the disintegration of the economy. In 1974, he suddenly announced that he had become a civilian and was to be known as U Ne Win. He now led a one-party 'socialist' state. In 1981 he retired as head of state but maintained political control as chairman of the Burma Socialist Programme Party, the country's only legal party. Regular purges of the military leadership, in which those exhibiting leadership qualities were eliminated, allowed Ne Win to retain power.

Ne Win harbours some bizarre beliefs and his superstitious convictions are legendary. He believes in *yedaya chay*, the old Burmese theory that fate can be outwitted by prompt action. On one occasion, he ordered the introduction of bank notes in denominations of 45 and 90 kyat on the grounds that they were

---

The BNA initially fought with the Japanese, but began to realize that the occupiers did not have their best interests at heart. The Japanese alienated the local population and throughout the country there were stories of Japanese cruelty. Aung San eventually dispatched an envoy to India to negotiate with the British – although his critics claim he was really only prompted to do this because the Japanese were losing the war elsewhere in Asia and he did not want to end up on the wrong side. In Mar 1945, under the leadership of Aung San, Burmese troops switched their allegiance to the Allies and participated in the final stages of the Allied victory, helping British General Slim and the 14th Army recapture Rangoon. The Japanese surrendered in Aug 1945 but as they de-

divisible by 9 – his lucky number. Many people lost their life-savings as a result. When his chief astrologer pronounced that the left side was unlucky and that he should "move the country more to the right", he directed that traffic should immediately change to driving on the right. According to some reports he ordered the demolition of the village at Pagan because he was embarrassed to be seen consulting Pagan's astrologers on such a regular basis (see page 599). Ne Win's behind-the-scenes influence was most recently seen during the 1993 National Convention; to Burma-watchers his hand was obvious in the choice of astrologically-sound numbers. It was convened on 9 January – a very auspicious date. A total of 702 delegates were invited (7+0+2=9) – but that only 699 attended was regarded as an astrological catastrophe.

Ne Win is said to have married 7 times. He has 4 children from Daw Khin May – better known as Kitty – who he married just after the coup in 1962. His eldest daughter, Sanda, is supposed to be his favourite. He is thought to live in the same house – a magnificent villa – as Sanda on Ady Road, on the shores of Inya Lake in Rangoon. She is known to be close to Major-General Khin Nyunt, Ne Win's protegé and the head of MI. When Kitty died in 1974, he married an academic, Daw Ni Ni Myint, then divorced her and married June Rose Bellamy (Yadana Nat Mai). She is an Australian great-granddaughter of King Mindon, penultimate monarch of Burma's Konbaung dynasty (see page 525). There was much speculation in the 1980s that Ne Win was interested in declaring himself King and his marriage to June Rose was probably calculated to legitimize his claim. On one occasion he went to great trouble to retrieve a statue of King Alaungpaya, founder of the last Dynasty of Konbaung, from London's Victoria & Albert Museum.

His marriage to June Rose did not last long and he remarried Daw Ni Ni Myint. In 1988 astrologers recommended he should take another wife and he is believed to have married an Arakanese girl in her mid-20s. Ne Win is now an octogenarian and rumours surface every so often that he is dead; other rumours suggest he is suffering from senile dementia. Calculating that his days were numbered, and having headed a brutal regime since 1962, Ne Win spent the 1980s making merit. He did this in the traditional manner employed by Burmese kings – he built a pagoda. His Maha Wizaya (Great Conquerer) Pagoda (see page 571) stands on the site of Signal pagoda near the Shwedagon in Rangoon. Although he no longer holds a title, Ne Win is deemed to be as influential in Burma today as Deng Xiao-ping is in China. Sources close to the old strong man say that he has prostrate cancer, and that he possibly suffered a stroke at the end of '93.

parted they too left a trail of destruction.

By the end of the war the Burmese economy was devastated. Pre-war Burma had been a wealthy colony but Burma suffered more than any other country in the region: its oil industry fell into disrepair and about a $\frac{1}{3}$ of all cultivated land went out of production. After the war the British tried to re-establish colonial rule, but the na-

tionalist movement, led by Aung San, proved too strong. In Sept 1946, a general strike forced the colonial government to the negotiating table and Aung San demanded independence. The wartime leadership of British Prime Minister, Sir Winston Churchill, came to an end and Clement Atlee's new Labour government in London was far more sympathetic to the cause of Burmese self-determination. A conference was held in London in Jan 1947 – at which minority groups were not represented – and the British dropped all opposition to Burmese independence. The support of the hill peoples was crucial to Aung San's plan to form a union and he signed the Panglong Agreement with tribal leaders. Under the terms of this treaty, ethnic minority groups would be allowed to secede from the union after 10 years. Each state was to have an elected council which was in charge of education and local taxation.

National elections were held in Apr 1947, Aung San and his AFPFL won a landslide majority – capturing 248 of the 255 seats. But on 19 Jul, a few months before Burma was to be granted full independence, Aung San and 5 of his ministers were assassinated while attending a meeting in the Secretariat in Rangoon. U-Saw, a right-wing prime minister in the pre-war colonial government was convicted of hatching the plot, and executed; he had hoped to create a leadership role for himself. It was a tragedy for Burma as Aung San seemed best equipped to unite the many different factions and minorities; had he lived, post-war Burmese history may have taken a very different course.

Independence

On 4 Jan 1948 at 0420 – an auspicious hour determined by Burmese astrologers – the Union Jack was lowered to the strains of *Auld Lang Syne* and U Nu, one of the early leaders of the student movement, became the first Prime Minister of independent Burma. It fell to U Nu to attempt to forge a national identity, build political institutions and rebuild the war-shattered economy. But Burma plunged immediately into chaos. Within 3 months, the Communists were in open revolt. The People's Volunteer Organization, a key component of the AFPFL split in 2, with the majority siding with the Communists. Muslim separatists rebelled in Arakan and the

Karen National Union (KNU), upset at the prospect of Burman domination, refused to be a part of independent Burma and unilaterally declared their own independence on 5 May 1948. A large number of Karen had converted to Christianity during the 19th century and sided with the British before and during the war. Other ethnic groups also revolted: within the first year U Nu's government faced 9 separatist insurrections.

Gradually the government regained military control – aided by the fact that the rebels were busy fighting each other as well as the government. By 1951, U Nu was finally in charge of the situation. He set about building a socialist state, nationalizing former British companies and expanding the health service and education. Elections were held in 1951 and 1956; both were won by U Nu's faction of the AFPFL. But in 1958 the party formally split and to avoid open revolt, U Nu invited his defence minister and army chief-of-staff, General Ne Win, to form a military caretaker government until elections could be held. When elections were finally held in 1960, U Nu won an overwhelming victory again – despite the split in the AFPFL. But rebel insurrections confounded his plans for a second time: by 1961 minority revolts by the Shans and Kachins were in full swing. Tensions were exacerbated when U Nu pushed a constitutional amendment through parliament making Buddhism the state religion, which alienated the Christian hilltribes, like the Karen, still further.

On 2 Mar 1962 the military engineered a surgically efficient – and almost bloodless – coup d'état, under the leadership of Ne Win. Government ministers and ethnic minority leaders were arrested: they had all been in Rangoon attending a conference aimed at resolving the secessionist insurrections. The constitution was swept aside and a 17-man Revolutionary Council (hand-picked by Ne Win) began to rule by decree, ending Burma's 14-year parliamentary democracy. The ideology of the military government – called the 'new order' – was set out in a communiqué entitled *The Burmese Way to Socialism*, published the month after the coup. The other seminal document of the regime was published in 1964: *The Correlation of Man and his Environment*, which was an eccentric mix of Marxism-Leninism and Theravada Buddhism.

State control was gradually extended over most aspects of Burmese life: industries were nationalized and the economy collapsed. The country entered a state of self-imposed isolation and the military government – which maintained rigid internal control – faced insurrection after insurrection from hilltribes and Communists. To mobilize popular support the Revolutionary Council formed the military Burma Socialist Programme Party (BSPP or *Lanzin*).

Five months after the government was installed, students protested against the military dictatorship. The next day the student union building was blown up by the army. Ne Win imprisoned all opposition politicians. U Nu was released in 1968 and demanded a return to democracy; he then travelled around the world, denouncing the Ne Win government before accepting asylum in Thailand where he formed the National United Liberation Front (NULF). The NULF rebels launched a series of raids across the Thai border – but in 1972 U Nu resigned from politics altogether. This came as a great relief to the government as the former Prime Minister had provided a focus for countless opposition groups.

In 1971 the Revolutionary Council announced plans to draw up a new constitution aimed at transferring power to civilian politicians. The following year Ne Win and 20 of his senior commanders in the military élite resigned their army posts and declared themselves the civilian Government of the Union of Burma.

The Socialist Republic of the Union of Burma came into existence on 3 Jan 1974, following the promulgation of a new constitution. Burma became a unitary state with effective power in the hands of the Burman majority at the centre and lip service was paid to minority rights. Political power was vested in the BSPP which was the only recognized party in the country; as its chairman, Ne Win became the head of the Council of State and the new President of Burma. Discontent with the state of the economy triggered a coup attempt in Jul 1976, led by junior military officers. Everyone who did not turn state's evidence was shot and General Tun U, the chief-of-staff was sentenced to 7 years' hard labour for failing to forewarn Ne Win. Because of growing political unrest, the BSPP was reorganized and tens of thousands of party members were expelled for 'being out of touch'; more than half the central committee was forced to resign. Over the course of the next year, the vacant places were gradually filled again by retired military officers.

Despite continued dissatisfaction and ongoing insurgencies (about 40% of the country was outside government control), Ne Win managed to bring the Buddhist *sangha* (order of monks) under his wing, giving Ne Win the confidence to declare an amnesty which allowed dissidents like U Nu to return to Burma in 1980. Ne Win resigned as president in 1981 but remained chairman of the BSPP and retained his grip on the leadership. By the mid-1980s his once self-sufficient country was on the verge of bankruptcy and in 1987 was conferred 'least-developed nation' status by the UN and international aid agencies. Economic mismanagement, poverty and the devaluation of the kyat helped spark the pro-democracy demonstrations of 1988 (see page 550).

Art and architecture

The only positive result of Burma's international isolation has been the preservation of its varied cultural traditions. Unlike most other countries in the region, it has not been invaded by Coca-Cola culture. In the late 1940s, former Prime Minister U Nu remarked: "We gained our independence without losing our self respect; we cling to our culture and our traditions and these we now hold to cherish and to develop in accordance with the genius of our people". Since Burmese independence, many minority groups have clung a little too tenaciously to their tribal cultures for the government's liking.

Burma was at the confluence of Indian and Chinese cultures; ethnically, most Burmese are more closely linked to the Chinese than the Indians – other than the Arakanese. However, Chinese influence in Burma is far less pronounced than it is in Indochina as Burma was so distant from Peking. (The 4 Chinese invasions from 1765 to 1769 under the Ch'ing dynasty failed.) Culturally, Indian influence has predominated. Burma adopted Pali, the Indian language of the Theravada Buddhist scriptures, and Buddhism was brought to Burma from India. Indian architecture provided the inspiration for most early Burmese monumental art and the Indian concept of kingship – rather than the Chinese Confucian bureaucracies – was a model for the Burmese dynasties. Burmese food is based on the Indian curry, and the most visually obvious of all Indian influences is the lungyi, the Burmese sarong.

The diffuse cultural traditions of Burma's various ethnic groups have influenced mainstream Burmese art; they in turn have been influenced by Burmese art. One of the earliest cultures was the Pyu. Early Chinese accounts talk of the wealth of the Pyu civilization and of the opulence of court life at Sri Kshetra. The king was carried on a golden litter, women wore silk and men and women were adorned with jewels. Inscriptions suggest that the Pyu were influenced by Indian culture. The Pyu left behind bronze and stone sculptures which indicate a high level of craftsmanship. Many pieces are similar in style to the late Gupta or post-Gupta style in India – Buddha statues are seated with their legs crossed and wearing tight clinging robes. Hindu statues dating from the same period show similarities with the Pallava period in S India.

The Mons created the next great Burmese civilization and developed a sophisticated culture, which was also deeply Indianized. For most of their history the Mons were Theravada Buddhists, but Hinduism later became more popular – little material evidence of the earlier Buddhist culture remains. The Mons were eventually absorbed into other states but continued to exert a strong cultural influence on other kingdoms – particularly Pagan. The Burmans founded Pagan in the 9th century and a large amount of high-quality sculpture and painting has survived. This period is usually regarded as the **Golden Age** of Burmese art. The art of Pagan was mainly connected with Theravada Buddhism: most remains are sculpted images of the Buddha. Crowned Buddha-figures appear for the first time during the Pagan period.

After Pagan fell to Kublai Khan in 1287, the stylistic variety of the **Buddha images** increased; most art historians speculate that this was due to the increased influence of the Siamese, or the Shans, or possibly because of the re-emergence of the Mons in the S. Traits of typical Burmese Buddhist figures became firmly established after the 13th century – fingers and toes are of equal length, tall projections (representing flames or lotus buds) crown the Buddha's head and the earlobes touch the shoulders. Towards the end of the 18th century a more naturalistic style arose in which the Buddha's robes were depicted in loose folds, fingers and toes were of unequal length and a wide band often decorated the forehead.

Some of the best relief work found in Burma is on the large gilded *sutra* chests, which are used to store the manuscripts of the sacred Buddhist texts. They often carry scenes from the Buddha's life. Another kind of temple furniture in which the Burmese excelled was red lacquerware (see page 549), usually with black figures and intricate ornamentation. The most common items were alms bowls to receive food offerings; many of these are also of beautiful design, with tiered and spired lids, like pagodas.

The Burmese arts fell into disarray during the British colonial period mainly because, with the demise of the monarchy in 1886, there was no longer any royal patronage. Burmese artists tended to adapt to English Victorian and Edwardian ideas of decoration. The magnificent wall paintings and frescoes at Pagan contrast sharply with the stagnation of contemporary Burmese painting, which, for the most part, still caters for 19th century English watercolour tastes. Woodcarving has also declined, and like lacquerware and embroidery, it has been imitated in Thailand; just S of Chiang Mai, for example, there are factories turning out 'Burmese handicrafts' for the tourist industry and for export to the West. Silversmiths in Rangoon and Mandalay are not in much demand these days either.

Most of the monumental remains in Burma are religious buildings. Buddhists lavish much of their surplus wealth on the construction and upkeep of stupas and temples – the surest way of attaining merit (see page 104). Because most secular structures – even palaces – were built of timber, bamboo and thatch, they have since rotted away.

The normal stupa is a tall structure incorporating a solid dome, surmounted by a *harmika* with a relic chamber set into the dome. Above the harmika is a pointed spire with *hti*, or honorific umbrellas of decreasing size set one above the other. Burmese architecture, which reached great and soaring beauty in the temples at Pagan, is now a lost art. A detailed account of the evolution of architectural styles at Pagan and the component parts of Burmese religious architecture starts on page 598. Only one or 2 Burmese architects have had a hand in any of the major buildings erected since World War II; most designs were submitted by foreign – particularly British – architects.

CULTURE AND LIFE

People

Burma's population was estimated at about 42 million in 1991. The greatest concentration is in the Irrawaddy delta region, where – along with Arakan and Tenasserim – the Burmans form the majority. The term 'Burman' refers to the largest and culturally dominant ethnic group in Burma, while 'Burmese' includes all ethnic groups within the Union of Burma – the ruling State Law and Order Restoration Council recognizes 135 nationalities. The upland areas are inhabited by hilltribes of which the

---

THE BURMESE FLAG: MINORITY STARS

The Burmese national flag symbolizes the country's minorities in an interesting way. The flag is red, to symbolize courage. In the top left-hand corner is a blue field, in the middle of which is a large white star. The star represents the whole country. Around this star are 5 smaller stars: one represents the Kachins, another the Shans, a 3rd the Karen and a 4th the Chins. The 5th star represents the largest group, the Burmans, who share the star with the Mons and Arakanese.

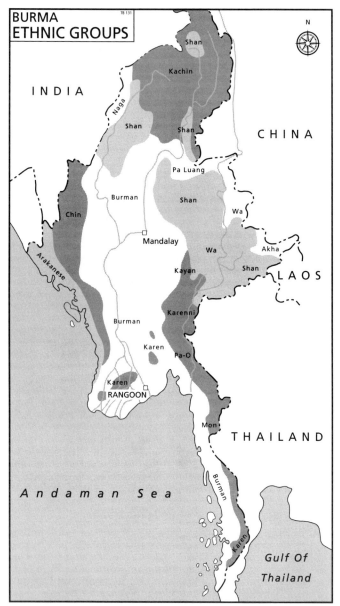

BURMA
ETHNIC GROUPS

N

INDIA

CHINA

LAOS

THAILAND

Andaman Sea

Gulf Of Thailand

Naga

Shan

Kachin

Shan

Shan

Pa Luang

Burman

Shan

Wa

Chin

Mandalay

Wa

Akha

Arakanese

Kayan

Shan

Karenni

Burman

Karen

Pa-O

Karen

RANGOON

Mon

Burman

Karen

THE KAREN LIBERATION STRUGGLE

The Karen National Liberation Army of the KNU has posed the most persistent security problem to the government and is now in its 5th decade. The KNU's Manerplaw headquarters backs on to the Thai border, and is about 300 km NE of Rangoon. Manerplaw is the capital of the self-declared independent state which the Karen call Kawthoolei ('the land of the flower that grows out of the ashes') and encompasses a number of villages nestled between the Salween and Moei rivers. The Karen, who fought for the British during World War II, felt betrayed by Britain, which refused to demarcate an independent Karen state before granting Burma its independence. Because of that, the Karen have fought what is possibly the longest-running war in the world.

In Nov and Dec 1991, there were clashes between the Karen and the Burmese Army as far W as the Irrawaddy delta region, not far from the capital itself. This was reported to have come as a shock to the government. For many years the government has been promising and predicting that the Karen resistance would soon be extinguished. In 1992 it became known that the Burmese Army had sworn to take Manerplaw by Armed Forces Day (27 Mar) and a long, bitter battle was fought in which the government forces took the strategic *Kwe Eik Daung* (Sleeping Dog Hill), which overlooks Manerplaw. All civilians were evacuated, Bo Mya appealed for UN intervention and analysts forecast the worst. But the Burmese Army failed to take the rebel stronghold and withdrew. Even if Rangoon does eventually capture the town, the fall of Manerplaw is unlikely to mark the end the war. Martin Smith, a writer on Burma, believes "the key for the Burmese Army is to be able to pacify the whole region and that will be very difficult, given the terrain of rugged mountains, deep jungle and fast-flowing rivers".

Karen are the most numerous.

There were 3 main migrations from the N into Burma:

1) The Mon-Khmer entered Burma mainly from the E and are now represented by a number of small tribes – the Wa, La, Tai, Loi, Palaung, Pale, Miao, Yao, Riang, En, Padaung and the Mon, who gained a foothold in the S of Burma.

2) The Tibeto-Burmans occupied the upper reaches of the Irrawaddy River and founded Pagan. They were then associated with a number of succeeding capitals at Toungoo, Ava, Amarapura, Sagaing and Mandalay. This group subdivides into:

i) the proto-Burmese such as the Toungoo, Yau, Kadu, Hpon, Lashi, Atsi and Arakanese

ii) the Chin-Kachins including the Chin, Kachin, Gauri, Sing-po and Duleng

iii) the Lolo including the Lolo, Lisu, Lahu, Muhso, Kwi, Moso, Kaw and Ako.

3) The Tai-Chinese migrated from Yunnan to the Shan states. It was this movement which broke up the Burmese civilization at Pagan and turned most of Upper Burma over to Shan control during the 13th and 15th centuries.

Today 68% of the population is Burman while the remaining population is divided into 5 main minority groups, each with its own history, language and culture. The most sizeable ethnic minorities are Shan 11%, Karen 7%, Kachin 6%, Arakanese 4% and Chin 2%. There are also many smaller groups like the Lahu, Wa, Akha and Lisu.

The Burmans

The central plains are the traditional home of the Burmans, the largest ethnic group in the country. They comprise about ⅔ of the population and are of Tibeto-Burman descent, having migrated from SW China. The Burmans gradually replaced or absorbed another Tibeto-Burman group, the Pyu, who occupied the central Irrawaddy valley and left important monuments at Sri Kshetra near Prome. The Burmans built their first and greatest capital at Pagan (849-1287) on the banks of the Irrawaddy – now one of the world's archaeological treasures (see page 595). Successive Burman capitals were built at Toungoo, Ava, Sagaing, Amarapura and Mandalay. While the Burmans are all Burmese, the converse is not true; the language Burmans speak is, however, called Burmese.

The Mon

Although the Mon were a powerful group in Burmese history they have largely been assimilated into Burman culture. There is an historical irony in this however, because many of the most important elements of Burman culture were originally derived from the Mon. It was also the Mon who introduced Theravada Buddhism to Burma along with the Indian (Pali) alphabet. The Mon are of Mon-Khmer descent and were linguistically closer to the Khmers of Cambodia than to Burmans. They had major cultural centres first at Prome and Thaton. Thaton, to the E of Rangoon, across the Gulf of Martaban, was a busy port through which the Mon developed strong ties with India. The Mon were later centred at Pegu which became an important trading centre.

The Shan

The Shan migrated from Nanchao in present-day Yunnan Province, SW China. They are of Tai descent – they are ethnic kinsfolk of the Tai and Lao – and speak a Tai dialect. Politically, the Shan enjoy greater autonomy than other minority groups and occupy the Shan pla-

teau. The Shan states form a large part of the Golden Triangle (see page 556) and opium poppy cultivation helps finance Shan military activity. Originally the plateau area was comprised of substates ruled by feudal princes or *sawbwas*. Whenever these sawbwas could bury their differences, they posed a serious threat to the rival Burman dynasties. Following the sacking of Pagan in 1287, the Shans nearly succeeded in creating their own empire, but internal rivalries prevented them from uniting into a cohesive political force. They did, however, expand to control central Burma for about 2 centuries. In 1959 the sawbwas signed an agreement with the Ne Win caretaker government, renouncing all their hereditary rights. Today the Shan area is called Shan State encompassing all the old Shan states. The Shan are historically the most autonomous and politically sophisticated group. The main party is the Shan State Progress Party (SSPP).

The 4 million people who live in Shan State belong to 32 different groups; these can be divided into 6 main ones – the Shan, Pa-O, Intha, Taungyoe, Danu and Pa Laung. Many tribespeople from all the different groups congregate at the regional periodic markets which rotate around the area over a 5-day period (see page 588).

The **Shan** are the most numerous and were the first immigrants to the region. As they are descended from Tai-Chinese stock they have a paler complexion than some other tribes. The Shan are traditionally traders but are also very artistic and are well known for their silverware and lacquerware. The traditional Shan dress is usually worn only on formal occasions now – most wear Burmese costume, although men still wear traditional baggy trousers. Their traditional dress includes a Chinese-style jacket with a turban, which is usually pink, blue or yellow. Shan women also wear turbans embroidered with gold or bright primary colours as well as a colourful striped lungyi and a tight-fitting jacket.

The **Pa-O** are the second most numerous tribe in the region and mainly live around Taunggyi. They are descended from Tibeto-Burman stock. The Pa-O are very religious, and although previously animist, most are now Buddhist. They are farmers and their main cash crop is leaves from the *cordia* trees, which are used for rolling cheroots (see page 590). The men wear similar trousers, jackets and turbans to the Shan but they are always black. The women wear lungyis, long sleeveless shirts and cropped long-sleeved jackets, which are also jet black, but with a brightly coloured turban.

The **Intha** people live around Inle Lake; *Intha* means 'sons of the lake'. Like the Pa-O, they are Tibeto-Burman, but they are thought to be descendants of the S Burmans, who migrated N during the reign of King Narapatisithu (1173-1210). The Intha are well known for their one-legged rowing technique, which the fishermen developed to enable them to keep 2 hands free for fishing. Because they do not have much fertile land, the Intha also developed a system of floating gardens which now provide most of the vegetables for the surrounding area (see page 591). The majority of the Intha are Buddhist. Most of the Intha wear Burmese costume – lungyis and open-necked shirts.

The **Taungyoe** tend to live in the hill regions above Inle lake and are also farmers of Tibeto-Burmese stock. There is a large group of Taungyoe in the Heho area. The Taungyoe wear a similar costume to the Pa-O but the women can be distinguished by the heavy rings below the knee. If they are married the bronze rings are just under the knee but if they are single they wear silver rings at the ankles.

The **Danu** – who are also of Tibeto-Burmese descent – live in the Pindaya Cave area (see page 593). The name *Danu* comes from *donake*, meaning 'brave archers'. In the 16th century the Danu were King Alaungpaya's archers and on returning from wars in Thailand settled in the Pindaya area. They are a farming people and speak Burmese, with a slightly different accent, and wear Burmese costume.

The **Pa Luang** are descended from Mon-Khmer stock and inhabit the Kalaw area; they were amongst the earliest inhabitants of Burma. They are famous for growing tea – unlike other tribes they have never grown opium. Their traditional dress is very colourful. The women wear white, green, pink, red and blue jackets and a red striped lungyi. They also wear cane rings around the waist when they are married and heavy strings of beads around their necks. The older women shave their heads and wear white hoods. Unlike other tribes the Pa Luang live in small longhouses – several families share a longhouse on stilts.

The Karen

If Karen legends are to be believed, this group originated somewhere around the Gobi Desert, but practically nothing is known of their early history. Half the Karen live in NW Thailand (see page 278), half in E Burma. They are the largest single minority in Burma. About 20% of the Karen are now Christian – most were converted by American missionaries at the beginning of this century. Karen mythology tells of a Great Book and a Teacher, which missionaries were quick to exploit. Their strong Christian background exacerbates the cultural rift between them and the Buddhist Burmans. The Karen group incorporates 11 smaller groups, including the Kayah (Red Karen), Karenni (Black Karen), Paku (White Karen), Pa-O and the Padaung (who live in the vicinity of Loikaw, Kayah State). The Karen National Union have been in armed opposition to the government since 1948 (see box).

Padaung womenfolk traditionally

wear an uncomfortable stack of rings around their necks, which physically elongates their necks – this has resulted in their being dubbed the 'giraffe women' or 'long-necked Karen'. Every year a Padaung girl would traditionally add new rings to her collection, until she got married, by which time her neck would be stretched. The practice is dying out, although some younger women still wear the rings. Traditionally, however, their necks and legs were literally encased in brass wire. The brass collar elongates the neck and apparently leads the head to shrink in size. The rings are also said to affect the shoulders which are compressed by the weight of the rings. Some say the custom began because Padaung men wanted to prevent invading tribes from kidnapping their women.

In the West, the Karen are one of the better known Burmese minorities as they were widely recruited by the British Army and fought against the Japanese during World War II. Because Burmese nationalists sided with the Japanese for most of the war (see page 527), the Karen were ostracized by other groups. The Karen National Liberation Army is one of the best organized of Burma's tribal insurgencies, and is under the leadership of Bo Mya (see above). The Karen independence struggle is mainly financed by tax revenue from the thriving smuggling business across the Thai border as well as from teak.

The Kachin

The Kachin are also a Tibeto-Burman people and originally migrated from W China, although more recently than the Burmans. They now occupy N Burma. They practice slash-and-burn agriculture (see page 29) and are skilled hunters. Most Kachin are animist but a significant number have converted to Christianity. The Kachin Independence Army (KIA) is the main party and has about 5000 regular fighters.

The Chin and the Naga

The Chin occupy the W mountains and are related to the Naga to the N – both are of Tibeto-Burmese stock. Both groups spread over the border into India. The Nagas have gained a certain notoriety because of their hard-fought guerilla war for independence in India. Both groups lead a more settled agricultural life than the Kachins. Many are still animist, although a number of Christian converts have begun to migrate away from the hills and into the valleys. Some Chin, like the neighbouring Nagas, practised headhunting until quite recently. The Chin have 44 related languages.

The Arakanese

The Arakanese have long been influenced by their proximity to India; they had independent kingdoms at Vesali until 1018 and then at Myohaung (1433-1784). Many are devout Buddhists (Rakhine). The main party is the National United Front of Arakan (NUFA). About $\frac{1}{5}$ of the Arakanese population is Muslim of Bengali descent; they are known as Rohingyas and have been persecuted over the past 200 years. The present government does not recognize the Rohingyas as one of Burma's 135 nationalities and has made a concerted effort to chase them out of the country (see page 543).

Smaller ethnic groups

The darker-complexioned, stocky **Wa** practiced headhunting as a part of their fertility rites until fairly recently; they are one of the better known of the smaller ethnic groups. About 30,000 Wa live along the border with China. The Beijing-supported Burma Communist Party recruited them to fight in their ranks against the Rangoon government.

There are also **Indian** and **Chinese** minorities in Burma – the former comprises both Hindus and Muslims. Large numbers of Indians settled in Burma when it became part of British India. In 1939 it was estimated that 58% of the population of Rangoon was Indian. Most of the Indian migrants were Chettiar moneylenders, who gained control of large areas of paddy land in the Irrawaddy Delta region during the Great Depression in the 1930s (see page 527). Some fled when growing resentment triggered riots against them. But until 1960, Burma still had a large Indian minority of over a million. The bulk subsequently left the country due to the military government's economic mismanagement. The present Indian population is now greatly reduced (about 2% of the total population) and is probably exceeded by the Chinese. The Chinese have mainly settled on the NE trade routes and along the great rivers. A large number of Chinese left in 1967 when there were anti-Chinese riots in Rangoon.

Insurgency

About a quarter of Burma's land area lies under the control of insurgent groups: it is a very divided Union. Many of the minorities feel subjugated politically, economically and culturally by the Burman majority. The resentment, which built up over centuries, has been aggravated by the events during World War II. The Karen remember massacres during the war; the Shan *sawbaws* (princes), the loss of their rights; the Kachin the loss of many of their villages to China under the border settlement of 1960; and the Rohingya Muslims, mainly in Arakan state, have been persecuted and repeatedly driven out of the country by a government which claims they do not exist. Some groups want independence, others just more autonomy. The main rebel offensives against the government began with the Karen in 1949, followed by the Shans in 1958 and the Kachin in 1961.

The concept of national loyalty is alien to many of these groups as so many straddle Burma's international frontiers. Some Shans live in China, Thailand and Laos for example, Kachins live in both Burma and China and Karens live on both sides of the Thai-Burmese border. Since independence in 1948, several groups have been engaged in protracted armed struggles against the government. (The total number of armed insurgents is estimated to be 26,000 under the National Democratic Front (NDF)). The existence of the insurgencies is partly due to the British colonial policy of divide and rule, which gave the groups some measure of autonomy. Today, tribal groups wield no political power – national policies are determined by the predominantly Burman government in Rangoon.

The government has tried to court some minorities, while it has remained in a constant state of war against others. While national unity is, for the most part, in the government's interests, some analysts speculate that the military junta relishes ethnic conflicts as they provide a rallying call for ethnic Burmans. The civil wars also serve to divert attention away from the military's heavy-handedness within the Burmese heartland. Commentators believe that today there are too many historical and emotional impediments to be overcome for the government to ever hope of unifying the country.

In the past few years, however, some insurgent groups have been 'bought over' by the government. This started with the Communist Party of Burma (CPB) which, until Apr 1989, had posed constant security problems. A sudden mutiny sent its leaders fleeing into China and ended the CPB's 41-year insurgency; the government promptly signed a peace treaty with the CPB mutineers, many of whom were heroin addicts. Similar peace deals were negotiated with smaller insurgent groups which had relied on the CPB for arms and ammunition. These included a brigade of the Kachin Independence Army (KIA) and the Shan State Army.

The rebels were awarded lucrative logging concessions and development aid in return for peace. Such policies have typified the government's way of dealing with insurrections: it has attempted to befriend smaller groups, while trying to obliterate the most powerful ones. The remaining 3 brigades of the KIA have come under mounting Chinese pressure to sit around the negotiating table with the SLORC. Talks between them were held in Jan and Mar 1993. The KIA wants the SLORC to talk to all the remaining rebel groups, which are loosely affiliated under the **Democratic Alliance of Burma**, along with elected members of the National League for Democracy (NLD) (see page 554), who fled following the 1990 election, and groups of students, who fled during and after the 1988 uprising. Rangoon is thought unlikely to want to do this, preferring to do deals with individual groups. But both the regime and the rebels are being urged by countries as diverse as the US, China, Australia and Thailand to start talking. Burma specialists point out that peace deals with insurgent groups would negate the need for Burma's quarter-of-a-million strong army. The junta in Rangoon would not feel secure without its huge military back-up.

The rebel coalition is headed by **Saw Bo Mya**, President of the Karen National Union (KNU) and is based at the Karen military headquarters at Manerplaw. The 'parallel government' of the NLD, which set up in Manerplaw in Dec 1990 has said that if it ever gets to form a government in Rangoon, the rights of tribal minorities will be respected. The NLD has suggested that it may try to reinstate Aung San's 1947 constitution, which guarantees eventual autonomy to ethnic minority groups within a federal framework, based on his 1947 Panglong Agreement with tribal leaders. In 1991 the Burmese government sent an ultimatum to tribal villages in frontline areas; it read: "if we hear of any guerrillas in the village, we will totally wipe it out".

Some analysts say political independence does not make much practical economic sense for tribal minorities as they would have few means of support. But much of Burma's oil, mineral and timber wealth – let alone opium – lies in tribal territories. This is another very good reason why the Burmese government has no wish to let them go. There are large jade deposits in N Burma and the Kachin Independence Army is partly funded through jade exports to China. The smuggling trade between Burma and Thailand has given Karen and Shan insurgents – who operate in the border regions – a secure economic base. By taxing shipments transiting their areas and by logging teak and mining precious stones for export, the rebel groups have developed sophisticated administrations. Lately, smuggling revenues have been undermined by Thai companies who have chosen to deal directly with Rangoon in the hope of securing more logging concessions and facilitating commercial joint-ventures.

The opium trade in the Shan and Kachin states provides funds for their armies as it did for the Burma Communist Party who were, until recently, operating in the remote N region. About half the heroin on America's streets comes from the Golden Triangle and Burma is by far the biggest producer (see page 556). Much of this area is controlled by independent opium warlords – the most powerful is **Chang Chi Fu** (alias Khun Sa) – 'the prince of death' – who runs one of the biggest opium-trafficking operations in the world. He has his own private army, called the Shan United Army. Other private armies operating in the Golden Triangle, which are mostly drugs-related, include the Kokang Army, the United Wa State Army and the Mong Tai Army. The other militia operating in the Golden Triangle is the Chinese nationalist Kuomintang-linked United Revolutionary Army.

The Shan states and some of the Karen territories along the Thai border are rich in teak. Thai logging companies – most connected to the Thai military – have the official approval of the Burmese government to negotiate with rebel groups to work in their territories. This agreement also benefits the Burmese government which badly needs foreign exchange. The logging roads have allowed the Burmese military better access to rebel-held areas, enabling it to remain on the offensive year round. The army has struck deals with Thai logging firms by which the timber companies build roads in exchange for lucrative logging concessions. Road construction teams were declared legitimate military targets by KNU leader Bo Mya in 1991.

Refugees

The net effect of the continued Burmese army offensive against ethnic minority groups has been a growing refugee problem. There are an estimated half-a-million displaced persons within Burma itself, but it was refugees pouring into neighbouring Bangladesh, India, Thailand and even China that has caused mounting international concern. There are known to be at least 400,000 refugees in neighbouring countries – although informal sources say the real figure is probably double that. All refugee groups tell similar stories of human rights abuses by the army. The number of Karen civilian refugees living in camps on the Thai-Burma border increased dramatically during the army's 1992 offensive on the KNU's Manerplaw headquarters. But the most serious refugee problem in recent years arose from the Rangoon regime's refusal to recognize the Muslims of Arakan state – who are known as Rohingyas – as one of Burma's national minorities.

There is said to be a Burman proverb which goes: "If you see a snake and an Arakanese, kill the Arakanese first".

There is a deep-seated loathing between the two. In the late 18th century, relations between Burma and British India became strained when King Bodawpaya chased tens of thousands of Rohingyas over the border into what is now Bangladesh. That was the first recorded mass-exodus of Rohingya refugees; more recently, about 200,000 flooded across Burma's 237 km-long border with Bangladesh in 1978. The Burmese government claimed it had been trying to stamp out illegal immigration from Bangladesh. The problem was resolved quickly and the refugees repatriated. But the same thing happened in 1991/1992 when another 260,000 escaped from well-documented persecution by the Burmese army. An Amnesty International report said: "Muslim men have been rounded up in large numbers and pressed into forced labour for the military, often as porters. They are ill-fed and abused, many are reported to have been beaten to death when they became too weak to carry their loads. Muslim women have been gang-raped in their homes, others have been held in army barracks and repeatedly raped." The men have also been forced to work as human mine-detectors.

The army has long exploited divisions between Arakan's Buddhist population (known as the Moghs) and the Rohingyas. Intervention by the UN eventually helped (but far from solved) the refugee problem and the government promised to curb the excesses of the armed forces. In May 1993, the UN High Commissioner for Refugees, Mrs Sadako Ogata, signed an agreement with the Bangladesh government providing for the repatriation of the refugees from camps around Cox's Bazaar. Many have already returned, but there is doubt over whether they have gone back voluntarily. The Arakan Rohingya Islamic Front, under the command of Nurul Islam, stepped up its attacks on the Burmese military in the wake of the

1991/92 refugee crisis. It is reportedly receiving arms and military training from former Afghan *mujahiddin* guerrillas and Muslim Filipino Moro rebels – both of whom rallied to the Islamic cause. There is also a second, more militant group, the Rohingya Solidarity Organisation (RSO) who claim to have a small army.

Religion

Buddhism is Burma's state religion and about 85% of the population is Buddhist – almost every hill-top in the country has a pagoda on it. Buddhism came to Burma in several stages; first to arrive were Indian merchants and missionaries who travelled to Burma and taught the scriptures. The Moghul emperor Asoka is said to have visited the Shwedagon Pagoda in around 260 BC. But Theravada Buddhism was only fully established in Burma after King Anawrahta came to the throne at Pagan in 1044 (see page 520). He was converted by a famous Mon monk called Shin Arahan.

The Burmese brand of Buddhism is unique as it incorporates **nat** – or spirit – worship. In the way the early Anglican Church adopted pagan vitality symbols such as holly, ivy and mistletoe, King Anawrahta tolerated spirit-worship in pagoda precincts in an attempt to fuse Buddhism and pre-Buddhist animism. He also decreed that Thagyamin, the king of gods and guardian-spirit of Buddhism, was to be added to the original 36 nats as their leader. After Thagyamin, the celestial lady, Thurthati, guardian of the Buddhist scriptures is the most popular nat. She is believed to be a Burmanization of Surasati, the Hindu goddess. Statues of her riding on the mythical hintha bird can often be found in temple stalls. The nats are the spirits of trees, rivers, stones, the ghosts of ancestors or Burmese versions of Hindu gods. The pantheon of Burmese nats is a mixed crew: there are deities as well as rogues and alcoholics. There is even one

nat who is an opium smoker. He is a local nat from central Burma by the name of U Min Kyaw. The 37 nats are capable of all kinds of mischief and have to be placated regularly. They are also capable, when appeased, of doing favours. Even devout Buddhists will go to nat seances where the spirits are believed to enter the bodies of trance-dancing mediums. Seance ceremonies – which can be quite spectacular – can often be seen at temple festivals. The nats have kept alive Burmese music, drama, dance and song. Natchins, songs in honour of the nats, are beautiful pieces of literature, comparable to the ballads of medieval Europe. Apart from temple festivals, nats may be offered special ceremonies, or kadaw-pwe, by private people who want to attract good fortune. These festivals are a release from daily life; alcohol flows abundantly and the Burmese lose their inhibitions and self-restraint and these ceremonies are often pandemonium. Offerings are made to the nats at every occasion: the first pillar of a house is never erected without an offering made to the nats; a road is made safe by tieing an offered bunch of flowers to the yoke of an ox cart or the mirror of a car. There is now a strong 'fundamentalist' movement in Burma which disregards Nat worship as superstitious.

The monastery is the focal point in a Burmese village. Monks are not only respected community leaders – they are also often healers, councillors, and teachers. Pagodas are beautifully maintained and families spend much of their hard-earned incomes on donations. They also offer food to the monks every morning, spend considerable sums on pilgrimages, and save up to cover the cost of their sons' initiation and ordination ceremonies. Traditionally the monastery was also the centre for education – *kyaung* is the Burmese word for a monastic school – which were commonplace until the British introduced a formal education system .

In Burma every boy must spend some time as a monk; initiation day (*shinbyu*) is considered one of the most important days in his life. The time and date of the shinbyu is set by the family astrologers, and the young boy is dressed in the finest silks and richest jewels his family can borrow or buy. His hair is allowed to grow long and tied into a topknot. The boy's father often goes deep into debt to provide a level of grandeur fit for a prince – for on initiation day the son is dressed to resemble Siddhartha, who later became Gautama, the Buddha. The boy is paraded around the village and visits all his relatives; at the induction ceremony, prayers are chanted, family snapshots are taken, and sometimes even video cameras are used to record the event. The ceremony is followed by as lavish a feast as the family can afford, for monks and guests (including any visitors who happen to stumble across the proceedings).

At the height of the festivities the boy's jewels come off, as do his locks and he puts on the orange or crimson robes of a monk, which symbolize his renunciation of worldly pleasures, following the example of the Buddha. As a monk he must beg for his food and he remains in the monastery for as long as his family can do without him. The period spent at the monastery provides religious education and merit for both the novice and his family. Novice ceremonies mostly take place during religious festivals – such as Thingyan – the New Year water festival – and Buddhist 'lent' – during the month of Waso (Jun/Jul) (see page 669). Novices and monks follow the 227 rules of the monastic code. After ordination they can return to the monastery at any time. Monks have 3 robes: the *ultarasanga*, which is wound round the upper body leaving the right shoulder bare; the *antaravasaka*, wound round the loins and reaching to the ankles and, over these 2 garments, a large rectangle of cloth called the *gaghati*, worn like a cloak.

Burmese nuns are not ordained and few women choose to follow a religious life. Monks are regularly fed as donors gain merit in offering food, but nuns have to beg for money. Although Burmese women have a respected place in Burmese society they are considered spiritually inferior and are often barred from entering the upper terraces of temples; nor are they permitted to put gold-leaf on the Mayamuni Image in Mandalay (see page 627). Women are believed to occupy a lowlier position in the cycle of birth and rebirth.

In Burma, merit-making counts for a

BURMESE NAMES

Family names are not used in Burma and it is impossible to determine a person's sex or marital status from their name. Boys and girls may have the same name, and women do not adopt their husband's name on marriage. Names reflect the day of the week a child is born – certain letters and consonants are divided up between the 8 planets (see page 568). The day of the week on which a Burmese is born also determines which corner of a pagoda platform the person should pray on. There is a complex system of titles which denote social standing: as an adult a man will be called *U* (pronounced *Oo*) – which literally translates as 'uncle', but is a respectful 'Mr'. A woman is called *Daw* or 'aunt'; *Ko* means 'elder brother', *Maung*, 'younger brother' and *Ma* 'sister'. Many Burmese have now adopted first names. Other common titles are connected with the military: *Bogyoke* means General – but is only used for the very top generals. *Bo* and *Bohmu* are also titles for army officers.

great deal – the best thing a Buddhist can possibly do is to build a pagoda – as this is thought to exemplify one's consideration for fellow men and is also evidence of detachment from worldly luxuries. Most of the kings of Pagan are thought to have achieved nirvana quite comfortably, thanks to their obsession with pagoda-building; by building stupas and temples, a king is also believed to make merit on behalf of his subjects. No special merit is to be gained from rebuilding someone else's pagoda, however. For ordinary people, who cannot afford to build pagodas, the easiest way to make merit is by gilding stupas and Buddha images. This happens throughout Burma, but the most remarkable example is the Mahamuni Image in Mandalay (see page 627) where so much gold-leaf has been applied to the statue that its features have been lost. A little square of gold-leaf costs about 10 kyat. In Mandalay, gold-leaf-making is a major industry.

Buddhism also occupies an important role at the national level. When political organizations were banned in the early period of colonial rule, Buddhist organizations became the focus of nascent nationalism (see page 527). Monks played a major role in the pre-independence period; one monk called Saya San led the first serious rebellion against the colonial regime in the early 1930s – although his uprising was brutally put down by the British and he was disrobed. There are more than 200,000 monks in Burma and they remain at the forefront of political resistance to the military government. Because of their reverential status in Burmese society, the army has been more reluctant to crack down on their political agitation. But the degree of monastic defiance in recent years has prompted less timidity from the ruling junta. On 8 Aug 1990, at a demonstration in Mandalay to commemorate the 8-8-88 uprising, 2 monks and 2 students were killed when the army opened fire. The monks contin-

ued to demonstrate in open defiance; they also excommunicated the government. The army countered by surrounding 133 temples and monasteries in Mandalay, cutting off water and electricity supplies until the disturbances subsided. About 150 monks were arrested. During their excommunication of the military, monks turned their begging bowls upside down and refused food from soldiers; they also mockingly knelt before them. *Thapeik hmauk* is the term used for a strike in Burma and literally translates as "turning the alms bowl upside down."

Language and literature

Several hundred languages and dialects are spoken in Burma by the various ethnic groups. Besides the indigenous languages, variations on Chinese dialects and South Asian languages are also spoken. Burmese is the national language and has been influenced by Pali and English. It is a tonal language – like Thai and Chinese – and has 32 consonants, 8 vowels and 4 diphthongs. The language is comprised of one-syllable words which are strung together to make longer or more complex constructions. As in Thai, slight variations in the tonal pronunciation of syllables can completely alter the sense of the word. An elaborate court language also evolved in Burma: addressing the king required the use of a special, flowery language – the king was known, for example, as 'Lord of the Sunrise'. The court language has mostly died out, although it is still spoken by a few people in Mandalay.

The earliest examples of written Burmese date from the early 12th century, mostly from Pagan. It was a Mon script, written from left to right without any spaces between the words. Prose writing was influenced by the Pali scriptures and retained this formal, religious association until the end of the 19th century, when the arrival of the printing press and contact with European literature altered its function. The first widely-read Burmese novel was published in 1904. The end of World War II and the attainment of independence in 1948 gave impetus to the novel as an art form and short story-writing became popular. Although a new bookstore (Inwa, Sule Pagoda Road, Rangoon) opened in 1993, foreign books are still censured and hard to get hold of. Burmese best sellers are also limited, and prices rise as copies become scarce. Paper quality of Burmese books is poor and so is the binding. There is a flourishing book binding business (31st and 32nd Streets, Rangoon), as it is customary to have your book rebound before reading it. Foreign books are photocopied and bound, as are most university and medical text books. There are no copyright laws in Burma. Books are so expensive in Burma, they are often rented out and most streets in Rangoon have a shop/rental store.

Burma's bestselling author is a 35 year old woman, "Fu", and many of her books are made into films. Her novels are mostly love stories, but she has been criticised for the topics of some of her books: living together without being married. Burmese cartoonists seem to have been granted a freedom of expression, which other artists do not have, cartoons in magazines and newspapers are often witty and daring in the way they portray Burmese society.

Dance, drama and music

The most popular form of entertainment in Burma is the *pwe* – an all-night extravaganza which combines song, dance and theatre. Slapstick comedy and satirical skits are interlaced with religious and historical plays (*zats* – see below). At temple *pwes* it is quite usual to see dancers in trance, possessed by the spirits of local nats. Nat dancers can be men or women. Nat *pwes* are mainly held by rich villagers who can afford to hire the orchestra and dancers. The nats often make outrageous demands for gifts and different nats have different predilections – some go around asking for money – others seem to prefer rum and whisky. Although *pwes* are intensely spiritual, they can also be extremely entertaining; they are highly charged frenetic occasions with the continuous background din of the orchestra. The popularity of the *pwe* has kept alive traditional music, dance and theatre.

The classical *zat* dramas are usually based on the Jataka tales or the Ramayana. Theatre is perhaps Burma's liveliest art. A national dance performance is organized every year at the national theatre (built by the Chinese). Each ethnic group is represented (to show that Myanmar is united). Traditional dancing can be seen at local festivals. Contemporary comedies – called *pyazats* – are most common in Rangoon. Pyazats have become unusual since 1888, when the government banned big gatherings of people; yet there are still theatre groups travelling around the country.

The *yokthe pwe*, or marionette theatre, has been enormously popular in Burma since the late 17th century. Aimed more at adults than children, the *yokthe pwe* was once Burma's major form of entertainment; master puppeteers used to enjoy an even higher social status than that accorded actors. Puppetry blossomed under royal patronage. Puppet shows were often part of the court reception for visiting embassies. There was an official post, Thabin wun, at the Burmese court for organising entertainment. Because of their popularity, Ahyoke Kyoka, the dance of the stringed ones, was even executed by court dancers. Shows were mainly reinacted Buddhist stories or scenes from the Ramayana (which took 45 nights to perform). Puppet faces were painted to conform to contemporary ideas of beauty, and characters which were natural enemies were never stored together. After the British annexation of Burma in 1886, the marionette theatre declined, as did many of the other arts which relied on royal patronage; it still survives however and can often be seen at temple fairs, local festivals or street pwe.

Traditional music is alive and well in Burma. Pwes are staged whenever there is something to celebrate – from weddings to funerals – and *zats* are usually performed during religious festivals. Both types of theatre involve song, dance and music and the cast is often supported by an 8-10 man *saing orchestra* (similar to Indonesian *gamelan*), dominated by percussion instruments. There are no written scores, so all the music is learnt by heart. Typical instruments include the *pattala* (xylophone), *kyee waing* (gongs), *yagwin* (cymbals), *palwe* (bamboo flute) and the *hne*, a wind instrument. An apprenticeship system ensures the music is passed down from generation to generation. The most interesting of the instruments is the circle of small horizontal metal gongs *or kyee waing*. To the Western ear, Burmese music is overly percussive and can sound tinny and unmelodious.

There are many professional dance troops in the country and several state schools teaching music and drama. Dancers are usually dressed in costumes which originated at the royal courts. The skirt is not the usual lungyi but a long split skirt with a train and dancing involves the rhythmic kicking away of the train. Most of the dances imitate the movements of the Burmese marionettes, popular in the royal courts during the 18th century, others are derived from classical Siamese dances; Ayutthaya's dancers were captured by the Burmese in 1767 and brought back to Ava. Thai classical *khon* and *lakhon* dance forms (see page 107) were used to form the basis of modern Myanmar dance. The Konbaung Dynasty (1783-1885) patronized masked dance dramas, which still survive today. Short dances are usually interspersed with routines by clowns who satirize contemporary politics – although these days they have to be careful.

Sport

Everywhere in Burma there are circles of young men playing *chinlon* – the national game and all-consuming male pastime. Chinlon – literally basketball – is played throughout the region, and is known in Thailand as *takraw* or (in Malaysia) *sepak raga*. A phenomenal demonstration of *chinlon* skills can be seen at the Karaweik Cultural Centre on Royal Lake, near the *Kandawgyi Hotel* in Rangoon (see page 576), where a girl with a long pigtail, in a brown nylon tracksuit (reputed to be the best chinlon-maestro in the land), performs acrobatics with the wicker balls to the beat of drums and traditional music. Rowing is a traditional Burmese sport. Rowers can sometimes be seen training on Kandawgyi and Inya lakes in Rangoon.

Crafts

Embroidery

Centuries of migration led Burma's hilltribes to develop portable art forms, and embroidery is one of their specialities. From early childhood a girl learns to sew and her needle-skills play an important role in helping her win a husband. Designs often reflect tribal legends, passed down the generations and geometric designs are stylized images of flowers, trees, rivers and mountains. *Kalaga* – or appliqué-work – in gold and sequins is common in Burma. These embroideries, often depicting figures from Buddhist mythology, are hung in temples or on bullock carts at festivals. Originally this type of appliqué-work was used for coffin covers for royalty and monks. Today, Mandalay's embroidery factories (see page 659) do a roaring trade in embroidered baseball hats, wall hangings, cushion covers, hats, bags and waistcoats for export to the West. The Mandalay factories also make traditional clothes for dancers.

Weaving

Mandalay and Amarapura are the most

important weaving centres and produce the *acheik*, the horizontal-weave patterned silk, once popular with royalty. This silk is still highly prized.

Lacquerware

Lacquered receptacles – mainly begging bowls – are used daily by monks in Burma and lacquerware was formerly in daily use by royalty too. It is the Burmese answer to everything from porcelain to plastic. Pagan is famous for its lacquerware, although the technique was probably imported from China, where it has a 3,000 year old history. The Burmese adopted the craft early in their history – Pagan is where the earliest-known surviving piece was unearthed; it is believed to date from 1274.

Traditionally the frame of a lacquerware item is made of woven bamboo which is then interwoven with horse hair – this makes it very flexible. Today many of the bases are wooden or just bamboo; high quality horse hair pieces are still made, but they are very expensive. But all in all, there are few shortcuts when it comes to making lacquerware. The base of the frame is coated with lacquer, which comes from the *thitsi* tree – found in N Burma – and is then coated with a second mixture of clay and lacquer together. The next layer is called *thayo* – ground bone ash – which is also mixed with lacquer; this is followed by a final layer of ground paddy husk mixed with lacquer. Between each layer, the item has to be dried for a week and then smoothed with a lathe before the next layer can be applied. The inside and the outside have to be painted separately. The piece is finally rubbed down with sesame oil and put on a hand-lathe and polished before being decorated.

On cheaper pieces the decorations are painted on; more expensive pieces the patterns engraved with a *kauk* blade and then the colour applied in separate stages. Red, green, yellow and gold are the traditional colours for lacquerware.

Blue and pink-painted pieces are modern. Many of the traditional designs are inspired by paintings on Pagan's temple walls. The best lacquerware is black, the next grade down is brown and yellow is inferior quality. Although Pagan is the main centre for lacquerware and has many lacquerware shops (see page 617), handicraft and antique shops throughout Burma sell it too. Good examples of traditional and antique lacquerware can be found at the Pagan Lacquerware Museum (see page 607), the Buddhist Art Museum in Rangoon (see page 573), the National Museum in Rangoon (see page 572), the Mandalay Museum (see page 626) and the Taunggyi Museum (see page 590).

Silverware

Silver objects were often put in relic chambers of pagodas and were a measure of wealth. Many early inscriptions list the cost of materials to construct pagodas and monasteries in tical of silver. Silver was also important in royal ceremonies: elephants wore silver bells round their necks and silver rings on their tusks. King Thirithuhamma, King of Mrauk-U, Arakan, had a silver howdah at his coronation in 1634. Silversmiths were often part of the booty of war. The Burmese and the hill tribes coveted silver and much of the silverware sold today is from tribal areas. Typical Burmese pieces are lime boxes, part of a betel set, with scenes from the jatakas inscribed round the sides.

Modern Burma

Politics

Poverty and political repression were the underlying factors which sparked the anti-government riots of 1988 that catapulted the otherwise dreamy capital of Rangoon into the international headlines. Initially, however, they were largely ignored in the West despite the fact there had been sporadic distur-

AUNG SAN SUU KYI

In Oct 1991, Aung San Suu Kyi (whose last name is pronounced *Chi*) was awarded the Nobel Peace Prize. Her prize citation said she had provided "one of the most extraordinary examples of civil courage in Asia in recent decades". Suu Kyi was born in 1945, the daughter of Aung San, the Burmese national hero who had negotiated independence from the British (see page 531). She never really knew her father – she was just 2 when he was assassinated. Aung San is to Burma what Mahatma Gandhi is to India – except for the fact that Aung San was a soldier, and founder of the Burmese Army. In contrast, Suu Kyi is committed to Gandhi's philosophy of non-violent protest; in every other way she is very much her father's daughter. In 1991, her husband, Michael Aris wrote: "There is a certain inevitability in the way she, like him, has now become an icon of popular hope and longing."

Suu Kyi left Burma in 1960 to join her mother in New Delhi where she was ambassador. She went on to read philosophy, politics and economics at Oxford before joining the United Nations in New York. On New Year's Day 1972, she married Michael Aris, an English academic and Tibetan specialist. There were conditions attached to the marriage: it was agreed that if destiny ever called her back to Burma, she would go. She joined her husband in Bhutan where she learned Tibetan, then learned Japanese in Kyoto; after that they returned to live in London where she became a post-graduate student at the School of Oriental and African Studies (SOAS). In Apr 1988 she left her husband and their 2 children and returned to Rangoon to nurse her mother who had suffered a stroke. It was Suu Kyi's first visit to Burma for 23 years.

When the demonstrations began to mount in the summer of 1988, Suu Kyi decided to enter politics, becoming the co-founder of Burma's main opposition party, the National League for Democracy (NLD). She made her first speech on the steps of the Shwedagon Pagoda to a crowd of at least 500,000; overnight she became the most popular person in Burma. She said: "I could not, as my father's daughter, remain indifferent to what was going on". Tens of thousands of people attended her mother's funeral in Jan 1989; by then Suu Kyi had the appeal of a film star, and had already become the focus of a personality cult. During early 1989 she campaigned throughout Burma . At one point during the

bances throughout 1987. But in Mar 1988, students from the Rangoon Institute of Technology became involved in a fight in a tea house and the army shot several students dead. Rallies and demonstrations continued through the following months as protests spread from Rangoon to other major towns. The flashpoint occurred on 8 Aug, when huge street demonstrations accompanied a general strike. The '8-8-88' protest culminated with the army firing into the crowds and led to similar demonstrations and massacres throughout the country in the days that followed. Universities, colleges

and schools were shut down. The demonstrations were brutally crushed by the army; most estimates put the number of casualties as high as 12,000 and 3,000-4,000 shot dead.

In late Jul, Ne Win had tactically resigned as party chairman amid mounting opposition against the one-party rule of the BSPP. Sein Lwin, nick-named the 'Butcher of Rangoon' for ordering riot police to fire into demonstrators, was appointed President, but resigned after just 18 days in office in the face of huge protests. He was succeeded by Dr Maung Maung, a long time

campaign, soldiers threatened to shoot her if she continued to lead a peaceful demonstration down a street in a provincial town. She refused to stop and the troops levelled their sights. Seconds later, an army major ordered his men to hold fire. The Burmese marvelled at her fierce courage in the face of military might – particularly in view of her delicate physique. Such incidents simply added to her popular appeal. Michael Aris later noted that: "The more she was attacked, the more people flocked to her banner. She brought overwhelming unity to a spontaneous, hitherto leaderless revolt."

On Martyr's Day (19 Jul) 1989, when Aung San and his cabinet are traditionally remembered, Suu Kyi decided to launch an unprecedented personal attack on General Ne Win, accusing him of ruining the country, and casting doubt on the junta's promise to transfer power to a civilian administration. This was more than the old dictator could stomach. The following day she was placed under house arrest – and was still there when this book went to press. It is not known whether she is allowed to listen to the radio. Outside her big white colonial bungalow on University Avenue, soldiers stand in 4 sentry boxes. Inside the compound Military Intelligence officers are frequently rotated as, in the words of one British journalist, they "were becoming too friendly with their brave, beautiful, bewitching captive." Her spirit does not appear to have been broken by years in detention, which included at least one lengthy hunger strike. People used to gather at the gates of her home in Rangoon to listen to her playing the piano – until it was removed in 1991.

When the NLD won a landslide at the polls on 27 May 1990, few voters had known anything about their candidates: it was a personal vote for the charismatic Suu Kyi, despite the fact that she had not been seen or heard of for 10 months. The government desperately wants her out of the country, but she has refused to leave, knowing that until she does, she will remain under house arrest. She is, however, free to go into permanent exile whenever she pleases. Junta leaders – probably prompted by the xenophobic Ne Win – have said that because she is married to a foreigner, Aung San Suu Kyi must never be permitted to hold power in Burma. Cartoons appeared in *The Working People's Daily* attacking her children for being only half-Burmese. Few Burmese need to be convinced of Suu Kyi's patriotism. As of June 1994, Suu Kyi was still being held under house arrest.

associate of Ne Win. He lasted just one month and his tenure as President was marked by daily demonstrations and strikes which by then had spread to over 50 towns and cities. Finally, on 18 Sept, General Saw Maung announced that the military had assumed power and had formed the State Law and Order Restoration Council (SLORC). About 10,000 students fled from the cities following the demonstrations and about half were still in jungle camps 4 years later along the Thai border.

Swedish journalist Bertil Lintner's book *Outrage* provides a blow-by-blow account of the events of 1988. Lintner is one of the regime's best-informed critics. The most telling review of *Outrage* appeared in *The Working People's Daily* in Rangoon. It described the book as "...a pot-pourri of maliciously selected misrepresentations, misinterpretations, fabrications and rumour-sourced disinformation about the Myanmar Naing-Ngan [Union of Burma] put together into book-form by past master of sensationalism, foreign journalist Bertil Lintner". A translation of his book became widely available in Rangoon, disguised behind a plain brown paper cover.

The SLORC

Since the coup d'état on 18 Sept 1988, Burma has been ruled by the State Law and Order Restoration Council, or the SLORC. The 19-man military junta, which ordered the streets to be cleared with bullets while promising free and fair elections, has been nationally and internationally condemned. In Burma the SLORC is known as *Nyain Wut Pipya* – which literally translates as "quiet, kneeling, lying flat" – which describes how the generals expect Burmese to behave. According to Bertil Lintner, "the country is ruled by corporals and sergeants who have become generals". Few of the SLORC's members – there are 23 of them now – have been educated beyond high school. General Saw Maung became chairman of the SLORC and Minister of Defence and Foreign Affairs following the 1988 'coup', but the man with the real influence was the dreaded intelligence chief, Major-General Khin Nyunt (see page 553).

For months after the SLORC takeover, *The Working People's Daily* carried prominent notices that the military junta was just a temporary administration which would hand the country over to a civilian administration just as soon as everything was in order. A typical notice read (under the headline Noble Desire):

"Although the State Law and Order Restoration Council has had to take over, due to unavoidable circumstances, the sovereign power of the State to prevent the Union from disintegration and for ensuring the safety and security of the lives, homes and property of the people, it wishes to retransfer State power to the people, in whom it was initially vested, through democratic means within the shortest time possible. Therefore, the entire people are urged to give all their co-operation to ensure the rule of law and for prevalence of peace and tranquility."

The Tatmadaw – the protector of the people

Among the first things a visitor notices on entering Burma are the huge red billboards emblazoned with white block capitals. American diplomats enjoy posing for snapshots beneath the one which faces their Rangoon embassy; it reads: "DOWN WITH THE MINIONS OF COLONIALISM". Most of these billboards, however, are advertising hoardings for Tatmadaw or the army. Near Pagan there is one which reads: "NEVER HESITATING, ALWAYS READY TO SACRIFICE BLOOD AND SWEAT IS THE TATMADAW"; outside Mandalay another says: "THE TATMADAW AND PEOPLE CO-OPERATE AND CRUSH ALL THOSE HARMING THE UNION". In 1992, many of the English translations on these signboards were painted out. The Tatmadaw have come to be known sarcastically throughout Burma as "Piyithu chin bat" a type of pickled vegetable, somewhat sour and stinks to high heaven.

The Burmese Army has grown dramatically in recent years. There are now estimated to be 350,000 troops and the final goal is believed to be a well equipped military machine of about 500,000 troops. The army is divided into 9 infantry divisions under 10 regional commands. It is supplied with weapons from China. An international arms embargo on Burma – which dissident groups have long been calling for – would probably have little more than a symbolic effect as China would be unlikely to respect it. The army has not found it difficult to recruit; living standards are so poor in many rural areas that men are pleased to earn a stable income of about 700 kyat a month. In 1990 there were reports that the army had recruited orphaned children from the countryside – even from the hilltribes – who are taught to regard the army as their family.

Army officers – who are exclusively

MILITARY INTELLIGENCE – SPY v. SPY

Rangoon's paranoid intelligentsia jokes that while George Orwell's novel *Burmese Days* is popular, the sequel is even better – *1984*. The recruitment drive by Military Intelligence (MI) since the 1988 demonstrations has given this black humour a ring of Orwellian truth, for in Burma, Big Brother really does watch you. MI chief Major-General Khin Nyunt's thought police have now infiltrated every section of a society which is seeped in fear. In the wake of the 1988 disturbances, an estimated 20,000 people disappeared. MI agents keep close tabs on the remaining elected 'politicians' from the National League for Democracy.

Colleges and universities – the hotbeds of unrest – have remained closed for much of the time since 1988; when they did reopen in 1991, there was reckoned to be a spy from the Division of Defence Services Intelligence for every 20 students.

Teachers and lecturers receive regular visits from MI. To avoid the fate of scores of their dissident colleagues, they are required to sign an undertaking to 'behave in a way befitting their status', a privilege which costs them 5 kyat. Students and their parents have had to give similar guarantees and assurances that they will pursue their education peacefully. Most students were so desperate to return to classes that they did not wish to further jeopardize their education.

In Burma's 250,000-300,000-strong army there is thought to be an agent for every 10 soldiers. Intelligence operatives – who are not blackmailed into spying – earn 750 kyat a month (US$125 at the official exchange rate, but a less princely US$11.50 at the more realistic black market rate) and a pension after 10 years. Khin Nyunt also has files on all his senior military colleagues detailing their black market business links with the gemstone and opium trade – information which can easily be used against them, should the need arise. Even in the top echelons of the military hierarchy there is mutual distrust.

Spies keep an eye on the *hnakaung shay* community too – the foreign 'long-noses' – to make sure they "do not instigate further disturbances" – as they were alleged to have done in 1988. When lottery ticket sellers set up opposite their front gates, foreign residents know they are under surveillance. The giant red and white sign boards at strategic locations in most towns and cities complement intelligence operations by extolling patriotic virtues and constantly reminding Burmese to "LOVE AND CHERISH THE MOTHERLAND" and to "SAFE-GUARD NATIONAL INDEPENDENCE". Perhaps more telling is the prominently placed board in Rangoon which reads: "ONLY WHERE THERE IS DISCIPLINE WILL THERE BE PROGRESS".

Burman – have come to expect a taste of the good life – a house, a car, cheap petrol and access to special shops. They enjoy enormous privileges: army wives go on shopping trips to Singapore and Bangkok and their children can afford to eat out in restaurants and travel abroad. Senior officers often go on to manage state-owned enterprises. The SLORC has been able to buy the continued loyalty of the armed forces thanks to its skill at plundering the country's natural resources. Nobel laureate and opposition leader Aung San Suu Kyi wrote that "fear of losing power corrupts those who wield it and fear of the scourge of power corrupts those subject to it".

The Tatmadaw sees enemies everywhere and is motivated by its determination to stamp out all existing political threats, whether from ethnic minorities, urban politicians, students or monks.

According to human rights groups like Amnesty International, Asia Watch and the Burma Action Group, the army regularly commits atrocities in ethnic minority areas, levying illegal taxes, stealing food and supplies and forcing villagers to work as ammunition porters. It has also been accused of using punitive 'scorched earth' tactics against villagers in contested areas.

Analysts have suggested that the days of Burma's international neutrality may be over. The army has too much to lose by transferring power to an elected civilian administration. If a democratic government ever does enter Rangoon's crumbling corridors of power, it will face an antagonistic army, which has been accorded too many privileges for too long and will not wish to see its power base eroded.

The 1990 election and its aftermath

US historian Josef Silverstein wrote: "The past 26 years of brutal totalitarian rule, incompetence, corruption and the withering of the economy have not stamped out the memory of the struggle for independence and the first 14 years of democratic rule in which diversity and choice were recognized and, in the main, respected". Perhaps the most remarkable thing about recent Burmese politics is that the SLORC allowed the 1990 election to be held at all. What was even more bizarre was that it was generally acknowledged to have been clean and fairly contested – there was little intimidation or vote tampering. Thai journalists covering the election joked that it was much cleaner than any Thai election. The trademark of National League for Democracy candidates had become the straw *topi*-style peasants' hat, the *kha-mut*, and it was reported that even on polling day, NLD supporters were openly wearing these hats to indicate voting intentions.

The SLORC seriously miscalculated. The government was humiliated and the NLD won 392 out of 485 seats – 82% of the 13 million votes cast – despite the fact that its 2 leaders, Aung San Suu Kyi and U Tin U had been detained since Jul 1989. The only areas the NLD failed to sweep were states where ethnic minority parties fielded candidates of their own. Many of these smaller political groups had reached an understanding with the NLD and formed the United Nationalities League for Democracy (UNLD).

But, as many had expected, the SLORC failed to honour its pledge and did not hand over power to the newly elected MPs. (It justifies its actions by claiming they are the saviours of the nation preventing it falling into Imperialist, or alternatively Communist, hands – only SLORC can avoid a disintegration of the Union of Burma). Instead, SLORC imprisoned at least 80 of them, including Aung San Suu Kyi and U Tin U, – as well as hundreds of their supporters – which caused the remainder to flee to Manerplaw, on the Thai border, where they set up a 'parallel' government-in-exile, called the National Coalition Government of the Union of Burma in Dec 1990. It was led by Sein Win, cousin of Aung San Suu Kyi. This parallel government has gained little international recognition or credibility. In the wake of the election, the SLORC cracked down on the Democratic Party for a New Society (DPNS), successor to the banned All Burma Students' Federation Union (ABSFU), which had been a key force in the uprising in 1988 and many other parties. Many leaders and members were arrested and others fled into the hills to Manerplaw and squalid jungle camps along the Thai border (hence the junta's concerted efforts to try and control Manerplaw). There are also about 1,500 students and activists in Bangkok who live in fear of being picked up by intelligence agents. By mid-1992, only 7 of the 200 parties which registered to contest the general election were still being allowed to function.

Musical chairs

In Apr 1992, when the SLORC suddenly announced that Aung San Suu Kyi's family could visit her in Rangoon, several other dissidents and NLD 'MPs' were released from detention – including the indomitable former Prime Minister U Nu. The previous week Prime Minister General Saw Maung had been replaced by army commander-in-chief and the SLORC vice-chairman, General Than Shwe. He joined the army after primary school and is not known for his leadership qualities. Saw Maung's replacement followed reports that he had suffered a nervous breakdown and had become increasingly unable to lead the country. He had begun to cause serious embarrassment to the government, due to his obsession with the kings of Pagan and their tyrannical ways. Real power is thought to be concentrated in the hands of intelligence chief Major-General Khin Nyunt, Ne Win's 'golden boy'. He is deeply resented by many high-ranking army officers due to his detailed intelligence files on all of them (see page 553).

Commentators played down the changes as 'old wine in a new bottle', and there is little prospect of the junta handing over power to a democratically elected civilian administration. In Sept 1992 the SLORC lifted the 2300-0400 curfew and about 1,300 political detainees have been released. In early 1993, 700 hand-picked delegates were invited by the generals to come to Rangoon for the long-promised national convention, whose purpose was to draft a new constitution to give SLORC some semblance of legitimacy. The 700 delegate conventon is merely a sham to rubber stamp a consitution already written by SLORC. A small minority of delegates were elected and the rest are representatives of social and economic groups whom SLORC can count upon. The increase in the junta's economic and political power over the past 2 years has not encouraged them to prepare a more liberal constitution. The new constitution being drafted not only gives the military a role in the executive, the legislative and the judiciary, and in all levels of government from the national to the local but also gives the armed forces complete autonomy in all military matters (including the defence budget) and the right to declare an emergancy and take power whenever they please. The draft document also lays down criteria for an executive President, with clauses that forbid anyone from becoming Head of State who has not been continuously resident in Burma for 20 years or whose parent or spouze is not a citizen. The clause thus excludes imprisoned opposition leader Aung San Suu Kyi, who is married to a Briton. The convention, meanwhile, has been adjourned and readjourned and the likelihood is that it will take years to complete. Dissidents – notably the Manerplaw-based parallel government – denounced the convention as a sham. The junta's latest political creation, a successor to failed pro-military political parties of the past, is the "non-political" Union Solidarity and Development Association (USDA), with civilian leaders to mobilise the population in support of the SLORC. Its activities include pro-government mass rallies in support of the new convention regularly reported in the Burmese press. Most of those attending these rallies are civil servants and school children given the day off.

In Feb 1993 the SLORC refused to allow a Nobel laureate's peace mission into Burma. The group included the Dalai Lama and Bishop Desmond Tutu. Their primary goal was to call for the release of Aung San Suu Kyi. Although they also called for the withdrawal of Burma's membership of the UN, the imposition of a strict arms embargo and

THE GOLDEN TRIANGLE AND THE SMACK
OF OFFICIAL COMPLICITY

In Mar 1992, government ministers from Burma, Laos and Thailand met in Bangkok to sign an agreement on the eradication of narcotics production and trafficking in the area where their borders meet, the notorious Golden Triangle. It was the first such meeting and was designed to boost the image of the 3 countries, which account for most of the world's heroin supply. Southeast Asian heroin now comprises about 80% of the drugs on America's streets, despite being overshadowed during the late-1980s by crack cocaine. Enforcement agents predict heroin will be the drug of the 1990s and even South and Central American producers are starting to cultivate opium poppies.

Burma, along with Pakistan, is the biggest raw opium producer in the world: a US State Department report in 1992 said it was producing about 2,300 tonnes of opium a year, which many consider a conservative estimate. Output has tripled since 1987, mainly in the N Shan and Kachin states. *The Far Eastern Economic Review* reports that : "While Burma remains the world's largest opium producer, with an annual yield that could meet the US market's demand of 60 tonnes 20 times over, Laos is also joining the big-time producer's club." Laos is estimated to produce around 300 tonnes a year – about 10 times as much as Thailand. Opium production in the Lao sector of the Golden Triangle was stepped up during America's secret war in Laos in the 1960s and 1970s. US and UN drug enforcement agencies believe that about 200 tonnes of refined heroin are exported each year from Burma.

The 1992 Bangkok agreement focused on plans for joint operations to eradicate poppy fields, heroin laboratories and opium caravans. But foreign anti-narcotics agents are sceptical about the level of commitment that can be expected – particularly from the Burmese government, which is known to launder profits from drugs money to help prop up the economy and line the pockets of military generals. Periodically the Burmese junta publicizes the supervised destruction of opium refineries and puts sacks of heroin on bonfires as part of a public relations drive to satisfy the demands of the foreign drug enforcement agencies. Thai officials – many of them connected with the military – are also involved in the alleged drugs trade. In 1992, Narong Wongwan, a nominee for the premiership following Thailand's general election, turned out to be on a US black-list due to his suspected drugs links.

Much of Burma's opium traffic passes along the old Burma Road (see page 528) into China's Yunnan province. In 1992, the Chinese authorities began cracking down much more effectively on both the refining and trafficking of heroin on its side of the border. On both sides of the frontier, heroin-addiction rates have reached alarming levels: a heroin fix is much cheaper than a bottle of beer. There has been an associated increase in infection by the HIV virus which causes AIDS. High-grade ('No. 4') heroin from the border region mostly finds its way to drugs syndicates in Hong Kong and from there goes to Europe, America and Australia. Opium also transits to Chiang Mai in N Thailand (Bangkok is a major international trafficking centre) and through Moulmein in the S of Burma, where it supplies the S Thai, Malaysian and Singapore markets. Singapore – where drug traffickers receive a mandatory death sentence – is still an international trans-shipment centre.

Following the Burmese Army's suppression of the pro-democracy demonstrations in 1988, the US government suspended its US$18 million-a-year drug enforcement project in Burma, in which it cooperated with the government in spraying defoliants on opium crops. Since then opium production has increased markedly, and former members of the now-disbanded Communist Party of Burma have emerged as the new drugs warlords, all with private armies and operating with the blessing of Rangoon. The most famous of the warlords is Khun Sa, 'the self-proclaimed king of opium' who the US drug enforcement agency has dubbed 'public enemy number one' because he is thought to provide the world with more than ⅔ of its heroin supply. Since 1990, Khun Sa may have been superceded by the new warlords who have been groomed by Burma's military government. Several new opium *sawbwas* are former commanders of rebel insurgencies who have been bought off by Rangoon: if they stop the fighting the government will leave their poppy fields alone.

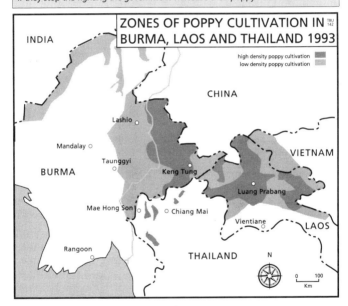

ZONES OF POPPY CULTIVATION IN BURMA, LAOS AND THAILAND 1993

an end to the 'constructive engagement' policy of Burma's neighbours. The government has been making small moves and improve its image abroad. The first person Aung San Suu Kyi was allowed to meet, outside her immediate family, since she was first placed under house arrest in 1989, was US Congressman Bill Richardson. Some political prisoners have also been released: 1,700 in 1993 according to Amnesty International. However, this still leaves over 1000 are still behind bars.

The rebel armies of ethnic groups along the borders have agreed to negotiate ceasefires with the government after years of guerilla warfare. The Wa, Pa-O National Organisation, Palaung, Kachin Independence Organisation, the Shan State Army have signed a ceasefire with SLORC on the condition that they be allowed to retain their arms and territory. The Karenni Nationalities People's Liberation Front are expected to sign a ceasefire agreement soon. The Karen rebels, based in the eastern town of Manerplaw, are still holding out. Although Bo Mya announced in Spring 1994 that he was willing to hold peace talks with the government, as are the Mons. While the patchwork peace process will probably result in a cessation of hostilities, analysts say fundemental differences between SLORC and the rebels must still be resolved before any long term solution can be reached. The minorities are advocating a modified version of the federal system that existed before the first military coup in 1962. SLORC, on the other hand, wants a system similar to China's – let the minorities do what they want within their respective areas as long as they do not interfere with national politics.

Despite ceasefire agreements, NGOs, which assist refugee camps along the Thai border, reported the refugee total in 1993 to be 72,139 – a 10% increase on the previous year. And there is no evidence that the status of Rohinga Muslims being repatriated across the Bangladesh border has changed. Aung San Suu Kyi's plight and the junta's appalling human rights record prevents the resumption of aid from international development agencies. Although Japan has started small-scale aid projects focussing on health and other humanitarian projects. It seems that the only hope now is for generational change within the army and thus the SLORC. By many accounts younger officers are better educated and more open to change than those in power at present. Splits within the army provide hope for Burmese at home and abroad. The army is believed to be split into 3 factions. The uncertainty, however, is which group will gain the favour of Burma's pro-democracy movement.

Economy

In the 19th and early 20th centuries, Burma was a wealthy British colony, thanks to its natural resources and fertile ricefields. Because of the fractious political climate in the wake of independence in 1948, there was no concerted effort to reconstruct the war-damaged economy. In the late 1950s private enterprise was encouraged – but following General Ne Win's 1962 coup d'état – more than 15,000 private enterprises were nationalized. Ne Win tried to build an industrialized socialist state, free from foreign exploitation and influence. The policies excluded all foreigners – including Europeans, Indians and Chinese – from the commanding heights of the economy. Thousands of Burma's prosperous Indian merchants and Chinese shopkeepers fled the country and the economy stagnated. Economic control was placed firmly in the hands of the central government which was almost exclusively Burman. The theories were based on the junta's seminal document, *The Burmese Way to Socialism*.

Only agriculture remained in private hands, although all produce had to be sold to the government for internal distribution and export. The economy was managed by soldiers who had no experience of business. Half the state budget was pumped into public sector industries; the value of goods produced represented a fraction of what was invested in their production. Agricultural production slumped, distribution networks collapsed, black markets emerged and smuggling increased; unemployment became a serious problem. Ethnic insurgencies emptied state coffers as defence expenditure soared. By the early 1970s the government was conceding that its economic policies had failed and some reforms were introduced, although they failed to revitalize the economy.

Eventually, in Jun 1974, riots broke out which were sparked by food shortages. Further riots erupted 6 months later when the body of U Thant – the Burmese Secretary-General of the United Nations, who had been killed in a plane crash – was returned to Burma. These were also attributed to the declining economic conditions, soaring corruption and resentment over the ostentatious lifestyle of the members of the junta. Student demonstrations broke out in 1976 and dissatisfaction even penetrated the ranks of the military élite, sparking a coup attempt by junior officers in Jul 1976. The riots in 1988 were also partly blamed on the economic situation.

Following the 1988 uprising, the regime did a U-turn, reversing its isolationist stance and creating an 'open-door policy'; a more market-oriented economic system was also adopted. But due to corruption, poor planning and the drain on resources resulting from the ongoing civil war, none of the economic systems of the post-independence era has worked. The military still controls many businesses and, unlike Vietnam, no one can even remember how a capitalist system operates. Factories are working at about 10% of their capacity. In order to pay for new construction projects the government simply ordered that more money should be printed, fuelling inflation. The blackmarket exchange rate soared as the political and economic situation deteriorated; by 1994 it reached 120 kyat to the US dollar, compared with the official exchange rate of 6.25 kyat.

The Far Eastern Economic Review reported that "whatever modest development official figures indicated, little seemed to filter down to the general population. Malnutrition, previously almost unknown in Burma, has become widespread in most of Rangoon's poorer neighbourhoods and elsewhere."

Burma is now ranked the 9th poorest country in the world, with an estimated average per capita income of about US$280 a year. The country is also saddled with a foreign debt of nearly US$5 billion. In 1987 the government was forced to go to the UN requesting 'Least Developed Country' status. Yet profits generated in the economy are pumped into defence expenditure. SLORC has steadily obtained modern weapons and military technology from around the world. Primarily from China, but also from France, Germany, Sweden and former Yugoslavia. China is helping remodel Burma's navy – still largely based on World War II-era petrol boats. Six first class attack craft were supplied in 1991 accompanied by 70 Chinese naval personnel to assist in training local crews and maintainence. Intelligence sources report Chinese technicians are helping build new bases at Hainggyi in the Irrawaddy delta near Bassein and in the Coco Islands, S of the Burmese mainland, including new Chinese-made radar equipment. In the 5 years to 1993, the army has expanded to 350,000 men. A popular saying in Rangoon is 'join the army if you want to get rich and have a priviledged life'. Recruiting is easy: Burma has thousands of unemployed. 4.8% of GDP is spent on defence (about $1.3 billion).

The economy is in a pitiful state. That's not what the SLORC would have people believe. In mid-May 1993 the Ministry of Planning came out with a 300-page report in which it claimed the economy had expanded by 11% the previous year. In reality Burma's economic output is 10% lower than it was in the mid-1980s. In 1994, the official inflation rate was running at 36%; the real rate is at least 60%, and for certain essential products, like rice and cooking oil, prices are doubling every year. Sharp price increases in rice has increased resentment toward SLORC. At government stores, government workers buy rice at 6 kyat per kilogram while it sells for anything up to 52 kyat in the markets. Similar policies favour the sale of petrol to civil servants. The official price is 4 kyats per litre but it sells for almost double on the black market. Car owners are rationed to 15 litres per week. Salaries in the public sector have not risen since 1989 while the prices of most daily necessities have roughly tripled in the same period. (A civil servant earns between 450 and 2,000 kyat a month; a chicken costs 200 kyat in the market). The state monopoly of the production and distribution of goods by rationing under Ne Win's administration led to the rise of nationwide black market, with huge disparities between official and unofficial prices. Corruption has become so rife, it is now an accepted way to supplement incomes. Only the military elite and their supporters can afford to live well. Giant military enterprises grouped under a Defence Services holding company, whose capital amounts to 10% of the GDP, now reap wealth and distribute privileges for a minority. For instance, when military officers retire, they are transferred to civil administration services, government-owned factories and embassies and are given the highest positions. As long as they remain loyal, their future is certain. Climbing the social/economic ladder is mainly a matter of loyalty to the military. Military displays of wealth are becoming more blatant: businessmen presented 30 cars as wedding gifts to the child of a senior SLORC general.

Worries about looming hyperinflation, together with the slowdown of economic output and general recession, prompted the UN to warn in a 1993 report, that if things didn't change soon, further social and political instability could follow. The report concluded that fundamental reforms were needed and that the first step in bringing the economy back into line is political stability and the introduction of a civilian government.

Despite widespread calls for economic sanctions against Burma, trade and investment have picked up in recent

years. The border with China only officially opened to trade in 1988 following an agreement between the 2 sides. Two-way trade quickly rose to at least US$1.5 billion a year – not including opium trafficking – and cheap Chinese goods have flooded into the country. Under SLORC's market reforms and liberalized border trade, entrepreneurs have flourished, especially in the Mandalay area (while the rest of Burma sinks into recession). Border trade with China is helping the Burmese economy to grow by as much as 6% per year. The army, collaborating closely with officials in China's neighbouring Yunnan province, encouraged Chinese businessmen to migrate to Burma. According to one local source, corrupt immigration officials began selling the papers of dead Burmese to business immigrants from China, Thailand and even Singapore. Arrivals with dubious connections soon set up shop. Lo Hsing Han, a former drug warlord whose death sentence for trafficking and high treason was suspended by Ne Win, has substantial investments in Mandalay. The 2 proprietors of the Lucky Hotel in Mandalay are related to the notorious Khun Sa, a Sino-Shan outlaw who commands a 6,500 man opium army in the NE. Along the China-Burma border, Chinese army sources report that the crack 99th Brigade has formed its own business arm – aptly named the 99th Co.

Foreign investment has also risen following new foreign investment legislation in 1988 which permits 100% foreign ownership. Investment is secretly flowing in from Malaysia, Singapore, Indonesia, the Philippines and Hong Kong - mainly from firms not accountable to share holders and eager for quick profits. Burma's wealth of natural resources is being plundered by the military government, which, in its desperation for foreign exchange, has farmed out lucrative fishing, logging and oil concessions as fast as it can. This has turned Burma into a free-for-all jamboree and the government has been unable to control and police the logging and fishing industries. Another major source of foreign exchange includes the annual Gems, Jade and Pearl Emporium which is held in Rangoon every Mar (see page 642). This raises about US$11 million a year for the government. Historical animosities between Burma and Thailand, for example, have been swept aside in the rush to get rich quick. The Burmese government is trying to revive the mining sector and has begun approving foreign participation in exploiting the country's mineral resources. Although prospects seem promising, civil war could hamper projects as many of the mineral-rich areas are controlled by rebel groups. The ridiculous official exchange rate is a major disincentive to foreign investors in Burma. The black market rate is as much as 20 times the official rate. But the big South Korean manufacturer, Daewoo, now has 3 factories, making electronics and clothing, around Rangoon. Pepsi have recently signed a joint venture with the government. The people of Rangoon have been drinking Pepsi at the rate of 11,000 cases per week, a pittance compared to other Asian capitals but astounding in the Burmese context. Pepsi wasn't even available until 1991, except for black market cans smuggled over the border from Thailand. But one manufacturer – Levi Strauss, the American clothing giant – pulled out of Burma in 1992 on the grounds that the country's human rights record did not shape up with the company's ethical investment code. To try and ease Burma's chronic power deficit, and to supply electricity to Thailand, the 2 countries have agreed on plans to build several hyrdo-electric dams: such as the $5 billion string of dams along the rivers on the Thai-Burmese border including a colossal 4,540 megawatt dam on the Salween River; a further 7 dams in the S (in Karen state), across the Kra River

in the southernmost tip of Burma; and 3 dams on the Moei Than Lwin River, one on the Nam Hkok River. There are also plans to build the Golden Square highway from Chaing Rai to Ta Lua via Kentung, and second highway from Chiang Khong in Thailand to Huey Sai in Laos, and eventually to Jinghong in China.

Agriculture

Although many people have migrated to towns and cities in search of work over the past decade, nearly 3/4 of Burma's 42 million population is rural and agriculture directly supports about 2/3 of the population. Burma used to be a major rice exporter – it is now hovering on the verge of being a rice importer. During the British colonial period, the Irrawaddy delta region became one of the most productive rice-bowls in Asia. Following General Ne Win's 1962 coup, tenant farmers rejoiced as landlords had their land confiscated and debts were cancelled. But they had to sell their rice to the government which sold it on the international market for 3 times the amount it paid the farmers. Within 10 years, the volume of rice exported had suffered a 12-fold decline from the heady days before World War II. Today, population pressure on farmland is growing – both among the indigenous groups, which practice slash-and-burn agriculture, and in the traditional rice-growing areas. SLORC's decision to give farmers greater freedom in choosing crops and partial deregulation of agricultural prices have marginally boosted output. But shortage of pesticides and fertilizers still limit production.

Timber

About half of Burma's land area is covered in forest, much of which is comprised of teak and other hardwoods. Burma has about 75% of the world's teak reserves – although it is disappearing fast. Many of the best known books written by British colonial residents were about the tough life of the teak-wallahs. In the days before World War II, there were said to be more than 5,000 elephants working Burma's teak forests. The elephants allowed selective logging to be practised and left minimal environmental impact compared with the bulldozers and trucks used today. Overlogging in neighbouring Thailand and then the imposition of a logging ban in 1989 led Thai companies to move into Burma. They used to deal exclusively with the tribal insurgent groups along the border – most notably the Karen – but more recently, they have begun to work directly with the Rangoon government, which is keen to award logging concessions as a means of earning sorely needed foreign exchange.

At least 20 Thai timber companies raced to exploit the highly lucrative contracts awarded by the SLORC. (They realise these concessions will not last and so are raping the forests for short term gains. A report in the *Financial Times* in 1990 estimated that all the teak forest will have disappeared within 15 years). More than 160,000 tonnes of teak logs and a further 500,000 tonnes of other hardwood logs were extracted by Thai logging firms every year. In 1991/92, Burma earned US$112 million from the exports of logs, processed wood and wood products to Thailand. Thai timber firms are closely associated with the Thai military which has long fostered links with the junta in Rangoon. The Thai logging companies are building logging roads into the jungle giving the Burmese army all weather routes to previously inaccessible insurgent areas. SLORC announced the end of all logging concessions in Burma at the end of 1993. This is a big set back for Thai companies, who have invested heavily in equipment and because Burma is the most accessible source for the vast amounts of wood needed to keep the Thai logging industry alive, since the

ban on logging in Thailand in 1989. Several theories have been put forward. One is that SLORC is upset by the fact that Thai logging companies have been paying a logging tax to ethnic forces along the border. From 1994, Burmese companies have been given logging concessions and can sell timber to Thai companies via Rangoon and all land routes have closed. The second theory is that SLORC simply wants to increase their income from the sale of natural resources. Thailand's recent co-operation with SLORC over ethnic minorities on the border has meant SLORC have relented on the total ban and contracts are being reviewed. The flash new International Business Centre in Rangoon is owned by the Forestry Ministry and built by a Singaporean company in return for logging rights.

The government has set targets for reafforestation, but their response is believed to be totally inadequate in comparison with the rate of logging. Environmentalists and Burmese opposition groups have begun to voice serious concern at the rate of deforestation.

Oil

International oil companies from America, Britain, The Netherlands, France, Australia, Japan, South Korea, Thailand and Malaysia have been awarded onshore and offshore exploration and production licences, mainly in the Tenasserim Peninsula. Before World War II, Burma was an important oil exporter – and was the birthplace of the Burmah Oil Company. Installations were sabotaged and destroyed during the war, but the surviving wells have been in use ever since – although production levels have declined. There are thought to be large untapped oil and gas reserves both on and offshore. But in Nov 1992, Petro-Canada completely withdrew from Burma having spent US$28 million over 3 years in fruitless exploration.

Tourism

In 1992 the military junta decided that the tourist industry was to provide the panacea to Burma's economic ailments by attracting 500,000 tourists a year. Private tour operators are setting up, old hotels are now being renovated and new ones built in joint ventures with private companies. Much of the finance comes from Japan, Singapore, South Korea and Hong Kong. China is also helping to build an international airport at Mandalay. To boost the tourist industry "Visit Myanmar year" is now being planned for 1997.

BURMA: FACT FILE

Geographic

Land area	677,000 sq km
Arable land as % of total	14.5%
Average annual rate of deforestation	0.3%
Highest mountain Hkakobo Razi	5,881 m
Average rainfall in Rangoon	2,500 mm
Average temperature in Rangoon	27°C

Economic

Income/person (1988)	US$200
GDP/person (PPP*, 1990)	US$659
GNP growth (/capita, 1965-1980)	1.6%
% labour force in agriculture	70%
Total debt (% GNP)	n.a.
Debt service ratio (% exports)	30.4%
Military expenditure (% GDP)	6%

Social

Population	43.7 million
Population growth rate (1960-91)	2.2%
Adult literacy rate	81.5%
Mean years of schooling	2.5 years
Tertiary graduate as % of age group	n.a.
Population in absolute poverty	15.3%
Rural population as % of total	75%
Growth of urban population (1960-92)	3%/year
Urban population in largest city (%)	32%
Televisions per 1,000 people	2

Health

Life expectancy at birth	56.9 years
Population with access to clean water	31%
Calorie intake as % of requirements	116%
Malnourished children under 5 years old	1.9 million
Contraceptive prevalence rate†	5%

* PPP = Purchasing Power Parity (based on what it costs to buy a similar basket of goods and services in different countries).
† % of women of childbearing age using contraception.

Source World Bank (1994) *Human development report 1994*, OUP: New York; and other sources.

RANGOON (YANGON)

When King Alaungpaya captured the riverside village of Dagon from the Mons in 1755, he rechristened it *Yangon* – 'the end of war'. It was a gloriously optimistic name for the little trading settlement that was to become the capital of Burma: less than a century later, Yangon was destroyed during the Second Anglo-Burmese War. In more recent times its streets ran with blood during the army's brutal crackdown on anti-government demonstrators in 1988. Over the years, the city has also been rocked by violent earthquakes and devastated by fires – in 1841 it burned to the ground and was rebuilt by King Tharrawaddy.

Modern downtown Rangoon suffers from decades of neglect – but therein lies its appeal. Its buildings are crumbling, their paintwork chipped and weather-beaten. Over-crowded teak-bodied Chevrolet buses, dating from the 1940s, still ply the pot-holed streets which are lined by fractured pavements. In recent years, migrants have flooded into the city from all over Burma and its population has more than trebled since the 1970s (to around 4 million). Rangoon's markets and streets are thronging with lungyi-clad traders and hawkers and the fact that the city is a disintegrating relic of the colonial age makes it one of the most fascinating capitals in Southeast Asia. One of the city's most famous landmarks, the *Strand Hotel*, has been restored at great expense. Its opulent trappings seem out of place in a city that has barely changed for half a century, and where tens of thousands of people live in squalor.

Rangoon was never a royal capital like Mandalay or a religious city like Pagan, although the original settlement of Dagon grew up around the magnificent Shwedagon Pagoda, which was – and remains – the focus of Burma's Buddhist faith. When the British captured Rangoon in 1852, it was still a jumble of thatched huts and when they united Upper and Lower Burma in 1885, after the Second Anglo-Burmese War, Rangoon became the capital. It was rebuilt from scratch, on a grid system, with wide boulevards and tree-lined streets. The British transformed Rangoon into the administrative centre for Further India; the river port was expanded and commerce became its raison d'être. Rangoon quickly grew into a booming entrepôt – trading in rice, oil and teak – and assumed a cosmopolitan air, attracting Indians, Chinese, Malays, Thais and Europeans. One traveller who visited it in 1912 wrote: "It was difficult immediately to grasp the paradox that the capital of Burma was not a Burmese city, but a trade emporium." Its cosmopolitan air evaporated after Burmese independence in 1948 and in 1962, following General Ne Win's seizure of power, Burma closed its doors to the outside world. There was an exodus of foreign

CLIMATE: RANGOON											
	Jan	Feb	Mar	Apr	May	Jun	Jul	Aug	Sep	Oct	Nov	Dec
Av Max (°C)	32	33	36	36	33	30	29	29	30	31	31	31
Av Min (°C)	18	19	22	24	25	24	24	24	24	24	23	19
Av Rain (mm)	3	5	8	51	307	480	582	528	394	180	69	10

Source: Pearce, E.A and Smith C.G. *The world weather guide*: Hutchinson, London

traders from Rangoon – other than a few groups which hung on in the markets of Chinatown and 'Little India'. Rangoon became an urban fossil, and for 3 decades has remained virtually untouched.

Rangoon's British-designed grid system was devised with the monsoons in mind. Shorter streets act as ventilators: they run roughly NE to SW – in the direction of the 2 prevailing winds. Rangoon is built on a spit and is surrounded by water on 3 sides: the Rangoon (or Hlaing) River to the S and W, and Pazundaung Creek, a tributary of the Rangoon River, to the E. The Rangoon River is navigable up to the capital and beyond, and most of Burma's imports and exports go through the city's docks. The main wharves and warehouses are opposite the *Strand Hotel*.

Places of interest

The **Shwedagon Pagoda** sits about 3 km NW of the centre on Singuttara Hill. The physical presence of the Shwedagon's golden stupa dominates Rangoon and its spiritual magnetism in turn dominates Burma, attracting tens of thousands of pilgrims each year. It is a visually impressive monument. The British writer, Somerset Maugham, when he visited Rangoon early this century, was moved to write that the Shwedagon was "like a sudden hope in the dark night of the soul". The pagoda dates back about 2,500 years and was built to house 8 sacred hairs of the Buddha. Its original shape has changed beyond all recognition over the centuries – it has remained in continuous use and has been periodically enlarged, restored and rebuilt.

Its bell-shaped superstructure, resting on a terraced base, is covered in about 60 tonnes of gold-leaf, which is constantly being replaced (100 sheets cost about 900 kyat). The gilded *hti*, on top, is hung with gold and silver bells and studded with rubies, sapphires and topaz. Even the gold and silver weather vane is decorated with 1,100 diamonds as well as precious and semi-precious stones; on it sits the diamond orb, encrusted with 4,350 diamonds and crowned with a 76 carat diamond. The priceless treasures of Burma's holiest shrine can only be marvelled at by visiting pilgrims, who donate around 10,000 kyat a day to pay for its upkeep. Walls, doors and stucco-work are continuously

---

THE SHWEDAGON'S DIVING BELLS

In 1612, Felipe de Brito, a Portuguese adventurer (see page 522), stole the 32-tonne bronze and brass bell which had been donated by King Dhammazedi in the 15th century. De Brito wanted to recast it into cannon and the bell was hauled down to the riverbank. But the boat ferrying it across the Rangoon River to the port at Syriam sank and the bell was lost. When the British seized Rangoon in 1825, during the First Anglo-Burmese war, they tried to take the 23-tonne *Maha Ganda* bell, which had been donated to the temple by King Hsinbyushin's son, Singu, 50 years earlier. It suffered the same fate. The bell tumbled off the boat and settled on the riverbed. The Burmese requested that should they be able to salvage it, the bell would be allowed to remain in the Shwedagon. To the amazement of colonial observers, the bell was retrieved and raised to the surface using bamboo floats. It was then returned to its rightful place in the NW corner of the pagoda platform. The British apparently learned from their mistake: the biggest of the Shwedagon's bells, the 42-tonne 3-toned bell donated by King Tharawaddy in 1841, still sits in its original resting place, in the NW corner of the terrace.

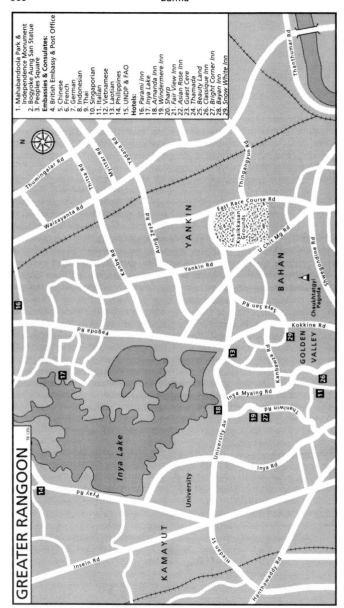

GREATER RANGOON

1. Mahabandoola Park &
2. Independence Monument
3. Bogyoke Aung San Statue
4. Peoples Square

Embassies & Consulates:
4. British Embassy & Post Office
5. Chinse
6. French
7. German
8. Indonesian
9. Thai
10. Singaporian
11. Italian
12. Vietnamese
13. Laotian
14. Philippines
15. UNDP & FAO

Hotels:
16. Parami Inn
17. Inya Lake
18. Amanda Inn
19. Windermere Inn
20. Sharp
21. Fair View Inn
22. Asian Rose Inn
23. Guest Care
24. Thamada
25. Beauty Land
26. Classique Inn
27. Bright Corner Inn
28. Bayan Inn
29. Snow White Inn

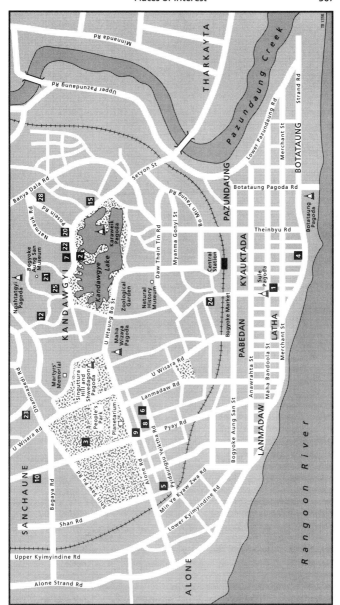

being torn down and replaced – although major renovations and architectural additions must now be approved by the Department of Archaeology.

The legend surrounding the pagoda's construction concerns 2 Burman merchants who travelled to India and met the Buddha under the sacred bodhi tree. They offered him cakes and honey and as a measure of his appreciation, the Buddha gave them 8 sacred hairs, plucked from his head. On the way home to Burma, 4 of the hairs were given away to kings en route, but the remaining 4 were presented to the local ruler in Dagon, King Okkalapa, who enshrined them on the holy Singuttara Hill. The story goes that when the site was later excavated, the golden casket containing the sacred relics was miraculously found to contain all 8 hairs.

The original pagoda was only 9m high. The Moghul emperor Asoka was its first notable pilgrim; he set the precedent by ordering its first restoration. Successive monarchs enlarged it over the years: King Byinnya-U of Pegu raised it to 22m in 1362 and Queen Shinsawbu of Pegu (1453-1472) built an even bigger Mon-style pagoda on top of it, which she gilded with her own weight in gold. Her son-in-law, King Dhammazedi later offered 4 times his, and his wife's, weight in gold, which was beaten into gold leaf and layered on the stupa. The Shwedagon expanded; every time

an earthquake struck – and there were several during the 16th century – it was restored and rebuilt. In 1774 it attained its present height of 107m. The main gilding of the stupa was undertaken during the reign of King Hsinbyushin (of Ava) in the late 18th century and the present 7-tiered, gold-plated *hti* was donated by King Mindon in 1871. Above the plinth there are 3 terraces, and above them rises the dome, shaped like an inverted begging-bowl. Higher still there are multiple mouldings, 2 bands of ornamental lotus designs and a gold-plated spire, shaped like a banana bud, on which sit the jewel-encrusted *hti* and weather vane.

There are 4 entrances to the Shwedagon. The main entrances are on the S and the E side, where there are bazaars with stallholders licensed to sell goods for pilgrims. The W stairway was closed for almost 80 years during the British colonial period. It was originally built by Ma May Gale, King Tharrawaddy's wife, but was destroyed by fire in 1931. The N stairway was built in 1460 by Queen Shinsawbu. The walkways lead out onto the 5.7 ha pagoda terrace, which is a forest of 64 mini-pagodas, temples and shrines with 4 larger pagodas in the centre of each side. British writer Aldous Huxley described the Shwedagon as having a "merry-go-round style of architecture," a sort of "sacred fun fair," where pilgrims now pose for family photo-

Day	Planet	Birth sign	Compass point
Monday	Moon	tiger	east
Tuesday	Mars	lion	south-east
Wednesday am	Mercury	elephant (tusked)	south
Wednesday pm	Rahu	elephant (tuskless)	north-west
Thursday	Jupiter	rat	west
Friday	Venus	guinea pig	north
Saturday	Saturn	dragon	south-west
Sunday	Sun	galon bird	north-east

graphs in front of the extravagant golden backdrop.

Around the terrace, at the 8 compass points, are the 8 planetary or birth posts; the Burmese leave offerings at their birth post, to appease the guardian spirit of their fate, which is represented by a planet and an animal. The Buddhist 8-day week is squeezed into the Gregorian 7-day week by dividing Wednesdays in 2 – Rahu, Wednesday afternoon, is believed to be the planet which causes solar eclipses.

On the main terrace are several pavilions (*tazaungs*) and resting places (*zayats*) with traditional tiered roofs. Visitors, like the pilgrims, should walk around the pagoda in a clockwise direction. Starting from the top of the S stairway, the most notable features are:

● The *Arakanese Prayer Pavilion*, with intricate woodcarvings, is in the SW corner of the platform (to the left of the reclining Buddha prayer hall). It was donated by pilgrims from Arakan. Virtually opposite are the figures of Mani Lamu and the King of the Nats (see page 544).

● The *Kassapa Adoration Hall*, on the W side of the stupa, was gutted by fire in 1931 and rebuilt 4 years later. The main image is Kassapa, the Third Buddha.

● Opposite the Kassapa is the *Two-Pice Tazaung* (pavilion), which was also gutted by fire in 1931; its construction was funded by the merchants of Rangoon market. The escalator here provides great entertainment for visiting pilgrims.

● The small pagoda in the NW corner is the *Eight-Day Pagoda*. It has 8 niches, each containing a Buddha, in between which are the figures of the 8 planetary birds and animals (see above).

● The *Maha Ganda Bell Pavilion*, which houses the 32-tonne Maha Ganda bell (see page 565), is behind the Eight-Day Pagoda, to the left of the pavilion containing a 9m-high Buddha image.

● The *Northern Adoration Hall*, on the N side of the stupa, is dedicated to Gautama, the historic Buddha, and contains his image. (The Bogyoke Aung San Martyr's Mausoleum (see page 571) can be reached from the N stairway).

● The *Hair Relics Well* – which is said to be fed by the Irrawaddy River so that its water level rises and falls with the tide – is in the *Sandawdwin Tazaung*, opposite the N adoration hall. The Buddha's hairs were washed in it before their enshrinement.

● Next to the Sandawdwin Tazaung is the *Maha Bodhi Pagoda* modelled on the Maha Bodhi Temple in Varanasi, India.

● The large *Elder* or *Naungdawgyi Pagoda*, in the NE corner, is where the sacred hair relics were first placed before being enshrined in the stupa's relic chamber.

● Right in the NW corner of the platform is the 1485 *Dhammazedi inscription* which relates the history of the Shwedagon in Pali, Mon and Burmese.

● King Tharawaddy's 42-tonne bell, cast in 1841, is in a prominent pavilion in the NW corner of the Shwedagon (see page 565).

● The elegant *Eastern Adoration Hall* was destroyed by fire in 1931 but has been rebuilt and contains a statue of the first Buddha, Kakusandha.

● The *Eastern Stairway* is lined with stalls selling religious paraphernalia.

● In the SE corner is a sacred bodhi tree, supposedly a cutting from the original tree under which the Gautama Buddha attained enlightenment.

● The museum is next to the S entrance and exhibits a rich collection of artefacts given to the pagoda by devotees. Also notable is a 19th century minister's gold coat.

The most interesting times to visit the Shwedagon are early morning and evening when the pagoda terrace is thronged with pilgrims. Tourists should enter from the S end. Admission: US$5; (5 kyat cam-

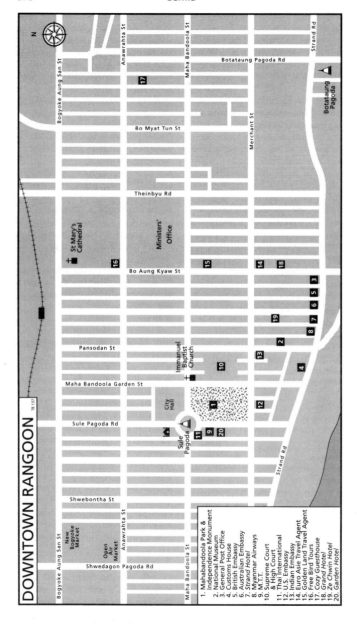

DOWNTOWN RANGOON

TB 137

1. Mahabandoola Park &
   Independence Monument
2. National Museum
3. General Post Office
4. Customs House
5. British Embassy
6. Australian Embassy
7. Strand Hotel
8. Myanmar Airways
9. M.T.T.
10. Supreme Court
    & High Court
11. Thai International
12. U.S. Embassy
13. Indian Embassy
14. Euro Asie Travel Agent
15. Golden Land Travel Agent
16. Free Bird Tours
17. Cozy Guesthouse
18. Grand Hotel
19. Ze Chwin Hotel
20. Garden Hotel

era fee which goes to the pagoda trustees fund). Open: 0400-2100 Mon-Sun. **Getting there**: bus 10 from Theinbyu Rd.

To the right of the S entrance to the Shwedagon is the new **Maha Wizaya Pagoda** (meaning 'great conqueror') built by General Ne Win in the 1980s. In a bid to make some much-needed merit, Burma's old military strongman began his 350 million kyat construction project with relish more befitting the kings of Pagan, which raised eyebrows over his supposed monarchic aspirations. The pagoda is hollow with a ceiling depicting Burmese constellations and a permanent display of pagoda styles through the ages.

There are several important sights to the N of the Shwedagon. **Martyrs' Mausoleum** is on the hill N of the pagoda, just off Shwegondine Road. It is the tomb of Bogyoke (General) Aung San, the father of the Burmese independence movement, and the 5 ministers assassinated with him on 19 Jul 1947 (see page 529).

Kyaukhtatgyi Pagoda ('six-storeyed') is NE of Shwedagon, on Shwegondine Road. The temple contains a gaudy, modern, 70m-long reclining Buddha, built in 1966, housed in a metal and corrugated iron pavilion. The image cost 5 million kyats – paid for entirely by public donation. The temple doubles as a monastery (there are over 600 monks) and a centre for the study of Buddhist manuscripts.

Ngahtatgyi (or Ngadatkyi) Pagoda ('five-storeyed') is S of Kyaukhtatgyi just off Shwegondine Road, in the Ashay Tawya Monastery. It houses a huge seated Buddha, known as the 5-storey Buddha. The abbot's house beside the pagoda is a brightly painted Chinese-style building. **Getting there**: bus 3 from city centre, 47 from Shwedagon.

Further S are the **Royal Lakes**. On the E side is the **Karaweik** stone boat, a concrete copy of a royal barge which is used as a restaurant and venue for cultural shows, see page 576. On the N shore is the **Bogyoke Aung San Park**, with a statue of Aung San. **Rangoon Zoo** is on the SW side of the lake; a miniature train runs round the grounds. It is a big zoo and animals on show can be fed by visitors; their living conditions are cramped. Open: 0600-1800 Mon-Sun.

The 48m-high golden dome of **Sule Pagoda**, on Sule Pagoda Road is the main landmark in central Rangoon. It stands in the middle of Rangoon's equivalent of London's Piccadilly Circus: the British used the temple as the nucleus of their grid pattern for the city, when it was rebuilt in the 1880s. The pagoda's peculiarity is its octagonal-shaped stupa, which retains its shape as it tapers to the spire. This relates to the division of the week into 8 days, each of which are represented by a planet and an animal or bird (see page 568). Sule Pagoda is believed to date back over 2,000 years, although its historical significance has been undermined by the haphazard construction of shrines and brash temple art. Like the Shwedagon, it was founded to house sacred hair relics. Two Buddhist missionaries from India, Sona and Uttara, are said to have presented one of the Buddha's hairs to Maha Sura, a minister in Dagon, who built the temple. It was originally known as *Kyaik Athok*, Mon for "the pagoda of the sacred hair relic". Its more recent name, Sule, refers to the Sule nat, guardian spirit of Singuttara Hill. The entrances are unimpressive but the temple platform is always busy. Sule Pagoda is notable for its profusion of fortune tellers.

Nearby is **City Hall** (on the corner of Sule Pagoda Road and Maha Bandoola St), a fine piece of British colonial architecture. Just to the SE is **Maha Bandoola Park**, named after a Burmese general from the First Anglo-Burmese war. The **Independence Monument** is at the centre of the park and represents Burma's 5 former semi-autonomous states, Shan, Kachin, Karen, Kayah and

Chin. Admission: 1 kyat. Facing the square on the E side are the old colonial **Supreme Court** and **High Court**.

South of the park on Pansodan St is the **National Museum**, formerly a bank, whose antique wooden lift would elsewhere be considered a museum piece in itself. The first display just inside the entrance is an impressive array of gold ornaments labelled: "Replicas of some royal regalia not returned by the British." Some Burmese booty was returned to Burma in 1964 as a gesture of goodwill during Ne Win's official visit to London, but many other royal treasures continue to gather dust in British museums. The museum's ground floor, however, brims with the belongings of the last 2 kings of Burma: King Thibaw's intricately carved ivory chair, white umbrellas, swords and royal robes, jewelled baskets, betelnut boxes and silver spitoons. Many pieces – such as the gold betel cup, betel box and arak goblet – are studded with rubies, diamonds and other precious stones. Letters from King Thibaw to Queen Victoria before the last Anglo-Burmese war in 1885 are also on display. The room is dominated by the 8m-tall, gilded **Lion Throne** (Sihasana Throne), which was originally in the Royal Palace at Mandalay and was used by King Thibaw, the last Burmese monarch. It was returned from the palace by the British in 1945, before everything else in it was destroyed, and returned by Lord Louis Mountbatten in 1948 following Burmese independence. On the same floor is a scale model of the Mandalay Royal Palace.

The 2nd floor contains a room of prehistoric artefacts (which are not labelled in English) as well as reproductions of cave paintings and some Neanderthal busts. There is also an array of 4th-1st century BC weaponry. On the same floor, there are 2 rooms with pieces from Pagan and Sri Kshetra. There is also a good display of statues and carvings from old monasteries as well as tapestry coffin covers, pipes, musical instruments, silverware and lacquerware. There is an informative display of sandstone and bronze Buddha images, showing their Indian and Indo-European influence, with Gupta features. The top floor has an exhibition of Burmese watercolours and modern oil paintings. Admission: US$4. Open: 1000-1530 Mon-Fri.

Just around the corner is the ***Strand Hotel*** originally one of the leading hotels in the East and regarded as "the finest hostelry east of Suez". It belonged to the Sarkie Brothers' hotel empire, which included Singapore's *Raffles* and Penang's *Eastern & Oriental*. The hotel, built in 1901 by John Dawood – a leading British entrepreneur in the late 19th century – has witnessed wars, revolutions and riots before its decaying grandeur came to the attention of a consortium of Hong Kong hoteliers. They struck a US$12.5 million deal with the state tourism corporation to do for the *Strand* what had been done to *Raffles* in Singapore. Developers have, at the expense of Burma's teak forests, managed to retain the charm of this national institution even though its ancient lifts and quaint original fittings, such as GEC fans and Victorian bathtubs, have been ripped out. Australian diplomats, whose embassy occupies another former annex of the Strand, say they have more bathrooms than any other embassy in the world: the offices occupy former hotel suites. The British-built **General Post Office** on the W side of the hotel now houses Myanmar Airways (internal flights only). The main dock area is almost opposite the *Strand*, you can cross the river here on rowing boats, or the regular passenger boats.

To the E of Strand Road on the waterfront is the **Botataung Pagoda**. 'Botataung' means 'one thousand officers' – a thousand soldiers were said to have constituted the guard of honour which received the Buddha relics donated by the king of Syriam. It is unusual in that visitors can enter the stupa, which is hollow. An Allied bomb completely destroyed the original pagoda in 1943, revealing a miniature golden stupa which contained Buddha relics and a hoard of treasure. An exact replica was rebuilt after the war. The central shrine contains the relics of the Buddha – they are actually kept in a safe below. The courtyard is not as busy as that of the Sule or Shwedagon pagodas but on the N side there is a large hall containing a Buddha image retrieved from Mandalay by the British, in front of which is one of the Buddha's hairs, rescued from the original Botataung stupa. The rotating model, depicting a scene from the life of the Buddha, is the latest ploy for attracting donations. There is a small market opposite the main E entrance.

On the N side of the city, between Inya Lake and the airport, is the **Kaba Aye Pagoda**, off Kaba Aye Pagoda Road. This 'World Peace Pagoda' was built in 1952 by U Nu, the first Prime Minister of independent Burma, for the Sixth Buddhist Synod in 1954-56. As the name suggests, it was dedicated to world peace. The pagoda is not particularly beautiful but is famous for the silver Buddha in the inner relic chamber weighing 500 kg. There are 5 entrances to the pagoda each with a 3m-tall Buddha image – representing the 4 past Buddhas and one future.

The other building erected for the Sixth Buddhist Synod is the extraordinary **Maha Pasan Guha**, an artificial cave, surrounded by 28 bodhi trees, and able to seat 10,000 people. Inside are 2,500 seats for members of the Sangha (the Buddhist monkhood) and a separate 7,500 for members of the audience. It is meant to resemble India's Satta Panni Cave, where the First Buddhist Synod was held shortly after the Buddha's death but looks more like a gym. The nearby Institute of Advanced Buddhist Studies is translating the entire Buddhist canon into English.

Not far from the Maha Pasan Guha is the **Buddhist Art Museum**, housed in a 1952 Art Deco-style building in the grounds. The dominant lotus window depicts all the attitudes of the Buddha. The museum's contents were collected by the archaeology department: begging bowls, palm leaf scriptures and 18th-20th century wooden Buddha images and a palm leaf Pali manuscript. There are also models showing the evolution of stupa shapes and examples of the 8 requisites of a Buddhist monk: an upper garment, underwear, girdle, robe, alms bowl, razor, needle and thread, a water strainer and a collection of rosary beads (*seitpadi*) used by celebrated monks. Open 0900-1630 Mon-Sun. The Ministry of Fine Arts is housed in the Chinese pagoda at the top of Kaba Aye Pagoda Rd; the house was built by a Chinese business tycoon at the beginning of the century.

Tours

Tour agencies offer various city tours and excursions. Prices quoted are for a single tourist – it is much cheaper in larger groups. Tours must usually be paid for in US dollars. *Introducing Rangoon*: 4 hrs, US$19; *Rangoon city tour* (morning, afternoon or evening): 3½ hrs, US$14-18; *Highlights of Rangoon*: 8 hrs, US$32; *Outside Rangoon*: 4 hrs, US$17; *Shwedagon* (evening): 2½ hrs, US$12; *Pegu*: 7 hrs, US$73; *Syriam*: 4½ hrs, US$32; *Twante*: 7 hrs, US$73. See page 578 for addresses of agents.

Festivals

Mar: *Gems and Pearls Emporium* (moveable) held at the *Inya Lake Hotel*; *Full Moon of Tabaung Festival* (moveable), one week long. Visitors come from all over Burma to visit the Shwedagon Pagoda. There are many stalls and sideshows.
Apr: *Thingyan* or *Burmese New Year* (moveable: public holiday) lasting 4-5

days, the streets of Rangoon are thronged with thousands of residents and visitors dousing each other with water and enjoying dance and music performances staged on roadside *mandats*.

May: *Kason Festival* (moveable) takes place at the Shwedagon Pagoda to commemorate Buddha's enlightenment.

Oct: *Thadingyut* (moveable), pagodas and houses throughout Rangoon are illuminated with candles to celebrate the end of lent.

Local infomation

● Orientation

Downtown Rangoon along the river front is the main hub of the city with most of the shops and restaurants. There are not many guesthouses in this area. Most of the places to stay are around the 2 lakes, where there is a lack of places to eat.

● Accommodation

Price guide
A+ US$200; A US$100-200; B US$50-100;
C under US$50.

Aware that its tourism industry cannot expand until more hotel rooms are built in Rangoon, the government has undertaken some major refurbishment projects with the help of foreign private-sector developers and private guesthouses are opening up all over the city. The price of rooms in private guesthouses can be bargained down, especially in the low season. A 4 star floating hotel is planned in Rangoon; it is a converted ship built in Finland in 1968. Prices of hotels/guesthouses in Rangoon include breakfast, unless otherwise stated.

A+ Strand, 92 Strand Rd, T 81533, a/c, coffee shop, restaurant, the *Strand* has been completely restored (see page 572).

B Arnanda Inn, 21 University Ave, Aungztya Lane, Bahan, T 31251, a/c, h/w, 4 large rooms in a well cared for family house, reasonably priced; **B Asian Rose Inn**, 9A Natmauk Ave, Tamwe, T 50942, a/c, h/w, restaurant on the balcony, only 7 rooms all spacious and clean, well-run in a quiet area with a garden, slightly more expensive than other family hotels in the area but worth the price, rec; **B Bagan Inn**, 29 Po Sein Rd, Tamwe, T 50489, a/c, h/w, restaurant set up for business men, clean but fea-

tureless; **B Bright Corner Inn**, 38 Bawdi Yeiktha (Windemere), Bahan, T 31958, a/c, h/w, only 4 rooms in a private house, family atmosphere although it is ideal for business men with a private meeting room, patio; **B Classique Inn**, 53B Golden Valley, Bahan, T 30954, a/c, h/w, rooms are nothing special but run by a friendly family who will cook guests meals, quiet area, rec; **B Cozy Guesthouse**, 126 52nd St, Pazundaung, T 91623, F 92239, a/c, h/w, 5 small clean rooms with separate bathroom, friendly, owner speaks English, best budget place downtown, rec; **B Guest Care**, 107a Dhammazedi Rd, Kamaryut, T 83171, F 73573, a/c, h/w, clean but sterile rooms with all facilities (including satellite TV), on the main road but has a small garden; **B Myanmar Holiday Inn**, 379 Maha Bandoola St, a/c, some rooms with private bathroom, clean and friendly, most central of the cheap guesthouses; **B Inya Lake**, Kaba Aye Pagoda Rd (9 km from centre), T 62858, a/c, restaurant, nice pool, built with Soviet aid in the 1960s and described as "the Russian bunker", mainly used by tour groups, the hotel is being completely refurbished by the developer who restored the *Strand Hotel*; **B Parami Inn**, 34 Parami Rd, Yankin, T 61002, F 89862, a/c, h/w, clean standard rooms, meals cooked on request, convenient for the airport and buses at Highway Gate but otherwise too far out of town; **B Sharp**, 3 Pho Sein Rd, Bahan, T 51865, a/c, h/w, restaurant, rooms nothing special and expensive but it does have a small swimming pool; **B Snow White Inn**, 12(B)1 Kokine Ave, Bahan, T 53156, F 89960, a/c, h/w, friendly (the owner's brother is a Burmese film star), but average rooms; **B Strand annexe**, Strand Rd, T 81530, a/c, restaurant, the annexe of the old *Strand Hotel* is run as a separate entity with none of the charm of the original, don't get this and the restored *Strand* confused; **B Summer Palace**, 160 University Ave, a/c, h/w, restaurant, run by the owners of *The Grand* and *Fair View*, and top of their "chain", Colonial-style house with pretty garden and lake, large rooms; **B Thamada**, 5 Signal Pagoda Rd, T 71499, some a/c, restaurant, 1960s-style hotel near the railway station, undergoing refurbishment; **B Windemere Inn**, Aungmingaung Ave, Thanlwin Rd, Kamayut, T 33846, F 89960, a/c, h/w, restaurant, friendly and well-run with free cars to the airport, they will also organize taxis downtown and tours round Burma, nice rooms and pretty garden make this one of the best value hotels in Rangoon, despite being a bit out of town, rec; **B-C** *Kandawgyi*, Kan Yeiktha Rd, T 82327, a/c, restaurant, old English boat club overlooking the Royal Lake, some rooms have pleasant views, also more expensive chalets right on the lake.

C *Fair View*, 16 Sawmaha St, Kandawgyi, Bahan, T 53526, F 83360, a/c, h/w, family house with attractive garden, clean rooms at the back, good option if you don't want to stay in town but book ahead, minibus shuttle downtown am and pm, breakfast not included in price; **C** *Garden Guesthouse*, 73 Sule Pagoda Rd, T 71516, fans only, restaurant, rooms are partitioned and have communal bathrooms, cheap but grubby; **C** *The Grand*, 108 Bo Aung Gyaw St, T 89460, F 83360, a/c, h/w, small rooms with no windows but clean and efficiently run, right in the centre of town; **C** *Pyin OO Lwin Guesthouse*, 183 Maho Bandoola Garden St (near Sule Pagoda), T 74005, clean, well-run and friendly, rec by travellers; **C** *Sakantha*, Rangoon Station, T 82975, some a/c, restaurant, many of the rooms are right next to the railway line; **C** *Zar Chi Win*, 1st Floor, 59 37th St (Lower Block), fan only, grotty rooms but the cheapest place to stay in Rangoon, car for hire for trips round Burma.

The only *YMCA*, Maha Bandoola/25 St, a/c, fan, restaurant, offers cheap accommodation (US$11 at the official rate) although it is not recommended.

● **Places to eat**

Price guide
♦♦♦♦ US$15+ (over 180 kyat); ♦♦♦ US$5-15 (120-180 kyat); ♦♦ US$2-5 (60-120 kyat); ♦ under US$2 (under 60 kyat).

Burmese: ♦♦♦♦*Khin Khin Gyi Restaurant*, Prome Rd, Myenigon, well prepared Burmese food in a friendly atmosphere, the owner is an artist and his works are displayed in the restaurant, there is a menu in English, but it is always possible to have a look at the food at the back, the restaurant is not easy to spot, it is next to *Moe Nat Hai* bar and restaurant; ♦♦♦*Karaweik*, E side of the Royal Lakes, in huge, 'floating', concrete replica of a royal barge, Government-run, but reasonable, cultural shows in the evenings, with Burmese buffet; ♦♦*Danubyu*, Upper Block 29th St, there are also several other small Burmese restaurants in this street; ♦♦*999 Shan Khauk Swe*, 130b 34th St (enter the street from behind the Town Hall or from Anowratha),

clean and cool, serves good quality Shan food: *mishé* (thick rice noodles), *shan kouq-swèh* (sticky rice noodles), *shan tàmin, tohu nwèh* (shan noodles with a warm tofu sauce) and *sichè kouq-swèh* (soft wheat noodles), all with a choice of pork or chicken, or vegetarian (*theq-thaq-luq*), closes at 7 pm; ♦♦*Shweba*, Aung Thu Ka, Shwegondine Rd, near Shwedagon Pagoda (opposite Resistance Park, take the small road down the side of a football pitch), good assortment of curries; ♦♦Burmese restaurant in 37th St (no name), good choice of food early evening but runs out quickly, popular; ♦*Kone Min Tua*, 7½ miles Prome Rd, serves *mohinga* until early afternoon.

Chinese: ♦♦♦♦*Golden View*, Shwedagon Pagoda Rd (right next to Ne Win's pagoda), open air restaurant with stunning views of Shwedagon, good Chinese fare with traditional Burmese country dance; ♦♦♦♦*Mya Kan Tha*, 70 Natmauk Rd, in a big house, to N of the royal lake, lobster is a speciality; ♦♦♦♦*The Man Restaurant*, Theinbyu St, rec by locals; ♦♦♦♦*The Panda*, 205 Wardan St, on corner of Keighley Rd and St, John's Rd, expensive, rec; ♦♦♦♦*Yadana Gardens*, S entrance, Shwedagon pagoda; ♦♦♦♦-♦♦♦*The Great Wall*, Pan Soe Dan St, large menu; ♦♦♦*7-Up Hot Pot*, Kokine Swimming Pool Rd, Mongolian cuisine; ♦♦♦*Furusato*, Shwegondine Rd, opposite Chincse temple, Japanese and Chinese food, not highly rated by foreign residents; ♦♦♦*Fu Sun*, 160 Kokkine, Kaba Aye Pagoda Rd, pavilion dining; ♦♦♦*Khun Loke*, 22nd St (between Maha Bandoola and Strand Rd); ♦♦♦*Lu Lu Chung*, 21 St; ♦♦♦*Palace*, 37th St; ♦♦♦*Pann Wut Yi*, 110 Bo Aung Kyaw St; ♦♦♦*Ruby*, 50 Bo Aung Kyaw St, seafood particularly good, rec; ♦♦♦*Yin Swe*, 137 University Ave, garden; ♦♦♦-♦*Nan Yu*, Pansodan St; ♦♦*69*, 21st St, Chinese and Burmese dishes, speciality is 100 year-old eggs; ♦♦*Haikhin*, Sule Pagoda Rd, (next to *Dagon Hotel*); *Dolphin*, next to boat club, good Chinese grub and live music.

Indian: ♦♦*Golden City*, 170 Sule Pagoda Rd, excellent Thali and Ohosa; ♦♦*Sule*, Sule Pagoda Rd, Thali. The Indian restaurant on 32nd St (it doesn't have a name) serves first class Thali, under US$1; ♦♦*Sunla*, 222 Anawratha Rd, good selection of curries.

International: the bigger hotels all have restaurants serving international dishes. ♦♦♦*Strand Restaurant*, Strand Hotel, a five star international-style menu which changes daily, the most expensive food in Burma;

♦*Green*, 205 Pansodan Rd, a/c snack bar with a good line in milk shakes; ♦*Strand Cafe*, *Strand Hotel*, serves a range of international snacks if you fancy a treat.

Other Asian cuisines: ♦♦♦*Salathai*, 56 Saya San Rd, T 50997.

Bakeries: *Shwe Myin Bakery*, opposite Tourist Department Stores, pizzas and pastries.

Foodstalls: A selection of teashops and food-stalls can be found throughout the downtown area and in the main markets selling snacks such as samosas, *ko-pyan-kyaw* (spring rolls) and for breakfast, *mohinga* (noodles with fish sauce). Locals rec the noodle stall on the corner of 21st St and Mahabandoola.

Yoghurt shop: *Nilar Win's*, 377 Maha Bandoola St (between 37 and 38 sts), delicious assortment of yoghurt shakes and fruit shakes, Nilar Win was a well known Burmese boxer – his pictures decorate the shop walls, under US$1.

● **Bars**
Kandawgyi Hotel, Kanyoikhta Rd, bar overlooks Royal Lake; *Strand Hotel*, Strand Rd, formerly a very popular old bar, being refurbished.

● **Airline offices**
Domestic flights must be paid for in dollars. Flights are always full and difficult to book. **Aeroflot**, 501-3 Prome Rd, 7th Mile, T 61066; **Air France**, 69 Sule Pagoda Rd, T 74199; **Biman** (Bangladesh), 106 Pansodan Rd, T 75882; **Myanmar Airways**, 104 Strand Rd, T 84566 (internal flights); **CAAC** (Air China), 67A Prome Rd, T 75714; **Air Indian**, 533 Merchant St, T 72410; **KLM** (Royal Dutch Airlines), 104 Strand Rd, T 74180; **Royal Nepal Airways**, 22 York Rd, T 71347; **SAS** (Scandinavian), 441-445 Tavoy House, Maha Bandoola St, T 75988; **Silk Air** (Singapore), Merchant/Pan Soe Dan sts, T 84600/81609; **Thai Airways**, 441 Tavoy House, Maha Bandoola St, T 75988/74922, next to Sule Pagoda.

● **Banks & money changers**
The main hotels will change money at the official rate (and will stamp exchange papers) as well as the banks listed below. Visitors are advised to refer to the section **Money and the black market** (see page 657). People's Bank, Rangoon Airport. **Union Bank of Burma**, 24/26 Sule Pagoda Rd.

● **Embassies & Consulates**
Rangoon is a cheap and quick place to get visas for China and India. **Australia**, 88 Strand Rd, T 80711; **Austria**, 16(G) Thallawaddy Rd, T 73098; **Belgium**, 15 Myayagon St, Kandawgalay, T 76505; **China**, 1 Pyidaungsu Yeiktha Rd, T 21280; **Denmark**, 65-A Kaba Aye Pasoda Rd, T 60883; **France**, 102 Pyidaungsu Yeiktha Rd, T 82122; **Germany**, 32 Natmauk Rd, T 50477; **India**, 545-547 Merchant St, T 82550; **Indonesia**, 100 Pyidaungsu Yeiktha Rd, T 81714; **Italy**, 3 Inya Myaing Rd, Golden Valley, T 30966; **Laos**, A-1 Diplomatic Quarters, Taw Win Rd, T 22482; **Malaysia**, 82 Pyidaungsu Yeiktha Rd, T 20248; **Netherlands**, 53/55 Maha Bandoola Garden St, T 71495; **Norway**, 65-A Kata Aye Pagoda Rd, T 60883; **Singapore**, 287 Prome Rd, T 33200; **Spain**, 563 Merchant St, T 80608; **Sweden**, 80 Strand Rd, T 81700; **Thailand**, 91 Prome Rd, T 21713; **Vietnam**, 40 Komin Kochin Rd, T 50361; **UK**, 80 Strand Rd, T 81700/2/3/8 (also looks after New Zealand and Swedish interests); **USA**, 581 Merchant St, T 82055.

● **Emergency telephone numbers**
Ambulance: T 192; **Fire**: T 191; **Police**: T 199.

● **Entertainment**
See *New Light of Myanmar* to find out what's on in Rangoon. Traditional Burmese entertainment has been stifled by censorship. *A-nyeint* performances (burlesque) and *nat-pwes* are few and far between. There are occasional pop concerts in the sports stadium or National Theatre by local groups.

Cinema: there are more than 50 cinemas in Rangoon, the following show English-language films: *Bayint*, 321 Bogyoke Aung San St; *Gon*, 223/229 Sule Pagoda Rd; *Pa Pa Win*, Sule Pagoda Rd; *Thamada*, 5 Signal Pagoda Rd; *Waziya*, 327 Bogyoke Aung San St; *Wizaya*, 224 U Wisara Rd.

Cultural Shows: *Karaweik Cultural Centre* on Royal Lake, not far from the *Kandawgyi Hotel*. The Karaweik (a mythical bird with a beautiful song) is a copy of a royal barge and is decorated with designs in glass mosaic, marble and mother-of-pearl. (Traditionally rowers weren't allowed on board the royal barge and was towed by smaller boats called hlaw sar.) Traditional Burmese music and dance: the show includes folk dance, puppet dances, religious rituals, traditional court dances and an acrobatic *chinlon* display. Performances usually only take place when requested by large tour groups; check with MTT. (Buffet supper available beforehand). Admission: 60 kyat. Tickets available at the door, or from MTT. Traditional country dance performances at *Golden View* restaurant (see page 575). Locals recommend dance show at the National Theatre; tickets available on the door.

Theatre: the open-air theatre was replaced by the National Theatre which stages occasional performances by visiting cultural troupes and fund-raising pop concerts. *State School of Music and Drama* (associated with the State School of Fine Art, Music and Dancing in Mandalay). Traditional Burmese arts are taught and demonstrated. Open to visitors but mainly supplies pplies cultural performers for diplomatic events. Closed in Apr.

● **Hospitals & medical services**
Diplomatic Hospital, Kyaikkasan Rd, T 50149. *Rangoon General Hospital*, Bogyoke Aung San St, T 81722 (ask for medical superintendent). *Infectious Disease Hospital*, Upper Pansodan St, T 72497. *University Hospital*, University Ave, T 31541. (Some embassies also have nurses; see **Health**, page 657.)

● **Immigration office**
In the Government Office on Strand Rd, T 85505.

● **International organizations**
UNIC, 6 Natmauk Rd, T 92622; **UNDCP**, 40 Thanlwin Rd, T 31582; **FAO**, 56 Shwethunggya Rd, T 31281; **UNDP**, 6 Natmauk Rd, T 92911; **WHO**, 39 Shwetaungyar Rd, T 31135; **UNICEF**, 132 University Ave Rd, T 31107.

● **Meditation Centres**
The best known meditation centres for foreigners in Rangoon are: *Mingun Meditation Centre*, *Mahasi Meditation Centre*, Hermitage Rd and the *International Meditation Centre* and *Chan Mye Yeiktha* (about 100m N of *Inya Lake Hotel* on Kaba Aye Pagoda Rd) the Sayadaw (abbot) U Janaka, speaks good English.

● **Post & telecommunications**
General Post Office: Strand Rd/80 Bo Aung Kyaw St (Poste Restante on the first floor). **Telephone and telegraph office**: Pansodan/Maha Bandoola St, fax and telex facilities. **Area code**: 01.

● **Private guides**
U Mya Win Maung, Me Da Wi Rd, Salain, T 64777, German and English; *U Soe Myint*, 137 38th St, T 85116, French; *Htay Htay Tin*, 92 Thunanda, T 81391, French and English; *Rose Martha*, 38 Eiksathaya St, Kauikmyaung, T 53109, English and Japanese.

● **Religious services**
Catholic: *St Mary Cathedral*, 372 Bo Aung Kyaw St, T 72662, service at 0900 every Sun; *St Augustine Church*, No 64 Inya Rd, services at 0715 and 0900 every Sun.

Hindu: *Sree Sree Siva Krishna*, 141 Pansodan St, service hrs 1000-1100 and 1500-2000 daily.

Jewish: there is a synagogue in 26th St where services are held when Jewish Communities gather.

Mosques: *Surti Sunny Jama Mosque*, Shwe Bontha St; *Narsapuri (Moja) Mosque*, 227 Shwe Bontha St; *Cholia Jama Mosque*, Bo Soon Pat St; service hours: noon prayer – 1230-1330 daily; evening prayer – 1645-1700 daily; Fri prayer – 1230-1330 (congregation).

Protestant: *Holy Trinity Cathedral*, 446 Bogyoke Aung San St, T 72326, service at 0830 every Sun; *Immanuel Baptist Church*, Maha Bandoola Garden St, T 75908, service at 0830 every Sun; *St John the Baptist American Church*, 113 Bo Aung Kyaw St, service at 0900 every Sun; *Judson Church*, Yangon University Estate, T 31509, service at 1600.

Sikh Temple: 256 Theinbyu St.

● **Shopping**
Antiques: *Mme Thair*, 220 Edwards St, antiques, lacquerware, beads, carvings; reckoned to be the best place for antiques. There is also a row of 4 small grey-painted shops selling lacquerware, brassware, gemstones, antique ships' clocks and gramophones (many of which are replicas) close to the *Inya Lake Hotel* on Kaba Aye Pagoda Rd. There is another group of similar shops a little further into town opposite the mosque and the Singapore Girl cake shop. The pieces are magnificent but incredibly expensive.

Books: the Burmese are voracious readers and there are bookstalls all over Rangoon. Few Western books find their way into Burma as government censors are strict and any book traded on the black market is a potentially 'dangerous' item; most literature branded 'subversive' by the government is, however, widely available. Burmese bookshops and the Burmese literary scene flourishes along 33rd St between Anawrahta and Bogyoke Aung San sts. The *Sa-pe Beikman* at 529 Merchant St sells official government books, propaganda, laws, translations etc. There are several bookshops opposite Bogyoke Zay Market on Bogyoke Aung San St and along Pansodan and

37th sts. *Pagan Bookshop*, 100 37th St, has a good selection of books on Burma in English.

Handicrafts: *Bogyoke Zay Market* (or Scotts Market), NW of Sule Pagoda, entrance on Bogyoke Aung San St. Wide range of merchandise, including lacquerware, ivory, teak, Shan bags, lungyis, mother-of-pearl and crushed shell boxes, monks' umbrellas, silver, watercolour cards, baskets. Visitors are advised to bargain hard. Closes 1700. At the S and E entrances to the Shwedagon Pagoda there are many stalls selling religious paraphernalia and puppets. *Rangoon Glass Factory*, Yogi Kyaung St, just off Insein Rd, NW of Inya Lake. Private enterprise; possible to watch glass-blowers at work; stall selling finished products. Open: 1000-1500 Mon-Fri. *Win Mar*, 150 Kaba Aye Pagoda Rd, some items on the tacky side.

Markets: *Bogyoke Zay Market* (see above); *New Bogyoke Market*, opposite, on the S side of the road, sells local produce, lungyis clothes, shoes – mainly Chinese imports – and hardware. *Indian market*, on the S side of Anawrahta St; spices, fruit and vegetables. *Chinese market*, few blocks W of Indian market, opposite General Hospital (Lan Ma Daw Rd). *Nyaung Pin Lay* is close to the main port area and mainly trades basic commodities from the delta and coastal regions, eg rice, salt, beans, pulses. The *Lammadaw Market* (or *Iron Market*) is Rangoon's main fish market and is only a short walk from *Nyaung Pin Lay*.

Precious stones: the *Tourist Department Store* (Diplomatic Store), just N of the Sule Pagoda on Sule Pagoda Rd, offers the best selection of gems. Purchases at the Tourist Department Store can only be made in foreign currency. (The store also has a small selection of handicrafts and sells imported brands of alcohol and cigarettes.) Open: 0930-1630 Tue-Sat. The government has a monopoly on gem stones and tourists are encouraged to shop here – stones bought without a certificate have been confiscated on departure (see **Customs**, page 658). There is also a government-run shop, near the Kataye Pagoda called the *Mayanmar Gems Emporium*. It is however possible to find some reasonably good quality stones in *Bogyoke Zay Market* although, unlike the Tourist Department Store, authenticity is not guaranteed. The goldsmiths and jewellers in Chinatown (the area around Latha St) also sell unset stones. Foreign residents say Bangkok is a better bet.

● **Sport**

Golf: a whole series of golf clubs have sprung up around Burma to entertain the nouveau riche and Japanese tourists. Most of the clubs are within easy reach of Rangoon. *City Golf Club*, Thiri Mingalar St, 10th Mile Instin, T 40086, even has its own resort hotel; *Yangon Golf Club*, Danyingone, Mingaladon, T 45563; *Myanmar Golf Club*, 9th Mile, Prome Rd, T 61702.

Swimming: *Inya Lake Hotel* or *Kokine Swimming Club*, 23 Saya San Rd.

● **Tour companies & travel agents**

Euro-Asie, 116 Bo Aung Kyaw St, Botataung (close to *Grand Hotel*), T 74640, F 84981, clued up on off the beaten track places, extending visas etc, good guides, rec; *Flying Dragon Tourism Business*, 337 Pyay Rd, Sanchaung Township; *Free Bird Tours*, 357 Bo Aung Gyaw St (upper block), T 94941, F 89960, the largest private operators in Burma, very efficient; *Golden Express*, 56 Wadan St, T 21479, also operate a small chain of good hotels in the main sightseeing areas; *Golden Land*, 214 (2A) Bo Aung Kyaw St, T 96074, F 61900, well organized, connected to MTT; *Journeys*, Room 38, 2nd Floor Suite, Building 4, 8th Mile Junction, Prome Rd, T 64275, F 89960; *Korea Myanmar*, 1 Wingaba St, Bahan Township; *Open Sesame*, Thirimingalar Rd, Kamayut, T 32890, F 89862; *Rubyland Tourism Services*, 90 Upper Pansodan St, Mingala Taungnyunt Township, T 81219, rec; *Thuriya Tours & Travels*, 47, Room 13, Bogalayzay St, Botataung Township; *U Chit Swe*, 21A Natmauk Lane 2, Tamwe Township; *View International*, 21A Natmauk Ave 2, Tamwe Township.

● **Tourist offices**

Myanmar Travels & Tours (MTT), 77-91 Sule Pagoda Rd, T 78376/75328/80321. Excursions, country and city tours, hotel room reservations, car hire, rail and air tickets and official currency exchange but not as efficient as private operators. Open: 0800-1730 Mon-Sun.

● **Transport**

Local Boat: ferries and riverboats from various piers (1-3 kyat).

Bus: frequent bus services round town, can be very crowded, but cheap. Most rides cost 1 kyat. Many local buses leave from outside the National Museum. (All are numbered in Burmese numerals.)

Bus 3: leaves from Latha Rd in China-Town,

between Mahabandoola and Anowratha. It also stops on Shwedagon Pagoda Rd by the new Bo Gyaw Market, just pass the crossing with Anowratha, and goes on the Shwedagon (stops at the S, W and N doors) and the Myenigon crossing.

Bus 7: goes from Shwedagon Pagoda Rd, between Mahabandoola and the Strand to South Okalappa. Stops at Kokaing, and goes up along Inya Lake (eastern side).

Bus 8: goes either from bo ta taung jetty (where boats leave to Syriam) or Mahabandoola Park eastern side (Barr St), to Insein along the Prome Rd, stops at Myenigon, Hle Dan. On its way back from Insein, goes up Mahabandoola all the way to Sule Pagoda.

Bus 9: leaves from Sule Pagoda Rd, western side of Mahabandoola park, and goes to Mingaladon (along Prome Rd), stops at Myenigon and Hle Dan, Inya Lake western side (just after Hle Dan), If you want to get to the airport, you will still have to take a taxi from the last stop.

Bus 12: One of the longest bus rides, from Htin Pon Ze, to Yankin, along University Ave and through Kokaing (eastern side of Inya Lake), it will take you through some typically Burmese parts of town. If you ride from the stop in front of Bo Gyaw Market on Bo Gyaw Aung San Rd, under the bridge, you will be going towards Htin Pon Ze. From the corner of Barr St and Anowratha or from the stop called Latha, on Anowratha (after crossing with Shwedagon Pagoda Rd), you will go towards Kokaing and Yankin.

Buses 14 and 5: go to the Peace Pagoda.

Bus 37: goes to the Shwedagon (from Sule Pagoda, 1 kyat).

Bus 38: goes to Thida Jetty for Syriam.

Bus 46: goes around the Royal Lakes (down Signal Pagoda Rd).

Bus 48: leaves from Thein Phyu St between 44th and 45th sts, goes to Insein along the Prome Rd.

Buses 51 and 9: go to the airport.

Taxi: fares should be negotiated before setting off. Blue Mazda 3-wheeler taxis are cheaper than large cars. Large cars to out-of-town destinations cost about US\$27/day. There are many private cars operating as unofficial taxis.

Train: circular rail route around the city, 2 hrs. Can hop on and off – a good way of seeing the suburbs.

Trishaw: Rangoon's back-to-back trishaws take 2 passengers; the fare should be settled before setting off. Price is usually worked out per head.

Air Mingaladon airport, 19 km NW of Rangoon. International connections with Bangkok, Dhaka, Hong Kong, Kunming, Jakarta, Moscow and Singapore but the most reliable are those to Bangkok and Singapore. Regular connections with Nyaung-U, Pagan; Heho, for Inle Lake/Taunggyi; Mandalay; Sandoway.

Train Just off Sule Rd. Regular connections with Mandalay, Prome, Thazi, Pegu.

Road Bus: main bus station is at Highway Gate, 8 km out, just N of the airport. Regular connections to all main cities and towns, air conditioned coach to Mandalay, 12 hrs.

AROUND RANGOON

Twante

Twante is best known for its pottery. Visitors can watch artists at work and then buy from a good, reasonably priced selection. **Getting there**: take a sampan from opposite the *Strand Hotel* across the river to the entrance of the Twante Canal; from there linecars leave every hour for Twante. Alternatively, Twante is a 2 hr boat trip down the canal. Boats leave from Twante jetty 2 km W of the *Strand Hotel*.

Syriam (Thanlyin)

The Arakanese seized Syriam in 1596 but realized that their only way of retaining the town was to gain the support of the Portuguese, who were busy establishing trading posts along the coast. The opportunistic Portuguese adventurer Felipe de Brito was dispatched to take charge of the customs house at Syriam; he quickly consolidated his position, building a brick customs house and a fort to protect it (you can still see Portuguese buildings in Syriam today). He then persuaded a Portuguese officer to expel the Arakanese governor. This done, he appointed himself governor and then left his officer, Ribeyro, in charge while he set sail for Goa, in an effort to secure the Portuguese Viceroy of India's support. While he was away, the Mons besieged the town for 8 months. Ribeyro put up a good defence and when de Brito returned with 6 ships, the Mons accepted him as King of Lower Burma in 1603 (see page 522).

The town thrived as a port until it was sacked in 1756 by King Alaungpaya, founder of the Third Burmese Empire, which promptly ended its days of glory. He laid out a new city at Rangoon which took the place of Syriam as the country's chief port. Today, Syriam's local economy depends on the Peoples' Brewery, the largest oil refinery in Burma, and rice production. Like many villages in the Irrawaddy Delta, the town has a large Indian population, descendants of labourers brought over from India by the British, during the Delta's rice-growing boom in the late 19th century. Many Indians were deported in the years following Burmese independence but the country's biggest concentration of ethnic Indians remains in Syriam.

Places of interest

The main sight is the **Kyaik Khauk Pagoda**, on a hill 3 km out of town to the S, on the way to Kuaktan. It has an imposing golden stupa, similar to the Shwedagon. The 2 tombs in front of the pagoda are of Burmese writers, Natshinnaung and Padethayaza, who wrote about ordinary people in the Ava period and were captured by the Mons.

The **Kyauktan Pagoda** or the **Ye Le Paya Pagoda**, meaning 'the pagoda in the middle of the river' is 21 km S of Syriam, on a tributary of the Rangoon River. Inside there are paintings of all the most important pagodas in Burma. **Getting there**: linecars from Syriam, 2-3 hr round-trip.

● **Transport Local Pony traps, trishaws, buses** and **linecars** mill around the ferry terminal. Ye Le Paya is too far for a pony and trap. **Taxis**: cost about 150-200 kyat/hr to charter, trishaws and ponycarts 40-60 kyat/hr. Prices should be negotiated in advance.
Road/Sea Bus: bus 9 or 12 from Bogyoke market in Rangoon, or bus 38 from Sule Pagoda Rd to Htinbonseik Jetty. **Ferry**: from there ferries leave every hour down the Pazundaung Creek and across the Rangoon River. Government-subsidized boats leave every hour on the hour, except for a 2 hr gap at lunch time. Last ferry back to Rangoon leaves 1800, 45 mins.

Pegu (Bago)

The 2 hr drive from Rangoon to Pegu is rather disappointing as the road was widened in 1991 and all the beautiful trees which lined it were chopped down. There are a few sights *en route*, however. The **War Cemetery**, at Htaukkyan (30 km N of the Mingaladon airport) is a memorial to the 27,000 Allied servicemen who died in World War II; it is beautifully maintained by the Commonwealth War Graves Commission. The **Naga-Yone**, past the cemetery, has 8 planetary posts (see page 568) with their guardian birds and animals and an unusual Buddha image, which is enwrapped by a cobra. The **Shwenyaung-bin** (Golden Banyan Tree), is an ancient tree on the road to Pegu, reputed, in local lore, to be home of nats, the guardian spirits of the highway. Passers-by often stop to make offerings, while owners take their new cars to the spot to be blessed. About an hour out of Rangoon you will pass Yebo on your left. This highly fortified town was built by the Chinese in case the Burmese military have to make a swift exit. According to locals, inside are helicopters ready and waiting to fly to the Chinese border.

In 573 AD, Thamala and Wimala, 2 Mon brothers of noble birth – who were excluded from the succession order – founded Pegu as an outpost of the Mon Thaton kingdom. The site, which was then on the Gulf of Martaban, had already been earmarked as the location of a great city by Gautama, the historic Buddha. According to legend, the Buddha rested on a small hillock and two hintha birds came before him in obeisance. He prophesied that 1,660 years after his death, a city would be established on that spot which would be a capital. Sure enough, Pegu developed into a prosperous port, while Thaton declined in importance.

In the 12th century, Pegu came under the rule of the Burmese kings of Pagan and remained under their sway until 1323 when it became the Mon capital. Its golden age was from 1385-1635, when it was the capital of the Mon kingdom of Lower Burma. In 1542, the King of Toungoo (which had become a prominent kingdom in the Sittang valley), who built up a huge, rich and powerful kingdom based at Pegu, almost the size of present-day Burma. His son and successor, Nandanaung, who came to the throne in 1581, was a feeble and paranoid ruler; suspecting some of his officers of complicity with the King of Ava, he had them burned to death, along with their wives and children. Nandanaung then waged war with Ava and then Siam, but sickened by the bloodshed, the people revolted and neighbouring kingdoms besieged the city.

Portuguese adventurer Felipe de Brito stepped into the breach in 1603; he occupied the desolated city for a decade, and declared himself King of Pegu (see page 522). Another Portuguese official, Fernand Mendez Pinto, who visited Pegu around this time wrote that the kingdom was "...the most abundant, and richest in gold, silver, and precious stones that may be found in any part of the world." After that, the King of Ava ruled his empire from Pegu but he grew tired of living in the decaying city; when the port began to silt up, he transferred his capital to Ava in 1635. Pegu was briefly re-established as the Mon capital in 1740 but was again destroyed in 1757 by King Alaungpaya, the founder of Burma's Konbaung dynasty and the Third Burmese Empire (see page 524). By 1795, Pegu had a population of less than 6,000. Alaungpaya's son, King Bodawpaya, undertook some restoration work in Pegu at the end of the 18th century. But by then the city was already losing its commercial raison d'être: in the early 1800s, the Pegu River had changed its course, cutting the city off from the sea, finally sealing its fate.

Places of interest
There is little of secular interest left standing in Pegu, apart from the remains of the old moated walls. The Mon-style **Shwemawdaw Pagoda** or 'Pagoda of the Great Golden God', on the N side of town, is one of the most venerated pagodas in Burma. It stands 114m high and is taller but similar in style to the Shwedagon Pagoda in Rangoon. The temple has a 1,000 year history: it was originally built by two merchants, Taphussa and Bhalita, to house some hair relics of the Buddha. A sacred tooth was added by King Anurama in 982 AD and another by King Rajadarit in 1385. Successive kings have added to the stupa's height: in 1385 it was raised to 86m by King Dhammazedi; in 1796 King Bodawpaya built a new *hti* (using jewels from his crown) and raised the height of the stupa to 90m.

Its architectural interest lies in its octagonal base and elaborate projections in the lower portion. The Shwemawdaw was severely damaged by earthquakes in 1912 and 1917 and completely destroyed by another earthquake in 1930. It was finally rebuilt between 1952 and 1954 in a slightly different style to the original and has a new diamond-studded hti, the stupa is covered with 1½ tonnes of gold. Over US$100 per day is collected from pilgrims to maintain the building. The stairways leading to the pagoda are guarded by huge white chinthes (temple lions), each containing a sitting Buddha in its mouth. There are 8 planetary prayer posts (see page 568) and a small museum of Buddha images of stone and bronze, varying ages and styles, rescued from the original pagoda after the 1930 quake. The 'bananabud' from the original stupa has been left on the platform in memory of the earthquake. Admission: US$2 (includes entrance to other pagodas in Pegu). Camera fee: 25 kyat. There is a small market at the bottom of the W entrance selling pagoda paraphernalia,

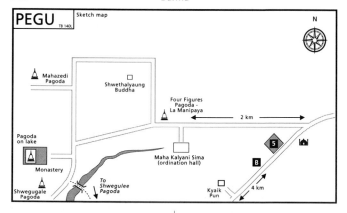

as well as a few tea shops. There is a busy shopping area, a few guesthouses (not open to tourists at the moment) and the post office on the S side of the pagoda.

To the E of the Shwemawdaw is **Hinthagone Hill**, with a small pagoda on top. The hill is originally said to have been an island. According to legend, the original pair of mythological hintha birds (see page 580) perched on this hill. There are models of them in front of the main shrine – the male bird is carrying the female. The pagoda is down at heel but there are interesting paintings of Buddha's life on the ceiling. The popular shrine, to the right as you go up, is to a local nat (or spirit).

Most of the other sights are the other side of town, on the road to Rangoon. The **Kalyani Sima**, or Ordination Hall, 1 km W of the station, was built in 1476 by King Dhammazedi, who was a fervent promoter of the Buddhist faith. The hall was the first of its kind in Burma and seems to have been built and rebuilt many times. The previous hall – dating from 1902 – was badly damaged by the 1930 earthquake; the present one was erected in 1954 and dedicated to its original purpose in a ceremony attended by former Prime Minister U Nu. To the W there are 10 huge stone pillars covered with inscriptions. These were set up by King Dhammazedi in 1476 to record the ceremony consecrating the sima. Their value lies in the detailed information on the early history of Buddhism in Burma that can be gleaned from the inscriptions. The language of the first 3 stones is Pali and the rest, Mon.

Pegu is probably most famous for its huge reclining Buddha image, the **Shwethalyaung Buddha**, 55m long and 16m high, which is a short walk NW of Kalyani Sima. A helpful board gives his vital statistics: ear 4.57m, sole of foot 7.77m, great toe 1.83m, and eyelid 2.29m. It was built by King Migadippa I in 994 AD, but fell into a state of disrepair. Five centuries later King Dhammazedi restored the image and King Bayinnaung maintained it until it lapsed into obscurity once again following the destruction of Pegu in 1757. The statue lay undisturbed for 125 years before being rediscovered in 1881 when the British were constructing the Rangoon-Pegu railway. It was restored to its former glory, and an open pavilion, rather like a railway station, was built over it in 1906. It is said to depict the Gautama Buddha on the eve of his attaining nirvana. It is a busy picnic site at the weekends and there are several tea shops round the entrance.

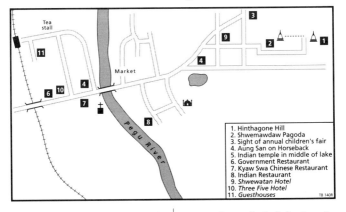

1. Hinthagone Hill
2. Shwemawdaw Pagoda
3. Sight of annual children's fair
4. Aung San on Horseback
5. Indian temple in middle of lake
6. Government Restaurant
7. Kyaw Swa Chinese Restaurant
8. Indian Restaurant
9. Shwewatan Hotel
10. Three Five Hotel
11. Guesthouses

Mahazedi Pagoda, close to the Shwethalyaung, was built by King Bayinnaung in 1560 to enshrine a tooth-relic brought from Ceylon – a duplicate of the sacred tooth at Kandy. Ten years after Pegu was conquered in 1599, the relics were moved to King Anaukhpetlun's capital in Toungoo. They were then transferred to Ava, and finally housed by King Thalun in the Kaunghmidaw Pagoda in Sagaing, near Ava. The building was destroyed by the 1930 earthquake and has been repaired – it is blindingly white. Only men can climb the stupa – ladies can walk around the platform. One of the most important is the **Shwegugale Pagoda** with its 64 seated Buddhas. It is a working monastery – visitors are requested not to wander round the monks' living quarters. There is a pretty pagoda in the middle of the lake beyond the monastery – Lamance peya. The small, and not very impressive, pagoda over the bridge is called Shwesugyi.

The Kyaikpun is 5 km from Pegu on the Rangoon road and sits on a tributary of the Pegu River. The entrance is just by the Kaikton ze Tawon meditation centre. It is a giant, 30m-high, version of the 4 seated Buddhas opposite the Hall of Ordination in Pegu; they sit back-to-back, facing the 4 points of the compass. It was also built by the religious King Dhammazedi in 1476. The Buddha on the W side was damaged by the 1930 earthquake. Note the interesting, but rather ramshackle, Indian temple – Sripalyandar Temple – on the road out to Kyoukpun.

Excursions

Kyaiktiyo Pagoda, 65 km E of Pegu on the railway line to Moulmein, is 20 km from Kyaiktiyo town. The 'Golden Rock' pagoda is in a spectacular location, perched on a huge, seemingly precarious boulder on the edge of a cliff. A Buddha hair is said to be enshrined in the pagoda, which was supposed to have been given to a hermit monk, who kept it in his top-knot. His last request was that the hair should be enshrined in a pagoda built on a rock, resembling his head. There are numerous legends about the pagoda, and the path up is lined with nat shrines. It is a tough climb to the top of the hill (but there is a popular belief that those who reach the top will grow rich) and the views are magnificent. There are porters at the bottom of the hill. Kyaiktiyo is only accessible in the dry season (Oct-Apr) and the extreme heat of Mar/Apr reduces the number of pilgrims who undertake the 8 hr climb. **Accommodation**: **B** *Kyaiktiyo*, at the top of the hill. There are guesthouses on top of the mountain. **Getting there**: by hired taxi or car from Pegu, US$55, or Rangoon (6 hrs). Kaiktiyo is accessible by car, two thirds of the way; it is an hours walk from this point to the top

Festivals
The annual *Shwemawdaw Festival* is in March/April.

Local information
● **Orientation**
The main road from the S takes you over the bridge and directly N to the Shwemawdaw. The town is along this main axis. The railway station, a few restaurants and the main indoor market are below the bridge. While the main hotel, as well as smaller guesthouses, and a local market are centred around the Shwemawdaw.

● **Accommodation**
B *Shwewahtun*, T 21263, a/c, no h/w, restaurant, is the only hotel open to foreigners, government-run, poorly maintained, the new block is in slightly better condition, and the rooms have h/w, quiet with a tatty garden.

● **Places to eat**
Kyawswa Restaurant, 6 Main Rd (W of Pegu River), Chinese, cheap and clean; and the *Kyaiktiyo Hotel*.

● **Shopping**
Pegu market, whose thatched roofs extend between the main road and the river, is full of local produce plus some handicrafts. The modern covered market next to it contains textiles and Chinese imports. There is a busy local market on the S side of the Shwemawdaw.

● **Transport**
80 km NE of Rangoon.

Local Taxis, ponycarts and **trishaws** wait outside the train station. Driver may give you a guided tour.

Train The 0500 departure from Rangoon allows plenty of time to visit most sights of interest in Pegu; the last train to Rangoon leaves at 2000 (2-3 hrs). Also connections to Mandalay, via Thazi (8 hrs).

Road Bus: buses leave from Highway Gate in Rangoon every half hour, 1½-2 hrs from 0430 onwards (3 hrs). It is advisable to book tickets one day in advance as buses can be very crowded; the return bus journey should be booked on arrival in Pegu. The bus station in

Pegu is ½ km S of town on the Rangoon road; there are linecars into town from here. **Taxi**: expensive, but many visitors prefer to take a taxi from Rangoon for the day as it allows much greater flexibility. A full-day return trip from Rangoon should cost about 1,500 kyats.

BASSEIN AND THE COAST

Bassein (Pathein)

The history of Bassein, a port city 190 km from Rangoon, dates back to when the Mons and the Burmese were fighting to gain control of the Irrawaddy Delta. The British East India Company set up a trading post at Bassein in the 17th century but it was raided by King Alaungpaya during the 18th century. In 1852, after the annexation of Lower Burma, the British established a garrison in the town and began to vigorously promote the cultivation of rice in the delta.

Bassein's importance diminished with the growth of Rangoon, but it remains the main town of the delta region and the principal market for the surrounding rice-growing area. Today the population includes Karen, Arakanese and many Indians, descended from Indian immigrant traders and farmers who migrated here during the British colonial era.

Bassein is the European pronunciation of Pathein, derived from the Burmese word for 'Muslim'. The town's specialities are its red monks' umbrellas, fish paste and halawa, a sticky cake of rice and sugar.

The main sight is the **Shwemokhtaw Pagoda**, the 'golden stupa', which is banded with concentric rings and has a soaring spire. It was built by a Muslim princess, Onmadandi – the Tazaung and Thayaounga Yaung pagodas are also attributed to her. The most recent addition to the city is **Ne Win's Pagoda**, modelled on Htilominlo Pagoda (see page 607).

Festivals Mar: *Tabaung* (moveable: full moon) is the main regional festival; boats leave Bassein for Mawdinsun Pagoda, on a beach on the far SW tip of the Irrawaddy Delta.

● **Accommodation B** *Pathein New Hotel*, Kanthonesint, T 21783; **C-D** *Pathein Hotel*, Pathein Monywa Rd, T 21162.

● **Places to eat** There is a governmen-run restaurant right on the river front; the good views make up for the average food.

● **Shopping** There is a daily market.

● **Transport** 190 km from Rangoon. **Road** Bassein is also accessible by car and river ferries (5-6 hrs).
    Sea Overnight boats leave Mawtin St jetty (about 2 km W of *Strand Hotel*), Rangoon between 1500 and 1700 (depending on the tide) and arrives at 0800 the next morning. More expensive tickets give access to the saloon at the top of the boat. Boats leave Bassein for Rangoon at a similar time and arrive in the capital the next morning.

Chaungtha

About 32 km across the tail of the Arakan Yoma mountain range is a small beach resort with miles and miles of golden deserted beach. **Accommodation: A** *Chaungtha Beach Hotel*, T 89589, fairly comfortable but basic bungalows. **Getting there**: By bus – connections from Bassein (2 hrs).

SOUTH OF RANGOON

Thaton

Thaton was the first great capital of the Mon kingdom and there are still some remains of the medieval fortifications. The Shwezayan Pagoda is thought to date back to the 5th century BC. The Thagyapaya Pagoda is known for its terracotta glazed tiles dating from the 11th and 12th centuries – the best examples are in the Kalyani Sima (ordination hall).

● **Transport Train** Connections with Rangoon (10 hrs).

Moulmein

On the Tennasserim coast, Moulmein was once an important port but has been superseded by Rangoon and Bassein. Most of Burma's teak was exported from here and some of the timber yards are still working.

The city is renowned for its seafood and beautiful pagodas. The **Uzina Pagoda** has exquisitely carved life-sized figures depicting Buddha's enlightenment. The **Kyaikthanlan Pagoda** was – in colonial times – better known as 'Kipling's Pagoda' after his lines:

> By the old Moulmein Pagoda lookin' lazy at the sea,
> There's a Burma girl a-settin, and I know she thinks o' me;
> For the wind is in the palm trees and the temple bells they say:
> "Come you back you British soldier; come you back to Mandalay!"

It has good views over the town. The **Mon Cultural Museum** has an eclectic collection of Mon musical instruments, 18th and 19th century statues and an old carved wooded screen from Mergui.

● **Accommodation B** *Mawlamyine*, Strand Rd, T 22560, a/c, nice restaurant with terrace.

● **Places to eat** *Min Thin*, on the jetty, Chinese fare.

Amherst

South of Moulmein is unchartered tourist country. Amherst was originally a seaside resort during the British colonial period. It is renowned for its pagoda which is separated from the mainland at high tide. The war cemetery, 64 km S of Setse, is the resting place of many prisoners of war forced by the Japanese to build the Burma-Thailand railway during World War II. Tavoy, the capital of Tenasserim, lies on the Thalween River. 20 km S is one of Burma's most beautiful stretches of beach. There are no hotels but tour companies organize stays in government bungalows

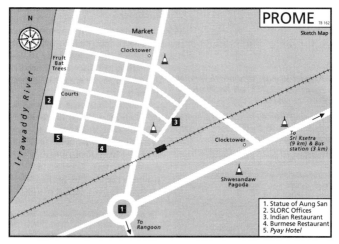

PROME TB 162

Sketch Map

N

Market

Clocktower

Fruit
Bat
Trees

Courts

Irrawaddy River

2

5

4

3

Clocktower

To
Sri Ksetra
(9 km) & Bus
station (3 km)

Shwesandaw
Pagoda

1

To
Rangoon

1. Statue of Aung San
2. SLORC Offices
3. Indian Restaurant
4. Burmese Restaurant
5. *Pyay Hotel*

Setse

There is a long sandy beach here; the water is muddy from the Salween river.

PROME AND SANDAWAY

Prome

Prome lies on the E bank of the Irrawaddy, near to some of Burma's newly developed oil fields. It is probably best known for the nearby archaeological site of Sri Ksetra. It is an important trading centre between Lower and Upper Burma and crossing point to Yakhine Yoma and Sandaway.

The **Shwesandaw Pagoda**, on the S side of town, is one of Burma's most holy sites – the Gautama Buddha is said to have preached a sermon here. The pagoda, a copy of the Shwedagon in Rangoon, dominates the top of the hill and views from here are impressive. There are several traditional wooden pavilions on the platform with impressive metalwork. The eastern entrance is dominated by an enormous Buddha statue. Halfway up the hill to the S is the **Bo Bo**

Aung Pagoda, a shrine to a mystic of the Konbaung dynasty and a leader of a Tantric sect.

Excursions

The archaeological site of **Sri Ksetra** is 8 km SE of Prome. It was the Pyu capital until the 8th century and was finally destroyed by King Anawrahta in 1057, and all the booty moved to his new capital at Pagan. A Chinese chronicle of the Tang dynasty paints a vivid picture of life at the Pyu capital around 800 AD: "The city wall, faced with green-glazed brick is 600 li in circumference and has 12 gates and pagodas at each of the four corners. Within there are more than 100 monasteries, all resplendent with gold, silver and cinnabar. Likewise the palace of the sovereign. The women wear their hair in a top-knot ornamented with flowers, pearls and precious stones and are trained in music and the dance. Having no oil, they use candles of perfumed beeswax. The people have a knowledge of astronomy and delight in the Law of the Buddha. At the age of 7, both boys and girls shave their heads and go to live at a monastery as novices until they are 20. If at this age they have not awakened to the religious life, they once again allow their hair to grow and return to town. The people deplore the taking of life. Their clothing is of cotton, for they maintain that silk should not be worn as it involves injury to the silkworm."

This large site has been excavated on and off for nearly 100 years. An impressive city wall (the road goes along part of it) and moat, which enclose 3 sides of Sri Ksetra, have been unearthed. There are also remains of several pagodas: Payamna, Payagy and Bawbawgyi, the most complete are outside the city wall. The cylindrical-shaped Bawbawgyi and conical-shaped Payagy and Payamna stupas with their commanding position over the plains were also used as lookout posts. The hollow-square Lemyethna and East Zegu temples, within the city walls, were prototypes for the temples at Pagan. At the centre of the archaeological zone is a small museum with a few, rather badly displayed and disappointing, exhibits including stone reliefs and covers of relic chambers excavated from the Pyu dynasty palace. There are out of focus photographs of the more important finds, which are in the National Museum in Rangoon and the Victoria and Albert Museum in London. Open: 0900-1600 Tue-Sun. The site has not been maintained and most of the remains are overgrown and hidden among the village buildings and farms. The temples are spread out over a large area (there is a map in the museum) and only worth the hike for real enthusiasts. **Getting there**: as the sites are spread over a wide area, it is best to hire a taxi in Prome.

● **Orientation** The centre of town is N of the Shwesandaw Pagoda along the river, where you will find the *Prome Hotel*, a few restaurants and the market.

● **Accommodation B** *Prome Hotel*, by the river.

● **Transport** 285 km N of Rangoon.
Road Bus: there are irregular connections with Rangoon. It is easier to hire a car (6 hrs).

Sandaway and Ngapali Beach

Ngapali

Just S of Sandaway is Burma's best known resort, although all along this coast are unspoilt sandy beaches fringed with coconut groves. It has not changed much since Maurice Collis' visit in 1923 on his way to take up his post as Deputy Commissioner of Sandaway for the Indian Civil Service: "The pleasures of Sandaway were very simple. The chief was to drive down to Ngapali beach and bathe... By the edge of the beach was a bungalow on posts with coconut palms waving over it, where you could stay as long as you liked. There was, however, nothing to do except bathe, walk along an incomparable sand, and sit in an armchair on the bungalow's veranda, dozing in the warm wind." (*Into Hidden Burma*). Most of the local villages thrive from the good fishing off the coast. Many wealthy Burmese generals and government ministers have holiday homes in Ngapali. The best time to go is between Oct and May.

● **Accommodation A** *New Ngapali Beach Hotel*, T 27; **B** *Ngapali Beach Hotel*, T 28.

● **Transport Air** There are regular flights between Rangoon and Sandaway (1 hr).
Road Bus: there are irregular connections from Prome – it is best to hire a car in Rangoon but it is a long and arduous journey – about 10 hrs. The road is good as far as Prome but deteriorates over the Yakhine Yoma towards Sandaway.
Sea Ferry: There are 3 ferry crossings per day across the Irrawaddy at Prome – the crossing is just S of the town.

Shan state – the biggest state in the Burmese union, bordering Thailand, Laos and China – has a population of around 4 million people who belong to a total of 32 different tribes. The rugged and mountainous state makes up part of the Golden Triangle, the largest opium poppy-producing area in Asia (see page 556). The government has fought continual ethnic insurgencies in the state for many years (see page 541) and because of the security problems, only this small part of Shan state is open to tourists. The people can be divided into 6 main ethnic groups (for more details, see page 538):

● The Shan, descended from Tai-Chinese stock and traditionally traders.
● The Pa-O, a Tibeto-Burman people, living around Taunggyi.
● The Intha, residents of the Inle lake area.
● The Taungyoe, of Tibeto-Burmese stock, living around Inle and Heho.
● The Danu, also Tibeto-Burmese people, living around Pindaya.
● The Pa Luang, a Mon-Khmer tribal people who live around Kalaw.

One of the most rewarding excursions in the Inle area is to one of the regional markets, at which many of the tribal people come to sell their produce. There is one going on somewhere every day of the week, but they rotate between different towns on a 5-day cycle:

1) Heho
2) Taunggyi, Floating Market Inle Lake, Aungban (near Kalaw)
3) Pwehela (on the way to Pindaya)
4) Kalaw and Shwenyaung
5) Nyaung Shwe and Pindaya

Taunggyi Shan State's administrative capital, which is perched on top of a precipitous escarpment. Inle Lake itself is reached from the town of Nyaung Shwe; the main sight is the Phaung Daw U pagoda which houses five 12th century Buddha images, although the lake is just as famous for its floating gardens and its 'one-legged fishermen'. To the W is Kalaw, a former British colonial hill station, which is surrounded by Palaung hilltribe villages. Pindaya, to the NE of Inle Lake, is famous for its Shweumin Pagoda – a cave temple which houses more than 6,000 Buddha images.

Taunggyi

The administrative capital of Shan state, 28 km NE of Inle Lake, has a population of about 150,000. The people of Taunggyi – who are predominantly Shan – regard themselves as so distinct from the Burmans that they talk about

INLE IN BLOOM

From Jan to Apr, Burma blossoms. Nowhere are flowering trees more dramatic than in the Inle area, where they line roadsides, provide startling splashes of colour in far-off fields, and grace the shores of the lake itself. First to flower is the tiger claw, with its orange blossoms, and the bompax trees which turn bright red: bompax flowers are boiled and eaten with Shan noodles. In Mar the jacaranda bursts into lilac blossom, followed closely by the flame of the forest (*Butea frondosa*), with its hanging clusters of scarlet flowers. The bougainvillaea blossom in Mar, as do white bohemia – the 'Hong Kong orchids', which are eaten as a salad (mixed with ground peanuts) after being boiled and chopped. In an explosive finale, the pink cassia blossoms – often mistaken for cherry – also come out in Mar.

'going down to Burma'. The town has mushroomed into the country's 4th largest centre after Rangoon, Mandalay and Moulmein. *Taunggyi* literally means 'big hill' – an understated description of the dramatic scarp slope on which the town stands. It was founded by Sir George Scott, superintendent of the Shan states in the early 1900s, as a hill station for over-heated colonial officials and their families; a few colonial buildings remain. Sited at 1,430m it has a much more temperate climate than the sultry plains below.

Shan princes came to Taunggyi to get a British education and Christian mis-

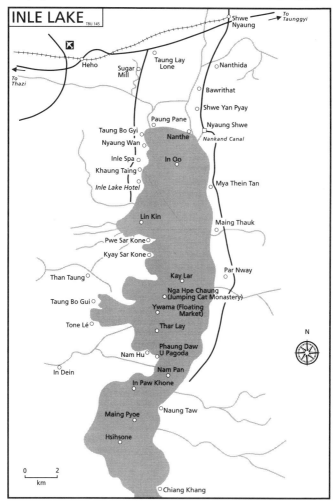

INLE LAKE TBU 145

To Taunggyi
Shwe Nyaung
Heho
To Thazi
Sugar Mill
Taung Lay Lone
Nanthida
Bawrithat
Shwe Yan Pyay
Paung Pane
Nyaung Shwe
Taung Bo Gyi
Nanthe
Nankand Canal
Nyaung Wan
In Oo
Inle Spa
Khaung Taing
Inle Lake Hotel
Mya Thein Tan
Lin Kin
Maing Thauk
Pwe Sar Kone
Kyay Sar Kone
Par Nway
Than Taung
Kay Lar
Nga Hpe Chaung (Jumping Cat Monastery)
Taung Bo Gui
Ywama (Floating Market)
Tone Lé
Thar Lay
Phaung Daw U Pagoda
Nam Hu
Nam Pan
In Dein
In Paw Khone
Maing Pyoe
Naung Taw
Hsihsone
N
0   2
km
Chiang Khang

sionaries, who headed into the hilltribe areas, used Taunggyi as their base. Today there are said to be more than 32,000 Roman Catholics in the diocese and the bishop is an old Italian Priest. Despite the fact that Burma was officially 'closed' from 1962, there were Western Catholic priests working at Taunggyi's St Joseph's Cathedral throughout. Two of them are buried in the graveyard; one had lived there for 64 years, the other for 47.

The town has a hectic daily market and a bigger regional market once every 5 days. Huge piles of *thanaka* bark (from the acacia tree) are sold in small packets; it is ground into a paste and worn by many Burmese women on their faces, who often apply it in intricate patterns. It protects the face from the sun and is the Burmese equivalent of vanishing cream, make-up and sun-tan lotion, all rolled into one. In March, the market sells huge avocados and strawberries. Mingala Market, to the S of Taunggyi's Russian Hospital, is a well known source of smuggled goods.

The **Taunggyi Museum**, on the Main St (near the *Taunggyi Hotel*), is in need of a spring clean. It contains a small collection of tribal costumes, weapons and artifacts as well as a collection of antique opium weights and musical instruments (including a snakeskin guitar). Next to the entrance there is a large ethnographic map 'showing the dwelling places of the natives' of Shan State which borders China, Laos and Thailand. Tourists are unlikely to get another chance to see the costumes of many of the more remote hilltribes as they are not allowed access to most of the war-torn state. A second, more interesting room, upstairs, has old Shan royal costumes and furniture, as well as portraits of previous kings on display. It also has a copy of the 1947 Panglong Agreement, a treaty of peace and co-operation between the interim government, headed by national hero Aung San, and the hilltribes. Open: 0900-1600 Mon-Fri.

Ma Op cheroot factory is near the Nyaung Shwe pool, N of the market. Taunggyi is the Havanna of Burma: its tobacco is sweet and is known throughout the country; the town's tobacco traders are among its wealthiest residents. Ma Op is the number one brand – the cheroot equivalent of 555 cigarettes – and the factory produces over a million a year. Ma Op herself is a rich and jolly Intha lady in her 60s. She employs 50 women who roll about 1,000 cheroots each and every day. They work 7 days a week (except for special market and full moon days) and get paid 2 kyat for every 100 produced – roughly the retail cost of 4 big cheroots. The cheroots are made from a mixture of dried tobacco and woodchips and are flavoured with tamarind and dried banana. Their filters are made from maize husks wrapped in old copies of the *Working People's Daily*, and finally they are rolled in dried green codia leaves. They are a surprisingly mild and aromatic smoke and burn for more than half an hour. Ma Op welcomes visitors to the factory and is likely to dispatch men with a bundle of her best cheroots which would take several weeks to smoke.

Local information
● Accommodation
There are several smaller hotels in the centre of town but they are not always open to foreigners, many of these are considerably cheaper than the *Taunggyi Hotel* but facilities are very basic. **B-C** *Taunggyi*, Tower Rd, T 21127/21302, just off the main street at the S end of town (near the museum), T 21127, restaurant, pleasant hotel in wooded grounds.

● Places to eat
Chinese: ♦♦♦*Coca Cola*, near Nan film studio at N end of town; ♦♦*Lyan You Hotel Restaurant*, Main St, mainly noodles, good selection of Burmese liquor; ♦♦♦*Maw Shwe Synn Restaurant*, Main St, good menu; ♦♦♦♦*Summer Prints*, E of Nan film studio, rec by locals.

International/Burmese: ♦♦♦*Taunggyi Hotel Restaurant*, European, Burmese and Chinese food, good spot for breakfast as it is one of the few places in Burma not serving insipid coffee.

Shan: *Daw Htwan* (or *Htun's*), noodle shop,

Thida St, Nyun Shwe Haw Gone quarter (behind the market), highly rec for breakfast or lunch, Shan exiles in Rangoon dream of Daw Htwan's Shan *hkankswe* (noodles), fried tofu and *weq-tha-kyin* (rice and pork).

● **Tourist offices**
MTT, *Taunggyi Hotel*.

● **Transport**
See General Information on Inle Lake area, page 593.

Local Taxis: small green taxis, cost around 20 kyat from the *Taunggyi Hotel* to the centre of town. **Pony & cart**: 20 kyat for short ride.

Nyaung Shwe and Inle Lake

The lake is nearly 100 km N to S but only 5 km wide and there are more than 200 villages on or around it, supporting a population of about 150,000. Most are Intha people (*Intha* means 'sons of the lake') who are of Mon rather than Shan descent, originally from SE Burma (see page 538).

The main lake town is **Nyaung Shwe** (Yaunghwe), 11 km from the Shwe Nyaung junction on the Heho-Taunggyi road and 1 km from the lake – although the main part of town is a bit further from the lake. Fifteen minutes from the market is an old Shan stilt palace, beautifully carved and constructed of teak. There is very little left of the interior, however. Open: 0900-1700 Mon-Fri.

The **Nankand Canal** from Nyaung Shwe goes down to the lake, which is only 4m deep. Inle's central portion is devoted to floating gardens and newly reclaimed land (see below). Travelling in a boat, parts of Inle seem more like a network of canals than an open lake. These channels are continually redredged by villagers and the army which co-opts local dredging parties every weekend. All the waterways are marked with whitewashed wooden railings and the round mile posts give it the appearance of a giant, flooded racecourse. With the mountains as a backdrop, Inle bears comparison with Kashmir's Dal Lake in India. Admission: US$50.

Inle's most unusual feature is its extraordinary 'one-legged fishermen', who have developed an original, eccentric method of rowing with one leg. With the other, they balance precariously on the back of their sampans, leaving their hands free to drop their tall conical nets over passing fish, which they can spot in the shallow lake. Another of Inle's unusual claims to fame is its floating gardens, which are built-up from strips of water hyacinth and mud, dredged from the lake bed, which breaks down into a rich humus; it take 50 years to produce a layer 1m thick. The floating allotments are anchored to the bottom with bamboo poles. Land is also reclaimed in this way, and parts of the lake have been reduced to a maze of canals around these plots. Most of the produce grown on the lake gardens is vegetables – mainly tomatoes and beans – and the codia leaf, which is used to roll tobacco and make cheroots. As well as being accomplished fishermen and market gardeners, the Intha are talented metalworkers, carpenters and weavers.

The best time to visit Inle Lake is during the Phaung Daw U festival (see below) or in Nov and Dec when the water lilies are flowering and the Hazy Blue Mountains surrounding the lake are not quite as hazy.

The main sight is **Phaung Daw U Pagoda** on the lake, one of the principal shrines in Burma (12 km from Nyaung Shwe). Phaung Daw is the name of the royal bird. The building dates from the 18th century but has been greatly altered over the years, and plans are afoot to further enlarge the complex (see model inside). It houses five 12th century Buddha images, which have completely lost their shape due to the fact that devotees are constantly plastering them with gold leaf. To the right of the main shrine there are 2 golden pedestals used to transport the images during the festival (the smaller one takes them to the **floating market** and the larger one carries them on the lake).

The boat used in the procession is housed in a shed in the complex. In 1965 at the annual Phaung Daw U festival, the royal boat capsized in a storm and the 4 images sank – this is all documented in a series of photographs in the pagoda. They were all salvaged and a statue of the royal bird was erected in the lake at the disaster site. There is a market beneath the pagoda selling local textiles, knives and assorted domestic wares and some antiques. Admission: US$5. Inle's famous floating market, at nearby **Ywama**, is held every 5 days. Just N of Ywama is the **Nga Hpe Chaung Monastery**, an old wooden building where the monks have trained their cats to show jump (it is known locally as Jumping Cat Monastery).

Inle Spa, N of the *Inle Hotel*, has a modest hot spring. Admission: 5 kyat for bath, 15 kyat for changing room. Open: daily.

Festivals

Oct: *Phaung Daw U festival* (moveable), four of the Buddha images from the Phaung Daw U Pagoda are rowed round the lake (one remains behind to guard the pagoda) in a copy of a royal *karaweik* on a tour of other pagodas around the lake. The barge is in the shape of the royal bird (which is akin to a giant chicken). There are boat races on the lake during the festival.

Nov: *Full moon of Tazaungmon* (moveable), following the harvest festival, donations are given to the local temples. Large procession; biggest in Taunggyi.

Local information
● **Accommodation**

B-C *Golden Express*, 19 Foungtawpyan Rd, Nyaung Shwe.

C *Inle Inn*, Yonegyi Rd, Nyaung Shwe, T 16, restaurant, friendly, well-run and nice rooms, popular with travellers so advisable to book, put on traditional puppet shows and serve Shan food; **C** *Inle Lake*, Khaung Taing, fan rooms only, restaurant, electricity 1800-2300, magnificent views across the lake, only a few rooms. A bar and a swimming pool are being constructed in the lake below the hotel.

● **Places to eat**

Burmese: ♦♦♦*Daw Aye Hla*, at the lake-end of Nyaung Shwe, near the teacher training school and the Russian hospital, rec by locals; *Inlay Inn*, near the market, Burmese food and puppet show; ♦♦♦*Khine Thazin*, near the teacher training school and Russian hospital.

Chinese: ♦♦♦*Naung Shwe*, on the Nankand Canal, government run, necessary to order in advance. ♦♦*Inn Thar Lay*, near Phaung Daw U Pagoda, fish and rice; *Inle Hotel Restaurant*, Burmese curries, standard dreadful food in a beautiful setting, overlooking the lake. There are long-term plans to build a floating restaurant on the lake below the hotel.

● **Tourist offices**

Naungshwe, Nankand Canal.

● **Transport**

See General information on Inle Lake area, page 593.

Local Boats: motorboats can be hired from MTT office in Nyaung Shwe (US$65/day). It is cheaper to take the boat trip from the *Inle Hotel*. There are also local ferries which criss-cross the lake.

Kalaw

A former British hill station on the rim of the Shan plateau. There are a large number of mock-Tudor colonial bungalows in Kalaw. There is a good regional market in the town every 5 days. A large community of Gurkhas, seconded to Kalaw in colonial days, still lives in the area. But this drowsy town is largely by-passed by commerce and most tourists. The Plateau area is inhabited by 60,000 Pa Laung tribespeople – who characteristically dress in blue jackets with red collars and skirts, around which are slung bamboo hoops (see page 539). There is a series of Pa Laung villages within about 10-15 km of Kalaw, and the walk through the hills is beautiful.

● **Accommodation** **A-B** *Kalaw*, 1 km out of town, restaurant, garden and tennis court, the hotel, like the *Candacraig* in Maymyo, retains much of its colonial charm with a solid teak staircase and doors, annexe cheaper.

● **Places to eat** There is a mediocre Chinese

restaurant in Kalaw. The restaurant at the *Kalaw Hotel* is OK.

● **Tour companies & travel agents** Paul can be contacted through his brother who works at the *Kalaw Hotel* (ask at the front desk). He can take more adventurous guests on treks into the hilltribe areas. His tours are strictly unofficial – but they are well worth the money (approx 600 kyats per day).

● **Transport** See General information on Inle Lake area, page 593.

Pindaya

39 km from the Aungban junction, Pindaya is a small town, centred round a lake, called Nattamiekan or Angels Lake, which looks rather like an Indian tank, with steps leading down into the murky water. The population is mainly comprised of Taungyoe and Danu people (page 539). Apart from its cool air and pretty setting, Pindaya's attraction is its cave complex.

The main sight is the **Shweumin Pagoda** – the 'Golden Cave Pagoda' – (also simply known as Pindaya Caves) on the steep hill behind the hotel. The limestone caves contain a maze of chambers with 6,226 Buddha statues – last counted in 1990; there are now so many that the temple has stopped accepting new ones. Some of the images are tiny, others are huge, and are made of white marble, bronze or plaster, coated with gold leaf. Most of the statues have been donated by devotees and pilgrims, and have been brought from all around the area. Behind the smaller stupa to the right of the entrance there are also several teakwood pillars, carved with small Buddhas. Some of the smaller caves within the complex serve as meditation chambers. The main stupa dates from the 12th century. It is a steep climb up to the cave but there is also a road to the entrance. The Pindaya Cave festival takes place in March, in which thousands of pilgrims converge on the small area below the caves. Everyone has something to sell from large watermelons to old clothes;

hundreds of people spend their time standing around watching videos. There are also stage performances of traditional dancing and Western-style rock music. Local Pindaya specialities on sale at the caves and in the town are potato snacks, Shan tea (sesame flavoured) and avocados at 1 or 2 kyat each. There is also a sweet called *thagya-kwe* or twisted sugar, a bit like nougat, which can be found drying outside houses in town. Take a torch. Admission to the caves: US$3. **NB**: the nearby Padah-Lin caves, in which traces of Neolithic settlement have been unearthed, are not accessible for tourists.

● **Accommodation** C *Pindaya*, Main St, 5 mins' walk from town on the road towards the caves, restaurant.

● **Places to eat** ♦♦♦*Kyanlike*, near the Banyan tree on the road into town, Chinese, reasonable.

● **Transport** See General information on Inle Lake area, below.

Local information on the Inle Lake area

● Banks & money changers

It is possible to change money at the official rate at government run hotels and MTT offices. Black market rates in the Inle area are considerably lower than in Rangoon, and unlike Rangoon, you have to go in active pursuit of business.

● Tourist offices

Heho Airport, Nyaung Shwe, Inle Lake and Taunggyi.

● Transport

Local Car hire: it is possible to hire cars or 4WD vehicles in Taunggyi.

Air Heho is the regional airport, 40 km from Taunggyi. Regular connections with Rangoon, Mandalay and Pagan every Sun, Tues and Fri.

Train The nearest train station which is open to tourists is Thazi (Shwenyaung station is closed to tourists). It is not possible to buy a ticket Thazi-Rangoon or Thazi-Mandalay: you have to pay the Rangoon-Mandalay full price fare. Because all tickets are sold on this basis, it is very difficult to get a seat at Thazi. Regular overnight connections with Rangoon and

Mandalay. There are additional trains every Sun, Tues and Fri.

Road Bus: regular public buses run from Taunggyi to Thazi 5 hrs, Mandalay 8 hrs, and Pagan 8 hrs. Prices fluctuate according to the cost of petrol.

Kengtung

The Maesai-Tacheileik border was previously only accessible for Thais and Burmese but it has recently been open to foreigners. The Burmese Government has officially sanctioned the border crossing to Tachelieik, but the Thais have not, so your passport is not officially stamped as leaving Thailand. The Burmese allow tour groups of up to 10 people to make the 167 km journey to Kengtung. The visa is only for 3 nights, 2 days and is liable to change at a moment's notice. Visitors must leave the border before 1000 so they reach Kengtung by nightfall. The border is open 0600-1800 Mon-Sun. It is obligatory to exchange US$100 for Burmese FEC on the border.

The road to Kengtung is in bad condition – a 4WD is advisable. However, the Thais are building a new road which should be completed by the end of 1994.

A smugglers outpost, the city is often compared to Chiang Mai 50 years ago before it was hit by tourism. It is and was an important Shan stronghold. Next to the main hotel, originally named the Kengtung, is the site of an old Shan palace demolished by the military in 1992 to build a car park. The Buddha image, Maha Myat Muni is the most sacred but other important temples are the Sun Sali, Sun Taung and Sun Lwe. The town is a treasure trove of traditional architecture with old-style houses with intricately designed wooden balconies so characteristic of Shan architecture.

● **Accommodation** Military governor, Brigadier Kyaw Win, believes there is future in tourism here and has turned his residence into a guesthouse. So, too, has the local police chief who lives next door.

● **Tour companies & travel agents** Several Thai tour companies run trips to the border: *Dits Travel*, Baanboran Hotel, Sop Ruak, T 716678, F 716680; *Diethelm*, Kian Gwan Bldg II, 140/1 Wireless Rd, Bangkok 10330, T 2559150, F 2560248.

● **Transport Road Car**: 6-7 hrs; petrol is available along the route.

PAGAN (BAGAN)

Sprawling across the arid flood plain of the Irrawaddy River, in the dusty heat haze of central Burma, stands Pagan – recently renamed Bagan – one of the most remarkable archaeological sites in Southeast Asia. As 2 centuries' accumulation of architectural master- pieces, Pagan ranks on a par with the region's other awe-inspiring religious monuments: Cambodia's Angkor Wat and Borobudur in Java. But at Pagan, there are 2,217 pagodas still standing and another 2,000-odd ruined temples – the remains of Burma's architectural Golden Age. Pagan was Burma's capital for 230 years, between the 11th and 13th centuries, and in those days there would also have been thousands of secular buildings such as palaces and houses. But because these were built of wood, all have long-since rotted away, leaving only the brick temples and pagodas.

Amazingly, all Pagan's monuments are concentrated in just 42 sq km on the left bank of the Irrawaddy River, known as the Pagan Plain. Through these temples and pagodas it is possible to trace the evolution of distinct architectural styles – from early Mon and Indian-inspired shapes (after the Late Pala style) to the classic Burmese stupa-design and the light and airy post-Mon temples. Pagan's documented history begins with its most famous temple-building king, Anawrahta, who came to the throne in 1044. He introduced Theravada Buddhism to the city – before the state religion was a mixture of Mahayana Buddhism and Brahmanism. Pagan's glory days ended abruptly with the invasion of the Mongul emperor Kublai Khan in 1287, after which the city was abandoned. Marco Polo, who arrived with the Tatar and Mongul raiders, was probably the first Westerner to set eyes on the city.

The Pagan plain is in the dry zone with only 640 mm of rain per year – and only supports a small population. Local farmers cannot grow rice but after the rains reap harvests of sesame, peanuts, corn and vegetables.

History

Pagan – whose name is thought to be a corruption of the Burmese *Pyu Ga Ma*, settlement of the Pyu – was most probably founded in 849 AD, at about the same time as many other Pyu cities in Upper and Middle Burma. There is thought to have been an even older Pyu city on the site though – legend has it that Pagan was settled from early in the first millenium. However, there are no architectural remains of the old Pyu pagodas. The earliest structure, dating from the late 9th century, is the Sarabha Gate (see page 603). The Buhpaya was the oldest surviving temple until it collapsed into the river in 1975. Architecturally, the city began to blossom in the reign of King Anawrahta (1044-1077), the 42nd ruler of the Pagan dynasty.

PAGAN VILLAGE TB 149

1. Lacquerware Museum & Training Centre
2. Pagan Museum & Archaeology Dept.
3. Myanmar Airways
4. Evergreen Restaurant, Cultural shows & Saratha Gate
5. Tourist Office
6. Site of Old Royal Palace
7. Nathlaung Kyaung
8. Bagan Hotel
9. Ayeyar Inn & boat trips
10. Thiripyitsaya Hotel
11. Co-op Hotel

Sketch Map

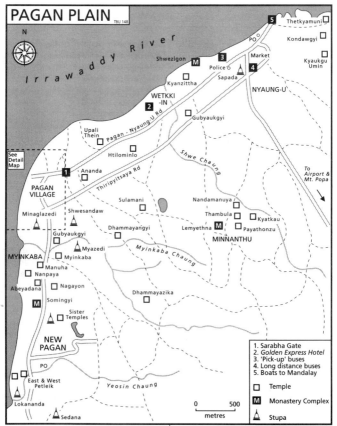

PAGAN PLAIN

TBU 14B

Irrawaddy River

N

See Detail Map

1. Sarabha Gate
2. *Golden Express Hotel*
3. 'Pick-up' buses
4. Long distance buses
5. Boats to Mandalay

☐ Temple
Ⓜ Monastery Complex
△ Stupa

0   500
metres

Labels on map:
Thetkyamuni, Kondawgyi, Kyaukgu Umin, Market, Shwezigon, Police, Sapada, NYAUNG-U, Kyanzittha, WETKKI-IN, Gubyaukgyi, Pagan - Nyaung-U Rd, Upali Thein, Htilominlo, Ananda, Thiripyitsaya Rd, Shwe Chaung, To Airport & Mt. Popa, PAGAN VILLAGE, Sulamani, Nandamanuya, Thambula, Kyatkau, Minaglazedi, Shwesandaw, Dhammayangyi, Lemyethna, Payathonzu, MINNANTHU, Gubyaukgyi, Myazedi, Myinkaba Chaung, MYINKABA, Manuha, Myinkaba, Nanpaya, Abeyadana, Nagayon, Dhammayazika, Somingyi, Sister Temples, NEW PAGAN, PO, East & West Petleik, Yeosin Chaung, Lokananda, Sedana

Pagan occupied a strategic location on the Irrawaddy and was an important crossroads for Mon, Chinese and Indian traders. The core of the city occupied a commanding position on the inside bend of the river, which formed part of Pagan's defences and flooded the moat – still visible around the Sarabha Gate.

From his base at Pagan, Anawrahta unified the whole country, conquering the Mon kingdom of Thaton in Lower Burma in 1057. Anawrahta had earlier become a zealous convert to Theravada Buddhism (see page 520), having met Shin Arahan, a missionary monk from Thaton. By besieging and destroying the Mon capital, Anawrahta obtained the Tripitaka scriptures of Theravada Buddhism which he had long coveted. Manuha, the deposed Mon king, had earlier refused to hand them over – Manuha and the rest of the Talaing royal family ended their lives as pagoda slaves in Pagan. The 30 sets of the Tripitaka were said to have been brought back to Pagan on 32 white elephants. Thaton's 30,000 inhabitants were also marched N to Pagan. Anawrahta then set about con-

MAIN PERIODS OF TEMPLE BUILDING IN PAGAN

Early Period: *circa* 850-1120

It is thought that Pagan was built on the site of an earlier Pyu city and prototypes of the early temples at Pagan have been found at the old Pyu capital of Sri Kshetra (near Prome, further S on the Irrawaddy River). The latter years of the early period are sometimes referred to as the Mon Period, as the temple and stupa designs were heavily influenced by the Mon artists and craftsmen captured by King Anawrahta following his conquest of Thaton in 1057.

King	Temples
PYUSAWATI c. 850	Buphaya, Sarabha Gate
THUGYI 931-964	Nathlaungkyaung
ANAWRAHTA 1044-1077	East & West Petleik, Kyaukgu Umin (added to by Narapatisithu), Lokananda, Manuha, Myinkaba*, Myazedi, Nanpaya, Pitakattaik, Shwesandaw, Shwezigon (finished by Kyanzittha)
KYANZITTHA 1084-1113	Abeyadana, Ananda, Kyanzittha Cave, Nagayon, Myinkaba Gabyaukgyi (built by Kyanzittha's son, Patothamya*

Middle Period: *circa* 1120-1170

By the end of the Early Period, builders were already experimenting with upper storeys. During the middle period, the multi-storey temple was further developed, with the inclusion of upper-level sanctuaries. The earlier Pyu and Mon influences gradually disappeared and a true 'Burmese' style of art and architecture began to develop.

ALAUNGSITHU I 1113-1169	Sister Temples, Shwegugyi, Thatbyinnyu
NARATHU (also known as Kalakya) 1169-1174	Dhammayangyi

Late Period: *circa* 1174-1300

Innovation and experimentation continued throughout the Late Period and the novel 5-faced ground plan was introduced. Pagan also remained open to N Indian influences – such as that of the Maha Bodhi Temple. The fascination with elevation ceased as builders tried to create something different.

NARAPATISITHU II 1174-1211	Gwadapalin (finished by Htilominlo), Hmyathat cave temple*, Sapada, Somingyi Monastery*, Sulamani, Thamiwhet cave temple*
HTILOMINLO (or Nadaungmya) 1211-1234	Htilominlo, Lemyethna, Maha Bodhi, Upali Thein, Wetkkyi-in Gubyaukgyi
KYAZWA 1235-1249?	Nandamanuya
UZANA 1249?-1255	Thambula
NARATHIHAPATI 1248-1287	Mingalazedi
Late 1200s	Kondawgyi*, Pyathonzu, Thetkyamuni*

* Denotes those whose dates of construction are uncertain.

verting his own people – who were mainly Mahayana Buddhists, Hindus and spirit worshippers – to Theravada Buddhism, with the help of orthodox monks from Thaton. He also used Mon architects and artists to build many of Pagan's great pagodas; Anawrahta's most famous monument is the Shwezigon Pagoda.

Twenty years after his victory over the Mon, Anawrahta was gored and killed by a wild buffalo. His son, Sawlu, succeeded him, but reigned just 7 years before he was killed and his half brother, Kyanzittha, seized the throne. Thousands of monuments were erected during Kyanzittha's 28-year reign. His grandson Alaungsithu, who succeeded him as King of Pagan, ruled for 45 years. A highly developed system of irrigation canals was built, allowing the 17 surrounding villages to grow enough rice to feed the capital. The empire began to weaken during the 13th century as the neighbouring Shan states grew in strength and Kublai Khan built up his Mongul army to the N. The Mongul Emperor – Genghis Khan's grandson, who had overthrown China's Sung dynasty 8 years earlier – finally stormed and took Pagan in 1287. King Narathihapati, the last king of Pagan, is said to have pulled down 10,000 buildings, so as to leave little for the Mongul invaders. As they approached the city, Narathihapati earned himself the epitaph 'He who fled from the Chinese'. The once-great capital was plundered, then abandoned to stand as a monument to the Buddhist renaissance.

Seven uneventful centuries after Kublai Khan's army overran and plundered Pagan, the city suffered another catastrophe. In 1975, Pagan – which stands on a geological fault-line – was at the epicentre of a major earthquake, measuring 6.5 on the Richter scale. The quake – and subsequent tremors – destroyed many of the smaller temples and most of the larger ones were damaged.

As stupas cracked and crumbled, relic chambers were split open, exposing gold and jewels and priceless Buddha images. The army was quickly dispatched to guard against looters and a curfew was imposed. The treasures that were removed and smuggled out of the country kept Bangkok's antiques market in business for over a decade. Even today, in Bangkok's River City shopping centre (see page 173), items from some of Pagan's pagodas and temples are for sale. The damaged temples were quickly restored and reconstructed, using traditional materials and skills, with UNESCO assistance.

Architecture

For Buddhists, the best way to make merit is to build a temple or stupa. The kings, noblemen and monks of Pagan, however, appear to have been obsessed with the idea. Royal temple-building, according to inscriptions, secured merit for the king's subjects as well as the king himself, guaranteeing them a shortcut to nirvana. Most of the monuments that have survived into the 20th century are religious structures built of brick and stucco. Much of Pagan's original vegetation would have been cut down to fire the brick kilns for the temples and stupas. The interiors of many of these monuments also contain intricate murals. There is plenty of evidence that there were once hundreds – if not thousands – of other, secular wooden buildings, which have now decayed. Dedicatory inscriptions in some of Pagan's temples, mention palaces, libraries and congregation halls.

Stupas – also known as ceityas or zedis (chedis) – are solid structures enshrining sacred relics, precious stones and images of the Buddha. The domes are tall, bell-shaped cylinders often with bands of ornamental moulding, and crowned with a *hti*, or umbrella. The ground plan is usually square although a 5-sided type developed in the late Pagan period. The terraces, designed to allow pilgrims to circumambulate the stupa, symbolize the tiered slopes of the cosmic Mount Meru. The terraces were also for pilgrims to view pictorial depictions of Buddhist texts emblazoned on glazed terracotta plaques – known as jataka plaques. These terraced plinths became increasingly elaborate over the centuries and the shape of the stupas evolved from early bulbous domes to the tall, tapered ones of later periods. The sealed relic chamber, or spiritual centre

---

NEW PAGAN, *CIRCA* 1990: A MOVING STORY

Until 1990 the main village on the Pagan Plain was Pagan itself – a small settlement inside the old city walls. To create a pristine, peasant-free, historical environment for tourists, and for 'archaeological reasons', Pagan's 5,000-7,000 residents were given one week's notice and then forcibly relocated to New Pagan, a soulless and treeless wilderness 5 km S of the old city. The government was good enough to lend the entire village one truck for a week; most people had to hire other vehicles, at considerable expense, to move the contents of their homes. To encourage the people to move, the government first cut electricity supplies to the village, then water supplies. After they had cut off the road to the local market, the military supervised the removals at gunpoint. Pagan's residents lost many years' worth of investments in hotel premises, restaurants, shops, lacquerware workshops and cellars, and houses. At least 4 people, who wrote letters of complaint to the Township Law and Order Restoration Council (the local version of the SLORC), were arrested and jailed; they were not given access to lawyers.

In compensation for the inconvenience of moving, the government gave each of the 1,000-odd families a rocky plot of land, 10 bags of cement, 30 sheets of corrugated tin roofing and 300 kyats. These materials were promptly resold on the black market to help finance the construction of traditional grass-roofed bamboo huts in New Pagan. In the new settlement, there is little shade and water and electricity supplies are erratic. There is a notable absence of tea shops, no sense of community and no jobs. The old settlement has now been razed to the ground – only the water tanks remain. The offices of Myanmar Travels & Tours and Myanmar Airways and one handicraft shop were allowed to stay put.

The reason behind the forced resettlement was ostensibly to allow the archaeological excavation of the site of the royal palace. The excavation of the site had been suggested by UNESCO (the United Nations Educational, Scientific and Cultural Organization) which met at Pagan in 1988. The actual village, however, was not on the site of the palace; since 1990, there has been no archaeological activity on the land formerly occupied by the village. Other explanations as to why the government was so keen to demolish the village have been suggested. Following the demonstrations and the military clamp-down in 1988 (there were protests both in Pagan and at nearby Nyaung-U), the military junta was not keen to have tourists mixing with or talking to locals. It may also have been to wipe out competition between private hostels and state hotels and restaurants. A more entertaining possibility, however, concerns the SLORC's top generals (most of whom are highly superstitious), who regularly come to Pagan to have their fortunes told by astrologers and for consultations with monks. One visiting journalist was told that the generals were embarrassed by the frequency of their visits and did not want locals to see how often they flew up from Rangoon.

THE MUDRAS OF THE PAGAN BUDDHAS

Most of Pagan's Buddha images can be classified into 6 main attitudes or mudras:
● Buddha in a sitting position, attaining enlightenment with the left hand in the lap, palm upward and the right hand touching the earth.
● Buddha in a sitting position, preaching his first sermon, with the thumb and index finger of the right hand touching a finger of the left hand (turning the Wheel of Law).
● Buddha meditating with both hands turned upwards, resting in his lap.
● Buddha in a standing position with the left hand extended in the posture of bestowing gifts and the right hand with palm outwards in the gesture of reassurance.
● Buddha in a standing position in the gesture of turning the Wheel of Law.
● Buddha reclining with his head supported by his right hand, representing his attainment of 'the point of final liberation'.

For more information on the mudras, see page 94.

of the stupa, lies at the core of the stupa, below ground level. The whole religious complex, and individual buildings within it, whether based around a stupa or a temple (see below) is known as a pagoda in Burma.

Temples evolved out of the solid mass of the stupa, the interior of which was opened up to house images of the Buddha, while the stupa itself was raised on a high plinth with staircases in the middle of each of the 4 sides. Temples come in 2 main types: the hollow square design and the central pillar design. Those built around a **hollow square** have just one entrance, usually a vaulted chapel and one Buddha image at the far end. They were the earliest types of temple and most are just one storey high. They mimicked the early Indian cave temples, which served as places for devotion, ritual and meditation.

The later temples had a square plan and were built around a **central pillar**. A Buddha image was placed around each side of the pillar, facing the 4 entrances. The walls of these temples are usually very thick to support the heavy superstructure. The later temples are better lit and have vaulted corridors around the central pillar, around which pilgrims would walk. The later ones

were also higher and often had monastic complexes attached to them. Their exteriors were decorated with bold stucco carvings on friezes and cornices, scrollwork on pilasters and flamboyant pediments on arches. The interiors were embellished with elaborate murals and the corridors lit by perforated windows. The remains of brick monasteries, or *oakkyaung*, which would originally have had wooden porches, are found within the precincts of larger temples.

Art

The exterior decoration of temples was an integral architectural feature at Pagan. Large areas of wall are left bare but the plinth, frieze, pilasters and the pediments above the archways are often elaborately decorated with stucco. Makaras are a common form of decoration, as are the half-human half-bird Hintha. Flame-arch pediments were frequently used to give an impression of greater elevation.

The main Buddha images are made of brick and stucco (the Thandawgya Image is a classic example, see page 604). Most of the stone sculptures were crafted to occupy the niches in the temple walls. Much of Pagan's sculpture was influenced by the Indian art of Bengal and Bihar of the 8th-12th centuries. It is possible to identify common features in many of the Pagan figures:

- Buddha images are seated cross-legged on a stylized lotus throne.

- Their hair is represented by spiral (or snail-shell) curls.

- The robe is lightly defined, the body is plump and the waist thin.

Images modelled in the pure Burmese style have a more drooping head, a short neck, thick torso and fingers of uniform length. Their ear-lobes touch the shoulders. Precious stones were often placed within the spiritually sensitive areas of the body – the head, chest, abdomen and upper arms – which accounts for the widespread vandalism of the statues. Images have been plundered for centuries: many statues have gaping holes in the stomach area. Pagan's archaeological office has, in recent years, removed many of the smaller remaining images from the temples and moulded replicas in concrete. The originals are now in the museum to prevent further thefts and vandalism.

The terracotta plaques found in many of Pagan's temples, depict episodes from the jataka stories. These record the previous lives of the Buddha, and the art form was of Indian origin – though developed by the Burmese into a distinctive style of their own. The plaques are different from the relief work found in other great Buddhist temples in the region. The earliest plaques are unglazed (eg those at the East and West Petleik), while the later ones are finished with a green glaze and a beaded border (eg those at the Ananda Temple). A total of 547 jatakas represent the previous lives of the Buddha.

Nearly all of Pagan's temples would originally have had wall paintings; many still survive. Most are murals, actually painted on the wall, rather than frescoes, which are painted on wet plaster. Typically, all the forms are outlined in black or red and the paintings have little or no perspective. Most depict the Jataka tales but some are also valuable historical records, portraying secular buildings as well as fashion, jewellery and furnishings of the period. The tops and bottoms of walls were often decorated with floral and geometric designs. Some of the best murals of the Pagan period can be seen at Gubyaukkyi, while the Abeyadana is distinctive with its Mahayanist paintings, which include portrayals of Vishnu, Siva and Indra.

Places of interest

The central area, in and around the old walled city of Pagan, has many of the most important and impressive temples – they are also the most accessible temples from the main hotels. The route starts with the Ananda temple, just outside the old walls, then follows around the inside of the city in a clockwise direction. Temples and pagodas spread across the Pagan plain, and are divided into those NE of Pagan proper; N and E of Nyaung-U; S of Pagan to Myinkaba; further S around Thiripyitsaya; and E of Pagan around Minnanthu.

In and around the city walls

The **Ananda** Temple, just E of the city wall, is distinguished by its golden stupas; as it is in constant use, it is kept in good repair. The British colonial official Sir Henry Yule, who visited Pagan in 1858 talked of the "sublimity" of the Ananda's architecture, which, he said excited "wonder, almost awe". Started in 1091 by King Anawrahta and finished by Kyanzittha, the Ananda inspired the temple-building of later Burmese kings. It is a central pillar-type temple: the central portion is a square block, each side of which is 53m long and 10.7m high. There are 4 large gabled portico entrances, giving the temple a cruciform structure. Above the base there are 6 receding terraces, crowned with a bee-

PAGAN HIGHLIGHTS

Ananda Temple, built by Pagan's prolific temple-builder, King Kyanzutha, in 1091, see page 601.

Thatbyinnyu Temple, dating from 1144; beautiful temple with views over the plain (most popular sunset spot), see page 605.

Pagan Museum, Buddha images and treasures from Pagan's stupas and temples, see page 606.

Gawdawpalin Temple, upper terraces are a good spot to watch the sunset over the Irrawaddy, see page 607.

Upali Thein, despite some deterioration, beautiful interior painting, see page 608.

Shwezigon Pagoda, with its golden stupa, is Pagan's biggest and most important temple, see page 608.

Mingalazedi Pagoda, built 3 years before the Mongul invasion; beautifully proportioned, with gentle flowing lines, see page 610.

Nanpaya Temple, for beautiful stone carving on interior pillars, see page 613.

Dhammayangyi Temple, one of the most imposing buildings on the plain, known for its fine brickwork, see page 615.

Sulamani Temple, a fine example of Pagan's Late Period, see page 615.

● Most of the main temples are signposted off the roads with yellow signs and the archaeology department's white plaques give basic information on the most important sites.

● Many of the temples are now locked to protect against thieves; some have watchmen who look after the key, or it is kept in the nearby village. For other temples, the key must be collected in advance from the Department of Archaeology next to the museum.

● Admission: US$10 to the archaeological zone, US$3 for every extra day exceeding 2 days, 2 nights. Tickets available at hotels, MTT offices and museums.

hive-like spire called a *sikhara*. The pinnacle is a tapering pagoda with a hti. Four smaller stupas, all copies of the central spire, are at the roof's corners. Two tiers of windows admit light into the interior, illuminating the narrow corridors inside the temple. The Ananda initiated the 'double terrace' style of temple at Pagan.

The Ananda's inner and outer corridors are full of niches, in which there are 1,424 Buddha statues in various postures. The most notable sculptures in the temple are the series of 80 reliefs in the 2 lower tiers of niches in the outer corridor, which illustrate the life of the Bodhisattva. On each face of the central cube there is a tall, arched alcove, each enshrining an imposing standing Buddha; the 4 Buddhas represent the Buddha's incarnations: Gautama faces W, Kakusandha N, Konagamana E and Kassapa S. Two of them date from the construction of the temple; the images on the E and S sides were destroyed in the 17th century and later rebuilt.

The W sanctum also enshrines life-size statues of King Anawrahta, and the missionary monk Shin Arahan from Thaton, who converted the king to Theravada Buddhism and died at the age of 81. In the porch on the S face, on a pedestal, there are stone footprints of the Buddha. The entrance to each porch is guarded by 2 door-keepers, seated on pedestals, in arched niches, topped with miniature spires. Each entrance to the main building is also guarded by an-

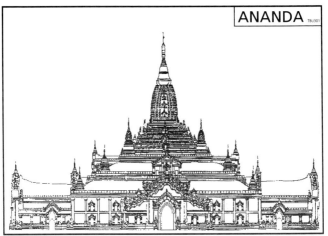

ANANDA TBU301

other set of door-keepers, in plaster-work, standing on low pedestals. The temple's lavish interior walls have been painted ochre and gold.

The base and terraces on the outside of the temple are ornamented with green-glazed terracotta tiles relating the jataka stories. Those on the W half of the base depict various monsters of Mara's army; the ones on the E side show devas, holding auspicious symbols, who are celebrating the Buddha's conquest of Mara. The jataka plaques on the lower terraces show just one scene, but the ones on the 4 upper-terraces are decorated with 389 different scenes, and are inscribed in Mon; these terraces are closed to the public to prevent theft. Inside the aisles of the 4 porches are stone sculptures depicting the 8 principle scenes of the Buddha's life. The *Ananda Pagoda festival* is during the full moon in Jan. Camera fee: 5 kyat.

Within the Ananda Temple compound is a small red-brick building, which is the monastery, or **Ananda Okkyaung**. Its walls are covered in well-preserved 18th century wall paintings depicting scenes from the Buddha's life and scenes from Pagan's history. Unlike

Pagan's earlier temple painters, these painters made much more use of colour combinations, light, shadow and perspective.

The **Sarabha Gate** (to the W of Ananda) and a few ruined walls are among the only surviving remnants of Pagan's secular architecture. The *Mahgiri nats*, Pagan's guardian spirits, still have their prayer niches in the gateway. These 2 nats, *Nga Tin De* (Mr Handsome) and his sister, *Shwemyethna* (Golden Face), are called Lords of the Great Mountain because they are believed to live on the sacred Mount Popa (see page 613). Originally the city wall had 12 gates, one for each month of the year, built by King Pyusawati in 850. The Department of Archaeology is rebuilding parts of the city wall and moat.

According to an 11th century Mon inscription – known as Kyanzittha's inscription – there was a royal **palace**, composed of a main pavilion surrounded by 4 minor ones, together with a throne room and audience hall. The archaeology department has excavated the site, which is close to the Pitakattaik (below), just within the city walls. The foundations are believed to date from

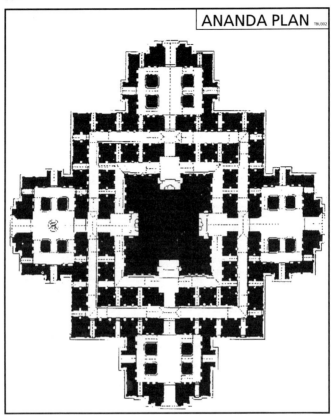

ANANDA PLAN TBU302

the Early Pagan Period, but there are also remnants of some later building.

The **Pitakattaik**, or library, is just off the main road, W of Sarabha Gate. It is said to have been built to house the 32 elephant-loads of scriptures bought by King Anawrahta from Thaton in 1057. It is 15m square and 18m high, with 3 entrances on the E side – 2 of which are now blocked up – and windows on the other sides. It is built like a temple, with a central cell, and is surrounded by a processional corridor. From this library it is possible to get an idea of what some of the other secular buildings must have looked like, although the Pitakattaik was altered by King Bodawpaya in 1783, who added finials to the corners of the 5 multiple roofs and plaster carvings above the entrances. Many of the monasteries of Pagan would have had similar libraries attached to them.

The 6m-high Buddha image just to the S of the Pitakattaik is known as the **Thandawgya Image**, which means 'within earshot of the royal voice' – it was close to the palace. It shows how most of the images in Pagan were built: the bulk of the statue was made from brick and stucco with a wooden shaft

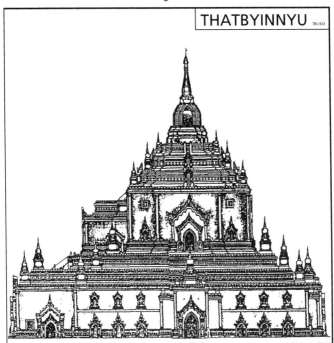

through the centre of the torso to fix it to the temple wall. The image was then covered in stucco, painted and sometimes gilded.

The **Shwegugyi** Temple, just to the W of the Pitakattaik, was built by King Alaungsithu in 1131 and straddles the earlier and middle periods of Pagan's architecture. Both the hall and the inner corridor have doorways and open windows, making it airy and well-lit. The arch-pediments, pilasters, plinth and cornice mouldings are decorated with fine stucco carvings. Inside there is a Pali inscription recording King Alaungsithu's religious aspirations and that the temple was completed in 7 months.

Thatbyinnyu, to the S of the Pitakattaik and the Thandawgya Image, was also built by King Alaungsithu in 1144. The magnificent temple stands within

the old city walls (to the SW of the Ananda) and is made up of 2 large storeys, the upper one set back above 3 intermediate terraces. Thatbyinnyu introduced the idea of putting a smaller 'hollow cube' on top of a larger Burman-style structure – earlier Mon-style temples were just one storey high. The main (E) entrance is unusually larger than the other 3; from it a stairway – guarded by 2 standing figures – leads to a corridor, which runs round the central core. At the top of the next flight of steps, which are built into the thick wall, more steps scale the outside of the temple to the upper storey. There is an enormous seated Buddha image in the upper sanctuary, which despite appearances, dates from the temple's construction. It has been continually re-gilded and rebuilt over the centuries. Thatbinnyu is famous for its fine brickwork, which is best exemplified by the wall at the back of the statue. The 1st and 2nd levels were once the residence of monks, the 3rd level housed Buddha images and the 4th, a library.

Access to the top of the upper storey is by another narrow flight of steps to the left of the shrine. The pinnacle consists of the usual sikhara, with a tapering stupa on top, which reaches to 62m – Pagan's highest. The mini-stupas, at the corners of the terraces, were badly damaged in the 1975 earthquake, but they have been well restored. There are spectacular views from its wide terraces – it is said to be possible to see 1,500 temples from the top – which makes the temple Pagan's most popular sunset spot. The Tuyan hills are clearly visible in the distance (beyond the fertilizer plant), and 60 km to the SE, is Mount Popa. For every 10,000 bricks used in the construction of Thatbinnyu, King Alaungsithu kept one aside, with which he built the little temple next door. Camera fee: 5 kyat.

From the top of Thatbinnyu it is possible to see the **Nathlaungkyaung Temple** to the SW. It is Pagan's only Hindu Vaishnavite temple and was probably built in the 10th century to serve Pagan's Indian community of merchants and craftsmen. Little is left of the original structure but inside there are alcoves which originally held brick and stucco images of Vishnu – the remains of one of these statues are in the main alcove. Some of the sculptures from this temple are in the Pagan Museum.

Patothamya, to the W of Thatbyinnyu and Nathlaungkyaung, is thought to date from the 10th century, although it is attributed to King Kyanzittha (1084-1113). It has a square main block and a rectangular vaulted hall on the E. The hall has 3 doorways with elegant pediments on the arches while each side of the main block has 5 perforated windows. The sanctuary is lit by skylights through shrines on the terraces above. In the corridor walls are niches enshrining stone Buddhas. The jataka paintings on the walls of the sanctuary have Mon captions below them. The temple is often locked to protect the murals and inscriptions. Above, there are 3 terraces; the bulbous dome has 12 vertical ribs and on top is the harmika – the casket containing the holy relics – and a 12-sided tapering finial.

Pagan Museum, to the W of Thatbyinnyu and near the Gawdawpalin, was built in 1979 and preserves many of the images and treasures exposed or damaged during the 1975 earthquake. In the main gallery is the Rosetta Stone, dating from 1113, which is inscribed in Pyu, Mon, Pali and Burmese allowing scholars to decode the Pyu script for the first time – it was previously indecipherable. It is also known as the **Myazedi Pillar** and was found at the pagoda of the same name, next to the Gubyaukgyi temple (see page 611) in 1917 by the German superintendent of archaeology in Pagan. One of the most interesting exhibits is a bronze lotus bud which opens up to reveal a tiny stupa with delicately carved figures of the Buddha at its base. Pagan was also famous for its dolomite carvings on display in the main room.

The museum houses a collection of 10th and 11th century Buddha images in the Statue Gallery. The Chinese-influenced pot-bellied Buddhas are a source of much amusement to visiting Burmese. It is said there are over 4 million Buddha images in Pagan – it is not hard to see why, if the scores of tiny images in relief on the stone slabs are included in the Buddha-count. A selection of jataka plaques are also on display. All items are labelled in English and dated. Next door to the Statue Gallery, replicas of particularly valuable statues are moulded from the originals; these will replace the originals in Pagan's temples to prevent theft.

The Department of Archaeology is

attached to the museum; its superintendent and staff can update visitors on
plans for restoration and renovation and
on the progress of various archaeological
digs. Since 1982, when restoration work
began, most has been funded by the
government and public donations, with
United Nations agencies supplying
technical assistance. Occasionally bilat-
eral donations are received for particular projects – Germany, for example, has
funded restoration work on the Ananda
Pagoda. Archaeological digs on the E
side of the city began in 1989, and excavations on the mound site of what is
presumed to be one of the wooden palaces got underway in May 1990. Despite
the mass-relocation of 5,000-7,000 of Pagan's residents in 1990 (see page 599),
there still appear to be no plans to start
archaeological excavations on the site of
the old village. Admission: US$4. Open:
0900-1630 Tues-Sun.

The **Gawdawpalin Temple**, to the N
of the museum, was mostly built during
the reign of King Narapatisithu but was
finished by his son, King Htilominlo.
The Gawdawpalin may have been built
for the purpose of royal ancestor worship as *gawdawpalin* means "platform to
which respect of homage is paid". The
temple is an example of the late period
of Pagan architecture, and, like Thatby-
innu, it is double-storeyed with the main
shrine on the upper level. A curvilinear
spire rises above the upper terraces and
is crowned by a slim tapering stupa.
Unfortunately the temple was near the
epicentre of the 1975 earthquake and
was badly damaged – its restoration
work is rather obvious. The Gawdawpalin is a good place to watch sunrises
and sunsets, with its views over the Irrawaddy. Camera fee: 5 kyat.

The **Maha Bodhi Temple**, NE of the
Gawdawpalin and just off the main
road, is a replica of the temple of the
same name at Bodhgaya in India's Bihar
state, which was built in 500 AD at the
site where Buddha achieved enlightenment. The Pagan version is typical of
India's Gupta Period and it is quite different from the standard bell-shaped
Burmese temples. There are very few
temples of this kind in Burma and was
built during the reign of King
Htilominlo (or Nadaungmya). It was the
first temple in which a large number of
Buddha images were placed in exterior
niches – previously they had been confined to interior chambers. Most of these
images are crude and rather disappointing close up: the whole temple is more
impressive from a distance.

The **Pagan Lacquerware Museum
& Training Centre** is on the way down
to the river and the Buphaya. The museum has good examples of early lacquerware: 15th century gilded glass
mosaic boxes and carved wooden doors.
Visitors can look around the training
centre to watch how lacquerware is
made. Closed: Apr. The shop has a good
selection of items made by the students,
all traditional designs. Well worth a
visit. If the museum is locked, the office
has a key.

According to legend, the **Buphaya
Temple**, which sits above the riverbank,
was built by the third king of Pagan,
Pyusawti (c.850), who found a way to get
rid of the *Bu* plant which infested the
riverbanks. He was rewarded by the then
King Thamuddarit, with the hand of his
daughter and the inheritance of the
throne. In commemoration of his good
fortune Pyusawati had the Buphaya pagoda built. The bulbous shape of the
stupa is suggestive of its Pyu origins but
it was totally destroyed in the 1975
earthquake. The temple has been reconstructed according to the original design. It is not particularly impressive.

North-east of Pagan

The **Htilominlo**, NE of Pagan proper, is
a 2-storey red-brick temple built by
King Htilominlo around 1211. He was
King Narapatisithu's son, which explains the similarity in style to the

VILLAGES

Myinkaba, to the S of Pagan, is well known for its bamboo 'cottage-industry'. The bamboo is floated down the Irrawaddy in the wet season from N Burma and made into walls for houses, roofing and is also used in Pagan's lacquerware industry.

Minnathu, to the E of Pagan, is an agricultural village which specializes in the production of sesame and peanut oil. The village is well worth a look around, if only to view its cow-driven sesame seed grinders.

Nyaung-U (also spelt Nyaung-Oo) is NE of Pagan, and the main settlement on the Pagan plain. Visitors arriving from the airport will drive through Nyaung-U – and past the nearby Shwezigon – on the way to hotels around Pagan itself. Nyaung-U is a busy, modern untidy town with a few friendly tea-shops and a big market every day.

New Pagan, see page 599, is spread out and rather characterless, small morning market.

Sulamani temple (see page 615). It is one of the larger temples of Pagan, reaching 46m and commands the road from Pagan to Nyaung-U. Like the Sulamani it is orientated E. There is an ambulatory at the base – the arched doorways and windows of which catch the morning and evening sunlight – and on the upper level, from which there are excellent views of the plain. The steps to the top are built into the thick walls on the E side. There are good examples of the original stucco decoration on the exterior.

Upali Thein, close to Htilominlo, on the other side of the road, is a good example of a sima or ordination hall. It is thought to have been founded in the mid-13th century and named after the monk, Upali. It is rectangular with a vaulted hall and an image of the Buddha at the W end. Its design is said to resemble many of Pagan's former wooden buildings. The low parapets, arch pediments and interior paintings date from the 18th century. Unlike the early panelled paintings, these are vivid murals – large and continuous, showing the renunciation of the world by past Buddhas and depicting the consecration of the hall by the king. It is closed to visitors, but special permission to visit it can be obtained from the Department of Archaeology (next to the museum).

The **Wekkyi-in Gubyaukgyi Temple**, with its pyramidal spire, lies S of the Shwezigon. It was known for its interior jataka paintings – some were removed by an archaeologist in 1899 – and dates from the early 13th century. Most temples in Pagan would have been painted inside as this one. This temple should not be confused with the Gubyaukgyi Temple near Myinkaba village.

The **Shwezigon Pagoda**, N of Pagan, about 500m from Nyaung-U, is the main centre of pilgrimage in Pagan. It is the greatest temple of King Anawrahta's reign. A sacred relic of the Buddha is supposed to have been put on the back of a white elephant by the king and the Shwezigon marks the spot where the elephant knelt down on the river bank (Shwezigon means golden stupa on a sandbank). Anawrahta is reputed to have started the building of this pagoda, but it was finished by his son, King Kyanzittha. It was repaired over the years by several kings but never very much altered – although pilgrims' donations have funded many additions to the temple platform. The Shwezigon is one of the most important pagodas in Burma as it is believed to contain the

SHWEZIGON PAGODA TBU306

Source: Ecole Français d'Extrême-Orient

Buddha's collar bone, his 'frontlet' bone and one of his teeth. It is also the first major monument built in Burmese, rather than the earlier Mon style, and the first pagoda to have nat images allowed within its precincts. The Shwezigon was a prototype for many later Burmese stupas.

The golden stupa rises from 5 terraces (3 square, 2 round) each symbolizing a different state of nirvana. Stairways from all sides lead to the top of the 3rd terrace. The terrace plinths are decorated with green-glazed jataka plaques – most of which are now weathered – which illustrate the former lives of the Buddha. The terraces are closed to the public to prevent theft of the plaques. The main stupa was partially destroyed by the earthquake in 1975 and the old *hti* sits at the right of the entrance

– it now rotates electronically with flashing lights and wishing bowls. Pilgrims armed with coins aim at the various bowls in the hope that they might win the lottery, become learned or pass their exams. On the N side there is a tiny hole in the pavement between the temple and the stupa which reflects the stupa when filled with water. The story goes that this little hole enabled visiting kings to view the top of the stupa without losing their ornate headgear.

On each of the 4 sides of the stupa, King Anawrahta built a small square temple for worshippers; each of these houses a standing Buddha in bronze – the largest surviving bronzes from Pagan. Anawrahta ordered all pagan statues to be brought into the temple to convert villagers to Buddhism. The 37 nats – many of which are riding mythological animals – are housed in an insignificant-looking building at the N-E corner of the pagoda precinct – originally they were on the lower terraces (almost Inca-looking). This building is also home to the earliest known figure of the god Indra in Burma. On the S side of the stupa there is a small pavilion with 2 statues of the local nats, Shwenyothin and his son Shwesaka. If you throw your coins into the bowls on the lucky "merry-go-round" you can free yourself "from 5 enemies": water, fire, the king, thieves, and those who hate you. In front of them is a wishing stone: when you pick it up the first time it should feel light; if it feels heavy the second time you pick it up, your wish will come true. The Shwezigon Pagoda's annual festival takes place in Nov during the full moon – it is a particularly exciting time to visit the temple. There are several stalls on the S and E sides.

A stone's-throw from the Shwezigon is the simple **Kyanzittha Cave Temple**, which served as a place of lodging for monks. Its long dark corridors are painted with murals, some of which depict the Mongul soldiers who invaded Pagan in 1287. The temple is believed to date from Anawrahta's or Kyanzittha's reign.

Close to Nyaung-U itself is the Sapada **Stupa**, a monument to Burma's good relations with Ceylon (Sri Lanka). Sapada, a Burmese monk, travelled to Ceylon for ordination and on his return to Pagan in 1181 erected this stupa to commemorate his visit. It is distinctively Sinhalese in style with its box-like relic chamber and circular stem.

North and east of Nyaung-U

Kyaukgu Umin Temple – or Rock Cave Tunnel – is to the E of Nyaung-U. This early temple is built into the side of a cliff, with a high archway forming the main entrance. Around the entrance are impressive friezes and decorated door jambs. Opposite, at the back of a large square hall, is a large statue of the Buddha seated on a lotus throne. There are also niches with stone reliefs and painted panels. A series of tunnels with meditation chambers have been excavated deep into the hillside. The main temple dates from the 11th century but the terraces and small stupa are believed to have been built by King Narapatisithu. It is dark inside; visitors should bring a torch.

The **Kondawgyi Temple** or 'Great Royal Mound' overlooks the Kyaukgu Umin. Similar in date and style to the Thetkyamuni temple, it is a square block with receding terraces mounted by a large stupa.

Close-by is the **Thetkyamuni Temple**; it has entrances on all 4 sides, but the main porched entrance is orientated to the W. The temple dates from the late 13th century and has some decipherable examples of contemporary wall paintings, based on the Jataka tales. The shrine paintings are not in such good condition.

Southeast of Nyaung-U are the **Thamiwhet** and **Hmyathat Cave Temples**: formed by the excavation of hillsides during the 12th and 13th centuries. The complex of passages and cells were created for monks as they were supposed to be conducive to prayer and meditation.

South of Pagan to Myinkaba

The **Mingalazedi Stupa**, S of Pagan and close to the *Thiripyitsaya Hotel*, with its soft, fluid lines, represents the height of Burmese pagoda architecture. It was built by King Narathihapati – 'the king who ran away from the Chinese' – in 1284, 3 years before Kublai Khan's invasion and the fall of Pagan. It is a well-proportioned pagoda and is noted for its beautiful terracotta jataka plaques around the terraces, which have been heavily eroded over the years. They are prized by the art world and many have been stolen; some are still for sale in antique shops in Bangkok's River City shopping complex. The small stupas at the corners of the stepped terraces are in the form of the *kalasa* – or sacred pot. On the top of the third terrace the 4 larger stupas balance the central stupa, which tapers to a pinnacle above the bell. The stairways enhance the soaring effect of the stupa.

The **Shwesandaw**, to the W of the Mingalazedi, was built by Anawrahta and has a strong Mon influence. The stupa has a more cylindrical bell, topped by moulded rings. The 5 receding terraces are accessible on all 4 sides by long flights of steps. There are also 2 octagonal bases immediately below the bell. It is believed to enshrine some sacred hairs of the Buddha, obtained from Pegu. It is also known as the Ganesh Pagoda as a stone figure of the Hindu elephant-god,

Ganesh (the patron god of the Mons), was originally placed at each corner of the stone terraces. A local monk donated money to have this stupa whitewashed, making it stand out rather too dramatically on the Pagan plain. (The only other white washed pagodas are the series of stupas which make up Min O Chan Tha.) Nearby is a brick building (Shinbinthalyaung temple) containing a reclining Buddha which is thought to date from the 11th century.

The **Gubyaukgyi Temple** on the N side of Myinkaba was built by Prince Rajakumar in 1113 and dedicated to his father, King Kyanzittha. Rajakumar commissioned a quadrilingual inscription in which he gave an account of his meritorious deeds and listed a chronology of the Pagan kings in Mon, Pali, Bur-

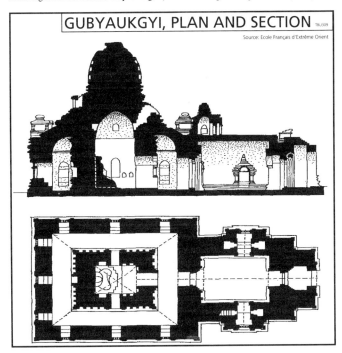

GUBYAUKGYI, PLAN AND SECTION TBU309
Source: Ecole Français d'Extrême Orient

KING NARATHU

It is difficult to imagine a nastier piece of work than King Narathu, the man responsible for the construction of the imposing Dhammayangyi temple, whose powerful shape dominates the Pagan plain. He ascended to the throne by murdering his father, King Alaungsithu, and then his elder brother, Minthinsaw. He then executed one of his wives – a beautiful Hindu princess from India – after she had displeased him. The homicidal Narathu built the temple as an act of atonement and in an effort to make some much-needed merit. Nonetheless, he decided to kill the architect once the temple had begun to take shape, to ensure that he could never build another like it.

According to Burmese chronicles, Narathu was assassinated before the Dhammayangyi was completed, just 2 years after he had seized the throne. His past misdeeds had finally caught up with him, for his assassins were 8 Indians, dispatched by his late wife's father. They came to Pagan disguised as Brahmin priests to avenge the execution of the princess. Narathu was remembered as *Kalagya Min* – 'He who was slain by Indians'. The Dhammayangyi temple he left behind is notable for its fine brickwork. But the temple's bricklayers fared only slightly better than the architect. King Narathu is said to have inspected their brickwork by testing the gaps with a pin; if it did not measure up to his standards he had the bricklayer's hands chopped off.

---

mese and Pyu. The Rosetta Stone (also known as the Myazedi Pillar) was found near the Myazedi Stupa, next to the temple, in 1917. It is now in the Pagan Museum (see page 606). The Gubyaukgyi has the characteristics of the earlier Mon temples, with a dark central shrine, a corridor lit by perforated stone windows and a large hall with its entrance facing E. The spire is straight-sided and tapered like that of the Maha Bodhi. The exterior is decorated with exquisite plaster carvings and the interior contains jataka paintings, including one of Gautama Buddha during his incarnation as a hermit. They are some of the earliest surviving paintings in Pagan, but many have been removed by collectors. There are 28 Buddhas, each sitting under a different tree. Each incarnation of the Buddha is believed to have achieved enlightenment under a different species of tree. The temple is often locked, but permission to visit it can be obtained from the Department of Archaeology, next to the museum.

The **Myazedi**, next to the Gubyaukgyi,

is said to have been built by Anawrahta in order to atone for the crime of killing his predecessor and half brother, Sokkade, in a duel for the throne in 1044. The low round terraces and an elongated bell show that it was built before the Mon-Buddhist influence on Pagan. It has been restored by donations but is heavily whitewashed and with a gilded stupa.

The **Manuha Temple**, just off the road on the S side of Myinkaba, was built by the captive King Manuha of Thaton, brought to Pagan by King Anawrahta in 1057 after his conquest of the Mon kingdom. Manuha is supposed to have sold his last jewels to build the temple. Inside are 3 Buddha images, cramped into a small space, symbolizing the king's captivity. The main gold statue has a 'heavy' chest, which is thought to represent the vanquished Manuha's misery. The reclining Buddha at the back of the main shrine lies in the death position, with the head to the N. The upper storey collapsed during the 1975 earthquake.

Next to the Manuha is the Hindu

THE MAHAGIRI NATS – A FAIRY TALE FROM OLD PAGAN

Once upon a time, during King Thinlikyaung of Thiripyitsaya's reign – in the 4th century – there was a good-looking blacksmith called Nga Tin De. He lived with his sister outside the capital. He was known as 'Mr Handsome' and was very popular with the locals, which made the king very jealous. The wicked king sent his men to kill Mr Handsome, but the blacksmith was warned in the nick of time and escaped into the woods. The king fell in love with Nga Tin De's beautiful sister, Shwemyethna (Golden Face). He soon married her and tricked her into persuading her brother to come out of hiding. But when Mr Handsome emerged, he was immediately captured by the king's guards, tied to a saga tree and burned alive. In despair, Golden Face threw herself into the flames and perished with her brother.

Following their violent deaths, the siblings became mischievous nats and lived in the saga tree. To pre-empt their mischief-making, King Thinlikyaung ordered the tree to be chopped down and thrown into the Irrawaddy. But this made his subjects very angry and they forced the king to fish the tree-trunk out of the river. Statues of Mr Handsome and Golden Face were carved from the saga wood and these were carried, with great pomp and ceremony, to the top of Mount Popa. For the next 700 years, every king, on his coronation, would climb Mount Popa and visit the 2 nats to appease them. Today the images of Mr Handsome and Golden Face, the Lords of the Great Mountain and the guardian spirits of Pagan, stand in the prayer niches that flank the ancient Sarabha Gate, at the entrance to the old walled city. Neither image does particular justice to the good-looking couple.

Nanpaya Temple. Some believe this was the prison of the captive Mon king, who is thought to have worked as a temple slave. Others attribute it to one of Manuha's descendants, who built it during the reign of King Narapatisithu on the site of Manuha's residence, in memory of him. It was obviously designed by Mon architects and craftsmen and is the only temple in Pagan built in sandstone and brick. It is thought to be the first free-standing 'cave' (or hollow square) temple at Pagan. The perforated windows are set in frames of pilasters on which rest arch-pediments, each enclosing a *kalasa* pot. Within the main shrine are 4 square stone pillars; 2 sides of each are carved with fantastic figures of seated Brahmas and the 2 other sides with ornate floral designs. Prior to their adoption of Theravada Buddhism, the Mons had been Hindu, hence the strong Brahman influence, particularly in the interior stone relief carvings. The Mons were well known for their stone carving, much of it is so intricate that it could have been carved from wood. Unfortunately the Brahmas have had their stomachs gouged out by treasure hunters. In the centre is a low square pedestal – there is no indication of what it originally supported.

The **Abeyadana Temple**, on the W side of the Myinkaba road S of the village, is ascribed to King Kyanzittha (1084-1113). It is believed to have been built on the spot where his wife, Abeyadana, came and waited for him when he was in hiding, after Kyanzittha had incurred the wrath of his half-brother, King Sawlu (1077-1084), whom he eventually deposed. It resembles the Nagayon (see below), but has 3 perforated windows on the walls of the main block and a bell-shaped stupa above the terraces instead of a *sikhara*, like that of the Nagayon. The bell is topped by a prominent *harmika* – or reliquary casket – and an octagonal tapering spire. A miniature stupa resembling the main spire stands at each corner of the first terrace; a *kalasa* pot stands on the second terrace and a corner crest on the upper terrace. In the sanctuary is a large image of a seated Buddha in brick. The paintings on the outer wall of the corridor represent Bodhisattvas while on the inner walls there are figures of Brahma, Vishnu, Siva and Indra. There are some surviving jataka paintings on the walls of the front hall. It is necessary to bring a torch to inspect these paintings; the temple is usually locked, but permission to visit it can be obtained form the Department of Archaeology.

Legend has it that the **Nagayon Temple** was built by King Kyanzittha on the spot he was given protection by a *naga* (serpent) in the course of his flight from King Sawlu, who he later overthrew. The temple has the usual hall, facing N, a dark corridor and an inner chamber. The pinnacle, in the shape of a mitre, stands above curvilinear roofs and square terraces with corner stupas. The main entrance has double pedimented gables. Within the hall are niches containing stone reliefs of the life of the Buddha. The hall and the corridor are paved with green-glazed stones. The corridor is ventilated with 5 perforated windows on each side. The outer walls of the shrine and the corridor walls have niches housing stone sculptures, depicting scenes from the Buddha's life. Paintings in the corridor depict similar scenes. Inside, there is a stucco image of the Buddha, double life size, under the hood of a huge naga. It is characteristic of the Mon style and is very similar to temples in India's Orissa region. The Nagayon was badly renovated after the 1975 earthquake.

Further south to Thiripyitsaya

The **Somingyi Monastery** is on the road between Myinkaba and New Pagan. It is one of the few brick-built monasteries on the Pagan plain – most were built of wood and did not survive. The ruined complex consists of a main hall, surrounded by a lobby to the E, a chapel to the W and small cells to the N and S. The chapel is a small, square, 2-storeyed building with a door opening on the E side, connecting it with the central hall by a passage.

Just S of the Somingyi are the **Sister Temples**. The elder sister, Sein Nyet Ama, built the temple in the 12th century. It is a typical square temple with entrances on all 4 sides, the E entrance being the main one. There are remnants of ornate stucco work. The younger sister, Sein Nyet Nyima, built the stupa, complete with guardian lions on the corners.

The **Lokananda** was built by King Anawrahta in 1059 and marks the S boundary of Pagan; Anawrahta built 4 stupas at the 4 corners of the city. It has a tall cylindrical bell similar to the Pyustyle stupa, and 3 octagonal terraces; the lower 2 can be reached by flights of steps on all 4 sides. Below the pagoda, there used to be an anchorage for large trading vessels, which was used when the water level was too low for them to dock at Pagan proper. The Lokananda has a modern compound, whitewashed stupa but good views of the river.

The twin Petleik pagodas, **East Petleik** and **West Petleik** are also attributable to King Anawrahta. These were half-buried by debris but when excavated, 2 tiers of unglazed terracotta tiles illustrating scenes from the jataka tales were recovered from around their bases. Originally, all 550 plaques were found in these temples, but many have been stolen over the years. The West Petleik is better-preserved. A vaulted corridor would originally have led around the base to house the jataka plaques (which have now been touched-up and repaired) and an entrance chamber facing

E at both pagodas. Both temples are usually locked, but tour guides normally bring keys with them.

East of Pagan

The **Dhammayangyi Temple**, to the SE of Pagan, is similar to the Ananda in plan, but is even bigger. It is an impressive structure and looks magnificent in the evening light. The temple was built by the notorious King Narathu. There are 4 main entrances, but only the outer corridors are accessible as the interior is blocked by brickwork for an unknown reason. Like the Ananda, the Dhammayangyi has large porticoes in the centre of all 4 sides, forming the shape of a Greek cross. The top of the central stupa crumbled in the 1975 earthquake; the staircase to the top is on the E side.

The **Sulamani Temple** is just beyond the Dhammayangyi and was built by King Narapatisithu. It is one of the first examples of the Late Period of temple architecture and, like the Dhammayangyi, has no dark chambers or deep alcoves. It is characterized by the use of smaller bricks, the perfection of its arches and its elaborate stucco-work. The Sulamani consists of 2 storeys, each crowned by terraces ornamented with parapets and small stupas at the corners. Each storey is a square with 4 porches facing the cardinal points; the porch on the E face is larger than the rest and was reserved for royalty. The upper storey is almost the same height as the lower storey and access is via 2 narrow flights of steps.

A vaulted corridor runs round the central pillar with a statue of the Buddha on each side. There is an image chamber in a recess on the E side of the central block, with another vaulted corridor running around it. The walls and vaults were originally covered with murals; those remaining mostly date from the 18th century, although the paintings on the ceiling are older. The building is well lit with doorways ornamented with flame arches – the stucco work at the

Sulamani is some of the best in Pagan. An enormous treasure-trove was discovered in the stupa of this temple following the 1975 earthquake. Unlike treasure from many of Pagan's other stupas which, along with Buddha heads and jataka plaques, has been smuggled out of the country and sold, the Sulamani's treasure has now been re-enshrined.

Around Minnanthu Village

The first temple to the N of Minnanthu is the whitewashed **Lemyethna**, meaning "Temple of the 4 Faces". The bright and airy temple was built in the early 13th century by a minister at the court of King Htilominlo in the style of Pagan's later temples. Unfortunately the original wall paintings have been whitewashed and modern murals painted over the top. This temple is still in regular use by local villagers.

Payathonzu, just N of the Lemyethna, is a group of 3 buildings joined by vaulted passages. The temple is of particular interest because of its Mahayanist and Tantric murals which suggests that Mahayana Buddhism was practised throughout the era, as this temple was built in the late 13th century. Two of the shrines are painted but not the third – possibly because the Monguls invaded before it could be finished. Note the bolder use of red in these later Pagan paintings. The temple is usually locked.

The next temple N of the village is **Thambula**. It is thought to have been built by Queen Thambula, wife of King Uzana. This later style temple is also well lit, making it easy to see the Chinese-influenced murals – note the Chinese-looking Buddhas, the ladies with Chinese hair styles and eyes, and the use of yellow.

A bit further N is the **Nandamanuya Temple** built by King Kyazwa. Some of the exterior stucco-work is still in good condition – such as the monster head on the left side of the entrance. There is a

Mahayana influence in the paintings and many of these floral designs are used on lacquerware. The paintings are very complete and the colour has survived well in many of the panels. The temple is usually locked.

Kyatkau is a cave monastery next door to Nandamanuya temple. A maze of tunnels and cells, the temple is still in use. A monk, U Narada, meditated in here for 40 years. He was highly respected locally and there are pictures of his funeral in 1988 in the monastery.

Excursions

The most popular excursion is up the Irrawaddy to **Nat Htaunt Kaung Monastery**. It is still inhabited by monks and has good woodcarvings, although much has been stolen. En route is **Selen** village, standing on another island in the middle of the Irrawaddy. **Getting there**: rowing boat (50 kyat pp): motor boat (500 kyat); the monastery can be reached by boat from the river bank, *Ayeyar Hotel*.

Mount Popa lies 60 km SE of Pagan. *Popa* means 'flower' in Sanskrit and is believed to be the sacred home of the nats – an extraordinary collection of deities, including spirits of trees, rivers, ancestors, and snakes. There is even a nat especially for the spirits of people who meet violent deaths. Originally there were numerous nats, but their official numbers have been restricted to the canonical number of 36, with the Buddha included as the 37th. Many adorn Burmese architecture (see Shwezigon page 608 and Sarabha Gate page 603). Perched on the volcanic peak (1,518m) are several pagodas and halfway up is the shrine to the Mahagiri nats – Nga Tin De and Shwemyethana, the brother and sister who guard the Sarabha Gate at Pagan. The path to the top starts at the monastery at the foot of the hill – it is possible to stay in the monastery, for a donation. The annual festival of the spirits is held in May/Jun.

Getting there: hire a jeep or pick up (US$30).

Festivals

Jan: *Ananda Pagoda's annual festival* (moveable) with dancing, music and stalls.

Nov: *Shwezigon Pagoda's annual festival* (moveable) – pilgrims travel from all over Burma; dancing, music and stalls.

Dec: *Annual Festival of the Spirits* – festivities in honour of the Mahagiri nats, Nga Tin De and Shwemyethana, whose home is Mount Popa (see above).

Local information

● **Orientation**

Pagan is 42 km square with several small villages. Nyaung-U is the main centre where buses and boats stop; the airport is close by. Most of the hotels are along the river around Old Pagan and restaurants along the main road between Nyaung-U and Old Pagan.

● **Accommodation**

At present, most of the accommodation is along the river around Pagan proper.

A-B *Golden Express Hotel*, Wetkyi-in.

B *Thiripyitsaya*, on the riverfront to the S side of the city wall, a/c, h/w, restaurant, pool (dirty), money-changing facilities (official rate), gift shop, bungalows/chalets, promoted as the "best hotel in Burma" but has a lot of catching up to do with the newly renovated *Strand* in Rangoon.

C *Ayeyar*, some a/c, no h/w, restaurant, beautiful garden with a view over the river, ask for rooms with a balcony and river view; bicycles for hire at 75 kyat/day; **C** *Bagan* (Than Te), near the *Thiripyitsaya*, a/c, some h/w, restaurant, landscaped grounds on the banks of the Irrawaddy, surrounded by chalets, riverfront chalets have a fine view; **C** *Co-Operative Hotel*, Old Pagan, fan only, restaurant (not rec), unkempt and basic, popular with travellers; **C** *Golden Express*, on the main road between Nyaung-U and Old Pagan, T 17, a/c and fan, friendly and well-run with clean rooms, garden, restaurant, serves European and Chinese food, best value for money in Pagan, rec. Over the next year other guesthouses are expected to open. *Aulng Mingala*, opposite *The Shwezigon*, cheaper guesthouse, is tatty but has character; *Myathidar Guesthouse*, New Pagan, family-run.

● Places to eat
Restaurants in all the hotels provide standard Burmese/European fare.

Pagan: ♦♦*Mya Ye Da Nar*, Wetkyi-in village (formerly in Old Pagan), Burmese/Chinese dishes; ♦♦*Ever Queen*, Old Pagan, friendly and the travellers hang out, mainly Chinese dishes, outside tables.

Between Nyaung-U and Pagan: ♦♦♦*Aye Yake Thar Yar*, opposite the Shwezigon just outside Nyuang-U, Burmese (2 hrs notice) and Chinese, rec; ♦♦*Myayadanar*, classic travellers fare – omelettes, shakes, toast and honey, also serves Chinese dishes and Burmese if ordered 1 hr in advance, small handicraft stall inside; ♦*Nation*, opposite Shwezigon, Chinese dishes and Burmese if pre-ordered, budget, rec.

New Pagan: ♦♦*River View Restaurant*, Chinese and Burmese dishes to order.

● Banks & money changers
At MTT next to Sarabha Gate, Pagan and at the *Thiripitsaya Hotel*.

● Entertainment
Cultural Show, in hall just outside city walls, starts 1830ish; **Zaw Gyi**, Pyan Saya Hla, next to *Ever Queen* restaurant, traditional puppet show, 1830. Marionette plays in a small theatre on 66th St (close to the intersection with 28th St).

● Shopping
There are small stalls selling lacquerware and antiques outside all the main temples, hotels, restaurants and the airport. Pagan is known for its lacquerware; you'll find the finest pieces here as well as a good range of antique items. Stalls also sell small antiques: tattoo sticks, door knockers, opium weights, betel nut cutters, bells and small brass statues.

Lacquerware: *Maung Aung Myan*, near Gubyaukgyi, Myinkaba. Family lacquerware shop. *Pagan Lacquerware School and Museum*, on road to the Irra Inn/Buphaya temple. High quality pieces made by the students can be bought at reasonable prices (not always open). *Shweaeinsi*, next to MTT, Pagan; lacquerware and handicrafts. Run as a cooperative but buys from other shops, so more expensive. *Thayar-Aye monastery*, Pagan, good selection at reasonable prices. *The Golden Tortoise*, New Pagan, the best in the area, selling top quality lacquerware, but as much of it is made to order there is often little choice

at the shop. Visitors can order items which the shop will pack for export. It is also a good place to see all the different stages of lacquerware production. Fixed price. *Shwe Sin*, next to *Golden Express Hotel*, good range and good quality. *U Ba Nyein & Son*, family shop near Ananda Pagoda; the shop was previously in the old town and they have plans to open a shop in New Pagan. *U Kan Htun-Daw Hla Myaing and Ma Moe Moe*, Ywar Thit Quarter, Pagan; family workshop – planning to open in New Pagan. Probably the best shop for smaller, more portable wares. *Maung Aung Myin*, Myinkata, good quality and large range of lacquerware. There are several small modern and antique lacquerware shops around Pagan's temples: the ones outside Thatbinnyu are reckoned to be the best but there are others around the Nanpaya and Manuha temples in Myinkaba and outside the Buphaya, Pagan.

Antique lacquerware: *Ma Khin Aye Han*, near Thatbinnyu. *Muang Muang*, Wetkyiginn village on way to Nyaung-U.

Handicrafts & antiques: there are stalls in the main entrances of the Ananda, Shwezigon and Htiminlo and outside Thatbinnyu (which are probably the best). 'Antiques' should be treated with a measure of suspicion. Tourists buying from stalls in the main temples are at risk of attack from manic salespeople; most are keen to engage in barter, exchanging statues or paintings for Bangkok T-shirts and copy-watches.

Markets: *Nyaung-U market* daily. If you accept gifts of thanaka from children they expect a present back.

● Tourist offices
MTT, next to Sarabha Gate, Pagan, T 89001.

● Transport
193 km from Mandalay, 430 km from Rangoon. Most visitors recommend hiring a car if you're going from Pagan to Mandalay or Inle Lake area (7 hrs) to avoid meeting connections at Thazi.

Local Bicycle hire: outside *Myayadanar Restaurant, Ayeyar Hotel, Golden Express Hotel* (15 kyat/hr, 75 kyat/day). **Boats**: small boats for hire from the jetty of the *Ayeyar Hotel* (200-300 kyat/hr). **Buses & pickups**: from Nyaung-U to Pagan New Town. **Horse & cart**: 200 kyat/day (dawn to dusk – with a generous siesta but much the best way to get around). MTT guides can help find an English-speaking driver.

Air Airport is at Nyaung-U, 10 km N of Pagan.

Regular connections with Mandalay and Rangoon, Heho and Chiang Mai, Thailand.

Train/Road Nearest station is Thazi, which is on the Mandalay-Rangoon line. Regular buses leave Thazi for Pagan via Meiktila, (see below).

Road Bus: buses leave from Nyaung-U. Connections with Mandalay and Taunggyi via Meiktila (6-7 hrs). The local bus leaves Nyaung-U at 0400 and arrives in Mandalay at 1400 (250 kyat). It is crowded. There are direct buses from Nyaung-U to Thazi (250 kyat) and Taunggyi (500 kyat), leaving at 0400.

Sea It only makes sense to travel downriver from Pagan to Mandalay as it can take anything from 2 to 3 days upstream. Visitors can only take the day boat which leaves Mandalay at 0600 and arrives at Naung-U in the evening.

There is an express boat on Thurs and Sun.

Thazi

There is very little to see in Thazi and for most travellers it is a stopping off point.

● **Accommodation C** *Moon Light*, Meiktila, Taunggyi Rd, T 56, nothing fancy; **D** *Red Star restaurant annex*, main street (close to the railway station), friendly but basic.

● **Transport Train** Thazi is on the Rangoon-Mandalay line. Regular connections with both cities.

　　Road Bus: from Thazi there are regular connections by bus/pick-up to Inle Lake and Pagan.

MANDALAY

Mandalay is not an old city: it was founded by King Mindon in 1857 and was previously called Yadanatin. He decided to fulfil a prophesy that a sacred centre would be built at the foot of Mandalay Hill on the 2,400th anniversary of the founding of the Buddhist faith. The Irrawaddy lies to the W of the former royal capital and the hazy Shan hills stand to the E. In 1861, Mindon moved his court, government and about 150,000 of his subjects to Mandalay from the previous capital at Amarapura. The elaborate carved teak buildings of the Golden Palace at Amarapura were all transported to Mindon's chosen location. The town was centred on the extravagant moated royal palace with its parapets, distinctive tiered guard towers and palaces of teak, lacquer, gilt and glass.

"Mandalay presented a series of violent contrasts: jewel-studded temples and gilded monasteries standing side by side with wattled hovels penetrated by every wind that blew; the haughty prince preceded by the respited murderer, his victor; the busy Chinaman next door to the gambling scum of the low country; the astrologer, learned in his mantras, over-persuaded by the glib talk of the Western adventurer... " (Shway Yoe, *The Burman: His Life and Notions*, 1882).

King Mindon was determined to ensure that his new city became the capital of the Buddhist world and the Fifth Buddhist Synod was held in Mandalay in 1879. It had long been the custom to bury people alive under the foundations of a new city or royal palace; the unfortunate victims were believed to become guardian spirits. King Mindon is said to have had 52 people buried beneath the 4 corners of the city. His antidote did not prove effective: 25 years after Mindon moved Mandalay, the British annexed Upper Burma following the Third Anglo-Burmese War, sending Mindon's son, King Thibaw and his wife, Queen Supayalat into exile in South India (there's a tomb to Queen Supayalat not far from the Shwedagon Pagoda in Rangoon). The palace became a barracks for the British colonial administration, and renamed Fort Dufferin. During World War II, after the British had fled back to neighbouring India, the Japanese 15th Army used the precincts of the magnificent royal palace as its high command centre for N Burma. In Allied bombing raids, it was the prime target, and was totally destroyed, along with a third of the city.

Today, despite the absence of the monarchy, Mandalay retains a few regal pretensions: some inhabitants still use the formal language of royal court and their manners are said to be the most polished in all of Burma. Because of its royal past, the city is also a centre for crafts, dance and music. But for a town whose name has romantic connotations – Mandalay has featured in the verse of

CLIMATE: MANDALAY											
	Jan	Feb	Mar	Apr	May	Jun	Jul	Aug	Sep	Oct	Nov	Dec
Av Max (°C)	28	31	36	38	37	34	34	33	33	32	29	27
Av Min (°C)	13	15	19	25	26	26	26	25	24	23	19	14
Av Rain (mm)	3	3	5	31	147	160	69	104	137	109	51	10

Source: Pearce, E.A and Smith C.G. *The world weather guide*: Hutchinson, London

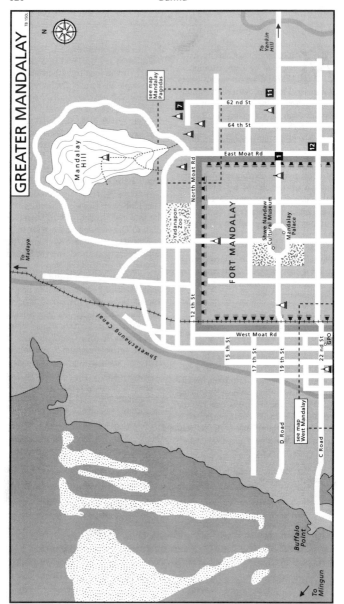

GREATER MANDALAY

TB 150L

N

To Yankin Hill

To Madaya

Shwetachaung Canal (Level)

Mandalay Hill

see map Mandalay Pagodas

62 nd St

64 th St

East Moat Rd

North Moat Rd

Yadanapon Zoo

FORT MANDALAY

Shwe Nandaw Cultural Museum

Mandalay Palace

12 th St

West Moat Rd

15 th St

17 th St

19 th St

22 nd St

GPO

D Road

C Road

see map West Mandalay

Buffalo Point

To Mingun

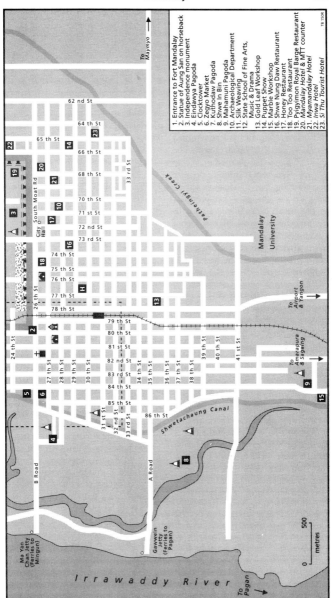

1. Entrance to Fort Mandalay
2. Statue of Aung San on horseback
3. Independence monument
4. Eindawya Pagoda
5. Clocktower
6. Zegyo Market
7. Kuthodaw Pagoda
8. Shwe In Bin
9. Mahamuni Pagoda
10. Archaeological Department
11. Silk Weaving
12. State School of Fine Arts,
    Music & Drama
13. Gold Leaf Workshop
14. Puppet Show
15. Marble Workshop
16. Shwe Nung Daw Restaurant
17. Honey Restaurant
18. Too Too Restaurant
19. Pyigyimon Royal Barge Restaurant
20. Mandalay Hotel & MTT counter
21. *Myamandalay Hotel*
22. *Inwa Hotel*
23. *Si Thu Tourist Hotel*

Rudyard Kipling – its dusty streets can be a disappointment. All that remains of its royal heritage is to be found in Rangoon's National Museum. Mandalay is now Burma's second largest city, with a population of over half a million. The city is an important river port, the start of the overland route to China and a big market centre for the surrounding area. The recent freedom of trade over the Burmese/Chinese border has turned Mandalay into a boom town: The Kokant Chinese have moved in. People now say Mandalay is Burma's premier city, not Rangoon. Mandalay is setting the pace for change – karaoke bars popped up all over the city a good 18 months before they took off in Rangoon. It is also an important religious centre: one quarter of the city is covered in monasteries and there are over 20,000 monks in Mandalay.

Places of interest

Although Mandalay is Burma's cultural centre, most of its buildings are postwar. All that now remains of Mandalay's (admittedly short) history was built by the last 2 kings of the Alaungpaya Dynasty – Mindon and Thibaw – and date from the middle of the 19th century – with one or 2 unspectacular exceptions. The sights are dotted around the city; the best way to get around is by trishaw.

Most of the N section of the city is dominated by the moated grounds of the **Royal Palace** – which is now known as **Fort Mandalay**. The palace was built in the early 1860s by King Mindon and was decorated with elaborate woodcarvings. The original buildings were very ornate and made of teak, which was carved, lacquered, gilded or covered with glass mosaics. The artist R Talbot Kelley, visiting Mandalay in 1905, saw "a collection of twenty or more separate buildings, all built of specially selected teak, brightly painted and gilded, and having the same upturned eaves and carved ornamenta-

tion common to all royal religious buildings in Burma. It has many audience chambers, in each of which is a carved and gilded throne. Above the principal one towers the lofty and elegant *pyathat* called by Burmans 'The centre of the universe!'..."

All Burmese royal palaces were built according to the same formula and when the capital was moved, the royal buildings were transported, in their entirety, to the new site. According to ancient custom, the palace roofs were meant to be made of silver or lead; in the end this proved too expensive: they were made of corrugated tin. The palace area was home to 5,000 people in Mindon's time.

After annexing Upper Burma, the British set up a provincial government in the old palace, renaming it Fort Dufferin. But the new colonial administration quickly undermined its own credibility when it established its headquarters in the palace's 7-roofed court house – only buildings with 9 roofs were considered suitable for rulers. The British also converted the Queen's royal reception room, the Lily Throne Room, into a clubhouse – known as the Upper Burma Club – and a picture of Queen Victoria was hung on the wall. This caused such resentment locally that the club was finally moved. Mandalay's Royal Palace was the last surviving example of royal Burmese wooden buildings; they were almost totally destroyed by fire following Allied bombing raids in World War II. Ironically, Japanese forces and Burmese collaborators had already crept out of the palace complex, escaping along a drain which led into the S moat. No trace is left of the splendour and pomp witnessed by foreign envoys to the royal court of Burma.

The palace is being partially reconstructed in concrete (at no small expense) by the present government, which gives some idea of what the original structures must have looked like. The reconstruction programme, which

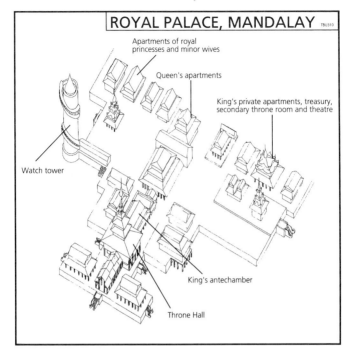

ROYAL PALACE, MANDALAY TBU310

Apartments of royal
princesses and minor wives

Queen's apartments

King's private apartments, treasury,
secondary throne room and theatre

Watch tower

King's antechamber

Throne Hall

has taken several years, is not without its critics. They charge that the undisclosed billions of kyats that have been spent would have been better invested in social welfare projects in what is one of the poorest countries in the world. A copy of the **Glass Palace** contains a display of the few remains salvaged from the old buildings. Open: 0930-1630 Tues-Sun. The **Shwe Nan Daw Cultural Museum** sounds as if it should be interesting but only has statues of important Burmese figures. Admission: US$3. The reconstructed watchtower, with its spiral stairway corkscrewing up the outside, can be climbed for 1 kyat. It is the symbol of Mandalay.

There is a scale model of the original palace buildings within the grounds, W of the old palace. It was made in 1952

from the original plans and is kept in an iron cage. The **Great Audience Hall**, with its 7 tiered golden spire, stood at the 'centre of the universe' – on the model of Brahmin-Buddhist cosmology – and was surrounded by other throne halls containing the Duck, Elephant, Deer and Lily thrones. The great hall has been reconstructed by local craftsmen who have assembled a reasonable replica of the intricately carved roof ornamentation. It has been repainted in vermilion lacquer-colour. In the original there were 133 apartments and dormitories, mainly to accommodate the king's 53 wives and his concubines.

The **Lion Throne**, several tonnes of regal regalia – including the royal ruby – had been stolen in an 1885 raid on the palace by British Colonel Sladdon. The booty was then 'lost' in transit. The throne finally turned up in London and was returned to the National Museum in Rangoon by Lord Louis Mountbatten at independence. It is still displayed there along with photographs of the palace (see page 572).

Within the palace grounds are the tombs of some members of the royal family, including King Mindon and his chief queen, Setkyadevi; these are in the NE corner. There is also a stone marking the spot where King Thibaw surrendered to the British. On the S side of the old palace grounds there is a monument to Burma's independence. The fort area is now used by the military – the *Tatmadaw* – and up to 10,000 troops are stationed within its walls. The palace area is not particularly exciting; it's a Sun afternoon playground for locals. Open: 0800-1800 Mon-Fri, sometimes closed Sat and Sun. Admission: US$5, tickets from the MTT desk at *Mandalay Hotel*. Entrance at the E gate of the fort.

The Folk Art Museum on 80th St (between 22nd and 24th sts) has a weird, and badly displayed assortment – carved wooden doors to a head man's house, hand loom, umbrellas and models of nats.

At the NE corner of the palace grounds around Mandalay Hill is a group of important sights. One of the most spectacular buildings in Mandalay – which gives some insight into the original grandeur of the erstwhile palace – is the **Shwe Nandaw Kyaung**, or 'Golden Palace Monastery' (to the right near the top of the E moat road). It is all that remains of King Mindon's palace. The Nathanon or Scented Palace was moved to the site in 1880 by King Thibaw after his father King Mindon had inauspiciously died in it. The building was thus spared the bombing which destroyed the main palace. It is made of carved teak with glass mosaic and is heavily gilded inside. Each pillar is a single trunk of teak, and the remains of the original lacquering and gilding can

still be seen on them. Hanging from the pillars are photographs of King Thibaw and his wife (the chief queen) and King Mindon – albeit a photograph of a painting – who had 49 wives. The Golden Palace is still in use as a monastery, and is now under its 4th abbot.

Around the ceiling are nats worshipping the Buddha. Inside are 2 halls: the main hall contains a copy of the Lion Throne, a Buddha image commissioned by King Thibaw (with the features of his father) and a golden couch used for meditation by the king. The second hall is partitioned off and used as a storeroom (it is not open to the public). The carvings of the 10 great jataka scenes on the outer walls are well preserved and still have some of their original gold leaf. They were only introduced when the palace became a monastery in 1880. Admission: US$3. Opposite the Shwe Nandaw, there is a new religious university for 500 monks.

Atumashi Kyaung, or 'Incomparable Monastery', next to the Shwe Nandaw Kyaung, is now a ruin. It was built by King Mindon in 1857, at vast expense, to house a valuable Buddha image – with a huge diamond on its head – as well as 4 sets of the Tripitaka scriptures. The building was of wood and covered with stucco. In 1885, the night after King Thibaw's surrender to British General Prendergast, the diamond was stolen. Five years later, a fire gutted the building. Only the masonry balustrade and staircases with elaborate stucco carvings remain. Westerners who saw the monastery before its demise were captivated by its beauty.

North of the Atumashi, near the S stairway to Mandalay Hill, is the **Kuthodaw Pagoda**. It was built in 1857 by King Mindon, and is a model of the Shwezigon Pagoda at Pagan (see page 608). Large teak carved doors, painted a rich vermilion (the S entrance still has the original doors) open onto an arcade and a small gold-topped stupa. On the S and

W sides are faded paintings of the palace gardens by a royal artist in 1892. This pagoda would not really figure on the Mandalay itinerary if it were not for its one claim to fame: row upon row of white miniature pagodas cover 5.3 ha in the temple's shaded grounds. These house 729 marble slabs inscribed (on both sides) with the entire Tripitaka. In the early 1870s, King Mindon commissioned 5,000 masons to carve the slabs, copying them from palm-leaf manuscripts, which took 8 years to complete. Originally the letters were inlaid with gold. This exercise was central to Mindon's plan to turn Mandalay into the centre of the Buddhist world – and as a show of prowess in the face of British expansionism which was threatening to erode his power. The project was also undertaken to fulfil the Buddha's prophesy that the faith would last 5,000 years. Mindon calculated that if the Tripitaka was recorded on stone – the first time in history that this had been accomplished – Buddhism would last at least that long. The inscribed stelae cover all the canons of Buddhism – the 3 pitakas: rules, philosophy and prayers.

In fitting with his vision for Mandalay, King Mindon convened the Fifth Buddhist Synod at his new capital in 1879. The whole work was read aloud without a pause – a task which occupied 2,400 monks for 6 months. It is the ambition of all monks to memorize the scriptures, but of the 300,000 monks in Burma today – 20,000 of whom reside in Mandalay – only 5 have managed it. The full scriptures take one monk around 2 years to recite. The oldest living monk to have memorised it all is now an octogenarian and resides in Mingun, and none of the others are younger than 50.

The **Sandamuni Pagoda**, W of the Kuthodaw and closer to the S stairway of Mandalay Hill, marks the spot where Prince Kanaung, King Mindon's younger brother and chosen successor, was assassinated in 1866. He was killed by 2 of Mindon's other sons who were aggrieved at being excluded from the succession. The pagoda contains an iron Buddha image, cast by King Bodawpaya of Amarapura in 1802 and moved by Mindon to his new capital in 1874. The Sandamuni houses marble slabs in the mini-stupas which are commentaries on the Tripitaka.

On the other side of the S stairway to Mandalay Hill is the **Kyauktawgyi Pagoda**. It was completed in 1878 by King Mindon and was originally styled on the Ananda Pagoda in Pagan. But the plan was interrupted by a palace rebellion in 1866, following the assassination of Prince Kanaung, and the Ananda design was dropped. The temple is well known for its Buddha image, carved out of a single block of pale green marble from the quarries of Sagyin, a few miles N of Mandalay. It was roughly hewn in the quarry and a canal was dug specially to bring the 800-tonne figure to Mandalay. It took 10,000 men 2 weeks to drag it to the pagoda. The Buddha's dress and shawl are inlaid with jewels... all of which are fake except the central diamond. Disappointing; gaudy decoration and the entrance is lined with tourist stalls. A week-long festival is held at the pagoda every Oct.

In 1945, it took a British Gurkha battalion a whole night to fight its way to the top of **Mandalay Hill** (236m), in the face of stiff Japanese resistance. Today, the hill's 1,729 steps take about 30 mins to climb (it is necessary to remove your shoes). The main stairway winds its way through a series of rather kitsch pagodas – there are 3 covered approaches to the hill. From a design perspective, Mandalay Hill ranks with Singapore's Tiger Balm Gardens as among the least tasteful pieces of landscape architecture in the region. The hill is scattered with shrines, many of which were the work of a pious hermit, U Khanti. Near the top of the hill stands the **Shweyattaw**, a huge image depict-

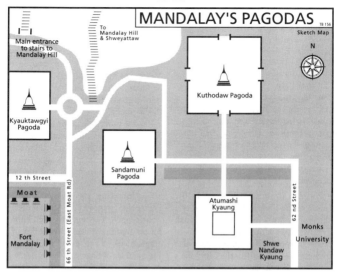

MANDALAY'S PAGODAS TB 156

Sketch Map

Main entrance to stairs to Mandalay Hill

To Mandalay Hill & Shweyattaw

N

Kyauktawgyi Pagoda

Kuthodaw Pagoda

12 th Street

Sandamuni Pagoda

Moat

62 nd Street

66 th Street (East Moat Rd)

Atumashi Kyaung

Monks University

Fort Mandalay

Shwe Nandaw Kyaung

ing the Buddha pointing towards the royal palace compound as the future centre of the capital. On this spot, the Buddha, accompanied by his disciple Ananda, is said to have prophesied the construction of a great religious city at the foot of the hill. It is an unusual image as the Gautama Buddha is normally portrayed in a mudra posture. From the top there is a good view over the town, the vast royal palace, and between the golf course and the river, to the W, the People's Brewery and Distillery, the national beer monopoly. On fine days the Shan Plateau can be seen to the NE, on the horizon beyond the military camp. It is possible to take a taxi to the top of the hill (500 kyats).

The main city of Mandalay is to the W and S of the palace grounds. Just off the W moat road on 24th St is the **Mandalay Museum** which houses an uninteresting collection of bits and pieces, including some royal garments which were probably those left behind by King Thibaw and Queen Supayalat when they were exiled by the British in 1885. Ad-

mission: US$3. Nearby, also on 24th St (between 82nd and 83rd sts), is the **Shwekyimyin Pagoda**. It was built in 1167 during the Pagan era by Prince Minshinzaw, an exiled son of King Alaungsithu. The temple still has the original Buddha image, which was consecrated in 1167, as well as a collection of gold, silver and crystal Buddha images – salvaged from the royal palace prior to the British occupation of Mandalay. Also on and around C Rd is the Zegyo Market, with a clocktower at its centre.

West of the market, and right on the riverbank at the end of C Rd (22nd St) is Kywezun – otherwise known as **Buffalo Point**. It is the main transit point for teak which is floated down the Irrawaddy; the logs are loaded onto ancient trucks using water buffalo. The trip down to Buffalo Point is highly recommended; the place belongs to another world, virtually unchanged in decades, and full of life. Apart from the odd truck, Bangkok must have looked like this a century ago. There is a small, but lively, market on the dyke nearby (built to protect the city from floods in the wet season).

To the S of C Rd is the interestingly named B Rd, which also runs E-W; to the W it becomes 26th St, which runs along the S moat. At its E end is the **Eindawya Pagoda**, built by King Pagan Min of Amarapura in 1847 on the site of his home before he became king. It is well proportioned and is gilded from top to bottom. The Buddha image is made from chalcedony, a combination of quartz and opal. The Eindawya Pagoda was the home of the 'Eindawya Column', a group of monks who briefly took over the running of the city in August 1988 when the country was in chaos. The Column was later broken up by the SLORC and its leaders arrested. Just E of the pagoda is the distinctive Zegyo Market (see page 631), which serves as a useful landmark.

Set Kyathiha Pagoda is S of Zegyo Market on 31st/85th sts. It contains a 5m-high bronze Buddha cast at Ava in 1814 by King Bagyidaw. It was moved to Amarapura by King Pagan in 1849 and brought to Mandalay in 1884. The pagoda had to be rebuilt after World War II, when it was badly damaged. The Bodhi tree at the entrance was planted by U Nu, the first Prime Minister of independent Burma.

Shwe In Bin, Pe Boke Ian St (S of 35th St) is one of the most interesting monasteries in Mandalay. A Chinese merchant, U Set Shwin, married a local Burmese lady and with his newly acquired fortune built a monastery for his religious wife. It is built of teak, has Burmese carved doors and paintings depicting General Prendergast negotiating with court ministers prior to King Thibaw's exile.

The **Mahamuni (or Arakan) Pagoda**, on 82nd St is in the S quarter of town on the road to Amarapura. The Arakanese – from Burma's W state, on the Bay of Bengal – discovered the Mahamuni Image in the jungle and restored it, keeping it in Arakan until 1784, where it acquired a magical aura and was revered as the guardian of the kingdom. Others believe it is an actual image of the Buddha himself. Archaeologists date it to around 146 AD during the reign of Chandra Suriya, when Buddhism spread to Arakan. In the 11th century, Pagan's King Anawrahta had raided Arakan with the intent of removing the Buddha to his capital, but failed to capture it. It was not until the late 18th century that 30,000 of King Bodawpaya's troops finally snatched it and brought it back to Amarapura where the king built a temple specially for it. A hundred years later, a fire destroyed the temple in which it was housed and it was then moved to the present site. The entrance arcade is packed with astrologers and palmists.

The 3.8m tall Mahamuni, or 'Great Sage', sits on a 2m-high podium covered in gold leaf in a posture symbolizing his calling the earth as witness in the face of temptation. The image is cast in bronze, but the original features have been blurred by millions of sheets of gold leaf which now form a layer more than 15 cm thick. The gilding covers the whole image other than the face itself – it even covers the chunks of ruby, sapphire and jade that originally adorned the chest and crown. There is a constant procession of pilgrims queueing up to cake the Buddha with tiny sheets of gold leaf which they buy for 10 kyat each. Women are not allowed into the inner sanctum and have to give their sheets of gold leaf to the men in charge of the Buddha's welfare. The image is believed to be alive – the face is said to have grown proportionally as the body has expanded under the layers of gold leaf. Photographs near the main shrine show the statue as it was 90 years ago, when the features were more precisely defined. The image's face is ceremonially washed every morning at 0500.

The Mahamuni Buddha image is the holiest shrine in Mandalay and greatly revered as it is believed to be a true likeness of the Gautama Buddha himself. The inner sanctum is very atmospheric, packed with worshippers and pilgrims praying, toying with their beads and chanting. The women's area is partitioned off, set back about 6m from the area where monks and laymen swarm around the image.

In the inner courtyard there are hundreds of stone slabs inscribed with copies of inscriptions recording religious endowments. Also within the precinct, N of the main pagoda, are 6 bronze figures: 2 warriors, 3 lions and a 3-headed elephant, all central to an extraordinary slice of history. They were brought from Arakan by King Bodawpaya at the same time as he captured the Mahamuni Image. The Arakanese King Razagyi had removed the statues from the Burmese kingdom of Pegu, 120 years earlier. The Burmese had originally taken them from the Siamese capital of Ayutthaya and the Siamese in their turn had looted them from Angkor Wat, Cambodia in 1431. The statues, which date from the 12th century, are said to possess healing powers – pilgrims can be seen touching the part of the statue that corresponds to the area of their affliction. The sheen on the metal suggests that the most common complaint in Mandalay is stomach ache.

The 1960s gallery on the far side of the courtyard has a series of paintings showing how Bodawpaya's army returned with the image. On the edge of the compound, steps lead up to a viewing balcony overlooking a gigantic neon-lit, technicolour, 3-dimensional map of the Buddhist world. Also in the complex is a small museum with a display of statues and Buddha images. The main entrance to the pagoda is busy with shops selling religious paraphernalia as well as lacquerware and embroidery. Admission: US$4.

The **artisan guilds** in the S of the city, not far from the Mahamuni Pagoda, are the backbone of Burma's craft industry. The guilds were set up by King Mindon when Mandalay was under construction. They are still going today and include alabaster, marble and wood-carving guilds, and others for bronze casting and the production of gold leaf.

A **silk weaving factory** can be visited on the corner of 62nd and 19th sts. Young girls sit in dimly lit rooms, making up rather gaudy designs in silk (all the dyes are synthetic now). There are 30 or so set designs and the girls learn to memorize 4 or 5 of them. In the days when the Royal Family was 500-strong, silk was much in demand. Today, however, almost all work is done to order and the client chooses the colours laid down by an astrological adviser.

Excursions

Amarapura, see page 632; **Ava**, see page 633; **Sagaing**, see page 635; river trip to **Mingun**, see page 637.

Festivals

Oct: *Elephant Dancing Festival* in Kyaukse (S of Mandalay).

Local information

● **Orientation**

The city is built on a grid, with numbered streets running N-S and E-W as well as 4 alphabetically named roads running from the centre of the city down to the left bank of the Irrawaddy. In 1981 a fire gutted the NW quarter of town, and this area is still being rebuilt. The town 'centre' is SW of the moat – centred around Zegyo market. Most of the guesthouses and restaurants are in this area and buses to surrounding towns leave from the market. The railway station is on the main road S, which also goes to the airport. The larger, more expensive, hotels are in the area to the S of the fort. The W is known as the 'town side' and the E the 'country side'.

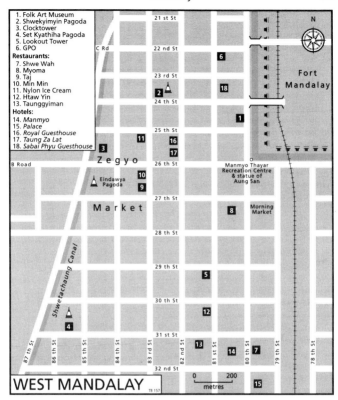

1. Folk Art Museum
2. Shwekyimyin Pagoda
3. Clocktower
4. Set Kyathiha Pagoda
5. Lookout Tower
6. GPO
Restaurants:
7. Shwe Wah
8. Myoma
9. Taj
10. Min Min
11. Nylon Ice Cream
12. Htaw Yin
13. Taunggyiman
Hotels:
14. *Manmyo*
15. *Palace*
16. *Royal Guesthouse*
17. *Taung Za Lat*
18. *Sabai Phyu Guesthouse*

21 st St
22 nd St
23 rd St
24 th St
25 th St
26 th St
27 th St
28 th St
29 th St
30 th St
31 st St
32 nd St

C Rd
B Road
Z e g y o
M a r k e t
Eindawya Pagoda
Shwetachaung Canal

Fort Mandalay
Manmyo Thayar Recreation Centre & statue of Aung San
Morning Market

87 th St
86 th St
85 th St
84 th St
83 rd St
82 nd St
81 st St
80 th St
79 th St
78 th St

WEST MANDALAY
TB 157

0   200
metres

● **Accommodation**

Dismal choice of hotels in Mandalay – the 'top' government hotels are all badly run – you are better off staying in cheaper, private guesthouses.

A-B *Tiger Hotel*, 628 82nd St (between 36th and 37th sts), T 23134, a/c, h/w, no charm but slightly better than government-run place in Mandalay; **A-B** *Hotel Venus*, 22 28th St (between 80th and 81st sts), T 25612.

B *Mandalay*, 26th St/3rd St, T 22499, a/c, restaurant, bar, MTT office, money-changing facilities, tour groups often stay at this hotel but it has gone downhill in recent years, there is talk of the *Mandalay* undergoing restoration in the next couple of years; **B** *In Wa*, near *Karaweik Restaurant*, one block from the SE corner of the moat, a/c, restaurant, copy of

Thiripyitsaya in Pagan, with teak floors and verandahs, it is known locally as the 'gold hotel' as its main patrons are wealthy local gemstone miners, best of the top end hotels.

C *Golden Express Hotel*, 43 9th St, same owners as the *Golden Express* in Pagan – one of the better bets in Mandalay; **C** *Mya Mandala*, 26B Rd, T 21283, a/c, restaurant, pool, better value than the Mandalay with its own – deserted – swimming pool, the outside sitting area, between the rooms and the dining area is a pleasant place for an evening drink; **C** *Sabai Phyu*, 58 81st St (between 25th and 26th sts), T 25377, a/c, basic rooms but clean, noisy as in the centre of town (quieter rooms on top floor), geared up for travellers with cars for hire, pet money changers, etc; **C** *Sapphire*, 223 83rd St (between 28th and 29th sts),

T 27327, attached bathroom, breakfast included, satellite TV, rec; **C Si Thu**, 29 65th St (between 30th and 31st sts), T 26201, fan only, family house in a small compound with only a few rooms, well kept and friendly, will cook meals on request, best value in Mandalay; **C Taung Za Lat**, 60 81st St, T 23210, opposite *Sabai Phyu* and much the same set up but not as friendly; **C Venus**, 28th St (between 80th and 81st sts), T 25612; **C Mandalay Royal Guesthouse** (moving location), clean, popular with travellers.

● **Places to eat**

Restaurants in the main hotels serve standard European and Burmese food.

Burmese: ♦♦♦*Aung San*, 82nd St, between 33rd and 34th sts, well known for its fried pork; ♦♦♦*Sa Kham Thar*, 24 72nd St (between 27th and 28th sts), slightly more expensive than average but has a terrace and garden, rec; ♦♦♦*Too Too*, 27th St, between 74th and 75th sts, considered best Burmese food in town, very popular with locals, delicious fish curry, but meat is not so good, arrive early, before food runs out, closing down 2000, rec; ♦♦*Sa Kham Thar*, good Burmese fare; ♦♦*Taung Gyi Mar*, 193, 31st St (between 81st and 82nd sts), don't be put off by surroundings, good selection of Shan dishes, run by a friendly family; *Ya Manya*, opposite railway station on 30th Rd, rec by locals for its Burmese breakfast, *Mo Hen Ngar*, comprised of hot-and-sour vegetable soup with onion and rice noodles laced with fish paste.

Chinese: (The whole of central Mandalay is now Chinatown since the Sino-Burmese drug war lords moved in.) ♦♦♦♦*Honey*, 70th St, (between 28th and 29th sts – N side of soccer stadium), the *Honey restaurant* – which advertises with big hand-painted pictures of 'honeys' is reckoned to be about the best in town with prices to match, outside eating area; ♦♦♦♦*Lucky Hotel*, 84th St, near 35th St, the first Chinese high-rise hotel, a roof-top restaurant has a bar, cabaret and sky-high prices (1 dish min); ♦♦♦♦-♦♦♦*Pyigyimon Royal Barge*, SE corner of moat, Chinese food, lots of fish, government-run, not rated by locals; ♦♦♦-♦♦*Htaw Yin*, 396 81st St (between 30th and 31st sts), large menu, ask to sit upstairs; ♦♦♦*Shan Family*, 80th St, between 28th and 29th sts, rec by locals; ♦♦♦*Shwe Nung Daw*, 110 73rd St (between 28th and 29th sts), clean, rec by locals; ♦♦*Min Min*, 194 83rd St, between 26th and 27th sts, Chinese and Burmese dishes, no beer; ♦♦*Shwe Let Yar*, 226 83rd St (between 27th and 28th sts), rec by travellers, average Chinese nosh, serves beer.

Foodstalls: Next to the railway station; 26th St near Zeygo market; *Hpeq-Htouq-Kyaw*, corner of 30th and 80th St, outdoor stall specializing in *hpeq-htonq-kyaw*, pork wrapped in dough and fried, then dipped in sauce of ginger and corriander, very popular in evenings, rec, (kosher versions available), 15 kyat per plate.

Indian: ♦♦*Everest*, 27th Rd (next to temple), good vegetarian Pungabi dishes, no beer; *Taj*, 194 83rd St (between 26th and 27th sts), Biriyani, Chinese dishes and Burmese food to order, friendly owner and reasonable nosh.

Shan: *Lashio Shan*, 23rd St, between 84th and 85th sts, full of Shan gem dealers, try the water lily root and a variety of sausages.

Snacks: *Nylon Ice Cream*, 83rd St, between 25th and 26th sts, home-made custard rec; *Flowers World Ice Cream*, 84th St, near Mahamuni Pagoda; ♦♦*Shells*, 26th St (between 81st and 82nd sts), good breakfasts.

● **Airline offices**

Myanmar Airways office on corner of 25th Rd and 80th St.

● **Banks & money changers**

Mandalay Hotel for currency exchange (official rate). The black market rate in Mandalay is often as good as or better than Rangoon's. **Myanma Economic Bank** is on 26th St (at the SW corner of the palace wall).

● **Entertainment**

State School of Fine Art, Music and Drama just off the E moat rd. Dances often based on stories from the life of Buddha and from the Hindu epic, the Ramayana. Visitors can watch students practising. Closed: Apr. *J Mandalay Marionettes*, Garden Villa Theatre, 66th St (between 26th and 27th sts).

● **Hospitals & medical services**

Mandalay's People's Hospital is one block from the railway station, near 77th St and 30th Rd.

● **Post & telecommunications**

General Post Office: near the intersection of 81st and 22nd sts. **Area code**: 02.

● **Shopping**

Mandalay has a strong tradition of handicrafts which originally supplied the royal courts. Many of the cottage handicraft industries are run by the same families.

Buddha images: in the area around Maha-muni Pagoda.

Gold Leaf & Ivory Workshops: group on 36th St, between 77th and 78th sts.

Handicrafts: most handicraft stalls are found around the Mahamuni temple. *Mann Shwe Gon*, 45 28th/73rd sts – a craft shop with a range of *kalaga* (tapestry), puppets, teak opium-scale boxes. Bargain hard or barter Western goods.

Marble: most of the marble-carvers are found on 84th St on the way out to Amarapura, about 1 km from the city centre.

Markets: *Zegyo Market*, on 84th St, 3 km N of Mahamuni Pagoda; one of Burma's biggest markets, designed by an Italian, Count Caldrari, who was first Secretary of the Mandalay municipality, in 1903. Primary market for Chins, Kachins and Shans. Local produce, hardware and black-market goods from Thailand. The building, whose style is reminiscent of 1960s-vintage Russian architecture, is eventually to be demolished and rebuilt with Burmese-style blocks. Part of it has already been knocked down to make way for redevelopment, which should finish in late 1993. There's a small, but lively, market – *Mingala Market* – on the corner of 73rd and 30th sts, it gets very busy in the evening. *Night market* on 84th St (between 26th and 28th sts), on the W side of the railway yard, starts 1800.

Precious stones: second rate stones in *Zegyo Market* (all the best stones are exported or sold to the Diplomatic Store in Rangoon for US dollars).

Silk weaving: Mandalay and Amarapura are the most important weaving centres in Burma and produce the famous *acheik* – horizontal weave patterned silk which was popular with royalty – and a highly prized silk (about 9,000 kyats for a length). *Daw Supplies & Son*, Eastern Town Nandawshei, Sagaingdan Quarter, factory and shop. Gets many VIP visitors. *Acheik Lunyargyaw* on 62nd St, off 19th St, T 22617, fine textiles; silk weavers in the street opposite the E entrance to Mandalay Palace. Or at Amarapura.

Tapestry (*kalaga*): *Tin Maung OO*, 26, 72nd St (W of Municipal Office) workshop and shop, good quality; *U Sein Myint*, 42 Sangha University Rd (62nd St), made *kalaga* for the UN HQ in New York, his house is a miniature museum for Burmese handicrafts; *Sein Win Myint*, 273 St (between 26th and 27th sts and

83rd and 84th sts, owner speaks good English.

Woodcarving: most of the woodcarvers are on 84th St, on the road out to Amarapura, close to the marble-carving area. Most of the carvings are sold in stalls around the Mahamuni Pagoda. *Pam Mya*, on road from Mandalay to Sagaing is renowned as a woodcarver and sculptor in Mandalay. Specializes in Buddha images. *U Win Maung*, 181/47 Htidan, Tampawaddy (just S of the Mahamuni) is directing the restoration of the palace and is probably the best wood carver.

● **Tourist offices**

MTT desk at the railway station, T 22541 (open 1400-1600 Mon-Sun) and at the palace. The main office is in the Mandalay Hotel, 26th St/3rd St, T 22540, open 0800-2000 Mon-Sun, ticket sales until 1400. Bookings, travel information and currency exchange.

● **Transport**

580 km N of Rangoon.

Local Bicycle rickshaw: prices negotiable, same price to take 2 people on one rickshaw, as 2 rickshaws with one on each. Rickshaw driver, Maung Maung Toe, based outside the *Mandalay Hotel* is a good source of information. Bargain on basis of 150 kyat/day; 20-30 kyat for trips from main hotels into town. Note that rickshaws cannot travel on all the roads. **Buses**: buses around town are very crowded. Most leave from Zegyo Market for areas surrounding Mandalay. Public buses going up Mandalay Hill leave from Mahamuni Pagoda (5 kyat). The buses stop running at 1700. **Car hire**: ask at hotels – especially cheaper ones around the market. **Pony cart**: best way to get around town; cheap: approximately 75 kyat for half a day. Drivers often act as guides. **Taxi**: there are usually taxis outside the main hotels and Zegyo market. Always negotiate fare in advance (around 60 kyat/hr). Probably the best way to see sights around Mandalay. *Thounbein* literally means '3 wheels' (like Thai *saamlor*): they are the small orange taxis which make a terrible noise – they have been banished from Rangoon because of the noise and air pollution they caused. Cheaper than taxis – about 500 kyat/day, dawn to dusk. **Tram**: a new tram system, opened in 1990, runs around the city. It was built at the instigation of General Ne Win who decided that the project would be sufficiently grandiose to upset an astrologer's prediction that his time in power would end after 26 years.

Air Airport is on the S side of town, on the Rangoon road. Regular connections with Rangoon and Nyaung-U, Pagan. Flights to Heho (for Inle Lake area), every Mon, Thur, Sat.

Train Station is in the S of Mandalay palace area, on 78th St. Ordinary trains leave for Rangoon daily; smarter 'special' trains leave on Mon, Thur, Sat. Leave Rangoon at 1700 and arrive Mandalay early the next morning (14 hrs).

Road Bus: regular connections with Pagan (2 hrs), Taunggyi (10 hrs) – a very uncomfortable journey.

Sea The downriver trip from Mandalay to Pagan takes a full day – it can take anything up to 2 or 3 days the other way. Not advisable during the dry season as boats can be marooned on sandbanks; others have sunk on collision with sandbanks in the dark. The twice-weekly boat leaves Mandalay from Minbu at 0500 and arrives at Pagan around 1830, Thur & Sun. There are also smaller boats, with deck-only seats.

AROUND MANDALAY

Amarapura

When King Bodawpaya came to the throne in 1782, he dismantled his capital at Ava and founded Amarapura on the advice of court astrologers. His grandson and successor, Bagyidaw, moved back to Ava in 1823. King Tharawaddy (1837-1846), who succeeded Bagyidaw, took the capital back to Amarapura and then Mindon Min founded Mandalay in 1857. One reason for his moving the capital from Amarapura was its susceptibility to flooding; boats could sail straight up to the city putting the royal capital within range of British artillery fire.

Unlike Mandalay, there is little indication of where the royal city once stood and all that remains are the 4 pagodas which marked the 4 corners of the city walls, the watch tower and the treasury building. The military now occupies the site of the original palace. The city was laid out in a square, with a moat surrounding the brick walls. There were 12 gates in the city walls, above which there would have been wooden pavilions. Most of the palace buildings were removed, in their entirety, to Mandalay by King Mindon. Even the bricks of the fort walls have been used for building roads and railway tracks locally.

Today Amarapura has a population of 26,000 whose main livelihood is weaving cotton and silk.

Places of interest

One of the main sights at Amarapura is the **U Bein Bridge** – a 1.2 km-long wooden bridge over the seasonal **Taungthaman Lake**, to the S of the city. It was built by the city's mayor, U Bein, in 1784 and used to have rest houses along its length. It is mainly constructed of teak planks salvaged from the ruins of the royal city of Ava. The lake dries up in winter, leaving fertile arable land for paddy farming and temporary brick factories. When the lake is full, the walkway is only a few feet above the surface. The sturdy teak pillars and the structural timbers are still strong, considering their age, although some of the planks are in need of replacement. King Pagin Min ordered the bridge to be built but charged the 'contractor', U Bein, with fraud for cutting corners by using beams and pillars from the former palace at Ava, which were abandoned when the capital moved to Amarapura. The bridge is an excellent place to meet monks from the nearby monastery and to sample toddy, a spirit distilled from the toddy palm and sold in the shelters. During the rainy season (Jul-Sept), it is possible to walk across the bridge and hire a rowing boat back. In the dry season a local delicacy, roasted paddy field rats, are sold on the bridge.

At the far end of the bridge there are several stalls in the shade of the trees – often selling local delicacies such as barbecued rats – and beyond them stands **Kyauktawgyi Pagoda**. It was built in 1847 by King Pagan Min and modelled on the Ananda Pagoda in Pagan. It is now in a rural area but the pagoda once marked the edge of Amarapura. There is one Buddha image inside carved from a single block of Sagyin marble, which looks almost like jade. Within the shrine there are 88 statues of the Buddha's disciples, as well as 12 *manusihas* – or mythical figures, half-man, half-beast. The walls of the porches are covered with 18th century paintings depicting scenes from Burmese life and other religious buildings from around the country. Taungthaman village is a typical Burmese village, without electricity, whose inhabitants make a living from weaving and selling toddy.

On the other side of the bridge is the **Mahagandayon** Monastery, the largest in Burma with over 1,000 monks during lent and about 700 at other times. It was founded in the early 1950s and follows the original teachings of the Buddha and has very high academic standards. Monks come from all over the country to study here.

The **Path Hto Dawgyi Pagoda,** near the S wall, outside the city, was built by King Bagyidaw in 1819. Scenes from the jataka stories cover the 3 lower terraces. There is also a large bronze bell in the precincts. Apart from this pagoda's size, it does not contain any relics and is not particularly noteworthy other than for the fact that it marks the SW corner of the old city of Amarapura.

Kwa Yen Chinese Temple nearby was built in 1773 by Chinese missionaries on a site granted to them by the king. The original building burned down in 1810 and its replacement went up in flames 19 years later. This structure dates from 1847. Its ornate classical Chinese-style roofs are typically gaudy but there is a collection of rather nice marble-topped tables in the courtyard. The temple is maintained by Mandalay's 20,000-strong Chinese business community. It is not necessary to take your shoes off in the temple precincts.

All that remains of the former royal palace of Amarapura is the yellow stuccoed treasury building and record office, which was built during the reign of King Tharrawaddy (1837-1846). Formerly it had been topped by a gilt pavilion which served as a belvedere – a room with a view. Nearby is the old watchtower and the tombs of King Bodawpaya and his grandson, King Bagyidaw.

Some of the villages around Amarapura are known for their weaving; the village of **Kyi Tun Khat** is renowned for its bronze Buddha statues.

Excursions

On the road S from Mandalay there is a turn-off to the right just before the Ava bridge, which leads to the **Shwekyet Yet** (Golden Cock Scratches) and **Shwekyet Kya** (Golden Cock Falls) pagodas, so called because the Buddha is reputed to have lived there in a previous incarnation. The Shwekyet Yet pagoda is a cluster of stupas clinging to a high cliff over the Irrawaddy. It is most beautiful at sunset when a boat can be hired (for about 30 kyat) to go on the river and watch the sun set behind the Ava bridge and Sagaing hills.

● **Transport** 12 km S of Mandalay.
Local Pony traps: can be hired for 75-100 kyat for a half-day.
Road Bus: bus 8 leaves from the Zegyo market (B Rd/84th St, Mandalay) every half-hour.

Ava (In-Wa)

Located at the confluence of the Irrawaddy and the Myitnge (Dokhtawadi) rivers, Ava lies to the SW of Amarapura. The city was founded by the Shan King Thadominbya in 1364 and it remained a royal capital for a good part of the next 5 centuries, until it was finally abandoned in favour of Amarapura in 1782. During its first 300 years, Ava continually came under attack from the Mons from Pegu and the Burmans from Toungoo, and was occupied, for a time, by both. Ava's classical name is Ratnapura, the 'City of Gems', and locally it is known as In-Wa.

After founding the city in 1364, King Thadominbya led an expedition against the Mons, who had established themselves at Pegu after the fall of Pagan in 1287, but he died on the way. Ava's war of attrition with the Mons of Pegu became a recurring theme. Thadominbya was succeeded by Minkyiswa-sawke, a descendant of Pagan's Anawrahta Dynasty, who extended Ava's suzerainty as far as Prome. He launched another invasion of Pegu – but it failed too and there followed decades of continued struggle between the 2 kingdoms, with the Burmans of Toungoo caught in the middle. Today, Burmese traditional drama still re-enacts these epic struggles between kings Minkhaung, his son Minye-kyawswa of Ava and King Razadarit of Pegu. Minkhaung died in 1422 and shortly afterwards, King Razadarit was killed on a hunting expedition; after their deaths there was a lull in the struggle for supremacy.

In the meantime the Burman kingdom of Toungoo was on the ascendency: it emerged as an important kingdom when Tabengshweti came to the throne in 1530. He led a successful attack on Pegu in 1533 and the Mon king fled to Prome. But King Tabinshweti followed up with a raid on Prome, and when it fell he was recognized as the undisputed ruler of Lower Burma. 22 years later, his son, King Bayinnaung went on to capture Ava, breaking the power of the Shan kings. Ava became a tributary state of the Burman Empire. Then, in 1636, Toungoo's King Thalun moved to Ava, and it became the capital of the Burman kingdom. But their power lasted just over a century: the Mons sacked and destroyed Ava in 1752, carrying off its king as captive to Pegu, marking the end of the Toungoo Dynasty.

The following year, Alaungpaya, a deputy in Shwebo, to the N of Ava, gathered local support in defiance of Ava's Mon conquerors, and retook the capital, sending the Mons fleeing for their lives. Alaungpaya declared himself king and founded the third and final Burmese dynasty, which he ruled from Shwebo and then Ava. His son, Hsinbyushin, made Ava his capital as did his successor, King Singu Min. When Bodawpaya came to the throne in 1782, he moved the capital to Amarapura, but the next king, Bagyidaw, moved back to Ava again. On many old European maps from this period, Burma was known as Ava. In 1838, the city was virtually destroyed by an earthquake and it was finally abandoned 3 years later by Shwebo Min, in favour of Amarapura.

The city is bounded on the N by the Irrawaddy and on the E by the Myitnge. On the S and W, a canal links the 2 rivers. Ava's fortifications are unlike those of any other Burmese city in that its walls are zig-zagged. The royal palace was not in the middle either – it was positioned in the NE quarter of the city. There were 3 periods of building at Ava, first by King Nyaungyan Min in 1597, then by King Hsinbyushin in 1763 and finally by King Bagyidaw in 1832. Today, there are villages within the city area and most of the ruins are overgrown. The remains of the moat and the fort walls can still be seen as can a small part of the palace and several pagodas.

Places of interest

The **Nanmyin**, in the NE section of the old city, is all that remains of Bagyidaw's palace. The upper part of the 30m-high masonry watch tower was destroyed by the 1838 earthquake. The lower part leans to one side, lending it the nickname of the 'leaning tower of Ava'.

The **Maha Aungmye Bonzan** monastery, was built by King Bagyidaw's chief queen for the royal abbot Nyaunggan Sayadaw (rumoured to have been her lover) in 1818. Constructed of brick and stucco, its design simulates that of wooden monasteries, with multiple roofs and a prayer hall with a 7-tiered superstructure. It has fine decorations and carvings. It was also damaged by the 1838 earthquake but was repaired by one of King Mindon's wives in 1873. Within the compound is the Adoniram Judson Memorial. Dr Judson was an American missionary who compiled the First Anglo-Burmese Bible. He was jailed on the site of the memorial stone during the First Anglo-Burmese War in 1824 – the Burmese did not distinguish between Americans and British – and died after being tortured. His name lives on in the Judson Baptist Church in Mandalay, which – according to the sign outside – "opposes liberalism, modernism, ecumenism, formalism and worldliness".

The city walls are in good repair near the **Gaung Say Daga**, or N gate. This 'Gate of the Hair-Washing', was where the king had his hair washed in a ceremony of public purification during the Thingyan Festival in April.

The **Bagaya Kyaung** monastery has ornate wood carvings, and is built of 267 teak posts. The main hall stands on a raised platform, separate from the monk's quarters, and is designed so that the space between the walls and roof allows air to circulate. It is set in the middle of the Le Daw Gyee – the royal ricefields.

Htilaingshin Pagoda was built by King Kyanzittha of Pagan.

A 15-min walk S of the old walled city are the ruins of the **Ava Fort**, built during the reign of King Mindon. It forms a triad with the Sagaing Fort on the opposite bank and the Thabyedan Fort near the Ava bridge. An old brick causeway leads from the S city gate towards the town of Tada-U, which is near Panya, and which, for a short time, was the capital of the early Shan kingdom.

● **Shopping Lacquerware**: there is a small factory within the old walled city, where black begging bowls are made.

● **Transport** 20 km SW of Mandalay.
Road Bus: bus 8 goes to Sagaing and passes through Amarapura and Ava.

Sagaing

Sagaing is on the right bank of the Irrawaddy, on the other side of the river from Ava, and is widely regarded as the religious centre of Burma. It is popularly known as 'Little Pagan' as the Sagaing ridge is crowded with around 600 pagodas and monasteries in which there are more than 3,000 monks. There are nearly 100 meditation centres in the Sagaing area.

After the fall of Pagan, Athinkhaya Sawyun, a Shan chieftain, founded Sagaing in 1315. It was the Shan capital for just 49 years, as King Thadominbya moved to Ava in 1364. Naungdawgyi, King Alaungpaya's eldest son, moved back to Sagaing for 4 years in the early 1760s but when he died, Ava reverted to being the capital. Many Burmese fled into the hills and caves in and around Sagaing when the Japanese invaded in 1942. The people – and monks – of Sagaing also suffered at the hands of the military in the brutal clamp-down on the 1988 anti-government demonstrations. Countless unidentified bodies were dumped in the Irrawaddy.

Places of interest

The 732m-long **Ava Bridge** is the only bridge in the whole country to cross the Irrawaddy River. Even though it is called the Ava Bridge it does not actually pass through Ava, but goes from Amarapura to Sagaing. It was built by the British in 1934 and was then blown up by them 8 years later – the central portion was sabotaged in a bid to stop the Japanese advance in 1942. This section was rebuilt, the 2 sides rejoined and the bridge reopened in 1954. It connects Ava with Sagaing, affording a good view of Ava's white pagoda, and the hills on the far bank. Photographing the bridge itself is strictly prohibited.

At the foot of the bridge are the ruins of **Thabyedan Fort**. Burmese forces mounted their final resistance here against British forces in the Third Anglo-Burmese war in 1886.

There is a good view of Sagaing from the bridge but the best vantage point to view Sagaing's sprawling forest of pagodas is from **Shin Bin Man Kai**, a hill overlooking the Irrawaddy, on which stands **Pon Nya Shin**, a golden pagoda. The hill can be climbed from a village known as Sagaing's Hton Bo Quarter – a good spot for sunset.

Htupayon was built by Narapatigyi (1443-1469) of Ava. Destroyed by the earthquake of 1838, King Pagan Min began reconstruction in 1849, but it was left unfinished when he was dethroned. It has a circular plan, with 3 concentric storeys with arched niches. In a nearby hut are a collection of stone engravings, which include the history of the Shan Prince Thonganbwa.

Aungmyelawka Pagoda is on the river by the hospital and close to the Htupayon. It was erected by Bodawpaya (1782-1819) on the site of his home before he became king. It is built of sandstone and based on Shwezigon Pagoda at Pagan. It is also known as the Eindawya Pagoda.

Ngadatkyi Pagoda, to the W of town, was built in 1657 by Pindale, who succeeded his father King Thalun and contains a large seated Buddha image. Pindale was unceremoniously dethroned by his brother in 1661 and a few weeks later was drowned together with his whole family. This was a fairly standard method of putting royalty to death so that no blood was spilt on the soil. The practice of disposing of all rival heirs was also fairly commonplace throughout Burmese history (see page 523).

Hsinmyashin Pagoda, the 'Elephant Pagoda', between Sagaing and Kaungmudaw, enshrines some relics from Ceylon (Sri Lanka) and was built by King Monhyin of Ava in 1429. Its gates are guarded by 6m-high pachyderms, which failed to protect it from an earthquake in 1485 (after which it was repaired) and another, which totally destroyed the pagoda in 1955. Its reconstruction has been progressing in recent years. The contents of its relic chamber – votive tablets and Buddha images – are on display.

There are hundreds of pagodas scattered over the Sagaing hills; some of the other more noteworthy ones are: the **Ponnyashin Zedi**, said to contain 2 relics of Buddha, the **Padamya Zedi**, built by a monk called Padugyi Thingayaza in 1300 and the **Onhmin Thonze** (Thirty Caves) pagoda which enshrine a large collection of Buddha images in a crescent-shaped colonnade on the hillside. The Tilawkaguru cave temple is said to have been built in 1672 by King Narawara of the second dynasty of Ava and contains rare mural paintings depicting scenes from the former incarnations of the Buddha.

Khaunghmudaw Pagoda is 10 km to the N of the town and is Sagaing's most important temple. It was built by King Thalun in 1636 and styled after a Ceylonese (Sri Lankan) pagoda in commemoration of the re-establishment of Ava as the royal capital. It was constructed to house tooth and hair relics formerly kept in the Mahazedi Pagoda in Pegu. It is composed of 3 circular terraces and a huge, brightly white-washed dome, which – at 46m high – is the biggest in the country. In local lore, the well-proportioned dome is said to represent the ample bosom of Thalun's chief queen. A marble inscription, 2.6m high, which records the details of the pagoda's construction, is well preserved in a masonry shed. In niches around the outside of the base are 120 images of nats. The main hall is like a Buddhist disco. Each entrance is studded with mirrors and coloured tiles and the images – which come from ruins in the area – are adorned with flashing green and red neon haloes.

In Nov, at the full moon, people come from 60 villages in the area to celebrate the Khaunghmudaw annual festival. There is a colourful pageant and involves lots of dressing-up. Pilgrims also come to celebrate the end of Buddhist lent at the pagoda. But apart from the occasional festival, the Khaunghmudaw is usually deserted; there is a Burmese saying which goes: "People prefer to worship in golden pagodas." Admission: US$3.

The Sagaing area – especially in Ywataung – is renowned for its silversmiths. **U Ba Thi Silversmith** factory, on the road from Sagaing to Khaungmudaw (just before the 53rd Light Infantry Battalion camp) has a workshop and shop specializing in the crafting of ceremonial silver bowls. U Ba Thi also has a shop at the *Inya Lake Hotel* in Rangoon.

● **Transport** 21 km SW of Mandalay.
Road Bus: from various stops in Mandalay, 29th St/83rd St.

Mingun

Having enlarged his kingdom to include Arakan, captured the Mahamuni Image and founded the capital at Amarapura, King Bodawpaya set about constructing the biggest pagoda in the world on the banks of the Irrawaddy. But on his death, in 1819, his project was abandoned. Bodawpaya's vast building site is now the main sight at Mingun, which is a favourite destination for locals from Mandalay. It is an enjoyable river trip. In the dry season there are fishing communities on the islands and the river is busy with boats transporting sand to Mandalay for building, and bamboo rafts floating downstream from the Chinese border areas for sale as roofing material.

Places of interest

On the W bank of the Irrawaddy, the **Mingun Pagoda** (also known as the Mantara Gyi Pagoda) would have been the biggest in Burma if it had been completed – it was to be 150m high. It was the brainchild of the mad King Bodawpaya (4th son of Alaungpaya) but was left unfinished after his death in 1819; it was also damaged by the 1838 earthquake. Even as it stands, it is the largest brick base in the world, the bottom terrace being a square, each side being 137m long. More than 20,000 Arakanese slaves were put to work on the pagoda. Each side is hollowed out to accommodate a small shrine in an archway. The only one now used faces the river. The terraces above the obelisk have small square panels which were intended to have glazed plaques on them showing scenes from the 5 Buddhist synods. About 500m S of the Mingun Pagoda is a small model (5m high), the Bodawpaya, designed as a working model for the real one.

The **Mingun bell** (to the N of the pagoda), weighing 90 tonnes, was cast by the lost-wax process on Nandaw Island, and commissioned by King Bodawpaya in 1790 for his big new pagoda. It was transported across the Irrawaddy on 2 boats (now in the Sagaing Fort Museum). The bell was originally hung on teak uprights, but these gave way during the 1838 earthquake. It is said to be the largest uncracked bell in the world – the biggest, although flawed, is in Moscow.

To the N of the pagoda is the **Hsinbyume Pagoda** (or the Myatheindan Pagoda), built by Bagyidaw (Bodawpaya's grandson) in 1816 in memory of his wife, Hsinbyume. It is in the form of the Sulamani Pagoda resting on Mount Meru, the centre of the earth according to Buddhist cosmography. The 7 terraces represent the 7 seas of Buddhist cosmology and around the terrace base are niches housing nats, ogres and nagas. The modern-looking image in the main shrine at the top of the pagoda hides a much older one.

On the river bank to the S is the **Settawya Pagoda**, which contains a marble footprint of the Buddha. Completed in 1811, it was the first pagoda built by King Bodawpaya in Mingun. There are several large monasteries at Mingun, one of which supports elderly men and women with no families (nearest the village jetty).

● **Transport** 12 km N of Mandalay.
Sea Take a boat from the Ma Yan Chan jetty at the end of B Road (26th St), which takes 1-1½ hrs to reach Mingun. Or you can hire your own boat for 700 kyat. There are two landing places; one is a 15 min walk across a field, the other is in the middle of the village. Last boat back to Mandalay departs 1600.

Kyaukse

Kyaukse is probably most famous for its **elephant dancing festival** in Oct and the entrance to the town is dominated by two elephant statues.

The town's most sacred pagoda is the **Shwemokhtaw**. Half way up Shwthalyaoung Hill is the Kyaukthinbaw, an unusual temple built in the shape of a ship. It is a meditation centre and is surrounded by 19 Buddha images called Labamuni which are supposed to bring worshippers great wealth.

Yankintaung

East of Mandalay is a sacred hill called Yankintaung, or 'Hill that is Free From Danger'. Of the Buddha's 547 previous incarnations 136 were spent as animals on this hill. People come especially to worship the four stone fish and the Buffalo stupa, surrounded by 8 statues of buffaloes to represent the Buddha's previous reincarnations as this creature.

Paleik

Paleik is comparable to Pagan with its 325 stupas. The best known temple Mwepaya or Snake Pagoda has a live python in the precinct. When the temple site was originally excavated 3 pythons were found curled round a Buddha statue. One of these pythons was female, and it's one of her offspring which inhabits the Mwepaya. The snake is fed every Saturday.

Maymyo

Maymyo (Pyin U Lwin) is Burma's best known colonial hill station and dates from the 1900s. The British called it Maytown, after Colonel May, who crushed a rebellion in the area after the Third Anglo-Burmese War in 1886. Maymyo served as the British colonial summer capital and the town was almost exclusively British. It stands on a plateau, 1,000m up in the Shan Hills, and is still a popular retreat for senior ministers and generals – Ne Win, for example, the old dictator of Burmese politics, has a summer house here. The Burmese army maintains a large garrison in Maymyo. A number of Indian and Nepali Gurkhas who entered the country with the British-Indian army live in Maymyo. The town is growing fast as it is on the main road. Lashio, the capital of northern Shan State and more significantly on the China road. With the increased trade with China, it is now an important outpost. Along the Lashio road there are lines of Japanese cars which are smuggled across the Chinese frontier. The Japanese impose a strict limit on the number of vehicles exported direct to China. To bypass this formality Japanese cars are sold via Burma.

Some parts of the town were badly damaged during World War II and have not been rebuilt; the rest of the town, with its brick and timber houses – complete with English-style gables, turrets and chimneys – remains as a ghost-like memento of empire. Most of the houses are mock-Tudor and have names like 'The Gables' and 'Fernside'. **Candacraig**, on a hill above the town, is the central attraction; it was the old R&R centre for the Bombay Burmah Trading Company, which logged teak in Upper Burma, and was built in 1905. It is often called the 'Thiri Myaing' or 'Magnificent corpse', and still serves English food including early morning tea. Even Maymyo's churches are classically de-

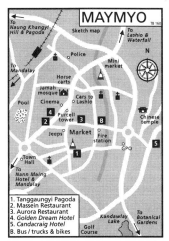

MAYMYO TB 160
Sketch map

To Naung Khangyi Hill & Pagoda

To Lashio & Waterfall

Police

To Mandalay

N

Mini market

Horse carts

Jamah mosque

Cars to Lashio

Pool

Cinema

Purcell tower

Chinese temple

Jeeps

Market

Fire station

GPO

Town Hall

To Nann Maing Hotel & Mandalay

Kandawlay Lake

To Botanical Gardens

Golf Course

1. Tanggaungyi Pagoda
2. Massein Restaurant
3. Aurora Restaurant
4. Golden Dream Hotel
5. Candacraig Hotel
B. Bus / trucks & bikes

signed and there are miniature stage-coaches acting as taxis around town. In some respects, it seems like the British never left.

The British planted petunias and hollyhocks in neat gardens while the rugby fields, botanical garden and a golf course were carved out of the jungle. The 140 ha **Botanical Gardens**, to the S of town, were laid out by Sir Harcourt Butler, former Governor of Burma. Turkish prisoners-of-war during the Crimean War were used to create the now very pleasant gardens of mature trees on slopes above the two lakes. The plants and trees are labelled in Latin, Burmese and English. A tranquil spot, except on high days and holidays when the gardens are crowded with locals. A sign on the main gate 'create garden promote happiness' prompts you to buy seeds from the small shop by the entrance.

Maymyo's temperate micro-climate means a wide range of fruit (including strawberries), vegetables and coffee can be grown – it is an important market gardening centre. Locals say the climate has changed over the last ten years; this cool retreat from the Burmese plains is becoming hotter, presumably as a result of deforestation. The variety of the produce in the daily **Maymyo market** is matched by the mixture of ethnic backgrounds of the traders. The covered area is full of stalls selling Chinese and Thai imports but behind this is a mass of smaller stalls with colourful displays of local produce. Stall 401 in the main market is run by Soe Moe a trader with perfect English. He buys antiques from hill villages and has collected an array of old watches, clocks, opium weights, puppets, tapestries and knives. He also fixes local trips for tourists. The **Taungaungyi Pagoda** next door is surprisingly neglected.

North on Circular Rd, over the railway line, is octagonal **Naung Kan Gyi Pagoda**, situated on a hill; a track leads to the covered steps which climb to the top, from which there are good views.

Excursions

Pwe Kauk Falls are 8 km NE of town on the Lashio Rd – not at all spectacular, although a favourite picnic spot for the locals. There's a good swimming spot with crystal clear water a bit further up river.

Anisakan Falls are 8 km SW of Maymyo; they are more impressive than Pwe Kauk and it is possible to swim. The walk back to Maymyo is a stiff uphill climb, taking about $1\frac{1}{2}$ hrs from the bottom of the hill to Anisakan and probably another 2 hrs back up the road to Maymyo. Or take a horse and cart from the clocktower.

Shibaa, a Shan village, 20 km out of town, is renowned for its puppet shows. Trips can be arranged by Soe Moe, stall 401, main market.

Local information
● **Orientation**

Maymyo is very spread although the market, train station, buses and restaurants are all central. Hotels are all a short ride away from the centre.

● **Accommodation**

A *Thiri-myaing* (*Candacraig*), Anawrahta Rd,

T 22112, restaurant, tennis court, large garden, the house had its heyday during the colonial period – it was built to resemble a scaled-down English mansion; used by the Bombay Burmah Trading Company as a 'chummery' – or bachelor quarters, since independence, the house has not been well maintained, but log fires are still lit in the lounge. Still the best place to stay in Maymyo. Often full as it only has 9 rooms so it's worth making a reservation. *Candacraig* and the '*myaing*' hotels used to be government resthouses, where the British Civil Service lived for half the year; **A-B** *Nanmyaing*, by the checkpoint on the way into Maymyo, T 22112, hot water, restaurant, is a more modern-looking and larger version of the *Candacraig*. It has marginally better service but is short on atmosphere. There are 4 other government hotels but they are only used when the above are full: **A** *Cherry Myaing*, Aing Daw Rd.

B *Gandamar Myaing*, Yuga St, most similar in style to the *Candacraig*; **B** *Thazin Myaing*, Aing Daw Rd; **B** *Yuzana Myaing*, Aing Daw Rd.

The **C** *Grace Hotel*, 114a Nanmyaing St, is a cheaper option but has none of the hill station atmosphere.

● **Places to eat**
The *Nanmyaing Hotel* serves English food (including roast beef and potatoes) as well as Burmese dishes. There are also a couple of reasonably priced **Chinese** restaurants: the *Shanghai*, Lashio Rd; the *Layngoon*, Lashio Rd, a bit further out of town and *Mg Sein*.

Indian: *Dream Merchant*, Site 4 Mandalay-Lashio Rd, Block 6, opposite *Mg Sein*, best Indian in town, serve *nambya* (unleavened bread), fresh butter and chapati.

● **Shopping**
Markets: *Maymyo market* is in the middle of town and offers everything from fresh strawberries to tribal souvenirs. The small shop by the clock tower sells interesting knick-knacks. *Dream Merchant*, Site 4 Mandalay-Lashio Rd, Block 6, has good selection of souvenirs.

● **Sport**
Maymyo Golf Club 18-hole course; another colonial relic. Golfers must produce evidence of their handicap; green fees: 100 kyat, clubs 100 kyat, shoes 50 kyat.

● **Tourist offices**
MTT office at Nanmyaing.

● **Transport**
67 km E of Mandalay.

Local *Myin-lay* are a peculiarity of Maymyo; they are brightly coloured horse-drawn carriages, probably a descendant of the Victorian cab. **Bicycles**: can be hired from hotels, from the Indian restaurant, *Dream Merchant*, or from stalls at the back of the market (3 kyat/hr).

Train Takes several hours from Mandalay on a very windy track: daily connection.

Road Linecar: taxis leave from Zegyo Market (84th St), Mandalay but the drivers wait until they have a load (usually every hr), last leaves about 1500, 2-3 hrs; hairpins and low gears.

At the end of January 1993, the SLORC opened up a land route to **Kengtung** in eastern Shan State from Mai Sai, in Thailand's northernmost Chiang Rai province. It is intended to eventually connect Thailand with China's Yunnan Province. Tourists can obtain passes to drive the 160 km to Kengtung from **Tachileik**, on the Burmese side of the border. It is the only way visitors can reach the otherwise inaccessible Burmese territory within the *Golden Triangle*. This road, which winds precipitously through the mountain ravines on rock-cut shelves, is a major smuggling route, not only for heroin and opium, but for Chinese and Shan girls, many of whom end up in Bangkok brothels. James Pringle, one of the few Western journalists to have made the trip to Kengtung, reported seeing chain gangs of shackled prisoners breaking stones to be used for building the road to China. Some of the prisoners are reported to be students, arrested during the 1988 uprising. Pringle quotes a Burma specialist in Bangkok as saying: "The Burmese military is so out of touch with the real world it does not seem to realise it is doing anything wrong, and is even allowing tourists to see this".

Lashio

Further to the NE of Maymyo is Lashio, from where the Burma Rd leads through

CLIMATE: LASHIO											
	Jan	Feb	Mar	Apr	May	Jun	Jul	Aug	Sep	Oct	Nov	Dec
Av Max (°C)	23	26	30	32	31	29	28	28	29	28	25	23
Av Min (°C)	8	9	13	17	19	21	21	21	20	18	13	9
Av Rain (mm)	8	8	15	56	175	249	305	323	198	145	69	23

Source: Pearce, E.A and Smith C.G. *The world weather guide*: Hutchinson, London

the hilltribe areas into the rugged Chinese province of Yunnan. With increased border trade with China, the centre of the Shan heartland is growing in importance and becoming a busy trading centre.

● **Transport Train** Connections from Maymyo (10 hrs).

Road Car: Soe Moe, stall 401 in the market at Maymyo, will fix permits and arrange transport to Maymyo; price depends on how easy it is to arrange permits through his army connections.

Monywa

About 36 km W of Mandalay Monywa is the commercial centre of the Chindwin Valley. It is an important transit point on the drug route between China and India and for goods coming down the Chindwin River. Monywa is otherwise known for the discovery of Anyatha man, believed the be as sold as Peking man and is in a pretty position right on the river. **Thanbokde Pagoda**, which boasts over 500,000 Buddha images vies for importance with **Bodhitahtaung Pagoda** known for its *one thousand bo trees*. **Mahaleydy** is an important teaching monastery with its 806 stone slabs inscribed with the Buddhist scriptures.

Excursions

Five miles out of Monywa on the Monywa-Mandalay road, you get to Myenay village. One mile E of Myenay you will find **Thanbodae Pagoda** with 582,357 Buddha images which were build in 1930. Four mile further E are **Boditataung** and **Alantaye** pagodas. **Kyauka-shweguni Pagoda** is 9 miles

E of Monywa. Each year at the end May, there is a pagoda festival here. It is the only pagoda in Monywa that faces N and is also famous for its lacquerware. A quarter of a mile from the pagoda is the river Tantaluk, a nice spot where the government is building bungalows for tourists.

Powintaung Across the river and 15 miles to the NE, several large Buddha images have been carved directly into the stone on the Powintaung hills.

Twintaung 21 miles N of Monywa you get to Budalin, 7 miles W to Budalin you will reach Twintaung, an extinct volcano with a lake in the middle. The weeds that grow in the lake are turned into spirulina, a vitamin widely used in Burma.

● **Accommodation B** *Monywa Hotel*, Ah-Lone Rd, T 21549.

● **Places to eat Burmese**: *Daw Tin On*, western part of town, near the town hall.

Chinese: *Pangyeyyi*, Bo Gyok Aung San Rd; *Paradise*, Bo Gyok Aung San Rd (middle block); *Ye Pau Restaurant* (floating restaurant), Shandaw Rd; *Shine*, Bo Gyok Aung San Rd.

● **Transport Road Bus**: irregular connections (8 hrs). **Car**: depending on access to the area cars can be hired in Mandalay (5 hrs).

Shwebo

At various times during the Konbaung (or Alaungpaya) dynasty the Burmese capital was based at Shwebo: King Naungdawgyi ruled from Shwebo from 1750 to 1760, as did his successor, Naungdawgyi, from 1760 to 1763. However, Burmese kings took their palaces with them and there is little left in Shwebo to mark its previous importance.

THE SLORC AND THE BLOOD-RED RUBY RACKET

The town of Mogok, high in the mountains, 115 km NE of Mandalay is one of the most strategically important towns in Burma: it is where most of the country's rubies are mined. For centuries rubies were the favoured stones of Burmese royalty, and Burma has some of the finest rubies in Asia. The gem was thought to have strong occult power; those who wore a ruby ring were believed to be invulnerable in battle. Today the mining at Mogok is controlled by the government under aegis of the Myanmar Gems Enterprise. The pockets of the SLORC's top brass are well known to be lined with the proceeds of gemstone smuggling. Precious stones, jade, opium and teak are among the few tangible commodities which afford Burma's generals an opportunity for corruption.

The ruby market is a major source of income for the SLORC; every year a big gem fair is staged at the *Inya Lake Hotel* in Rangoon, where stones are auctioned to international buyers. The fair attracts a high-living and dubious clientele – during the 1970s and 80s, former Philippines President Ferdinand Marcos and his wife, Imelda, were regularly spotted at it. Nearly every Feb, word spreads on the Bangkok rumour-mill that the SLORC has clamped down on tourism after visa applications are delayed or rejected. In reality, the reason is that most of Rangoon's hotel rooms are full of international gem-dealers – who are a much more lucrative breed than tourists – until hotel capacity is increased. Feb is not a good month to plan a visit to Rangoon. In 1993, at the 30th annual gem emporium, the SLORC auctioned off more than US$17 million-worth of gemstones and sold US$4 million of gold jewellery and jade carvings.

Mogok

This town is famous for its jade and ruby mines – mogok means ruby. The mines are in rugged mountainous country and important government territory because of its potential wealth.

Arakan

Arakan is predominantly Muslim; its people were the focus of international concern in 1992 when 200,000 of them fled into neighbouring Bangladesh, to refugee camps at Cox's Bazar.

Sittwe

The Muslim city of Akyab (Sittwe) stands on a small island at the end of a spit of land jutting into the Bay of Bengal. It was originally built by the British after the annexation of Arakan in 1826 and has several buildings dating from that period.

● **Accommodation** *Gisspar Guesthouse*, in the centre of town.

● **Transport Air** Connection with Rangoon.

CLIMATE: SITTWE												
	Jan	Feb	Mar	Apr	May	Jun	Jul	Aug	Sep	Oct	Nov	Dec
Av Max (°C)	27	29	31	32	32	30	29	29	30	31	29	27
Av Min (°C)	15	16	20	24	26	25	25	25	25	24	22	17
Av Rain (mm)	3	5	10	51	391	1151	1400	1133	577	287	130	18

Source: Pearce, E.A and Smith C.G. *The world weather guide*: Hutchinson, London

MRAUK-U

The last royal capital of Rakhine is renowned for its archaeological remains, wall paintings of Indian influence and scenic beauty. It is popularly known as the 'Golden City'. It lies at the head of a tributary of the Kaladan River, about 60 km from Sittwe on the coast. Myohaung, as it is known today, is a simple market town. In the Myohaung area you may come across local hill tribe people called the *thet* and can be recognized by their large earrings.

History

The first kingdom of the Rakhine dynasty was based ruled by King Vasudeva. He married a local princess and became the head of a powerful kingdom. His son, Marayu, conquered Vesali and founded Dhanyawaddy on the Thari River in 3000 BC. Several dynasties were based on this site until 326 AD.

The Chandra dynasty, founded by King Mahataing Chandra, moved from Dhanywaddy to Vesali on the advice of his astrologers in 327 AD. The city prospered as a river port and established foreign trade. Local legends tell of thousands of vessels laden with merchandise calling at Vesali annually. The kingdom was Buddhist and the Mahamuni image formed the centre of religious worship. Early inscriptions also tell of two missionaries introducing a new religion and images of Brahma, Vishnu and Siva have also been found in local shrines at Vesali. Despite invasions by the Shans, Vesali continued to flourish until 1018. King Minbeeloo was assassinated by a nobel in 1078 and the royal family fled to Pagan. According to tradition a large army was sent from Pagan to restore King Letyaminnan, the true descendant, to the throne in 1103. He built a temporary city at Launggret and then settled at nearby Parein. In 1251, on the advice of his astrologers, King Alaw-

marphyu, reinstated Launggret reinstated as the capital of his kingdom.

The Kaladan River was originally navigable to this area, and it was a meeting point of roads E and W. With high rainfall the surrounding area was also a rich rice growing region. Launggret was based on the plains but King Minsawmon decided its position was indefensible and the city had been ruined by invaders. Mrauk-U was an obvious choice, naturally well defended by surrounding ridges and the king's astrologers foretold the prosperity of the city. The city was founded in 1430 AD. City walls were built in the gaps between the natural barriers and a maze-like chain of lakes and moats were constructed for protection and to supply fresh drinking water. The city became an important commercial centre and the seat of the Rakhine dynasty until 1785.

Places of interest

Beside the pagodas, the city walls, moats, ramparts, watch towers and forts are still visible. If you get a chance, the archaeological museum is worth a visit for its 15th and 16th century Buddha images. **The palace** was the centre of the ancient city and was built to the same traditional pattern as Burmese palaces. The walls can be seen today but the original teak building have long disappeared. The stone walls were erected by King Minbin (1531-53). According to Father Manrique, a Portuguese monk, "there were 3 enclosures which rose in tiers, each bounded by a thick stone wall. ... The main audience hall and the private apartments were situated in the innermost square. ... They were of teakwood, lacquered and gilded, the roofs carved with figures and rising in spires. ... The audience hall with its great wooden pillars of such length and symmetry that one would be astonished that

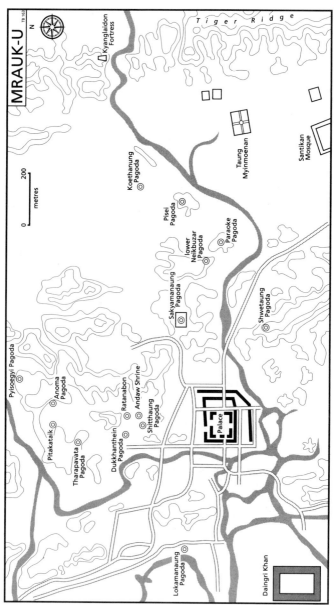

MRAUK-U

TB 163

N

Tiger Ridge

Kyanglaidon Fortress

Taung Myinmoenan

Santikan Mosque

0 200
metres

Koethanung Pagoda

Pisei Pagoda

Paraoke Pagoda

lower Neikbuzar Pagoda

Sakyamanaung Pagoda

Shwetaung Pagoda

Pyisoegyi Pagoda

Anoma Pagoda

Pitakattaik

Ratanabon

Andaw Shrine

Shitthaung Pagoda

Tharapavata Pagoda

Dukkhanthein Pagoda

Palace

Lokamanaung Pagoda

Daingri Khan

trees so lofty and straight could exist." Manique was conducted into a room "which was panelled with scented timber, such as sandalwood and eaglewood". Passing through these perfumed chambers he came to a pavilion known as the 'House of Gold', the walls of which were plated with gold. Along the ceiling was a golden creeper with many gourds moulded in the same metal and leaves of emeralds and grapes of garnets. In the same chamber were 7 idols of gold.

The Northern Side

About 1 km N of the palace site is the **Shitthaung Pagoda**, or the shrine of 80,000 images. It was built in 1535 by King Minbin, one of the most powerful rulers of the Mrauk-U dynasty, in celebration of the successful defeat of the Portuguese. It is said that the pagoda was built by 1,000 architects and work-

SHITTAUNG PAGODA

SHITTHAUNG PAGODA PLAN

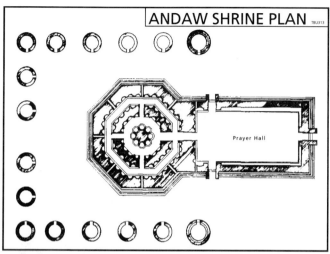

ANDAW SHRINE PLAN TBU313

Prayer Hall

men over a year. It is probably the most famous temple here and renowned for its Buddha images and reliefs.

There are 2 small sandstone pagodas on the first platform: the octagonal **Ne Htwet Para** (Sun Rise Pagoda) and the stupa **Ne Win Para** (Sun Set Pagoda). The central platform is dominated by a wooden prayer hall, which housed innumerable Buddha images. By the entrance is a stone pillar inscribed with Rakhine characters and a statue of King Minbin. The central pagoda is 27m high and is surrounded by smaller copies between which is a stone slab sculpted with nagas, mythical birds and beasts. The shrine is surrounded by a gallery with Buddha images in the outer wall.

The **Shitthaung Pillar** is to the N of the Shitthaung Pagoda and is said to have been brought here by King Minbin from Vesali, an earlier Rakhine capital. Three sides of the pillar are inscribed with Sanskrit and list the kings who ruled ancient Rakhine. It is believed to have been a lintel.

The **Andaw Shrine** is to the NE of the Shitthaung. It was built by King Min

Hla Raza in 1521 to enshrine a tooth-relic of the Buddha, which was bought from Sri Lanka by King Minbin. King Minrazagyi rebuilt the shrine in 1596. The sandstone shrine is octagonal and encircled by smaller brick pagodas. A gallery runs round the main shrine with thousands of niches with Buddha images carved into the walls. On the E side is the main prayer hall.

Further N stands the **Ratanabon Pagoda**, built by King Minkhamaung and his chief queen Shin Htway in 1612, and is impressive by its massiveness. Unfortunately, the central sandstone stupa, and surrounding stupas, were badly damaged in World War II. It is completely undecorated, uncharacteristic for Rakhine. The lions protecting the outer pagoda walls are still standing.

King Minphalaung built the **Dukkhanthein** (or Htaukkanthein) **Pagoda** in 1571 to the W of Ratanabon. It is approached by massive stone stairways on all four sides. The bell-shaped central dome is similar to the Shitthaung but an arch on the eastern side admits light into the central chamber.

DUKKHANTHEIN PAGODA CROSS SECTION TBU314

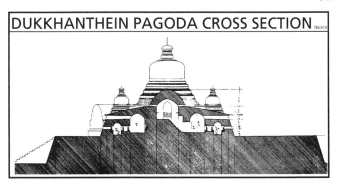

DUKKHANTHEIN PAGODA PLAN TBU315

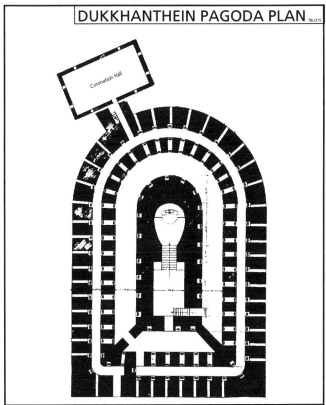

Coronation Hall

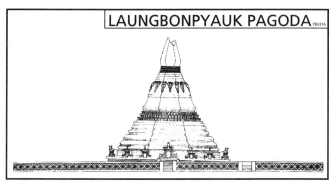

LAUNGBONPYAUK PAGODA TBU316

The pagoda is renowned for its sculpture in the inner passages – especially the seated ladies offering lotus buds to the Buddha. These ladies have 64 different kinds of hairstyles and were modelled on the wives of noblemen. These inner walls are also punctuated with 140 niches holding Buddha statues.

To the NW is the **Lemyetnha or Four Faced Pagoda**, built by King Minsawmon (the first king of Mrauk-U dynasty) in 1430. Along with the nearby Myatanzaung pagodas and the Mokseiktaw, it was built when the city was established. The Mokseiktaw has a well preserved library and a famous footprint of the Buddha.

The **Laungbonpyauk Pagoda** was built in 1525 by King Minkhaungraza. The sculptures on the inner wall are particularly fine: at the centre of each is a rosette containing 8 coloured clay tablets. The façade also has exquisite carvings.

According to local records, the rather neglected **Htuparyon Pagoda** was erected by King Minranaung, the sixth king of the Mrauk-U dynasty in 1494. It was rebuilt in 1613 by King Minkhamaung. The four corners are guarded by manotethiha, or lions with 2 heads. It was an important pagoda – the site of victory and prosperity – and was traditionally visited by kings after their coronations.

On a hill between Htuparyon and Mokseiktaw is the **Tharapavata Pagoda**. A buddha image was found here with inscriptions dating back to the 4th century. Just to the N is the **Pitakataik**, or library, donated by King Minphalaung in 1591. It housed the Buddhist scriptures, supposedly the 30 sets of the Triptika which King Narapatigyi (1638-1645) received from Sri Lanka. Just to the N of the library are remains of the old city wall and moat.

Further E is the **Pyisoegyi Pagoda**, which also has a library decorated with fine sculptures. Pyisoegyi means 'head of state' and it was believed to have been donated. Further E is the Minthami water gate, which was opened to fill the Tharikonboung moat in times of war.

All that remains of the **Anoma Pagoda** is a Buddha statue and a finely decorated pedestal. The original pagoda was donated by Princess Anowzaw, daughter of King Salingathu (1494-1501). The Minpaung Pagoda to the S was built by King Minkhamaung and his chief queen, Shin Htway, in 1640. The pagoda walls are decorated with fantastic figures of dragons. The bell-shaped temple to the S is the Mahabodhi Shwegu and is renowned for the carving in its inner corridors. The stone sculptures around the pedestal of the main

THE PITAKATAIK FAÇADE _{TBU317}

image are held to be some of the best Rakhine sculpture. The two temples to the S, Ratanasanraway and Ratanamhankin, were built by King Basawphyu in 1468. The latter is renowned for its carvings of birds, ogres, lotus and griffin. Further E is the Ratanmanaung donated in 1652 by King Candathudhammaraza. The field to the E is called Laykhinpyin meaning archery. It was the training ground for the Rakhine archers.

Eastern Side

The **Sakyamanaung Pagoda**, NE of the palace site, stands out because of its unusual shape and the two giants which guard the western gate. On a hill to the S is the Wuninattaung, the oldest site in Mrauk-U. The Wuntinattaung inscription found here is an important cultural link as the script resembled the Pali inscriptions found at Srikstra from the 6th and 7th century. To the E is the Winmana paddy storehouse, one of 40 in the inner city used to store rice; it was originally surrounded by walls and moats. The Neikbuza pagodas on the hill to the E were all built by King Min Saw Oo in 1527.

To the SE of the lower Neikbuzar Pagoda is the **Paraoke Pagoda** built by King Minphalaung in 1571. After building the Dukkhanthein Pagoda the king was advised by astrologers to donate an-

SAKYAMANAUNG PAGODA (NORTHERN SIDE)

TBU318

other pagoda to prevent disintegration of his kingdom. 'Oake' means to control the whole country.

The **Pisei Pagoda** to the NE was built in 1123 by King Kawliya and houses a relic of the Buddha. It is an important Buddhist shrine. Koethanung means 90,000 and the **Koethanung Pagoda** to the N is supposed to have contained a large number of Buddha images. It was built by King Mintaikkha, son of King Minbin, in 1553. It is one of the largest temples at Mrauk-U and is similar in style to his father's temple, Shitthaung Pagoda although the workmanship is not as good. Traditionally the kings celebrated their head washing in a small tank, Udawsaykan, to the NE. Kings usually stayed in a small temporary palace originally on the site. On the W side

was the elephant training camp for the Rakhine elephant army. **Kyanglaidon Fortress** on Tiger Ridge parallel to the Lemro River was one of the most important defense points.

To the S of the palace site are the remains of the **Taung Myinmoenan**, another palace. Within the palace walls were 5 islands, each surrounded by a small moat. The palace or 'Golden House' was on the central island. It is called the Golden House as the central hall was supposed to have been gilded. The king and his chief queen stayed here for important ceremonies. The governors from the provinces stayed on the surrounding islands and were taken in to the Golden House in a gilded boat. They drank the sacred water in the presence of the king to show their loyalty.

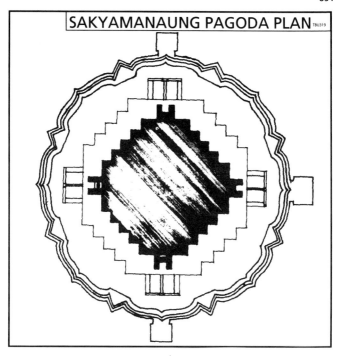

SAKYAMANAUNG PAGODA PLAN TBU319

The nearby **Santikan Mosque** was built by Muslim followers of King Minsawmon in 1429 after campaigns abroad.

Southern Side

On top of a small hill, the **Shwetaung Pagoda** is one of the most prominent temples to the S of the palace site. It is believed to have been built by King Mindon in 1531. Nearby are some remaining Burmese fortifications from the first Anglo-Burmese War in 1824. Beyond this temple to the S is a large man-made lake called Anomakan. It was originally a moat but now supplies fresh water to the area. Beyond the lake are the Myataung and Laythataung fortresses and another lake – Letsekan. To the N of the lake is the largest Buddha image in Mrauk-U, all of 4m high. It was donated by King Tazarta in 1515. King Minbin built a shrine to cover the image before one of his military campaigns in India. Unfortunately the shrine is now in ruins.

Western Side

The **Lokamanaung Pagoda** was built by King Candathudhammaraza in the late 17th century. It was an important pagoda as it was at the start of the 'gold' and 'silver' roads to Vesali and Mahamuni. The nearby Parabaw got its name from the image it houses. According to legend the image was salvaged from the river, hence the name Parabaw meaning 'out of water'. The Daingripet, a former European settlement, is on the other bank of the Aungdat Creek. The European Quarter was outside the city walls and flourished from the 16th to the 17th centuries. King Thirithudhammaraza even allowed Father Manrique to build a Christian church in the area.

The area to the SW of the palace site was protected by a narrow ridge and the Launggret Creek. Ramparts and forts, such as Aungmingala, were built along the slope. The Thongyaiktasu Shrine on the ridge has good views over the Letsekan Valley.

Excursions

30 km from Mrauk-U are the remains of the old Rakhine capitals, **Launggret** and **Parein**. Most of the buildings have disappeared but there is a huge stone slab on top of Taungmawtaung Hill. The inscriptions on the slab describe King Kawliya's (1118-1123) donations. Although the slab is nothing much to look at, the view from the top of the hill is worth the climb. From here you can see the original palace site, the Nandawgon, and city of Launggret to the S.

About 16 km S of Launggret is the **Kadothein Shrine**, discovered in the jungle in 1890. Kadothein was built by King Candavizaya in 1720 and is covered in ornamental designs. There are 8 huge boulders engraved with figures, the only ones of this kind in the area.

10 km to the N of Mrauk-U is one of the earliest Rakhine cities, **Vesali**. It was founded by King Mahataing Candra in 327. According to local inscriptions it was called Vesali Kyaukhlayga, the City with Stone Stairs. The city was an important river port and the stairs led to the docks on the river; they can still be seen at low tide. The present village of Vesali is on the original palace site, which remains unexcavated. To the N of the village is the Vesali image, donated by the chief queen, Thupabadevi, in 327. There are few remains of other important sites in the area: the Shwedaunggyi, or great golden hillock to the N; Sanghayana Hill, supposedly the site of the fourth Buddhist Synod; and Thingyaingtaung, an old burial site.

Dhanyawaddy, 34 km N of Mrauk-U, is another ancient Rakhine city. Its heyday was from 580 BC to 326 AD. It was believed to have been founded by King Sandasuriya but there is some disagreement between archaeologists. There are walls and fortifications still remaining. The city had an inner and outer area. The inner city was a special site for the royal family. The outer walls enclosed the paddy fields so that in times of siege there was an assured food supply. The fields were irrigated by a complex system of tanks and channels, which can be seen in aerial photographs of the region.

The **Mahamuni Shrine**, one of the most renowned Buddhist sites in Burma, is at the NE corner of the old palace site. It was built to house the Mahamuni image (now in Mandalay, see page 627), believed to be an actual likeness of the Gautama Buddha. Because of its religious importance, it was sought as a prize by neighbouring kings and after several attempts was finally captured by King Bodawpaya in the 18th century. On the first platform you can still see the library built by King Minkhari in 1439, a tank dug by King Sandasuriya and an ordination hall. The Buddha is believed to have rested under the Banyan tree on the second platform, and so it is surrounded by small shrines. On the central platform is the chamber where the Mahamuni image was once kept.

● **Accommodation** E *Myantheingy Guesthouse*, basic but friendly, good restaurant.

● **Transport Local** Most of the pagodas can be visited on **horse and cart** but for trips further afield hire a **jeep**.

Sea Boat: to Mrauk-U (Myohaung) (100 kyat). It is possible to get to Mrauk-U in a day from Rangoon, but if stuck stay at the *Gisspar Guesthouse* in Sittwe.

INFORMATION FOR VISITORS

Before you go

Entry requirements

Regulations for tourists and businessmen are in a constant state of flux. The advice given below was checked in 1994, but visitors must be ready for the possibility that new, or altered, regulations have come into force since then.

● **Visas**

At the time of going to press, tourists are eligible for a 28 day visa to Burma. Visas cost US$12 and take 48 hrs to process at the Burmese Embassy in Bangkok.

Visas can be obtained at any of Burma's consulates or embassies abroad, the Bangkok Embassy (132 Sathorn Nua Rd) being the one most frequently used by tourists. Procuring a visa can take anything up to 48 hrs from embassies outside the region. Two application forms are required along with 3 passport photographs; occasionally tourists are also asked to show their return ticket. Extended stays are rarely given – you must have a good reason such as joining a Burmese language course or going to a meditation centre. Meditation visas for foreign yogis can be obtained by writing to: Buddhasana, Niaggaha Organization, Mahasi Meditation Centre, 16 Thatana Rd, Rangoon. This organization runs full-time meditation courses which run for 6-12 weeks. Visas can be extended in Rangoon; apply through tour agents (approx US$40)

● **Vaccinations**

Cholera and yellow fever vaccinations are required if you have been in an affected area in the 9 days prior to arrival. A vaccination against typhoid is advisable. Anti-malarial drugs are essential, although Rangoon is said to be malaria-free.

● **Representation overseas**

Australia, 22 Arkana Street, Canberra ACT 2600, T 062 733811, F 61-6 273.4357; **Bangladesh**, 89 (B) Rd No 41, Banani Model Town, Dhaka 13, T 2 601 915, F 88-2 883740; **Canada**, 85, Range Rd, Apartment No. 902-903, The Sandringham, Ottawa, Ontario, KIN 816, T 613 232-6434, F 1-613 232-6435; **China** No. 6, Dong Zhi MenWai Street, Chaoyang District, Beijing, T 1 532 1584, F 86-1 532.1344; **France**, 60 Rue De Courcelles, 3rd Floor, 75008 Paris, T 1 4225 5695, F 33.1 42.56.49.41; **Germany**, Schumann Str. 112, 5300 Bonn 1, T 0228 210091, F 49-228 219316; **Hong Kong**, Room No. 2424, Sun Hung Kai Centre, No. 30, Harbour Rd, Wanchai, Hong Kong, T 5 8913329, F 852 8386597; **India**, No. 3/50 f, Nyaya Marg, Chanakyapuri, New Delhi 110021, T 11 600251, F 91-11 6877.942; **Indonesia**, 109 Jalan Haji Agus Salim, Jakarta, T 21 320 440, F 62-21 327.204; **Israel**, No.19, Yona Street, Ramat Gan, Tel Aviv, T 03 783151, F 972-3 780484; **Italy**, Via Vincenzo Bellini 20, Interno 1, 00198 Rome, T 6 8549374, F 39-6 8413167; **Japan**, 8-26, 4 Chome, Kita-Shinagawa, Shinagawa-Ku, Tokyo, T 03 441-9291-5, F 81-3 447.7394; **Laos**, Sok Paluang Rd, P.O. Box II, Vientiane, T 2789, F 2789; **Malaysia**, 5, Taman U Thant

Satu, 55000 Kuala Lumpur, T 3 242 4085, F 60-3 2480049; **Nepal**, Chakupat, Patan Gate, Lalitpur, Kathmandu, T 521 788, F 97-71 521788; **Pakistan**, No. 12/1, Street 13, F-7/2, Islamabad, T 51 820 123, F 92-51 820.123; **Philippines**, DAO II Bldg, 4th Floor, 104, Alvardo Street, Legaspi Village, Makati, Metro Manila, T 2 817 2373, F 63-2 8175895; **Russia**, 41 UL Gertsena, Moscow, T 291 05 34, F 7-95 2910165; **Singapore**, 15 St. Martin's Drive, Singapore 102, T 2358763, F 65 23559635; **Sri Lanka**, 17 Skelton Garden, Colombo 5, T 1 587 608, F 94-1 580460; **Switzerland**, Permanent Mission to the UN, 47, Avenue Blanc, 1202 Geneva, T 022 7317540, F 41-22 7384882; **Thailand**, 132, North Sathorn Rd, Bangkok 10500, T 02 233 2237, F 66-2 236.6898; **UK**, 19 A Charles Street, London W1X 8ER, T 071-629 6966, F 071-629 4169; **USA**, 2300 S Street NW, Washington DC 20008, T (202) 332-9044, F (202) 332 9046, and 10 East 77th Street, New York NY 10021, T (212) 535 1310; **Vietnam**, Building No. A3, Ground Floor, Van Phuc, Diplomatic Quarters, Hanoi, T 53369, F (84-4) 52404.

● **Travelling in Burma**

In 1992 the military junta decided that the tourist industry was to provide the panacea to Burma's economic ailments by attracting 50,000 tourists a year. The reality is somewhat different. Burma is scraping about 20,000 tourists a year, and does not have the infrastructure to cope with more. Any increase in numbers in the years to come will not only depend on political developments but also on capacity.

Many tourists are put off by the ruling junta and the expense and restrictions on travel. The former has not changed but travel restrictions have eased up somewhat.

There are no problems travelling to the main tourist destinations:

1) Rangoon area: Rangoon city proper, Pegu, Syriam, Twante;

2) Central Burma: Prome, Sandaway (access by air only);

3) Inle Lake area: Taunggyi, Nyang Shwe, Inle Lake, Kalaw, Pindaya;

4) Pagan area: Pagan archaeological site, Mount Popa, Meiktila, Thazi;

5) Mandalay area: Mandalay city proper, Sagaing, Amarapura, Ava, Mingun, Maymyo.

However, other areas are often restricted, although regions are opening up to tourists all the time. Restrictions will depend on government control of these more remote areas.

Some tourists will find they can reach their destination without any problem while others will be stopped by the military en route. If you want to travel to these 'restricted' areas, you must travel with a registered guide, organized through tour companies. Travel plans must be made well in advance in order for the agency to get the permits required (10-12 days). Agencies can be contacted beforehand with details of the areas you want to visit plus a copy of your passport, Burmese visa and 3 passport photographs. As yet few private tour operators have offices abroad so it is best to contact agencies in Rangoon by fax, telex, phone or by letter. Leave plenty of time to arrange trips.

A deposit of US$50 per person is usually required on confirmation of the tour. Full payments must be made 3/4 weeks prior to arrival; tour companies will give you instructions of where to pay the money.

Travelling on a tour in Burma does not mean that you have to put up with 10 or 20 other tourists; it is possible to go alone with a registered guide. However, the fewer the people, the more expensive the tour. Registered guides all have to undergo a 6 month government training and usually know their 'stuff'. They will also interpret in places where English is not spoken. See **Tours** below for examples of prices.

In main towns, ie Rangoon, Mandalay, Maymyo, Taungguyi travellers will often come across a 'Mr Fixit' who will be able to organize trips to restricted areas. He will, depending on the situation, be able to grease the right palms and always has a 'friend' with a car for hire.

To save hassles with transport, travellers often hire cars in Mandalay to get around the main sights in Pagan and the Inle Lake area. This is a good way to travel if you want to save time and be more flexible. It should cost around US$100 for a car from Mandalay to Pagan but prices vary depending on the cost of petrol.

● **Private v Government**

The government is trying to eke dollars out of tourists to Burma to fill its coffers. If you don't want to support the current regime there are ways of putting your money into private hands:

1) Stay in private hotels/guesthouses rather than government-run institutions (they are often better anyway, see page 662);

2) Eat in private restaurants rather than government-run ones (the food tends to be authentic and fresh in private restaurants);

3) Travel by bus, linecar or hire cars where possible; Myanmar Airways and trains are run by the government (it is usually cheaper and more flexible to use privately run transport options);

4) Use private-run tour operators as opposed to MTT (privately organized tour companies are usually more efficient and less restrictive);

5) Buy from private shops/stalls rather than government-run shops (you cannot bargain in government shops, so it is usually cheaper to buy from private operators).

If you want to find out more about the situation in Burma, contact The Burma Action Group, Collins Studio, Collins Yard, Islington Green, London N1 2XU. The Burma Action Group suggest travellers interested in making an anti-government statement while in Burma should: visit U Thant's tomb and leave flowers; wear Aung Sang Suu Kyi T shirts; bring books, magazines and medicines (with careful instructions).

Tours

It is possible to purchase Burma package tours in the US, Europe and Australasia, but they are cheaper to organize in Bangkok or through agents in Rangoon. There are many travel and tour agents specializing in Burma – but top 'brandname' packages are expensive.

The cheapest 7-night tours, which include the return flight from Bangkok to Rangoon cost around US$350 and take in the main tourist attractions – Rangoon, Mandalay and Pagan. Bangkok-based travel agents offer short tours (5-6 days) from Chiang Mai to Pagan and Mandalay; they are highly recommended, although expensive (US$600+). The companies offering these tours are *Asia Voyage* and *Diethelm Travel*. Tours to 'restricted' areas in Burma tend to be more expensive. A 5 day tour to Arakan (from Rangoon) for a single traveller with a guide costs US$400, including return flight to Sittwe, all transport, hotels and food.

● **Tour agents**
In Burma: There are now 120 registered agents in Rangoon. The smaller agents often use the facilities of the larger companies but offer a more personalized service. The well-established tour companies in Rangoon are: *Euro-Asie*, 116 Bo Aung Kyaw St, Botataung, T 74640, F 84981; *Free Bird Tours*, 357 Bo Aung Gyaw St (upper block), T 94941, F 89960; *Golden Express*, 56 Wadan St, T 21479; *Golden Land*, 214 (2A) Bo Aung

Kyaw St, T 96074, F 61900; *Open Sesame*, Thirimingalar Rd, Kamayut, T 32890, F 89862; *Rubyland Tourism Services*, 90 Upper Pansodan St, Mingala Taungnyunt Township, T 81219.

In Bangkok: All agents offer similar tours. Some of Bangkok's more reputable companies specializing in tours to Burma are listed below: *Apex*, CCT Bldg, 4th Floor, 109 Surawong Rd, T 2381207, F 2376898; *Asia Voyage*; *Crossworld*, 293/3 Surawong Rd, T 2349800, F 2368370; *Diethelm Travel*, Kian Gwan Bldg II, 140/1 Witthayu Rd, T 2559150, F 2560248; *Exotissimo*, 21/17 Sukhumvit, Soi 4, T 2545240, F 2547683, also branch in Chiang Mai (see below); *Future World*, 604/3 Phanthip Plaza, T 2522818; *M K Ways*, 18/4 Saint Louis Soi 3, Sathorn Tai Rd, T 2122532, F 2545583, also a branch at 57/11 Witthayu Rd; *Orientours*, 8/25-28 Soi 16 (Soi Sam-Mit), Sukhumvit Rd, F 2546000; *Skyline Travel Service*, 491/39-40 Silom Plaza (2nd Floor), Silom Rd, T 2359780/ 2359781, F 2366585; *Siam Wings*, 173/1-3 Surawong Rd, T 2534757- 8/2532807-8, F 2366808; *Tour East*, 10th Floor, Rajapark Bldg, 163 Asoke Rd, T 2593160, F 2583236; *White Elephant Travel*, 1091/121-2 Chaivadee Bldg, Phetburi Rd, Metro Trade Centre.

In Chiang Mai: *Exotissimo*, 54-56 Tha Pae Rd, T (053) 236237, F 235095.

In Singapore: *Albatros Travel*, 05-11 Orchard Towers, 400 Orchard Rd, T 7327222; *Anglo-French Travel*, 10-03 Asia Chambers, 20 McCallum St, T 2224222; *Express Service Enterprise*, 01-03 Hotel Grand Central, 22 Cavenagh Rd, T 7349288, F 7376567; *German-Asian Travel*, 126 Telok Ayer St, T 2215539, F 2214220; *Guthric Detico*, 41 6th Ave, F 4683484; *Sea-Sun Cruises*, Seafix Co, 31-02, 78 Shenton Way, F 2218705; *Transinex*, 08-07 Golden Wall Centre, 89 Short St, T 3383733.

● **Outside the region**
Australia: *Tour East*, 99 Walker St, 12th Flr, North Sydney. **France**: *Jet Tours/(Club Med)*, Paris. **Germany**: *Studiosus Reisen*, Postfach 201942, D-80019 München, T 089 500 600, F 089 502 1541; *Tour East*, Goethestr 30/3, D-6000 Frankfurt 1. **Italy**: *Granniviaggi*. **Japan**: *Saiyu Travel*, Shinsekai Bldg, 5th Floor, 2-2 Kanda Jimbocho, Chiyoda-ku, Tokyo, T 32371391/32371396; *SSK Trading Corp*, 3939 – 1 Okazaki Hiratsuka – City, Kanagawa, F 0463 582733. **Netherlands**: *Baobab*

Travel, Haarlemmerstraat 24-26, 1013 ER Amsterdam, F 020 624 54 01. **Spain**: *Anosluz*, Club de Viajeros, Rodriguez San Pedro 2, Oficina 1202, 28015 Madrid, F 5939181; *Dimensiones*, Jacometre 30, 4 Planta 11, Madrid, T 531 5185, F 521 4254. **Switzerland**: *Intercable*, IM Bosch 37, CH 6331, Hurrenberg; *Kuoni Tours* Zurich. **UK**: *Andrew Brock Travel*, UK, T 0572 821330; *Equinox Travel*, Kingsmead House, 250 Kings Rd, London; *Explore Worldwide*, T 0252 344161; *Mergui Travels and Tours*, 36 Sisters Ave, London SW11 5SQ, T/F 071-223 8987; *One World Tours*, 80 Stuart Rd, London SW19, T 081-946 6295; *Regent Travel*, 15 John St, Bristol, T (0272) 211711; *Top Deck*, Top Deck House, 131-135 Earls Court Rd, London SW5, T (071) 244 8641, F (071) 373 6201; *Tour East*, King's Lodge, 28 Church St, Epsom, Surrey KT17 4ZP, T 372-739799, F 372 739824; *Visit Burma*, 5 White Croft Close, Connahts Quay, Deeside, Clwyd, T 0244 822815, birdwatching tours. **USA**: *S&J Travel Agency*, 36526 Bottlebrush Ct, Newark, CA 94560, F 415 792 7176; *Tour East*, 1960 East Grand Ave, Suite 800, El Segundo, California.

● **Tourist information**

The main tourist office in the country is Myanmar Travels & Tours (MTT) in Rangoon (77-79 Sule Pagoda Rd). There are branch offices in Mandalay, Pagan and Taunggyi. MTT is state-run and can only provide basic information (street plans of Rangoon and Mandalay); some of the MTT tour guides, however, are very well informed. MTT sells tickets for main sights, which are paid for in US$ (or the kyat equivalent at the official rate). Government-run hotels and the museums in Rangoon and Mandalay also sell these tickets.

When to go

● **Best time to visit**

Nov to the end of Feb, in the cool season, when temperatures are around 16-21°C. But because this is the most popular time to go, it is also difficult to confirm bookings for hotels and travel. Hill stations are quite cool at this time. Tourists should also note that Rangoon's annual international gem fair in Feb/Mar regularly results in an accommodation crisis (see page 642). Mar and Apr are dry but very hot – temperatures rise as high as 45°C in Pagan. **NB**: do not arrive in Bangkok during Chinese New Year, hoping to get a Burmese visa in 48 hrs. Many Bangkok travel agents close for the duration of the festivities.

● **Clothing**

Shorts and short skirts are considered immodest forms of dress. Cool trousers and longish skirts are recommended – as is a hat. Sweaters might be needed for the evenings in the hill stations. Traditional dress is the *lungyi* (see *shopping*, above), similar to the Malaysian *sarong*, and a blouse called the *eingyi*. The lungyi is worn shorter in the countryside for working in the ricefields. Men usually wear a collarless shirt and a short waist-length jacket. Traditional male headwear, the *gaung-baung*, is only worn on special occasions.

The women's lungyi is tied at the side whereas the men's lungyi is knotted in the middle. The women's ceremonial lungyi is called a *hta-mein*. It is similar to an orthodox lungyi but overlaps at the front and has a train at the back. The graceful management of this train while walking and dancing was considered an important accomplishment for women. It is now only worn by female Burmese dancers. Since there are no pockets in a lungyi, the Shan bag, slung over the shoulder has become a universal accessory.

Health

● **Vaccinations**

Hepatitis, typhoid, tetanus and polio vaccinations are also recommended. It is necessary to have evidence that you have been vaccinated against yellow fever if coming from an infected area.

● **Malaria**

Malaria is endemic in much of Burma; anti-malarial medication and repellents are strongly recommended.

● **Food & water**

Do not eat raw vegetables, or fruit which you cannot peel yourself. It is highly inadvisable to drink tap water unless it has been boiled for at least 15 mins. Dehydration can be a problem; visitors are advised to bring some electrolyte rehydration powder with them.

● **Medical facilities**

Although Burmese doctors are well-trained, drug stocks are poor. It is advisable for tourists to contact their embassies, should they suddenly fall ill. Some (such as the Australian embassy) have their own clinics and a nurse. They will always be able to recommend the best course of action. Unofficial medical care like this must be paid for in US dollars. Health insurance with emergency air ambulance provision is worthwhile. The main hospitals in Rangoon are *Diplomatic Hospital*, Kyaikkasan Rd, T 50149; *Rangoon General Hospital*, Bogyoke Aung San St, T 81722 (ask for medical superintendent); *Infectious Disease Hospital*, Upper Pansodan St, T 72497.

Money

● **Currency**

Burma's currency unit is the kyat (pronounced 'chat'); notes come in unhelpful (but cosmologically sound) denominations of 1, 5, 10, 15, 45, 90 and 200. New 500, 100, 50 and 20 kyat notes were issued in Spring 1994. There are 100 pyas to the kyat but the coins are virtually worthless and rarely seen. Blissful economic mismanagement has meant that while the official exchange rate is pegged at around 6 kyat to US$1, the purchasing power of the dollar on the black market can be more than 20 times that (120-130 kyat in 1994). The demand for hard currency has resulted in what economists call 'the dollarization' of the urban economy.

● **US$/FECs**

Fortunately, the booming black market is relatively painless and profitable and nobody seems to get into trouble for using it. But tourists confronted by ominous-looking currency declaration and exchange control forms on entering Burma are liable to worry about bending or breaking rules. Foreign independent travellers are supposed to exchange a minimum of US$200 (or the equivalent) at the official rate. You will be given foreign exchange certificates (FECs) in return (a similar system to China). Those on tours with everything – transport and full board – included in the cost of a pre-paid package, do not need to change any money at the official rate on arrival. US$1=1 foreign exchange certificate (FEC) unit. Certificates are issued in 3 denominations equivalent to US$10, US$5 and US$1. All hotel bills, air fares and some rail fares have to be paid in hard currency (ie US$ or FECs) and have to be declared on exchange control forms. You should have changed hard currency at the official rate for at least the same amount declared on your exchange control form (although exchange control forms are rarely checked on departure).

● **Cash and travellers' cheques**

Cash and travellers' cheques can be exchanged at the official rates at the airport, Myanmar Travels and Tours offices and at government-run hotels. Any unused FECs cannot be exchanged on departure unless you have exchanged more than US$200 into FEC's on your trip. However FEC's can be exchanged on the black market in main cities at slightly less than the US$ rate.

● **Black market**

US$ are easily exchanged on the black market. Other currencies can also be exchanged on the black market, for example Thai baht and pounds Sterling, but the rates are not usually as good. You do not generally have to look far to exchange money – most people will be approached before they even leave the airport. However you are usually better off waiting until you get into town when you know the going rate. The best place to do a quick transaction is at Bogyoke Zay Market in Rangoon. Note larger notes get better rates. The black market rate is highest in Rangoon but generally drops 5-10 kyats once outside the capital (the exception being Mandalay). Bundles of old notes are still occasionally touted on the black market in the hope they can be palmed off on some naive tourist.

NB: it is important to set US$6 aside for airport departure tax, as airport officials conveniently never have change. Tourists who forget about this tax and change all their money on the black market are the bane of foreign consular divisions in Rangoon. It is also important to avoid being left with piles of kyat after your trip. Remaining kyat must be surrendered on departure and you only get a quarter of their official value in exchange – an extremely bad deal. Because the kyat is not a convertable currency, it cannot be exchanged outside Burma.

Getting there

● **Entry points**

Rangoon is the main point of entry, although some companies run trips to Mandalay and Pagan from Chiang Mai. The *Myanmar Information for Tourists* states tour groups can enter Burma overland from the Yunnan, China border and from Thailand from Tachilek, Myawaddy, Three Pagodas Pass and Kawthaung. Thailand and Burma have signed an agreement to build a bridge linking Mae Sot and Myawaddy. In practise these borders open and close irregularly, and tourists should check before departure.

● **Air**

Several international carriers fly to Burma: Myanma Airways International, Biman (links with Hanoi and Dhaka), CAAC (Air China), Garuda (Jakarta), Hong Kong, Thai Airways International and Silk Air (Singapore). Daily connections with Bangkok on Myanmar Airways International (now a joint venture with Royal Brunei) and Thai. Myanmar Airways International (ø4,200); Thai Airways (ø5,800). **NB**: you must confirm your outward bound flight on arrival.

Procedure on arriving:

1) Visas and passports are checked at immigration.

2) Independent travellers must change US$300 at the exchange desk (see page 607).

3) Declaration forms are examined at customs.

Procedure on leaving:

1) Pay airport tax (US$6) at counter just inside main door to airport; you will need to show your air ticket and passport.

2) Check in at relevant airline counter; you will need your airport tax receipt.

3) Passport and embarkation cards are checked at immigration.

4) Luggage is inspected before going into waiting area.

● **Customs**

Officially, all items of jewellery, cameras and foreign currency must be declared at customs and currency declaration forms. Very occasionally, items are checked off against this list on departure, to ensure they have not been sold on the black market. This is a rare occurrence however.

Duty-free allowance 400 cigarettes, 2 litre of spirits and half a litre of perfume. Cigarettes and spirits are in great demand in Burma and it is possible to make a profit in kyat on the black market (see page 659).

Currency regulations Foreign currency is accepted from the following countries: USA, United Kingdom, Canada, Germany, France, Switzerland, Australia, Singapore, Malaysia, Hong Kong and Japan. Black market exchange dealers have a preference for US dollars. Foreign currency brought into the country should (officially) be entered on currency control forms on arrival (see page 657). Currency transactions within Burma should also be entered on these forms by authorized exchange agents. The forms must be presented on departure. Tourists are (officially) expected to exchange around US$200 while in Burma – but even the government tacitly concedes that these regulations are ludicrous in view of the differential on the black market.

Export restrictions Gemstones can only be bought at government-controlled outlets such as the Tourist Department Store in Rangoon (where value for money is often not as good as Bangkok). It is inadvisable to smuggle black market gemstones out of the country as they will be confiscated if found. The export of Buddha images and antiques requires a special licence.

When you arrive

● **Airport information**

Mingaladon Airport is 19 km NW of Rangoon. Facilities at the airport include a MTT information office, restaurant upstairs from the arrivals area, money-changing facilities, post office, souvenir shop.

Transport to town Bus: from the main road (5 kyat). **Taxi**: taxis into Rangoon cost about US$6.

● **Airport tax**

US$6 for all international flights. Visitors should set aside a US$5 bill and a US$1 bill in advance as there is never any change available at the airport. (See also Money and the black market, page 657.)

RED FACES ON THE BLACK MARKET

Faced with a massive counterfeit operation, the government withdrew all 100 kyat notes from circulation in 1985. Because little advance notice was given and communications in Burma are so poor, many people lost a fortune, having been left with their life savings in worthless bills. Many families now prefer to protect their savings by investing in gemstones. In 1987, following demonetization, the government abolished 25, 35 and 75 kyat notes and introduced 45 and 90 kyat notes. Astronomers had told the superstitious General Ne Win that 9 was his lucky number. This fitted in with the general's regal pretensions: past kings of Burma were obsessed with the number 9 – King Mindon, for example, had 9 royal white umbrellas and 9-tiered roofs on his palace.

● **Conduct**
See Thailand section, page 494.

● **Cost of living**
Visitors staying in top hotels and eating in hotel restaurants will probably spend US$200-300 per day. Those staying in standard hotels should expect to spend around US$50 per day and travellers staying in cheaper accommodation and eating in local restaurants might be able to live on US$40 per day.

● **Hours of business**
Government offices: 0930-1600, Mon-Fri. **Banks**: 1000-1400, Mon-Fri. **Shops** in the cities are open Mon-Sun; opening and closing hours vary. **Restaurants**: most close by 2100. **Myanmar Travels & Tours (MTT)**: 0800-2000, Mon-Sun.

● **Official time**
$6\frac{1}{2}$ hrs ahead of GMT.

● **Safety**
Burma is generally a lot safer for tourists than it is for the Burmese. The government does not allow tourists to travel to areas which they consider militarily insecure; tourists have rarely been victims of civil crime – other than those who have been stung on the black market. The most dangerous thing visitors are likely to encounter is Russell's Viper – one of the world's deadliest snakes. It is worth taking particular care in and around old pagodas – particularly in Pagan – where sun warmed bricks and cool crevices provide perfect living conditions for snakes. Scorpions are also a problem in Burma and visitors are advised to shake out shoes after leaving pagoda complexes and in the morning.

● **Selling duty-free on the black market**
While some precautions are necessary in informal currency transactions, officialdom turns a blind eye to the black market in spirits and cigarettes. Johnny Walker Red Label Scotch and 555 or Marlboro' cigarettes command premium rates. If Bangkok or Chiang Mai airport duty free shops have sold out of these brands (as is often the case) most other brand names will be rewarded with profits. Designer T-shirts, watches, cosmetics, cameras and walkmans are also readily saleable. **But beware**: if you have declared any of these items on entering the country and you are found to be leaving without them, you may have to pay for them at their declared value. These forms are rarely scrupulously checked on departure though.

● **Shopping**
Antiques: it is possible to buy brass and bronze opium weights, folding scales, temple bells, tattoo sticks, door knockers, betel nut cutters, brass statues, wooden boxes as well as antique lacquerware; in Rangoon there are some shops selling items such as ships' clocks and gramophones (see page 577). Religious antiques cannot be shipped out of the country without obtaining proper documentation – although a large number of Burmese antiques are being smuggled out of the country and appear in Bangkok antique shops (see page 174).

Copperware and brassware: Cottage industry in Mandalay.

Embroidery: The best embroidery is found in Mandalay. Burmese embroidery is now found worldwide made into baseball hats, waistcoats and cushions. Originally the sequinned, appliquéd embroidery was used in funerary ceremonies as coffin covers.

Gems: rubies, jade and sapphires mostly come from the northern mines of Mogok, 115 km NE of Mandalay and Mogaung. Also aquamarine, topaz, amethysts and lapis lazuli. Gemstones

BURMESE NAMES

Burmese names are usually made up of two or three syllables, e.g. Tin Win, or Khin Maung Aye. A few names have one or four. The syllables usually carry auspicious or affectionate meanings. Here are some favourite name syllables:

traditional roman spelling	pronounced	meaning
Tin, Tinn	*Tin*	survivor
Win, Wynn	*Win*	radiant
Naing	*Nain*	victor
Thein, Thane	*Thàyn*	100,000
Than	*Thàn*	million
Khin, Kin	*Kin*	loving, loved
Hla	*Hlá*	pretty
Myint	*Myín*	noble
Kyi, Kyee	*Jchee*	clear
Kyi, Jee	*Jcheè*	big
Shwe	*Shway*	gold
Lay, Le	*Lày*	little
Aye, E	*Ày*	calm
Maung	*Maun*	brother
Kyaw	*Jchaw*	famous
Sein	*Sayn*	diamond
Mya	*Myá*	emerald

Burmese tradition is to have individual names, not family names. So someone named Aye Aye Shwe might have a father named Hla Maung and a mother named Khin Than Myint. A few parents imitate western customs by incorporating an element of their own name into their children's names.

Children are called by their name as it stands, and so are some young women, but normally when you talk to or about adults you put a prefix before the name:

traditional roman spelling	used for
U (pronounced *Oò*)	men
Daw	women
Ko	young men (student age)
Ma (pronounced *Má*)	young women (student age) and girls
Maung	boys

So the members of the fictitious family mentioned above would be Ma Aye Aye Shwe, U Hla Maung and Daw Khin Than Myint.

---

should be bought at government-approved shops only (see Tourist Department Store/Diplomatic Store, page 578), otherwise you risk having them confiscated on leaving the country.

Lacquerware: while most articles are made for practical domestic purposes, a wide variety of products can be found. The most common are *kunit* (betel nut boxes), *lahpetok* (receptacle boxes), cheroot boxes and *bu* (storage containers), but even big *sadaik* (manuscript chests) can be bought. Burmese lacquerware is now being copied in Chiang Mai, Thailand but Thai copies tend to be heavier than Burmese pieces and are not as carefully finished.

Mother-of-pearl: originally popular for decorating palace interiors, mother-of-pearl goods – necklaces, boxes etc, come from the Tenerassim region.

Shan shoulder bags: can be found in Rangoon and Taunggyi.

Silverware: dates back to the 13th century. Now mostly produced near Sagaing.

Textiles: local textiles now face stiff competition from cheap imported fabrics smuggled into Burma from neighbouring countries.

Weaving: silk *lungyis* are often made to order. The colours in an individual's lungyi is determined by his or her horoscope. Specially-made lungyis are often expensive – more than 5,000 kyat. Cotton lungyis are made in several patterns, which are associated with different parts of the country. The purple/green/black 'tartan' pattern comes from Kachin state and 'tartan' lungyis became a uniform for politicians of the National League for Democracy in the run-up to the elections in 1990; they were worn with white shirts.

Woodcarvings: Mandalay is the main centre.

NB: film is difficult to buy in Burma and is often past its sell-by date; visitors should try to bring a stock of film into the country with them.

● **Tipping**
Tipping is not encouraged in Burma, although it is quite common in hotels and restaurants. Small gifts are welcomed, especially if you are invited to visit someone's home for a meal. Gifts particularly appreciated are lipsticks, ballpoint pens, T-shirts, paperback books, and postcards (for Britons, pictures of Piccadilly Circus, Nelson's Column, Buckingham Palace, the Queen and Princess Diana go down very well). Disposable cameras are also highly appreciated: they cost about ฿250 in Bangkok.

It is normal to tip guides – without tips it is hard for them to make a living.

● **Voltage**
220 volts, 50 cycles; current fluctuates alarmingly and can cause problems with electrical equipment.

● **Weights and measures**
As in neighbouring India, the Indian-English terms *lakh* and *crore* are widely used in Burma – mainly in the context of money. One lakh is 100,000; a crore is 100 lakhs, or 10 million. In markets, rice and flower is usually sold by volume rather than weight; the normal standard measuring unit is an empty condensed milk can. Other commonly used weights and measures include:

    1 viss (peith-tha) = 1,633g
    1 tical = 16.33g
    1 cubit (tong) = 46 cm
    1 span (htwa) = 23 cm

Where to stay

● **Accommodation**
Hotels in Burma are generally quite expensive and the choice is limited. Hotels and guesthouses tend to get booked up quickly. All hotels have to be paid for in hard currency (US$ or FECs) – except for the very cheapest guesthouses (see below). Several of the big hotels in Rangoon are being totally refurbished. All government hotels are run to the same standard with rarely functioning air conditioners, sporadic hot water and a hotel restaurant serving European/Burmese food. There is sometimes a small single occupancy surcharge; there is also a 10% service charge. Since Spring 1994, some government hotels

HOTEL CLASSIFICATIONS

A+: US$200+ Only *The Strand* falls into this category at the moment but more top international-style hotels are planned. You will only find the top end hotels in Rangoon.

A: US$100-200 Burmese hotels backed by foreign capital, these hotels offer a/c, rooms with attached bathrooms, restaurant and bar, some business services, ie a fax, room service, laundry service, television in room showing satellite TV. Neither standards, nor facilities are as good as their Bangkok counterparts. You will only find hotels in this bracket in Rangoon, although there are hotels planned in Mandalay.

B: US$50-100 Hotels in this bracket will have a/c, rooms with attached bathrooms, h/w, laundry service and a restaurant. Most government-run hotels will fall into this bracket or the top of those in C.

C: under US$50 There are a few privately-run guesthouses/hotels which fall into this category and the lower end of the government-run hotels. Facilities are basic: fan or a/c, h/w (if you're lucky), some rooms with attached bathroom, some hotels will have restaurants, in privately-run hotels the family might well offer to cook meals. Standards vary considerably depending on the owners. Cheaper hotels, where travellers are allowed to stay, are only found in the main tourist destinations.

have been leased to entrepreneurs so standards should improve.

Travellers are only allowed to stay in hotels/guesthouses registered with MTT. Tourists are able to stay in private hotels/guesthouses not registered with MTT at the discretion of hotel owners. These are also basic. Private hotels are usually a bit cheaper, and definitely better value, than their government-run counterparts. However, they cannot afford to radically reduce their rates as government taxes are so high. There are private hotels/guesthouses in all major tourist destinations: Rangoon, Mandalay, Nyaung-U and New Pagan, Taunggyi and Yanshwe.

Food and drink

Food

Burmese food is generally disappointing – especially in comparison with Thailand. Many restaurants serve Indian, Chinese or European food; Burmese food is harder to come by and usually has to be ordered in advance. Burmese restaurants tend to close early, 1900-2000. In Rangoon many hotel and restaurant menus are printed in English. Hotel food tends to be poor in government-run establishments – often a disastrous mix between Burmese and European.

In small restaurants outside Rangoon and Mandalay expect to pay 20-40 kyat for a meal. The choice of restaurants outside the main cities is limited, and only Burmese and local dishes are available (although Chinese restaurants are common in towns). In larger cities, like Rangoon and Mandalay, there is a wide range of cuisines. The standard of restaurants is also higher, as are the prices. In top restaurants in Rangoon expect to pay 70-100 kyat for a meal.

The staples of typical Burmese cuisine are rice and rice noodles; these are traditionally served in a large bowl placed in the centre of the low table. Burmese curries, unlike Indian curries, use only a few spices and herbs – garlic and onions, tomatoes, coriander, ginger, tumeric, salt and hot chilli peppers, which are all fried in peanut oil. *Hin* is curry; *kyatnarhin* is chicken curry, *ametha hnat*, beef curry and *ngathalauk*, fish curry. Portions of curries are often small, you are supposed to fill yourself up with rice. A clear soup, or *hingho*, nearly always accompanies the meal. Food is always served at room temperature. Dishes are usually served with *ngapi ye* – fermented fish or shrimp

paste. The more upmarket fish paste, *balachaung*, is made with dried shrimps and garlic (it is related to the Malaysian *belacan*). Balachaung is not supposed to be taken out of the country as it is red and is therefore an easy way to smuggle rubies. The tiny chillipadis, which lace many dishes, are known as *kala au* – which translates as "the chillies which make Indian men cry". They are very hot. Seafood is exported from Burma and items such as *kyar-pazun* (tiger prawns) regularly appear on menus even far inland.

● **Meat dishes**

Weq-tha chow – sweet pork – a favourite – pork is meant to be very good in Burma.
Weq-tha-paung – stewed pork soup.
Jcheh tha hin – chicken curry.
Jcheh tha jow – fried chicken.
Jcheh tha thoq – chicken salad with onions.
Sey-ta hin – goat curry.
Ameh-tha – beef, but beef is rarely served in restaurants since many Burmese buddhist do not eat beef.
Beh-tha-hin – duck curry.

● **Fish dishes**

Gna-talaung paung – stewed fish – typically Burmese fish, tastes a bit like Sardines, since it is stewed, the bones have gone soft and can be eaten too.

Gna-pan mwe – shredded fish (no bones at all), cooked in chilli, garlic and ginger.

Gna-min – butter fish – usually served in a spicy tomato based sauce.

Bazun si-pien – prawns in oil and onions. Prawns can be very big, usually from the river.

Bazun thoq – small prawn salad.

Gna-chouq-jow – dried fried fish.

Gna-pi jow – fried fish paste with chilli – a Burmese favourite.

Gna-talaung u – fish roe – usually cooking in oil and onions.

● **Vegetable dishes**

Peh-dji-naq – large yellow butter beans – can be ordered as a vegetarian dish.

Cheh-hin-kha-dee jow – bitter gourds

Kha-yin-dee naq – aubergines.

Byan-boo jow – corn.

Ah-loo – potatoes.

Gazun yweh – spinach tasting leaf, often translated as water cress here.

Gazun-yweh-hmoe – same as above with mushrooms.

Chin baung – sour leaf that tastes a bit like sorrel, often cooked with bamboo shoots.

● **Salads (***thoq***)**

Burmese are fond of those salads (*thoq*), to be eaten with rice or without. Salty, sometimes spicy. The base for salad is peanuts, sesame seeds, pea powder, fried onions and garlic, peanut oil and tamarind juice.

Min-khwa-yweh thoq – type of water cress.

Salad yweh thoq – lettuce leaves in Burmese style (in season).

Kha-yin-jchin-dee thoq – tomato salad.

Lapeh thoq – pickled tea leaves – only found in Burma, usually eaten after the meal, though can also be had with rice. Best in Mandalay.

Jchin thoq – pickled ginger – also eaten after a meal.

● **Soups**

Peh-kala hin – lentil soup with vegetables.

Thi-zon-hin-jcho – vegetable sour soup.

Beh-tha-paung-hin-jcho – stewed duck soup.

Peh-dji-hin-jcho – yellow butter bean soup.

● **Noodles**

Mohinga – fermented rice noodles, served in a spicy fish soup with an onion and ginger base. the Burmese love *mohinga* they eat in the street at every hour of the day.

On-no-khauk-swe – wheat noodles served in a coconut milk soup, with chicken and duck egg.

Drink

Tap water is not safe to drink unless it has been thoroughly boiled. *Lapetgye* – Burmese or Chinese tea – is available at restaurants and teahouses; it is served free of charge. Teahouses mainly serve strong, sweet and milky tea (made with condensed milk). Pickled tea, or *letpet*, is also popular. Soft drinks are not hard to find: imported cans of Coke or Sprite are expensive and sometimes cost more than 50 kyats, while locally produced soda water or sickly sweet green lemonade costs 10-15 kyats a bottle. Bottled drinking water is 20-28 kyat per bottle.

Mandalay beer is a light but malty brew, made by the People's Brewery and Distillery in the original British-built brewery, which has been operating since 1886. The quality is said to have gone down hill since 1988 and as the country's only brewery it has also had problems meeting demand. The price of Mandalay beer varies considerably: it is around 40 kyat/bottle in government-run outlets and 80-100 kyats elsewhere; it is too expensive for the average Burmese to afford. Imported alcohol is normally only available at hotel bars, although black market Johnnie Walker is an ubiquitous ornament in shops, bars and private homes. **Mandalay Rum** is not very strong; it claims to be "finely flavoured" and "mellow throughout". In bars and restaurants, spirits are measured in "pegs" – a quaint colonial hangover. A peg is a double; single measures are known as smalls.

Getting around

● **Air**

Myanma Airways runs Fokker 27s (turboprops) and F-28s (jets) on internal routes – the former had a spate of fatal crashes in the mid-1980s which were attributed to pilot error, not lack of maintenance. Although their cabin fittings are falling apart, the F-28s, have a more reliable record. One foreign diplomat in Rangoon cautions against using the airline at all, saying: "Our advice to those planning to travel by plane is 'Don't'". Most tourists do, however, travel by plane; train journeys take too long, particularly in view of visa restrictions.

There are regular services connecting Rangoon with Mandalay, Nyaung-U (Pagan) and Heho (Inle Lake) as well as Sandoway (although Arakan is a politically sensitive part of the country). Tickets have to be paid for in US dollars. Schedules are unreliable and flights are notoriously difficult to book and tourists have sometimes been forced to forego their seats when government officials require them at short notice. Return tickets can be purchased but return flights can only be confirmed at the destination. Tickets can be purchased in Bangkok but reservations can only be made in Burma.

● **Internal flight prices**

From Rangoon (Yangon):	US$
Bhamo	129
Heho	85
Kale Myo	116
Katha	127
Kentung	102
Kyaupyu	66-78
Lashio	110
Loikaw	55
Mandalay	100
Moulmein	32-37
Myeik (Mergui)	87-98
Myitkyina	148-165
Pagan	90
Sittwe	78-88
Tachilek	98
Tavoy	80
Twante	47-84

● **Train**

Train tickets can be booked through MTT or through the main station ticket offices and are supposed to be paid for at the official rate. Most travellers book tickets to Thazi or Mandalay through MTT at the official rate, but most other train rides can be bought at the station and paid for in kyats. Tickets can be booked on T 74027. Rail fares are cheap compared with air fares and 'upper class', first class and 'ordinary class' are available; tourists are not expected to travel on the latter. First class seats are reserved and recline, ordinary class is unreserved. Smarter 'special' trains run between Rangoon and Mandalay on Mon, Thur and Sat (US$38). Trains are slow and travel times unpredictable. Overnight trains are very noisy and dusty. Travel agents are reluctant to sell tickets to Thazi, most travellers buy a ticket to Mandalay and jump off at Thazi. There is always plenty to eat on the trains as vendors hop on and off at stations.

Train fares

From Rangoon:	US$
Amherst	25
Kyaiktiyo Pagoda	12
Mandalay	30-38
Moulmein	25
(For Inle Lake and Pagan)	25
Pegu	8

Prome	15
Thaton	15
Thazi	30
Ye	32

● **Road**

In 1974 General Ne Win decided that it would be more auspicious if Burma changed to driving on the right – although outside the main towns this becomes irrelevant.

Bus The buses that operate in Burma – particularly those in Rangoon – are extinct almost everywhere else in the world. The ones in Rangoon are 1940s-vintage Chevrolets with brightly painted teak bodies; they are invariably overcrowded, with passengers hanging off them. Long-distance buses run all over the country and are the cheapest form of 'transport' – although they are also very crowded, uncomfortable and unreliable.

Linecars Some areas now have pick-ups called linecars – rather like the Thai songthaew with bench seats in the back. They are faster and more reliable than the buses. Bus/pick-up prices vary considerably from one week to the next. If bus owners can buy petrol from government outlets it only costs 16 kyat per gallon; if they have to buy it on the black market it can cost up to 250 kyat per gallon and fares are adjusted accordingly. Mandalay-Pagan and Pagan-Inle Lake usually costs 250 kyat. People with private vehicles hoard petrol in the run-up to the water festival in Apr (those who own jeeps cruise up and down the streets for 3 days) and fares tend to escalate at that time. Bus fares can be paid for in kyat.

Bus fares:

From Rangoon:	Kyat
Pegu	30
Mandalay	700 (a/c coach)
Prome	150
Twante	20

From Mandalay:	Kyat
Lashio	35

From Thazi:	Kyat
Kyaiktiyo	175
Moulmein	150
Nyaung-U	30
Taunggyi	30
Thaton	30

Car hire Private cars can also be hired in main cities. Hotels can usually organize car hire. Long distance trips should cost around US$35 per day for the car. The price will go up if areas are considered difficult to get to (ie 'restricted'

USEFUL BURMESE WORDS & PHRASES

Many people in Burma can speak English well, and others remember a bit from schooldays. All staff in immigration, customs, tourist shops and hotels are English speakers. However, everyone is appreciative if visitors show they have made an effort to learn the language.

Spelling & pronunciation

Burmese is written in its own script and there is no standard method of writing Burmese words in roman letters. In the following notes read:

ee as in *see*	ay as in *day*	eh as in *men*	a as in *bra*	aw as in *law*
oh as in *go*	oo as in *too*	in as in *pin*	ai as in *Thai*	an as in *man*
ou as in *sound*	u as in *put*	å as in *about*		

Read *bp gk dt jch zs* as sounds midway between the first and second consonants (so *dtee* is between *d* and *t*, like a foreigner's pronunciation of *tea*). *Th* is pronounced as in English. Words ending in *-n* are pronounced as in French *vin, son* etc. And *q* stands for a glottal stop, as in Cockney *the caq saq on the maq*. Burmese also has tones: read *à, á* and *aq* on a higher pitch than *a*, and likewise for other vowels.

Hello and goodbye

Among themselves people use a variety of greetings phrases ("Where are you going?" "I see you've arrived" etc), but in schools, and sometimes to foreigners, they may say *Min-gålaba*. The reply is the same. On leaving say *Thwà-ba-òhn-meh* ("I'll be getting along now") or less formally *Thwà-meh-naw?* ("I'm going now – OK?"). The response is *Gkaùn-ba-bee* ("Fine" "OK"). You can preface your farewell with *Thwà-zåya sheé-ba-deh* ("I have to go now").

Useful words and phrases

Thanks	*Jchày-zoò dtin-ba-deh* or *Jchày-zoò-bèh*
– You're welcome	*– Yá-ba-deh* or *Gkayq-zsá måsheé-ba-boò*
– Sorry	*– Sàw-reè-bèh*
– That's all right	*– Yá-ba-deh* or *Gkayq-zsá måsheé-ba-boò*
No thanks or That's enough	*Dtaw-ba-bee*
Just a minute	*Kånà-làe*
Have you finished?	*Bpeè-bee-là?*
– Yes ("I have finished")	*– Bpeè-bee*
– No ("I haven't finished")	*– Måbpeè-thày-ba-boò*
I'm happy to have met you	*Dtwáy-yá-da wùn-tha-ba-deh*
– I'm happy too (woman speaking)	*– Jchåmá-lèh wùn-tha-ba-deh*
– I'm happy too (man speaking)	*– Jchånaw-lèh wùn-tha-ba-deh*
How are you?	*Nay-gkaùn-yéh-là?* literally ("Are you well?")
– Fine	*– Nay-gkaùn-ba-deh* literally ("I am well")
What is your name?	*Nan-meh beh-loh kaw-dhålèh?*
– It is Mary	*– Mary-ba*

areas) or for longer trips (ie to Pagan or Inle Lake from Mandalay). For a 5-day trip a car should cost around US$450. For local trips you should pay US$20-25 per day. Cars are always hired with drivers and you are nearly always asked to pay in hard currency.

● Boat

River boats travel the entire length of the Irrawaddy, although in the dry season, sand banks make river journeys hazardous. The best trip to take by boat in Burma is from Mandalay down the Irrawaddy to Pagan; it takes 13-15 hrs (see page 632). It is also possible to travel by boat from Rangoon to Syriam (see page 580) from Mandalay to Mingun (see page 638) from Rangoon to Twante, Pagan to Rangoon (although this trip is time consuming) and Rangoon to Bassein. Fares are cheap – it costs between 50-150 kyat from Mandalay to Pagan, depending which class you travel. Towns on rivers will always have private boats to hire for short hops. Rowing boats are cheaper than motor boats (approx 300-400 kyat/hr, depending on price of petrol) but can only be used for nearby sights.

● Other local transport

Taxis Taxis can easily be found in most towns

'Asking for' words

What's this?	*Da ba-lèh?*
– It's a mango	*– Thầyeq-thì*
What's that called?	*Èh-da beh-loh kaw-thầlèh?*
– It's called Ee-jcha-gkwày	*– Ee-jcha-gkwày-lóh kaw-ba-deh*
Please say that again	*Taq-bpyàw-ba-òhn*

Asking the way

I want to go to ...	*... thwà-jin-ba-deh*
How do I get there?	*Beh-lo thwà-yá-mầlèh?*
– Go this way	*– Dee-beq thwà-ba*
– Go straight	*– Dtéh-dèh thwà-ba*
Is it far?	*Wày-dhầlà?*
– It is a bit far	*– Nèh-nèh wày-ba-deh*
– It's not far	*– Mầwày-ba-boò*

Restaurants

Please give me/us ...	*... pày-ba*
Have you got any ...?	*Pầlin sheé-thầlà?*
– Yes, I have	*– Sheé-ba-deh* ("I have")
– No, I haven't	*– Mầsheé-ba-boò* ("I haven't")
We want to settle up	*Paiq-san shìn-meh*
How much does it come to?	*Beh-louq jchá-thầlèh?*

Numbers

0	thohn-nyá	10	dtầseh
1	dtiq	20	hnầseh
2	hniq	30	thòhn-zeh
3	thòhn	40	lày-zeh
4	lày	100	dtầya
5	ngà	200	hnầya
6	chouq	300	thòhn-ya
7	kun-niq	400	lày-ya
8	shiq	1,000	dtầtoun
9	gkò	10,000	dtầthoùn
		100,000	dtầthàyn
		1,000,000	dtầthàn

– there are no long-distance taxis. Always negotiate the price before setting off; saloon taxis should cost around 200 kyat/hr. Small Mazda taxis in Rangoon and **thoun-bein** (three-wheelers) in Mandalay are cheaper (about 120 kyat/hr).

Horse-drawn cart Mainly found in Pagan, Mandalay and Maymyo, cost about 200 kyat/day.

Trishaw Bicycle trishaws are used in Mandalay and Rangoon, cost about 250 kyat/day or 20-30 kyat for short trips around town.

Communications

● Language

More than 80 different dialects are spoken in Burma, with all the different tribal minorities having their own dialects. The national language is Burmese; it uses an extraordinary-looking script which is based on strings of circles and is related to Tamil script. English is no longer as widely spoken as it used to be, although in the towns and cities there is never much difficulty finding someone who speaks reasonable English. Under British colonial rule, English was the medium of instruction but following independence it was dropped from the school curriculum. In 1981 English was reinstated on the national curriculum after Ne Win's daughter Sanda failed her English examinations abroad.

● Postal services

Aerograms – 6 kyat to all destinations. Postcards – 3 kyat (anywhere), letters: 5 kyat (Europe), 6 kyat (US).

Counting

one glass of water	*yay dtåkweq*
two cups of coffee	*kaw-pee hnåkweq*
two bottles of Coke	*Kouq thòhn-pålìn*
two plates of fish curry	*ngå-hìn hnåpwèh*
one plate of rice	*tåmìn dtåbpwèh*

Items without a unit of quantity are counted by -*goó* (sometimes pronounced *koó*)

two cakes	*gkeiq hnåkoó*
three dumplings	*bpouq-see thòhn-goó*
four paratas	*bpålata lày-goó*

Shops

How much is this?	*Da beh-louq-lèh?*
– It's 8 kyats	*– Shiq-jchaq-bpa*
That's too expensive	*Zày myà-ba-deh*
I'll give you 6 kyats	*Chouq-jchaq pày-meh*
Would that be all right?	*Yá-målà?*
– OK	*– Gkaùn-ba-bee*
– No it wouldn't	*– Måyá-ba-boò*
– It's too little	*– Nèh-ba-deh*
– Give me 7 kyats	*– Kun-nåjchaq pày-ba*
OK	*Gkaùn-ba-bee*
It's too small	*Thày-deh*
It's too big	*Jcheè-deh*
I'll look around elsewhere – OK?	*Jcheé-òhn-meh-naw?*

Basic vocabulary

beef	*åmèh-thà*	pork	*weq-thà*
chicken	*jcheq-thà*	post office	*zsa-daiq*
curry	*hìn*	prawn	*båzun*
doctor	*såya-wun*	restaurant	*tåmìn-zain*
fish	*ngà*	rice	*tåmìn*
hotel	*ho-dteh*	room	*åkàn*
hospital	*sày-yohn*	toilet	*ein-tha*
noodles	*kouq-swèh*	vegetarian	*theq-thaq-luq*
police station	*yèh-ta-ná*		

● **Telephone services**

Local: the city code for Rangoon is 01; Mandalay is 02; Pagan is 35 and Taunggyi is 81. Local calls are free of charge. Call 101 to book inland calls.

International: the country code is 95. International calls can be made from major hotels and from the Central Telegraph Office in Rangoon (Pansodan/Maha Bandoola roads; open 0700-2000 Mon-Sun). The international service has improved, but is still poor due to major deficiencies in the domestic network. All international calls have to go through the operator: 131 to book an overseas or inland trunk call between 0700 and 1900. Connections take a very long time. Telex facilities are also available at the Central Telegraph Office, as well as in some major hotels.

Entertainment

● **Newspapers**

Newspapers are a product of Western influence. The first English-language newspaper was started in British Burma in 1836 and the first Burmese-language paper rolled off the presses in Arakan in 1873. After the 1962 military coup, the press was restricted and quickly became the mouthpiece of the government. Rangoon has six daily newspapers, two of which are English-language papers: *The Working People's Daily* – which in 1993 was rechristened *Myanmar Alin*, or 'New Light of Burma', after a pre-1962 publication – takes most of its information from Western or Asian news agencies. Newspaper reports of events inside Burma are highly selective and should be taken with a pinch of salt; the pages of *Myanmar Alin* are filled with rants against the BBC and are padded out with endless transcripts of the latest landmark speech by a member of the junta.

● Radio

Burmese Broadcasting Service (BBS) operates for 16 hrs of the day and has news in English at 0830, 1300 and 2115. Most of the broadcasting is in Burmese, although there are some programmes in minority dialects. Burmese themselves rely mainly on the BBC World Service and Voice of America to bring them news of what is happening in Burma; both of these stations have Burmese-language services which broadcast daily.

● Television

Burma's first TV station started operating in 1981 with the assistance of the Japanese. There are about 2 hrs of broadcasting a day, in the evenings. Many of the programmes are in English. The most popular programme is pre-recorded English first division football from 1240-1430 every Saturday. Transmissions are sponsored by 555 and usually show the previous year's FA Cup qualifiers.

Warning Many people were jailed for their links with foreign journalists in the run-up to the 1988 riots. In 1990 a Burmese Military Intelligence mole who had infiltrated the Burmese service of the BBC World Service in London was dismissed from his job. Information passed by him to MI in Rangoon had been instrumental in the arrest of Nay Min, a Burmese lawyer and secret source of reports on the 1988 uprising. He was sentenced to 14 years' hard labour by a military tribunal. Foreign diplomats report that he has been badly beaten and has suffered internal injuries.

Holidays and festivals

The government runs on the Gregorian calendar but religious and cultural festivals are regulated by the **Burmese calendar**, which is counted from 638 AD. The Burmese calendar is lunar-based. The Buddhist era dates from 544 BC, the agreed date of the Buddha's attainment of nirvana. Each pagoda has its own birthday festival and its favourite *nat* (see page 544) to honour. If a festival is due at one of the most important pagodas, pilgrims travel vast distances to attend the festival.

Burma still uses a lunar calendar. On the centre of the masthead of *The Working People's Daily*, for example, the date in the centre of the

page might be '14th Waxing of Tagu, 1353' or '6th Waning of Tazaungmon, 1353', the year corresponding to the Buddhist Era (BE). Most festivals (*pwes*) take place on or around the full moon. Business – including MTT – fortunately operates on the Gregorian system.

Jan: *Independence Day* (4th: public holiday) week-long festivities; celebrated all over the country with boat races on the Royal Lake, Rangoon and the palace moat, Mandalay.

Feb: *Union Day* (12th: public holiday) in honour of the founding of the Union of Burma in 1947. Parade in Rangoon of representatives of Burma's various ethnic groups in traditional costumes. *Htamane* (moveable: new moon) rice-harvest festival.

Mar: *Farmers' (or Peasants') Day* (2nd: public holiday) anniversary of General Ne Win's military take-over in 1962, marked by parades. *Dry Season Festival* (10th: public holiday). *Armed Forces (Resistance) Day* (27th: public holiday) celebrated with fireworks and parades; although the Tatmadaw (see page 552) has given the Burmese people little cause to celebrate in recent years.

Apr: *Thingyan (water festival)* (moveable: public holiday) similar to Songkran in Thailand; Thagyamin, king of the nats, descends to earth to bring blessings for the new year. Buddhist New Year is celebrated by much water-throwing – a tradition most enthusiastically observed in Mandalay. Traditionally a small bowl of scented water was thrown over passers-by to "cleanse" them; now anything goes. Revellers are armed with everything from buckets to firehoses. People from all over Burma travel to the city for the simple pleasure of getting soaked, driving around in World War II vintage open-topped Willy Jeeps and watching traditional dancers and bad rock bands performing late into the night on streetside stages. The festival has not yet been hooliganized as it has in parts of Thailand and there are never many tourists around. At night, once the water-throwing deadline is passed at 1800 (no-one breaks this unwritten rule), the streets of Mandalay are host to a huge city-wide open-air party which stops dead at curfew time (2300), when soldiers come and spoil the fun. A visit to Mandalay during Thingyan is highly recommended – but visitors are advised to be very careful with cameras. Buddha images and pagodas are cleaned for New Year's Day. The exact time the Lord of the Nats descends to earth is calculated by astrologers. The stars on New Year's Eve also provide the basis for predictions about the coming year – such as whether the rains will be good. There are similar festivals in Laos, Cambodia and Thailand.

May: *Workers' Day* (1st: public holiday). *Kason* (or pouring-water-on-the- banyan-tree Festival) (moveable – full moon: public holiday) is the Buddha's birthday; banyan trees get a soaking to celebrate the Buddha's enlightenment under one. Procession in temples.

Jul: *Waso* (moveable: public holiday) commemorates the Buddha's first sermon and the beginning of Buddhist lent. New robes are offered to the monks and gifts taken to pagodas. *Thadingyut* (Buddhist Lent) and the beginning of a 3-month period of prayer and contemplation by Buddhists. During this time monks are not supposed to travel and marriages and pwes should not take place. *Martyr's Day* (19th: public holiday) in memory of Bogyoke Aung San, independent Burma's first Prime Minister, assassinated in 1947 (see page 529).

Sept: during Sept, boat races are held on rivers and lakes throughout Burma: it is known as the *Tawthalin* festival. The most spectacular procession is at Inle Lake (see page 592).

Oct: *Thadingyut* (end of Buddhist Lent) – or festival of lights (moveable) celebrates the end of Buddhist lent and means weddings and other celebrations can now take place. Oil lamps are lit for 3 days. Robe-giving ceremonies throughout October when monks' robes are presented to monasteries.

Nov. *National Day* (11th: public holiday). *Tazaungmon* (moveable: full moon); weaving festival in which teams of unmarried girls engage in weaving competitions, making new robes for monks in the light of the full moon.

Dec: *Spirit-honouring festivals* are held during the full moon. *Christmas Day* (25th, public holiday).

Further reading

Aung San Syu Kyi (1991) *Aung San of Burma*, Kiscadale; Aung San Suu Kyi (1991) *Freedom from Fear*, Penguin ; Aung San Suu Kyi (1993) *Towards a True Refuge*, Oxford; Aung-Thwin, Michael (1985) *Pagan: the origins of modern Burma*, University of Hawaii Press: Honolulu; Aye Saung (1989) *Burman in the back row: autobiography of a Burmese rebel*, White Lotus: London and Bangkok; Boucaud, Andre & Louis (1989) *Burma's Golden Triangle on the trail of the opium warlords*, Asia 2000; Cady, John F. (1958) *A history of modern Burma*, Cornell University Press: Ithaca; Foucar, E.C.V. (1963) *Mandalay the golden*, Dennis Dobson: London; Lintner, Bertil (1990) *Outrage: Burma's struggle for democracy*, White Lotus: London and Bangkok. This book, a definitive and emotive account of the 1988 uprising has been printed in Burmese and is available in Burma in brown paper covers, under-the-counter; Lowry, John (1974) *Burmese Art*, Victoria & Albert Museum: London; O'Connor (1907) *Mandalay and other cities of the past in Burma*, Hutchinson: London; McCoy, Alfred W (1991) *The Politics of Heroin: CIA complicity in the global drugs trade*, Lawrence Hill Books: New York; Smith, Martin (1991) *Burma*, Zed Books: London; Steinberg, David (1982) *Burma: a socialist nation of Southeast Asia*, Westview Press: Boulder, Colorado; Taylor, Robert, *The state in Burma*, University of Hawaii Press: Honolulu; Thaw, Aung *Historical sites in Burma*, Ministry of Union Culture; Toke Gale U *Burmese timber elephant*, Trade Corporation: Rangoon.

Acknowledgements

Cas Bylhott (Netherlands), Russell Murdoch (UK), Elaine Kovacs (UK), Pter Oray (UK) Violaine Brisou (France).

TEMPERATURE CONVERSION TABLE

°C	°F	°C	°F	°C	°F	°C	°F	°C	°F
1	34	11	52	21	70	31	88	41	106
2	36	12	54	22	72	32	90	42	108
3	38	13	56	23	74	33	92	43	109
4	39	14	57	24	75	34	93	44	111
5	41	15	59	25	77	35	95	45	113
6	43	16	61	26	79	36	97	46	115
7	45	17	63	27	81	37	99	47	117
8	46	18	64	28	82	38	100	48	118
9	48	19	66	29	84	39	102	49	120
10	50	20	68	30	86	40	104	50	122

The formula for converting °C to °F is: °C x 9 ÷ 5 + 32 = °F

WEIGHTS AND MEASURES

Metric
Weight:
1 kilogram (kg) = 2,205 pounds
1 metric ton = 1.102 short tons
= 0.984 long ton

Length:
1 millimetre (mm) = 0.03937 inch
1 metre = 3.281 feet
1 kilometre (km) = 0.621 mile

Area:
1 hectare = 2.471 acres
1 square km (km^2) = 0.386 sq mile

Capacity:
1 litre = 0.220 Imperial gallon
= 0.264 US gallon
(5 Imperial gallons are approximately equal to 6 US gallons)

Volume:
1 cubic metre (m^3) = 35.31 cubic feet
= 1.31 cubic yards

British and US

1 pound (lb) = 454 grams
1 short ton (2,000lb) = 0.907 metric ton
1 long ton (2,240lb) = 1.016 metric tons

1 inch = 25.417 millimetres
1 foot (ft) = 0.305 metre
1 mile = 1.609 kilometres

1 acre = 0.405 hectare
1 square mile (sq mile) = 2,590 km^2

1 Imperial gallon = 4.546 litres
1 US gallon = 3.785 litres

1 cubic foot (cu ft) = 0.028 m^3
1 cubic yard (cu yd) = 0.765 m^3

GLOSSARY

T = Thailand, **C** = Cambodia, **V** = Vietnam, **L** = Laos, **B** = Burma

A

Amitabha	the Buddha of the Past (see Avalokitsvara)
Amphoe	district; administrative division below the province (see page 63) (T)
Amulet	protective medallion (see page 142)
Ao	bay (T)
Arhat	a person who has perfected himself; images of former monks are sometimes carved into arhat
Avadana	Buddhist narrative, telling of the deeds of saintly souls
Avalokitsvara	also known as Amitabha and Lokeshvara, the name literally means 'World Lord'; he is the compassionate male Bodhisattva, the saviour of Mahayana Buddhism and represents the central force of creation in the universe; usually portrayed with a lotus and water flask

B

Bai sema	boundary stones marking consecrated ground around a Buddhist bot (see page 92)
Ban	village; shortened from muban (T and L)
Baray	artificial lake or reservoir (C)
Batik	a form of resist dyeing
Bhikku	Buddhist monk
Bilu	an ogre; Burmese version of the dvarapala (B)
Bodhi	the tree under which the Buddha achieved enlightenment (*Ficus religiosa*)
Bodhisattva	a future Buddha. In Mahayana Buddhism, someone who has attained enlightenment, but who postpones nirvana to help others reach it.
Bonze	term for a Buddhist monk, used in Burma (B)
Bot	Buddhist ordination hall, of rectangular plan, identifiable by the boundary stones placed around it; an abbreviation of ubosoth (see page 92) (T)
Brahma	the Creator, one of the gods of the Hindu trinity, usually represented with four faces, and often mounted on a hamsa
Brahmin	a Hindu priest
Bun	to make merit
Byauk	'variegated'; describes a temple with a colourfully painted interior (B)

C

Caryatid	elephants, often used as buttressing decorations
Ceityas	stupa (B)
Celadon	pottery ware with blue/green to grey glaze (see page 174) (T)
Chakri	the current royal dynasty in Thailand. They have reigned since 1782 (T)

Champa	rival empire of the Khmers, of Hindu culture, based in present day Vietnam
Changwat	province (see page 63) (T)
Chao	title for Lao and Thai kings (T and L)
Chat	honorific umbrella or royal multi-tiered parasol
Chedi	from the Sanskrit *cetiya* (Pali, *caitya*) meaning memorial. Usually a religious monument (often bell-shaped) containing relics of the Buddha or other holy remains. Used interchangeably with stupa (see pages 89-90)
Chenla	Chinese name for Cambodia before the Khmer era
Chinlon	The Burmese equivalent of the Thai sport *takraw*; a rattan ball is hit over a net using any part of the body except the hands (see page 548) (B)
Chinthe	Guardian temple lion (see page 581) (B)
Chofa	'sky tassel' on the roof of wat buildings (T)
CPT	Communist Party of Thailand (T)

D

Deva	a Hindu-derived male god
Devata	a Hindu-derived goddess
Dharma	the Buddhist law
Dipterocarp	family of trees (Dipterocarpaceae) characteristic of Southeast Asia's forests
Dok sofa	literally, 'bucket of flowers'. A frond-like construction which surmounts temple roofs in Laos. Over 10 flowers signifies the wat was built by a king (L)
Dvarapala	guardian figure, usually placed at the entrance to a temple

F

Farang	Westerner (T)
Funan	the oldest Indianised state of Indochina and precursor to Chenla

G

Ganesh	elephant-headed son of Siva
Garuda	mythical divine bird, with predatory beak and claws, and human body; the king of birds, enemy of naga and mount of Vishnu
Gautama	the historic Buddha
Geomancy	the art of divination by lines and figures
Gopura	crowned or covered gate, entrance to a religious area

H

Hamsa	sacred goose, Brahma's mount; in Buddhism it represents the flight of the doctrine
Hang yaaw	long-tailed boat, used on canals (T)
Harmika	box-like part of a Burmese stupa that often acts as a reliquary casket (B)
Hat	beach (T)

Hinayana	'Lesser Vehicle', major Buddhist sect in Southeast Asia, usually termed Theravada Buddhism (see page 40)
Hintha	mythical bird (B)
Hong	swan (T)
Hor kong	a pavilion built on stilts where the temple drum is kept (T and L)
Hor takang	bell tower (see page 92) (T and L)
Hor tray/trai	library where manuscripts are stored in a Lao or Thai temple (see page 92) (T and L)
Hti	'umbrella' surmounting Burmese temples, often encrusted with jewels (B)

I

Ikat	tie-dyeing method of patterning cloth (see page 282)
Indra	the Vedic god of the heavens, weather and war; usually mounted on a 3 headed elephant

J

Jataka(s)	the birth stories of the Buddha; they normally number 547, although an additional 3 were added in Burma for reasons of symmetry in mural painting and sculpture; the last ten are the most important

K

Kala (makara)	literally, 'death' or 'black'; a demon ordered to consume itself; often sculpted with grinning face and bulging eyes over entranceways to act as a door guardian; also known as kirtamukha
Kalasa	the sacred pot from which temple plinths at Pagan, Burma often take their profile (B)
Kathin/krathin	a one month period during the eighth lunar month when lay people present new robes and other gifts to monks
Ketumula	flame-like motif above the Buddha head
Khao	mountain (T)
Khlong	canal (T)
Khruang	amulet (see page 142) (T)
Kinaree	half-human, half-bird, usually depicted as a heavenly musician
Kirtamukha	see kala
Koh	island (T)
Koutdi	see kuti
Krating	wild bull, most commonly seen on bottles of *Red Bull* (Krating Daeng) stimulant drink (T)
Krishna	incarnation of Vishnu
Kuti	living quarters of Buddhist monks in a temple complex (T and L)
Kyaung	monastery, or school (B)

L

Laem	cape (as in bay) (T)
Lak muang	city pillar (T)
Lakhon	traditional Thai classical music (T)
Laterite	bright red tropical soil/stone commonly used in construction of Khmer monuments (see page 88)
Linga	phallic symbol and one of the forms of Siva. Embedded in a pedastal shaped to allow drainage of lustral water poured over it, the linga typically has a succession of cross sections: from square at the base through octagonal to round. These symbolise, in order, the trinity of Brahma, Vishnu and Siva
Lintel	a load-bearing stone spanning a doorway; often heavily carved
Lokeshvara	see Avalokitsvara
Lungyi	Burmese sarong, worn by men and women (B)

M

Mahabharata	a Hindu epic text written about 2,000 years ago
Mahayana	'Greater Vehicle', major Buddhist sect (see page 40)
Maitreya	the future Buddha
Makara	a mythological aquatic reptile, somewhat like a crocodile and sometimes with an elephant's trunk; often found along with the kala framing doorways
Mandala	a focus for meditation; a representation of the cosmos
Mara	personification of evil and tempter of the Buddha
Matmii	Northeastern Thai and Lao cotton ikat (T and L) (see page 331)
Mat mi	see matmii
Meru	sacred or cosmic mountain at the centre of the world in Hindu-Buddhist cosmology; home of the gods (see page 207)
Mon	race and kingdom of southern Burma and central Thailand from 7-11th century
Mondop	from the sanskrit, *mandapa*. A cube-shaped building, often topped with a cone-like structure, used to contain an object of worship like a footprint of the Buddha
Muang	administrative unit in Laos and town in Thailand. In Laos, the system, based on local governors, was established by King Samenthai in the 14th century (T and L)
Muban	village, usually shortened to ban (T and L)
Mudra	symbolic gesture of the hands of the Buddha (see page 94)

N

Naga	benevolent mythical water serpent, enemy of Garuda
Naga makara	fusion of naga and makara
Nalagiri	the elephant let loose to attack the Buddha, who calmed him
Namtok	waterfall (T)
Nandi/nandin	bull, mount of Siva
Nang thalung	shadow play/puppets (see page 112) (T)

Nat	a Burmese spirit or god. There are 37 in total, which are local spirits, famous people who have died, or are borrowed from Hindu mythology (B)
Nikhom	resettlement village (T)
Nirvana	release from the cycle of suffering in Buddhist belief; 'enlightenment'

P

Pa kama	Lao men's all purpose cloth usually woven with checked pattern (L and T)
paddy/padi	unhulled rice
Pagoda	in Burma this Western term has evolved to describe a stupa or zedi; in Vietnam it corresponds with a Mahayana Buddhist temple (B and V)
Pali	the sacred language of Theravada Buddhism
Parvati	consort of Siva
Pha sin	tubular piece of cloth, similar to sarong (T and L)
Phi	spirit
Phnom/ phanom	Khmer for hill/mountain (C)
Phra sinh	see pha sin
Pradaksina	pilgrims' clockwise circumambulation of holy structure
Prah	sacred
Prang	form of stupa built in Khmer style, shaped like a corncob (see page 88)
Prasada	stepped pyramid (see prasat)
Prasat	residence of a king or of the gods (sanctuary tower), from the Indian prasada (see page 88)
Pwe	Burmese festival (see page 547) (B)

Q

| Quan Am | Chinese goddess (Kuan-yin) of mercy (see page 324) |

R

Rahu	Burmese planet which causes eclipses (B)
Rai	unit of measurement, 1ha = 6.25rai (T)
Rama	incarnation of Vishnu, hero of the Indian epic, the *Ramayana*
Ramakien	Thai and Lao version of the *Ramayana* (see page 134) (T and L)
Ramayana	Hindu romantic epic, known as *Ramakien* in Thailand (see page 134)

S

Saamlor	three-wheeled bicycle taxi (T)
Sakyamuni	the historic Buddha
Sal	the Indian sal tree (*Shorea robusta*), under which the historic Buddha was born
Sala	open pavilion (T)
Sangha	the Buddhist order of monks

Sawankhalok	type of ceramic (see page 208) (T)
Sawbwas	Shan feudal lords (B)
Seitpadi	rosary beads used by important monks in Burma (B)
Sema	see bai sema (T)
Shwe	gold (B)
Sikhara	beehive-like spire, usual in Burmese temples (B)
Singha	mythical guardian lion
Siva	the Destroyer, one of the three gods of the Hindu trinity; the sacred linga was worshipped as a symbol of Siva
Sofa	see dok sofa
Songthaew	'two rows': pick-up truck with benches along either side (T)
Sravasti	the miracle at Sravasti when the Buddha subdues the heretics in front of a mango tree
Stele	inscribed stone panel
Stucco	plaster, often heavily moulded
Stupa	chedi (see page 90)

T

Talaat	market (T)
Tambon	a commune of villages (T)
Tam bun	see bun
Tavatimsa	heaven of the 33 gods at the summit of Mount Meru
Tazaungs	small pavilions found within Burmese temple complexes (B)
Tham	cave (T)
Thanaka	a paste worn by many Burmese women on their faces; it is ground from the bark of the acacia tree (B)
Thanon	street in Lao and Thai (T and L)
That	shrine housing Buddhist relics, a spire or dome-like edifice commemorating the Buddha's life or the funerary temple for royalty; peculiar to Laos and parts of Northeastern Thailand (T and L)
Thein	Burmese ordination hall (see page 92 for Thai equivalent) (B)
Theravada	'Way of the Elders'; major Buddhist sect also known as Hinayana Buddhism ('Lesser Vehicle') (see page 40)
Traiphum	the three worlds of Buddhist cosmology – heaven, hell and earth
Trimurti	the Hindu trinity of gods: Brahma, the Creator, Vishnu the Preserver and Siva the Destroyer
Tripitaka	Theravada Buddhism's Pali canon
Tuk-tuk	motorised three-wheeled taxi (T)
Tukata	doll (T)

U

Ubosoth	see bot
Urna	the dot or curl on the Buddha's forehead, one of the distinctive physical marks of the Enlightened One
Usnisa	the Buddha's top knot or 'wisdom bump', one of the physical marks of the Enlightened One

V

Vahana	'vehicle', a mythical beast, upon which a deva or god rides
Viharn	from Sanskrit *vihara*, an assembly hall in a Buddhist monastery; may contain Buddha images and is similar in style to the bot (see page 92)
Vishnu	the Protector, one of the gods of the Hindu trinity, generally with four arms holding a disc, conch shell, ball and club

W

Wai	Thai greeting, with hands held together at chin height as if in prayer (T)
Wat	Buddhist 'monastery' with religious and other buildings (see page 92) (T)

Z

Zat	Classical Burmese dramas, usually based on the *Ramayana* (see page 547) (B)
Zayat	prayer pavilion found in Burmese temple complexes (B)
Zedi	Burmese term for a stupa (B)

MAPS

TINTED BOXES

682

BURMA

INDEX

R

S

Y